MORMON DOCTRINE

MORMON DOCTRINE

BY

BRUCE R. MCCONKIE

SECOND EDITION

Bookcraft
Salt Lake City, Utah

1979

Lithographed in the United States of America
PUBLISHERS PRESS
Salt Lake City, Utah

PREFACE

This work on *Mormon Doctrine* is designed to help persons seeking salvation to gain that knowledge of God and his laws without which they cannot hope for an inheritance in the celestial city.

Since it is impossible for a man to be saved in ignorance of God and his laws, and since man is saved no faster than he gains knowledge of Jesus Christ and the plan of salvation, it follows that men are obligated at their peril to learn and apply the true doctrines of the gospel.

This gospel compendium will enable men, more effectively, to "teach one another the doctrine of the kingdom"; to "be instructed more perfectly in theory, in principle, in doctrine, in the law of the gospel, in all things that pertain unto the kingdom of God, that are expedient" for them "to understand." (D. & C. 88:77-78.)

For the work itself, I assume sole and full responsibility.

Salt Lake City, Utah
June 1, 1958

—Bruce R. McConkie

SECOND EDITION

From the time the first copies came from the press, this compendium of *Mormon Doctrine* has found a wide and gratifying acceptance among doctrinal students in all parts of the Church. In publishing this Second Edition, as is common with major encyclopedic-type works, experience has shown the wisdom of making some changes, clarifications, and additions.

Salt Lake City, Utah
September 1, 1966

Bruce R. McConkie

ABBREVIATIONS

Scriptural references are abbreviated in a standard and self-identifying way.

Other books are cited by author and title, except that the following oft-cited works are referred to by title only:

Little, James A., & Richards, Franklin D., *Compendium;*

Roberts, Brigham H., *Outlines of Ecclesiastical History;*

Smith, Joseph, *History of the Church,* vols. 1 to 6;

> *Lectures on Faith;*
>
> *Teachings of the Prophet Joseph Smith* (cited as *Teachings*);

Smith, Joseph F., *Gospel Doctrine;*

Smith, Joseph Fielding, *Doctrines of Salvation,* vols. 1 to 3;

> *Essentials in Church History;*
>
> *Man: His Origin and Destiny;*
>
> *Progress of Man;*
>
> *Way to Perfection;*

Talmage, James E., *Articles of Faith;*

Taylor, John, *Gospel Kingdom;*

> *Mediation and Atonement;*

Woodruff, Wilford, *Discourses of Wilford Woodruff;*

Young, Brigham, *Discourses of Brigham Young* (cited as *Discourses*)

To Oscar W. McConkie, my father, a pillar of spiritual strength, a scriptorian and theologian; and to Vivian R. McConkie, my mother, a saintly and spiritual soul whose example and teachings have been Christ-like.

A

AARON.

See AARONIC PRIESTHOOD, AARONITES, LEVI, MELCHIZEDEK, MOSES, PRESIDING BISHOP, PRIESTHOOD, SONS OF MOSES AND AARON. To *Aaron* goes the honor—as a perpetual memorial through all generations—of having his name used to identify the lesser, Levitical, or Aaronic Priesthood. (D. & C. 84:18-27; 107:1, 20.) As a possessor of the Melchizedek Priesthood, Aaron held a position of prominence and leadership among the elders. (Ex. 18:12; John Taylor, *Items on Priesthood,* p. 5.) Indeed, with Moses, Nadab, Abihu, and 70 of the elders of Israel, Aaron saw the God of Israel before the existence of the Aaronic order; and when "Moses went up into the mount of God," Aaron and Hur were left in a position of presidency over the other elders. (Ex. 24.) But when the law of carnal commandments was "added" to the gospel "because of transgressions," then Aaron and his sons were chosen to bear that priesthood by which the lesser law was administered. (Gal. 3.) Aaron's position then became comparable to that of the Presiding Bishop of the Church. (John Taylor, *Items on Priesthood,* pp. 5-6.)

Also before the institution of the Levitical Priesthood, Aaron was chosen by the Lord to act as a minister with and a spokesman for Moses, his younger brother. (Ex. 4; 5; 6; 7; 8; 9; 10; 11; 12; 16.) After the beginning of the Aaronic order, Aaron and his sons after him were anointed priests unto Israel. (Ex. 28; 29; 30; Num. 3; 4.)

Aaron's call to the Levitical ministry stands as the perfect example of the choosing of legal administrators to do the Lord's work; ever since that day, the legality of priestly administration has been determined by whether the professing minister was "called of God, as was Aaron" (Heb. 5:4; D. & C. 27:8; 132:59), that is, by revelation and ordination, and with the full approval of the body of the Lord's true worshipers.

AARONIC PRIESTHOOD.

See AARON, AARONITES, BISHOPS, DEACONS, JOHN THE BAPTIST, KEYS, LAW OF MOSES, LEVITES, MELCHIZEDEK PRIESTHOOD, ORDINATIONS, PRIESTHOOD, PRIESTHOOD OF ELIAS, PRIESTHOOD OFFICES, PRIESTHOOD QUORUMS, PRIESTS, QUORUM PRESIDENTS, TEACHERS. When the Lord first gave the law of carnal commandments, the preparatory gospel, to school Israel for a future time when again they could enjoy the gospel fulness, of necessity a lesser

9

order of priesthood was conferred to administer the lesser law. (Heb. 7:12; *Inspired Version,* Ex. 34:1-2.) This lesser priesthood (D. & C. 85: 11) was conferred upon Aaron and his sons after him (Ex. 28; 29; 30; Lev. 1:11; 3:2; 13:2; Num. 18), as "an everlasting priesthood throughout their generations." (Ex. 40:15; Num. 25:10-13.) It was also conferred upon substantially the whole house of Levi who were between 30 and 50 years of age. (Num. 3; 4.) Hence it is called the *Aaronic or Levitical Priesthood;* the two names are synonymous. (D. & C. 107:1, 6, 10.)

Aaron and his sons after him held the *keys* of the Aaronic Priesthood and acted in the full majesty and power of this Levitical order; many of their functions were comparable to those of bishops and priests in this dispensation. Though the rest of the ordained Levites held the fulness of the Aaronic Priesthood (Heb. 7:5) and participated in the offering of sacrifices, they did not hold the keys of the Aaronic ministry; many of their functions were comparable to those of teachers and deacons in this dispensation. (Num. 3; 4; 2 Chron. 29; Mal. 3:3; D. & C. 13; *Doctrines of Salvation,* vol. 3, pp. 111-114.)

From Aaron to John the Baptist the hereditary nature of the Levitical Priesthood "was in active operation." (*Teachings,* pp. 318-319; D. & C. 84:18, 26-27, 30; 107:13.) This priesthood in that day was conferred solely upon worthy members of the special lineage chosen to receive it; it came to individuals by descent, because of father and because of mother, as contrasted with the Melchizedek Priesthood which was "without father, without mother, without descent." (Heb. 7:3.) John the Baptist "was a descendant of Aaron" and held the keys of the Aaronic Priesthood. (*Teachings,* pp. 272-273.) There was no Aaronic Priesthood among the Nephites prior to the ministry of the resurrected Lord among them, for none of the tribe of Levi accompanied the Nephite peoples to their promised land.

Few members of the tribe of Levi gathered with the fold of Israel in the meridian of time; few have come back to the fold of their fathers in this dispensation; and there were none among the Nephites to whom our Lord ministered. Consequently, beginning in the day of the primitive Church the lesser priesthood was spread out among the body of the people and was no longer confined exclusively to the chosen lineage. When the latter-day kingdom is perfected, and when the other tribes of Israel are gathered and receive their blessings under the hands of Ephraim, the first to gather (D. & C. 133:26-35), then the sons of Levi again will stand forth in the majesty of their calling and "offer again an offering unto the Lord in righteousness." (D. & C. 13.)

John the Baptist, as a resurrected personage, came to Joseph Smith and Oliver Cowdery on the 15th of

May, 1829, and made the first conferral of Levitical Priesthood in this dispensation. (D. & C. 13; 27:8.) Since then, as the needs of the ministry warranted, the offices of bishop, priest, teacher, and deacon, have all been revealed as part of this Aaronic ministry.

The Priesthood of Aaron "is called the lesser priesthood . . . because it is an appendage to the greater, or the Melchizedek Priesthood, and has power in administering outward ordinances." (D. & C. 107:13-14.) Though it is a lesser priesthood, it is yet one of great majesty and power. It holds "the keys of the ministering of angels," meaning that those who hold it and are faithful have the key whereby they can open the door to the receipt of visitations from heavenly messengers. (D. & C. 13; 84:26-27; 107:20.) Faith, repentance, and baptism—comprising as they do the preparatory gospel—fall within its province, though the laying on of hands for the gift of the Holy Ghost is not a prerogative that attends it.

Perfection does not come by the Levitical order, and this lesser priesthood is not received with an oath. (Heb. 7:11, 21; *Teachings*, p. 323.) But it is a preparatory priesthood, the Priesthood of Elias, the schooling ministry, which prepares its worthy and faithful ministers for the oath and covenant and perfection that appertain to the Melchizedek order. That those who train themselves to receive the Melchizedek Priesthood, by magnifying their callings in the Aaronic Priesthood, must be true and faithful and worthy for the final receipt of the greater priesthood is self-evident. Indeed, one of the reasons the Lord destroyed Korah and his band of Levites was that they, *being unworthy*, sought "the high priesthood also." (*Inspired Version,* Num. 16.)

AARONITES.

See AARON, AARONIC PRIESTHOOD, LEVITES, SONS OF MOSES AND AARON. Descendants of Aaron, specially honored as the priests of Israel, were called *Aaronites*. (1 Chron. 12:27; 27:17.) Descent and genealogical proof thereof were of vital importance. "The children of the priests," when the temple was to be rebuilt in Jerusalem, "sought their register among those that were reckoned by genealogy, but they were not found: therefore were they, as polluted, put from the priesthood." (Ezra 2:61-63; Neh. 7:63-65.)

ABADDON.

See APOLLYON, DESTROYER, DEVIL, HELL. This expression, of Hebrew origin, was used by John as a name for Satan. (Rev. 9:11.) It is the same as the Greek *Apollyon* and means literally *the Destroyer*. It was used anciently to mean *hell*, as shown in the marginal reading of Psalm 88:11.

ABOMINABLE CHURCH.

See CHURCH OF THE DEVIL.

11

ABOMINATION OF DESOLA-
TION.
See ABOMINATIONS, SECOND
COMING OF CHRIST, SIGNS OF THE
TIMES. Daniel spoke prophetically
of a day when there would be "the
abomination that maketh desolate"
(Dan. 11:31; 12:11), and the phrase
was recoined in New Testament
times to say, "the *abomination of
desolation,* spoken of by Daniel the
prophet." (Matt. 24:15.) Aside from
the prophetic setting and relying
solely on the plain meaning of
words, we would conclude that this
phrase (abomination of desolation)
would have reference to some great
act or status of corruption and be-
foulment, of contamination and filthiness, which would bring to pass
destruction, ruination, devastation,
desolation.

Such is the case. These conditions of desolation, born of abomination and wickedness, were to occur
twice in fulfilment of Daniel's words.
The first was to be when the Roman
legions under Titus, in 70 A.D., laid
siege to Jerusalem, destroying and
scattering the people, leaving not
one stone upon another in the desecrated temple, and spreading such
terror and devastation as has seldom
if ever been equalled on earth. Of
those days Moses had foretold that
the straitness of the siege would
cause parents to eat their own children and great loathing and evil to
abound. (Deut. 28.)

And of the same events our Lord
was led to say: "For then, in those
days, shall be great tribulation on

the Jews, and upon the inhabitants
of Jerusalem, such as was not before sent upon Israel, of God, since
the beginning of their kingdom until
this time; no, nor ever shall be sent
again upon Israel. . . . And except
those days should be shortened,
there should none of their flesh be
saved." (Jos. Smith 1:12-20.)

Then, speaking of the last days,
of the days following the restoration
of the gospel and its declaration "for
a witness unto all nations," our
Lord said: "And again shall the
abomination of desolation, spoken
of by Daniel the prophet, be fulfilled." (Jos. Smith 1:31-32.) That
is: Jerusalem again will be under
siege ("For I will gather all nations
against Jerusalem to battle");
again the severity of the siege and
the extremities of brutal conflict,
born of wickedness and abomination, will lead to great devastation
and desolation ("and the city shall
be taken, and the houses rifled, and
the women ravished; and half of
the city shall go forth into captivity"). (Zech. 14.) It will be during
this siege that Christ will come,
the wicked will be destroyed, and
the millennial era commenced.

In a general sense, this expressive
designation, abomination of desolation, also describes the latter-day
terrors to be poured out upon the
wicked wherever they may be. And
so that the honest in heart may
escape these things, the Lord sends
his missionaries forth to raise the
warning voice, to declare the glad
tidings of the restoration, lest "des-

olation and utter abolishment" come upon them. The elders are commanded to reprove "the world in righteousness of all their unrighteous and ungodly deeds, setting forth clearly and understandingly the desolation of abomination in the last days." (D. & C. 84:114, 117.)

Also: "Go forth among the Gentiles for the last time, as many as the mouth of the Lord shall name, to bind up the law and seal up the testimony, and to prepare the saints for the hour of judgment which is to come; That their souls may escape the wrath of God, the *desolation of abomination which awaits the wicked, both in this world and in the world to come.*" (D. & C. 88:84-85.)

ABOMINATIONS.

See ABOMINATION OF DESOLATION, CHURCH OF THE DEVIL, SIGNS OF THE TIMES, SIN, WICKEDNESS. Those practices which are so vile, hateful, and detestable as to excite and deserve loathing are called *abominations.* Idolatory and every form of sex immorality, for instance, are so classified. (Lev. 18.)

ABRAHAMIC COVENANT.

See ADOPTION, CELESTIAL MARRIAGE, CHILDREN OF THE COVENANT, COVENANTS, EXALTATION, GATHERING OF ISRAEL, HOPE OF ISRAEL, MELCHIZEDEK PRIESTHOOD, NEW AND EVERLASTING COVENANT, RESTORATION OF THE GOSPEL. Abraham first received the gospel by baptism (which is the covenant of sal-

vation); then he had conferred upon him the higher priesthood, and he entered into celestial marriage (which is the covenant of exaltation), gaining assurance thereby that he would have eternal increase; finally he received a promise that all of these blessings would be offered to all of his mortal posterity. (Abra. 2:6-11; D. & C. 132: 29-50.) Included in the divine promises to Abraham was the assurance that Christ would come through his lineage, and the assurance that Abraham's posterity would receive certain choice, promised lands as an eternal inheritance. (Abra. 2; Gen. 17; 22:15-18; Gal. 3.)

All of these promises lumped together are called the *Abrahamic covenant.* This covenant was renewed with Isaac (Gen. 24:60; 26: 1-4, 24) and again with Jacob. (Gen. 28; 35:9-13; 48:3-4.) *Those portions of it which pertain to personal exaltation and eternal increase are renewed with each member of the house of Israel who enters the order of celestial marriage;* through that order the participating parties become inheritors of all the blessings of Abraham, Isaac, and Jacob. (D. & C. 132; Rom. 9:4; Gal. 3; 4.)

To fulfil the covenant God made with Abraham — having particular reference to the fact that the literal seed of his body would be entitled to the blessings of the gospel, the priesthood, celestial marriage, and eternal life (Abra. 2:10-11)—a number of specific and particular things must take place in the last days.

The gospel must be restored, the priesthood be conferred again upon man, the keys of the sealing power given again to mortals, Israel gathered, and the Holy Ghost must be poured out upon the Gentiles. All this has, of course, already taken place or is in process of fulfilment. (1 Ne. 14:5-7; 15:12-20; 19:14-17; 22:3-25; 2 Ne. 6:6-12; 9:1-2; 10:7-15; 11:5; 29:1; 3 Ne. 15; 20; 21; Ether 13:1-13.) This is the very day when the identity of those "who are heirs according to the covenant" (D. & C. 52:2), who are "lawful heirs, according to the flesh" (D. & C. 86:8-11), is being made known.

To the Nephites the resurrected Lord proclaimed: "Ye are of the house of Israel; and ye are of the covenant which the Father made with your fathers, saying unto Abraham: And in thy seed shall all the kindreds of the earth be blessed. The Father having raised me up unto you first, and sent me to bless you in turning away every one of you from his iniquities; and this because ye are the children of the covenant—And after that ye were blessed then fulfilleth the Father the covenant which he made with Abraham, saying: In thy seed shall all the kindreds of the earth be blessed—*unto the pouring out of the Holy Ghost through me upon the Gentiles,* which blessing upon the Gentiles shall make them mighty above all, unto the scattering of my people, O house of Israel. And they shall be a scourge unto the people of this land. Nevertheless, when they shall have received the fulness of my gospel, then if they shall harden their hearts against me I will return their iniquities upon their own heads, saith the Father. And I will remember the covenant which I have made with my people; and I have covenanted with them that I would gather them together in mine own due time, that I would give unto them again the land of their fathers for their inheritance, which is the land of Jerusalem, which is the promised land unto them forever, saith the Father." (3 Ne. 20:25-29.)

As a sign—"that ye may know the time when these things shall be about to take place"—the Lord said that a free nation would be set up on the American continent, that the gospel would be restored, and that the Book of Mormon would come forth. "And when these things come to pass that thy seed shall begin to know these things—it shall be a sign unto them, that they may know that the work of the Father hath already commenced unto the fulfilling of the covenant which he hath made unto the people who are of the house of Israel." (3 Ne. 21.)

ABRAHAMIC DISPENSATION.
See DISPENSATIONS.

ABRAHAM'S BOSOM.
See PARADISE, SPIRIT WORLD.

Our Lord, in the parable of Lazarus and the rich man, uses the term *Abraham's bosom* to mean paradise. Abraham, the friend of God, not at that time having been resurrected, was continuing his life in the paradise of God, the same place to which the righteous beggar went. (Luke 16:19-31.) The expression connotes the close fellowship and harmony that exists among the righteous in the paradisiacal sphere of peace and rest.

ABRAHAM'S CHILDREN.

See ADOPTION, CHILDREN OF THE COVENANT, ISRAEL, TRIBES OF ISRAEL. "We be Abraham's seed," the Jews said; and so they were in the literal sense. But in the gospel sense *Abraham's children* are those who do the works of Abraham, for their blood is thereby cleansed and purified as was Abraham's, and they are adopted into his lineage. (Abra. 2:8-11; D. & C. 84:33-41; 132:29-33; *Teachings*, pp. 149-150.) Hence, our Lord replied to the Jews, "If ye were Abraham's children, ye would do the works of Abraham. . . . Ye do the deeds of your father. . . . Ye are of your father the devil, and the lusts of your father ye will do." (John 8:31-47.)

ABSOLUTION.

See FORGIVENESS.

ABSTINENCE.

See WORD OF WISDOM.

ABYSS.
See BOTTOMLESS PIT.

ACCOUNTABILITY.

See AGENCY, BAPTISM, INFANT BAPTISM, ORIGINAL SIN THEORY, SALVATION OF CHILDREN, TEMPTATION, YEARS OF ACCOUNTABILITY. Personal *accountability* for all of one's acts underlies the whole gospel plan and is the natural outgrowth of the law of free agency. Without such personal responsibility free agency could not operate, for neither rewards nor punishments would follow the exercise of agency. And if there were no rewards or punishments, there would be no salvation or damnation, and so the whole plan of salvation would vanish away. (2 Ne. 2:11-16.) But contrary to the false doctrine which denies personal responsibility for sin, and says instead that men are predestined to salvation or damnation, the Lord has said that men will be punished for their own sins (Second Article of Faith; *Articles of Faith*, pp. 52-73), and that they will be judged according to the deeds done in the flesh. (Rev. 20:12.)

Accordingly, men are accountable for all their acts both temporal and spiritual. (D. & C. 42:32; 104:13.) Accountability for civic and governmental acts is included. "We believe that governments were instituted of God for the benefit of man; and that he holds men accountable for their acts in relation to them, both in making laws and administering

15

them, for the good and safety of society." (D. & C. 134:1.) In fact the Lord established the constitution of the United States, "That every man may act in doctrine and principle pertaining to futurity, according to the moral agency which I have given unto him, that every man may be accountable for his own sins in the day of judgment." (D. & C. 101:77-80.)

ACTS OF GOD.

See GOD, JUDGMENTS OF GOD, SIGNS OF THE TIMES. Common custom designates the calamities of nature as *acts of God.* In courts of law, for instance, floods, earthquakes, volcanic eruptions, hailstorms, and the like, since they apparently are wholly outside the realm of human control, are called acts of God. This view of things is particularly offensive to those branches of modern Christendom which specialize in the false view that Deity is light, love, and goodness and never manifests himself except through attributes of this sort.

In actuality the hand of the Lord is seen in all things including the calamities of nature. He has given laws unto all things, including the forces of nature; and by these laws those forces are operated, governed, and controlled. (D. & C. 88:42-45.) One of these laws is that the righteousness or wickedness of men directly affects the operation of the forces of nature. Crops grow for the righteous who pay tithing. (Mal.

3:7-12.) The rains come and the productivity of the soil is enhanced when men keep the commandments. (Lev. 26:3-5.) By listening to the whisperings of the Spirit, many righteous persons have been led out of the paths of impending calamities; conversely, when the fulness of the Lord's wrath has rested upon wicked cities and nations, the inhabitants of those places have been placed in the way of "acts of God" which would destroy them. These things are seen in the whole record of God's dealings with men.

ADAM.

See ADAM-GOD THEORY, ADAMIC LANGUAGE, ADAM-ONDI-AHMAN, ANCIENT OF DAYS, BATTLE OF THE GREAT GOD, EVE, FALL OF ADAM, FIRST FLESH, FIRST MAN, FORBIDDEN FRUIT, MICHAEL THE ARCHANGEL, PRE-EXISTENCE. WAR IN HEAVEN. Our knowledge about *Adam,* and the exalted station held by him in the eternal providences of the Almighty, begins with an understanding of his pre-existent work and mission. By his diligence and obedience there, as one of the spirit sons of God, he attained a stature and power second only to that of Christ, the Firstborn. None of all the billions of our Father's children equalled him in intelligence and might, save Jesus only. He sat in the council of the gods in the planning of the creation of this earth, and then, under Christ, participated in the creative enterprise. (Abra. 3:22-

26.) He was foreordained to come to earth as the father of the human race, and when Lucifer and one-third of the hosts of heaven rebelled, Adam (with the exalted title of Michael the Archangel) led the hosts of the righteous in the war in heaven. (Rev. 12:7-9.)

"And the first man of all men have I called Adam," the Lord says, "which is many." (Moses 1:34; 3:7; 6:45; Abra. 1:3; 1 Ne. 5:11; D. & C. 84:16.) That is, Adam was placed on earth as the first of the human family and given a name which signifies *many* as pertaining to the greatness of the posterity which should flow from him.

As to the manner in which Adam was placed on earth, the First Presidency of the Church (Joseph F. Smith, John R. Winder, and Anthon H. Lund) has given us this plain statement: "He took upon him an appropriate body, the body of a man, and so became a 'living soul.' ... All who have inhabited the earth since Adam have taken bodies and become souls *in like manner.* ... Man began life as a human being, in the likeness of our Heavenly Father. True it is that the body of man enters upon its career as a *tiny germ or embryo, which becomes an infant,* quickened at a certain stage by the spirit whose tabernacle it is, and the child, after being born, develops into a man. There is nothing in this, however, to indicate that the original man, *the first of our race, began life as anything less than a man, or less than the human*

germ or embryo that becomes a man." (*Man: His Origin and Destiny,* p. 354.)

Adam's great part in the plan of redemption was to fall from the immortal state in which he first existed on earth and thus bring mortality and death into the world. This he did, bringing temporal and spiritual death into the world, from the effects of which deaths the atonement of Christ was foreordained as a ransom. After the fall, Adam and Eve became the parents of all living. (Moses 5:11; D. & C. 27:11; 1 Ne. 5:11; 2:23-25.) We are his descendants and there are no persons who have ever lived on earth who have not had this same ancestry. "He is the father of the human family; ... [the] head of the human family." (*Teachings,* p. 157.)

Father Adam was one of the most noble and intelligent characters who ever lived. He began his earth life as a son of God, endowed with the talents and abilities gained through diligence and obedience in pre-existence. He is the head of all gospel dispensations (*Teachings,* pp. 167-169), the presiding high priest (under Christ) over all the earth; presides over all the spirits destined to inhabit this earth (*Teachings,* pp. 157-159); holds the keys of salvation over all the earth; and will reign as Michael, our prince, to all eternity. (D. & C. 78: 16.) He was baptized (Moses 6:64-66), married for eternity, for death had not yet entered the world (Moses 3:21-25), had the fulness of

17

the gospel (Moses 5:57-59), and following 930 years of existence after the fall went on to the paradise of God to await a glorious resurrection with Christ and the righteous saints. He has returned to earth in our day, bringing keys and authorities to the Prophet Joseph Smith (D. & C. 128:21); will soon preside at the great Adam-ondi-Ahman council (D. & C. 116); and finally will reign over his righteous posterity in the Patriarchal Order to all eternity. (*Doctrines of Salvation,* vol. 1, pp. 90-106.)

ADAM-GOD THEORY.

See ADAM, ANCIENT OF DAYS, BIRTHRIGHT, CELESTIAL MARRIAGE, EXALTATION, GOD, GODHOOD, MICHAEL THE ARCHANGEL, PATRIARCHAL CHAIN, PATRIARCHAL ORDER, PLURALITY OF GODS. Cultists and other enemies of the restored truth, for their own peculiar purposes, sometimes try to make it appear that Latter-day Saints worship *Adam* as their Father in heaven. In support of their false assumptions, they quote such statements as that of President Brigham Young to the effect that Adam is our father and our god and the only god with whom we have to do. This statement, and others of a similar nature, is perfectly consistent and rational, when viewed in full gospel perspective and understood in the light of the revelations relative to the patriarchal chain binding exalted beings together. Full and detailed explanations of all important teachings on these points are readily available. (*Doctrines of Salvation,* vol. 1, pp. 96-106.)

Faithful members of the Church worship the Father, in the name of the Son, by the power of the Holy Spirit, and view Adam in his proper high place as the pre-existent Michael, the first man and presiding high priest (under Christ) over all the earth for all time, and as the one who will again lead the armies of heaven in the final great war with Lucifer. There is a sense, of course, in which Adam is a god. But so also, in the same sense, are Abraham, Isaac, and Jacob; Moses and all the ancient prophets; Peter, James, and John; and all the righteous saints of all ages, including those of both high and low degree.

All exalted beings become joint-heirs with Christ and inherit the fulness of the Father's kingdom. Having entered in at the gate of celestial marriage, and having pressed forward in righteousness, overcoming all things, they pass by the angels and the gods "to their exaltation and glory in all things. . . . Then shall they be gods, because they have no end; therefore shall they be from everlasting to everlasting, because they continue; then shall they be above all, because all things are subject unto them. Then shall they be gods, because they have all power, and the angels are subject unto them." (D. & C. 132:19-20.) Of all these Adam is the chief, presiding (under

Christ and the Father) in the patriarchal order over all the rest. There is no mystery about this doctrine except that which persons ignorant of the great principles of exaltation and unfriendly to the cause of righteousness have attempted to make.

ADAMIC DISPENSATION.
See DISPENSATIONS.

ADAMIC LANGUAGE.
See BOOK OF REMEMBRANCE, GAZELAM, LANGUAGES, TONGUES. In the beginning God gave Adam a language that was pure, perfect, and undefiled. This *Adamic language,* now unknown, was far superior to any tongue which is presently extant. For instance, the name of God the Father, in this original language, is *Man of Holiness,* signifying that he is a Holy Man and not a vague spiritual essence. (Moses 6:57.)

This first language spoken by mortals was either the celestial tongue of the Gods or such adaptation of it as was necessary to meet the limitations of mortality; and Adam and his posterity had power to speak, read, and write it. (*Way to Perfection,* pp. 60-69.) In writing of the saints in the day of the first man, Moses says: "And a book of remembrance was kept, . . . in the language of Adam, for it was given unto as many as called upon God to write by the spirit of inspiration; And by them their children were

taught to read and write, having *a language which was pure and undefiled."* (Moses 6:5-6.) The beauty and power of this Adamic language is indicated by a statement made by Moroni to the Lord about the Brother of Jared (who spoke the original and pure language): "Thou madest him that *the things which he wrote were mighty even as thou art, unto the overpowering of man to read them."* (Ether 12:24.)

During the millennium, it appears that men will again have power to speak and write the Adamic language. Of that day the Lord says he will "turn to the people *a pure language,* that they may all call upon the name of the Lord, to serve him with one consent." (Zeph. 3:9.) In some instances when the saints speak in tongues, the language impressed upon them by the power of the Spirit is the pure Adamic tongue.

ADAM-ONDI-AHMAN.
See ADAM, AHMAN, GARDEN OF EDEN, MILLENNIUM, SECOND COMING OF CHRIST, SIGNS OF THE TIMES. *Adam* was the first man of all men; *Ahman* is one of the names by which God was known to Adam. *Adam-ondi-Ahman,* a name carried over from the pure Adamic language into English, is one for which we have not been given a revealed, literal translation. As near as we can judge—and this view comes down from the early brethren who associated with the Prophet Joseph Smith, who was the first one to use the

name in this dispensation—*Adam - ondi - Ahman means the place or land of God where Adam dwelt.*

Apparently the area included was a large one; at least, the revelations speak of the *land,* the *valley,* and the *mountains of* Adam - ondi - Ahman. They tell us that Christ himself "established the foundations of Adam-ondi-Ahman" (D. & C. 78: 15-16), and that it included the place now known as Spring Hill, Daviess County, Missouri. (D. & C. 116.)

Far West, Missouri, also appears to be included in the land of Adam-ondi-Ahman. On April 17, 1838, the Lord commanded his saints to assemble at Far West, which place, he said, was holy ground; and there they were to build a city. (D. & C. 115.) By July 8 of that year, William Marks and Newel K. Whitney had not left their temporal concerns in Kirtland, Ohio, and were not assembling with the saints coming to Zion. In rebuking them the Lord said this: "Is there not room enough on the *mountains of Adam-ondi-Ahman,* and on the plains of Olaha Shinehah, or *the land where Adam dwelt,* that you should covet that which is but the drop, and neglect the more weighty matters? Therefore, come up hither unto the land of my people, even *Zion.*"

William Marks was told that he was to "preside in the midst of my people in the city of Far West," and Newel K. Whitney was told to "come up to the *land of Adam-ondi-Ahman,* and be a bishop unto my people." (D. & C. 117.)

The early brethren of this dispensation taught that the Garden of Eden was located in what is known to us as the land of Zion, an area for which Jackson County, Missouri, is the center place. In our popular Latter-day Saint hymn which begins, "Glorious things are sung of Zion, Enoch's city seen of old," we find William W. Phelps preserving the doctrine that *"In Adam-ondi-Ahman, Zion rose where Eden was."* And in another hymn, written by the same author in the days of the Prophet Joseph Smith, we find these expressions:

This earth was once a garden place,
    With all her glories common,
And men did live a holy race,
And worship Jesus face to face,
    In Adam-ondi-Ahman.

We read that Enoch walk'd with God,
    Above the power of mammon,
While Zion spread herself abroad,
And Saints and angels sang aloud,
    In Adam-ondi-Ahman.

Her land was good and greatly blest,
    Beyond old Israel's Canaan;
Her fame was known from east to west,
Her peace was great, and pure the rest
    Of Adam-ondi-Ahman.

Hosannah to such days to come—
　The Savior's second coming,
When all the earth in glorious bloom,
Affords the Saints a holy home,
　Like Adam-ondi-Ahman.

One of the greatest spiritual gatherings of all the ages took place in the Valley of Adam-ondi-Ahman some 5,000 years ago, and another gathering—of even greater importance relative to this earth's destiny —is soon to take place in that same location. Our revelations recite: "Three years previous to the death of Adam, he called Seth, Enos, Cainan, Mahalaleel, Jared, Enoch, and Methuselah, who were all high priests, with the residue of his posterity who were righteous, into the valley of Adam-ondi-Ahman, and there bestowed upon them his last blessing.

"And the Lord appeared unto them, and they rose up and blessed Adam, and called him Michael, the prince, the archangel. And the Lord administered comfort unto Adam, and said unto him: I have set thee to be at the head; a multitude of nations shall come of thee, and thou art a prince over them forever. And Adam stood up in the midst of the congregation; and, notwithstanding he was bowed down with age, being full of the Holy Ghost, predicted whatsoever should befall his posterity unto the latest generation." (D. & C. 107:53-56.)

At that great gathering Adam offered sacrifices on an altar built for the purpose. A remnant of that very altar remained on the spot down through the ages. On May 19, 1838, Joseph Smith and a number of his associates stood on the remainder of the pile of stones at a place called Spring Hill, Daviess County, Missouri. There the Prophet taught them that Adam again would visit in the Valley of Adam-ondi-Ahman, holding a great council as a prelude to the great and dreadful day of the Lord. (*Mediation and Atonement,* pp. 69-70.) At this council, all who have held keys of authority will give an accounting of their stewardship to Adam. Christ will then come, receive back the keys, and thus take one of the final steps preparatory to reigning personally upon the earth. (Dan. 7:9-14; *Teachings,* p. 157.)

ADDRESSES.
　See SERMONS.

ADJURATION.
　See EXORCISM.

ADMINISTERING TO THE SICK.
　See ADMINISTRATIONS.

ADMINISTRATIONS.
　See CONSECRATION OF OIL, FAITH, HEALINGS, LAYING ON OF HANDS. "Is any sick among you? let him call for the elders of the

church; and let them pray over him, anointing him with oil in the name of the Lord: And the prayer of faith shall save the sick, and the Lord shall raise him up." (Jas. 5:14-16.) These words of James aptly summarize the practice of the Church in all ages where *administrations* are concerned. (D. & C. 42:43-44; 66:9; Mark 5:23; 6:5; 16:18; Luke 4:40-41; 13:11-13; Acts 28:8.) Administrations are of two parts: *anointings* and *sealings;* both performances are accompanied by the laying on of hands.

It is the policy of the Church that administering to the sick should be done at the request of the sick person or someone vitally concerned, so that it will be done in answer to faith. Those called to perform the ordinance should encourage the sick person to rely on the Lord's promise, *"Whatsoever thing ye shall ask the Father in my name, which is good, in faith believing that ye shall receive, behold, it shall be done unto you."* (Moro. 7:26.) If need be the sick person should be encouraged to keep the commandments so that he can have faith and be entitled to the blessings of the Lord.

In the performance of the administration, one of the elders should anoint the sick person with oil on or near the crown of the head, for the restoration of his health. Ordinarily he should not seal the anointing. Pure olive oil which has been consecrated for the anointing and healing of the sick in the household of faith should be used. Taking consecrated oil internally, or using it for anointing or rubbing afflicted parts of the body, is not part of the ordinance of administering to the sick.

After the anointing two or more elders should lay their hands on the head of the sick person, and with one of them acting as voice, seal the anointing. The one speaking should offer such prayers, pronounce such blessings, give such promises, say such things, and rebuke the affliction—all as the Spirit of the Lord may dictate.

Ordinarily one administration is sufficient for one illness, although in serious cases, or where other circumstances seem to dictate the propriety of such, a sick person may be administered to several times during one illness. It is also the common practice, if a sick person has recently been anointed, for those performing a second administration merely to give the sick person a blessing in the authority of the priesthood. In an emergency, where only one elder is present or available, he may either give the sick person a blessing or he can both anoint and seal in a formal administration.

Ordinances of administration with actual healings resulting therefrom are one of the evidences of the divinity of the Lord's work. Where these are, there is God's kingdom; where these are not, there God's kingdom is not. Sincere investigators must necessarily beware of the devil's substitutes of the true ordinances.

ADONAI.

See CHRIST, LORD. In the Old Testament record, Christ is frequently referred to under the Hebrew word *Adonai*—a term having reference to *God,* meaning literally *my Lord,* but usually translated as *Lord.*

ADOPTION.

See BORN AGAIN, ISRAEL, JOINT-HEIRS WITH CHRIST, SONS OF GOD, SONS OF MOSES AND AARON. By the *law of adoption* those who receive the gospel and obey its laws, no matter what their literal blood lineage may have been, are adopted into the lineage of Abraham. (Abra. 2: 9-11.) "The effect of the Holy Ghost upon a Gentile," the Prophet says, "is to purge out the old blood, and make him actually of the seed of Abraham." Such a person has "a new creation by the Holy Ghost." (*Teachings,* pp. 149-150.) Those who magnify their callings in the Melchizedek Priesthood are promised that they will be "sanctified by the Spirit unto the *renewing of their bodies.* They become the *sons of Moses and of Aaron* and the seed of Abraham." (D. & C. 84:33-34.)

Indeed, the faithful are adopted into the family of Christ; they become "the *children of Christ, his sons, and his daughters*"; they are "*spiritually begotten,*" for their "hearts are changed through faith on his name," thus being "born of him," becoming "his sons and his daughters." (Mosiah 5:7.) Paul explained the doctrine of adoption by saying, "As many as are led by the Spirit of God, they are the sons of God," because they receive "the Spirit of adoption," being or becoming Israelites, "to whom pertaineth the adoption." (Rom. 8:14-24; 9:4; Gal. 4:5; Eph. 1:5.)

ADORATION.
See WORSHIP.

ADULTERY.

See DAMNATION, FORNICATION, SEX IMMORALITY, SIGN-SEEKING, TELESTIAL LAW. 1. "Thou shalt not commit *adultery.*" (Ex. 20:14; Deut. 5:18; D. & C. 42:24.) Sex immorality stands next to murder in the category of personal crimes; it is "most abominable above all sins save it be the shedding of innocent blood or denying the Holy Ghost." (Alma 39:5.) Anciently the penalty therefor was death; "the adulterer and the adulteress shall surely be put to death." (Lev. 20:10; Deut. 22:21-29.)

In the initial day of judgment, at the Second Coming of our Lord, Christ "will be a swift witness . . . against the adulterers," and they shall be burned as stubble. (Mal. 3:5; 4:1.) Adulterers shall be cast down to hell to suffer the vengeance of eternal fire; and their eventual destiny—after suffering the torments of the damned until the second resurrection—shall be that of the telestial kingdom. (D. & C. 76:103-106.) They shall not inherit the kingdom of God. (1 Cor. 6:9-11.)

Adultery opens the flood gates of wickedness in general. Physical disease, divorce, illegitimacy, violence, broken homes, and a host of evils always attend adulterous acts. There never was an adulterer, for instance, who was not also a liar; the two always go together. Adulterers are sign-seekers (Matt. 12:39; 16:4); their spirits are diseased so as to hinder them in recognizing and accepting the gospel truths and thus becoming heirs of salvation.

Adulterous acts are born spiritually before they are committed temporally; they proceed out of the heart. (Matt. 15:19; Mark 7:21.) As a man "thinketh in his heart, so is he." (Prov. 23:7.) Therefore, "whosoever looketh on a woman to lust after her hath committed adultery with her already in his heart." (Matt. 5:27-28; 3 Ne. 12:17-28.) "He that looketh on a woman to lust after her, or if any shall commit adultery in their hearts, they shall not have the Spirit, but shall deny the faith and shall fear." (D. & C. 63:16.)

When the day comes that men live again—as they did in the golden era of Nephite history—the perfect law of marriage, then "whoso shall marry her who is divorced" shall be guilty of adultery. (3 Ne. 12:31-32; Matt. 5:31-32.) "Whosoever putteth away his wife, and marrieth another, committeth adultery: and whosoever marrieth her that is put away from her husband committeth adultery." (Luke 16:18; Matt. 19:9.)

Is it possible to repent of adultery and gain forgiveness of sins so as to be saved in the celestial kingdom of God? *Yes* in most cases; *No* in some. Forgiveness with resultant celestial salvation depends upon the light and knowledge of the one guilty of the grossly wicked adulterous relationship. Worldly people who repent with all their hearts, accept baptism, and then conform to the Lord's law shall be saved even though guilty of adultery before accepting the truth. (1 Cor. 6:9-11; 3 Ne. 30.)

Speaking to members of the Church in 1831—prior to the restoration of the temple covenants and ceremonies—the Lord said: "Thou shalt not commit adultery; and he that committeth adultery, and repenteth not, shall be cast out. But he that has committed adultery and repents with all his heart, and forsaketh it, and doeth it no more, thou shalt forgive; But if he doeth it again, he shall not be forgiven, but shall be cast out." (D. & C. 42:24-26.)

After a person has advanced in righteousness, light, and truth to the point that the fulness of the ordinances of the house of the Lord have been received so that he has been sealed up unto eternal life, and his calling and election has been made sure, then as expressed

24

in the Prophet's language, the law is: "If a man commit adultery, he cannot receive the celestial kingdom of God. Even if he is saved in any kingdom, it cannot be the celestial kingdom." (*History of the Church,* vol. 6, p. 81; *Doctrines of Salvation,* vol. 2, pp. 92-94.)

2. In a spiritual sense, to emphasize how serious it is, the damning sin of idolatry is called *adultery.* When the Lord's people forsake him and worship false gods, their infidelity to Jehovah is described as whoredoms and adultery. (Jer. 3: 8-9; Hos. 1:2; 3:1.) By forsaking the Lord, his people are unfaithful to their covenant vows, vows made to him who symbolically is their Husband.

ADVENT.
See SECOND COMING OF CHRIST.

ADVERSARY.
See AGENCY, DEVIL, SATAN. This name for Satan signifies that he is the enemy of all righteousness, opposes every good thing with evil, and is the arch foe of every upright person. Endowed with agency, he came out in open rebellion in pre-existence and has ever since been the chief antagonist of every righteous cause, "For it must needs be, that there is an opposition in all things." (2 Ne. 2:11.) "Be sober, be vigilant," Peter said, "because your *adversary* the devil, as a roaring lion, walketh about, seeking whom he may devour." (1 Pet. 5:8.)

ADVERSITIES.
See AFFLICTIONS.

ADVOCACY.
See ADVOCATE, ATONEMENT OF CHRIST, EXPIATION, INTERCESSION, MEDIATION, PROPITIATION, RECONCILIATION. Our Lord acts according to the *law of advocacy* or intercession in pleading the cause of his faithful saints before the tribunals of eternity. (D. & C. 45:3-4.)

ADVOCATE.
See ADVOCACY, ATONEMENT OF CHRIST, CHRIST, EXPIATOR, INTERCESSOR, MEDIATOR, PARACLETE, PROPITIATOR, RECONCILER. Christ is the *Advocate* with the Father, meaning that he pleads the cause of the righteous in the courts above. (D. & C. 29:5; 32:3; 62:1; 110:4; Moro. 7:28; 1 John 2:1.) "Listen to him who is the advocate with the Father, who is pleading your cause before him—Saying: Father, behold the sufferings and death of him who did no sin, in whom thou wast well pleased; behold the blood of thy Son which was shed, the blood of him whom thou gavest that thyself might be glorified; Wherefore, Father, *spare these my brethren that believe on my name, that they may come unto me and have everlasting life.*" (D. & C. 45:3-5.)

AFFLICTIONS.
See PATIENCE, SIGNS OF THE

25

TIMES, TRIBULATIONS. *Afflictions,* including sorrow, adversity, tribulation, calamity, and trouble—all these are the common lot of mankind; they are an essential part of this probation. "Be patient in afflictions." (D. & C. 31:9; 66:9.)

Frequently afflictions are imposed as a result of disobedience, and they could be avoided by righteousness. If Zion, for instance, "observe not to do whatsoever I have commanded her," the Lord said, "I will visit her according to all her works, with sore afliction, with pestilence, with plague, with sword, with vengeance, with devouring fire." (D. & C. 97:26; 101:1-9.)

AGENCY.

See FREEDOM, KNOWLEDGE, LAW, LIGHT OF CHRIST, PLAN OF SALVATION, PREDESTINATION, PRE-EXISTENCE. *Agency* is the ability and freedom to choose good or evil. It is an eternal principle which has existed with God from all eternity. The spirit offspring of the Father had agency in pre-existence and were thereby empowered to follow Christ or Lucifer according to their choice. (Moses 4:3; D. & C. 29:36-37.) It is by virtue of the exercise of agency in this life that men are enabled to undergo the testing which is an essential part of mortality. (Moses 3:17; 4:3; 7:32; Abra. 3:25-28.)

Four great principles must be in force if there is to be agency: 1. Laws must exist, laws ordained by an Omnipotent power, laws which can be obeyed or disobeyed; 2. Opposites must exist—good and evil, virtue and vice, right and wrong—that is, there must be an opposition, one force pulling one way and another pulling the other; 3. A knowledge of good and evil must be had by those who are to enjoy the agency, that is, they must know the difference between the opposites; and 4. An unfettered power of choice must prevail.

Agency is given to man as an essential part of the great plan of redemption. As with all things appertaining to this plan, it is based on the atoning sacrifice of Christ. As Lehi expressed it: *"Because that they are redeemed from the fall they have become free forever, knowing good from evil; to act for themselves* and not to be acted upon, save it be by the punishment of the law at the great and last day, according to the commandments which God hath given. Wherefore, *men are free according to the flesh;* and all things are given them which are expedient unto man. And *they are free to choose liberty and eternal life, through the great mediation of all men,* or to choose captivity and death, according to the captivity and power of the devil; for he seeketh that all men might be miserable like unto himself." (2 Ne. 2:26-30; 10:23; Alma 13:3; Hela. 14:31.)

Agency is so fundamental a part of the great plan of creation and redemption that if it should cease, all other things would vanish away.

"All truth is *independent* in that sphere in which God has placed it, *to act for itself,* as all intelligence also; *otherwise there is no existence."* (D. & C. 93:30.) Expanding and interpreting this revealed principle, Lehi said: *"It must needs be, that there is an opposition in all things. If not so, . . . righteousness could not be brought to pass, neither wickedness, neither holiness nor misery, neither good nor bad.* Wherefore, all things must needs be a compound in one; wherefore, if it should be one body it must needs remain as dead, having no life neither death, nor corruption nor incorruption, happiness nor misery, neither sense nor insensibility. Wherefore, it must needs have been created for a thing of naught; wherefore there would have been no purpose in the end of its creation. Wherefore, this thing must needs destroy the wisdom of God and his eternal purposes, and also the power, and the mercy, and the justice of God.

"And if ye shall say there is no law, ye shall also say there is no sin. If ye shall say there is no sin, ye shall also say there is no righteousness. And if there be no righteousness there be no happiness. And if there be no righteousness nor happiness there be no punishment nor misery. And if these things are not there is no God. And if there is no God we are not, neither the earth; for there could have been no creation of things, neither to act nor to be acted upon; where-

fore, all things must have vanished away." (2 Ne. 2:11-14; D. & C. 29:39.)

Agency is the philosophy of opposites, and because these opposites exist, men can reap either salvation or damnation by the use they make of their agency. If it were not for the law of agency, there could be no judgment according to works and consequently no rewards or punishments. "Choose ye this day, to serve the Lord God who made you" (Moses 6:33), is the voice of the Lord to all people of all ages. (Alma 30:8; Josh. 24:15.)

Satan "sought to destroy the agency of man" (Moses 4:3), an eventuality which would have made the attainment of salvation impossible, and accordingly he was cast out of heaven. Two great agencies on earth pattern their courses in accordance with Lucifer's program of compulsion and seek to deny the inalienable right of agency to men. These are the church of the devil and the communistic dictatorships, both of which prosper proportionately as they are able to withhold truth from their adherents and compel them through fear to conform to the "religious" and "party" lines. On the other hand, it is the will of the Lord that all agencies, governments included, should be so ordained "That every man may act in doctrine and principle pertaining to futurity, according to the moral agency which I have given unto him, *that every man may be accountable for his own sins in the day of judg-*

ment." (D. & C. 101:78.)

Churches which teach that men are predestined to gain salvation or damnation, according to the election of God, regardless of the acts of the individual, find no place in their theology for the true doctrine of agency. Their reasoning is to this effect: Why is there any need for agency, so as to be able to perform good works leading to salvation, if your salvation is determined by Deity on the basis of predestination regardless of works? Thus the false doctrine of predestination begets the false doctrine that men are not free to work out their own salvation, as such is made possible through the atoning sacrifice of Christ. The Church of England, for instance, in its Articles of Religion, under the heading of "Free Will," says: "The condition of Man after the fall of Adam is such, that he cannot turn and prepare himself, by his own natural strength and good works, to faith, and calling upon God: Wherefore we have no power to do good works pleasant and acceptable to God, without the grace of God by Christ preventing us, that we may have a good will, and working with us, when we have that good will." (*Book of Common Prayer,* p. 663.)

Agency, of course, is exercised in accordance with law. Once a *final* choice has been made, there is no turning back to seek the opposite goal. Men may exercise their agency to repent and turn to the Lord in this life, in which event they will be saved. But if they choose to rebel against the light and work wickedness, they will be damned. And once they are damned, there is no power of choice left whereby they can alter their course and gain salvation. If men choose to commit suicide, for instance, they will continue to have agency in hell, but they will not be able to use it to gain their lives back again. The purpose of this life is to test men, to see if they will take the bodies which have been given them, and by the righteous exercise of agency make those bodies fit abodes for the Spirit of God.

AGE OF ACCOUNTABILITY.
See YEARS OF ACCOUNTABILITY.

AGE OF RESTORATION.
See TIMES OF RESTITUTION.

AGNOSTICISM.
See APOSTASY, ATHEISM, GOD, INFIDELS. *Agnosticism* is the doctrine that God is not known and cannot be known. It is the concept that his existence can be neither proved nor disproved, and hence it neither affirms nor denies that existence. To the agnostics God is unknown and unknowable because they are unwilling to accept as proof the evidence of revelation and spiritual manifestations. Unless this is done no man can come to a knowledge of God, for "the things of God knoweth no man, but the

Spirit of God. . . . The natural man receiveth not the things of the Spirit of God: for they are foolishness unto him: neither can he know them, because they are spiritually discerned." (1 Cor. 2:11-14.) Similarly agnosticism rejects any knowledge about the ultimate origin of the universe.

From the gospel standpoint, agnostics are properly classified as being in opposition to the truth. However much they may claim to be neutral by neither affirming nor denying eternal truths, yet that very neutrality makes them enemies of God. In the ultimate analysis there is no such thing as neutrality. "He that is not with me is against me; and he that gathereth not with me scattereth abroad." (Matt. 12:30.)

AHMAN.

See GOD, MAN OF HOLINESS, SON OF MAN. In the pure language spoken by Adam—and which will be spoken again during the millennial era (Zeph. 3:9)—the name of God the Father is *Ahman,* or possibly *Ah Man,* a name-title having a meaning identical with or at least very closely akin to *Man of Holiness.* (Moses 6:57.) God revealed himself to Adam by this name to signify that he is a *Holy Man,* a truth which man must know and comprehend if he is to become like God and inherit exaltation. (1 John 3:1-3; D. & C. 132: 19-24.)

"There is one revelation," Orson Pratt said, "that this people are not generally acquainted with. I think it has never been published, but probably will be in the Church History. It is given in questions and answers. The first question is, 'What is the name of God in the pure language?' The answer says, '*Ahman.*' 'What is the name of the Son of God?' Answer, '*Son Ahman*—the greatest of all the parts of God excepting *Ahman.*' 'What is the name of men?' '*Sons Ahman,*' is the answer. 'What is the name of angels in the pure language?' '*Angloman.*'

"This revelation goes on to say that Sons Ahman are the greatest of all the parts of God excepting Son Ahman and Ahman, and that Angloman are the greatest of all the parts of God excepting Sons Ahman, Son Ahman and Ahman, showing that the angels are a little lower than man." (*Journal of Discourses,* vol. 2, p. 342.)

Since God revealed himself to Adam by certain names, we might suppose that those names, or variants of them, would be preserved among succeeding generations, even though people coming later developed false religions. It is, also, not uncommon for important names to be carried from one language to another by transliteration rather than translation. Hence, it is of more than passing interest to note that the Egyptians worshiped a deity, considered by them to be supreme, whose name bears a striking resemblance to that of the true

God, as his name was recorded in the Adamic language. The Egyptian deity *Ammon,* or *Amon,* or *Amen* (who corresponds to Zeus of the Greeks and Jupiter of the Romans) was first worshiped as the local deity of Thebes; he was shown as a ramheaded god of life and reproduction. Later, united with the sun-god to become a supreme deity, he was known as *Amen-Ra,* with the other gods as his members or parts.

It is also interesting to note that *Amen,* a transliterated word which is the same in Egyptian, Hebrew, Latin, Greek, Anglo-Saxon, and English, is one of the names of Christ. Speaking to John on the Isle of Patmos, our Lord said: "These things saith the Amen, the faithful and true witness, the beginning of the creation of God." (Rev. 3:14.)

ALCHEMY.
See MAGIC, OCCULTISM, SORCERY. *Alchemy* is the great medieval science which, bordering on magic and sorcery, had as its objectives to transmute base metals into gold, to discover the universal cure for diseases, and to prolong life indefinitely.

ALCOHOLIC BEVERAGES.
See STRONG DRINKS.

ALLELUIA.
See HALLELUJAH.

ALMIGHTY.
See ALMIGHTY GOD.

ALMIGHTY GOD.
See CHRIST, FATHER IN HEAVEN, GOD, LORD, LORD OMNIPOTENT, OMNIPOTENCE. Both the Father and the Son, being omnipotent Gods, are designated by the name-titles, *Almighty* (Gen. 49:25; Rev. 1:8; 2 Ne. 23:6; Hela. 10:11; D. & C. 84:96; 121:33), *Almighty God* (Gen. 17:1; 28:3; 1 Ne. 17:48; D. & C. 20:21; 87:6; 88:106), *Lord Almighty* (D. & C. 84:118; 2 Cor. 6:18), and *Lord God Almighty* (Rev. 4:8; 11:17; 21:22; D. & C. 109:77; 121:4; 1 Ne. 1:14; 2 Ne. 9:46.) These designations signify that these holy beings have all power and unlimited might. A deep sense of reverence is implicit in the use of each name-title.

ALMSGIVING.
See CHURCH WELFARE PLAN, DOLE, EMPLOYMENT, IDLENESS, WORK. *Almsgiving* is the contribution of free gifts to relieve the poor; the spirit that attends such a course is of God and finds its highest manifestation in the organized charitable enterprises of his earthly kingdom. Paul, for instance, in his day, carried alms to the poor saints in Jerusalem (Acts 24:17), he having first assembled the contributions from the saints in Macedonia and Achaia. (Acts 11:29; Rom. 15:25-28.) In modern times the major portion of the almsgiving of the saints is admin-

istered through the great Church Welfare Plan.

Giving alms is not an optional thing; it is a command of the Lord. (Luke 11:41; 12:31-34.) "Verily, verily, I say that *I would that ye should do alms unto the poor,"* our Lord said to his Nephite saints, "but take heed that ye do not your alms before men to be seen of them; otherwise ye have no reward of your Father who is in heaven. Therefore, when ye shall do your alms do not sound a trumpet before you, as will hypocrites do in the synagogues and in the streets, that they may have glory of men. Verily I say unto you, they have their reward. But when thou doest alms let not thy left hand know what thy right hand doeth; That thine alms may be in secret; and thy Father who seeth in secret, himself shall reward thee openly." (3 Ne. 13:1-4; Matt. 6:1-4.)

Prayers are answered for those who freely give alms to the poor, but the heavens are sealed where the petitions of those who do not give alms are concerned. *"If ye turn away the needy, and the naked, and visit not the sick and afflicted, and impart of your substance, if ye have, to those who stand in need—I say unto you, if ye do not any of these things, behold, your prayer is vain, and availeth you nothing, and ye are as hypocrites who do deny the faith."* (Alma 34:28; Acts 10; D. & C. 88:2; 112:1.)

ALPHA AND OMEGA.

See ALPHUS, BEGINNING AND END, CHRIST, ETERNITY TO ETERNITY, EVERLASTING TO EVERLASTING, FIRST AND LAST, OMEGUS. Christ bears the title *Alpha and Omega.* (D. & C. 19:1; 63:60; 68:35; 75:1; 81:7; 112:34; 132:66; Rev. 1:8-17; 21:6; 22:13.) These words, the first and last letters of the Greek alphabet, are used figuratively to teach the timelessness and eternal nature of our Lord's existence, that is, that "from eternity to eternity he is the same, and his years never fail." (D. & C. 76:4.)

ALPHUS.

See ALPHA AND OMEGA, CHRIST, OMEGUS. One of the name-titles of Christ is *Alphus* (D. & C. 95:17), a derivative of the Greek *Alpha*. Use of this title emphasizes our Lord's high status of godhood in pre-existence; he was God from eternity; by diligence and obedience, while yet a Spirit Being, he became "like unto God" the Father. (Abra. 3:22-24.)

ALTARS.

See SACRIFICES, TEMPLES. In the days when sacrifices were required as part of true divine worship, they were offered on raised earth or stone structures called *altars*. Noah (Gen. 8:20), Abraham (Gen. 12:7), and Lehi (1 Ne. 2:7), for instance, built altars and offered sacrifices upon them. Altars were also found in the temples and perhaps in other holy structures, at which God was

31

worshiped (Alma 15:17), and where the faithful came "to call on his name and confess their sins before him." (Alma 17:4.) Today, as anciently, temples contain altars at which sacred ordinances, including celestial marriage, are performed. John saw a "golden altar" in heaven before the throne of God. (Rev. 6:9; 8:3; 9:13.)

AMEN.

See AHMAN, CHRIST, PRAYER.
1. In Hebrew *amen* means *truly, certainly, faithfully;* in English it means *so be it;* and it has always had a distinctively religious usage. Saying *amen* is a proper means of making solemn affirmation (Rev. 1:18; 22:20); it is an utterance used in confirming agreements (1 Kings 1:36); prayers and sermons are properly so ended (Matt. 6:13); those who hear and concur in prayers and sermons should add their own *amen* (1 Cor. 14:16); indeed, by saying *amen* concurrence is given to any worshipful utterance, sermon, or solemn declaration. (D. & C. 88:135; Ps. 106:48; Rev. 5:13-14; 19:4.) There are about a score of instances in which the term is found in the Bible, nearly twice that many in the Book of Mormon, and nearly every revelation in the Doctrine and Covenants is so closed.

As a result of unrighteousness, it is "Amen to the priesthood" of a man, meaning that his priesthood comes to an end, as far as being a power which would assure the

bearer of eternal life is concerned. (D. & C. 121:33-46.)
2. One of Christ's names is *Amen* (Rev. 3:14), a title given to show that it is in and through him that the seal of divine affirmation is placed on all the promises of the Father.

AMERICA.

See AMERICAN INDIANS, CONSTITUTION OF THE UNITED STATES, INALIENABLE RIGHTS, SIGNS OF THE TIMES. *America,* meaning the United States of America, is the Gentile nation established on the Western Hemisphere in the last days "by the power of the Father," so that the true Church might be set up and preserved among men. The American nation as such—with all its freedoms, rights, and constitutional guarantees—came into being and continues to exist so that a proper religious climate would prevail for the restoration and spread of the gospel. (3 Ne. 21.)

AMERICAN INDIANS.

See BOOK OF MORMON, JAREDITES, JEWS, MEDICINE MEN, MULEKITES, NEPHITES AND LAMANITES, TRIBES OF ISRAEL. When Columbus discovered America, the native inhabitants, the *American Indians* as they were soon to be designated, were a people of mixed blood and origin. Chiefly they were Lamanites, but such remnants of the Nephite nation as had not been destroyed had, of course, mingled with the Lamanites. (1 Ne. 13:30; 2 Ne. 3:1-3; 9:53; Alma 45:13-14; D. & C. 3:16-19.) Thus the Indians were Jews by nationality (D. & C. 57:4), their forefathers having come out from Jerusalem, from the kingdom of Judah. (2 Ne. 33:8-10.)

Thus also they were of the House of Israel. Lehi was of the tribe of Manasseh (Alma 10:3), Ishmael of the tribe of Ephraim, and Mulek of the tribe of Judah. (Hela. 8:20-22.) We have no knowledge of the tribal affiliation of Zoram, and it is possible that other tribes may have been represented in the colony that accompanied Mulek. It was primarily the tribes of Benjamin and Judah which made up the kingdom of Judah, but there may have been a sprinkling of all the tribes intermingled with them.

The American Indians, however, as Columbus found them also had other blood than that of Israel in their veins. It is possible that isolated remnants of the Jaredites may have lived through the period of destruction in which millions of their fellows perished. It is quite apparent that groups of orientals found their way over the Bering Strait and gradually moved southward to mix with the Indian peoples. We have records of a colony of Scandinavians attempting to set up a settlement in America some 500 years before Columbus. There are archeological indications that an unspecified number of groups of people probably found their way from the old to the new world in pre-Columbian times. Out of all these groups would have come the American Indians as they were discovered in the 15th century.

Since the days of the Spanish conquests and colonizations of Mexico and South America, there has been further dilution of the pure Lamanitish blood. But with it all, for the great majority of the descendants of the original inhabitants of the Western Hemisphere, the dominant blood lineage is that of Israel. The Indians are repeatedly called Lamanites in the revelations to the Prophet, and the promise is that in due course they "shall blossom as the rose" (D. & C. 49:24), that is, become again a white and delightsome people as were their ancestors a great many generations ago.

AMUSEMENTS.
See RECREATION.

ANARCHY.
See SIGNS OF THE TIMES.

ANATHEMA.
See DAMNATION, EXCOMMUNICATION. *Anathema* is a Greek word meaning *accursed*. Hence, a person or thing cursed by God or his authority, as for instance one who has been excommunicated, is anathema. (Rom. 9:3.) "Wo unto them who are cut off from my church, for the

same are overcome of the world."
(D. & C. 50:8.)

Paul's statement, "If any man love not the Lord Jesus Christ, let him be *Anathema Maranatha"* (1 Cor. 16:22), probably means, ". . . let him be accursed until the Lord comes." *Maranatha,* an Aramaic word meaning, *O our Lord, come,* appears to have been used by the primitive saints as a watchword or salutation by which they reminded each other of the promised Second Coming. Paul's statement, "The Lord is at hand" (Philip. 4:5), and John's, "Even so, come, Lord Jesus" (Rev. 22:20), carry the same hope and encouragement.

ANATHEMA MARANATHA.
See ANATHEMA.

ANCESTORS.
See GENEALOGICAL RESEARCH.

ANCIENT OF DAYS.
See ADAM, ADAM-GOD THEORY, ADAM-ONDI-AHMAN, BIRTHRIGHT, MICHAEL THE ARCHANGEL, PATRIARCHAL ORDER. Having particular reference to his position as the patriarchal head of the human family —the first man, "the first and oldest of all, the great, grand progenitor"— Adam is known as the *Ancient of Days.* (D. & C. 27:11; *Teachings,* pp. 157-159, 167-169.) In this capacity he will yet sit in formal judgment upon "ten thousand times ten

thousand" of his posterity, and before him at Adam-ondi-Ahman will be brought the Son of Man to receive "dominion, and glory, and a kingdom, that all people, nations, and languages, should serve him." (Dan. 7:9-14.)

ANGEL.
See CHRIST, MESSENGER OF SALVATION, MESSENGER OF THE COVENANT. Our Lord is called *The Angel* by Jacob in the blessing which he gave to Ephraim and Manasseh. "God, before whom my fathers Abraham and Isaac did walk, the God which fed me all my life long unto this day, *The Angel* which redeemed me from all evil, bless the lads," he said. (Gen. 48: 15-16.) The Inspired Version makes no change in this statement, although a number of other matters in connection with the same occurrences are changed in that more perfect version. Obviously the meaning is that Christ is the *Messenger of Salvation, the Messenger of the Covenant* (Mal. 3:1), *the One carrying out his Father's will.* (Moses 4:2.)

It may be that the King James translators were attempting to use language in the same way when they recorded the experience of Moses at the burning bush in these words: "And *the angel* of the Lord appeared unto him in a flame of fire out of the midst of a bush. . . . And . . . God called unto him out of the midst of the bush, and said,

... I am the God of thy father, the God of Abraham, the God of Isaac, and the God of Jacob." (Ex. 3:2-6.)

It was not an angel in the usual sense of the word but the Lord Jesus who appeared to Moses in the bush. The passage is more meaningful if the term *The Angel* is interpreted in the same sense in which Jacob used it. In this instance the Inspired Version concurs by changing the account to read, "The *presence of the Lord* appeared unto him, in a flame of fire in the midst of a bush" (*Inspired Version,* Ex. 3:2), thus showing that what the King James Version calls *The Angel* is *The Lord.*

ANGEL OF LIGHT.
See DEVIL.

ANGEL OF THE BOTTOMLESS PIT.
See BOTTOMLESS PIT, DEVIL. John used this expressive language, *angel of the bottomless pit,* to describe Satan, having particular reference to his status as the *king of hell,* the ruling authority over those cast into the pit which is hell. (Rev. 9:11.)

ANGELS.
See ANGEL, ANGEL OF THE BOTTOMLESS PIT, ANGLO-MAN, ARCHANGELS, GUARDIAN ANGELS, KEYS OF THE MINISTERING OF ANGELS, MICHAEL THE ARCHANGEL, MINISTERING OF ANGELS, PLURALITY OF GODS, PRE-EXISTENCE, RECORDING ANGELS, RESURRECTION, SERVANTS OF GOD, SPIRIT CHILDREN, TRANSLATED BEINGS. God's messengers, those individuals whom he sends (often from his personal presence in the eternal worlds), to deliver his messages (Luke 1:11-38); to minister to his children (Acts 10:1-8, 30-32); to teach them the doctrines of salvation (Mosiah 3); to call them to repentance (Moro. 7:31); to give them priesthood and keys (D. & C. 13; 128:20-21); to save them in perilous circumstances (1 Ne. 3:29-31; Dan. 6:22); to guide them in the performance of his work (Gen. 24:7); to gather his elect in the last days (Matt. 24:31); to perform all needful things relative to his work (Moro. 7:29-33)—such messengers are called *angels.*

These messengers, agents, angels of the Almighty, are chosen from among his offspring and are themselves pressing forward along the course of progression and salvation, all in their respective spheres. The following types of beings serve the Lord as angels:

1. *Pre-existent Spirits.*—Before men were first placed on this earth, there was war in heaven. "Michael and his *angels* fought against the dragon; and the dragon fought and his angels." (Rev. 12:7.) All the angels here involved were the spirit children of the Father. The angel who appeared to Adam, the first man, and asked him why he was offering sacrifices apparently was one of these spirits from pre-exist-

35

ence (Moses 5:6-8), for no angels minister to this earth except those who belong to it (D. & C. 130:5), and up to that time no one had been either translated or resurrected.

2. *Translated Beings.*—Many righteous persons in the early days of the earth's history were translated. (*Inspired Version,* Gen. 14:26-36.) Enoch and the whole city of Zion were among these. (Moses 7:18-69.) These translated personages became "ministering *angels* unto many planets." (*Teachings,* p. 170.) Many of the angels who ministered to righteous men anciently, without question, were translated beings. The Three Nephites, after their translation, became "as the angels of God" (3 Ne. 28:30), and have continued to minister and appear unto mortal men from time to time. John the Revelator ministered as a translated being to the Prophet and Oliver Cowdery in connection with the restoration of the Melchizedek Priesthood. (D. & C. 7; 27:12-13.) It could well be that Paul had translated beings in mind when he said that "some have entertained angels unawares." (Heb. 13:2.)

3. *Spirits of Just Men Made Perfect.*—Part of the "innumerable company of *angels*" in "the heavenly place" are the "spirits of just men made perfect." (D. & C. 76:66-69; Heb. 12:22-24.) These are the spirits of men who have worked out their salvation, but are awaiting the day of the resurrection. (D. & C. 129.)

4. *Resurrected Personages.*—Many instances of ministration by resurrected *angels* have occurred since the coming forth of our Lord from the tomb. (Matt. 27:52-53; Hela. 14:25.) These angels, having bodies of flesh and bones (D. & C. 129), have played an indispensable part in the restoration of the gospel. Peter, James (D. & C. 27:12-13; 128:20), John the Baptist (D. & C. 13), Moroni, Michael, Gabriel, Raphael (D. & C. 128:20-21), Moses, Elijah, and Elias (D. & C. 110:11-16; 133:54-55) all came to earth as resurrected personages to confer their keys, powers, and authorities again upon men. Moses and Elijah, who in the first instance had been translated, "were with Christ in his resurrection." (D. & C. 133:55.)

It is of these angels, and others of like righteousness, that the revelation says: "Then shall the angels be crowned with the glory of his might, and the saints shall be filled with his glory, and receive their inheritance and be made equal with him" (D. & C. 88:107), meaning that these worthy saints and angels shall receive exaltation. They shall be gods. But those angels who did not abide in the fulness of the gospel law shall, after their resurrection, continue as "angels of God forever and ever." Such group shall be "ministering servants, to minister for those who are worthy of a far more, and an exceeding, and an eternal weight of glory." (D. & C. 132:16-17.)

5. *Righteous Mortal Men.*—Even certain righteous mortal men are called *angels* in the revelations.

36

The King James Version gives an account of "two angels" rescuing Lot from Sodom. In the account these angels are called "men" and the wicked inhabitants of Sodom so considered them. (Gen. 19.) The Inspired Version tells us that actually there were "three angels," and that these "angels of God" in reality "were holy men." (*Inspired Version,* Gen. 19.)

Also in the King James Version, the Lord is quoted as saying such things as, "Unto the *angel* of the church of Ephesus write" (Rev. 2:1) such and such, meaning that the message should be written to the bishop or presiding elder, such individual being designated as an angel. (Rev. 2:8, 12, 18; 3:1, 7, 14.) In the Inspired Version this rather unusual usage of the name angel is changed so that the quotation reads, "Unto the *servant* of the church of Ephesus write." (*Inspired Version,* Rev. 2:1, 8, 12, 18; 3:1, 7, 14.) This inspired rendition more accurately accords with the manner in which we ordinarily use words today.

ANGELS OF THE DEVIL.
See DEVILS.

ANGEL'S TIME.
See TIME.

ANGER.
See GNASHING OF TEETH, INDIGNATION, WRATH. As with nearly all strong emotions or passions, *anger* is manifest both in righteousness and in unrighteousness. Always there is a sense of displeasure attending it, and usually this is accompanied by a feeling of antagonism, excited by a sense of injury or insult.

Righteous anger is an attribute of Deity. His anger is everlastingly kindled against the wicked. (D. & C. 1:13; 5:8; 60:2; 63:11, 32; 84:24.) Similarly, an inspired man might speak or act in righteous anger, as when Moses broke the tablets upon which the Ten Commandments were written, or as when our Lord drove the money changers from the temple.

But where man is concerned there is peril in anger, and the fear is ever present that the emotion and passion attending it will be exercised in unrighteousness. *"Can ye be angry, and not sin?"* Paul asked. (*Inspired Version,* Eph. 4:26.) "Whosoever is angry with his brother *without a cause,"* our Lord said in the Sermon on the Mount, "shall be in danger of the judgment." (Matt. 5:22.)

ANGLO-MAN.
See AHMAN, ANGELS. Because angels are of the same race as man and God, it is with perfect logic that in the pure language spoken by Adam, they were designated as *Anglo-man.* This is in harmony with the Adamic designation of God as *Ahman,* of the Son as *Son Ah-*

man, and of men generally as *Sons Ahman.*

ANGUISH.

See CONSCIENCE, HELL, REMORSE, SORROW. Both the righteous and the wicked suffer *anguish* of soul, meaning excruciating distress and extreme pain of body and mind. The righteous suffer anguish in this life because of the sins and rebellion of their brethren. (1 Ne. 17:47; 2 Ne. 26:7; Mosiah 25:11; Alma 8:14; Morm. 6:16.) Christ himself suffered until blood came from every pore, so great was "his anguish for the wickedness and the abominations of his people." (Mosiah 3:7.)

The wicked and rebellious may suffer some anguish of conscience in this life (Alma 38:8; D. & C. 124:52), but the great penalty for their rebellion is in the future. Of such a person, King Benjamin said: "If that man repenteth not, and remaineth and dieth an enemy to God, the demands of divine justice do awaken his immortal soul to a *lively sense of his own guilt,* which doth cause him to shrink from the presence of the Lord, and doth fill his breast with guilt, and pain, and anguish, which is like an unquenchable fire, whose flame ascendeth up forever and ever." (Mosiah 2:38; Rom. 2:9.)

ANIMAL MAGNETISM.
See SPIRITUALISM.

ANIMALS.

See CREATION, EVOLUTION, PRE-EXISTENCE, RESURRECTION. *Animals,* birds, fowls, fishes, plants, and all forms of life occupy an assigned sphere and play an eternal role in the great plan of creation, redemption, and salvation. They were all created as spirit entities in pre-existence. (Moses 3:1-9.) When first placed on earth in the Garden of Eden, they were immortal. The revealed record, speaking of the edenic day, specifies: "All things which were created must have remained in the same state in which they were after they were created; and they must have remained forever, and had no end." (2 Ne. 2:22.) Such would have been the continuing condition had there been no fall of Adam, but Adam and all forms of life were subject to the fall and have been living on earth in their mortal states ever since.

At the Second Coming, when the earth is taken back to its edenic state, "every corruptible thing, both of *man,* or of the *beasts* of the field, or of the *fowls* of the heavens, or of the *fish* of the sea, that dwells upon all the face of the earth, shall be consumed. . . . And in that day the enmity of man, and the enmity of beasts, yea, the enmity of all flesh, shall cease from before my face." (D. & C. 101:24-26.) Then finally, all these forms of life will come up in the resurrection, "in their destined order or sphere of creation, in the enjoyment of their eternal felicity." (D. & C. 77:3.)

ANIMAL SACRIFICES.
See SACRIFICES.

ANNIHILATION.
See CREATION, DEATH, ELEMENTS, SPIRIT ELEMENT. There is no such thing as *annihilation,* no such thing as matter or element of any sort going out of existence. The elements are eternal; they may be organized and reorganized, but they cannot be destroyed. (D. & C. 93:33; *Teachings,* pp. 350-352.)

ANNUNCIATION.
See CHRIST, MARY, VIRGIN BIRTH. Gabriel's appearance to Mary to make solemn announcement of the coming birth of our Lord is referred to as the *Annunciation.* (Luke 1:26-38.)

ANOINTED ONE.
See CHRIST, MESSIAH. Literally interpreted the Hebrew *Messiah* means *Anointed One,* and accordingly Christ is the Anointed One. (Ps. 2; Acts 4:23-30.) He was the Anointed of the Father to carry the eternal truths of salvation to the living and the dead. (Isa. 61:1-3; Luke 4:16-32; Acts 10:38.)

ANOINTINGS.
See TEMPLE ORDINANCES.

ANOINTING WITH OIL.
See ADMINISTRATIONS.

ANTHEMS.
See MUSIC.

ANTHROPOMORPHIC GOD.
See GOD. Strictly speaking *anthropomorphism* is the conception that God has human attributes and characteristics; hence, people who profess to worship a personal God are sometimes said to believe in an *anthropomorphic God.* Actually, of course, man was created in God's image, not God in man's. But since man is the inheritor of the physical form and, to some extent, the attributes and characteristics of Deity, it follows that Deity has the same form and the fulness of the attributes enjoyed by men, and so in a rather inaccurate sense it may be agreed that the true God is an anthropomorphic Being.

ANTHROPOMORPHISM.
See ANTHROPOMORPHIC GOD.

ANTICHRISTS.
See APOSTASY, CHRIST, CHURCH OF THE DEVIL, DEVIL, FALSE CHRISTS, MAN OF SIN. An *antichrist* is an opponent of Christ; he is one who is in opposition to the true gospel, the true Church, and the true plan of salvation. (1 John

2:19; 4:4-6.) He is one who offers salvation to men on some other terms than those laid down by Christ. Sherem (Jac. 7:1-23), Nehor (Alma 1:2-16), and Korihor (Alma 30:6-60) were antichrists who spread their delusions among the Nephites.

"Many deceivers are entered into the world, who confess not that Jesus Christ is come in the flesh. This is a deceiver and an antichrist." (2 John 7.) "Who is a liar but he that denieth that Jesus is the Christ?" John asked. *"He is an antichrist, that denieth the Father and the Son."* (1 John 2:22.) Though many modern day religionists profess to believe in Christ, the fact is they do not accept him as the literal Son of God and have not turned to him with the full knowledge and devotion necessary to gain salvation. "Whosoever receiveth my word receiveth me," he said, "and *whosoever receiveth me, receiveth those, the First Presidency, whom I have sent,* whom I have made counselors for my name's sake unto you." (D. & C. 112:20.)

The saints in the meridian of time, knowing there would be a great apostasy between their day and the Second Coming of our Lord, referred to the great apostate church as the anti-christ. "Little children, it is the last time," John said, "and as ye have heard that antichrist shall come, even now are there many antichrists; whereby we know that it is the last time." (1 John 2:18.) "And every spirit that confesseth not that Jesus Christ is come in the flesh is not of God: and this is that spirit of antichrist, whereof ye have heard that it should come; and even now already is it in the world." (1 John 4:3.) This great antichrist which is to stand as the antagonist of Christ in the last days, and which is to be overthrown when he comes to cleanse the earth and usher in millennial righteousness, is the church of the devil (Rev. 13; 17), with the man of sin at its head. (2 Thess. 2:1-12.)

APOCALYPSE.
See BIBLE, ESCHATOLOGY, REVELATION. Anything viewed as a prophetic revelation is an *apocalypse.* The name comes from a Greek word meaning *revelations;* the book of Revelation in the Bible is called the *Apocalypse.* Much apocalyptic literature is also found in other parts of the Bible as well as in all of the standard works of the Church.

Uninspired scholars theorize that apocalyptic writings are attempts on the part of the prophets to escape from reality, to hold out future and ethereal hopes of better things to people who are presently bound down by the turmoil and strife of this life. Actually, of course, these so-called apocalyptic records are not hidden from the understanding of those who have the same spirit of revelation which rested upon the original prophets. (2 Pet. 1:20-21.) They are part of the Lord's revelation of his eternal plan of salvation.

APOCRYPHA.

See BIBLE, CANON OF SCRIP-
TURE, INSPIRED VERSION OF THE
BIBLE, KING JAMES VERSION OF
THE BIBLE, LOST SCRIPTURE, NEW
TESTAMENT, OLD TESTAMENT,
SCRIPTURE, STANDARD WORKS.
Scholars and Biblical students have
grouped certain apparently scriptural Old Testament writings,
which they deem to be of doubtful
authenticity or of a spurious nature, under the title of the *Apocrypha*. There has not always been
agreement as to the specific writings which should be designated
as apocryphal, but the following
are now generally so listed: 1st
and 2nd Esdras (sometimes called
3rd and 4th Esdras, because in
the Douay Bible, Ezra is 1st Esdras, and Nehemiah, 2nd Esdras);
Tobit; Judith; the rest of the chapters of Esther; Wisdom of Solomon;
Wisdom of Jesus the Son of Sirach
or Ecclesiasticus; Baruch and the
Epistle of Jeremiah; additional parts
of Daniel, including the Song of the
Three Holy Children, the History of
Susanna, and the History of the
Destruction of Bel and the Dragon;
Prayer of Manasses; 1st and 2nd
Maccabees (called in the Douay
Version, 1st and 2nd Machabees).

These apocryphal writings were
never included in the Hebrew Bible,
but they were in the Greek Septuagint (the Old Testament used by
the early apostles) and in the Latin
Vulgate. Jerome, who translated the
Vulgate, was required to include
them in his translation, though he
is quoted as having decided they
should be read "for example of life
and instruction of manners" and
should not be used "to establish
any doctrine." Luther's German
Bible grouped the apocryphal books
together (omitting 1st and 2nd Esdras) at the end of the Old Testament under the heading: "Apocrypha: these are books which are
not held equal to the sacred scriptures, and yet are useful and good
for reading."

The Apocrypha was included in
the King James Version of 1611, but
by 1629 some English Bibles began
to appear without it, and since the
early part of the 19th century it has
been excluded from almost all protestant Bibles. The American Bible
Society, founded in 1816, has never
printed the Apocrypha in its Bibles,
and the British and Foreign Bible
Society has excluded it from all but
some pulpit Bibles since 1827.

From these dates it is apparent
that controversy was still raging as
to the value of the Apocrypha at the
time the Prophet began his ministry.
Accordingly, in 1833, while engaged
in revising the King James Version
by the spirit of revelation, the
Prophet felt impelled to inquire of
the Lord as to the authenticity of
the Apocrypha. From the answer it
is clear that the books of the Apocrypha were inspired writings in the
first instance, but that subsequent
interpolations and changes had perverted and twisted their original

contexts so as to leave them with doubtful value.

Speaking of the Apocrypha the Lord says: "There are many things contained therein that are true, and it is mostly translated correctly; There are many things contained therein that are not true, which are interpolations by the hands of men. Verily, I say unto you, that it is not needful that the Apocrypha should be translated. Therefore, whoso readeth it, let him understand, for the Spirit manifesteth truth; And whoso is enlightened by the Spirit shall obtain benefit therefrom; And whoso receiveth not by the Spirit, cannot be benefited. Therefore it is not needful that it should be translated." (D. & C. 91.)

There are certain Oriental Christian churches which have in their Bibles or other ecclesiastical literature some added apocryphal writings of Jewish origin. These books are supposed to have been written between 200 B.C. and 100 A.D. Those written in *Hebrew* are: Testaments of the Twelve Patriarchs, Psalms of Solomon, Lives of the Prophets. Those written in *Aramaic* are: Jubilees, Testament of Job, Enoch, Martyrdom of Isaiah, Paralipomena of Jeremiah, Life of Adam and Eve, Assumption of Moses, Syriac Baruch, Apocalypse of Abraham. Those written in *Greek* are: Letter of Aristeas, Sibylline Oracles three, four, and five; 3rd and 4th Maccabees, Slavic Enoch, Greek Baruch.

Obviously, *to gain any real value from a study of apocryphal writings, the student must first have an extended background of gospel knowledge, a comprehensive understanding of the standard works of the Church, plus the guidance of the Spirit.*

APOLLYON.

See ABADDON, DESTROYER, DEVIL. This is one of the names of Satan. It is of Greek origin and means literally *the Destroyer*. *Abaddon* is the Hebrew equivalent. (Rev. 9:11.)

APOSTASY.

See ABOMINATIONS, AGNOSTICISM, ANATHEMA, ANTICHRISTS, ATHEISM, BLASPHEMY, BROADMINDEDNESS, CARD PLAYING, CELIBACY, CHRISTENDOM, CHRISTENING, CHRISTIANITY, CHRISTMAS, CHURCH OF THE DEVIL, CLINIC BAPTISMS, CREEDS, DAMNATION, DARK AGES, DARKNESS, DEVIL, DOCTRINE, EASTER, EUCHRIST, EVOLUTION, EXCOMMUNICATION, EXTREME UNCTION, FALLEN MAN, FALSE CHRISTS, FALSE GODS, GAMBLING, GNOSTICISM, GOD AS A SPIRIT, GOSPEL, GOSPEL HOBBIES, GOVERNMENT OF GOD, HELL, HERESY, IDOLATRY, IGNORANCE, INFANT BAPTISM, INQUISITIONS, KINGCRAFT, MAN OF SIN, MINISTERIAL TITLES, MURDERERS, MYTHOLOGY, OBEDIENCE, PERSECUTION, PHILOSOPHY, POLYTHEISM, PRIESTCRAFT,

PROFANITY, REBELLION, RELIGIOUS SYNCRETISM, REORGANIZED CHURCH OF JESUS CHRIST OF LATTER DAY SAINTS, RESTORATION OF THE GOSPEL, RIGHTEOUSNESS, SCATTERING OF ISRAEL, SECOND COMING OF CHRIST, SECRET COMBINATIONS, SEX IMMORALITY, SHRINES, SIGN OF THE CROSS, SIGNS OF THE TIMES, SIN, SONS OF PERDITION, SORCERY, SPIRITUALISM, TELESTIAL LAW, TEMPTATION, UNKNOWN GOD, WAR, WICKEDNESS, WITCHCRAFT, WORSHIP OF IMAGES. From Adam to the present, the whole history of the world has been one recurring instance of personal and group *apostasy* after another. To Adam the Lord gave the true gospel and the true government so that all matters pertaining to this mortal sphere could be governed and arranged in harmony with the order of heaven. Apostasy consists in the abandonment and forsaking of these true principles, and all those who do not believe and conform to them are in a apostate condition, whether they are the ones who departed from the truth or whether they inherited their false concepts from their apostate fathers.

Apostate peoples were swept off the earth by the universal flood in Noah's day, but immediately the process of apostatizing began again, and soon there were apostate individuals, groups, peoples, nations, and religions. The Lord's handdealings with men have always been designed to keep the faithful from the treason of apostasy and to encourage those who do not have the fulness of truth to come to the light and reap the blessings of obedience.

Blessings have always attended conformity to true principles, while cursings have been the fruit of apostasy. The scattering of Israel, for example, took place because that people forsook their God and the true principles he had revealed to them. Their gathering takes place as they return to him and begin to live his laws. (Jer. 16:10-21.)

In the meridian of time our Lord personally restored his gospel and, through the ministry of his apostolic witnesses, offered its saving truths to all men. (Mark 1:14-15; 16:14-18.) He did not, however, restore the true order of political government; that was reserved for a future millennial era. (Acts 1:6-8.) Consequently men remained in subjection to man-made governments, but had the opportunity to accept the saving truths of pure religion. The great apostasy which is of importance and concern to men in this day is the one which took place when men departed from the pure Christianity which was restored in the meridian of time.

This universal apostasy began in the days of the ancient apostles themselves (2 Pet. 2:1-2); and it was known to and foretold by them. Paul recorded specifically that the Second Coming would not be until this great falling away took place. (2 Thess. 2:1-12.) He warned of the "perilous times" that should come "in the last days"; times when men would have "a form of godliness," but would deny "the power thereof"; times when they would be "Ever learning, and never able to come to the knowledge of the truth" (2 Tim. 3:1-7); times in which they would be turned "from the truth . . . unto fables." (2 Tim. 4:1-4.) Our Lord foretold the perplexities, calamities, and apostate wickedness of these same days. (Matt. 24; Mark 13; Luke 21.)

With the loss of the gospel, the nations of the earth went into a moral eclipse called the Dark Ages. Apostasy was universal. "Darkness covereth the earth, and gross darkness the minds of the people, and all flesh has become corrupt before my face." (D. & C. 112:23.) And this darkness still prevails except among those who have come to a knowledge of the restored gospel. (*Doctrines of Salvation*, vol. 3, pp. 265-326.)

No better descriptions are to be found of the conditions of false latter-day churches than those recorded prophetically by Nephite prophets. Nephi said: "In the last days, or in the days of the Gentiles —yea, behold *all the nations* of the Gentiles and also the Jews, both those who shall come upon this land and those who shall be upon other lands, yea, even upon all the lands of the earth, behold, they *will be drunken with iniquity and all manner of abominations.*" (2 Ne. 27: 1.) He spoke in detail of the many churches; of their pride, worldly learning, and denial of miracles; of their "envyings, and strifes, and malice"; of the secret combinations of the devil which commit murders and iniquities; of their priestcrafts and iniquities (2 Ne. 26:20-29); of the ministers who "shall teach with their learning, and deny the Holy Ghost, which giveth utterance"; and of their "false and vain and foolish doctrines." (2 Ne. 28.)

Moroni described the direful apostasy that would prevail in the day of the coming forth of the Book of Mormon. That volume "shall come in a day," he said, "when the power of God shall be denied, and *churches become defiled and be lifted up in the pride of their hearts;* yea, even in a day when leaders of churches and teachers shall rise in the pride of their hearts, even to the envying of them who belong to their churches. . . . Yea, it shall come in a day when *there shall be great pollutions upon the face of the earth; there shall be murders, and robbing, and lying, and deceivings, and whoredoms, and all manner of abominations;* when there shall be many who will say, Do this, or do that, and it mattereth not, for the Lord will uphold such at the last day. But wo unto such, for they are in the gall of bitterness and in the bonds of iniquity. Yea, it shall come in a day when *there shall be churches built up that shall say: Come unto me, and for your money you shall be forgiven of your sins.*

"O ye wicked and perverse and stiffnecked people, why have ye built up churches unto yourselves to get gain? Why have ye transfigured the holy word of God, that ye might bring damnation upon your souls? ... *Your churches, yea, even every one, have become polluted because of the pride of your hearts.* For behold, ye do love money, and your substance, and your fine apparel, and the adorning of your churches, more than ye love the poor and the needy, the sick and the afflicted. *O ye pollutions, ye hypocrites, ye teachers, who sell yourselves for that which will canker, why have ye polluted the holy church of God?* Why are ye ashamed to take upon you the name of Christ? Why do ye not think that greater is the value of an endless happiness than that misery which never dies—because of the praise of the world? Why do ye adorn yourselves with that which hath no life, and yet suffer the hungry, and the needy, and the naked, and the sick and the afflicted to pass by you, and notice them not? Yea, why do ye build up your secret abominations to get gain, and cause that widows should mourn before the Lord, and also orphans to mourn before the Lord, and also the blood of their fathers and their husbands to cry unto the Lord from the ground, for vengeance upon your heads?" (Morm. 8:28-41.)

To the extent that worldliness, false doctrine, and iniquity are found among the saints, they too partake of the spirit of the great apostasy. Speaking of men in the last days Nephi said: "They have all gone astray save it be a few, who are the humble followers of Christ; nevertheless, *they are led, that in many instances they do err because they are taught by the precepts of men.*" (2 Ne. 28:14.) It follows that if members of the Church believe false doctrines; if they accept false educational theories; if they fall into the practices and abominations of the sectarians; if they use tea, coffee, tobacco or liquor; if they fail to pay an honest tithing; if they find fault with the Lord's anointed; if they play cards; if they do anything contrary to the standards of personal righteousness required by the gospel—then to that extent they are in personal apostasy and need to repent.

Since truth is always in harmony with itself, and since all true saints "speak the same thing," have "no divisions" among them, and are "perfectly joined together in the same mind and in the same judgment" (1 Cor. 1:10-13), it follows that where there are divisions and contention there apostasy is present.

If modern churches do not conform to the New Testament pattern of the true Church, then the nonconforming organizations are apostate. This simple test of the authenticity of any church claiming to be the Lord's may be made by finding answer to such questions as: Where is there a church that has (according to the New Testament pattern) some combination of the names of Christ as its name?

Where is there a church claiming to have priesthood of both the Aaronic and Melchizedek orders, as set forth in the New Testament? Where are there apostles, prophets, seventies, and all the officers put in the Church by our Lord? Where do we find all of the gospel ordinances, among others—baptism for the dead, the laying on of hands for the gift of the Holy Ghost, and administering to the sick?

Where are the true New Testament doctrines taught: That the plan of salvation consists in faith, repentance, baptism, gaining the gift of the Holy Ghost, and enduring in good works to the end; that there are degrees of glory in the eternal worlds; that the gospel is preached in the spirit world; that there was to be a universal apostasy, followed by an era of restoration; that the gospel was to be returned to earth by angelic ministration; that Israel was to be gathered in a day subsequent to New Testament times; and so forth? Where are all these New Testament doctrines taught? And above all, where are the gifts of the Spirit, the signs, visions, miracles, and marvelous works that, without respect of persons, "shall follow them that believe"? (Mark 16:17.) For those who are honest and sincere in their search, it is not difficult to find out whether there has been a universal apostasy, and if so, where the truth is today.

APOSTATE CULTS.

See SECTS.

APOSTATES.
See APOSTASY.

APOSTLE.
See APOSTLES, CHRIST. Christ is the great *Apostle* of the Church. (Heb. 3:1.) This means, not that he held the ordained office of apostle in the Melchizedek Priesthood, but that he himself stands as a special witness of his own divine mission. "I am the Son of God" is the witness he bears of himself. (John 10: 36; D. & C. 45:52.)

APOSTLES.
See APOSTOLIC FATHERS, APOSTOLIC SUCCESSION, DISCIPLES, JUDGES, MELCHIZEDEK PRIESTHOOD, PRIESTHOOD, PRIESTHOOD OFFICES, PROPHETS, TESTIMONY. 1. An *apostle* is a special witness of the name of Christ who is sent to teach the principles of salvation to others. He is one who knows of the divinity of the Savior by personal revelation and who is appointed to bear testimony to the world of what the Lord has revealed to him. *Every elder in the Church is or should be an apostle;* that is, as a minister of the Lord and as a recipient of personal revelation from the Holy Ghost, every elder has the call to bear witness of the truth on all proper occasions. Indeed, *every member of the Church should have*

apostolic insight and revelation, and is under obligation to raise the warning voice. (D. & C. 88:81; Mosiah 18:9.)

In September, 1832, (nearly two and a half years before there were any ordained apostles in the Church) the Lord said to certain missionaries: "You are mine apostles, even God's high priests." (D. & C. 84:63-64.) In fact, Joseph Smith became an apostle in the spring of 1820, as a result of the First Vision, even before priesthood was conferred upon him through the ministration of Peter, James, and John; and after the Church was established, the Lord ordained (*meaning decreed*) that he continue to serve in this high apostolic station. (D. & C. 20:1-4; 21:1; 27:12; *Doctrines of Salvation,* vol. 3, pp. 144-149.)

Men are saved by giving heed to the words of the prophets and apostles sent among them and are damned for failure to heed the inspired testimony. (D. & C. 1:14.) And as with nearly all things, the devil offers a spurious substitute to deceive men. These "are false apostles, deceitful workers, transforming themselves into the apostles of Christ." (2 Cor. 11:13.) But faithful members of the Church have the assurance that they shall sit in judgment, "And liars and hypocrites shall be proved by them, and they who are not apostles and prophets shall be known." (D. & C. 64:37-39; Rev. 2:2.)

2. In the ordained sense, an apostle is one who is ordained to the office of apostle in the Melchizedek Priesthood. Ordinarily those so ordained are also set apart as members of the Council of the Twelve and are given all of the keys of the kingdom of God on earth. This apostleship carries the responsibility of proclaiming the gospel in all the world and also of administering the affairs of the Church. Christ "chose twelve, whom also he named apostles" (Luke 6:13), and upon their shoulders the burden of the kingdom rested after he ascended to his Father. (1 Cor. 12:28.) The original Twelve in latter-days were selected by revelation by the Three Witnesses to the Book of Mormon. (D. & C. 18:26-47.)

The Twelve Disciples among the Nephites ministered in an ordained apostolic capacity. (3 Ne. 18; 19; 27; 28.) In writing about the Book of Mormon, the Prophet said that it "tells us that our Savior made his appearance upon this continent after his resurrection; that he planted the gospel here in all its fulness, and richness, and power, and blessing; that they had *apostles,* prophets, pastors, teachers, and evangelists; the same order, the same priesthood, the same ordinances, gifts, powers, and blessings as were enjoyed on the eastern continent." (*History of the Church,* vol. 4, p. 538.)

APOSTLES CREED.

See APOSTASY, ATHANASIAN CREED, CREEDS, NICENE CREED.

According to tradition—the source of authority for so many false doctrinal and historical conclusions for which there is neither evidence nor proof—this creed dates back to apostolic times. The legend is that it was formulated by the Twelve Apostles "on the day of Pentecost, while still under the direct inspiration of the Holy Ghost," each of the group contributing to the final result. As to the actual origin of the creed, however, some Catholic historians trace it to a baptismal confession in use in Southern Gaul not earlier than the latter part of the 5th century. Others claim to find indications that an older form of the creed was in use in Rome as early as the middle of the 2nd century.

The creed professes to recite briefly "the fundamental tenets of Christian belief." There have been many versions in many places, all differing somewhat from each other. (*Catholic Encyclopedia,* vol. 1, pp. 629-632.) The modern version, as published in Catholic manuals of devotion is:

"I believe in God, the Father Almighty, Creator of heaven and earth; and in Jesus Christ, His only Son, our Lord, who was conceived by the Holy Ghost, born of the Virgin Mary, suffered under Pontius Pilate, was crucified, died, and was buried, He descended into hell; the third day He rose again from the dead; He ascended into heaven, sitteth at the right hand of God, the Father Almighty; from thence He shall come to judge the living and the dead I believe in the Holy Ghost; the Holy Catholic Church; the communion of Saints; the forgiveness of sins; the resurrection of the body; the life everlasting. Amen."

APOSTLESHIP.
See APOSTLES.

APOSTOLIC DISPENSATION.
See DISPENSATIONS.

APOSTOLIC FATHERS.
See APOSTASY, APOSTLES, APOSTOLIC SUCCESSION, SCRIPTURE, STANDARD WORKS. Those religious writers who followed closely on the heels of the early apostles are called the *apostolic fathers.* They did not write by way of revelation or commandment, as the apostles did, and their writings are not scripture. But because they had opportunity to record their views on church government, organization, and doctrine in a day when the apostasy was not yet complete, such views are of real value in the study of primitive Christianity.

"In addition to the New Testament books, a certain number of writings of the first two hundred years of the Christian Era of authors who had known the apostles, the 'Church Fathers,' have survived. They include (1) The Letter of Clement of Rome, anonymous, but attributed to Clement, written about

96 A.D.; (2) The Letters of Ignatius of Antioch, martyred, according to Eusebius, 108 A.D., in Rome; (3) The Teachings of the Twelve or the Didache, anonymous, discovered by Bryennios in 1875 in the Patriarchal Library of Jerusalem at Constantinople; (4) The Letter of Barnabas, really anonymous, written probably during the first century; (5) The Letter of Polycarp, martyred, according to Eusebius, in 166-167 A.D.; (6) The Shepherd of Hermas, written by Hermas, brother of Pius who was bishop of Rome about 148 A.D.; and (7) Fragments of Papias.

"The difference in value between the books of the New Testament and the writings of the Apostolic Fathers is very striking. It is difficult to understand how so great a change could have occurred in so short a time. 'Until the death of the Apostles the deposit of revelation was progressively enriched, as Saint Paul writes: "the mystery of Christ has not been made known in other ages to the sons of man so clearly as it has now been revealed to the holy apostles and prophets (Eph. 3: 4-5)"; after the death of the apostles, no new enrichment will be made.' (Lebreton et Zeiller (Catholique), L'Eglise Primitive, p. 321.)" (James L. Barker, *Protestors of Christendom,* pp. 23-24.)

APOSTOLIC LETTERS.
  See EPISTLES.

APOSTOLIC SUCCESSION.
  See APOSTLES, APOSTOLIC FATH-

ERS, ASSISTANT PRESIDENT OF THE CHURCH, FIRST PRESIDENCY, KEYS OF THE KINGDOM. Every apostle who is set apart as a member of the Council or Quorum of the Twelve is given the keys of the kingdom. (D. & C. 112:14-32; *Discourses of Wilford Woodruff,* pp. 71-77.) Since keys are the right of presidency and the kingdom of God on earth is the Church, it follows that each apostle so set apart receives the inherent power and authority to preside over the Church and direct all of its affairs. The fulness of these keys can be exercised only in the event an apostle becomes the senior apostle of God on earth, for unless he does there will always be someone above him to direct his labors. The senior apostle is always chosen and set apart as the President of the Church, and through this system of *apostolic succession,* the Lord has made provision for the continuation and preservation of his kingdom on earth. (*Doctrines of Salvation,* vol. 3, pp. 144-159.)

The quorum of the First Presidency is the supreme governing body of the Church, but the Twelve form a quorum "equal in authority and power" to them, meaning that when there is no First Presidency of three men, then the Twelve become the First Presidency in that they can then exercise all of the power and authority previously reserved to the Presidency. In the same sense the Seventy (meaning the first quorum of the Seventy, a body of 70 men) form a quorum equal in authority to that of the Council of the Twelve. (D. & C. 107:22-30.)

"The duty of the Twelve Apostles of the Church," President Joseph F. Smith said, "is to preach the gospel to the world, to send it to the inhabitants of the earth and to bear testimony of Jesus Christ the Son of God, as living witnesses of his divine mission. That is their special calling, and they are always under the direction of the Presidency of the Church of Jesus Christ of Latter-day Saints when that presidency is intact, and there is never at the same time two equal heads in the Church—never. The Lord never ordained any such thing, nor designed it. There is always a head in the Church, and if the Presidency of the Church are removed by death or other cause, then the next head of the Church is the Twelve Apostles, until a Presidency is again organized of three presiding high priests who have the right to hold the office of First Presidency over the Church." (*Gospel Doctrine,* 5th ed., pp. 177-178.)

Apostolic succession was also the Church order in the meridian of time. The New Testament records, however, are so fragmentary that we cannot trace the events in detail which transpired in that day. But enough has been preserved to give a reasonably clear picture of what took place. Our Lord called and ordained the original Twelve, giving the keys of the kingdom to each member of the quorum. (Matt. 16: 19; 18:18; John 15:16.) Paul taught plainly that the apostles were to continue in the true Church until the millennial era, that age in which all men will be converted and in which the necessity will no longer exist for sending the gospel message to the world. (Eph. 4:11-16; Jer. 31: 31-34.)

Matthias replaced Judas in the Council of the Twelve. (Acts 1:15-16.) "Paul was an ordained apostle, and without question he took the place of one of the other brethren in that Council." (*Doctrines of Salvation,* vol. 3, p. 153; 1 Tim. 2:7; 2 Tim. 1:11; Tit. 1:1.) Barnabas (Acts 14:14) and "James the Lord's brother" (Gal. 1:19), neither of whom were numbered among the original Twelve, are also named apostles.

With the coming of the great apostasy, vacancies no longer were filled in the Council of the Twelve, and when the last apostle ceased to minister among mortals, the keys of the kingdom no longer were exercised, and the so-called Christian Church was no longer the Lord's Church. Vacancies were also filled in the Nephite Twelve until the day in which apostasy overtook that branch of the house of Israel. (4 Ne. 14.)

APPARTITIONS.
See GHOSTS.

APPENDAGES TO THE PRIESTHOOD.
See PRIESTHOOD OFFICES.

ARCHANGELS.

See ANGELS, GABRIEL, MICHAEL THE ARCHANGEL, RAPHAEL. An *archangel* is a chief angel. Michael (Adam) is the only one so designated in the scriptures proper. (D. & C. 29:26; 88:112; 107:54; 128:21; 1 Thess. 4:16; Jude 9.) And certainly he is the chief of all angels, the head (under Christ) of the heavenly heirarchy.

The Hebrew celestial hierarchy, however, is said to consist of seven archangels. The names of two of these, Michael and Gabriel, are found in the Bible and in latter-day revelation. (Jude 9; Luke 1:5-38; D. & C. 128:21.) The name of a third, Raphael, is found in the apocryphal book of Tobias and in the Doctrine and Covenants. (Tob. 12: 15; D. & C. 128:21.) The names of the other four—Uriel, Raguel, Sariel, and Jerahmeel—are found in the so-called Book of Enoch, a non-canonical, apocalyptic work. (Enoch 21.) Apocryphal sources give the names of the last three as Izidkiel, Hanael, and Kepharel.

In reality, we know very little about the organization that exists among angelic beings; that a perfect, proper, and complex organization does exist is obvious, but the positions held by the various ministers in that celestial hierarchy have not been revealed in our day.

ARCHENEMY.

See DEVIL.

ARGUMENTS.

See CONTENTION.

ARK OF NOAH.

See FLOOD OF NOAH.

ARMAGEDDON.

See BATTLE OF ARMAGEDDON.

ARMIES OF HEAVEN.

See GOD OF BATTLES, MICHAEL THE ARCHANGEL, WAR, WAR IN HEAVEN. Those who follow Christ and fight for righteousness in the great battles of eternity are soldiers in the *armies of heaven.* Michael led these forces in preexistence when Lucifer rebelled and there was war in heaven. (Rev. 12: 7-8; D. & C. 29:36-38.) Our Lord himself is described by John as leading "the armies which were in heaven" in the great battle of Armageddon. (Rev. 19:11-21.)

It is Michael who "shall gather together his armies, even the hosts of heaven" so they can fight "the battle of the great God," in which Lucifer and his angels shall be cast out eternally. (D. & C. 88:111-116.) In a sense, those who are fighting for righteousness here and now are also soldiers in the armies of heaven; though, for the moment, they are fighting a losing battle against the forces of sin, eventual triumph is assured.

ARTICLE ON MARRIAGE.

See CELESTIAL MARRIAGE, DOCTRINE AND COVENANTS, MANIFESTO, PLURAL MARRIAGE, SCRIPTURE. As early as 1832 the Lord revealed to the Prophet the doctrine of celestial marriage, including also the principle of plurality of wives. This was before the restoration of the sealing keys, and so the Lord did not command either the practice of eternal marriage or the practice of the added order of plurality of wives at that time. Monogamy and civil marriage remained and were, at that time, the order of the Church. The revelation setting forth the higher law of temple marriage was not recorded; the doctrine was not taught except in private to some of the leading brethren of the Church; and it was not practiced.

In 1835, in connection with the approval of the first edition of the Doctrine and Covenants for publication, and in the absence of the Prophet, Oliver Cowdery wrote an *article on marriage.* The article, dealing with civil and monogamous marriage—that is, with the then accepted marriage discipline of the Church—though not particularly a wise and proper presentation of the Church's views even on matters pertaining to civil marriage, was accepted by the people and approved for publication in the same book with the revelations. It was clearly understood by all concerned, however, that the article on marriage was not a revelation, that it contained Oliver Cowdery's views and not necessarily those of the Prophet, and that it was merely a statement of policy bearing on the system of civil marriage then prevailing in the Church and in the world.

When the Prophet returned and learned of the action taken relative to the publication of the article on marriage, he was greatly troubled. However, knowing that up to that date the new and everlasting covenant of marriage had only been revealed in principle, that there was as yet no command to practice it, and that the power and keys had not been restored whereby marriages could be solemnized so they would endure for eternity, he let the action stand. The higher order was to come later.

Then in 1836 Elijah came and restored the sealing power, the power to bind on earth and have it sealed eternally in the heavens. (D. & C. 110:13-16; 132:45-47.) At a still later date, temple endowments and other ordinances were revealed —all of which are a necessary prelude to the performance of an eternal marriage, a marriage between one man and one woman, or between one man and more than one women, as the case may be. After these things the practice of celestial marriage, including plurality of wives, was commanded. In 1843 the previously revealed doctrine of celestial marriage (including plurality of wives) was recorded for the first time; added truths were also stated in the revelation as finally recorded, as for instance a reference to the fact that the keys of sealing now had been given and also special instruction to Emma Smith relative to plural marriage. (D. & C. 132:45-47, 51-55.)

There was, of course, no opportunity to add the revelation on marriage to a new edition of the Doctrine and Covenants until after the saints came west. Temple endowments, celestial marriage, and plural marriage had all been practiced in Nauvoo, but being higher, sacred ordinances their practice had not as yet been announced to the world. After the saints came west the restored order of marriage discipline was taught publicly, and in due course the revelation on marriage was published. Obviously it was good sense to delete from the Doctrine and Covenants the article on marriage because it had application to a lesser order, an order that prevailed before the full law had been restored.

The Reorganized Church of Jesus Christ of Latter Day Saints has tried to make it appear that the article on marriage was the only approved order of the Church and that the revelation on marriage was a spurious one authored by Brigham Young. The facts, of course, destroy their specious claims. An understanding of the historical sequences involved and of the doctrinal principles relative to the sealing power make the truth very clear. (*Doctrines of Salvation,* vol. 3, pp. 195-198.)

ARTICLES OF FAITH.

See CREEDS, FIRST PRINCIPLES OF THE GOSPEL, PEARL OF GREAT PRICE, SCRIPTURE. Joseph Smith wrote 13 brief statements which have become known as the *Articles of Faith,* statements which summarize some of the basic doctrines of the Church. These Articles of Faith are scripture and are published as part of the Pearl of Great Price.

For brevity, clearness, and forthrightness of doctrinal presentation, they are unexcelled. When compared with the muddled creeds formulated by the supposedly greatest religious thinkers of Christendom—creeds born amid the strife, bitterness, and debates of councils that struggled at length over every word and comma—the Articles of Faith, coming forth as the spontaneous and inspired writing of one man, are a marked evidence of the spirit of revelation that rested upon the Prophet.

These articles, of course, do not attempt to summarize all of the basic doctrines of the gospel. Indeed, one of the articles itself specifies that God "will yet reveal many great and important things" pertaining to his kingdom. (Ninth Article of Faith.) For example, the Articles of Faith are silent on such things as celestial marriage, salvation for the dead, temple work in all its phases, the resurrection, and degrees of glory in the eternal worlds.

ASCENSION DAY.

See CHRIST, ASCENSION OF CHRIST, EASTER. Since our Lord ascended in dramatic manner to his Father 40 days after his resurrection, it has become traditional among sectarians to celebrate the Thursday, 40 days after Easter, as *ascension day*. But since Easter is only the traditional day of his resurrection, it follows that ascension day is not the actual day of his formal return to his Father.

ASCENSION OF CHRIST.

See ASCENSION DAY, CHRIST, SECOND COMING OF CHRIST. Our Lord, after his resurrection, ascended to his Father and received the glory which was his before the world was. (John 16:28; 17:5.) Immediately following his resurrection, he said to Mary: *"Touch me not; for I am not yet ascended to my Father:* but go to my brethren, and say unto them, *I ascend unto my Father,* and your Father; and to my God, and your God." (John 20:17.) Thereafter he appeared to the disciples in the upper room and said, "Handle me, and see; for a spirit hath not flesh and bones, as ye see me have" (Luke 24:39), from which it is supposed that during the interval he had ascended to his Father.

During the period of 40 days while he continued to minister as a resurrected Being among his disciples in Jerusalem (Acts 1:3), it is presumed that he ascended to his Father many times. But the particular instance which is commonly referred to as the *ascension of Christ* is that formal occasion on the mount of Olivet when he took leave in dramatic form from his disciples. "While they beheld," the record avers, "he was taken up; and a cloud received him out of their sight. And while they looked stedfastly toward heaven as he went up, behold, two men stood by them in white apparel; Which also said, Ye men of Galilee, why stand ye gazing up into heaven? this same Jesus, which is taken up from you into heaven, shall so come in like manner as ye have seen him go into heaven." (Acts 1:9-11.)

It should be noted particularly that he here ascended as a tangible Being, a Personage having that body of flesh and bones which those who beheld him go up had theretofore handled and felt and which had eaten food in their presence. (Luke 24:36-43.) After this formal ascension, our Lord ministered personally again on earth both to Paul and others in the old world and to chosen prophets in modern times. (Acts 9:1-9; 22:6-16; Rev. 1:13-18; Jos. Smith 2:16-20; D. & C. 110:1-10.)

The Book of Mormon record says "that soon after the ascension of Christ into heaven he did truly manifest himself unto" the Nephites. (3 Ne. 10:18; 11:12.) It would appear that from the manner in which Book of Mormon prophets speak of the ascension (Mosiah 18:2; Alma 40:20), that they have reference to his ascension immediately following his resurrection and not to that formal occasion 40 days after which *later* became known among Christian peoples as the ascension. Viewing the time differences between the old and new worlds, there would be no reason why he should not have ministered as a resurrected Being among the Nephites during the same interval in which he was continuing his resurrected walk with his followers in Jerusalem.

ASHES.
See SACKCLOTH AND ASHES.

ASHTORETH (ASHTAROTH).
See BAAL (BAALIM), FALSE GODS. As Baal was the supreme male deity of the Phoenician and Canaanitish nations, so Ashtoreth (Ashtaroth) was their supreme female deity. She was the so-called goddess of love and fertility, whose licentious worship pleased Israel in her apostate periods. (Judges 2:13; 10:6; 1 Sam. 7:3-4; 12:10.)

ASSEMBLIES.
See SOLEMN ASSEMBLIES.

ASSISTANT PRESIDENT OF THE CHURCH.
See APOSTLES, APOSTOLIC SUCCESSION, FIRST PRESIDENCY, LAW OF WITNESSES, PRESIDENT OF THE CHURCH. Oliver Cowdery was with the Prophet when the priesthood and keys necessary for the full restoration of the gospel and the establishment of the dispensation of the fulness of times were conferred. (D. & C. 13; 27:12; 110:11-16.) He held the keys jointly with the Prophet. At the formal organization of the Church the Prophet was sustained as the *first elder* and Oliver Cowdery as the *second elder* (D. & C. 20:2-3), that is, they were first and second from the standpoint of pre-eminence, or presiding authority. Then as the Church grew, and when the full organization was revealed, Oliver Cowdery was made the *Assistant* (or *Associate*) President of the Church.

As the Assistant President, Oliver ranked second in authority to the Prophet. He stood ahead of the Counselors in the First Presidency and ahead of the Council of the Twelve. In explaining the nature of the office of Assistant President, the Prophet said: *"The office of Assistant President is to assist in presiding over the whole Church, and to officiate in the absence of the President,* according to his rank and appointment, viz.: President Cowdery, first; President [Sidney] Rigdon, second; and President [Frederick G.] Williams, third, as they were generally called. The office of this priesthood is also to act as spokesman, taking Aaron for an example. The virtue of the above priesthood is to hold the keys of the kingdom of heaven or of the Church militant." (*Manuscript*

55

History of the Church, Book A, Chap. 1; *Essentials in Church History,* pp. 179-180.) Thus if the Prophet had died, Oliver Cowdery would have been the President of the Church.

After Oliver Cowdery fell from his high status, Hyrum Smith the Patriarch was chosen by revelation to succeed to the position of Assistant President and to stand as a joint witness with the Prophet of the truth of the restoration. (D. & C. 124:94-96.) When these two joint Presidents of the Church sealed their testimonies with their blood, the full operation of the keys of the kingdom rested with the Twelve, and Brigham Young, the senior apostle, became the ranking officer of the Church. Since the kingdom was then fully established and the two witnesses had left a binding testimony, it was no longer necessary to continue the office of Assistant President. Accordingly, the office is not found in the Church today. (*Doctrines of Salvation,* vol. 1, pp. 210-222.)

ASSISTANTS TO THE TWELVE.

See GENERAL AUTHORITIES, HIGH PRIESTS, PRIESTHOOD OFFICES. From time to time as the needs of the ministry require, those holding the keys of the kingdom call worthy and qualified brethren to serve in administrative positions in the Church. *Assistants to the Twelve,* with appointments to serve as General Authorities, have been

so called. They are high priests, not apostles, and serve pursuant to the revelation which says: "Other officers of the church, who belong not unto the Twelve, neither to the Seventy, are not under the responsibility to travel among all nations, but are to travel as their circumstances shall allow, notwithstanding they may hold as high and responsible offices in the church." (D. & C. 107:98.)

ASSOCIATE PRESIDENT OF THE CHURCH.

See ASSISTANT PRESIDENT OF THE CHURCH.

ASTROLOGERS.

See ASTROLOGY.

ASTROLOGY.

See ASTRONOMY, DIVINATION, FORTUNE TELLING, SORCERY. A form of divination and fortune telling akin to sorcery, *astrology* is a pseudo science that pretends to divulge the influence of the stars upon human affairs; it is a false science that claims to foretell earthly events by means of the positions and aspects of these heavenly luminaries. It is, of course, one of Satan's substitutes for the true science of astronomy and for the true principle of receiving revelation of future events from divine sources.

Ancient uninspired peoples were frequently deluded by the snares of the *astrologers* among them (Isa. 47; Dan. 1:20; 2:27; 4:7; 5:7), but it is difficult to understand why people in modern and supposedly enlightened and civilized nations should submit to these same stargazing absurdities. Enlightened people in and out of the Church shun them for the abominations they are.

ASTRONOMY.

See CREATION, EARTHS. *Astronomy* is the science which treats of the celestial bodies, their creation, magnitudes, motions, constitution, and the like. It is falsely supposed in the world that this is a modern science, that through our telescopes and by other means we have discovered for the first time some of the great truths relative to the sidereal heavens and the infinite number of spheres that roll through them. In reality the greatest astronomers of all time lived in the early ages of the earth and received their knowledge by revelation from the Creator, Maker, and Organizer of all things.

Moses saw many earths—all created by Deity; all rolling in space at his command; all controlled by his law, "by which they move in their times and their seasons" (D. & C. 88:7-13, 41-50); all inhabited by men and women who are redeemed with immortality and offered eternal life through the power of the Father. (Moses 1:27-39.) Enoch was equally aware of these endless creations and their equally endless inhabitants. (Moses 7:29-36.) Perhaps many prophets and righteous men have known of these things.

But, as far as our records reveal, Abraham stands pre-eminent as the greatest astronomer of all the ages. He saw, recorded, and taught the truths relative to the creation of the earth; of the movements and relationships of the sun, moon, and stars; and of the positions and revolutions of the various spheres in the sidereal heavens. (Abra. 3; 4; 5; *History of the Church,* vol. 2, p. 286.) When the Lord comes again, he will reveal all things (D. & C. 101:32-34); then the perfect knowledge of astronomy will be had again, and the faithful will know all things about all the creations of him who is omnipotent.

ATHANASIAN CREED.

See APOSTASY, APOSTLES CREED, CREEDS, NICENE CREED. Of all the major creeds, the so-called *Athanasian* is by far the most incomprehensible and difficult to understand. Of it Elder James E. Talmage says: "It would be difficult to conceive of a greater number of inconsistencies and contradictions expressed in words as few." (*Articles of Faith,* p. 48.)

Strangely, it is the one creed which its defending apologists feel called upon to praise for its clarity, lucidity, and plainness. Their official statement describes it as "a short, clear exposition of the doctrines of the Trinity and the Incarnation, with a passing reference to several other dogmas." They promulgate it as a "summary of Catholic Faith," and as a document that "is approved by the Church as expressing its mind on the fundamental truths with which it deals." They eulogize "the compactness and lucidity of its statements," which "make it highly prized," and say that it "states in a very plain and precise way what the Catholic Faith is concerning the important doctrines of the Trinity and the Incarnation." Authorship of the creed is unknown, although Catholic authorities lean to the view that it was written by some less prominent person sometime after the day of Athanasius (296-373 A.D.).

Enlightened persons can judge for themselves whether this creed sheds light upon or blankets with darkness the truths it attempts to define. This is the official Catholic version of the creed:

"Whosoever will be saved, before all things it is necessary that he hold the Catholic Faith. Which Faith except everyone do keep whole and undefiled, without doubt he shall perish everlastingly. And the Catholic Faith is this, that we worship one God in Trinity and Trinity in Unity. Neither confounding the Persons, nor dividing the Substance. For there is one Person of the Father, another of the Son, and another of the Holy Ghost. But the Godhead of the Father, of the Son and of the Holy Ghost is all One, the Glory Equal, the Majesty Co-Eternal. Such as the Father is, such is the Son, and such is the Holy Ghost. The Father Uncreate, the Son Uncreate, and the Holy Ghost Uncreate. The Father Incomprehensible, the Son Incomprehensible, and the Holy Ghost Incomprehensible. The Father Eternal, the Son Eternal, and the Holy Ghost Eternal and yet they are not Three Eternals but One Eternal. As also there are not Three Uncreated, nor Three Incomprehensibles, but One Uncreated, and One Incomprehensible. So likewise the Father is Almighty, the Son Almighty, and the Holy Ghost Almighty. And yet they are not Three Almighties but One Almighty.

"So the Father is God, the Son is God, and the Holy Ghost is God. And yet they are not Three Gods, but One God. So likewise the Father is Lord, the Son Lord, and the Holy Ghost Lord. And yet not Three Lords but One Lord. For, like as we are compelled by the Christian verity to acknowledge every Person by Himself to be God and Lord, so are we forbidden by the Catholic Religion to say, there be Three Gods or Three Lords. The Father is made of none, neither created, nor begotten. The Son is of the Father alone; not made, nor created, but begotten. The Holy Ghost is of the Father, and of the Son: neither made, nor created, nor begotten, but proceeding.

"So there is One Father, not Three Fathers; one Son not Three Sons; One Holy Ghost, not Three Holy

Ghosts. And in this Trinity none is afore or after Other, None is greater or less than Another, but the whole Three Persons are Co-eternal together, and Co-equal. So that in all things, as is aforesaid, the Unity in Trinity, and the Trinity in Unity is to be worshipped. He therefore that will be saved, must thus think of the Trinity.

"Furthermore, it is necessary to everlasting Salvation, that he also believe rightly the Incarnation of our Lord Jesus Christ. For the right Faith is, that we believe and confess, that our Lord Jesus Christ, the Son of God, is God and Man.

"God, of the substance of the Father, begotten before the worlds; and Man of the substance of IIis mother, born into the world. Perfect God and Perfect Man, of a reasonable Soul and human Flesh subsisting. Equal to the Father as touching His Godhead, and inferior to the Father as touching His Manhood. Who, although He be God and Man, yet He is not two, but One Christ. One, not by conversion of the Godhead into Flesh, but by taking of the Manhood into God. One altogether, not by confusion of substance, but by Unity of Person. For as the reasonable soul and flesh is one Man, so God and Man is one Christ. Who suffered for our salvation, descended into Hell, rose again the third day from the dead. He ascended into Heaven, He sitteth on the right hand of the Father, God Almighty, from whence

he shall come to judge the quick and the dead. At whose coming all men shall rise again with their bodies, and shall give account for their own works. And they that have done good shall go into life everlasting, and they that have done evil into everlasting fire. This is the Catholic Faith, which except a man believe faithfully and firmly, he cannot be saved." (*Catholic Encyclopedia,* vol. 2, pp. 33-34.)

ATHEISM.

See AGNOSTICISM, APOSTASY, DEISM, GOD, INFIDELS, THEISM. *Atheism* is the disbelief in or denial of the existence of God. Such takes various forms, and there are many degrees of atheism. In the absolute sense, it is doubtful if there is such a person as an atheist, for even though one denies the traditionally taught concept of Deity, yet he probably worships at some other shrine as, for instance, the shrine of false intellectuality. At the other extreme, those who profess belief in the sectarian God are in a position at least akin to atheism for their God is defined in effect as an immaterial nothing.

Reasoning along this line Orson Pratt wrote: "There are two classes of atheists in the world. One class denies the existence of God in the most positive language; the other denies his existence in duration or space. One says 'There is no God'; the other says 'God is not *here or there,* any more than he exists *now*

59

and *then.'* The infidel says 'God does not exist anywhere.' The immaterialist says 'He exists *nowhere.'* The infidel says, 'There is no such substance as God.' The immaterialist says 'There is such a substance as God, but it is *without parts.'* The atheist says 'There is no such substance as *spirit.'* The immaterialist says 'A spirit, though he lives and acts, occupies no room, and fills no space in the same way and in the same manner as matter, not even so much as does the minutest grain of sand.' The atheist does not seek to hide his infidelity; but the immaterialist, whose declared belief amounts to the same thing as the atheist's, endeavors to hide his infidelity under the shallow covering of a few words. . . . *The immaterialist is a religious atheist; he only differs from the other class of atheists by clothing an indivisible unextended nothing with the powers of a God. One class believes in no God; the other believes that Nothing is god and worhips it as such."* (Cited, *Articles of Faith,* p. 465.)

ATHLETIC GAMES.
See RECREATION.

ATONEMENT OF CHRIST.
See ADVOCACY, ADVOCATE, BLOOD ATONEMENT DOCTRINE, CHRIST, ETERNAL LIFE, EXPIATION, EXPIATOR, FALL OF ADAM, GOSPEL, GRACE OF GOD, IMMORTALITY, INTERCESSION, MEDIATION, PROPITIATION, PROPITIATOR, RECONCILIATION, RECONCILER, REDEMPTION, REPENTANCE, SACRAMENT, SACRIFICES, SALVATION, SALVATION BY GRACE, SYMBOLISMS. Nothing in the entire plan of salvation compares in any way in importance with that most transcendent of all events, the atoning sacrifice of our Lord. It is the most important single thing that has ever occurred in the entire history of created things; it is the rock foundation upon which the gospel and all other things rest. Indeed, all "things which pertain to our religion are only appendages to it," the Prophet said. (*Teachings,* p. 121.)

The doctrine of the *atonement* embraces, sustains, supports, and gives life and force to all other gospel doctrines. It is the foundation upon which all truth rests, and all things grow out of it and come because of it. Indeed, the atonement is the gospel. In recording the Vision, the Prophet wrote: "And this is the gospel, the glad tidings, which the voice out of the heavens bore record unto us—That he came into the world, even Jesus, to be crucified for the world, and to bear the sins of the world, and to sanctify the world, and to cleanse it from all unrighteousness; That through him all might be saved whom the Father had put into his power and made by him." (D. & C. 76:40-42.) To the Nephites the resurrected Lord spoke similarly: "Behold I have given unto you my gospel, and this is the gospel which I have given unto you—that I came into the world to do the will of my Father, because my Father sent me. And my Father sent me that I might be lifted up upon the cross." (3 Ne. 27:13-14.)

Salvation comes because of the atonement. Without it the whole plan of salvation would be frustrated and the whole purpose behind the creating and populating of the earth would come to naught. With it the eternal purposes of the Father will roll forth, the purpose of creation be preserved, the plan of salvation made efficacious, and men will be assured of a hope of the highest exaltation hereafter. (*Doctrines of Salvation,* vol. 1, pp. 121-138.)

"Redemption cometh in and through the Holy Messiah," Lehi taught, "for he is full of grace and truth. Behold he offereth himself a sacrifice for sin, to answer the ends of the law, unto all those who have a broken heart and a contrite spirit; and unto none else can the ends of the law be answered. Wherefore, how great the importance to make these things known unto the inhabitants of the earth, that they may know that there is no flesh that can dwell in the presence of God, save it be through the merits, and mercy, and grace of the Holy Messiah, who layeth down his life according to the flesh, and taketh it again by the power of the Spirit, that he may bring to pass the resurrection of the dead, being the first that

should rise. Wherefore, he is the firstfruits unto God, inasmuch as he shall make intercession for all the children of men; and they that believe in him shall be saved." (2 Ne. 2:6-9.)

One of the greatest sermons of all the ages, preached by an angel from heaven on the subject of the atonement, includes these words: "As in Adam, or by nature, they fall, even so the blood of Christ atoneth for their sins. And moreover, I say unto you, that there shall be no other name given nor any other way nor means whereby salvation can come unto the children of men, only in and through the name of Christ, the Lord Omnipotent. For behold he judgeth, and his judgment is just; . . . salvation was, and is, and is to come, in and through the atoning blood of Christ, the Lord Omnipotent. For the natural man is an enemy to God, and has been from the fall of Adam, and will be, forever and ever, unless he yields to the enticings of the Holy Spirit, and putteth off the natural man and becometh a saint through the atonement of Christ the Lord, and becometh as a child, submissive, meek, humble, patient, full of love, willing to submit to all things which the Lord seeth fit to inflict upon him, even as a child doth submit to his Father." (Mosiah 3:16-19.)

A knowledge of two great truths is essential to an understanding of the doctrine of the atonement: 1. The fall of Adam; and 2. The divine

Sonship of our Lord.

Adam's fall brought spiritual and temporal death into the world. *Spiritual death* is to be cast out of the presence of the Lord (2 Ne. 9:6) and to die as pertaining to things of righteousness, or in other words things of the Spirit. (Hela. 14:15-18.) *Temporal death* or natural death is the separation of body and spirit, the body going back to the dust from which it was created and the spirit to a world of waiting spirits to await the day of the resurrection.

To atone is to ransom, reconcile, expiate, redeem, reclaim, absolve, propitiate, make amends, pay the penalty. Thus the atonement of Christ is designed to ransom men from the effects of the fall of Adam in that both spiritual and temporal death are conquered; their lasting effect is nullified. The spiritual death of the fall is replaced by the spiritual life of the atonement, in that all who believe and obey the gospel law gain spiritual or eternal life—life in the presence of God where those who enjoy it are alive to things of righteousness or things of the Spirit. The temporal death of the fall is replaced by the state of immortality which comes because of the atonement and resurrection of our Lord. The body and spirit which separated, incident to what men call the natural death, are reunited in immortality, in an inseparable connection that never again will permit the mortal body to see corruption. (Alma 11:37-45; 12:16-18.) *Immortality* comes as a free gift, by the grace of God alone, without works of righteousness. *Eternal life* is the reward for "obedience to the laws and ordinances of the Gospel." (Third Article of Faith.)

"Adam fell that men might be; and men are, that they might have joy," Lehi says. "And the Messiah cometh in the fulness of time, that he may redeem the children of men from the fall." (2 Ne. 2:25-26.) "The atonement," King Benjamin explains, "was prepared from the foundation of the world for all mankind, which ever were since the fall of Adam, or who are, or who ever shall be, even unto the end of the world." (Mosiah 4:7.)

And Moroni taught that God "created Adam, and by Adam came the fall of man. And because of the fall of man came Jesus Christ, even the Father and the Son; and because of Jesus Christ came the redemption of man. And because of the redemption of man, which came by Jesus Christ, they are brought back into the presence of the Lord; yea, this is wherein all men are redeemed, because the death of Christ bringeth to pass the resurrection, which bringeth to pass a redemption from an endless sleep, from which sleep all men shall be awakened by the power of God when the trump shall sound; and they shall come forth, both small and great, and all shall stand before his bar, being redeemed and loosed from this eternal band of death, which death is a temporal death. And then cometh the judgment of the Holy One upon them; and then cometh the time that he that is filthy shall be filthy still; and he that is righteous shall be righteous still; he that is happy shall be happy still; and he that is unhappy shall be unhappy still." (Morm. 9:12-14.)

And thus the Lord says that because of the atonement, and following the "natural death," man is "raised in immortality unto eternal life, even as many as would believe; And they that believe not unto eternal damnation; for they cannot be redeemed from their spiritual fall, because they repent not." (D. & C. 29:43-44.)

If there had been no atonement of Christ (there having been a fall of Adam!), then the whole plan and purpose connected with the creation of man would have come to naught. If there had been no atonement, temporal death would have remained forever, and there never would have been a resurrection. The body would have remained forever in the grave, and the spirit would have stayed in a spirit prison to all eternity. If there had been no atonement, there never would have been spiritual or eternal life for any persons. Neither mortals nor spirits could have been cleansed from sin, and all the spirit hosts of heaven would have wound up as devils, angels to a devil, that is, as sons of perdition.

Jacob, brother to righteous Nephi, has left us these inspired words: "For as death hath passed upon all men, to fulfil the merciful plan of the great Creator, there must needs be a power of resurrection, and the resurrection must needs come unto man by reason of the fall; and the fall came by reason of transgression; and because man became fallen they were cut off from the presence of the Lord. Wherefore, it must needs be an infinite atonement— save it should be an infinite atonement this corruption could not put on incorruption. Wherefore, the first judgment which came upon man must needs have remained to an endless duration. And if so, this flesh must have laid down to rot and to crumble to its mother earth, to rise no more. O the wisdom of God, his mercy and grace! For behold, if the flesh should rise no more our spirits must become subject to that angel who fell from before the presence of the Eternal God, and became the devil, to rise no more. And our spirits must have become like unto him, and we become devils, angels to a devil, to be shut out from the presence of our God, and to remain with the father of lies, in misery, like unto himself." (2 Ne. 9:6-9; D. & C. 29:39-41.)

Children and others who have not arrived at the years of accountability are automatically saved in the celestial kingdom by virtue of the atonement. "Little children are whole, for they are not capable of committing sin," the Lord says, "wherefore the curse of Adam is taken from them in me, that it hath no power over them." (Moro. 8:8; D. & C. 29:

46-50; Mosiah 15:25; *Teachings,* p. 107.) The curse of Adam includes both temporal and spiritual death, and accordingly neither of these is binding upon children and those who have "no understanding" (D. & C. 29:50), that is, those who are not accountable. All such will be raised in immortality and unto eternal life.

Christ is the only person ever to be born in the world who had power to bring to pass the resurrection of himself or anyone else and to atone for the sins of any living being. This is because he had life in himself; he had the power of immortality by divine inheritance. The atonement came by the power of God and not of man, and to understand it one must believe that our Lord was literally the Son of God (an immortal Personage) and of Mary (a mortal woman). From his mother he inherited mortality, the power to lay down his life, to die, to permit body and spirit to separate. From his Father he inherited the power of immortality, the power to keep body and spirit together, or voluntarily having permitted them to separate, the power to unite them again in the resurrected state.

This power he exercised, becoming the firstfruits of them that slept, and in a way incomprehensible to mortal man, he had the power to pass the effects of this resurrection on to all living creatures. "I lay down my life, that I might take it again," he said. "No man taketh it from me, but I lay it down of myself. I have power to lay it down, and I have power to take it again. This commandment have I received of my Father." (John 10:17-18.)

Amulek bore this testimony: "I do know that Christ shall come among the children of men, to take upon him the transgressions of his people, and that he shall atone for the sins of the world; for the Lord God hath spoken it. For it is expedient that an atonement should be made; for according to the great plan of the Eternal God there must be an atonement made, or else all mankind must unavoidably perish; yea, all are hardened; yea, all are fallen and are lost, and must perish except it be through the atonement which it is expedient should be made. For it is expedient that there should be a great and last sacrifice; yea, *not a sacrifice of man,* neither of beast, neither of any manner of fowl; for *it shall not be a human sacrifice; but it must be an infinite and eternal sacrifice. Now there is not any man that can sacrifice his own blood which will atone for the sins of another.* . . . Therefore there can be nothing which is short of an *infinite atonement* which will suffice for the sins of the world." (Alma 34: 8-12.)

When the prophets speak of an *infinite* atonement, they mean just that. Its effects cover all men, the earth itself and all forms of life thereon, and reach out into the endless expanses of eternity. "The word *atonement,"* it is written in the *Compendium,* "signifies deliverance, through the offering of a ransom, from the penalty of a broken law. The sense is expressed in Job 33:24: 'Deliver him from going down to the pit: I have found a ransom.' As effected by Jesus Christ, it signifies the deliverance, through his death and resurrection, of the earth and everything pertaining to it, from the power which death has obtained over them through the transgression of Adam. . . . Redemption from death, through the sufferings of Christ, is for all men, both the righteous and the wicked; for this earth, and for all things created upon it." (*Compendium,* pp. 8-9.)

Because of the atonement and by obedience to gospel law men have power to become the sons of God in that they are spiritually begotten of God and adopted as members of his family. They become the sons of God and joint-heirs with Christ of the fulness of the Father's kingdom. (D. & C. 39:1-6; 76:54-60; Rom. 8:14-17; Gal. 3:1-7; 1 John 3:1-4; Rev. 21:7.) Now our Lord's jurisdiction and power extend far beyond the limits of this one small earth on which we dwell. He is, under the Father, the Creator of worlds without number. (Moses 1:33.) And through the power of his atonement the inhabitants of these worlds, the revelation says, "are begotten sons and daughters unto God" (D. & C. 76:24), which means that the atonement of Christ, being literally and truly infinite, applies to an infinite number of earths.

Those who have ears to hear, find this doctrine taught in the following scripture: "And we beheld the glory of the Son, on the right hand of the Father, and received of his fulness," the Prophet says in recording the Vision, "And saw the holy angels, and them who are sanctified before his throne, worshiping God, and the Lamb, who worship him forever and ever. And now, after the many testimonies which have been given of him, this is the testimony, last of all, which we give of him: That he lives! For we saw him, even on the right hand of God; and we heard the voice bearing record that he is the Only Begotten of the Father—That by him, and through him, and of him, the *worlds* are and were created, and *the inhabitants thereof are begotten sons and daughters unto God."* (D. & C. 76:20-24.)

In addition to the plain meaning of this passage, we have an explanation of it given by the Prophet Joseph Smith. He paraphrased, in poetical rhyme, the entire record of the Vision, and his words covering this portion were:

"I beheld round the throne holy
  angels and hosts,
And *sanctified beings from worlds
  that have been,*
In holiness worshipping God and the
  Lamb,
  For ever and ever. Amen and
  amen.

"And now after all of the proofs
 made of him,
By witnesses truly, by whom he
 was known,
This is mine, last of all, that he
 lives; yea, he lives!
And sits on the right hand of God
 on his throne.

"And I heard a great voice bearing
 record from heav'n,
He's the Saviour and Only Be-
* gotten of God;*
By him, of him, and through him,
* the worlds were all made,*
Even all that careen in the heav-
* ens so broad.*

"Whose inhabitants, too, from the
* first to the last,*
Are sav'd by the very same Sav-
* iour of ours;*
And, of course, are begotten God's
* daughters and sons*
By the very same truths and the
* very same powers."*
(*Millennial Star,* vol. 4, pp. 49-55.)

ATTRIBUTES OF GOD.
 See FAITH.

AUSTERE MAN.
 See CHRIST, JUDGE OF ALL THE
EARTH, JUSTICE. In the parable of
the pounds, the slothful servant who
did not put his money to usury justified himself because he feared the
Lord who was an austere man. In
answer the Lord—who is Christ, the
Judge of all the earth—agreed that
he was an *Austere Man,* a man who
would mete out justice to all men

and impose severe penalties for sins
of omission as well as those of commission. (Luke 19:12-27.)

AUTHORITIES.
 See GENERAL AUTHORITIES.

AUTHORITY IN THE MINIS-
TRY.
 See PRIESTHOOD.

AUTHORIZED VERSION OF
THE BIBLE.
 See KING JAMES VERSION OF THE
BIBLE.

AUTHOR OF SALVATION.
 See ATONEMENT OF CHRIST,
CHRIST, PLAN OF SALVATION, SAL-
VATION. Christ is the *Author of
Salvation.* This means that he
made salvation available to all men
in that he worked out the infinite
and eternal atonement. Paul's
statement that Christ is "the
author of eternal salvation unto all
them that obey him" (Heb. 5:9),
as the marginal reading shows,
means that he is the "cause" thereof; that is, salvation is possible
because of his atoning sacrifice;
without this sacrifice there would
be no salvation. Paul's other statement that Christ is "the author and
finisher of our faith" (Heb. 12:2),
also according to the marginal reading, means that he is the "leader"
in the cause of salvation.
 Christ is not the Author of Salvation in the sense that he created

the plan of salvation, nor in the sense that he supposedly presented a plan of his own in the councils in heaven, which plan the Father supposedly adopted in preference to a less desirable one formulated by Lucifer. Rather *the Father is the Author of the plan of salvation,* a plan which began to operate long before Christ was ever chosen to be the Redeemer.

Thus when the Father presented his own plan in the pre-existent council, he asked for volunteers from whom he could choose a Redeemer to be born into mortality as the Son of God. Lucifer offered to become the Son of God on condition that the terms of the Father's plan were modified to deny men their agency and to heap inordinate reward upon the one working out the redemption. Christ, on the other hand, accepted the Father's plan in full, saying, "Father, thy will be done, and the glory be thine forever." Our Lord was then foreordained to a mission which in due course he fulfilled, which mission enabled him to make salvation available to all men. (Moses 4:1-4; Abra. 3:22-28.)

AUXILIARY ORGANIZATIONS. *See* CHURCH ORGANIZATION, GENERAL AUXILIARY OFFICERS, MUTUAL IMPROVEMENT ASSOCIATIONS, PRIESTHOOD, PRIMARY ASSOCIATION, RELIEF SOCIETY, SUNDAY SCHOOL. There are in the Church the following *auxiliary organizations:* Relief Society, Sunday School, Primary, Young Men's Mutual Improvement Association, and Young Women's Mutual Improvement Association. These units of church government are aids and helps to the priesthood. (1 Cor. 12:28.) They serve in a subsidiary, subordinate, subservient, and ancillary position to the priesthood; their purposes are to supplement the work being done by the priesthood quorums. (*Gospel Doctrine,* 5th ed., pp. 383-400.)

Auxiliary organizations are created to meet particular needs and problems that exist from time to time. Much of their work is temporary in that it ceases when the particular need ceases, or it will be absorbed in due course by the priesthood organizations. "We expect to see the day, if we live long enough (and if some of us do not live long enough to see it, there are others who will)," President Joseph F. Smith said, "when every council of the priesthood in the Church of Jesus Christ of Latter-day Saints will understand its duty; will assume its own responsibility, will magnify its calling, and fill its place in the Church, to the uttermost, according to the intelligence and ability possessed by it. *When that day shall come, there will not be so much necessity for work that is now being done by the auxiliary organizations, because it will be done by the regular quorums of the priesthood. The Lord designed and comprehended it from the be-*

ginning, and he has made provision in the Church whereby every need may be met and satisfied through the regular organizations of the priesthood. It has truly been said that the Church is perfecly organized. The only trouble is that these organizations are not fully alive to the obligations that rest upon them. When they become thoroughly awakened to the requirements made of them, they will fulfil their duties more faithfully, and the work of the Lord will be all the stronger and more powerful and influential in the world." (*Gospel Doctrine,* 5th ed.', pp. 159-160.)

B

BAAL (BAALIM).

See ASHTORETH (ASHTAROTH), BEELZEBUB, FALSE GODS. Numerous Old Testament references recite apostate Israel's worship of *Baal* and *Baalim* (plural of Baal). It was the priest of Baal, for instance, with whom Elijah had his dramatic contest in the days of Ahab and Jezebel. (1 Kings 18.) Baal was the supreme male deity of the Phoenician and Canaanitish nation. It is likely that there were, in practice, many Baals or gods of particular places, the worship of whom was licentious in nature, *Baalzebub* (the same name as *Beelzebub* or *Satan*) was the name of the god of one particular group. (2 Kings 1:3.)

BABEL.
See JAREDITES.

BABE OF BETHLEHEM.

See CHRIST, CHRIST CHILD. It is common among Christian people to refer to the Infant Jesus as the *Babe of Bethlehem,* an appellation applied because of his birth in Bethlehem. (Micah 5:2; Matt. 2:1-10; Luke 2:1-20.)

BABIES.
See STILLBORN CHILDREN.

BABYLON.
See CHURCH OF THE DEVIL, SECOND COMING OF CHRIST, WORLD. Anciently *Babylon* was the chief and capital city of the Babylonian empire. Founded by Nimrod and built astride the Euphrates, it is claimed to have been one of the largest and most magnificent cities of all time. The name is the Greek form of *Babel* and

means *confusion*. The city was taken by Cyrus and again by Alexander the Great and has now become a desolate heap as prophesied by Isaiah and Jeremiah. (Isa. 13:19-22; Jer. 51.)

As the seat of world empire, Babylon was the persistent persecutor and enemy of the Lord's people. It was to escape the imminent destruction of Jerusalem by Nebuchadnezzar's Babylonian hordes that Lehi and his family were led to the new world. To the Lord's people anciently, Babylon was known as the center of iniquity, carnality, and worldliness. Everything connected with it was in opposition to all righteousness and had the effect of leading men downward to the destruction of their souls.

It was natural, therefore, for the apostles and inspired men of New Testament times to apply the name *Babylon* to the forces organized to spread confusion and darkness in the realm of spiritual things. (Rev. 17; 18; D. & C. 29:21; Ezek. 38; 39.) In a general sense, the wickedness of the world generally is Babylon. (D. & C. 1:16; 35:11; 64:24; 133:14.)

As Babylon of old fell to her utter destruction and ruin, so the great and abominable church together with all wickedness shall be utterly destroyed when the Lord comes. Before that great day the servants of the Lord are calling, "Go ye out from Babylon" (D. & C. 133:5, 7), for the time is not far distant when "BABYLON THE GREAT, THE MOTHER OF HARLOTS AND ABOMINA-

TIONS OF THE EARTH" (Rev. 17:5) shall receive her foreordained doom, and an angel shall proclaim the fateful judgment: "Babylon is fallen, is fallen, that great city, because she made all nations drink of the wine of the wrath of her fornication." (Rev. 14:8.)

BACKBITING.
See GOSSIPING. To *backbite* is to slander one who is not present. It is a wicked, evil practice, hated of God and fostered by Satan. (Ps. 15:3; Rom. 1:30; 2 Cor. 12:20.) It is the express appointment of the teachers in the Aaronic Priesthood —as part of their mission to do home teaching—to see that there is no *backbiting* in the Church. (D. & C. 20:54.)

BACKSLIDING ISRAEL.
See APOSTASY.

BAPTISM.
See ACCOUNTABILITY, BAPTISMAL FONT, BAPTISM FOR THE DEAD, BAPTISM OF FIRE, BORN AGAIN, CHRIST, CLINIC BAPTISMS, FAITH, GIFT OF THE HOLY GHOST, HOLY GHOST, INFANT BAPTISM, JOHN THE BAPTIST, ORIGINAL SIN THEORY, PLAN OF SALVATION, REDEMPTION, REPENTANCE, SACRAMENT, SALVATION, SALVATION OF CHILDREN, YEARS OF ACCOUNTABILITY. *Baptism* by immersion under the hands of a legal administrator, one em-

powered to bind on earth and seal in heaven, is the initiatory ordinance into the Church on earth and the celestial kingdom in the world to come. (D. & C. 20:68-74; 2 Ne. 9:23-24.) It is of two kinds: 1. *Baptism in water* by the power of the lesser or Aaronic Priesthood; and 2. *Baptism of the Spirit* by the power of the greater or Melchizedek Priesthood. (Mark 1:1-8; Luke 3:16; Acts 19:1-6; D. & C. 20:38-60; *Articles of Faith,* pp. 120-170.)

The gospel is the new and everlasting covenant by means of which God, on his own terms, offers salvation to man. Baptism is the formally appointed means and ordinance which the Lord has provided so that man can signify his personal acceptance of all of the terms and conditions of the eternal gospel covenant. Thus in baptism, which as part of the gospel is itself a new and an everlasting covenant (D. & C. 22), man covenants to abide by all of the laws and requirements of the whole gospel.

As summarized by Alma at the waters of Mormon, the contractual obligations assumed by men as part of the covenant of baptism are: 1. "To come into the fold of God," that is, to join the Church of Jesus Christ, the Church which is God's kingdom on earth; 2. "To be called his people," meaning to "Take upon you the name of Christ" (D. & C. 18:17-25); 3. "To bear one another's burdens, that they may be light"; 4. "To mourn with those that mourn"; 5. To "comfort those that stand in need of comfort"; 6. "To stand as witnesses of God at all times and in all things, and in all places that ye may be in, even until death"; and 7. To agree to serve God and keep his commandments.

The Lord, as his part of the bargain, covenants that if men will do these things, then he will: 1. "Pour out his Spirit more abundantly upon" them, that is, they will receive the baptism of fire and the companionship of the Holy Ghost; and 2. They shall "be redeemed of God, . . . numbered with those of the first resurrection," and "have eternal life." (Mosiah 18:7-10.)

Baptism serves four purposes: 1. It is for the remission of sins. (D. & C. 13; 19:31; 20:37; 33:11; 49:13; 68:27; 84:27, 64, 74; 107:20.) 2. It admits the repentant person to membership in the Church and kingdom of God on earth. (D. & C. 20:37, 71-74.) 3. It is the gate to the celestial kingdom of heaven, that is, it starts a person out on the straight and narrow path which leads to eternal life. (2 Ne. 9:23-24; 31:13-21.) 4. It is the means whereby the door to personal santification is opened. "Repent, all ye ends of the earth, and come unto me and be baptized in my name," the resurrected Lord proclaimed to the Nephites, *"that ye may be sanctified by the reception of the Holy Ghost, that ye may stand spotless before me at the last day."* (3 Ne. 27:20.)

When the Church and kingdom is fully organized and operative, one baptism suffices for any one person.

There is no need for and no ordinance of rebaptism in the Church. Excommunicated persons must of course be baptized a second time if they are to be restored to fellowship in the kingdom. If there were no record or proof that a person had been baptized, it would be necessary to perform the ordinance over again.

Joseph Smith and Oliver Cowdery were, of course, baptized for the remission of sins on May 15, 1829 (Jos. Smith 2:66-75), and were baptized again for admission to the Church on April 6, 1830. (*History of the Church,* vol. 1, pp. 75-78.) Their first baptism could not admit them to membership in an organization which did not exist at the time the ordinance was performed. A similar situation once prevailed among the Nephites. (3 Ne. 7:18-26; 19:7-15.) Many of the saints in this dispensation were baptized a second time after they arrived in the Salt Lake Valley. (*Doctrines of Salvation,* vol. 2, pp. 332-337.)

Some different reasons exist as to the need for baptism in the case of our Lord, he being without sin and in need of no repentance. His expression to John was, "Suffer it to be so now: for thus it becometh us to fulfil all righteousness." (Matt. 3:15.) Nephi explains that Christ did fulfil all righteousness in being baptized in that: 1. He humbled himself before the Father; 2. He covenanted to be obedient and keep the Father's commandments; 3. He had to be baptized to gain admission to the celestial kingdom; and 4. He

set an example for all men to follow. (2 Ne. 31:4-11.)

Our Lord's baptism "showeth unto the children of men the straightness of the path, and the narrowness of the gate, by which they should enter, he having set the example before them." (2 Ne. 31:9.) If even the King of the kingdom could not return to his high state of pre-existent exaltation without complying with his own eternal law for admission to that kingdom, how can any man expect a celestial inheritance without an authorized and approved baptism? Indeed, so invarying is the eternal law which states, "Except a man be born of water and of the Spirit, he cannot enter into the kingdom of God" (John 3:5), that this holy baptismal ordinance must be performed vicariously for accountable persons who departed this life unbaptized but who would have complied with the law had the privilege been afforded them. Hence we have the doctrine of *baptism for the dead.* (1 Cor. 15:29.)

As an everlasting covenant, baptism began on this earth with Adam (Moses 6:64-67) and has continued ever since whenever the Lord has had a people on earth. (D. & C. 20:23-28; 84:26-28.) It was not a new rite introduced by John the Baptist and adopted by Christ and his followers. The. Jews were baptizing their proselytes long before John, as is well attested from secular sources. The Inspired Version of the Bible, the Book of Moses being a part thereof, contains ample evidence of the practice of baptism in Old Testament times. The part of the Book of Mormon of the pre-Christian Era contains some of the best information we have relative to this eternal law.

As with other doctrines and ordinances, apostate substitutes of the real thing are found both among pagans and supposed Christians. Perverted forms of baptism were common among the mystery religions of the old world. (Milton R. Hunter, *Gospel Through the Ages*, pp. 192-226.) Some of the churches of modern Christendom deny the necessity of baptism and talk in terms of salvation coming by the mere act of confessing Christ with one's lips. Others, not comprehending the mercies of Christ and the power of his atonement, enlarge the doctrine to include children who have not arrived at the years of accountability.

True water baptisms are performed by legal administrators who immerse the candidate in water. The symbolic representation thus adhered to bears record of the death, burial, and resurrection of Christ. (Rom. 6:1-12.) Baptism is also symbolical of a new birth, with the same elements—water, blood, and spirit—being present as are found in the first birth. (Moses 6:59-60) These elements were also present in the circumstances surrounding the atoning sacrifice of our Lord. (John 19:28-37; 1 John 5:5-12.) Thus through this

ordinance attention is also focused on that most transcendent of all events. It goes without saying that sprinkling or pouring, where supposed baptisms are concerned, do not conform to the Lord's law.

BAPTISMAL FONTS.
See BAPTISM, BAPTISM FOR THE DEAD. Any appropriate body of water of sufficient size—be it stream, lake, ocean, or artificial body—may properly be used for baptismal purposes. Baptisms in a bath tub are not proper; there must be ample room for both parties to go down into the water. Many Latter-day Saint church buildings have especially built *baptismal fonts.* Artistic paintings and archaeological discoveries both in the Americas and in the old world show such fonts as having been in use in ancient times also. (Milton R. Hunter, *Archaeology and the Book of Mormon,* vol. 1, pp. 89-92.)

In our day, baptisms for the dead can be performed only in temples. (D. & C. 124:28-35.) Fonts for such purposes should be constructed only in the basements or lower portions of such buildings. (D. & C. 128:12-13.)

BAPTISM FOR THE DEAD.
See BAPTISM, PLAN OF SALVATION, SALVATION, SALVATION FOR THE DEAD, SECOND CHANCE THEORY, SPIRIT PRISON, SPIRIT WORLD,

TEMPLE ORDINANCES, TEMPLES, VICARIOUS ORDINANCES. Based on the eternal principle of vicarious service, the Lord has ordained *baptism for the dead* as the means whereby all his worthy children of all ages can become heirs of salvation in his kingdom. Baptism is the gate to the celestial kingdom, and except a man be born again of water and of the Spirit he cannot gain an inheritance in that heavenly world. (John 3:3-5.) Obviously, during the frequent periods of apostate darkness when the gospel light does not shine, and also in those geographical areas where legal administrators are not found, hosts of people live and die without ever entering in at the gate of baptism so as to be on the path leading to eternal life. For them a just God has ordained baptism for the dead, a vicarious-proxy labor. (D. & C. 124:28-36; 127; 128; 1 Cor. 15:29.)

Baptisms for the dead were not performed in pre-meridian dispensations. But since our Lord preached to the spirits in prison, organizing his kingdom among them, these and other vicarious temple ordinances have been performed. The dispensation of the fulness of times is the great era of vicarious ordinance work, a work which will continue during the millennial era until it has been performed for every living soul entitled to receive it. (*Doctrines of Salvation,* vol. 2, pp. 100-196.)

BAPTISM OF FIRE.

See BAPTISM, BORN AGAIN, GIFT OF THE HOLY GHOST, HOLY GHOST, SANCTIFICATION, SANCTIFIER. To gain salvation every accountable person must receive two baptisms. They are baptism of water and of the Spirit. (John 3:3-5.) The baptism of the Spirit is called the *baptism of fire and of the Holy Ghost.* (Matt. 3:11; Luke 3:16; 2 Ne. 31:13-14; 3 Ne. 11:35; 12:1-2; Morm. 7:10; D. & C. 20:41; 33:11; 39:6.) By the power of the Holy Ghost—who is the Sanctifier (3 Ne. 27:19-21)—dross, iniquity, carnality, sensuality, and every evil thing is burned out of the repentant soul as if by fire; the cleansed person becomes literally a new creature of the Holy Ghost. (Mosiah 27:24-26.) He is born again.

The baptism of fire is not something in addition to the receipt of the Holy Ghost; rather, it is the actual enjoyment of the gift which is offered by the laying on of hands at the time of baptism. "Remission of sins," the Lord says, comes *"by baptism and by fire, yea, even the Holy Ghost."* (D. & C. 19:31; 2 Ne. 31:17.) Those who receive the baptism of fire are *"filled as if with fire."* (Hela. 5:45.)

There have been, however, exceptional and miraculous instances when literal fire has attended the baptism of the Spirit. After the baptism of the Nephite disciples, "they were filled with the Holy Ghost and with fire. And behold, they were encircled about as if it were by fire; and it came down from heaven, and the multitude did witness it, and did bear record." (3 Ne. 19:13-14.) Similar manifestations occurred on the day of Pentecost (Acts 2:1-4) and among a group of Lamanite converts. (Hela. 5; 3 Ne. 9:20.)

BAPTIST.
See JOHN THE BAPTIST.

BASTARDS.
See SONS OF GOD. Since a *bastard* is an illegitimate child, one born out of wedlock, Paul aptly and pointedly uses the term to describe those who are *not* sons of God, who have not been adopted into the family of God as joint-heirs with Christ. (Heb. 12:5-8.) According to his terminology there are sons on the one hand and bastards on the other. The sons inherit the fulness of the Father's kingdom; the bastards—never having been born of God—are cast out of the eternal family as though they were illegitimate; they become "servants, to minister for those who are worthy of a far more, and an exceeding, and an eternal weight of glory." (D. & C. 132:16.)

BATTLE OF ARMAGEDDON.
See GOG AND MAGOG, MILLENNIUM, SECOND COMING OF CHRIST, SUPPER OF THE GREAT GOD, WAR. Some 60 air miles north of Jerusalem lies the ancient city of *Megid-*do (now called Tell el-Mutesellim). In its north-central Palestinian location, Megiddo overlooks the great plain of Esdraelon, an area of some 20 by 14 miles in which many great battles took place anciently. Megiddo is the older Hebrew form of *Armageddon* or *Har-Magedon* meaning the Mount or Hill of Megiddo, or the Hill of Battles; it is "the valley of *Megiddon*" mentioned in Zechariah. (Zech. 12:11.)

At the very moment of the Second Coming of our Lord, "all nations" shall be gathered "against Jerusalem to battle" (Zech. 11; 12; 13; 14), and the *battle of Armageddon* (obviously covering the entire area from Jerusalem to Megiddo, and perhaps more) will be in progress. As John expressed it, "the kings of the earth and of the whole world" will be gathered "to the battle of that great day of God Almighty, . . . into a place called in the Hebrew tongue Armageddon." Then Christ will "come as a thief," meaning unexpectedly, and the dramatic upheavals promised to accompany his return will take place. (Rev. 16:14-21.) It is incident to this battle of Armageddon that the Supper of the Great God shall take place (Rev. 19:11-18), and it is the same battle described by Ezekiel as the war with Gog and Magog. (Ezek. 38; 39; *Doctrines of Salvation,* vol. 3, p. 45.)

BATTLE OF THE GREAT GOD.
See GOD OF BATTLES, GOG AND

MAGOG, MICHAEL THE ARCHANGEL, WAR. After the millennium, Satan "shall be loosed for a little season, that he may gather together his armies. And Michael, the seventh angel, even the archangel, shall gather together his armies, even the hosts of heaven. And the devil shall gather together his armies; even the hosts of hell, and shall come up to battle against Michael and his armies. And then cometh the *battle of the great God;* and the devil and his armies shall be cast away into their own place, that they shall not have power over the saints any more at all." (D. & C. 88:111-115.) This final great battle, in which evil spirits, mortal men, and resurrected personages all participate, will be the end of war as far as this earth is concerned. Then the earth shall be celestialized and become the abode of the righteous forever. (D. & C. 88:16-31, 116.)

BEARING FALSE WITNESS.

See GOSSIPING, LAW OF WITNESSES, LIARS, TEN COMMANDMENTS. 1. "Thou shalt not *bear false witness* against thy neighbour." (Ex. 20:16.) "Thou shalt not raise a false report: put not thine hand with the wicked to be an unrighteous witness." (Ex. 23:1.) Witnesses who wilfully testify falsely are liars and perjurers and will be rewarded accordingly. Many false witnesses came forth to testify against Jesus when the Jews sought his life. (Mark 14:53-65.) Gossiping and the spreading of false and idle rumors about a person is a form of bearing false witness.

2. To testify falsely about the truths of salvation, or to claim truth and verity for a false system of salvation, is also to *bear false witness.* According to the Lord's system, almost all things are established in the mouths of witnesses. Apostles and seventies, for instance, are given the special calling of standing as especial witnesses of the name of Christ. Every member of the Church is obligated to be a witness of the restoration. Those, however, who teach false doctrines are bearing false witness; and those who claim, falsely, that salvation is found in some system other than the very one ordained by Deity are bearing record of that which is not true—and along with all false witnesses will be rewarded according to their deeds.

BEELZEBUB.

See BAAL (BAALIM), DEVIL. This name for Satan signifies his position as the prince or chief of the devils. It is the same name (Baalzebub) as was given to an ancient heathen god. (2 Kings 1:3.) In their rebellion against light, the ancient Jews applied the name *Beelzebub* to Christ (Matt. 10:25), and also said that he cast out devils by the power of Beelzebub. (Matt. 12:22-30.)

BEGGARS.

See ALMSGIVING, CHURCH WELFARE PLAN, POOR. Kindness and

help toward *beggars* is a basic principle of pure religion. It frequently happens that temporal prosperity has no relationship to righteousness or the lack of it. Wars, disasters, calamities, prolonged illness, or any of a number of circumstances beyond human control, might turn the most affluent persons into beggars.

In the Lord's view, men are judged by what they are and not what they have. Blind Bartimaeus, who begged on the Jericho road, and the beggar at the pool of Siloam both had faith to receive their sight. (Mark 10:46-52; John 9.) Upon his death the beggar Lazarus was carried by the angels to the paradise of Abraham's bosom. (Luke 16:19-31.) And it was a beggar, lame from his mother's womb, who obeyed Peter's God-given command: "In the name of Jesus Christ of Nazareth rise up and walk." (Acts 3; 4.) Poor people have ever been the recipients of special prophetic solicitude, and the law made special provision for their poverty and destitute circumstances. (Lev. 19:10; 25:25; Ps. 69:33.)

King Benjamin spoke feelingly to his people of their responsibility to love and serve God and their fellow men, saying that if they did, then, "Ye yourselves will succor those that stand in need of your succor; ye will administer of your substance unto him that standeth in need; and *ye will not suffer that the beggar putteth up his petition to you in vain,* and turn him out to perish. Perhaps thou shalt say: The man has brought upon himself his misery; therefore I will stay my hand, and will not give unto him of my food, nor impart unto him of my substance that he may not suffer, for his punishments are just—But I say unto you, O man, whosoever doeth this the same hath great cause to repent; and except he repenteth of that which he hath done he perisheth forever, and hath no interest in the kingdom of God. For behold, *are we not all beggars? Do we not all depend upon the same Being, even God, for all the substance which we have,* for both food and raiment, and for gold, and for silver, and for all the riches which we have of every kind? And behold, even at this time, ye have been calling on his name, and begging for a remission of your sins. And has he suffered that ye have begged in vain?" (Mosiah 4:16-20.)

BEGINNING.

See BEGINNING AND END, CREATION, PRE-EXISTENCE. There is no such thing as an ultimate *beginning,* a time prior to which there was nothing, any more than there ever can be an ending, a time past which there will be nothing. "The elements are eternal." (D. & C. 93:33.) Spirit element (that is, "the intelligence of spirits") always existed. "Is it logical to say that the intelligence of spirits is immortal, and yet that it had a beginning?" the Prophet asked. *"The intelligence of spirits had no beginning, neither will it have an end.* That is good logic. That which has a beginning may have an end." (*Teachings,* pp. 353-354.)

Such scriptural assertions as, "I was in the beginning with the Father, and am the Firstborn; ... Ye were also in the beginning with the Father" (D. & C. 93:21-23), simply mean that all the spirit offspring of the Father were with him in pre-existence. Spirit entities as such, in their organized form as the offspring of Deity, have not existed as long as God has, for he is their Father, and he begat them as spirits.

Thus there are two principles: 1. That "man was also in the beginning with God," meaning that the spirits of men were created, begotten, and organized, that they came into being as spirits at the time of their spirit birth; and 2. That "intelligence, or the light of truth, was not created or made, neither indeed can be" (D. & C. 93:29), meaning that spirit element, "the intelligence of spirits," the substance from which they were created as entities, has always existed and is as eternal as God himself. This is the correct meaning and purport of the scriptures and of the Prophet's explanation of the *immortal spirit,* as found in the King Follett Sermon. (*Teachings,* pp. 352-354.)

Similarly, the expression, "In the beginning God created the heaven and the earth" (Gen. 1:1), means there was a time of commencement as far as the earth in its present organized or created form is concerned. But the elements from which the creation took place are eternal and therefore had no beginning.

BEGINNING AND END.
See ALPHA AND OMEGA, CHRIST, ETERNITY TO ETERNITY, EVERLASTING TO EVERLASTING, FIRST AND LAST. Christ is the *Beginning and the End.* (D. & C. 35:1; 38:1; 45:7; 54:1; 61:1; 84:120; Rev. 1:8-17; 21:6; 22:13.) These are English words having substantially the same meaning as the Greek *Alpha and Omega.* The thought conveyed is one of timelessness, of a being who is the Beginning and the End because his "course is one eternal round, the same today as yesterday, and forever." (D. & C. 35:1.) He was God "in the beginning" (John 1:1-3); he is God now; he will be God in the "end," that is to all eternity. The *beginning* is the pre-existent eternity that went before; the *end* is the immortal eternity that is to come.

BEL.
See BAAL (BAALIM), FALSE GODS. *Bel* was the chief god of Babylon, probably the sun god of both the Assyrians and the Babylonians. He was essentially identical with the Phoenician and Canaanitish god *Baal,* also called *Belus.* The Lord promised to confound and punish Bel (Jer. 50:2; 51:44), "for I am God, and there is none else." (Isa. 45:22; 46:1-2.)

BELIAL.

See DEVIL, FALSE GODS, SONS OF BELIAL. *Belial* is one of the names of Satan and has particular reference to the fact that he is the personification of evil and lawlessness. The literal meaning of the term is *worthlessness* with an especial connotation of *recklessness* and *lawlessness.* Paul made use of this name of Satan in this persuasive language: "What fellowship hath righteousness with unrighteousness? and what communion hath light with darkness? And what concord hath Christ with Belial? or what part hath he that believeth with an infidel? And what agreement hath the temple of God with idols?" (2 Cor. 6:14-18.)

BELIEF.

See BELIEVERS, CHRIST, FAITH, GOD, MIRACLES, OBEDIENCE, REPENTANCE, SALVATION, TESTIMONY, TRUTH. 1. In nearly every instance, the scriptures use *belief* as a synonym for *faith.* The two terms are interchangeable; they mean the same thing, are gained in the same way, and the same effects flow from them. The Prophet adopted this usage in the *Lectures on Faith;* and accordingly, no one has faith in Christ who does not believe that he is the Son of God, nor does a person believe in Christ in the full sense without having faith in him. Faith is belief, and belief is faith. To illustrate: Two blind men besought Jesus to restore their sight. *"Believe*

ye that I am able to do this?" he asked; and receiving an affirmative, "Yea, Lord," in reply, "Then touched he their eyes, saying, According to your *faith* be it unto you. And their eyes were opened." (Matt. 9:27-31; Rom. 10:13-17.)

Belief in Christ is essential to salvation. (John 12:34-50; 17:21; Rom. 9:33; 10:8-9; Heb. 10:39; D. & C. 20:29; 29:43-44; 84:74; Moses 6:52.) The gifts of the Spirit come because of belief (Mark 16:16-18; D. & C. 58:64; 68:8-12; 84:64-74); miracles are wrought and the dead are raised because of it (Matt. 8:13; Mark 5:35-43; John 11:11-46); and "all things are possible to him that believeth." (Mark 9:23-24.) *"He that believeth on me,"* the Lord said, *"the works that I do shall he do also; and greater works than these shall he do;* 14:12.) In this connection, it is important to note the explanation of the Prophet that *"the greater works which those that believed on his name were to do were to be done in eternity, where he was going and where they should behold his glory."* (*Lectures on Faith,* p. 66.)

"Repent all ye ends of the earth, and come unto me," Christ said in summarizing the plan of salvation, "and believe in my gospel, and be baptized in my name; for he that believeth and is baptized shall be saved; but he that believeth not shall be damned; and signs shall follow them that believe in my name." (Ether 4:18.)

Belief in the various truths that

must be accepted if salvation is to be won, cannot be parceled out in such a way as to accept one essential truth and reject another. All phases of the doctrines of salvation are so intertwined with each other that it is not possible to believe one part without also believing all parts of which knowledge has been gained. Thus no one can believe in Christ without believing in his Father also. (Matt. 11:27; John 5:23; 6:44; 12:44-46; 14:1, 6.) And no one can accept Christ without accepting the prophets who testify of him. "He that believeth not my words believeth not my disciples," the Lord said. "But he that believeth these things which I have spoken, him will I visit with the manifestations of my Spirit, and he shall know and bear record. . . . *He that will not believe my words will not believe me—that I am; and he that will not believe me will not believe the Father who sent me.*" (Ether 4:10-12.)

"Had ye believed Moses," he also said, "ye would have believed me: for he wrote of me. But if ye believe not his writings, how shall ye believe my words?" (John 5:46-47.) "Believe in Christ and deny him not," Nephi said, "for by denying him ye also deny the prophets and the law." (2 Ne. 25:28.) To prosper, the saints must both "believe in the Lord" and also "believe his prophets." (2 Chron. 20:20; John 15:1-11.)

No one in our day who has an understanding of the Book of Mormon can believe in Christ unless he also believes the Book of Mormon. Speaking of that record, Nephi says: *"If ye shall believe in Christ ye will believe in these words, for they are the words of Christ."* (2 Ne. 33:10.) Similarly, people who have an understanding of both the Book of Mormon and the Bible cannot believe the one without believing the other also. In speaking of the Bible and Book of Mormon, the Prophet Mormon said, "If ye believe that ye will believe this also." (Morm. 7:8-9.)

The same principle applies to the acceptance of Joseph Smith as a Prophet. President Brigham Young taught: "There is not that being that ever had the privilege of hearing the way of life and salvation set before him as it is written in the New Testament, and in the Book of Mormon, and in the book of Doctrine and Covenants, by a Latter-day Saint, that can say that Jesus lives, that his gospel is true, and at the same time say that Joseph Smith was not a Prophet of God. That is strong testimony, but it is true. No man can say that this book [laying his hand on the Bible] is true, is the word of the Lord, is the way, is the guideboard in the path, and a charter by which we may learn the will of God; and at the same time say, that the Book of Mormon is untrue; if he has had the privilege of reading it, or of hearing it read, and learning its doctrines. There is not that person on the face of the earth who has had the privilege of learning the gospel of Jesus Christ from these two books, that can say that one is true, and the other is false. No Latter-day Saint, no man or woman, can say the Book of Mormon is true, and at the same time say that the Bible is untrue. If one be true, both are; and if one be false, both are false. If Jesus lives, and is the Savior of the world, Joseph Smith is a Prophet of God, and lives in the bosom of his father Abraham. Though they have killed his body, yet he lives and beholds the face of his Father in Heaven; and his garments are pure as the angels that surround the throne of God; and no man on the earth can say that Jesus lives, and deny, at the same time, my assertion about the Prophet Joseph. This is my testimony, and it is strong." (*Discourses,* new ed., p. 459.)

2. In a few scriptural instances, *belief* is used to signify mental assent to a proposition whether the matter assented to is true or false. This usage gives belief no similarity whatever to faith. This kind of belief may or may not be predicated on truth, and salvation does not result from it. Thus the devils "believe, and tremble" (Jas. 2:19), for they know who Christ is and await with awful foreboding their destined fate. And thus also an apostate world has turned to "strong delusion," as for instance by accepting the false doctrines of the day, causing them to "believe a lie: That they all might be

damned who believed not the truth, but had pleasure in unrighteousness." (2 Thess. 2:11-12.)

BELIEFS.
See DOCTRINE.

BELIEVERS.
See BELIEF, BELIEVING BLOOD, BRETHREN, CHRISTIANS, CHURCH OF JESUS CHRIST OF LATTER-DAY SAINTS, DISCIPLES, HEATHENS, MORMONS, PROPHETS, SAINTS, TESTIMONY, TRUTH. 1. Those who believe in Christ, who accept his doctrines, and who cleave unto the disciples whom he sends to declare those doctrines and to administer the ordinances of salvation are called *believers*. All others are *unbelievers* or *nonbelievers*. Believers have views founded on truth; acceptance of apostate doctrines, of false scientific theories, or of error in any field, makes a person a nonbeliever. Believers accept the fulness of the gospel and reject all theories and views inharmonious with it; they are the saints of God, members of the sheepfold of Christ.

There are, of course, many devout people in all churches who believe in Christ and seek to do his will, insofar as their knowledge of him permits them so to do. But until they receive the truth and light revealed in latter-days and until they gain the personal revelation which follows enjoyment of the gift of the Holy Ghost, their belief and understanding cannot be perfected.

Thus, in the full sense, the *faithful* members of the Church of Jesus Christ of Latter-day Saints are the only true believers in the world today, just as the apostolic converts of the early Christian Era were the only true believers in that day. (D. & C. 74:5.) Similarly, the Nephites in their day (4 Ne. 36) and the saints in the various dispensations have been the true believers. Men are saved by belief, damned by unbelief (D. & C. 68:9; 84:74; 112:29), or in other words believers are saved, unbelievers are damned.

2. As used by so-called Christian people generally, the term *believers* means those who accept what the world considers Christianity to be without reference to the truth or falsity of the divergent doctrines and views espoused. In a like sense, one could speak of *believers* in *Mohammedanism,* or in *evolution,* or in *communism,* or in any philosophy which is or serves as a religion to the person accepting it.

BELIEVING BLOOD.

See ADOPTION, BELIEF, FAITH, FOREORDINATION, ISRAEL, PREEXISTENCE. This is a figurative expression commonly used to designate the aptitude and inclination of certain persons to accept and believe the principles of revealed religion. In general, the Lord sends to earth in the lineage of Jacob those spirits who in pre-existence developed an especial talent for spirituality and for recognizing truth. Those born in this lineage, having the blood of Israel in their veins and finding it easy to accept the gospel, are said to have *believing blood.*

Since much of Israel has been scattered among the Gentile nations, it follows that millions of people have mixed blood, blood that is part Israel and part Gentile. The more of the blood of Israel that an individual has, the easier it is for him to believe the message of salvation as taught by the authorized agents of the Lord. This principle is the one our Lord had in mind when he said to certain Jews: "I am the good shepherd, and know my sheep, and am *known of mine.* . . . But ye believe not, because ye are not of my sheep, as I said unto you. *My sheep hear my voice,* and I know them, and *they follow me.*" (John 10:14, 26-27.)

BELOVED.

See BELOVED SON.

BELOVED SON.

See CHRIST, ONLY BEGOTTEN SON, SON, SON OF GOD. *"This is My Beloved Son. Hear Him!"* (Jos. Smith 2:17.) These are the words by which the Father introduces the Son and commands men to hearken to his teachings. (Matt. 3:17; 17:5; Mark 1:11; Luke 3:22; D. & C. 93:

15; 2 Ne. 31:11; 3 Ne. 11:7; 21:20.) Christ is the Beloved Son, which signifies his favored, preferential, *Chosen*, and *Beloved* status (Moses 4:2), and also his divine Sonship.

BENEDICTION.
See PRAYER.

BEREAVEMENT.
See MOURNING.

BETROTHAL.
See ESPOUSAL.

BETTING.
See GAMBLING.

BIBLE.
See APOCALYPSE, APOCRYPHA, BOOK OF MORMON, CANON OF SCRIPTURE, DOCTRINE AND COVENANTS, EPISTLES, GOSPELS, INSPIRED VERSION OF THE BIBLE, LOST SCRIPTURE, MORMON BIBLE, NEW TESTAMENT, OLD TESTAMENT, PEARL OF GREAT PRICE, SCRIPTURE, SIGNS OF THE TIMES, STANDARD WORKS, STICK OF EPHRAIM. That portion of the writings of inspired men in the old world which, in the providences of the Almighty, has been handed down from age to age until modern times is called the *Bible*. These writings in their original form were perfect scripture; they were the mind and will of the Lord, his voice to his chosen people and to all who would hear it. (D. & C. 68:4.) That they have not come down to us in their perfect form is well known in the Church and by all reputable scholars. Only a few fanatics among the sects of Christendom close their eyes to reality and profess to believe in what they call *verbal revelation,* that is, that every word and syllable in some version or other of the Bible is the exact word spoken by Deity.

"I believe the Bible as it read when it came from the pen of the original writers," the Prophet said. *"Ignorant translators, careless transcribers, or designing• and corrupt priests have committed many errors."* (*Teachings,* p. 327; Eighth Article of Faith.) Nephi recorded that the Bible, in its original form, "contained the plainness of the gospel of the Lord." After it had passed through the hands of "a great and abominable church, which is most abominable above all other churches," however, he saw that "many plain and precious things "were deleted, in consequence of which error and falsehood poured into the various churches. (1 Ne. 13.)

Yet with it all, the Bible is a book of books. It has enlightened and influenced the Christian world generally as no other book has ever done. Such measure of truth as was preserved in its pages (as soon as this truth became known to people generally) was instrumental in bringing to pass the Renaissance and of laying the foundation for the restoration of the gospel. When the Bible is read under the guidance of the Spirit, and in harmony with the many latter-day revelations which interpret and make plain its more mysterious parts, it becomes one of the most priceless volumes known to man. "He who reads it oftenest will like it best, and he who is acquainted with it, will know the Hand [of the Lord] wherever he can see it," the Prophet taught. (*Teachings,* p. 56.)

In its present form, the Bible is divided into Old and New Testaments and has a total of 66 books within its covers. These books contain doctrinal, historical, prophetic, and poetic materials of transcendent worth. Members of the Church are commanded to teach the principles of the gospel "which are in the Bible." (D. & C. 42:12.)

One of the great heresies of modern Christendom is the unfounded assumption that the Bible contains all of the inspired teachings now extant among men. Foreseeing that Satan would darken the minds of men in this way, and knowing that other scripture would come forth in the last days, Nephi prophesied that unbelieving Christians would reject the new revelation with the cry: "A Bible! A Bible! We have got a Bible, and there cannot be any more Bible."

And then he recorded this answering proclamation from the Lord: *"Thou fool, that shall say: A Bible,* *we have got a Bible, and we need no* *more Bible.* Have ye obtained a Bible save it were by the Jews? Know ye not that there are more nations than one? Know ye not that I, the Lord your God, have created all men, and that I remember those who are upon the isles of the sea; and that I rule in the heavens above and in the earth beneath; and I bring forth my word unto the children of men, yea, even upon all the nations of the earth? *Wherefore murmur ye, because that ye shall receive more of my word?"* (2 Ne. 29.)

BIBLE VERSIONS.
See KING JAMES VERSION OF THE BIBLE.

BIGAMY.
See SEX IMMORALITY.

BIGOTRY.
See TOLERANCE. *Bigotry*—that is, blind, obstinate, intolerant, and unreasoning adherence to a particular view—has no place among the true saints. They have the truth; their doctrines will bear investigation; there is no reason to close the mind against light and inquiry where any principle of the gospel is concerned.

BILL OF DIVORCEMENT.
See DIVORCE.

BILL OF RIGHTS.

See CONSTITUTION OF THE UNITED STATES, FREEDOM, INALIENABLE RIGHTS, LIBERTY. The first 10 amendments to the constitution of the United States are called the *bill of rights*. Their purpose is to protect men in their inalienable rights (such as life and liberty) by guaranteeing civil rights (such as trial by jury). Federal guarantees of freedom of speech, of worship, and of the press are found in the bill of rights. Obviously the establishment and spread of the gospel is facilitated by such legal guarantees.

BINDING.

See SEALINGS.

BIRDS.

See ANIMALS.

BIRTH.

See BEGINNING, BIRTH CONTROL, BIRTHDAYS, BIRTHRIGHT, BORN AGAIN, SPIRIT CHILDREN, STILLBORN CHILDREN. All men were first born in pre-existence as the literal *spirit offspring* of God our Heavenly Father. This birth constituted the beginning of the human ego as a conscious identity. By the ordained procreative process our exalted and immortal Father begat his spirit progeny in pre-existence. "All men and women are in the similitude of the universal Father and Mother, and are literally the sons and daughters of Deity," President Joseph F. Smith and his associates in the First Presidency declared. (*Improvement Era,* vol. 13, pp. 75-81.)

True, as Joseph Smith taught, man "is a self-existent being," for "the intelligence of spirits is immortal," and "had no beginning." (*Teachings,* pp. 352-354.) That is to say the bodies of Deity's spirit children were created from the existing spirit element just as the spirit bodies of the progeny of future exalted beings will be organized from the same substance. Abraham referred to the spirit children of our Father as "the intelligences that were organized before the world was." (Abra. 3:22.)

Christ, destined to be the Only Begotten Son in mortality, was the first spirit offspring in pre-existence. He "is the Firstborn among all the sons of God—the first begotten in the spirit, and the Only Begotten in the flesh. He is our elder brother." (*Improvement Era,* vol. 13, pp. 75-81.) "I was in the beginning with the Father, and am the Firstborn; . . . Ye were also in the beginning with the Father," he has revealed. (D. & C. 93:21-23.)

When the spirit children of the Father pass from his presence into this mortal sphere, a *mortal birth* results. Again by the ordained procreative process a body is provided, but this time it is made from the dust of this earth, that is, from the natural elements which appertain to this temporal sphere. Three things are necessary to effect every mortal birth. They are: water, blood, and spirit—the same elements found in every rebirth into the fellowship of God's kingdom. (Moses 6:59.)

Since Adam, all who have been born into the world have come as the offspring of mortal parents, excepting only the Lord Jesus. He came into the world as the Son of a mortal mother and an Immortal Father, thus inheriting the power both to lay down his life and to take it again in immortality. (John 10:10-18.)

Birth into this life is a great blessing in that it furthers the eternal advancement of the obedient. Those who fight the truth and come out in open rebellion against God, however, would have remained better off had they never been born. (D. & C. 76:32.) Their punishment will be so severe that the privilege of progression offered through mortal birth becomes a curse unto them.

"And wo be unto him that will not hearken unto the words of Jesus, and also to them whom he hath chosen and sent among them; for whoso receiveth not the words of Jesus and the words of those whom he hath sent receiveth not him; and therefore he will not receive them at the last day; *And it would be better for them if they had not been born.* For do ye suppose that ye can get rid of the justice of an offended God, who hath been trampled under feet of men, that thereby salvation might

come?" (3 Ne. 28:34-35.) These, also, would have been better off to have remained in pre-existence, never chancing the probation of mortality.

BIRTH CONTROL.

See BIRTH, SPIRIT CHILDREN. In the beginning the Lord commanded man to be fruitful and multiply and fill the earth with posterity, thus providing bodies for the hosts of pre-existent spirits. (Gen. 1:28.) "Marriage is ordained of God . . . that the earth might answer the end of its creation; And that it might be filled with the measure of man, according to his creation before the world was made." (D. & C. 49:15-17.)

President Brigham Young stated the position of the Church relative to *birth control* in these words: "There are multitudes of pure and holy spirits waiting to take tabernacles, now what is our duty? To prepare tabernacles for them; to take a course that will not tend to drive those spirits into the families of the wicked, where they will be trained in wickedness, debauchery, and every species of crime. *It is the duty of every righteous man and woman to prepare tabernacles for all the spirits they can."* (*Discourses,* new ed., p. 197.)

President Joseph F. Smith has said in relation to this question: "Those who have taken upon themselves the responsibility of wedded life should see to it that they do not abuse the course of nature; that they do not destroy the principle of life within them, nor violate any of the commandments of God. The command which he gave in the beginning to multiply and replenish the earth is still in force upon the children of men. Possibly no greater sin could be committed by the people who have embraced this gospel then to prevent or to destroy life in the manner indicated. We are born into the world that we may have life, and we live that we may have a fulness of joy, and if we will obtain a fulness of joy, we must obey the law of our creation and the law by which we may obtain the consummation of our righteous hopes and desires—life eternal." (*Gospel Doctrine*, 5th ed., pp. 276-277.)

Also: "I regret, I think it is a crying evil, that there should exist a sentiment or a feeling among any members of the Church to curtail the birth of their children. I think that is a crime wherever it occurs, where husband and wife are in possession of health and vigor and are free from impurities that would be entailed upon their posterity. I believe that where people undertake to curtail or prevent the birth of their children that they are going to reap disappointment by and by. I have no hesitancy in saying that I believe this is one of the greatest crimes of the world today, this evil practice." (*Rel. Soc. Mag.*, vol. 4, p. 318.)

Today the cry is heard in some quarters that these statements calling upon parents to provide bodies for the spirit hosts of heaven are outmoded. Massive birth control programs are being sponsored on a national and international scale. Fears are expressed that the earth cannot support the number of people that unrestricted births will bring. But God's decree and the counsel of the prophets remain unchanged. The real need is not to limit the number of earth's inhabitants, but to learn how to care for the increasing hosts which the Lord designs should inhabit this globe before the last allocated spirit has been sent here to gain a mortal body. Amid all the cries and pressure of the world, the position of the true Church remains fixed. God has commanded his children to multiply and fill the earth, and the earth is far from full.

BIRTHDAYS.

See BIRTH, FAMILY REUNIONS. The custom of having special celebrations on the anniversaries of one's birth appears to have originated in most ancient times. Biblical reference is made to the birthday celebrations of the Egyptian Pharaoh who honored Joseph (Gen. 40:20) and of King Herod (Matt. 14:6), who ordered the beheading of John the Baptist.

Quite likely the custom of commemorating *birthdays* started with divine approval in the days of Adam. At least Adam and all the ancient prophets, knowing the importance of man's stepping from pre-existence into mortality, might well have taken occasion to cement family solidarity and renewed desires for righteousness in connection with birthdays. Family reunions—which ofttimes serve the same purpose and also are a means of encouraging genealogical research—are frequently and appropriately held on the birthday anniversaries of a prominent member of the family.

Importance of accurate knowledge of the time of one's birth is seen in the command that the saints are to have their children baptized when eight years of age. (D. & C. 68:25.) It is the practice of the Church, also, to ordain worthy young men to certain offices in the priesthood at specified ages. Similarly, in ancient times, the divine order was to name and perform the rite of circumcision on the 8th day after birth. (Gen. 17:11; Luke 2:21.)

BIRTHRIGHT.

See BIRTH, FOREORDINATION, PRE-EXISTENCE, PRIESTHOOD. It appears that anciently under the Patriarchal Order certain special blessings, rights, powers, and privileges—collectively called the *birthright*—passed from the father to his *firstborn son.* (Gen. 43:33.) In later ages special blessings and prerogatives have been poured out upon *all* the worthy descendants of some who gained special blessings and birthrights anciently. (3 Ne. 20:25-

27.) Justification for this system, in large part, lies in the pre-existent preparation and training of those born in the lines destined to inherit preferential endowments.

Christ, the *Firstborn* among all the spirit offspring of the Father, attained the eminence of godhood while yet in pre-existence and was there foreordained as the Savior and Redeemer of mankind. Adam, Abraham, Moses, Joseph Smith, and all the prophets, numbered among the noble and great in the pre-existent eternities, were also foreordained and sent to earth in the lineage and at the times when their talents and abilities were most needed in the furtherance of the plans of the Almighty. Indeed, as taught by Moses, the whole house of Israel was so chosen and so sent to earth. (Deut. 32:7-8.)

From Adam to Noah the presiding representative of the Lord on earth held the joint office of patriarch and high priest—a calling conferred successively from father to son. Similar rights were held by Abraham, Isaac, Jacob and others of the patriarchs in their respective days. Abraham was promised that from his day on all who would receive the gospel would be accounted his seed and that his descendants after him would have right, *by lineage,* to the same priesthood he had gained. (Abra. 2:6-11.) Certain righteous persons were thus destined to receive the priesthood because they were *"lawful heirs, according to the flesh."* (D. & C. 86: 8-10.) *It was their birthright.*

Special birthright blessings and priesthood pre-eminence have remained in the lineage of Jacob. Reuben, his firstborn, lost the birthright because of iniquity, and it passed to Joseph (1 Chron. 5:1-2) and through him to Ephraim. "I am a father to Israel," the Lord said, "and Ephraim is my firstborn." (Jer. 31:9.) This preferential status enjoyed by Ephraim among his fellow tribes in Israel has continued to our day. Predominantly Ephraim, among all the tribes of Israel, has so far been gathered into the fold of the true Shepherd. When the lost tribes return, they shall come to the children of Ephraim to receive their crowns of glory. (D. & C. 133:26-34.)

From Aaron to the coming of John the Baptist, the high priests in Israel served in their presiding offices (of the Aaronic order) because they were descendants of Aaron. The office of Presiding Bishop in the Church today is of comparable hereditary nature, although the Lord has not so far designated the lineage in which the right to such office rests. (D. & C. 68:14-24.) The right to hold the Levitical Priesthood anciently was limited to the sons of Levi, who thus gained their priesthood prerogatives by birth. In the meridian of time our Lord altered this system and spread this Aaronic order of authority among worthy male members of the Church generally. (1 Tim. 3:1-13.)

The office of Patriarch to the Church is also a hereditary office.

It is conferred upon "the oldest man of the blood of Joseph or of the seed of Abraham" (*Teachings*, p. 151), that is, the oldest man of the exact patriarchal lineage in Israel. Joseph Smith, Sr., father of the Prophet, was the first to hold this office in latter-day Israel, with Hyrum, his oldest living son, gaining the birthright upon his father's death. (*Doctrines of Salvation*, vol. 3, pp. 162-169.)

Lineage alone does not guarantee the receipt of whatever birthright privileges may be involved in particular cases. Worthiness, ability, and other requisites are also involved. Jacob prevailed over his older brother Esau because "Esau despised his birthright." (Gen. 25: 24-34; 27; Rom. 9:10-12.) The Lord placed Ephraim (the younger) before Manasseh to fulfil his own purposes (Gen. 48); and Nephi, junior in point of birth to Laman and Lemuel, was made a ruler and a teacher over them, a circumstance that became the cause of much contention for many generations. (1 Ne. 2:22; 16:37-38; 18:10; 2 Ne. 5:3, 19; Mosiah 10:11-17.)

Civil and governmental prerogatives have also been determined down through the ages on the birthright principle. Many of the kings of Israel and of Judah rose to their positions of temporal eminence by inheritance from their fathers. King Mosiah, on this continent, prevailed upon his people to adopt a system of rule by judges

88

to avoid the evils of this system of civil rule. (Mosiah 29.) Monarchies and empires in general have had laws of succession patterned after the ancient patriarchal system, and problems of property rights in feudal and caste systems have often been regulated in accordance with laws of primogeniture.

BISHOP.

See CHRIST, GOOD SHEPHERD, OVERSEERS. Christ is "the Shepherd and *Bishop*" of the souls of the saints, by which is meant that he is the Overseer who has led the saints to salvation through his atoning sacrifice. (1 Pet. 2:21-25.)

BISHOPRIC.

See BISHOPS, OVERSEERS, PRESIDING BISHOP, PRIESTHOOD OFFICES. 1. Any office or position of major responsibility in the Church, any office of overseership under the supervision of which important church business is administered, is a *bishopric*. Thus the church affairs administered by a bishop are his bishopric. Thus, also, members of the Council of the Twelve—who hold the keys of the kingdom and are empowered to regulate all the affairs of the Church—serve in their bishopric. (D. & C. 114; Acts 1:20.)

2. A *ward bishopric,* a quorum of three high priests, consists of a bishop and two counselors. They are set apart to preside over and direct the affairs of the kingdom in a particular ward. (D. & C. 107:74.) They are "to feed the church of God." (Acts 20:28.) Ward clerks are not members of bishoprics. In the absence of a literal descendant of Aaron, the *Presiding Bishopric* consists of three high priests of the Melchizedek Priesthood. (D. & C. 68:14-24; 107:13-17, 68-76.)

BISHOPS.

See AARONIC PRIESTHOOD, BISHOP, BISHOPS COURT, BISHOPS STOREHOUSES, BRANCH PRESIDENTS, JUDGES IN ISRAEL, OVERSEERS, PASTORS, PRESIDING BISHOP, SHEPHERDS. One of the ordained offices in the Aaronic Priesthood is that of *bishop*. (D. & C. 20:67.) Those so ordained and set apart to serve either in the Presiding Bishopric or as ward bishops are called to preside over the Aaronic Priesthood. A ward bishop is the president of the Aaronic Priesthood in his ward and is also the president of the priests quorum. (D. & C. 107:87-88.) The office of a bishop is also an appendage "belonging unto the high priesthood." (D. & C. 84:29.)

In his Aaronic Priesthood capacity a bishop deals primarily with temporal concerns (D. & C. 107:68); as the presiding high priest in his ward, however, he presides over all ward affairs and members. A bishop is a common judge in Israel (D. & C. 107:74); it is his right to have the gift of discernment, the power to discern all other spiritual gifts, "lest there shall be any among you professing and yet be not God." (D. & C. 46:27.)

"A bishop must be blameless, as the steward of God; not selfwilled, not soon angry, not given to wine, no striker, not given to filthy lucre; But a lover of hospitality, a lover of good men, sober, just, holy, temperate; Holding fast the faithful word as he hath been taught, that he may be able by sound doctrine both to exhort and to convince the gainsayers." (Tit. 1:7-9; 1 Tim. 3:1-7.)

BISHOPS COURT.
See BISHOPS, CHURCH COURTS, DISFELLOWSHIPMENT, ELDERS COURT, EXCOMMUNICATION, JUDGES IN ISRAEL. As common judges in Israel, bishops sit in judgment on their ward members. (D. & C. 42:78-93; 64:40; 102:2; 107:71-75.) Not only do they discern the personal righteousness of their ward members—calling them to positions of responsibility, approving them for temple recommends, priesthood ordinations, and the like—but when iniquity arises they are bound to hear confessions and to call in question the fellowship and membership of such members. When a formal *bishops court* is held, the bishop is the judge, with his counselors concurring in the judgment unless some iniquity is manifest in it.

BISHOPS STOREHOUSES.
See BISHOPS, CONSECRATION, UNITED ORDER, CHURCH WELFARE PLAN. To help bishops discharge their obligation to care for the temporal needs of the poor the Lord has directed the building, stocking, maintenance, and use of *bishops storehouses*. (D. & C. 42:30-36; 51:9-20; 58:24, 37; 70; 72:9-16; 78:3-7; 82:15-24; 83; 90:22-23; 101:96.) These are operated as part of the Church Welfare Plan.

BLACK MAGIC.
See MAGIC.

BLASPHEMY.
See APOSTASY, CHRIST, PROFANITY, REVERENCE, UNPARDONABLE SIN. *Blasphemy* consists in either or both of the following: 1. Speaking irreverently, evilly, abusively, or scurrilously against God or sacred things; or 2. Speaking profanely or *falsely* about Deity.

Among a great host of impious and sacrilegious speaking that constitute blasphemy are such things as: Taking the name of God in vain; evil-speaking about the Lord's anointed; belittling sacred temple ordinances, or patriarchal blessings, or sacramental administrations; claiming unwarranted divine authority; and promulgating with profane piety a false system of salvation.

Accordingly blasphemy is a sign of apostasy (2 Tim. 3:2); and the great apostate church which is not the Lord's Church is described as reveling in blasphemy. (Rev. 13:1-8.) When our Lord performed healings (Matt. 9:3) and announced himself as the Son of God, he was accused by the Jews of blasphemy (Matt. 26:63-65; Mark 14:61-64; John 10:22-38)—a charge that would have been true, if his witness had not been true and his power divine.

In ancient Israel blasphemy against the name of the Lord was an offense punishable with death by stoning. (Lev. 24:16.) Blasphemy against the Holy Ghost—which is falsely denying Christ after receiving a perfect revelation of him from the Holy Ghost—is the unpardonable sin. (Matt. 12:31-32; Mark 3:28-29; D. & C. 132:27.)

BLASPHEMY AGAINST THE HOLY GHOST.
See UNPARDONABLE SIN.

BLESSING OF CHILDREN.
See ORDINANCES, SALVATION OF CHILDREN. "Every member of the church of Christ having children is to bring them unto the elders before the church, who are to lay their hands upon them in the name of Jesus Christ, and bless them in his name." (D. & C. 20:70.) Ordinarily this command is complied with through the ordinance of *blessing of children,* although it might also be complied with in connection with confirmation and bestowal of the Holy Ghost. It is the practice of the Church to perform the ordinance of the blessing of children in fast meetings a few weeks after the birth of the child. At that time the child is formally and officially given a name, and the proper church records are made so that the necessary genealogical data will be preserved.

The blessing of children is not an ordinance of salvation; children are saved through the atoning sacrifice of Christ without ordinances. This was fully understood by the ancient apostles, for when the people brought "little children" to Jesus, "that he should put his hands on them and pray, . . . the disciples rebuked them, saying, *There is no need, for Jesus hath said, Such shall be saved.* But Jesus said, Suffer little children to come unto me, and forbid them not, for of such is the kingdom of heaven. And he laid hands on them" (*Inpsired Version,* Matt. 19:13-15.)

BLESSING ON THE FOOD.
See PRAYER.

BLINDNESS.
See DEAFNESS.

BLOCK TEACHERS.
See HOME TEACHERS.

BLOOD.

See FLESH AND BLOOD.

BLOOD ATONEMENT DOC-
TRINE.

See ATONEMENT OF CHRIST,
CALLING AND ELECTION SURE,
CHRIST, FLESH AND BLOOD. From
the days of Joseph Smith to the
present, wicked and evilly-disposed
persons have fabricated false and
slanderous stories to the effect that
the Church, in the early days of
this dispensation, engaged in a
practice of *blood atonement* whereunder the blood of apostates and
others was shed by the Church as
an atonement for their sins. These
claims are false and were known
by their orignators to be false.
There is not one historical instance
of so-called blood atonement in
this dispensation, nor has there
been one event or occurrence
whatever, of any nature, from
which the slightest inference arises
that any such practice either existed or was taught.

There are, however, in the sermons of some of the early church
leaders some statements about the
true doctrine of blood atonement
and of its practice in past dispensations, for instance, in the days of
Moses. By taking one sentence on
one page and another from a succeeding page and even by taking a
part of a sentence on one page and
a part of another found several
pages away—all wholly torn from

context—dishonest persons have
attempted to make it appear that
Brigham Young and others taught
things just the opposite of what
they really believed and taught.

Raising the curtain of truth on
this false and slanderous bluster of
enemies of the Church who have
thus wilfully chosen to fight the
truth with outright lies of the bas-
est sort, the true doctrine of blood
atonement is simply this:

1. Jesus Christ worked out the
infinite and eternal atonement by
the shedding of his own blood. He
came into the world for the purpose
of dying on the cross for the sins of
the world. By virtue of that atoning
sacrifice immortality came as a free
gift to all men, and all who would
believe and obey his laws would in
addition be cleansed from sin
through his blood. (Mosiah 3:16-19;
3 Ne. 27:19-21; 1 John 1:7; Rev. 5:
9-10.)

2. But under certain circumstances there are some serious sins
for which the cleansing of Christ
does not operate, and the law of
God is that men must then have
their own blood shed to atone for
their sins. Murder, for instance, is
one of these sins; hence we find the
Lord commanding capital punishment. Thus, also, if a person has so
progressed in righteousness that his
calling and election has been made
sure, if he has come to that position
where he knows "by revelation and
the spirit of prophecy, through the
power of the Holy Priesthood" that
he is sealed up unto eternal life (D.

& C. 131:5), then if he gains forgiveness for certain grievous sins, he must "be destroyed in the flesh," and "delivered unto the buffetings of Satan unto the day of redemption, saith the Lord God." (D. & C. 132:19-27.)

President Joseph Fielding Smith has written: "Man may commit certain grievous sins—*according to his light and knowledge*—that will place him beyond the reach of the atoning blood of Christ. If then he would be saved, he must make sacrifice of his own life to atone—so far as in his power lies—for that sin, for the blood of Christ alone under certain circumstances will not avail. . . . Joseph Smith taught that there were certain sins so grievous that man may commit, that they will place the transgressors beyond the power of the atonement of Christ. If these offenses are committed, then the blood of Christ will not cleanse them from their sins even though they repent. Therefore their only hope is to have their own blood shed to atone, as far as possible, in their behalf." (*Doctrines of Salvation,* vol. 1, pp. 133-138.)

This doctrine can only be practiced in its fulness in a day when the civil and ecclesiastical laws are administered in the same hands. It was, for instance, practiced in the days of Moses, but it was not and could not be practiced in this dispensation, except that persons who understood its provisions could and did use their influence to get a form of capital punishment written into the laws of the various states of the union so that the blood of murderers could be shed.

BLOOD OF ISRAEL.
See BELIEVING BLOOD.

BOASTING.
See PRIDE, REJOICING, SIGNS OF THE TIMES, VAINGLORY, VANITY. *Boasting* is of two kinds: either righteous, or unrighteous; either in the arm of flesh, or in the Lord and his gracious goodness and power. "He that glorieth, let him glory in the Lord," Paul said in summing up a sermon on boasting, "For not he that commendeth himself is approved, but whom the Lord commendeth." (2 Cor. 10:7-18; Ps. 44:8.) Ammon spoke similarly: "I do not boast in my own strength, nor in my own wisdom; but behold, my joy is full, yea, my heart is brim with joy, and I will rejoice in my God. Yea, I know that I am nothing; as to my strength I am weak; therefore I will not boast of myself, but I will boast of my God, for in his strength I can do all things. . . . Therefore, let us glory, yea, we will glory in the Lord; yea, we will rejoice for our joy is full; yea, we will praise our God forever. Behold, *who can glory too much in the Lord?*" (Alma 26:8-16, 35.)

Boasting in the arm of flesh, one of the commonest of all sins among worldly people, is a gross evil; it is a sin born of pride, a sin that creates a frame of mind which keeps men from turning to the Lord and accepting his saving grace. When a man engages in self exultation because of his riches, his political power, his worldly learning, his physical prowess, his business acumen, or even his works of righteousness, he is not in tune with the Spirit of the Lord. Salvation itself comes by the grace of God, "Not of works," that is not of the performances and outward display of the law, "lest any man should boast." (Eph. 2:4-22; Rom. 3:27.) As King Benjamin asked, after explaining the goodness of God and the comparative nothingness of men, "Of what have ye to boast?" (Mosiah 2:17-26.)

Even when the righteous glory in the Lord, certain very definite restrictions attend their godly boasting. The elders are to proclaim against evil spirits, but "Not with railing accusation, that ye be not overcome, neither with boasting nor rejoicing, lest you be seized therewith." (D. & C. 50:32-33.) Spiritual gifts are poured out abundantly upon the true saints. "But a commandment I give unto them," the Lord says, "that they shall not boast themselves of these things, neither speak them before the world; for these things are given unto you for *your* profit and for salvation." (D. & C. 84:73.) "Talk not of judgments, neither boast of faith nor of mighty works." (D. & C. 105:24.)

BONDAGE.

See ABRAHAM'S CHILDREN, AGENCY, APOSTASY, CASTE SYSTEM, FREEDOM, INALIENABLE RIGHTS, LIBERTY. *Bondage* and captivity of every sort are of the devil; the gospel is "the perfect law of liberty" (Jas. 1:25); it is the truth that makes men free. (John 8:32.) The saints should free themselves from the bondage of debt. (D. & C. 19:35; 104:83-84.) In a perfect Christian society there would be no serfdom or slavery, for "it is not right that any man should be in bondage one to another." Bondage curtails free agency, thus interfering with a man's power to work out his salvation. (D. & C. 101:78-79.)

There is no bondage like the bondage of sin and no darkness like the darkness of rebellion against the truth. (John 8:31-46; Gal. 5:1.) "And the whole world lieth in sin, and groaneth under darkness and under the bondage of sin. And by this you may know they are under the bondage of sin, because they come not unto me. For whoso cometh not unto me is under the bondage of sin." (D. & C. 84:49-51.)

BOND-SERVANTS.
See SLAVERY.

BOOK OF ABRAHAM.
See PEARL OF GREAT PRICE.

BOOK OF COMMANDMENTS.

See DOCTRINE AND COVENANTS, REVELATION, SCRIPTURE, STANDARD WORKS. As early as the summer of 1830, the Prophet began to copy and prepare the revelations he had received for eventual publication. At a conference held in Hiram, Ohio, on November 1st and 2nd, 1831, it was decided the revelations should be compiled and published under the title, *Book of Commandments.* The Lord gave approval to the project by revealing a preface for the book. (D. & C. 1.)

It was at this conference that some of the elders questioned the language in the revelations, causing the Lord to give the revealed tests whereby the divinity of the revelations might be known. "Seek ye out of the Book of Commandments, even the least that is among them," the Lord said, "and appoint him that is the most wise among you; Or, if there be any among you that shall make one like unto it, then ye are justified in saying that ye do not know that they are true; But if ye cannot make one like unto it, ye are under condemnation if ye do not bear record that they are true. For ye know that there is no unrighteousness in them, and that which is righteous cometh down from above, from the Father of lights." (D. & C. 67:6-9.) William E. McLellin attempted to write a revelation equal to the least of those the Lord had given and failed miserably.

By July 20, 1833, most of the Book of Commandments had been set in type under the direction of W. W. Phelps. On that date the printing plant in Independence, Missouri, was destroyed by a mob, and only a few copies of the forms of the unfinished book were salvaged. Only a score or so copies are known to be in existence now. The last statement in the publication is, "The rebellious are not of the blood of Ephraim," thus ending the book in the middle of verse 36 of section 64 of the Doctrine and Covenants as presently published.

Thereafter a committee headed by the Prophet was appointed to continue the work necessary to get the revelations published. Their labors were completed, and they reported to a general assembly of the Church, at Kirtland, Ohio, August 17, 1835. The revelations so compiled and approved, and some other matters, were published under the title Doctrine and Covenants. (*Doctrines of Salvation,* vol. 3, pp. 192-198.)

Between the time of the publication of the Book of Commandments in 1833 and the Doctrine and Covenants in 1835, the Prophet, as moved upon by the Spirit of the Lord, inserted some additional revealed truths in the revelations and in an instance or two clarified the existing language. This procedure, of course, was in perfect harmony with the two principles: 1. That revelations are necessarily given to men "after the manner of their language" (D. & C. 1:24); and 2.

That the Lord always reveals line upon line, precept upon precept, here a little and there a little, adding more light and knowledge as rapidly as that already received is known and practiced. (D. & C. 98: 12; 128:21.) The various revelations were divided into *chapters* in the Book of Commandments and into *sections* in the Doctrine and Covenants, and some personal revelations were not carried over into the latter publication but are to be found in the *History of the Church.* Divisions into verses and punctuation was, of course, changed as between the two publications.

BOOK OF ENOCH.

See LOST SCRIPTURE, REVELATION, SCRIPTURE. One of the things yet to come forth in the last days is the *Book of Enoch.* This record contains the prophecies made by Adam at Adam-ondi-Ahman when he "predicted whatsoever should befall his posterity unto the latest generation." (D. & C. 107:56-57.) From the account in the Book of Moses we know that Enoch performed one of the greatest and most spectacular works of any prophet. (Moses 6; 7.) How much the Book of Enoch contains relative to his ministry and teachings we can only speculate. It appears from Paul's writings that he had information about Enoch which is not contained in the Old Testament as we have that document. (Heb. 11:5.) Jude recorded in

his epistle a prophecy made by Enoch, thus indicating that some of Enoch's writings may have been extant in New Testament times. (Jude 14:15.)

BOOK OF JOSEPH.

See BRASS PLATES, LOST SCRIPTURE, PEARL OF GREAT PRICE, REVELATION, SCRIPTURE. Two papyrus rolls were acquired by the Prophet in connection with the Egyptian mummies purchased from Michael H. Chandler. One roll was translated and is now published as the Book of Abraham. Translation of the other roll, which contained the writings of Joseph who was sold into Egypt, apparently was never completed. Enough was known of this *Book of Joseph,* however, for Oliver Cowdery to write that it contained doctrine relative to the creation, the fall of man, the nature of the Godhead, and the final judgment. (Milton R. Hunter, *Pearl of Great Price Commentary,* pp. 1-40.)

Nephi says that there were not many prophecies greater than those which Joseph wrote; that many of them concerned the Nephites and Lamanites; and that "they are written upon the plates of brass." (2 Ne. 4:1-3.) Some of these prophecies are quoted in the Book of Mormon (2 Ne. 3; 25:21; Alma 46:24); some were restored by the Prophet in the Inspired Version of the Bible. (*Inspired Version,* Gen. 50:24-38.)

As to the papyrus rolls which the Prophet had, after his death they fell into the hands of apostates and enemies of the Church. As far as is known they were destroyed in the great Chicago fire in 1871. But the day shall come when the Book of Joseph shall be restored and its contents shall be known again. This we know because the Brass Plates themselves are yet to be translated and sent forth "unto every nation, kindred, tongue, and people." (Alma 37:3-5.)

BOOK OF LIFE.

See BOOK OF REMEMBRANCE, BOOK OF THE LAW OF GOD, CELESTIAL BODIES, ETERNAL LIFE, JUDGMENT DAY, OBEDIENCE, RECORDING ANGELS, TELESTIAL BODIES, TERRESTRIAL BODIES. 1. In a real through figurative sense, the *book of life* is the record of the acts of men as such record is written in their own bodies. It is the record engraven on the very bones, sinews, and flesh of the mortal body. That is, every thought, word, and deed has an affect on the human body; all these leave their marks, marks which can be read by Him who is Eternal as easily as the words in a book can be read.

By obedience to telestial law men obtain telestial bodies; terrestrial law leads to terrestrial bodies; and conformity to celestial law—because this law includes the sanctifying power of the Holy Ghost—results in the creation of a body which is clean, pure, and spotless, a celestial body. (D. & C. 88:16-32.) When the book of life is opened in the day of judgment (Rev. 20:12-15), men's bodies will show what law they have lived. The Great Judge will then read the record of the book of their lives; the account of their obedience or disobedience will be written in their bodies.

2. In a literal sense, the *book of life,* or *Lamb's book of Life,* is the record kept in heaven which contains the names of the faithful and an account of their righteous covenants and deeds. (D. & C. 128:6-7; Ps. 69:28; Rev. 3:5; 21:27.) The book of life is the book containing the names of those who shall inherit eternal life; it is the book of eternal life. (Dan. 12:1-4; Heb. 12:23; D. & C. 76:68; 132:19.) It is "the book of the names of the sanctified, even them of the celestial world." (D. & C. 88:2.) Names of faithful saints are recorded in the book of life while they are yet in mortality. (Luke 10:20; Philip. 4:3; *Teachings,* p. 9.) But those names are blotted out in the event of wickedness. (Rev. 13:8; 17:8; 22:19.)

BOOK OF MORMON.

See AMERICAN INDIANS, BIBLE, BRASS PLATES, CUMORAH, DOCTRINE AND COVENANTS, GOLD PLATES, GOSPEL, JAREDITES, JEWS, JOSEPH SMITH THE PROPHET, LAMANITE CURSE, LOST SCRIPTURE, MAHONRI MORIANCUMER, MORMON BIBLE, MORMONISM,

MORMONS, MORONI, MULEKITES, NEPHITES AND LAMANITES, PEARL OF GREAT PRICE, QUETZELCOATL, SCRIPTURE, SIGNS OF THE TIMES, STANDARD WORKS, STICK OF EPHRAIM, TESTIMONY, THREE NEPHITES, URIM AND THUMMIM, WITNESSES OF THE BOOK OF MORMON. That holy document known as the *Book of Mormon* is a volume of sacred scripture which was known anciently and has been revealed anew in modern times. It contains the fulness of the everlasting gospel (D. & C. 20:9; 42:12; 135:3) and an abridged account of God's dealings with the ancient inhabitants of the American continents from about 2247 B.C. to 421 A.D.

The original records, which were compiled and abridged to form the Book of Mormon as presently constituted, were written on metallic plates by prophets who were commanded to keep records of God's dealings with them and their peoples. These records preserved a true knowledge of God, of the mission and ministry of his Son, and of the doctrines and ordinances of salvation. Incidental to these gospel truths much information was also preserved relative to the history and the social, economic, cultural, educational, governmental, and other conditions that existed among Book of Mormon peoples.

During the latter part of the 4th century A.D., Mormon, a prophet-general, made a compilation and abridgment of the records of the people of Lehi, a Jew who led a colony of his family and friends from Jerusalem to their American promised land in 600 B.C. Mormon's son Moroni added a few words of his own to the record and also abridged, in very brief form, the records of a nation of Jaredites who had migrated to America at the time of the confusion of tongues when the tower of Babel was built. The records of these two great peoples, preserved on the Gold Plates, were translated by Joseph Smith and are known as the Book of Mormon. The main part of the work deals with the period from 600 B.C. to 421 A.D. during which the Nephite, Lamanite, and Mulekite civilizations flourished.

Moroni, the last prophet to possess the ancient and sacred writings, hid them up in the hill Cumorah. Then in modern times, in fulfilment of John's apocalyptic prophecy (Rev. 14:6-7), Moroni, now resurrected, delivered the plates to Joseph Smith. Miraculously, by means of the Urim and Thummim, in not to exceed two months translating time, the Prophet put the ancient record into English. Since then it has been translated and published in scores of other languages. (*Doctrines of Salvation*, vol. 3, pp. 209-226.)

Purposes of the Book of Mormon are: 1. To bear record of Christ, certifying in plainness and with clarity of his Divine Sonship and mission, proving irrefutably that he is the Redeemer and Savior; 2. To teach the doctrines of the gospel in such a pure and perfect way that the plan of salvation will be clearly revealed; and 3. To stand as a witness to all the world that Joseph Smith was the Lord's anointed through whom the foundation was laid for the great latter-day work of restoration.

Almost all of the doctrines of the gospel are taught in the Book of Mormon with much greater clarity and perfection than those same doctrines are revealed in the Bible. Anyone who will place in parallel columns the teachings of these two great books on such subjects as the atonement, plan of salvation, gathering of Israel, baptism, gifts of the Spirit, miracles, revelation, faith, charity, (or any of a hundred other subjects), will find conclusive proof of the superiority of Book of Mormon teachings.

On November 28, 1841, following a meeting with the Twelve Apostles, the Prophet wrote in his journal: *"I told the brethren that the Book of Mormon was the most correct of any book on earth, and the keystone of our religion, and a man would get nearer to God by abiding by its precepts, than by any other book."* (History of the Church, vol. 4, p. 461.) On another occasion he said: *"Take away the Book of Mormon and the revelations, and where is our religion? We have none."* (*Teachings*, p. 71.)

We "believe the Book of Mormon to be the word of God." (Eighth Article of Faith.) The book is true and was translated correctly. By revelation the Lord said of Joseph Smith: "He has translated the book, even that part which I have commanded him, and *as your Lord and your God liveth it is true."* (D. & C. 17:6.) "We . . . have seen the plates," the three witnesses testified, "and we also know that *they have been translated by the gift and power of God, for his voice hath declared it unto us;* wherefore we know of a surety that *the work is true."* (Testimony of Three Witnesses, *Book of Mormon.*)

There are numerous Biblical and other ancient prophecies foretelling the coming forth of, and various things pertaining to, the Book of Mormon. (Moses 7:59-62; Ps. 85:11; Isa. 29: 45:8; Ezek. 37:15-28; John 10:16; Rev. 14:6-7; 2 Ne. 3; *Inspired Version,* Gen. 50:24-38.) Since its publication many archaeological discoveries have been made, particularly in Central and South America, which bear out some known facts relative to ancient Book of Mormon civilizations. (Milton R. Hunter, *Archaeology and the Book of Mormon.*)

But the great and conclusive evidence of the divinity of the Book of Mormon is the testimony of the Spirit to the honest truth seeker. Moroni promised: "When ye shall receive these things, I would exhort you that ye would ask God, the Eternal Father, in the name of Christ, if these things are not true; and if ye shall ask with a sincere heart, with real intent, having faith in Christ, he will manifest the truth of it unto you, by the power of the Holy Ghost." (Moro. 10:4.)

BOOK OF MOSES.
See PEARL OF GREAT PRICE.

BOOK OF REMEMBRANCE.
See BOOK OF LIFE, BOOK OF THE LAW OF GOD, GENEALOGICAL RESEARCH, RECORD KEEPING. Adam kept a written account of his faithful descendants in which he recorded their faith and works, their righteousness and devotion, their revelations and visions, and their adherence to the revealed plan of salvation. To signify the importance of honoring our worthy ancestors and of hearkening to the great truths revealed to them, Adam called his record a *book of remembrance*. It was prepared "according to the pattern given by the finger of God." (Moses 6:4-6, 46.)

Similar records have been kept by the saints in all ages. (Mal. 3: 16-17; 3 Ne. 24:15-16.) Many of our present scriptures have come down to us because they were first written by prophets who were following Adam's pattern of keeping a book of remembrance. The Church keeps similar records today (D. & C. 85) and urges its members to keep their own personal and family books of remembrance.

BOOK OF REVELATION.
See APOCALYPSE.

BOOK OF THE LAW OF GOD.
See BOOK OF LIFE, BOOK OF REMEMBRANCE, CHURCH HISTORIAN AND RECORDER, GENEALOGICAL RESEARCH, RECORD KEEPING. Those records kept by the Church showing the names, genealogies, and faith and works of those to be remembered by the Lord in the day when eternal inheritances are bestowed upon the obedient are, taken collectively, called the *book of the law of God*. Such records contain both the law of God and the names of those who keep that law. They are in effect a church book of remembrance. (D. & C. 85.)

BOOK OF THE NAMES OF THE SANCTIFIED.
See BOOK OF LIFE.

BORN AGAIN.
See BAPTISM, BAPTISM OF FIRE, BIRTH, CONVERSION, GIFT OF THE HOLY GHOST, GIFTS OF THE SPIRIT, HOLY GHOST, HOLY SPIRIT OF PROMISE, SONS OF GOD, SPIRITUAL DEATH, SPIRITUAL LIFE. To gain salvation in the celestial kingdom men must be *born again* (Alma 7:14); born of water and of the Spirit (John 3:1-13); born of God, so that they are changed from their "carnal and fallen state, to a state of righteousness," becoming new creatures of the Holy Ghost. (Mosiah 27:24-29.) They must become newborn babes in Christ (1 Pet. 2:2); they must be

"spiritually begotten" of God, be born of Christ, thus becoming his sons and daughters. (Mosiah 5:7.)

The first birth takes place when spirits pass from their pre-existent first estate into mortality; the second birth or birth "into the kingdom of heaven" takes places when mortal men are born again and become alive to the things of the Spirit and of righteousness. The elements of water, blood, and Spirit are present in both births. (Moses 6:59-60.) The second birth begins when men are baptized in water by a legal administrator; it is completed when they actually receive the companionship of the Holy Ghost, becoming new creatures by the cleansing power of that member of the Godhead.

Mere compliance with the formality of the ordinance of baptism does not mean that a person has been born again. No one can be born again without baptism, but the immersion in water and the laying on of hands to confer the Holy Ghost do not of themselves guarantee that a person has been or will be born again. The new birth takes place only for those who actually enjoy the gift or companionship of the Holy Ghost, only for those who are fully converted, who have given themselves without restraint to the Lord. Thus Alma addressed himself to his "brethren of the church," and pointedly asked them if they had "spiritually been born of God," received the Lord's image in their countenances, and

had the "mighty change" in their hearts which always attends the birth of the Spirit. (Alma 5:14-31.)

Those members of the Church who have actually been born again are in a blessed and favored state. They have attained their position, not merely by joining the Church, but through faith (1 John 5:1), righteousness (1 John 2:29), love (1 John 4:7), and overcoming the world. (1 John 5:4.) *"Whosoever is born of God doth not continue in sin; for the Spirit of God remaineth in him; and he cannot continue to sin, because he is born of God, having received that holy Spirit of promise." (Inspired Version,* 1 John 3:9.)

BORN IN SIN.

See Conceived in Sin.

BOTTOMLESS PIT.

See ANGEL OF THE BOTTOMLESS PIT, HADES, HELL, PIT, SHEOL, SPIRIT PRISON. In an attempt to convey in imperfect, mortal language the infinite intensity of the sufferings of those cast into the pit (that is, into hell), John spoke not simply of the pit, but of the *bottomless pit.* (Rev. 9:1-2, 11; 11:7; 17:8; 20:1-3.) The bottomless pit is the *depths of hell.* It is not a literal pit without a bottom, for such is a contradiction in terms. But it is a pit or prison where the inhabitants suffer, as mortals view suffering, to an infinite, unlimited, or bottomless extent. Referring to finite inability to comprehend the vastness of the suffering of those reaping the full measure of this status, the revelation says: "The end, the width, the height, the depth, and the misery thereof, they understand not, neither any man except those who are ordained unto this condemnation." (D. & C. 76:48.)

BOWING DOWN.
See OBEISANCE.

BRAGGING.
See BOASTING.

BRANCH.
See CHRIST, GOD OF ISRAEL, HOLY ONE OF ISRAEL, KING OF ISRAEL, ROOT OF DAVID, STEM OF JESSE. Christ is the *Branch,* a name applied in ancient Israel to point attention to the great truth that the promised Messiah would come in the lineage of Israel and of David, that he would be a branch or part of that illustrious line. Through Jeremiah the Lord said: "Behold, the days come, saith the Lord, that I will raise unto David a righteous Branch, and a King shall reign and prosper, and shall execute judgment and justice in the earth. In his days Judah shall be saved, and Israel shall dwell safely: and this is his name whereby he shall be called, THE LORD OUR RIGHTEOUSNESS." (Jer. 23:5-6; 33:15-17; Isa. 11:1-5; Zech. 3:8-10; 6:12-15.)

BRANCHES.
See BRANCH PRESIDENTS, CHURCH ORGANIZATION, DISTRICTS, MISSIONS, STAKES, TRUE VINE, WARDS. In the stakes, congregations of saints which are not large and stable enough to form wards are organized into *branches,* presided over by a branch president. The larger and more powerful branches, those with considerable stability and local leadership, are called *independent branches*. They operate as nearly like a regular ward as their circumstances permit. *Dependent branches* are usually smaller and less endowed with local leadership; they receive help in their programs from some other ward or branch, upon which they are dependent.

All the congregations of saints, no matter how strong and stable, which are located within the districts of missions are called *branches*. Several branches comprise a district. When one or more mission districts are chosen as an area in which to form a stake, the main branches involved become wards, while the lesser branches remain as either independent or dependent branches.

BRANCH PRESIDENCY.
See BRANCH PRESIDENTS.

BRANCH PRESIDENTS.
See BISHOPS, BRANCHES. Presiding officers in branches are *branch presidents*. They hold the keys of

their ministry, are assisted by two counselors (thus forming a *branch presidency*), and are comparable to bishops in their sphere of service.

BRANCH TEACHERS.
See HOME TEACHERS.

BRANCH TEACHING.
See HOME TEACHERS.

BRASS PLATES.
See BOOK OF MORMON, GOLD PLATES, LOST SCRIPTURE, OLD TESTAMENT. When the Lord led Lehi and his colony out from Jerusalem, they were required to take with them the *Brass Plates* of which Laban had been the custodian. These plates—which Nephi acquired through his faith, works, and zeal (1 Ne. 3; 4)—were a volume of sacred scripture. They contained a record of God's dealings with men from the beginning down to that day. They were "the record of the Jews" (1 Ne. 3:3.), a record of many of the prophecies from the beginning down to and including part of those spoken by Jeremiah. On them was the law of Moses, the five books of Moses, and the genealogy of the Nephite forbears. (1 Ne. 3:3, 20; 4:15-16; 5:11-14.)

There was more on them than there is in the Old Testament as we now have it. (1 Ne. 13:23.) The prophecies of Zenock, Neum, Zenos, Joseph the son of Jacob, and probably many other prophets were preserved by them, and many of these writings foretold matters pertaining to the Nephites. (1 Ne. 19:10, 21; 2 Ne. 4:2, 15; 3 Ne. 10:17.)

The value of the Brass Plates to the Nephites cannot be overestimated. By means of them they were able to preserve the language (1 Ne. 3:19), most of the civilization, and the religious knowledge of the people from whence they came. (1 Ne. 22:30.) By way of contrast, the Mulekites, who were led out of Jerusalem some 11 years after Lehi's departure, and who had no record equivalent to the Brass Plates, soon dwindled in apostasy and unbelief and lost their language, civilization, and religion. (Omni 14-18.)

From prophet to prophet and generation to generation the Brass Plates were handed down and preserved by the Nephites. (Mosiah 1:16; 28:20; 3 Ne. 1:2.) At some future date the Lord has promised to bring them forth, undimmed by time and retaining their original brightness, and the scriptural accounts recorded on them are to "go forth unto every nation, kindred, tongue, and people." (Alma 37:3-5; 1 Ne. 5:18-19.)

BRAZEN SEA.
See BAPTISM, BAPTISMAL FONTS, TEMPLES. In Solomon's Temple a large *molten sea* of brass was placed on the backs of 12 brazen oxen, these oxen being symbolical of the 12 tribes of Israel. (1 Kings 7:23-

26, 44; 2 Kings 16:17; 25:13; 1 Chron. 18:8.) This *brazen sea* was used for performing baptisms for the living. There were no baptisms for the dead until after the resurrection of Christ.

It must be remembered that all direct and plain references to baptism have been deleted from the Old Testament (1 Ne. 13) and that the word *baptize* is of Greek origin. Some equivalent word, such as *wash,* would have been used by the Hebrew peoples. In describing the molten sea the Old Testament record says, *"The sea was for the priests to wash in."* (2 Chron. 4:2-6.) This is tantamount to saying that the priests performed baptisms in it.

In this temple building dispensation the Brethren have been led by the spirit of inspiration to pattern the baptismal fonts placed in temples after the one in Solomon's Temple.

BRAZEN SERPENT.

See ATONEMENT OF CHRIST, CHRIST, ORDINANCES, SYMBOLISMS. To typify Christ and point attention to the salvation which would come because he would be lifted up on the cross, Moses (as commanded by the Lord) made a *brazen serpent* and lifted it up on a pole. Then those of the children of Israel who were bitten by poisonous serpents were healed by looking upon the serpent, while those who re-fused to look died of the poisonous bites. (Num. 21:4-9.) This performance was a ceremony in Israel which was intended to show the people that by looking to Christ they would be saved with eternal life, but by refusing to look to him they would die spiritually. (John 3:14-15; Alma 33:19-22; Hela. 8:14-15.) The brazen serpent was kept as a symbol in Israel until the time of Hezekiah, who broke it in pieces to keep apostate Israel of his day from burning incense to it. (2 Kings 18:4.)

BREAD AND WATER.
See SACRAMENT.

BREAD AND WINE.
See SACRAMENT.

BREAD OF LIFE.
See CHRIST, LIGHT OF CHRIST, MANNA, SACRAMENT, SYMBOLISMS. Christ is the *Bread of Life.* Just as manna was showered down as bread from heaven to save ancient Israel from starvation and temporal death, so Christ came down from heaven to give living bread and living water to all men so that they might gain

everlasting life. (John 4:10-38; 6:30-65.)

BREASTPLATE.

See URIM AND THUMMIM.

BREATH OF LIFE.

See LIFE, LIGHT OF LIFE, PRE-EXISTENCE, SPIRIT CHILDREN. Literally, the *breath of life* is the air we breathe, for without this man and all air-breathing creatures would die. The Mosaic account of the creation says that "the Lord God formed man of the dust of the ground, and breathed into his nostrils the breath of life; and man became a living soul." (Gen. 2:7; Moses 3:7.) Similarly, when the Lord created the beasts and fowls, he "breathed into them the breath of life," and they also became "living souls." (Moses 3:19; Gen. 6:17.)

In a figurative sense the expression breath of life is frequently used to mean the life of man. Ezekiel says, in speaking of the resurrection of the house of Israel, "Thus saith the Lord God unto these bones; Behold, I will cause breath to enter into you, and ye shall live." (Ezek. 37:5-10.) This is a figurative way of saying that the spirit will again enter the body. Actually, as Abraham's account of the creation points out, there is a distinction between the spirit and the breath of life. "And the Gods formed man from the dust of the ground," this record states, "and took his spirit

(that is, the man's spirit), and put it into him; and breathed into his nostrils the breath of life, and man became a living soul." (Abra. 5:7.) Paul also speaks of God's giving both "life, and breath" (Acts 17: 25) to all, thus making an apparent distinction between the two things.

BRETHREN.

See BELIEVERS, DISCIPLES, MORMONS, PROPHETS, SAINTS. All men are brothers in the sense of being the spirit offspring of Deity. But those who join the true Church, who take upon themselves the name of Christ, who are adopted into the family of Jesus Christ, becoming his sons and his daughters, thus become brothers and sisters in a special spiritual sense. (Mosiah 5:7.) Hence, all believers collectively or any group of them in particular are called the *brethren.* (Acts 14:2; 15:33, 40.) They are members of the great brotherhood of Christ. In a spirit of love and fellowship members of the Church commonly and properly call each other *brother* and *sister.*

Our Lord gave graphic expression to this spiritual usage of the term *brethren* when, being told that his mother and literal brothers desired to see him, he asked: "Who is my mother? and who are my brothers?" In answer, "He stretched forth his hand toward his disciples, and said, Behold my mother and my brethren! *For whosoever shall do the will of my*

Father which is in heaven, the same is my brother, and sister, and mother." (Matt. 12:46-50.)

BRIDE.
See BRIDE OF THE LAMB.

BRIDEGROOM.
See BRIDE OF THE LAMB, CHRIST, ESPOUSAL, HUSBAND, MARRIAGE SUPPER OF THE LAMB. Christ is the *Bridegroom* (Matt. 9:15; Mark 2:19; Luke 5:34; John 3:29), who shall take the Church as his bride and celebrate the glorious occasion at the marriage supper of the Lamb. Our Lord's parable of the 10 virgins teaches the need of the saints to be ready at the coming of the Bridegroom. (Matt. 25:1-13.) Similarly, he has said in this day: "Be faithful, praying always, having your lamps trimmed and burning, and oil with you, that you may be ready at the coming of the Bridegroom—For behold, verily, verily, I say unto you, that I come quickly." (D. & C. 33: 17-18; 88:92; 133:10, 19.)

BRIDE OF THE LAMB.
See BRIDEGROOM, CHRIST, ESPOUSAL, HUSBAND, MARRIAGE SUPPER OF THE LAMB, NEW JERUSALEM. Both the New Jerusalem, which shall come down from God out of heaven, and The Church of Jesus Christ of Latter-day Saints are called the *Bride of*

the lamb and the *Lamb's wife.* (Rev. 21:2, 9-10; 22:17; D. & C. 109:72-74.) The bride celebrates the marriage supper with the Bridegroom, her Husband, and is cherished and honored by him. To the millennial saints the Lord promises: "As the bridegroom rejoiceth over the bride, so shall thy God rejoice over thee." (Isa. 62:5.)

BRIGHAMITES.
See JOSEPHITES.

BRIGHT AND MORNING STAR.
See CHRIST, EXALTATION. Christ is the *Bright and Morning Star.* (Rev. 22:16.) In speaking of a man as a star the meaning is that he is a person of brilliant qualities, who stands out pre-eminently among his fellows. Thus to single out our Lord as the Bright and Morning Star, the last bright luminary of the night to give way before the rising sun, is to testify that he is pre-eminent over all his brethren, that he is the Son of God in whom all fulness and perfection dwell.

In this connection, and having in mind that those who gain eternal life shall be joint-heirs with Christ, it is interesting to note that such exalted persons are promised that they shall receive the morning star, that is, reach a state of pre-eminence and perfection themselves. (Rev. 2:26-28.) "And they that be wise shall shine as the brightness of the firmament; and they that turn many to righteousness as the stars for ever and ever." (Dan. 12:3.) Peter's statement about the day star arising in the hearts of certain of the saints, has reference also to those who shall inherit the fulness of all things. (2 Pet. 1:19.)

BRIMSTONE.
See FIRE AND BRIMSTONE.

BROAD-MINDEDNESS.
See CONVERSION, GOSPEL, TESTIMONY, TOLERANCE, TRUTH. From the generally accepted and worldly standpoint, *broad-mindedness* consists in entertaining liberal opinions and in having tolerant views, particularly on religious matters. Those who so classify themselves take pride in *not* accepting any particular creed or following any selected dogma; they suppose that theirs is a broad perspective which makes them receptive to all truth; invariably they reach the conclusion that all religions are equally true and equally false and that salvation, if there is such a thing, is not found in, through, or because of any one of them in particular.

It is not difficult to see how this sort of broad-mindedness comes into being. When inquiring and scientific minds delve into the narrow and bigoted creeds of the apostate sects of Christendom, it is not surprising that they rebel against those dogmas falsely set forth as the tenets of true religion. If this modern broad-mindedness leads to an open-minded state in which men investigate and receive the true principles of revealed religion, it has served a beneficial purpose. But if it results in an aversion and contempt for all religions, the restored Church of our Lord included, it leaves the scientific-minded person no better off than the bigoted adherent to the narrow creeds of the apostate world.

In a very real sense this worldly broad-mindedness is of the devil, not of God. Lucifer is willing and anxious that men believe any and every conceivable notion so long as they do not accept Joseph Smith and the restoration. *The devil is the most broad-minded person in all eternity;* he is tolerant to every view, particularly those leading to ungodly practices. *"Wide is the gate, and broad is the way, that leadeth to destruction,* and many there be which go in thereat." (Matt. 7:13.)

In the true gospel sense of the word, however, broad-mindedness is the state of mind of those who know the truths of the gospel, who reject the false creeds of the day, and who walk in the light of revealed truth. The broad-minded man is the one who knows that baptism is essential to salvation and celestial marriage to exaltation; he is the one who knows the truth. In the eternal sense it is narrow-minded to reject the laws and ordinances of the gospel, for they are the way and means whereby men can go on without limit, restraint, or curtailment in attaining perfection and enjoying eternal progression.

BROKEN HEART.
See CONTRITE SPIRIT.

BROTHERHOOD OF MAN.
See FATHER IN HEAVEN.

BROTHERLY LOVE.
See LOVE.

BROTHER OF JARED.
See MAHONRI MORIANCUMER.

BUFFETINGS OF SATAN.
See DAMNATION, DEVIL, FIRE AND BRIMSTONE, HELL. To be turned over to the *buffetings of Satan* is to be given into his hands; it is to be turned over to him with all the protective power of the priesthood, of righteousness, and of godliness removed, so that Lucifer is free to torment, persecute, and afflict such a person without let or hindrance. When the bars are down, the cuffs and curses of Satan, both in this world and in the world to come, bring indescribable anguish typified by burning fire and brimstone. The damned in hell so suffer.

Those who broke their covenants in connection with the United Order in the early days of this dispensation were to "be delivered over to the buffetings of Satan until the day of redemption." (D. & C. 78:12; 82:20-21; 104:9-10.) A similar fate (plus destruction in the flesh) is decreed against those who have been sealed up unto eternal life so that their callings and elections have been made sure and who thereafter turn to grievous sin. (D. & C. 131:5, 132:19-26.)

BURIALS.
See FUNERALS.

BURNING.
See SECOND COMING OF CHRIST.

C

CAIN.
See DEVIL, HAM, MASTER MAHAN, NEGROES, PERDITION, SONS OF PERDITION, UNPARADONABLE SIN. Though he was a rebel and an associate of Lucifer in pre-existence,

and though he was a liar from the beginning whose name was *Perdition, Cain* managed to attain the privilege of mortal birth. Under Adam's tutelage, he began in this life to serve God. He understood the gospel and the plan of salvation, was baptized, received the priesthood, had a perfect knowledge of the position and perfection of God, and talked personally with Deity. Then he came out in open rebellion, fought God, worshiped Lucifer, and slew Abel.

Cain's sacrifice was rejected because it was offered at Satan's command, not the Lord's; it was not and could not be offered in faith for "he could have no faith, or could not exercise faith contrary to the plan of heaven." (*Teachings,* pp. 58-59.)

As a result of his rebellion, Cain was cursed and told that "the earth" would not thereafter yield him its abundance as previously. In addition he became the first mortal to be cursed as a son of perdition. As a result of his mortal birth he is assured of a tangible body of flesh and bones in eternity, a fact which will enable him to rule over Satan. The Lord placed on Cain a mark of a dark skin, and he became the ancestor of the black race. (Moses 5; Gen. 4; *Teachings*, p. 169.)

CALAMITIES.
See SIGNS OF THE TIMES.

CALLING AND ELECTION SURE.

See CELESTIAL KINGDOM, CELESTIAL MARRIAGE, CHURCH OF THE FIRSTBORN, DAUGHTERS OF GOD, ELECTION OF GRACE, ETERNAL LIFE, ETERNAL LIVES, EXALTATION, FULNESS OF THE FATHER, GODHOOD, JOINT-HEIRS WITH CHRIST, SALVATION, SECOND COMFORTER, SONS OF GOD. Those members of the Church who devote themselves wholly to righteousness, living by every word that proceedeth forth from the mouth of God, make their *calling and election sure.* That is, they receive the more sure word of prophecy, which means that the Lord seals their exaltation upon them while they are yet in this life. Peter summarized the course of righteousness which the saints must pursue to make their calling and election sure and then (referring to his experience on the Mount of Transfiguration with James and John) said that those three had received this more sure word of prophecy. (2 Pet. 1.)

Joseph Smith taught: "After a person has faith in Christ, repents of his sins, and is baptized for the remission of his sins and receives the Holy Ghost (by the laying on of hands), which is the first Comforter, then let him continue to humble himself before God, hungering and thirsting after righteousness, and living by every word of God, and the Lord will soon say unto him, *Son, thou shalt be exalted.* When the Lord has thoroughly proved him, and finds that the man is determined to serve him at all hazards, then the man will find his calling and election made sure, then it will be his privilege to receive the other Comforter." To receive the other Comforter is to have Christ appear to him and to see the visions of eternity. (*Teachings,* pp. 149-151.)

Thus, as the Prophet also said, "The more sure word of prophecy means a man's knowing that he is sealed up unto eternal life, by revelation and the spirit of prophecy, through the power of the Holy Priesthood." (D. & C. 131:5.) Those so favored of the Lord are sealed up against all manner of sin and blasphemy except the blasphemy against the Holy Ghost and the shedding of innocent blood. That is, their exaltation is assured; their calling and election is made sure, because they have obeyed the fulness of God's laws and have overcome the world. Though such persons "shall commit any sin or transgression of the new and everlasting covenant whatever, and all manner of blasphemies, and if they commit no murder wherein they shed innocent blood, yet they shall come forth in the first resurrection, and enter into their exaltation." (D. & C. 132:26.)

The Lord says to them: "Ye shall come forth in the first resurrection; . . . and shall inherit thrones, kingdoms, principalities, and powers, dominions, all heights and depths." (D. & C. 132:19.) The Prophet, for one, had this seal placed upon him. That is, he knew "by revelation and the spirit of prophecy, through the power of the Holy Priesthood," that he would attain godhood in the world to come. To him Deity said: "I am the Lord thy God, and will be with thee even unto the end of the world, and through all eternity; for verily *I seal upon you your exaltation, and prepare a throne for you in the kingdom of my Father, with Abraham your father."* (D. & C. 132:49.)

It should be clearly understood that these high blessings are not part of celestial marriage. "Blessings pronounced upon couples in connection with celestial marriage are conditioned upon the subsequent faithfulness of the participating parties." (*Doctrines of Salvation,* vol. 2, pp. 46-47.)

CALVARY.

See GOLGOTHA.

CANCELLATION OF SEALINGS.

See CELESTIAL MARRIAGE, SEALINGS. Properly speaking there is no such thing as a *temple divorce;* divorces in this day are civil matters handled by the courts of the land. But following a civil divorce of persons who have been married for eternity in the temples, if the circumstances are sufficiently serious to warrant it, the President of the Church has power to *cancel the sealings* involved. He holds the keys and power both to bind and loose on earth and in heaven. (Matt. 16:19; D. & C. 132:46; *Doctrines of Salvation,* vol. 2, p. 84.)

·CANON OF SCRIPTURE.

See APOCRYPHA, BIBLE, BOOK OF MORMON, DOCTRINE AND COVENANTS, LOST SCRIPTURE, PEARL OF GREAT PRICE, SCRIPTURE, STANDARD WORKS. Such Biblical writings as are accepted by any substantial part of Christianity, as inspired and authentic, are considered by their acceptors as the *canon of scripture.* Other supposedly sacred Biblical writings which are not so accepted are designated as *apocryphal* by those who reject them. What is accepted as canonical by one group may be thrust aside as apocryphal by another. Books of the Apocrypha itself may be listed as canonical by those who accept them as authentic and inspired writings. Canonizing is generally considered as complete when some formal council, convention, or other official church assemblage officially adopts a particular work. Thus, applying Biblical standards to revelations in general, the standard works of the Church may be said to be canonical books.

Canonizing, as understood and practiced in the Christian world, has nothing whatever to do with the truth or falsity of a particular writing. A revelation is true if it came from God, false if it did not. If a true revelation is deleted from the body of compiled revelations, yet the discarded truths remain in force, and those who reject them are condemned.

Inspired writing is true if the Holy Ghost rests upon its author at the time of the writing, and unless that Spirit authors or inspires the choice of words used, the resultant language is not scripture. Any true document may subsequently be changed and perverted by uninspired men. But if the spirit of revelation is present in the body of the priesthood or of the Church, and if that inspired body votes to accept a writing as true and binding upon its members, then that action is a witness on earth and in heaven of the validity of the scriptural writing involved.

CAPTAIN OF SALVATION.

See ATONEMENT OF CHRIST, AUTHOR OF SALVATION, CAPTAIN OF THE LORD'S HOST, CHRIST, SALVATION. Christ is the *Captain of Salvation* (Heb. 2:10), meaning that he is the leader, chief officer, and agent who made salvation available to his brethren through his atoning sacrifice.

CAPTAIN OF THE LORD'S HOST.

See ARMIES OF HEAVEN, CAPTAIN OF SALVATION, CHRIST, GOD OF BATTLES, LORD OF HOSTS, MICHAEL THE ARCHANGEL. 1. Christ himself is the chief soldier in his own army; as *Commander,* he carries the title *Captain of the Lord's Host.* By this name he appeared to Joshua, who seeing "him with his sword drawn in his hand," and hearing him say, "As captain of the host of the Lord am I now come, . . . Joshua fell on his face to the earth, and did worship, and said unto him, What saith my lord unto his servant? And the captain of the Lord's host said unto Joshua, Loose thy shoe from off thy foot; for the place whereon thou standest is holy." (Josh. 5:13-15.) What further direction was then given has not been preserved for us.

It is profitable to compare this appearance of our Lord to Joshua with his appearance to Moses in the burning bush at which time the ground also was hallowed by the personal presence of Deity (Ex. 3), and also to compare it with the ministry of the angel whom John attempted to worship, but was restrained with the command: "See thou do it not: . . . worship God." (Rev. 19:9-11.) Among righteous messengers from the spirit realms, none but Deity will accept worship from mortals, and none but the Lord himself hallows a spot so that mortals are commanded to remove their shoes.

2. Although not in those words so named in the scriptures, Michael or Adam may also properly be designated, *Captain of the Lord's Host,* for he, under Christ, led the armies of heaven when Lucifer rebelled (Rev. 12:7-9), and he, under Christ, will again lead the hosts of heaven in "the battle of the great God," when Lucifer and his hosts are cast out eternally. (D. & C. 88:111-116.)

CARD PLAYING.

See APOSTASY, GAMBLING, RECREATION. President Joseph F. Smith has stated the position of the Church with reference to *card playing* in these words: "Card playing is an excessive pleasure; it is intoxicating and, therefore, in the nature of a vice. It is generally the companion of the cigaret and the wine glass, and the latter lead to the poolroom and the gambling hall. . . . Few indulge frequently in card playing in whose lives it does not become a ruling passion. . . . *A deck of cards in the hands of a faithful servant of God is a satire upon religion. . . . Those who thus indulge are not fit to administer in sacred ordinances.* . . . The bishops are charged with the responsibility for the evil, and it is their duty to see that it is abolished. . . . No man who is addicted to card playing should be called to act as a ward teacher; such men cannot be consistent advocates of that which they do not themselves practice.

"The card table has been the scene of too many quarrels, the birthplace of too many hatreds, the occasion of too many murders to admit one word of justification for the lying, cheating spirit which it too often engenders in the hearts of its devotees. . . .

"Card playing is a game of chance,

112

and because it is a game of chance it has its tricks. It encourages tricks; its devotees measure their success at the table by their ability through devious and dark ways to win. It creates a spirit of cunning and devises hidden and secret means, and cheating at cards is almost synonymous with playing at cards." (*Gospel Doctrine*, 5th ed., pp. 328-332.)

Members of the Church should not belong to bridge or other type of card clubs, and they should neither play cards nor have them in their homes. By cards is meant, of course, the spotted face cards used by gamblers. To the extent that church members play cards they are out of harmony with their inspired leaders. Innocent non-gambling games played with other types of cards, except for the waste of time in many instances, are not objectionable.

CARNALITY.

See BORN AGAIN, CORRUPTION, DEVILISHNESS, FALLEN MAN, FALL OF ADAM, MORTALITY, SENSUALITY. Since the fall, all men have become carnal, sensual and devilish by nature. (Moses 5:13; 6:49; Alma 42:10; Mosiah 16:1-4; D. & C. 20:20.) In this fallen state they are subject to the lusts, passions, and appetites of the flesh. They are spiritually dead, having· been cast out of the presence of the Lord; and thus "they are without God in the world, and they have gone con-

trary to the nature of God." They are in a "carnal state" (Alma 41:10-11); they are of the world. *Carnality* connotes worldliness, sensuality, and inclination to gratify the flesh.

To be saved men must forsake carnality and turn to the things of the Spirit. They "must be born again; yea, born of God, changed from their carnal and fallen state, to a state of righteousness, being redeemed of God, becoming his sons and daughters." (Mosiah 27:25.) All accountable persons who have not received the truth and the spiritual re-birth that attends such reception are yet in a carnal state. (Mosiah 4:2; 16:1-4; 26:4; Alma 22:13; 4:10-15.)

Even members of the Church who have not forsaken the world, and who have not bridled their passions (Alma 38:12), are yet in a carnal state. "Ye are yet carnal," Paul said to the Corinthian Saints, "for whereas there is among you envying, and strife, and divisions, are ye not carnal, and walk as men?" (1 Cor. 3:3; Mosiah 3:19.) "To be carnally minded is death; but to be spiritually minded is life and peace. Because the carnal mind is enmity against God." (Rom. 8:6-7; 2 Ne. 9:39.)

CARPENTER'S SON.

See CHRIST, SON OF GOD, SON OF JOSEPH. In a spirit of unbelief and derision, the citizens of our Lord's own community referred to him as the *Carpenter's Son.* (Matt. 13:53-58; Mark 6:1-6; Luke 4:16-29.) Joseph, his foster father, earned his daily bread through carpentry, and Jesus himself was schooled in that trade.

CASTE SYSTEM.

See BONDAGE, PRE-EXISTENCE, SLAVERY, TRIBES OF ISRAEL. In one sense of the word, *caste systems*— that is, the formation of hereditary classes within the social organization—are contrary to gospel principles of equality and fair treatment. This is so when these systems impose restrictions, slavery, and denial of natural rights upon members of any caste.

God is no respecter of persons, and inalienable rights are the natural heritage of all mankind (D. & C. 98:5); persons in every nation, caste, and class of society are entitled, as of right, to be put in a position where they can exercise the "moral agency" which the Lord has given them, so that they can be accountable for their "own sins in the day of judgment." (D. & C. 101:78.) Certainly the caste systems in communist countries and in India, for instance, are man made and are not based on true principles.

However, in a broad general sense, caste systems have their root and origin in the gospel itself, and when they operate according to the divine decree, the resultant restrictions and *segregation* are right and proper and have the approval of the Lord. To illustrate: Cain, Ham, and the whole negro race have been cursed with a black skin, the mark of Cain, so they can be identified as a caste apart, a people with whom the other descendants of Adam should not intermarry. (Gen. 4; Moses 5.) The whole house of Israel was chosen as a peculiar people, one set apart from all other nations (Ex. 19:5-6; Deut. 7:6; 14:2); and they were forbidden to marry outside their own caste. (Ex. 34:10-17; Deut. 7:1-5.) In effect the Lamanites belonged to one caste and the Nephites to another, and a mark was put upon the Lamanites to keep the Nephites from intermixing with and marrying them. (Alma 3:6-11.)

All this is not to say that any race, creed, or caste should be denied any inalienable rights. But it is to say that Deity in his infinite wisdom, to carry out his inscrutable purposes, has a caste system of his own, a system of segregation of races and peoples. The justice of such a system is evident when life is considered in its true eternal perspective. It is only by a knowledge of pre-existence that it can be known why some persons are born in one race or caste and some in another.

Segregation and caste systems will continue on in a future eternity; the righteous will go to paradise and the wicked to hell; and finally all men will be segregated into kingdoms—each separate from

114

the others—according as their works have been.

CASTING LOTS.
See LOTS.

CATHEDRALS.
See CHAPELS, MEETINGHOUSES, TABERNACLES, TEMPLES. In some churches of the world the particular church building containing the *cathedra,* or chair of the bishop, is called a *cathedral.* Since these houses of worship have normally been the largest, most ornate, and by far the most costly of all places of religious assembly, it has become common in the sectarian world to refer to all large and important church buildings as cathedrals. The Latter-day Saints, however, do not build cathedrals; indeed, the erection and inordinate adorning of expensive and elaborate meetinghouses for church worship is one of the signs of the great apostasy. (Morm. 8:37.)

CAVE MAN.
See EVOLUTION.

CELESTIAL BODIES.
See CELESTIAL GLORY, CELESTIAL KINGDOM, CELESTIAL LAW, CELESTIAL SPIRITS, EXALTATION, SALVATION. By obedience to celestial law men gain *celestial bodies,* bodies which are sanctified by the Spirit. (D. & C. 84:33; 88:16-32; Alma 13:12; 3 Ne. 27:19-21.) They become new creatures of the Holy Ghost, having been born again. (Alma 5.) Their renewed bodies are just as different from bodies still in their carnal state as the bodies of the various animals, fowls, and fishes differ from each other. (1 Cor. 15:39-42.) Those who have gained celestial bodies will, in the resurrection, receive back "the same body which was a natural body" (D. & C. 88:28), that is their celestial bodies will be immortalized and then they will gain admission to the celestial kingdom.

CELESTIAL CITY.
See NEW JERUSALEM.

CELESTIAL DAY.
See DAY.

CELESTIAL EARTH.
See EARTH.

CELESTIAL GLORY.
See CELESTIAL BODIES, CELESTIAL KINGDOM, CELESTIAL LAW, CELESTIAL SPIRITS, EXALTATION, SALVATION. If a man obeys celestial law in this life, he obtains a celestial body and spirit. In the resurrection these are received back again quickened by a *celestial glory,* thus qualifying him to go to a celestial kingdom where alone

celestial glory is found. (D. & C. 88:16-32.) Mortal man has no concept of the glory of that world. Those who finally attain it are persons "whose bodies are celestial, whose glory is that of the sun, even the glory of God, the highest of all, whose glory the sun of the firmament is written of as being typical." (D. & C. 76:70; 1 Cor. 15:40-42.)

Exaltation consists in gaining a fulness of celestial glory. (D. & C. 132:19-20.) Those so attaining will receive "a fulness of the glory of the Father" and be glorified in Christ as he is in the Father. (D. & C. 93:16-20.) The Prophet said that in the resurrection the righteous "shall rise again to dwell in everlasting burnings in immortal glory, not to sorrow, suffer, or die any more; but they shall be heirs of God and joint-heirs with Jesus Christ." (*Teachings* p. 347.)

CELESTIAL KINGDOM.

See CELESTIAL BODIES, CELESTIAL GLORY, CELESTIAL LAW, CELESTIAL MARRIAGE, CELESTIAL SPIRITS, EXALTATION, HEAVEN, KINGDOM OF GOD, KINGDOM OF HEAVEN, KINGDOMS OF GLORY, MANSIONS, SALVATION, TELESTIAL KINGDOM, TERRESTRIAL KINGDOM. Highest among the kingdoms of glory hereafter is the *celestial kingdom*. It is the kingdom of God, the glory thereof being typified by the sun in the firmament. (D. & C. 76: 50-70, 92-96; 1 Cor. 15:39-42.) The Prophet has left us this record of a glorious occurrence that took place in the Kirtland Temple on January 21, 1836: "The heavens were opened upon us, and I beheld the celestial kingdom of God, and the glory thereof, whether in the body or out I cannot tell. I saw the transcendent beauty of the gate through which the heirs of that kingdom will enter, which was like unto circling flames of fire; also the blazing throne of God, whereon was seated the Father and the Son. I saw the beautiful streets of that kingdom, which had the appearance of being paved with gold." (*Teachings,* p. 107.)

An inheritance in this glorious kingdom is gained by complete obedience to gospel or celestial law. (D. & C. 88:16-32.) By entering the gate of repentance and baptism candidates find themselves on the strait and narrow path leading to the celestial kingdom. By devotion and faithfulness, by enduring to the end in righteousness and obedience, it is then possible to merit a celestial reward. (2 Ne. 31:17-21.)

No unclean thing can enter this kingdom, and the plan of salvation is the system whereby men are washed and cleansed, whereby they are "sanctified by the reception of the Holy Ghost," and thus enabled to stand spotless before the Lord. (3 Ne. 27:19-21.) "The sanctified" are "them of the celestial world." (D. & C. 88:2.)

"In the celestial glory there are three heavens or degrees," and in the same sense that baptism starts a person out toward an entrance into the celestial world, so celestial marriage puts a couple on the path leading to an exaltation in the highest heaven of that world. (D. & C. 131:1-4; 132.)

CELESTIAL LAW.

See CELESTIAL BODIES, CELESTIAL GLORY, CELESTIAL KINGDOM, CELESTIAL MARRIAGE, CELESTIAL SPIRITS, CONSECRATION, GOSPEL, LAW, OBEDIENCE. That law by obedience to which men gain an inheritance in the kingdom of God in eternity is called *celestial law.* It is the law of the gospel, the law of Christ, and it qualifies men for admission to the celestial kingdom because in and through it men are "sanctified by the reception of the Holy Ghost," thus becoming clean, pure, and spotless. (3 Ne. 27:19-21.)

"And they who are not sanctified through the law which I have given unto you, even the law of Christ," the Lord says, "must inherit another kingdom, even that of a terrestrial kingdom, or that of a telestial kingdom. For *he who is not able to abide the law of a celestial kingdom cannot abide a celestial glory.*" (D. & C. 88:21-22.) Those who have the companionship of the Holy Ghost and are guided thereby in their lives are "able to abide the law of a celestial kingdom," including the law of consecration or anything else the Lord might ask of them. They are the ones who—"united according to the union required by the law of the celestial kingdom" (D. & C. 105:1-5)—will build up Zion in the last days.

CELESTIAL MARRIAGE.

See ARTICLE ON MARRIAGE, CALLING AND ELECTION SURE, CELESTIAL KINGDOM, CHURCH OF THE FIRSTBORN, CIVIL MARRIAGE, DAUGHTERS OF GOD, ETERNAL LIFE, ETERNAL LIVES, EXALTATION, FULNESS OF THE FATHER, GODHOOD, JOINT-HEIRS WITH CHRIST, PLURAL MARRIAGE, SALVATION, SALVATION FOR THE DEAD, SEALING POWER, SONS OF GOD. Marriages performed in the temples for time and eternity, by virtue of the sealing keys restored by Elijah, are called *celestial marriages.* The participating parties become husband and wife in this mortal life, and if after their marriage they keep all the terms and conditions of this order of the priesthood, they continue on as husband and wife in the celestial kingdom of God.

If the family unit continues, then by virtue of that fact the members of the family have gained eternal life (exaltation), the greatest of all the gifts of God, for by definition exaltation consists in the continuation of the family unit in eternity. Those so inheriting are the sons and daughters of God, the members of his family, those who have made their callings and elections sure.

They are joint-heirs with Christ to all that the Father hath, and they receive the fulness of the glory of the Father, becoming gods in their own right. (D. & C. 132; *Doctrines of Salvation,* vol. 2, pp. 58-99.)

Baptism is the gate to the celestial kingdom; celestial marriage is the gate to an exaltation in the highest heaven within the celestial world. (D. & C. 131:1-4.) To gain salvation after baptism it is necessary to keep the commandments of God and endure to the end (2 Ne. 31:17-21); to gain exaltation after celestial marriage the same continued devotion and righteousness is required. Those who have been married in the temples for eternity know that the ceremony itself expressly conditions the receipt of all promised blessings upon the subsequent faithfulness of the husband and wife.

Making one's calling and election sure is in *addition* to celestial marriage and results from undeviating and perfect devotion to the cause of righteousness. Those married in the temple can never under any circumstances gain exaltation unless they keep the commandments of God and abide in the covenant of marriage which they have taken upon themselves.

Celestial marriage is a holy and an eternal ordinance; as an order of the priesthood, it has the name the *new and everlasting covenant of marriage.* Adam was the first one on this earth to enter into this type of union, and it has been the Lord's order in all ages when the fulness of the gospel has been on earth. Its importance in the plan of salvation and exaltation cannot be overestimated. *The most important things that any member of The Church of Jesus Christ of Latter-day Saints ever does in this world are: 1. To marry the right person, in the right place, by the right authority; and 2. To keep the covenant made in connection with this holy and perfect order of matrimony—thus assuring the obedient persons of an inheritance of exaltation in the celestial kingdom.*

CELESTIAL SPIRITS.

See CELESTIAL BODIES, CELESTIAL GLORY, CELESTIAL KINGDOM, CELESTIAL LAW, EXALTATION, SALVATION. Those who by full obedience to gospel requirements develop celestial bodies, gain at the same time *celestial spirits.* Then in the resurrection, when "the same body which was a natural body," (that is, the renewed body, the body sanctified by the Spirit, the celestial body) is received back again, "they who are of a *celestial spirit*" are quickened by a celestial glory and go on to an inheritance in a celestial kingdom. (D. & C. 88:28.)

CELESTIAL TIME.

See TIME.

CELIBACY.

See APOSTASY, CELESTIAL MAR-

RIAGE, EUNUCHS, HARLOTS. Some persons in some of the churches in the world are bound by vows of *celibacy* whereunder they agree to remain unmarried. Celibacy is not of God, whose law is that "Marriage is honourable in all" (Heb. 13:4), and that men should "Be fruitful, and multiply, and replenish the earth." (Gen. 1:28.)

Many who practice celibacy do so out of an excessive religious devotion and with the idea in mind that they are serving their Maker. In reality they are forsaking some of the most important purposes of their creation for a man-made, uninspired system. Indeed, Paul says of this practice of celibacy that it consists in "giving heed to seducing spirits, and doctrines of devils." (1 Tim. 4:1-3.)

In this connection it is interesting to note that it is to Paul that advocates of celibacy turn in a fruitless search to find scripture justifying their unnatural mode of living. Paul himself was married. Of this there is no question. He had the sure promise of eternal life; his calling and election had been made sure (*Teachings,* p. 151)—which, according to God's eternal laws, could not have been unless he had first entered into the order of celestial marriage. (D. & C. 131; 132.)

However, Paul wrote some things to the Corinthian Saints which have been interpreted by some to mean that he was unmarried and that he thought it preferable if others did not marry. It may well be that his expressions on marriage, as found in the King James Version of the Bible (1 Cor. 7), have come to us in changed and perverted form, as compared to what he originally wrote. Some changes and clarifications have been made in the Inspired Version. But even as the record stands, it does not support celibacy; and when it is read in harmony with the rest of the scriptures (which always should be done in interpreting passages), it is found to teach quite the reverse.

It is apparent that the Corinthians had written Paul and had said to him, "It is good for a man not to touch a woman." Paul replied, in the Lord's name, writing by way of commandment, *"Let every man have his own wife, and let every woman have her own husband."* Then he announced that the Lord had ceased to speak and that he would give some personal opinions, in an attempt to solve some difficult cases. He does not record what the cases were; obviously they had been in the letter the Corinthians wrote him; and to get a fair perspective of his answer, we would need to know the exact questions involved. However, from latter-day revelation we do know that the questions pertained to circumcision, the law of Moses, marrying out of the Church, and the false tradition that little children are conceived in sin and hence are unholy. (D. & C. 74.)

Paul then gives it as his opinion (plainly saying that it is a personal view and not the voice of the Lord) that certain persons should not marry. It may be that he was referring to some particular persons for whom it would have been unwise to contract marriages. Knowing what he did about the doctrine of celestial marriage and exaltation, it is unthinkable that he would have counseled against marriage, except in some peculiar circumstance. There might be cases today in which individuals should not marry, but it is not the general rule, and the principle of not marrying is not the doctrine of the Church now any more than it was in his day. (*Inspired Version,* 1 Cor. 7.) If we knew the situation about which Paul wrote, and had a full transcript of his actual words, there would be no ambiguity as to his meaning and doctrine.

Indeed, it is to some of Paul's other writings that we turn for direct confirmation of the everlasting principle of eternal marriage, as for instance his epigrammatic statement, "Neither is the man without the woman, neither the woman without the man, *in the Lord.*" (1 Cor. 11:11.)

CEREMONIES.
See ORDINANCES.

CHAINS OF HELL.
See DAMNATION, GATES OF HELL, HELL. Those who "harden their hearts" against gospel truths soon become engulfed in total spiritual darkness in which "they know nothing concerning" God and "his mysteries; and then they are taken captive by the devil, and led by his will down to destruction. Now this is what is meant by the *chains of hell.*" (Alma 12:9-11.)

When persons are thus finally bound, there is no longer hope of reprieve; they suffer the second death and are "chained down to an everlasting destruction" (Alma 12:17), "from whence there is no deliverance." (2 Ne. 28:19, 22.) But as these chains begin to encircle the mind, closing out light and truth degree by degree, there is still the chance of escape through repentance and righteousness. (2 Ne. 1:13, 23; 9:45; Alma 5:7, 9; 13:30; 26:14.)

The angels who kept not their first estate are destined to inherit everlasting darkness; for them there is no escape from the chains of hell. (D. & C. 38:5; 2 Pet. 2:4; Jude 6.)

CHANCE.
See LAW.

CHAPELS.
See CATHEDRALS, MEETINGHOUSES, TABERNACLES, TEMPLES. Strictly speaking a *chapel* is a subordinate place of worship in a more elaborate church building; it is a room, recess, or cell containing an altar and located in a cathedral or other church building. The assembly halls in which services of wor-

ship are held in Latter-day Saint meetinghouses are commonly called chapels, though the term does not fully apply. To speak of the ward chapel when ward meetinghouse is meant is not the best usage of terms.

CHAPLAINS.

Clergymen on official duty with the armed services or who are employed by public institutions are commonly called *chaplains*. The title is not one that pertains to the Church or the gospel, and those who so serve are appointed by military or civil power and have no divine commission, unless, as occasionally happens, one of the elders of Israel serves in such a capacity.

CHARITY.

See ALMSGIVING, CHRIST, FAITH, HOPE, LOVE, PERFECTION, RELIEF SOCIETY, SALVATION, WELFARE PLAN. Above all the attributes of godliness and perfection, *charity* is the one most devoutly to be desired. Charity is more than love, far more; it is everlasting love, perfect love, the pure love of Christ which endureth forever. It is love so centered in righteousness that the possessor has no aim or desire except for the eternal welfare of his own soul and for the souls of those around him. (2 Ne. 26:30; Moro. 7:47; 8:25-26.)

"Above all things," the Lord says, "clothe yourselves with the bond of charity, as with a mantle, which is the bond of perfectness and peace." (D. & C. 88:125; Col. 3:14.) "Above all things have fervent charity among yourselves," Peter said to the saints, "for charity shall cover the multitude of sins." (1 Pet. 4:8.) Charity is the crowning virtue, "the end of the commandment" (1 Tim. 1:5); "And now abideth faith, hope, charity, these three; but the greatest of these is charity." (1 Cor. 13:13.)

Charity is an essential qualification for the ministers of Christ (D & C. 4:5); no one can assist in the Lord's work without it (D. & C. 12:8; 18:19); and the saints of God are commanded to seek and attain it. (D. & C. 121:45; 124:116; 2 Ne. 33:7-9; Alma 7:24; 1 Cor. 16:14; 1 Tim. 4:12; 2 Tim. 2:22; Tit. 2:2; 2 Pet. 1:7.) Charity is a gift of the Spirit which must be gained if one is to have salvation. "There must be faith," Moroni writes, "and if there must be faith there must also be hope; and if there must be hope there must also be charity. And *except ye have charity ye can in nowise be saved in the kingdom of God;* neither can ye be saved in the kingdom of God if ye have not faith; neither can ye if ye have no hope." (Moro. 10:20-21.)

To Moroni the Lord said: "Faith, hope and charity bringeth unto me —the fountain of all righteousness," and Moroni replied to the Lord (being, of course, moved upon by the Holy Ghost): "I remember that thou hast said that *thou hast loved the world, even unto the laying down of thy life for the world,* that thou mightest take it again to prepare a place for the children of men. And now I know that *this love which thou hast had for the children of men is charity;* wherefore, *except men shall have charity they cannot inherit that place which thou hast prepared in the mansions of thy Father."* (Ether 12:28, 33-34.)

Both Paul and Mormon wrote of charity in similar language. Either they both had the same words of some earlier prophet before them or the Holy Ghost revealed the same truths to them in almost the same words. Mormon's language included these statements: "If a man be meek and lowly in heart, and confesses by the power of the Holy Ghost that Jesus is the Christ, he must needs have charity; for if he have not charity he is nothing; wherefore he must needs have charity. And charity suffereth long, and is kind, and envieth not, and is not puffed up, seeketh not her own, is not easily provoked, thinketh no evil, and rejoiceth not in iniquity but rejoiceth in the truth, beareth all things, believeth all things, hopeth all things, endureth all things. Wherefore, my beloved brethren, if ye have not charity, ye are nothing, for *charity never faileth. Wherefore, cleave unto charity, which is the greatest of all, for all things must fail—But charity is the pure love of Christ, and it endureth forever;* and whoso is found possessed of it at the last day, it shall be well

with him. Wherefore, my beloved brethren, pray unto the Father with all the energy of heart, that ye may be filled with *this love, which he hath bestowed upon all who are true followers of his Son, Jesus Christ;* that ye may become the sons of God; that when he shall appear we shall be like him, for we shall see him as he is; that we may have this hope; that we may be purified even as he is pure." (Moro. 7:44-48.)

CHARMS.
See MAGIC.

CHASTENING.
See CHASTISEMENT, LOVE, PUNISHMENT, REPENTANCE, SECOND ESTATE. By a process of *chastening* the Lord helps prepare his saints for salvation. It is one of his ways of turning erring souls to paths of righteousness. As varying situations require, chastening may include rebukes for misconduct or subjection to trials and afflictions. It may even take the form of chastisement, meaning corporal punishment.

Men are chastened for their sins (D. & C. 58:60; 61:8; 64:8; 75:7; 93:50; 97:6; 103:4; 105:6; 1 Ne. 16:25), to bring them to repentance (D. & C. 1:27; 98:21), because the Lord loves them. (D. & C. 95:1-2; Hela. 15:3; Rev. 3:19.) Chastening is designed to try the faith and patience of the saints (Mosiah 23:21), and those who endure it well gain eternal life.

"For whom the Lord loveth he chasteneth, and scourgeth every son whom he receiveth. If ye endure chastening, God dealeth with you as with sons; for what son is he whom the father chasteneth not? But if ye be without chastisement, whereof all are partakers, then are ye bastards, and not sons. Furthermore we have had fathers of our flesh which corrected us, and we gave them reverence: shall we not much rather be in subjection unto the Father of spirits, and live? For they verily for a few days chastened us after their own pleasure; but he for our profit, that we might be partakers of his holiness. Now no chastening for the present seemeth to be joyous, but grievous: nevertheless afterward it yieldeth the peaceable fruit of righteousness unto them which are exercised thereby." (Heb. 12:6-11; Job 5:17; Prov. 3:11.)

Chastening is both mental and physical. The Lord and his prophets may rebuke and counsel people for their benefit. (1 Ne. 16:39.) And the Lord may send calamities upon the people to soften their hearts so they will become more receptive to his will. "Except the Lord doth chasten his people with many afflictions, yea, except he doth visit them with death and with terror, and with famine and with all manner of pestilence, they will not remember him." (Hela. 12:3; D. & C. 87: 6.) *"And my people must needs be chastened until they learn obedi-ence, if it must needs be, by the things which they suffer."* (D. & C. 101:6.)

"Verily I say unto you, concerning your brethren who have been afflicted, and persecuted, and cast out from the land of their inheritance"—the Lord is speaking of those driven from their homes in Jackson County by the mobs—"I, the Lord, have suffered the affliction to come upon them, wherewith they have been afflicted, in consequence of their transgressions; Yet I will own them, and they shall be mine in that day when I shall come to make up my jewels. Therefore, they must needs be chastened and tried, even as Abraham, who was commanded to offer up his only son. *For all those who will not endure chastening, but deny me, cannot be sanctified."* (D. & C. 101:1-5.)

CHASTISEMENT.

See CHASTENING, PUNISHMENT. When the chastening of the Lord takes the form of corporal punishment, it is called *chastisement.* (D. & C. 95:1; 103:1-4; Lev. 26:28.) Those who will not bear chastisement are not worthy of salvation. (D. & C. 136:31.)

One of the great Messianic prophecies foretold that our Lord would bear in his own body the wounds of chastisement. "He was wounded for our transgressions, he was bruised for our iniquities: the chastisement of our peace was upon him;

and with his stripes we are healed." (Isa. 53:5.)

CHASTITY.
See MODESTY, REPENTANCE, SEX IMMORALITY. *Chastity,* meaning virtue and sexual purity, is that state of moral purity which is "most dear and precious above all things." (Moro. 9:9.) On the other hand, sexual sins are "most abominable above all sins save it be the shedding of innocent blood or denying the Holy Ghost." (Alma 39:5.)

Loss of virtue is too great a price to pay even for the preservation of one's life—better dead clean, than alive unclean. Many is the faithful Latter-day Saint parent who has sent a son or a daughter on a mission or otherwise out into the world with the direction: "I would rather have you come back in a pine box with your virtue than return alive without it." *"I, the Lord God, delight in the chastity of women. And whoredoms are an abomination before me; thus saith the Lord of Hosts."* (Jac. 2:28.)

CHEERFULNESS.
See DESPAIR, HOPE, JOY, LAUGHTER, REJOICING. One of the frequent bits of counsel, comfort, and solace coming from God to his people is, "Be of good cheer." (John 16:33; Acts 27:22, 25; 2 Ne. 10:23; Alma 17:31; 3 Ne. 1:13; D. & C. 61:36; 68:6; 78:18; 112:4.) That is, the saints are exhorted to raise their spirits, to increase their hope of better days, to be comforted in their sorrows, gladdened in their successes, and made to rejoice in general. True *cheerfulness* is born of righteousness, for in right living there can be no remorse of conscience.

CHERUB.
See CHERUBIM.

CHERUBIM.
See ANGELS, HIERARCHY, SERAPHIM. Apparently a *cherub* is an angel of some particular order or rank to whom specific duties and work are assigned. That portion of the Lord's word which is now available among men does not set forth clearly either the identity or work of these heavenly beings. The concept of sectarian scholars that they are "mythological living creatures," who filled for the Hebrew people the same position that the griffins did for the Hittites, is utterly false. (Griffins were supposed to be winged sphinxes having the bodies of lions and the heads and wings of eagles, and they were in fact mythological creatures.)

In English, the plural of cherub is *cherubs;* in Hebrew, the plural is *cherubim,* except that the King James Version of the Bible erroneously translates the plural as

124

cherubims. The Book of Mormon (Alma 12:21; 42:2-3), the Pearl of Great Price (Moses 4:31), and the Inspired Version of the Bible (Ex. 25:20-22), give the plural as *cherubim*. When Adam and Eve were cast out of Eden, it was "cherubim and a flaming sword" which kept them from partaking of the tree of life so they would have lived forever in their sins. (Moses 4:31.)

As seen in the vision of Ezekiel (Ezek. 1; 10; 11); as placed over the mercy seat in the tabernacle in the wilderness (Ex. 25:17-22; 37:6-7); as decorations on the curtains and veil of this tabernacle (Ex. 21:1, 31); as embroidered on the veil of Solomon's Temple (2 Chron. 3:14); as decorating the base whereon the molten sea rested (1 Kings 7:23-29); and as placed in the holy of holies of that magnificent temple (1 Kings 6:23-30; 8:6-7; 2 Chron. 3:10; 5:7-8; Heb. 9:1-5)—the cherubim were shown with wings. There are, of course, no angels (cherubim included) who have wings. Their usage in these instances was symbolical; as with certain beasts seen in vision by John, the presence of wings was "a representation of power, to move, to act, etc." (D. & C. 77:4.)

The statement that the Lord "rode upon a cherub" is figurative; it means, as the balance of the sentence explains, that "he was seen upon the wings of the wind." (2 Sam. 22:11; Ps. 18:10.) Cherubs and the wind both have wings in the same sense and in no other.

CHIEF SHEPHERD.
See GOOD SHEPHERD.

CHILDREN.
See SALVATION OF CHILDREN.

CHILDREN OF ABRAHAM.
See ISRAEL.

CHILDREN OF BELIAL.
See SONS OF BELIAL.

CHILDREN OF CHRIST.
See SEED OF CHRIST.

CHILDREN OF DISOBEDIENCE.
See CARNALITY, CHILDREN OF LIGHT, DEVILISHNESS, DISOBEDIENCE, SENSUALITY, WORLD. Those persons who walk after the manner of the world, following their carnal, sensual, and devilish desires, are referred to as the *children of disobedience*. (Eph. 2:2.) They are followers or disciples of disobedience and are also variously designated as "children of transgression" (Isa. 57:4), "children of this world" (Luke 16:8; 20:34), "children of wrath" (Eph. 2:3), "children of the kingdom of the devil" (Alma 5:25), and "the children of them which killed the prophets." (Matt. 23:31.) They revel in the lusts of their "father the devil." (John 8:33-56.) As servants of sin themselves, they

fight the living oracles (D. & C. 121:17), and the wrath of God will in due course rest upon them. (Eph. 5:6; Col. 3:6.)

CHILDREN OF EPHRAIM.

See TRIBES OF ISRAEL.

CHILDREN OF GOD.

See SONS OF GOD.

CHILDREN OF ISRAEL.

See TRIBES OF ISRAEL.

CHILDREN OF JACOB.

See TRIBES OF ISRAEL.

CHILDREN OF JUDAH.

See JEWS.

CHILDREN OF LIGHT.

See LIGHT, LIGHT OF THE WORLD, SAINTS, SECOND COMING OF CHRIST. By accepting the gospel and thus coming out of darkness into the marvelous light of Christ (1 Pet. 2:9), men become the *children of light.* (John 12:36; Col. 1:12.) They are then followers or disciples of light and truth. The saints are commanded to "walk as children of light." (Eph. 5:8.) If they do, they have the promise that the great and dreadful day of the Lord will not overtake them as a thief in the night. (1 Thess. 5:1-6; D. & C. 106:4-5.)

CHILDREN OF THE COVENANT.

See ADOPTION, CELESTIAL MARRIAGE, GOSPEL, ISRAEL, NEW AND EVERLASTING COVENANT, SONS OF GOD. According to the terms of the covenant which God made with Abraham, all of the literal seed of that great prophet are entitled to receive the gospel, the priesthood, and all of the ordinances of salvation and exaltation. (Abra. 2:9-11; D. & C. 86:8-11.) When any of those descendants do receive all of these things, "They become the sons of Moses and of Aaron and the seed of Abraham, and the church and kingdom, and the elect of God." (D. & C. 84:34.) They are then *children of the covenant,* that is, they are inheritors of the fulness of the blessings appertaining to the new and everlasting covenant which is the gospel. "Ye are the children of the covenant" (3 Ne. 20:24-27), our Lord told the Nephites among whom he ministered, a distinction which the faithful saints of this dispensation also enjoy. Rebellious descendants of Abraham are not his children in the special sense that is intended by the designation children of the covenant. (John 8:33-59.)

CHILDREN OF THE KINGDOM.

See CHURCH OF JESUS CHRIST OF LATTER-DAY SAINTS, KINGDOM OF GOD, SAINTS. Our Lord's Church is the kingdom of God on earth. Faithful members of that

Church, those who adhere to the standards of the kingdom, are the *children of the kingdom.* (Matt. 13:38.) They are followers or disciples of the Master because they believe the gospel of the kingdom. Special blessings are reserved for them (D. & C. 41:6), and they are commanded to bring forth fruit mete for the Father's kingdom. (D. & C. 84:58-59.) Children of the kingdom eventually "shall sit down with Abraham, and Isaac, and Jacob, in the kingdom of heaven." (Matt. 8:11-12.)

CHILDREN OF THE PROPHETS.

See ADOPTION, CHILDREN OF THE COVENANT, PROPHETS, SEED OF CHRIST. Those who follow in the footsteps of the prophets, who believe as they believed and live as they lived, are the *children of the prophets.* (D. & C. 84:33-34.) They are children in the sense of being followers or disciples, and they may also be their literal seed. (3 Ne. 20:25-27; Acts 3:25.) However, the rebellious literal seed cut themselves off from the blessings of their fathers, and they become the children of the devil rather than the children of the prophets. (John 8:33-59.)

CHILDREN OF ZION.

See CHILDREN OF LIGHT, CHILDREN OF THE KINGDOM, ZION. Those who seek the welfare of Zion, whose desires and strivings are that Zion may be built up and her glory spread through all the earth, are the *children of Zion.* Since the great latter-day Zion is to be built up by the Church and kingdom of God on earth, it follows that the children of Zion are members of that divine institution. (D. & C. 84:56-58; 101:41, 81-85; 103:35.)

CHOCOLATE.

See WORD OF WISDOM.

CHOSEN ONE.

See CHRIST, ELECTION OF GRACE. Christ is the *Chosen One.* (Moses 4: 2; 7:39.) By this is meant that from the beginning, because of devotion, obedience, and righteousness, he was chosen by the Father to play the chief part in the great creative and redemptive enterprises of Deity.

CHOSEN SEED.

See ELECT OF GOD.

CHRIST.

See ADONAI, ADVOCACY, ADVOCATE, ALMIGHTY GOD, ALPHA AND OMEGA, ALPHUS, AMEN, ANGEL, APOSTLE, ASCENSION OF CHRIST, ATONEMENT OF CHRIST, AUSTERE MAN, AUTHOR OF SALVATION, BABE OF BETHLEHEM, BEGINNING AND END, BELOVED SON, BISHOP,

BLASPHEMY, BLOOD ATONEMENT DOCTRINE, BRANCH, BRAZEN SERPENT, BREAD OF LIFE, BRIDEGROOM, BRIDE OF THE LAMB, BRIGHT AND MORNING STAR, CAPTAIN OF SALVATION, CAPTAIN OF THE LORD'S HOST, CARPENTER'S SON, CHOSEN ONE, CHRIST AS THE FATHER, CHRIST CHILD, CHRISTENDOM, CHRISTHOOD, CHRISTIAN ERA, CHRISTIANITY, CHRISTIANS, CHRISTMAS, CHURCH OF JESUS CHRIST OF LATTER-DAY SAINTS, COUNSELOR, CREATOR, CROSS, CRUCIFIED ONE, CRUCIFIXION, DELIVERER, DESIRE OF ALL NATIONS, DOOR OF THE SHEEP, ELDER BROTHER, ELIAS, ETERNAL LIFE, EXALTATION, EXEMPLAR, EXPIATION, EXPIATOR, FAITH, FALL OF ADAM, FALSE CHRISTS, FATHER IN HEAVEN, FIRST AND LAST, FIRSTBORN, GALILEAN, GOD; GOD OF ABRAHAM, ISAAC, AND JACOB; GOD OF BATTLES, GOD OF GODS, GOD OF ISRAEL, GOD OF JESHURUN, GOD OF NATURE, GOD OF SPIRITS, GOD OF THE WHOLE EARTH, GOD OF TRUTH, GOOD SHEPHERD, GOSPEL, GREAT I AM, HEIR OF GOD, HIGH PRIEST, HOLY, HOLY GHOST, HOLY MESSIAH, HOLY ONE, HOLY ONE OF GOD, HOLY ONE OF ISRAEL, HOLY ONE OF JACOB, HOLY ONE OF ZION, HUSBAND, IMMANUEL, INCARNATE GOD, INTERCESSION, INTERCESSOR, JAH, JEALOUS, JEHOVAH, JESUS, JESUS OF NAZARETH, JOINT-HEIRS WITH CHRIST, JUDGE OF ALL THE EARTH, JUSTIFICATION, JUST ONE, KEEPER OF THE GATE, KEY OF DAVID, KING, KING OF GLORY, KING OF HEAVEN, KING OF ISRAEL, KING OF KINGS, KING OF THE JEWS, KING OF ZION, LAMB OF GOD, LAW, LAWGIVER, LIGHT OF CHRIST, LIGHT OF LIFE, LIGHT OF THE WORLD, LION OF TRIBE OF JUDAH, LOGOS, LORD, LORD GOD, LORD OF GLORY, LORD OF HOSTS, LORD OF LORDS, LORD OF SABAOTH, LORD OF THE HARVEST, LORD OF THE SABBATH, LORD OF THE VINEYARD, LORD OMNIPOTENT, LORD OUR RIGHTEOUSNESS, MANNA, MARRIAGE SUPPER OF THE LAMB, MARY, MASTER, MEDIATION, MEDIATOR, MELCHIZEDEK, MESSENGER BEFORE THE LORD, MESSENGER OF SALVATION, MESSENGER OF THE COVENANT, MESSIAH, MESSIAHSHIP, MESSIANIC PROPHECIES, MESSIAS, MINISTER OF SALVATION, MOSES, MOST HIGH, NAME OF CHRIST, NAZARENE, OMEGUS, OMNIPOTENCE, OMNIPRESENCE, OMNISCIENCE, ONLY BEGOTTEN, OUR LORD, PARABLES, PARACLETE, PASSION OF CHRIST, PERSONIFICATION, PLAN OF SALVATION, POTENTATE, POTTER, PRE-EXISTENCE, PRINCE OF PEACE, PROPHET, PROPHET OF THE HIGHEST, PROPHETS, PROPITIATION, PROPITIATOR, PURIFIER, QUETZALCOATL, RABBI, RECONCILIATION, RECONCILOR, REDEEMER, REDEMPTION, REFINER, REST OF THE LORD, RESTORER, RESURRECTION, RESURRECTION AND THE LIFE, RISEN LORD, ROCK OF HEAVEN, ROOT OF DAVID, RULER, SALVATION, SANCTIFICATION, SAVIOR, SECOND ADAM, SECOND COMING OF

CHRIST, SEED OF CHRIST, SERVANT, SHILOH, SIGN OF JONAS, SIGN OF THE CROSS, SON, SON AHMAN, SON OF DAVID, SON OF GOD, SON OF JOSEPH, SON OF MAN, SON OF MARY, SON OF RIGHTEOUSNESS, SON OF THE ETERNAL FATHER, SON OF THE EVERLASTING GOD, SON OF THE HIGHEST, SON OF THE LIVING GOD, SONG OF THE LAMB, SPIRIT OF TRUTH, STEM OF JESSE, STONE OF ISRAEL, SYMBOLISMS, TESTATOR, TETRAGRAMMATON, THEOPHANIES, TRUE VINE, TRUTH, UNPARDONABLE SIN, VIRGIN BIRTH; WAY, TRUTH, AND LIFE; WORD OF GOD, YAHWEH, YOKE OF CHRIST. As far as man is concerned, all things center in *Christ*. He is the Firstborn of the Father. By obedience and devotion to the truth he attained that pinnacle of intelligence which ranked him as a God, as the Lord Omnipotent, while yet in his pre-existent state. As such he became, under the Father, the Creator of this earth and of worlds without number; and he was then chosen to work out the infinite and eternal atonement, to come to this particular earth as the literal Son of the Father, and to put the whole plan of redemption, salvation, and exaltation in operation.

Through him the gospel, all saving truths, and every edifying principle have been revealed in all ages. He is the Eternal Jehovah, the promised Messiah, the Redeemer and Savior, the Way, the Truth, and the Life. By him immortality and eternal life become realities, and through his grace and goodness salvation is possible for all who will believe and obey.

He was born into this world as the Son of Mary (inheriting from her the power of mortality) and as the Son of Man of Holiness (inheriting from him the powers of immortality). In this life he received not of the fulness at the first, but went from grace to grace until, in the final triumph of the resurrection, he gained the fulness of all things; and all power was given him both in heaven and on earth. He has all truth, all power, all knowledge; he comprehends all things, is infinite in all his attributes and powers; and he has given a law unto all things.

In due course he will come again, in power, dominion, and glory to reign with righteous men on earth a thousand years. Thereafter, with the righteous saints, he shall reign to all eternity as King of Kings, Lord of Lords, and God of Gods. To his holy name, both now and forever, be ascribed glory and honor, power, riches, and dominion, and an eternal fulness of all things for endless ages.

If the sectarian world, or even the spiritually unenlightened in the Church, had the slightest concept of the dominion, exaltation, and pre-eminence of our Lord both in pre-existence, during his mortal ministry, and now that he has returned to his Father, it would seem little short of direful and presumptuous blasphemy to them. Words, either written or spoken, cannot convey such a realization; it can only come by the revelations of the Spirit. This work on *Mormon Doctrine* deals in a most fragmentary way with him, his laws, and his doctrines. The well over 200 separate articles cross-referenced under the heading *Christ* deal briefly with his names, ministry, mission, and exalted position in the eternal scheme of things.

CHRIST AS THE FATHER.

See BORN AGAIN, CHRIST, CREATOR, FATHER IN HEAVEN, SON OF GOD, SONS OF GOD. Although Christ—the Firstborn in the spirit and the Only Begotten in the flesh —is the Son of God the Father, and as such is a separate and distinct personage from the Father, yet there are three senses in which *Christ is called the Father.* These are clearly set forth in a document entitled, "The Father and the Son: A Doctrinal Exposition by the First Presidency and the Twelve." (*Articles of Faith*, pp. 465-473; *Man: His Origin and Destiny*, pp. 117-129.)

1. Christ is the Father in the sense that he is the Creator, the Maker, the Organizer of the heavens and of the earth, and all things that in them are. (Isa. 9:6; 2 Ne. 19:6; Mosiah 15:4; 16:15; Alma 11:

38-39; Ether 4:7.)

2. He is the Father of all those who are born again (Mosiah 27:24-29), who "are begotten sons and daughters unto God" through his atoning sacrifice (D. & C. 76:24), who are "spiritually begotten" through faith, thus becoming "his sons and his daughters." (Mosiah 5:7.)

3. He is the Father by what has aptly been termed divine investiture of authority. That is, since he is one with the Father in all of the attributes of perfection, and since he exercises the power and authority of the Father, it follows that everything he says or does is and would be exactly and precisely what the Father would say and do under the same circumstances.

Accordingly, the Father puts his own name on the Son and authorizes him to speak in the first person as though he were the Father. This is similar to the situation in which Christ puts his name on an angel so that the designated heavenly ministrant can speak in the first person as though he were Christ himself. (Rev. 1:1; 19:9-10; 22:8-14.) Thus it is that our Lord can begin a revelation by saying, "Listen to the voice of Jesus Christ," and shortly thereafter speak of "mine Only Begotten" (D. & C. 29:1, 41-46), such latter expression being made by Christ, but under that divine investiture of authority which permits him to speak as though he were the Father. (D. & C. 93:3-5; Mosiah 15:1-5.)

CHRIST CHILD.

See BABE OF BETHLEHEM, CHRIST. Among Christian people it is common to refer to the youthful Son of Deity as the *Christ Child,* he of course having been born and having grown to maturity as other men do. (Matt. 2:19-23; Luke 1:76.) Though as a youth he had unusual mental and spiritual capacity (Luke 2:41-52), yet according to the customs and laws of the time he was in subjection to his parents. The Prophet inserted this revealed truth in the *Inspired Version* of the Bible. "Jesus grew up with his brethren, and waxed strong, and waited upon the Lord for the time of his ministry to come. And he served under his father, and *he spake not as other men, neither could he be taught; for he needed not that any man should teach him.*" (*Inspired Version,* Matt. 3: 24-25.)

CHRISTENDOM.

See APOSTASY, CHRIST, CHRISTIANITY, CHRISTIANS. That portion of the world in which so-called Christianity prevails—as distinguished from heathen or Mohammedan lands—is called *Christendom.* The term also applies to the whole body of supposed Christian believers; as now constituted this body is properly termed *apostate Christendom.*

CHRISTENING.

See APOSTASY, BLESSING OF CHILDREN, INFANT BAPTISM. In modern Christendom the ceremony of baptizing and naming a child is called *christening.* Obviously this practice, including as it does the false practice of infant baptism, is contrary to revealed truth. In the Lord's Church infant children are named in blessings given by the elders, but this is not accompanied by infant baptism and is not properly called christening.

CHRISTHOOD.

See APOSTASY, CHRIST, JOINT-HEIRS WITH CHRIST. There is only one Christ, because there is only one Son of God, only one Only Begotten, only one person ever born into the world with life in himself, with the power to lay down his life and to take it up again. (John 10: 11-18.) False doctrines found in some cults to the effect that a number of persons have attained *Christhood* or the state of being a Christ are direful perversions of the truth. They are the devil's substitute for the true doctrine which teaches that men may become joint-heirs with Christ.

CHRISTIAN ERA.

See CHRIST, CHRISTIANITY. On the false assumption that Christianity had its beginning with our Lord's mortal ministry, his birth was chosen to mark the beginning of the so-called *Christian Era.* Though there is considerable controversy and uncertainty among scholars of the world as to the actual year of Christ's birth, the revelation given on the day the Church was organized in this dispensation apparently intends to convey the thought that he was born April 6, B.C. 1. (D. & C. 20:1.)

CHRISTIANITY.

See CHRIST, CHRISTIANS, DISPENSATIONS. *Christianity* is the religion of the Christians. Hence, true and acceptable Christianity is found among the saints who have the fulness of the gospel, and a perverted Christianity holds sway among the so-called Christians of apostate Christendom. In these circles it is believed and taught that Christianity had its beginning with the mortal ministry of our Lord. Actually, of course, Adam was the first Christian, for both he and the saints of all ages have rejoiced in the very doctrines of salvation restored to earth by our Lord in his ministry.

CHRISTIANS.

See BELIEVERS, BRETHREN, CHRIST, CHRISTIANITY, CHURCH OF JESUS CHRIST OF LATTER-DAY SAINTS, DISCIPLES, MORMONS, PROPHETS, SAINTS. True believers in Christ, both in America among the Nephites and in the old world beginning in apostolic times, were called *Christians*. (Alma 46:13-16; 48:10; Acts 11:26; 26:28; 1 Pet. 4: 16.) Probably the name was applied

first in derision, but it found ready acceptance among the members of the Church because they rejoiced in the privilege of taking upon themselves "the name of Christ, or Christians." (Alma 46:15.)

As the day of the great apostasy set in, the term Christian continued to be applied to the supposed followers of Christ, even though in reality they had departed from the true doctrines. Today those who purport to believe in Christ though they may not actually accept him as the Son of God, are called Christians.

The first Nephite reference to Christians in the Book of Mormon is dated about 73 B.C. in what the sectarian world would call the pre-Christian era. But since the doctrine of Christ has been taught in successive dispensations from the days of Adam to the present, either the very name Christian or some equally expressive synonym has been applied to the saints of the Most High of all ages.

CHRISTMAS.

See APOSTASY, CHRIST, EASTER, EPIPHANY. Modern day Christians celebrate December 25th as an annual church festival and as the traditional day of our Lord's mortal birth. Special gifts and greetings are common, and both *Christmas* itself and the whole yuletide season often take on an air of commercialism and worldliness. Apparently Christ was born on the day corresponding to April 6 (D. & C. 20:1),

but the saints nevertheless join in the wholesome portions of the Christmas celebration. Christmas becomes to them an ideal opportunity to renew their search for the true Spirit of Christ and to center their attentions again on the true doctrine of his birth as the Son of an Immortal Father, a fact that enabled him to work out the infinite and eternal atonement.

CHRIST'S PASSION.

See PASSION OF CHRIST.

CHURCH.

See CHURCH OF JESUS CHRIST OF LATTER-DAY SAINTS, CHURCH OF THE DEVIL, CHURCH OF THE FIRSTBORN, DISPENSATIONS, GOSPEL, KINGDOM OF GOD, MORMONISM. Our Lord's true *Church* is the formal, official organization of believers who have taken upon themselves the name of Christ by baptism, thus covenanting to serve God and keep his commandments. (D. & C. 10:67-69; 18:20-25.) It is literally the kingdom of God on earth (D. & C. 65; 84:34; 136:41), and as such its affairs are administered by apostles, prophets, and other legal administrators appointed by Christ the King. (1 Cor. 12:27-29.) It is the congregation or assembly of saints who have forsaken the world by accepting the gospel, a formal society of converted persons and not the unorganized spiritual vagary termed the Christian Church by sectarianism.

The Church was first organized on earth in the days of Adam, with that great patriarch standing as its first president, the presiding high priest over God's earthly kingdom. The common sectarian notion that the day of Pentecost is the birthday of the Christian Church is a false heresy. Whenever the gospel has been on earth, it has been taught and administered in and through Christ's Church. The Church or kingdom as organized in the meridian of time by our Lord and his apostolic ministers was a restored Church.

With the coming of the great apostasy the primitive Church was lost, and the various churches or societies which have since grown up bear no particular similiarity to the original. This reality is frankly accepted by impartial theologians whether in the Church or out of it. One eminent author has written: "As God permits men to mar the perfection of his designs in their behalf, and as men have both corrupted the doctrines and broken the unity of the Church, we must not expect to see the Church of Holy Scripture actually existing in its perfection on earth. It is not to be found, thus perfect, either in the collected fragments of Christendom, or still less in any one of these fragments; though it is possible that one of those fragments more than another may approach the scriptural and apostolic ideal which existed only until sin, heresy, and schism,

had time sufficiently to develop themselves to do their work." (*Smith's Bible Dictionary,* vol. 1, p. 458.)

It has always been common to refer to the Church as the *kingdom.* Matthew so speaks more than a score of times. (Matt. 13:24.) But the term *Church* itself has also always been used, though possibly more frequently in some ages than in others. "The church, in ancient days," for instance, chose to call the higher priesthood after the name of Melchizedek. (D. & C. 107:3-4.) Some 600 years before Christ, Nephi spoke of "the brethren of the church" (1 Ne. 4:26), though the name *Church* is not found in the Old Testament as we now have that document.

Matthew is the only gospel author in whose writings the term has been preserved, and it appears over 100 additional times in the balance of the New Testament. It is found about 230 times in the Book of Mormon with about 191 of these occurring between 600 B. C. and 34 A. D. and the other two score or so being in the period after the ministry of the resurrected Lord among the Nephites. The Doctrine and Covenants contains about 500 references to the Church or churches.

Those who join the true Church and keep their covenants gain salvation in the celestial kingdom of God. (D. & C. 10:55, 69.) In the true Church there will be apostles, prophets, true doctrinal teachings, revelation, visions, miracles, healings, the ministering of angels, and all of the gifts of the Spirit. (Mark 16:14-20; 1 Cor. 12; 13; 14; 3 Ne. 27; Morm. 8; 9; Moro. 7; 8; D. & C. 46.) Where these things are found, there is the true Church; where these things are not found, there the true Church is not.

CHURCH COURTS.

See BISHOPS COURT, COMMON COUNCIL OF THE CHURCH, DISFELLOWSHIPMENT, ELDERS COURT, EXCOMMUNICATION, FIRST PRESIDENCY, HIGH COUNCIL, HOME TEACHERS, JUDGES IN ISRAEL. Being the kingdom of God on earth and having a perfect organization, provision is made in the Church for the trial of transgressors against church standards and for the settlement of disputes between church members and groups. It is the practice of the Church for home teachers (or other specially assigned brethren) to investigate alleged transgression and then, if necessary, bring charges against accused persons, either before a bishops court or a stake presidency and high council. Both of these courts have original jurisdiction in all cases, but a bishops court may not impose a penalty of excommunication upon a holder of the Melchizedek Priesthood. Persons tried by a bishops court may appeal to the stake presidency and high council, and from there appeals may be taken to the First Presidency of the Church.

In practice most church trials

deal with alleged transgression, excommunication being the supreme penalty that may be imposed. (D. & C. 134:10.) On occasion, however, temporal matters have been decided by church courts as in the case of President John Taylor's calling a Common Council of the Church to decide water disputes between persons living in different stakes. (*Gospel Kingdom,* pp. 201-202.) Indeed, the framework is so formed that all types of cases might be handled by church courts.

CHURCH HIERARCHY.
  See HIERARCHY.

CHURCH HISTORIAN AND RECORDER.
  See BOOK OF REMEMBRANCE, BOOK OF THE LAW OF GOD, CLERKS, HISTORY, JOURNALS, RECORD KEEPING. Record keeping and the writing of history is so essential a part of the gospel plan that it would be done automatically by prophets and others even if there were no commandments requiring it. From the very beginning, whenever prophets received revelations, such necessarily were recorded and preserved so they could be studied and obeyed. Joseph Smith kept a daily journal, which of course included the revelations he received, and this journal has become the six volume *History of the Church.*
  On the very day the Church was organized in this dispensation the Lord commanded his people to keep records. (D. & C. 21:1.) Oliver Cowdery, who already had been acting as amanuensis to the Prophet, became the first *Church Historian and Recorder.* When he was called to other work, John Whitmer was chosen by revelation to "keep a regular history" of the Church (D. & C. 47:1), "a history of all the important things which he shall observe and know concerning my church," the Lord said. Also: "Let my servant John Whitmer travel many times from place to place, and from church to church, that he may the more easily obtain knowledge—Preaching and expounding, writing, copying, selecting, and *obtaining all things which shall be for the good of the church, and for the rising generations* that shall grow up on the land of Zion, to possess it from generation to generation, forever and ever." (D. & C. 69; 85.)
  This gathering, recording, compiling, and collecting of historical data is continuing in the Church today. The *Church Historian's Office* is a great repository of original journals and documents; of books about the Church and its affairs; of the historical records of ward, stakes, missions, and quorums; of statistical data revealing the faith and works of the saints; and of the sermons and doctrinal teachings of church members. Church histories are the most important and accurate in existence. It is interesting to note that pur-

suant to revelation and commandment this office keeps copies of the scurrilous, false, and libelous histories that are published about the Church and the Lord's people. (D. & C. 123; *Doctrines of Salvation,* vol. 2, pp. 197-204.)

CHURCH HISTORIAN'S OFFICE.

See CHURCH HISTORIAN AND RECORDER.

CHURCH OF CHRIST.

See CHRIST, CHURCH, CHURCH OF JESUS CHRIST OF LATTER-DAY SAINTS, MORMONS. One or more of the names of Christ has always been used in the formal name of the Church. The revelation commanding the Prophet to organize the Church in this dispensation speaks of it as the *Church of Christ.* (D. & C. 20:1.) Similar usage is found in the Book of Mormon. (Mosiah 18:17; 3 Ne. 26:21; 28:23; 4 Ne. 26, 29; Moro. 6:4.) In due course, however, the Lord giving his revelations line upon line and precept upon precept, the official and formal name of the Church was specified, that is, *The Church of Jesus Christ of Latter-day Saints.* (D. & C. 115: 3-4.)

CHURCH OF ENOCH.

See CHURCH OF THE FIRSTBORN, EXALTATION, TRANSLATED BEINGS. All the inhabitants of Zion—being devoted members of the Lord's Church, with Enoch at their head— were translated and taken to heaven. (Moses 7:69.) Their callings and elections were made sure, and they were all assured of membership in the Church of the Firstborn and of an inheritance of exaltation in the eternal worlds. Those so favored were, of course, with Christ in his resurrection. (D. & C. 133:54-56.) They are spoken of as "the general assembly and *church of Enoch"* (D. & C. 76:67,) and all those who gain exaltation will be joined with them.

CHURCH OF JESUS CHRIST OF LATTER-DAY SAINTS.

See CHRIST, CHURCH, CHURCH OF CHRIST, DISPENSATION OF THE FULNESS OF TIMES, GOSPEL, JOSEPH SMITH THE PROPHET, KINGDOM OF GOD, MISSIONARIES, MORMONISM, RESTORATION OF THE GOSPEL, SIGNS OF THE TIMES. To his earthly kingdom in the dispensation of the fulness of times the Lord has given the formal name, *The Church of Jesus Christ of Latter-day Saints.* (D. & C. 115:3-4.) This Church is "the only true and living church upon the face of the whole earth" (D. & C. 1:30), the only organization authorized by the Almighty to preach his gospel and administer the ordinances of salvation, the only Church which has power to save and exalt men in the hereafter. Membership in this divine institution is a pearl of great price.

With the appearance of the Father and the Son to the Prophet in the spring of 1820, the final great gospel dispensation had its beginning. Thereafter angels ministered to the Prophet, he received many revelations, the Book of Mormon (which itself contains the fulness of the gospel) was translated, and the keys and power of the priesthood were restored.

In about June, 1829, Peter, James, and John conferred upon Joseph Smith and Oliver Cowdery the Melchizedek Priesthood, the keys of the kingdom of God (meaning the Church), and the keys of the dispensation of the fulness of times. (D. & C. 27:12-13; 65; 128: 20.) Acting by revelation and commandment, in the power and authority of the priesthood and keys so conferred upon them, and in the name of Him whose we are, on the 6th day of April, 1830, the Prophet and his associates organized again on earth the Lord's own Church. (D. & C. 20.)

The Lord's hand was in the work, and he decreed the ultimate and final triumph of the work so begun. (D. & C. 65; Dan. 2:44.) From that day the Church began to grow and the gospel message to roll forth. Guidance and direction was received line upon line and precept upon precept. Each part of the doctrine and of the organization was made manifest as occasion required.

After every key, power, and authority had been restored, after the foundation of the great latter-day work was securely laid, the Prophet and Patriarch sealed their testimony with their own blood and were taken on to continued glory and dominion in the realms of the Spirit. (D. & C. 135.) But the work they had commenced continued to progress, carrying with it the assurance that eventually the knowledge of God would cover the earth as the waters cover the sea and every living soul would be converted to the truth. (Isa. 11:9.)

This newly organized Church is the same in every essential particular as the Church of the Lamb has been in all ages past when it has been found among men. It conforms, for instance, to the New Testament pattern of the Lord's Church. In it is found the same authority, the same organization, the same ordinances, the same teachings and doctrines that were found in the primitive Church. And the same gifts of the Spirit—revelations, visions, miracles, healings, the ministering of angels, tongues, and a host of others—as were poured out upon the ancient saints are again showered in equal measure upon the modern saints, the members of the Lord's own Church and kingdom.

CHURCH OF THE DEVIL.

See APOSTASY, BABYLON, DEVIL, KINGDOM OF THE DEVIL, SECOND COMING OF CHRIST, WORLD. The titles *church of the devil* and *great and abominable church* are used to identify all churches or organizations of whatever name or nature—whether political, philosophical, educational, economic, social, fraternal, civic, or religious —which are designed to take men on a course that leads away from God and his laws and thus from salvation in the kingdom of God.

Salvation is in Christ, is revealed by him from age to age, and is available only to those who keep his commandments and obey his ordinances. These commandments are taught in, and these ordinances are administered by, his Church. There is no salvation outside this one true Church, the Church of Jesus Christ. There is one Christ, one Church, one gospel, one plan of salvation, one set of saving ordinances, one group of legal administrators, "One Lord, one faith, one baptism." (Eph. 4:5.)

Any church or organization of any kind whatever which satisfies the innate religious longings of man and keeps him from coming to the saving truths of Christ and his gospel is therefore not of God.

Hence we find our Lord saying, "He that is not with me is against me; and he that gathereth not with me scattereth abroad." (Matt. 12:30.) And hence we find Alma inviting the wicked to repent and join the true Church of Christ and become the sheep of the Good Shepherd. "And now if ye are not the sheep of the good shepherd, of what fold are ye?" he asks. "Behold, I say unto you, that the devil is your shepherd, and ye are of his fold; and now, who can deny this? Behold, I say unto you, whosoever denieth this is a liar and a child of the devil." (Alma 5:39; Jos. Smith 2:19.)

Iniquitous conditions in the various branches of the great and abominable church in the last days are powerfully described in the Book of Mormon. (2 Ne. 28; Morm. 8:28, 32-33, 36-38; D. & C. 10:56.) Nephi saw the "church which is most abominable above all other churches" in vision. He "saw the devil that he was the foundation of it"; and also the murders, wealth, harlotry, persecutions, and evil desires that are part of this organization. (1 Ne. 13:1-10.)

He saw that this church took away from the gospel of the Lamb many covenants and many plain and precious parts; that it perverted the right ways of the Lord; that it deleted many teachings from the Bible; that it was "the mother of harlots"; and finally that the Lord would again restore the gospel of salvation. (1 Ne. 13:24-42.)

Similar visions were given to John as recorded in the 17th and 18th chapters of Revelation. He saw this evil church as a whore ruling over peoples, multitudes, nations and tongues; as being full of blasphemy, abominations, filthiness, and fornication; as having the name, "MYSTERY, BABYLON THE GREAT, THE MOTHER OF HARLOTS AND ABOMINATIONS OF THE EARTH"; as drunken with the blood of the saints; as revelling in wealth and the delicacies of the earth; as making merchandise of all costly items and of "slaves, and souls of men." And then John, as did Nephi, saw the fall and utter destruction of this great church whose foundation is the devil.

In this world of carnality and sensuousness, the great and abominable church will continue its destructive course. But there will be an eventual future day when evil shall end, "and the great and abominable church, which is the whore of all the earth, shall be cast down by devouring fire." (D. & C. 29:21; Ezek. 38; 39; 1 Ne. 22:23; Rev. 18.) Before that day, however, desolations will sweep through the earth and the various branches of the great and abominable church "shall war among themselves, and the sword of their own hands shall fall upon their own heads, and they shall be drunken with their own blood." (1 Ne. 22:13-14; 14:3.)

The resurrected Christ gave to the Nephites this test whereby they might distinguish the true Church from any other: 1. It would be called in his name, for "how be it my church save it be called in my name?" he said. 2. It would be built upon his gospel, that is, the eternal plan of salvation with all its saving powers and graces would be had in it. 3. The Father would show forth his works in it, meaning that miracles, righteousness, and every good fruit would abound in it. 4. It would not be hewn down and cast into the fire as must surely come to pass

with the great and abominable church. "If it be not built upon my gospel, and is built upon the works of men, or upon the works of the devil, verily I say unto you they have joy in their works for a season, and by and by the end cometh, and they are hewn down and cast into the fire, from whence there is no return." (3 Ne. 27:4-12.)

CHURCH OF THE FIRSTBORN.
See CELESTIAL MARRIAGE, CHURCH OF ENOCH, CHURCH OF JESUS CHRIST OF LATTER-DAY SAINTS, DAUGHTERS OF GOD, EXALTATION, FULNESS OF THE FATHER, GODHOOD, JOINT-HEIRS WITH CHRIST, SALVATION, SONS OF GOD. Members of The Church of Jesus Christ of Latter-day Saints who so devote themselves to righteousness that they receive the higher ordinances of exaltation become members of the *Church of the Firstborn.* Baptism is the gate to the Church itself, but celestial marriage is the gate to membership in the Church of the Firstborn, the inner circle of faithful saints who are heirs of exaltation and the fulness of the Father's kingdom. (D. & C. 76:54, 67, 71, 94, 102; 77:11; 78:21; 88:1-5; Heb. 12:23.)

The Church of the Firstborn is made up of the sons of God, those who have been adopted into the family of the Lord, those who are destined to be joint-heirs with Christ in receiving all that the Father hath. "If you keep my commandments you shall receive of his fulness, and be glorified in me as I am in the Father; . . . And all those who are begotten through me are partakers of the glory of the same, and are the church of the Firstborn." (D. & C. 93:20-22; *Doctrines of Salvation*, vol. 2, pp. 9, 41-43.)

CHURCH ORGANIZATION.

See AUXILIARY ORGANIZATIONS, BRANCHES, GENERAL AUTHORITIES, GENERAL AUXILIARY OFFICERS, HIERARCHY, MISSIONS, PRIESTHOOD OFFICES, PRIESTHOOD QUORUMS, STAKES, WARDS. Basically, *church organization* is the same in all ages; the same organization that existed in the primitive Church prevails now. (Sixth Article of Faith.) Whenever the Church has been fully established on earth, the priesthood, the keys of the kingdom, and the apostolic power have been manifest. In such periods there have always been prophets, evangelists, pastors, and teachers. (Eph. 4:11-14.)

But God's earthly kingdom is always organized in such a manner as to serve most ideally the needs of the people under the conditions that exist in the particular age. Hence, provision is made for "helps, governments," quorums, auxiliary organizations, committees, boards, and special administrative units to satisfy special needs. (1 Cor. 12:28.) In the last days, worldly conditions and the complexities of civilization being what they are, the church organization is probably more extended and intricate than in any previous dispensation.

Church organization is always given by revelation. One of the great evidences of the need of contemporary revelation is the fact that changing social, economic, industrial, and other conditions, warrant changes in the helps and governments appended to the great basic and unchanging church organization.

Over the whole Church the First Presidency presides; each group of General Authorities acts under the direction of the Presidency in an assigned sphere. From time to time special auxiliaries, committees, and organizations are set up to serve the whole Church.

For administrative purposes the Church is divided into *stakes* and *missions*. Each stake (composed of *wards* and *branches*) is so organized as to carry on the full program of the Church; each mission (composed of *districts* which in turn are composed of *branches*) adapts itself to the circumstances prevailing in it and carries on as much of the church program as possible. Priesthood quorums and the auxiliary organizations function within the stakes, wards, branches, missions, and districts. Groups of stakes are combined to form *regions* or *districts,* for the purpose of administering various programs, as for instance the welfare program and the work in the temples.

The Church maintains an extensive educational program that includes universities, colleges, schools, seminaries, and institutes of religion. Since the kingdom of God on earth is concerned with temporal as well as eternal salvation, there are of course banking, insurance, industrial, agricultural and other business enterprises in which the Church has an interest.

CHURCH SECURITY PROGRAM.

See CHURCH WELFARE PLAN.

CHURCH STANDARDS.

See OBEDIENCE.

CHURCH WELFARE PLAN.

See ALMSGIVING, BISHOPS STOREHOUSES, CONSECRATION, DEBT, DESERET INDUSTRIES, DOLE, EMPLOYMENT, FAST OFFERINGS, IDLENESS, POOR, RELIEF SOCIETY, SELF-RELIANCE, STEWARDSHIPS, THRIFTINESS, UNITED ORDER, USURY, WORK. The *Church Welfare Plan* is that part of the gospel which is designed under our present economic circumstances to care for the temporal needs of the saints and to do it on the basis of gospel principles. Welfare work and principles as such are not new; in every dispensation there have been tithes, offerings, cooperative enterprises, united orders, or whatever arrangements were needed under conditions as they then existed.

But the present organization for handling welfare matters, first set up in 1936, is the particular one geared to the present needs and faith of the saints. Indeed, the fact that the saints do have adequate procedures for caring for the temporal well-being of the poor among them is one of the evidences of the divinity of the great latter-day work. Modern revelation is required to apply the eternal welfare principles to the intricacies of modern civilization.

"Our primary purpose," said the First Presidency with reference to the newly formulated welfare arrangements, "was to set up, in so far as it might be possible, a system under which the curse of idleness would be done away with, the evils of a dole abolished, and independence, industry, thrift and self-respect be once more established amongst our people. The aim of the Church is to help the people to help themselves. Work is to be re-enthroned as the ruling principles of the lives of our Church membership." (Conf. Rep., Oct., 1936, p. 3.)

The doctrine of Church Welfare is that "the responsibility for one's economic maintenance rests (1) upon himself, (2) upon his family, and (3) upon the Church, if he is a faithful member thereof." (*Welfare Handbook,* pp. 1-2.)

Man has been placed on earth to work out his salvation both temporally and spiritually. If all that had been needed for his eternal progression was spiritual in nature, this earth life would not have been necessary. Accordingly, "No true Latter-day Saint will, while physically able, voluntarily shift from himself the burden of his own support. So long as he can, under the inspiration of the Almighty and with his own labors, he will supply himself with the necessities of life." (*Welfare Handbook*, p. 2.)

In keeping with this principle, the saints are counseled to get out of debt, free themselves from mortgages, live within their incomes, save a little, have on hand enough food and clothing and where possible fuel also for a least a year ahead, plant gardens, farm farms, and use wisdom and inspiration in all their temporal pursuits.

When a member of the Church is unable to care for his own temporal needs, the responsibility for such falls upon his relatives. "If any provide not for his own, and specially for those of his own house, he hath denied the faith, and is worse than an infidel." (1 Tim. 5:8.) But if the just wants and needs of a church member cannot be supplied through his own efforts or by his family, then the Church itself steps in, draws on the bishops storehouses and the fast offering contributions, and cares for the temporal needs of the poor person. Wherever possible those receiving welfare assistance work for what they receive. The necessary food, clothing, fuel, and other items are almost all produced by the Church on the hundreds of great welfare projects operated by various wards, stakes, and welfare regions.

CIRCUMCISION.

See ABRAHAMIC COVENANT, BAPTISM, COVENANTS, SALVATION OF CHILDREN. In token and remembrance of the everlasting covenant made by God with Abraham, Deity instituted the *law of circumcision*. As revealed to Joseph Smith, the circumstances and conditions calling forth the revelation of this law of circumcision were these: "My people have gone astray from my precepts, and have not kept mine ordinances, which I gave unto their fathers," the Lord said to Abraham, "And they have not observed mine anointing, and the burial, or baptism wherewith I commanded them; But they have turned from the commandment, and taken unto themselves the washing of children, and the blood of sprinkling; And have said that the blood of the righteous Abel was shed for sins; and have not known wherein they are accountable before me.

"But as for thee, behold, I will make my covenant with thee, and thou shalt be a father of many nations. *And this covenant I make, that thy children may be known among all nations.* Neither shall thy name any more be called Abram, but thy name shall be called Abraham; for, a father of many nations have I made thee. And I will make thee exceedingly fruitful, and I will make nations of thee, and kings shall come of thee, and of thy seed. *And I will establish a covenant of circumcision with thee,* and it shall be my covenant between me and thee, and thy seed after thee, in their generations; *that thou mayest know for ever that children are not accountable before me until they are eight years old.* And thou shalt observe to keep all my covenants wherein I covenanted with thy fathers; and thou shalt keep the commandments which I have given thee with mine own mouth, and I will be a God unto thee and thy seed after thee. And I will give unto thee and thy seed after thee, a land wherein thou art a stranger; all the land of Canaan, for an everlasting possession; and I will be their God.

"And God said unto Abraham, Therefore thou shalt keep my covenant, thou and thy seed after thee, in their generations. And this shall be my covenant which ye shall keep between me and thee and thy seed after thee; *every man child among you shall be circumcised. And ye shall circumcise the flesh of your foreskin; and it shall be a token of the covenant betwixt me and you.* And he that is eight days old shall be circumcised among you, every man child in your generations; He that is born in the house, or bought with money of any stranger, which is not of thy seed. He that is born in thy house, and he that is bought with thy money, must needs be circumcised, and *my covenant shall be in your flesh* for an everlasting covenant. And the uncircumcised man child, whose flesh of his foreskin is not circumcised, that soul shall be cut off from his people, he hath broken my covenant." (*Inspired Version,* Gen. 17:4-20.)

One of the provisions of this law of circumcision was that it should be practiced by the chosen seed, to identify and distinguish them, until the day of the mortal ministry of Christ. From Abraham to the meridian of time, the gospel and such of the laws of salvation as were revealed in any period were reserved almost exclusively for the seed of Abraham in whose flesh the token of circumcision was found.

But beginning in the meridian of time the Lord's eternal plans called for sending the gospel to all the world; the Gentile nations were to be invited to come to Christ and be heirs of salvation. The laws of salvation were to be offered to those in whose flesh the token of the everlasting covenant was not found. Christ himself limited his ministry to the house of Israel; "I am not sent but unto the lost sheep of the house of Israel," he said. (Matt. 15:24.) But he sent his apostolic ministers to preach to all men (Mark 16:15), it being pointedly revealed to Peter that the gospel was for Gentiles as well as Jews. (Acts 10.) Accordingly, the need for the special token in the flesh no longer existed, and so circumcision as a gospel ordinance was done away in Christ.

Mormon received this revelation: "Little children are whole, for they are not capable of committing sin; wherefore the curse of Adam is taken from them in me, that it hath no power over them; and *the law of circumcision is done away in me.*" (Moro. 8:8.) The disciples in the Old World received a similar revelation and with the approval of the Holy Ghost discontinued the practice of circumcision, rejecting the doctrine of those who claimed that circumcision was still essential to salvation. (Acts 15.) Paul, the apostle to the Gentiles, of necessity had to write and teach much about circumcision so that his converts would understand that it was done away in Christ. (Rom. 2; 3; 4; 1 Cor. 7:19; Gal. 5:6; 6:15; Col. 2:11; 3:11.)

By the time of Paul the apostate Jews, as with the people of Abraham's day, had lost the knowledge "that children are not accountable . . . until they are eight years old." (*Inspired Version,* Gen. 17:11.) Rather they had a tradition that little children were unholy and that circumcision was essential to their cleansing. Those thus circumcised were then "brought up in subjection to the law of Moses," and giving "heed to the traditions of their fathers," they "believed not the gospel of Christ, wherein they became unholy." (D. & C. 74.) It was while struggling to solve this difficult problem that Paul gave some of his counsel on marriage, which counsel can only be understood in the light of the then existing circumcision difficulties. (1 Cor. 7.)

CITY OF ENOCH.
See ZION.

CITY OF ZION.
See ZION.

CIVIL GOVERNMENTS.
See APOSTASY, CONSTITUTION OF THE UNITED STATES, GOVERNMENT OF GOD, INALIENABLE RIGHTS, KINGDOM OF GOD, PATRIOTISM, THEOCRACY (THEARCHY). The first government on earth was a theocracy. But as apostasy set in and men rejected the direct rule of God through his prophets, governments of men were created. Except for short periods of time and among limited groups of people, *civil governments* have held sway ever since. These earthly governments have had varying degrees of merit, depending on the manner in which they have been organized and the integrity and ability of their rulers.

But all nations have been used by the Lord to accomplish his inscrutable purposes. (*Doctrines of Salvation,* vol. 3, pp. 313-326.) Egypt saved the house of Jacob in an age of famine. (Gen. 46; 47; 48; 49; 50.) Cyrus the unbelieving Persian ruler was called of God to accomplish a particular work with ancient Israel. (Isa. 44:28; 45:1-4.) The constitution of the United States was established by the Lord as an aid to the perpetuation of freedom among the American people. (D. & C. 101:76-80.)

With the restoration of the gospel, however, the government of God began again to be established on earth. So far that government operates only in spiritual things, but in due course the Lord will make a full end of all nations. (D. & C. 87:6.) Then civil government as found in all the kingdoms of this present world will cease, and the theocratic millennial administration will begin in which the government of God will be both spiritual and temporal. (D. & C. 38:20-22.) Pending that glorious day the saints are commanded to obey the laws of the land, to be subject to the powers that be (D. & C. 58:20-22), and to uphold, sustain, and support constitutional laws and wise leaders. (D. & C. 98:4-10.)

CIVILIZATION.

See APOSTASY, DARK AGES, EVOLUTION, GOSPEL, GOVERNMENT OF GOD, PRIESTHOOD, RIGHTEOUSNESS. As part of the false educational theories of the day, it is generally believed and taught that *civilization* has reached its highest point in the 20th century and that the civilizations of the past were far beneath present standards. Measured solely from the stand-point of inventions, engineering achievements, and industrial development, this is true. But when every form of social development and culture, of arts, letters, and refinement, and of moral uprightness is included in the meaning of civilization, then it becomes apparent that many of the civilizations of the past have far exceeded our own.

Adam began his mortal life as a son of God. (Moses 6:22.) He and Eve and their posterity wrote and spoke the pure Adamic language, a language far more perfect and powerful than any now had on earth. (Moses 6:5-8.) They had the gospel, celestial marriage, a perfect government, communion with God and angels, and they walked in the light of continual revelation. Similar conditions prevailed for 365 years in the City of Zion; indeed, so perfect was the civilization of that people that the Lord came and dwelt with them. (Moses 7.) Among the Nephites for 200 years a godly society prevailed. There is no question but what literature, art, culture, refinement, morality, and every form of social intercourse in these ancient times far exceeded anything that has evolved among worldly kingdoms. During the millennium the most advanced social development ever known on earth will take place; civilization will then reach its zenith as far as mortal beings are concerned.

But even among worldly kingdoms, there have been civilizations of the past which have surpassed ours in selected fields. Can we equal today the literary excellence of the King James Bible or of Shakespeare? What art are we producing that compares with the paintings of the old masters? Do we have musicians today that excel Beethoven, Bach, Brahms, Mendelssohn, and Mozart?

CIVIL LAW.
See CIVIL GOVERNMENTS.

CIVIL MARRIAGE.
See CELESTIAL MARRIAGE. Among Latter-day Saints the term *civil marriage* means a marriage performed solely by civil authority as distinguished from an *eternal* or a *celestial marriage,* which is performed both by civil authority and by that power which binds on earth and seals eternally in the heavens. Civil marriages are performed by man's authority and last until death or divorce separates the parties; celestial marriages are by God's authority, and the unions endure in time and in eternity.

For those who are not qualified and worthy to enter into the Lord's order of matrimony, civil marriages are proper and honorable and there is no sin attached to the relationship that results from them. But for a true saint, one who loves the Lord and has in his heart the hope of eternal life, no marriage will prove satisfactory but one that is eternal. President Joseph F. Smith expressed the feelings of those who believe and know the truth when he said that he would rather go himself to the grave than associate with a woman outside the new and everlasting covenant of marriage. (Conf. Rep., Oct. 1909, pp. 5-6.)

CLEANLINESS.
See BAPTISM, FORGIVENESS, HOLINESS, PURITY, SANCTIFICATION. Since no *unclean* thing can inherit the kingdom of heaven (Alma 11:37; 3 Ne. 27:19-21; Moses 6:57), and since all accountable men have committed sin and are therefore unclean (Rom. 3:23; 5:12), it follows that all who gain salvation must undergo a *cleansing process.* This process is one of repentance and baptism (D. & C. 76:52; Alma 7:14), one that enables the cleansing power of the Holy Ghost to transform the human soul from an unclean to a *clean* state (Moro. 6:4), one that enables the penitent person to wash his garments in the blood of the Lamb. (Alma 5:21-27.)

Our Lord came into the world for the purpose of cleansing and sanctifying men through the power of his atoning sacrifice. (D. & C. 76:41; Morm. 9:6.) This cleaning power is offered only on conditions of obedience to his laws. (D. & C. 29:17.) *"If we walk in the light, as he [God] is in the light,"* John said, *"we have fellowship one with another, and the blood of Jesus Christ his Son cleanseth us from all sin. If we* say that we have no sin, we deceive ourselves, and the truth is not in us. If we confess our sins, he is faithful and just to forgive us our sins, and to cleanse us from all unrighteousness." (1 John 1:6-9.)

After their baptism the Lord commands his saints to continue to seek *cleanliness* of life and spirit with all their power. "Be ye clean that bear the vessels of the Lord." (D. & C. 38:42; 133:5; 3 Ne. 20:41; Isa. 52:11.) "Let all things be done in cleanliness before me." (D. & C. 42:41.) "Entangle not yourselves in sin, but let your hands be clean, until the Lord comes." (D. & C. 88:86.) "Cleanse your hands, ye sinners; and purify your hearts ye double minded." (Jas. 4:8.)

Those who love the Lord desire to cleanse and perfect their lives: To themselves they say: "Let us cleanse ourselves from all filthiness of the flesh and spirit, perfecting holiness in the fear of God." (2 Cor. 7:1.) "Create in me a clean heart, O God; and renew a right spirit within me;" is their cry. (Ps. 51:10.) They desire to worship God with pure hearts and clean hands (2 Ne. 25:16); to work miracles among their fellowmen in this life (3 Ne. 8:1); to be clean in the day of judgment (Alma 5:19; 24:15); to be cleansed from mortality to immortality (3 Ne. 28:36); to enjoy the eternal presence of their God (Ps. 24:1-5); to be possessors of all things. (D. & C. 50:28-29.) They know that the Lord is pleased only with the clean. (D. & C. 38:8-10; 66:3.)

When men accept the truth and embark on the Lord's errand, acting as his ministers, they thereby assume the responsibility for the blood and sins of those over whom they preside or to whom they are sent with the Lord's message. This burden is removed from the Lord's agents only on the condition that they magnify their callings and faithfully discharge the duties imposed upon them. (Ezek. 33; 34.) Thus though their faithfulness the elders have power to become clean from the blood and sins of this generation. (D. & C. 88:74-75, 85; 109:42; 112:33; 135:5; Ether 12:37.)

CLERGY.
See MINISTERIAL TITLES, MINISTERS. In the sectarian world, the *clergy* is the whole body of so-called ordained ministers; those ordained to the ministry (as they suppose) are called *clergymen*. The ministry involved differs so radically from the Lord's true ministry that the terms *clergy* and *clergymen* are not ordinarily applied by the true Church to its own ministers.

CLERGYMEN.
See CLERGY.

CLERKS.
See CHURCH HISTORIAN AND RECORDER, RECORD KEEPING. Since record keeping is such an important

part of church operation, qualified and able persons are chosen and set apart to serve as *clerks* and *secretaries* in all of the organizations of the Church. Among others, *stake clerks* assist stake presidencies, *ward clerks* aid bishoprics, *quorum secretaries* carry much of the priesthood load, and *auxiliary organization secretaries* preserve the records of those units.

CLINIC BAPTISMS.

See APOSTASY, BAPTISM, INFANT BAPTISM. "Baptisms by pouring or sprinkling were exceptional in the early ages of the Christian Church. They were called *clinic baptisms,* because administered as a rule to the sick, who could not be taken from their beds to be immersed; but they were rare, and were regarded only as quasi-baptisms." (Orson F. Whitney, *Saturday Night Thoughts,* pp. 252-253.)

COCOA.
See WORD OF WISDOM.

COFFEE.
See HOT DRINKS.

COLA DRINKS.
See WORD OF WISDOM.

COMBINATIONS.
See SECRET COMBINATIONS.

COMFORTER.

See HOLY GHOST, PARACLETE, SECOND COMFORTER. The Holy Ghost is the *Comforter.* (John 14:26-27; *Teachings,* pp. 149-150.) This name-title is given to the third member of the Godhead to signify his mission of bringing solace, love, peace, quiet enjoyment, and comfort to the saints. Scriptures setting forth the consolation and encouragement which spring up in the hearts of the righteous by the power of the Holy Ghost frequently speak of him as the *Comforter.* Moroni, writing of "the visitation of the Holy Ghost," says that this *"Comforter filleth with hope and perfect love."* (Moro. 8:26.)

By gaining the testimony of Jesus men find peace, rest, and comfort. This testimony comes by the power of the Holy Ghost. Thus it is the Comforter who testifies of Christ (John 15:26); it is "the Comforter, which manifesteth that Jesus was crucified by sinful men for the sins of the world" (D. & C. 21:9); it is "the Comforter" which is "shed forth upon" men "for the revelation of Jesus Christ" (D. & C. 90:11); it is "the Comforter" who "knoweth all things, and beareth record of the Father and of the Son." (D. & C. 42:17.)

By gaining light and knowledge from heaven, men attain a prelude of that peace and quiet enjoyment which is found in a future heaven. Thus it is "the Comforter, which showeth all things, and *teacheth the peaceable things of the king-*

dom" (D & C. 39:6; 36:2); it is the Comforter who gives revelation and guidance to the disciples (D. & C. 24:5; 31:11; 52:9; 79:2; 90:14); it is by the power of the Comforter that the Lord's agents teach the gospel, even being given in the very hour the words they shall speak (D. & C. 28:1; 50:14, 17; 75: 10; 124:97); and it is by the Comforter that inspired men write (D. & C. 47:4) and speak and prophesy. (D. & C. 42:16.) Our Lord's promise to his ancient disciples was that the Comforter would "bring all things" to their "remembrance" (John 14:26), and it was by this power that the scriptures were written.

COMMANDER.

See CAPTAIN OF THE LORD'S HOST.

COMMANDMENTS.

See AGENCY, COVENANTS, GOSPEL, LAW, OBEDIENCE, RIGHTEOUSNESS, TEN COMMANDMENTS. Those things which men are directed to do to attain peace in this life and gain eternal life in the world to come are collectively called the *commandments*. They are the laws, ordinances, covenants, contracts, statutes, judgments, decrees, revelations, and requirements which come to man from God. They are "the words of eternal life," with reference to which it is proclaimed: *"You shall live by every word that*

proceedeth forth from the mouth of God." (D. & C. 84:43-44.)

It is God's right to command; he is not restricted to sending requests or petitions. He made us; we belong to him; in his infinite wisdom he orders us to do what will further our interests and his. By obedience we are blessed. Failure to obey denies us the blessing and makes us guilty of the additional sin of ingratitude.

"If thou wilt enter into life, keep the commandments," was our Lord's succinct statement to the rich young man. (Matt. 19:17.) "If ye love me, keep my commandments," he said to his disciples. (John 14:15.) "For this is the love of God, that we keep his commandments: and *his commandments are not grievous,"* John wrote. (1 John 5:3.) *"Let us hear the conclusion of the whole matter: Fear God, and keep his commandments: for this is the whole duty of man."* (Eccles. 12:13.)

COMMON CONSENT.

See AGENCY, KEYS OF THE KINGDOM, REVELATION. Administrative affairs of the Church are handled in accordance with the law of *common consent*. This law is that in God's earthly kingdom, the King counsels what should be done, but then he allows his subjects to accept or reject his proposals. Unless the principle of free agency is operated in righteousness men do not progress to ultimate salvation in the heavenly kingdom hereafter. Accordingly, church officers are selected by the spirit of revelation in those appointed to choose them, but before the officers may serve in their positions, they must receive a formal sustaining vote of the people over whom they are to preside. (D. & C. 20:60-67; 26:2; 28; 38:34-35; 41:9-11; 42:11; 102:9; 124:124-145.)

Revelations given of God through his prophets, however, are not subject to an approving or sustaining vote of the people in order to establish their validity. Members of the Church may vote to publish a particular revelation along with the other scriptures, or the people may bind themselves by covenant to follow the instructions found in the revealed word. But there is no provision in the Lord's plan for the members of the Church to pass upon the validity of revelations themselves by a vote of the Church; there is nothing permitting the Church to choose which of the revelations will be binding upon it, either by a vote of people or by other means.

Revelation is revelation. When the Lord speaks, he has spoken. His word is to be accepted and obeyed if men expect to receive salvation. To reject the word of the Lord is to reject the Lord himself to that extent. This is the case with members of the so-called Reorganized Church of Jesus Christ of Latter Day Saints. They have selected, by a vote of their people, which of the revelations they will accept and which they will reject. Naturally revelations dealing with salvation for the dead, temple work,

and celestial marriage find no part in their philosophy, and in consequence they deny themselves the blessings offered in these revelations.

COMMON COUNCIL OF THE CHURCH.

See CHURCH COURTS, FIRST PRESIDENCY. The supreme tribunal in the Church is the *Common Council of the Church,* which consists of the First Presidency of the Church and 12 high priests chosen by them to assist as counselors. "This is the highest council of the church of God, and a final decision upon controversies in spiritual matters. There is not any person belonging to the church who is exempt from this council of the church. And inasmuch as a President of the High Priesthood shall transgress, he shall be had in remembrance before the *common council of the church,* who shall be assisted by twelve counselors of the High Priesthood; And their decision upon his head shall be an end of controversy concerning him. Thus, none shall be exempted from the justice and the laws of God, that all things may be done in order and in solemnity before him, according to truth and righteousness." (D. & C. 107:76-84.)

Presumably the First Presidency would choose the Council of the Twelve to serve as the 12 high priests, but in one case in the days of President John Taylor, they

chose brethren who were not among the General Authorities but who were experts in the matters scheduled to come before the Council. In that case water rights were involved. (*Gospel Kingdom,* pp. 201-202.)

COMMON ENEMY.

See DEVIL. This designation of Satan describes his position as the general enemy of all mankind. No accountable persons are free from his wiles. (D. & C. 29:47.)

COMMON JUDGE IN ISRAEL.

See JUDGES IN ISRAEL.

COMMON PROPERTY.

See UNITED ORDER.

COMMOTIONS.

See SIGNS OF THE TIMES.

COMMUNISM.

See CHURCH OF THE DEVIL, SECRET COMBINATIONS. Basically and chiefly, *communism* is a form of false religion; it is one of the major divisions of the church of the devil. It denies God and Christ; belittles Christianity; runs counter to the moral and ethical standards of religion and decency; denies men their agency; wrenches from them their inalienable rights; and swallows the individual and his well-being up in the formless mass of the state.

Communism is also a political movement, one that fosters and promotes world revolution, and has as its aim the subjugation of all free peoples and nations. It necessarily is a dictatorship of the severest and most ruthless type.

The position of the Church relative to communism is stated by the First Presidency in these words: "With great regret we learn from credible sources, governmental and others, that a few Church members are joining, directly or indirectly, the communists and are taking part in their activities.

"The Church does not interfere, and has no intention of trying to interfere, with the fullest and freest exercise of the political franchise of its members, under and within our Constitution which the Lord declared: 'I established . . . by the hands of wise men whom I raised up unto this very purpose,' (D. & C. 101:80) and which, as to the principles thereof, the Prophet dedicating the Kirtland Temple, prayed should be 'established forever.'

"But communism is not a political party nor a political plan under the Constitution; it is a system of government that is the opposite of our Constitutional government, and it would be necessary to destroy our government before communism could be set up in the United

States.

"Since communism, established, would destroy our American Constitutional government, to support communism is treasonable to our free insitutions, and no patriotic American citizen may become either a communist or supporter of communism.

"To our Church members we say: Communism is not the United Order, and bears only the most superficial resemblance thereto; communism is based upon intolerance and force, the United Order upon love and freedom of conscience and action; communism involves forceful despoliation and confiscation, the United Order voluntary consecration and sacrifice.

"Communists cannot establish the United Order, nor will communism bring it about. The United Order will be established by the Lord in his own due time and in accordance with the regular prescribed order of the Church.

"Furthermore, it is charged by universal report, which is not successfully contradicted or disproved, that communism undertakes to control, if not indeed to proscribe the religious life of the people living within its jurisdiction, and that it even reaches its hand into the sanctity of the family circle itself, disrupting the normal relationship of parent and child, all in a manner unknown and unsanctioned under the Constitutional guarantees under which we in America live. Such interference would be contrary to

the fundamental precepts of the gospel and to the teachings and order of the Church.

"Communism being thus hostile to loyal American citizenship and incompatible with true Church membership, of necessity no loyal American citizen and no faithful Church member can be a communist.

"We call upon all Church members completely to eschew communism. The safety of our divinely inspired Constitutional government and the welfare of our Church imperatively demand that communism shall have no place in America." (*Improvement Era,* vol. 39, p. 488.)

COMPASSION.

See KINDNESS, MERCY. True *compassion* for one's fellow men is a mark of a true saint. It consists in sorrow for their sufferings, in having pity and sympathy for them, and in exhibiting mercy, tenderness and kindness towards them. Indeed, one of the specific covenants taken by those who accept fellowship with the saints is to mourn with those that mourn, comfort those that stand in need of comfort, and bear the burdens of each other. (Mosiah 18:8-9.) Standing counsel to the saints is: "Be ye all of one mind, having compassion one of another, love as brethren, be pitiful, be courteous." (1 Pet. 3:8.) "Be ye kind one to another, tenderhearted, forgiving one another, even as God for Christ's sake hath forgiven you." (Eph. 4:32.)

Jesus himself set the perfect example of compassion; as James said, "The Lord is very pitiful, and of tender mercy." (Jas. 5:11.) This was in no instance better illustrated than in his ministry among the Nephites. "Behold, my bowels are filled with compassion towards you," he told them. "Have ye any that are sick among you? Bring them hither. Have ye any that are lame, or blind, or halt, or maimed, or leprous, or that are withered, or that are deaf, or that are afflicted in any manner? Bring them hither and I will heal them, for I have compassion upon you; my bowels are filled with mercy." (3 Ne. 17:6-7.)

COMPULSION.

See AGENCY, FREEDOM, INALIENABLE RIGHTS, SALVATION. *Compulsion* involves the use of coercion or force. It is the opposite of free agency. Neither salvation, the attainment of godly virtues, nor eternal progression can be forced upon an individual. In the pre-existent counsels, Lucifer sought to deny men their agency and compel them to be saved, a proposal that would not and could not work. God deals in agency, Lucifer in compulsion. To the extent that men are not free to choose their own governments, beliefs, faiths, associates, employment, and the like, the will of Satan is overruling the will of Deity in the world.

CONCEIVED IN SIN.

See INFANT BAPTISM, ORIGINAL SIN THEORY, SALVATION OF CHILDREN, YEARS OF ACCOUNTABILITY. Are all little children *conceived in sin?* Such is the teaching of those churches which practice infant baptism, such baptism being performed, as they contend, to free the newborn infant from the taint of original sin. It is true that there are scriptures which say that children are conceived in sin. But do they mean what those who practice infant baptism claim they do?

When David was groaning under the crushing burden of those personal sins which caused him to lose his exaltation (D. & C. 132:39), he pleaded for mercy with such cries as: "Have mercy upon me. . . . My sin is ever before me. . . . Behold, I was shapen in iniquity; and in sin did my mother conceive me. . . . Hide thy face from my sins, and blot out all mine iniquities. . . . Deliver me from bloodguiltiness." (Ps. 51.) From the entire context it should be clear that David is not teaching that he came into this world burdened with the sin of Adam, so that without the cleansing of infant baptism his soul would be lost, but rather that he had been born into a world of sin and temptation that was greater than he could bear, and hence he seemed to think that the Lord should act leniently toward him.

Perhaps when David wrote the expression, "conceived in sin," he was familiar with a more ancient scripture which used the same words. In any event, the expression is found in scriptures that date back to Adam's day—found, however, in a context that makes the whole doctrine involved stand out clearly.

"And our father Adam spake unto the Lord, and said: Why is it that men must repent and be baptized in water? And the Lord said unto Adam: Behold *I have forgiven thee thy transgression in the Garden of Eden.* Hence came the saying abroad among the people, That *the Son of God hath atoned for original guilt, wherein the sins of the parents cannot be answered upon the heads of the children, for they are whole from the foundation of the world.* And the Lord spake unto Adam, saying: *Inasmuch as thy children are conceived in sin, even so when they begin to grow up, sin conceiveth in their hearts, and they taste the bitter, that they may know to prize the good. And it is given unto them to know good from evil; wherefore they are agents unto themselves,* and I have given unto you another law and commandment. Wherefore teach it unto your children, that all men, everywhere must repent, or they can in nowise inherit the kingdom of God." (Moses 6:53-57.)

In other words, though children are born into a world where sin is present so that they can be tried and tested and use their own agency, yet there is no "original guilt" attaching to them, and the sins of the parents cannot be answered upon their heads.

It is a false and unholy perversion of the true doctrine to suppose that innocent children come into the world with any taint of original sin. *"Marriage is honourable in all, and the bed undefiled."* (Heb. 13:4.) Parents are commanded to multiply and fill the earth with posterity. (D. & C. 49:15-17.) "Children are an heritage of the Lord." (Ps. 127:3.) "Little children are whole, for they are not capable of committing sin; wherefore the curse of Adam is taken from them in me," the Lord said, with Mormon adding, "Little children are alive in Christ." (Moro. 8:8, 12.)

CONCUBINES.

See CELESTIAL MARRIAGE, PLURAL MARRIAGE. In modern times a *concubine* is a woman who cohabits with a man without being his wife. But "from the beginning of creation," all down through the history of God's dealings with his people, including those with the house of Israel, concubines were legal wives married to their husbands in the new and everlasting covenant of marriage. (D. & C. 132:1, 37-39, 65.)

Anciently they were considered to be *secondary wives,* that is, wives who did not have the same standing in the caste system then prevailing as did those wives who were not called concubines. There were no concubines connected with the practice of plural marriage in this dispensation, because the caste system which caused some wives to be so designated did not exist.

CONCUPISCENCE.
See SEX IMMORALITY.

CONDEMNATION.
See DAMNATION.

CONDESCENSION OF GOD.
See GOD, GRACE OF GOD, ONLY BEGOTTEN SON, SALVATION BY GRACE. After asking the question, "Knowest thou the *condescension of God*," an angel showed Nephi the virgin who was to be "the mother of the Son of God, after the manner of the flesh." Nephi saw that "she was carried away in the Spirit . . . for the space of a time," and that she then appeared "bearing a child in her arms, . . . even the Son of the Eternal Father." Then with the exclamation, "Look and behold the condescension of God," the angelic ministrant showed Nephi many of the major incidents in the mortal ministry of the Lamb of God, including the fact that "he was lifted up upon the cross and slain for the sins of the world." (1 Ne. 11:13-36.)

Thus the condescension of God (meaning the Father) consists in the fact that though he is an exalted, perfected, glorified Personage, he became the personal and literal Father of a mortal Offspring born of mortal woman. And the condescen-sion of God (meaning the Son) consists in the fact that though he himself is the Lord Omnipotent, the very Being who created the earth and all things that in it are, yet being born of mortal woman, he submitted to all the trials of mortality, suffering "temptations, and pain of body, hunger, thirst, and fatigue, even more than man can suffer, except it be unto death" (Mosiah 3:5-8), finally being put to death in a most ignominious manner.

CONFERENCES.
See DISTRICTS, FAST MEETINGS, SACRAMENT MEETINGS, SOLEMN ASSEMBLIES, TESTIMONY MEETINGS, WORSHIP. 1. Latter-day Saints assemble periodically in various *conferences* "to worship the King, the Lord of hosts" (Zech. 14:16-19); to be built up in faith, testimony, and desires of righteousness; to transact the business of the Church; to sustain the officers whom the Lord has appointed to administer the affairs of his kingdom; and to receive, from those appointed so to serve, the counsel, inspiration, and revelation needed in both temporal and spiritual fields.

Conferences are far more than religious conventions in which views are expressed, differences resolved, and policies adopted. Rather they consist in a series of meetings at which the mind and will of the Lord is manifest to the people by the mouths of his servants. The Church being a kingdom, not a democracy, instruction and direction comes from above; it does not originate with the citizens but with the King. Songs, prayers, sermons, testimonies, reports, and sometimes recreational undertakings are woven into conference schedules.

2. In the early days of this dispensation, the ecclesiastical units in missions, which units are now called *districts,* were called *conferences.*

CONFESSION.

See FORGIVENESS.

CONFIRMATION.

See BAPTISM, GIFT OF THE HOLY GHOST, LAYING ON OF HANDS. In the name of Christ and the authority of the Melchizedek Priesthood, baptized persons are *confirmed* members of The Church of Jesus Christ of Latter-day Saints. As part of this ordinance of *confirmation* the gift of the Holy Ghost is bestowed. (D. & C. 20:38-43; 33:15.) It is also proper for the legal administrators performing the ordinance to give expression, as led by the Spirit, to a few brief words of blessing promise, counsel, and exhortation.

CONFORMITY.

See OBEDIENCE.

CONFUSION OF TONGUES.

See LANGUAGES.

CONGREGATIONS.

See WARDS.

CONJURATION.

See EXORCISM.

CONJURE MAN.

See MAGIC, MEDICINE MEN, WITCHCRAFT, WITCH DOCTORS. In some localities, particularly the West Indies and Southern United States, a witch, practitioner of magic, or witch doctor is called a *conjure man or woman. Conjuration* includes the practice of magic and the summoning of evil spirits by invocation or incantation.

CONSCIENCE.

See AGENCY, GIFT OF THE HOLY GHOST, LIGHT OF CHRIST. Every person born into the world is endowed with the light of Christ (Spirit of Christ or of the Lord) as a free gift. (D. & C. 84:45-48.) By virtue of this endowment all men automatically and intuitively know right from wrong and are encouraged and enticed to do what is right. (Moro. 7:16.) The recognizable operation of this Spirit in enlightening the mind and striving to lead men to do right is called *conscience.* It is an inborn consciousness or sense of the moral goodness or blameworthiness of one's conduct, intentions, and character, together with an instinctive feeling or obligation to do right or be good.

Members of the Church are entitled to the enlightenment of the light of Christ and also to the guidance of the Holy Ghost. If they so live as to enjoy the actual gift of the Holy Ghost, then their consciences are also guided by that member of the Godhead. (Rom. 9:1.)

Every man's conscience is pure and clean at birth. (D. & C. 93: 38.) But after an individual arrives at the years of accountability his conscience begins to be blackened by his sins. Because of disobedience one's conscience is "seared with a hot iron" (1 Tim. 4:2); it becomes weak and defiled. (1 Cor. 8:7; Tit. 1:15.)

Wickedness invariably leads to remorse of conscience (Alma 29:5; 42:18), and those so smitten tremble under a consciousness of their own guilt and filthiness before the Lord. (Alma 12:1; 14:6; Morm. 9:3-4; John 8:9.) But men are commanded to purge their consciences from dead works (Heb. 9:14), to gain "peace of conscience" through "a remission of their sins." (Mosiah 4:3.) Paul (Acts 23:1; 2 Tim. 1:3; Heb. 13:18), King Benjamin (Mosiah 2:15, 27), and Joseph Smith (D. & C. 135:4), list themselves among those whose consciences were not burdened with regret or remorse. "The free exercise of conscience" is one of the inalienable rights of man, and governments are obligated to enact and administer such laws as will preserve this right. (D. & C. 134:2-5.)

CONSCIOUSNESS.
See MIND.

CONSECRATION.
See CHURCH WELFARE PLAN, STEWARDSHIPS, TITHING, UNITED ORDER. Righteous saints in all ages have *consecrated* their time, talents, strength, properties, and monies to the establishment of the Lord's work and kingdom in their respective days. As circumstances have required, these saints—having set their hearts on righteousness and having actually put first in their lives the things of God's kingdom—have been and are called upon to serve on missions, colonize wilderness areas, build temples, go to the ends of the earth on the Lord's errand, magnify calls in the ministry, and contribute of their means in the great welfare and building projects of the Church.

In practice and as a general thing, church members now are being called upon to consecrate only portions (usually relatively small portions) of their total substance for use in the furtherance of the Lord's interests. However, an attempt was made in the early days of this dispensation to live the *law of consecration* in full. The vehicle through which the attempt was made to live the financial and monetary portions of this law was called the United Order.

As then attempted, practice of the full law of consecration called for the saints to consecrate, transfer, and convey to the Lord's agent all of their property "with a covenant and a deed which cannot be broken." (D. & C. 42:30; 58:35.) They were then given stewardships to use for their own maintenance, with all surpluses reverting back to the Lord's storehouses. Because of greed, avarice, and the worldly circumstances in which they found themselves, the saints did not achieve great success in the practice of this law, and in due course the Lord withdrew from them the privilege of so conducting their temporal affairs.

Many of the underlying principles which were part of the law of consecration, however, have been retained and are still binding upon the Church. Those touching church finances, as summarized by President J. Reuben Clark, Jr., are: "1. Worldly riches should not be sought for. 2. Every man should esteem his brother as himself. 3. The Church should care for the temporal needs of those whom the Lord called into church service. 4. The worldly goods of the members, beyond family necessities, should be made available for the Lord's work. 5. The Church should see that its poor were cared for." (Albert E. Bowen, *The Church Welfare Plan,* p. 6.)

Practice of the law of consecration is inextricably intertwined with the development of the attributes of godliness in this life and the attainment of eternal life in the world to come. "The law pertaining to material aid is so formulated that the carrying of it out necessitates practices calculated to root out human traits not in harmony with requirements for living in the celestial kingdom and replacing those inharmonious traits with the virtues and character essential to life in that abode." (Bowen, *The Church Welfare Plan,* p. 13.) "For if you will that I give you a place in the celestial world, you must prepare yourselves by doing the things which I have commanded you and required of you." (D. & C. 78:7.)

That the full law of consecration will yet again be practiced is well known. It is a celestial law, "And Zion cannot be built up unless it is by the principles of the law of the celestial kingdom; otherwise I cannot receive her unto myself." (D. & C. 105:5.) In this connection it should be remembered that man cannot live a higher law until he is first able to abide a lesser law; he will not consecrate all of his properties, unless he is first willing to consecrate a portion; and he cannot live the perfect law of consecration unless he first abides perfectly the law of tithing.

CONSECRATION OF OIL.

See ADMINISTRATIONS. Before oil is used in administering to the sick it should be *consecrated,* dedicated, and set apart, by those holding the Melchizedek Priesthood, for the anointing of the sick in the household of faith. (Jas. 5:14-16.) It is the oil and not the container that is being consecrated, and there is no impropriety in consecrating the oil in a large container and thereafter pouring it into smaller vessels. A good grade of pure olive oil should be used, and after it has been consecrated, it should not be commingled with any ointments or used indiscriminately.

CONSTITUTIONAL LAW.

See CONSTITUTION OF THE UNITED STATES.

CONSTITUTION OF THE UNITED STATES.

See BILL OF RIGHTS, CIVIL GOVERNMENTS, FREEDOM, INALIENABLE RIGHTS, KINGDOM OF GOD, LIBERTY, SIGNS OF THE TIMES. Our federal *constitution* is the supreme law of the land. It is the written instrument embodying the fundamental organic laws and principles governing the American nation, and it has the following essential characteristics:

1. The constitution was ordained and established by the people, not by the states, not by a select group of autocrats who seized power, not by any outside governmental power. The whole philosophy of constitutional government is that all sovereign power rests with the body of the people and that by the free exercise of their agency they elect to delegate certain powers and functions to the governmental bodies set up by them.

2. It is a written document, not an accumulation of traditions, customs, or legal interpretations. It is capable of specific interpretation and encourages a course of stability and uniformity of action where governmental affairs are concerned.

3. A framework of government is established by it. Powers are divided between legislative, executive, and judicial branches of government, thus creating an ideal system of checks and balances where the possible exercise of autocratic powers is concerned.

4. In the constitution are listed the specific powers and authorities delegated to the government and to the particular branches of the same. The government has no rights; it has duties only. It is ordained to serve the people. The constitution contains the written instructions of the sovereign people to their chosen servants; it is the circuit by which the people transmit part of their power to their government.

5. Express provision is made in the constitution for the preservation of the natural rights of man: (a) by specifically delegating to the national government the things

159

it can do; (b) by pointedly reserving to the people all rights and the performance of all acts not so delegated; and (c) by expressly denying the federal government power to interfere with the people's use of certain named rights such as freedom of speech.

6. Means are, of course, provided for the constitution's own change and amendment.

In the providences of the Almighty, the constitution of the United States was established to serve an even greater purpose than that of setting up a stable government under which freedom would prevail. It was designed to do far more than guarantee the preservation of natural and inalienable rights to the American people. The constitution came forth to prepare the way for the restoration of the gospel, the fulfilling of the covenants God made with ancient Israel, and the organization of the Church and kingdom of God on earth in the last days.

America was to be a land of liberty upon which no kings should rule. (2 Ne. 10:11-14.) The nation to possess it was to "be free from bondage, and from captivity, and from all other nations." (Ether 2:12.) The Gentiles were to "be established in this land, and be set up as a free people by the power of the Father," so that the Book of Mormon might come forth to the people and the covenants made with ancient Israel be fulfilled. (3 Ne. 21:4.) "And for this purpose have I established the Constitution of this land, by the hands of wise men whom I raised up unto this very purpose, and redeemed the land by the shedding of blood." (D. & C. 101:80; 109:54.)

"The constitution of the United States is a glorious standard," the Prophet said, "it is founded in the wisdom of God. It is a heavenly banner; it is to all those who are privileged with the sweets of liberty, like the cooling shades and refreshing waters of a great rock in a thirsty and weary land. It is like a great tree under whose branches men from every clime can be shielded from the burning rays of the sun.

"We say that God is true; that the constitution of the United States is true; that the Bible is true; that the Book of Mormon is true; that the Book of Covenants is true; that Christ is true; that the ministering angels sent forth from God are true, and that we know that we have an house not made with hands eternal in the heavens, whose builder and maker is God." (*Teachings,* pp. 147-148.)

CONTENTION.

See DEBATES, WAR. *Contention* consists in debating, quarreling, and disputing about some contested matter. Disputation, debates, dissensions, arguments, controversies, quarrels, and strife or contention of any sort have no part in the gospel; they are of the devil. The gospel is one of peace, harmony, unity, and agreement. In it argument and debate are supplanted by discussion and study. Those who have the Spirit do not hang doggedly to a point of doctrine or philosophy for no other reason than to come off victorious in a disagreement. Their purpose, rather, is to seek truth by investigation, research, and inspiration. "Cease to contend one with another," the Lord has commanded. (D. & C. 136:23; Tit. 3:9.)

The Nephite disciples had disputed among themselves about the doctrine of baptism. To them the Lord revealed the true doctrine and then said: "Thus shall ye baptize. And there shall be no disputations among you, as there have hitherto been; neither shall there be disputations among you concerning the points of my doctrine, as there have hitherto been. For verily, verily I say unto you, *he that hath the spirit of contention is not of me, but is of the devil, who is the father of contention,* and he stirreth up the hearts of men to contend with anger, one with another. Behold, this is not my doctrine, to stir up the hearts of men with anger, one against another; but this is my doctrine, that such things should be done away." (3 Ne. 11:28-30.)

CONTINENCE.
See PASSIONS.

CONTINUATION OF THE LIVES.
See ETERNAL LIVES.

CONTINUATION OF THE SEEDS.
See ETERNAL LIVES.

CONTRACTS.
See COVENANTS.

CONTRITE SPIRIT.
See HUMILITY, MEEKNESS, PENITENCE, REMORSE, REPENTANCE. To have a broken heart and a contrite spirit is to be broken down with deep sorrow for sin, to be humbly and thoroughly penitent, to have attained sincere and purposeful repentance. Such a status is a condition precedent to a valid baptism and consequent membership in the earthly kingdom of God. (D. & C. 20:37; 3 Ne. 9:20; 12:19; Moro. 6:2.) Acquirement of a broken heart and a contrite spirit is thus essential to salvation. (Hela. 8:15; Ps. 34:18; D. & C. 97:8.) Indeed, it was primarily for those in this condition of heart and mind that the very atoning sacrifice of Christ was worked out. (2 Ne. 2:7; D. & C. 21:9.) And the sacrifice the Lord, in turn, requires of his saints is that they offer him a broken heart and a contrite spirit. (D. & C. 59:8; 3 Ne. 9:20; Ps. 51: 17.)

The Lord's Spirit is sent forth to enlighten the contrite (D. & C. 136: 33), and they are the ones who gain the gift of the Holy Ghost. (D. & C. 55:3.) In fact, special blessings are repeatedly showered forth upon them. (D. & C. 52:15; 56:7, 17-18; Isa. 66:2; Ether 4:15.) The wicked on the other hand, are condemned because they do not "come unto Jesus with broken hearts and contrite spirits." (Morm. 2:14.)

CONTRITION.
See CONTRITE SPIRIT.

CONTROVERSY.
See CONTENTION.

CONVERSION.
See BORN AGAIN, FAITH, GIFT OF THE HOLY GHOST, GIFTS OF THE SPIRIT, HOLY GHOST, PROPHECY, REVELATION, TESTIMONY, TRUTH. 1. In a broad, general sense *conversion* consists in changing one's views or beliefs to conform to a pattern of thinking which was unacceptable prior to the time of the conversion. There is one Biblical instance of such usage. (Acts 3:19.)

2. In the full gospel sense, however, *conversion* is more—far more —than merely changing one's belief from that which is false to that which is true; it is more than the acceptance of the verity of gospel truths, than the acquirement of a testimony. To convert is to change from one status to another, and gospel conversion consists in the transformation of man from his fallen and carnal state to a state of saintliness.

A convert is one who has put off the natural man, yielded to the enticings of the Holy Spirit, and become "a saint through the atonement of Christ the Lord." Such a person has become "as a child, submissive, meek, humble, patient, full of love, willing to submit to all things which the Lord seeth fit to inflict upon him, even as a child doth submit to his father." (Mosiah 3:19.) He has become a new creature of the Holy Ghost: the old creature has been converted or changed into a new one. He has been born again: where once he was spiritually dead, he has been regenerated to a state of spiritual life. (Mosiah 27:24-29.) In real conversion, which is essential to salvation (Matt. 18:3), the convert not only changes his beliefs, casting off the false traditions of the past and accepting the beauties of revealed religion, but he changes his whole way of life, and the nature and structure of his very being is quickened and changed by the power of the Holy Ghost.

Peter is the classic example of how the power of conversion works on receptive souls. During our Lord's mortal ministry, Peter had a testimony, born of the Spirit, of the divinity of Christ and of the great plan of salvation which was in Christ. "Thou art the Christ, the Son of the living God," he said, as the Holy Ghost gave him utterance. (Matt. 16:13-19.) When others fell away, Peter stood forth with the apostolic assurance, "We believe and are sure that thou art that Christ, the Son of the living God." (John 6:69.) Peter knew, and his knowledge came by revelation.

But Peter was not converted, because he had not become a new creature of the Holy Ghost. Rather, long after Peter had gained a testimony, and on the very night Jesus was arrested, he said to Peter: *"When thou art converted, strengthen thy brethren."* (Luke 22:32.) Immediately thereafter, and regardless of his testimony, Peter denied that he knew Christ. (Luke 22:54-62.) After the crucifixion, Peter went fishing, only to be called back to the ministry by the risen Lord. (John 21:1-17.) Finally on the day of Pentecost the promised spiritual endowment was received; Peter and all the faithful disciples became new creatures of the Holy Ghost; they were truly converted; and their subsequent achievements manifest the fixity of their conversions. (Acts 3; 4.)

It is interesting to note also that the Latter-day Twelve, long after they had testimonies of the gospel, and more than two years after their calls to the apostleship, were promised that if they would be faithful they would yet be converted. (D. & C. 112:12-13.)

CORRUPTION.

See CARNALITY, DEATH, DEVILISHNESS, INCORRUPTION, MORTALITY, SENSUALITY. 1. Mortal bodies are corruptible bodies; that is, they are subject to physical change and decay. *Corruption* means mortality; incorruption means immortality. Speaking of the resurrection, Abinadi said, *"This mortal shall put on immortality, and this corruption shall put on incorruption."* (Mosiah 16:10; 2 Ne. 9:7; Alma 40:2; 41:4; 1 Cor. 15:42-54.)

2. *Corruption* is also used to signify the decay and change that will take place after death. Thus David recorded the Lord's promise that he would not suffer his Holy One to see corruption (Ps. 16:10), a promise amply fulfilled in Christ as both Peter (Acts 2:27) and Paul (Acts 13:30-37) testified.

3. The term is further used with reference to the wicked, depraved, and dissolute acts of those who are steeped in iniquity. "He that soweth to his flesh shall of the flesh reap *corruption;* but he that soweth to the Spirit shall of the Spirit reap life everlasting," Paul says (Gal. 6:8); and it is by thus sowing to the Spirit that the saints have "escaped the corruption that is in the world through lust." (2 Pet. 1:4.)

COUNCIL IN HEAVEN

See AGENCY, FOREORDINATION, HEAVEN, PLAN OF SALVATION, PREEXISTENCE, WAR IN HEAVEN. There were many meetings, conferences, *councils,* and schooling sessions held among the Gods and their spirit offspring in pre-existence. Among other things, at these various assemblages, plans were made for the creation and peopling of this earth and for the redemption and salvation of the offspring of Deity. The spirit children of the

Father were then taught the terms and conditions of the plan of salvation and were given opportunity to accept or reject the Father's proposals.

Joseph Smith speaks of "the head of the Gods" calling "a council of the Gods" to arrange for the creation and peopling of the earth. (*Teachings,* pp. 348-349.) He also speaks of "the grand council of heaven" in which those destined "to minister to the inhabitants of the world" were "ordained" to their respective callings. (*Teachings,* p. 365.)

Ordinarily, perhaps, when the saints speak of the *council in heaven,* they have in mind the solemn session (at which, apparently, all of the pre-existent hosts were present) when the Father made formal announcement of his plan of redemption and salvation. It was then explained that his spirit children would go down to earth, gain bodies of flesh and blood, be tried and tested in all things, and have opportunity by obedience to come back again to the Eternal Presence. It was then explained that one of the spirit children of the Father would be chosen to be the Redeemer and work out the infinite and eternal atonement. And it was then that the Father sent forth the call which said in substance and effect: Whom shall I send to be my Son in mortality? Who will go down, be born with life in himself, and work out the great atoning sacrifice by which immortality will come to all men and eternal life be assured to the obedient?

Two mighty spirits answered the call and volunteered their services. Christ said, in effect: Here am I, send me; I will be thy Son; I will follow thy plan; and "thy will be done, and the glory be thine forever." But Lucifer sought to amend the plan of the Father and to change the proffered terms of salvation. "Behold, here am I, send me," he said, "I will be thy son, and I will redeem all mankind, that one soul shall not be lost, and surely I will do it; wherefore give me thine honor." (Moses 4:1-4.) When the Father said, "I will send the first," then Lucifer was angry, kept not his first estate, rebelled, and he and one-third of the hosts of heaven were cast out down to earth to become the devil and his angels. (Abra. 3:25-28; D. & C. 29:36-40.)

COUNCIL OF THE TWELVE.

See APOSTOLIC SUCCESSION.

COUNSELOR.

See CHRIST, MAN OF COUNSEL. Christ, the Son of Man of Counsel (Moses 7:35), bears the name-title *Counselor.* Isaiah so designates him in one of the great Messianic prophecies. (Isa. 9:6-7.) The name bears record of his pre-eminent position among men where the exercise of deliberate judgment and prudence are concerned. *His counsel is: Come unto me and be saved.*

COUNSELORS.

See CHURCH ORGANIZATION, PRESIDENCY. In nearly all instances of presidency, the Lord vests the keys and power in a president who is assisted, aided, and counseled by two *counselors*. Such is the case with the First Presidency, with stake presidencies, ward bishoprics, branch presidencies, quorum presidencies (except in case of seventies), auxiliary organizations, and the Presiding Bishopric (except when a literal descendant of Aaron holds the keys of this ministry).

The keys of presidency center in the president; counselors are set apart to aid him, to give him their views and judgment on all matters that properly come before the presidency. But the final decision rests with the president, and counselors are obligated to sustain and support that decision (no matter what counsel they have given prior to the final determination), unless some iniquity is manifest which requires an appeal to higher authority.

In reaching decisions, however, full weight should be given to the views of counselors. President Joseph F. Smith said: "I propose that my counselors and fellow presidents in the First Presidency shall share with me in the responsibility of every act which I shall perform in this capacity. I do not propose to take the reins in my own hands to do as I please; but I propose to do as my brethren and I agree upon, and as the Spirit of the Lord manifests to us. . . . The Lord never did intend that one man should have all power, and for that reason he has placed in his Church, presidents, apostles, high priests, seventies, elders and the various officers of the lesser priesthood, all of which are essential in their order and place according to the authority bestowed on them. The Lord never did anything that was not essential or that was superfluous. There is a use for every branch of the priesthood that he has established in his Church. We want every man to learn his duty, and we expect every man will do his duty as faithfully as he knows how, and carry off his portion of the responsibility of building up Zion in the latter-days." (*Gospel Doctrine,* 5th ed. pp. 176-177.)

COUNSELS OF GOD.

See COMMANDMENTS, COUNSELOR, COUNSELORS, OBEDIENCE, PLAN OF SALVATION. The *counsels of God* include: 1. His purposes and plan, the great system he has ordained whereby men may gain immortality and eternal life; and 2. Such commandments, admonitions, warnings, advice, and instruction as he gives to enable men to gain peace here and salvation hereafter.

Speaking of God's counsels as synonymous with his purposes and plans, Peter said that "Jesus of Nazareth, a man approved of God," was crucified and slain "by the determinate counsel and foreknowledge of God." (Acts 2:22-23.) That is, as the primitive saints said in a prayer to God, those who crucified Christ had done what God's hand and his "counsel determined before to be done." (Acts 4:23-30.)

Speaking of Deity's counsels, having reference to his commandments, our Lord said "the Pharisees and lawyers rejected the counsel of God against themselves" because they did not submit to John's baptism. (Luke 7:30.)

All of the Lord's counsels are eternal and immutable. (Heb. 6:17.) They stand forever. (Ps. 33:11.) Those who reject them "shall perish." (2 Ne. 9:28.) "Seek not to counsel the Lord, but to take counsel from his hand. For behold, ye yourselves know that he counseleth in wisdom, and in justice, and in great mercy, over all his works." (Jac. 4:10; Alma 29:8; 37:12.) "Counsel with the Lord in all thy doings, and he will direct thee for good." (Alma 37:37.)

COURTESY.

See KINDNESS, TACTFULNESS. *Courtesy* is a natural outgrowth of the refining influence of the Spirit of the Lord. It presupposes the presence of kindness and an inherent consideration for the comfort and well-being of others. Peter summed up the doctrine of the Church in this field by saying simply: "Be courteous." (1 Pet. 3:8.)

COVENANTS.

See ABRAHAMIC COVENANT, CHILDREN OF THE COVENANT, COMMANDMENTS, GOSPEL, MEDIATOR, NEW AND EVERLASTING COVENANT, NEW TESTAMENT, OLD TESTAMENT. In the gospel sense, a *covenant* is a binding and solemn compact, agreement, contract, or mutual promise between God and a single person or a group of chosen persons. (D. & C. 5:3, 27-28; 54:4.) Since God is a party to every gospel covenant, it follows that his mind and will must be known with respect to the particular contractual relationship involved. Hence, covenants come only by revelation, and no person or group of persons enters into a gospel covenant except on the basis of direct revelation from God.

It follows that, as far as men now living are concerned, the only ones who have entered into covenants with the Lord are the members of The Church of Jesus Christ of Latter-day Saints. Their prophets are the only spiritual leaders receiving revelation for the Church and the world, and the saints themselves are the only ones enjoying the companionship of the Holy Ghost so that personal revelation may be received. Ancient and modern scriptures contain a record of many of the covenants of the past and the present. (1 Ne. 13:23-26; *Doctrines of Salvation,* vol. 1, pp. 152-156.)

The *new and everlasting covenant* is the fulness of the gospel and embraces within its terms and conditions every other covenant that Deity ever has made or ever will make with men. (D. & C. 132: 5-7; 133:57.) The provisions of this covenant are that if men will believe, repent, be baptized, receive the Holy Ghost, and endure in righteousness to the end, they shall have an inheritance in the celestial world.

All of the terms and conditions of the new and everlasting covenant are accepted by individual men incident to their baptism under the hands of a legal administrator. In effect, by baptism, an individual signs his name to the *contract of salvation.* If, after the baptism, a person keeps the covenant of baptism (which is to endure in faith to the end), his salvation is assured. (2 Ne. 31; Mosiah 18:8-10.)

In the ordinance of the sacrament men renew the covenant made in the waters of baptism, receiving again the assurance that they shall have the Spirit to be with them in this life (D. & C. 20:77-79), as well as an inheritance of eternal life in the world to come. (John 6:54.) They, on their part, agree again to keep the commandments.

Ordination to office in the Melchizedek Priesthood and entering into that "order of the priesthood" named "the new and everlasting covenant of marriage" are both occasions when men make the *covenant of exaltation,* being promised through their faithfulness all that the Father hath. (D. & C. 131:1-4; 84:39-41; 132; Num. 25:13.)

Tithing is a covenant by conformity to which men are assured temporal and spiritual blessings. (Mal. 3:7-12; D. & C. 119.) Sabbath observance is a covenant between God and his people through all their generations. (Ex. 31:16; D. & C. 59:9-20.) The word of wisdom is a covenant, conformity to which assures both strength of body and a special spiritual endowment. (D. & C. 89.) The United Order with its principles of consecration was and is to be entered by the saints by covenant (D. & C. 42:30; 78:11; 82: 11, 15, 21; 104:4), a covenant assuring the faithful of a celestial reward. (D. & C. 105:3-5.) In the temples the faithful enter into many covenants pertaining to exaltation. And so it goes, the more faithful and devoted a person is, the more of the covenants of the Lord he is enabled to receive, until he receives them in full and his calling and election is made sure.

Special covenants have often been made for special purposes to particular persons or groups. The Lord covenanted with Noah never to destroy the earth again by flood, and he set the rainbow as a token of such covenant. (Gen. 9:12-13.) To Abraham he gave the covenant of circumcision to remain in force with the chosen lineage until it was fulfilled in Christ. (Gen. 17: 11-14; Moro. 8:8.) To Lehi the covenant was vouchsafed that America should be a land of inheritance for his seed forever. (2 Ne. 1.) A similar promise came to the saints in this day. (D. & C. 38:20.) As part of the great Abrahamic covenant, a special land inheritance was offered Israel. (Gen. 17.) The Book of Mormon is a new covenant binding upon the Latter-day Saints, that is, having received this ancient record as a divine book, they are bound to conform to its teachings and follow its counsels. (D. & C. 84:57.)

To remember and keep the covenants is a standing obligation resting upon the Lord's people. (D. & C. 33:14; 35:24; 42:13, 78; 97:8.) Nothing is ever appointed or required of any of the saints which is "contrary to the church covenants." (D. & C. 28:12; 68:24; 107:63.) All gospel teaching is to be "according to the covenants." (D. & C. 107:89.) Those who keep their covenants have the Lord's promise, given with "an immutable covenant," that all things shall work together for their good. (D. & C. 98:3.) Every member of the Church should subscribe, without any mental reservation whatever, to this revealed statement: *"And this shall be our covenant—that we will walk in all the ordinances of the Lord."* (D. & C. 136:2-4.) "Blessed are they who have kept the covenant and observed the commandment, for they shall obtain mercy." (D. & C. 54:6.)

COVETOUSNESS.
See DESIRES, TEN COMMANDMENTS, WICKEDNESS. 1. To covet is to have an eager, extreme, and un-godly desire for something. The presence of *covetousness* in a human soul shows that such person has not overcome the world and is not living by gospel standards of conduct. Coveting is such a serious offense, and it is so imperative that man overcome all tendencies thereto, that the Lord condemned it in the Ten Commandments. (Ex. 20: 17; Mosiah 13:24.)

Many other revelations also condemn covetousness. "Thou shalt not covet thy neighbor's wife; . . . *thou shalt not covet thine own property.*" (D. & C. 19:25-26; 88: 123; 136:20.) "Beware of covetousness: for a man's life consisteth not in the abundance of the things which he possesseth." (Luke 12:15.) In commanding men to repent "of all their covetous desires," the Lord asked, "What is property unto me? saith the Lord." (D. & C. 117:4, 8.) For leaders in his earthly kingdom the Lord seeks men who hate covetousness. (Ex. 18:21.)

Covetousness on the part of the saints in the early days of this dispensation was one of the reasons the Lord permitted persecutions to come upon them. (D. & C. 98:20; 101:6; 104:4, 52-53.) The covetous shall not inherit the kingdom of God. (1 Cor. 6:9-11; Eph. 5:5.)

2. Paul used the term *covet* in an approved and righteous sense in connection with his counsel relative to the gifts of the Spirit. To signify the intense, eager desire the saints should have to attain these gifts, he commanded: "Covet earnestly the

best gifts" (1 Cor. 12:31) and, "Covet to prophesy." (1 Cor. 14:39)

CREATION.

See ANNIHILATION, CREATOR, DAY, EARTH, EARTHS, ELEMENTS. To *create is* to *organize*. It is an utterly false and uninspired notion to believe that the world or any other thing was created out of nothing or that any created thing can be destroyed in the sense of annihilation. *"The elements are eternal."* (D. & C. 93:33.)

Joseph Smith, in the King Follett sermon, said: "You ask the learned doctors why they say the world was made out of nothing; and they will answer, 'Doesn't the Bible say He *created* the world?' And they infer, from the word create, that it must have been made out of nothing. Now, the word create came from the word *baurau,* which does not mean to create out of nothing; it means to *organize;* the same as a man would organize materials and build a ship. Hence we infer that *God had materials to organize the world out of chaos—* chaotic matter, which is element, and in which dwells all the glory. *Element had an existence from the time he had. The pure principles of element are principles which can never be destroyed; they may be organized and reorganized, but not destroyed. They had no beginning, and can have no end."* (*Teachings,* pp. 350-352.)

Christ, acting under the direction of the Father, was and is the Creator of all things. (D. & C. 38:1-4; 76:22-24; John 1:1-3; Col. 1:16-17; Heb. 1:1-3; Moses 1; 2; 3.) That he was aided in the creation of this earth by "many of the noble and great" spirit children of the Father is evident from Abraham's writings. Unto those superior spirits Christ said: "We will go down, for there is space there, and *we will take of these materials, and we will make an earth whereon these may dwell."* (Abra. 3:22-24.) Michael or Adam was one of these. Enoch, Noah, Abraham, Moses, Peter, James, and John, Joseph Smith, and many other "noble and great" ones played a part in the great creative enterprise. (*Doctrines of Salvation,* vol. 1, pp. 74-75.)

This earth was not the first of the Lord's creations. An infinite number of worlds have come rolling into existence at his command. Each is an *earth;* many are inhabited with his spirit children; each abides the particular law given to it; and each will play its part in the redemption, salvation, and exaltation of that infinite host of the children of an Almighty God. The Lord has said that his work and glory is to bring to pass immortality and eternal life for his children on all the inhabited worlds he has created. (Moses 1:27-40; 7:29-36; D. & C. 88:17-26.)

Such details of the creative process and of the order of events in it as have been revealed pertain only to this earth. (Moses 1:35.) In

the temple we receive the clearest understanding of what took place and how it was accomplished. Abraham has left us an account of the planning and decisions of the Creators "at the time that they counseled among themselves to form the heavens and the earth." (Abra. 4; 5.)

In the books of Moses and Genesis we have revealed accounts of the actual physical creation of the earth. The 2nd chapter of Moses and the 1st chapter of Genesis give the events which occurred on the successive creative days. (Ex. 20:8-11.) Then the 3rd chapter of Moses and the 2nd chapter of Genesis—by way of interpolation, amplification, and parenthetical explanation—recount the added truth that all things were created spiritually "before they were naturally upon the face of the earth."

There is no revealed account of the spirit creation, only this explanatory interpolation that all things had been created in heaven at a previous time. That this prior spirit creation occurred long before the temporal or natural creation is evident from the fact that spirit men, men who themselves were before created spiritually, were participating in the natural creation. (*Doctrines of Salvation,* vol. 1, pp. 72-78.)

CREATOR.

See CHRIST, CREATION, FATHER IN HEAVEN, WORD OF GOD. Both the Father and the Son bear the title, *Creator.* (Moses 1; 2; 3; *Teachings,* p. 190.) The creative work itself is actually done by the Son, as he is directed by and uses the power of the Father. Hence the scriptures speak of Christ as the Creator of this world and of worlds without number. (Moses 7:29; John 1:1-3; Col. 1:16-17; Heb. 1:1-3; D. & C. 38:1-4; 76:22-24.) In his creation of this earth he was assisted by Michael and other noble and great spirits. (Abra. 3:22-24.)

CREEDS.

See APOSTASY, APOSTLES CREED, ATHANASIAN CREED, NICENE CREED. From the earliest era of apostate Christianity, the leaders of the then existing church—no longer finding revelation available and incapable of speaking by the power of the Holy Ghost so as to have the resultant record vouchsafed as authoritative scripture—sought other ways of settling religious and philosophical disputes and of establishing authoritative doctrine. By the 4th century formal documents called *creeds* had been formulated, adopted by councils, and the dogmas expressed in them imposed upon the church, insofar as the political power of the moment was able to enforce such an imposition.

These creeds—modified and changed from time to time to suit the whims and views of various emperors, philosophers, and politically powerful segments of the apostate

church—eventually became the accepted standards and guides in religious matters. They are considered authoritative declarations of belief. Numerous versions have been preserved to this day which form in large part the present doctrinal foundation upon which the Catholic and Protestant churches rest.

The most charitable thing that can be said of them is that they are man made. Neither their authors, the councils which adopted them, nor those who presently accept them, make any claim that revelation or inspiration was present in their formulation and promulgation, although attempts are made to show that the various articles in them conform to the teachings of the scriptures.

Actually the spirit which imposed them on the people in early days was from beneath. Joseph Smith, writing by way of inspiration concerning the persecution, tyranny, and oppression imposed upon the saints in his day said that such was "supported and urged on and upheld by the *influence of that spirit which hath so strongly riveted the creeds of the fathers, who have inherited lies, upon the hearts of the children, and filled the world with confusion.*" (D. & C. 123:7.)

The major creeds, in large measure, deal with the Godhead; they describe the members of that holy trinity as being three-in-one, incomprehensible, unknowable, uncreated, incorporeal, and without body, parts, or passions. Names of the members of the Godhead are applied to vague forces or essences that have little resemblance to the true Beings whom men are commanded to worship.

In prophetic vision Jeremiah foresaw this forsaking of the truth about God and recorded that those in the latter-days who would return to the truth would say: "Surely our fathers have inherited *lies, vanity,* and *things wherein there is no profit.*" Then he summed up what men had done in their creeds by saying: "*Shall a man make gods unto himself, and they are no gods?*" (Jer. 16:19-20.)

When the Father and the Son appeared to Joseph Smith to usher in the dispensation of the fulness of times, the young Prophet asked which of all the sects was right and which he should join. In answer he was told to "join none of them, for they were all wrong; and the Personage who addressed me," he explained, "said that *all their creeds were an abomination in his sight.*" (Jos. Smith 2:19.)

"I cannot believe in any of the creeds of the different denominations," the Prophet once said, "though all of them have some truth. I want to come up into the presence of God, and learn all things; but *the creeds set up stakes,* and say, 'Hitherto shalt thou come, and no further,' which I cannot subscribe to." (*Teachings,* p. 327.) Each creed, he said on another occasion, "was conceived in ignorance, and brought forth in folly—a cobweb of yesterday!" (*Teachings*, p. 203.)

CREMATION.

See DEATH, FUNERALS, GRAVES. *Cremation* of the dead is no part of the gospel; it is a practice which has been avoided by the saints in all ages. The Church today counsels its members not to cremate their dead. Such a procedure would find gospel acceptance only under the most extraordinary and unusual circumstances. Wherever possible the dead should be consigned to the earth, and nothing should be done that is destructive of the body; that should be left to nature, "for dust thou art, and unto dust shalt thou return." (Gen. 3:19.)

CRIME.

See SIGNS OF THE TIMES.

CRITICS.

See HIGHER CRITICISM.

CROSS.

See CHRIST, CRUCIFIED ONE, CRUCIFIXION, SIGN OF THE CROSS.
1. Among the Assyrians, Persians, Phoenicians of Carthage, Egyptians, Greeks, and Romans, the *cross* was an instrument of execution. From earliest times the eventual crucifixion and death of our Lord upon the cross was revealed to holy prophets. (Moses 7:

55; 1 Ne. 11:33; 19:10-13; 2 Ne. 6:9; 10:3-7; 25:13; Mosiah 3:9; 15:7.) The gospel authors detail many of the events and circumstances incident thereto. (Matt. 26; 27; 28; Mark 14; 15; 16; Luke 22; 23; 24; John 18; 19; 20; 21.) And after his resurrection, our Lord said that the very reason he came into the world was to fulfil the will of the Father in being lifted up upon the cross. (3 Ne. 27:13-15.)
2. Because of its association with our Lord, the *cross* has come to have symbolic meanings for those who profess belief in his atoning blood. Paul properly used the *cross of Christ* to identify to the mind the whole doctrine of the atonement, reconciliation, and redemption. (1 Cor. 1:17-18; Gal. 6:12-14; Eph. 2: 8-21; Philip. 2:5-9; 3:18; Col. 1:20; 2:14; Heb. 12:2.)

In succeeding centuries, the churches which came into being through an intermingling of pagan concepts with the true apostolic Christianity developed the practice of using symbolic crosses in the architecture of their buildings and as jewelry attached to the robes of their priests. Frequently this practice of dwelling on the personal death struggle of our Lord has caused these churches to put sculptured representations of Christ on their crosses, thus forming so-called *crucifixes*. All this is inharmonious with the quiet spirit of worship and reverence that should attend a true Christian's remembrance of our Lord's sufferings and death. In fact, the revealed symbolism to bring these things to the attention of true worshipers is found in the ordinance of the sacrament.

3. Growing out of the crucifixion of Christ is the concept that any great affliction or trial that comes upon the saints does in itself constitute a *cross* they must bear as part of their obligation to overcome the world. Thus the saints—knowing that Christ "for the joy that was set before him endured the cross, despising the shame, and is set down at the right hand of the throne of God" (Heb. 12:2)—are themselves strengthened to withstand all trials and persecutions which come upon them in the gospel cause. Such afflictions or trials are regarded as crosses which test Christian patience or virtue. (2 Ne. 9:18; Jac. 1:8.)

4. Similarly, the gospel cause commands every man to take up his *cross* and follow him who carried his own cross to Golgotha. That is, the saints are to carry the cross of service and consecration, the cross of devotion and obedience. "If any man will come after me, let him deny himself, and take up his cross and follow me," our Lord said. "And now *for a man to take up his cross, is to deny himself all ungodliness, and every worldly lust, and keep my commandments.*" (*Inspired Version*, Matt. 16:25-26.)

CROSS OF CHRIST.
See CROSS.

CROWNS.
See EXALTATION, KING, KINGS, PRIESTESSES, PRIESTS, THRONES. Those who gain exaltation in the highest heaven of the celestial world shall wear *crowns*. Perhaps literal crowns may be worn on occasion—emblematic of their victory over the world and signifying that they rule and reign as kings and queens in the eternal house of Israel. But at all times they will be "crowned with honor, and glory, and immortality, and eternal life." (D. & C. 75:5.)

In the gospel sense, a crown is the sign and symbol of eternal exaltation and dominion, of godhood in the kingdom of God. Our Lord has been seen in vision wearing "a golden crown" (Rev. 14:14; 6:2; 19:12), and those surrounding the throne of Deity have been seen similarly identified. (Rev. 4:4, 10.) Paul speaks of such persons as having "an incorruptible" crown (1 Cor. 9:25) and as inheriting "a crown of righteousness" (2 Tim. 4:8); James says they "shall receive the crown of life, which the Lord hath promised to them that love him" (Jas. 1:12); John records a similar affirmation (Rev. 2:10); and Peter speaks of receiving "a crown of glory that fadeth not away." (1 Pet. 5:4.) The crowns so spoken of are crowns of eternal life (D. & C. 66:12), of eternal lives (D. & C. 132:55), of celestial glory. (D. & C. 101:65.)

By keeping the commandments and enduring in righteousness to the end the saints overcome the world and gain crowns of glory in eternity. Hence the counsel: *"Hold that fast which thou hast, that no man take thy crown."* (Rev. 3:11.)

CRUCIFIED ONE.
See CHRIST, CROSS, CRUCIFIXION. Christ is the *Crucified One*— a title used by Christians generally when they desire to point attention to the horrible and painful death by crucifixion which he suffered on the cross.

CRUCIFIX.
See CROSS.

CRUCIFIXION.
See CHRIST, CROSS, CRUCIFIED ONE, PASSION OF CHRIST. Few if any forms of execution are or could be more painful and agonizing than that of *crucifixion*—a form of taking life in which the condemned person has his hands and feet nailed or bound to a cross of execution, after which he is left to suffer inexpressible pain and torture until the spirit finally leaves the mangled and broken body. When crucified persons were nailed rather than bound to the cross, the nails ordinarily were driven through the feet and wrists (or both hands and wrists) so that the weight of the body could be sustained. Our Lord was, of course, nailed rather than tied to the cross. (Isa. 22:21-25.)

Crucifixion was the form of death

chosen from the beginning for Christ, that in his death, having descended below all things, he might in his resurrection ascend above all things. (D. & C. 88:6; 122:8; Eph. 4:9-10.) Long before his earthly ministry, holy prophets foresaw his crucifixion on the cross. (Moses 7: 55; 1 Ne. 19:10-13; 2 Ne. 6:9; 10:3-5; 25:13; Mosiah 3:9; 15:7.)

After his resurrection our Lord showed his disciples in Jerusalem and the host of Nephite Saints on this continent the nail marks in his hands and in his feet. (Luke 24:36-43; 3 Ne. 11:14-19.) At the Second Coming these same wounds will stand as a witness to the Jews that he is the Crucified One, their King whom they rejected in the meridian of time. (D. & C. 45:51-52; Zech. 12: 10; 13:6.)

CRUELTY.
See PERSECUTION.

CRYING.
See WEEPING.

CRYSTAL BALLS.
See PEEP STONES.

CULTS.
See SECTS.

CUMORAH.
See BOOK OF MORMON, GOLD

174

PLATES. Both the Nephite and Jaredite civilizations fought their final great wars of extinction at and near the *Hill Cumorah* (or *Ramah* as the Jaredites termed it), which hill is located between Palmyra and Manchester in the western part of the state of New York. It was here that Moroni hid up the gold plates from which the Book of Mormon was translated. (Morm. 6; Ether 15.) Joseph Smith, Oliver Cowdery, and many of the early brethren, who were familiar with all the circumstances attending the coming forth of the Book of Mormon in this dispensation, have left us pointed testimony as to the identity and location of Cumorah or Ramah. (*Doctrines of Salvation*, vol. 3, pp. 232-241.)

CURSINGS.

See ANATHEMA, BLASPHEMY, OATHS, OBEDIENCE, WOES. Just as obedience and righteousness bring blessings, so wickedness and rebellion result in *cursings*. (D. & C. 104:1-8.) *"Instead of blessings, ye, by your own works, bring cursings, wrath, indignation, and judgments upon your own heads, by your follies, and by all your abominations, which you practise before me, saith the Lord."* (D. & C. 124:48.) As Moses explained in great detail to ancient Israel, the curses flowing from disobedience pertain to both temporal and spiritual matters. Famine, pestilence, plague, disease, slavery, poverty, war, and death are all sent of God as curses upon Israel for failure to keep the commandments. (Deut. 27; 28; 29; 30.)

Cursings are the opposite of blessings, and the greater the opportunity given a people to earn blessings, the more severe will be the cursings heaped upon them, if they do not measure up and gain the proffered rewards. Failure to pay tithing, for instance, brings condemnation upon the covenant people, whereas the people of the world—not being specifically obligated to keep this law—do not suffer the same penalties for non-tithe paying. (Mal. 3:7-12.) "Hearken and hear, O ye my people, saith the Lord and your God, ye whom I delight to bless with the greatest of all blessings, ye that hear me; and *ye that hear me not will I curse, that have professed my name, with the heaviest of all cursings."* (D. & C. 41:1.)

Those who persecute the saints shall be cursed with the damnation of hell. (D. & C. 121:11-25.) To those on his left hand the Lord shall say: "Depart from me, ye cursed, into everlasting fire, prepared for the devil and his angels." (D. & C. 29:28, 41; Matt. 25:40.)

Cursings as well as blessings may be administered by the power and authority of the priesthood (D. & C. 124:93), but the Lord's earthly agents are sent forth primarily to bless and not to curse, and no curse should ever be decreed except by direct revelation from the Lord commanding such to be done. The true spirit of the gospel is exemplified in the counsel, "Love your enemies, bless them that curse you, do good to them that hate you, and pray for them which despitefully use you, and persecute you." (Matt. 5:44.) "Bless, and curse not." (Rom. 12:14.)

President Joseph F. Smith explained, when speaking of the priesthood: "It is the same power and priesthood that was committed to the disciples of Christ while he was upon the earth, that whatsoever they should bind on earth should be bound in heaven, and that whatsoever they should loose on earth should be loosed in heaven, and whosoever they blessed should be blessed, and *if they cursed, in the spirit of righteousness and meekness before God, God would confirm that curse; but men are not called upon to curse man-*

kind; that is not our mission; it is our mission to preach righteousness to them. It is our business to love and to bless them, and to redeem them from the fall and from the wickedness of the world. This is our mission and our special calling. God will curse and will exercise his judgment in those matters. 'Vengeance is mine,' saith the Lord, and 'I will repay.' (Rom. 12:19.) We are perfectly willing to leave vengeance in the hands of God and let him judge between us and our enemies, and let him reward them according to his own wisdom and mercy." (*Gospel Doctrine,* 5th ed., p. 140.)

To curse in unrighteousness is in itself a serious crime. Through Moses the Lord decreed: "He that curseth his father, or his mother, shall surely be put to death." (Ex. 21:17; Lev. 20:9; Prov. 20:20; Matt. 15:4; Mark 7:10.)

D

DAMNATION.

See DEVIL, ETERNAL DAMNATION, FIRE AND BRIMSTONE, HELL, KINGDOMS OF GLORY, RESURRECTION, SALVATION, SIN, SONS OF PERDITION, SPIRIT PRISON, SPIRITUAL DEATH, UNPARDONABLE SIN. The opposite of salvation is *damnation,* and just as there are varying degrees and kinds of salva-

tion, so there are degrees and kinds of damnation. There is a "greater damnation" (Matt. 23:14) and, obviously, a lesser damnation. Literally, to be damned is to be condemned, and the scriptures speak of the damned as: 1. Those who are thrust down to hell to await the day of the *resurrection of damnation;* 2. Those who fail to gain an inheritance in the celestial kingdom or kingdom of God; 3. Those who become sons of perdition; and 4. Those who fail to gain exaltation in the highest heaven within the celestial world, even though they do gain a celestial mansion in one of the lower heavens of that world.

Accordingly, we find the Lord saying of the wicked and those who persecute his saints that, "a generation of vipers shall not escape the damnation of hell." (D. & C. 121: 23; Matt. 22:33.) The disobedient are damned (D. & C. 42:60; Hela. 12:26; 3 Ne. 26:5); likewise those who reject Christ (D. & C. 49:5); those who do not believe the gospel (D. & C. 68:9; Mark 16:16); those who, having believed, are not baptized (D. & C. 84:74; 112:29); and those who having been baptized do not endure in faith unto the end. "If they will not repent and belive in his name, and be baptized in his name, and endure to the end, they must be damned; for the Lord God, the Holy One of Israel, has spoken it." (2 Ne. 9:24.) Believers in the doctrines of modern Christendom will reap damnation to their souls (Morm. 8; Moro. 8), as will also members of the Church who partake unworthily of the sacrament. (3 Ne. 18:28-29; 1 Cor. 11: 29.) The rejection of any covenant, the gospel, celestial marriage, or any other, assures the rebellious person of damnation. (D. & C. 132: 4, 6, 27.)

It is very evident that church membership alone will not keep an individual from one degree of damnation or another. It was of his saints, members of his kingdom or Church on earth, that the Lord said: "Behold, it is not meet that I should command in all things; for he that is compelled in all things, the same is a slothful and not a wise servant; wherefore he receiveth no reward. Verily I say, men should be anxiously engaged in a good cause, and do many things of their own free will, and bring to pass much righteousness; For the power is in them, wherein they are agents unto themselves. And inasmuch as men do good they shall in nowise lose their reward. But he that doeth not anything until he is commanded, and receiveth a commandment with doubtful heart, and keepeth it with slothfulness, the same is damned." (D. & C. 58:26-29.)

DANCING.
See MUTUAL IMPROVEMENT ASSOCIATIONS, RECREATION. Two extreme and opposite views are held by people of the world with reference to *dancing*. In some sects of Christendom even the most circumspect and wholesome dancing is banned as immoral and ungodly; in other circles, dancing is so twisted and perverted as to make it a vulgar caricature of the wholesome recreational pursuit that should result from friendly association between the sexes.

Under proper circumstances and supervision dancing is a wholesome, edifying, and clean amusement having the specific approval of the Lord. By the mouth of Brigham Young the Lord revealed: "If thou art merry, praise the Lord with singing, with music, with dancing, and with a prayer of praise and thanksgiving." (D. & C. 136:28.) "To every thing there is a season, and a time to every purpose under the heaven: . . . A time to weep, and a time to laugh; a time to mourn, and a time to dance." (Eccles. 3:1-8.)

Dances should be properly conducted, supervised, and chaperoned. Church standards of dress and conduct must prevail. It is unwise to dance a whole evening (or a major part of it) with the same person. Dating by the very young and immature is discouraged. Attendance at *public dances,* as distinguished from those sponsored by the Church, schools, or other private organizations often lead to disastrous consequences. Prolonging dances past midnight when the next day is the Sabbath or to the early hours of the morning on any day should not be permitted. Tobacco and liquor have no place at a proper dance. Church dances should be opened and closed with prayer.

DARK AGES.

See APOSTASY, CHURCH OF THE DEVIL, DARKNESS. That period of about 1000 years which lasted from the fall of the Roman Empire to the age of the Renaissance is called the *Dark Ages.* During this near-millennium the light of learning and truth almost went out. Progress was nil. Men and nations sank into illiteracy and ignorance.

Why should such universal retrogression take place? Historians struggle without success to find an explanation. Plainly and simply put, the fact is that the pall of darkness that overcast the earth during all those years was part of the great apostasy from the truth. The gospel brings light and truth, fosters learning, encourages education, promotes scientific research, grants freedom of thought and word—all for the very reason that the gospel is true and has nothing to fear either from error or from any new truth that may be learned or discovered. But when churches, governments, or organizations of any nature come into power, which are founded on falsehood and error rather than on truth, such organizations must impose restraints upon learning and education, otherwise men might become enlightened and end up throwing off their shackles.

The hold of Lucifer is always more secure when truth and light are rejected, when men forget how to read and write, and when they can be held in bondage to those who practice priestcrafts. It was not until the age of the Renaissance that light, truth, and learning again began to prevail on earth. (*Progress of Man,* pp. 178-195.)

DARKNESS.

See APOSTASY, DARK AGES, DEVIL, LIGHT, LIGHT OF CHRIST. In the gospel sense, *darkness*—the opposite of light—reigns where there is ignorance, iniquity, and apostasy. Light is of God, darkness of the devil; Christ is the true light, Lucifer the fountain of gross darkness and apostasy. "I am the light which shineth in darkness, and the darkness comprehendeth it not," our Lord said. (D. & C. 6:21; John 1:5.) "God is light, and in him is no darkness at all." (1 John 1:5.)

Where the true gospel of Christ is, there is light; and where that gospel is not found, darkness reigns. "The whole world lieth in sin, and groaneth under darkness and under the bondage of sin, . . . because they come not unto me," the Lord said. (D. & C. 84:49-54.) "Darkness covereth the earth, and gross darkness the minds of the people." (D. & C. 112:23.) The kingdom of the devil is "full of darkness." (Rev. 16: 10.) And men "love darkness rather than light, because their deeds are evil." (D. & C. 10:21; John 3:19.) But when men repent and heed the call of Christ, they thereby come "out of darkness into his marvellous light." (1 Pet. 2:9; 1 Thess. 5:4; 1 John 2:9.)

By following Christ men have power to chase darkness from their midst and to come to the fulness of the light. (D. & C. 50:23-29.) "I am the light of the world: he that followeth me shall not walk in darkness, but shall have the light of life." (John 8:12.) "Yet a little while is the light with you. Walk while ye have the light, lest darkness come upon you: for he that walketh in darkness knoweth not whither he goeth. . . . I am come a light into the world, that whosoever believeth on me should not abide in darkness." (John 12:35, 46.)

If, after receiving the truth, men then apostatize and turn to unrighteousness, the darkness that envelopes them is deeper than it was before they came into the light. If "the light that is in thee be darkness!" (Matt. 6:22-23; Luke 11:33-36; D. & C. 88:67.) Similarly, though they do not apostatize, the saints who do not magnify their callings "are walking in darkness at noon-day." Further: *"If you keep not my commandments, the love of the Father shall not continue with you, therefore you shall walk in darkness."* (D. & C. 95:6, 12.)

DAUGHTERS OF GOD.

See ADOPTION, CELESTIAL MARRIAGE, CHURCH OF THE FIRSTBORN, EXALTATION, FULNESS OF THE FATHER, GODHOOD, JOINT-HEIRS WITH CHRIST, PRE-EXISTENCE, SALVATION, SERVANTS OF GOD, SONS OF GOD. All women are the daughters of God because of their pre-existent birth as female spirits. However, the designation *daughters of God*, as used in the revelations, has a far more pointed meaning than this. Just as men who pursue a steadfast course toward exaltation become the sons of God while in this life, so women who walk hand-in-hand in obedience with them become the daughters of God. (D. & C. 25:1; 76:24; Mosiah 5:7.)

The temple ordinances, including celestial marriage, precede attainment of that membership in the household of God which makes one a daughter. Those who are adopted as daughters in this life will, if they continue faithful, gain exaltation in the world to come. (*Doctrines of Salvation,* vol. 2, pp. 64-65.)

DAY.

See CREATION, LAST DAY, LAST DAYS, NIGHT, SABBATH, SEASONS, TIME. 1. One period of the earth's revolution on its axis (24 hours) is called a *day.* (Gen. 7:24.) Hebrew days were calculated "from even unto even" (Lev. 23:32), meaning from sunset to sunset. The *Lord's day* is the first day of the week. (D. & C. 59:9-14.)

2. That period between dawn and dark is the *day* as distinguished from the *night.* (Gen. 8:22; Ps. 19:2.) "Are there not twelve hours in the day?" (John 11:9.)

3. A *day* is a specified age, time, or period. (Job 19:25.) "Now is the time and the day of your salvation. . . . For behold, this life is the time for men to prepare to meet God." (Alma 34:31-32.) We are fast approaching "the day when the Lord shall come." (D. & C. 1:10.)

4. The Mosaic and Abrahamic accounts of the creation recite that this earth was created in six days and that on the 7th the Lord rested. (Gen. 1; 2; Moses 2; 3; Abra. 4; 5.) Several revelations throw light upon the meaning of the term *day* as it is used in connection with the Lord's great creative enterprises. The Lord told Abraham, "by the Urim and Thummim, that Kolob was after the manner of the Lord, according to its times and seasons in the revolutions thereof; that *one revolution was a day unto the Lord, after his manner of reckoning, it being one thousand years* according to the time appointed unto that whereon thou standest. This is the reckoning of the *Lord's time,* according to the reckoning of Kolob." (Abra. 3:4.)

Following this revealed definition of a day unto the Lord, Abraham recorded the events of the successive days of the creation of the earth. Then he wrote: "Now I, Abraham, saw that *it was after the Lord's time, which was after the time of Kolob;* for as yet the Gods had not appointed unto Adam his reckoning." (Abra. 5:13.) Thus the *celestial day* (which was used in the creation) was 1000 years in length measured in terms of time as it is reckoned on this earth. This accords with Peter's recitation that "one day is with the Lord as a thousand years, and a thousand years as one day" (2 Pet. 3:8), and also with revealed time-periods as these have been made known through Joseph Smith. (D. & C. 77.)

5. That period of time between the loss of the true Church in the early part of the Christian Era and its restoration in modern times is scripturally measured in what have been termed *prophetic days*. John specified that this period of prolonged apostate darkness would prevail for 1260 days (Rev. 12:6), that is for 42 months (Rev. 13:5), or in other words "for a time, and times, and half a time." (Rev. 12:14; Dan. 7:25.) Obviously these 1260 days ended when the Church was restored in the latter-days. Interesting attempts have been made by some scholars to identify the exact period covered by these 42 months. (J. M. Sjodahl, *The Reign of Antichrist*, pp. 70-71.)

DAY OF BURNING.
See SECOND COMING OF CHRIST.

DAY OF INDIGNATION.
See SECOND COMING OF CHRIST.

DAY OF JUDGMENT.
See JUDGMENT DAY.

DAY OF PENTECOST.
See EASTER, GIFT OF THE HOLY GHOST, HOLY GHOST, PASSOVER, TONGUES. In ancient Israel "the feast of weeks" (Ex. 34:22; Deut. 16:10), or "the feast of harvest" (Ex. 23:16), or "the day of the first-fruits" (Num. 28:26), was celebrated 50 days after the Passover. This occasion, from the Greek word *Pentekoste* (meaning 50th) was known as the *day of Pentecost.* It was on this day of Jewish celebration, in the year our Lord was resurrected, that the promised endowment of the Holy Spirit was first enjoyed in the Christian Era. Some sects of Christendom observe Pentecost or *Whitsuntide* as a solemn feast seven weeks or 50 days after Easter, counting both Easter and Pentecost in the 50.

During his mortal ministry our Lord gave his disciples the gift of the Holy Ghost, which is the right to the constant companionship of that member of the Godhead based on faithfulness. (John 20:22.) But as long as Jesus was with them, the actual enjoyment of the gift was withheld. (John 7:39; 14:26; 15:26-27; 16:7-15; Acts 1:8.) Fulfilment of the promise came on the day of Pentecost; with miraculous majesty attending, the gift of tongues and of interpretation was poured out upon a great multitude and many conversions were made. (Acts 2:1-17.)

This occasion is falsely considered by the sectarian world generally to be the beginning of the Christian Church. In reality the Church had existed in previous dispensations, but even as pertaining to the meridian of time, the Church had been an organized and formal body during the lifetime of the Master.

Pentecostal outpourings of the

Spirit have occurred many times in many dispensations. One of these great latter-day Pentecostal periods was in connection with the dedication of the Kirtland Temple. For a period of weeks, the visions of eternity were opened to many, angels visited in the congregations of the saints, the Lord himself was seen by many, and tongues and prophecy were multiplied. (*History of the Church,* vol. 2, pp. 379-436.) On Sunday, March 27, 1836, in the dedicatory service itself, an almost exact repetition of the events of the New Testament day of Pentecost took place. "Brother George A. Smith arose and began to prophesy," the Prophet recorded, "when a noise was heard like the sound of a rushing mighty wind, which filled the Temple, and all the congregation simultaneously arose, being moved upon by an invisible power; many began to speak in tongues and prophesy; others saw glorious visions; and I beheld the Temple was filled with angels, which fact I declared to the congregation. The people of the neighborhood came running together (hearing an unusual sound within, and seeing a bright light like a pillar of fire resting upon the Temple), and were astonished at what was taking place." (*History of the Church,* vol. 2, p. 428.)

DAY OF REDEMPTION.
See SECOND COMING OF CHRIST.

DAY OF REST.
See SABBATH.

DAY OF THE LORD.
See SECOND COMING OF CHRIST.

DAY OF TRANSFIGURATION.
See TIMES OF REFRESHING.

DAY OF VENGEANCE.
See SECOND COMING OF CHRIST.

DAY OF VISITATION.
See SECOND COMING OF CHRIST.

DAY OF WRATH.
See SECOND COMING OF CHRIST.

DEACONESSES.
See APOSTASY, DEACONS. In some branches of modern Christendom a woman who is chosen or assigned to assist in church work is called a *deaconess.* In reality there is no such office either in the priesthood or in the Church, and the designation is not so much as found in the scriptures. Its usage by some Christian churches of the day is one of the evidences of the great apostasy.

DEACONS.

See AARONIC PRIESTHOOD, DEA-
CONESSES, LEVITES, PRIESTHOOD,
PRIESTHOOD OFFICES, PRIESTHOOD
QUORUMS, QUORUM PRESIDENTS.
One of the ordained offices in the
Aaronic Priesthood is that of a
deacon. (D. & C. 20:60.) This
office, the lowest in the priesthood
hierarchy (D. & C. 88:127), is an
appendage to the lesser priesthood.
(D. & C. 84:30.) Deacons are "appointed to watch over the church,
to be standing ministers unto the
church." (D. & C. 84:111.) They
are to assist the teachers in all their
duties (which includes home teaching), and are "to warn, expound,
exhort, and teach, and invite all to
come unto Christ," although they
can neither "baptize, administer the
sacrament, or lay on hands." (D. &
C. 20:57-60.) Among other things, it
is the practice of the Church to as-
sign them to pass the sacrament,
perform messenger service, act as
ushers, keep church facilities in good
repair, go home teaching, and perform special assignments at the
direction of the bishopric. Many
of their assigned functions are comparable to those performed by the
Levites of old. (*Doctrines of Salvation,* vol. 3, pp. 111-114.)

It is the practice of the Church
in this dispensation—a practice dictated by the needs of the present
day ministry and confirmed by the
inspiration of the Spirit resting
upon those who hold the keys of the
kingdom—to confer the Aaronic
Priesthood upon worthy young men
who are 12 years of age and to ordain them to the office of a deacon
in that priesthood. Notwithstanding the fact that this is the lowest
priesthood office, it is yet a high
and holy one in God's kingdom. In
the meridian of time the needs of
the ministry were such that adult
brethren were ordained deacons.

"The deacons," Paul wrote, must
"be grave, not doubletongued, not
given to much wine, not greedy of
filthy lucre; Holding the mystery of
the faith in a pure conscience. And
let these also first be proved; then
let them use the office of a deacon,
being found blameless. Even so
must their wives be grave, not
slanderers, sober, faithful in all
things. Let the deacons be the husbands of one wife, ruling their children and their own houses well.
For they that have used the office
of a deacon well purchase to themselves a good degree, and great
boldness in the faith which is in
Christ Jesus." (1 Tim. 3:8-13.)

DEAD WORKS.

See GOOD WORKS, SALVATION.
Dead works are those unauthorized
religious acts which men do in the
false hope of gaining salvation
through their performance. They
are works without life, works which
never gain the ratifying seal of approval from the Spirit and which do
not lead to eternal life. They are
not of God. All apostate ordinances
and performances are of this sort.

After the law given to Moses

was fulfilled in Christ, every ordinance or ritual imitative of what legal administrators had done in righteousness when the law was in force became a dead work. Ordinances—such as baptism (though it may imitate the true mode, immersion)—are dead works when performed by sectarian churches. (D. & C. 22.) Believing in and relying on infant baptism is "putting trust in dead works." (Moro. 8:23.) The religious performances of those outside the true Church of Christ are dead works, from which they are commanded to repent. (Heb. 6:1; 9:14.)

DEAFNESS.

See APOSTASY, SPIRITUALITY. *Spiritual deafness* describes the state of those who are lacking in spirituality, whose spirit ears are not attuned to the whisperings of the still small voice of the Spirit. Similarly, *spiritual blindness* is the identifying mark which singles out those who are unable to see the hand of God manifest in the affairs of men. Such have "unbelief and blindness of heart" (D. & C. 58:15); they are "hard in their hearts, and blind in their minds." (3 Ne. 2:1.)

Of the unbelieving Jews our Lord said, "They seeing see not; and hearing they hear not, neither do they understand. . . . For this people's heart is waxed gross, and their ears are dull of hearing, and their eyes they have closed; lest at any time they should see with their eyes, and hear with their ears, and should understand with their heart, and should be converted, and I should heal them." (Matt. 13:10-17.) "And wo unto the deaf that will not hear; for they shall perish. Wo unto the blind that will not see; for they shall perish also." (2 Ne. 9:31-32.)

The gathering of Israel in the last days shall consist in bringing together "the blind people that have eyes, and the deaf that have ears," that is, the spiritually blind and deaf shall come to a knowledge of the things of God and they shall see and hear. (Isa. 43.) In large part the opening of the eyes of the blind and the unstopping of the ears of the deaf shall take place by means of the Book of Mormon. "And in that day shall the deaf hear the words of the book, and the eyes of the blind shall see out of obscurity, and out of darkness." (Isa. 29:18.)

DEATH.

See ANNIHILATION, ATONEMENT OF CHRIST, FALL OF ADAM, FUNERALS, MILLENNIUM, MORTALITY, MOURNING, RESURRECTION, SPIRITUAL DEATH, TRANSLATED BEINGS. There is no such thing as *death* in the sense of annihilation, in the sense that matter ceases to exist or that living things cease to have a conscious identity. Death is merely a change from one status or sphere of existence to another. In a sense the spirit children of

God die (as pertaining to their life in the presence of the Father) when the transition from the pre-existent sphere to this life is made. That is, they die as pertaining to their pre-mortal life, but they are born as pertaining to mortality.

When the scriptures speak of death, however, they ordinarily mean the *natural* or *temporal* death. (D. & C. 29:42-43; Alma 11: 42; 12:16, 24; 42:8; Morm. 9:13.) This death consists in the separation of the eternal spirit from the mortal body so that the body is left to go back to the dust or element from which it was created (meaning organized), and the spirit is left to sojourn in a world of waiting spirits until the day of the resurrection. (Rev. 20:13; 2 Ne. 9:10-15.)

In the case of translated beings and the righteous persons who shall live during the millennial era, death and the resurrection shall take place instantaneously. They shall be changed from mortality to immortality in the twinkling of an eye, the spirit never having occasion to separate from the body, and in their cases this change is called *death*. (D. & C. 63:49-52; 3 Ne. 28.) But it is not death according to the most common usage of the word. (D. & C. 101:29-31; Isa. 65:20.)

"Death hath passed upon all men, to fulfil the merciful plan of the great Creator." (2 Ne. 9:6.) It is one of the most important and desirable events that can transpire in the eternal existence of the spirit off-spring of Him who ordained the great plan of mercy of which it is a part. It is just as important to die as to be born, for the spirit to leave the body as for it to enter that same body. Mortality is a necessary prelude to immortality; it is by passing the test of this life that men obtain eternal life in the world to come. If there had been no creation, there could have been no fall. If there had been no fall, there could have been no birth into mortality. If there were no mortality, there would be no death. And without death there would be no resurrection, and hence no immortality or eternal life. Thus to do away with death would frustrate the whole plan of redemption. (2 Ne. 9:6-16.)

Death began, as far as this earth is concerned, after and as a result of the fall of Adam. There was no death for man or for any form of life until after Adam transgressed. (2 Ne. 2:22; *Doctrines of Salvation,* vol. 1, pp. 107-120.) Death will cease, as far as this earth is concerned, when every person and created thing has been raised in immortality and when the earth itself has become an immortal sphere. (D. & C. 29:22-29; 77:1-3; 88:16-32; 130:9.)

By faith the dead are sometimes raised, meaning that the spirit is called back to inhabit again the mortal body. (3 Ne. 7:19; 19:4; 4 Ne. 5; 1 Kings 17:17-23; Matt. 9: 18-26; Mark 5:21-43; Luke 7:11-17, 22; 8:41-56; John 11:1-46; Acts 9: 36-43; 20:9-12.) Such persons pass through the natural or temporal death twice. In due course, also, all men will be raised from the dead and live in an immortal state. (Alma 11:41; 12:8.)

There is no fear of death in the hearts of the righteous. True, they properly seek to live as long as the Lord will permit them so to do. When the time of departure comes, they go in peace. But with the wicked it is not so, for "the sting of death is sin." (1 Cor. 15:56.) "Those that die in me shall not taste of death," the Lord says, "for it shall be sweet unto them; And they that die not in me, wo unto them, for their death is bitter." (D. & C. 42:46-47; Alma 40:23-26.)

DEBATES.
See CONTENTION. Except under very unusual circumstances, *debates* play no part in the approved system of presenting the message of salvation to the world or of persuading members of the Church to accept a particular doctrine or view. Almost always a debate entrenches each contestant and his sympathizers more firmly in the views already held. "Debates, envyings, wraths, strifes, backbitings, whisperings, swellings, tumults"—all these Paul describes as evil. (2 Cor. 12:20; Rom. 1:29.)

Rather, the Lord has directed, the elders are to "declare glad tidings," that is, explain, expound, and teach the message of the restoration. "And thou shalt do it with all humility," he directs, "trusting in me, *reviling not against revilers. And of tenets thou shalt not talk.*" (D. & C. 19:29-31.) There are to be no arguments about peculiar doctrinal concepts that people may have; the elders are simply to explain their message and bear testimony of its truthfulness.

If a situation arises in which the elders cannot in honor refuse a challenge to debate an issue, as when by withdrawing from the discussion they would lose their investigators, then it may be proper to go ahead and engage in the debate or discussion. In such instances, if the elders are as informed as they should be, they always come off victorious. The truth is with the saints, and truth will stand of its own self.

DEBT.
See CHURCH WELFARE PLAN, USURY. 1. Speaking of the eternal plan of salvation, all men are and ever will be *indebted* to Christ for all that they have and are. As King Benjamin said: "In the first place, he hath created you, and granted unto you your lives, for which ye are indebted unto him. And secondly, he doth require that ye should do as he hath commanded you; for which if ye do, he doth immediately bless you; and therefore he hath paid you. And ye are still indebted unto him, and are, and will be, forever and ever." (Mosiah 2:23-24.)

In lesser degrees, men are in-

debted for various great blessings to their parents, to the church officers who serve them, to the missionaries who brought them the gospel, to friends who succor them in time of need, to the martyrs of freedom, and to all those who have poured out their strength and energy in marking this wicked world a better place in which to live.

2. Speaking of financial *indebtedness* to other men, the standing counsel of the Church is that the saints, ever and always, should seek to be free from debt.

Financially indebted persons usually are yoked down with the burden of interest payments. President J. Reuben Clark, Jr., said in a General Conference of the Church: "Interest never sleeps nor sickens nor dies; it never goes to the hospital; it works on Sundays and holidays; it never takes a vacation; it never visits nor travels; it takes no pleasure; it is never laid off work nor discharged from employment; it never works on reduced hours; it never has short crops nor droughts; it never pays taxes; it buys no food; it wears no clothes; it is unhoused and without home and so has no repairs, no replacements, no shingling, plumbing, painting, or whitewashing; it has neither wife, children, father, mother, nor kinfolk to watch over and care for; it has no expense of living; it has neither weddings nor births nor deaths; it has no love, no sympathy; it is as hard and soulless as a granite cliff. Once in debt, interest is your companion every minute of the day and night; you cannot shun it or slip away from it; you cannot dismiss it; it yields neither to entreaties, demands, or orders; and whenever you get in its way or cross its course or fail to meet its demands, it crushes you." (Conf. Rep., Apr., 1938, p. 103.)

President Joseph F. Smith gave this direction as to how to get out of debt: "One of the best ways that I know of to pay my obligations to my brother, my neighbor, or business associate, is for me first to pay my obligations to the Lord. I can pay more of my debts to my neighbors, if I have contracted them, after I have met my honest obligations with the Lord, than I can by neglecting the latter; and you can do the same. *If you desire to prosper, and to be free men and women and a free people, first meet your just obligations to God, and then meet your obligations to your fellowmen.*" (*Gospel Doctrine*, 5th ed., pp. 259-260.)

DECEITFULNESS.
  See LIARS.

DECEIVINGS.
  See SIGNS OF THE TIMES.

DECEPTION.
  See LIARS.

DECREES.
See COMMANDMENTS.

DEDICATION.
See DEVOTION.

DEDICATION OF BUILDINGS.
See DEDICATION OF GRAVES, MEETINGHOUSES, PRAYER, TEMPLES. It is the practice of the Church to *dedicate* to the Lord all temples, meetinghouses, schools, welfare buildings, and other structures which are prepared for use in carrying out the great programs of the Church. Not infrequently individual members of the Church also dedicate to the cause of righteousness their own homes, and occasionally even their business enterprises.

The essential part of any dedicatory service is the formal prayer of dedication. In general the purpose is to hallow and consecrate the building for the particular purpose for which it was constructed. Temples and meetinghouses, being houses of worship, are given to the Lord as his houses. Dedication of private homes normally includes petitions for special blessings upon the members of the family and covenants on their part to serve the Lord and use the means at their disposal for the rolling forth of his work. No building is ever dedicated unless it is free from debt.

DEDICATION OF GRAVES.
See CREMATION, DEATH, FUNERALS, GRAVES, MOURNING. It is the accepted practice of the Church —based on precedent and guided by the spirit of revelation in those whom God has chosen to lead the Church—to dedicate the graves of faithful saints who depart this life. *Dedication of graves* is an ordinance of the gospel and is performed in the name of Christ and in the authority of the Melchizedek Priesthood. The dedicatory prayer should contain such expressions of thanksgiving, such words of comfort to the bereaved, such assurances (or petitions) for the protecting care of Divine Providence over the grave as the Spirit may indicate to the one performing the dedication.

Graveside prayers, which do not involve the exercise of the Melchizedek Priesthood, and which merely recite expressions of thanksgiving and request such petitions as seem proper, are sometimes offered instead of dedicatory prayers. If bodies are cremated, funeral services may of course be held, but the disposition of the ashes would normally make unnecessary the offering of either a dedicatory or graveside prayer.

DEDICATORY PRAYERS.
See PRAYER.

DEGREES OF GLORY.
See KINGDOMS OF GLORY.

DEISM.
See ATHEISM, GOD, HENOTHEISM, MONOTHEISM, POLYTHEISM, THEISM. *Deism* is the partial acceptance of God, that is, deists profess to believe in him as the Creator of the world and the final judge of men, but they reject the idea that he rules over or guides men during the interval between the creation and the judgment. Deists assert a disbelief in Christianity.

DEITY.
See GOD, FALSE GODS. As commonly used by Christian peoples, *Deity* means *God,* with no attempt being made to distinguish between the personages of the Father, Son, or Holy Ghost. The word deity itself connotes a condition of divinity, or of divine nature or rank. References to other than the true and living God are ordinarily couched in such expressions as *pagan deities, false deities, or tribal deities.*

DELIVERER.
See CHRIST, KING, MESSIAH, REDEEMER, SAVIOR. Christ is the *Deliverer* (2 Sam. 22:1-4; Ps. 18:1-3; 40:17; 70:5), a designation akin to Savior or Redeemer. Some references to him as the Deliverer lay stress on temporal deliverance from present enemies (Ps. 144:1-2), and this seems to have been the concept firmly lodged in the popular mind in the day of his mortal ministry. What the ancient Jews failed to realize was that any temporal deliverance effected by him was but symbolical of the far greater spiritual redemption to be effected when the great Deliverer, through his atoning sacrifice, turned away ungodliness from those in Jacob who accepted him as their Redeemer. (Isa. 59:20-21; Rom. 11:25-26.)

DELUSION.
See APOSTASY, HALLUCINATIONS. Almost the whole modern world is enveloped in a state of apostasy, darkness, and *delusion.* This is the day of which Paul wrote: "God shall send them strong delusion, that they should believe a lie: That they all might be damned who believed not the truth, but had pleasure in unrighteousness." (2 Thess. 2:11-12.)

Modern delusion is not limited to what is generally classified as the religious field; it is found in social, philosophical, political, and governmental realms, and in the speculative and theoretical parts of modern sciences. Every false belief, no matter where found, is a delusion; every belief and philosophy of whatever nature that leads men away from God, the gospel, and the principles of freedom which appertain to these, is a delusion.

DEMIGOD.

See GOD. By adding the prefix *demi,* meaning *half,* to the word *God* gives us the title *demigod,* meaning literally *half-god.* Accordingly in pagan religions a demigod is assumed to be a divine or semi-divine being who is the offspring of a deity and a mortal. The interesting thing about this is that there are so many pagan legends in which gods are supposed to have cohabited with mortals with offspring of one kind or another being brought forth. Obviously these beliefs, encountered among apostate peoples, had their origin in the true account, first revealed to Adam, that God in due course would father his Only Begotten in the flesh.

DEMOCRACY IN THE CHURCH.

See COMMON CONSENT.

DEMONS.

See DEVIL, DEVILS, WAR IN HEAVEN. Devils are *demons,* the spirit beings cast out of heaven for rebellion. (Rev. 12:7-9.) "We are surrounded by demons," the wicked Nephites cried, "yea, we are encircled about by the angels of him who hath sought to destroy our souls." (Hela. 13:37.) *Demonism* is belief in demons; a *demoniac* is one thought to be possessed of an evil spirit.

DENOMINATIONS.

See SECTS.

DENTISTS.

See PHYSICIANS.

DEPENDENT BRANCHES.

See BRANCHES.

DEPRESSION.

See SIGNS OF THE TIMES.

DESERET.

See BOOK OF MORMON, JAREDITES. *Deseret* is the Jaredite name for honey bee. (Ether 2:3.) Brigham Young and his followers first named their new intermountain empire the *territory of Deseret* after this unique Book of Mormon name. The name has since been applied to many businesses and enterprises in the Utah area, and the beehive, as a symbol of industry, is part of the great seal of the state of Utah.

DESERET INDUSTRIES.

See WELFARE PLAN. One of the agencies of the Church Welfare Plan, *deseret industries* is a business enterprise designed to provide employment and aid in the economic rehabilitation and support of persons who have suffered economic reverses. Commercial items are manufactured, repaired, and sold on the retail market through various deseret industry stores.

DESERET SUNDAY SCHOOL UNION.

See SUNDAY SCHOOL.

DESIRE OF ALL NATIONS.

See CHRIST, DESIRES, SECOND COMING OF CHRIST. Christ is the *Desire of All Nations.* "For thus saith the Lord of hosts; Yet once, it is a little while, and I will shake the heavens, and the earth, and the sea, and the dry land; And I will shake all nations, and the desire of all nations shall come." (Hag. 2: 5-9; Heb. 12:25-29.) This prophecy has reference to the Second Coming of Christ. It is true that there may be a few righteous saints in all nations who will be looking forward with desire for the return of their Lord, but the nations of peoples as a whole will not have any such desires. The meaning of the promise, as the marginal reading shows, is that our Lord's return will bring *desirable things* for the nations.

DESIRES.

See COVETOUSNESS, DESIRE OF ALL NATIONS. In the eternal perspective, men are rewarded according to their *desires.* Righteous desires lead to peace here and salva-

tion hereafter; lustful desires guarantee sorrow, remorse of conscience and final damnation. (2 Chron. 15: 1-15; Ps. 37:4; Eph. 2:3; Alma 29: 4-5; 41:5-6.)

The whole doctrine of salvation for the dead is based on the principle that men will be judged according to the desires of their hearts; that is, if in this life they do not have opportunity to live a law and gain a blessing, yet by virtue of certain vicarious performances the blessing will be gained by those whose desires are right. (*Teachings,* p. 107.)

DESOLATIONS.

See SIGNS OF THE TIMES.

DESPAIR.

See CHEERFULNESS, HOPE, INIQUITY, REJOICING. *Despair* is a feeling of hopelessness and futility, a feeling that there is no chance for continued progression, or forgiveness, or salvation. The Spirit of the Lord sheds forth cheerfulness and hope; the spirit of the devil casts men into despair and despondency. "And if ye have no hope ye must needs be in despair; and *despair cometh because of iniquity.*" (Moro. 10:22.) Though the saints may be perplexed, they are not in despair. (2 Cor. 4:8.)

DESPONDENCY.

See DESPAIR.

191

DESTINY.

See FOREORDINATION.

DESTROYER.

See ABADDON, APOLLYON, DESTRUCTION OF THE SOUL, DEVIL. This name for Satan signifies that his great labor is to destroy the souls of men. Incident thereto he rejoices in bringing to pass temporal, spiritual, and mental ruin and waste of all degrees. William W. Phelps, in daylight vision, saw the *destroyer* riding in power upon the face of the Missouri River; and thereupon the Lord revealed to the Prophet the perils to be wrought upon the waters in the last days by the destroyer. (D. & C. 61.)

DESTRUCTION OF THE SOUL.

See ANNIHILATION, DESTROYER, HELL, SOUL, SPIRITUAL DEATH. Souls of the wicked are *destroyed,* meaning that they enter the wide gate and traverse the broad way leading to hell. (Matt. 7:13-14; 10: 28; Rom. 9:22; Philip. 3:19; 1 Thess. 1:9; 2 Pet. 2:1; 3:16; Alma 5:7; 12:6, 16, 36; 3 Ne. 14:13-14.) The *destruction of the soul* consists in the inheritance of spiritual death in hell and not in the annihilation of the spirit. There is no such thing in all the economy of God as a soul or spirit ceasing to exist as such. (*Doctrines of Salvation,* vol. 2, pp. 227-228.)

By definition, "the death of the spirit" is for the spirit to die as to

things pertaining to righteousness and consequently reap the damnation of hell. (2 Ne. 9:10-12.) Utter spiritual *ruin* is thus imposed upon the soul; it is a *lost soul,* one that has not filled the measure of its creation. Lucifer's self-imposed mission is to destroy the souls of men (D. & C. 10:27), and his own ultimate destruction will come when he and his angels are cast into the lake of fire. (D. & C. 19:3; 2 Ne. 9:16.)

DEVIL.

See ABADDON, ADVERSARY, AGENCY, ANGEL OF THE BOTTOMLESS PIT, APOLLYON, BEELZEBUB, BELIAL, CAIN, CHURCH OF THE DEVIL, COMMON ENEMY, DEMONS, DESTROYER, DEVILS, DRAGON, EVIL ONE, GOD OF THIS WORLD, HELL, LUCIFER, MASTER MAHAN, PERDITION, PRINCE OF DEVILS, PRINCE OF POWER OF THE AIR, PRINCE OF THIS WORLD, SATAN, SERPENT, SON OF THE MORNING, SONS OF BELIAL, SONS OF PERDITION, SPIRITUAL DEATH, TEMPTER. The *devil* (literally meaning *slanderer*) is a spirit son of God who was born in the morning of pre-existence. (D. & C. 76:25-26.) Endowed with agency, the free power of choice, he chose the evil part from the beginning, thus placing himself in eternal opposition to the divine will. He was "a liar from the beginning." (D. & C. 93:25.)

Obviously he gained for himself great executive and administrative ability and had a sufficiently compelling personality to influence for ill a myriad host of other spirit offspring of the Father. His position was one of great power and authority. He was "an angel of God" who "became a devil, having sought that which was evil before God." (2 Ne. 2:17; D. & C. 76:25.)

When the plan of salvation was presented—the plan whereunder the spirit children of the Father would be enabled to gain tangible bodies and, if faithful in all things, progress to a like status with their Father—and when the need for a Redeemer was explained, Satan offered to come into the world as the Son of God and be the Redeemer. "Behold, here am I, send me," he said. "I will be thy son." But then, as always, he was in opposition to the full plan of the Father, and so he sought to amend and change the terms of salvation; he sought to deny men their agency and to dethrone God. "I will redeem all mankind, that one soul shall not be lost, and surely I will do it; wherefore give me thine honor," he continued. (Moses 4:1-4.)

With the rejection of his offer and the choosing of the Beloved Son to be the Redeemer, Satan made open warfare against the Lord. "Wherefore, because that Satan rebelled against me, and sought to destroy the agency of man, which I, the Lord God, had given him, and also, that I should give unto him mine own power; by the power of mine Only Begotten, I caused that he should be cast down; And he became Satan, yea, even the devil, the father of all lies, to deceive and to blind men, and to lead them captive at his will, even as many as would not hearken unto my voice." (Moses 4:3-4.) "A third part of the hosts of heaven" joined the rebellion; "And they were thrust down, and thus came the devil and his angels." (D. & C. 29:36-38; Rev. 12:4-9; Abra. 3:27-28.)

Those thus cast out are denied bodies forever. They are sons of perdition, and with Lucifer, their father, they are in eternal opposition to all righteousness. By them all men are tempted, enticed, and encouraged to leave the paths of truth, walk in darkness, and become carnal, sensual, and devilish. (Moses 6:49.) This opposition is used by the Lord, as part of his plan, to test and try men. In mortality the overcoming of opposition is an essential part of progression and advancement. (2 Ne. 2.)

One of Satan's greatest aims, as he works his nefarious schemes among men, is to get them "to worship him." (Moses 1:12; 6:49.) His success in this venture is phenomenal. As the god of this world, he has the support and, though they may not consciously realize it, the adoration and worship of all those who live after the manner of the world. God our Father is worshiped in and through compliance with his commandments and in no other way. The same is true of Satan.

As the organization through which formal adoration may be given him, Satan has founded his own church, the church of the devil, the "church which is most abominable above all other churches." (1 Ne. 13; 14; Rev. 17; 18.) Nephi says: "I beheld this great and abominable church; and I saw the devil that he was the foundation of it." (1 Ne. 13:6.) Of those adhering to this apostate organization, John says, "They worshipped the dragon" (Rev. 13:4), that is, the devil. False worship is worship of devils, as Paul said, "The things which the Gentiles sacrifice, they sacrifice to devils, and not to God: and I would not that ye should have fellowship with devils." (1 Cor. 10:20; Rev. 2:9; 9: 20.)

Satan's influence is also manifest in the world through governmental powers, particularly those in which dictatorship and compulsion are the rule. Political philosophies, as those which spread communistic and socialistic ideologies, are his propaganda vehicles. Those educational philosophies which deny Christ, and the divine origin of man as an offspring of God, are spawned and sponsored by Satan. Secret combinations, evil oath-bound organizations, criminal gangs, and groups of every sort which run counter to the principles of the gospel of salvation, are organizations founded, sponsored, and used by the devil.

Unfortunately, because even the worst and most evil organizations have some truth and good in them (otherwise they could not continue to prosper even under worldly conditions), even some of the "very elect" are deceived to the point that they support aims and programs of these devil-born groups. But "God hath said a man being evil cannot do that which is good; . . . For behold, a bitter fountain cannot bring forth good water; neither can a good fountain bring forth bitter water; wherefore, a man being a servant of the devil cannot follow Christ; and if he follow Christ he cannot be a servant of the devil." (Moro. 7:5-20.)

In decrying the teachings of false ministers, "false apostles, deceitful workers," Paul said, "Satan himself is transformed into an angel of light. Therefore it is no great thing if his ministers also be transformed as the ministers of righteousness; whose end shall be according to their works." (2 Cor. 11:13-15; 2. Ne. 9:9.)

Korihor is an illustration of such false ministers. After being confounded by Alma, he said: "Behold, the devil hath deceived me; for he appeared unto me in the form of an angel, and said unto me: Go and reclaim this people, for they have all gone astray after an unknown God. And he said unto me: There is no God; yea, and he taught me that which I should say. And I have taught his words; and I taught them because they were pleasing unto the carnal mind; and I taught them, even until I had much success, insomuch that I verily believed that they were true; and for this cause I withstood the truth, even until I have brought this great curse upon me." (Alma 30:53.)

As part of the testing incident to mortal existence, man for the moment has forgotten the great truths which were commonplace to him in pre-existence. Thus Satan's power over men is a result of his superior knowledge. He does not, however, have intelligence. "Light and truth," which is intelligence, "forsake that evil one." (D. & C. 93:37.)

Shortly, when the millennial era arrives, Satan will be bound, and for a thousand years he will "deceive the nations no more." Thereafter, he will "be loosed a little season" (Rev. 20:2-3) to gather together the hosts of hell preparatory to "the battle of the great God," as a result of which he "and his armies shall be cast away into their own place, that they shall not have power over the saints any more at all." (D. & C. 88:114.)

In eternity, "they who are filthy shall be filthy still; wherefore, they who are filthy are the devil and his angels; and they shall go away into everlasting fire, prepared for them; and their torment is as a lake of fire and brimstone, whose flame ascendeth up forever and ever and has no end." (2 Ne. 9:16.)

DEVILISHNESS.
See CARNALITY, CORRUPTION, DEVIL, FALLEN MAN, MORTALITY,

SENSUALITY. All forms of wickedness, all rebellion and evil, are sponsored by the devil. Any degree of wickedness is a degree of *devilishness*. "He that committeth sin is of the devil." (1 John 3:8; Moro. 7:17.) Any persons over whom the devil has power, who subject themselves to him, who submit to his enticements (following the carnal and sensual allurements of the world), are devilish. Such was the status of Adam after his spiritual death and before he was born again to righteousness. When "he partook of the forbidden fruit and transgressed the commandment, . . . he became subject to the will of the devil, because he yielded unto temptation." (D. & C. 29:40.)

Abinadi defined the status of the wicked by saying: "They are carnal and devilish, and the devil has power over them; yea, even that old serpent that did beguile our first parents, which was the cause of their fall; which was the cause of all mankind becoming carnal, sensual, devilish, knowing evil from good, subjecting themselves to the devil." (Mosiah 16:3.)

DEVILS.
See DEMONS, DEVIL, EVIL SPIRITS, FALSE SPIRITS, PRE-EXISTENCE, PRINCE OF DEVILS, SONS OF BELIAL, SONS OF PERDITION. *Devils* are the spirit beings who followed Lucifer in his war of rebellion in pre-existence. They comprise one-third of those spirit children of the

Father who were destined to pass through a mortal probation on this earth. (D. & C. 29:36-41; Rev. 12:3-9.) They were cast down to earth, and have been forever denied physical bodies, a fact which causes them to seek habitation in the bodies of other persons. By the power of faith and the authority of the priesthood, devils are frequently cast out of such afflicted persons. (Mark 1:23-34; 16:15-17.)

As followers of Satan, who is Perdition, they are sons of perdition; they are demons, angels of the devil, his evil ministers and servants. (2 Ne. 9:9.) Their ultimate destiny is to go away into everlasting fire where "their torment is as a lake of fire and brimstone, whose flame ascendeth up forever and ever and has no end." (2 Ne. 9:16; D. & C. 29:28.)

DEVOLUTION.

See EVOLUTION. *Devolution* is the opposite of evolution; in the biological sense it means the degeneration of species. According to God's law there is no such thing as the development of higher forms of life from lower orders of creation anymore than lower orders degenerate from higher. In each instance living things bring forth after their own kind (Moses 2), each form of life remaining "in the sphere" in which God created it. (Moses 3:9.)

Speaking of the degrees of civilization and decency found within nations in successive ages, it is clear that there have been instances of great *national devolution* or degeneracy. The American Indians, in their tribal and degenerate state, were the descendants of the highly civilized Nephite civilization that prevailed on the American continent for nearly 200 years after the ministry of Christ in the Western Hemisphere. So-called cave men and the like were all degenerate descendants of the highly civilized men who peopled the earth beginning with Adam, the father of civilization.

DEVOTION.

See CONSECRATION, OBEDIENCE, RIGHTEOUSNESS, WORSHIP, ZEAL. True *devotion* consists in a man loving and worshiping Deity with all his heart, and with all his might, mind, and strength. It presupposes that he will keep the commandments, walk uprightly, serve in the Church with an eye single to the glory of God, and put first in his life the things of God's kingdom. True devotion to the end gives an absolute guarantee of eternal salvation.

DEVOUTNESS.

See DEVOTION.

DIARIES.

See JOURNALS.

DICTATORSHIP.
See KINGCRAFT.

DILIGENCE.
See DEVOTION, DUTY, ENDUR-
ING TO THE END, OBEDIENCE,
WORK, ZEAL. To endure to the end
requires *diligence*—that is, pure
dogged determination, persever-
ance, application to duty, zeal,
industry, heed to counsel. Continuing diligence in church service is a
mark of testimony, conversion, and
spiritual stability. "Be ye doers of
the word, and not hearers only."
(Jas. 1:22.)

DISASTERS.
See SIGNS OF THE TIMES.

DISCERNING OF SPIRITS.
See FALSE SPIRITS.

DISCERNMENT.
See EVIL, FALSE SPIRITS, GIFTS
OF THE SPIRIT, GOOD, LIGHT OF
CHRIST. To all men in some degree
and to the faithful saints in particular is given the spirit, gift, and power of *discernment*. This ability is
conferred upon people generally by
the operations of the light of Christ
(Moro. 7:12-18), but in addition the
faithful saints receive discerning
power through revelation from the
Holy Ghost. (D. & C. 63:41.)

In its most important aspect,
discernment is used to distinguish
between good and evil (Moro. 7:12-
18), between the righteous and the
wicked (D. & C. 101:95; Mal. 3:18;
3 Ne. 24:18), between the false or
evil spirits and those spirits who
truly manifest the things of God.
(D. & C. 46:23; 1 Cor. 12:10.) In
its fullest manifestation the gift of
the discerning of spirits is poured
out upon presiding officials in God's
kingdom; they have it given to
them to discern all gifts and all
spirits, lest any come among the
saints and practice deception. (D. &
C. 46:27.)

There is no perfect operation of
the power of discernment without
revelation. Thereby even "the
thoughts and intents of the heart"
are made known. (D. & C. 33:1;
Heb. 4:12.) Where the saints are
concerned—since they have received
the right to the constant companionship of the Holy Ghost—the
Lord expects them to discern, not
only between the righteous and the
wicked, but between false and true
philosophies, educational theories,
sciences, political concepts, and social schemes. Unfortunately, in
many instances, even good men
hearken to "the tradition of their
fathers" (D. & C. 93:39) and rely
on the learning of the world rather
than the revelations of the Lord,
so that they do not enjoy the full
play of the spirit of discernment.

DISCIPLES.
See APOSTLES, BELIEVERS,
BRETHREN, PROPHETS, SAINTS. 1.

Anyone who believes the doctrine, teachings, or philosophy of another and who follows that teacher is his *disciple*. He stands as a learner, a devotee of the one whose concepts he accepts. Thus we read of the disciples of John the Baptist (Mark 2:18; Luke 11:1; John 1:35; 3:25), of Moses (John 9:28), and of the Pharisees. (Mark 2:18.)

2. All the saints from the day of Adam to the present have been *disciples of Christ*. (Isa. 8:16; Matt. 27:57; John 19:38; Acts 9:36; 11:26.) Those who believe the false doctrines of Christendom consider themselves to be true disciples, yet by their false beliefs and evil works they are not so classed by Him whose judgment shall prevail.

Scriptural tests establishing true discipleship include: 1. Believing the true doctrines of Christ (Ether 4:10-12); 2. Obeying the principles of the gospel (John 8:31); 3. Having "love one to another" (John 13:35); 4. Accepting the message and aiding the work of the missionaries (D. & C. 84:87-91); and 5. Bringing forth works of righteousness. (John 15:4-8.)

3. The apostolic ministers chosen to labor among the Jews, and also those who rendered similar service among the Nephites, are called "the *twelve disciples*." (Matt. 20:17; 3 Ne. 19:4.)

DISCIPLINE.
See CHASTENING.

DISCOURSES.
See SERMONS.

DISEASES.
See DEATH, HEALINGS, HEALTH, PHYSICIANS, SIGNS OF THE TIMES, WORD OF WISDOM. Since the fall, man's body has been subject to *sickness and disease,* these being essential parts of the probationary experiences that go with mortality. We may suppose that for the first 2000 years of man's sojourn on earth that diseases and bodily illness were far less prevalent than has been the case since. During that early period man enjoyed a higher degree of physical perfection than he does now; his body was then so constituted as to resist plague, infection, and corruption, and to live for near 1000 years. (Moses 6; D. & C. 107:43-53.)

But since the day in which man's age was set by the Lord at threescore and ten (Ps. 90:10), disease germs and physical ills have been more effective in their attacks. Both the Bible and the Book of Mormon give many accounts of diseases and of healings by the power of faith. During the dark ages disease frequently reached plague proportions.

These same ills are still with us, and as medical science provides a cure for one afflication another takes its place. Indeed, one of the final great signs of the times, an event just preceding the Second Coming, is that "an overflowing scourge, . . . a desolating sickness shall cover the land." (D. & C. 45: 31.) During the millennium, however, disease will be utterly banished from the earth; man's body will then be changed so that no germ or plague can affect it; and there will be no death as we now know it. (D. & C. 101:23-31.)

Disease comes both because of failure to obey the laws of health and because of failure to keep the other commandments of God. Righteous persons frequently become ill and suffer bodily afflictions simply because they have been exposed to disease, and the contaminating germs have power over their bodies. Sometimes by faith the righteous escape plagues that are sweeping the land; and often, having become sick, the gift of healing restores the obedient to full physical well-being.

But when the Lord's people rebel, he sends diseases upon them. To disobedient Israel came this curse: "The Lord will smite thee with the botch of Egypt, and with the emerods, and with the scab, and with the itch, whereof thou canst not be healed. The Lord shall smite thee with madness, and blindness, and astonishment of heart. . . . The Lord will make thy plagues wonderful, and the plagues of thy seed, even great plagues, and of long continuance, and sore sicknesses, and of long continuance. Moreover he will bring upon thee all the diseases of Egypt, which thou wast afraid of, and they shall cleave unto thee.

Also every sickness, and every plague, which is not written in the book of this law, them will the Lord bring upon thee, until thou be destroyed." (Deut. 28:27-28, 59-61; Mosiah 17:16; Alma 15:3-5.) On the other hand, the promise was that by obedience all this would be avoided. (Ex. 15:26; Deut. 7:15; 28.)

DISFELLOWSHIPMENT.

See CHURCH COURTS, EXCOMMUNICATION. Transgressions which do not seem in mercy and justice to warrant excommunication may properly result in the lesser punishment of *disfellowshipment*. Under these circumstances the transgressor retains his membership in the Church, but the hand of fellowship is withdrawn, and the offender is denied full participation in the Church and the full blessings of the gospel. He is not admitted to priesthood meetings or to an assembly of church officers. He cannot hold any office in the Church or exercise his priesthood in any way. He may attend the public meetings of the Church (the same as a non-member may), but he is not entitled to speak, pray, partake of the sacrament or otherwise participate in any meeting. Following repentance and conformity to the standards of the Church, a disfellowshiped person may again receive the full blessings of the Church.

DISHONESTY.

See LIARS.

DISOBEDIENCE.

See CHILDREN OF DISOBEDI-
ENCE, OBEDIENCE, REBELLION.
Nonconformity to divine standards
of personal righteousness constitutes *disobedience.* All men are
either obedient or disobedient; they
either keep the commandments or
fail to do so; either neglect or refusal to conform to gospel standards classifies a person as a rebel.

Disobedience is of the devil.
"That wicked one cometh and taketh away light and truth, through
disobedience, from the children of
men, and because of the traditions
of their fathers." (D. & C. 93:39.)
By disobedience men gain membership in the kingdom of the devil, as
he operates it on earth, in the spirit
world, and among the resurrected
rebels of eternity. The most violent
and destructive of all disobedience
is the complete and open rebellion
against light and truth which makes
a person a son of perdition. Those
who love darkness rather than
light, their deeds being evil, "receive their wages of whom they list
to obey." (D. & C. 29:45.)

DISPENSATION OF THE FUL-NESS OF TIMES.

See CHURCH OF JESUS CHRIST
OF LATTER-DAY SAINTS, DISPENSA-
TIONS, GOSPEL, JOSEPH SMITH THE
PROPHET, KEYS OF THE KINGDOM,
NEW AND EVERLASTING COVE-
NANT, PRIESTHOOD, RESTORATION
OF THE GOSPEL, REVELATION,
SECOND COMING OF CHRIST, SIGNS
OF THE TIMES. The final great dispensation of the gospel is known
as the *dispensation of the fulness
of times,* or in other words the time
of the fulness of times, or the dispensation of the fulness of dispensations. That is, as rivers flow into
an ocean, all the dispensations of
the past flow into this final great
dispensation. It is the time, age,
or era which is made up of all the
dispensations of the earth's history. It is the age in which the
Lord will "gather together in one all
things in Christ, both which are
in heaven, and which are on earth."
(Eph. 1:10; D. & C. 27:13.)

Every key, power, and authority
ever dispensed from heaven to men
on earth, which is necessary for
their eternal salvation, has already
been restored in this dispensation.
(D. & C. 110:11-16; 112:14-32; 128:
18-21.) All of the knowledge that
has ever been revealed (plus some
held in reserve to be revealed
initially in the last days) will in
due course come to light in this
final dispensation. (D. & C. 101:32-
34; 121:26-32; 124:41; 128:18.)

DISPENSATIONS.

See CHURCH OF JESUS CHRIST OF
LATTER-DAY SAINTS, DISPENSATION
OF THE FULNESS OF TIMES, GOS-
PEL, NEW AND EVERLASTING COVE-
NANT, PRIESTHOOD, REVELATION.
Gospel *dispensations* are those per-
iods of time during which the Lord
reveals or dispenses the doctrines
of the gospel to men so that reliance

need not be placed on past ages for this saving knowledge. If the priesthood and keys have not come down by proper descent from a previous dispensation, these also must necessarily be conferred upon men again by the opening of the heavens.

Since the gospel, "the power of God unto salvation" (Rom. 1:16), was first revealed to Adam, we speak of the *Adamic dispensation* as the first from the standpoint of time. (Moses 5:57-59.) Thereafter, the saving knowledge and powers of the gospel, as Paul expressed it, were "revealed from faith to faith" (Rom. 1:17), that is from era of faith to era of faith or from dispensation to dispensation.

In the providences of the Almighty, Adam stands at the head of all dispensations, he being the presiding high priest (under Christ) over all the earth. (*Teachings,* pp. 157-158.) "Adam holds the keys of the dispensation of the fulness of times; i.e., the dispensation of *all the times* have been and will be revealed through him from the beginning to Christ, and from Christ to the end of the dispensations that are to be revealed. . . . This, then, is the nature of the priesthood; every man holding the presidency of his dispensation, and *one man holding the presidency of them all, even Adam;* and Adam receiving his presidency and authority from the Lord." (*Teachings,* pp. 167-169.) It appears that Abel, acting under the direction of his father Adam, held the keys of the first dispensation.

(*Teachings,* p. 169.)

When we speak of the great gospel dispensations, we generally have in mind those given to *Adam, Enoch* (Moses 6; 7), *Noah* (Moses 8), *Abraham* (Abra. 2:6-11; Gal. 3:6-8, 18), *Moses* (D. & C. 84:17-28); the *apostles* in the meridian of time (Matt. 16:18-19; 18:18; D. & C. 27:12-13; 128:20), and to *Joseph Smith* and his associates. (D. & C. 112:14-32.) The keys and powers exercised by the Lord's prophets in each of these ancient dispensations have been conferred upon men in this final dispensation, for in "the fulness of times," the Lord says, "I will gather together in one all things, both which are in heaven, and which are on earth." (D. & C. 27:13; Eph. 1:10.)

But there have also been many other gospel dispensations in the course of the Lord's dealings with his children. It is very evident that *John the Baptist* (Luke 7:24-30; John 1:19-37; D. & C. 84:26-28), the *Jaredites* (Ether 1:41-43; 3:6-16), the *Nephites* (1 Ne. 2:2-4), *Lehi and Nephi* who lived at the time of the coming of the Savior (Hela. 10:3-17; 11:19-23; 3 Ne. 7:15-19; 9: 15-22; 11:7-40), and the *Ten Tribes* whom Christ visited after his resurrection (3 Ne. 16:1-4) all had dispensations of the gospel. (*Doctrines of Salvation,* vol. 1, pp. 160-164.)

We know that Esaias, Gad, Jeremy, Elihu, Caleb, and Jethro all lived between Abraham and Moses and all enjoyed the fulness of the blessings of the gospel. (D. & C.

84:6-13.) What peoples they ministered to and whether they had dispensations of the gospel are truths yet to be revealed. Paul speaks of having a dispensation of the gospel (1 Cor. 9:17; Eph. 3:2; Col. 1:25), but apparently this is only in the sense that present day apostles have received one, in that the Lord has given them revelation of his mind and will, and in that they hold the keys of the dispensation in which they live. (D. & C. 112:14-32.)

DISPUTATIONS.
   See CONTENTION.

DISSENTERS.
   See APOSTASY.

DISSENTIONS.
   See CONTENTION.

DISTRICT PRESIDENCY.
   See DISTRICT PRESIDENTS.

DISTRICT PRESIDENTS.
   See DISTRICTS, MISSIONS, STAKE PRESIDENTS. Presiding officers in foreign mission districts are *district presidents*. They hold the keys of their ministry, are assisted by two counselors (thus forming a *district presidency*), and are comparable to stake presidents in their sphere of service. In the stake missions, those

chosen to preside over areas of the mission and to supervise the proselyting labors of their fellow missionaries are also called *district presidents*.

DISTRICTS.
   See BRANCHES, CHURCH ORGANIZATION, MISSIONS, STAKES. Missions are divided into ecclesiastical areas called *districts*. In stake and regional missions these areas are merely locales in which the proselyting work is carried forward. In foreign missions they are comparable to stake areas and are presided over by a district president. The church programs normally carried on in the stakes are, insofar as possible, made available to the saints living in the districts.
   Temple districts are church areas made up of a number of stakes and/or missions whose members are asked to perform their temple ordinances in an assigned temple.

DIVINATION.
   See FORTUNE TELLING, NECROMANCY, OCCULTISM, PROPHECY, SORCERY, WITCHCRAFT. True religion provides for a revelation of future events by prophets sent of God. False religions—whose ministers have no communion with Deity —frequently imitate the true practice by engaging in *divination*. This practice is an attempt to foretell the future by augeries, omens,

presages, or forebodings. Among primitive peoples it frequently meant interpreting dreams or other signs or seeking peculiarities in the entrails of sacrificial victims. A *diviner* is one who attempts to foretell the future by divination. Soothsayers act by the "spirit of divination." (Acts 16:16-18.) The Lord's people are commanded not to engage in divination of any sort. (Deut. 18:9-14.)

DIVINERS.

See DIVINATION.

DIVINITY.

See GODHOOD.

DIVORCE.

See CANCELLATION OF SEALINGS, CELESTIAL MARRIAGE, CIVIL MARRIAGE. In the gospel view all marriages should be eternal, and *divorce* should never enter the picture. But since all men—as a result of apostasy and iniquity—are not living (and in their present states cannot live) the full and perfect gospel law, the Lord permits divorce and allows the dissolution of the marriage union. Under the law of Moses, divorce was permitted because the people were not able to live the high gospel standard which would abolish it. (Lev. 21:7, 14; Deut. 24:1-4.)

As revealed both to the Jews and to the Nephites, the terms of the perfect marriage system include this teaching: "It hath been written, that whosoever shall put away his wife, let him give her a writing of divorcement. Verily, verily, I say unto you, that whosoever shall put away his wife, saving for the cause of fornication, causeth her to commit adultery; and whoso shall marry her who is divorced committeth adultery." (3 Ne. 12:31-32; Matt. 5:31-32.)

When the Pharisees raised the divorce issue to tempt him, our Lord taught them the eternity of the marriage covenant, ("What therefore God hath joined together, let not man put asunder"), told them that Moses permitted divorce because of the hardness of their hearts, but explained that from the beginning it had not been so ordained. Then it appears he went into the house and gave special and added instruction to "his disciples." For them the law was: "Whosoever shall put away his wife, and marry another, committeth adultery against her. And if a woman shall put away her husband, and be married to another, she committeth adultery." (Mark 10:2-12.) Also to his disciples he said: "All men cannot receive this saying, save they to whom it is given. . . . He that is able to receive it, let him receive it." (Matt. 19:3-12; *Doctrines of Salvation,* vol. 2, pp. 80-85.)

Even in the Church today the saints do not abide by the full and perfect law. It is somewhat as it was in the days of Moses; divorce is permitted because of the hardness of the hearts of the people, and the Lord permits his agents to exercise the power to loose as well as the power to bind. Under our circumstances divorced persons who remarry are not always guilty of the crimes they would be if the highest gospel standards were in force.

DOCTORS.
See PHYSICIANS.

DOCTRINE.
See ARTICLES OF FAITH, CREEDS, GOSPEL, SALVATION, SERMONS, TRUTH. *Doctrines* are teachings. They are classified as true or false. *True doctrines* come from God, the source and fountain of all truth, and are the teachings and concepts found in the gospel. *False doctrines* are from beneath. Their effect is to pervert, change, and alter revealed truth, so that by obeying false directions men will fall short of salvation in the celestial world.

True doctrines are always found in the Lord's true Church because the channel of communication between God and his people is open. False doctrines abound in churches which deny contemporary revelation and consequently have no sure way of checking various views and concepts to see if they conform to the mind and will of Deity. There is, of course, much truth in all churches, but those churches which do not have the fulness of the gospel, have much error and falsehood intermingled with such truths as they happen to have. And the fulness of salvation can come to those only who believe and conform to the fulness of the Lord's revealed doctrines.

Gospel doctrine is synonymous with the truths of salvation. It comprises the tenets, teachings, and true theories found in the scriptures; it includes the principles, precepts, and revealed philosophies of pure religion; prophetic dogmas, maxims, and views are embraced within its folds; the Articles of Faith are part and portion of it, as is every inspired utterance of the Lord's agents.

The doctrines of salvation are recorded in the scriptures. (2 Tim. 3: 14-17.) The Book of Mormon has come forth in this day so that men might "learn doctrine." (Isa. 29:24; 2 Ne. 27:35.) The Bible and the Book of Mormon "shall grow together, unto the confounding of false doctrines." (2 Ne. 3:12.) So that the "true points" of the Lord's doctrine might be known again, the gospel has been restored (D. & C. 10:62); and these true points of doctrine are now found in the true Church. (D. & C. 11:16.) The true doctrine of Christ is that all men must come unto him, gain faith, repent, be baptized, receive the Holy Ghost, and endure in faith to the end in order to gain salvation. (2 Ne. 31:17-21; 3 Ne. 11:29-41; D. & C. 10:67; 68:25.)

Conversion to the truth comes by accepting true doctrine. (1 Ne. 15:15; 3 Ne. 21:6.) Those so converted are expected to "speak . . . by doctrine" (1 Cor. 14:6); to "teach one another the doctrine of the kingdom" (D. & C. 88:77); to "be perfected in the understanding of their ministry, in theory, in principle, and in doctrine" (D. & C. 97:14); to "act in doctrine" (D. & C. 101:78); and to learn more doctrine by revelation from heaven. (D. & C. 121:45-46.)

In the final analysis the truth of doctrine can only be known by revelation gained as a result of obedience. "My doctrine is not mine, but his that sent me," our Lord proclaimed. "If any man will do his will, he shall know of the doctrine, whether it be of God, or whether I speak of myself." (John 7:16-17.)

Apostles and prophets have been set in the Church for the purpose of teaching and identifying true doctrine, lest men be "tossed to and fro, and carried about with every wind of doctrine." (Eph. 4:11-14.) If a church has no prophets and apostles, then it has no way of knowing whether its doctrines are true or false. "Whosoever transgresseth, and abideth not in the doctrine of Christ, hath not God. He that abideth in the doctrine of Christ, he hath both the Father and the Son." (2 John 9.)

False doctrine is of the devil (1 Tim. 4:1; D. & C. 10:63; 46:7), and men who preach it do so "for the sake of riches and honor." (Alma 1:16.) There is no salvation in believing or teaching false doctrines. "In vain they do worship me, teaching for doctrines the commandments of men." (Matt. 15:9; Mark 7:7; Jos. Smith 2:19.) An apostate age is identified as one in which men "will not endure sound doctrine." (2 Tim. 4:3.)

Apostasy is born of the teaching of false doctrine. Nephi described our present religious world by saying, "There shall be many which shall teach . . . false and vain and foolish doctrines," and by specifying that "Because of pride, and because of false teachers, and false doctrine, their churches have become corrupted." Speaking of the whole world, he said: "They have all gone astray save it be a few, who are the humble followers of Christ; nevertheless, *they are led, that in many instances they do err because they are taught by the precepts of men.*" Then he added this awful interdiction: *"And all those who preach false doctrines, . . . wo, wo, wo be unto them, saith the Lord God Almighty, for they shall be thrust down to hell!"* (2 Ne. 28:8-15.)

DOCTRINE AND COVENANTS.

See ARTICLE ON MARRIAGE, BIBLE, BOOK OF COMMANDMENTS, BOOK OF MORMON, COVENANTS, DOCTRINE, LECTURES ON FAITH, LOST SCRIPTURE, MANIFESTO, PEARL OF GREAT PRICE, REVELATION, SCRIPTURE, STANDARD

WORKS, URIM AND THUMMIM. That volume of latter-day scripture which contains selections from the revelations given to Joseph Smith and his successors in the Presidency of the Church is called the *Doctrine and Covenants.* Certain parts of these revelations were published in Independence, Missouri, in 1833 under the title *Book of Commandments,* but mob violence destroyed the printing press and stopped the work at that time. By 1835, however, a new and enlarged selection of revelations had been made by the Prophet, and the first edition of the Doctrine and Covenants came off the press.

Thereafter, of course, written revelations continued to be received. After the saints came west, Elder Orson Pratt was commissioned and directed by the First Presidency to prepare an up-to-date edition of the Doctrine and Covenants for publication. This volume, the one now in use, containing additional revelations and being divided into sections and verses, was first published in 1876.

As now constituted the Doctrine and Covenants contains 136 sections or chapters to which are appended an Official Declaration, commonly called the *Manifesto.* Most of these sections came to Joseph Smith by direct revelation, the recorded words being those of the Lord Jesus Christ himself. (D. & C. 29.) The power of the Holy Ghost was manifest in the receipt of all the revelations. Some came

by the whisperings of the Spirit to the Prophet (D. & C. 20); some were received by means of the Urim and Thummim (D. & C. 3); others are the recorded words of angelic ministrants (D. & C. 2); others are accounts of visions (D. & C. 76); a few are inspired epistles of the Prophet (D. & C. 128); a few others contain inspired items of instruction (D. & C. 131); one is an article setting forth church beliefs relative to governments and laws in general (D. & C. 134); one is an inspired announcement of the martyrdom of the Prophet and patriarch (D. & C. 135); and, since its adoption in 1890, the Official Declaration (or Manifesto) of President Wilford Woodruff has been published in the Doctrine and Covenants.

Early editions of the Doctrine and Covenants also contained the Lectures on Faith and an article on marriage by Oliver Cowdery. These items were not revelations, were never so considered, and are no longer published in the same volume as the revelations. (*Doctrines of Salvation,* vol. 3, pp. 192-202.)

Perhaps no other book is of such great worth to the saints as is the Doctrine and Covenants. It is their book, the voice of God in their day. The revelations therein are true, and men are commanded to search them. (D. & C. 1:37-39.)

But all of the written revelations received in this day are not in this volume. The revelations setting forth the temple ordinances and other sacred matters are not published to the world. Many revelations were received by the Prophet for individuals, and these are not included in the published record. There are some accounts of visions and revelations recorded in the *History of the Church* which are not published with the Doctrine and Covenants. On January 21, 1836, for instance, the Prophet saw in vision the Father and the Son in the celestial kingdom and heard the voice of God make the great proclamation relative to salvation for the dead. (*Teachings,* p. 107.) President Joseph F. Smith and others of the Presidents of the Church have received written revelations since the day of the Prophet which have been accepted by their brethren but never ordered published with the Doctrine and Covenants. (*Gospel Doctrine,* 5th ed., pp. 472-477.)

DOCTRINE OF ELIAS.
See ELIAS.

DOGMAS.
See DOCTRINE.

DOLE.
See ALMSGIVING, CHURCH WELFARE PLAN, EMPLOYMENT, IDLENESS, WORK. Attempts to gain one's temporal livelihood by means of a *dole*—that is, through charitable gifts of money or food—either from the government, the Church, or some other social organization, violate the divine command that men should work for what they get and that the idler should not eat the bread nor wear the garment of the laborer. (Gen. 3:19; D. & C. 42: 42.) The practice of supporting the poor by means of a dole is not the Lord's way of caring for their temporal needs.

DOOMSDAY.
See JUDGMENT DAY.

DOOR.
See DOOR OF THE SHEEP.

DOOR OF THE SHEEP.
See CHRIST, GOOD SHEPHERD, KEEPER OF THE GATE, PERSONIFICATION; WAY, TRUTH, AND LIFE. Christ is the *Door,* or the *Door of the Sheep.* By so designating himself, he teaches that no one can enter his sheepfold either in time or in eternity without his approval. He personally stands ever on guard to reject the ungodly. (2 Ne. 9:41-43.) He is the *Way.* "By me if any man enter in, he shall be saved, and shall go in and out, and find pasture," he said. (John 10:7-9.)

DOUAY VERSION OF THE BIBLE.
See KING JAMES VERSION OF THE BIBLE.

DOUBT.

See BELIEF, FAITH. Where the gospel is concerned, *doubt* is an inclination to disbelieve the truths of salvation, a hesitancy to accept the revealed will of the Lord; it is a state of uncertainty in mind with reference to the doctrines of the gospel. Faith and belief are of God; doubt and skepticism are of the devil.

There is no excuse for not knowing and believing true principles for the Lord has ordained the way whereby all may come to a knowledge of the truth. Doubt comes from failure to keep the commandments. "O then despise not, and wonder not, but hearken unto the words of the Lord, and ask the Father in the name of Jesus for what things soever ye shall stand in need. *Doubt not, but be believing,* and begin as in times of old, and come unto the Lord with all your heart, and work out your own salvation with fear and trembling before him." (Morm. 9:27; Matt. 21:21.)

DRAGON.

See DEVIL, SERPENT. Dragons belong to the serpent family; they are fabulous monsters, often represented as winged serpents breathing fire. Traditionally fierce and relentless in combat, it is possible that later-age concepts of them grew from memories of the preflood dinosaurs. In any event, the term *dragon* was applied with great propriety by John to Satan. (Rev. 12; 13:2-4; 16:13; 20:2.) As the fiercest and most dreaded of serpents, the name is certainly appropriate for the most fierce and relentlessly wicked of all beings.

DREAMS.

See HOLY GHOST, REVELATION, TRANCES, VISIONS. An inspired *dream* is a vision given to a person while he sleeps. "Behold, I have dreamed a dream; or, in other words, I have seen a vision," Lehi said. (1 Ne. 8:2.) All inspired dreams are visions, but all visions are not dreams. Visions are received in hours of wakefulness or of sleep and in some cases when the recipient has passed into a trance; it is only when the vision occurs during sleep that it is termed a dream. (Isa. 29:17; Dan. 2; 7; 1 Ne. 1:16; Alma 30:28.)

As with other visions, inspired dreams foretell future events (Gen. 37:5; 40:5, 8; 41:15); the Lord appears to men in dreams (Gen. 28:10-22; 31:24; 1 Kings 3:5; 1 Ne. 2:1-2; 3:2); angels appear and minister to faithful persons in their dreams (Gen. 31:11; Matt. 1:20; 2:13, 19); prophetic warnings are given by this means (Ether 9:3); and symbolic representations portrayed in dreams teach marvelous truths. (1 Ne. 8; 9; 10; 15:21.) Inspired dreams are the fruit of faith; they are not given to apostate peoples. (1 Sam. 28:6, 15.)

DRUGS.

See WORD OF WISDOM.

DRUIDISM.

See GHOSTS, MAGIC, SORCERY, WITCHCRAFT. *Druidism* is one of the ancient apostate religions which, as far as is known, specialized in magic, conjuration, and the like. It prevailed during the dark ages in Britain, Ireland, and Gaul.

DRUNKENNESS.

See WORD OF WISDOM. *Drunkenness,* or intoxication in any degree, is an evil abomination in the sight of the Lord. "Cease drunkenness," is his decree. (D. & C. 136:24.) "Strong drinks are not for the belly, but for the washing of your bodies." (D. & C. 89:7.) The Second Coming shall catch the drunkards unawares to their destruction. (Luke 21:34.) They shall not be saved in the kingdom of God, unless, as is the case where all evils and abominations are concerned, they repent and walk soberly and uprightly before the Lord. (Gal. 5:19-21.) In a spiritual sense drunkenness means apostasy. (Isa. 29:9-10; Rev. 17:2; 18:3.)

DUST.

See DEATH, ELEMENTS, GRAVES. Those natural elements that make up the physical earth are sometimes referred to in the scriptures as *dust.* Thus Adam was created from the dust of the ground meaning that the physical body which he received was created from the elements of the earth. (Gen. 2:7; Moses 3:7; Abra. 5:7; D. & C. 77:12.) Similarly all men are created from the dust of the earth; that is, the elements organized into a mortal body are assembled together through the birth process. (Moses 6:69.)

Figuratively, dust means the *grave* or *death* as in such expressions as: "By the sweat of thy face shalt thou eat bread, until thou shalt return unto the ground—for thou shalt surely die—for out of it wast thou taken: for *dust thou wast, and unto dust shalt thou return.*" (Moses 4:25; Gen. 3:19.) "Sleep in the dust." (D. & C. 63:51; Job 7:21.) David's Messianic prophecy foretelling our Lord's death, says he should be brought "into the *dust of death*" (Ps. 22:15), though, as elsewhere prophesied (Ps. 16:10), the body of the Lord did not see corruption, that is, did not go back to the dust in the literal sense.

The Book of Mormon is, of course, repeatedly referred to in the scriptures as a *voice from the dust.* (Isa. 29:4; 2 Ne. 3:19-20; 26:15-16; 27:9; 33:13; Morm. 8:23-26; Moro. 10:27.) Such statements as, "Awake! and arise from the dust" (2 Ne. 1:14, 21, 23; Mosiah 4:2), are figures of speech, signifying that those addressed should rise above carnal, petty, groveling things and stand forth in the strength of the Spirit as men of character. Similar prophetic calls to Jerusalem to shake herself from the dust (2 Ne. 8:25; 3 Ne. 20:37; Moro. 10:31) are calls for her to come back from her downtrodden position of obscurity to the high eminence she should occupy in the eternal scheme of things. The Book of Mormon expression that men are "less than the dust of the earth," as the context shows, has reference to the fact that the dust is obedient to the commands of the Creator, whereas men rebel against his will.

DUST STORMS.
See SIGNS OF THE TIMES.

DUTY.
See DILIGENCE, OBEDIENCE,

THANKSGIVING. In consequence of the innumerable blessings showered upon them by their Creator and Redeemer, men are morally bound to conform their lives to the divine will. It is their *duty* to keep the commandments. (Eccles. 12:13; Luke 17:10.)

By entering into the various gospel covenants and accepting positions in the Church, they also assume specific obligations and duties in the performance of which they are enabled to work out their salvation. "Wherefore, now let every man learn his duty, and to act in the office in which he is appointed, in all diligence." (D. & C. 107:99-100.)

E

EARTH.
See CREATION, DUST, EARTHS, ELEMENTS, WORLD. This *earth* or planet which we inhabit was created as a place where we could gain our physical bodies and undergo the probation of mortality. Not only does it play an important part in the plan whereunder men may work out their salvation, but the earth itself is subject to certain laws of progression and salvation because of which it eventually will become a fit abode for exalted beings. This earth was created as a living thing, and the Lord ordained

that it should live a celestial law. It was baptized in water and will receive the baptism of fire; it will die, be resurrected and attain unto a state of celestial exaltation. In the course of its eternal existence, it is destined to pass through certain stages of existence. (*Doctrines of Salvation,* vol. 1, pp. 72-89; Parley P. Pratt, *Voice of Warning,* ch. 5.)

1. SPIRIT EARTH.—We may suppose, as is the case with all other forms of life, that this earth was created first as a spirit, and that it was thereafter clothed upon with

tangible, physical element. We know that the Creators planned all things incident to the creation in advance; and that all things were created "spiritually, before they were naturally upon the face of the earth." (Moses 3:5-9; Abra. 4:31; 5:3-5.)

2. EDENIC EARTH.—Following its physical creation, the earth was pronounced *good*. It was in a *terrestrial or paradisiacal* state. There was no death either for man or for any form of life, and "all the vast creation of animated beings breathed naught but health, and peace, and joy." (2 Ne. 2:22; *Voice of Warning,* pp. 89-91.)

3. TELESTIAL EARTH.—When Adam fell, the earth fell also and became a mortal sphere, one upon which worldly and carnal people can live. This condition was destined to continue for a period of 6,000 years, and it was while in this state that the earth was baptized in water. (D. & C. 77:6-7, 12; *Man: His Origin and Destiny,* pp. 415-436, 460-466.)

4. TERRESTRIAL EARTH.—"We believe . . . that the earth will be *renewed* and receive its *paradisiacal glory.*" (Tenth Article of Faith.) Thus, the earth is to go back to the primeval, paradisiacal, or terrestrial state that prevailed in the days of the Garden of Eden. Accompanying this transition to its millennial status the earth is to be burned, that is, receive its baptism of fire. It will then be a new heaven and a new earth, and again health, peace,

and joy will prevail upon its face. (D. & C. 101:23-32; Isa. 65:17-25; Mal. 3:1-6; 4:1-6; *Man: His Origin and Destiny,* pp. 380-397.)

5. CELESTIAL EARTH.—Following the millennium plus "a little season" (D. & C. 29:22-25), the earth will die, be resurrected, and becoming like a "sea of glass" (D. & C. 130:7), attain unto "its sanctified, immortal, and eternal state." (D. & C. 77:1-2.) Then the poor and the meek—that is, the godfearing and the righteous—shall inherit the earth; it will become an abiding place for the Father and the Son, and celestial beings will possess it forever and ever. (D. & C. 88:14-26, 111.)

EARTHQUAKES.

See EARTH, SIGNS OF THE TIMES. Since the earth has been in its present fallen or telestial state, it has been subject to *earthquakes*. These are part of the Lord's plan; they come by his power and fulfil his purposes. By them he delivers his servants from perils, destroys the wicked, and leaves a sign that his hand has been in transcendent events. (Hela. 12:7-17.)

Earthquakes attended the delivery from prison of Paul and Silas in the old world, of Lehi and Nephi in the new. (Acts 16:25-26; Hela. 5: 27.) Both the crucifixion and the resurrection of our Lord were attested by earthquakes. (Matt. 27:54; 28:2.) Among the Nephites the quakings and destructions at the time of the crucifixion were so extensive that the whole face of the land was changed and the wicked and rebellious were destroyed. (3 Ne. 8; 9:1-14; 10:9-10.)

Earthquakes are given as one of the signs of the times; they foreshadow the Second Coming. (Matt. 24:7; Mark 13:8; Luke 21:11; D. & C. 45:33; 87:6.) By them the testimony of the Lord's power is borne to the people of the earth. (D. & C. 43:25; 88:89), and when the glorious Second Coming itself arrives there will be "a great earthquake, such as was not since men were upon the earth, so mighty an earthquake, and so great." (Rev. 16:18-20; 6:12-17; 8:5; 11:12-15, 19; Zech. 14:4-5; D. & C. 133:22-25.)

EARTHS.
See EARTH. We are blessed with the knowledge that ours is not the only inhabited *earth.* Rather, Christ acting under the direction of the Father is the Creator of *worlds without number.* Moses was permitted to see many of these earths, to learn that they are inhabited by the spirit children of the Father, and to receive the revelation that it is the Lord's work and glory to bring to pass the immortality and eternal life of the inhabitants of all these earths. (Moses 1:27-41; D. & C. 76:22-24; John 1:1-5; Heb. 1:1-4; *Doctrines of Salvation,* vol. 1, pp. 72-74.) Our particular earth, the one to which Christ was sent to work out

the infinite and eternal atonement, has seen greater wickedness among her inhabitants than has been the case on any earth. (Moses 7:29-36.)

EASTER.
See ATONEMENT OF CHRIST, CHRIST, CHRISTMAS, PASSOVER, RESURRECTION. *Easter* is the church festival celebrated by Christians in commemoration of the resurrection of our Lord. The lone scriptural reference to it (Acts 12:4) should have been translated *Passover* from the Greek *pascha* found in the original. The name *Easter* comes from the Norse goddess *Eastre* whose festival was observed at the vernal equinox. In 325 A.D. the Council of Nicea determined that Easter among Christians should be celebrated the first Sunday after the full moon on or following the vernal equinox.

Obviously, Easter as now celebrated has come into being as a compromise between pagan and apostate Christian views, and obviously it does not pretend to be the anniversary of the actual resurrection of Christ. Nonetheless the true saints gladly take it as an appropriate occasion on which to turn their attentions to the infinite and eternal atonement of Christ as such was climaxed by his coming forth as the firstfruits of them that slept.

ECCLESIA.
See CHURCH.

ECONOMIC TURMOIL.
See SIGNS OF THE TIMES.

EDEN.
See GARDEN OF EDEN.

EDIFICATION.
See EDUCATION, GIFT OF THE HOLY GHOST, GOSPEL, KNOWLEDGE, LIGHT OF CHRIST, TEACHERS. *Edification* is education in uplifting and enlightening things. To edify a person is to teach, instruct, and benefit him in the moral and religious fields. Gospel principles and practices are designed to mellow and edify true believers so that they may become saints in very deed. It is the duty of the saints to "instruct and edify each other." (D. & C. 43:8; 84:106, 110; 136:24; 1 Thess. 5:11.)

Those who teach in church organizations are specifically commanded to speak so that "all may be edified." (D. & C. 88:122, 137.) Quorum officers are to edify those over whom they preside. (D. & C. 107:85.) Indeed, apostles, prophets, pastors, evangelists, teachers, and all church officers, have been appointed of God, "For the perfecting of the saints, for the work of the ministry, for the edifying of the body of Christ." (Eph. 4:11-16, 29.)

Things that are edifying are of God and lead to salvation; unedifying things are from beneath and lead to damnation. When the Spirit of the Lord is present, then "he that preacheth and he that receiveth, understand one another, and both are edified and rejoice together. *And that which doth not edify is not of God, and is darkness.*" (D. & C. 50:22-23.) "Charity edifieth." (1 Cor. 8:1.) "He that prophesieth speaketh unto men to edification, and exhortation, and comfort. He that speaketh in an unknown tongue edifieth himself; but he that prophesieth edifieth the church." (1 Cor. 14:3-4.) Unfortunately, there is much in the world in the way of teaching, doctrine, literature, music, art, and recreation that is not edifying and in consequence leads men away from righteousness.

EDUCATION.
See EDIFICATION, IGNORANCE, KNOWLEDGE, RELIGIOUS EDUCATION, TEACHERS, WISDOM. In the broad sense of the word, the process of living on earth, of seeking to work out one's salvation with fear and trembling before God, is in itself a course of *education;* it is a system of training, study, and discipline whereby the mental and moral powers are schooled and prepared for graduation into the eternal realms.

Also in the gospel sense, *education* consists in gaining a knowledge of God and the saving truths of the gospel. No man can be saved in ignorance of Jesus Christ and the laws of salvation. (John 17:3; D. & C. 131:6.) Accordingly, the saints are under command to "teach one another the doctrine of the king-

213

dom," to learn all expedient "things that pertain unto the kingdom of God," and to gain a knowledge of countries, kingdoms, sciences, arts, and every form of learning, so that they can both work out their own salvation and carry the message of salvation to the Lord's other children. (D. & C. 88:77-81.)

Education is gained primarily from the Spirit of the Lord by revelation and secondarily from study, research, and investigation. Those who lack wisdom are commanded to ask of God who giveth liberally to all the faithful. (D. & C. 46:7; Jas. 1:5-7.) "Let him that is ignorant learn wisdom by humbling himself and calling upon the Lord his God, that his eyes may be opened that he may see, and his ears opened that he may hear; For my Spirit is sent forth into the world to enlighten the humble and contrite, and to the condemnation of the ungodly." (D. & C. 136:32-33.)

In view of the Latter-day Saint perspective of the importance of education in the eternal scheme of things, it has inevitably followed that schools, colleges, universities, and secular learning have prospered wherever the influence of the saints has been felt. Many surveys and studies have shown that there is a higher degree of literacy and high scholastic attainment among members of the Church than among any other similar group in the world.

EGO.
See SPIRIT BODIES.

EGYPTUS.
See CAIN, HAM, NEGROES. Two women of note, a mother and her daughter, both carried the name *Egyptus*. The mother, a descendant of Cain, was the wife of Ham; the daughter was the mother of Pharaoh, the first ruler of Egypt. Abraham says that in the Chaldean tongue Egyptus "signifies that which is forbidden," meaning apparently that Ham married outside the approved lineage. (Abra. 1:20-27; Gen. 6:2.)

EIGHT WITNESSES.
See WITNESSES OF THE BOOK OF MORMON.

ELDER BROTHER.
See CHRIST, FATHER IN HEAVEN, FIRSTBORN, PRE-EXISTENCE. Christ is literally our *Elder Brother*. Since all men are the personal spirit children of the Father, and since Christ was the Firstborn spirit offspring, it follows that he is the Elder Brother of all men.

ELDERS.
See MELCHIZEDEK PRIESTHOOD, MISSIONARIES, PRIESTHOOD, PRIESTHOOD OFFICES, PRIESTHOOD QUORUMS, QUORUM PRESIDENTS. 1. In ancient times when tribal and governmental affairs were more fully centered in the family, and when those affairs were partly and sometimes wholly regulated ac-

cording to a patriarchal system, especial deference was given to the older men, and they were referred to as the *elders*. No special priesthood endowment or office was involved. Rather, the designation singled out those whose maturity, experience, and judgment made them natural leaders whose counsel and direction was highly esteemed.

People both in and out of the earthly kingdom of God designated their mature leaders and rulers as elders. Thus when Joseph went up to bury his father, Jacob, there went with him "the elders of his house, and all the elders of the land of Egypt." (Gen. 50:7.) This usage of the term elders was common among the Jews in the meridian of time. There are more than a score of such references in Matthew, Mark, Luke, and Acts. (Matt. 15:2; Mark 7:3; Luke 9:22; Acts 4:5.)

2. One of the ordained offices in the Melchizedek Priesthood is that of an *elder*. (D. & C. 20:60; 55:2; 107:7; Acts 14:23; Tit. 1:5.) This office grows out of and is an appendage to the higher priesthood. (D. & C. 84:29; 107:5.) As far as we know, there were no ordained elders in the Church until the day of Moses, just as there was no Aaronic Priesthood until that day.

There were, of course, ordained elders in ancient Israel (Ex. 24:9-11; Num. 11:16), among the Nephites both in their early and latter history (Alma 4:7, 16; 6:1; Moro. 3:1; 4:1; 6:1, 7), and among the

meridian saints. In New Testament usage the term is a translation of the Greek *presbyter*. (1 Tim. 5:1, 17, 19.) The ordination of elders in modern times began with Joseph Smith and Oliver Cowdery on April 6, 1830. (*Doctrines of Salvation,* vol. 3, pp. 146-147.)

Elders are ministers of Christ; they are called to administer in spiritual things (D. & C. 107:12), "To teach, expound, exhort, baptize, and watch over the church; And to confirm the church by the laying on of the hands, and the giving of the Holy Ghost. . . . The elders are to conduct the meetings as they are led by the Holy Ghost, according to the commandments and revelations of God." (D. & C. 20:42-45; 46:2.) They are to preach the gospel (D. & C. 53:3), teach from the scriptures (D. & C. 42:12), administer to the sick (D. & C. 42:43-52; Jas. 5:14-15), function in the church court system (D. & C. 42:80), and perform any duty that can be done by a holder of the lesser priesthood. (D. & C. 20:38-67.)

3. *Elder* is the title given all holders of the Melchizedek Priesthood whether the individuals concerned are or have been ordained to the *office* of elder or not. (D. & C. 20:38; 1 Pet. 5:1; 2 John 1; 3 John 1.) Thus if a priest in the Aaronic Priesthood had the Melchizedek Priesthood conferred upon him and was ordained a seventy or high priest, though he would never be ordained to the office of

an elder, yet he would be known by that title.

ELDERS COURTS.

See EXCOMMUNICATION. In the missions of the Church where there are no bishoprics or regularly organized high councils to try transgressors against the Lord's laws, the proper church officers form *elders courts* by appointing several Melchizedek Priesthood holders so to serve. These courts exercise jurisdiction similar to that of high councils in the stakes.

ELDERS OF ISRAEL.

See ELDERS.

ELECT.

See ELECT OF GOD.

ELECTION OF GRACE.

See AGENCY, CALLING AND ELECTION SURE, FOREORDINATION, GRACE OF GOD, ISRAEL, PREDESTINATION, PRE-EXISTENCE. As part of the new song the saints will sing when they "see eye to eye" and the millennial era has been ushered in will be these words, "The Lord hath redeemed his people, Israel, According to the *election of grace,* Which was brought to pass by the faith And covenant of their fathers." (D. & C. 84:98-102; Rom. 11:1-5.) This election of grace is a very fundamental, logical, and important part of God's dealings with men through the ages. To bring to pass the salvation of the greatest possible number of his spirit children the Lord, in general, sends the most righteous and worthy spirits to earth through the lineage of Abraham and Jacob. This course is a manifestation of his grace or in other words his love, mercy, and condescension toward his children.

This election to a chosen lineage is based on pre-existent worthiness and is thus made "according to the foreknowledge of God." (1 Pet. 1:2.) Those so grouped together during their mortal probation have more abundant opportunities to make and keep the covenants of salvation, a right which they earned by pre-existent devotion to the cause of righteousness. As part of this election, Abraham and others of the noble and great spirits were chosen before they were born for the particular missions assigned them in this life. (Abra. 3:22-24; Rom. 9.)

As with every basic doctrine of the gospel, the Lord's system of election based on pre-existent faithfulness has been changed and perverted by an apostate Christendom. So absurd have been the false conclusions reached in this field that millions of sincere though deceived persons have devoutly believed that in accordance with the divine will men were pre-destined to receive salvation or damnation which no act on their part could change. (*Teachings,* p. 189.)

Actually, if the full blessings of

salvation are to follow, the doctrine of election must operate *twice.* First, righteous spirits are elected or chosen to come to mortality as heirs of special blessings. Then, they must be called and elected again in this life, an occurrence which takes place when they join the true Church. (D. & C. 53:1.) Finally, in order to reap eternal salvation, they must press forward in obedient devotion to the truth until they make their "calling and election sure" (2 Pet. 1), that is, are "sealed up unto eternal life." (D. & C. 131:5.)

ELECT LADY.

See DAUGHTERS OF GOD, ELECTION OF GRACE, ELECT OF GOD. An *elect lady* is a female member of the Church who has already received, or who through obedience is qualified to receive, the fulness of gospel blessings. This includes temple endowments, celestial marriage, and the fulness of the sealing power. She is one who has been elected or chosen by faithfulness as a daughter of God in this life, an heir of God, a member of his household. Her position is comparable to that of the elders who magnify their callings in the priesthood and thereby receive all that the Father hath. (D. & C. 84:38.)

In the early days of this dispensation Emma Smith, the Prophet's wife, was in such complete harmony with the Lord's program that he forgave her of her sins and ad-dressed her as an elect lady. (D. & C. 25:1-3; *History of the Church,* vol. 4, p. 552.) John the Beloved used a similar salutation to certain chosen women in his day. (2 John 1, 13.) Just as it is possible for the very elect to be deceived, and to fall from grace through disobedience, so an elect lady, by failing to endure to the end, can lose her chosen status.

ELECT OF GOD.

See CHURCH OF THE FIRSTBORN, ELECTION OF GRACE, ELECT LADY, SAINTS, SONS OF GOD. The *elect of God* comprise a very select group, an inner circle of faithful members of The Church of Jesus Christ of Latter-day Saints. They are the portion of church members who are striving with all their hearts to keep the fulness of the gospel law in this life so that they can become inheritors of the fulness of gospel rewards in the life to come.

As far as the male sex is concerned, they are the ones, the Lord says, who have the Melchizedek Priesthood conferred upon them and who thereafter magnify their callings and are sanctified by the Spirit. In this way, "They become the sons of Moses and of Aaron and the seed of Abraham, and the church and kingdom, and the elect of God." They keep "the oath and covenant which belongeth to the priesthood," and are rewarded with the fulness of the Father's kingdom. (D. & C. 84:33-41.)

To gain this elect status they must be endowed in the temple of the Lord (D. & C. 95:8), enter into that "order of the priesthood" named "the new and everlasting covenant of marriage" (D. & C. 131: 1-4), and overcome by faith until, as the sons of God, they merit membership in the Church of the Firstborn. (D. & C. 76:50-70, 94-96.) The elect of God are the chosen of God; and he has said: *"There are many who have been ordained among you, whom I have called but few of them are chosen."* (D. & C. 95:5; 121:34-40.)

This is the day in which the Lord is gathering his elect, those who hear his voice and harden not their hearts (D. & C. 29:7), from the four quarters of the earth (D. & C. 33:6), so that if they continue to abide in his word, they shall have an eventual salvation in his presence. This is the day of which the Lord spoke: "I will bring forth a seed out of Jacob, and out of Judah an inheritor of my mountains: and *mine elect shall inherit it, and my servants shall dwell there."* (Isa. 65:9.) The coming millennial day is one in which the "elect shall long enjoy the work of their hands" (Isa. 65: 22), for the earth and the fulness thereof shall then be theirs.

ELEMENTS.

See CREATION, DUST, IMMORTALITY, MORTALITY, SIGNS OF THE TIMES, SOUL, SPIRIT ELEMENT. Those natural or earthy substances of which the earth in all its parts is composed and which make up the physical or temporal bodies of all created things are called *elements*. They are of the earth, earthy (1 Cor. 15:44-48); they are to be distinguished from the more pure and refined substances of which spirit matter is composed. (D. & C. 131: 6-7.) "The elements are eternal," the Lord says; and when they are organized into a mortal body, those elements become the tabernacle of the eternal spirit that comes from pre-existence. Also, "The elements are the tabernacle of God," meaning that the Spirit of the Lord will dwell in the hearts of righteous men. In the resurrection "spirit and element" are "inseparably connected," thus assuring immortality to the soul. (D. & C. 93:33-35.) It follows that elements which are mortal now are destined to become immortal elements hereafter.

One of the signs of the times is that the elements (meaning weather conditions and such things as bring about earthquakes and the like) shall be in commotion in the last days. (D. & C. 88:87-92.) When the Lord comes, the elements (meaning the earth itself and all that composes it) shall melt with fervent heat, and all things shall be made new. (D. & C. 101:25; 2 Pet. 3:10-12; 3 Ne. 26:3; Morm. 9:2.) And finally, when this earth becomes a celestial sphere, the natural elements of which it is composed will become immortal and eternal. (D. & C. 77:1; 88:16-32; 130:9.)

ELEVENTH HOUR.

See LAST DAYS, RESTORATION OF THE GOSPEL, SIGNS OF THE TIMES. Based on the common verity that there are 12 hours in the day (John 11:9), the expression *eleventh hour,* used figuratively to apply to the earth's history, has reference to the latter-days. In the vineyard, those who were employed during the 11th hour were paid the same as those whose services had commenced with the rising sun. (Matt. 20:1-16.) One application of this parable is that those called to Christ's service in the latter-days will inherit equally with Adam and Abraham, though those ancient prophets have long since gone to their exaltation. (D. & C. 132:29-37; 133:54-56.) In sending forth his ministers in this dispensation the Lord said: "It is the eleventh hour, and the last time that I shall call laborers into my vineyard." (D. & C. 33:3.)

ELIAS.

See AARONIC PRIESTHOOD, ELIJAH THE PROPHET, JOHN THE BAPTIST, JOSEPH SMITH THE PROPHET, PRIESTHOOD OF ELIAS, RESTORATION OF THE GOSPEL. Many scriptures use the term *Elias* in connection with vital doctrinal explanations. Some of these passages have come to us in garbled and fragmentary form. Various of them use the word to mean wholly different and divergent things. Much confusion and uncertainty would be avoided if gospel students would note carefully the distinguishable differences in the various usages of this important though unusual word. The following different meanings of the designation *Elias* are of scriptural record: 1. ELIAS OF ABRAHAM'S DAY.—As part of the restoration of all things, a prophet named *Elias* came to Joseph Smith and Oliver Cowdery on April 3, 1836, and committed unto them the dispensation of the gospel of Abraham. The scriptural account of this glorious event specifies: "Elias appeared, and committed the dispensation of the gospel of Abraham, saying that in us and our seed all generations after us should be blessed." (D. & C. 110:12.)

Now what was the *gospel of Abraham?* Obviously it was the commission, the mission, the endowment and power, the message of salvation, given to Abraham. And what was this? It was a divine promise that both in the world and out of the world his seed should continue "as innumerable as the stars; or, if ye were to count the sand upon the seashore ye could not number them." (D. & C. 132:30; Gen. 17; Abra. 2:1-12.)

Thus the gospel of Abraham was one of celestial marriage (including plurality of wives); it was a gospel or commission to provide a lineage for the elect portion of the pre-existent spirits, a gospel to provide a household in eternity for those who live the fulness of the celestial law. This power and commission is what Elias restored, and as a consequence, the righteous among all future generations were assured of the blessings of a continuation of the seeds forever, even as it was with Abraham of old. (D. & C. 132.)

This committing to man of the gospel of Abraham, of the great commission which he had, should not be confused with the *spirit of Elias* or the *doctrine of Elias.* The commission which the man Elias conferred was *not* an authorization either to operate in the spirit of Elias or to preach the gospel. The spirit of Elias had been manifest long *before* the man Elias came. The commission to preach the gospel was restored by Peter, James, and John in 1829, and the gospel had been preached for nearly seven years *before* Elias came. In their mortal ministry, Peter, James, and John had been given this commission: "Go ye into all the world, and preach the gospel to every creature." (Mark 16:15.) In other words, the *gospel of Peter, James and John,* their great commission, was to preach the gospel of salvation. When they came in modern times that, among other things, was what they restored.

We have no information, at this time, as to the mortal life or ministry of Elias. Apparently he lived in the days of Abraham, but whether he was Abraham, or Melchizedek, or some other prophet, we do not know.

2. ELIAS A NAME FOR ELIJAH.—

Elias is the greek form of Elijah. This leads to some confusion and the necessity of determining whether Elijah or someone else is meant in each passage where the name Elias appears. Such a determination is not difficult, however, when the full doctrine of Elias and Elijah is understood.

3. SPIRIT AND DOCTRINE OF ELIAS.—Joseph Smith taught that a preparatory work, one that lays a foundation for a greater work, one that goes before to prepare the way for a greater which is to come, is a work performed by the *spirit of Elias.* This principle is called the *doctrine of Elias.* The Prophet explained that *the spirit and doctrine of Elias pertain to the Aaronic Priesthood only.* He used himself as an example, saying that he worked by the spirit of Elias from the time he received the Aaronic Priesthood (which is a preparatory priesthood) until the Melchizedek Priesthood was restored. In the same way John the Baptist, he explained, served in the spirit and power of Elias; that is, as our Lord's forerunner, serving in the lesser priesthood, he prepared the way for a greater work.

Work done by authority of the Melchizedek Priesthood is not performed in accordance with the spirit of Elias. To distinguish between the spirit of Elias and a higher power, the Prophet said that a man could be baptized by the spirit of Elias, but he could not receive the Holy Ghost by that power, and "any man that comes, having the spirit and power of Elias, he will not transcend his bounds." (*Teachings,* pp. 335-341.)

4. ELIAS OF THE RESTORATION. —According to the plan and program of the Lord, the dispensation of the fulness of times is "the times of restitution of all things, which God hath spoken by the mouth of all his holy prophets since the world began." (Acts 3:21.) This restoration is to be effected by *Elias.* Before the winding up of the Lord's work, the promise is: "Elias truly shall first come, and restore all things." (Matt. 17:11.) With these ancient scriptures before us, these questions arise: Who is the promised Elias who was to come and restore all things? Has this work of restoration taken place? Or is it something that is yet future?

Correcting the Bible by the spirit of revelation, the Prophet restored a statement of John the Baptist which says that *Christ is the Elias who was to restore all things. (Inspired Version,* John 1:21-28.) By revelation we are also informed that *the Elias who was to restore all things is the angel Gabriel* who was known in mortality as Noah. (D. & C. 27:6-7; Luke 1:5-25; *Teachings,* p. 157.) From the same authentic source we also learn that *the promised Elias is John the Revelator.* (D. & C. 77: 9, 14.) Thus there are three different revelations which name Elias as being *three different persons.* What are we to conclude?

By finding answer to the question, by whom has the restoration been effected, we shall find who Elias is and find there is no problem in harmonizing these apparently contradictory revelations. Who has restored all things? Was it one man? Certainly not. Many angelic ministrants have been sent from the courts of glory to confer keys and powers, to commit their dispensations and glories again to men on earth. At least the following have come: Moroni, John the Baptist, Peter, James, and John, Moses, Elijah, Elias, Gabriel, Raphael, and Michael. (D. & C. 13; 110; 128:19-21.) Since it is apparent that no one messenger has carried the whole burden of the restoration, but rather that each has come with a specific endowment from on high, it becomes clear that *Elias is a composite personage. The expression must be understood to be a name and a title for those whose mission it was to commit keys and powers to men in this final dispensation.* (*Doctrines of Salvation,* vol. 1, pp. 170-174.)

5. JOHN THE BAPTIST AN ELIAS. —No better illustration is found in the revelations of one who acted in the spirit and power of Elias—and yet who expressly disavowed any claim to being the Elias who was to restore all things—than that seen in the ministry of John the Baptist. Gabriel foretold that John would go before the Lord "in the spirit and power of Elias" (Luke 1:17); and

the skeptical and unbelieving Jews —knowing that *Elijah* was to come again and that *Elias* was to restore all things—made pointed inquiry of John to determine if he claimed to fulfil ancient predictions in this field.

"And this is the record of John, when the Jews sent priests and Levites from Jerusalem, to ask him: Who art thou? *And he confessed, and denied not that he was Elias;* but confessed, saying: I am not the Christ. And they asked him, saying: *How then art thou Elias?* And he said, *I am not that Elias who was to restore all things.* And they asked him, saying, Art thou that prophet? And he answered, No. . . . And they asked him, and said unto him: Why baptizest thou then, if thou be not the Christ, nor Elias who was to restore all things, neither that prophet? John answered them, saying: I baptize with water, but there standeth one among you, whom ye know not; He it is of whom I bear record. *He is that prophet, even Elias, who, coming after me, is preferred before me,* whose shoe's latchet I am not worthy to unloose, or whose place I am not able to fill; for he shall baptize, not only with water, but with fire, and with the Holy Ghost." (*Inspired Version,* John 1:21-28.)

After Moses and Elijah (Elias) had appeared on the Mount of Transfiguration, our Lord's "disciples asked him, saying, Why then say the scribes that Elias must *first*

come?" That is, the scribes knew that Elias (Elijah) was to *precede* the coming of the Lord, and yet here Peter, James, and John had seen the heavenly visitant come *after* the Lord had been manifest among the people.

"And Jesus answered and said unto them, Elias truly shall first come, and restore all things, as the prophets have written. And again I say unto you that Elias has come already, concerning whom it is written, Behold, I will send my messenger, and he shall prepare the way before me; and they knew him not, and have done unto him, whatsoever they listed. Likewise shall also the Son of Man suffer of them. But I say unto you, Who is Elias? Behold, this is Elias, whom I send to prepare the way before me. Then the disciples understood that *he spake unto them of John the Baptist, and also of another who should come and restore all things, as it is written by the prophets.*" (*Inspired Version,* Matt. 17:9-14; *Doctrines Salvation,* vol. 2, pp. 108-112.)

ELIJAH THE PROPHET.

See CALLING AND ELECTION SURE, KEYS OF THE KINGDOM, SALVATION, SALVATION FOR THE DEAD, SAVIORS ON MOUNT ZION, SEALING POWER, SECOND COMING OF CHRIST, SIGNS OF THE TIMES. For dramatic manifestations and the visible exhibition of divine power, the ministry of *Elijah the*

Prophet scarcely has an equal. He sealed the heavens, was fed by the ravens, extended the widow's barrel of meal and cruse of oil, raised the dead, destroyed the priests of Baal, called down fire from heaven on at least three occasions, fasted 40 days and nights, was attended frequently by angelic ministrants, and finally was translated and taken up into heaven without tasting death. (1 Kings 17; 18; 2 Kings 1; 2.)

Centuries later Malachi prophesied that Elijah would return before the great and dreadful day of the Lord. (Mal. 4:5-6.) With Moses, another translated being, he appeared to Peter, James, and John on the Mount of Transfiguration to give those apostolic ministers the keys of the kingdom. (Matt. 17:1-13; *Teachings*, p. 158.) During the night of September 21st-22nd, 1823, Moroni told Joseph Smith that the Lord would soon reveal unto him the priesthood by the hand of Elijah the Prophet (Jos. Smith 2:29-39); and on April 3, 1836, Elijah came (in fulfilment of the promises of Malachi and Moroni) to Joseph Smith and Oliver Cowdery, in the Kirtland Temple, and conferred upon them the keys of the sealing power. (D. & C. 110:13-16.)

Because Elijah has come in this dispensation, the fulness of salvation is again available for the *living* and the *dead.* He "was the last prophet that held the keys of the priesthood" in ancient Israel, the Prophet said. His latter-day mission was to "restore the authority and deliver the keys of the priesthood, in order that *all the ordinances* may be attended to in righteousness. . . . Why send Elijah? Because he holds the keys of the authority to administer in *all the ordinances* of the priesthood; and without the authority is given, the ordinances could not be administered in righteousness." (*Teachings,* p. 172.)

"The spirit, power, and calling of Elijah is," the Prophet also taught, *"that ye have power to hold the key of the revelations, ordinances, oracles, powers and endowments of the fulness of the Melchizedek Priesthood and of the kingdom of God on the earth; and to receive, obtain, and perform all the ordinances belonging to the kingdom of God, even unto the turning of the hearts of the fathers unto the children, and the hearts of the children unto the fathers, even those who are in heaven. . . .*

"This is the spirit of Elijah, that we redeem our dead, and connect ourselves with our fathers which are in heaven, and seal up our dead to come forth in the first resurrection; and here we want the power of Elijah to seal those who dwell on earth to those who dwell in heaven. This is the power of Elijah and the keys of the kingdom of Jehovah." (*Teachings,* pp. 337-338.)

"How shall God come to the rescue of this generation?" the Prophet asked. "He will send Elijah the Prophet. . . . Elijah shall reveal the covenants to seal the hearts of the fathers to the children, and the children to the fathers. The anointing and sealing is to be called, elected, and made sure." (*Teachings,* p. 323.)

ELOHIM.
See FATHER IN HEAVEN, GOD, JEHOVAH. 1. *El,* as the Hebrew word for God or Divine Being, is used in various Hebrew word combinations to identify Deity and to reveal particular things about him. Thus *El Elyon* means *the Highest God, the Possessor or Creator of heaven and earth* (Gen. 14:19); *El Shaddai* signifies *God Almighty* (Gen. 17:1); *El Elohe Yisrael* is the *God of Israel.* (Gen. 33:20.)

Elohim is the plural of the Caananite *El* or the Hebrew *Eloah;* consequently, its literal meaning is *Gods.* Accordingly, as the Prophet pointed out, such Old Testament passages as, "In the beginning God (Elohim) created the heaven and the earth" (Gen. 1:1), should more properly be translated, "In the beginning the head of the Gods brought forth the Gods," and they created the heavens and the earth. (*Teachings,* pp. 370-371.)

2. *Elohim,* plural word though it is, is also used as the exalted name-title of God the Eternal Father, a usage that connotes his supremacy and omnipotence, he being God above all Gods. (The Father and the Son: A Doctrinal Exposition by the First Presidency and the

Twelve, cited, *Articles of Faith,* pp. 465-473; 1 Cor. 8:6.)

ELVES.
See GHOSTS.

ELYSIUM.
See PARADISE. According to Greek mythology, *Elysium* or the *Elysian Fields* is the name given the abode of the blessed after death. This concept, found among an apostate people, was obviously an outgrowth of the true gospel doctrine, taught from the beginning, relative to paradise.

EMBLEMS.
See SYMBOLISMS.

EMMANUEL.
See IMMANUEL.

EMPERORS.
See KINGCRAFT.

EMPLOYMENT.
See CHURCH WELFARE PLAN, DOLE, IDLENESS, STEWARDSHIPS, WORK. As part of man's mortal probation, he is being tested with reference to temporal things. The obligation to earn his bread in the sweat of his face necessitates *employment.* (Gen. 3:19.) The gospel requires that man work in temporal

as well as spiritual pursuits to gain salvation. Flocks and herds, farms and vineyards, industries and business ventures, are all part and portion of the gospel plan; the manner in which man acts with reference to them affects not only his temporal well-being, but his eternal salvation. "Thou shalt not be idle; for he that is idle shall not eat the bread nor wear the garments of the laborer." (D. & C. 42:42.)

Provision is made in the great Welfare Plan of the Church for priesthood quorums and other church organizations to aid their members in finding employment and in bettering inadequate existing employment.

ENCHANTMENTS.
See SORCERY.

ENDING.
See BEGINNING.

ENDLESS.
See CHRIST, ETERNAL, ETERNAL DAMNATION, ETERNAL LIFE, ETERNITY, EVERLASTING, GOD, ONE ETERNAL ROUND. 1. That which goes on forever and has no end is *endless*. For instance: The eternal, unending duration of time is *endless time;* the infinite, limitless expanse of space is *endless space*. Similarly there is no end to matter, element, or any of the at-

tributes of perfection which make up the personalities of exalted beings. In the hymn, "If You Could Hie to Kolob," Elder William W. Phelps teaches very effectively the endless nature of all good things:

If you could hie to Kolob
  In the twinkling of an eye,
And then continue onward
  With that same speed to fly,
D'ye think that you could ever,
  Through all eternity,
Find out the generation
  Where Gods began to be?

Or see the grand beginning,
  Where space did not extend?
Or view the last creation,
  Where Gods and matter end?
Methinks the Spirit whispers,
  "No man has found 'pure space,'
Nor seen the outside curtains,
  Where nothing has a place."

The works of God continue,
  And worlds and lives abound;
Improvement and progression
  Have one eternal round.
There is no end to matter,
  There is no end to space;
There is no end to spirit;
  There is no end to race.

There is no end to virtue;
  There is no end to might;
There is no end to wisdom;
  There is no end to light.
There is no end to union;
  There is no end to youth;
There is no end to priesthood;
  There is no end to truth.

There is no end to glory;
   There is no end to love;
There is no end to being;
   There is no death above.
There is no end to glory;
   There is no end to love;
There is no end to being;
   There is no death above.

2. *Endless,* used as a noun and not as an adjective, is one of the names of God and signifies his unending, eternal continuance as the supreme, exalted ruler of the universe. "Behold, I am the Lord God Almighty, and *Endless* is my name," he said, "for I am without beginning of days or end of years; and is not this endless?" (Moses 1: 3; 7:35.) *"Endless is my name"* he said to the Prophet. (D. & C. 19: 10.) By using his name Endless and by combining it with other terms, the Lord has revealed some very significant truths in the scriptures. For instance: Endless life means God's life; "Endless punishment is God's punishment." (D. & C. 19:12.)

ENDLESS DAMNATION.
See ETERNAL DAMNATION.

ENDLESS FATHER.
See ETERNAL FATHER.

ENDLESS GOD.
See ETERNAL GOD.

ENDLESS HELL.
See ETERNAL DAMNATION.

ENDLESS LIFE.
See ETERNAL LIFE.

ENDLESS PUNISHMENT.
See ETERNAL DAMNATION.

ENDLESS TORMENT.
See ETERNAL DAMNATION.

END OF THE EARTH.
See EARTH.

END OF THE WORLD.
See WORLD.

ENDOWMENTS.
See CALLING AND ELECTION SURE, CELESTIAL MARRIAGE, CHURCH OF THE FIRSTBORN, DAUGHTERS OF GOD, ETERNAL LIFE, ETERNAL LIVES, EXALTATION, FULNESS OF THE FATHER, GODHOOD, JOINT-HEIRS WITH CHRIST, SALVATION FOR THE DEAD, SEALING POWER, SONS OF GOD, TEMPLES, VICARIOUS ORDINANCES. Certain special, spiritual blessings given worthy and faithful saints in the temples are called *endowments,* because in and

through them the recipients are endowed with power from on high. They receive an education relative to the Lord's purposes and plans in the creation and peopling of the earth and are taught the things that must be done by man in order to gain exaltation in the world to come. They place themselves in a position to receive the sanctifying and cleansing power of the Holy Ghost, thus becoming clean and spotless before the Lord. So sacred and holy are the administrations performed that in every age when they have been revealed, the Lord has withheld them from the knowledge of the world and disclosed them only to the faithful saints in houses and places dedicated and selected for that purpose. (D. & C. 95:8-9; 124:25-41; Luke 24:59.)

All temple ordinances, except baptism for the dead, pertain to exaltation in the celestial kingdom and not merely to admission to that world. When the Prophet first administered the endowment in this dispensation he said it embraced "all those plans and principles by which anyone is enabled to secure the fulness of those blessings which have been prepared for the Church of the Firstborn." (*Teachings,* p. 237.) These sacred ordinances are administered for the living and on a proxy basis for the dead also. (*Doctrines of Salvation,* vol. 2, pp. 252-257.)

Elder James E. Talmage, in *The House of the Lord,* a work published by the Church in 1912, gives the following data on endowments: "The temple endowment, as administered in modern temples, comprises instruction relating to the significance and sequence of past dispensations, and the importance of the present as the greatest and grandest era in human history. This course of instruction includes a recital of the most prominent events of the creative period, the condition of our first parents in the Garden of Eden, their disobedience and consequent expulsion from that blissful abode, their condition in the lone and dreary world when doomed to live by labor and sweat, the plan of redemption by which the great transgression may be atoned, the period of the great apostasy, the restoration of the gospel with all its ancient powers and privileges, the absolute and indispensable conditions of personal purity and devotion to the right in present life, and a strict compliance with gospel requirements. . . .

"The ordinances of the endowment embody certain obligations on the part of the individual, such as covenant and promise to observe the law of strict virtue and chastity, to be charitable, benevolent, tolerant and pure; to devote both talent and material means to the spread of truth and the uplifting of the race; to maintain devotion to the cause of truth; and to seek in every way to contribute to the great preparation that the earth may be made ready to receive her King, the Lord Jesus. With the taking of each covenant and the assuming of each obligation a promised blessing is pronounced, contingent upon the faithful observance of the conditions.

"No jot, iota, or tittle of the temple rites is otherwise than uplifting and sanctifying. In every detail the endowment ceremony contributes to covenants of morality of life, consecration of person to high ideals, devotion to truth, patriotism to nation, and allegiance to God. The blessings of the House of the Lord are restricted to no privileged class; every member of the Church may have admission to the temple with the right to participate in the ordinances thereof, if he comes duly accredited as of worthy life and conduct." (*The House of the Lord,* pp. 99-101.)

ENDOWMENTS FOR THE DEAD.
See SALVATION FOR THE DEAD.

ENDURING TO THE END.
See OBEDIENCE, PLAN OF SALVATION, SALVATION, STRAIGHT AND NARROW PATH. Baptism is the gate which puts the converted Christian on the straight and narrow path which leads to eternal life. To gain the promised inheritance in the celestial world it is necessary to travel the length of the path, a course of travel which consists in obedience to the laws and principles of the gospel. This process is

called *enduring to the end,* meaning the end of mortal life. (D. & C. 20:29; 3 Ne. 27:19-21.)

Speaking to members of the Church who have already repented and been baptized, Nephi says: "Ye must press forward with a steadfastness in Christ, having a perfect brightness of hope, and a love of God and of all men. Wherefore, if ye shall press forward, feasting upon the word of Christ, and endure to the end, behold, thus saith the Father: Ye shall have eternal life. And now, behold, my beloved brethren, this is the way; and there is none other way nor name given under heaven whereby man can be saved in the kingdom of God." (2 Ne. 31:20-21.)

ENOCHIAN DISPENSATION.
See DISPENSATIONS.

ENSIGN TO THE NATIONS.
See GATHERING OF ISRAEL, RESTORATION OF THE GOSPEL, ZION. Many ancient prophecies foretold that in the last days the Lord would set up an *ensign to the nations,* a standard to which Israel and the righteous of all nations might gather. (Isa. 5:26; 11:10-12; 18:3; 30:17-26; 31:9; 49:22; 62:10; Zech. 9:16.) This ensign is the new and everlasting covenant, the gospel of salvation (D. & C. 49:9); it is the great latter-day Zion (D. & C. 64:41-43); it is The Church of Jesus Christ of Latter-day Saints.

ENTITIES.
See PRE-EXISTENCE.

ENVIRONMENT.
See HEREDITY, PRE-EXISTENCE.
Two obligations face the saints
where the matter of *environment* is
concerned: 1. To create for themselves and their families the most
wholesome and edifying environment possible, so there will be less
chance of any member of the family circle being lost through transgression; and 2. To rise above
every unwholesome enviromental
situation that may be encountered
during the course of this mortal
probation.

When the spirit offspring of God
pass from pre-existence to mortality, they bring with them the talents, capacities, and abilities
acquired during a long existence
and experience in their first estate.
At the time of mortal birth all
children are innocent and pure.
Then as they begin to become accountable, they are swayed by "the
tradition of their fathers." (D. & C.
93:38-39.) Their lives and destinies
are shaped and altered by their
environment—the circumstances,
external surroundings, and influences in which they find themselves. The command to bring up
children in light and truth includes
a requirement to create for them a
wholesome environment.

One of the great purposes of this
mortal probation is to test and try
men, to see if they will keep the

commandments and walk in the
light no matter what environmental enticements beckon them away
from the straight and narrow path.
(1 John 2:15-17.) The prayer, "lead
us not into temptation, but deliver
us from evil" (Matt. 6:13), is a petition that we may be kept from such
unwholesome environmental circumstances as to be overcome by
them.

It is axiomatic that the saints
should establish peace and love in
their families; engage in wholesome recreation only; perform their
daily labors in the cleanest and
most wholesome environment possible; associate with proper com-
panions always; and seek to live
under those surroundings and influences that breathe the spirit of
righteousness and faith. Constant
association with that which is low
and vulgar inevitably leads to the
debasement of the human soul.

EONS.
See ETERNITY.

EPIPHANY.
See APOSTASY, CHRISTMAS. According to tradition it is supposed
that the wise men from the east
came to Jerusalem and found the
newly born Son of God 12 days after his birth. Hence portions of the
sectarian world celebrate *Epiphany*
(Twelfthtide or Twelfth-day) on
January 6. This is the traditional
and customary end to the Christ-

mas season.

It appears from Matthew's account, however, that in reality the wise men came two or three years after the birth of our Lord. It was a "young child," not a baby, they were seeking; he was found in a "house," not a manger; and Herod "sent forth, and slew all the children that were in Bethlehem, and in all the coasts thereof, from two years old and under, according to the time which he had diligently enquired of the wise men." (Matt. 2.) Those who had not reached the third anniversary of their births were "two years old and under." The true Church, of course, pays no heed to Epiphany and conducts no celebration thereon.

EPISTLES.

See BIBLE, EPISTLES OF COMMENDATION, GOSPELS, NEW TESTAMENT, SCRIPTURE. In the New Testament there are 21 *epistles* or letters written by inspired writers to persons or groups. In their original forms they were perfect scripture, and they were written by the authors whose names they bear, the specious speculations of higher criticism to the contrary notwithstanding. Their authorship and inspiration are attested to by references made to them and quotations taken from them in the sermons of the Prophet and in latter-day revelation itself.

Purpose of the epistles is to bear record of Christ (and in this sense they are apostolic letters), to teach the principles of the gospel, and to exhort the saints to that personal righteousness which leads to salvation. As with the other books of the Bible, they were preserved by Divine Providence to come forth and form a part of that book of books.

Sections 121, 122, 123, 127, and 128 of the Doctrine and Covenants are epistles written under the spirit of inspiration by the Prophet. Sidney Rigdon was commanded by revelation to write an epistle to the Church to solicit funds "to purchase lands for an inheritance for the children of God." (D. & C. 58: 51.) The First Presidency has taken frequent occasion, particularly in the early days of the Church, to send epistles to portions or all of the Latter-day Saints. Frequent Book of Mormon reference is found to epistles, which were formal letters dealing with affairs of state and of the Church. (Alma 54:4; 55: 3; 56:1; 57:1.)

EPISTLES OF COMMENDATION.

See EPISTLES, RECOMMENDS. It appears from 2 Cor. 3:1 that the practice prevailed among the primitive saints of introducing faithful members of the Church from one group of saints to another by means of *epistles of commendation* or letters of commendation. That is, the saints were commended, introduced, or recommended to the various local churches by these written certifications. These would correspond to "recommends" in modern times.

EQUALITY.

See CONSECRATION, EQUITY, EXALTATION, JOINT-HEIRS WITH CHRIST, RESPECT OF PERSONS, UNITED ORDER. 1. Under conditions of full gospel *equality,* perfect fairness and equity would prevail in every sphere of life. All persons similarly situated would be treated exactly the same as all other such persons; all would enjoy and possess the same things. Perfect impartiality would reign, for "there should be an equality among all men." (Mosiah 27:3; Alma 1:26.) By way of illustration, the gospel message itself is and should be freely available to all men. (Third Article of Faith.) The Lord "inviteth them all to come unto him and partake of his goodness; and he denieth none that come unto him, black and white, bond and free, male and female; and he remembereth the heathen; and *all are alike unto God,* both Jew and Gentile." (2 Ne. 26:33.)

Perfect equality does not now prevail, either in the world or in the Church. But when life is perfected among the saints and when the highest gospel law is lived, then both temporal and spiritual equality will prevail. Temporal adjustments under the principles of consecration will make "every man equal according to his circum-stances and his wants and needs." (D. & C. 51:3; 82:17.) *"In your temporal things you shall be equal, and this not grudgingly, otherwise the abundance of the manifestations of the Spirit shall be withheld."* (D. & C. 70:14.) *"For if ye are not equal in earthly things ye cannot be equal in obtaining heavenly things."* (D. & C. 78:3-7.)

2. Exalted beings will enjoy *eternal equality* in their high celestial status. "And he makes them equal in power, and in might, and in dominion." (D. & C. 76:95.) "And then shall the angels be crowned with the glory of his might, and the saints shall be filled with his glory, and receive their inheritance and be made equal with him." (D. & C. 88:107.) In other words, they all enjoy exaltation; all live the same kind of life; all exercise the same power, the power of God; all are possessed of the same Spirit, the Spirit of truth; all are gods and have eternal increase; all are joint-heirs with Christ, possessing all things with him, and being inheritors of all that the Father hath.

EQUITY.

See EQUALITY, JUSTICE, MERCY, RIGHTEOUSNESS. *Equity* is the principle which tempers the harshness of justice. Equity dictates that the law shall be administered according to its spirit and not merely its letter. (D. & C. 102:16; 134:3; Hela. 3: 20; 3 Ne. 6:4.) It is an attribute of Deity (Ps. 98:9; 99:4; Alma 9:26), the companion of justice and mercy, and the friend of righteousness. One of the great Messianic prophecies says of our Lord: "With righteousness shall he judge the poor, and reprove with equity for the meek of the earth." (Isa. 11:4.)

ERA.
See DISPENSATIONS.

ERA OF RESTORATION.
See TIMES OF RESTITUTION.

ERRORS.
See APOSTASY.

ESCHATOLOGY.
See BOTTOMLESS PIT, CELESTIAL KINGDOM, HEAVEN, HELL, IMMORTALITY, JUDGMENT DAY, MILLENNIUM, PARADISE, RESURRECTION, SECOND COMING OF CHRIST, SONS OF PERDITION, SPIRIT WORLD, TELESTIAL KINGDOM, TERRESTRIAL KINGDOM. Under the pretense of studying *eschatology*—doctrines concerning the ultimate destiny of mankind—uninspired Biblical scholars speculate, quibble, and deny the plain meaning of the revelations about death, immortality, the resurrection, the day of judgment, the Second Coming of Christ, and related matters. It is common among these sectarian scholars to attempt to show the evolution of these doc-

trines from prophet to prophet; to point out the supposedly contradictory and confusing views expressed by prophets in different ages, by Jesus himself, and by the New Testament writers; and finally to conclude their mental and theological flights of fantasy without reaching any sound conclusion about things which are to them impenetrable mysteries.

The fact is, of course, that all of these so-called eschatological doctrines have been known and taught from the beginning; the gospel of salvation is not something that has been formulated in the minds of men item by item as new light has dawned in succeeding ages. One prophet did not modify or change what a previous inspired man had uttered. And the spiritually enlightened have no difficulty in determining the meaning of all that God has revealed about the ultimate destiny of his children.

ESPECIAL WITNESSES.
See SEVENTIES.

ESPOUSAL.
See BRIDEGROOM, BRIDE OF THE LAMB, CELESTIAL MARRIAGE. Ancient marriage customs in Israel provided for a formal *espousal* or betrothal which preceded the marriage proper. In effect the espousal marked the beginning of the marriage ceremony, though as much as a year might elapse between it

and the marriage proper. Though the espoused woman was still dependent on her father, she was considered as consecrated to her future husband, was denied to all others, and was virtually regarded as his wife. (Deut. 22:23-24.) Thus Joseph being espoused to Mary and finding her with child planned to put her away privily until Gabriel commanded otherwise. (Matt. 1:18-25; Luke 1:27; 2:5.) Unfaithfulness on the part of an espoused woman was adultery (D. & C. 132:63), punishable anciently by death. (Deut. 22:23-24.)

In a figurative sense, the saints are espoused to Christ. "I have espoused you to one husband, that I may present you as a chaste virgin to Christ," Paul wrote to the Corinthians. (2 Cor. 11:1-4.) By keeping the vows of their espousal, the saints become the bride of the Lamb (Rev. 19:7-9), who is the Bridegroom (D. & C. 33:17) and Husband. (Isa. 54:5.)

ESTATES OF MAN.
See FIRST ESTATE.

ETERNAL.
See CHRIST, ENDLESS, ETERNAL DAMNATION, ETERNAL FATHER, ETERNAL GOD, ETERNAL LIFE, ETERNITY, EVERLASTING, GOD, ONE ETERNAL ROUND. 1. One of the names of God is *Eternal;* to Enoch the Lord said, "Eternal is my name" (Moses 7:35), using this designation as a noun and not as an adjective. This name of Deity signifies that he is "infinite and eternal, from everlasting to everlasting the same unchangeable God." (D. & C. 20:17.) In fact, members of the godhead, possessing the same characteristics and attributes, are "infinite and eternal, without end." (D. & C. 20:28, 77, 79; 121:32; 128:23.)

The Lord uses his name Eternal to teach with specific accurateness certain great principles of revealed truth. Thus the kind of life he lives (which, of course, is God's life) is called *eternal life* (meaning exaltation); and the kind of punishment which is dealt out to transgressors by him is called *eternal punishment,* a name having reference to the type and not the duration of the penalty imposed.

2. That which is of infinite duration, which goes on forever and has no end is *eternal,* endless, everlasting. Using the term in this sense the revelations teach that "The elements are eternal" (D. & C. 93:33), and that there are such things as *eternal glory* (D. & C. 76:6), *eternal felicity* (D. & C. 77:3), and *eternal joy.* (D. & C. 109:76.)

3. *Eternal* is also used to mean the opposite of *temporal,* the opposite of that which pertains to *time* and *mortality.* This is a temporal world in which we now live; hereafter we shall gain places in the eternal worlds. (D. & C. 76:86; 121:2; 132:55, 63.) The earth itself is now passing through "its temporal

existence"; hereafter it is to be sanctified, become immortal, and gain an "eternal state." (D. & C. 77:1-6.) Any views expressed by man through his own power consist of natural or mortal words; in contrast, words spoken by the power of the Holy Ghost, being the Lord's words (D. & C. 68:1-4), are "eternal words." (D. & C. 85:7.)

ETERNAL DAMNATION.

See DAMNATION, DEVIL, ETERNAL LIFE, FIRE AND BRIMSTONE, HELL, KINGDOMS OF GLORY, PUNISHMENT, RESURRECTION, SALVATION, SIN, SONS OF PERDITION, SPIRIT PRISON, SPIRITUAL DEATH, UNPARDONABLE SIN. To denote the severity and extent of the condemnation falling upon those whose feet slip from the straight and narrow path, and who do not repent and return to righteousness, the Lord couples the word *eternal* with the term *damnation*. There are three distinct senses in which the expression *eternal damnation* is used.

1. *Eternal damnation* is the opposite of eternal life, and all those who do not gain eternal life, or exaltation in the highest heaven within the celestial kingdom, are partakers of eternal damnation. Their *eternal condemnation* is to have limitations imposed upon them so that they cannot progress to the state of godhood and gain a fulness of all things.

They "remain separately and singly, without exaltation, . . . *to all eternity;* and from henceforth are not gods, but are angels of God *forever and ever.*" (D. & C. 132:17.) Their kingdom or progress has an "end," and they "cannot have an increase." (D. & C. 131:4.) Spirit children are denied to them to all eternity, and they inherit "the deaths," meaning an absence of posterity in the resurrection. (D. & C. 132:16-25.)

They are never redeemed from their spiritual fall and taken back into the full presence and glory of God. Only the obedient are "raised in immortality unto eternal life." The disobedient, "they that believe not," are raised in immortality "unto *eternal damnation;* for they cannot be redeemed from their spiritual fall, because they repent not." (D. & C. 29:42-44.)

2. *Eternal damnation* is also used to specify the punishment of those who come forth in the *resurrection of damnation* (John 5:29), meaning those who are destined to inherit the telestial kingdom and those who will be cast out to reign with the devil and his angels as sons of perdition. (D. & C. 76:30-49, 81-112; 88:100-102.)

After the angel had taught King Benjamin the basic truths relative to Christ's atoning sacrifice and the salvation that flows therefrom, these words were spoken relative to the teachings given: "They shall stand as a bright testimony against this people, at the judgment day; whereof they shall be judged, every man according to his works, whether they be good, or whether they be evil. And if they be evil they are consigned to an awful view of their own guilt and abominations, which doth cause them to shrink from the presence of the Lord into a state of misery and *endless torment,* from whence they can no more return; therefore they have drunk *damnation* to their own souls. . . . And their torment is as a lake of fire and brimstone, whose flames are unquenchable, and whose smoke ascendeth up forever and ever." (Mosiah 3:24-27.)

Abinadi uses the term *endless damnation* similarly, to refer to the resurrected state of all the rebellious, those who come forth in the resurrection of the unjust, those who refused to repent when the gospel was offered to them but who chose to go their own carnal ways, receiving eventually an inheritance in the telestial kingdom. Though they attain a kingdom of glory, yet to all eternity they are damned, cannot go where God and Christ are (D. & C. 76:112), and are never completely free from the lingering remorse that always follows the loss of opportunity.

These are Abinadi's words: "This mortal shall put on immortality, and this corruption shall put on incorruption, and shall be brought to stand before the bar of God, to be judged of him according to their works whether they be good or whether they be evil—If they be good, to the resurrection of endless life and happiness; and if they be evil, to the *resurrection of endless damnation,* being delivered up to the devil, who hath subjected them, which is *damnation*—Having gone according to their own carnal wills and desires; having never called upon the Lord while the arms of mercy were extended towards them; for the arms of mercy were extended towards them, and they would not; they being warned of their iniquities and yet they would not depart from them; and they were commanded to repent and yet they would not repent." (Mosiah 16:10-12.)

The last persons to come forth in the resurrection of damnation will be the sons of perdition. "They shall go away into everlasting punishment, which is endless punishment, which is eternal punishment, to reign with the devil and his angels in eternity, where their worm dieth not, and the fire is not quenched, which is their torment— And the end thereof, neither the place thereof, nor their torment, no man knows; Neither was it revealed, neither is, neither will be revealed unto man, except to them who are made partakers thereof; Nevertheless, I, the Lord, show it by vision unto many, but straightway shut it up again; Wherefore, the end, the width, the height, the depth, and the misery thereof, they understand not, neither any man except those who are ordained unto this condemnation." (D. & C. 76: 44-49.)

3. *Eternal damnation* is used

further to specify the torment and anguish to which the spirits of the wicked are heir in the spirit prison as they await the day of their resurrection. This type of eternal damnation ceases when the offender has finally come forth in the resurrection. In this sense, eternal damnation is the type, kind, and quality of torment, punishment, or damnation involved rather than the duration of that damnation. In other words, *eternal* is the name of the kind of punishment involved, just as it is the name of the kind of life referred to in the expression *eternal life*. Eternal punishment is, thus, the kind of punishment imposed by God who is *Eternal,* and those subject to it may suffer therefrom for either a short or a long period. After their buffetings and trials cause them to repent, they are freed from this type of eternal damnation.

"And surely every man must repent or suffer, for I, God, am endless," the Lord says. "Wherefore, I revoke not the judgments which I shall pass, but woes shall go forth, weeping, wailing and gnashing of teeth, yea, to those who are found on my left hand. Nevertheless, it is not written that there shall be no end to this torment, but it is written *endless torment.* Again, it is written *eternal damnation;* wherefore it is more express than other scriptures, that it might work upon the hearts of the children of men, altogether for my name's glory. . . . Behold, I am endless, and the pun-ishment which is given from my hand is endless punishment, for Endless is my name. Wherefore— *Eternal punishment is God's punishment. Endless punishment is God's punishment.*" (D. & C. 19:4-12.)

ETERNAL DEATHS.
See ETERNAL LIVES.

ETERNAL FATHER.
See CHRIST AS THE FATHER, ETERNAL, ETERNAL GOD, FATHER IN HEAVEN, GOD. On very formal occasions, as in the revealed sacramental prayers, Deity is addressed as, "God, the *Eternal Father.*" (D. & C. 20:77-79.) This exalted and sacred name-title combines in one expression the concept of God as an Eternal, exalted Being and his position as the personal Father of the spirits of all men. In the sense in which Christ is called the *Everlasting Father* (Isa. 9:6), he is also the *Eternal Father,* for he is both Eternal and (in special ways) the Father.

ETERNAL FIRE.
See FIRE AND BRIMSTONE.

ETERNAL GOD.
See CHRIST, ETERNAL, ETERNAL FATHER, ETERNITY TO ETERNITY, EVERLASTING FATHER, EVERLASTING GOD, EVERLASTING TO EVERLASTING, GOD. Both the Father

and the Son carry the exalted name-title, *Eternal God*. Both are exalted Beings and as such are Eternal; both are from everlasting to everlasting, with all that this phrase connotes; both are beyond finite comprehension in power, dominion, godly attributes, and eternal glory. (D. & C. 121:32.) By their eternal grace men have been created, redeemed, and placed as possible heirs of all things.

ETERNAL HELL.
See ETERNAL DAMNATION.

ETERNAL INCREASE.
See ETERNAL LIVES.

ETERNAL JUDGE.
See JUDGE OF ALL THE EARTH.

ETERNAL KING.
See KING.

ETERNAL LIFE.
See BOOK OF LIFE, CALLING AND ELECTION SURE, CELESTIAL KINGDOM, CELESTIAL MARRIAGE, CHURCH OF THE FIRSTBORN, DAUGHTERS OF GOD, ETERNAL DAMNATION, ETERNAL LIVES, EXALTATION, FULNESS OF THE FATHER, GODHOOD, IMMORTALITY, JOINT-HEIRS WITH CHRIST, RICHES OF ETERNITY, SALVATION, SONS OF GOD. As used in the scriptures, *eternal life* is the name given to the kind of life that our Eternal Father lives. The word *eternal,* as used in the name *eternal life,* is a noun and not an adjective. It is one of the formal names of Deity (Moses 1:3; 7:35; D. & C. 19:11) and has been chosen by him as the particular name to identify the kind of life that he lives. He being God, the life he lives is God's life; and his name (in the noun sense) being Eternal, the kind of life he lives is eternal life. Thus: *God's life is eternal life; eternal life is God's life*—the expressions are synonymous.

Accordingly, eternal life is not a name that has reference only to the unending duration of a future life; immortality is to live forever in the resurrected state, and by the grace of God all men will gain this unending continuance of life. But only those who obey the fulness of the gospel law will inherit eternal life. (D. & C. 29:43-44.) It is "the greatest of all the gifts of God" (D. & C. 14:7), for it is the kind, status, type, and quality of life that God himself enjoys. Thus those who gain eternal life receive exaltation; they are sons of God, joint-heirs with Christ, members of the Church of the Firstborn; they overcome all things, have all power, and receive the fulness of the Father. They are gods.

ETERNAL LIVES.
See CELESTIAL MARRIAGE,

CHURCH OF THE FIRSTBORN, DAUGHTERS OF GOD, ETERNAL LIFE, EXALTATION, FULNESS OF THE FATHER, GODHOOD, JOINT-HEIRS WITH CHRIST, SALVATION, SONS OF GOD. Those who gain eternal life (exaltation) also gain *eternal lives,* meaning that in the resurrection they have eternal *"increase," "a continuation of the seeds,"* a *"continuation of the lives."* Their spirit progeny will "continue as innumerable as the stars; or, if ye were to count the sand upon the seashore ye could not number them." (D. & C. 131:1-4; 132:19-25, 30, 55.)

"Except a man and his wife enter into an everlasting covenant and be married for eternity, while in this probation, by the power and authority of the holy priesthood," the Prophet says, "they will cease to increase when they die; that is, they will not have any *children after the resurrection."* Then with reference to those who have been properly sealed in marriage and who have thereafter endured in righteousness until their callings and elections were made sure by revelation he adds: "But those who are married by the power and authority of the priesthood in this life, and continue without committing the sin against the Holy Ghost, [their callings and elections having been made sure through perfect devotion to the truth, they] will continue to increase and have *children in the celestial glory."* (*Teachings,* pp. 300-301.)

The opposite of eternal lives is *eternal deaths.* Those who come up separately and singly in the resurrection and who therefore do not have spirit children eternally are said to inherit "the deaths." (D. & C. 132:16-17, 25.)

ETERNAL ONE.
See GREAT I AM.

ETERNAL PROGRESSION.
See CELESTIAL KINGDOM, CELESTIAL MARRIAGE, CHURCH OF THE FIRSTBORN, DAUGHTERS OF GOD, ETERNAL LIFE, ETERNAL LIVES, EXALTATION, FULNESS OF THE FATHER, GODHOOD, JOINT-HEIRS WITH CHRIST. Endowed with agency and subject to eternal laws, man began his progression and advancement in pre-existence, his ultimate goal being to attain a state of glory, honor, and exaltation like the Father of spirits. During his earth life he gains a mortal body, receives experience in earthly things, and prepares for a future eternity after the resurrection when he will continue to gain knowledge and intelligence. (D. & C. 130:18-19.) This gradually unfolding course of advancement and experience—a course that began in a past eternity and will continue in ages future —is frequently referred to as a course of *eternal progression.*

It is important to know, however, that for the overwhelming majority of mankind, eternal progression has very definite limitations.

In the full sense, eternal progression is enjoyed only by those who receive exaltation. Exalted persons gain the fulness of the Father; they have all power, all knowledge, and all wisdom; they gain a fulness of truth, becoming one with the Father. All other persons are assigned lesser places in the mansions that are prepared, and their progression is not eternal and unlimited but in a specified sphere. There will be truths such persons never learn, powers they never possess. They are "ministering servants, to minister for those who are worthy of a far more, and an exceeding, and an eternal weight of glory," and they so continue "to all eternity, and . . . forever and ever." (D. & C. 132:16-17.)

Those who gain exaltation, having thus enjoyed the fulness of eternal progression, become like God. It should be realized that God is not progressing in knowledge, truth, virtue, wisdom, or any of the attributes of godliness. He has already gained these things in their fulness. But he is progressing in the sense that his creations increase, his dominions expand, his spirit offspring multiply, and more kingdoms are added to his domains. (*Doctrines of Salvation,* vol. 1, pp. 5-10.)

ETERNAL PUNISHMENT.
See ETERNAL DAMNATION.

ETERNAL ROUND.
See ONE ETERNAL ROUND.

ETERNAL TORMENT.
See ETERNAL DAMNATION.

ETERNITY.
See ETERNAL, ETERNITY TO ETERNITY, IMMORTALITY, MORTALITY, PRE-EXISTENCE, RESURRECTION, RICHES OF ETERNITY, TIME. In general, *eternity* refers to the eternal worlds, to the spheres of existence outside the realm of time, those outside the temporal limitations circumscribing mortal life on this earth. Spirit beings and immortal persons live in *eternity;* mortal man lives in *time.* Eternity goes on forever and is of infinite duration; time is of finite proportions, beginning for each person at birth and ending at death. (D. & C. 38:12, 20; 39:22; 72:3; 109:24; 132:17.) Properly performed priesthood ordinances are binding in time and in eternity. (D. & C. 132:7, 18-19, 49.) Faithful saints are promised the riches and the wonders of eternity (D. & C. 38:39; 67:2; 68:31; 76:8; 78:18); the sons of perdition are destined to go "with the devil and his angels in eternity." (D. & C. 76:33, 44.)

Because he is an eternal Being, God dwells "in the high and holy place" in eternity. He is "the high and lofty One that inhabiteth eternity, whose name is Holy." (Isa. 57:15.) He "sitteth upon his throne, . . . is in the bosom of eternity, . . . in the midst of all things." (D. & C. 88:13.) And it is he who "looked upon the wide expanse of eternity, and all the seraphic hosts of heaven, before the world was made." (D. & C. 38:1.)

ETERNITY TO ETERNITY.

See CHRIST, ENDLESS, ETERNAL, ETERNAL FATHER, ETERNAL GOD, ETERNAL LIFE, ETERNITY, EVERLASTING, EVERLASTING TO EVERLASTING, IMMORTALITY, ONE ETERNAL ROUND, PRE-EXISTENCE, RESURRECTION. As men view things from their mortal perspective, there was a *past eternity* and there will be a *future eternity*. The past eternity embraced the sphere of eternal existence which all men had as the spirit offspring of exalted Parents in pre-existence. The future eternity will be that eternal sphere in which the righteous, having gained both immortality and eternal life, will themselves become exalted Parents and have a continuation of the seeds forever and ever. (D. & C. 132:19-25.) In this sense, eternity becomes a measure of eternal "time." Those past ages when all men dwelt in the presence of their Eternal Father were one eternity, and those future ages when these spirit children will have gone on to exaltation, having spirit children of their own, will be another eternity.

Having in mind this eternal, unending repetition of the eternal plan of creation, redemption, and salvation, it is plain what our Lord meant when he said he was "from all eternity to all eternity" (D. & C. 39:1), and also when he said of himself, "From eternity to eternity he is the same, and his years never fail." (D. & C. 76:4.) In other words Christ, as an eternal, exalted Being, never varies; from one eternity to the next he is the same. From pre-existence to pre-existence his course goes on in one eternal round, and so will it be with all exalted beings. Those who become gods will then be from eternity to eternity, everlastingly the same, always possessing the fulness of all things and multiplying their race without end. (*Doctrines of Salvation,* vol. 1, pp. 10-12.)

ETHICS.

See CHRIST, CHRISTIANITY, LIGHT OF CHRIST. Principles of right conduct are called *ethics*. Ethical principles grow out of the teachings of Christianity; some of them are instilled into the consciences of men by the light of Christ. The only real superiority of the apostate sects of Christendom over their more openly pagan counterparts is the fact that the Christian sects (though rejecting the doctrines, ordinances, and powers of the gospel) have nonetheless preserved many of the ethical teachings of Christ and the apostles.

The more gospel doctrines accepted by a particular people, the higher are their ethical standards. Thus the highest manifestation of ethical achievement is found among the true saints.

EUCHARIST.

See APOSTASY, SACRAMENT, SACRAMENTS. One of the sacraments of the Catholic Church is the *Eucharist*. As administered by them this is not the correct form of the true ordinance of the sacrament of the Lord's Supper. The chief feature of the Eucharist—according to their teaching—is that bread and wine, on the principle of transubstantiation, turn literally into the flesh and blood of our Lord. (James Cardinal Gibbons, *The Faith of Our Fathers*, pp. 235-250.)

EUNUCHS.

See CELIBACY. In a passage of uncertain accuracy and meaning, our Lord said: "There are some *eunuchs*, which were so born from their mother's womb: and there are some eunuchs, which were made eunuchs of men: and there be eunuchs, which have made themselves eunuchs for the kingdom of heaven's sake." (Matt. 19:12.) Apparently those who made themselves eunuchs were men who in false pagan worship had deliberately mutilated themselves with the expectancy that such would further their salvation. It is clear that such was not a true gospel requirement of any sort. There is no such thing in the gospel as willful emasculation; such a notion violates true principles of procreation and celestial marriage.

Eunuchs who are righteous and keep the commandments are heirs of the fulness of the Father's kingdom. (Isa. 56:1-8.) One of the most dramatic conversions and baptisms recorded in the scripture is that of the eunuch by Philip. (Acts 8:26-39.)

EVANGELICAL MINISTERS.
See EVANGELISTS.

EVANGELISTS.

See MELCHIZEDEK PRIESTHOOD, MISSIONARIES, PATRIARCHAL BLESSINGS, PATRIARCHAL ORDER, PATRIARCHS, PATRIARCH TO THE CHURCH, PRIESTHOOD, PRIESTHOOD OFFICES, PRIESTHOOD QUORUMS. 1. "An *evangelist* is a patriarch," the Prophet said, "even the oldest man of the blood of Joseph or of the seed of Abraham. Wherever the Church of Christ is established in the earth, there should be a patriarch for the benefit of the posterity of the saints, as it was with Jacob in giving his patriarchal blessing unto his sons." (*Teachings*, p. 151; Gen. 49; Acts 21:8; Eph. 4:11-14; 2 Tim. 4:5.)

Stake patriarchs are chosen pursuant to the following revelation: "It is the duty of the Twelve, in all large branches of the church, to ordain evangelical ministers, as they shall be designated unto them by revelation." (D. & C. 107:39.) The office of *Evangelist* or *Patriarch to the Church* is hereditary; it "was confirmed to be handed down from father to son, and rightly belongs to the literal descendants of the chosen seed, to whom the promises were made." (D. & C. 107:40-53.)

2. Having lost the true knowledge of the priesthood and its offices, and knowing nothing of patriarchal blessings as a necessary part of church administration, the false traditions of the sectarian world have applied the designation *evangelist* to traveling preachers, missionaries, and revivalists. The sectarian theory is that evangelists travel to spread the gospel. This usage of the term is so widespread that even in the Church it is not inappropriate to speak of the evangelical work of missionaries.

EVE.

See ADAM, FORBIDDEN FRUIT, WOMAN. Scant knowledge is available to us of *Eve* (the wife of Adam) and her achievements in pre-existence and in mortality. Without question she was like unto her mighty husband, Adam, in intelligence and in devotion to righteousness, during both her first and second estates of existence. She was placed on earth in the same manner as was Adam, the Mosaic account of the Lord creating her from Adam's rib being merely figurative. (Moses 3:20-25.)

Eve was the first woman; she became the mother of the whole human race, her very name signifying "mother of all living." (Moses 4:26; 1 Ne. 5:11.) Strictly speaking it was she who first partook of the forbidden fruit, with the resultant change in the physical body from a state of immortality to mortality. Adam thereafter partook in order to comply with the command to multiply and fill the earth with posterity. "Adam was not deceived, but the woman being deceived was in the transgression." (1 Tim. 2:14.)

Before the fall Eve was sealed to Adam in the new and everlasting covenant of marriage, a ceremony performed by the Lord before death entered the world and therefore one destined to last forever. (Moses 3:20-25.) After the fall the Lord said to her: "I will greatly multiply thy sorrow and thy conception. In sorrow thou shalt bring forth children, and thy desire shall be to thy husband, and he shall rule over thee." (Moses 4:22.)

One of the most perfect summaries of the plan of salvation ever given fell from the lips of Eve: "Were it not for our transgression," she said, "we never should have had seed, and never should have known good and evil, and the joy of our redemption, and the eternal life which God giveth unto all the obedient." (Moses 5:11.) Indeed, Eve is a joint-participant with Adam in all his ministry, and will inherit jointly with him all the blessings appertaining to his high state of exaltation.

EVERLASTING.

See CHRIST, ENDLESS, ETER-

NAL, ETERNAL LIFE, ETERNITY TO ETERNITY, EVERLASTING GOD, EVERLASTING TO EVERLASTING, GOD, ONE ETERNAL ROUND. 1. In the same sense in which one of the Lord's names is *Endless* and another *Eternal,* so *Everlasting* is also an appellation of Deity. (Moses 1:3; 7:35; D. & C. 19:10.) He is called the *Everlasting God* (Gen. 21:33; Isa. 9:6; 40:28; Jer. 10:10; Rom. 16:26; D. & C. 133:34), signifying that he endures forever, for "his years never fail." (D. & C. 76:4.)

Everlasting, used thus, is a noun and not an adjective; it is the name of the kind, status, and quality of existence enjoyed by an everlasting Being. Accordingly, *everlasting life* (a synonym for endless life and eternal life) is the name of the kind of life that God lives, or in other words everlasting life is exaltation. (Matt. 19:29; John 3:16, 36; 5:24; 6:40, 47.)

2. *Everlasting* is also used to signify the eternal, lasting, and enduring nature of some particular thing. For instance: the "everlasting covenant" (D. & C. 1:15), "the everlasting gospel" (D. & C. 36:5), "songs of everlasting joy" (D. & C. 45:71), "an everlasting inheritance" (D. & C. 57:5), "the everlasting hills." (D. & C. 133:31.)

EVERLASTING COVENANT.

See NEW AND EVERLASTING COVENANT.

EVERLASTING DAMNATION.

See ETERNAL DAMNATION.

EVERLASTING FATHER.

See CHRIST, CHRIST AS THE FATHER, ETERNAL, EVERLASTING, EVERLASTING GOD, FATHER IN HEAVEN, GOD. One of Isaiah's great Messianic prophecies names Christ as "The *everlasting Father*" (Isa. 9:6), an expression having reference both to our Lord's everlasting godhood and to the special senses in which he stands as the Father. Since God the Father is both an everlasting Being and the Father of the spirits of men, he also may properly be called the *Everlasting Father.*

EVERLASTING GOD.

See CHRIST, ETERNAL GOD, ETERNITY TO ETERNITY, EVERLASTING FATHER, EVERLASTING TO EVERLASTING, GOD. Both the Father and the Son are known by the sacred name-title, *Everlasting God.* (Gen. 21:33; Isa. 9:6; 40:28; Jer. 10:10; Rom. 16:26; D. & C. 133:34.) Carrying as it does a connotation of eternal continuance and unending existence, this designation of Deity points up the sharp contrast between the living Gods and the false and temporary gods of the world.

EVERLASTING GOSPEL.

See GOSPEL.

EVERLASTING HELL.
See ETERNAL DAMNATION.

EVERLASTING KING.
See KING.

EVERLASTING LIFE.
See ETERNAL LIFE.

EVERLASTING PUNISHMENT.
See ETERNAL DAMNATION.

EVERLASTING TO EVERLAST-
ING.
See ENDLESS, ETERNAL, ETER-
NAL LIFE, ETERNITY, ETERNITY
TO ETERNITY, EVERLASTING, EVER-
LASTING FATHER, EVERLASTING
GOD, EXALTATION, FULNESS OF THE
FATHER, IMMORTALITY, ONE ETER-
NAL ROUND, PRE-EXISTENCE, RES-
URRECTION. By gaining exaltation
—which includes the fulness of the
Father and "a continuation of the
seeds forever and ever"—men become "gods, because they have no
end; therefore shall they be from
everlasting to everlasting, because
they continue." (D. & C. 132:19-20.)
That is, those who gain eternal increase, who have unending spirit
children in the resurrection, have
thereby become from everlasting to
everlasting. Because of their eternal progeny they continue everlastingly without end; from eternity
to eternity they are the same; and
being perfected and exalted beings,
their course never varies, nor is
there shadow of turning to the right
or the left.

Our Eternal Father, of course,
now has this kind of an existence.
"There is a God in heaven," the
revelation says, of him "who is infinite and eternal, from everlasting
to everlasting the same unchangeable God." (D. & C. 20:17; 109:77.)
Christ also describes himself as being "from everlasting to everlasting." (D. & C. 61:1; Ps. 90:2; *Doctrines of Salvation,* vol. 1, pp. 10-
12.)

EVERLASTING TORMENT.
See ETERNAL DAMNATION.

EVIL.
See AGENCY, DEVIL, EVIL ONE,
EVIL SPIRITS, GOOD, SIN, WICKED-
NESS. *Evil* is the opposite of good;
it consists in disobeying the laws of
God. It is of the devil. Everything
which is fostered, inspired, and
spread forth by the power of the
Evil One is in its nature evil. Accordingly, evil is that which is morally corrupt, wicked, and bad;
which neither edifies nor enlightens; which chooses darkness and
secrecy to cover its doings; which is
destructive of faith, good morals,
and godly virtues; which is in opposition to all righteousness; which
leads away from God and from salvation. Evil is sin, transgression,
unrighteousness, wickedness.

Philosophers and certain religionists are forever seeking to find the origin and purpose of evil, but until they accept the gospel truths, they will never succeed. To understand the nature and source of evil, together with its place in the eternal scheme of things, it is necessary to know the basic truths of the great plan of salvation.

As far as men on this earth are concerned, evil had its beginning in pre-existence. The Eternal Father begat spirit children, ordained laws to enable them to progress, and endowed them with agency. Disobedience to those laws was in its nature evil, and consequently without the possibility of committing evil there could be no hope of progression toward exaltation. Lucifer and one-third of the spirit hosts of heaven chose evil rather than good, failed to exercise their agency in righteousness, and finally coming out in open rebellion against the Lord, they were cast out onto the earth and denied bodies. (Moses 4:1-4; Abra. 3:24-28; D. & C. 29:36-40; Rev. 12:7-13.)

Continuing their rebellion against God, their self-appointed mission is to entice men to violate the laws of God and thereby commit evil and be damned. Thus, as far as this mortal life is concerned, Lucifer is the author and creator of evil. "That which is evil cometh of the devil; for the devil is an enemy unto God, and fighteth against him continually, and inviteth and enticeth to sin, and to do that which is evil continually." (Moro. 7:12.)

"Let no man say when he is tempted, I am tempted of God: for God cannot be tempted with evil, neither tempteth he any man." (Jas. 1:13.)

The presence of evil in this world, with the ever present possibility that each accountable person may do that which is evil, becomes a basic reality without which the great plan of salvation would not operate. "It must needs be, that there is an opposition in all things," Lehi said. (2 Ne. 2:11.) Without virtue in contrast to vice, good as the opposite of bad, and evil as the opponent of righteousness, men would not be able to overcome the lusts of the flesh and thus work out their own salvation in the kingdom of God. Thus the *existence* but not the *partaking* of evil is essential to the attainment of salvation.

As part of the gospel plan, men are commanded: "Forsake all evil and cleave unto all good" (D. & C. 98:11); "cease to do evil" (D. & C. 124:116); "Keep yourselves from evil." (D. & C. 136:21.) "Deliver us from evil," is the approved petition for divine grace as it is found in the Lord's prayer. (Matt. 6:13.)

"The wicked," those "who are evil," those who choose "evil works rather than good," shall be thrust down to hell to suffer the torments of the damned until they have paid the penalty for their evil deeds. (Alma 40:13-14.) At the end of their imprisonment they shall come forth in the resurrection of

245

the unjust to receive a telestial inheritance. (D. & C. 76:17, 105-106.)

EVIL ONE.

See DEVIL, EVIL, EVIL SPIRITS. Satan is the *Evil One,* a name-title signifying that he is the embodiment of all evil and all wickedness, that he is in opposition to all righteousness, and that he is the *father of lies* and the author of evil. (2 Ne. 4:27; 9:28; Alma 46:8; Hela. 12:4; Ether 8:25.) "Light and truth forsake that evil one." (D. & C. 93:37.) His mission is "to destroy the souls of men." (Hela. 8:28.) Sorceries, witchcrafts, magics, and every form of evil abomination are wrought by "the power of the evil one." (Morm. 1:19.)

EVIL SPIRITS.

See DEMONS, DEVILS, DIVINATION, EVIL, EVIL ONE, EXORCISM, GHOSTS, MAGIC, NECROMANCY, SIN, SORCERY, S P I R I T U A L I S M, TEMPTATION, WITCHCRAFT. Lucifer is not alone; one-third of the spirit hosts of heaven, having been cast out with him, stand at his side to do his bidding. Their mission is to make war with the saints and to destroy the souls of all men. (Rev. 12.) Obviously there are many *evil spirits* available to seduce and lead astray each person on earth.

Acting in conformity with laws which exist, evil spirits have power to tempt men, to entice them to work wickedness, and to induce them to do those things which are carnal, sensual, and devilish. Revelations come to men just as easily from devils as they do from holy sources. By rebellion and wickedness men may commune with evil spirits, whereas by obedience and righteousness they might have seen angels and had the communion of the Holy Spirit. All these things are governed by law.

Evil spirits control much of the so-called religious worship in the world; for instance, the great creeds of Christendom were formulated so as to conform to their whispered promptings. They have played a substantial part in the formulation of the philosophies of the world; so-called scientific theories have been influenced by them. By hearkening to their promptings, leaders of nations have led their peoples into wars and every sort of evil.

Whether they know it or not, Satan is and has been the master of all who live after the manner of the world. Stalin, for instance (though he may not have been aware of the source of his ideas), seemed to have been influenced by evil spirits in the direction of the murderous and barbarous course he pursued both in his home Russia and in the nations of the earth.

To his saints the Lord says: "Ye are commanded in all things to ask of God, who giveth liberally; and that which the Spirit testifies unto you even so I would that ye should do in all holiness of heart, walking uprightly before me, considering the end of your salvation, doing all things with prayer and thanksgiving, *that ye may not be seduced by evil spirits, or doctrines of devils, or the commandments of men; for some are of men, and others of devils."* (D. & C. 46:7.)

EVOLUTION.

See ADAM, ATONEMENT OF CHRIST, CREATION, EARTH, EARTHS, FALLEN MAN, FALL OF ADAM, FIRST MAN, GOD, MILLENNIUM, PRE-EXISTENCE. Of the several theories, postulated in one age or another to explain (without the aid of revelation) the origin of man and the various forms of life, none has taken such hold or found such widespread acceptance as the relatively modern so-called theory of *organic evolution.* Stated generally, this theory assumes that over long periods of times, and through a series of changes, all present living organisms or groups of organisms have acquired the morphological and physiological characters which distinguish them. The theory assumes that all present animals and plants have their origin in other pre-existing types, the distinguishable differences being due to modifications in successive generations. One or more common origins for all forms of life are assumed.

From the day of their first announcement, these theories of organic evolution found themselves in conflict with the principles of revealed religion as such are found recorded in the scriptures and expounded by inspired teachers. (*Doctrines of Salvation,* vol. 1, pp. 139-151.)

President John Taylor wrote as follows: "The animal and vegetable creations are governed by certain laws, and are composed of certain elements peculiar to themselves. This applies to man, to the beasts, fowls, fish and creeping things, to the insects and to all animated nature; each one possessing its own distinctive features, each requiring a specific sustenance, each having an organism and faculties governed by prescribed laws to perpetuate its own kind. So accurate is the formation of the various living creatures that an intelligent student of nature can tell by any particular bone of the skeleton of an animal to what class or order it belongs.

"These principles do not change, as represented by evolutionists of the Darwinian school, but the primitive organisms of all living beings exist in the same form as when they first received their impress from their Maker. . . . If we take man, he is said to have been made in the image of God, for the simple reason that he is a son of God; and being his son, he is, of course, his offspring, an emanation from God, in whose likeness, we are told, he is made. He did not originate from a chaotic mass of matter, moving or inert, but came forth possessing, in an embryotic state, all the faculties and powers of a God.

And when he shall be perfected, and have progressed to maturity, he will be like his Father—a God; being indeed his offspring. As the horse, the ox, the sheep, and every living creature, including man, propagates its own species and perpetuates its own kind, so does God perpetuate his. . . .

"Paul, in speaking on the resurrection, refers to the different qualities of flesh as follows: 'But God giveth it a body as it hath pleased him, and to every seed his own body. *All flesh is not the same flesh:* but there is one kind of flesh of men, another flesh of beasts, and another of fishes, and another of birds.' (1 Cor. 15:38-39.)

"These different qualities seem to be inherent in the several species, as much so as the properties of silver, gold, copper, iron, and other minerals are inherent in the matter in which they are contained, whilst herbs, according to their kind, possess their specific properties, or as the leading properties of earth, air, and water, are distinct from one another; and hence, on physiological grounds, this principle being admitted, and it cannot be controverted, *it would be impossible to take the tissues of the lower, or, indeed, of any order of fishes, and make of them an ox, a bird, or a man;* as impossible as it would be to take iron and make it into gold, silver, or copper, or to produce any other changes in the laws which govern any kind of matter. And when the resurrection and exalta-

tion of man shall be consummated, although more pure, refined and glorious, yet will he still be in the same image, and have the same likeness, without variation or change in any of his parts or faculties, except the substitution of spirit for blood." (*Mediation and Atonement,* pp. 160-161.)

This aptly expressed and plainly worded statement from President John Taylor expresses the same views and perspective found in the writings and sermons of Joseph Smith, Brigham Young, Orson Pratt, Parley P. Pratt, Charles W. Penrose, and many of our early day inspired writers. (*Man: His Origin and Destiny,* pp. 1-563.)

The First Presidency of the Church (Joseph F. Smith, John R. Winder, and Anthon H. Lund), in November, 1909, issued a formal pronouncement under the title, "The Origin of Man," in which, as they expressed it, is set forth "the position held by the Church" upon the subject of evolution. After explaining the scriptural passages relative to the creation and pre-existence, this document concludes:

"Adam, our great progenitor, 'the first man,' was, like Christ, a pre-existent spirit, and like Christ, he took upon him an appropriate body, the body of a man, and so became a 'living soul.' The doctrine of the pre-existence, revealed so plainly, particularly in latter-days, pours a wonderful flood of light upon the otherwise mysterious problem of man's origin. It shows that man, as a spirit, was begotten and born of heavenly parents, and reared to maturity in the eternal mansions of the Father, prior to coming upon the earth in a temporal body to undergo an experience in mortality. It teaches that all men existed in the spirit before any man existed in the flesh, and that *all who have inhabited the earth since Adam have taken bodies and become souls in like manner.*

"It is held by some that Adam was not the first man upon this earth, and that the original human being was a development from lower orders of the animal creation. These, however, are the theories of men. The word of the Lord declares that Adam was 'the first man of all men' (Moses 1:34), and we are therefore in duty bound to regard him as *the primal parent of the race.* It was shown to the brother of Jared that all men were created in the beginning after the image of God; and whether we take this to mean the spirit or the body, or both, it commits us to the same conclusion: *Man began life as a human being, in the likeness of our heavenly Father.*

"True it is that the body of man enters upon its career as a tiny germ or embryo, which becomes an infant, quickened at a certain stage by the spirit whose tabernacle it is, and the child, after being born, develops into a man. There is nothing in this, however, to indicate that the original man the

first of our race, began life as anything less than a man, or less than the human germ or embryo that becomes a man.

"Man, by searching, cannot find out God. Never, unaided, will he discover the truth about the beginning of human life. The Lord must reveal himself, or remain unrevealed; and the same is true of the facts relating to the origin of Adam's race—God alone can reveal them. Some of these facts, however, are already known, and what has been made known it is our duty to receive and retain.

"The Church of Jesus Christ of Latter-day Saints, basing its belief on divine revelation, ancient and modern, proclaims man to be the direct and lineal offspring of Deity. God himself is an exalted man, perfected, enthroned, and supreme. By his almighty power he organized the earth, and all that it contains, from spirit and element, which exist co-eternally with himself. He formed every plant that grows, and every animal that breathes, each after its own kind, spiritually and temporally—'that which is spiritual being in the likeness of that which is temporal, and that which is temporal in the likeness of that which is spiritual.' He made the tadpole and the ape, the lion and the elephant; but he did not make them in his own image, nor endow them with Godlike reason and intelligence. Nevertheless, the whole animal creation will be perfected and perpetuated in the hereafter, each class in its 'destined order or sphere.' and will enjoy 'eternal felicity.' That fact has been made plain in this dispensation. (D. & C. 77:3.)

"Man is the child of God, formed in the divine image and endowed with divine attributes, and even as the infant son of an earthly father and mother is capable in due time of becoming a man, so the undeveloped offspring of celestial parentage is capable, by experience through ages and aeons, of evolving into a God." (*Man: His Origin and Destiny,* pp. 354-355.)

Obviously there never will be a conflict between truths revealed in the realm of religion and those discovered by scientific research. Truth is ever in harmony with itself. But if false doctrines creep into revealed religion, these will run counter to the discovered truths of science; and if false scientific *theories* are postulated, these ultimately will be overthrown by the truths revealed from Him who knows all things.

Sometimes persons having a knowledge of the revealed truths of salvation and of the evolutionistic theories of the day keep these two branches of knowledge divided between separate mental compartments. Their purpose seems to be to avoid resolving the obvious conflicts which otherwise would arise. Truth, however, is truth, and ultimately every believing person must channel his mental processes so that proper choices are made as be-

tween the truths of salvation and the theories of men. Perhaps it will be profitable to list a few of the basic, revealed truths concerning the origin and destiny of man and of all life—truths which are not taken into consideration by evolutionists in their theorizing and which, in most instances, are diametrically opposed to the speculative conclusions reached by them.

1. GOD: CREATOR AND RULER OF MANY WORLDS.—While it is true that evolutionists may be divided between theistic and atheistic groups, yet most of those professing belief in God consider him to be an indefinable force, essence, or power of an incomprehensible nature. According to revelation, however, he is a personal Being, a holy and exalted Man, a glorified, resurrected Personage having a tangible body of flesh and bones, an anthropomorphic Entity, the personal Father of the spirits of all men. (D. & C. 130:22-23; Moses 6: 51, 57; Abra. 3:22-24; Jos. Smith 2: 16-19.)

This Person, in whose image and likeness man is created, has ordained the same plan of creation and salvation for this earth, and all the varieties of life on its face, that he has ordained with reference to the infinite number of worlds elsewhere created by him. (Moses 1; D. & C. 76:22-24.) Obviously the eternal truths concerning the nature of the true God and his creative enterprises have received no consideration in the formulation of the theory of organic evolution.

2. PRE-EXISTENCE.—Life did not originate on this earth; it was transplanted from other and older spheres. Men are the literal spirit children, spirit offspring, of the Eternal Father; they were born to him as his spirit progeny, as spirit entities having bodies made of a more pure and refined substance than that comprising these mortal tabernacles.

Further, *every form of life had a spirit existence in that eternal world before it came to dwell naturally upon the face of the earth;* and that prior existence, for all forms of life, was one in which the spirit entity had the exact form and likeness of its present temporal body. Animals, plants, fowls, fishes, all forms of life existed as spirit entities in pre-existence; their number, extent, variety, and form were known with exactitude before ever the foundations of this earth were laid. They were all destined to live in their time and season upon this particular globe. (Moses 3:1-9; D. & C. 77:1-2.) *There was no chance whatever connected with the creative enterprises.* All things were foreknown to that God who fathered man in his own image and who created all other forms of life for the benefit and blessing of man. Evolutionary speculation takes no account of any such revealed knowledge as this.

3. EARTH CREATED IN A PARADISIACAL STATE.—This earth, when first it rolled forth from the Creator's hand, was in a paradisiacal or terrestrial state. This condition, which does not now prevail, will be restored when the earth is "renewed" (made new again) and receives its paradisiacal glory. (Tenth Article of Faith.)

In its primeval, edenic state all of the earth's surface was in one place (Moses 2:9); thorns, thistles, briars and noxious weeds had not yet begun to grow on it; rather, all plant and animal life was desirable, congenial, and designed to provide for man (earth's crowning inhabitant) a fruitful, peaceful garden in which to dwell. It was not a condition attained by progressive, creative evolvement from less propitious situations; it was creation in its glory, beauty, and perfection; hence, the Lord God pronounced it "very good." The fall to present conditions was to come later. (Parley P. Pratt, *Voice of Warning,* chapter 5.)

Bearing on this general theme that the earth was created in its glory and perfection, in a higher type of existence than it now enjoys, is the revealed fact that, as is the case with man, *the earth itself is passing through a plan of salvation.* It was created (the equivalent of birth); it fell to its present mortal or telestial state; it was baptized by immersion, when the universal flood swept over its entire surface (Ether 13:2-11); it will be baptized by fire (the equivalent of baptism of the Spirit) in the day when it is renewed and receives its paradisiacal glory; it will die; and finally it will be quickened (or resurrected) and become a celestial sphere. Evolutionary theories take no account of any of this.

4. TEMPORAL CREATION OF MAN AND ALL LIFE.—*Adam and Eve and all forms of life, both animal and plant, were created in immortality; that is, when first placed on this earth, all forms of life were in a state of immortality.* There was no death in the world; death entered *after* the fall. All things existed in a state of primeval innocence. If conditions had not changed, death would not have entered the picture. Instead, as the revelations express it, "All things which were created must have remained in the same state in which they were after they were created; and they must have remained forever, and had no end." (2 Ne. 2:22.)

The recorded teachings of many of the early brethren of the Church bear this same testimony. Orson Pratt, for instance, has left us such apt expressions as these: "When the Lord made the fowls of the air, and the fishes of the sea, to people the atmospheric heavens, or the watery elements, these fowls and fishes were so constructed in their nature as to be capable of eternal existence. . . . *Man, when he was first placed upon this earth, was an immortal being, capable of eternal endurance; his flesh and bones, as well as his spirit, were immortal and eternal in their nature; and it was just so with all the inferior*

creation—the lion, the leopard, the kid, and the cow; it was so with the feathered tribes of creation, as well as those that swim in the vast ocean of waters; all were immortal and eternal in their nature; and the earth itself, as a living being, was immortal and eternal in its nature. . . . The earth was so constructed that it was capable of existing as a living being to all eternity, with all the swarms of animals, fowls, and fishes that were first placed upon the face thereof. . . . If there had been no sin, our father Adam would at this day have been in the Garden of Eden, as bright and as blooming, as fresh and as fair, as ever, together with his lovely consort Eve, dwelling in all the beauty of youth." (*Man: His Origin and Destiny,* pp. 388-396.)

After this temporal creation, this creation of all forms of life in a state of immortality, the Lord God issued the decree that all created life should *remain* in the *sphere* in which it was after it was created. Further, having in mind the coming fall and consequent entrance of death and mortality into the world, the Lord in that first primeval day commanded that all forms of life, after mortality entered the picture, should bring forth posterity, *each after its own kind.* (Moses 2; 3.) These principles accord with the one announced by Paul that "All flesh is not the same flesh: but there is one kind of flesh of men, another of beasts, another of fishes, and another of birds." (1 Cor.

15:39.)

If the revelations are true which say that all life was created in immortality, then evolutionary theorries which necessarily assume there was *always death* in the world are false.

5. FALL OF ADAM AND ALL THINGS.—Before the fall there was neither death nor procreation. Plants, animals, and man would have continued living forever unless a change of condition overtook them; and in their then immortal condition they could not have reproduced, each after its own kind. *Death and procreation pertain to mortality,* that is, to the status and type of existence attained by all forms of life subsequent to the fall.

Lehi said: "If Adam had not transgressed he would not have fallen, but he would have remained in the garden of Eden. And all things which were created must have remained forever, and had no end. And they would have had no children; wherefore they would have remained in a state of innocence, having no joy, for they knew no misery; doing no good, for they knew no sin. But behold, all things have been done in the wisdom of him who knoweth all things. Adam fell that men might be; and men are, that they might have joy. And the Messiah cometh in the fulness of time, that he may redeem the children of men from the fall." (2 Ne. 2:22-26.)

Eve expressed the same truth in this language: "Were it not for our transgression we never should have had seed, and never should have known good and evil, and the joy of our redemption, and the eternal life which God giveth unto all the obedient." (Moses 5:11.)

Adam's fall brought temporal (natural) and spiritual death into the world. The temporal or natural death means that body and spirit separate, the spirit going to a world of waiting spirits to await the day of the resurrection, the body returning to the dust, the primal element, from which it was taken. The effects of this fall passed upon all created things. "Adam was appointed Lord of this creation," Orson Pratt says, "a great governor, swaying the scepter of power over the whole earth. When the governor, the person who was placed to reign over this fair creation, had transgressed, all in his dominion had to feel the effects of it, the same as a father or a mother, who transgresses certain laws, frequently transmits the effects thereof to the latest generations." (*Man: His Origin and Destiny,* p. 395.)

Thus when man fell, the earth fell together with all forms of life on its face. Death entered; procreation began; the probationary experiences of mortality had their start. Before this fall there was neither mortality, nor birth, nor death, nor—for that matter—did Adam so much as have blood in his veins (and the same would be true for other forms of life), for blood is an element pertaining only to mortality. (*Man: His Origin and Destiny*, pp. 362-365; *Doctrines of Salvation*, vol. 1, pp. 76-77.)

Obviously, the whole doctrine of the fall, and all that pertains to it, is diametrically opposed to the evolutionary assumptions relative to the origin of species.

6. ATONEMENT OF CHRIST.—Our Lord's atoning sacrifice is the cornerstone on which the whole gospel of salvation rests. For this atonement to come to pass, two things were necessary: 1. Christ had to come into the world as the literal Son of an immortal, personal Father, a Father who had life in himself and from whom his offspring in mortality would inherit power over death (John 10:7-18); 2. The fall of Adam had to introduce temporal and spiritual death into the world, for the atonement in its very nature was designed to ransom all things that fell from the effects of that fall. All forms of life are ransomed from the temporal effects of the fall in that they are resurrected and become immortal.

Now if Adam did not fall and bring death into the world, there would be no need for the atoning sacrifice of Christ. If there were no atonement to ransom fallen beings and creatures from the effects of the fall, there would be no resurrection, no immortality, no salvation, no eternal life; and if all these things should vanish away, we could discard God himself, and our faith would be vain.

7. ADAM'S PLACE IN PLAN OF SALVATION.—Father Adam was the mightiest and most intelligent spirit son of God, save Jesus (Jehovah) only, among all the pre-existent hosts destined to come to this earth. (D. & C. 78:15-16.) When there was war in heaven following Lucifer's rebellion, Adam led the armies of the righteous in casting out the rebels. (Rev. 12:7-10.) When the populating of the earth was to commence, Adam came to fill his foreordained mission and stand as the first man of all men. He was placed in the Garden of Eden, fell in due course from his state of immortality and innocence, and became the first mortal flesh on earth. (Moses 2; 3.) There were no pre-Adamites. Any assumption to the contrary runs counter to the whole plan and scheme of the Almighty in creating and peopling this earth.

As a mortal man, Adam held the priesthood, had the fulness of the gospel, heard the voice of God and saw his face, received the ministration of angels, held the keys of the kingdom, enjoyed the gifts of the Spirit, was an intelligent and wise as any man (save Jesus only) who has ever lived; and, finally, having filled the full measure of his creation, he has gone on to his exaltation and glory in all things, and he will reign as a prince and ruler over his posterity forever. He and other men of his day enjoyed abundant spiritual endowments and possessed physical bodies superior to those of any men now on earth. Many, including Adam, lived nearly a thousand years on earth. (Moses 6; D. & C. 107:40-52.)

It is vain to belittle Adam and attempt to place him but a step ahead of some lower form of creature. Revelation speaks to the contrary. And, of course, the reasoning that concerns us here is: No Adam, no fall; no fall, no atonement; no atonement, no true religion, no purpose in life.

8. AGE OF THE EARTH.—Evolutionary theories assume that hundreds of millions of years were involved, first in the creation of the earth as a habitable globe, and again in the evolution of spontaneously generated, single celled forms of life into the complex and multitudinous forms of life now found on its face. We have rather specific scriptural indications that the creative period was of relatively short duration. The record says: "It was after the Lord's time, which was after the time of Kolob" (one day on which planet is equal to a thousand years of our time); "for as yet the Gods had not appointed unto Adam his reckoning." (Abra. 5:13.)

However, for our present purposes, it is sufficient to know that the time element since mortal life began on earth is specifically and pointedly made known. We are now nearing the end of the 6th thousand years of this earth's "continuance, or its temporal existence," and the millennial era will commence "in the beginning of the seventh thousand years." (D. & C. 77.) That is, we are approaching the end of the 6th of the periods of one thousand years each, all of which periods have occurred since the fall, since the earth became temporal, since it gained its telestial status, since it became the natural earth that we know, since death and mortality entered the scene. Thus the period during which birth, and life, and death have been occurring on this earth is less than 6,000 years.

9. FUTURE DESTINY OF THE EARTH AND LIFE THEREON.—According to evolutionary theories, life will continue on this sphere with such changes, mutations, and developments as circumstances and environment require. Actually, however, future events involving the earth and all living things thereon will be as dramatic and divergent from what finite intellects might assume as past events have been. Our knowledge of these future events—events in no sense harmonious with progressive evolutionary development—gives us an entirely different perspective relative to the origin and development of species than the one assumed by evolutionists.

For instance: Evolutionary theories have no place in them for the imminent Second Advent of our Lord, a coming which will usher in the millennial era of peace. These theories give no consideration to the revealed facts that the elements are to melt with fervent heat when Christ comes; that "every corruptible thing, both of man, or of the beasts of the field, or of the fowls of the heavens, or of the fish of the sea, that dwells upon all the face of the earth, shall be consumed" (D. & C. 101:24); that the earth will then be renewed, returning again to that paradisiacal state which prevailed before the fall; that the enmity of man and of beasts will cease; and that there will be no more death as we know it, men living instead (freed from disease and sickness) until they are an hundred years old when they will be changed to immortality in the twinkling of an eye. (D. & C. 101:23-32.)

Further: These theories take no account of the resurrection from the dead, that eventual status when all men (and all forms of life, every living thing that has ever breathed the breath of life, every animal, fish, fowl, or what have you!) will come forth as immortal, resurrected beings and creatures. (D. & C. 29:22-26; 77:1-3.) Nor do these theories give consideration to the fact that this earth itself is to pass through changes equivalent to death and resurrection, finally becoming a celestial sphere which will burn like the sun in the firmament, a planet on whose surface only celestial beings will then be able to live. (D. & C. 88:14-28; 130:7-9.)

How weak and puerile the intellectuality which, knowing that the Lord's plan takes all forms of life from a pre-existent spirit state, through mortality, and on to an ultimate resurrected state of immortality, yet finds comfort in the theoretical postulates that mortal life began in the scum of the sea, as it were, and has through eons of time evolved to its present varieties and state! Do those with spiritual insight really think that the infinite Creator of worlds without number would operate in this way?

10. EVOLUTION AND SPIRITUAL THINGS IN GENERAL.—Merely to list the basic doctrines of the gospel is to point out the revealed truths which are inharmonious with the theories of organic evolution and which were not taken into account by those who postulated those theories. In addition to the considerations so far mentioned attention might be given to revelation, visions, and angelic ministrations; to miracles, signs, and gifts of the Spirit; to the enjoyment of the gift of the Holy Ghost by the faithful; to the truths comprising the plan of salvation; to the decreed judgment according to works, and the ultimate assignment of all resurrected men to kingdoms or degrees of glory hereafter.

There is no harmony between the truths of revealed religion and the theories of organic evolution.

EXALTATION.
See CALLING AND ELECTION SURE, CELESTIAL KINGDOM, CELESTIAL MARRIAGE, CHURCH OF

THE FIRSTBORN, DAUGHTERS OF GOD, ENDOWMENTS, ETERNAL LIFE, ETERNAL LIVES, ETERNAL PROGRESSION, FULNESS OF THE FATHER, GODHOOD, IMMORTALITY, JOINT-HEIRS WITH CHRIST, KINGS, PERFECTION, PLURALITY OF GODS, PLURAL MARRIAGE, PRIESTESSES, PRIESTHOOD, PRIESTS, QUEENS, REDEMPTION, SALVATION, SEALING POWER, SECOND COMFORTER, SERVANTS OF GOD, SONS OF GOD. Celestial marriage is the gate to *exaltation,* and exaltation consists in the continuation of the family unit in eternity. Exaltation is eternal life, the kind of life which God lives. Those who obtain it gain an inheritance in the highest of three heavens within the celestial kingdom. (D. & C. 131:1-4.)

They have eternal increase, a continuation of the seeds forever and ever, a continuation of the lives, eternal lives; that is, they have spirit children in the resurrection, in relation to which offspring they stand in the same position that God our Father stands to us. They inherit in due course the fulness of the glory of the Father, meaning that they have all power in heaven and on earth. (D. & C. 76:50-60; 93:1-40.) *"Then shall they be gods,* because they have no end; therefore shall they be from everlasting to everlasting, because they continue; then shall they be above all, because all things are subject unto them. Then shall they be gods, because they have *all power,* and the angels are subject unto

them." (D. & C. 132:16-26; *Doctrines of Salvation,* vol. 2, pp. 35-79.)

Although *salvation* may be defined in many ways to mean many things, in its most pure and perfect definition it is a synonym for *exaltation.* This was the way in which the Prophet used it when he left us this inspired explanation: "Where shall we find a prototype into whose likeness we may be assimilated, in order that we may be made partakers of life and salvation? or, in other words, *where shall we find a saved being?* for if we can find a saved being, we may ascertain without much difficulty what all others must be in order to be saved. We think that it will not be a matter of dispute, that two beings who are unlike each other cannot be saved; for whatever constitutes the salvation of one will constitute the salvation of every creature which will be saved; and if we find one saved being in all existence, we may see what others must be, or else not be saved.

"We ask, then, where is the prototype? or where is the saved being? We conclude, as to the answer of this question, there will be no dispute among those who believe the Bible, that it is *Christ:* all will agree in this, that *he is the prototype or standard of salvation;* or, in other words, that *he is a saved being.* And if we should continue our interrogation and ask how it is that he is saved, the answer would be—because *he is a just and holy*

257

being; and if he were anything different from what he is, he would not be saved; for *his salvation depends on his being precisely what he is and nothing else;* for if it were possible for him to change, in the least degree, so sure he would fail of salvation and lose all his dominion, power, authority and glory, which consitute salvation; for *salvation consists in the glory, authority, majesty, power and dominion which Jehovah possesses and in nothing else; and no being can possess it but himself or one like him."*

After quoting many passages of scripture, the record of the Prophet's teachings continues: "These teachings of the Savior most clearly show unto us the *nature of salvation,* and what he proposed unto the human family when he proposed to save them—that *he proposed to make them like unto himself, and he was like the Father, the great prototype of all saved beings; and for any portion of the human family to be assimilated into their likeness is to be saved;* and to be unlike them is to be destroyed; *and on this hinge turns the door of salvation."* (*Lectures on Faith,* pp. 63-67.)

EXALTATION FOR THE DEAD.
See SALVATION FOR THE DEAD.

EXALTATION OF CHILDREN.
See SALVATION OF CHILDREN.

EXALTED MAN.
See AHMAN.

EXCELLENCE.
See PERFECTION.

EXCOMMUNICATION.
See ANATHEMA, APOSTASY, CHURCH COURTS, DISFELLOWSHIP-MENT, RESTORATION OF FORMER BLESSINGS. Whenever, as is presently the case, there is a separation of Church and state, then the highest punishment which the Church can impose upon its members is *excommunication.* This consists in cutting the person off from the Church so that he is no longer a member. Every blessing of the gospel is thereby lost, and unless the excommunicated person repents and gains his church status again, he cannot be saved in the celestial kingdom. (1 Tim. 1:20; Matt. 18:15-19; 1 Cor. 5:1-5.)

Apostasy, rebellion, cruelty to wives and children, immorality, and all crimes involving moral turpitude, are among those which warrant excommunication. The Lord imposes upon church officers the responsibility to handle every such case of transgression. If there is honest contrition of soul, frank confession of sin, and complete repentance therefrom, the transgressor's membership is not taken from him. But "him that repenteth not of his sins, and confesseth them not," the Lord says, "ye shall bring before the church, and do with him as the scripture saith unto you, either by commandment or by revelation. And this ye shall do that God may be glorified—not because ye forgive not, having no compassion, but that ye may be justified in the eyes of the law, that ye may not offend him who is your lawgiver—Verily I say, for this cause ye shall do these things." (D. & C. 64:12-13.)

"The way of transgressors is hard." (Prov. 13:15.) When they turn from the light, their curse is far worse than it would have been had they never known the truth. (D. & C. 41:1; 76:29-37; 82:1-7; 104:8-9; 121:13-25.) But if they have not sinned unto death, and if they do repent, there is yet hope. By baptism, entrance can again be gained into the Church of our Lord, and following testing and faithfulness all their former blessings may be restored.

EXEMPLAR.

See CHRIST. Christ is the great *Exemplar*. With reference to "all covenants, contracts, bonds, obligations, oaths, vows, performances, connections, associations, or expectations" (D. & C. 132:7)—that is, in *all* things—he leads the way and sets an example for his brethren. "Follow thou me," is his cry. (2 Ne. 31:10.) "What manner of men ought ye to be?" he asked; and then answered: "Verily I say unto you, even as I am." (3 Ne. 27:27.)

EXHORTATIONS.
See SERMONS.

EXORCISM.

See DEVILS, SORCERY, SPIRITUALISM. In imitation of the true order whereby devils are cast out of people, false ministers (having no actual priesthood power) attempt to cast them out by *exorcism*. This ungodly practice was probably more common anciently than it is now, because few people today believe either in miracles or in the casting out of literal devils. But over the years it has not been uncommon for so-called priests to attempt to expel evil spirits from persons or drive them away from particular locations by incantations, conjuration, or adjuration. Commonly some holy name is used in these false rituals.

Having seen Paul cast out devils in the power and majesty of his priesthood, "certain of the vagabond Jews, *exorcists,* took" it upon themselves to imitate the divine practice. Commanding the devil to come out of a possessed person, they said: "We adjure you by Jesus whom Paul preacheth." Thereupon the devil said to the seven sorcerers who so acted: "Jesus I know, and Paul I know; but who are ye?" Then "the man in whom the evil spirit was leaped on them, and overcame them, and prevailed against them, so that they fled out of that house naked and wounded." (Acts 19:11-16.) This scriptural account is symbolical of the final overthrow of all those who practice exorcism.

EXORCISTS.
See EXORCISM.

EXPIATION.
See ADVOCACY, ATONEMENT OF CHRIST, EXPIATOR, INTERCESSION, MEDIATION, PROPITIATION, RECONCILIATION. Our Lord's atoning sacrifice complied with the *law of expiation* in that, through his suffering and death, a way and means was provided so that the guilt and sins of the faithful might be extinguished. Expiation is the act of making satisfaction or atonement for sin; it is the extinguishing of guilt by suffering or penalty. This is the very thing which Christ did for all men, on conditions of repentance, when he took upon himself the sins of the world.

EXPIATOR.
See ADVOCATE, ATONEMENT OF CHRIST, CHRIST, EXPIATION, INTERCESSOR, MEDIATOR, PROPITIATOR, RECONCILER. Christ is the great *Expiator,* the one whose sufferings and death paid the penalty for the sins of those who believe

and obey the laws of the gospel. An expiator is one who expiates or extinguishes guilt by suffering the prescribed penalty, thus atoning or making complete satisfaction where the broken law is concerned.

EXTREME UNCTION.
See ADMINISTRATIONS, APOSTASY, SACRAMENTS, UNCTION. One of the sacraments of the Catholic Church is called *Extreme Unction.* It is administered by a priest to one in danger of death and includes both the application of oil to his organs of sense and the recital of prayers. It is a false form of the true ordinance of administering to the sick, which true ordinance is effective in healing the sick in the household of faith. But this substitute practice is in a very real sense an anointing unto death and not unto life. According to the official Catholic explanation, it is "spiritual medicine which diminishes the terrors of death, comforts the dying Christian, fortifies the soul in its final struggle, and purifies it for its passage from time to eternity." (James Cardinal Gibbons, *The Faith of Our Fathers,* pp. 314-316.)

EXULTATION.
See BOASTING.

F

FABLES.

See APOSTASY, DOCTRINE, HERESY. All false doctrines are *fables.* That is, they are stories which have been imagined, fabricated, and invented as opposed to the gospel which is real and true. (2 Pet. 1:16.) Apostasy consists in turning from true doctrine to fables. Paul said: "The time will come when they will not endure sound doctrine; but after their own lusts shall they heap to themselves teachers, having itching ears; And they shall turn away their ears from the truth, and shall be turned unto fables." (2 Tim. 4:1-4; 1 Tim. 1:3-4; 4:7.)

FAIRIES.

See GHOSTS.

FAIRNESS.

See JUSTICE.

FAITH.

See BAPTISM, BELIEF, CHARITY, CHIRST, FIRST PRINCIPLES OF THE GOSPEL, GIFTS OF THE SPIRIT, GOD, HOLY GHOST, HOPE, KNOWLEDGE, LECTURES ON FAITH, MIRACLES, OBEDIENCE, PLAN OF SALVATION, REPENTANCE, SALVATION, TESTIMONY, TRUTH. In teaching the laws and principles surrounding the subject of *faith,* Joseph Smith outlined his presentation under three heads: 1. "Faith itself—what it is"; 2. "The object on which it rests"; and 3. "The effects which flow from it."

By way of definition, the Prophet taught that faith is "the first principle' in revealed religion, and the foundation of all righteousness." After quoting Paul's affirmation, "Now faith is the substance of things hoped for, the evidence of things not seen" (Heb. 11:1), he said, "From this we learn that faith is the assurance which men have of the existence of things which they have not seen, and the principle of action in all intelligent beings." Continuing his analysis, the Prophet affirmed: "Faith is . . . the moving cause of all action in . . . intelligent beings. And as faith is the moving cause of all action in temporal concerns, so it is in spiritual. . . . But faith is not only the principle of action, but of *power* also, in all intelligent beings, whether in heaven or on earth. . . . *Faith, then, is the first great governing principle which has power, dominion, and authority over all things; by it they exist, by it they are upheld, by it they are changed, or by it they remain, agreeable to the will of God.* Without it there is no power, and without power there could be no creation nor existence. . . . How would you define faith in its most unlimited sense? It is the first great governing principle which has power, dominion, and authority over all things." (*Lectures on Faith,* pp. 1-8.)

Faith is based on truth and is preceded by knowledge. Until a person gains a knowledge of the truth he can have no faith. Alma said, "Faith is not to have a perfact knowledge of things; therefore if ye have faith ye hope for things which are not seen, *which are true.*" (Alma 32:21; Ether 12:6.) Thus *faith is a hope in that which is not seen which is true,* and accordingly it can enter the heart of man only after he has received the truth.

Faith unto life and salvation centers in Christ. There is no salvation in that general principle of faith alone, that moving cause of action, which causes the farmer to plant his seed with the unseen hope that it will bear grain. But there is faith unto salvation when Christ is the focal point in which the unseen hope centers. Accordingly the Prophet explained "that three things are necessary in order that any rational and intelligent being may exercise faith in God unto life and salvation." These he named as: 1. "The idea that he actually exists"; 2. "A *correct* idea of his character, perfections, and attributes"; and 3. "An actual knowledge that the course of life which he is pur-

suing is according to his will."

It follows that *a knowledge of the true and living God is the beginning of faith unto life and salvation,* "for faith could not center in a being of whose existence we have no idea, because the idea of his existence in the first instance is essential to the exercise of faith in him." (*Lectures on Faith,* p. 33.) So a belief in a false god can engender no faith in the human breast. If a person believes that an idol is God, or that Deity is a power or essence that fills the immensity of space, or if he has any other false concept, he estops himself from gaining faith, because faith is a hope in that which is not seen which is true. *Faith and truth cannot be separated; if there is to be faith, saving faith, faith unto life and salvation, faith that leads to the celestial world, there must first be truth.*

Not only is a true knowledge of God a condition precedent to the acquirement of this faith, but *faith can be exercised only by those who conform to the principles of truth which come from the true God who actually exists.* For instance, the Prophet, discoursing upon the great plan of redemption and the sacrifices offered to typify the atoning sacrifice of our Lord, explained that Abel's sacrifice was accepted because it conformed to the true pattern. Then he said: "Cain offered of the fruit of the ground, and was not accepted, because *he could not do it in faith, he could have no faith, or could not exercise faith contrary to the plan of heaven. . . .* As the sacrifice was instituted for a type, by which man was to discern the great Sacrifice which God had prepared, to offer a sacrifice contrary to that, *no faith could be excised,* because redemption was not purchased in that way, nor the power of the atonement instituted after that order; consequently, *Cain could have no faith;* and whatsoever is not of faith, is sin." (*Teachings,* p. 58.) On this same principle no one can exercise faith, saving faith, faith unto life and salvation, in infant baptism, or in any ordinance or performance that does not conform to revealed truth, for no faith can be exercised "contrary to the plan of heaven."

The Prophet summarizes the *character of God* under six headings: 1. "He was God before the world was created, and the same God that he was after it was created"; 2. "He is merciful and gracious, slow to anger, abundant in goodness, and . . . he was so from everlasting, and will be so to everlasting"; 3. "He changes not, neither is there variableness with him, and . . . his course is one eternal round"; 4. "He is a God of truth, and cannot lie"; 5. "He is no respecter of persons"; and 6. "He is love." (*Lectures on Faith,* p. 39.) And any ideas men have relative to these characteristics must be true, if faith is to result.

As pertaining to the *attributes of God,* the Prophet said: "The real design which the God of heaven had in view in making the human family acquainted with his attributes, was, that they, through the ideas of the existence of his attributes, might be enabled to exercise faith in him, and, through the exercise of faith in him, might obtain eternal life; for *without the idea of the existence of the attributes which belong to God the minds of men could not have power to exercise faith in him* so as to lay hold upon eternal life. The God of heaven, understanding most perfectly the constitution of human nature, and the weakness of men, knew what was necessary to be revealed, and what ideas must be planted in their minds in order that they might be enabled to exercise faith in him unto eternal life." The attributes of God are listed as: *Knowledge; Faith or Power; Justice; Judgment; Mercy; and Truth..* (*Lectures on Faith,* pp. 42-49.)

Relative to the *perfections of God,* the record says: "What we mean by perfections is, the perfections which belong to all the attributes of his nature." (*Lectures on Faith,* p. 50.) That is, the perfection of God consists in his possession of all knowledge, all power, all truth, and the fulness of all good things. (D. & C. 93:6-34.)

Accordingly, if a person accepts the false heresy that God is progressing or increasing in any of these attributes, that is, does not now possess them in their fulness and perfection, he places a bar across the path leading to a full measure of faith. "Without the knowledge of *all things,*" for instance, as the Prophet expresses it, "God would not be able to save any portion of his creatures; for it is by reason of the knowledge which he has of *all things,* from the beginning to the end, that enables him to give that understanding to his creatures by which they are made partakers of eternal life; and *if it were not for the idea existing in the minds of men that God had all knowledge it would be impossible for them to exercise faith in him.*" (*Lectures on Faith,* p. 44; *Doctrines of Salvation,* vol. 1, pp. 1-17.) Obviously those who suppose there is a power or being greater than God (a necessary corollary of the false notion that God is gaining new knowledge or new truth or more power), cannot have full faith in God because there is always the chance that the new knowledge will reverse the order of the past or that the greater power will rescind the eternal decrees of God.

Faith is a gift of God bestowed as a reward for personal righteousness. It is always given when righteousness is present, and the greater the measure of obedience to God's laws the greater will be the endowment of faith. Hence the Prophet says that to acquire faith men must gain the actual knowledge "that the course of life which they pursue is according to the will of God, in order that they may be enabled to

exercise faith in him unto life and salvation. This knowledge supplies an important place in revealed religion; for it was by reason of it that the ancients were enabled to endure as seeing him who is invisible. *An actual knowledge to any person, that the course of life which he pursues is according to the will of God, is essentially necessary to enable him to have that confidence in God without which no person can obtain eternal life.* It was this that enabled the ancient saints to endure all their afflictions and persecutions, and to take joyfully the spoiling of their goods, *knowing* (not *believing* merely) that they had a more enduring substance." (*Lectures on Faith,* p. 57; Heb. 10: 34.)

Miracles, signs, the gifts of the Spirit, the knowledge of God and godliness, and every conceivable good thing—all these are the *effects of faith;* all of these come because faith has become the ruling force in the lives of the saints. Conversely, where these things are not, faith is not.

In Moroni's language, the reason why God "ceaseth to do miracles among the children of men is because that they dwindle in *unbelief,* and depart from the right way, and know not the God in whom they should trust. Behold, I say unto you that *whoso believeth in Christ, doubting nothing, whatsoever he shall ask the Father in the name of Christ it shall be granted him;* and this promise is unto all, even unto the ends of the earth. For behold, thus said Jesus Christ, the Son of God, unto his disciples who should tarry, yea, and also to all his disciples, in the hearing of the multitude: Go ye into all the world, and preach the gospel to every creature; And he that believeth and is baptized shall be saved, but he that believeth not shall be damned; *And these signs shall follow them that believe*—in my name shall they cast out devils; they shall speak with new tongues; they shall take up serpents; and if they drink any deadly thing it shall not hurt them; they shall lay hands on the sick and they shall recover; *And whosoever shall believe in my name, doubting nothing, unto him will I confirm all my words, even unto the ends of the earth.*" (Morm. 9: 20-25; Mark 16:15-20.)

Mormon taught similarly: "By the ministering of angels, and by every word which proceedeth forth out of the mouth of God, men began to exercise faith in Christ; and thus by faith, they did lay hold upon every good thing; and thus it was until the coming of Christ. And after that he came men also were saved by faith in his name; and by faith, they become the sons of God. And as sure as Christ liveth he spake these words unto our fathers, saying: *Whatsoever thing ye shall ask the Father in my name, which is good, in faith believing that ye shall receive, behold, it shall be done unto you.*" Mormon then says that Christ "claimeth all

those who have faith in him; and they who have faith in him will cleave unto every good thing."

Then, after showing that miracles and the ministering of angels are an eternal part of the gospel of Christ, he asks: "Have angels ceased to appear unto the children of men? Or has he withheld the power of the Holy Ghost from them? Or will he, so long as time shall last, or the earth shall stand, or there shall be one man upon the face thereof to be saved? Behold I say unto you, Nay; for it is by faith that miracles are wrought; and it is by faith that angels appear and minister unto men; wherefore, *if these things have ceased wo be unto the children of men, for it is because of unbelief, and all is vain. For no man can be saved, according to the words of Christ, save they shall have faith in his name; wherefore, if these things have ceased, then has faith ceased also; and awful is the state of man. . . . If ye have not faith in him then ye are not fit to be numbered among the people of his church.*" (Moro. 7:25-39.)

"When faith comes," the Prophet said, *"it brings its train of attendants with it—apostles, prophets, evangelists, pastors, teachers, gifts, wisdom, knowledge, miracles, healings, tongues, interpretation of tongues, etc. All these appear when faith appears on the earth, and disappear when it disappears from the earth; for these are the effects of faith, and always have, and al-*

ways will, attend it. For where faith is, there will the knowledge of God be also, with all things which pertain thereto—revelations, visions, and dreams, as well as every necessary thing, in order that the possessors of faith may be perfected, and obtain salvation; for God must change, otherwise faith will prevail with him. And he who possesses it will, through it, obtain all necessary knowledge and wisdom, until he shall know God, and the Lord Jesus Christ, whom he has sent—whom to know is eternal life." (Lectures on Faith, pp. 70-71.)

Again: "Because faith is wanting, the fruits are. No man since the world was had faith without having something along with it. The ancients quenched the violence of fire, escaped the edge of the sword, women received their dead, etc. By faith the worlds were made. A man who has none of the gifts has no faith; and he deceives himself, if he supposes he has. Faith has been wanting, not only among the heathen, but in professed Christendom also, so that tongues, healings, prophecy, and prophets and apostles, and all the gifts and blessings have been wanting." (Teachings, p. 270.)

"Miracles are the fruits of faith," the Prophet said on another occasion. "Faith comes by hearing the word of God. If a man has not faith enough to do one thing, he may have faith to do another: if he cannot remove a mountain, he may heal the sick. Where faith is there

will be some of the fruits: all gifts and power which were sent from heaven, were poured out on the heads of those who had faith." (History of the Church, vol. 5, p. 355.)

Showing that miracles and signs follow faith and do not precede it, Moroni said: "Faith is things which are hoped for and not seen; wherefore, dispute not because ye see not, for ye receive no witness until after the trial of your faith. For it was by faith that Christ showed himself unto our fathers, after he had risen from the dead; and he showed not himself unto them until after they had faith in him; wherefore, it must needs be that some had faith in him, for he showed himself not unto the world. But because of the faith of men he has shown himself unto the world, and glorified the name of the Father, and prepared a way that thereby others might be partakers of the heavenly gift, that they might hope for those things which they have not seen. Wherefore, ye may also have hope, and be partakers of the gift, if ye will but have faith. Behold it was by faith that they of old were called after the holy order of God. Wherefore, by faith was the law of Moses given. But in the gift of his Son hath God prepared a more excellent way; and it is by faith that it hath been fulfilled. For if there be no faith among the children of men God can do no miracle among them; wherefore, he showed not himself until after their faith. . . .

And neither at any time hath any wrought miracles until after their faith; wherefore they first believed in the Son of God." (Ether 12:6-18; Heb. 11.)

To gain faith men must first have knowledge; then as their faith increases, they come to a state where it is supplanted by perfect knowledge; and in any field in which perfect knowledge has been gained, "faith is dormant." (Alma 32:21-34.) For instance, a man first comes to a knowledge of the nature and kind of being that Christ is, and he thereby is enabled to gain faith in him. As a result he gains further knowledge about Christ as an effect of faith and by revelation from the Holy Ghost. This knowledge and this faith both increase, supplementing each other, until by the power of faith the veil is rent, the man sees Christ and gains a perfect knowledge of him. Then, as Alma expresses it, "in that thing" his "faith is dormant" (Alma 32:34), although in other things his faith may not yet have blossomed forth into perfect knowledge.

The Brother of Jared is one who followed this course until he saw the Lord. As Moroni explained it, *"Because of the knowledge of this man he could not be kept from beholding within the veil; and he saw the finger of Jesus, which, when he saw, he fell with fear; for he knew that it was the finger of the Lord; and he had faith no longer, for he knew, nothing doubting. Wherefore, having this perfect knowledge*

of God, he could not be kept from within the veil; therefore he saw Jesus; and he did minister unto him." Indeed, "The Lord could not withhold anything from him, for he knew that the Lord could show him all things." (Ether 3:19-26.)

"And there were many whose faith was so exceeding strong, even before Christ came, who could not be kept from within the veil, but truly saw with their eyes the things which they had beheld with an eye of faith, and they were glad." (Ether 12:19.) Today as anciently the same effects flow from faith. "It is the privilege of every elder to speak of the things of God," the Prophet said, "and *could we all come together with one heart and one mind in perfect faith the veil might as well be rent today as next week, or any other time."* (*Teachings,* p. 9; D. & C. 93:1.)

FAITH AND WORKS.
See GOOD WORKS.

FAITHFULNESS.
See RIGHTEOUSNESS.

FALLEN MAN.
See ATONEMENT OF CHRIST, CARNALITY, DEVILISHNESS, FALL OF ADAM, MAN, MORTALITY, SENSUALITY, SPIRITUAL DEATH, WORLD. After the fall of Adam, man became carnal, sensual, and devilish by nature; he became *fallen man.*

(Moses 5:13; 6:49; Mosiah 16:1-4; Alma 42:10; D. & C. 20:20.) All accountable persons on earth inherit this fallen state, this probationary state, this state in which worldly things seem desirable to the carnal nature. Being in this state, "the natural man is an enemy to God," until he conforms to the great plan of redemption and is born again to righteousness. (Mosiah 3:19.) Thus all mankind would remain lost and fallen forever were it not for the atonement of our Lord. (Alma 42:4-14.)

FALL OF ADAM.

See ADAM, ATONEMENT OF CHRIST, CORRUPTION, DEATH, FALLEN MAN, MORTALITY, SPIRITUAL DEATH. Adam, our first parent (1 Ne. 5:11), a "son of God" (Moses 6:22), was first placed on earth as an immortal being. His coming was the crowning event of the creation; and as with him, so with every department of creation—immortality reigned supreme. (2 Ne. 2:22.) There was no death, no mortality, no corruption, no procreation. Blood did not flow in Adam's veins, for he was not yet mortal, and blood is an element that pertains exclusively to mortality. (Gen. 9:2-6; Lev. 17:10-15; *Man: His Origin and Destiny*, pp. 362-364; Joseph Fielding Smith, *Church History and Modern Revelation*, vol. 1, p. 231.) Radical changes were in the offing for man, the earth, and all forms of life when the fall came.

In that first edenic day, Adam was still in the presence of God, with whom he walked and talked and from whom he received counsel and commandments. (Moses 3; 4.) He had temporal life because his spirit was housed in a temporal body, one made from the dust of the earth. (Abra. 5:7.) He had spiritual life because he was in the presence of God and was alive to the things of righeousness or of the Spirit. He had not yet come to that state of mortal probation in which are found the testings and trials requisite to a possible inheritance of eternal life. As yet the full knowledge of good and evil had not been placed before him; and, what was tremendously important in the eternal scheme of things, he could have no children.

But all these conditions, in the providences of the Almighty, were soon to change. According to the foreordained plan, Adam was to fall; that is, "in the wisdom of him who knoweth all things" (2 Ne. 2: 24), Adam was to introduce mortality and all that attends it, so that the opportunity for eternal progression and perfection might be offered to all the spirit children of the Father.

In conformity with the will of the Lord, *Adam fell both spiritually and temporally*. Spiritual death entered the world, meaning that man was cast out of the presence of the Lord and died as pertaining to the things of the Spirit which are the things of righteousness. Temporal death also entered the world, meaning that man and all created things became mortal, and blood became the life preserving element in the natural body. In this mortal condition it became possible for the body and the spirit to separate, a separation which by definition is the natural or temporal death. (Alma 42:6-12; D. & C. 29:40-42.)

In this state of mortality, subject to both spiritual and temporal death, man thus was in a position to be examined relative to his worthiness to inherit eternal life. He became subject to corruption, disease, and all the ills of the flesh. Spiritually he was required to walk by faith rather than by sight; a knowledge of good and evil could now come to him by actual experience; and being mortal he could now have children, thus providing bodies for the pre-existent hosts. "Adam fell that men might be." (2 Ne. 2:19-25; Moses 5:11; 6:45-48; *Doctrines of Salvation,* vol. 1, pp. 107-120.)

Behold, he is in the desert; go not forth: behold, he is in the secret chambers; believe it not." (Matt. 24: 23-27; Mark 13:21-23; Jos. Smith 2:21-26.)

Since then untold millions have worshiped before the thrones of false Christs. Some deluded fanatics have bowed before persons professing to be saviors or to have the power to confer salvation. Other hosts of misguided souls have trekked to desert monasteries, to mountain hermitages, to Jesuit retreats, and to the meeting places of secret cults—all acting under the specious asumption that in the place of their choice they would find Christ. Still others have made money, power, worldly learning, political preferment, or the gratification of sensual lusts their God. And virtually all the millions of apostate Christendom have abased themselves before the mythical throne of a mythical Christ whom they vainly suppose to be a spirit essence who is incorporeal, uncreated, immaterial, and three-in-one with the Father and Holy Spirit.

FALSE CHRISTS.

See ANTICHRISTS, APOSTASY, CHRIST, SALVATION. Our Lord during his ministry foretold that in the coming eras of apostate darkness there would arise false prophets and *false Christs* who would deceive many, even if it were possible the very elect. Then he counseled: "If they shall say unto you,

FALSE DOCTRINE.

See DOCTRINE.

FALSE DOCTRINES.

See HERESY.

FALSE GODS.

See APOSTASY, CREEDS, FALSE

CHRISTS, GOD, IDOLATRY, UN-KNOWN GOD. As pertaining to this universe, there are three Gods: the Father, Son, and Holy Ghost. All other supposed deities are *false gods*.

However, the mere worship of a god who has the proper scriptural names does not assure one that he is worshiping the true and living God. The true names of Deity, for instance, are applied to the false concepts of God found in the apostate creeds of the day. "There is but one only living and true God who is infinite in being and perfection," the Presbyterian *Confession of Faith* correctly recites, and then proceeds to describe a false god who is *"without body, parts, or passions,* immutable, immense, eternal, *incomprehensible,"* and so forth. (*Doctrines of Salvation,* vol. 1, p. 2.)

From the beginning of history the great masses of men have worshiped false gods. Those who believe the creeds of Christendom profess to worship an incomprehensible, unknowable, immaterial essence that fills the immensity of space and is everywhere and nowhere in particular present. Heathen and pagan peoples in all ages have worshiped idols; the liberal Athenian philosophers paid homage to what they called, "The Unknown God." (Acts 17:22-31.) There are those who set their whole hearts on learning, money, power, and the like, until these things become in effect their god. *There is no salva-tion in the worship of false gods.* For such false worship the Lord imposed the death penalty in ancient Israel. (Deut. 13:6-11.)

FALSE GOSPELS.
See GOSPEL.

FALSEHOOD.
See LIARS.

FALSE PREACHERS.
See SERMONS.

FALSE PROPHETS.
See PROPHETS.

FALSE RELIGIONS.
See CHURCH OF THE DEVIL.

FALSE SPIRITS.
See DEVILS, DISCERNMENT, EVIL SPIRITS, GIFTS OF THE SPIRIT, LIGHT OF CHRIST. *Two spirits are abroad in the earth—one is of God, the other of the devil.* The spirit which is of God is one that leads to light, truth, freedom, progress, and every good thing; on the other hand, the spirit which is of Lucifer leads to darkness, error, bondage, retrogression, and every evil thing. One spirit is from above, the other from beneath; and that which is from beneath never allows more light or truth or freedom to exist

than it can help. All religion, philosophy, education, science, governmental control—indeed, all things—are influenced and governed by one or the other (in some cases, part by one and part by the other) of these spirits. (Moro. 7.)

It should be understood that these two influences in the world are manifest through the ministrations of actual spirit personages from the unseen world. The power and influence wielded by Satan is exercised through the host of evil spirits who do his bidding and who have power, according to laws that exist, to impress their wills upon the minds of receptive mortals. On the other hand, much of the power and influence of Deity is exercised by and manifest through spirit beings who appear and give revelation and guidance as the Lord's purposes may require. In general, the more righteous and saintly a person is, the easier it will be for him to receive communications from heavenly sources; and the more evil and corrupt he is, the easier will it be for evil spirits to implant their nefarious schemes in his mind and heart.

The problem that most men have is to discern the spirits, so that they may know what is of God and what is not. The gift of discernment, that is the "discerning of spirits," is itself one of the gifts of the Spirit which comes from God. (1 Cor. 12:10; D. & C. 46:23.) "Believe not every spirit," John counseled, "but try the spirits whether they are of God: because many false prophets are gone out into the world." (1 John 4:1.)

How can we try the spirits? By what tests shall it be known whether they are of God or the devil? If a messenger appears from the unseen world, how shall we know whether he is a good spirit or an evil spirit? When a revelation is received is it one born of light or darkness? When trances, visions, tongues, enchantments, miracles, and related things come to view, are they from above or beneath? When a philosophy is taught, a doctrine preached, a religion proclaimed, an educational theory espoused, how shall we know whether it is true or false?

"We may look for angels and receive their ministrations," the Prophet said, "but *we are to try the spirits and prove them,* for it is often the case that men make a mistake in regard to these things. God has so ordained that when he has communicated, no vision is to be taken but what you see by the seeing of the eye, or what you hear by the hearing of the ear. *When you see a vision pray for the interpretation; if you get not this, shut it up; there must be certainty in this matter.* An open vision will manifest that which is more important. *Lying spirits are going forth in the earth. There will be great manifestations of spirits, both false and true. . . . Not every spirit, or vision, or singing, is of God."* (*Teachings,* pp. 161-162.)

As part of a long discussion of true and false spirits, and in explaining how they may be distinguished, the Prophet also said: *"No man can do this without the priesthood, and having a knowledge of the laws by which spirits are governed; for as no man knows the things of God, but by the Spirit of God, so no man knows the spirit of the devil, and his power and influence, but by possessing intelligence which is more than human, and having unfolded through the medium of the priesthood the mysterious operations of his devices. . . .*

"A man must have the discerning of spirits before he can drag into daylight this hellish influence and unfold it unto the world in all its soul-destroying, diabolical, and horrid colors; for nothing is a greater injury to the children of men than to be under the influence of a false spirit when they think they have the Spirit of God. Thousands have felt the influence of its terrible power and baneful effects. Long pilgrimages have been undertaken, penances endured, and pain, misery and ruin have followed in their train; nations have been convulsed, kingdoms overthrown, provinces laid waste, and blood, carnage and desolation are habiliments in which it has been clothed.

"As we have noticed before, the great difficulty lies in the ignorance of the nature of spirits, of the laws by which they are governed, and the signs by which they may be known; *if it requires the Spirit of God to know the things of God; and the spirit of the devil can only be unmasked through that medium, then it follows as a natural consequence that unless some person or persons have a communication, or revelation from God, unfolding to them the operation of the spirit, they must eternally remain ignorant of these principles;* for I contend that if one man cannot understand these things but by the Spirit of God, ten thousand men cannot; it is alike out of the reach of the wisdom of the learned, the tongue of the eloquent, the power of the mighty. And we shall at last have to come to this conclusion, *whatever we may think of revelation, that without it we can neither know nor understand anything of God, or the devil;* and however unwilling the world may be to acknowledge this principle, it is evident from the multifarious creeds and notions concerning this matter that they understand nothing of this principle, and it is equally as plain that *without a divine communication they must remain in ignorance."* (*Teachings,* pp. 204-206.)

It follows that the discerning of spirits is and can be practiced in righteousness only where the true Church and kingdom of God is found. In the final analysis, it takes apostles, prophets, priesthood, the gift of the Holy Ghost, and a knowledge of God's laws and the manner in which he operates, in order to separate the spirits into their two opposing camps. Only where these things are found can error be segregated from truth, because only there are the channels of revelation open.

FALSE TEACHERS.
See PROPHETS.

FALSE WITNESSES.
See LIARS.

FALSE WORSHIP.
See WORSHIP.

FAMILIAR SPIRITS.
See SPIRITUALISM.

FAMILY.
See CELESTIAL MARRIAGE, FAMILY ORGANIZATIONS, FAMILY REUNIONS, HOME, PATRIARCHAL CHAIN, PATRIARCHAL ORDER, TRIBES OF ISRAEL. Among the saints the *family* is the basic unit of the Church and of society, and its needs and preservation in righteousness take precedence over all other things. True family organization is patriarchal in nature; it is patterned after that organization which exists in heaven (Eph. 3:15); it always consists of a husband and wife who have entered into the new and everlasting covenant of mar-

riage; and if the couple so united are blessed with children, they too become members of the family.

Adam and Eve set a proper and righteous pattern for all of their descendants. As husband and wife, married by God himself while yet in the Garden of Eden (Gen. 2:22-25), they became the first family—an eternal family, for there was no death. Then came the fall, mortality began, the power of procreation was given, and Adam and Eve added children to their family. They and such of their children as abode in the truth have since gone on in immortality and glory, and now as resurrected beings, parents and children together, comprise an eternal family unit in celestial glory. The same is true of Abraham, Isaac, and Jacob, and the faithful saints who were with Christ in his resurrection. (D. & C. 132: 29-37.)

Eternal families have their beginning in celestial marriage here in mortality. Faithful members of them continue in the family unit in eternity, in the highest heaven of the celestial world, where they have eternal increase. (D. & C. 131: 1-4; 132:16-32.) Perfect peace and a full endowment of all good graces attend such eternal families. By obedience to the laws of the gospel (which are celestial laws), Latter-day Saint families begin here and now to enjoy much of that peace, joy, love, and charity which will be enjoyed in eternal fulness in the exalted family unit.

It is also common to speak of the descendants of a common ancestor as members of a family; the descendants of President Joseph F. Smith, through all their generations, for instance, make up his family. Similarly, there is the family of Israel and of Abraham. The Church itself, composed of a gathered remnant of Israel, is a family. And as with individual families, so with these great patriarchal groups, faithful members of them will continue on as members of these great patriarchal families in eternity.

FAMILY ORGANIZATIONS.

See BOOK OF REMEMBRANCE, FAMILY, FAMILY REUNIONS, GENEALOGICAL RESEARCH. Church members who are descendants of common ancestors should form *family organizations.* These organizations serve four particular purposes:

1. They create family solidarity and honor the patriarchal system. Desires to work righteousness are enhanced, and members of the rising generations are encouraged to keep the commandments and look forward to temple marriages and the fulness of the blessings of the priesthood.

2. They make it possible for large groups of saints, having a common purpose, to pool their skills and means in organized genealogical research. Incident to this research the preparation of family histories is a proper and desirable enterprise.

3. They keep current family genealogical data.

4. They make recreational opportunities available to groups bound together by a common tie.

FAMILY PRAYER.
See PRAYER.

FAMILY REUNIONS.

See FAMILY, FAMILY ORGANIZATIONS, RECREATION. In keeping with the spirit of love and unity which should always exist in Latter-day Saint families, it is proper for families, both large and small, to hold frequent *family reunions.* Regular family organizations, as an aid in carrying out their important work, should hold these affairs from time to time. Sunday is not a proper day for family reunions.

FAMINES.

See APOSTASY, CHURCH WELFARE PLAN, SIGNS OF THE TIMES. 1. *Famines* involving general scarcity of food and resulting in hunger and starvation, have been of frequent occurrence among nearly all peoples. Such are among the probabionary experiences ordained for the testing and trial of man. Sometimes they have come upon the rebellious; often both the righteous and the wicked have suffered under their curse.

They are one of the ways the

Lord has of humbling his children so they will seek him and his help in their temporal concerns. "How oft have I called upon you . . . by the voice of famines and pestilences of every kind," he says. (D. & C. 43:25.) Famines are among the signs of the times, and the great Church Welfare Plan is designed to help free men from the effects of them.

2. *Spiritual famines* are periods of apostasy from the truth. "Behold, the days come, saith the Lord God, that I will send a famine in the land, not a famine of bread, nor a thirst for water, but of hearing the words of the Lord: And they shall wander from sea to sea, and from the north even to the east, they shall run to and fro to seek the word of the Lord, and shall not find it." (Amos 8:11-12.)

FANATICISM.

See GOSPEL HOBBIES, ZEAL. *Fanaticism* is the devil's substitute for and perversion of true zeal. It is exhibited in wildly extravagant and overzealous views and acts. It is based either on unreasoning devotion to a cause, a devotion which closes the door to investigation and dispassionate study, or on an over emphasis of some particular doctrine or practice, an emphasis which twists the truth as a whole out of perspective.

Through the ages religious fanatics have fought and died on the field of battle in false causes; in the Church there are those who became fanatics on such things as the Word of Wisdom, even to the point that they teach against the use of white bread, white flour, refined sugar, chocolate, and sometimes even milk, eggs, and cheese. *Stable and sound persons are never fanatics; they do not ride gospel hobbies.*

FAST DAY.

See FASTING, FAST MEETINGS, FAST OFFERINGS. In partial compliance with the Lord's command that his saints are to continue in fasting and prayer (D. & C. 88:76), the Church designates one day each month (ordinarily the first Sunday of the month) as a *fast day.* "The law to the Latter-day Saints, as understood by the authorities of the Church," President Joseph F. Smith said, "is that food and drink are not to be partaken of for 24 hours, 'from even to even,' and that the saints are to refrain from all bodily gratification and indulgences. Fast day being on the Sabbath, it follows, of course, that all labor is to be abstained from." (*Gospel Doctrine,* 5th ed., p. 243.) Most members of the Church when fasting eat the evening meal on Saturday and then abstain from food and drink until the evening meal on Sunday.

FASTING.

See FAST DAY, FAST MEETINGS,

FAST OFFERINGS, PRAYER, TESTIMONY. As President Joseph F. Smith expressed it, *fasting* consists in the complete abstinence from "food and drink." (*Gospel Doctrine,* 5th ed., p. 243.) Fasting, with prayer as its companion, is designed to increase spirituality; to foster a spirit of devotion and love of God; to increase faith in the hearts of men, thus assuring divine favor; to encourage humility and contrition of soul; to aid in the acquirement of righteousness; to teach man his nothingness and dependence upon God; and to hasten those who properly comply with the law of fasting along the path to salvation.

Many specific reasons for fasting are found in the scriptures. It is a general obligation imposed by revelation upon church members in good standing. (D. & C. 59:13-14; 88:76; Luke 5:33-35; 2 Cor. 6:5; 11:27.) It is itself a form of the true worship of God. (Luke 2:37; Acts 9:9; Alma 45:1; 4 Ne. 12.) It is proper to fast for the sick (2 Sam. 12:16); for special blessings (Mosiah 27:22-23); to gain a testimony (Alma 5:46); to gain revelation (Alma 17:3; 3 Ne. 27:1; Ex. 34:28; Deut. 9:9, 18); for the conversion of nonmembers to the truth (Alma 6:6; 17:9); for guidance in the choice of church officers (Acts 13:3); as an accompaniment of righteous mourning and sorrow (Alma 28:2-6; 30:2; Hela. 9:10); as a means of sanctifying one's soul (Hela. 3:35); and for guidance along the path leading to salvation. (Omni 26.) Temples are houses of fasting. (D. & C. 88:119; 95:16; 109:8, 16.) To be acceptable fasting must conform to the Lord's law and not be done for hypocritical reasons. (Matt. 6:16-18; 3 Ne. 13:16-18.)

"Compliance with the law of the fast," President Joseph F. Smith said, "would call attention to the sin of over eating, place the body in subjection to the spirit, and so promote communion with the Holy Ghost, and insure a spiritual strength and power which the people of the nation so greatly need. As fasting should always be accompanied by prayer, this law would bring the people nearer to God, and divert their minds once a month at least, from the mad rush of worldly affairs and cause them to be brought into immediate contact with practical, pure, and undefiled religion—to visit the fatherless and the widow, and keep themselves unspotted from the sins of the world." (*Gospel Doctrine,* 5th ed., pp. 237-238.)

Extended fasts are proper on some special occasions. Moses (Ex. 34:28), Elijah (1 Kings 19:8), and Christ (Matt. 4:2) each fasted for 40 days and nights. But ordinarily 24 hours should suffice, and those called upon to fast should be of such an age and in such a sound condition of health that no impairment of mental or physical well-being will result.

President Joseph F. Smith explained: "The Lord has instituted the fast on a reasonable and intelligent basis, and none of his works are vain or unwise. His law is perfect in this as in other things. Hence, those who can are required to comply thereto; it is a duty from which they cannot escape; but let it be remembered that the observance of the fast day by abstaining 24 hours from food and drink is not an absolute rule, it is no iron-clad law to us, but it is left with the people as a matter of conscience, to exercise wisdom and discretion. Many are subject to weakness, others are delicate in health, and others have nursing babies; of such it should not be required to fast. Neither should parents compel their little children to fast. I have known children to cry for something to eat on fast day. In such cases, going without food will do them no good. Instead, they dread the day to come, and in place of hailing it, dislike it; while the compulsion engenders a spirit of rebellion in them, rather than a love for the Lord and their fellows." (*Gospel Doctrine,* 5th ed., p. 244.)

FAST MEETINGS.

See FASTING, FAST OFFERINGS, SACRAMENT MEETINGS, TESTIMONY MEETINGS. In every gospel dispensation it has been the practice of the saints to *"meet together oft, to fast and to pray, and to speak one with another concerning the welfare of their souls."* (Moro.

6:5.) In this dispensation, it is the practice of the Church to designate one sacrament meeting a month as a *fast meeting*. In these meetings it is proper to invite members of the congregation to express themselves by way of testimony, doctrine, confession, exhortation, or the like, each member arising to speak as he may be led by the Spirit. Special fasts are held by families, groups of missionaries, or others as special occasions require.

FAST OFFERINGS.

See CHURCH WELFARE PLAN, FASTING, OBLATIONS, POOR, TITHING. One of the chief purposes of organized fasting by the Church is to enable the saints to contribute the food thus saved, or its equivalent in money, to the care of the poor. Isaiah decried the ostentatious and hypocritical fasting practices of ancient Israel, and then gave them this word from the Lord: *"Is not this the fast that I have chosen? . . . Is it not to deal thy bread to the hungry, and that thou bring the poor that are cast out to thy house? when thou seest the naked, that thou cover him; and that thou hide not thyself from thine own flesh?"* (Isa. 58:6-8.)

"It is, therefore, incumbent upon every Latter-day Saint," President Joseph F. Smith said, "to give to his bishop, on fast day, the food that he or his family would consume for the day, that it may be given to the poor for their benefit and blessing; or, in lieu of the food, that its equivalent amount, or, if the person is wealthy, a liberal donation, in money, be so reserved and dedicated to the poor." (*Gospel Doctrine,* 5th ed., p. 243; Mal. 3:8.)

FATHERHOOD OF GOD.
See FATHER IN HEAVEN.

FATHER IN HEAVEN.

See ELDER BROTHER, ETERNAL LIVES, FIRSTBORN, GOD, GODHEAD, HOLY FATHER, MOTHER IN HEAVEN, PRE-EXISTENCE, SPIRIT CHILDREN. God the Eternal Father, our *Father in Heaven,* is an exalted, perfected, and glorified Personage having a tangible body of flesh and bones. (D. & C. 130:22.) The designation *Father* is to be taken literally; it signifies that the Supreme Being is the literal Parent or Father of the spirits of all men. (Heb. 12:9.) All men, Christ included, were born as his children in pre-existence. (D. & C. 93:21-23; Moses 1; 2; 3; 4; Abra. 3:22-28.) This is the reason men are commanded to approach Deity in prayer by saying, "Our Father which art in heaven." (Matt. 6:9.)

It is only by understanding the real and literal sense in which God is our Father that we are able to understand what is meant by the *Fatherhood of God* and the *Brotherhood of Man.* In addition to the fact that all men are brothers in the sense that all have descended from Adam, they are also brothers in that they have the same personal Father who begat them in the spirit. Our Lord had reference to this when he said, "Go to my brethren, and say unto them, I ascend unto my Father, and your Father; and to my God, and your God." (John 20:17.)

FATHER OF LIES.

See CAIN, DEVIL. Both Satan and Cain bear the title *father of lies,* both having been liars from the beginning. (2 Ne. 9:9; Moses 5: 18-27.) The name signifies authorship and sponsorship of all that is dishonest and which leads away from the truth. In a similar sense Satan is the *master of sin* (Mosiah 4:14) and the father of secret combinations and every evil thing. (2 Ne. 26:22; Hela. 6:26; Moro. 7:12.)

FATHER OF LIGHTS.

See FATHER IN HEAVEN, GOD, HOLY FATHER, LIGHT OF CHRIST. "God is light, and in him is no darkness at all." (1 John 1:5.) That is, he is the embodiment, author, and source of light, or in other words the *Father of Lights.* (Jas. 1:17.) Similarly, Lucifer is the *Father of Darkness,* of apostasy, iniquity, and every evil thing.

FATHER OF SPIRITS.
See FATHER IN HEAVEN.

FEAST OF THE PASSOVER.
See PASSOVER.

FICTION.
See FABLES.

FIGURATIVE EXPRESSIONS.
See SYMBOLISMS.

FILTHINESS.
See SEX IMMORALITY.

FILTHY LUCRE.
See RICHES.

FIRE.
See BAPTISM OF FIRE, FIRE AND BRIMSTONE, SECOND COMING OF CHRIST. Use of *fire* in a miraculous manner has often attended the Lord's dealings with men. "Cherubim and a flaming sword" (Moses 4:31; Gen. 3:24) barred Adam from returning to his edenic home. A pillar of fire guided ancient Israel by night (Ex. 13:21-22; Ps. 78:14), and the fires on her sacrificial altars were never permitted to go out. (Lev. 6:13.) Elijah called down fire from heaven in his contest with the priests of Baal (1 Kings 18), and also to consume the soldiers sent by Ahab to arrest him. (2 Kings 1.) And at the time of Elijah's translation, "a chariot of fire, and horses of fire," appeared to transport him "by a whirlwind into heaven." (2 Kings 2:11.)

Heavenly fire has often been used by the Lord in giving miraculous manifestations to his prophets. (Gen. 15:17; Ex. 3:2; 24:17; 1 Ne. 1:6.) Lehi and Nephi, sons of Helaman, "were encircled about as if by fire, . . . and were not burned," as a means of protecting them in their ministry, a miracle soon expanded to embrace "about three hundred souls." (Hela. 5:23-49.) Fire from heaven encircled groups of worshipers in connection with the ministry of the resurrected Lord among the Nephites (2 Ne. 17:23-24; 19:13-14), and the Three Nephite disciples were cast into fiery furnaces and came out unharmed. (3 Ne. 28:21; 4 Ne. 32; Morm. 8:24.) Similar protection was given Shadrach, Meshach, and Abednego when Nebuchadnezzar had them cast into a fiery furnace so hot that it slew the handlers who carried out the deed. (Dan. 3.)

Indeed the power of God is so abundantly manifest through fiery demonstrations that Paul wrote, "Our God is a consuming fire." (Heb. 12:29; Deut. 4:24.) And the Prophet taught that God dwells in everlasting burnings, as will all the righteous who gain exaltation. (*Teachings,* p. 347; Isa. 33:14-16.)

As pertaining to the righteous, the term fire is used to indicate a purifying, cleansing agent, but where the wicked are concerned it is used to signify destruction and the severity of eternal torment. The scriptures speak of the receipt of the gift of the Holy Ghost as a *baptism of fire,* meaning that sin and iniquity are burned out of the repentant person as though by fire. (3 Ne. 9:20.)

The revelations also speak of the day when the Lord's vineyard shall be burned, a day when the righteous shall be preserved, but one in which every corruptible thing shall be consumed, in which the elements shall melt with fervent heat and all things shall become new. (D. & C. 101:23-25; Mal. 3; 4.) That is the day in which the tares shall be burned (D. & C. 101:66), in which the Lord will "consume the wicked with unquenchable fire." (D. & C. 63:32-34, 54; Matt. 3:12; Luke 3:17.) Finally, all those who suffer the second death shall suffer the vengeance of *eternal fire* (D. & C. 63:17; 76:44, 105); their torment shall be "as a lake of fire and brimstone, whose flame ascendeth up forever and ever." (Alma 12:17.)

FIRE AND BRIMSTONE.
See ETERNAL DAMNATION, FIRE, SECOND COMING OF CHRIST, SONS OF PERDITION, SPIRITUAL DEATH 1. In ancient days the wickedness and abominations practiced in Sodom, Gomorrah, Admah, and Zeboim became so great that the Lord utterly destroyed those cities by raining *fire and brimstone* upon them. (Gen. 10:19; 19:24-25; Hos. 11:8; Luke 17:29.) Similar destruction awaits the wicked in the day of vengeance, the great and dreadful day of the Lord, for the Lord will again rain upon the ungodly fire and brimstone from heaven. (Ezek. 38:22; Rev. 9:17-18; D. & C. 29:21.)

Brimstone is sulfur, an easily melted, very inflammable mineral which burns with a blue flame and emits a suffocating odor. "It is found in great abundance near volcanoes. The soil around Sodom and Gomorrah abounded in sulphur [sulfur] and bitumen." (*Peloubet's Bible Dictionary,* p. 100.)

Nothing is quite so destructive of present mortal life as fire and brimstone. Living things as we know them cannot exist where these elements are found. Nor is productivity thereafter to be found in soil cursed with brimstone. Indeed, when the Lord sought to impress upon ancient Israel the curse of disobedience, he said that plagues and sickness would come upon their land until "the whole land thereof is brimstone, and salt, and burning, that it is not sown, nor beareth, nor any grass groweth therein, like the overthrow of Sodom, and Gomorrah, Admah, and Zeboim, which the Lord overthrew in his anger, and in his wrath." (Deut. 29:22-23; Job 18:15; Ps. 11:6; Isa. 30:33.)

2. The nature of burning brimstone is such that it perfectly symbolized to the prophetic mind the eternal torment of the damned. Accordingly we read that the wicked are "tormented with *fire and brimstone*" (Rev. 14:9-11; 19:20; 20:10),

or in other words that "their torment is *as* a lake of fire and brimstone, whose flame ascendeth up forever and ever and has no end." (2 Ne. 9:16; Alma 12:17.) This burning scene, a horrifying "lake of fire and brimstone," symbolizes "endless torment" (2 Ne. 9:19, 26; 28:23; Jac. 6:10; Alma 14:14; D. & C. 76:36); those who find place therein are subject to the second death. (Jac. 3:11; D. & C. 63:17.) They suffer the vengeance of eternal fire. (D. & C. 29:28; 43:33; 76: 44, 105.) When the sons of perdition come forth in the resurrection, they "rise to that resurrection which is as the lake of fire and brimstone." (*Teachings*, p. 361.)

FIRES.
See SIGNS OF THE TIMES.

FIRMAMENT.
See CREATION. As used in the scriptures, *firmament* means *expanse.* The firmament of heaven is the expanse of heaven; it refers, depending upon the context, to either the atmospheric or the sidereal heavens. (Gen. 1; Moses 2; Abra. 4.) It is not true, as has been falsely supposed, that the ancient prophets believed that the firmament was a solid arch between the lower and upper waters in which the stars were set as so many stones in gold or silver. Such was rather the false view of the church in the dark ages. (*Man: His Origin and Destiny,* pp. 468-474.)

FIRST AND LAST.
See ALPHA AND OMEGA, BEGINNING AND END, CHRIST, ETERNITY TO ETERNITY, EVERLASTING TO EVERLASTING. Christ is the *First and the Last.* (D. & C. 110:4; Isa. 41:4; 44:6; 48:12; Rev. 1:8-17; 2:8; 22:13.) These terms are descriptive of his eternal timelessness; he is God everlastingly. As the *First,* the thought is conveyed that he is pre-eminent above all the earth's inhabitants, both from the standpoint of time (he being the Firstborn in the spirit), and from the standpoint of power and dominion (he having become a God in the beginning). As the *Last,* the concept is revealed that he will go on as God, continuing to enjoy his full pre-eminence, to all eternity, everlastingly without end.

FIRSTBORN.
See CHRIST, CHURCH OF THE FIRSTBORN, FATHER IN HEAVEN, FIRST ESTATE, MOTHER IN HEAVEN, ONLY BEGOTTEN SON, SPIRIT BIRTH, SPIRIT BODIES, WORD OF GOD. Christ is the *Firstborn,* meaning that he was the first Spirit Child born to God the Father in pre-existence. (D. & C. 93:21; John 1:1-5; Rom. 8:29; Col. 1:15.) He is also the *Firstborn from the Dead,* which signifies that he was the first person resurrected. (Col. 1:18.)

FIRSTBORN FROM THE DEAD.
See FIRSTBORN.

FIRST COMFORTER.
See HOLY GHOST.

FIRST COUNCIL OF THE SEVENTY.
See GENERAL AUTHORITIES, PRIESTHOOD OFFICES, SEVENTIES. Each quorum of seventy is presided over by seven presidents called a *council*. The *First Council of Seventy* (sometimes called the First Seven Presidents of Seventy) presides over the first quorum of seventy and in addition over all quorums and all seventies. Members of the First Council hold the keys of presidency over the seventies, are General Authorities of the Church, and act under the direction of the Council of the Twelve. As with all councils of seventy, all members are equal in responsibility and presidency, though the 7th president (meaning the senior of the group) presides over the others. (D. & C. 107:93-97.)

FIRST ESTATE.
See PRE-EXISTENCE, SECOND ESTATE. Both Abraham and Jude speak of pre-existence as our *first estate,* that is, it was the first time we lived as conscious identities. The spirits who were faithful in that first estate earned the right to be born into this world and get mortal bodies, bodies which would become the eternal habitation of the spirit after the resurrection. (Abra. 3:22-28.) But the rebellious pre-existent spirits, "the angels which kept not their first estate" (Jude 6), have been denied bodies and the probationary experiences of this *second estate* of mortality.

FIRST FLESH.
See ADAM, FALLEN MAN, FALL OF ADAM, FIRST MAN, FLESH, FORBIDDEN FRUIT. Animals, fowls, fishes, and all forms of life were created by the Lord with tangible, physical bodies of flesh and bones and were duly placed on this earth. (Moses 2; 3.) When all other forms of life had been created naturally upon the face of the earth, and when all things were in readiness, the crowning creative enterprise of the Almighty was undertaken. Man was formed from the dust of the earth and placed here in a physical body of flesh and bones to rule as governor over all other creatures.

Yet the revealed account of the creation specifies that man was "the *first flesh* upon the earth." (Moses 3:7.) The meaning of this is clear when two things are remembered: 1. That all things, man included, were first created in immortality. There was no death in the world either for man or for any form of life until after the fall. (2 Ne. 2:22.) 2. That the word *flesh,* as used by the Lord and his prophets in scores of scriptures, means *mortality.* Adam fell and brought mortality into the world. Thereafter the effects of his fall passed on all created things. Adam thus became literally, not only the first man, but the first flesh (meaning mortal flesh) on earth. (*Doctrines of Salvation,* vol. 1, pp. 77-78; 107-120.)

FIRSTLINGS OF FLOCK.
See SACRIFICES.

FIRST MAN.
See ADAM, FALLEN MAN, FALL OF ADAM, FIRST FLESH, MAN. "Adam, who was the son of God" (Moses 6:22), was "the *first man of all men.*" (Moses 1:34; 3:7; 6:45; Abra. 1:3; D. & C. 84:16; 1 Ne. 5:11; 1 Cor. 15:45; *Inspired Version, Luke* 3:45; *Man: His Origin and Destiny,* pp. 348-355.) *There were no pre-Adamites;* the great archangel Michael, who descended from the courts of glory to be the father of the human race, was appointed to be the father of all living. Indeed, Adam and Eve were not able to have children and provide bodies for the spirit children of the Father until *after* the fall. (2 Ne. 2: 22; Moses 5:11.)

This first man, from the standpoint of ancestry and lineage, is also first in point of pre-eminence, power, and position. He stands next to Christ; holds the "keys of salvation" (D. & C. 78:16); and (under Christ) is the presiding high priest over all the earth. (*Teachings,* p. 158.)

FIRST PRESIDENCY.
See HIGH PRIESTS, PRESIDENT OF THE CHURCH, PRIESTHOOD, PRIESTHOOD QUORUMS, PROPHETS, REVELATORS, SEERS. From ancient times the supreme, directing power and authority over the Church and kingdom has rested with "a quorum of three presidents . . . who were ordained after the order of Melchizedek, and were righteous and holy men." (D. & C. 107:29.) "Three Presiding High Priests, chosen by the body, appointed and ordained to that office, and upheld by the confidence, faith, and prayer of the church, form a quorum of the *Presidency* of the Church." (D. & C. 107:22.)

As "the Presidency of the High Priesthood," they "always" hold "the keys of the kingdom" (D. & C. 81:2), and "have a right to officiate in all the offices in the church." (D. & C. 107:9.) They are *"the highest council of the church of God,* and a final decision upon controversies in spiritual matters. There is not any person belonging to the church who is exempt from this council of the church." (D. & C. 107:80-81.)

Death of the President of the Church dissolves the First Presidency, his two counselors then ceasing to function as members of that supreme body. As Joseph Smith expressed it: "The Twelve are not subject to any other than the First Presidency, viz., myself, Sidney Rigdon, and Frederick G. Williams, who are now my Counselors, and *where I am not, there is no First Presidency over the Twelve."* (*Teachings,* pp. 105-106.)

FIRST PRINCIPLES OF THE GOSPEL.

See FAITH, GOSPEL, MYSTERIES, PLAN OF SALVATION, REPENTANCE. "It is *the first principle of the gospel,"* the Prophet taught, "to know for a certainty the character of God, and to know that we may converse with him as one man converses with another." (*Teachings,* p. 345.) After this principle comes that of the divine mission and atoning sacrifice of our Lord, and out of these two grow faith and repentance and all of the basic and fundamental truths which must be accepted and lived to gain peace in this life and eternal reward in the life to come.

The Prophet also said: "The fundamental principles of our religion are the testimony of the apostles and prophets, concerning Jesus Christ, that he died, was buried, and rose again the third day, and ascended into heaven; and all other things which pertain to our religion are only appendages to it. But in connection with these, we believe in the gift of the Holy Ghost, the power of faith, the enjoyment of the spiritual gifts according to the will of God, the restoration of the house of Israel, and the final triumph of truth." (*Teachings,* p. 121.)

Thus the first principles of the gospel, the basic doctrines of salvation, are the fundamental truths that have been revealed in plainness as distinguished from the mysteries, those things which have not as yet been unfolded in their clarity and perfection to mortal man. The Articles of Faith contain a summarization of some, but not all, of the basic and first principles of the gospel.

Speakers and teachers are obligated to confine their expressions to the doctrines that have been revealed in plainness. They are to "preach Jesus Christ and him crucified" (*Teachings,* p. 109), and to "declare the first principles, and let mysteries alone." (*Teachings,* p. 292.)

FIRST RESURRECTION.
See RESURRECTION.

FIRST SEVEN PRESIDENTS OF SEVENTY.
See FIRST COUNCIL OF THE SEVENTY.

FIRST VISION.
See DISPENSATION OF THE FULNESS OF TIMES, GODHEAD, JOSEPH SMITH THE PROPHET, RESTORATION OF THE GOSPEL, REVELATION, SACRED GROVE, THEOPHANIES, VISIONS, WENTWORTH LETTER. That glorious theophany which took place in the spring of 1820 and which marked the opening of the dispensation of the fulness of

times is called the *First Vision.* It is rated as first both from the standpoint of time and of pre-eminent importance. In it Joseph Smith saw and conversed with the Father and the Son, both of which exalted personages were personally present before him as he lay enwrapped in the Spirit and overshadowed by the Holy Ghost.

This transcendent vision was the beginning of latter-day revelation; it marked the opening of the heavens after the long night of apostate darkness; with it was ushered in the great era of restoration, "the times of restitution of all things, which God hath spoken by the mouth of all his holy prophets since the world began." (Acts 3:21.) Through it the creeds of Christendom were shattered to smithereens, and because of it the truth about those Beings whom it is life eternal to know began again to be taught among men. (John 17:3.) With this vision came the call of that Prophet who, "save Jesus only," was destined to do more "for the salvation of men in this world, than any other man that ever lived in it." (D. & C. 135:3.) This vision was the most important event that had taken place in all world history from the day of Christ's ministry to the glorious hour when it occurred.

Our knowledge of God's dealings with his children from the days of Adam to the present leads us to believe that both the Father and the Son have been manifested to other prophets in other ages. Jos-

eph Smith, himself, on at least two other occasions saw these heavenly Beings in vision (D. & C. 76:22-24; *Teachings,* p. 107), and Stephen beheld them as the murderous mob stoned him to death. (Acts 7:54-60.) Indeed, it is the privilege of those who attain the Second Comforter to have the Son "manifest the Father" unto them. (*Teachings,* pp. 149-151; John 14:23; D. & C. 130:3.) But our account of the First Vision is the only plain scriptural record now extant which details the personal appearance of the Father and the Son to mortal man.

"Believing the word of God," the Prophet wrote in the Wentworth Letter, "I had confidence in the declaration of James—'If any of you lack wisdom, let him ask of God, that giveth to all men liberally, and upbraideth not; and it shall be given him.' (Jas. 1:5.) I retired to a secret place in a grove, and began to call upon the Lord; while fervently engaged in supplication, my mind was taken away from the objects with which I was surrounded, and *I was enwrapped in a heavenly vision, and saw two glorious Personages, who exactly resembled each other in features and likeness,* surrounded with a brilliant light which eclipsed the sun at noon day. They told me that all religious denominations were believing in incorrect doctrines, and that none of them was acknowledged of God as his Church and kingdom: and I was expressly commanded 'to go not after them,'

at the same time receiving a promise that the fulness of the gospel should at some future time be made known unto me." (*History of the Church,* vol. 4, p. 536.)

"I saw a pillar of light exactly over my head, above the brightness of the sun, which descended gradually until it fell upon me," the Prophet also wrote. "When the light rested upon me *I saw two Personages, whose brightness and glory defy all description, standing above me in the air.* One of them spake unto me, calling me by name, and said, pointing to the other—*This is My Beloved Son. Hear Him!*

"My object in going to inquire of the Lord was to know which of all the sects was right, that I might know which to join. No sooner, therefore, did I get possession of myself, so as to be able to speak, than I asked the Personages who stood above me in the light, which of all the sects was right—and which I should join. I was answered that I must join none of them, for they were all wrong; and the Personage who addressed me said that all their creeds were an abomination in his sight; that those professors were all corrupt; that: 'they draw near to me with their lips, but their hearts are far from me; they teach for doctrines the commandments of men, having a form of godliness, but they deny the power thereof.' He again forbade me to join with any of them; and many other things did he say

unto me." (Jos. Smith 2:16-20.)

When Joseph Smith, then but a youth in his 15th year, went into the Sacred Grove to seek answer to the Spirit-inspired question, "which of all the sects was right," he carried with him the mental vagaries taught in the creeds of the day as to the personality of God. He supposed, as was then universally taught in apostate Christendom, that God was a three-in-one Spirit that filled the immensity of space, incorporeal, uncreated, immaterial, without body, parts, or passions. When he returned from that sacred spot, he had the sure knowledge—for his eyes had seen and the Holy Ghost (whose power had also been felt on that sacred occasion) had born record to his soul—that the Father and the Son were two glorified Personages in the express image of each other. (D. & C. 130:22.)

If this inexperienced youth had been seeking to fabricate some great spiritual experience, he never in the world would have come back with a story that struck irreconcilably at all the creeds of Christendom and all the teachings he himself had so far received from his parents and others. In an attempt to deceive he might have said that an angel appeared, or that some other miraculous event transpired, but never would it have occurred to him to rock the whole religious foundation of the Christian world with such a startling claim as that which he did make.

And now—wonder of wonders!—those who have attained greater spiritual enlightenment than was then prevalent discover that the new revelation about God's personality is the same which was from the beginning; it is the same truth to which all the prophets bear record.

But even if, by some inconceivable miracle, this one youth—in defiance of all the learning and teachings of the religious world—had stumbled upon the truth that God was a personal Being, yet no rational mind would expect him to record the events incident to the First Vision so that those occurrences would be in perfect harmony with the laws of mediation, intercession, and advocacy. For instance, if he had said that the Father taught him certain truths (rather than saying that the Father introduced the Son and that the Son gave the actual direction to him), such would have shown his story to be false. Inexperienced as he was, he could not have known that by God's eternal law it is everlastingly ordained that all revelation comes through Christ and that the Father never does more than introduce and bear record of the Son.

Evidences of the reality of the First Vision might be multiplied, but the greatest proofs that it took place are the whisperings of the Spirit to the devout truth seekers and the establishment and triumph of The Church of Jesus Christ of Latter-day Saints, the Church which is founded and grounded on the testimony that Joseph Smith saw God and was in literal reality chosen to be his mighty latter-day Prophet.

FISH.
See ANIMALS.

FLATTERY.
See IDLE WORDS, LIARS. *Flattery* is the act of ingratiating oneself into another's confidence by excessive praise, or by insincere speech and acts. It includes the raising of false and unfounded hopes; there is always an element of dishonesty attending it.

Flattery is a tool of Satan (D. & C. 10:25-29); he uses it to lead souls to destruction. (2 Ne. 28:22.) Ministers of false religions obtain the support of their congregations in large measure by flattery, in that by appeals to vanity and through other means they hold out false hopes of salvation to their worshipers. For instance: Certain saved-by-grace-alone fanatics flatter their followers into believing they can be saved through no act other than confessing Christ with their lips. Other professors of religion flatter their adherents into believing there will be a final harmony of all souls with God and that none will be damned. Still others flatter their disciples with the false belief that forgiveness of sins comes from confession alone, or that souls may be redeemed from so-called purgatory by purchased prayers. "Flattery," the Prophet said, is "a deadly poison." (*Teachings,* p. 137.)

FLESH.

See CARNALITY, CORRUPTION, DEVILISHNESS, FALLEN MAN, FIRST FLESH, FLESH AND BLOOD, FLESH AND BONES, MORTALITY, SENSUALITY. Since *flesh* as we know it is all *mortal flesh,* and since fallen or mortal man is carnal, sensual, and devilish by nature (Moses 5:13; Mosiah 3:19), the prophetic mind has always chosen the term flesh to signify the carnality and sensuality common to unregenerate human kind. "The *works of the flesh,*" as Paul lists them, "are these; Adultery, fornication, uncleanness, lasciviousness, Idolatry, witchcraft, hatred, variance, emulations, wrath, strife, seditions, heresies, Envyings, murders, drunkenness, revellings, and such like: of the which I tell you before, as I have also told you in time past, that they which do such things shall not inherit the kingdom of God." (Gal. 5:19-21.)

"Though we walk in the flesh," Paul also says, "we do not war after the flesh" (2 Cor. 10:3), that is, though we are in the world (of mortality), we are not of the world. Manifestly the saints are to "abstain from fleshly lusts, which war against the soul" (1 Pet. 2:11),

"hating even the garment spotted by the flesh." (Jude 23.)

FLESH AND BLOOD.

See FLESH, FLESH AND BONES, MORTALITY. "The life of the flesh is in the blood" (Lev. 17:11), that is, the mortal body lives only so long as the blood is present. Spill the blood and mortality ceases. Hence, *flesh and blood means mortality.* Our Lord's statement to Peter, "Flesh and blood hath not revealed it unto thee, but my Father which is in heaven" (Matt. 16:17), meant that no mortal person or power had given Peter his testimony; it had come from the Father by revelation. "Flesh and blood," Paul says, "cannot inherit the kingdom of God; neither doth corruption inherit incorruption." (1 Cor. 15:50.) In other words: Mortality cannot inherit a celestial world, for that is the dwelling place of immortal, incorruptible beings.

FLESH AND BONES.

See FLESH, FLESH AND BLOOD, IMMORTALITY, RESURRECTION, SPIRITUAL BODIES. In the same sense that *flesh and blood* is used to signify *mortality, flesh and bones* is the scriptural phrase meaning *immortality,* the state after the resurrection when all men will have spiritual bodies. Thus, appearing to his disciples after his resurrection, our Lord said: "Handle me, and see; for a spirit hath not flesh and bones, as ye see me have." (Luke 24:39.) In exactly the same sense, "The Father has a body of flesh and bones as tangible as man's" (D. & C. 130:22), for he too is a resurrected, immortal Being.

FLOOD OF NOAH.

See BAPTISM. In the days of Noah the Lord sent *a universal flood* which completely immersed the whole earth and destroyed all flesh except that preserved on the ark. (Gen. 6; 7; 8; 9; Moses 7:38-45; 8; Ether 13:2.) "Noah was born to save seed of everything, when the earth was washed of its wickedness by the flood." (*Teachings,* p. 12.) This flood was the baptism of the earth; before it occurred the land was all in one place, a condition that will again prevail during the millennial era. (D. & C. 133:23-24.)

There is no question but what many of the so-called geological changes in the earth's surface, which according to geological theories took place over ages of time, in reality occurred in a matter of a few short weeks incident to the universal deluge. (*Man: His Origin and Destiny,* pp. 414-436.)

FLOODS.

See SIGNS OF THE TIMES.

FORBIDDEN FRUIT.

See ADAM, EVE, FALL OF ADAM.

Our first parents, Adam and Eve, were first created in a state of immortality; there was no death in the world as things were then organized. (2 Ne. 2:22.) While in their immortal state they were commanded to multiply and fill the earth with posterity. (Moses 2:28.) They were also told that of every tree in the Garden of Eden they might eat excepting only the tree of the knowledge of good and evil.

For disobedience to this command death (*or in other words mortality*) was to enter the world. (Moses 3:17.) In order to have children it was necessary that they become mortal; and so in accordance with the divine plan they partook of the *forbidden fruit,* death and mortality entered the world, and the bodies of our first parents were so changed as to permit them to have offspring and thus fulfil the purposes of the Lord in the creation of the earth. (D. & C. 29:40-44; Moses 5:11; 2 Ne. 2:22-25.)

What the real meaning is of the expression forbidden fruit has not been revealed, and it is profitless to speculate. It is sufficient for us to know that Adam and Eve broke the law which would have permitted them to continue as immortal beings, or in other words they complied with the law which enabled them to become mortal beings, and this course of conduct is termed eating the forbidden fruit.

One thing we do know definitely: *The forbidden fruit was not sex sin.* The view that immoral indulgence on the part of our first parents constituted the forbidden fruit is one of the most evil and wicked heresies in apostate Christendom. Adam and Eve were married for eternity by the Lord himself before the fall, and the command given them to have children was one directing the begetting of children in legal and lawful wedlock. (Moses 3:20-25.)

FOREIGN MISSIONS.
See MISSIONS.

FOREORDINATION.

See AGENCY, ELECTION OF GRACE, PREDESTINATION, PRE-EXISTENCE, RACES OF MEN. To carry forward his own purposes among men and nations, the Lord *foreordained* chosen spirit children in pre-existence and assigned them to come to earth at particular times and places so that they might aid in furthering the divine will. These pre-existence appointments, made "according to the foreknowledge of God the Father" (1 Pet. 1:2), simply designated certain individuals to perform missions which the Lord in his wisdom knew they had the talents and capacities to do.

The mightiest and greatest spirits were foreordained to stand as prophets and spiritual leaders, giving to the people such portion of the Lord's word as was designed for the day and age involved. Other spirits, such as those who laid the foundations of the American nation, were appointed beforehand to perform great works in political and governmental fields. In all this there is not the slightest hint of compulsion; persons foreordained to fill special missions in mortality are as abundantly endowed with free agency as are any other persons. By their foreordination the Lord merely gives them the opportunity to serve him and his purposes if they will choose to measure up to the standard he knows they are capable of attaining.

Alma taught the great truth that every person who holds the Melchizedek Priesthood was foreordained to receive that high and holy order in the pre-existent councils of eternity. "This is the manner after which they were ordained," he says. They were "called and prepared from the foundation of the world *according to the foreknowledge of God,* on account of their exceeding faith and good works [while yet living in pre-existence]; in the first place [that is, in pre-existence] being left to choose good or evil; therefore they having chosen good, and exercising exceeding great faith, are called with a holy calling, yea, with that holy calling which was prepared with, and according to, a preparatory redemption for such." Thus, he explains, Melchizedek Priesthood holders have been "prepared

from the foundation of the world" for their high callings. The Lord has prepared them *from eternity to all eternity, according to his foreknowledge of all things."* (Alma 13:3-9.)

Speaking of foreordination to spiritual callings, the Prophet Joseph Smith said: *"Every man who has a calling to minister to the inhabitants of the world was ordained to that very purpose in the Grand Council of heaven before this world was.* I suppose that I was ordained to this very office in that Grand Council." (*Teachings,* p. 365.) Abraham saw the hosts of pre-existent spirits. "And among all these," he recorded, "were many of the *noble and great ones; And God saw these souls that they were good,* and he stood in the midst of them, and he said: *These I will make my rulers;* for he stood among those that were spirits, and he saw that they were good; and he said unto me: *Abraham, thou art one of them; thou wast chosen before thou wast born."* (Abra. 3:22-23.)

Jeremiah records a similar truth relative to his foreordination to be "a prophet unto the nations" (Jer. 1:5), and Moses taught that the whole host of spirits born in the lineage of Jacob were before appointed to come through that chosen line. (Deut. 32:7-8.) It was because of their pre-existent training, election, and foreordination that Christ was able to say of certain chosen ones, "My sheep hear my voice, and I know them, and they follow me." (John 10:27.)

There is scriptural record of many other instances of specific foreordination. Christ, himself, was before chosen to come to this life as the Son of God and Redeemer of the world (Moses 4:1-4; Abra. 3:27; 1 Pet. 1:19-20), "the Lamb slain from the foundation of the world." (Rev. 13:8.) Mary, the mother of our Lord, was before named for her sacred mission (1 Ne. 11:18-20; Mosiah 3:8; Isa. 7:14), and John the Baptist received a pre-mortal commission to prepare the way for the first coming of the Son of Man. (1 Ne. 10:7-10; Isa. 40:3; Matt. 3:3.) The Twelve who in their mortal life were destined to follow our Lord were seen in vision by Nephi nearly 600 years before the assigned day of their mortal missions. (1 Ne. 11:29, 34-36.)

Joseph who was sold into Egypt spoke prophetically of Moses, and Joseph Smith, and others, both by name and by describing the foreordained missions to be performed by them, hundreds of years before the destined birth of those concerned into mortality. (2 Ne. 3.) John the Beloved's name, apostolic call, and mission as the great Revelator were revealed to Nephi long before John's birth. (1 Ne. 14:19-29.) In pre-existence, before Jacob or Esau were born as mortal beings, the Lord decreed, "The elder shall serve the younger." (Rom. 9:10-12.) The temporal rule of Cyrus and the mission he was to perform as it affected the Lord's Israel, was foretold by Isaiah long before the birth of that earthly ruler. (Isa. 44:28; 45.) The mission of Columbus to bring the American nations to the knowledge of the old world, and the Lord's dealings with the Gentile nations which should inhabit the areas thus re-discovered, was all foreknown and foreordained. (1 Ne. 13.)

And what is true of these great leaders and episodes in the history of the Lord's religious and civic dealings with mankind is also true of other political and religious leaders and other great historical events. "I am God," the Lord said, "and there is none like me, *Declaring the end from the beginning, and from ancient times the things that are not yet done,* saying, My counsel shall stand, and I will do all my pleasure." (Isa. 46:9-10.)

FORGIVENESS.

See BAPTISM, REPENTANCE, SACRAMENT, SIN. *Forgiveness,* which includes divine pardon and complete remission of sins, is available, on conditions of repentance, for all men except those who have sinned unto death. (D. & C. 42:18, 79; 64:7.) For such there is no forgiveness, neither in this world nor in the world to come. (D. & C. 76: 32-34; 132:27; Matt. 12:31-32.) To accountable persons in the world, remission of sins comes by repentance and baptism of water and of the Spirit. For those who have once been cleansed in this way and who thereafter commit sin—but not unto death—(and all members of the Church are guilty of sin, in either greater or lesser degree) the *law of forgiveness* embraces the following requirements:

1. GODLY SORROW FOR SIN.— This includes an honest, heartfelt contrition of soul, a contrition born of a broken heart and a contrite spirit. It presupposes a frank, personal acknowledgment that one's acts have been evil in the sight of Him who is holy. There is no mental reservation in godly sorrow, no feeling that perhaps one's sins are not so gross or serious after all. It is certainly more than regret either because the sin has been brought to light or because some preferential reward or status has been lost because of it. Paul said: "Godly sorrow worketh repentance to salvation, . . . but the sorrow of the world worketh death." (2 Cor. 7:10.)

2. ABANDONMENT OF SIN.—This means to stop doing what is wrong, to cease completely from one's evil acts, to flee from iniquity both of thought, word, and deed. "Put away the evil of your doings from before mine eyes," saith the Lord, "cease to do evil; Learn to do well." (Isa. 1:16-17.) "By this ye may know if a man repenteth of his sins—behold, he will *confess* them and *forsake* them." (D. & C. 58:43.)

3. CONFESSION OF SIN.—To gain forgiveness all sins must be confessed to the Lord. The sinner

must open his heart to the Almighty and with godly sorrow admit the error of his ways and plead for grace. *"I, the Lord, forgive sins unto those who confess their sins before me and ask forgiveness, who have not sinned unto death."* (D. & C. 64:7.)

Further, those sins which involve moral turpitude—meaning serious sins for which the court procedures of the Church could be instituted so that a person's fellowship or membership might be called in question—such sins must be confessed to the proper church officer. "To whom should confession be made?" President Stephen L Richards asked. *"To the Lord,* of course, whose law has been violated. *To the aggrieved person or persons,* as an essential in making due retribution if that is necessary. And then certainly to the *Lord's representative,* his appointed judge in Israel, under whose ecclesiastical jurisdiction the offender lives and holds membership in the kingdom.

"Is the offender justified in bypassing his immediate church authority and judge, and going to those who do not know him so well to make his confession? Almost universally, I think the answer should be No, for the local tribunals are in position to know the individual, his history and environs far better than those who have not had close contact with him, and in consequence the local authorities have a background which will enable them to pass judgment with more justice, and also mercy, than might be reasonably expected from any other source. It follows that *it is the order of the Church for confession to be made to the bishop,* which entails heavy and exacting responsibilities on the part of the bishop, the first of which is that every confession should be received and held in the utmost confidence. A bishop who violates such a sacred confidence is himself guilty of an offense before God and the Church. Where it becomes necessary to take counselors into his confidence, as it frequently does, and where it is necessary to organize tribunals, the bishop should inform the confessor, and if possible obtain his permission so to do.

"Why is confession essential? First, because the Lord has commanded it, and secondly, because the offender cannot live and participate in the kingdom of God, to receive the blessings therefrom, with a lie in his heart.

"Now the confessed offender is not left without hope, for he can obtain forgiveness by following the course outlined, and by forsaking sins comparable to that committed, as well as all other sin, and living before the Church and the Lord in such manner as to win approbation of both. The offender who has brought stigma and affront to the ward, the stake or the mission should seek the forgiveness of those he has thus offended. That may be had at times through the presiding authorities of the various divisions of the Church. At other times it may be appropriate and quite necessary to make amends for public offenses and seek forgiveness before organizations of the people. The judges of Israel will determine this matter." (Conf. Rep., Apr., 1954, pp. 10-13.)

It should be clear that bishops and other church officers, when confessions are made to them, do not forgive sins except in the sense that they forgive them as far as the Church is concerned; they remit any penalty which the Church on earth might impose; they adjudge that repentant persons are worthy of full fellowship in the earthly kingdom.

Normally a period of *probation* is involved before the earthly agent determines to refrain from instituting the procedures whereunder church penalties are imposed. "This probation serves a double purpose," President Richards says. "First, and perhaps most important, it enables the offender to determine for himself whether he has been able to so master himself as to trust himself in the face of ever-recurring temptation; and secondly, to enable the judges to make a more reliable appraisement of the genuineness of repentance and worthiness for restored confidence." (Conf. Rep., Apr., 1954, p. 12.)

Actual and ultimate forgiveness comes only from the Lord in heaven. He of course on occasions forgave sins during his ministry (Matt. 9:2-8), and he has by revelation in modern times announced that certain persons were free from sin. (D. & C. 29:3; 31:5; 36:1; 50:36; 60:7.) The Prophet Enos received a personal revelation telling him his sins were forgiven. (Enos 4-8.) Similar revelations might come at any time to the Lord's earthly agents, in which instances they could and would remit the sins of the repentant persons. But in the true sense it would be the Lord forgiving the sins, though he acted through the agency of his servants the prophets. (D. & C. 132:46-47; John 20:23.)

Unless practiced and regulated in strict harmony with the divine will, the gospel requirement of confession can easily degenerate into a system which has the practical effect of inviting and enticing men to commit sin. By leaving the impression in men's minds that mere vocal recitation of past sins to the appointed church officer—without the attendant contrition of heart and the future righteousness of life—will suffice to cleanse the sinner, it is obvious that many persons will not be restrained from the commission of sin. Further, this true doctrine and law of confession stands in sharp contrast to the customs and practices found in the world in which churches say to their adherents, as Moroni expressed it: "Come unto me, and for your money you shall be forgiven of your sins." (Morm. 8:32.)

4. RESTITUTION FOR SIN.—Restitution means restoration; it is to

return the stolen property, to make amends for the offense committed, to repair the damage done, to compensate for hardships imposed by one's acts. Ordinarily restitution is made to the aggrieved party, but full compliance with this requirement is not always possible; virtue destroyed cannot be brought back. Where literal and actual restitution cannot be made, still all possible compensation must be given so that the one seeking forgiveness will have complied with the law to the extent of his ability.

5. OBEDIENCE TO ALL LAW.— Complete forgiveness is reserved for those only who turn their whole hearts to the Lord and begin to keep all of his commandments— not just those commandments disobeyed in the past, but those in all fields. *"He that repents and does the commandments of the Lord shall be forgiven."* (D. & C. 1:32.) "I will forgive you of your sins with this commandment—that you remain steadfast in your minds in solemnity and the spirit of prayer, in bearing testimony to all the world of those things which are communicated unto you." (D. & C. 84:61.)

Necessarily a part of this full compliance with divine law includes forgiveness of one's neighbor of his trespasses. (Luke 11:1-4; 3 Ne. 13:9-15.) "Forgive us our debts, as we forgive our debtors." (Matt. 6:9-15.) *"Forgive, and ye shall be forgiven."* (Luke 6:37.) "My disciples, in days of old, sought occasion against one another and forgave not one another in their hearts; and for this evil they were afflicted and sorely chastened. Wherefore, I say unto you, that ye ought to forgive one another; for he that forgiveth not his brother his trespasses standeth condemned before the Lord; for there remaineth in him the greater sin. *I, the Lord, will forgive whom I will forgive, but of you it is required to forgive all men.* And ye ought to say in your hearts—let God judge between me and thee, and reward thee according to thy deeds." (D. & C. 64:8-11.)

At what times and under what circumstances do men gain forgiveness of their sins? Manifestly, they attain this reward at any time when they are in complete harmony with the divine will, that is at any time when they have complied with the Lord's law whereunder they are enabled to become pure and spotless before him.

Initially and primarily, accountable and worthy persons gain forgiveness of their sins when a valid and authoritative baptism is performed for them. The very ordinance of baptism is ordained, among other reasons, so that men may gain a remission of their sins through it. Thus the resurrected Lord taught the Nephites: "And no unclean thing can enter into his [the Father's] kingdom; therefore nothing entereth into his rest save it be those who have washed their garments in my blood, because of their faith, and the repentance of all their sins, and their faithfulness unto the end. Now this is the commandment: *Repent, all ye ends of the earth, and come unto me and be baptized in my name, that ye may be sanctified by the reception of the Holy Ghost, that ye may stand spotless before me at the last day."* (3 Ne. 27:19-20.)

Mere performance of the formal rite or ordinance of baptism, standing alone and without full compliance with the law on the part of the converted persons, does not put the Lord's cleansing power into operation. No blessing ever accrues to men except as a result of full compliance with the law upon which its receipt is predicated. (D. & C. 130:20-21.) Accordingly, Moroni counseled: *"See that ye are not baptized unworthily; see that ye partake not of the sacrament of Christ unworthily; but see that ye do all things in worthiness,* and do it in the name of Jesus Christ, the Son of the living God; and if ye do this, and endure to the end, ye will in nowise be cast out." (Morm. 9:29.) Ordinances and performances are performed in worthiness when the recipients of the blessings have so lived that the ratifying seal of the Spirit attends what is done. (D. & C. 132:7.)

Thus baptisms performed for worthy persons and in accordance with the revealed law, actually cleanse the baptized persons. Their sins are washed away in the waters of baptism; they are burned out of their souls through the baptism of fire. The revealed law governing baptismal worthiness is this: *"All those who humble themselves before God, and desire to be baptized, and come forth with broken hearts and contrite spirits, and witness before the church that they have truly repented of all their sins, and are willing to take upon them the name of Jesus Christ, having a determination to serve him to the end, and truly manifest by their works that they have received of the Spirit of Christ unto the remission of their sins, shall be received by baptism into his church."* (D. & C. 20:37.)

When converted persons are baptized for the remission of sins, the sacred baptismal ordinance is designed to free them from past and future sins. Those sins committed after baptism are forgiven whenever members of the Church, by full compliance with the law of forgiveness, again get themselves in the same state of righteousness and purity previously attained in connection with their baptisms.

Provision, accordingly, is found in the gospel for worthy members of the Lord's Church to renew the covenants made in the waters of baptism and to receive again into their lives the promises of peace in this life and eternal life hereafter that were given them when they accepted membership in the kingdom.

In the covenant of baptism, among other things, men promise: 1. To remember the death, burial, and resurrection of their Lord—the very ordinance itself being so ordained as to symbolize these things; 2. "To take upon them the name of Jesus Christ"; and 3. To "serve him and keep his commandments." In return, the Lord on his part promises: 1. That he will "pour out his Spirit more abundantly" upon such persons; and 2. That they shall "have eternal life." (Mosiah 18:8-10; D. & C. 20:37.)

Now precisely and identically this same covenant is made by persons who partake of the sacrament. In other words, if they have been baptized (thus making the covenant of baptism), and if they then partake of the sacrament, they are renewing or making again the very covenant which brought remission of sins to them. Each time baptized members of the Church partake of the bread and water of the Lord's Supper, they most solemnly promise: 1. To remember the body of the Son of God which was crucified for them; 2. To take upon them the name of the Son; and 3. To "always remember him and keep his commandments which he has given them." In return, as his part of the covenant, the Lord promises: 1. That the saints shall "have his Spirit to be with them"; and 2. That they shall have "eternal life . . . at the last day." (D. & C. 20:75-79; John 6:54.)

It is an axiomatic gospel verity that the Spirit of the Lord will not dwell in an unclean tabernacle. (1 Cor. 3:16-17; 6:19; Mosiah 2:37;

Alma 7:21; 34:36; Hela. 4:24.) The Spirit will not come to a man unless and until he is prepared by personal righteousness to have the companionship of that member of the Godhead. Thus to be worthy of baptism men must "witness before the church that they have truly repented of all their sins" (D. & C. 20:37), and precisely the same thing is involved in their preparation to partake worthily of the sacrament. In other words, as a result of worthy baptism men stand clean before him if they fulfil the full law involved in partaking of the sacrament, for in each instance they are rewarded with the companionship of the Spirit, which companionship they cannot have unless they are cleansed and purified from sin.

There are also other sacred occasions on which men are privileged to ascend to those spiritual heights where they gain the justifying approval of the Spirit for their conduct and as a consequence are forgiven of their sins. James named the ordinance of administration to the sick as one of these. "Is any sick among you?" he asked, "let him call for the elders of the church; and let them pray over him, anointing him with oil in the name of the Lord: And the prayer of faith shall save the sick, and the Lord shall raise him up; *and if he have committed sins, they shall be forgiven him.*" (Jas. 5:14-15.) That is, the person who by faith, devotion, righteousness, and personal worthiness, is in a position to be healed, is also in a position to have the justifying approval of the Spirit for his course of life, and his sins are forgiven him, as witnessed by the fact that he receives the companionship of the Spirit, which he could not have if he were unworthy.

In principle, what is here stated with reference to the sacrament and the ordinance of administration to the sick, applies to any other course of spiritual preparation which persons undergo, if that course of life is such as to get them in harmony with the Spirit of the Lord. One of the beauties of this doctrine is that in and through it repeated opportunities are given to sinners—and all men are sinners to a greater or lesser degree, whether they are in the Church or out of it—to repent and get their lives in such accord with the divine will that they may become heirs of salvation.

In the final analysis, men are not saved unless they have struggled and labored through repentance and the attainment of forgiveness to the point that they stand clean and spotless before the judgment bar, for "no unclean thing can inherit the kingdom of heaven." (Alma 11:27.)

FORNICATION.
See ADULTERY, DAMNATION, SEX IMMORALITY, TELESTIAL LAW. 1. Illicit sexual intercourse on the part of an unmarried person is called *fornication*. It is one of the grossest types of sex immorality, ranking close to adultery in wickedness. Men are commanded to abstain therefrom (1 Thess. 4:3), with the dire decree that unrepentant fornicators shall not inherit the kingdom of God. (1 Cor. 6:9-11.) The saints are "not to company with fornicators" (1 Cor. 5:9-13), unless such a person has repented with all his heart and gained forgiveness for his debasing crime. (D. & C. 42:74-77.)

2. In a spiritual sense, infidelity to and a forsaking of the true God for false gods is also called *fornication*. (2 Chron. 21:5-11.)

FORTUNE TELLERS.
See FORTUNE TELLING.

FORTUNE TELLING.
See ASTROLOGY, DIVINATION, NECROMANCY, SOOTHSAYERS, SORCERY, SPIRITUALISM. As practiced in modern times, *fortune telling* falls into two categories: 1. Frivolous attempts to amuse by pretending to foretell the future under circumstances which are recognized by all concerned as mere entertainment; and 2. Serious attempts to foretell and prognosticate future occurrences by using occult or hidden powers, or at least, through devious and concealed means, to make recipients of the messages believe such have come from

sources or through arrangements by which the future can be made known.

These serious attempts at fortune telling are of the devil and are in effect often accepted as a substitute for the true principle and practice of receiving revelation and guidance from a divine source. Frivolous fortune telling games played at parties are relatively innocent past-times, but real attempts to foretell the future and to delineate the destiny and fate of persons or groups by *palmistry, phrenology, cards, tea leaves, horoscopes,* or any other astrological device—all these are contrary to revealed truth.

To Babylon the Lord sent this message: For thy crime of self-exaltation, and "for the multitude of thy sorceries, and for the great abundance of thine enchantments," thou shalt be destroyed. Then, in mocking vein, he challenged: "Stand now with thine enchantments, and with the multitude of thy sorceries, wherein thou hast laboured from thy youth. . . . Let now the astrologers, the stargazers, the monthly prognosticators, stand up, and save thee from these things that shall come upon thee." Then the Lord decreed that these fortune tellers "shall be as stubble; the fire shall burn them; they shall not deliver themselves from the power of the flame." (Isa. 47.) True it is that serious fortune telling has no part in God's kingdom.

FOWLS.
See ANIMALS.

FREE AGENCY.
See AGENCY.

FREEDOM.
See AGENCY, CIVIL GOVERNMENT, CONSTITUTION OF THE UNITED STATES, INALIENABLE RIGHTS, LIBERTY, TRUTH. *Freedom* is the power and ability to choose for oneself the course one will follow in all fields of activity. It is an inalienable right with which man has been endowed by his Creator. (D. & C. 98:4-8.)

Freedom is based on truth, and no man is perfectly free unless he has knowledge of and abides in the truth. "Ye shall know the truth, and the truth shall make you free." (John 8:32.) As long as man's beliefs, or any part of them, are based on error, he is not completely free, for the chains of error bind his mind. Freedom also results from righteousness because the captivity of sin is bondage. "Whosoever committeth sin is the servant of sin" (John 8:34), "for of whom a man is overcome, of the same is he brought in bondage." (2 Pet. 2:19.)

Freedom of conscience, the freedom to worship God according to the dictates of one's own conscience, is the greatest of all freedoms. (Eleventh Article of Faith; Alma 1:17; 21:22; 30:9.) The gospel gives freedom to men (Gal. 5:1), and the gospel itself is free. (Matt. 10:8; Rev. 21:6; 22:17; 2 Ne. 26:25-28.)

This American nation has been established by the Lord as the champion of freedom in the last days. (D. & C. 101:76-80.) The ancient promise was that the inhabitants of this land should "be set up as a *free people* by the power of the Father" (3 Ne. 21:4), so that the gospel could be restored and the Lord's great latter-day work accomplished. The freedoms guaranteed under our constitutional government should belong "to all mankind." (D. & C. 98:4-10.) Eventually they will, for freedom shall be enthroned during the millennial era. "Ye shall have no laws but my laws when I come" (D. & C. 38:22), the Lord says, and his law is "the perfect law of liberty." (Jas. 1:25.)

FRIENDS OF GOD.

See SERVANTS OF GOD.

FRUITS.

See GOOD WORKS.

FULNESS OF THE FATHER.

See CELESTIAL MARRIAGE, CHURCH OF THE FIRSTBORN, DAUGHTERS OF GOD, EXALTATION, GODHOOD, JOINT-HEIRS WITH CHRIST, SALVATION, SONS OF GOD. The expression *fulness of the*

Father has reference to his position of power, glory, perfection, and godhood. The "fulness of the glory of the Father" consists in the possession of "all power, both in heaven and on earth." (D. & C. 93:16-17.) God is an exalted Man, and exaltation consists in having the fulness of all powers, all attributes, and all perfections. (D. & C. 76; 93; 132.)

The plan of exaltation is one whereunder those who fill the full measure of their creation are able to progress to that state wherein they will gain the fulness of the Father. Christ is the Exemplar; he went from grace to grace until finally after the resurrection he gained the fulness of all things, including the fulness of truth, knowledge, and power. (Matt. 28:18; D. & C. 93:6-30.)

Obedience to the whole law of the whole gospel, including the crowning ordinance of celestial marriage, is the way whereby the fulness of the Father may be gained. Those so married, who keep their covenants, shall go on "to their exaltation and glory in all things, . . . which glory shall be a *fulness* and a continuation of the seeds forever and ever. Then shall they be gods." (D. & C. 132:6, 19-20; *Doctrines of Salvation*, vol. 2, pp. 24, 44-45, 62-63.)

Joseph Smith taught: "All those who keep his [the Father's] commandments shall grow up from grace to grace, and become heirs of the heavenly kingdom, and joint-heirs with Jesus Christ; possessing the same mind, being transformed into the same image or likeness, even the express image of him who fills all in all; being filled with the *fulness of his glory,* and become *one in him,* even as the Father, Son and Holy Spirit are one. . . . As the Son partakes of the *fulness of the Father* through the Spirit, so the saints are, by the same Spirit, to be partakers of the *same fulness,* to enjoy the *same glory;* for as the Father and the Son are one, so, in like manner, the saints are to be one in them. Through the love of the Father, the mediation of Jesus Christ, and the gift of the Holy Spirit, they are to be heirs of God, and joint-heirs with Jesus Christ." (*Lectures on Faith,* pp. 50-52; 3 Ne. 28:10-11.)

FULNESS OF THE GENTILES.
See SIGNS OF THE TIMES.

FULNESS OF THE GOSPEL.
See GOSPEL.

FULNESS OF TIMES.
See DISPENSATION OF THE FULNESS OF TIMES.

FUNERALS.
See CREMATION, DEATH, DEDICATION OF GRAVES, GRAVES, MOURNING. Religious services or *funerals* held in connection with death are designed for the comfort, blessing, and edification of the living; they have no effect whatever on the reward or condemnation of the departed. They are proper occasions on which to preach the truths of salvation; to testify of the reality of the resurrection; to give comfort, solace, and counsel to the bereaved; to hold forth the assurance of immortality for all men and the hope of eternal life for those who have kept the faith; to mention the good qualities and achievements of the departed. The practice of wiping out every fault and magnifying every seeming virtue of faithless persons, as soon as they are dead, however, leaves the false impression that acceptance of the gospel and complete obedience to its standards while in this life are not important. Extravagant statements, promises, or assurances—unless clearly dictated by the Spirit—should not be made at funerals.

GABRIEL.
See ANGELS, ARCHANGELS, ELIAS, KEYS OF THE KINGDOM.

To play his part in the great restoration of all things, *Gabriel* came in modern times and conferred the keys of his dispensation upon Joseph Smith. As with other angelic ministrants to this earth, Gabriel also spent his mortal probation here. He is Noah, the one who stands next to Michael or Adam in the priesthood hierarchy. (*Teachings,* p. 157.)

We have Biblical evidence that Gabriel ministered to Daniel (Dan. 8:16; 9:21); and that he appeared to Zacharias, the father of John the Baptist, and to Mary, the mother of our Lord. (Luke 1:5-38.) There is no foundation for the common sectarian tradition that it is he who will blow his horn to herald the resurrection. Rather, as appears from latter-day revelation, it will be Michael the archangel who shall sound the trump at the great and coming day. (D. & C. 88: 106-116.)

GADIANTON ROBBERS.
See SECRET COMBINATIONS.

GALILEAN.
See CHRIST, JESUS OF NAZARETH. Christ is called the *Galilean* (Matt. 21:11; Luke 23:5-7; John 7:41-42), because he lived in the city of Nazareth in the Roman province of Galilee. His prophetic powers were belittled by the Jews on the specious contention that "out of Galilee ariseth no prophet." (John 7:52.)

GAMBLING.
See APOSTASY, CARD PLAYING, LOTTERIES, RAFFLES. *Gambling* is the playing or gaming for money or other stakes with a view to getting something for little or nothing; elements of luck and chance are always present—all of which, when taken together, form a system which is not of God.

Gambling is in opposition to the divine will; it is a wicked, evil practice, destructive of the finer sensitivities of the soul. No matter how cloaked or disguised, and no matter how professedly worthy an accompanying money raising scheme may be, gambling is morally wrong and will be avoided by all who are saints in deed.

Clubs, civic organizations, fraternal groups, governments, and sometimes even some churches, sponsor, support, approve, or conduct various gambling enterprises as part of their fund raising programs. Such sponsorship has no sanctifying or transforming power. Gambling is gambling, and is to be shunned, no matter where it is found.

In every concern of life the element of chance is present, and this fact of itself does not classify an enterprise as gambling. "The element of chance enters very largely into everything we undertake," President Joseph F. Smith said, "and it should be remembered that the spirit in which we do things decides very largely whether we are gambling or are entering into legitimate business enterprise." (*Gospel Doctrine,* 5th ed., p. 326.)

GAMES OF CHANCE.
See GAMBLING.

GAMING.
See GAMBLING.

GARDEN OF EDEN.
See ADAM, ADAM-ONDI-AHMAN, DEATH, FALL OF ADAM, MILLENNIUM, NEW HEAVEN AND NEW EARTH. Adam and Eve, when first created, were placed in the *Garden of Eden,* by which is meant they were given a home "eastward in Eden," in a garden which the Lord had planted on an earth which was paradisiacal in nature. (Gen. 2; 3; Moses 3; 4.) As things were then constituted, death had not entered the world either for Adam and Eve or for any living creature; there was no procreation; and all things were in a state of pristine innocence and beauty. (2 Ne. 2:19-25.) It was the fall which brought death, mortality, and all the present vicissitudes of life to man on earth. This glorious garden was located on the American continent "where the City Zion, or the New Jerusalem, will be built." (*Doctrines of Salvation,* vol. 3, p. 74.)

At the Second Coming of our Lord, "the earth will be renewed and receive its paradisiacal glory" (Tenth Article of Faith), that is, it will return again to the edenic state and millennial conditions will exist. Of this restoration Isaiah said: "For the Lord shall comfort Zion: he will comfort all her waste places; and he will make her wilderness like Eden, and her desert like the garden of the Lord; joy and gladness shall be found therein, thanksgiving, and the voice of melody." (Isa. 51:3; Ezek. 36:35.)

GARMENTS.
Garments are various articles of clothing used to dress the body. They may be worn for utilitarian or religious purposes or both. The Lord made "coats of skins" for Adam and Eve to cover their nakedness. (Gen. 3:21.) Special ceremonial and "holy garments" were worn by Aaron and the priests. (Ex. 28; Lev. 16; Ezek. 42:14.) Garments worn by angels are "pure and white above all other whiteness." (D. & C. 20:6.) To avoid pride, garments of mortals should be "plain, and their beauty the beauty of the work of thine own hands." (D. & C. 42:40-42.)

Much that is sacred and symbolical is taught by reference to garments. Kings and rulers were identified anciently by their robes of scarlet and purple; such a robe was placed on Christ in mocking derision by the soldiers. (Matt. 27:28-31; John 19:2-5.) When our Lord comes again, as a sign of impending judgment, he "shall be red in his apparel, and his garments like him that treadeth in the wine-vat." (D. & C. 133:46-51; Isa. 63:1-6.) It was the ancient custom to tear one's garments as a token of great sorrow or abject humility, a custom so hypocritically abused that Joel commanded: "Rend your heart, and not your garments." (Joel 2:13.) It was also the practice to sit in sackcloth and ashes as a token of great sorrow and mourning. (Gen. 37:34.)

It was an ancient practice for the Lord's prophets to take off their garments and shake them as a sign that they were rid of the blood and sins of those to whom they had been sent to testify. (2 Ne. 9:44; Jac. 1:19; 2:2; Mosiah 2:28; Morm. 9:35.) Similar symbolism is used in latter-day revelation: "Cleanse your hearts and your garments, lest the blood of this generation be required at your hands," the Lord says. (D. & C. 112:33; 88:85; 135:5.)

Clean garments are a sign of cleanliness, perfection, and salvation. To gain salvation men must wash their garments in the blood of the Lamb. (1 Ne. 12:10; Alma 5:21-27; 7:25; 13:11-12; 3 Ne. 27:19; Rev. 6:11; 7:9-17.) Speaking of the saints, at the dedication of the Kirtland Temple, the Prophet prayed: "That our garments may be pure, that we may be clothed upon with robes of righteousness, with palms in our hands, and crowns of glory upon our heads, and reap eternal joy for all our sufferings." (D. & C. 109:76.)

"Thou hast a few names . . . which have not defiled their garments; and they shall walk with me in white: for they are worthy. He that overcometh, the same shall be clothed in white raiment." (Rev. 3:4-5.) *"Behold, I come as a thief. Blessed is he that watcheth, and keepeth his garments, lest he walk naked, and they see his shame."* (Rev. 16:15.)

GATES OF HELL.
See CHAINS OF HELL, HELL. Lucifer leaves the *gates of hell* wide open so that all who will yield to his enticements can enter that abode of darkness and sorrow. The path of sin leads to the gates of hell; unrepentant persons carry their own sins which are the tickets of admission granting entrance through those mammoth gates.

Figuratively, these gates beckon to the unwary, inviting them to enter, and these gates of hell are said to *prevail* against those who by sin cast their lot with Lucifer and thus go to hell. But those who accept the gospel, join the Church, live in righteousness and faith, and endure to the end, have the promise that the gates of hell shall not prevail against them. (D. & C. 10:69; 17:8; 18:5; 21:6; 33:13; 98:22; 3 Ne. 11:39.) To Peter the Lord said that the gates of hell should never prevail against the rock of revelation. (Matt. 16:18.)

304

GATE TO EXALTATION.
See CELESTIAL MARRIAGE.

GATE TO SALVATION.
See BAPTISM.

GATHERING OF ISRAEL.
See ISRAEL, JEWS, LOST TRIBES OF ISRAEL, MOSES, SCATTERING OF ISRAEL, TRIBES OF ISRAEL. Through her establishment as a nation, her ancient dispersion among all the peoples of the earth, and her latter-day gathering together again, the world is viewing the *miracle that is Israel.* Scattered when she forsook the Lord, rejected his statutes, and turned to unrighteousness, Israel is now being gathered as she turns back to the true God of her fathers, stands fast again in the everlasting gospel covenant, and turns her heart to righteousness. (*Teachings,* pp. 84-85, 92-93, 183, 231-232; *Articles of Faith,* pp. 328-344.)

"*As general as was the scattering of Israel so must the gathering be. If the dispersion was over all the earth, and among all nations, so the gathering must be out of all nations, and from all parts of the earth.*

"When we reflect that it is 32 centuries since the enemies of Israel began to oppress them in the land of Canaan; that about one-third of the time they were a people in that land, they were, more or less, in bondage to their enemies; that 700 years before the coming of Christ the Ten Tribes were scattered throughout western Asia; that we have no record that any have as yet returned to the land of their inheritance; that nearly 600 years before Christ the Babylonish captivity took place, and that, according to the Book of Esther only a part of the Jews ever returned, but were scattered through the 127 provinces of the Persian empire; that Asia was the hive from which swarmed the nomadic tribes who overran Europe; that at the destruction of Jerusalem by the Romans the Jews were scattered over the known world; we may well ask the question, *Does not Israel today constitute a large proportion of the human family?* With this comprehensive view of the subject of the scattering, we the better understand such passages as the following: '*I will gather the remnant of my flock out of all countries whither I have driven them.*' (Jer. 23:3.)" (*Compendium,* p. 90.)

The gathering of Israel is first *spiritual* and second *temporal.* It is *spiritual* in that the lost sheep of Israel are first "restored to the true church and fold of God," meaning that they come to a true knowledge of the God of Israel, accept the gospel which he has restored in latter-days, and join The Church of Jesus Christ of Latter-day Saints. It is *temporal* in that these converts are *then* "gathered home to the *lands of their inheritance,* and . . . established in *all their lands of prom-*

ise" (2 Ne. 9:2; 25:15-18; Jer. 16:14-21), meaning that the house of Joseph will be established in America, the house of Judah in Palestine, and that the Lost Tribes will come to Ephraim in America to receive their blessings in due course. (D. & C. 133.)

However, the temporal gathering of Israel will not be completed before the Second Coming of the Son of Man. "I beheld that the church of the Lamb, who were the saints of God," Nephi recorded relative to the last days, "were also upon *all the face of the earth;* and their dominions upon the face of the earth were *small,* because of the wickedness of the great whore." (1 Ne. 14:12.) The erection by the Church of temples in distant lands is further evidence that all the hosts of Israel who are gathered into the spiritual fold will not be assembled temporally. But in due course "the Son of Man shall come, and he shall send his angels before him with the great sound of a trumpet, and they shall gather together the *remainder* of his elect from the four winds, from one end of heaven to the other." (Jos. Smith 1:37.)

The purpose of the gathering of Israel is twofold: 1. To put the peoples of living Israel in that environment where they may the better work out their salvation, where they may have the Gentile and worldly views erased from them, and where they may be molded into that pattern of perfect right-eousness which will please the Almighty; and 2. To enable the gathered remnants of the chosen lineage to build temples and perform the ordinances of salvation and exaltation for their Israelitish ancestors who lived when the gospel was not had on earth.

"It was the design of the councils of heaven before the world was," the Prophet taught, "that *the principles and laws of the priesthood should be predicated upon the gathering of the people in every age of the world.* Jesus did everything to gather the people, and they would not be gathered, and he therefore poured out curses upon them. Ordinances instituted in the heavens before the foundation of the world, in the priesthood, for the salvation of men, are not to be altered or changed. All must be saved on the same principles.

"It is for the same purpose that God gathers together his people in the last days, to build unto the Lord a house to prepare them for the ordinances and endowments, washings and anointings, etc. One of the ordinances of the house of the Lord is baptism for the dead. God decreed before the foundation of the world that that ordinance should be administered in a font prepared for that purpose in the house of the Lord." (*Teachings,* p. 308.)

That Israel cannot be gathered in the latter-days, in fulfilment of the host of ancient prophecies, without revelation and direction from on high is evident to every thoughtful person. Accordingly, the Lord restored the ancient covenants again and sent Moses to deliver the keys of the gathering of Israel and the leading of the Ten Tribes from the land of the north. (D. & C. 110:11.) By virtue of these keys the Prophet and his successors, each in turn, have held the directive and presiding authority relative to this great work. The Lord has set his hand the second time to gather his people (D. & C. 133), and they are now beginning to assemble from all nations at the mountain of the Lord's house. (Isa. 2:2-4.) In due course all Israel will be gathered and the other tribes will receive their blessings from Ephraim whose status is that of the firstborn. (D. & C. 133; Jer. 31:9.)

The fact of the gathering of Israel, under the direction of the President of the Church who holds the keys, is one of the great evidences of the divine calling of The Church of Jesus Christ of Latter-day Saints. Any church which does not understand the doctrine of the kingdom being restored to Israel in an age after New Testament times (Acts 1:6) cannot be the Lord's Church.

The glory of Israel's latter-day gathering is beginning to appear, and it will not be long before the Ten Tribes will return (D. & C. 133) and all things incident to this great work will be fulfilled. Then the Lord's promise as given by Jeremiah will find complete fulfilment: "Behold, the days come, saith the Lord, that it shall no more be said, The Lord liveth, that brought up the children of Israel out of the land of Egypt; But, The Lord liveth, that brought up the children of Israel from the land of the north, and from all the lands whither he had driven them: and I will bring them again into their land that I gave unto their fathers." (Jer. 16:14-15.)

GAZELAM.

See ADAMIC LANGUAGE, JOSEPH SMITH THE PROPHET. Strange and unusual names were placed by the Prophet in some of the early revelations so that the individuals whom the Lord was then addressing would not be known to the world. The purpose for keeping these identities secret from their enemies having long since passed, the true names are now found in the Doctrine and Covenants.

Two of the names which identified the Prophet himself were *Gazelam* and *Enoch*. (D. & C. 78:9; 82:11; 104:26, 43, 45, 46.) Presumptively these and other names used at the same time have particular meanings, which are not now known to us.

With reference to the name Gazelam, it is interesting to note that Alma in directing Helaman to preserve both the Urim and Thummim and the plates containing the

Book of Ether, says that such record will be brought to light by the Lord's servant *Gazelem,* who will use "a stone" in his translation work. (Alma 37:21-23.) It may be that *Gazelem* is a variant spelling of *Gazelam* and that Alma's reference is to the Prophet Joseph Smith who did in fact bring forth part at least of the Ether record. Or it could be that the name Gazelem (Gazelam) is a title having to do with power to translate ancient records and that Alma's reference was to some Nephite prophet who brought the Book of Ether to light in the golden era of Nephite history.

GEHENNA.

See HADES, HELL, SHEOL, SPIRIT PRISON, TARTARUS. Outside Jerusalem, to the south and west, lies the *Valley of Hinnom* or *Gehenna.* In the days of Isaiah and Jeremiah, infants were sacrificed to Molech at a *Topheth* or high place built in this valley, causing it to take on a sinister significance and be called "the valley of slaughter." (2 Kings 23:5, 10; 2 Chron. 28:3; 33:6; Isa. 30:33; Jer. 7:31-34; 19:6, 11-15.) Thereafter Gehenna was further desecrated as a garbage and rubbish heap and as a place where bodies of criminals were thrown out; to help prevent pestilence, ever-burning fires were kept smoldering in this infested refuse.

Under these conditions, it was natural for the prophetic mind to use the term *gehenna* to signify the burnings, torment, anguish, and unspeakable horrors of hell. Our Lord himself made frequent use of gehenna to signify hell and its attendant horrors. (Matt. 5:22; 29:30; Mark 9:43-47; Luke 12:5; Jas. 3:6.) His statement, "Where their worm dieth not, and the fire is not quenched" (Mark 9:48), becomes even more expressive when viewed in the light of the numerous crawling things and perpetual burnings of that Gehenna of which his hearers had personal knowledge.

GENEALOGICAL RESEARCH.

See ELIJAH THE PROPHET, FAMILY ORGANIZATIONS, SALVATION FOR THE DEAD, SIGNS OF THE TIMES, VICARIOUS ORDINANCES. Before vicarious ordinances of salvation and exaltation may be performed for those who have died without a knowledge of the gospel, but who presumably would have received it had the opportunity come to them, they must be accurately and properly identified. Hence, *genealogical research* is required.

To aid its members in intelligent and effective research, the Church maintains in Salt Lake City one of the world's greatest *genealogical societies.* Much of the genealogical source material of various nations of the earth has been or is being microfilmed by this society; millions of dollars is being spent; and a reservoir of hundreds of millions of names and other data about people who lived in past generations is available for study.

GENEALOGICAL SOCIETY.

See GENEALOGICAL RESEARCH.

GENERAL AUTHORITIES.

See APOSTLES, APOSTOLIC SUCCESSION, ASSISTANTS TO THE TWELVE, FIRST COUNCIL OF THE SEVENTY, FIRST PRESIDENCY, GENERAL AUXILIARY OFFICERS, HIERARCHY, PATRIARCH TO THE CHURCH, PRESIDING BISHOP. In order of their precedence, beginning at the top, the *general authorities* of the Church include members of: The First Presidency, Council of the Twelve, the Patriarch to the Church, Assistants to the Twelve, First Council of the Seventy, and Presiding Bishopric. These brethren are all delegated general *administrative* authority by the President of the Church. That is, they are called to preach the gospel, direct church conferences, choose other church officers, perform ordinations and settings apart, and handle the properties and interests of the Church generally. The labors of their ministries are not confined to stake, ward, or regional areas, but they have general jurisdiction in all parts of the Church.

Some general authorities are empowered to do one thing and some another. All are subject to the strict discipline the Lord always imposes on his saints and those who preside over them. The positions they occupy are high and exalted. But the individuals who hold these offices are humble men like their brethren in the Church. So well qualified and trained are the members of the Church that there are many brethren who could —if called, sustained, and set apart —serve effectively in nearly every important position in the Church.

Though general authorities are authorities in the sense of having power to administer church affairs, they may or may not be authorities in the sense of doctrinal knowledge, the intricacies of church procedures, or the receipt of the promptings of the Spirit. A call to an administrative position of itself adds little knowledge or power of discernment to an individual, although every person called to a position in the Church does grow in grace, knowledge, and power by magnifying the calling given him.

GENERAL AUXILIARY OFFICERS.

See AUXILIARY ORGANIZATIONS, GENERAL AUTHORITIES, GENERAL BOARDS, HIERARCHY, PRIESTHOOD OFFICES. Heads of the various auxiliary organizations are sustained as the *general auxiliary officers* of the Church. The Relief Society, Young Women's Mutual Improvement Association, and Primary Association are each presided over by a president and two counselors, forming a general presidency; the Deseret Sunday School Union and the Young Men's Mutual Improvement Association are each presided over by a general superintendent and two assistants, forming a general superintendency. These offices are filled with qualified and worthy brethren and sisters who are called, for a time and a season, to preside over and govern the affairs of their respective organizations. The keys of such presidency are conferred upon them for the periods of their calls.

GENERAL BOARDS.

See AUXILIARY ORGANIZATIONS, CHURCH ORGANIZATION, GENERAL AUXILIARY OFFICERS, STAKE BOARDS. Each auxiliary organization is supervised by its general officers, assisted by a *general board*. These boards, made up of specialists in the various fields of auxiliary organization work, help initiate, plan, and prepare the programs which are put into operation in the various stakes. The boards are counseling and advisory bodies. They train and encourage stake and ward workers, but do not preside over or direct the church service of these local officers.

GENERATION.

See GENEALOGICAL RESEARCH, RECORD KEEPING, SECOND COMING OF CHRIST. Since *generation* means the act of producing or begetting offspring, a generation of people is composed of those who descend from the same parents. The statement, "This is the book of the generations of Adam" (Gen. 5:1), means in effect, "This is the book of the descendants of Adam," or "This is the genealogy of those who sprang from Adam."

In the sense of reproducing itself, a generation is about 30 or 40 years. (Job 42:16; 1 Ne. 12:11-12.) In the sense of measuring time by the lives of men, a generation, since the Abrahamic day, has been about 100 years. (Gen. 15:13-16; Ex. 12: 40; 4 Ne. 18, 22.) From this standpoint of measurement, a generation from the time of Adam to the flood would have been nearly 1000 years. (Gen. 5.) A generation may be measured in terms of the life of the oldest persons who live in a particular period. (D. & C. 45:30-31; 84: 4-5.) It may also refer to all contemporary people living in a given age. (D. & C. 5:8-10.)

GENTILE FULNESS.

See SIGNS OF THE TIMES.

GENTILES.

See ADOPTION, GATHERING OF ISRAEL, HEATHENS, ISRAEL, JEWS, SCATTERING OF ISRAEL, SIGNS OF THE TIMES. Various meanings have been attached to the name *Gentiles* in different ages, depending on the historical setting or the doctrinal teachings involved. Literally the meaning is, "of the same clan or race," and Biblical revisions frequently substitute the word *nations* in its place.

The descendants of Noah's son Japheth were called Gentiles (Gen. 10:1-5), and in this sense the descendants of Shem (ancestor of Abraham) and of Ham (father of the negro race) would not be Gentiles. In the days of Abraham, the term was used to refer to those nations and peoples who had not descended from him, with the added assurance that all Gentiles who should receive the gospel would be adopted into the lineage of Abraham and be accounted his seed. (Abra. 2:9-11.) The Prophet taught that those so adopted became literally of the blood of Abraham. (*Teachings,* pp. 149-150.) In the days of ancient Israel, those not of the lineage of Jacob were considered to be Gentiles, although the Arabs and other races of Semitic origin who traced their lineage back to Abraham would not have been Gentiles in the strict Abrahamic use of the word.

After the Kingdom of Israel was destroyed and the Ten Tribes were led away into Assyrian captivity, those of the Kingdom of Judah called themselves Jews and designated all others as Gentiles. It is this concept that would have been taught to Lehi, Mulek and the other Jews who came to the Western Hemisphere to found the great Nephite and Lamanite civilizations.

It is not surprising, therefore, to find the Book of Mormon repeatedly speaking of Jew and Gentile as though this phrase marked a division between all men; to find the United States described as a Gentile Nation (1 Ne. 13; 3 Ne. 21); and to find the promise that the Book of Mormon would come forth "by way of the Gentile." (Title page of Book of Mormon; D. & C. 20:9.)

Actually, of course, the house of Israel has been scattered among all nations, and Joseph Smith (through whom the Book of Mormon was revealed) was of the Tribe of Ephraim. At the same time the Prophet was of the Gentiles, meaning that he was a citizen of a Gentile Nation and also that he was not a Jew. Members of the Church in general are both of Israel and of the Gentiles. Indeed, the gospel has come forth in the last days in the *times of the Gentiles* and, in large measure, will not go to the Jews until the *Gentile fulness* comes in. (D. & C. 45:28-30.)

Having in mind the principle that Gentiles are adopted into the lineage of Israel when they accept the gospel, and that those who fail to believe the truths of salvation (no matter what their lineage) lose any preferential status they may have had, it is not inappropriate in our day to speak of members of the Church as Israelites and unbelievers as Gentiles.

GHOSTS.

See EVIL SPIRITS, HOLY GHOST, SORCERY, SPIRIT BODIES, WITCHCRAFT. 1. Properly, a *ghost* is a spirit. In death the spirit leaves the body, or in other words the body gives up the ghost. (Gen. 49: 33; Acts 5:10; Jac. 7:20-21.) Of our Lord's death, the scripture says he "yielded up the ghost." (Matt. 27: 50; Hela. 14:21.) In referring to the third member of the Godhead the terms *Holy Ghost* and *Holy Spirit* are used interchangeably.

2. As part of the mythology and false worship of apostate Christendom—particularly during the dark ages—the true concept of *ghosts* was perverted so that disembodied spirits (ghosts) were conceived of as being hideous and horrible denizens of an unseen world who occasionally appeared in bodily likeness to torment and frighten mortals.

Along with this twisting of the truth, concepts arose relative to *apparitions, goblins, specters, spooks, sprites, elves, fairies,* and the like. Though these various mythological phantoms do not exist in reality, belief in them arose initially out of the true doctrine of ghosts and other actual beings of the unseen world. Such appearances of spirit beings (supposed to be goblins, specters, and the like) as have actually occurred, probably, have been appearances of devils who never had a body rather than of disembodied ghosts.

GIFT OF PROPHECY.
See PROPHECY.

GIFT OF THE HOLY GHOST.

See BAPTISM OF FIRE, BORN AGAIN, CONFIRMATION, HOLY GHOST, LAYING ON OF HANDS, SPIRIT OF THE LORD, SPIRITUAL LIFE. "There is a difference between the Holy Ghost and the gift of the Holy Ghost," the Prophet taught. (*Teachings,* p. 199.) As the third member of the Godhead, the Holy Ghost is a Personage of Spirit; the gift of the Holy Ghost, however, is the right, based on faithfulness, to the constant companionship of that member of the Godhead. It is the right to receive revelation, guidance, light, and truth from the Spirit. "The presentation or 'gift' of the Holy Ghost," President Joseph F. Smith said, "simply confers upon a man the right to receive at any time, when he is worthy of it and desires it, the power and light of truth of the Holy Ghost, although he may often be left to his own spirit and judgment." (*Gospel Doctrine,* 5th ed., pp. 60-61.)

Joseph Smith explained: "Cornelius received the Holy Ghost before he was baptized, which was the convincing power of God unto him of the truth of the gospel, but he could not receive the gift of the Holy Ghost until after he was baptized. Had he not taken this sign or ordinance upon him, the Holy Ghost which convinced him of the truth of God, would have left him. Until he obeyed these ordinances and received the gift of the Holy Ghost, by the laying on of hands, according to the order of God, he could not have healed the sick or commanded an evil spirit to come out of a man, and it obey him." (*Teachings,* p. 199.)

In similar manner, in this day, many nonmembers of the Church, "by the power of the Holy Ghost" (Moro. 10:4-5), learn that the Book of Mormon is true, or that Joseph Smith is a Prophet of God, but unless they repent and are baptized that flash of testimony leaves them. They never receive the continuing, renewed assurance that comes from the companionship of that Spirit Being whose mission it is to whisper truth to the spirits within men. (*Teachings,* pp. 198-199.)

Further, the fact that a person has had hands laid on his head and a legal administrator has declared, "Receive the Holy Ghost," does not guarantee that the gift itself has actually been enjoyed. The gift of the Holy Ghost is the *right* to have the constant companionship of the Spirit; the actual *enjoyment* of the gift, the *actual receipt of the companionship* of the Spirit, is based on personal righteousness; it does not come unless and until the person is worthy to receive it. The Spirit will not dwell in an unclean tabernacle. (1 Cor. 3:16-17; 6:19.) Those who actually enjoy the gift or presentment of the Holy Ghost are the ones who are born again, who have become new creatures of the Holy Ghost. (Mosiah 27:24-26.)

Even a righteous person is often left to himself so that he does not at all times enjoy the promptings of revelation and light from the Holy Ghost. "Every elder of the Church who has received the Holy Ghost by the laying on of hands, by one having authority, has power to confer that gift upon another; it does not follow that a man who has received the presentation or gift of the Holy Ghost shall always receive the recognition and witness and presence of the Holy Ghost himself; or he may receive all these, and yet the Holy Ghost not tarry with him, but visit him from time to time (D. & C. 130:23); and neither does it follow that a man must have the Holy Ghost present with him when he confers the Holy Ghost upon another, but he possesses the gift of the Holy Ghost, and it will depend upon the worthiness of him unto whom the gift is bestowed whether he receives the Holy Ghost or not." (*Gospel Doctrine,* 5th ed., p. 61.)

GIFT OF TONGUES.
See Tongues.

GIFTS OF GOD.
See Gifts of the Spirit.

GIFTS OF THE SPIRIT.

See FAITH, GIFT OF THE HOLY GHOST, HEALINGS, HOLY GHOST, MIRACLES, PROPHECY, SAINTS, SIGNS, TONGUES, VISIONS. By the grace of God—following devotion, faith, and obedience on man's part —certain special spiritual blessings called *gifts of the Spirit* are bestowed upon men. Their receipt is always predicated upon obedience to law, but because they are freely available to all the obedient, they are called gifts. They are signs and miracles reserved for the faithful and for none else.

Moroni says that the gifts of God come from Christ, by the power of the Holy Ghost and by the Spirit of Christ. (Moro. 10.) In other words, the gifts come by the power of that Spirit who is the Holy Ghost, but the Spirit of Christ (or light of Christ) is the agency through which the Holy Ghost operates.

Their purpose is to enlighten, encourage, and edify the faithful so that they will inherit peace in this life and be guided toward eternal life in the world to come. Their presence is proof of the divinity of the Lord's work; where they are not found, there the Church and kingdom of God is not. The promise is that they shall never be done away as long as the earth continues in its present state, except for unbelief (Moro. 10:19), but when the perfect day comes and the saints obtain exaltation, there will be no more need for them. As Paul expressed it, "When that which is perfect is come, then that which is in part shall be done away." (1 Cor. 13.)

Faithful persons are expected to seek the gifts of the Spirit with all their hearts. They are to "covet earnestly the best gifts" (1 Cor. 12: 31; D. & C. 46:8), to "desire spiritual gifts" (1 Cor. 14:1), "to ask of God, who giveth liberally." (D. & C. 46:7; Matt. 7:7-8.) To some will be given one gift; to others, another; and "unto some it may be given to have all those gifts, that there may be a head, in order that every member may be profited thereby." (D. & C. 46:29.)

From the writings of Paul (1 Cor. 12; 13; 14), and of Moroni (Moro. 10), and from the revelations received by Joseph Smith (D. & C. 46), we gain a clear knowledge of spiritual gifts and how they operate. Among others, we find the following gifts named either in these three places or elsewhere in the scriptures: the gift of knowing by revelation "that Jesus Christ is the Son of God, and that he was crucified for the sins of the world" (D. & C. 46:13), and also the gift of believing the testimony of those who have gained this revelation; the gifts of testimony, of knowing that the Book of Mormon is true, and of receiving revelations; the gifts of judgment, knowledge, and wisdom; of teaching, exhortation, and preaching; of teaching the word of wisdom and the word of knowledge; of declaring the gospel and of ministry; the gift of faith, including power both to heal and to be healed; the gifts of healing, working of miracles, and prophesy; the viewing of visions, beholding of angels and ministering spirits, and the discerning of spirits; speaking with tongues, the interpretation of tongues, the interpretation of languages, and the gift of translation; the differences of administration in the Church and the diversities of operation of the Spirit; the gift of seership, "and a gift which is greater can no man have." (Mosiah 8:16; Alma 9:21; D. & C. 5:4; 43:3-4; Rom. 12:6-8.) And these are by no means all of the gifts. In the fullest sense, they are infinite in number and endless in their manifestations.

GLADNESS.
See JOY.

GLASS.
See URIM AND THUMMIM.

GLORYING.
See BOASTING.

GNASHING OF TEETH.
See ANGER, WEEPING. In the literal sense, the *gnashing of teeth* consists in grinding and striking the teeth together in anger. This expressive act, indicative of hate and violent animosity, was adopted by the prophets as the proverbial way of portraying the intensity of the weeping, wailing, and sorrow of the ungodly. Wicked men gnash their teeth at the anointed of the Lord in this life. (Job 16:9; Ps. 35:16; 37:12; 112:10; Mark 9:18; Acts 7:54; Alma 14:21.) Then in eternity the wicked are cast into hell where there is weeping, and wailing, and gnashing of teeth. (Mosiah 16:2; Alma 40:13; D. & C. 19:5; 85:9; 101:9; 124:8, 52; 133:73; Matt. 8:12; 13:42, 50; 22:13; 24:51; 25:30; Luke 13:28.)

GNOLAUM.
See GNOLOM. In what appears to be a case of transliteration from the Egyptian of the Book of Abraham, the Prophet Joseph Smith has added the word *gnolaum* to the English language. Its meaning is substantially synonymous with our word *eternal.* Speaking of "two spirits" the Lord said to Abraham, as the Prophet has translated it, that they "have no beginning; they existed before, they shall have no end, they shall exist after, for *they are gnolaum, or eternal.*" (Abra. 3:18.)

The Lord revealed a similar truth to the Prophet by saying: "Intelligence, or the light of truth, was not created or made, neither indeed can be." (D. & C. 93:29.) And the Prophet taught the same truth when he said that "the mind or the intelligence which man possesses is coequal [coeternal] with

God himself. . . . The intelligence of spirits had no beginning, neither will it have an end." (*Teachings,* p. 353.) Thus, *intelligence, or the light of truth,* that is the *spirit element* which Abraham says was organized to form *intelligences* or *spirit children,* was not created or made. (Abra. 3:23.) It has existed forever, and will exist to all eternity, for it is *gnolaum,* or *eternal.*

GNOLOM.

See GNOLAUM. Joseph Smith used this word in his famous King Follett sermon in describing the punishment of those who commit the unpardonable sin. Like *gnolaum,* it is peculiar to Latter-day Saint theology, and appears to have the same root origin.

The Prophet said: "There have been remarks made concerning all men being redeemed from hell; but I say that those who sin against the Holy Ghost cannot be forgiven in this world or in the world to come; they shall die the second death. *Those who commit the unpardonable sin are doomed to Gnolom—to dwell in hell, worlds without end.* As they concoct scenes of bloodshed in this world, so they shall rise to that resurrection which is as the lake of fire and brimstone. Some shall rise to the everlasting burnings of God; for God dwells in everlasting burnings, and some shall rise to the damnation of their own filthiness, which is as exquisite a torment as the lake of fire and brimstone." (*Teachings,* p. 361.)

GNOSTICISM.

See AGNOSTICISM, APOSTASY, CREEDS, FALSE GODS. *Gnosticism* is one of the great pagan philosophies which antedated Christ and the Christian Era and which was later commingled with pure Christianity to form the apostate religion that has prevailed in the world since the early days of that era. Its chief interest to the gospel student lies in the fact that the gnostic concept of God, in large part, was the one adopted by the early church councils, with the result that modern Christians, as acceptors of these early creeds, are worshiping with a false concept of God to which Christian names have been given.

"The Gnostics taught that there existed from eternity," Elder B. H. Roberts explains, "a Being that embodied within himself all the virtues; a Being who is the purest light and is *diffused throughout boundless space* which they called Pleroma." In due course a celestial family was created, the members of which were called *Aeons.* One of these Aeons created the earth, formed man with a vicious body, and tried to overthrow "the authority of the supreme God." Salvation to the Gnostics consisted in restoring liberty to the "spirits now imprisoned in bodies," by dissolving the "fabric of the world."

"When the followers of this philosophy became converted to Christianity, they looked upon Jesus Christ and the Holy Ghost as the latest Aeons or emanations from the Deity, sent forth to emancipate men from the tyranny of matter by revealing to them the true God, to fit them—through perfect knowledge—to enter the sacred Pleroma. In connection with this, however, some of these Christian Gnostics held that Jesus had no body at all, but was an unsubstantial phantom that constantly deceived the senses of those who thought they associated with him. Others of them said there doubtless was a man called Jesus, born of human parents, upon whom one of the Aeons, called Christ, descended at his baptism, having quitted the Pleroma for that purpose; but who, previous to the crucifixion of the man Jesus, withdrew from him and returned to Deity." (*Outlines of Ecclesiastical History,* pp. 183-194.)

GOBLINS.
See GHOSTS.

GOD.
See ALMIGHTY GOD, CHRIST, CONDESCENSION OF GOD, CREATOR, CREEDS, ELOHIM, ENDLESS, ETERNAL, EXALTATION, FALSE GODS, FATHER IN HEAVEN, FATHER OF LIGHTS, GOD AS A SPIRIT, GODHOOD; GOD OF ABRAHAM, ISAAC,

AND JACOB; GOD OF BATTLES, GOD OF GODS, GOD OF ISRAEL, GOD OF NATURE, GOD OF SPIRITS, GOD OF THE WHOLE EARTH, GOD OF TRUTH, GRACE OF GOD, HIGHEST, HOLY FATHER, HOLY GHOST, IDOLATRY, LORD, MAN OF COUNSEL, MAN OF HOLINESS, MOST HIGH, MOTHER IN HEAVEN, OMNIPOTENCE, OMNIPRESENCE, OMNISCIENCE, ONLY BEGOTTEN SON, PERSONIFICATION, PLURALITY OF GODS, RIGHTEOUSNESS, SALVATION, SON OF GOD, THEOPHANIES, UNKNOWN GOD. There are three *Gods*—the Father, Son, and Holy Ghost—who, though separate in personality, are united as one in purpose, in plan, and in all the attributes of perfection. Thus anything, in these fields, which is revealed with reference to any of them is equally true of each of the others; and hence no attempt need be made in these fields to distinguish between them.

By definition, God (generally meaning the Father) is the one supreme and absolute Being; the ultimate source of the universe; the all-powerful, all-knowing, all-good Creator, Ruler, and Preserver of all things. Of him, when considering the object upon which faith rests, the Prophet observes "that God is the only supreme governor and independent Being in whom all fulness and perfection dwell; who is omnipotent, omnipresent, and omniscient; without beginning of days or end of life; and that in him every good gift and every good principle dwell; and that he is the Father of lights; in him the principle of faith dwells independently, and he is the object in whom the faith of all other rational and accountable beings centers for life and salvation." (*Lectures on Faith,* p. 9.)

"There is a God in heaven, who is infinite and eternal, from everlasting to everlasting the same unchangeable God, the framer of heaven and earth, and all things which are in them." (D. & C. 20: 17.) He is not a progressive being in the sense that liberal religionists profess to believe; he was not created by man; and he was not a God of vengeance and war in Old Testament times and a God of love and mercy in a later New Testament era. He is the same yesterday, today, and forever.

God is known only by revelation; he stands revealed or remains forever unknown. He cannot be discovered in the laboratory, or by viewing all immensity through giant telescopes, or by cataloging all the laws of nature that do or have existed. A knowledge of his powers and the laws of nature which he has ordained does not reveal his personality and attributes to men in the true gospel sense. Certainly a knowledge of these laws and powers enables man to learn truths which are faith promoting and which help him to understand more about Deity; but saving knowledge of God comes only by revelation from the Holy Ghost as a consequence of obedience to the laws and ordinances of the gospel.

Man's purpose in life is to learn the nature and kind of being that God is, and then, by conformity to his laws and ordinances, to progress to that high state of exaltation wherein man becomes perfect as the Father is perfect. (Matt. 5:48; *Teachings,* pp. 342-362.)

GOD ALMIGHTY.
See ALMIGHTY GOD.

GOD AS A SPIRIT.
See APOSTASY, CREEDS, GOD. False creeds teach that God is a spirit essence that fills the immensity of space and is everywhere and nowhere in particular present. In a vain attempt to support this doctrine, formulated by councils in the early days of the great apostasy, it is common for apologists to point to the statement in the King James Bible which says, *"God is a Spirit."* (John 4:22-24.) The fact is that this passage is mistranslated; instead, the correct statement, quoted in context reads: "The hour cometh, and now is, when the true worshippers shall worship the Father in spirit and in truth; for the Father seeketh such to worship him. *For unto such hath God promised his Spirit.* And they who worship him, must worship in spirit and in truth." (*Inspired Version,* John 4:25-26.)

However, it is true that God may be said to be a Spirit, but this statement must be understood to mean that he is a Spirit in the same sense that a resurrected *man is a spirit*. When the apostles, beholding the resurrected Lord, "were terrified and affrighted, and supposed that they had seen a spirit" (Luke 24:36-43), there was not the slightest intimation that the "spirit" was a vaporous nothingness that filled immensity. Spirits are personages. God the Father is a glorified and perfected Man, a Personage of flesh and bones (D. & C. 130:22), in which tangible body an eternal spirit is housed. It is in this sense that God is a Spirit.

GODHEAD.

See CHRIST, FATHER IN HEAVEN, GOD, GODHOOD, HOLY GHOST, PLURALITY OF GODS. Three glorified, exalted, and perfected personages comprise the *Godhead* or supreme presidency of the universe. (*Doctrines of Salvation,* vol. 1, pp. 1-55.) They are: God the Father; God the Son; God the Holy Ghost. (First Article of Faith.) "Everlasting covenant was made between three personages," the Prophet said, "before the organization of this earth, and relates to their dispensation of things to men on the earth; these personages, according to Abraham's record, are called God the first, the Creator; God the second, the Redeemer; and God the third, the witness or Testator." (*Teachings,* p. 190.)

Though each God in the Godhead is a personage, separate and distinct from each of the others, yet they are "one God" (Testimony of Three Witnesses in Book of Mormon), meaning that they are united as one in the attributes of perfection. For instance, each has the fulness of truth, knowledge, charity, power, justice, judgment, mercy, and faith. Accordingly they all think, act, speak, and are alike in all things; and yet they are three separate and distinct entities. Each occupies space and is and can be in but one place at one time, but each has power and influence that is everywhere present. The oneness of the Gods is the same unity that should exist among the saints. (John 17; 3 Ne. 28:10-11.)

Perhaps no better statement defining the Godhead and showing the relationship of its members to each other has been written in this dispensation than that given by the Prophet Joseph Smith in the *Lectures on Faith*. "There are two personages who constitute the great, matchless, governing, and supreme, power over all things, by whom all things were created and made, that are created and made, whether visible or invisible, whether in heaven, on earth, or in the earth, under the earth, or throughout the immensity of space. They are the Father and the Son—the Father being a personage of spirit

[meaning that he has a spiritual body which by revealed definition is a resurrected body of flesh and bones (1 Cor. 15:44-45; D. & C. 88:27)], glory, and power, possessing all perfection and fulness; the Son, who was in the bosom of the Father, a personage of tabernacle, made or fashioned like unto man, or being in the form and likeness of man, or rather man was formed after his likeness and in his image; he is also the express image and likeness of the personage of the Father, possessing all the fulness of the Father, or the same fulness with the Father; being begotten of him, and ordained from before the foundation of the world to be a propitiation for the sins of all those who should believe on his name, and is called the Son because of the flesh, and descended in suffering below that which man can suffer; or, in other words, suffered greater sufferings, and was exposed to more powerful contradictions than any man can be.

"But, notwithstanding all this, he kept the law of God, and remained without sin, showing thereby that it is in the power of man to keep the law and remain also without sin; and also, that by him a righteous judgment might come upon all flesh, and that all who walk not in the law of God may justly be condemned by the law, and have no excuse for their sins.

"And he being the Only Begotten of the Father, full of grace and truth, and having overcome, received a fulness of the glory of the Father, possessing the same mind with the Father, which mind is the Holy Spirit, that bears record of the Father and the Son, and these three are one; or, in other words, these three constitute the great, matchless, governing and supreme, power over all things; by whom all things were created and made that were created and made, and these three constitute the Godhead, and are one; the Father and the Son possessing the same mind, the same wisdom, glory, power, and fulness— filling all in all; the Son being filled with the fulness of the mind, glory, and power; or, in other words, the spirit, glory, and power, of the Father, possessing all knowledge and glory, and the same kingdom, sitting at the right hand of power, in the express image and likeness of the Father, mediator for man, being filled with the fulness of the mind of the Father; or, in other words, the Spirit of the Father, which Spirit is shed forth upon all who believe on his name and keep his commandments.

"And all those who keep his commandments shall grow up from grace to grace, and become heirs of the heavenly kingdom, and joint-heirs with Jesus Christ; possessing the same mind, being transformed into the same image or likeness, even the express image of him who fills all in all; being filled with the fulness of his glory, and become

one in him, even as the Father, Son and Holy Spirit are one." (*Lectures on Faith,* pp. 50-51.)

GODHOOD.

See CELESTIAL MARRIAGE, CHURCH OF THE FIRSTBORN, DAUGHTERS OF GOD, ETERNAL LIFE, ETERNAL LIVES, EXALTATION, FULNESS OF THE FATHER, JOINT-HEIRS WITH CHRIST, PLURALITY OF GODS, SALVATION, SONS OF GOD. That exaltation which the saints of all ages have so devoutly sought is *godhood* itself. Godhood is to have the character, possess the attributes, and enjoy the perfections which the Father has. It is to do what he does, have the powers resident in him, and live as he lives, having eternal increase. (D. & C. 132:17-20, 37.) It is to know him in the full and complete sense, and no one can fully know God except another exalted personage who is like him in all respects. Those attaining the supreme height are sons of God (D. & C. 76:50-60); they receive the fulness of the Father and find membership in the Church of the Firstborn (D. & C. 93:17-22); they are joint-heirs with Christ (Rom. 8:14-18), inheriting with him all that the Father hath. (D. & C. 84:33-51.) They are gods. (Ps. 82:1, 6; John 10:34-36; *Doctrines of Salvation,* vol. 2, pp. 35-79; *Gospel Kingdom,* pp. 27-30.)

Joseph Smith said: "God himself was once as we are now, and is an exalted man, and sits enthroned in yonder heavens!. . . I am going to tell you *how God came to be God.* We have imagined and supposed that God was God from all eternity. I will refute that idea, and take away the veil, so that you may see. . . . It is the first principle of the gospel to know for a certainty the character of God, and to know that we may converse with him as one man converses with another, and that he was once a man like us; yea, that God himself, the Father of us all, dwelt on an earth, the same as Jesus Christ himself did; and I will show it from the Bible. . . .

"Here, then, is eternal life—to know the only wise and true God; and *you have got to learn how to be gods yourselves,* and to be kings and priests to God, the same as all gods have done before you, namely, by going from one small degree to another, and from a small capacity to a great one; from grace to grace, from exaltation to exaltation, until you attain to the resurrection of the dead, and are able to dwell in everlasting burnings, and to sit in glory, as do those who sit enthroned in everlasting power. . . . [Such persons are] heirs of God and joint-heirs with Jesus Christ. What is it? To inherit the same power, the same glory and the same exaltation, until you arrive at the station of a god, and ascend the throne of eternal power, the same as those who have gone before." (*Teachings,* pp. 345-347.)

Again: "Every man who reigns in celestial glory is a god to his dominions." (*Teachings*, p. 374.)

GOD OF ABRAHAM, ISAAC, AND JACOB.

See CHRIST, GOD, GOD OF IS-RAEL, GREAT I AM, JEHOVAH. 1. Christ is the *God of our Fathers, the God of Abraham, Isaac, and Jacob.* (D. & C. 136:21-22; Ex. 3:1-16.) It was he who appeared to and covenanted with Abraham (Abra. 2:6-11), who was the one by whom salvation should come (1 Ne. 6:4), and who was destined in due course to come into the world and be crucified for the sins of the world. (1 Ne. 19:7-17.)

2. Since Abraham, who had the fulness of the gospel, worshiped both the Father and the Son, Peter and others have taken occasion, quite properly, to refer to the Father also as the *God of our Fathers, the God of Abraham, Isaac, and Jacob.* (Acts 3:13; 5:30; 22:14.)

GOD OF BATTLES.

See BATTLE OF THE GREAT GOD, CHRIST, GOD, LORD OF HOSTS, WAR. Christ is the *God of Battles.* (D. & C. 98:23-48; 105:14.) Anciently he commanded his people to engage in righteous wars (Ex. 23:27-33; 1 Sam. 15:2-3), and whenever they were so engaged, he was entreated of them and fought their battles. (1 Chron. 5:20; 2 Chron. 20:15; 32:7-8.) The whole Nephite history is one of the Lord giving frequent direction to them in their battles, whenever they sought such guidance in faith. In the day of his Second Coming the promise is that he again will fight the battles of his saints, "as when he fought in the day of battle." (Zech. 14:1-5; Ezek. 38; 39; Zeph. 3:8.) Despite the false sensitivities of those who cannot conceive of the meek and lowly Nazarene as a *Man of War* (Ex. 15:3), yet the inspired answer to the query: Who is the King of Glory? is, "The Lord strong and mighty, and Lord mighty in battle." (Ps. 24:8.)

GOD OF GODS.

See EXALTATION, GOD, KING OF KINGS, LORD OF LORDS. "*Every man who reigns in celestial glory is a god to his dominions,*" the Prophet said. (*Teachings*, p. 374.) Hence, the Father, who shall continue to all eternity as the God of exalted beings, is a *God of Gods.* Further, as the Prophet also taught, there is "*a God above the Father of our Lord Jesus Christ. . . . If Jesus Christ was the Son of God, and John discovered that God the Father of Jesus Christ had a Father,* you may suppose that he had a Father also. Where was there ever a son without a father? . . . Hence if Jesus had a Father, can we not believe that *he* had a Father also?" (*Teachings*, pp. 370, 373.) In this way both the Father and the Son, as also all exalted

beings, are now or in due course will become Gods of Gods. (*Teachings,* pp. 342-376.)

GOD OF HOSTS.
See LORD OF HOSTS.

GOD OF ISRAEL.
See CHRIST, GOD, ISRAEL, STONE OF ISRAEL. Christ is the *God of Israel* (1 Ne. 19:7-17; 3 Ne. 11:7-17), the *God of Jacob* (Ps. 146:5; Isa. 2:3; D. & C. 136:21), the *Lord God, the Mighty One of Israel* (D. & C. 36:1), *the Lord God of the Hebrews.* (Ex. 3:18.) These names signify both that he came of Israel himself and also his personal, attentive care toward that chosen race. They point to his "great goodness toward the house of Israel, which he hath bestowed on them according to his mercies, and according to the multitude of his loving kindnesses." (Isa. 63:7-9; D. & C. 133:52-53.)

GOD OF JACOB.
See GOD OF ISRAEL.

GOD OF JESHURUN.
See CHRIST, GOD OF ISRAEL. Christ is the *God of Jeshurun* (Deut. 33:26), meaning that he is the God of Israel. Jeshurun or Jesurun, translated as *upright one,* is used by Moses and Isaiah as a

symbolical name for Israel. (Deut. 32:15; 33:4-5; Isa. 44:2.)

GOD OF NATURE.
See CHRIST, GOD. Many who do not profess belief in God as he is revealed in the scriptures, or even as he is described in the false creeds of sectarianism, yet recognizing that law prevails in the universe and among all forms of life, speak of the manifestations of this law as the *God of Nature.* In reality, Christ is the God of Nature (1 Ne. 19:12), for it is in and through his almighty power that all things are created, upheld, governed, and controlled.

GOD OF OUR FATHERS.
See GOD OF ABRAHAM, ISAAC, AND JACOB.

GOD OF SPIRITS.
See CHRIST, FATHER IN HEAVEN, GOD, PRE-EXISTENCE. Our Father in Heaven (Matt. 6:9) is the *God of Spirits* (Num. 16:22; 27:16) *or the Father of Spirits* (Heb. 12:9), meaning that he is the literal Parent of the Spirit Christ and of all other spirits. Inasmuch, however, as Christ attained Godhood while yet in pre-existence, he too stood as a God to the other spirits, but this relationship was not the same one of personal parenthood that prevailed between the Father and his offspring.

GOD OF THE WHOLE EARTH.
See CHRIST, GOD OF ISRAEL. Christ is the *God of the Whole Earth* (Isa. 54:5; 3 Ne. 11:14), an appellation he carries to bear record of his universal interest in all men and their salvation. He is not alone the God of the Jews, or of Israel, or of the Latter-day Saints, but of the whole earth and all life on its face.

GOD OF THIS WORLD.
See CHILDREN OF DISOBEDIENCE, DEVIL, WORLD. This *world* of carnality and lust, of every lascivious and evil thing, belongs to Satan. He created it; he is its father and its god. All those who belong to it—all those who are carnal, sensual, and devilish—are his children, the children of disobedience. The earth itself is the Lord's, and he is its ruler; but the world (the corrupt society on earth) is under the rule of him who is the *god of this world.* "If our gospel be hid," Paul wrote, "it is hid to them that are lost: In whom the god of this world hath blinded the minds of them which believe not, lest the light of the glorious gospel of Christ, who is the image of God, should shine unto them." (2 Cor. 4:3-4.)

GOD OF TRUTH.
See CHRIST, PERSONIFICATION, TRUTH; WAY, TRUTH, AND LIFE. Christ is a *God of Truth* (Ex. 34:6; Deut. 32:4; Ps. 31:5), meaning he is the embodiment and personification of truth. In the same sense he is the God of grace, mercy, love, righteousness, charity, integrity, and all of the attributes of godliness.

GODS.
See PLURALITY OF GODS.

GOD'S LIFE.
See ETERNAL LIFE.

GOD'S TIME.
See TIME.

GOD-STORY.
See GOSPEL.

GOD THE LORD.
See LORD GOD.

GOG AND MAGOG.
See ARMIES OF HEAVEN, BATTLE OF ARMAGEDDON, BATTLE OF THE GREAT GOD, MILLENNIUM, SECOND COMING OF CHRIST, SUPPER OF THE GREAT GOD, WAR. 1. Our Lord is to come again in the midst of the battle of Armageddon, or in other words during the course of the great war between Israel and *Gog and Magog.* At the Second Coming all the nations of the earth are to be engaged in battle, and

the fighting is to be in progress in the area of Jerusalem and Armageddon. (Zech. 11; 12; 13; Rev. 16: 14-21.) The prophecies do not name the modern nations which will be fighting for and against Israel, but the designation Gog and Magog is given to the combination of nations which are seeking to overthrow and destroy the remnant of the Lord's chosen seed.

The 38th and 39th chapters of Ezekiel record considerable prophetic detail relative to this great war. It should be noted that it is to take place "in the latter years"; that it will be fought in the "mountains of Israel" against those who have been gathered to the land of their ancient inheritance; that the land of Israel shall be relatively unprotected, a "land of unwalled villages"; that Gog and Magog shall come "out of the north parts" in such numbers as "to cover the land" as a cloud; that the Lord will then come, and all men shall shake at his presence; that there will be such an earthquake as has never before been known, which will throw down the mountains; that there will be pestilence, blood, fire, and brimstone descend upon the armies; that the forces of Gog and Magog will be destroyed upon the mountains of Israel; that the Supper of the Great God shall then take place as the beasts and fowls eat the flesh and drink the blood of the fallen ones (Rev. 19:17-18; D. & C. 29:18-21); and that the house of Israel will be seven months burying the dead and seven years burning the discarded weapons of war.

In the light of all this and much more that is prophetically foretold about the final great battles in the holy land, is it any wonder that those who are scripturally informed and spiritually enlightened watch world events with great interest as troubles continue to foment in Palestine, Egypt, and the Near East?

2. *Gog and Magog,* those nations which combine as the assailants of God's plans and purposes, will also come up in war and rebellion in the final battle of the Great God which is to take place at the end of the millennium plus a short season of preparation. (*Doctrines of Salvation,* vol. 3, p. 45.) John describes this war as follows: "And when the thousand years are expired, Satan shall be loosed out of his prison, And shall go out to decieve the nations which are in the four quarters of the earth, Gog and Magog, to gather them together to battle: the number of whom is as the sand of the sea. And they went up on the breadth of the earth, and compassed the camp of the saints about, and the beloved city: and fire came down from God out of heaven, and devoured them." (Rev. 20:7-9; D. & C. 88:111-116.)

GOLD.

See RICHES.

GOLDEN RULE.

"All things whatsoever ye would that men should do to you, do ye even so to them: for this is the law and the prophets." (Matt. 7:12; 3 Ne. 14:12.) This perfect code for personal conduct, taken from our Lord's sermon on the mount, is commonly referred to as the *Golden Rule,* a name which attempts to point up the transcendent wisdom of the counsel involved. Sometimes the Golden Rule is paraphrased to say: Do unto others, as you would have them do unto you.

GOLDEN TEXT.

See JUSTICE, LOVE, MERCY. "What doth the Lord require of thee, but to do justly, and to love mercy, and to walk humbly with thy God?" (Mic. 6:8.) To signify the inherent beauty and worth of these words they are often referred to as the *golden text* of the Old Testament. Unfortunately they are interpreted by many to mean that it is not necessary to believe any particular principles of the gospel or to submit to baptism and the ordinances of salvation. The real truth is, of course, that no man can walk humbly with his God unless he keeps the counsels of that God including the direction to repent and join the true kingdom; and no one is even subject to the terms and provisions of the law of mercy until he has first attained that saving grace which is offered through the atoning sacrifice of our Lord.

GOLD PLATES.

See BOOK OF MORMON, BRASS PLATES, CUMORAH, SEALED BOOK. As we now have it, the Book of Mormon is a translation of a portion of the *Gold Plates*. These plates came into being in the following way: Nephi made two sets of plates which are known as the *Large Plates of Nephi* and the *Small Plates of Nephi.* Upon the Large Plates he abridged the records of his father, Lehi, and began a detailed history of his people, including their wars, contentions, the reign of their kings, and their genealogy. The Small Plates he reserved for sacred writings, prophecies, and things pertaining to the ministry. (1 Ne. 1:17; 9; 19:1-6; 2 Ne. 4:14; 5:30, 33; Jac. 1:1-4.) These plates were handed down from prophet to prophet, and by about 130 B.C., some 370 years after Lehi left Jerusalem, the Small Plates were full. (Omni 30.)

Mormon made the *Plates of Mormon* on which he abridged the Large Plates of Nephi and to which he added without abridgment the Small Plates of Nephi. (Words of Morm. 1-11.) Both Mormon and Moroni wrote some things of their own on the Plates of Mormon, and Moroni also wrote on them an abridgment of Jaredite history taken from the *Plates of*

Ether. Thus when the Gold Plates were placed in the Hill Cumorah, they contained a record of both the Nephites and the Jaredites.

Joseph Smith said that "each plate was six inches wide and eight inches long, and not quite so thick as common tin," that they were "filled with engravings, in Egyptian characters," and that they were bound together with three rings, forming a volume "something near six inches in thickness, a part of which was sealed." (*History of the Church,* vol. 4, p. 537; Morm. 9: 32-34.) Orson Pratt says two-thirds of the volume was sealed (*Journal of Discourses,* vol. 3, p. 347), George Q. Cannon that only one-third was sealed. (George Q. Cannon, *Life of Joseph Smith,* new ed., p. 45.)

Moroni deposited the plates in the Hill Cumorah in about 421 A.D., and then as a resurrected being revealed the hiding place to the Prophet on September 22, 1823. Four years later the Prophet was permitted to obtain possession of them, but the actual translation of the portion we now have as the Book of Mormon did not take place until between April 7 and June 11, 1829. Thereafter the plates were returned to the custody of Moroni. (Jos. Smith 2:27-65; D. & C. 27:5; *Doctrines of Salvation,* vol. 3, pp. 215-226.) In the Lord's own due time the plates shall be returned and the sealed portion translated and published to the world. This shall not take place, however, until

men exercise faith to the extent that the Brother of Jared did. (Ether 4.)

GOLGOTHA.

See CHRIST, CRUCIFIED ONE, CRUCIFIXION. *Golgotha* is the Hebrew name of the place outside of Jerusalem where our Lord was crucified; it corresponds to *Calvary* which was taken from the Greek. The apparent literal meaning of both names is, *place of a •skull.* Matthew, Mark, and John speak of Golgotha (Matt. 27:33; Mark 15:22; John 19:17) as the place of crucifixion; Luke names it as Calvary. (Luke 23:33.) Each of the gospel accounts speaking of Golgotha is so worded in the Inspired Version as to show that the name means *a place of burial.* (*Inspired Version,* Matt. 27:35; Mark 15:25; John 19: 17.) The inference is that Golgotha or Calvary may have been in an elevated location, but none of the accounts name it as either a hill or a mount. (Mark 15:40; Luke 23:49.) The actual location is unknown.

GOOD.

See AGENCY, EVIL, GOOD WORKS. *Good* is the opposite of evil. It is of God and consists in obedience to his laws and conformity to his mind and will. That is good which is edifying, enlightening, and uplifting; which furthers the cause of liberty and truth; which speeds the spread of revealed truth to the peoples of the world; which leads to the acquirement of faith, hope, charity, love, and all godly virtues; which is harmonious with the moral order of the universe; which guides men to keep the commandments of God, to grow in grace, and to work out their salvation. The opposites of all these things are evil.

"All things which are good cometh of God. . . . That which is of God inviteth and enticeth to do good continually; wherefore, every thing which inviteth and enticeth to do good, and to love God, and to serve him, is inspired of God." (Moro. 7:12-13.)

GOOD BOOK.
See BIBLE.

GOOD SHEPHERD.
See CHRIST, PASTORS. Christ is the *Shepherd* (Gen. 49:24; Ps. 23; 1 Pet. 2:25; Morm. 5:17), the *Chief Shepherd* (1 Pet. 5:4), the *Great Shepherd* (Heb. 13:20), the *True Shepherd* (Hela. 15:13), the *Shepherd of Israel* (Ps. 80:1), the *Good Shepherd*. (D. & C. 50:44; John 10:7-18; Alma 5:38-60; Hela. 7:18.) His saints are the sheep; his sheepfold is the Church of Jesus Christ; and the day will come when there will be "one God and one Shepherd over all the earth" (1 Ne. 13:41), "and he shall feed his sheep, and in him they shall find pasture." (1 Ne. 22:25.)

For a pastoral people the symbolism attending all this is perfect. "Behold, the Lord God will come with strong hand, and his arm shall rule for him: behold, his reward is with him, and his work before him. *He shall feed his flock like a shepherd: he shall gather the lambs with his arm, and carry them in his bosom, and shall gently lead those that are with young.*" (Isa. 40:10-11; Jer. 31:10.)

The parable of the lost sheep (Matt. 18:12-13; Luke 15:3-7) and the commands: "Feed my lambs. . . . Feed my sheep" (John 21:15-17) exemplify the standing orders he has given his other shepherds.

GOOD WORKS.
See ENDURING TO THE END, EVIL, FAITH, GOOD, OBEDIENCE, RELIGION, SALVATION BY GRACE, WORK. By believing the truths of salvation, repenting of his sins, and being baptized in water and of the Spirit, the seeker after salvation places himself on the strait and narrow path which leads to eternal life. (2 Ne. 31.) Thereafter his progress up the path is achieved by the performance of *good works*.

After joining the Church, the commandment is: "Ye must press forward with a steadfastness in Christ, having a perfect brightness of hope, and a love of God and of all men. Wherefore, *if ye shall press forward, feasting upon the word of Christ, and endure to the end, behold, thus saith the Father: Ye shall have eternal life."* (2 Ne. 31: 20.) None attain salvation "save it be those who have washed their garments in my blood, because of their faith, and the repentance of all their sins, and their *faithfulness unto the end,"* was Christ's message to the Nephites. (3 Ne. 27:19.)

Salvation comes in and through and because of the atoning sacrifice of our Lord. It is through his grace that all men are redeemed from death and offered the chance to "work out," in addition, an inheritance in the celestial world. (Philip. 2:12.) Thus it is that men are not saved in "the kingdom of heaven" by merely confessing the Lord Jesus with their lips, but rather by doing the will of the Father which is in heaven. (Matt. 7:21-22.) And thus it is that they must be "doers of the word, and not hearers only." (Jas. 1:22.)

Remission of sins comes in the first instance by repentance and baptism, but it is retained by continued good works. King Benjamin taught: "For the sake of *retaining a remission of your sins* from day to day, that ye may walk guiltless before God—I would that ye should impart of your substance to the poor, every man according to that which he hath, such as feeding the hungry, clothing the naked, visiting the sick and administering to their relief, both spiritually and temporally, according to their wants." (Mosiah 4:26.) Indeed the very religion of the saints consists in visiting the fatherless and the widows in their affliction, and in keeping oneself unspotted from the world. (Jas. 1:26.)

Peter counseled the baptized saints: "Giving all diligence, add to your faith virtue; and to virtue knowledge; And to knowledge temperance; and to temperance patience; and to patience godliness; And to godliness brotherly kindness; and to brotherly kindness charity." (2 Pet. 1:5-7.) The immortal sermon of James on good works includes these statements: "What doth it profit, my brethren, though a man say he hath faith, and have not works? can faith save him? . . . Faith, if it hath not works, is dead, being alone. . . . For as the body without the spirit is dead, so faith without works is dead also." (Jas. 2:14-26.)

Joseph Smith taught: "Let truth and righteousness prevail and abound in you; and in all things be temperate; abstain from drunkenness, and from swearing, and from all profane language, and from everything which is unrighteous or unholy; also from enmity, and hatred, and covetousness, and from every unholy desire. Be honest one with another." (*Teachings,* p. 129.)

Again: "If you wish to go where God is, you must be like God, or possess the principles which God possesses, for if we are not drawing towards God in principle, we are going from him and drawing towards the devil. . . . If God should speak from heaven, he would command you not to steal, not to commit adultery, not to covet, nor deceive, but be faithful over a few things. As far as we degenerate from God, we descend to the devil and lose knowledge, and without knowledge we cannot be saved, and while our hearts are filled with evil, and we are studying evil, there is no room in our hearts for good, or studying good. *Is not God good? Then you be good; if he is faithful, then you be faithful.* Add to your faith virtue, to virtue knowledge, and *seek for every good thing."* (*Teachings,* pp. 216-217.)

"Be not deceived; God is not mocked: for whatsoever a man soweth, that shall he also reap. For he that soweth to his flesh shall of the flesh reap corruption; but he that soweth to the Spirit shall of the Spirit reap life everlasting. *And let us not be weary in well doing:* for in due season we shall reap, if we faint not. As we have therefore opportunity, let us do good unto all men, especially unto them who are of the household of faith." (Gal. 6:7-10.)

This doctrine of good works—a doctrine that men, based on the atoning sacrifice of Christ, must work out their own salvation in the kingdom of God—though abundantly attested to in the Bible, is flatly rejected by many churches in modern Christendom. In its place they teach such things as that men are saved through the ordinances of the church alone; or by the mere act of confessing with the lips the divinity of the Lord Jesus; or that they are justified through faith alone, without works, though good works are then said to follow as a fruit of faith; or that they are predestined to salvation by the election of grace regardless of the presence or absence of good works, though here again good works are said to be pleasing to God in the case of those already justified, but not in the case of those not so chosen and favored.

Some of these false concepts, about good works and the obtaining of salvation because of righteousness and obedience, are formally and ponderously set forth by the Church of England, for instance, in three of its Articles of Religion.

Article 2, entitled, "Of the Justification of Man," reads: "We are accounted righteous before God, only for the merit of our Lord and Saviour Jesus Christ by Faith, and not for our own works or deservings: Wherefore, that *we are justified by Faith alone is a most wholesome Doctrine,* and very full of comfort." It should be remembered that those who believe this doctrine also believe that men are predestined by God's election to salvation or damnation, regardless of any act of their own.

Article 12, entitled, "Of Good Works," states the case further in these words: "Albeit that Good Works, which are the fruits of Faith, and follow *after* Justification, cannot put away our sins, and endure the severity of God's Judgement; yet are they pleasing and acceptable to God in Christ, and do spring out necessarily of a true and lively Faith; insomuch that by them a lively Faith may be as evidently known as a tree discerned by the fruit."

Then in Article 14, entitled, "Of Works before Justification," this strange and unusual doctrine is presented: *"Works done before the grace of Christ, and the Inspiration of his Spirit, are not pleasant to God, forasmuch as they spring not of faith in Jesus Christ, neither do they make men meet to receive grace, or* (as the School-authors say) deserve grace of congruity: *yea rather, for that they are not done as God hath willed and commanded them to be done, we doubt not but they have the nature of sin."* (*Book of Common Prayer,* pp. 663-664.)

In other words, according to this teaching, men are elected to salvation by the grace of Christ, through no act of their own; they are thereby received into a so-called state of justification, meaning that their status and condition meets God's approval; their righteousness or good works plays no part in this; if after they are justified, they perform good works, such is pleasing to God; it not, no matter, for they will be saved anyway; and if they should live upright lives and perform good works when they are not among those elected to salvation, but among those predestined to be damned, then the very good works which they perform

partake of "the nature of sin." In effect, this teaching is that righteousness is sin in the lives of those predestined to be damned. It is difficult to imagine how the pure doctrines of Christ could be more completely garbled and perverted than they have been in this instance.

GOSPEL.

See ATONEMENT OF CHRIST, CHRIST, CHURCH, CHURCH OF JESUS CHRIST OF LATTER-DAY SAINTS, DISPENSATION OF THE FULNESS OF TIMES, DISPENSATIONS, FIRST PRINCIPLES OF THE GOSPEL, LAW OF MOSES, MORMONISM, NEW AND EVERLASTING COVENANT, PLAN OF SALVATION, PRIESTHOOD, RESTORATION OF THE GOSPEL, REVELATION, SAINTS, SALVATION, SALVATION FOR THE DEAD, SIGNS OF THE TIMES, TESTIMONY, TRUTH. The *gospel* of Jesus Christ is the plan of salvation. It embraces all of the laws, principles, doctrines, rites, ordinances, acts, powers, authorities, and keys necessary to save and exalt men in the highest heaven hereafter. It is the covenant of salvation which the Lord makes with men on earth.

Literally, gospel means good tidings from God or God-story. Thus it is the glad tidings or good news concerning Christ, his atonement, the establishment of his earthly kingdom, and a possible future inheritance in his celestial presence. "And this is the gospel," the Prophet recorded by way of revelation, "the glad tidings, which the voice out of the heavens bore record unto us—That he came into the world, even Jesus, to be crucified for the world, and to bear the sins of the world, and to sanctify the world, and to cleanse it from all unrighteousness; That through him all might be saved whom the Father had put into his power and made by him." (D. & C. 76:40-42.)

Ministering among the Nephites after his resurrection, our Lord proclaimed: "Behold I have given unto you my gospel, and this is the gospel which I have given unto you—that I came into the world to do the will of my Father, because my Father sent me. And my Father sent me that I might be lifted up upon the cross; and after that I had been lifted up upon the cross, that I might draw all men unto me, that as I have been lifted up by men even so should men be lifted up by the Father, to stand before me, to be judged of their works, whether they be good or whether they be evil—And for this cause have I been lifted up; therefore, according to the power of the Father I will draw all men unto me, that they may be judged according to their works.

"And it shall come to pass, that whoso repenteth and is baptized in my name shall be filled; and if he endureth to the end, behold, him will I hold guiltless before my Father at that day when I shall stand to judge the world. And he that endureth not unto the end, the same is he that is also hewn down and cast into the fire, from whence they can no more return, because of the justice of the Father. And this is the word which he hath given unto the children of men. And for this cause he fulfilleth the words which he hath given, and he lieth not, but fulfilleth all his words.

"And no unclean thing can enter into his kingdom; therefore nothing entereth into his rest save it be those who have washed their garments in my blood, because of their faith, and the repentance of all their sins, and their faithfulness unto the end. Now this is the commandment: Repent, all ye ends of the earth, and come unto me and be baptized in my name, that ye may be sanctified by the reception of the Holy Ghost, that ye may stand spotless before me at the last day. Verily, verily, I say unto you, this is my gospel." (3 Ne. 27: 13-21; D. & C. 39:5-6.)

In the broadest sense, all truth is part of the gospel; for all truth is known to, is ordained by, and comes from Deity; and all truth is aidful to progression and advancement. But in the high spiritual sense in which the term is used in the revelations, the gospel is concerned with those particular religious truths by conformity to which men can sanctify and cleanse their own souls, thus gaining for themselves salvation in the eternal worlds.

Gospel principles were first made known to men in pre-existence, and the progression made there was as a result of obedience to them. Then beginning with Adam, the first man, gospel dispensations have been given to men from time to time by the Almighty. Two true gospels are spoken of in the revelations and have been revealed to men as occasions have warranted; one is the *fulness of the everlasting gospel* (Rev. 14:6; D. & C. 14:10), the other is the *preparatory gospel.* (D. & C. 84:26-27.)

The *fulness of the gospel* consists in those laws, doctrines, ordinances, powers, and authorities needed to enable men to gain the fulness of salvation. Those who have the gospel fulness do not necessarily enjoy the fulness of gospel knowledge or understand all of the doctrines of the plan of salvation. But they do have the fulness of the priesthood and sealing power by which men can be sealed up unto eternal life. *The fulness of the gospel grows out of the fulness of the sealing power and not out of the fulness of gospel knowledge.*

On the other hand, *the preparatory gospel* is a lesser portion of the Lord's saving truths, a portion which prepares and schools men for a future day when the fulness of the gospel may be received, a portion which of itself is not sufficient to seal men up unto eternal life or assure them an inheritance in the celestial world. The prepara-tory gospel "is the gospel of repentance and of baptism, and the remission of sins, and the law of carnal commandments." (D. & C. 84:27.) It is a gospel system administered by the lesser or Aaronic Priesthood. When the power to bestow the Holy Ghost is enjoyed, which power is reserved for holders of the Melchizedek Priesthood, then the fulness of the gospel is manifest. John the Baptist administered the preparatory gospel; Christ came with the fulness of the Melchizedek Priesthood and restored the fulness of the gospel. (John 1:26-27; Acts 19:1-6.)

Our revelations say that the Book of Mormon contains the fulness of the gospel. (D. & C. 20:9; 27:5; 42:12; 135:3.) This is true in the sense that the Book of Mormon is a record of God's dealings with a people who had the fulness of the gospel, and therefore the laws and principles leading to the highest salvation are found recorded in that book. In the same sense the Bible and the Doctrine and Covenants contain the fulness of the gospel.

As President John Taylor expressed it, the scriptures "are simply records, histories, commandments, etc. The gospel is a living, abiding, eternal, and unchangeable principle that has existed co-equal [i.e. coeval] with God, and always will exist, while time and eternity endure, wherever it is developed and made manifest." (*Gospel Kingdom,* p. 88.) The fulness of the gospel cannot be preserved in the written word. *The scriptures bear record of the gospel, but the gospel itself consists in the power of the priesthood and the possession of the gift of the Holy Ghost.*

Just as there are false teachers, false religions, false prophets, and false Christs, so there are *false gospels.* Paul proclaimed that all who preached any gospel except that received "by the revelation of Jesus Christ" should be accursed. (Gal. 1:6-12.) And the revealed test whereby the true gospel may be identified is that revelations, visions, miracles, signs, apostles, prophets, and all the gifts of the Spirit will always be found in connection with it. (Mark 16:14-20.) Where these signs are found, there is the gospel of Christ; where these signs are not found, there the gospel of Christ is not.

"And if it so be that the church is built upon my gospel," the Lord says, "then will the Father show forth his own works in it. But if it be not built upon my gospel, and is built upon the works of men, or upon the works of the devil, verily I say unto you they have joy in their works for a season, and by and by the end cometh, and they are hewn down and cast into the fire, from whence there is no return." (3 Ne. 27:10-11.) The true gospel of Jesus Christ was restored to earth in the last days through the instrumentality of Joseph Smith. It is found only in The Church of Jesus Christ of Latter-day Saints.

GOSPEL COVENANTS.
See COVENANTS.

GOSPEL DISPENSATIONS.
See DISPENSATIONS.

GOSPEL HOBBIES.
See FANATICISM, OBEDIENCE, ZEAL. Salvation is won in and through conformity to the whole gospel plan and not by specializing and centering on some chosen field as though that field were the gospel. Religious or *gospel hobbies* are dangerous signs of spiritual instability; they lead to fanaticism and sometimes even to apostasy and the consequent loss of eternal life.

"Don't have hobbies," President Joseph F. Smith counseled. "Hobbies are dangerous in the Church of Christ. They are dangerous because they give undue prominence to certain principles or ideas to the detriment and dwarfing of others just as important, just as binding, just as saving as the favored doctrines or commandments.

"Hobbies give to those who encourage them a false aspect of the gospel of the Redeemer; they distort and place out of harmony its principles and teachings. The point of view is unnatural. Every principle and practice revealed from God is essential to man's salvation, and to place any one of them unduly in front, hiding and dimming all others is unwise and dangerous; it jeopardizes salvation, for it darkens our minds and beclouds our understandings. Such a view, no matter to what point directed, narrows the vision, weakens the spiritual perception, and darkens the mind, the result of which is that the person thus afflicted with this perversity and contraction of mental vision places himself in a position to be tempted of the evil one, or, through dimness of sight or distortion of vision, to misjudge his brethren and give way to the spirit of apostasy. He is not square with the Lord.

"We have noticed this difficulty —that saints with hobbies are prone to judge and condemn their brethren and sisters who are not so zealous in the one particular direction of their pet theory as they are. The man with the Word of Wisdom only in his brain, is apt to find unmeasured fault with every other member of the Church who entertains liberal ideas as to the importance of other doctrines of the gospel.

"There is another phase of this difficulty—the man with a hobby is apt to assume an 'I am holier than thou' position, to feel puffed up and conceited, and to look with distrust, if with no severer feeling, on his brethren and sisters who do not so perfectly live that one par-

ticular law. This feeling hurts his fellow servants and offends the Lord." (*Gospel Doctrine*, 5th ed., pp. 116-117.)

GOSPEL OF ABRAHAM.
See ELIAS.

GOSPEL ORDINANCES.
See ORDINANCES.

GOSPEL PRINCIPLES.
See DOCTRINE.

GOSPELS.
See BIBLE, BOOK OF MORMON, CHRIST, GOSPEL, INSPIRED VERSION OF THE BIBLE, NEW TESTAMENT, SCRIPTURE, STANDARD WORKS. Our Lord promised certain of his disciples that the Holy Ghost would teach them all things and would bring to their remembrances all that the Master had taught them. (John 14:26; 15:26-27; 16:7-15.) Under this spirit of inspiration and revelation, portions of our Lord's teachings and some of the historical events attending his birth, life, ministry, and death were recorded. Accounts written by Matthew, Mark, Luke, and John have been preserved, and because they deal with the gospel or glad tidings which Christ preached, they are known as the *gospels*. The first three, dealing in general with the same teachings and historical

events, are called the *synoptic gospels*. The book of Third Nephi in the Book of Mormon is sometimes called the *fifth gospel*.

Many volumes have been written by the scholars of the world analyzing, comparing, dissecting, and criticizing the gospels. As is always the case when "the things of God" are subjected to evaluation by "the spirit of man" (1 Cor. 2:11-16), the conclusions reached are, in the main, false, speculative, and destructive of faith.

It is true that the four New Testament gospels do present different aspects of our Lord's personality and teachings. It appears that Matthew was directing his gospel to the Jews. He presents Christ as the promised Messiah and Christianity as the fulfilment of Judaism. Mark apparently wrote with the aim of appealing to the Roman or Gentile mind. Luke's gospel presents the Master to the Greeks, to those of culture and refinement. And the gospel of John is the account for the saints; it is pre-eminently the gospel for the Church, for those who understand the scriptures and their symbolisms and who are concerned with spiritual and eternal things. Obviously such varying approaches have the great advantage of presenting the truths of salvation to people of different cultures, backgrounds, and experiences. But the simple fact is that all of the gospel authors wrote by inspiration, and all had the same purposes: 1. To testify of the divine Sonship of our Lord; and 2. To teach the truths of the plan of salvation.

None of the gospels profess to do more than present a fragmentary account of the life and teachings of Christ. But such matters as were recorded were true and correct as they first came from the pens of the inspired authors. The gospels, as first written, were perfect scripture because they were inspired of the Holy Ghost. (D. & C. 68:4.) But since that primitive day, some of their beauty has been lost by translation from language to language, and also "many plain and precious things" (1 Ne. 13:23-35) have been deleted and changed by evil and uninspired persons. Yet, with it all, for literary excellence and the preservation of inspired teachings, the gospels as they now stand in the King James Version of the Bible, excel almost all other written matters.

GOSPEL SCHOLARSHIP.
See KNOWLEDGE.

GOSPEL STANDARDS.
See OBEDIENCE.

GOSSIPING.
See BEARING FALSE WITNESS, IDLE WORDS, LIARS. *Gossip* ordinarily consists in talebearing, in spreading scandal, in engaging in familiar or idle conversation deal-

ing personally with other people's affairs. Frequently the reports are false; almost always they are so exaggerated and twisted as to give an unfair perspective; and in nearly every case they redound to the discredit of the persons under consideration. It follows that gossip is unwholesome, serves no beneficial purpose, and should be shunned.

GOVERNMENT OF GOD.

See APOSTASY, CHURCH OF JESUS CHRIST OF LATTER-DAY SAINTS, CONSTITUTION OF THE UNITED STATES, GOVERNOR, INALIENABLE RIGHTS, KINGDOM OF GOD, MILLENNIUM, PRIESTHOOD, THEOCRACY (THEARCHY). Adam and his posterity were subject to the *government of God.* They had the priesthood, the Church of Jesus Christ, and the kingdom of God on earth—the officers of which administered in both civil and ecclesiastical affairs. In those days God made the laws, revealed them to his servants, and they administered them by the spirit of inspiration. As man began to fall away from the truth, however, various groups usurped the powers of government; the rule that had been legitimate and righteous became illegitimate, and errors and weaknesses crept in. The righteous saints, however, from Adam to the flood continued in subjection to Him whose right it is to rule and enjoyed the protection and blessings of God's own government.

After the flood God again commenced administering the affairs of men through his own government, but again apostasy was the order of the day; soon the governments of men prevailed in all parts of the earth. But among selected portions of men the Lord continued to rule. The patriarchs, the house of Israel, and the Nephites—all these from time to time enjoyed theocratic government.

Since the final Nephite degeneracy and destruction, as far as we know, there has been no people on earth who have been under direct civil and ecclesiastical control of the true government of God. Rather Church and state have been separated and administered by separate agencies, except in instances when apostate priesthoods have imposed false religions and governments upon nations.

However, in a limited degree God has continued to govern in and through the existing and recognized powers of the various nations. Kings have been exalted to thrones and then thrust from their high positions to further his eternal purposes. Nations have risen and fallen; floods, famines, and desolations have been sent to alter the course of history; groups of people have been guided to discover and populate new lands and continents; and all things have been so arranged that the Lord's purposes would prevail. Israel was freed from Egyptian bondage; the nations of Canaan were driven out;

the Roman Empire was overthrown; Columbus was led to American soil; the hand of Deity was over the American colonists; the American nation was set up with its constitutional guarantees of freedom; and nations rose and fell as directed by an omnipotent power. Indeed, Daniel in revealing and in interpreting Nebuchadnezzar's dream had forecast both the history of nations and the final setting up, in the last days, of the kingdom of God again on earth. (Dan. 2; *Progress of Man*, pp. 9-519.)

With the restoration of the gospel and the setting up of the ecclesiastical kingdom of God on earth, the restoration of the true government of God commenced. Through this Church and kingdom a framework has been built through which the full government of God will eventually operate. With the ushering in of the millennial era the present ecclesiastical kingdom will be expanded into a political kingdom also, and then both civil and ecclesiastical affairs will be administered through it. Then there will be two great world capitals, and the law shall go forth from Zion and the word of the Lord from Jerusalem. (Isa. 2:1-4.)

Pending that glorious day, the Lord's plan calls for a complete separation of Church and state; no religious organization, whether true or false, is to dictate affairs of state; if such were permitted, false religions would prevail, for they are in the majority and will continue to be until the wicked are swept off the earth by the millennial cleansing.

GOVERNOR.

See CHRIST, GOVERNMENT OF GOD, KING, RULER. Christ is the *Governor,* the Ruler, the King, the One whose right it is to reign. Micah prophesied that in Bethlehim would "he come forth" who was "to be ruler in Israel; whose goings forth have been from of old, from everlasting." (Mic. 5:2.) This prophecy as understood and quoted by the Jews was that out of Bethlehem "shall come a Governor, that shall rule my people Israel." (Matt. 2:6.) When the government of God is perfected during the millennium, he shall indeed stand as Governor, and "Of the increase of his government and peace there shall be no end." He shall reign "upon the throne of David," and shall order and establish his kingdom "with judgment and with justice from henceforth even for ever." (Isa. 9:7.)

GRACE OF GOD.

See CONDESCENSION OF GOD, ELECTION OF GRACE, GOD, LOVE, MERCY, SALVATION BY GRACE. *God's grace* consists in his love, mercy, and condescension toward his children. All things that exist are manifestations of the grace of God. The creation of the earth, life itself, the atonement of Christ, the plan of salvation, kingdoms of immortal glory hereafter, and the supreme gift of eternal life—all these things come by the grace of him whose we are.

Grace is granted to men proportionately as they conform to the standards of personal righteousness that are part of the gospel plan. Thus the saints are commanded to "grow in grace" (D. & C. 50:40), until they are sanctified and justified, "though the grace of our Lord and Savior Jesus Christ." (D. & C. 20:30-32.) Grace is an attribute of perfection possessed by Deity (D. & C. 66:12; 84:102), and Christ himself "received grace for grace" until finally he gained the fulness of the Father. The same path to perfection is offered to man. "If you keep my commandments," the Lord says, "you shall receive of his fulness, and be glorified in me as I am in the Father; therefore, I say unto you, you shall receive grace for grace." (D. & C. 93:6-20.)

GRATITUDE.
See THANKSGIVING.

GRAVEN IMAGES.
See WORSHIP OF IMAGES.

GRAVES.
See CREMATION, DEDICATION OF GRAVES, DEATH, DUST, FUNERALS, MOURNING, SHEOL. Since the *grave* is the resting place of the mortal remains of deceased loved ones, common Christian decency and respect for the tender feelings of the mourners dictate that the site be chosen wisely and that it be properly maintained. This feeling seems to have been in the hearts of inspired men of old. Abraham selected and purchased a burial place for Sarah with great care and ceremony. (Gen. 23; 25:8-10.) Joseph of Arimathea apparently had his own tomb selected and prepared in advance, and into it the body of our Lord was lain. (Luke 23:50-56.)

But a grave site is not, and was never intended by the Lord to be, a monument or a shrine or a place of recurring religious meditation. It is not a locale for worship or a place to pay inordinate devotion to the memory of the departed. These things breed ancestor worship and other apostate misconceptions as to the real position of death and burial in the plan of salvation. Repeated and excessive placing of flowers on graves partakes of this spirit. Obviously the Egyptian pyramids, apparently built as tombs for powerful Pharaohs, went far beyond any reasonable reverence or respect which should have been paid to deceased rulers.

There is, of course, nothing in a grave except the dust, the element, from which the mortal body was made. The spirit continues to live and is in a world of spirits awaiting the day of the resurrection. In that glorious day the graves will be opened, and the bodies of all men will be rescued from death. (2 Ne. 9:6-16.)

GRAVESIDE PRAYERS.
See DEDICATION OF GRAVES.

GREAT AND ABOMINABLE CHURCH.
See CHURCH OF THE DEVIL.

GREATER PRIESTHOOD.
See MELCHIZEDEK PRIESTHOOD.

GREAT I AM.
See CHRIST, ETERNITY TO ETERNITY, EVERLASTING TO EVERLASTING. Christ is the Great I AM, the I AM, the I AM THAT I AM, meaning that he is the Eternal One, the One "who is from all eternity to all eternity" (D. & C. 39:1; Ex. 3:14), the God who is "from everlasting to everlasting" (Ps. 90:2), whose course is one eternal round and who never varies or changes. (1 Ne. 10:17-20.) "From eternity to eternity he is the same, and his years never fail" (D. & C. 76:4), for he is the I AM. When he said to the Jews, for instance, "Before Abraham was, I am" (John 8:58), it was the same as saying, "Before Abraham, was I AM, the Everlasting God, he 'whose goings forth have been from of old, from everlasting.'" (Mic. 5:2.)

GREAT JUDGE.
See JUDGE OF ALL THE EARTH.

GREAT SHEPHERD.
See GOOD SHEPHERD.

GREAT SPIRIT.
See FALSE GODS, GOD. According to Lamanite traditions, God is the Great Spirit. It is obvious that by this designation the Lamanites had in mind a personal being, for King Lamoni mistakenly supposed that Ammon was the Great Spirit. (Alma 18:2-28; 19:25-27.) Both Ammon and Aaron, using the same principle of salesmanship applied by Paul on Mars Hill (Acts 17:22-31), taught that the Great Spirit was the God who created the heavens and the earth. (Alma 18:8-29; 22:8-11.) This same Lamanite concept that God is the Great Spirit has existed among the American Indians in modern times.

GREEDINESS.
See ALMSGIVING, CHARITY, POOR, RICHES, SELFISHNESS. Since mortal man is being tested to see if he will seek the riches of eternity rather than the transitory wealth of the world, it follows that greediness—the avaricious grasping for an unreasonable amount of this world's goods—is a sin. (Prov. 1:19; 15:27; 21:26; Ezek. 22:12; Eph. 4:19; 1 Tim. 3:3, 8; Judge 11.) The idle poor who lay hold on other

men's goods because their "eyes are full of greediness" are condemned by the Lord. (D. & C. 56:17.) Similar condemnation rests upon the saints who "seek not earnestly the riches of eternity, but their eyes are full of greediness." (D. & C. 68:31.)

Perhaps the most scathing denunciation of greediness ever written is found in Isaiah's excoriation of the wickedness of apostate ministers. He describes them a *blind watchmen, "greedy dogs which can never have enough, . . . shepherds that cannot understand,"* ignorant ministers interested only in *"gain."* (Isa. 56:9-12.) This description accords perfectly with the angelic pronouncement to Nephi: "Behold the gold, and the silver, and the silks, and the scarlets, and the fine-twined linen, and the precious clothing, and the harlots, are the desires of this great and abominable church." (1 Ne. 13:8.)

GRIEF.

See MOURNING, SORROW, WEEPING. All men, as a necessary part of their mortal training, suffer *grief* (D. & C. 123:7), our Lord himself being no exception. (Isa. 53:3-4; Mosiah 14:3-4.) Grief is a poignant sorrow for some definite cause, as for instance the grief of righteous parents because of the waywardness of their children. (1 Ne. 18:17.) "This is thankworthy," in Peter's wise language, "if a man for conscience toward God endure grief, suffering wrongfully. For what glory is it, if, when ye be buffeted for your faults, ye shall take it patiently? but if, when ye do well, and suffer for it, ye take it patiently, this is acceptable with God." (1 Pet. 2:19-20.)

GUARDIAN ANGELS.

See ANGELS, GIFT OF THE HOLY GHOST, LIGHT OF CHRIST, MINISTERING OF ANGELS, RECORDING ANGELS. There is an old and false sectarian tradition to the effect that all men—or if not that, at least the righteous—have *guardian angels,* heavenly beings of some sort who attend them and exercise some sort of preserving and guarding care. It is true that there are many specific instances in which angels, by special assignment, have performed particular works whereby faithful people have been guarded and preserved. The angel of the Lord's presence saved Israel (Isa. 63:7-9), and an angel preserved Daniel when he was cast into the den of lions, for instance. (Dan. 6:22.)

But to suppose that either all men or all righteous men have heavenly beings acting as guardians for them runs counter to the basic revealed facts relative to the manner in which the Lord exercises his benevolent watchfulness over his mortal children. The fact that angels have intervened to preserve someone in a particular peril does not establish the fact that all peo-

341

ple generally have guardian angels, anymore than the fact that angels have ministered to selected prophets would prove that angels have ministered to all men.

Actually the preserving care of the Lord is exercised through the Light of Christ. (D. & C. 84:44-48; Moro. 7:12-19.) Every person born into the world is endowed with the guidance and enlightenment of this power. By following its promptings God-fearing persons frequently are guarded against evils. Members of the Church, in addition, have the gift of the Holy Ghost, a special heavenly endowment whereby they may receive such guidance and enlightenment as will result in their being guarded and preserved in perilous circumstances. (D. & C. 8:2-4.)

Expressions of patriarchs or others relative to guardian angels must be interpreted either as figurative statements or as utterances having reference to special instances of guarding care of a miraculous nature, instances comparable to Daniel's experience in the lion's den. (*Doctrines of Salvation,* vol. 1, pp. 49-54.)

H

HADES.

See GEHENNA, HELL, SPIRIT PRISON, TARTARUS. In Greek the word for hell is *hades;* it is a place of outer darkness where the spirits of the wicked go at death to await the day of their eventual resurrection. Sorrow, anguish, and "the fiery indignation of the wrath of God" attend those cast down to this fate. (Alma 40:13-14; Luke 16:23.)

HAILSTORMS.
See SIGNS OF THE TIMES.

HALLELUJAH.

See HOSANNA, JAH, PRAYER, REVERENCE, THANKSGIVING, WORSHIP. *Hallelujah* (also rendered, *halleluiah, alleluia, alleluiah*) is a Hebrew word meaning *praise Jah,* or *praise ye Jehovah,* or, when anglicized, *praise ye the Lord.* It is a liturgical ejaculation urging all to join in praise of Jehovah, as in the Christian hymn, "Christ the Lord is risen today, Alleluia," or as in such scriptural exultations as, "Alleluia: for the Lord God omnipotent reigneth." (Rev. 19:1-6.) Many of the Psalms begin or end with Hallelujah, translated, "Praise ye the Lord." (Psalm 104; 106; 111;

112; 113; 115; 116; 117; 135; 146; 147; 148; 149; 150.)

been able to do so since June, 1978.

HALLUCINATIONS.

See DELUSION, SPIRITUALISM, VISIONS. Opponents of gospel truths sometimes deride the saints with the false charge that the visions and spiritual manifestations received by the prophets are *hallucinations,* that is, that as a result of disordered nerves or mental derangement the manifestations, though seen, do not in reality exist. Actually a spiritual manifestation could be an hallucination; or either Deity or the devil could give an actual vision; or in the absence of anything at all, still a false claim to spiritual communion could be made. Man's problem, at the peril of his own salvation, is to determine the reality and source of spiritual communications.

HAM.

See CAIN, EGYPT, NEGROES, PRE-EXISTENCE, PRIESTHOOD. Through *Ham* (a name meaning *black*) "the blood of the Canaanites was preserved" through the flood, he having married Egyptus, a descendant of Cain. (Abra. 1:20-27.) Ham was cursed, apparently for marrying into the forbidden lineage, and the effects of the curse passed to his son, Canaan. (Gen. 9:25.) Ham's descendants include the Negroes, who originally were barred from holding the priesthood but have

HAPPINESS.

See JOY.

HAREM.

See PLURAL MARRIAGE. Under Moslem practices the wives and female relatives of a Mohammedan are a *harem.* From the Christian standpoint harems are frequently associated with sensuality and excess—a perspective that no doubt was and is justified in many instances. But harems have no part in the gospel. The Mohammedan practice of plural marriage is an apostate perversion of a true principle once properly in force among their ancestors.

HARLOTS.

See CHURCH OF THE DEVIL, SEX IMMORALITY. Literally an *harlot* is a prostitute; figuratively it is any apostate church. Nephi, speaking of harlots in the literal sense and while giving a prophetic description of the church of the devil, recorded that he "saw the devil that he was the foundation of it," that he "saw many harlots," and that among other things "the harlots" were "the desires of this great and abominable church." (1 Ne. 13:6-8.) Then, speaking of harlots in the figurative sense, he designated it as "the mother of harlots."

(1 Ne. 13:34; 14:15-17.)

John saw and recorded similar things. He wrote of the great and abominable church as "the great whore that sitteth upon many waters," and specified that "upon her forehead was a name written, MYSTERY, BABYLON THE GREAT, THE MOTHER OF HARLOTS AND ABOMINATIONS OF THE EARTH." (Rev. 17:1-5.)

HARMONY.

See PEACE, UNITY, Gospel *harmony* consists in that agreement in belief, action, feeling, and sentiment which—born of the Spirit—unites the saints as one. It is a gift of the Spirit, a special endowment to the saints. The gospel does not bring and is not intended to bring either peace or harmony to the world in its present telestial state. "Think not that I am come to send peace on earth," our Lord said. "I came not to send peace, but a sword. For I am come to set a man at variance against his father, and the daughter against her mother, and the daughter in law against her mother in law. And a man's foes shall be they of his own household." (Matt. 10:34-36.) But the gospel is designed to bring and does in fact bring inner peace and harmony to the believing soul —a harmony which enables the convert to unite perfectly in spirit with the saints of all ages. Righteous harmony in the full godly sense prevails only in the congre-

gations of the saints and in the homes of the faithful families of Israel.

HATRED.

See LOVE, PERSECUTION. *Hate* is the opposite of love; in its full force it is to abhor, abominate, and detest; in lesser degree it is merely to dislike or regard with displeasure. *Hatred* is a proper and holy emotion when channeled properly. "Hate the evil, and love the good." (Amos 5:15.)

Manifestations of perfect hatred are shown forth by Deity himself. "I the Lord love judgment, I hate robbery," he says. (Isa. 61:8.) One of the best statements in the Proverbs is: "These six things doth the Lord hate: yea, seven are an abomination unto him: A proud look, a lying tongue, and hands that shed innocent blood, An heart that deviseth wicked imaginations, feet that be swift in running to mischief, A false witness that speaketh lies, and he that soweth discord among brethren." (Prov. 6:16-19.)

Like persecution, hatred is the heritage of the faithful. Our Lord told the Twelve: "Ye shall be hated of all men for my name's sake." (Matt. 10:22; 24:9.) Such a reaction to the Lord's ministers should cause no surprise, as he said: "If the world hate you, ye know that it hated me before it hated you. If ye were of the world, the world would love his own: but because ye are not of the world, but I have chosen you out of the world, therefore the world hateth you." (John 15:18-19; 17:14.)

Proper hatred on the part of the saints must be against evil and not people. The gospel standard is: "Love your enemies, bless them that curse you, do good to them that hate you, and pray for them which despitefully use you, and persecute you." (Matt. 5:44; Luke 6:27.)

HAUNTED HOUSES.
See GHOSTS.

HEALINGS.
See ADMINISTRATIONS, FAITH, GIFTS OF THE SPIRIT, MIRACLES, PRIESTHOOD, SIGNS. 1. Miracles whereby diseases are cured and whereby physical and mental health are conferred by divine power are called *healings*. For instance, our Lord in his mortal ministry went "forth amongst men, working mighty miracles, such as healing the sick, raising the dead, causing the lame to walk, the blind to receive their sight, and the deaf to hear, and curing all manner of diseases." (Mosiah 3:5.)

Faithful men in all ages—deriving their power from that God who is "the same yesterday, today, and forever," in whom "there is no variableness neither shadow of changing," who is "a God of miracles" (Morm. 9:9-10)—have wrought as Christ did, healing the sick, raising the dead, and curing all manner of diseases, for the Lord works "by healings." (3 Ne. 29:6.)

Healings come because of faith. (D. & C. 35:9.) They are gifts of the Spirit (1 Cor. 12:9, 28, 30), some persons having "faith to be healed," others being endowed with "faith to heal." (D. & C. 46:19-20.) Healings are among the signs that follow true believers (D. & C. 84:68; 124:98), and the faithful elders have power to perform healings whenever it is required of them by those who have faith to be healed. (D. & C. 24:13-14.) As with other signs and miracles, if there are no healings among church members, such people are not the saints of God. And as with certain other miracles, the devil has power to perform some acts in imitation of the Lord's power.

2. Even more important than the healing of mentally and physically afflicted persons is the *spiritual healing* of those who have been dead to the things of righteousness. Those so healed are restored to a state of purity, integrity, and righteousness. Their healing comes about through conversion to the truth and adherence to the principles of righteousness. Thus there is the scriptural promise that Christ "shall rise from the dead, with healing in his wings; and all those who shall believe on his name shall be saved in the kingdom of God." (2 Ne. 25:13; 26:9; Mal. 4:2.) That is, spiritual sickness and

spiritual death vanish for those who turn to him through whose atoning sacrifice all men have power to become whole spiritually, or in other words to be healed from every spiritual malady that would keep them out of the celestial world. Thus the Lord's call to all men is, *"Return unto me, and repent of your sins, and be converted, that I may heal you."* (3 Ne. 9:13; Hos. 14:4.)

HEALTH.

See DEATH, DISEASES, HEALINGS, PHYSICIANS, WORD OF WISDOM. Joseph Smith taught that "it is the will of God that man should repent and serve him in *health,* and *in the strength and power of his mind,* in order to secure his blessings." (*Teachings,* p. 197.) Ordinarily a healthy, vigorous person is in a far better position to work out his own salvation and to be an effective instrument in rolling forth the great purposes of Deity. Accordingly, the Lord has given the Word of Wisdom and many other laws of health by obedience to which diseases may be avoided, health secured, and strength of mind and body increased. Many of the requirements of the Mosaic law were specifically revealed in order to enable a people, situated as the Israelites then were, to enjoy health and avoid plagues. (Lev. 11; 12; 13; 14; 15; Deut. 23:10-14.)

In addition to obeying the laws of health, however, physical well-being comes as a result of obedience to all of the commandments. To Israel the Lord promised: "If thou wilt diligently hearken to the voice of the Lord thy God, and wilt do that which is right in his sight, and wilt give ear to his commandments, and *keep all his statutes,* I will put none of these diseases upon thee, which I have brought upon the Egyptians: for I am the Lord that healeth thee." (Ex. 15: 26; Deut. 7:15; Alma 9:22; D. & C. 89:18-21.) On the other hand, it is by disobedience to God's laws that diseases and afflictions come. (Deut. 28:27-28, 59-61; Mosiah 17: 16; Alma 15:3-5.)

Those who keep the commandments, in addition to being thereby preserved in health and strength, will have power, by faith, when disease comes to be healed by the power of God.

HEART.

See CONTRITE SPIRIT.

HEATHENS.

See FALSE GODS, GENTILES, IDOLATRY. Frequent Biblical passages speak of the *heathen nations,* meaning in general those peoples and nations worshiping idols and false gods. The term is used similarly in latter-day revelation. The Lord speaks of redeeming the heathen nations during the millennium (D. & C. 45:54); of the tolerable status of the heathen in the day of judgment (D. & C. 75:22); and of teaching the gospel to "the heathen nations, the house of Joseph" in that future day when his arm is revealed in power. (D. & C. 90:9-11.)

The *heathens* are those who do not even profess a knowledge of the true God as record is borne of him in the scriptures. They worship idols or other gods that are entirely false as distinguished from so-called Christian peoples who attempt to worship the Lord, but who have totally false concepts of the nature and kind of being that he is.

HEAVEN.

See ARMIES OF HEAVEN, CELESTIAL KINGDOM, FIRMAMENT, HELL, KEYS OF THE KINGDOM, KINGDOM OF GOD, KINGDOM OF HEAVEN, KINGDOMS OF GLORY, PARADISE, SPIRIT WORLD, TELESTIAL KINGDOM, TERRESTRIAL KINGDOM, TRANSLATED BEINGS. 1. Scriptural usage applies the term *heaven* to the *atmospheric heavens* that surround the earth or planet on which mortal man lives. Thus we read of "the thunder of heaven" (D. & C. 87:6), "the fowls of heaven" (D. &. C. 89:14; 117:6), and the "new heavens and a new earth" at the beginning of the millennium (Isa. 65:17) and again in that day when the earth becomes an abode for celestial beings. (D. & C. 29:23.)

2. In an infinitely broader sense *heaven,* the area surrounding our globe, is expanded to include the *sidereal heavens* which fill the immensity of space. Thus we find frequent reference to "the stars of the heaven" (Gen. 22:17), and also such inspired statements as: "The heavens declare the glory of God; and the firmament sheweth his handywork." (Ps. 19:1.)

3. Obviously the place where God dwells is *heaven,* for he is our Father in Heaven. (Matt. 6:9.) Accordingly all men, being his spirit offspring in pre-existence, came down from heaven when their earth lives began. (John 6:38.) There was, of course, "war in heaven" (Rev. 12:7-9) when Lucifer and "a third part of the hosts of heaven" (D. & C. 29:36) rebelled, were cast out, and did "as lightning fall from heaven." (Luke 10:18.)

4. The place where translated beings dwell is called *heaven,* although they are not in the presence of God. (D. & C. 110:13; 2 Kings 2:11.) "Their place of habitation is that of a terrestrial order" where they perform certain assigned duties pending the time when they shall be taken "into the presence of God and into an eternal fulness." (*Teachings,* p. 170.)

5. Paradise may be said to be *heaven* in the sense that heaven is a place of peace, rest, and solace where the righteous go at death. (Alma 40:11-14; Luke 16:19-31.) Paradise is not heaven, however, in the sense of being an ultimate and eternal abode of the righteous, for

those in paradise are awaiting the day of their resurrection and assignment to a mansion of glory in the eternal world.

6. All of the kingdoms of glory— whether celestial, terrestrial, or telestial—are sometimes called *heaven*. Thus, prefacing his record of the vision of the degrees of glory, the Prophet wrote: "From sundry revelations which had been received, it was apparent that many important points touching the salvation of man had been taken from the Bible, or lost before it was compiled. It appeared self-evident from what truths were left, that if God rewarded every one according to the deeds done in the body, the term *heaven*, as intended for the saints' eternal home, must include more kingdoms than one." (D. & C. 76, section heading.)

7. In its most important sense, *heaven is the celestial kingdom of God*. This is the sense in which it is used, without exception, by prophets and inspired men when they teach the doctrines of salvation and exhort their fellow men to conform to those laws whereby salvation may be won. Amulek, for example, said: *"No unclean thing can inherit the kingdom of heaven; therefore, how can ye be saved, except ye inherit the kingdom of heaven? . . . And these are they that shall have eternal life, and salvation cometh to none else."* (Alma 11:37-40.) "In the celestial glory there are *three heavens* or degrees." (D. & C. 131:1.) Those

who gain the highest are inheritors of exaltation.

HEAVENLY CITY.
See NEW JERUSALEM.

HEAVENLY FATHER.
See FATHER IN HEAVEN.

HEBREWS.
See ISRAEL, JEWS. Two postulates are suggested as to the origin of the name *Hebrew*: one, that it is derived from *eber*, "beyond, on the other side," Abraham and his posterity being so named to distinguish them from the races living on the other side of the Euphrates River; the other, that it embraces the descendants of Eber or Heber, one of the ancestors of Abraham. (Gen. 10:24.)

Abraham and Joseph were called Hebrews (Gen. 14:13; 39:14-18), and then during the entire pre-Christian Era the whole house of Israel, including the members of all the tribes, were so designated. Thus the Nephites were Hebrews, and if the same terminology were considered apt today, the Latter-day Saints would bear the same title. Since the Jews were the chief known portion of Israel at the dawn of the Christian Era, and since most people consider them to be the house of Israel itself, it has become common in modern times

to use the name Hebrew as a synonym for Jew.

HEIR OF GOD.

See CHRIST, JOINT-HEIRS WITH CHRIST. Christ is the *Heir of God.* (Matt. 21:33-41; Mark 12:1-12; Luke 20:9-18; Rom. 4:13-14; Heb. 1:1-4.) By virtue thereof he was entitled to inherit and he did receive all that the Father had. He gained every endowment, quality, attribute, perfection, power, and possession, so that "in him dwelleth all the fulness of the Godhead bodily." (Col. 2:9.) He has received the "fulness of the glory of the Father." (D. & C. 93:4-20; Col. 1: 19.)

HEIRSHIP.

See JOINT-HEIRS WITH CHRIST.

HEIRS OF PROMISE.

See CHILDREN OF THE COVENANT.

HELL.

See ANGUISH, BOTTOMLESS PIT, CHAINS OF HELL, DAMNATION, ESCHATOLOGY, GATES OF HELL, GEHENNA, GRAVES, H A D E S, HEAVEN, IMMORTALITY, JUDGMENT DAY, MILLENNIUM, OUTER DARKNESS, PARADISE, PUNISHMENT, RESURRECTION, SHEOL, SONS OF PERDITION, SPIRIT PRISON, SPIRITUAL DEATH, SPIRIT WORLD, TARTARUS, TELESTIAL KINGDOM, TELESTIAL LAW, UNPARDONABLE SIN.
1. That part of the spirit world inhabited by wicked spirits who are awaiting the eventual day of their resurrection is called *hell.* Between their death and resurrection, these souls of the wicked are cast out into outer darkness, into the gloomy depression of sheol, into the hades of waiting wicked spirits, into hell. There they suffer the torments of the damned; there they welter in the vengeance of eternal fire; there is found weeping and wailing and gnashing of teeth; there the fiery indignation of the wrath of God is poured out upon the wicked. (Alma 40:11-14; D. & C. 76:103-106.)

Hell will have an end. Viewing future events, John saw that "death and hell delivered up the dead which were in them: and they were judged every man according to their works." (Rev. 20:13.) Jacob taught that this escape from death and hell meant the bringing of the body out of the grave and the spirit out of hell. "And this death of which I have spoken, which is the spiritual death," he said, "shall deliver up its dead; which *spiritual death is hell;* wherefore, death and hell must deliver up their dead, and *hell must deliver up its captive spirits,* and the grave must deliver up its captive bodies, and the bodies and the spirits of men will be restored one to the other." (2 Ne. 9:10-12.) It was in keeping with this principle for David to re-

349

ceive the promise: *"Thou wilt not leave my soul in hell."* (Ps. 16:10; Acts 2:27.)

After their resurrection, the great majority of those who have suffered in hell will pass into the telestial kingdom; the balance, cursed as sons of perdition, will be consigned to partake of endless wo with the devil and his angels. Speaking of the telestial kingdom the Lord says: "These are they who are thrust down to hell. These are they who shall not be redeemed from the devil *until* the last resurrection, until the Lord, even Christ the Lamb, shall have finished his work. . . . These are they who are cast down to hell and suffer the wrath of Almighty God, *until* the fulness of times." (D. & C. 76:84-85, 106.) As to the sons of perdition, the revelation says that after their resurrection, "they shall return again to their own place" (D. & C. 88:32, 102), that is, they shall go back to dwell in the lake of fire with Perdition and his other sons. Thus those in hell "are the rest of the dead; and they live not again until the thousand years are ended, neither again, until the end of the earth." (D. & C. 88:101.)

Statements about an everlasting and endless hell (Hela. 6:28; Moro. 8:13), are to be interpreted in the same sense as those about eternal and endless punishment. (D. & C. 19:4-12; 76:44, 105.)

Who will go to hell? This query is abundantly answered in the scriptures. Since those going to a telestial kingdom travel to their destination through the depths of hell and as a result of obedience to telestial law, it follows that all those who live a telestial law will go to hell. Included among these are the carnal, sensual, and devilish—those who live after the manner of the world. Among them are the sorcerers, adulterers, whoremongers (D. & C. 76:103), false swearers, "those that oppress the hireling in his wages," the proud, "and all that do wickedly." (Mal. 3; 4; 2 Ne. 9:27-39; 26:10.)

Several specific groups of wicked persons are singled out to receive the prophetic curse that their destination is the fires of hell. *"The wicked shall be turned into hell, and all the nations that forget God,"* David proclaimed. (Ps. 9:17.) Sex sin is rewarded with the torments of hell. (2 Ne. 9:36; Prov. 7:6-27.) *"Wo unto all those that discomfort my people, and drive, and murder, and testify against them, saith the Lord of Hosts; a generation of vipers shall not escape the damnation of hell."* (D. & C. 121:23.) Such also is the fate of liars (2 Ne. 9:34), of *"all those who preach false doctrines"* (2 Ne. 28:15), of those who believe the damnable doctrine of infant baptism (Moro. 8:14, 21), of the rich who will not help the poor (D. & C. 104:18; Luke 16:19-31), and of those who heap cursings on their fellow men. (Matt. 5:22; 3 Ne. 12:22.) *"The sectarian world are going to hell by hundreds, by thous-*

ands and by millions," the Prophet said. (*History of the Church,* vol. 5, p. 554.)

To catch souls in his snares and then drag them down to hell is the plan and program of the devil. (D. & C. 10:26; Alma 30:60.) One of his latter-day wiles is to persuade men that there is neither a devil nor a hell and that the fear of eternal torment is baseless. (2 Ne. 28:21-23.) But Christ, who holds "the keys of hell and of death" (Rev. 1:18), and can therefore control and abolish them, has power to save and redeem men from hell. (2 Ne. 33:6; Alma 19:29; 26:13-14.) This he does on conditions of repentance and obedience to his laws. But the unrepentant "would be more miserable to dwell with a holy and just God, under a consciousness of" their "filthiness before him, than" they "would to dwell with the damned souls in hell." (Morm. 9:4.)

2. After death and hell have delivered up the bodies and captive spirits which were in them, then, as John foresaw, "death and hell were cast into the lake of fire." (Rev. 20:14.) This lake of fire, a figure symbolical of eternal anguish and wo, is also called *hell,* but is a hell reserved exclusively for the devil and his angels which includes the sons of perdition. (D. & C. 29:38; 88:113; 2 Pet. 2:4.)

Speaking of this hell, and writing of events to take place after the resurrection and the judgment, and thus of a day after those going to a telestial kingdom have come out of their hell, Jacob says: "And assuredly, as the Lord liveth, for the Lord God hath spoken it, and it is his eternal word, which cannot pass away, that they who are righteous shall be righteous still, and they who are filthy shall be filthy still; wherefore, they who are filthy are the devil and his angels; and they shall go away into everlasting fire, prepared for them; and their torment is as a lake of fire and brimstone, whose flame ascendeth up forever and ever and has no end." (2 Ne. 9:16.)

Thus, for those who are heirs of some salvation, which includes all except the sons of perdition (D. & C. 76:44), hell has an end, but for those who have wholly given themselves over to satanic purposes there is no redemption from the consuming fires and torment of conscience. They go on forever in the hell that is prepared for them.

HENOTHEISM.

See ATHEISM, DEISM, GOD, MONOTHEISM, POLYTHEISM, THEISM. *Henotheism* is the belief in and worship of one God without at the same time denying that others can with equal truth worship different gods. It is falsely taught in the sectarian world that Abraham, for instance, was a *henotheist,* that is, that he worshiped the Almighty, but that at the same time he considered that other nations could worship their own gods with equally beneficial results. This apostate view is erroneously considered to be one step advanced from polytheism and one step behind the final type of monotheism that was in process of evolving.

HEREDITY.

See ENVIRONMENT, PRE-EXISTENCE. In his eternal providences and omniscient wisdom, an Almighty Deity has ordained laws whereby the characteristics and qualities of parents are transmitted to their descendents. From a mortal viewpoint this is called *heredity*. From an eternal perspective it is the Lord's way of sending through particular lineages the very spirits who have developed the mental, spiritual, and other qualifications entitling them so to be born. The complexities and intricacies of the laws prevailing in this field are beyond finite capacity to comprehend.

HERESY.

See APOSTASY, DOCTRINE, ORTHODOXY, TRUTH. In the true gospel sense, any opinion or doctrine in opposition to the revealed word of the Lord as recorded in the standard works of the Church and as taught by The Church of Jesus Christ of Latter-day Saints is an *heresy*. The issue is not how many people may believe a teaching; it is whether the doctrine is true or false. (2 Pet. 2:1.) The whole Chris-

tian world, in the days of the Prophet, believed falsely that God was a mystical spirit essence that filled the immensity of space and was everywhere and nowhere in particular present—all of which proved only that they were all *heretics,* that the apostasy was universal. Heresy is false doctrine.

Even members of the true Church are guilty of the crime of heresy to the extent that they accept false views which do not accord with the revealed word. "For there must be also heresies among you, that they which are approved may be made manifest among you." (1 Cor. 11:19; Gal. 5:20.) One of the purposes of this mortal probation is to see how much of the truth men will believe when they walk by faith rather then by sight. There is no salvation in a false doctrine.

HERITAGE.

See CHURCH OF JESUS CHRIST OF LATTER-DAY SAINTS, PECULIAR PEOPLE, SAINTS. The saints of God, the house of Israel, his chosen and peculiar people are the *Lord's heritage.* He has chosen them as his inheritance, as "a special people unto himself, above all people that are upon the face of the earth." (Deut. 7:6; Ex. 19:6; 1 Pet. 2:5, 9.) Peter counseled the elders: "Feed the flock of God which is among you, taking the oversight thereof, not by constraint, but willingly; not for filthy lucre, but of a ready mind; Neither as being lords over *God's heritage,* but being ensamples to the flock." (1 Pet. 5:2-3; D. & C. 58:17.)

HETERODOXY.
See ORTHODOXY.

HIERARCHY.
See EQUALITY, GENERAL AUTHORITIES, PRIESTHOOD, PRIESTHOOD OFFICES. Among the saints of God perfect brotherhood and equality in all things does or should exist. (D. & C. 78:3-7; 105:3-6.) There are no low or mean persons; all are the children of a loving Father; all are candidates for salvation; and the Almighty is no respecter of persons. Yet the Church is a kingdom, a theocracy, a complex organization operated by many officers serving in divers capacities.

To maintain discipline and carry the work forward, of necessity there must be high and low offices; seniority must exist between those holding the same office; and the decisions of those holding higher positions must prevail over the views of their brothers who hold lesser positions. Each General Authority has his own rank and position; ward bishops are subject to and give due deference to their stake presidents; counselors in presidencies do not rank with those whom they assist; and so it is throughout the whole organization of the Church. The great body of administrative officers—each successive group serving according to rank and precedence—form a complex and perfect *hierarchy.* (D. & C. 107.)

This same system prevails in heavenly realms. A great *celestial hierarchy* prevails. God stands at the head, with spirits, angels, and exalted personages each ranking in their respective, assigned positions and spheres.

HIGH COUNCIL.
See CHURCH COURTS, STAKE PRESIDENTS, TRAVELING PRESIDING HIGH COUNCIL. In each stake a *high council* composed of 12 high priests is organized to serve as a judicial and administrative body. With the stake presidency directing their considerations, *high councilors* assist in the trial of cases properly brought before them. (D. & C. 102; 107:37.) Their work in the administrative field is to aid and assist the stake presidency in regulating the various church affairs and programs in the stake.

HIGH COUNCILORS.
See HIGH COUNCIL.

HIGHER CRITICISM.
See APOSTASY, BIBLE, EVOLUTION, REVELATION, SCRIPTURE. In modern times, the uninspired Biblical scholars of the world—men

without faith, without revelation, without the gift of the Holy Ghost, without a knowledge of the plan of salvation; men who do not accept Christ as the literal Son of God—have studiously dissected the Bible so as, in effect, to destroy its divine authenticity. Their work is called *higher criticism,* though as has aptly been said it should more accurately be called *destructive criticism.*

Theories of the *higher critics*—based as they are on speculative evolution, on speculative archeological deductions, and on pure imagination—include such conclusions as:

That the books of the Bible (particularly the earlier Old Testament books) are not the revealed mind and will of the Lord, but rather they are the compilations of various authors and scribes who edited and wove together the myths of pre-historic peoples;

That the Pentateuch or five books of Moses were compiled long after the day of Moses from four earlier (and now unavailable) accounts—the "J" (Jehovistic), the "E" (Elohistic), the "P" (Priestly), and "D" (Deuteronomistic);

That the Book of Isaiah, for instance, was authored by two, three, or four different persons living at different times;

That as a result of the manner in which the Bible came into being, it abounds in errors, contradictions, and recorded myths, and that it is not inspired in the sense that it came by revelation from God;

That early man could neither read nor write and was not endowed with the same intellectual capacity which the evolutionary processes have now given him;

That such Biblical accounts as pertain to the creation, fall of Adam, Garden of Eden, flood of Noah, and confusion of tongues grew out of Assyrian and Babylonian myths and were incorporated into the Hebrew scriptures by ignorant or unenlightened scribes who thereby gave to myths the sanctity of revelation;

That the earliest religion came into being as part of the evolutionary development of man, that it included the worship of many gods, and that the concept of one supreme Deity was only gradually accepted by the Hebrew peoples.

To a greater or lesser extent these false theories are accepted and taught in every sectarian church in Christendom. They are interwoven in nearly every article found in the Bible dictionaries commonly used by sectarian Christians. They are part and portion of the promised universal apostasy which the prophets specified would prevail in the last days. Occasionally some of these views are even found in the true Church and creep into lessons and class discussions. In the final analysis they are doctrines of the devil, doctrines which destroy faith and prevent acceptance of the full gospel of salvation.

Latter-day Saints who have

gained testimonies of the divinity of the Lord's great latter-day work know that the theories of the higher critics are false. Scores of direct revelations given to the Prophet Joseph Smith deny, categorically and bluntly, the theories of these critics. For instance, the Book of Mormon establishes the divinity of Isaiah's writings; the Book of Moses and the Book of Abraham set forth the truth about God's ancient dealings with the people from the days of Adam down; and many sections in the Doctrine and Covenants pointedly refute the specific claims of the higher critics. An excellent analysis of higher criticism is found on pages 490-515 of *Man: His Origin and Destiny* by President Joseph Fielding Smith.

HIGHER PRIESTHOOD.
See MELCHIZEDEK PRIESTHOOD.

HIGHEST.
See FATHER IN HEAVEN, GOD, MOST HIGH, SON OF THE HIGHEST. To the Father, "the highest of all" (D. & C. 76:70), is ascribed the name, the *Highest* (Ps. 87:5; Luke 1:32-35, 76; 2:14; 6:35; 19:38), thus signifying that he is exalted above all others in standing, rank, dignity, power, and all things. Of the Father, he who is "the Son of the Highest" (Luke 1:32) proclaimed: "My Father is greater than I." (John 14:28.)

HIGH PRIEST.
See AUTHOR OF SALVATION, CHRIST, HIGH PRIESTS. "Christ is the great *High Priest*." (*Teachings*, p. 158; Heb. 3:1.) "Thou art a priest for ever after the order of Melchizedek," are the words of one of the great Messianic prophecies. (Ps. 110:4; Heb. 5:5-11; 7:14-17.) The designation of our Lord as the great High Priest points to his position as the chief minister of salvation, as the author of salvation in the sense of having worked out the infinite and eternal atonement. (Heb. 2:1-18; 5.)

HIGH PRIESTESSES.
See HIGH PRIESTS, PRIESTESSES, PRIESTHOOD. There is no such thing in the true Church as a *high priestess*. Where this office is found in a church, it is an unauthorized and apostate innovation. Women do not hold the priesthood.

HIGH PRIESTLY PRAYER.
See PRAYER.

HIGH PRIESTS.
See HIGH PRIEST, HIGH PRIESTESSES, MELCHIZEDEK PRIESTHOOD, PRESIDENT OF THE CHURCH, PRIESTHOOD, PRIESTHOOD OFFICES, PRIESTHOOD QUORUMS, PRIESTS, QUORUM PRESIDENTS. 1. God's chief representative on earth, the one who holds the highest spiritual position in his kingdom in any age,

is called *the high priest*. This special designation of the chief spiritual officer of the Church has reference to the administrative position which he holds rather than to the office to which he is ordained in the priesthood. When these high priests served under the law of Moses, they were ordained priests of the Aaronic order. (Lev. 21:10; 2 Kings 22:4.) However, since there were times in ancient Israel when the Melchizedek Priesthood was on earth—as in the days of Elijah—there may have been instances when the high priests held the higher priesthood. Among the Nephites (Alma 4:4, 18), and in the Church today this presiding high priest holds the ordained office of high priest of the Melchizedek order. (D. & C. 107:22, 66.) In the meridian of time the apostate Jews were in subjection to their self-appointed high priests. (Matt. 26:3, 51, 57; Acts 23:4.) In accordance with the governmental arrangements existing in particular periods, some of the high priests would have exercised secular as well as ecclesiastical powers.

2. One of the ordained offices in the Melchizedek Priesthood is that of a *high priest*. (D. & C. 20:67.) This office grows out of and is an appendage to the higher priesthood. (D. & C. 107:5.) Beginning in Adam's day, whenever the Church has been organized and the fulness of the gospel has been had by men, there have been high priests. (D. & C. 107:53; Alma 13.) These breth-

ren have been called to minister in spiritual things (D. & C. 107:18), to travel and preach the gospel (D. & C. 84:111), to perfect the saints and do all the things that a seventy, elder, or holder of the Aaronic Priesthood can do. (D. & C. 68:19.)

HILL CUMORAH.
See CUMORAH.

HISTORY.
See BOOK OF REMEMBRANCE, CHURCH HISTORIAN AND RECORDER, JOURNALS, RECORD KEEPING. *History* is a written account of past events, a record of human progress and experience; it generally deals with those events affecting nations and peoples; and it is usually accompanied by a philosophical explanation of the causes behind the events. It is a guide to progress and an aid to civilization. (*Doctrines of Salvation,* vol. 2, pp. 197-200.)

Contrary to what is generally assumed, and notwithstanding the fact that our libraries bulge with countless volumes of so-called history, very little is actually known of much of the real history of the world. Many historical events are nearly or completely unknown to modern scholars. From the standpoint of profane records, almost nothing is known of man's origin; of his early life on earth; of the nations, kingdoms, and peoples that lived more than three or four thousand years ago; of the ancient inhabitants of the American continent; or even of the peoples of northern Europe and of the orient in ancient and medieval times.

Laying revealed history aside— where do we find the true story of the creation? Where is the record that identifies Adam and Eve as intelligent, superior beings who are the actual progenitors of all men? Who knows anything of the 365 year history of the City of Enoch, or of the fact it was taken up into heaven? What is known of the fact that the continents and islands were all in one place until some 4000 or so years ago and that they were then divided? Who knows about the universal flood? The confusion of tongues at the tower of Babel? What of the great Jaredite and Nephite nations that flourished on the American continent for some 2500 years? And what was taking place on this continent 1000 years before Columbus? Where are the lost tribes of Israel? Where did our Lord go when he ministered to them in the meridian of time? How many times have the Father and the Son appeared to men? What visions and revelations have been lost to our knowledge?

Indeed, what is the real truth about what is going on in some communist countries today? And such histories as we do have, are they slanted as communists slant history? What histories shall we believe where Mormon history is concerned? Those written by the enemies of the saints or by their friends? Shall we accept civil war histories by northern or southern sympathizers?

From the beginning to now, the real history of the world has either been lost or so twisted and perverted that our present knowledge falls far short of the real truth about past events. When the real history of the world is written —as it will be by the spirit of inspiration—it will show God's dealings with men, the place the gospel has played in the rise and fall. of nations, and how eras of darkness and degeneracy have resulted from apostasy from the way of the Lord.

HOBBIES.
See GOSPEL HOBBIES.

HOLINESS.
See CLEANLINESS, HOLY, HOLY GHOST, HOLY MESSIAH, HOLY ONE, HOLY ONE OF GOD, HOLY ONE OF ISRAEL, HOLY ONE OF JACOB, HOLY ONE OF ZION, MAN OF HOLINESS, PURITY, RIGHTEOUSNESS, SANCTIFICATION. By compliance with the laws and ordinances of the gospel, the saints have power to attain a state of perfect *holiness* before the Lord. (D. & C. 60: 7.) Such a state is one of spiritual life, of godliness, of unimpaired innocence and proved virtue. "Through the shedding of the blood of Christ," the obedient gain a remission of their sins and "become

holy, without spot." (Moro. 10:32-33; 3 Ne. 28:39; D. & C. 133:35.)

"Sanctify yourselves therefore, and *be ye holy:* for I am the Lord your God." (Lev. 20:7.) "Practise virtue and holiness before me." (D. & C. 38:24.) "Bind yourselves to act in all holiness before me." (D. & C. 43:9.) "Continue in faith and charity and holiness with sobriety." (1 Tim. 2:15; 2 Cor. 7:1; Eph. 1:4; Heb. 12:10-14; D. & C. 20:69; 21:4; 46:7.)

Scores of different things pertaining to the Church and kingdom are referred to in the scriptures as being *holy,* including lands, laws, prophets, performances, priesthoods, and the like. Sacred and holy mysteries of the kingdom are offered to men only when they have shown by a holy walk and conversation that they are prepared to receive them. (Alma 12:9-11.) Strict command is laid upon the Lord's ministers to "Give not that which is holy unto the dogs." (Matt. 7:6; 3 Ne. 14:6.)

HOLY.

See CHRIST, HOLINESS, HOLY MESSIAH, HOLY ONE, HOLY ONE OF GOD, HOLY ONE OF ISRAEL, HOLY ONE OF JACOB, HOLY ONE OF ZION, MAN OF HOLINESS. One of Christ's names is *Holy,* using the designation in the noun sense and not as an adjective. Thus Isaiah entoned: "Thus saith the high and lofty One that inhabiteth eternity, whose name is *Holy.*" (Isa.

57:15.) Obviously the purpose of the name is to convey to man the concept of the supreme holiness and perfection embodied in him who is the Son of Man of Holiness. (Moses 6:57.)

HOLY CITY.
See NEW JERUSALEM.

HOLY FATHER.
See FATHER IN HEAVEN, GOD, HOLY ONE OF GOD, MAN OF HOLINESS, MINISTERIAL TITLES. 1. This sacred title, *Holy Father,* is an appropriate and proper way to address God the Father. In the revealed dedicatory prayer of the Kirtland Temple, the Father is so designated seven times. (D. & C. 109:4, 10, 14, 22, 24, 29, 47.) The title bears record both of Deity's holy and perfected status and his position as the Parent of the spirits of men.

2. In the Catholic Church the designation *Holy Father* is a title applied to the Pope. Such usage is inappropriate.

HOLY GHOST.
See BAPTISM OF FIRE, BORN AGAIN, CHRIST, COMFORTER, CONFIRMATION, GIFT OF THE HOLY GHOST, GIFTS OF THE SPIRIT, GOD, GODHEAD, HOLY SPIRIT OF PROMISE, LAYING ON OF HANDS, LIGHT OF CHRIST, PARACLETE, REVELATION, REVELATOR, SANCTIFIER,

SIGN OF THE DOVE, SPIRIT OF THE LORD, SPIRIT OF TRUTH, SPIRITUAL LIFE, TESTATOR, TESTIMONY. 1. The *Holy Ghost* is the third member of the Godhead. He is a Personage of Spirit, a Spirit Person, a Spirit Man, a Spirit Entity. He can be in only one place at one time, and he does not and cannot transform himself into any other form or image than that of the Man whom he is, though his power and influence can be manifest at one and the same time through all immensity. (D. & C. 130:22-23; *Teachings,* p. 190, 275-276; *Gospel Doctrine,* 5th ed., pp. 59-62.)

He is the Comforter, Testator, Revelator, Sanctifier, Holy Spirit, Holy Spirit of Promise, Spirit of Truth, Spirit of the Lord, and Messenger of the Father and the Son, and his companionship is the greatest gift that mortal man can enjoy. His mission is to perform all of the functions appertaining to the various name-titles which he bears. Because he is a Spirit Personage, he has power—according to the eternal laws ordained by the Father—to perform essential and unique functions for men. In this dispensation, at least, nothing has been revealed as to his origin or destiny; expressions on these matters are both speculative and fruitless.

2. Sometimes the designation *Holy Ghost* is used to mean, not the Individual or Person who is a member of the Godhead, but the *power or gift* of that Personage.

After Philip had baptized some converts in Samaria, Peter and John were sent unto them, "Who, when they were come down, prayed for them, that they might receive the Holy Ghost: (For as yet he was fallen upon none of them: only they were baptized in the name of the Lord Jesus.) Then laid they their hands on them, and they received the Holy Ghost." (Acts 8:12-17.) Similarly Paul found some converts in Ephesus who supposed they had been baptized by a legal administrator. To them Paul said, "Have ye received the Holy Ghost since ye believed?" Finding they were misinformed as to their church status, Paul arranged for a proper baptism. Then "when Paul had laid his hands upon them, the Holy Ghost came on them; and they spake with tongues, and prophesied." (Acts 19:1-7.) In both of these instances the scriptures speak of receiving the Holy Ghost, meaning the receipt and enjoyment following baptism of the gift and power of the Holy Ghost. Nephi spoke similarly when he said that the Holy Ghost "is the gift of God unto all those who diligently seek him, as well in times of old as in the time that he should manifest himself unto the children of men." (1 Ne. 10:17.)

HOLY INTERPRETERS.
See URIM AND THUMMIM.

HOLY KISS.
See SALUTATIONS.

HOLY MESSIAH.
See CHRIST, HOLY, HOLY ONE, HOLY ONE OF GOD, HOLY ONE OF ISRAEL, HOLY ONE OF JACOB, HOLY ONE OF ZION, MESSIAH. Christ is called by his name, the *Holy Messiah,* when the purpose is to bring to mind both his holy and perfected state and his position as Deliverer and King. (2 Ne. 2:6, 8.)

HOLY ONE.
See CHRIST, HOLINESS, HOLY, HOLY ONE OF GOD, HOLY ONE OF ISRAEL, HOLY ONE OF JACOB, HOLY ONE OF ZION. Christ is the *Holy One,* a designation signifying that he is a holy, pure, sanctified Person, One who was and is without sin, who had no need for repentance, and who stands perfect in all things. "I am the Lord, your Holy One, the creator of Israel, your King." (Isa. 43:15; 49:7; Ps. 16:10; Acts 2:27; 3:14; 13:35; 2 Ne. 9:20, 41; 3 Ne. 26:5; Morm. 9:5, 14; D. & C. 78:16.) "Holy, holy, holy, is the Lord of hosts: the whole earth is full of his glory." (Isa. 6:3.) "Holiness unto the Lord" will be emblazoned on useful items of every sort in that millennial day when the Holy One reigns personally upon the earth. (Zech. 14:20-21.)

HOLY ONE OF GOD.
See CHRIST, HOLY, HOLY ONE, HOLY ONE OF ISRAEL, HOLY ONE OF JACOB, HOLY ONE OF ZION. To couple the concept of Christ's holiness with the pointed realization that he came forth from and is the Son of God, he is called the *Holy One of God.* It was by this name that a devil addressed him, when that unclean spirit was commanded to leave his enforced tenancy in a stolen tabernacle. (Mark 1:24; Luke 4:34.)

HOLY ONE OF ISRAEL.
See CHRIST, GOD OF ISRAEL, HOLY, HOLY ONE, HOLY ONE OF GOD, HOLY ONE OF JACOB, HOLY ONE OF ZION. Christ is the *Holy One of Israel,* an appellation signifying that he is both the embodiment of holiness and the God of Israel who came into the world through the lineage of that chosen people. This particular name was in constant and popular usage anciently. It is found 40 times in the Book of Mormon and over 30 in the Old Testament, but it is not found of record in either the New Testament or the Doctrine and Covenants. (2 Ne. 25:29; 30:2; Omni 26; Ps. 89:18; Isa. 43:14; Ezek. 39:7.)

HOLY ONE OF JACOB.
See CHRIST, GOD OF ISRAEL, HOLY, HOLY ONE, HOLY ONE OF

GOD, HOLY ONE OF ISRAEL, HOLY ONE OF ZION. References to Christ as the *Holy One of Jacob* have substantially the same meaning as those which designate him as the Holy One of Israel. (Isa. 29:23; 2 Ne. 27:34.) They invite attention to our Lord's holiness and his position as the God of Jacob, a God who was born in the flesh as the literal descendant of that ancient patriarch.

HOLY ONE OF ZION.

See CHRIST, HOLY, HOLY ONE, HOLY ONE OF GOD, HOLY ONE OF ISRAEL, HOLY ONE OF JACOB, ZION. To speak of Christ as the *Holy One of Zion* is to point attention both to his holiness and to the especial and personal relationship that exists between him and his Zion. (D. & C. 78:15.) When the perfect Zion—composed solely of the pure in heart (D. & C. 97:21) —is again established on earth, then the presence of the Lord will be felt there as his presence was found in the ancient city of that name. (Moses 7:16-19, 62-64.)

HOLY ORDER OF GOD.
See MELCHIZEDEK PRIESTHOOD.

HOLY PRIESTHOOD AFTER THE ORDER OF THE SON OF GOD.
See MELCHIZEDEK PRIESTHOOD.

HOLY SCRIPTURES.
See BIBLE.

HOLY SPIRIT.
See SPIRIT OF THE LORD.

HOLY SPIRIT OF PROMISE.
See GIFT OF THE HOLY GHOST, HOLY GHOST, JUSTIFICATION. The *Holy Spirit of Promise* is the Holy Spirit *promised* the saints, or in other words the Holy Ghost. This name-title is used in connection with the sealing and ratifying power of the Holy Ghost, that is, the power given him to ratify and approve the righteous acts of men so that those acts will be binding on earth and in heaven. "All covenants, contracts, bonds, obligations, oaths, vows, performances, connections, associations, or expectations," must be sealed by the Holy Spirit of Promise, if they are to have "efficacy, virtue, or force in and after the resurrection from the dead; for all contracts that are not made unto this end have an end when men are dead." (D. & C. 132: 7.)

To seal is to *ratify,* to *justify,* or to *approve.* Thus an act which is sealed by the Holy Spirit of Promise is one which is ratified by the Holy Ghost; it is one which is approved by the Lord; and the person who has taken the obligation upon himself is justified by the Spirit in the thing he has done.

The ratifying seal of approval is put upon an act only if those entering the contract are worthy as a result of personal righteousness to receive the divine approbation. They "are sealed by the Holy Spirit of promise, which the Father sheds forth upon all those who are *just and true*." (D. & C. 76:53.) If they are not just and true and worthy the ratifying seal is withheld.

When any ordinance or contract is sealed by the Spirit, it is approved with a promise of reward, provided unrighteousness does not thereafter break the seal, remove the ratifying approval, and cause loss of the promised blessing. (*Doctrines of Salvation*, vol. 1, p. 55; vol. 2, pp. 94-99.) Seals are placed on contracts through righteousness.

The operation and power of the Holy Spirit of Promise is best illustrated by the ordinance and contract of baptism. An unworthy candidate for baptism might deceive the elders and get the ordinance performed, but no one can lie to the Holy Ghost and get by undetected. Accordingly, the baptism of an unworthy and unrepentant person would not be sealed by the Spirit; it would not be ratified by the Holy Ghost; the unworthy person would not be justified by the Spirit in his actions. If thereafter he became worthy through repentance and obedience, the seal would then be put in force. Similarly, if a worthy person is baptized, with the ratifying approval of the Holy Ghost attending the performance, yet the seal may be broken by subsequent sin.

These principles also apply to every other ordinance and performance in the Church. Thus if both parties are "just and true," if they are worthy, a ratifying seal is placed on their temple marriage; if they are unworthy, they are not justified by the Spirit and the ratification of the Holy Ghost is withheld. Subsequent worthiness will put the seal in force, and unrighteousness will break any seal.

Even if a person progresses to that state of near-perfection in which his calling and election is made sure, in which he is "sealed up unto eternal life" (D. & C. 131:5; 132:18-26), in which he receives "the promise . . . of eternal life" (D. & C. 88:3-4), in which he is "sealed up unto the day of redemption" (D. & C. 124:124; Eph. 1:13) —yet with it all, these great promises are secured only if the "performances" are sealed by the Holy Spirit of Promise.

HOLY WRIT.
See SCRIPTURE.

HOMAGE.
See OBEISANCE.

HOME.
See CELESTIAL MARRIAGE, EXALTATION. It is common to speak

362

of the Latter-day Saint *home,* meaning not just the dwelling place of the family, but the family institution itself. This usage considers a Mormon home to be one bound together for eternity by the sealing power of the priesthood; one in which love abounds because all members of the family believe and obey the gospel law; one in which the father holds the priesthood, blesses his wife and children, and stands as a true patriarch to his posterity; one where there are daily family prayers, where charity, faith, and devotion abound, where there is chastity and perfect cleanliness of mind and body; one from which young men go forth as missionaries to carry the message of salvation to our Father's other children; one in which all the members serve in the Church, keep the commandments of God, and enjoy the rich outpourings of the Spirit. It is in and through the eternal family (or as is colloquially said, the home) that men gain perfect peace in this life and a hope of eternal life hereafter.

HOME TEACHERS.
See CHURCH COURTS, PRIESTHOOD, TEACHERS, WARDS. Upon the priesthood bearers rests the obligation "to preach, teach, expound, exhort"; to "visit the house of each member, exhorting them to pray vocally and in secret and attend to all family duties; . . . to watch over the church always, and

be with and strengthen them; And see that there is no iniquity in the church, neither hardness with each other, neither lying, backbiting, nor evil speaking." (D. & C. 20:42-54.)

To aid them in the discharge of these responsibilities, it is the practice of the Church to send priesthood brethren out as *home teachers* to visit the homes of all church members each month. These brethren go out two by two, frequently one holding the lesser priesthood going with a possessor of the Melchizedek Priesthood. When this *home teaching* is done properly, it complies with all phases of the revelation, brings about conversion to the truth, increases righteousness among the saints, and leads souls to eternal salvation.

HOMICIDE.
See MURDERERS.

HOMOSEXUALS.
See SEX IMMORALITY.

HONESTY.
See INTEGRITY, LIARS, TRUTH, UPRIGHTNESS. Perfect *honesty* is one of the invarying characteristics exhibited by all who are worthy to be numbered with the saints of God. Honest persons are fair and truthful in speech, straightforward in their dealings, free from deceit, and above cheat-

ing, stealing, misrepresentation, or any other fraudulent action. Honesty is the companion of truth, dishonesty of falsehood; honesty is of God, dishonesty of the devil, for he was a liar from the beginning. (D. & C. 93:52; 2 Ne. 2:18.)

All men are commanded to be honest as one of the requisites for working out their salvation. (D. & C. 51:9; 97:8; Rom. 13:13; 2 Cor. 13:7; Philip. 4:8; 1 Thess. 4:12; Heb. 13:18; 1 Pet. 2:12; Thirteenth Article of Faith.) Those who are honest in heart readily accept the gospel and its truths. (D. & C. 8:1; 11:10; 135:7.) Honest men should be sought for to administer the civil law. (D. & C. 98:10.)

HONOR.

See OBEISANCE, REVERENCE, WORSHIP. To honor another person is to hold him in high esteem, to accord him respectful regard because of his high worth; in the case of Deity these feelings are coupled with reverential worship and necessarily presuppose that God is deserving of all glory and adulation because he has almighty power. His honor is his power. (D. & C. 29:36.)

Who is deserving of honor? Paul answers: "Unto the King eternal, immortal, invisible, the only wise God, be honour and glory for ever and ever." (1 Tim. 1:17; 6:16.) And with his view all the prophets accord. (Rev. 5:13; 7:12; 19:1; D. & C. 20:36; 65:6; 76:119; 84:102; 109:

77.) Further: "All men should honour the Son, even as they honour the Father. He that honoureth not the Son honoureth not the Father which hath sent him." (John 5:23.)

Exalted beings who become like God shall inherit all the honors of his kingdom. (D. & C. 43:25; 75:5; 124:55; 128:12, 23.) Those who serve as his prophets among men are deserving of attention and honor. (Matt. 13:57; Mark 6:4; John 4:44.) "Honour thy father and thy mother"; such is a divine decree that has been repeated over and over again by the Lord's prophets. (Ex. 20:12; Deut. 5:16; Matt. 15:4; 19:19; Mark 7:10; 10:19; Luke 18:20; Eph. 6:2; 1 Ne. 17:55; Mosiah 13:20.) "Honour all men. Love the brotherhood. Fear God. Honour the king." (1 Pet. 2:17; Rom. 13:7.)

Men receive honors either from God or from their fellow men. As far as the recipients are concerned, in the eternal perspective, the honors of men count for nothing. They may result in some transitory glory in this world, but in eternity no honors will remain except those conferred by Deity. *"I receive not honour from men,"* our Lord said. (John 5:41; Alma 60:36.) *"If I honour myself, my honour is nothing: it is my Father that honoureth me; of whom ye say, that he is your God."* (John 8:54.) Similarly, no man is able to take any honor of the priesthood or the gospel unto himself; they are gifts bestowed by the Almighty. (Heb. 5: 4.)

How is it possible to gain honor from God? "If any man serve me, let him follow me; and where I am, there shall also my servant be: *if any man serve me, him will my Father honour.*" (John 12:26.) "I, the Lord, am merciful and gracious unto those who fear me, and delight to honor those who serve me in righteousness and in truth unto the end." (D. & C. 76:5.) Honor is the reward of obedience.

HOPE.

See CHARITY, DESIRES, ETERNAL LIFE, FAITH, HOPE OF ISRAEL, PRISONERS OF HOPE, SALVATION. As used in the revelations, *hope* is the desire of faithful people to gain eternal salvation in the kingdom of God hereafter. It is not a flimsy, ethereal desire, one without assurance that the desired consummation will be received, but a desire coupled with full expectation of receiving the coveted reward. Paul, for instance, was not hesitant in affirming that he lived, "In hope of eternal life, which God, that cannot lie, promised before the world began" (Tit. 1:2), and Peter assured all the elect that "by the resurrection of Jesus Christ from the dead," their "lively hope" of "an inheritance incorruptible, and undefiled, and that fadeth not away, reserved in heaven" for the saints, had been renewed or "begotten" again. (1 Pet. 1:1-5.)

Hope is always centered in Christ (Ps. 31:24; 42:5, 11; 43:5; 146:5); it always pertains to salvation in the kingdom of God (Lam. 3:26; Acts 24:15; Rom. 8:24-25; Heb. 11:1; Col. 1:5, 23); and without hope there can be no salvation. Speaking to the Lord, Moroni said: "Thou hast prepared a house for man, yea, even among the mansions of thy Father, in which man might have a more excellent hope; wherefore *man must hope, or he cannot receive an inheritance in the place which thou hast prepared.*" (Ether 12:32.)

There is only one true hope (Eph. 4:4), "that blessed hope" (Tit. 2:13), and the saints are commanded to acquire it. (D. & C. 6: 19; Alma 7:24.) It is one of the essential qualifications for those who labor in the ministry (D. & C. 4:5); none can assist in the Lord's work without it. (D. & C. 12:8; 18:19); those who have it are not ashamed of the testimony they bear (Rom. 5:5); rather, they are commanded to "be ready always to give an answer to every man" for the hope that is in them. (1 Pet. 3:15.)

Hope is born of righteousness. "The hope of the righteous shall be gladness: but the expectation of the wicked shall perish." (Prov. 10:28; 14:32.) The hope of the wicked "shall be as the giving up of the ghost." (Job 11:20.) Hope is found through the gospel; the scriptures themselves have been recorded that men "might have hope" (Rom. 15:4); and angels minister unto man to confirm that hope. (D. & C. 128:21.) And those who gain the full hope of eternal life purify themselves even as Christ is pure. (1 John 3:1-3.)

Faith and hope are inseparable. Hope enables men to have faith in the first instance and then because of faith that hope increases until salvation is gained. *"How is it that ye can attain unto faith, save ye shall have hope?"* Mormon asks. "And what is it that ye shall hope for? Behold I say unto you that *ye shall have hope through the atonement of Christ and the power of his resurrection, to be raised unto life eternal,* and this because of your faith in him according to the promise. Wherefore, *if a man have faith he must needs have hope; for without faith there cannot be any hope.* And again, behold I say unto you that he cannot have faith and hope, save he shall be meek, and lowly of heart. If so, his faith and hope is vain, for none is acceptable before God, save the meek and lowly in heart." (Moro. 7:40-44.)

Moroni quoted the words of Ether who said: "By faith all things are fulfilled—Wherefore, *whoso believeth in God might with surety hope for a better world, yea, even a place at the right hand of God, which hope cometh of faith,* maketh an anchor to the souls of men, which would make them sure and steadfast, always abounding in good works, being led to glorify God." Then Moroni explained that "faith is things which are hoped for and not seen," and said that Christ had revealed himself to men, "that they might hope for those things which they have not seen. Wherefore, *ye may also have hope, and be partakers of the gift, if ye will but have faith."* (Ether 12:3-9.) Hope thus is one of the gifts of the Spirit. "Now the *God of hope* fill you with all joy and peace in believing," Paul prayed for the Roman Saints, "that ye may *abound in hope, through the power of the Holy Ghost."* (Rom. 15:13.)

HOPELESSNESS.
See DESPAIR.

HOPE OF ISRAEL.
See CHRIST, HOPE, ISRAEL, NEW JERUSALEM, RESURRECTION. An eternal inheritance in an eternal promised land was the *hope of Israel.* Paul, who found himself persecuted and in chains "for the hope of Israel" (Acts 28:20), said to King Agrippa: "I stand and am judged for *the hope of the promise made of God unto our fathers:* Unto which promise our twelve tribes, instantly serving God day and night, *hope* [in a day yet future] *to come.* For which hope's sake, king Agrippa, I am accused of the Jews. *Why should it be thought a thing incredible with you, that God should raise the dead?"* (Acts 26:6-8.)

The hope of Israel, from olden days and through all her generations, was that the house and people and nation of Israel would be eternal, that through the resurrection they would inherit their promised land forever. (Acts 23:6; 24:15, 21.) Abraham, Israel's father, was promised the land of Canaan for himself and his posterity forever (Gen. 12:1-10), but during his lifetime Abraham never actually received his inheritance. (Acts 7.) The hope of Israel was that Abraham and his posterity would yet enter into their promised inheritance.

David kept Israel in remembrance of their future hope by saying: *"Evildoers shall be cut off: but those that wait upon the Lord, they shall inherit the earth. For yet a little while, and the wicked shall not be: yea, thou shalt diligently consider his place, and it shall not be. But the meek shall inherit the earth; and shall delight themselves in the abundance of peace."* (Ps. 37:9-11.) Our Lord renewed this same promise during his mortal ministry. (Matt. 5:5.) Isaiah recorded the words of the Lord Jehovah, *"Thy dead men shall live, together with my dead body shall they arise. Awake and sing, ye that dwell in dust:* for thy dew is as the dew of herbs, and *the earth shall cast out the dead."* (Isa. 26:19.)

The Lord set Ezekiel "down in the midst of the valley which was full of bones," and had him foretell in detail relative to the resurrection. "Son of man," the Lord then said to him, *"these bones are the whole house of Israel:* behold, they say, *Our bones are dried, and our hope is lost:* we are cut off for our parts. Therefore prophesy and say unto them, Thus saith the Lord God; Behold, O my people, *I will open your graves, and cause you to come up out of your graves, and bring you into the land of Israel.* And ye shall know that I am the Lord, when I have opened your graves, O my people, and brought you up out of your graves. And shall put my spirit in you, and ye shall live, and *I shall place you in your own land:* then shall ye know that I the Lord have spoken it, and performed it, saith the Lord." (Ezek. 37:1-14.)

Paul said of Abraham and the prophets that they "looked for a city which hath foundations, whose builder and maker is God," but that "These all died in faith, *not having received the promises,* but having seen them afar off, and were persuaded of them, and embraced them, and confessed that they were strangers and pilgrims on the earth. For they that say such things declare plainly that *they seek a country, . . . a better country, that is, an heavenly."* (Heb. 11:8-16.)

The triumph and hope of Israel is yet future. In part it will be realized during the millennial era, but the final inheritance, the fulfilment of the hope in the eternal sense, will come after this earth becomes a celestial sphere, for in that day "the poor and the meek of the earth shall inherit it." (D. & C. 88:17.)

HOROSCOPES.
See FORTUNE TELLING.

HOSANNA.
See HALLELUJAH, HOSANNA SHOUT, PRAYER, REVERENCE, SALVATION, THANKSGIVING, WORSHIP. Hosanna—a word of Hebrew origin, meaning literally, save now, or save we pray, or save we beseech thee—is both a chant of praise and glory to God and an entreaty for his blessings. It is taken from the 118th Psalm, and was the exulting cry of the multitude as our Lord rode triumphantly into Jerusalem over the palm branches of his well-wishers. "Hosanna to the son of David," they cried, "Blessed is he that cometh in the name of the Lord; Hosanna in the highest." (Matt. 21:9-15; Mark 11:9-10; John 12:13.) Their song of prayer and praise thus rendered was almost verbatim what their forbears had sung in Messianic vein of the "stone which the builders refused" who yet became "the head stone of the corner." (Ps. 118:22-26.)

HOSANNA SHOUT.
See HOSANNA, SOLEMN ASSEMBLIES, TEMPLES. At the dedicatory services of temples and in certain other solemn assemblies, the saints follow the pattern set by the Prophet Joseph Smith at the dedication of the Kirtland Temple and give the hosanna shout. (History of the Church, vol. 2, pp. 427-428.) While standing, ordinarily with faces toward the east, and while waving white handkerchiefs with each word or phrase of praise, the united congregation exults:

Hosanna, Hosanna, Hosanna,
To God and the Lamb;
Hosanna, Hosanna, Hosanna,
To God and the Lamb;
Hosanna, Hosanna, Hosanna,
To God and the Lamb;
Amen, Amen, Amen!

HOT DRINKS.
See STRONG DRINKS, WORD OF WISDOM. What is meant by the expression hot drinks as such is found in the revealed command: "Hot drinks are not for the body or belly"? (D. & C. 89:9.) Many of the early Brethren in this dispensation have left statements indicating that tea and coffee were the drinks involved. Joseph Smith, himself, is quoted as having taught: "I understand that some of the people are excusing themselves in using tea and coffee, because the Lord only said 'hot drinks' in the revelation of the Word of Wisdom. Tea and coffee are what the Lord meant when he said 'hot drinks.'" (John A. Widtsoe, The Word of Wisdom, pp. 75-92.)

Speaking of the meaning of hot drinks, Hyrum Smith made this explanation: "There are many who wonder what this can mean—whether it refers to tea, or coffee, or not. I say it does refer to tea and coffee. Why is it that we are frequently so dull and languid? It is because we break the Word of Wisdom, disease preys upon our system, our understandings are darkened, and we do not comprehend the things of God; the devil takes advantage of us, and we fall into temptation." (*Times and Seasons*, vol. 3, p. 800.)

Elder James E. Talmage has left us this very excellent analysis: "We are consistent and in harmony with the spirit of the revelation in affirming that hot drinks as specified in the Word of Wisdom comprised the common beverages then and, less exclusively, since, taken hot. The commonest of these were and are tea and coffee, but the inhibition applies further to the drinking of any liquids at a high temperature. It should be remembered that the Lord's warning against the use of these drinks antedated by many years the discovery of the really injurious nature of thein and caffein, which are the poisonous alkaloids present in tea and coffee, and of the specific physical derangements from divers other physiological effects of these beverages.

"Tea and coffee, therefore, are the principal substances forbidden in the Word of Wisdom as hot drinks, just as alcoholic liquors are interdicted as strong drinks. Modern science has demonstrated that tea and coffee are bad for the body whether imbibed hot or cold, and also that alcoholic beverages are injurious whether malted, vinous, or distilled. The comprehensiveness of the terms used in the revelation is definite and effective.

"As demonstrated by chemical and medical science today, tea and coffee are harmful to the body on account of their poisonous nature, and, when drunk hot, on account of positive interference with the digestive processes, and lasting injury to the tissues of the stomach. Under normal conditions of eating, digestion begins in the mouth. By mastication saliva is mixed with the food, and the particular effect is that of eventually transforming certain insoluble substances, notably starch, into soluble compounds such as dextrose and glucose, which belong to the family of sugars. Within the stomach other chemical changes are wrought through the agency of the gastric juice. Now, it has long been known, and is today accepted as an undisputed fact, that high temperature hinders, and boiling heat destroys the efficacy of the ptyalin of the saliva and the pepsin of the gastric juice. It should be noted in this connection that temperatures far below the heat of the body also interfere with the action of both ptyalin and pepsin; and therefore the taking of iced drinks with meals is to be deprecated." (*Improvement Era,* vol. 20, p. 556.)

HOUSE OF ISRAEL.
See TRIBES OF ISRAEL.

HOUSE OF JACOB.
See TRIBES OF ISRAEL.

HOUSE OF PRAYER.
See TEMPLES.

HOUSE OF THE LORD.
See TEMPLES.

HUMAN SACRIFICES.
See SACRIFICES.

HUMAN SLAVERY.
See SLAVERY.

HUMILITY.
See MEEKNESS, PATIENCE. All progress in spiritual things is conditioned upon the prior attainment of *humility.* Pride, conceit, haughtiness, and vainglory are of the world and stand as a bar to the receipt of spiritual gifts.

We are commanded to be humble. (D. & C. 105:23; 112:10; 124:97, 103; Jas. 4:6, 10.) "Always retain in remembrance, the greatness of God, and your own nothingness, and his goodness and long-suffering towards you, unworthy creatures," King Benjamin taught, "and *humble yourselves even in the depths of humility,* calling on the name of the Lord daily, and standing steadfastly in the faith." (Mosiah 4:11.)

Humility must accompany repentance to qualify a person for baptism (D. & C. 20:37); it is required of all engaged in gospel service (D. & C. 12:8); is an essential attribute for all who embark in the service of God (D. & C. 4:6); precedes the acquiring of wisdom from the Spirit (D. & C. 136:32-33); is needed to qualify the righteous to see God (D. & C. 67:10); and without it no one can gain entrance to the kingdom of God hereafter. (2. Ne. 9:42.)

HUSBAND.
See BRIDEGROOM, BRIDE OF THE LAMB, CHRIST, MARRIAGE SUPPER OF THE LAMB. *Christ* (the Bridegroom) shall claim his bride (the Church), celebrate the marriage supper, and become the *Husband* of his wife. (Isa. 54:5; Jer. 31:32; Eph. 5:23; Rev. 19:7-9; 21:2.) As a Husband he shall deal intimately, with tenderness and compassion, toward the remnant of his people who have returned to enjoy millennial rest with him.

HUSBANDMAN.
See TRUE VINE.

HYMNS.
See MUSIC.

HYPNOTISM.
See SORCERY, WITCHCRAFT. In answer to the question, "Shall we practice *hypnotism,*" President Francis M. Lyman of the Council of the Twelve wrote: "Hypnotism is a reality, and though some who claim to have this mysterious power are only tricksters, yet others do really hypnotize those who submit to them. From what I understand and have seen, I should advise you not to practice hypnotism. For my own part I could never consent to being hypnotized or allowing one of my children to be. The free agency that the Lord has given us is the choicest gift we have. As soon, however, as we permit another mind to control us, as that mind controls its own body and functions, we have completely surrendered our free agency to another; and so long as we are in the hypnotic spell—and that is as long as the hypnotist desires us to be—we give no consent in any sense whatever to anything we do. The hypnotist might influence us to do good things, but we could receive no benefit from that, even if we remembered it after coming out of the spell, for it was not done voluntarily. The hypnotist might also influence us to do absurd and even shocking, wicked things, for his will compels us." (*Era,* vol. 6, p. 420.).

Reputable doctors sometimes use hypnotherapy, a limited form of hypnotism, in connection with the practice of their profession. Their sole apparent purpose is to relieve pain and aid patients in perfecting their physical well-being. It is claimed that there are many people who have been benefited materially by this practice and that the ills normally attending hypnotical practices have not resulted. This medical practice of hypnotism obviously does not carry the same opprobrium that attaches to hypnotism in general.

HYPOCRISY.
See APOSTASY, WICKEDNESS. In the true gospel sense, *hypocrisy* consists either in the false assumption of virtue, righteousness, and goodness, or in the false assumption of the right and power to preach the principles of the gospel.

Thus if a person knows what is right and makes open profession of conforming thereto and yet does not in reality live the gospel law, he is a *hypocrite.* Hypocrisy is to profess religion and not practice it. If a teacher advocates the payment of tithing, but does not himself pay an honest tithing, he is a hypocrite. If a person prays and seeks temporal and spiritual blessings from the Lord, and then turns away the naked and needy and fails to visit the sick and afflicted, he is a hypocrite. He has professed religion, but not practiced it. (Alma 34:17-29.)

Our Lord said: "Wo unto you, scribes and Pharisees, hypocrites! for ye are like unto whited sepulchres, which indeed appear beautiful outward, but are within full of dead men's bones, and of all uncleanness. Even so ye also outwardly appear righteous unto men, but within ye are full of hypocrisy and iniquity." (Matt. 23:27-28; Isa. 32:6.)

Thus also those who profess to be lights to the world and to lead people in the paths of righteousness, but who are not in reality the Lord's true legal administrators, are hypocrites, in consequence of their false assumption of authority. In other words, as specified in both the Bible and the Book of Mormon, ministers in the false churches of Christendom are called hypocrites. (Morm. 8:38; 1 Tim. 4:1-4.)

Hypocrites shall be damned. "Wo unto them that are deceivers and hypocrites, for, thus saith the Lord, I will bring them to judgment. . . . The hypocrites shall be detected and shall be cut off, either in life or in death, even as I will." (D. & C. 50:6-8; 101:90; 124:8.)

I AM.
    See GREAT I AM.

I AM THAT I AM.
    See GREAT I AM.

IDEAS.
    See MIND.

IDIOCY.
    See YEARS OF ACCOUNTABILITY.

IDLENESS.
    See CHURCH WELFARE PLAN, DOLE, EMPLOYMENT, IDLE WORDS,

WORK. Neither temporal nor spiritual salvation can be gained without work, and *idleness* is a grievous sin. *Idlers*—those who waste time in doing nothing, who are lazy, indolent, slothful—"shall be had in remembrance before the Lord." (D. & C. 68:30-31.) "Let every man be diligent in all things. And the idler shall not have place in the church, except he repent and mend his ways." (D. & C. 75:29.) One of the reasons the Lord destroyed Sodom was for her sin of "abundance of idleness." (Ezek. 16:49.) Idleness and abominable practices always go together; for such the Lamanites were cursed. (1 Ne. 12:23; 2 Ne. 5: 24.) Idleness breeds idolatry. (Alma

1:32.)

Idleness in both temporal and spiritual pursuits must be overcome by those who seek salvation. "Thou shalt not idle away thy time," the Lord says, "neither shalt thou bury thy talent that it may not be known." (D. & C. 60:13; 90:31.) "Cease to be idle." (D. & C. 88:124.) "Refrain from idleness." (Alma 38:12.) Those called to the ministry are not to be idle, but are to labor with their might. (D. & C. 75:3.)

IDLERS.
See IDLENESS.

IDLE THOUGHTS.
See THOUGHTS.

IDLE WORDS.
See FLATTERY, GOSSIPING, JUDGMENT DAY, LIGHT SPEECHES, PROFANITY, THOUGHTS. Man will be judged by his words. (Alma 12:14.) They reveal what is in his heart, "for out of the abundance of the heart the mouth speaketh. A good man out of the good treasure of the heart bringeth forth good things: and an evil man out of the evil treasure bringeth forth evil things. But I say unto you, That every *idle word* that men shall speak, they shall give account thereof in the day of judgment. For by thy words thou shalt be justified, and by thy words thou shalt be con-

demned." (Matt. 12:34-37; Luke 6:45.)

Idle words take many forms: foolish talking and jesting (Eph. 5:4), light speeches (D. & C. 88: 121), curses (Jas. 3:9), profane and vain babblings (1 Tim. 6:20), fables and endless genealogies (1 Tim. 1: 6), profanity, vulgar stories, blasphemy, and the like.

"How vain and trifling," the Prophet said, "have been our spirits, our conferences, our councils, our meetings, our private as well as public conversations—too low, too mean, too vulgar, too condescending for the dignified characters of the called and chosen of God." (*Teachings,* p. 137.) "If any man offend not in word, the same is a perfect man, and able also to bridle the whole body. . . . Who is a wise man and endued with knowledge among you? let him shew out of a good conversation his works with meekness of wisdom." (Jas. 3:2-13.)

IDOLATERS.
See IDOLATRY.

IDOLATRY.
See APOSTASY, FALSE GODS, GOD, UNKNOWN GOD, WORSHIP OF IMAGES. Idol worship prevails among nearly all uncivilized, pagan peoples and also to a degree and in a sense among portions of those who are supposedly enlightened by Christianity and modern civilization. Pagans and others frequently

373

worship graven images, or idols of wood, stone, or metal.

However sincere men may be in their views, they cannot gain salvation by worshiping idols, images, or false gods of any kind. Eternal life is attained through a knowledge of "the only true God, and Jesus Christ whom" he hath sent. (John 17:3.) Men are commanded "that they should love and serve him, the only living and true God, and that he should be the only being whom they should worship." (D. & C. 20:19.) "Thou shalt not make unto thee any graven image, or any likeness of any thing that is in heaven above, or that is in the earth beneath, or that is in the waters under the earth: Thou shalt not bow down thyself to them, nor serve them." (Ex. 20:4-5.)

Akin to these most obvious types of *idolatry* is the worship of money, power, worldly learning, the gratification of lust, and the like.

IDOLS.
See IDOLATRY.

IDUMEA.
See SECOND COMING OF CHRIST. *Idumea* or Edom, of which Bozrah was the principal city, was a nation to the south of the Salt Sea, through which the trade route (called the King's Highway) ran between Egypt and Arabia. The Idumeans or Edomites were a wicked non-Israelitish people; hence, traveling through their country symbolized to the prophetic mind the pilgrimage of men through a wicked world; and so, Idumea meant the world.

In two graphic passages outlining the destructions incident to the Second Coming, Isaiah speaks of the sword of judgment falling upon Idumea or Edom, and in one of them he specifies that the Lord's garments shall be red as he comes from Bozrah (Isa. 34; 63), all of which destructions are confirmed by latter-day revelation (D. & C. 133), as also is the fact that Idumea is the world. (D. & C. 1:36.)

IGNORANCE.
See EDUCATION, KNOWLEDGE, TRUTH. An *ignorant* person is one who is uninformed and lacking in knowledge. *Ignorance* is both general and specific. A person who lacks the common knowledge that everyone should possess is ignorant in the general sense; if he is merely uninformed on some particular matter, he is ignorant in the particular sense. Where the gospel is concerned, though everyone is ignorant on many specific doctrinal points, yet none of the saints should be ignorant of the general, basic truths of salvation. *Where the opportunity to gain knowledge exists, ignorance is a sin.*

In large part the worship of

apostate Christendom is performed in ignorance, as much so as was the worship of the Athenians who bowed before the Unknown God, and to whom Paul said: "Whom therefore ye ignorantly worship, him declare I unto you." (Acts 17: 22-34.) But where the sectarians are concerned they have the Bible, and in spite of the creeds of their fathers they have an obligation to replace ignorance with light and truth. Unless they do so, they are not blameless before God. (Mosiah 3:20-22.)

Joseph Smith's inspired statement, "It is impossible for a man to be saved in ignorance" (D. & C. 131:6), means in ignorance of Jesus Christ and the saving truths of the gospel. It has no reference whatever to ignorance of specialized scientific or historical truths. Salvation comes through the knowledge of God and his laws and not through the learning of the world. (John 17:3; 1 Cor. 1:17-31; 2.)

An especial obligation rests upon the saints to overcome ignorance and gain knowledge of the truth. "Let him that is ignorant," the Lord said through Brigham Young, "learn wisdom by humbling himself and calling upon the Lord his God, that his eyes may be opened that he may see, and his ears opened that he may hear; For my Spirit is sent forth into the world to enlighten the humble and contrite, and to the condemnation of the ungodly." (D. & C. 136: 32-33.)

ILLEGITIMACY.
See SEX IMMORALITY.

ILLITERACY.
See APOSTASY.

ILLNESS.
See DISEASES.

IMAGES.
See WORSHIP OF IMAGES.

IMAGINATION.
See THOUGHTS.

IMMACULATE CONCEPTION THEORY.
See CHRIST, MARY, ORIGINAL SIN THEORY, VIRGIN BIRTH. From the moment of her conception, Mary, the mother of our Lord, in the false Catholic view of things, is deemed to have been free from the stain of original sin. This supposed miraculous event is called the doctrine of the *immaculate conception.* After reciting the universal prevalence of so-called original sin, Cardinal Gibbons says: "The Church, however, declares that the Blessed Virgin Mary was exempted from the stain of original sin by the merits of our Savior Jesus Christ; and that, consequently, she was never for an instant subject to the dominion of Satan. This is what is meant by

the doctrine of the Immaculate Conception." (James Cardinal Gibbons, *The Faith of Our Fathers*, p. 220.) The virgin birth has reference to the birth of Christ and is a true doctrine; the immaculate conception has reference to the birth of Mary and is a false doctrine.

IMMANENCE.
See LIGHT OF CHRIST.

IMMANENT GOD.
See LIGHT OF CHRIST.

IMMANUEL.
See CHRIST, VIRGIN BIRTH. Christ is *Immanuel, Emmanuel,* the *King Immanuel* (D. & C. 128: 22), signifying literally, *God is with us.* This designation, used by Isaiah in a great Messianic prophecy (Isa. 7:14), alluded to by Micah as referring to the birth of our Lord (Mic. 5:3), and specifically named by Matthew as having reference to the Virgin Birth (Matt. 1:18-25), signifies that Christ as God would be born into mortality of a virgin and would be with men to save and redeem them.

IMMATERIALISM.
See ATHEISM.

IMMERSION.
See BAPTISM.

IMMODESTY.
See SEX IMMORALITY.

IMMORALITY.
See SEX IMMORALITY.

IMMORTALITY.
See ATONEMENT OF CHRIST, ELEMENTS, ETERNAL LIFE, FALL OF ADAM, FLESH AND BONES, INCORRUPTION, KINGDOMS OF GLORY, MORTALITY, SALVATION, SALVATION BY GRACE, SPIRITUAL BODIES, REDEMPTION, RESURRECTION. 1. Adam and all forms of life were first created in *immortality*. There was no death in the world until after the fall. (2 Ne. 2:22-24.) When Adam fell, becoming the first mortal flesh on earth (Moses 3:7), mortality and the consequent death that flows from such a status of existence passed upon all forms of life. (*Doctrines of Salvation,* vol. 1, pp. 72-127.) This *original immortality* was designed to continue only until the fall; it was not to be of unending duration; it ceased when mortality began.

2. *Immortality* is to live forever in the resurrected state with body and spirit inseparably connected. The Lord's work and glory is to

bring to pass both the immortality and the eternal life of man (Moses 1:39): all are resurrected to a state of immortality, those who believe and obey the gospel plan go on "in immortality unto eternal life." (D. & C. 29:42-43.) Immortality is a free gift which comes by grace alone without works on man's part; eternal life, "the greatest of all the gifts of God" (D. & C. 14:7), results from "obedience to the laws and ordinances of the Gospel." (Third Article of Faith; 1 Cor. 15:42-54; 2 Tim. 1:10; *Doctrines of Salvation,* vol. 2, pp. 4-10, 24, 309-310.)

Immortality is not a gift reserved for man alone. Every living thing will come forth in the resurrection with immortality (D. & C. 29:22-25), and even the earth itself, when quickened with a celestial glory, will become an *immortal globe.* (D. & C. 77:1; 88:16-26.)

IMMORTAL SOUL.
See SOUL.

IMPARTIALITY.
See JUSTICE.

IMPS.
See DEVILS.

IMPURITY.
See CLEANLINESS.

INALIENABLE RIGHTS.
See AGENCY, BILL OF RIGHTS, CONSTITUTION OF THE UNITED STATES, FREEDOM, LIBERTY, LIGHT OF CHRIST. As a natural and automatic inheritance from their Creator, all men are born into the world with certain *inalienable rights,* rights which cannot be surrendered, transferred, or alienated. The Declaration of Independence lists *life, liberty,* and the *pursuit of happiness* as among these. In the full sense they include every natural and inherent right necessary for the working out of one's salvation in the kingdom of God. Freedom of thought and of worship, freedom of speech and of preaching the gospel, freedom to investigate the truth, to worship God according to the dictates of one's own conscience, to earn a temporal livelihood—these are among our inalienable rights.

In its declaration of belief regarding governments and laws in general, the Church has put its official stamp of approval upon the political philosophy of inalienable rights. (D. & C. 134:5.) These rights belong to all mankind, no matter under what government they live, and as far as the American nation is concerned, the constitution of the United States is designed to protect men in their rights and privileges. (D. & C. 98:4-10.)

INCANTATIONS.
See EXORCISM, MAGIC, SORCERY, WITCHCRAFT, By *incantations* is meant the use of spells or verbal charms, which are chanted, spoken,

or sung, as part of the ritual of magic. They are in effect the formula by which devils are supposed to be exorcised and by which sorceries are practiced. (Rev. 18:23.)

INCARNATE GOD.

See CHRIST, ONLY BEGOTTEN SON. Christ is the *Incarnate God.* That is, he is the Lord Omnipotent, a God "from all eternity to all eternity," and yet he came down from heaven and dwelt "in a tabernacle of clay." (Mosiah 3:5.) Though he had attained Godhood, yet he was thereafter invested with flesh and took upon himself the bodily nature and form of a mortal man. (Mosiah 15.) "I was in the world and made flesh my tabernacle, and dwelt among the sons of men," he said. (D. & C. 93:4; John 1:1-5, 14.)

INCARNATION.

See INCARNATE GOD.

INCOMMUNICABLE NAME.

See TETRAGRAMMATON.

INCONTINENCE.

See PASSIONS.

INCORRUPTION.

See CORRUPTION, IMMORTALITY, MORTALITY, RESURRECTION, SPIR-ITUAL BODIES. As used in the scriptures, *incorruption* is descriptive of the status of physical perfection enjoyed by immortal beings. Mortal bodies are corruptible; they are subject to change and decay, eventually deteriorating and going back to the mortal element from which they were created. Thus in the resurrection they will be raised from an earthly state of corruption to a heavenly state of incorruption. Disease, pain, decay, and physical deformity will all vanish away. (2 Ne. 9:7; Mosiah 16:10; Alma 40:2; 41:4; 1 Cor. 15:42-54.)

INDEBTEDNESS.

See DEBT.

INDEPENDENCE.

See AGENCY, BONDAGE, CHURCH WELFARE PLAN, DEBT, FREEDOM. Temporal and economic *independence* is essential if there is to be absolute freedom of worship. (D. & C. 44.) Anyone whose support comes from another person or agency is to a greater or lesser degree subject to the will and control of the supporting power. Hence the Lord revealed the principles of consecration, stewardships, storehouses, and the united order, so that, as he said, "the church may stand independent above all other creatures beneath the celestial world." (D. & C. 78:14.)

INDEPENDENT BRANCHES.
See BRANCHES.

INDIANS.
See AMERICAN INDIANS.

INDIGNATION.
See ANGER, WRATH. Righteous *indignation* is an attribute of Deity. It consists in a deep, intense, and righteous anger aroused by the mean, shameful, petty, and wicked acts of men. For instance: "It shall come to pass, because of the wickedness of the world, that I will take vengeance upon the wicked, for they will not repent; for the cup of mine indignation is full." (D. & C. 29:17; 35:14; 43:26; 56:1; 87:6; 88:88; 97:24; 101:10-11; 109:52; 124:52.) Indignation is poured out as a result of wickedness (D. & C. 124:48); it is avoided when men keep the commandments. (D. & C. 98:22, 47.)

Righteous indignation also swells up in the hearts of the prophets because of the wickedness of the world and because professing saints partake of the spirit of rebellion of the world. Indignation coming from anger, which has been aroused in unrighteousness, is to be shunned; it is a passion to be bridled.

INDUSTRIOUSNESS.
See WORK.

INFANT BAPTISM.
See ACCOUNTABILITY, ATONEMENT OF CHRIST, BAPTISM, CLINIC BAPTISMS, ORIGINAL SIN THEORY, REDEMPTION, REPENTANCE, SALVATION, SALVATION OF CHILDREN, STILLBORN CHILDREN, YEARS OF ACCOUNTABILITY. *Infant baptism* (*pedo-baptism*) is the practice of performing what is considered to be the ordinance of baptism for children, ordinarily for babies, who have not arrived at the years of accountability. Few practices constitute so gross a perversion of true Christian doctrine as does infant baptism, because the philosophical basis upon which it rests is one that denies the efficacy of the atoning sacrifice of Christ. Infant baptism assumes that all men are born in sin and that to be cleansed from this original sin they must be baptized; that is, its practice denies one of the most basic of all gospel truths, "That the Son of God hath atoned for original guilt, wherein the sins of the parents cannot be answered upon the heads of the children, for they are whole from the foundation of the world." (Moses 6:54.)

Actually, baptism is a spiritual rebirth into the kingdom of God (meaning both the Church on earth and the celestial kingdom in heaven), and since little children are already alive in Christ because of his atoning sacrifice, they do not need to born again to spiritual things. Further: Baptism follows repentance and is for the remission of sins, and because little children cannot sin and have no need of repentance, the false practice of infant baptism is of no avail. (*Doctrines of Salvation,* vol. 2, pp. 49-57.)

Among a host of pointed denunciations of infant baptism, Mormon said: "It is solemn mockery before God, that ye should baptize little children. . . . He that supposeth that little children need baptism is in the gall of bitterness and in the bonds of iniquity; for he hath neither faith, hope, nor charity; wherefore, should he be cut off while in the thought, he must go down to hell. For awful is the wickedness to suppose that God saveth one child because of baptism, and the other must perish because he hath no baptism. Wo be unto them that shall pervert the ways of the Lord after this manner, for they shall perish except they repent. . . . He that saith that little children need baptism denieth the mercies of Christ, and setteth at naught the atonement of him and the power of his redemption. Wo unto such, for they are in danger of death, hell, and an endless torment." (Moro. 8:5-26.)

INFIDELITY.
See SEX IMMORALITY.

INFIDELS.
See AGNOSTICISM, APOSTASY,

ATHEISM. Those who do not belong to an accepted system of religion are classed as *infidels.* Thus to Christians all non-Christians are infidels; and to Mohammedans all non-Mohammedans are so designated. Unfaithfulness to Christianity or to the marriage vows of chastity are also classed as *infidelity.*

INFINITE GOD.
See OMNIPOTENCE.

INFORMATION.
See KNOWLEDGE.

INGRATITUDE.
See ATONEMENT OF CHRIST, THANKSGIVING. Among all sins, none is so prevalent as the sin of *ingratitude.* It consists in failure to keep the commandments of God. Men have been "bought with a price" (1 Cor. 6:20; 7:23; 2 Pet. 2:1), the price of the blood and suffering of our Lord. Because they have been so purchased, they are redeemed from death and have opportunity to gain eternal life. Since they now belong to the Lord, he having paid so great a price for them, it is his right to expect them to keep the commandments. By failing to do so they manifest gross ingratitude for all that has been done for them. (*Doctrines of Salvation,* vol. 1, pp. 131-133.)

INIQUITY.

See DESPAIR, SIGNS OF THE TIMES, SIN, WICKEDNESS. *Iniquity* is sin, wickedness, unrighteousness; it results from disobedience, is of the devil, leads to hell, destroys men's souls; it is the great chain which keeps men in the prison of darkness, away from the saving light of the gospel.

This is the day when "the world is ripening in iniquity" (D. & C. 18:6), when the promise is being fulfilled that "iniquity shall abound" (D. & C. 45:27), when "the whole earth groans under the weight of its iniquity." (D. & C. 123:7.) "And the rebellious shall be pierced with much sorrow; for their iniquities shall be spoken upon the housetops, and their secret acts shall be revealed." (D. & C. 1:3.)

INITIATIVE.

See AGENCY. *Initiative,* the self-reliance and energy to undertake new enterprises and to do the work ahead, is a wholesome and uplifting characteristic. It is not meet that men should be commanded in all things. They are expected to make such wise use of their agency as to "be anxiously engaged in a good cause, and do many things of their own free will, and bring to pass much righteousness." (D. & C. 58:26-29.)

INNOCENCE.

See BAPTISM, CLEANLINESS, SALVATION OF CHILDREN, YEARS OF ACCOUNTABILITY. In the gospel sense, *innocence* is the state of purity and freedom from sin which men must possess to gain salvation in the kingdom of God. (Alma 11:37.) Little children live in a state of perfect innocence and consequently are saved without works on their part. *"Every spirit of man was innocent in the beginning; and God having redeemed man from the fall, men became again, in their infant state, innocent before God."* (D. & C. 93:38.) But "those who are accountable and capable of committing sin, . . . they must repent and be baptized, and humble themselves *as their little children,* and they shall all be saved with their little children." (Moro. 8:10.)

INQUISITIONS.

See APOSTASY, CHURCH OF THE DEVIL, DARK AGES, HERESY. In the Roman Catholic Church the systematic pursuit of heresy and the punishment of heretics is called *inquisition.* "The Inquisition," as defined in the *Encyclopedia Britannica,* is "the name given to the ecclesiastical jurisdiction dealing both in the middle ages and in later times with the detection and punishment of heretics and all persons guilty of any offence against Catholic orthodoxy. (Lat. *inquisitio,* an inquiry.)

"It is incorrect to say that the Inquisition made its appearance in the 13th century complete in all its principles and organs. It was the result of, or rather one step in, a process of evolution, the beginnings of which are to be traced back to the fourth century at least." (*Encyclopedia Britannica,* 1946 ed., vol. 12, p. 377.)

In the primitive Church there was no such thing as an inquisition; such runs counter to the whole principle of free agency. Excommunication or disfellowshipment were then the supreme penalties imposed upon heretics. But as the darkness of the great apostasy began to cover the earth, and as Lucifer gained an increasingly strong control over the minds of men, he began to introduce the principles of compulsion and unrighteousness which he had championed in the war in heaven.

By the 12th century formal inquisitions were underway in various nations. These tyrannical and evil ecclesiastical courts—on the merest breath of suspicion—imprisoned, burned at the stake, and confiscated the properties of untold thousands who were falsely or otherwise suspected of unorthodox beliefs. Even down to the 19th century in some places (1834 in Spain), these inquisitions were institutions of murder, plunder, and confiscation.

These inquisitions were particularly effective in France, Italy, and Spain, although from 1480 on the Spanish Inquisition was more of a national than a papal institution. Less inquisitorial tyranny was manifest in England, Germany, and the Balkan states. In Mexico City, in the national archives, there are now more than 1500 large, dictionary-size volumes recording the cases tried in the Mexican Inquisition, an extension of the Spanish Inquisition.

Although the confiscation of the real and personal property of heretics was a lesser punishment than life imprisonment and death, it was, in a very real sense, the practice which caused the civil powers to uphold the actions of these iniquitous papal courts. Properties were usually divided between the papacy and the state. As the Britannica says, "Confiscation was, indeed, most profitable to the secular princes, and there is no doubt that the hope of considerable gain was what induced many princes to uphold the inquisitorial administration, especially in the days of the decay of faith. The resistance of the south of France to the Capetian monarchs was to a large extent broken owing to the decimation of the bourgeoisie by the Inquisition and their impoverishment by the extortions of the" confiscating officers. (*Encyclopedia Britannica,* 1946 ed., vol. 12, pp. 377-383.)

INSANITY.
See YEARS OF ACCOUNTABILITY.

INSIGHT.
See DISCERNMENT.

INSPIRATION.

See GIFT OF THE HOLY GHOST, REVELATION. *Inspiration* is a form and degree of revelation. It is revelation that comes from the still small voice, from the whisperings of the Spirit, from the promptings of the Holy Ghost. All inspiration is revelation, but all revelation does not come by inspiration alone. The difference is one of kind and degree. The appearance of God to a mortal or the opening of the visions of eternity to him, though attended by inspiration, are in fact revelation of a higher order.

"I will tell you in your mind and in your heart, by the Holy Ghost, which shall come upon you and which shall dwell in your heart," the Lord says. Then he adds: "Now, behold, this is the spirit of revelation." (D. & C. 8:2-3.) It is also the spirit of inspiration; these two are one and the same in this kind of a case. Members of the Church have the gift of the Holy Ghost, which is the right and power, based on faithfulness, to have the constant companionship of that member of the Godhead, that is, it is the right and power to walk in the light of continuous inspiration and revelation.

INSPIRED VERSION OF THE BIBLE.

See APOCRYPHA, BIBLE, BOOK OF MORMON, DOCTRINE AND COVENANTS, KING JAMES VERSION OF THE BIBLE, LOST SCRIPTURE, PEARL OF GREAT PRICE, REVELATION, SCRIPTURE, STANDARD WORKS. As all informed persons know, the various versions of the Bible do not accurately record or perfectly preserve the words, thoughts, and intents of the original inspired authors. (Eighth Article of Faith; 1 Ne. 13.) In consequence, at the command of the Lord and while acting under the spirit of revelation, the Prophet corrected, revised, altered, added to, and deleted from the King James Version of the Bible to form what is now commonly referred to as the *Inspired Version of the Bible.* (D. & C. 35:20; 42:56-60; 45:60-61; 73:3-4; 93:53; 94:10; 104:58; 124:89.)

This inspired revision of the ancient scriptures was never completed by the Prophet, and up to the present time none of his successors have been directed by the Lord to carry the work forth to its final fruition. President George Q. Cannon has written: "On the 2nd day of February, 1833, the Prophet completed, *for the time being,* his inspired translation of the New Testament. No endeavor was made at that time to print the work. It was sealed up with the expectation that it would be brought forth at a later day with other of the scriptures. Joseph did not live to give to the world an authoritative publication of these translations. But the labor was its own reward, bringing in the performance a special blessing of broadened comprehension to the Prophet and a general blessing of enlightenment to the people through his subsequent teachings."

Again: "We have heard President Brigham Young state that the Prophet before his death had spoken to him about *going through the translation of the scriptures again and perfecting it upon points of doctrine which the Lord had restrained him from giving in plainness and fulness at the time of which we write.*" (George Q. Cannon, *Life of Joseph Smith,* new ed., pp. 147-148; *History of the Church,* vol. 1, p. 324; Sidney B. Sperry, *Knowledge is Power,* pp. 9-61.)

Such changes as the Prophet made in the Bible were done, in the main, by *topics* or *subjects.* He did not go from Genesis to Revelation and make all needed corrections in every passage as he came to it. True, in many passages all necessary changes were made; in others he was "restrained" by the Spirit from giving the full and clear meaning. As with all revealed knowledge, the Lord was offering new truths to the world, "line upon line, precept upon precept; here a little, and there a little." (D. & C. 128:21.) Neither the world nor the saints generally were then or are now prepared for the fulness of Biblical knowledge. The Lord was operating in conformity with the principle explained by Alma: "It is given unto many to know the mysteries of God; nevertheless they are laid under a strict command that they shall not impart

only according to the portion of his word which he doth grant unto the children of men, according to the heed and diligence which they give unto him." (Alma 12:9.)

Such Biblical revisions as have been made may be used with safety, and parts of these are now published by the Church in its standard works. The first 151 verses of the Old Testament, down to Genesis 6:13, are published as the Book of Moses in the Pearl of Great Price. But as restored by the Prophet the true rendition contains about 400 verses and a wealth of new doctrinal knowledge and historical data. The revised 24th chapter of Matthew is also found in the Pearl of Great Price.

Most of the Prophet's corrections were made in Genesis, Matthew, Mark, Luke, and the first six chapters of John. Some important doctrinal changes were made in Exodus and other Old Testament books. Very little was done in Acts, but a reasonable number of corrections were made in the various Epistles and in Revelation. In all cases where major changes were made, the student with spiritual insight can see the hand of the Lord manifest; *the marvelous flood of light and knowledge revealed through the Inspired Version of the Bible is one of the great evidences of the divine mission of Joseph Smith.*

The fact that some changes were made in a particular passage or chapter does not mean that all needed corrections were given even in that portion of the Bible. Important changes were made in several thousand verses, but there are yet thousands of passages to be revised, clarified, and perfected. After his work of revision, the Prophet frequently quoted parts of the King James Version, announced that they contained errors, and gave clarified translations —none of which he had incorporated into his prior revisions of the Bible.

There will be a not too distant day when all necessary changes shall be made in the Bible, and the Inspired Version—as then perfected—shall go forth to the world. It is with the full Biblical account as it is with the full Book of Mormon record—both are now hidden from the world and will so remain until, as the Lord said: "I shall see fit in mine own wisdom to reveal all things unto the children of men." (2 Ne. 27:22.)

INSTINCT.
See INTUITION, LIGHT OF CHRIST, MIND. *Instinct,* as found in men and animals, is the natural and involuntary urging to some particular action. Reason and intelligence, as men ordinarily define these terms, do not seem to be involved. Rather, whenever a particular stimuli is given, an automatic or instinctive action results.

Actually what men call instinct is simply one of the manifestations of the Light of Christ. It is through this light or power that the Lord "giveth life to all things," and it is by this means that "all things are governed." (D. & C. 88:13.) Thus as part of the implanting of life in living creatures, this same light ordains instinctive actions and reactions to preserve and perpetuate that life.

INSTITUTES OF RELIGION.
See RELIGIOUS EDUCATION.

INTEGRITY.
See HONESTY, JUSTICE, RIGHTEOUSNESS. The complete development of man's moral character in conformity with principles of justice and uprightness is termed *integrity.* A man of integrity is sound, incorruptible, and particularly strict about fulfilling the trusts reposed in him by others. *The highest manifestation of integrity is exhibited by those who conform their conduct to the terms of those gospel covenants and promises which they have made.* Integrity goes hand in hand with uprightness and righteousness, and the Lord loves those who have integrity of heart. (D. & C. 124:15, 20.) "The integrity of the upright shall guide them" (Prov. 11:3), and "The just man walketh in his integrity: his children are blessed after him." (Prov. 20:7.)

INTELLECT.

See MIND.

INTELLECTUALITY.

See MIND, PRE-EXISTENCE, SPIRITUALITY. Those powers of the mind by which men are enabled to know, reason, and think are collectively called the *intellect. Intellectuality* is the measure of the intellect, the degree of mentality a person has, the extent of one's ability to use his mind.

There is no sufficient secular explanation for the mind of man. Such understanding is found only in the gospel. By compliance with divine law the agency-endowed spirit children of the Eternal Father developed talents and abilities along various lines, including the power to think, reason, and understand. The measure of intellectuality thus earned by obedience to law is the exact amount which men have at the time of their birth into mortality. Accordingly some men have great mental ability in one field and some in another.

All accountable persons have sufficient innate capacity to know right from wrong and to work out their salvation in the kingdom of God. But it is spirtuality, not intellectuality, which is of prime importance in the salvation of man. Intellectuality of itself has no saving virtue; it is only when it is coupled with spirituality that the greatest benefits result.

INTELLIGENCE.

See INTELLIGENCES, KNOWLEDGE, LIGHT, RIGHTEOUSNESS, SPIRIT ELEMENT, TRUTH, WISDOM.
1. In the gospel sense, *intelligence* is far more than the capacity to know and understand, and the intelligent man is one who does more than acquire knowledge. "The glory of God is intelligence, or, in other words, light and truth," the Lord says. "Light and truth forsake that evil one." (D. & C. 93: 36-37.) Thus intelligence is the light and truth which comes from Christ who is the way, the life, the light, and the truth of the world.

Knowledge can be obtained and used in unrighteousness; Satan gains his power on this principle. But intelligence presupposes the wise and proper use of knowledge, a use that leads to righteousness and the ultimate attainment of exaltation. The devil has tremendous power and influence because of his knowledge, but he is entirely devoid of the least glimmering of intelligence. An intelligent person is one who applies his knowledge so as to progress in the things of the Spirit; he glories in righteousness. (*Way to Perfection*, pp. 225-231.) "Whatever principle of intelligence we attain unto in this life, it will rise with us in the resurrection. And if a person gains more knowledge and intelligence in this life through his diligence and obedience than another, he will have so much the advantage in the world to come." (D. & C. 130:18-19.)

2. *Intelligence,* or light and truth, is also used as a synonymn for *spirit element.* Scriptures using both terms speak of the self-existent nature of the substance involved. (D. & C. 93:29; 131:7-8.) Abraham calls the pre-existent spirits "the intelligences that were organized before the world was" (Abra. 3:22) because the intelligences were organized intelligence or in other words the spirit bodies were born from spirit element.

INTELLIGENCES.
See INTELLIGENCE, PRE-EXISTENCE, SPIRIT BIRTH, SPIRIT BODIES, SPIRIT CHILDREN, SPIRIT ELEMENT. Abraham used the name *intelligences* to apply to the spirit children of the Eternal Father. The intelligence or spirit element became intelligences after the spirits were born as individual entities. (Abra. 3:22-24.) Use of this name designates both the primal element from which the spirit offspring were created and also their inherited capacity to grow in grace, knowledge, power, and intelligence itself, until such intelligences, gaining the fulness of all things, become like their Father, the Supreme Intelligence. (*Teachings,* p. 354.)

INTEMPERANCE.
See PASSIONS.

INTENTS OF THE HEART.
See THOUGHTS.

INTERCESSION.
See ADVOCACY, ATONEMENT OF CHRIST, EXPIATION, INTERCESSOR, MEDIATION, PROPITIATION, RECONCILIATION. To Christ, the Father has given "power to make *intercession* for the children of men" (Mosiah 15:8), that is, he has the role of interceding, of mediating, of praying, petitioning and entreating the Father to grant mercy and blessings to men. (Rom. 8:34; Heb. 7:25.) Lehi said: "He shall make intercession for all the children of men; and they that believe in him shall be saved. And because of the intercession for all, all men come unto God; wherefore, they stand in the presence of him, to be judged of him according to the truth and holiness which is in him." (2 Ne. 2:9-10.)

One of the great Messianic prophecies foretold that Christ would make "intercession for the transgressors." (Isa. 53:12; Mosiah 14:12.) His great *Intercessory Prayer,* excerpts of which are found in the 17th chapter of John, with some of the same petitions later being repeated on behalf of the Nephites (3 Ne. 19), is one of the chief illustrations of his pleadings on behalf of his brethren.

Further, the Spirit of Christ "maketh intercession for us with groanings which cannot be uttered"

(Rom. 8:26-27), or, as the Prophet more aptly phrased it, "The Spirit maketh intercession for us with striving which cannot be expressed." (*Teachings*, p. 278.) It is, of course, the Light of Christ and not the Holy Ghost which strives with men. And even as Christ makes intercession for all men, so his saints should supplicate, pray, and intercede before the throne of Grace in behalf of all men with a view to hastening the purposes of the Lord among men. (1 Tim. 2:1.)

INTERCESSOR.

See ADVOCATE, ATONEMENT OF CHRIST, CHRIST, EXPIATOR, INTERCESSION, MEDIATOR, PROPITIATOR, RECONCILER. Christ is the great *Intercessor*, the One who intercedes and mediates between God and men. His advocacy, prayers, petitions, and entreaties are made for all men and especially for those who love and serve him. (John 17; 3 Ne. 19.)

INTERCESSORY PRAYER.

See INTERCESSION.

INTEREST.

See USURY.

INTERPRETATION OF TONGUES.

See TONGUES.

INTOLERANCE.

See TOLERANCE.

INTOXICATION.

See DRUNKENNESS.

INTUITION.

See CONSCIENCE, DISCERNMENT, DIVINATION, GIFT OF THE HOLY GHOST, INSTINCT, LIGHT OF CHRIST. Philosophers use the term *intuition* to describe a truth or rule of conduct that is known automatically and without reasoning. By this is meant that whatever knowledge is involved was received by some indefinable insight or spiritual perception. Thus all accountable persons, innately within themselves and independent of any outward teaching, know that it is wrong to commit murder.

Actually this knowledge comes to man from God as a free gift by the operation of the Light of Christ, the same Spirit which "giveth light to every man that cometh into the world." (D. & C. 84:46.) The saints who enjoy the gift and companionship of the Holy Ghost might also know things intuitively by revelation from that member of the Godhead, and persons who have subjected themselves to Lucifer might have information given them intuitively by the evil powers of divination.

INVENTIONS.

See SIGNS OF THE TIMES.

INVOCATIONS.

See PRAYER.

ISHMAELITES.

See BOOK OF MORMON, NEPH-
ITES AND LAMANITES. 1. That portion of the Lamanites who were
lineal descendants of the sons of
Ishmael were sometimes called
Ishmaelites. (Jac. 1:13-14; 4 Ne.
37-39.) Ishmael himself was a righteous man who believed the revelation of the Lord and who died
before Lehi's colony divided into
Nephite and Lamanite groups. (1
Ne. 16:34-35.)

2. Ishmael was the son of Abraham and Hagar and the progenitor of a posterity of *Ishmaelites*
that "shall not be numbered for
multitude." (Gen. 16:7-12; 17:20.)
"The sons of Ishmael peopled
the north and west of the Arabian
peninsula, and supposedly formed
the chief element of the Arab nation, the wandering Bedouin tribes.
They are now mostly Mohammedans, who look to him as their
spiritual father, as the Jews look to
Abraham. Their language, which
is generally acknowledged to have
been the Arabic commonly so
called, has been adopted with insignificant exceptions throughout
Arabia." (*Peloubet's Bible Dictionary,* p. 278.)

ISRAEL.

See ADOPTION, BELIEVING
BLOOD, ELECTION OF GRACE, FORE-
ORDINATION, GATHERING OF IS-
RAEL, GENTILES, HEBREWS, JEWS,
LEVITES, LOST TRIBES OF ISRAEL,
NEPHITES AND LAMANITES, PAT-
RIARCHAL CHAIN, RACES OF MEN,
SCATTERING OF ISRAEL, SIGNS OF
THE TIMES, TRIBES OF ISRAEL.
1. Jacob's name was changed to
Israel, "for as a prince," the divine
decree announced, "hast thou
power with God and with men, and
hast prevailed." (Gen. 32:24-30;
35:9-13; Hos. 12:1-5.) Literally, the
name Israel means *contender with
God,* the sense and meaning indi-
cating one who has succeeded in
his supplication before the Lord,
who has enlisted as a *soldier of
God,* who has become a *prince of
God.*

2. By divine command the name
was applied to the 12 tribes collectively. (Gen. 49:28; Ex. 3:16.)
Hundreds of millions of persons
have thus been Israelites, heirs of
the promises made to their fathers.
This great host, called while on
earth to be a peculiar people (Ex.
19:5-6; Deut. 14:2; 1 Pet. 2:9.),
were also a separate and distinct
group in pre-existence. (Deut. 32:
7-9.) Those mortal Israelites who
are faithful in all things, who obey
the full law of the gospel, will continue on as members of the house of
Israel in a future eternity, there
ruling as kings and priests forever
in the patriarchal chain.

3. Those who accept the gospel
become of the *house of Israel* regardless of what their literal blood
ancestry may have been. Because
the blood of Israel has been scattered among the Gentile nations,
nearly all who come into the

Church are in greater or lesser degree of the house of Israel literally. But if someone whose blood was wholly of Gentile lineage were converted, he would be adopted into the lineage of Abraham and Jacob and become of the house of Israel. (Abra. 2:9-11.)

That this adoption involves a literal change in the convert's blood was plainly taught by the Prophet. The Holy Ghost, he said, "is more powerful in expanding the mind, enlightening the understanding, and storing the intellect with present knowledge, of a man who is of the literal seed of Abraham, than one that is a Gentile, though it may not have half as much visible effect upon the body; for as the Holy Ghost falls upon one of the literal seed of Abraham, it is calm and serene; and his whole soul and body are only exercised by the pure spirit of intelligence; while the effect of the Holy Ghost upon a Gentile, is to *purge out the old*

blood, and make him actually of the seed of Abraham. That man that has none of the blood of Abraham (naturally) must have a new creation by the Holy Ghost." (*Teachings,* pp. 149-150.)

In the same way in which Gentiles by righteousness are adopted into the house of Israel—so that the promises made to Abraham, Isaac, and Jacob become their inheritance—those who are literally of the house of Jacob may lose their blessings by unrighteousness. *"They are not all Israel, which are of Israel,"* Paul said, for "They which are the children of the flesh, these are not the children of God." (Rom. 9:6-8.)

ISRAELITES.
See TRIBES OF ISRAEL.

ISRAELITISH COVENANT.
See ABRAHAMIC COVENANT.

J

JACK-MORMONS.
See MORMONS. Mormons who are lukewarm, indifferent to their covenants, not valiant in defense of the faith, who are members of the Church in name but not in deed, are sometimes colloquially called *Jack-Mormons.* Those in this category, unless they repent and keep the commandments, shall fail to gain an inheritance in the celestial world even though their

names have been listed on the records of the Church in this life. (D. & C. 76:79.)

JACOB.
See ISRAEL.

JACOBITES.
See BOOK OF MORMON, NEPHITES AND LAMANITES. That portion of the Nephites who were lineal descendants of Jacob the younger brother of Nephi were sometimes called *Jacobites.* (Jac. 1:13-14; 4 Ne. 37-39.)

JAH.
See CHRIST, JEHOVAH, LORD, YAHWEH. *Jah* (Hebrew *Yah*) is a contracted form of Jehovah, Jahveh, or Yahweh—all of which names have reference to Christ, the God of Israel. "Sing unto God, sing praises to his name: extol him that rideth upon the heavens *by his name JAH,* and rejoice before him." (Ps. 68:4.) In a number of Old Testament passages use of the name *Jah* to designate *Jehovah,* who is Christ (D. & C. 110:1-10), have been translated Lord. (Ex. 15:2; 17:16; 89:8; Isa. 38:11.)

JAHWEH.
See YAHWEH.

JAREDITES.
See BOOK OF MORMON, MAHONRI MORIANCUMER. Those who were descendants of Jared and his associates—a chosen people whose language was preserved by faith at the time of the confusion of tongues, when the people attempted to build the Tower of Babel—were called *Jaredites.* An abridgment of their history and of the Lord's dealings with them is contained in the Book of Ether. Some of the greatest heavenly manifestations ever vouchsafed to man were given to the Brother of Jared. (Ether 1; 2; 3; 4.)

JAREDITISH DISPENSATIONS.
See DISPENSATIONS.

JEALOUS.
See CHRIST, PERSONIFICATION. To keep ever before his people the exacting and exclusive devotion which he requires of them, and acting on the principle of personification, our Lord uses the word *Jealous* as one of his names. "For thou shalt worship no other god: for the Lord, *whose name is Jealous,* is a jealous God." (Ex. 34:14.) Among other things, use of this name is a complete refutation of the sectarian heresy (found in the creeds) that Deity is devoid of passions. (Ex. 20:5; Deut. 4:24; 5:9; 6:15; Josh. 24:19.)

JEHOVAH.

See ADONAI, CHRIST, ELOHIM, GREAT I AM, JAH, LORD, TETRA- GRAMMATON, YAHWEH. Christ is *Jehovah;* they are one and the same Person. The word *Jehovah* itself is the anglicized form of the Hebrew *Yahweh,* which refers to the God of Israel. To Abraham the Lord said: "I am the Lord thy God. . . . My name is Jehovah." (Abra. 2:7-8.) Later he revealed himself to Moses and others by the same name. (*Inspired Version,* Ex. 6:3; Ps. 83:18; Isa. 12:2.) In general, in the King James version of the Bible, the name Jehovah has been translated *Lord.*

The death and resurrection of Jehovah (and the consequent res- urrection of all men) is foretold in Isaiah in these words: "In the Lord JEHOVAH is everlasting strength. . . . Thy dead men shall live, *to- gether with my dead body shall they arise.* Awake and sing, ye that dwell in dust: for thy dew is as the dew of herbs, and *the earth shall cast out the dead.* . . . The earth also shall disclose her blood, and shall no more cover her slain." (Isa. 26:3, 19, 21.)

In this dispensation Christ ap- peared to Joseph Smith and Oliver Cowdery under his name Jehovah and accepted the Kirtland Temple as a house of the Lord. In this revealed account his appearance is described in detail. (D. & C. 110:1- 10.) It is interesting to note that comparable detailed descriptions were given of the appearance of the *God of Israel* to Moses and the elders of Israel (Ex. 24:9-10), and of the appearance of *Christ* to John the Revelator. (Rev. 1:13-18.)

JESUS.

See CHRIST, JESUS OF NAZARETH. Taken from the Hebrew *Yeshua, Jesus* is a masculine personal name meaning *Jehovah is salvation or deliverance;* and accordingly, with supreme propriety, it was chosen and revealed as the personal name of our Lord. (Luke 1:31.) This name—also found as *Jeshua, Josh- ua,* and *Jehoshua*—apparently was a common one among the ancient Jews. Variants of the name include *Hosea, Hoshea,* and *Oshea* —all meaning *deliverance.*

Though it was a common name anciently, its use by the Lord God Omnipotent as his personal name has given it a sacred connotation for all succeeding generations. (Acts 2:36.) Accordingly its pro- fane and repetitious use is not in keeping with the true spirit of reverence and worship.

JESUS OF NAZARETH.

See CHRIST, GALILEAN, JESUS, NAZARENE. Because he lived in Nazareth of Galilee, Christ was referred to by friend and foe alike as *Jesus of Nazareth.* (Matt. 21:11; Mark 1:24; Luke 18:37; 24:19; Acts 3:6.)

JEWS.

See GENTILES, HEBREWS, ISRAEL, KINGDOM OF ISRAEL, NEPHITES AND LAMANITES, SIGNS OF THE TIMES, TRIBES OF ISRAEL. Although the term *Jew* comes from the Hebrew *yehudi,* "one belonging to Judah," it has always been used to identify a much larger group than those who are of the tribe of Judah. Citizens of the *Kingdom of Judah,* no matter what their tribal affiliation, were called *Jews* or sometimes *Judeans.* Lehi and Ishmael, though descendants of Joseph, were Jews (*Doctrines of Salvation,* vol. 3, pp. 262-264; 2 Ne. 30:4; 33:8); Paul was a Jew, but his tribe was Benjamin (Acts 21:37-39; 22:3; Rom. 11:1; Philip. 3:5); and the present day Lamanites, a remnant who descended from Lehi of old, are Jews. (D. & C. 19:27; 57:4.) Christ was a Jew, and he taught that "salvation is of the Jews" (John 4:22), meaning that through that chosen race had come the prophets, the priesthood, and the Redeemer himself. Our present Bible, for instance, has come to us by way of the Jews. (2 Ne. 29.)

Rebellious Jews opposed our Lord in his ministry and finally brought about his crucifixion. Thereafter they were scattered among all nations, but when they "begin to believe in Christ" and turn to righteousness, they will be gathered back into the true sheepfold. (2 Ne. 30:7; 25:15-18; 1 Ne. 19:13-17.) The conversion of the Jews as a people, however, will not take place until after the Second Coming of the Son of Man. (D. & C. 45:51-53; Zech. 12:10-14; 13:6.)

JHVH, JHWH.

See TETRAGRAMMATON.

JOHN THE BAPTIST.

See AARONIC PRIESTHOOD, BAPTISM, ELIAS, RESTORATION OF THE GOSPEL. Few prophets rank with *John the Baptist.* Among other things, his ministry was foretold by Lehi (1 Ne. 10:7-10), Nephi (1 Ne. 11:27; 2 Ne. 31:4-18), and Isaiah (Isa. 40:3); Gabriel came down from the courts of glory to announce John's coming birth (Luke 1:5-44); he was the last legal administrator, holding keys and authority under the Mosaic dispensation (D. & C. 84:26-28); his mission was to prepare the way before, baptize, and acclaim the divine Sonship of Christ (John 1); and in modern times, on the 15th of May, 1829, he returned to earth as a resurrected being to confer the Aaronic Priesthood upon Joseph Smith and Oliver Cowdery. (Jos. Smith 2:66-75; D. & C. 13.)

Asked about our Lord's statement, "Among those that are born of women there is not a greater prophet than John the Baptist: but he that is least in the kingdom of God is greater than he" (Luke 7:28), the Prophet Joseph Smith explained: "First. He was entrusted with a divine mission of preparing the way before the face of the Lord. Whoever had such a trust committed to him before or since? No man.

"Secondly. He was entrusted with the important mission, and it was required at his hands, to baptize the Son of Man. Whoever had the honor of doing that? Whoever had so great a privilege and glory? Whoever led the Son of God into the waters of baptism, and had the privilege of beholding the Holy Ghost descend in the form of a dove, in witness of that administratration? . . .

"Thirdly. John, at that time, was the only legal administrator in the affairs of the kingdom there was then on the earth, and holding the keys of power. The Jews had to obey his instructions or be damned, by their own law; and Christ himself fulfilled all righteousness in becoming obedient to the law which he had given to Moses on the mount, and thereby magnified it and made it honorable, instead of destroying it. The son of Zacharias wrested the keys, the kingdom, the power, the glory from the Jews, by the holy anointing and decree of heaven."

In explaining how the least in the kingdom of heaven was greater than John, the Prophet said: "Whom did Jesus have reference to as being the least? Jesus was looked upon as having the least claim in God's kingdom, and [seemingly] was least entitled to their

credulity as a prophet; as though he had said—*'He that is considered the least among you is greater than John—that is I myself.'*" (*Teachings,* pp. 275-276.)

JOINT-HEIRS WITH CHRIST.

See CELESTIAL MARRIAGE, CHURCH OF THE FIRSTBORN, DAUGHTERS OF GOD, EXALTATION, FULNESS OF THE FATHER, GODHOOD, SALVATION, SONS OF GOD. As the literal Son of God—the Firstborn in the spirit, the Only Begotten in the flesh—Christ is the natural *heir* of his Father. It thus became his right to inherit, receive, and possess all that his Father had. (John 16:15.) And his Father is possessor of all things: the universe; all power, wisdom, and goodness; the fulness of truth and knowledge; and an infinity of all good attributes. By heirship and by obedience, going from grace to grace, the Son attained these same things. (D. & C. 93:5-17.)

By obedience to the fulness of gospel law, righteous men are adopted into the family of God so that they also become heirs, *joint-heirs with Christ* (Rom. 8:14-18; Gal. 3:26-29; 4:1-7), inheritors of all that the Father hath. (D. & C. 84:33-41.) In his famous King Follett Sermon, speaking of those who "shall be heirs of God and joint-heirs with Jesus Christ," the Prophet asked what their glory should be. Answering his own query, he described joint-heirship as inheriting *"the same power, the same glory and the same exaltation, until you arrive at the station of a God, and ascend the throne of eternal power,* the same as those who have gone before." (*Teachings,* p. 347.)

A joint-heir is one who inherits equally with all other heirs including the Chief Heir who is the Son. Each joint-heir has an equal and an undivided portion of the whole of everything. If one knows all things, so do all others. If one has all power, so do all those who inherit jointly with him. If the universe belongs to one, so it does equally to the total of all upon whom the joint inheritances are bestowed.

Joint-heirs are possessors of all things. (D. & C. 50:26-28.) All things are theirs for they have exaltation. (D. & C. 76:50-60.) They are made "equal" with their Lord. (D. & C. 88:107.) They gain all power both in heaven and on earth and receive the fulness of the Father, and all knowledge and truth are theirs. (D. & C. 93:15-30.) They are gods. (D. & C. 132:20.) Celestial marriage is the gate to this high state of exaltation. (*Doctrines of Salvation,* vol. 2, pp. 24, 35-39; D. & C. 131:1-4; 132.)

JOSEPHITES.

See BOOK OF MORMON, NEPHITES AND LAMANITES, REORGANIZED CHURCH OF JESUS CHRIST OF LATTER DAY SAINTS. 1. That por-tion of the Nephites who were lineal descendants of Joseph the younger brother of Nephi were sometimes called *Josephites.* (Jac. 1:13-14; 4 Ne. 37-39.)

2. It has been a common practice, over the years, for representatives of the Reorganized Church of Jesus Christ of Latter Day Saints to call themselves *Josephites* and to call the members of the true Church *Brighamites.* Their objective, of course, is to make it appear that they follow the Prophet Joseph Smith, but that the saints who came west with Brigham Young are following some other course. This claim is wholly untrue; Joseph Smith, under Christ, was the first earthly head of The Church of Jesus Christ of Latter-day Saints as that Church is now organized and functioning among men. Church members should not be so gullible as to go along with nomenclature which furthers the claims and interest of a false organization. (*Doctrines of Salvation,* vol. 1, p. 261.)

JOSEPH SMITH THE PROPHET.

See BOOK OF MORMON, CHURCH OF JESUS CHRIST OF LATTER-DAY SAINTS, DISPENSATION OF THE FULNESS OF TIMES, ELIAS, FIRST VISION, GAZELAM, GOSPEL, MORMONISM, NEW AND EVERLASTING COVENANT, PROPHETS, RESTORATION OF THE GOSPEL. In the providences of Almighty God, and according to the plan before ordained in the councils of eternity, *Joseph Smith, Jr.,* was born into mortality, December 23, 1805. As a pre-existent spirit he had ranked with Adam and Abraham; he was one of the noble and great ones of whom Abraham wrote (Abra. 3:22-23), a truth which President Joseph F. Smith also saw in vision. (*Gospel Doctrine*, 4th ed., p. 601.) In that prior existence, by diligence and obedience, he gained the spiritual stature and capacity which entitled him to be foreordained to stand as the head of the greatest of all gospel dispensations. (*Teachings,* p. 365.)

So great was his assigned mission, with reference to the "restitution of all things" (Acts 3:21), that holy prophets spoke of him, by name, thousands of years before his mortal birth. (2 Ne. 3.) And as to the mighty work to be started by him—there are as many prophecies foretelling it as there are about any other single subject, not even excepting the host of prophetic utterances about our Lord and his redemptive sacrifice.

In the spring of 1820, when the hour had come for the opening of the final gospel dispensation, young Joseph, then $14^1/_2$ years of age beheld in glory the Father and the Son. Thereafter Moroni visited him; he received, translated, and published the ancient Nephite record; other messengers came bringing keys, power, priesthood, and authority; revelations in great number were showered upon him; and by the power and commandment of the Lord Omnipotent he organized again on earth God's literal kingdom, The Church of Jesus Christ of Latter-day Saints. Finally, having done all things well —as had been before ordained and appointed—he sealed his testimony with his blood; was taken home to that God who gave him breath; and now—enthroned in eternal glory—he continues his appointed labors on the Lord's errand.

To the Church the Lord commanded: "Give heed unto all his words and commandments which he shall give unto you as he receiveth them, walking in all holiness before me; *For his word ye shall receive, as if from mine own mouth, in all patience and faith.*" (D. & C. 21:4-5.)

Joseph Smith's greatness lies in the work that he did, the spiritual capacity he developed, and the witness he bore of the Redeemer. Since the keys of salvation were restored to the Prophet, it is in and through and because of his latter-day mission that the full redemptive power of the Lord has again become available to men. It is because the Lord called Joseph Smith that salvation is again available to mortal men. *"Joseph Smith, the Prophet and Seer of the Lord, has done more, save Jesus only, for the salvation of men in this world, than any other man that ever lived in it."* (D. & C. 135:3.)

JOURNALS.

See BOOK OF REMEMBRANCE, RECORD KEEPING. Members of the Church should keep accurate family records of births, marriages, deaths, blessings of children, baptisms, ordinations, and items of this sort which pertain to their own welfare and which may be of benefit to posterity. There is no particular obligation to keep a daily *journal* or diary, but special worthwhile events should be recorded and preserved. (*Doctrines of Salvation,* vol. 2, pp. 204-206.)

JOY.

See CHEERFULNESS, REJOICING, SALVATION. "Men are, that they might have *joy*." (2 Ne. 2:25.) That is, the very purpose of man's creation is to enable him to gain joy; it is the object and end of existence. The process of acquiring this joyful state of happiness began in pre-existence. It was there that "all the sons of God shouted for joy" (Job 38:7) at the prospect of coming to earth and undergoing the probationary experiences thereof.

Here in mortality men gain joy only by obedience to gospel law, the gospel itself being the "good tidings of great joy, which shall be to all people." (Luke 2:10.) Indeed, the great results of gospel obedience are "righteousness, and peace, and joy in the Holy Ghost." (Rom. 14:17.) *"Happiness is the object*

and design of our existence," the Prophet said, *"and will be the end thereof, if we pursue the path that leads to it; and this path is virtue, uprightness, faithfulness, holiness, and keeping all the commandments of God."* (*Teachings,* pp. 255-256.)

Joy is a gift of the Spirit. It comes from the Holy Ghost, is granted to those who gain a remission of their sins (Mosiah 4:3, 20; Alma 22:15), and there is great joy in heaven when sinners repent. (Luke 15:7; D. & C. 18:13-16.) It is in the Lord that the saints rejoice (Ps. 97:12), and he in turn rejoices over the righteous. (Deut. 30:9.) In the latter-days Israel "shall come to Zion, singing with songs of everlasting joy." (D. & C. 45:71; 66:11; 101:18; 109:39; 133:33; Isa. 51:11.)

Obtaining exaltation consists in gaining a fulness of joy; it is to enter into the joy of the Lord. (D. & C. 51:19.) The saints are to "reap eternal joy" for all their sufferings (D. & C. 109:76), though their joy is not to be full in this life. (D. & C. 101:36.) A fulness of joy is found only among resurrected, exalted beings. (D. & C. 93:33.) "Those who have died in Jesus Christ may expect to enter into all that fruition of joy when they come forth, which they possessed or anticipated here." (*Teachings,* p. 295.) Christ himself endured all things, including the cross, "for the joy that was set before him" (Heb. 12:2), and he has obtained a fulness of joy. (3 Ne. 17:20; 28:10.)

JUDAH.

See JEWS.

JUDEANS.

See JEWS.

JUDGE OF ALL THE EARTH.

See CHRIST, JUDGES, JUDGMENT, JUDGMENT DAY, JUDGMENTS OF GOD. Christ is the *Judge of all the Earth*, "For the Father judgeth no man, but hath committed all judgment unto the Son." (John 5:22; Ps. 50:6; Acts 10:42.) His judgment is administered with perfect justice (Isa. 9:7); "with righteousness shall he judge the poor, and reprove with equity for the meek of the earth." (Isa. 11:4.) "As I hear, I judge," he said, "and my judgment is just; because I seek not mine own will, but the will of the Father which hath sent me." (John 5:30.) In the coming day of judgment, when He judges whose judgment is just, perfect justice will be administered to all men. "Shall not the Judge of all the earth do right?" (Gen. 18:25; Ps. 94:1-2.)

JUDGES.

See JUDGE OF ALL THE EARTH, JUDGES IN ISRAEL, JUDGMENT, JUDGMENT DAY. Men are "their own *judges*" in the sense that they elect "to do good or do evil," consequently obtaining certain kinds of bodies and attributes, both of which they will have restored to them again in the resurrected state. (Alma 41; D. & C. 88:16-32.) But there will also be judges who dispense justice to others. Christ is the great and eternal Judge of all. (John 5:22; Acts 10:42.) "Ye must all stand before the judgment-seat of Christ," Mormon wrote, "yea, every soul who belongs to the whole human family of Adam; and ye must stand to be judged of your works, whether they be good or evil." (Morm. 3:20.)

Under Christ, selected agents and representatives shall sit in judgment upon specified peoples and nations. Scriptural intimations indicate that there will be a great judicial hierarchy, each judge acting in his own sphere of appointment and in conformity with the eternal principles of judgment which are in Christ. When John wrote of that day of judgment incident to the Second Coming of our Lord, he said: *"I saw thrones, and they sat upon them, and judgment was given unto them."* (Rev. 20:4.)

Our Lord promised his 12 apostolic ministers in Jerusalem that when he came in glory, they also should "sit upon twelve thrones, judging the twelve tribes of Israel." (Matt. 19:28; Luke 22:30.) "It hath gone forth in a firm decree, by the will of the Father, that mine apostles, the Twelve which were with me in my ministry at Jerusalem, shall stand at my right hand at the day of my coming in a pillar of fire, being clothed with robes of righteousness, with crowns upon their heads, in glory even as I am, *to judge the whole house of Israel, even as many as have loved me and kept my commandments, and none else."* (D. & C. 29:12.)

Some 600 years before the first coming of our Lord, an angel told Nephi, "The twelve apostles of the Lamb . . . are they who shall judge the twelve tribes of Israel; wherefore, the twelve ministers of thy seed shall be judged of them; for ye are of the house of Israel. And these twelve ministers whom thou beholdest shall judge thy seed." (1 Ne. 12:9-10.) Then to those 12 Nephite ministers, the resurrected Lord said: *"Ye shall be judges of this people, according to the judgment which I shall give unto you, which shall be just.* Therefore, what manner of men ought ye to be? Verily I say unto you, even as I am." (3 Ne. 27:27; Morm. 3:19.)

Nor is this principle of placing eternal judgment in the hands of the Lord's agents, who have undergone the testing of mortality along with those who are to be judged, limited to the Jewish and Nephite Twelves. Paul said that the saints should judge both the world and angels (1 Cor. 6:2-3); and the faithful elders have this promise relative to those who reject their testimony, "Know this, that *in the day of judgment you shall be judges of that house, and condemn them;* And it shall be more tolerable for the heathen in the day of judg-

ment, than for that house." (D. & C. 75:21-22; Matt. 10:14-15.) Daniel has left us the assurance that when the Ancient of Days sits in that great council at Adam-ondi-Ahman that then judgment will be given to the saints of the Most High. (Dan. 7:22.)

We have every reason to expect that the saints and the world will be judged by the apostles and prophets sent to carry the message of salvation to them; and that the great hierarchal chain of judgment with Christ at the head, will include Adam and the prophets of all ages, Peter and the apostles of all ages, and all the elders of the kingdom of all ages who have kept their covenants, died in the faith, and who are entitled therefore, as the Lord said, "to receive a crown of righteousness, and to be clothed upon, even as I am, to be with me, that we may be one" (D. & C. 29: 13.)

JUDGES IN ISRAEL.

See BISHOPS, BISHOPS COURT, ISRAEL, JUDGES, JUDGMENT. From Moses to Samuel, Israel was governed by *judges*. While Israel was still in the wilderness, Moses was the chief judge, who heard the hard causes, standing "for the people to God-ward," and under him were judges of thousands, of hundreds, of fifties, and of tens. (Ex. 18.) Seventy elders also stood with him to bear the burdens of the people. (Num. 11.) Proportionately as Israel was faithful, this system prevailed until Saul was anointed king. Then the civil power was vested in the kings while the spiritual powers remained in the prophets who governed the Church.

From the death of King Mosiah to the ministry of Christ among them, the Nephites were also ruled by judges. (Mosiah 29.) Alma the younger was elected as the first Chief Judge, and he was also the presiding High Priest over the Church. After he left the judgment seat to devote himself exclusively to the work of the ministry, the civil and ecclesiastical powers were vested in separate hands. (Alma 4.)

In this day, in civil matters the saints are subject to the powers that be, and will so continue until He rules whose right it is. But in ecclesiastical matters, the Lord has restored his system of judges with the bishop being the *judge in Israel,* having power, as it was anciently, "to divide the lands of the heritage of God unto his children; And to judge his people by the testimony of the just, and by the assistance of his counselors, according to the laws of the kingdom which are given by the prophets of God." (D. & C. 58:14-22; 64:37-40.) Eventually, in the millennial day, the judges in Israel will again have both civil and ecclesiastical jurisdiction, for the Lord has promised his saints that they shall have no laws but his laws when he comes. (D. & C. 38:22.)

Speaking of the great latter-day era of restoration, of the day when "Zion shall be redeemed with judgment, and her converts with righteousness," the Lord made this promise to Israel: "I will restore thy judges as at the first, and thy counselors as at the beginning: afterwards thou shalt be called, The city of righteousness, the faithful city." (Isa. 1:26-27.) Thus the fact that judges have been restored in Israel becomes one of the great evidences of the divinity of the Lord's latter-day work. Where the Lord's judges are, there is his kingdom; where these judges are not, there the earthly kingdom of God is not.

JUDGMENT.

See EQUITY, JUDGE OF ALL THE EARTH, JUDGES, JUDGES IN ISRAEL, JUDGMENT DAY, JUDGMENTS OF GOD, JUSTICE, RIGHTEOUSNESS. *Judgment* consists in the power to arrive at a wise and righteous decision and in the execution of that decision, to the blessing of the righteous and the condemnation of the wicked. It is an attribute of Deity. "The Lord is a God of judgment." (Isa. 30:18.) "The Lord shall endure for ever: he hath prepared his throne for judgment. . . . The Lord is known by the judgment which he executeth." (Ps. 9:7, 16.) "Righteousness and judgment are the habitation of his throne." (Ps. 97:2.) "He is the Rock, his work is perfect: for all his ways are judgment: a God of truth and without iniquity, just and right is he." (Deut. 32:4.) "I will execute judgment: I am the Lord." (Ex. 12:12; Ps. 89:14; Isa. 61:8.) "Judgment goeth before the face of him who sitteth upon the throne and governeth and executeth all things." (D. & C. 88:40.)

Men must have knowledge of the attribute of judgment in God if they are to have faith and gain salvation. "Without the idea of the existence of this attribute in the Deity," the Prophet says, "it would be impossible for men to exercise faith in him for life and salvation, seeing that it is through the exercise of this attribute that the faithful in Christ Jesus are delivered out of the hands of those who seek their destruction; for if God were not to come out in swift judgment against the workers of iniquity and the powers of darkness, his saints could not be saved; for it is by judgment that the Lord delivers his saints out of the hands of all their enemies, and those who reject the gospel of our Lord Jesus Christ. But no sooner is the idea of the existence of this attribute planted in the minds of men, than it gives power to the mind for the exercise of faith and confidence in God, and they are enabled by faith to lay hold on the promises which are set before them, and wade through all the tribulations and afflictions to which they are subjected by reason of the persecution from those who know not God, and obey not the gospel of our Lord Jesus Christ, believing that in due time the Lord will come out in swift judgment against their enemies, and they shall be cut off from before him, and that in his own due time he will bear them off conquerors, and more than conquerors, in all things." (*Lectures on Faith,* pp. 45-46.)

Judgment is manifest in all of the Lord's doings. "Zion shall be redeemed," for instance, "with judgment, and her converts with righteousness." (Isa. 1:27.) To aid in perfecting their lives, men are commanded to "seek judgment" (Isa. 1:17) of the kind administered by the Lord, having ever before them the realization, "For with what judgment ye judge, ye shall be judged." (Matt. 7:2.)

JUDGMENT BAR.
See JUDGMENT DAY.

JUDGMENT DAY.
See BOOK OF LIFE, CELESTIAL LAW, ESCHATOLOGY, JUDGE OF ALL THE EARTH, JUDGES, JUDGMENT, JUDGMENTS OF GOD, MILLENNIUM, RESURRECTION, SECOND COMING OF CHRIST, SIGNS OF THE TIMES, SPIRIT WORLD, TELESTIAL LAW, TERRESTRIAL LAW, WORLD. 1. Whenever the judgments of God are poured out upon men, it is a *day of judgment,* a day of vengeance, a day when in a very realistic sense the books have been

401

opened, the condemned persons found wanting, and a just punishment meted out to them.

Inspired history abounds in illustrations of this type of judgment day. For the entire population of the earth, except those on the ark, the flood of Noah was a day of judgment and destruction. (Gen. 7: 11-24; 1 Pet. 3:20-21.) Judgment day came to Sodom and Gomorrah when the Lord rained fire and brimstone upon them (Gen. 18; 19), and it came to Pharaoh and his Egyptian hosts when they were subjected to the plagues and were finally drowned in the Red Sea. (Ex. 7; 8; 9; 10; 11; 14.) Korah and his band stood before the judgment bar when the earth opened and swallowed them, and their 14,700 sympathizers who died of the plague were likewise judged and found wanting. (Num. 16.)

It was judgment day for the Amalekites when Israel, at the Lord's command, utterly destroyed them and all their property. (1 Sam. 15.) The rebellious Nephites destroyed in the tempests, earthquakes, whirlwinds, and fires at the time of the crucifixion faced their judgment day. (3 Ne. 8; 9; 10.) People in the world today, suffering in the wars and perils the Lord has decreed should prevail in the last days (D. & C. 63:32-36), are similarly called upon to face a day of judgment.

2. Death itself is an initial *day of judgment* for all persons, both the righteous and the wicked. When the spirit leaves the body at death, it is taken home to that God who gave it life, meaning that it returns to live in the realm of spiritual existence. (Eccles. 12:7.) At that time the spirit undergoes a partial judgment and is assigned an inheritance in paradise or in hell to await the day of the first or second resurrection. The righteous go to paradise, "a state of happiness, . . . a state of rest, a state of peace, where they shall rest from all their troubles and from all care, and sorrow." The wicked are "cast out into outer darkness; there shall be weeping, and wailing, and gnashing of teeth, and this because of their own iniquity, being led captive by the will of the devil." (Alma 40:11-14; Luke 16:19-31.)

3. Christ's Second Coming will be a *day of judgment* for all those then living and for the righteous dead (and in a sense for the wicked dead also). "When the Son of man shall come in his glory, and all the holy angels with him, then shall he sit upon the throne of his glory: And before him shall be gathered all nations: and he shall separate them one from another, as a shepherd divideth his sheep from the goats: And he shall set the sheep on his right hand, but the goats on the left." (Matt. 25:31-46.)

"I will come near to you to judgment," the Lord says, speaking of his Second Coming, "and I will be a swift witness against the sorcerers, and against the adulterers, and against false swearers, and against those that oppress the hireling in his wages, the widow, and the fatherless, and that turn aside the stranger from his right, and fear not me, saith the Lord of hosts." (Mal. 3:5.)

That is the day when every person then living shall find answer to the queries, "Who may abide the day of his coming? and who shall stand when he appeareth?" In that day "he shall sit as a refiner and purifier" (Mal. 3:2-3); "all the proud, yea, and all that do wickedly" (Mal. 4:1), shall be burned as stubble. "And every corruptible thing, both of man, or of the beasts of the field, or of the fowls of the heavens, or of the fish of the sea, that dwells upon all the face of the earth, shall be consumed." (D. & C. 101:24.)

"I have trodden the winepress alone, and have brought judgment upon all people," our Lord will say at the day of his Second Coming. To the wicked that judgment day is a "day of vengeance"; to the righteous it is a year of redemption, for they shall abide the day. (D. & C. 133:50-53.)

Of the judgment to take place at the Second Coming, John wrote: "I saw thrones, and they sat upon them, and judgment was given unto them: and I saw the souls of them that were beheaded for the witness of Jesus, and for the word of God, and which had not worshipped the beast, neither his image, neither had received his mark upon their foreheads, or in their hands; and they lived and reigned with Christ a thousand years." The wicked, he saw, "lived not again until the thousand years were finished." (Rev. 20:3-6; D. & C. 88:95-99.)

4. After all men have been resurrected the day of the great *final judgment* will come. Every living soul shall then stand before God, the books will be opened, and the dead will be judged out of those things written in the books, according to their works. (Rev. 20:11-15.) "And it shall come to pass," Jacob said, "that when all men shall have passed from this first death unto life, insomuch as they have become immortal, they must appear before the judgment-seat of the Holy One of Israel; and then cometh the judgment, and then must they be judged according to the holy judgment of God." (2 Ne. 9:15-16.)

5. Though there are specific times and formal occasions designated as days of judgment, in the final analysis every day is a *day of judgment* for every person, and every man is his own judge. By obedience to celestial, terrestrial, or telestial law men thereby develop celestial, terrestrial, or telestial bodies, which particular kind of bodies are then restored to them in the resurrection. (D. & C. 88:16-33.)

"It is requisite with the justice of God that men should be judged according to their works," Alma says, "and if their works were good in this life, and the desires of their hearts were good, that they should also, at the last day, be restored unto that which is good. And if their works are evil they shall be restored unto them for evil." (Alma 41:3-4.) The kind of body gained in this life and restored to a person in the resurrection determines the degree of glory inherited in eternity. Thus men are "their own judges," Alma concludes, for by their daily acts they judge or choose "whether to do good or do evil." (Alma 41:7.)

It is very evident that men will not have to await the day of final judgment—the formal occasion when every living soul will stand before the judgment bar, an event that will not take place until the last soul has been resurrected—to learn their status and the degree of glory they are to receive in eternity. Those who are living a telestial law will be swept off the earth at the Second Coming. (D. & C. 101:24; Mal. 3; 4.) Those who come forth in the morning of the first resurrection, who "are Christ's, the first fruits," will have celestial bodies and go to a celestial kingdom. "Those who are Christ's at his coming" will come forth with terrestrial bodies and go to a terrestrial kingdom. Similarly those coming forth in the beginning of the second resurrection will have telestial bodies and go to a telestial kingdom, while the sons of perdition, the last to be resurrected, will have bodies capable of receiving no glory and will be cast out with the devil and his angels forever. (D. & C. 88:98-102.)

No one has yet been resurrected with any kind of a body except a celestial. Those who were with Christ in his resurrection will all have eternal inheritance in his celestial presence. (D. & C. 133:54-56.) Though there is yet to be a day of formal judgment for all men, yet there is no question, for instance, of the reward that Abraham, Isaac, and Jacob will receive in that day. "They have entered into their exaltation, according to the promises, and sit upon thrones, and are not angels but are gods," the revelation records. (D. & C. 132:29-37.) The same is true of Adam, Enoch, Noah, Moses, and the faithful saints from the beginning to the day of Christ.

JUDGMENT SEAT OF CHRIST.
See JUDGMENT DAY.

JUDGMENTS OF GOD.
See ABOMINATION OF DESOLATION, ACTS OF GOD, GOD, JUDGMENT DAY, JUSTICE, SIGNS OF THE TIMES. In all ages the Lord pours out his *judgments* upon the children of disobedience. Famines, captivity, plagues, floods, lightnings, hailstorms, pestilences, tempests, earthquakes, wars, fire and brimstone raining from heaven —all these and infinitely more are sent of God upon men who forsake him and his laws. (Lev. 26; Deut.

28; 29; 30; 3 Ne. 8; 9; 10; D. & C. 43:25; 63:32-33; 88:88-91.) Obviously these judgments come upon peoples and nations to punish them for their rebellion and to humble them that peradventure they will turn to righteousness. And obviously also a righteous minority group may be called upon to suffer with those who are receiving a just reward for their unholy deeds. (*Teachings,* pp. 162-163; Dan. 11:35.)

Though the judgments of God consist in outpourings of wrath and vengeance upon those immediately subject to them, as they affect the great body of the Lord's children (both those in pre-existence and those in mortality), they are acts of mercy. What a curse it would have been, for instance, for righteous pre-existent spirits to have been sent to earth as the children of the inhabitants of Sodom and Gomorrah where every evil abomination was enthroned. What chance would they have had to walk in the paths of uprightness?

JUSTICE.

See EQUALITY, EQUITY, HONESTY, INTEGRITY, JUDGMENT, JUSTIFICATION, MERCY, RIGHTEOUSNESS, SALVATION FOR THE DEAD, UPRIGHTNESS. That which conforms to the mind and will of God and is righteous and proper before him is *just.* A just punishment, for instance, is one that is deserved because the recipient violated the law, thus meriting the particular penalty that always accompanies violation of that law. *Justice* deals with the unbending, invariable results that always and ever flow from the same causes. It carries a connotation of righteousness, fairness, impartiality. It embraces the principle and practice of just dealing, of conformity to a course of perfect rectitude, of adherence to a standard of complete integrity.

Justice is one of the attributes of God. "Publish the name of the Lord," Moses proclaimed, "ascribe ye greatness unto our God. He is the Rock, his work is perfect: for all his ways are judgment: a God of truth and without iniquity, *just* and right is he." (Deut. 32:3-4.) *"Justice* and judgment are the habitation of thy throne: mercy and truth shall go before thy face," the psalmist wrote. (Ps. 89:14.) "There is no God else beside me," the Lord says, "a *just* God and a Saviour." (Isa. 45:21; Zeph. 3:5; Zech. 9:9; Rev. 15:3-4.)

Both faith in God and salvation in his kingdom are attainable because of the justice of God and because men gain a knowledge of this particular attribute of Deity. "It is also necessary, in order to the exercise of faith in God unto life and salvation," the Prophet taught, "that men should have the idea of the existence of the attribute *justice* in him; for without the idea of the existence of the attribute justice in the Deity men could not have confidence sufficient to place themselves under his guidance and direction; for they would be filled with fear and doubt lest the judge of all the earth would not do right, and thus fear or doubt, existing in the mind, would preclude the possibility of the exercise of faith in him for life and salvation. But when the idea of the existence of the attribute justice in the Deity is fairly planted in the mind, it leaves no room for doubt to get into the heart, and the mind is enabled to cast itself upon the Almighty without fear and without doubt, and with the most unshaken confidence, believing that the judge of all the earth will do right." (*Lectures on Faith,* p. 45.)

According to the terms and conditions of the great plan of redemption, *justice demands that a penalty be paid for every violation of the Lord's laws.* This necessarily must be so or this mortal existence could not fulfil its purpose as a probationary and preparatory state. Since mortal man is on probation to prepare himself for eternity, and since he is endowed with the great gift of free agency, it follows that he must be held accountable for his disobedience. Otherwise this sphere of existence would not provide the test nor give the experience which would qualify him to return to the presence of God hereafter.

Now, all mankind is in a fallen state and has pursued a course of disobedience; therefore, in the mercy of God, a way must be pro- vided "to appease the demands of justice" and escape the just penalties attached to disobedience. The way of escape is through the atonement of our Lord, the redemption that is thus offered taking effect "only on conditions of repentance."

After setting forth how this great "plan of mercy" operates, Alma reasoned as follows: "Now, repentance could not come unto men except there were a punishment, which also was eternal as the life of the soul should be, affixed opposite to the plan of happiness, which was as eternal also as the life of the soul. Now, how could a man repent except he should sin? How could he sin if there was no law? How could there be a law save there was a punishment? Now, there was a punishment affixed, and a just law given, which brought remorse of conscience unto man. Now, if there was no law given—if a man murdered he should die— would he be afraid he would die if he should murder? And also, if there was no law given against sin men would not be afraid to sin. And if there was no law given, if men sinned what could justice do, or mercy either, for they would have no claim upon the creature?"

Then Alma returns to his explanation as to how the law of mercy and of justice is made operative because of repentance and the atoning sacrifice of our Lord. "But there is a law given, and a punishment affixed," he says, "and a repentance granted; which repentance, mercy claimeth; otherwise, justice claimeth the creature and executeth the law, and the law inflicteth the punishment; if not so, the works of justice would be destroyed, and God would cease to be God. . . . Behold, justice exerciseth all his demands, and also mercy claimeth all which is her own; and thus, none but the truly penitent are saved." (Alma 42; D. & C. 88: 40.)

Thus it is that the justice of God divides "the wicked from the righteous," the wicked going to an "awful hell," to suffer the eternal torment of the second death, and the righteous going to the kingdom of God. (1 Ne. 15:30-35; Jac. 6:10; Mosiah 2:38; Alma 12:32; D. & C. 88:35.) Justice and judgment are the penalty affixed for disobedience (D. & C. 82:4); none are exempt from the justice of God (D. & C. 107:84); and perfect justice will be administered to all men in the day of judgment. (2 Ne. 9:46.)

Perhaps no doctrine of the gospel better illustrates the eternal justice of God than the doctrine of salvation for the dead. Only a small part of the earth's inhabitants have so much as heard the name of Christ during their mortal probations, with only a yet smaller portion of them having opportunity to accept the fulness of the principles of salvation. And yet in the wisdom and justice of the Omnipotent, every soul will have a just and fair opportunity to hear the gospel preached and accept its saving truths.

Speaking about the justice of the great Lawgiver as such is manifest in the doctrine of salvation for the dead, the Prophet said: "While one portion of the human race is judging and condemning the other without mercy, the Great Parent of the universe looks upon the whole of the human family with a fatherly care and paternal regard; he views them as his offspring, and without any of those contracted feelings that influence the children of men, causes 'his sun to rise on the evil and on the good, and sendeth rain on the just and on the unjust.' (Matt. 5:45.) He holds the reigns of judgment in his hands; he is a wise Lawgiver, and will judge all men, not according to the narrow, contracted notions of men, but 'according to the deeds done in the body whether they be good or evil,' or whether these deeds were done in England, America, Spain, Turkey, or India. He will judge them, 'not according to what they have not, but according to what they have,' those who have lived without law, will be judged without law, and those who have a law, will be judged by that law.

"We need not doubt the wisdom and intelligence of the great Jehovah; he will award judgment or mercy to all nations according to their several deserts, their means of obtaining intelligence, the laws by which they are governed, the facilities afforded them of obtaining correct information, and his inscrutable designs in relation to the human family; and when the designs of God shall be made manifest, and the curtain of futurity be withdrawn, we shall all of us eventually have to confess that the Judge of all the earth has done right." (*Teachings,* p. 218.)

JUSTIFICATION.

See HOLY SPIRIT OF PROMISE, SALVATION BY GRACE, SANCTIFICATION. In summarizing the plan of salvation, Adam taught: "By the water ye keep the commandment; by the Spirit ye are *justified,* and by the blood ye are sanctified." (Moses 6:60.) And on the day the Church was organized in this dispensation, writing by way of revelation, the Prophet recorded: "We know that *justification* through the grace of our Lord and Savior Jesus Christ is just and true." (D. & C. 20:30.) Compliance with this basic doctrine of the gospel, the law of justification, is thus essential to salvation. Indeed, one of the great religious contentions among the sects of Christendom is whether men are justified by faith alone, without works, as some erroneously suppose Paul taught (Acts 13:38-39; Rom. 3:19-28; 4:5; 5:1-10; Gal. 2:15-21; 2 Ne. 2:5), or whether they are justified by works of righteousness as James explained. (Jas. 2:14-26.)

What then is the law of justification? It is simply this: "All covenants, contracts, bonds, obligations, oaths, vows, performances, connec-

tions, associations, or expectations" (D. & C. 132:7), in which men must abide to be saved and exalted, must be entered into and performed in righteousness so that the Holy Spirit can justify the candidate for salvation in what has been done. (1 Ne. 16:2; Jac. 2:13-14; Alma 41:15; D. & C. 98; 132:1, 62.) *An act that is justified by the Spirit is one that is sealed by the Holy Spirit of Promise, or in other words, ratified and approved by the Holy Ghost.* This law of justification is the provision the Lord has placed in the gospel to assure that no unrighteous performance will be binding on earth and in heaven, and that no person will add to his position or glory in the hereafter by gaining an unearned blessing.

As with all other doctrines of salvation, justification is available because of the atoning sacrifice of Christ, but it becomes operative in the life of an individual only on conditions of personal righteousness. As Paul taught, men are not justified by the works of the Mosaic law alone any more than men are saved by those works alone. The grace of God, manifest through the infinite and eternal atonement wrought by his Son, makes justification a living reality for those who seek righteousness. (Isa. 53:11; Mosiah 14:11.)

JUST ONE.

See CHRIST, HOLY ONE, JUSTICE. Christ is the *Just One* (Acts 3:14), signifying that perfect justice, equity, judgment, and impartiality are embodied in his person.

JUVENILE DELINQUENCY.
See SIGNS OF THE TIMES.

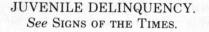

KEEPER OF THE GATE.

See CHRIST, DOOR OF THE SHEEP, PEARLY GATES; WAY, TRUTH, AND LIFE. Christ is the *Keeper of the Gate.* He it is who shall admit men into the presence of the Father. (D. & C. 132:12.) He opens the gate to the righteous and bars it to the wicked. Sectarian traditions placing Peter or anyone else as guardian of the pearly gates are false, for *Christ "employeth no servant there; and there is none other way save it be by the gate; for he cannot be deceived, for the Lord God is his name."* (2 Ne. 9:41-43.)

KEY OF DAVID.

See CHRIST, KEYS, KEYS OF SALVATION, KEYS OF THE KINGDOM, MESSIANIC PROPHECIES, SON OF DAVID. From the day of Adam the term *key* has been used by inspired writers as a symbol of power and authority. Keys are the right of presidency, and the one holding them holds the reigns of government within the field and sphere of his appointment. In ancient Israel, David was a man of blood and battle whose word was law and whose very name was also a symbol of power and authority. Accordingly, when Isaiah sought to convey a realization of the supreme, directive control and power resident in our Lord, the Son of David, he spoke these words in the Lord's name: "And *the key of the house of David* will I lay upon his shoulder; so he shall open, and none shall shut; and he shall shut, and none shall open." (Isa. 22:22.) Centuries later, speaking of himself, our Lord said to John: "These things saith he that is holy, he that is true, he that hath *the key of David,* he that openeth, and no man shutteth; and shutteth, and no man openeth." (Rev. 3:7.) Thus, the *key of David* is the absolute power resident in Christ whereby his will is expressed in all things both temporal and spiritual.

KEYS.

See CHURCH OF JESUS CHRIST OF LATTER-DAY SAINTS, KEYS OF SALVATION, KEYS OF THE KINGDOM, KEYS OF THE MINISTERING OF ANGELS, KINGDOM OF GOD, KINGDOM OF HEAVEN, PRIESTHOOD. Two different usages of the term *keys* are found in the revelations. One has reference to the directive powers whereby the Church or kingdom and all its organizations are governed, the *keys of the kingdom* being the powers of presidency. The other usage refers to the means provided whereby something is revealed, discovered, or made manifest. Thus Joseph Smith and Oliver Cowdery were given the keys to translate and bring hidden scriptures to light. (D. & C. 6:24-28.) And thus Joseph held "the keys of the mysteries, and the revelations which are sealed" (D. & C. 28:7; 35:18; 64:5), meaning that he had the power and means at his disposal to bring these things to light and reveal them to the world.

Similarly the higher priesthood "holdeth the key of the mysteries of the kingdom, even the key of the knowledge of God" (D. & C. 84:19-22), for it is only in and through and because of that priesthood that the mysteries of the kingdom can be learned and the knowledge of God obtained. The keys of the ministering of angels are resident in the Aaronic Priesthood (D. & C. 13; 107:20), and the Melchizedek Priesthood holds "the keys of all the spiritual blessings of the church —To have the privilege of receiving the mysteries of the kingdom of heaven, to have the heavens opened unto them, to commune with the general assembly and church of the Firstborn, and to enjoy the communion and presence of God

the Father, and Jesus the mediator of the new covenant." (D. & C. 107:18-19.)

President Joseph F. Smith said: *"What is a key? It is the right or privilege which belongs to and comes with the priesthood to have communication with God.* Is not that a key? Most decidedly. We may not enjoy the blessings, or key, very much, but the key is in the priesthood. *It is the right to enjoy the blessing of communication with the heavens, and the privilege and authority to administer in the ordinances of the gospel of Jesus Christ, to preach the gospel of repentance, and of baptism by immersion for the remission of sins.* That is a key. You who hold the priesthood have the key or the authority, the right, the power or privilege to preach the gospel of Jesus Christ, which is the gospel of repentance and of baptism by immersion for the remission of sins." (*Gospel Doctrine,* 5th ed., p. 142.)

KEYS OF SALVATION.
See CHRIST, EXALTATION, KEYS, KEYS OF THE KINGDOM, SALVATION, SEALING POWER. Those having power to open the door to salvation are said to hold the *keys of salvation,* that is they are able to make salvation available to other men. These keys center in Christ, for salvation comes in and through his name only (Mosiah 3: 16-18), and he directs how this

great gift may be obtained and by whom.

Adam, as the presiding high priest over the earth, holds "the keys of salvation under the counsel and direction of the Holy One" (D. & C. 78:16), and accordingly all the affairs of the kingdom of God on earth for all ages are administered under Adam's direction and supervision. Under him the heads of the various dispensations and the prophets called in those eras have had power to administer salvation to men. (D. & C. 7.) The President of The Church of Jesus Christ of Latter-day Saints holds the keys of salvation for all men now living because he is the only one by whose authorization the sealing power of the priesthood can be used to seal men up to salvation and exaltation in the kingdom of God. (D. & C. 132:7.)

KEYS OF THE KINGDOM

See ADAM-ONDI-AHMAN, CHURCH OF JESUS CHRIST OF LATTER-DAY SAINTS, ELIAS, ELIJAH THE PROPHET, GABRIEL, JOHN THE BAPTIST, JOSEPH SMITH THE PROPHET, KEYS, KEYS OF SALVATION, KEYS OF THE MINISTERING OF ANGELS, KINGDOM OF GOD, KINGDOM OF HEAVEN, MICHAEL THE ARCHANGEL, MOSES; PETER, JAMES, AND JOHN; PRIESTHOOD, RAPHAEL. Keys are the right of presidency, the directing, controlling, governing power. The *keys of the kingdom* are the power,

right, and authority to preside over the kingdom of God on earth (which is the Church) and to direct all of its affairs.

President Joseph F. Smith taught: "Every man ordained to any degree of the priesthood has this authority delegated to him. *But it is necessary that every act performed under this authority shall be done at the proper time and place, in the proper way, and after the proper order. The power of directing these labors constitutes the keys of the priesthood.*

"In their fulness, the keys are held by only one person at a time, the Prophet and President of the Church. He may delegate any portion of this power to another, in which case that person holds the keys of that particular labor. Thus, the president of a temple, the president of a stake, the bishop of a ward, the president of a mission, the president of a quorum, each holds the keys of the labors performed in that particular body or locality. His priesthood is not increased by this special appointment, for a seventy who presides over a mission has no more priesthood than a seventy who labors under his direction; and the president of an elders quorum, for example, has no more priesthood than any member of that quorum. But he holds the power of directing the official labors performed in the mission or the quorum, or in other words, the keys of that division of that work. So it is throughout all the ramifications of the priesthood—a distinction must be carefully made between the general authority and the directing of the labors performed by that authority." (*Gospel Doctrine,* 5th ed., p. 136.)

Through the ages various prophets have held various keys, by virtue of which they have been empowered to use their priesthood to perform specified labors. Adam holds the keys of presidency over all dispensations and is the presiding high priest (under Christ) over all the earth. (D. & C. 78:16; *Teachings,* pp. 157-158, 169.) Noah stands next to Adam in priesthood authority (*Teachings,* p. 157), and after these two come all the heads of the different gospel dispensations, together with a host of other mighty prophets. For example: Elijah held the keys of the sealing power in ancient Israel (D. & C. 27:9; 110:13-16; Mal. 4:5-6), as did Nephi the son of Helaman among the Nephites in the early years of the Christian Era. (Hela. 10:4-10.) One man named Elias held the keys of authority in the days of Abraham (D. & C. 110:12), while to another bearing the same name has been "committed the keys of bringing to pass the restoration of all things spoken by the mouth of all the holy prophets since the world began, concerning the last days." (D. & C. 27:6.)

Moroni holds "the keys of the record of the stick of Ephraim" (D. & C. 27:5); John the Baptist the keys of the Aaronic Priesthood and the gospel of repentance (D. & C. 13; 84:26-28); Moses those whereby the priesthood may be used to gather Israel and lead the Ten Tribes from the lands of the north (D. & C. 110:11); Peter, James, and John hold the keys of the kingdom and of the dispensation of the fulness of times (D. & C. 27:12-13; 128:20); and Raphael (whose mortal identity has not been revealed) holds the keys of his dispensation. (D. & C. 128:21.)

All of these and others—"divers angels, from Michael or Adam down to the present time"—have come in the last days, "all declaring their dispensation, their rights, their *keys,* their honors, their majesty and glory, and the power of their priesthood." (D. & C. 128:21.) Thus Joseph Smith and his successors have been and are possessors of all of the keys of the kingdom of heaven, even as these were held by Peter and the ancient apostles (Matt. 16:19; 18:18), and accordingly those so endowed have power to govern all the affairs of the earthly kingdom and direct the administration of all the ordinances of salvation and exaltation **for worthy recipients. (D. & C. 35:25; 42:69; 65; 90:2-3; 97:14; 115: 19.)**

"The keys of the kingdom, . . . belong always unto the Presidency of the High Priesthood" (D. & C. 81:2), and only one man on earth at a time, the President of the Church, can exercise them in their fulness. (D. & C. 132:7.) This necessarily must be so because keys are the right of presidency and there cannot be two equal heads, otherwise the Lord's house would not be a house of order but of confusion. (D. & C. 132:8-12.) All of the keys of the kingdom, however, are conferred upon every man sustained as a member of the Council of the Twelve. (D. & C. 112:14-34; 124:128.) Thus when a member of the Council of the Twelve becomes the senior apostle of God on earth, he can exercise in their fulness the keys which theretofore have lain dormant in him. (*Doctrines of Salvation*, vol. 3, pp. 125-159.)

The keys of the kingdom—the right and power to govern the Lord's affairs for and on his behalf —have been held by prophets in all ages, but when the Lord comes to reign personally upon the earth during the millennial era, he will take back the keys. Those who have held them will make an accounting to him of their stewardships at the place called Adam-ondi-Ahman, at which gathering Christ will receive "dominion, and glory, and a kingdom, that all people, nations, and languages, should serve him." (Dan. 7:13-14.) Eventually in the celestial day, "the keys of the kingdom shall be delivered up again unto the Father." (*Inspired Version*, Luke 3:8.)

KEYS OF THE MINISTERING OF ANGELS.
See AARONIC PRIESTHOOD, ANGELS, KEYS, KEYS OF THE KINGDOM. In the same sense that the Melchizedek Priesthood holds "the key of the knowledge of God" (D. & C. 84:19), and "of all the spiritual blessings of the church" in that holders of that priesthood may "have the heavens opened unto them" and "enjoy the communion and presence of God the Father, and Jesus the mediator of the new covenant" (D. & C. 107:18-19), so the Aaronic Priesthood holds the *keys of the ministering of angels.* (D. & C. 13; 84: 26-27; 107:20.) That is, the Aaronic Priesthood opens the door to the ministering of angels, or in other words, those holding the lesser priesthood are in a position to have angels minister unto them. Wilford Woodruff, for instance, said: "I had the administration of angels while holding the office of a priest." (*Discourses of Wilford Woodruff,* p. 298.)

KEYS OF THE PRIESTHOOD.
See KEYS OF THE KINGDOM.

KEYSTONE OF MORMONISM.
See BOOK OF MORMON.

KINDNESS.
See LOVING-KINDNESS. In their pursuit of godly graces the saints are exhorted, "And *be ye kind* one to another, tenderhearted, forgiving one another, even as God for Christ's sake hath forgiven you." (Eph. 4:32; D. & C. 4:6; 121:42.) Kindness embraces an interest in

another's welfare and a disposition to be helpful. The kind are tender, gracious, benevolent, well-disposed, and exhibit sympathy and humaneness toward their fellow men.

KING.

See CHRIST, GOVERNOR, KINGDOM OF GOD, KING OF GLORY, KING OF HEAVEN, KING OF ISRAEL, KING OF KINGS, KING OF THE JEWS, KING OF ZION, LAWGIVER, LORD, RULER. Christ is the *King.* (Ps. 5:2; 10:16; 44:4; 47:6-7; 89:18; Isa. 6:5; 43:15; Jer. 23:5; 46:18; 1 Tim. 1:17.) By this is meant that he is the Ruler, Lawgiver, and Sovereign in whom all power rests. As King he rules over the heavens and the earth and all things that are in them (Alma 5:50); and also, in a particular sense, he rules over the kingdom of God on earth which is the Church and over the kingdom of God in heaven which is the celestial kingdom.

KINGCRAFT.

See CIVIL GOVERNMENTS, KINGDOM OF GOD, LAWS OF THE LAND, THEOCRACY (THEARCHY). Earthly kings rule and reign by man's power and not by divine right. Their thrones, in the first instance, were set up by the power of the sword, are bathed in blood, and shall tumble to the earth when the Almighty makes "a full end of all nations." (D. & C. 87:6.)

There have been and are upright and just kings and queens who have and do serve as the titular or real heads of their respective governments. Many of these, as Victoria of Great Britain, have served useful and beneficial purposes under the systems of government prevailing in their realms. They have been symbols of unity and patriotism, have used their influence to have wise laws enacted, the rights and privileges of the people protected, and have set examples of moral and sober conduct worthy of emulation.

But the system of kingly government itself, no matter how talented or noble an individual occupant of the throne may be, does not make the best form of government, one in which the instinctive and automatic concern of government is to look after the best interests of the body of the people. It is inherent in the nature of even the best and most ideal kingly systems that special privilege and questionable adulation be heaped upon those in the ruling class.

As a matter of fact, the important and real blessings which flow from good government, as it is administered in countries subject to kings, come in the main in spite of the kingly system and not because of it. In Great Britain, for instance, the rights and privileges of all the people are held sacred, not because of the kings who have ruled and reigned in successive ages, but because over the years the people have demanded and received a magna carta, a bill of rights, parliamentary powers, and a great host of common law guarantees of freedom.

Now that these freedoms and powers are relatively secure, the monarchy is more of a symbol and less of a power than has traditionally been the case. Democratic principles must be adopted and followed even in a monarchy—and such is the case in Great Britain— if the people are to have good government and be preserved in their rights.

It is true that the Lord on occasions, in the pre-Christian Era, administered righteous and theocratic government through kings, but no such approved kingly government has existed among men for some 2000 years. Such a system, in which the king is the Lord's representative, is patterned after the true kingdom of God and is proper government, but even then the moment an unrighteous king gains the throne, the blessings and freedoms of such a system die out. As King Mosiah said, "Because all men are not just it is not expedient that ye should have a king or kings to rule over you. For behold, *how much iniquity doth one wicked king cause to be committed, yea, and what great destruction!*" (Mosiah 29.) Pending the day in which He shall again reign, whose right it is, the saints are obliged to be subject to the powers that be.

KINGDOM OF EPHRAIM.
See KINGDOM OF ISRAEL.

KINGDOM OF GOD.
See CELESTIAL KINGDOM, CHURCH OF JESUS CHRIST OF LATTER-DAY SAINTS, COMMON CONSENT, KEYS OF THE KINGDOM, KINGDOM OF HEAVEN, MILLENNIUM. 1. The Church of Jesus Christ of Latter-day Saints as it is now constituted is the *kingdom of God on earth.* Nothing more needs to be done to establish the kingdom. (D. & C. 35:27; 38:9, 15; 50:35; 62:9; 65; 136:41.) The kingdom is here, and it is the same kingdom which Daniel said would be set up in the last days. (Dan. 2:44-45.) This same kingdom has been set up in past ages whenever the gospel has been on earth, for the plan of salvation is the gospel of the kingdom. The Church and kingdom are one and the same.

Joseph Smith taught: "Some say the kingdom of God was not set up on the earth until the day of Pentecost, and that John did not preach the baptism of repentance for the remission of sins; but I say, in the name of the Lord, that the kingdom of God was set up on the earth from the days of Adam to the present time. Whenever there has been a righteous man on earth unto whom God revealed his word and gave power and authority to administer in his name, and where there is a priest of God—a minister who has power and authority from God to administer in the ordinances of the gospel and officiate in the priesthood of God, there is the kingdom of God. . . .

"Where there is no kingdom of God there is no salvation. What constitutes the kingdom of God? Where there is a prophet, a priest, or a righteous man unto whom God gives his oracles, there is the kingdom of God; and where the oracles of God are not, there the kingdom of God is not. . . .

"Whenever men can find out the will of God and find an administrator legally authorized from God, there is the kingdom of God; but where these are not, the kingdom of God is not. All the ordinances, systems, and administrations on the earth are of no use to the children of men, unless they are ordained and authorized of God; for nothing will save a man but a legal administrator; for none others will be acknowledge either by God or angels." (*Teachings,* pp. 271-274.)

The Church (or kingdom) is not a democracy; legislation is not enacted by the body of people composing the organization; they do not make the laws governing themselves. The Church is a kingdom. The Lord Jesus Christ is the Eternal King, and the President of the Church, the mouthpiece of God on earth, is the earthly king. All things come to the Church from the King of the kingdom in heaven, through the king of the kingdom on earth.

There is, of course, the democratic principle of common consent whereunder the people may accept or reject what the Lord offers to them. Acceptance brings salvation; rejection leads to damnation.

2. During the millennium the *kingdom of God* will continue on earth, but in that day it will be both an *ecclesiastical* and a *political* kingdom. That is, the Church (which is the kingdom) will have the rule and government of the world given to it. When inspired teachers speak of the future setting up of the kingdom of God on earth, they have reference to the millennial day when "The kingdoms of this world are become the kingdoms of our Lord, and of his Christ; and he shall reign for ever and ever." (Rev. 11:15.) Daniel also saw the day when "the saints of the most High shall take the kingdom, and possess the kingdom for ever, even for ever and ever." (Dan. 7:18, 22, 27.) The Prophet prayed that the present ecclesiastical kingdom of God on earth might roll forth that the future political and millennial kingdom of God on earth might come. (D. & C. 65; *Doctrines of Salvation,* vol. 1, pp. 229-246.)

3. In the eternal worlds, *the celestial kingdom is the kingdom of God,* and that kingdom does not reach down to include either a terrestrial kingdom or a telestial kingdom. (D. & C. 20:29; Moses 6:57; 2 Ne. 9:18, 23; Luke 13:28-29; John 3:3-5.) The gospel is de-

signed to prepare men for an inheritance in the celestial kingdom of God; persons can gain admittance to the lower kingdoms without obedience to the law of Christ. (D. & C. 88:16-29.)

Deity is, of course, the ruler, governor, and creator of all kingdoms of glory. Those going to terrestrial or telestial kingdoms will go to realms which are his and which he has provided. But since the whole gospel system is one of preparing men for a celestial inheritance, it is that particular part of the eternal worlds that is the kingdom of God in the true and full sense.

KINGDOM OF HEAVEN.

See CELESTIAL KINGDOM, CHURCH OF JESUS CHRIST OF LATTER-DAY SAINTS, HEAVEN, KEYS OF THE KINGDOM, KINGDOM OF GOD, MILLENNIUM, PARABLES. 1. *The kingdom of heaven* is the celestial kingdom of God, the place where our Father in Heaven dwells, the highest glory in eternity, the place where faithful saints go, if they endure in righteousness to the end. (D. & C. 6:37; 10:55; 58:2; Alma 11:37-40; Matt. 7:21-23.)

2. There is a kingdom of heaven both in heaven and on earth. Whenever the Lord's true Church is on earth—possessing as it does the power and way whereby man may gain the kingdom of heaven in the eternal worlds—that Church on earth is also called the *kingdom*

of heaven. Thus in the meridian of time, as the foundations of Christianity were being laid again among men, our Lord, his apostles, and John the Baptist, all went forth with the message: "Repent ye: for the kingdom of heaven is at hand." (Matt. 3:2; 4:17; 10:7.) That is, repent and come into the Church, for it is the kingdom of heaven on earth.

In line with this the Lord gave Peter and all the apostles "the keys of the kingdom of heaven" (Matt. 16:19; 18:18), meaning that they were given the directive and controlling power over the kingdom which is the Church. The same pattern has been followed in this dispensation. Elders have gone out proclaiming repentance, "for the kingdom of heaven is at hand" (D. & C. 33:10; 39:19; 42:7), and the keys of the kingdom have again been committed unto man on earth. (D. & C. 65:1-2; 81:1-2.)

When our Lord spoke in parables, saying, "The kingdom of heaven is likened" unto such and such, he was saying the same thing as though he had used the words, "The Church of Jesus Christ is likened" unto such and such. (Matt. 13.)

When used as a designation of the earthly Church, the term *kingdom of heaven* is a synonym for the appellation *kingdom of God,* as such title applies also to the earthly government of God as found in his Church.

3. *Kingdom of heaven* is also

used to identify the political kingdom that will be set up on earth during the millennial era, the kingdom that will reign over all the earth when the Lord has made a full end of all nations. (D. & C. 65; 87:6.) It is for this hallowed kingdom that the righteous pray when they plead, "Thy kingdom come." (Matt. 6:10; *Doctrines of Salvation,* vol. 1, pp. 229-230.)

KINGDOM OF ISRAEL.

See ISRAEL, KINGDOM OF GOD, LOST TRIBES OF ISRAEL, TRIBES OF ISRAEL. Beginning with the reign of Saul (about 1095 B.C.), Israel became a kingdom and so continued until her final destruction as a nation. After the death of Solomon (about 975 B.C.), however, the kingdom was divided. The tribe of Judah and part of the tribe of Benjamin, maintaining their allegiance and following Rehoboam, son of Solomon, became known as the *Kingdom of Judah;* the rest of the Israelites, commonly called the *Ten Tribes,* followed Jeroboam and were known as the *Kingdom of Israel,* or sometimes as the *Kingdom of Ephraim,* after their most prominent tribe.

Two and a half centuries later (about 721 B.C.), the Ten Tribes were taken captive by Shalmanezer and were transplanted as a people into Assyria. From thence, in due course, they were led away into the north countries, and being lost to the knowledge of men (1

Ne. 22:4), have been designated since as the *Lost Tribes.* In 600 B.C. Lehi and others left Jerusalem to begin their journey to the Americas; shortly thereafter, Nebuchadnezzar overran Jerusalem, destroyed the *Kingdom of Judah,* and carried the remaining remnants of Israel into Babylonian bondage. Seventy years later, under Cyrus the Persian, they were permitted to return to their native habitats and to rebuild the Temple at Jerusalem, where they continued to be known as the people of Israel although in reality they were somewhat less than two of the tribes of that once mighty nation. (*Articles of Faith,* pp. 314-316.) It was among the descendants of this part of Israel that our Lord ministered while in mortality.

On the occasion of the resurrected Lord's formal ascension to his Father, he was asked by the apostles: "Lord, wilt thou at this time restore again the kingdom to Israel?" (Acts 1:6.) His questioners, familiar with the prophetic assurances of the restoration of Israel to all her former glory and prominence, were obviously anxious to have that triumphant day grow out of their ministry. This restoration of the kingdom of Israel, however, as they were told then and on other occasions, was to take place as part of the "restitution of all things" (Acts 3:19-21) in the last days.

On April 6, 1830, the *ecclesiastical kingdom of God* on earth was set up, an occurrence which constituted the real beginning of the restoration of the kingdom to Israel. This ecclesiastical kingdom will continue to flourish and grow until the Second Coming. Then with the ushering in of the millennium, the Lord will make a full end of all nations (D. & C. 87:6) and the *political kingdom* also will be given to Israel. In that day, saith the Lord, "I will make them one nation in the land upon the mountains of Israel; and one king shall be king to them all: and they shall be no more two nations, neither shall they be divided into two kingdoms any more at all: Neither shall they defile themselves any more with their idols, nor with their detestable things, nor with any of their transgressions: but I will save them out of all their dwellingplaces, wherein they have sinned, and will cleanse them: so shall they be my people, and I will be their God." (Ezek. 37:22-23.) In that day, as Isaiah foretold, "The envy also of Ephraim shall depart, and the adversaries of Judah shall be cut off: Ephraim shall not envy Judah, and Judah shall not vex Ephraim." (Isa. 11:13.)

KINGDOM OF JUDAH.
See KINGDOM OF ISRAEL.

KINGDOM OF THE DEVIL.
See CHURCH OF THE DEVIL, DEVIL, HELL, PERDITION. Just as there is a kingdom of God both on earth and in heaven, so there is a *kingdom of the devil* both on earth and in hell. Just as the kingdom of God on earth is The Church of Jesus Christ of Latter-day Saints, "the only true and living church upon the face of the whole earth" (D. & C. 1:30), so the kingdom of the devil is the church of the devil, the great and abominable church, the combination of powers and forces which lead men away from heaven and toward hell. And just as the kingdom of God in heaven is the celestial world, where saved persons go, so the kingdom of the devil in the spirit realms is that eternal hell whose inhabitants suffer the torments of the damned.

Where there is a kingdom, there must be a king who ordains laws, rules over subjects, and governs those who inhabit his organized domain. So Deity rules and reigns on the one hand and the devil on the other; and so the earthly head of the Lord's work is the President of the true Church, and the leaders of the devil's earthly kingdom are all those who lead the organized agencies which direct men away from God and salvation and toward Lucifer and damnation.

Membership in the Lord's kingdom on earth is designed to qualify and prepare men for an inheritance in his kingdom in eternity, which inheritance is obtained by those who are faithful and true in all things. Similarly membership in the devil's kingdom on earth—unless its citizens repent, forsake carnal paths, and turn to the Lord—leads to hell and damnation and an ultimate inheritance in some kingdom other than the celestial.

Describing the kingdom of the devil as such is established on earth among men, and foretelling its fate at the Second Coming of our Lord, Nephi said: "And the righteous need not fear, for they are those who shall not be confounded. But it is *the kingdom of the devil, which shall be built up among the children of men, which kingdom is established among them which are in the flesh*—For the time speedily shall come that *all churches which are built up to get gain, and all those who are built up to get power over the flesh, and those who are built up to become popular in the eyes of the world, and those who seek the lusts of the flesh and the things of the world, and to do all manner of iniquity;* yea, in fine, *all those who belong to the kingdom of the devil* are they who need fear, and tremble, and quake; they are those who must be brought low in the dust; they are those who must be consumed as stubble; and this is according to the word of the prophet." (1 Ne. 22:22-23.)

KINGDOMS OF GLORY.

See CELESTIAL KINGDOM, HEAVEN, KINGDOM OF GOD, KINGDOM OF HEAVEN, MANSIONS, SALVATION, TELESTIAL KINGDOM, TERRESTRIAL KINGDOM. Contrary to the views found in the uninspired teachings and creeds of modern Christendom, there are in eternity *kingdoms of glory* to which all resurrected persons (except the sons of perdition) will eventually go. These are named: *celestial, terrestrial,* and *telestial*—the glory of each being beyond mortal comprehension. (D. & C. 76; 1 Cor. 15:39-42; Rev. 21.)

However, only the celestial kingdom is the kingdom of God where the faithful saints will gain their eternal inheritance. All who fall short of the glory of eternal life will in greater or lesser degree be damned (even though they dwell in a kingdom of glory), for their eternal progress will be limited, and they can never go on to an eternal fulness in the Father's presence. (D. & C. 132:16-17.)

Rewards granted individuals in eternity will vary between and within kingdoms. Only those who are sealed in the new and everlasting covenant of marriage and who thereafter keep the terms and conditions of that covenant will attain the highest of three heavens within the celestial kingdom. (D. & C. 131:1-4.) Inhabitants of the telestial kingdom will differ in glory among themselves "as one star differs from another star in glory." (D. & C. 76:98; 1 Cor. 15:41.) Similar variations will exist among inheritors of the terrestrial kingdom. (D. & C. 76:71-79.)

Revealed statements that those quickened with a portion of the glory of the respective kingdoms shall then receive a fulness of the glory concerned, mean (for instance) that no one can gain admission to the celestial kingdom unless by obedience to celestial law he has obtained a celestial body. (D. & C. 88:16-32.) The glory to be received by individuals in the kingdoms of glory hereafter will be in direct proportion to their obedience and diligence in this life (D. & C. 130:18-19), for all men will be judged in accordance with their particular works. (Rev. 20:13.)

KINGDOMS OF THIS WORLD.
See CIVIL GOVERNMENTS.

KING FOLLETT SERMON.
See JOSEPH SMITH THE PROPHET, SERMONS. At the April, 1844, conference of the Church the Prophet Joseph Smith preached his greatest sermon and one of the greatest sermons ever delivered by mortal man. Speaking before 20,000 saints, while moved upon by the Holy Ghost, he delivered the funeral sermon of Elder King Follett, in which he revealed the nature and kind of being that God is and told how man, as a joint-heir with Christ, may become like the Father. (*Teachings,* pp. 342-362.)

Commenting on this mighty discourse Elder B. H. Roberts said: "The Prophet lived his life in crescendo. From small beginnings, it rose in breadth and power as he neared its close. As a teacher he reached the climax of his career in this discourse. After it there was but one thing more he could do—seal his testimony with his blood. This he did three months later." (*Teachings,* p. 356, fn.)

KING IMMANUEL.
See IMMANUEL.

KING JAMES VERSION OF THE BIBLE
See APOCRYPHA, BIBLE, BOOK OF MORMON, CANON OF SCRIPTURE, DOCTRINE AND COVENANTS, INSPIRED VERSION OF THE BIBLE, LOST SCRIPTURE, MORMON BIBLE, PEARL OF GREAT PRICE, SCRIPTURE, STANDARD WORKS. Various versions of the Bible have found common usage among portions of the earth's inhabitants from time to time. Among them are these: The *Septuagint* was the Greek version of the Old Testament used by the Greek speaking world from the 3rd century B.C. down through the formative period of the Christian Church. It is said to be the version used by the early apostles and, according to tradition, was prepared by 70 learned Jews of Alexandria, hence the name *Septuagint* meaning *Version of the Seventy.* The *Vulgate* was a Latin version of the Bible prepared by Jerome under a commission re-

ceived from the Pope in 382 A.D. It was in common use for over a thousand years; the Gutenberg Bible, published in 1452 A.D., was the first printed edition of the Vulgate.

Wycliffe's Bible, the first English version of the whole Bible, was translated from the Vulgate beginning in 1382. *Tyndale* translated the New Testament and parts of the Old, his New Testament of 1525 being the first one ever published in English. A great part of his translation is retained in the *Authorized Version. Coverdale's Bible* of 1535 was the first complete English printing. *Luther's* German translation was forthcoming about the same time. Other early English versions included *Matthew's* in 1537, *Taverner's* in 1539, the *Great Bible* of 1539, the *Geneva Bible* of 1557 (also called the *Breeches Bible* from its use of the word "breeches" in Genesis 3: 7), the *Bishop's Bible* of 1568, and finally the *King James* or *Authorized Version* in 1611.

The *Douay Bible* is the English version of the old Vulgate. First published in 1609-10 it is the Roman Catholic version for English speaking peoples. Since the King James Bible, there has been published, among Protestant peoples, the *Revised Version* (in 1881) and the *Revised Standard Version* (completed in 1952). There have also been many published translations by individuals. (J. Paterson Smyth, *How We Got Our Bible,* pp. 1-153.)

Not all versions of the Bible are or have been of equal worth. In large measure the hand of the Lord has been manifest in the preservation of his word among men. Though translators and custodians of Bible manuscripts have enjoyed unabridged agency in their work, those of some ages have been endowed with greater inspiration and the possessors of more integrity than those of other ages. The great perversion of the scriptures, in which many plain and precious truths were deleted by evilly disposed persons (1 Ne. 13), took place primarily in the early centuries of the Christian Era. The English translations preceding the Authorized Version were preparatory in nature, that is, they paved the way and laid the groundwork for the literary, historical, and doctrinal masterpiece which was to come forth under the aegis of King James.

Certainly the King James Version is by all odds the greatest of the completed English translations. Scholars universally acclaim it as containing as forceful, direct, and majestic prose as has ever been coined in the English language. But more important than this, it was the version of the Bible which was preserved for use by his Prophet who should lay the foundations of the mighty work of latter-day restoration. Joseph Smith read, respected, reverenced, and taught the King James Version.

"as far as it is translated correctly." (Eighth Article of Faith.) Whenever he found Biblical quotations in the Book of Mormon (they having been copied from the brass plates and preserved by the Nephite prophets), he rendered them into English in the exact language of the King James Version, except in instances in which the language of that version did not convey accurately the original thought. It was on the King James Version that the Prophet worked when he corrected portions of the Bible by the spirit of revelation, always preserving the existing language unless a thought change was necessary.

English versions that have come forth since the King James Version, and particularly the Revised Standard Version, have been translated by individuals and groups some of whom have questioned the divinity of Christ and his mission. As a consequence, there are passages in many of these versions which have been so altered as to leave in question our Lord's Divine Sonship and other basic doctrines of the gospel. It is no wonder that the King James Version has been and remains the official version of The Church of Jesus Christ of Latter-day Saints. This official usage most assuredly will not be changed until such time as the Lord directs that the needed corrections in the Inspired Version be completed. (J. Reuben Clark, Jr., *Why the King James Version,* pp. 1-441.)

KING OF GLORY.

See CHRIST, KING, LORD OF GLORY. Christ is the *King of Glory* (Ps. 24), a title signifying his status as King and Ruler and also the transcendent glory that attends him and his marvelous works.

KING OF HEAVEN

See CHRIST, HEAVEN, KING, MELCHIZEDEK. Christ is the *King of Heaven* (2 Ne. 10:14; Alma 5:50; Dan. 4:37) or *Heavenly King* (Mosiah 2:19), titles which bear record of his high and exalted kingly status. Melchizedek, the great high priest and prototype of the Son of God, was also called the *King of Heaven,* meaning King of Peace, by his people. (*Inspired Version,* Gen. 14:36.)

KING OF ISRAEL.

See CHRIST, HOLY ONE OF ISRAEL, KING. Christ is the *King of Israel* (Isa. 44:6; John 1:49; 12:13), meaning both that he as the Eternal King would be born of the lineage of Israel and that he would rule on the throne of David over the house of Israel forever. (Luke 1:31-33.)

KING OF JACOB.

See KING OF ISRAEL.

KING OF KINGS.

See CHRIST, GOD OF GODS, KING, KINGS, LORD OF LORDS. Christ is the *King of Kings* (1 Tim. 6:15; Rev. 17:14; 19:11-16), a title signifying far more than the mere fact that he as the *Eternal King* holds dominion over mere earthly kings. Rather, those who gain exaltation are ordained kings and queens, priests and priestesses, in which positions they shall exercise power and authority in the Lord's eternal kingdoms forever. (Rev. 1:6; 5:10.) Christ as the chief of all exalted beings continues to hold dominion and sway over these other exalted kings and saints and consequently reigns as King of Kings and *King of Saints* forever. (Rev. 15:3.)

KING OF SAINTS.

See KING OF KINGS.

KING OF THE JEWS.

See CHRIST, JEWS, KING. Though rejected and crucified by them, Christ was and is the *King of the Jews*. Messianic prophecies had foretold the glorious reign of a great King, the King of Israel. (Zech. 9:9-10.) The Jews were looking forward to a temporal reign in which all nations of the earth would go up from year to year "to worship the King, the Lord of hosts," in Jerusalem (Zech. 14:16-21), an event which in reality is to occur during the millennium when Christ, the King, reigns personally on earth. (Tenth Article of Faith.)

Accordingly, when our Lord came ministering among the Jews and proclaiming his divine Sonship, the great query in the minds of the people was whether this was the promised King. He was believed to be of the lineage of David. (Matt. 1:1-16; Luke 3:23-38.) On one occasion the people sought to make him king by force. (John 6:15.) On another the multitudes hailed him publicly as the King of Israel. (Matt. 21:1-11; Luke 19:28-40; John 12:12-16.) Pilate asked him:"Art thou the King of the Jews?" to which query he received an affirmative answer, with the qualifying explanation: "My kingdom is not of this world" (John 18:33-37; Luke 23:1-4), a doctrine that our Lord had also taught previously. (Luke 22:24-30.) Then Pilate, when the Jews chanted, "We have no king but Caesar," ordered the crucifixion and the placing of a writing above our Lord's head reading: "JESUS OF NAZARETH THE KING OF THE JEWS." (John 19:14-22.)

At the Second Coming the Jews shall be converted, recognize him whom they crucified, and "lament because they persecuted their king." (D. & C. 45:51-53; Zech. 12:10-14; 13:6.)

KING OF ZION.

See CHRIST, KING, ZION. Christ is the *King of Zion* (Moses 7:53), a title signifying his high status as the King who shall reign over his chosen Zion forever. During the millennium, after the return of Enoch's Zion of old, the Lord will reign personally on earth, and he will be King and Lawgiver to his saints. (D. & C. 38:21-22; 45:59.)

KINGS.

See CALLING AND ELECTION SURE, CELESTIAL MARRIAGE, ENDOWMENTS, EXALTATION, MELCHIZEDEK PRIESTHOOD, PRIESTESSES, PRIESTS, QUEENS. Holders of the Melchizedek Priesthood have power to press forward in righteousness, living by every word that proceedeth forth from the mouth of God, magnifying their callings, going from grace to grace, until through the fulness of the ordinances of the temple they receive the fulness of the priesthood and are ordained *kings and priests.* Those so attaining shall have exaltation and be kings, priests, rulers, and lords in their respective spheres in the eternal kingdoms of the great King who is God our Father. (Rev. 1:6; 5:10.)

KNEELING IN WORSHIP.
See PRAYER.

KNOWLEDGE.
See CHRIST, FAITH, GOSPEL, HOLY GHOST, IGNORANCE, INTELLIGENCE, PROPHECY, REVELATION, SALVATION, TESTIMONY, TRUTH, WISDOM. Gospel *knowledge* deals primarily with a clear perception of the truths about God and his laws, the laws governing his dealings with his offspring, the laws which if obeyed will enable these offspring to gain salvation in the presence of God. In a lesser sense gospel knowledge deals with all truth, for all truth comes from God, and in the ultimate sense it is all part of the gospel.

Knowledge is an attribute of Deity and is possessed by him in its fulness. "Known unto God are all his works from the beginning of the world." (Acts 15:18.) "Remember the former things of old: for I am God, and there is none else; I am God, and there is none like me, Declaring the end from the beginning, and from ancient times the things that are not yet done, saying, My counsel shall stand, and I will do all my pleasure." (Isa. 46: 9-10.)

An understanding that God knows all things, and that there is nothing which he does not know, is essentially necessary for man to have in order to exercise faith and gain salvation. As the Prophet said: "Without the *knowledge of all things* God would not be able to save any portion of his creatures; for it is by reason of the knowledge which he has of all things, from the beginning to the end, that enables him to give that understanding to his creatures by which they are made partakers of eternal life; and if it were not for the idea existing in the minds of men that God had all knowledge it would be impossible for them to exercise faith in him." (*Lectures on Faith*, p. 44.) Not only does the Father know all things, but so likewise does the Son (D. & C. 38:2; 93:26), and the Holy Ghost. (D. & C. 35:19; 42:17.)

The process of gaining exaltation consists in growing in knowledge until a state of godhood is reached. "The relationship we have with God," the Prophet said, "places us in a situation to advance in knowledge. He has power to institute laws to instruct the weaker intelligences, that they may be exalted with himself, so that they might have one glory upon another, and all that knowledge, power, glory, and intelligence, which is requisite in order to save them in the world of spirits." (*Teachings*, p. 354.)

All types of knowledge however are not of equal worth, all do not reward the acquirer with equal progress toward exaltation. Knowledge of the arts and sciences—of mathematics, chemistry, history, medicine, and the like—have no direct and immediate bearing on the attainment of salvation. Of themselves they do not prepare a man for or lead him to a celestial inheritance, but they may school and train him in such a way that he will be more susceptible to the reception of saving truth or more capable to understand it.

But it is *the knowledge of God and his laws that leads to high reward in the hereafter.* (2 Ne. 9: 28-29, 42.) If the righteous man has knowledge of temporal things, so much the better, for he can use that knowledge in furthering the spread of the particular knowledge that does have saving value. And it is for this reason that the saints are commanded to seek knowledge in all fields. (D. & C. 88:77-81, 118; 93:53; *Doctrines of Salvation*, vol. 1, pp. 290-306.)

It is the knowledge of God that brings salvation. "And this is life eternal, that they might know thee the only true God, and Jesus Christ, whom thou hast sent." (John 17:3; D. & C. 93:6-28; 132: 24.) When the Prophet said, "A man is saved no faster than he gets knowledge," he had reference not to the *worldly knowledge* flowing from research, but to the *eternal knowledge* coming by revelation, "for it needs revelation to assist us," he continued, "and give us *knowledge of the things of God.*" (*Teachings*, p. 217.) Similarly, when he said, "It is impossible for a man to be saved in ignorance" (D. & C. 131:6), he meant *there could be no salvation in ignorance of Jesus Christ and the saving principles of the gospel.* "The principle of knowledge is the principle of salvation," he said on another occasion. "This principle can be comprehended by the faithful and diligent; and every one that does not obtain knowledge sufficient to be saved will be condemned.

The principle of salvation is given us through the knowledge of Jesus Christ." (Teachings, p. 297.)

One of the signs of the times is that at "the time of the end: many shall run to and fro, and knowledge shall be increased" (Dan. 12: 4); that men shall be "Ever learning, and never able to come to the knowledge of the truth." (2 Tim. 3:7.) But *the saints are expected to specialize in the knowledge of the truth, the knowledge that makes known the mysteries of the kingdom and the wonders of eternity* (D. & C. 76:1-10), *the knowledge that will rise with them in the resurrection and be of such a nature as to give them advantage in the world to come.* (D. & C. 130:18-19.) *This kind of knowledge is a result of righteousness and comes by revelation.* (John 7:17.)

The Holy Ghost is the revealer of saving knowledge. "God shall give unto you knowledge by his Holy Spirit, yea, by the unspeakable gift of the Holy Ghost," the revelation says, even knowledge "that has not been revealed since the world was until now; Which our forefathers have awaited with anxious expectation to be revealed in the last times, which their minds were pointed to by the angels, as held in reserve for the fulness of their glory; A time to come in the which nothing shall be withheld, whether there be one God or many gods, they shall be manifest." (D. & C. 121:26-28.)

In fact, the Melchizedek Priest- hood *is the key to the knowledge of God* because it is in and through that priesthood that men receive the gift of the Holy Ghost. (D. & C. 84:19.) And those who grow in the knowledge of God until they gain a "perfect knowledge of God" cannot be kept within the veil and they are permitted to see the Lord. (Ether 3:19-20, 25; D. & C. 93:1.)

All men who gain exaltation eventually arrive at the status where they have all truth and know all things. (D. & C. 93:26-28.) But this is not gained in a moment; it is a long process of advancement and education. "We consider that God has created man with a mind capable of instruction, and a faculty which may be enlarged in proportion to the heed and diligence given to the light communicated from heaven to the intellect," Joseph Smith said, "and that *the nearer man approaches perfection, the clearer are his views,* and the greater his enjoyments, till he has overcome the evils of his life and lost every desire for sin; and like the ancients, arrives at that point of faith where he is wrapped in the power and glory of his Maker and is caught up to dwell with him. But we consider that this is a station to which no man ever arrived in a moment: he must have been instructed in the government and laws of that kingdom by proper degrees, until his mind is capable in some measure of comprehending the propriety, justice, equality, and consistency of the same." (*Teachings*, p. 51.)

KOLOB.

See ASTONOMY. *Kolob* means "the first creation." It is the name of the planet "nearest to the celes-

tial, or the residence of God." It is "first in government, the last pertaining to the measurement of time. . . . One day in Kolob is equal to a thousand years according to the measurement of this earth." (Book of Abraham, pp. 34-35; Abra. 3:3-9.)

L

LABOR TROUBLES.
See SIGNS OF THE TIMES.

LADY.
See ELECT LADY.

LAKE OF FIRE AND BRIMSTONE.
See FIRE AND BRIMSTONE.

LAMANITE CURSE.
See APOSTASY, BOOK OF MORMON, NEPHITES AND LAMANITES, RACES OF MEN, SPIRITUAL DEATH. Because they rebelled against the truth, a twofold *curse* came upon the Lamanites:

1. They were cut off from the presence of the Lord and thus died spiritually. Scales of darkness covered their eyes because they did not accept the saving principles of the gospel. They became apostates and the descendants of apos-

tates. (1 Ne. 2:21-24; 2 Ne. 4:4-6; Alma 9:13-14.)

2. "After they had dwindled in unbelief," that is, after they had forsaken the Church and the gospel, "they became a dark, and loathsome, and a filthy people, full of idleness and all manner of abominations." (1 Ne. 12:23.) So that they "might not be enticing" unto the Nephites, "the Lord God did cause a skin of blackness to come upon them." (2 Ne. 5:20-25; Alma 3:14-16.)

During Book of Mormon times the curse fell upon Laman, Lemuel, the sons of Ishmael, the Ishmaelitish women, the descendants of all these, and upon all who were "led away by the Lamanites," and who mingled their seed with the seed of that people. (Alma 3:6-10.)

Then near the close of the 4th century after Christ, Mormon prophesied of yet greater curses to come upon the seed of the then warring nations. "This people shall be scattered, and shall become a dark, a filthy, and a loathsome people, beyond the description of that which ever hath been amongst us, yea, even that which hath been among the Lamanites, and this because of their unbelief and idolatry." (Morm. 5:15; D. & C. 3:16-20.)

During periods of great righteousness, when groups of Lamanites accepted the gospel and turned to the Lord, the curse was removed from them. Thousands of Lamanites were converted "and the curse of God did no more follow them" in the days of Aaron and Ammon and their brethren. (Alma 23:5-9, 17-18.) Some 20 years before the personal ministry of Christ among them, the curse was removed from a group of Lamanite converts and they became white like the Nephites. (3 Ne. 2:15-16.) From the time of Christ's ministry among them until nearly 200 A.D. there were no Lamanites for all had become "the children of Christ, and heirs to the kingdom of God." (4 Ne. 17-20, 38.)

When the gospel is taken to the Lamanites in our day and they come to a knowledge of Christ and of their fathers, then the "scales of darkness" shall fall from their eyes; "and many generations shall not pass away among them, save they shall be a white and delightsome people." (2 Ne. 30:6.) Finally, before the judgment bar of God, all who have been righteous, Lamanites and Nephites alike, will be free from the curse of spiritual death and the skin of darkness. (Jac. 3:5-9.)

LAMANITES.
See NEPHITES AND LAMANITES.

LAMB OF GOD.
See ATONEMENT OF CHRIST, CHRIST, SACRIFICES, SONG OF THE LAMB. Christ is "the *Lamb of God,* which taketh away the sin of the world." (John 1:29, 36; D. & C. 76:85; 88:106; 1 Ne. 13.) He is "the Lamb slain from the foundation of the world" (Rev. 13:8), the "lamb without blemish and without spot: Who verily was foreordained before the foundation of the world" (1 Pet. 1:19) to be the Savior and Redeemer, the One who would work out the infinite and eternal atonement. As a Lamb, he was sacrificed for men, and salvation comes because of the shedding of his blood. (Mosiah 3:18.) Those who gain salvation are the ones who "have washed their robes, and made them white in the blood of the Lamb." (Rev. 7:14; 12:11; 1 Ne. 12:11; Alma 13:11; 34:36; 3 Ne. 27:19; Morm. 9:6; Ether 13:10-11.)

In honor of the Lamb, a great choir of 100,000,000 voices of the redeemed shall sing this new song (Rev. 5:9-13):

Thou wast slain,
And hast redeemed us to God by
thy blood

*Out of every kindred, and tongue,
and people, and nation;
And hast made us unto our God
kings and priests:
And we shall reign on the earth. . . .
Worthy is the Lamb that was slain
To receive power, and riches, and
wisdom,
And strength, and honour, and
glory, and blessing. . . .
Blessing, and honour, and glory,
and power,
Be unto him that sitteth upon the
throne,
And unto the Lamb for ever and
ever.*

LAMB'S BOOK OF LIFE.
See BOOK OF LIFE.

LAMB'S WIFE.
See BRIDE OF THE LAMB.

LAMENTATION.
See MOURNING.

LANGUAGE OF ADAM.
See ADAMIC LANGUAGE.

LANGUAGE OF PRAYER.
See PRAYER.

LANGUAGES.
See ADAMIC LANGUAGE,
TONGUES. It is reasonable to suppose that in the approximately
1757 years between the fall and
the *confusion of tongues* at the
tower of Babel there would have
been some perversion and change
in the pure language of Adam. This
would have been particularly pronounced among early apostate
groups. It is clear, however, that
all people who lived during that
early period could understand each
other, for in a general sense, "The
whole earth was of one language,
and of one speech." (Gen. 11:1.)

Following the confounding of
the *language* of the people (Gen.
11:9), only the Jaredites retained
a tongue patterned after that of
Adam. (Ether 1:33-43; 12:24.) All
others had their language confounded. Since that day there
obviously have been many language
and dialect changes. The King
James Version of the Bible has
been one of the great stabilizing
influences in the English language.
One of the chief reasons for giving
the gift of tongues is to enable the
elders to teach the gospel to those
of different languages.

LARCENY.
See STEALING.

LARGE PLATES OF NEPHI.
See GOLD PLATES.

LASCIVIOUSNESS.
See SEX IMMORALITY.

LAST DAY.

See JUDGMENT DAY, LAST DAYS, WORLD. A great day of judgment, a day of dividing the sheep from the goats, a day when the inhabitants of all nations will be placed on the Lord's right hand or on his left, will take place at his Second Coming. (Matt. 25:31-46.) This is called *"the last great day of judgment"* which is to take place "at the end of the world" as that world is known to us. (D. & C. 19:3.) It is the last day of preparation, of probation, for those who will then be judged; but life and days as such will continue, for there is no end to either. The *last day* is the one of which the revelation speaks when it says: "In the beginning of the seventh thousand years will the Lord God sanctify the earth, and complete the salvation of man, and *judge all things,* and shall redeem all things, except that which he hath not put into his power." (D. & C. 77:12.) After this last day, the last day of this earth's continuance in its present mortal status, life will continue on during the millennial era.

LAST DAYS.

See SECOND COMING OF CHRIST, SIGNS OF THE TIMES. Our earth was originally created in a paradisiacal state; with Adam's fall and consequent expulsion from Eden, the earth also fell and became mortal. When our Lord comes to usher in the millennium, "We be-lieve . . . that the earth will be renewed and received its paradisiacal glory." (Tenth Article of Faith.) To and including the millennial period, the earth enjoys a "continuance" or "temporal existence" of 7,000 years duration. (D. & C. 77:6, 12.) That period of time just preceding the millennium is named the *last days*. It is the specified time, period, or age in which the necessary prerequisites to the Second Coming will occur. The last days are the days of the dispensation of the fulness of times, the days when the signs of the Second Coming are shown forth, the days of "restitution of all things, which God hath spoken by the mouth of all his holy prophets since the world began." (Acts 3:21.) We are now living in that period of time, and the great restitution (or restoration) is in process.

LAST JUDGMENT.
See JUDGMENT DAY.

LAST SUPPER.
See SACRAMENT.

LATIN VULGATE.
See KING JAMES VERSION OF THE BIBLE.

LATTER-DAY REVELATION.
See REVELATION.

431

LATTER-DAY SAINTS.
See MORMONS.

LAUGHTER.

See CHEERFULNESS, JOY, LIGHT-MINDEDNESS, LIGHT SPEECHES, REVERENCE, SOLEMNITY. 1. Joyful *laughter* meets with divine approval, and when properly engaged in, it is wholesome and edifying. Incident to the normal experiences of mortality, there is "A time to weep, and a time to laugh." (Eccles. 3:4.) Our Lord taught: "Blessed are ye that weep now: for ye shall laugh." (Luke 6:21, 25.)

Our Lord's ministers, however, are commanded: "Cast away your idle thoughts and your *excess* of laughter far from you." (D. & C. 88:69.) Their main concerns should be centered around "the solemnities of eternity" (D. & C. 43:34), with laughter being reserved for occasional needed diversion. Laughter on the sabbath day is expressly curtailed (D. & C. 59:15), and while worshiping and studying in the school of the prophets, the elders were commanded to abstain "from all laughter." (D. & C. 88:121.) This same abstinence should prevail in sacrament meetings and in all solemn assemblies.

2. *Laughter* is also used to connote: (a) *skepticism,* as illustrated by the reactions of Abraham and Sarah to the promise of Isaac's birth (Gen. 17:17; 18:13-15; 21:6); and (b) *scorn and derision,* as when the righteous are mocked for their good deeds and intentions. (Alma 26:23; 2 Kings 19:21; Neh. 2:19; Job 12:4; Matt. 9:24; Mark 5:40; Luke 8:53.) This kind of laughter is inspired of and practiced by the devil. When calamities befall the inhabitants of the earth, "the devil laugheth, and his angels rejoice." (3 Ne. 9:2.) At the Second Coming of Christ, "they that have laughed"—in this scornful and derisive manner—"shall see their folly. And calamity shall cover the mocker, and the scorner shall be consumed." (D. & C. 45:49-50.)

There is, of course, righteous scorn and derision as well as evil, and accordingly the Lord and his saints properly laugh at the wicked. (Ps. 37:13; 52:6.) "He that sitteth in the heavens shall laugh: the Lord shall have them in derision." (Ps. 2:4.)

LAW.

See CELESTIAL LAW, CHRIST, GOSPEL, LAWGIVER, LAW OF MOSES, LAWS OF THE LAND, LIGHT OF CHRIST, OBEDIENCE, RIGHTEOUSNESS, TELESTIAL LAW, TEN COMMANDMENTS, TERRESTRIAL LAW. 1. Christ is the *Law* (3 Ne. 15:9), meaning that he is the personification and embodiment of law; that acting in the power and authority of his Father he has given a law to all things (D. & C. 88:42); that he himself governs and is governed by law; that the Light of Christ is the "law by which all things are governed" (D. & C. 88:

13); that it is he who gave the law of Moses, and the law of the gospel, and the laws of science, and all laws that ever have been or ever will be revealed.

2. All things are governed by *law;* nothing is exempt. In the eternal perspective there is no such thing as chance; in the divine economy the same invarying result always flows from the same cause. These principles are immutable, eternal, everlasting; they apply to all things both temporal and spiritual. "Unto every kingdom is given a law; and unto every law there are certain bounds also and conditions." Christ "hath given a law unto all things, by which they move in their times and their seasons; And their courses are fixed, even the courses of the heavens and the earth, which comprehend the earth and all the planets." (D. & C. 88:38, 42-43.)

Once a law has been ordained, it thereafter operates automatically; that is, whenever there is compliance with its terms and conditions, the promised results accrue. The law of gravitation is an obvious example. Similarly, compliance with the law of faith always brings the gifts of the Spirit. By obedience to celestial law men automatically qualify for a celestial inheritance in eternity; by open rebellion against law, they automatically assure themselves of a place in a kingdom which is not a kingdom of glory. (D. & C. 88:21-34.)

3. Generally throughout the scriptures the term *law* has reference to "the law of the Lord." (Ps. 1:1-2.) That is, it means the statutes, judgments, and principles of salvation revealed by the Lord from time to time. In ancient Israel, for instance, the law was the law of Moses—which was a preparatory gospel, a law of restrictions and ordinances. To us the law is the law of Christ—which is the fulness of the gospel or "the perfect law of liberty." (Jas. 1:25.)

There is no whim, chance, or caprice in the operation of gospel law. Divine blessings always result from obedience to the law upon which their receipt is predicated. (D. & C. 130:20-21.) "For all who will have a blessing at my hands shall abide the law which was appointed for that blessing, and the conditions thereof, as were instituted from before the foundation of the world. . . . Will I appoint unto you, saith the Lord, except it be by law, even as I and my Father ordained unto you, before the world was? I am the Lord thy God; and I give unto you this commandment—that no man shall come unto the Father but by me or by my word, which is my law, saith the Lord." (D. & C. 132:5-12.)

"The law of the Lord is perfect, converting the soul: the testimony of the Lord is sure, making wise the simple. The statutes of the Lord are right, rejoicing the heart: the commandment of the Lord is pure, enlightening the eyes. The fear of the Lord is clean, enduring for ever: the judgments of the Lord are true and righteous altogether. More to be desired are they than gold, yea, than much fine gold: sweeter also than honey and the honeycomb. Moreover by them is thy servant warned: and in keeping of them there is great reward." (Ps. 19:7-11.)

LAWFUL HEIRS ACCORDING TO THE FLESH.
See MELCHIZEDEK PRIESTHOOD.

LAWGIVER.
See CHRIST, GOSPEL, JUDGE OF ALL THE EARTH, KING, LAW OF MOSES, RULER, SHILOH. Christ is the *Lawgiver* (D. & C. 38:22; 45:59; 64:13; Gen. 49:10; Jas. 4:12); "he hath given a law unto all things." (D. & C. 88:42.) "I am the law," he said. (3 Ne. 15:9.) "The Lord is our judge, *the Lord is our lawgiver,* the Lord is our king; he will save us." (Isa. 33:22.)

LAW OF CARNAL COMMAND-MENTS.
See LAW OF MOSES.

LAW OF CONSECRATION.
See CONSECRATION.

LAW OF FORGIVENESS.
See FORGIVENESS.

LAW OF MOSES.
See AARONIC PRIESTHOOD, GOSPEL, LEVITES, MOSES, SALVATION BY GRACE. To Moses the Lord first gave the higher priesthood and revealed the fulness of the gospel. But Israel rebelled and manifest such gross unworthiness that their God took from them the power whereby they could have become a kingdom of priests and of kings and gave them instead a lesser law, a law of carnal commandments, a preparatory gospel, a schoolmaster to bring them to Christ and the fulness of his gospel. He gave them instead the *law of Moses.* (D. & C. 84:17-28; Gal. 3; Heb. 4:2; *Inspired Version,* Ex. 34:1-2.)

Moses received by revelation many great gospel truths, as for instance the Ten Commandments recorded in the 20th chapter of Exodus. These gospel truths, being eternal in their nature, are part of the fulness of the everlasting gospel; they have always been in force in all dispensations. They are part of "the law of Christ." (D. & C. 88:21.) But the particular things spoken of in the scriptures as the law of Moses were the ordinances and performances that were "added because of transgressions." (Gal. 3:19.) They were the "divers washings, and carnal ordinances, imposed on them until the time of reformation." (Heb. 9:10.) They were "the law of commandments contained in ordinances." (Eph. 2:15.) In great detail they are recorded in Exodus, Leviticus, Numbers, and Deuteronomy, and were preserved on the brass plates which the Nephites took with them. (1 Ne. 4:15-16.)

Abinadi said that the law of Moses was given to point the attention of the people forward to Christ and that all things in it "were types of things to come." Israel was given, he said, "a very strict law; for they were a stiff-necked people, quick to do iniquity, and slow to remember the Lord their God; Therefore there was a law given them, yea, a law of performances and of ordinances, a law which they were to observe strictly from day to day, to keep them in remembrance of God and their duty towards him." (Mosiah 13:27-32.) Paul said "the law was our schoolmaster to bring us unto Christ." (Gal. 3:24.) It was "the law of carnal commandments" (D. & C. 84:27; Heb. 7:16) because it was given to teach those belonging to the chosen race to bridle their passions, to overcome the lusts of the flesh, to triumph over carnal things, and to advance to the place where the Spirit of the Lord could have full flow in their hearts.

Salvation is in Christ and not in the law of Moses. *"Salvation doth not come by the law alone,"* Abinadi explained, "and were it not for the atonement, which God himself shall make for the sins and iniquities of his people, . . . they must unavoidably perish, notwithstanding the law of Moses." (Mosiah 13:27-28.) Rather, as Nephi taught, the law was given to prove to the people "the truth of the coming of Christ; for, *for this end hath the law of Moses been given;* and all things which have been given of God from the beginning of the world, unto man, are the typifying of him." (2 Ne. 11:4.) Paul also found it necessary to teach with great force that men are saved by the grace of God, "Not of works," that is, the works of the law of Moses. (Eph. 2.)

At any time in ancient Israel when the Melchizedek Priesthood was operative and when the people were enjoying its blessings—even though they continued to keep the formalities of the law of Moses— the law itself became dead to them. The Nephites, for instance, prior to the ministry of our Lord among them, had only the Melchizedek Priesthood, and during that entire 600 year period they kept the law of Moses. (2 Ne. 5:10; Jar. 5; Mosiah 2:3.) They, of course, had the fulness of the gospel, and thus Nephi recorded: "It is by grace that we are saved, after all we can do. And, notwithstanding we believe in Christ, we keep the law of Moses, and look forward with steadfastness unto Christ, until the law shall be fulfilled. For, for this end was the law given; wherefore *the law hath become dead unto us, and we are made alive in Christ because of our faith; yet we keep the law because of the commandments."* (2 Ne. 25:23-25.)

In Christ the law of Moses, that is, the law of carnal commandments, was fulfilled. The great and eternal gospel truths revealed through Moses remained in force, but the lesser law that had pointed the attention of the people forward to the coming of the Lord became a dead letter. "Think not that I am come to destroy the law or the prophets," our Lord proclaimed. "I am not come to destroy but to fulfil; For verily I say unto you, one jot nor one tittle hath not passed away from the law, but in me it hath all been fulfilled." (3 Ne. 12:17-18.)

"Behold, I say unto you that *the law is fulfilled that was given unto Moses.* Behold, I am he that gave the law, and I am he who covenanted with my people Israel; therefore, the law in me is fulfilled, for I have come to fulfil the law; therefore it hath an end. Behold, I do not destroy the prophets, for as many as have not been fulfilled in me, verily I say unto you, shall all be fulfilled. And because I said unto you that old things have passed away, I do not destroy that which hath been spoken concerning things which are to come. For behold, the covenant which I have made with my people is not all fulfilled; but the law which was given unto Moses hath an end in me. Behold, I am the law, and the light. Look unto me, and endure to the end, and ye shall live; for unto him that endureth to the end will I give eternal life." (3 Ne. 15:4-9.)

LAW OF THE MOURNER.
See MOURNING.

LAW OF WITNESSES.
See AARONIC PRIESTHOOD, ASSISTANT PRESIDENT OF THE CHURCH, DISPENSATIONS, KEYS OF THE KINGDOM, MELCHIZEDEK PRIESTHOOD, PRIESTHOOD, RESTORATION OF THE GOSPEL, WITNESSES OF THE BOOK OF MORMON. Whenever the Lord has established a dispensation by revealing his gospel and by conferring priesthood and keys upon men, he has acted in accordance with the *law of witnesses* which he himself ordained. This law is: "In the mouth of two or three witnesses shall every word be established." (2 Cor. 13:1; Deut. 17:6; 19:15; Matt. 18:15-16; John 8:12-29.)

Never does one man stand alone in establishing a new dispensation of revealed truth, or in carrying the burden of such a message and warning to the world. In every dispensation, from Adam to the present, two or more witnesses have always joined their testimonies, thus leaving their hearers without excuse in the day of judgment should the testimony be rejected.

Joseph Smith, for instance, conformed perfectly to the law of witnesses in that someone else was always with him when priesthood or keys were being conferred by heavenly messengers. Both he and Oliver Cowdery had the Aaronic

Priesthood conferred upon them by John the Baptist (D. & C. 13); both were present when Peter, James, and John brought back the Melchizedek Priesthood (D. & C. 20:2-3; 27:12-13); both were present when Elias, Moses, and Elijah came with the keys of their dispensations (D. & C. 110:11-16); and so it was with reference to every key, power, and authority that the Lord restored anew in this final dispensation—someone was always with the Prophet so that two witnesses could leave a binding testimony to the world.

It was to fulfil perfectly the law of witnesses that Hyrum Smith was chosen to replace Oliver Cowdery when he fell from grace. And when the time came to seal the testimony of the Lord's witnesses with their own blood, both testators went to their death in Carthage Jail so that their testimony is in full force for all men. (*Doctrines of Salvation,* vol. 1, pp. 203-228.)

LAWS.
See COMMANDMENTS.

LAWS OF THE LAND.
See CIVIL GOVERNMENTS, CONSTITUTION OF THE UNITED STATES, KINGCRAFT, LAW, OBEDIENCE, THEOCRACY (THEARCHY). In a perfect theocracy, when the government of God functions as the Lord

originally ordained, both civil and spiritual laws are ordained by God and are administered through his agents. It was so in the days of Adam; it will be so in the millennium. But because of apostasy, men have declined to be governed by God directly and have set up instead civil governments of their own. Inspiration and divine guidance have been manifest in the creation of some of these civil governments as in the case of the United States. However, this inspiration has not made the government of the United States synonymous with the government of God, and so today we find civil law administered by men and spiritual law by the Church. Under present conditions there is and should be a complete separation of Church and state, and as long as such a separation continues, the saints are and should be subject to the *laws of the land.* (D. & C. 134.)

"Let no man break the laws of the land," the Lord said, speaking of the laws prevailing in the United States, "for he that keepeth the laws of God hath no need to break the laws of the land. Wherefore, be subject to the powers that be, until he reigns whose right it is to reign, and subdues all enemies under his feet." (D. & C. 58:21-22.) Paul gave similar counsel, even for the autocratic governments of his day. (Rom. 13:1-7; Tit. 3:1.)

Obviously, however, situations can arise in which civil power can command an act which so sets at naught the Lord's decrees as to require his saints to follow his law rather than the lesser worldly requirement. When commanded to preach no more in the name of Christ, Peter and John replied: "Whether it be right in the sight of God to hearken unto you more than unto God, judge ye. For we cannot but speak the things which we have seen and heard." (Acts 4:13-21.) Similarly, Daniel continued to worship the true God, though the law prohibited prayer to any but Darius (Dan. 6), and the three Hebrew captives continued their proper worship though their rebellion against Nebuchadnezzar's law meant the fiery furnace for them. (Dan. 3.)

LAYING ON OF HANDS.

See ADMINISTRATIONS, CONFIRMATION, GIFT OF THE HOLY GHOST, ORDINATIONS. Special blessings, anointings, sealing of anointings, confirmations, ordinations, callings, healings, offices, and graces are conferred by the *laying on of hands* by the Lord's legal administrators. As with all of the Lord's prescribed procedural requisites, the proffered blessings come only when the designated formalities are observed. (*Teachings,* pp. 198-199.)

Following baptism in water, the bestowal of the Holy Ghost takes place by the laying on of hands of the elders. (D. & C. 20:41, 58, 68; 35:6; 49:13-14; Acts 8:14-19; 19:1-7; 1 Tim. 4:14; 2 Tim. 1:6.) Those who receive this conferral, in a very real sense, have the hand of the Lord laid upon them. For instance, to Edward Partridge the Lord said: *"I will lay my hand upon you by the hand of my servant* Sidney Rigdon, and you shall receive my Spirit, the Holy Ghost, even the Comforter, which shall teach you the peaceable things of the kingdom." (D. & C. 36:1-2.)

"According to the order of God," ordination to offices in the priesthood is performed by the laying on of hands. (Alma 6:1; Acts 6:5-6; 1 Tim. 5:22.) Setting apart to positions of presidency, administration, or special responsibility comes in the same way. (Fifth Article of Faith; Num. 27:18-23; Deut. 34:9.) Formal blessings are conferred by the laying on of hands (D. & C. 20:70; Matt. 19:13-15; Acts 9:17), and the healing of the sick and the casting out of devils are oftentime accomplished in accord with this same formality. (D. & C. 42:44; 66:9; Mark 5:23; 6:5; 16:18; Luke 4:40-41; 13:11-13; Acts 28:8; Jas. 5:14-16.)

LAY MINISTRY.
See MINISTERS.

LECTURES.
See SERMONS.

LECTURES ON FAITH.

See DOCTRINE AND COVENANTS, FAITH, SCHOOL OF THE PROPHETS. From 1835 to 1921 all editions of the Doctrine and Covenants contained some lesson material called the *Lectures on Faith*. These lectures, seven in number, were prepared by the Prophet for study in the school of the elders in Kirtland in 1834-1835, and also for publication in the Doctrine and Covenants. They were not themselves classed as revelations, but in them is to be found some of the best lesson material ever prepared on the Godhead; on the character, perfections, and attributes of God; on faith, miracles, and sacrifice. They can be studied with great profit by all gospel scholars. (*Doctrines of Salvation*, vol. 2, pp. 303-304; vol. 3, p. 194.)

LEGAL ADMINISTRATORS.

See MINISTERS.

LEGENDS.

See MYTHOLOGY.

LEISURE.

See RECREATION.

LEMUELITES.

See BOOK OF MORMON, NEPHITES AND LAMANITES. That portion of the Lamanites who were lineal descendants of Lemuel the older brother of Nephi were sometimes called *Lemuelites*. (Jac. 1:13-14; 4 Ne. 37-39.)

LESSER PRIESTHOOD.

See AARONIC PRIESTHOOD.

LETTERS OF COMMENDATION.

See EPISTLES OF COMMENDATION.

LEVI.

See AARON, AARONIC PRIESTHOOD, LEVITES, MELCHIZEDEK, MOSES, TRIBES OF ISRAEL. As the 3rd son of Jacob and Leah, *Levi* stands as the head of one of the tribes of Israel. (Gen. 29:34.) For their valiance in defending the cause of righteousness, as for instance in the matter of the molten calf (Ex. 32), the qualified, male descendants of Levi were chosen to hold the priesthood and serve as the Lord's ministers in Israel. (Num. 3; 4; 8.)

LEVITES.

See AARONIC PRIESTHOOD, AARONITES, LEVI, SACRIFICES. In a general sense, all of the descendants of Levi are *Levites*, just as all of the descendents of Ephraim are *Ephraimites*. Moses and Aaron were Levites in this sense. But since the Levites, as a tribe, were honored with the lesser priesthood, it was common to speak of the ordained, adult, male members of the tribe as the *Levites.* These priesthood bearers were chosen as the Lord's ministers "instead of the firstborn of all the children of Israel," and Aaron and his sons presided over them. (Num. 8.) Charge of the tabernacle of the congregation was given to them. (Num. 3; 4.) They participated in the offering of sacrifices (2 Chron. 29), lived on the tithes of the people (Num. 18), and did not receive an inheritance of land with the other tribes. (Josh. 18:7.) Members of this tribe will again in this final dispensation offer their traditional sacrifices to the Lord as part of the restoration of all things. (D. & C. 13; *Teachings,* pp. 172-173.)

LEVITICAL ORDER.
See AARONIC PRIESTHOOD.

LEVITICAL PRIESTHOOD.
See AARONIC PRIESTHOOD.

LEVITY.
See LAUGHTER.

LEWDNESS.
See SEX IMMORALITY.

LIAHONA.
See BOOK OF MORMON, WITNESSES OF THE BOOK OF MORMON. Lehi found in his tent door a ball or director or compass, made of fine brass and curious workmanship, on which there were two spindles to point the course the Nephites should follow in the wilderness. Also from time to time messages were written on it by divine power giving counsel and guidance. This divine compass, called the *Liahona,* worked according to the faith of the Nephites, and its use typified the faith which men must have to follow the words of Christ which lead to eternal life. (1 Ne. 16:10, 26-30; 2 Ne. 5:12; Mosiah 1:16; Alma 37:38-45.) It was handed down from generation to generation among the Nephites, was hid up with the gold plates, and was seen by Joseph Smith and the Three Witnesses in this dispensation. (D. & C. 17:1.)

LIARS.
See BLASPHEMY, DEVIL, HONESTY, TRUTH. In the general dealings of men, those who knowingly utter or act out falsehoods are *liars.* This is also true in the gospel sense. But according to scriptural standards the sin of *lying* also branches out to include a much larger group of persons. Scripturally, *anything that in its nature is untrue and is therefore designed to deceive is a lie. Those who believe in false doctrines are thus guilty of believing a lie, and those who propagate these untruths are guilty of lying.*

For instance: The creeds of apostate Christendom teach untruths about God, and the scriptures say that those who accept these creeds "have inherited lies." (Jer. 16:16-21.) Those who accept any of the doctrines of the apostate churches are said to "believe a lie." (2 Thess. 2:1-12.) The process of apostasy consists in changing "the truth of God into a lie." (Rom. 1:25.) Alma taught that all who do not hearken to the voice of "the good shepherd" are part of the devil's fold, and then he added, "whosoever denieth this is a liar." (Alma 5:38-40.) Sherem confessed, after being smitten, "I have lied unto God; for I denied the Christ." (Jac. 7:19; Alma 12:3.) False teachers are liars. (Rev. 2:2.) Conversely, Moroni concluded some of his expositions of the truth by saying, "I lie not." (Moro. 10: 26-27.) In other words, *to teach true doctrine is to tell the truth, and to teach false doctrine is to lie.*

Particular obligation rests upon members of the true Church to walk in the truth which they have espoused and to keep themselves free from errors, falsehoods, and untruths. Certainly their false outward profession of that godliness or saintliness which should attend church membership becomes a living lie if they do not walk in the light. John taught: "He that saith, I know him [Christ], and keepeth not his commandments, is a liar, and the truth is not in him. . . . Who is a liar but he that denieth that Jesus is the Christ?" (1 John 2:4, 22.) "If any man say, I love God, and hateth his brother, he is a liar." (1 John 4:20; 5:10.)

Since truthfulness is an attribute that is perfected in Deity, it follows that God is a Being who cannot lie. (D. & C. 62:6; Enos 6; 3 Ne. 27:18; Ether 3:12; Titus 1:2; Heb. 6:18.) Similarly, "the Spirit speaketh the truth and lieth not." (Jac. 4:13.) Lucifer, on the other hand, "was a liar from the beginning" (D. & C. 93:25), "is the father of all lies" (2 Ne. 2:18; 9:9; Ether 8:25; John 8:44), and entices men to become liars. (2 Ne. 28:8.) But men are commanded by the Lord not to lie (D. & C. 10:25-28; 42:21; 3 Ne. 26:32; Col. 3:9), for liars "shall be thrust down to hell" (2 Ne. 9:34), shall suffer the second death (D. & C. 63:17; Rev. 21:8), and receive a final inheritance in the telestial kingdom. (D. & C. 76: 103.) In Nephite times liars were also punished by the civil law (Alma 1:17), and there are some civil and criminal proceedings today based on deceit and fraud. (D. & C. 42:86.)

LIBERTY.

See AGENCY, CIVIL GOVERNMENTS, CONSTITUTION OF THE UNITED STATES, FREEDOM, GOSPEL, INALIENABLE RIGHTS. Perfect *liberty,* the free power of choice, is found only where there is adherence to gospel principles. The gospel is "the perfect law of liberty." (Jas. 1:25; 2:12.) By accepting the gospel, men become partakers of "the glorious liberty of the children of God" (Rom. 8:21), liberty from the bondage of sin, the darkness of error, the lusts of the flesh. "Where the Spirit of the Lord is, there is liberty." (2 Cor. 3:17.) "Stand fast therefore in the liberty wherewith Christ hath made us free," Paul counseled, "and be not entangled again with the yoke of bondage." (Gal. 5:1; D. & C. 88:86.)

This American nation, in the providences of the Almighty, is "a land of liberty" (2 Ne. 10:11), to be inhabited by "a free people." (3 Ne. 21:4.) The Israelitish words, "Proclaim liberty throughout all the land unto all the inhabitants thereof" (Lev. 25:10), were aptly chosen by the early American patriots to be cast on the Liberty Bell. The constitution of the United States is designed to guarantee liberty and all inalienable rights to "all the inhabitants" of this choice land. (D. & C. 98:4-9; 101: 76-80; 109:54.)

LICENTIOUSNESS.
See SEX IMMORALITY.

LIES.
See LIARS.

LIFE.
See BREATH OF LIFE, DEATH, ETERNAL LIFE, INTELLIGENCE, LIGHT OF CHRIST, LIGHT OF LIFE, PRE-EXISTENCE, SOUL, SPIRIT CHILDREN, SPIRITUAL DEATH, SPIRITUAL

LIFE. The *life* of the body is in the soul; that is, the conscious, sentient, knowing, intelligent part of the human personality is resident in the spirit, in the eternal part of man, in the part which is the literal offspring of an Omnipotent Father. And as it is with man, so it is with animals, fowls, fishes, and every living creature, and even with the earth itself— all have life; and in each instance the life is resident in the spirit part of the created thing, for "all things were before created; but spiritually were they created and made." (Moses 3:7.) Life is manifest in four distinct states of existence.

1. PRE-EXISTENT LIFE.—*Life* began with the birth of the spirit in pre-existence; it began when the spirit element (or intelligence) was so arranged as to become one of "the intelligences that were organized before the world was." (Abra. 3:22.) Any notion or theory that life, or ego, or agency, existed for each individual prior to the time of the spirit birth is pure speculation, wholly unsupported by any correctly understood and properly interpreted scripture. Life began for man and for all created things at the time of their respective spirit creations. Before that there were only the spirit elements from which the Almighty would in due course create life. In the sense that spirits never die or go out of existence, life is unending or eternal. (*Improvement Era,* vol. 13, pp. 75-81.)

2. MORTAL LIFE.—It is this state

of existence to which reference is usually made when the term *life* is used. Mortal life consists in the temporary union of body and spirit. The natural or temporal death is brought to pass by the separation of body and spirit. In this sense life ceases when death comes. Thus the revelations speak of the end of life (D. & C. 19:25, 32), of preserving the life of some (D. & C. 25:2; 63:3), and of laying down one's life in the gospel cause. (D. & C. 98:13-14.) Life and death are set forth as two opposite things (D. & C. 50:5, 8), and men are expected while in this life to gain knowledge and intelligence so that their acquirements can be restored to them in the life to come. (D. & C. 130:18-19.)

In the sense that mortality is the great probationary period of eternal existence, in the sense that "this life is the time for men to prepare to meet God" (Alma 34:32), this life becomes the most important part of all eternity. In it we take the final examination for all the life we lived in pre-existence, and in it we take the entrance examination which will determine the kingdom of glory we shall inherit in the life hereafter.

But in the sense that spiritual realities and qualifications far excel temporal things in importance, this life is not of great worth as compared with the gospel and salvation. "All they who suffer persecution for my name, and endure in faith," the Lord says, "though they are called to lay down their lives for my sake yet shall they partake of all this glory [that of the millennial era]. Wherefore, fear not even unto death; for in this world your joy is not full, but in me your joy is full. Therefore, care not for the body, neither the life of the body; but care for the soul, and for the life of the soul." (D. & C. 101:35-37; 103:27-28.) Our Lord, of course, "gave his own life" as part of the great plan of redemption. (D. & C. 34:3.) "Greater love hath no man than this, that a man lay down his life for his friends." (John 15:13.)

It was also in accordance with this principle, which compares the relative worth of temporal and spiritual things, that our Lord said to the Nephite Twelve: "Take no thought for your life, what ye shall eat, or what ye shall drink; nor yet for your body, what ye shall put on. Is not the life more than meat, and the body than raiment?" (3 Ne. 13:25; Matt. 6:25.)

"The life of the flesh is in the blood" (Lev. 17:11), meaning that according to the laws which are ordained, mortal life ceases when the blood is shed. But in the full and eternal sense, life exists in the world in and through and because of Christ. He is the life of the world. (D. & C. 10:70; 12:9; 34:2; 39:2; 45:7; 3 Ne. 9:18; 11:11; Ether 4:12; John 1:4; 14:6.) "In him was the life of men and the light of men." (D. & C. 93:9.) Except for the light of Christ, the life-giving power which proceeds from his presence fo fill the immensity of space (D. & C. 88:12), life and being would cease. He is literally the light of the world and the life of the world in that life and light come because of him and without him they would not exist.

3. LIFE IN THE SPIRIT WORLD. —At death the eternal spirit merely steps out of the mortal tabernacle and enters a world of waiting spirits to await the day of the resurrection. The spirit, which lived before in pre-existence, lives on after death. In this sense, there is no death and there are no dead. Our departed fellow mortals only seem dead unto us because they have gone into another realm of existence where we can no longer see and associate with them.

4. IMMORTAL LIFE.—By definition, as we most generally use the term, immortality is to live forever in a resurrected state, body and spirit being inseparably connected. There is no end to life. Christ, for instance, is "without beginning of days or end of life." (D. & C. 78:16.) Resurrected beings "shall not any more see death." (D. & C. 88:116.)

LIFE OF THE WORLD.
See LIGHT OF LIFE.

LIGHT.
See GOSPEL, INTELLIGENCE, LIGHT OF CHRIST, LIGHT OF LIFE, LIGHT OF THE WORLD, OBEDIENCE, SALVATION, TRUTH. Gospel *light* is the mental and spiritual enlightenment from God which enables men to receive truth and knowledge and gain salvation. Light is an attribute of Deity and shines forth from him; in him it is found in its fulness and perfection. "God is light, and in him is no darkness at all" (1 John 1:5); he is "the Father of lights." (Jas. 1:17.)

Christ is the light of the world, and the gospel is his message of light and salvation to all men. "I have sent mine everlasting covenant into the world," he said, speaking of the restoration of the gospel, "to be a light to the world, and to be a standard for my people, and for the Gentiles to seek to it." (D. & C. 45:9.) Where the gospel is there is light; where the gospel is not darkness prevails. In telling his disciples the signs of his Second Coming, our Lord said: "When the times of the Gentiles is come in, a light shall break forth among them that sit in darkness, and it shall be the fulness of my gospel." (D. & C. 45:28-29, 36.) The light of the great latter-day Church is "a standard for the nations." (D. & C. 115:5; 124:9.)

Whenever the gospel is on earth, it is the true light. (1 John 2:8.) Those who accept the gospel of Christ are thus called "out of darkness into his marvellous light." (1 Pet. 2:9; Alma 26:3, 15.) Paul was sent to the Gentiles, "To open their eyes, and to turn them from darkness to light" (Acts 26:18), "the light of the glorious gospel of Christ, . . . the light of the knowledge of the glory of God." (2 Cor. 4:4-6.) Those who accept the gospel have their souls "illuminated by the light of the everlasting word." (Alma 5:7.) Our Lord "brought life and immortality to light through the gospel." (2 Tim. 1:10.)

On the other hand, those who reject the gospel reject the light and continue to walk in darkness. (Hela. 13:29.) "Because they yield unto the devil and choose works of darkness rather than light, therefore they must go down to hell." (2 Ne. 26:10.) "And this is the condemnation, that light is come into the world, and men loved darkness rather than light, because their deeds were evil. For every one that doeth evil hateth the light, neither cometh to the light, lest his deeds should be reproved. But he that doeth truth cometh to the light, that his deeds may be made manifest, that they are wrought in God." (John 3:19-21; D. & C. 10:21; 29:45; 93:31-32.)

Those who reject the light after they have received it are more to be condemned than those who have never known the truth. (D. & C. 41:1.) "For of him unto whom much is given much is required; and he who sins against the greater light shall receive the greater condemnation." (D. & C. 82:3; Alma 9:23; 45:12.) Sons of perdition are those who have known the fulness of light and have then come out in

open rebellion against the Author of light. (D. & C. 76:31-49; *Teachings,* pp. 357-358.) Light forsakes any who are unrepentant, and they lose even that which they may have received. (D. & C. 1:33.) Satan is the king of darkness; light flees from him. (D. & C. 93:36-37.)

Light comes from God (2 Ne. 31:3), and the cry of righteous men has always been, "O send out thy light and thy truth: let them lead me." (Ps. 43:3.) The Lord's word is a light to the path of the faithful (Ps. 119:105), and men are commanded to "walk in the light of the Lord." (Isa. 2:5; John 11:9-10; 12:35.) Parents are commanded to bring up their children "in light and truth." (D. & C. 93:40-42.) Light is a protection against evil of every sort, and the saints should "put on the armour of light." (Rom. 13:12.)

There are two great scriptural tests which show whether men have the light and are walking therein, one pertaining to beliefs, the other to conduct. Isaiah challenged false teachers with this test: "To the law and to the testimony: if they speak not according to this word, it is because there is no light in them." (Isa. 8:20.) And John, speaking particularly to members of the Church, those upon whom "the true light now shineth," said: "He that saith he is in the light, and hateth his brother, is in darkness even until now. He that loveth his brother abideth in the light, and there is none occasion of stumbling in him. But he that hateth his brother is in darkness, and walketh in darkness, and knoweth not whither he goeth, because that darkness hath blinded his eyes." (1 John 2:8-11.)

Light leads to salvation; it edifies and uplifts. *"And that which doth not edify is not of God, and is darkness. That which is of God is light; and he that receiveth light, and continueth in God, receiveth more light; and that light groweth brighter and brighter until the perfect day."* (D. & C. 50:23-24.) *"And if your eye be single to my glory, your whole bodies shall be filled with light, and there shall be no darkness in you; and that body which is filled with light comprehendeth all things."* (D. & C. 88:67.) "In me shall all mankind have light, and that eternally, even they who shall believe on my name." (Ether 3:14.) "If we walk in the light, as he is in the light, we have fellowship one with another, and the blood of Jesus Christ his Son cleanseth us from all sin." (1 John 1:7.) The saved shall walk in the light forever (Rev. 21:24) and rejoice in the light of the countenance of their God. (Ps. 4:6; D. & C. 88:56, 58; 3 Ne. 19:25.)

LIGHT-MINDEDNESS.

See LAUGHTER, LIGHT SPEECHES, RECREATION, SOLEMNITY. In connection with his command to build a house of God and conduct a school of the prophets therein, the Lord commanded his ministers to cease from light speeches, laughter, and *light-mindedness.* (D. & C. 88:121.) Obviously the elders of Israel, while engaged on the Lord's solemn and sober business, must avoid those trifling and frivolous things which make up light-mindedness. Theirs is an awesome responsibility while so engaged, for they are dealing with the souls of men. The divine injunction here given is not to be construed to enjoin proper and wholesome relaxation and recreational activities. These latter have the Lord's approval. (D. & C. 136:28.)

LIGHTNINGS.
See SIGNS OF THE TIMES.

LIGHT OF CHRIST.

See CHRIST, CONSCIENCE, HOLY GHOST, LIGHT, LIGHT OF LIFE, LIGHT OF THE WORLD, SPIRIT OF THE LORD. Christ is "the true light that lighteth every man that cometh into the world." (D. & C. 93:2; John 1:9.) This enlightenment is administered to all men through the Spirit of Christ, or the Spirit of the Lord, or the Light of truth, or the *light of Christ*—all of which expressions are synonymous. This Spirit fills the immensity of space, is in all things, and is not to be confused with the Personage of Spirit known as the Holy Ghost (or Spirit of the Lord). (*Doctrines of Salvation,* vol. 1, pp. 38-54.)

The light of Christ is the Spirit of the Lord which leads men to accept the gospel and join the Church so that they may receive the gift of the Holy Ghost. Men are commanded to "live by every word that proceedeth forth from the mouth of God. For the word of the Lord is truth, and whatsoever is truth is light, and whatsoever is light is Spirit, even the Spirit of Jesus Christ. And the Spirit giveth light to every man that cometh into the world; and the Spirit enlighteneth every man through the world, that hearkeneth to the voice of the Spirit." (D. & C. 84:44-46.) Those who hearken to this Spirit come into the Church, receiving "of the Spirit of Christ unto the remission of their sins." (D. & C. 20:37; 84:47-48; Alma 19:6; 26:3; 28:14.) Men are born again by following the light of Christ to the point where they receive the actual enjoyment of the gift of the Holy Ghost. (Mosiah 27:24-31; Alma 36.)

It is because of the light of Christ that all men know good from evil and enjoy the guidance of what is called *conscience.* (Moro. 7:12-19.) It is the Spirit by means of which God is omnipresent; it is the light which enables Christ to be in all things, and through all thing, and round about all things. It gives life to all things, is the law by which they are governed, and the power of God is manifest through it. (D. & C. 88:6-13.)

LIGHT OF LIFE.

See LIFE, LIGHT, LIGHT OF CHRIST, LIGHT OF THE WORLD.
1. Christ is the *light of life.* Life exists in and through and because of the light of Christ—"The light which is in all things, which giveth life to all things, which is the law by which all things are governed." (D. & C. 88:13.) Without this light of life, the planets would not stay in their orbits, vegetation would not grow, men and animals would be devoid of "the breath of life" (Gen. 2:7), and life would cease to exist. (D. & C. 88:50.)

2. Christ is also the *light of life* in a special sense for those who obey his gospel law. "In him was life; and the life was the light of men." (John 1:4.) "I am the light of the world: he that followeth me shall not walk in darkness, but shall have the light of life." (John 8:12.)

LIGHT OF THE WORLD.

See CHRIST, EXEMPLAR, LIGHT, LIGHT OF CHRIST, LIGHT OF LIFE.
1. Christ is the light (John 1:7-9; 12:35-36, 46), "the light which shineth in darkness, and the darkness comprehendeth it not" (D. & C. 6:21; 10:58; 11:11; 34:2; 39:2; 45:7; John 1:5), "a light which cannot be hid in darkness" (D. & C. 14:9); "I will be a light unto them forever, that hear my words." (2 Ne. 10:14; Ps. 27:1.) He is the *light of the world* (John 8:12; 9:5), "the life and light of the world"

(D. & C. 10:70; 11:28; 12:9; 34:2; 39:2; 45:7; Mosiah 16:9; Alma 38:9; 3 Ne. 9:18; 11:11); "in him was the life of men and the light of men." (D. & C. 93:9.) He was "A light to lighten the Gentiles" (Luke 2:32; Isa. 42:6), and it was foretold of those among whom he should minister: "The people that walked in darkness have seen a great light: they that dwell in the land of the shadow of death, upon them hath the light shined." (Isa. 9:2; 51:4; Hosea 6:5.)

When our Lord says, "I am the light, and the life, and the truth of the world" (Ether 4:12), he is teaching that he is the source of life, light, and truth; that he sets the perfect example in their use; and that all men must look to him for these things. "Behold, I am the law, and the light. *Look unto me,* and endure to the end, and ye shall live; for unto him that endureth to the end will I give eternal life." (3 Ne. 15:9.) "Behold I am the light; I have set an example for you." (3 Ne. 18:16.) Those who gain eternal life shall walk in the light of their Lord forever. (Isa. 60:19-20; Rev. 21:23; 22:5.)

2. Faithful saints are also the *light of the world.* "Ye are the light of the world," our Lord said to his ancient disciples. "Let your light so shine before men, that they may see your good works, and glorify your Father which is in heaven." (Matt. 5:14-16; 3 Ne. 12:14-16.) "Ye are my disciples; and ye are a light unto this people." (3 Ne. 15:12.) "Hold up your light that it may shine unto the world. Behold *I am the light which ye shall hold up—that which ye have seen me do."* (3 Ne. 18:24.)

John the Baptist "was a burning and a shining light" (John 5:35); Paul and Barnabas were sent to be a light to the Gentiles (Acts 13:47), as are also the elders in this day. (D. & C. 86:11.) Indeed, the elders are "set to be a light unto the world, and to be the saviors of men" (D. & C. 103:9), and church officers are set to be "a light unto the church." (D. & C. 106:8.) False teachers are those who "set themselves up for a light unto the world, that they may get gain and praise of the world; but they seek not the welfare of Zion." (2 Ne. 26:29.)

LIGHT OF TRUTH.
See INTELLIGENCE.

LIGHT SPEECHES.
See IDLE WORDS, LAUGHTER, LIGHT-MINDEDNESS, RECREATION, SACRAMENT MEETINGS, SOLEMNITY. *Light speeches,* loud speech, laughter, and light-mindedness were forbidden in the school of the prophets, the school where the officers and ministry of the Church were to be taught. (D. & C. 88:118-141.) That was an occasion when "the solemnities of eternity" (D. & C. 43:34) should rest upon the minds

of all who participated. In principle it would be well if this same sobriety and decorum attended where sacrament and other sacred church meetings are concerned. Entertainment, levity, frivolity, and trifling matters are highly offensive to the Spirit on sacred and solemn occasions. Sacrament meetings are not occasions of laughter and joking, but for serious consideration of the eternal principles of salvation, and anything else is of questionable propriety. Speakers who deliver light, frivolous talks on these occasions depart from the true and proper spirit of the meeting and might well ponder the Lord's injunction against using idle words. (Matt. 12:36.)

LINEAGE.
See PATRIARCHAL BLESSINGS.

LION OF THE TRIBE OF JUDAH.
See CHRIST, SHILOH, SON OF DAVID, STEM OF JESSE. Christ is the *Lion of the Tribe of Judah.* (Rev. 5:5.) When Father Jacob gave Judah his patriarchal blessing, Judah was likened both to a lion's whelp and to an old lion and was promised that the sceptre should not depart from his descendants until the coming of Christ. (Gen. 49:8-12.) Accordingly, to denominate our Lord as the Lion of the Tribe of Judah is to point to his position as a descendant of Judah, to his membership in that tribe from which kings were chosen to reign, and also to show his status as the most pre-eminent of all that house, as the one who bore the banner of the tribe so to speak.

LIQUOR.
See WORD OF WISDOM.

LIVING ORACLES.
See ORACLES.

LOGOS.
See APOSTASY, CHRIST, CREEDS, WORD OF GOD. Among the pagan philosophies extant in the early days of the Christian Era was one called the *New Platonic,* a philosophy based primarily on the views of Plato. "Everything which exists in heaven or in earth, except Deity and unorganized matter, according to Plato's philosophy, had a beginning—there was a time when it did not exist; but there never was a time when the idea, that is, the form or plan of the thing, did not exist in the mind of Deity. This idea or intelligence existing with God from all eternity, is what Plato called the *Logos*—the word or intelligence of Deity." (*Outlines of Ecclesiastical History,* pp. 186-193.)

In that early period of the Christian Era, when pagan philosophies were being mingled with the doctrines of the gospel to form the apostate Christianity, attempts

449

were made to harmonize these theories of men with the gospel concept of Christ being the *Word of God.* It was out of these attempts, and the consequent squabbling over the rank of the so-called *Logos* in the Trinity, that the early councils drafted the creeds which have since been the basis for the false sectarian notions about Deity.

LONG-SUFFERING.
See PATIENCE.

LORD.

See ADONAI, CHRIST, FATHER IN HEAVEN, GOD, JEHOVAH, JESUS, LORD GOD, LORD OF GLORY, LORD OF HOSTS, LORD OF LORDS, LORD OF SABAOTH, LORD OF THE SABBATH, LORD OMNIPOTENT, LORD OUR RIGHTEOUSNESS. 1. Both the Father and the Son, as omnipotent and exalted personages, are commonly known by the name-title *Lord.* (Ps. 110:1; Matt. 22:41-46.) Embraced within this appellation is the concept that they are supreme in authority and sovereign over all, that they are the rulers and governors of all things. Since it is Christ in particular, however, through whom Deity operates where men and their affairs are concerned, it follows that most scriptural references to the Lord have reference to him. (D. & C. 76:1; Isa. 43:14; 49:26; Luke 2:11; Acts 10:36; Philip. 2:11.)

2. There are about 150 Biblical instances in which the name *lord* is given to men, the intent being to convey especial honor or reverence on the one so designated. Similar usage prevails in the British caste system in this day.

LORD ALMIGHTY.
See ALMIGHTY GOD.

LORD GOD.

See CHRIST, GOD, LORD. By uniting the sacred names *Lord* and *God* into such reverential combinations as *God the Lord* or *Lord God* (Moses 3:4), superlative expression is made of the majesty, omnipotence, and glory of Deity. These names—used, as the various scriptural contexts show, with reference to both the Father and the Son—are also sometimes expanded to be, among others: *Lord God of Abraham* (Gen. 28:13), *Lord God of Israel* (Ex. 32:27), *Lord God of Elijah* (2 Kings 2:14), *Lord God of our fathers* (2 Chron. 20:6), *Lord God of hosts,* (1 Kings 19:10), and *Lord God Almighty* (Rev. 4:8; 11:17; 15:3; 16:7; D. & C. 109:77; 121:4.)

LORD GOD ALMIGHTY.
See ALMIGHTY GOD.

LORD GOD OF THE HEBREWS.
See GOD OF ISRAEL.

LORD JEHOVAH.
See JEHOVAH.

LORD JESUS.
See JESUS.

LORD OF GLORY.
See CHRIST, KING OF GLORY, LORD. Christ is the *Lord of Glory* (1 Cor. 2:8; Jas. 2:1), a name given him to signify the transcendent glory which attends him in his capacity of Lord of all.

LORD OF HOSTS.
See BATTLE OF THE GREAT GOD, CHRIST, LORD, LORD OF SABAOTH, ROCK OF HEAVEN. Christ is the *Lord of Hosts* (1 Chron. 17:24; Ps. 24:10; Isa. 6:5; Zech. 14:16-17; Mal. 1:14), meaning that he is a man of war (Ex. 15:3), a God of battles (Ps. 24:8), a leader of his saints in days of conflict and carnage. It was so anciently; it is so today; it will be so in the future, particularly in the coming battle of the great day of God Almighty. (Zech. 14:3; Rev. 16:14; 20:8.) There are more than 50 Book of Mormon references which speak of the Lord of Hosts, an equal number in the Old Testament, and a dozen such references in the Doctrine and Covenants.

LORD OF LORDS.
See CHRIST, EXALTATION, GOD, GODHOOD, GOD OF GODS, KING OF KINGS, LORD, PLURALITY OF GODS. Both the Father and the Son are properly known by the title *Lord of Lords,* a designation that means literally what it says. (Deut. 10:12-22; 1 Tim. 6:15; Rev. 17:14; 19:16.) The purpose of this name is not simply to reveal that Christ, for instance, is the Lord of mortal persons who are ranked as lords, but rather it is to show that he is Lord and God to others who themselves also are Lords and Gods in their own right. Thus Abraham, Isaac, and Jacob (among others) "have entered into their exaltation, according to the promises, and sit upon thrones, and are not angels but are *gods.*" (D. & C. 132:29, 37.) Since exalted beings themselves become Lords and Gods, and since they still stand in subjection to Christ their Lord and their God, it follows that he is a Lord of Lords. Whatever is true of him is also true of his Father, and in due course it will be true of all exalted beings.

LORD OF SABAOTH.
See CHRIST, LORD, LORD OF HOSTS. Christ is the *Lord of Sabaoth.* (Isa. 1:9; Rom. 9:29; Jas. 5:4; D. & C. 87:7; 88:2; 98:2.) *Sabaoth* is a Hebrew word meaning *hosts* or *armies;* thus, *Jehovah Sabaoth* means the *Lord of Hosts.* Also, as revealed to the Prophet, "The Lord of Sabaoth, . . . is by interpretation, the creator of the

first day, the beginning and the end." (D. & C. 95:7.)

LORD OF THE HARVEST.

See CHRIST, LORD, LORD OF THE VINEYARD. Christ is the *Lord of the Harvest* (Matt. 9:36-38); the elders of Israel are the laborers who thrust in their sickles to reap (D. & C. 4); the harvest is one of souls, souls who shall have eternal life. (Matt. 13:24-30; D. & C. 86: 1-7.) "He that reapeth receiveth wages, and gathereth fruit unto life eternal." (John 4:35-36.)

LORD OF THE SABBATH.

See CHRIST, LORD, SABBATH. Christ is the *Lord of the Sabbath* (Mark 2:23-28; Luke 6:1-12); he gave it, and he directs what men must do thereon to be saved. (Ex. 16:29; D. & C. 59:9-20.) The Sabbath bears record of Christ: from Adam to Moses it was the 7th day to signify that our Lord rested on that day from his creative labors (Ex. 20:8-11); from Moses to Christ, the Sabbath day was a different day each year to commemorate our Lord's leading of the children of Israel out of bondage (Deut. 5:12-15); and from the apostolic day until now, the Sabbath has been the first day of the week to point attention to our Lord's resurrection on his holy day.

LORD OF THE VINEYARD.

See CHRIST, LORD, LORD OF THE HARVEST. In the parable of the laborers in the vineyard, Christ is the *Lord of the Vineyard* who sends forth laborers to prune and work in his vineyard. (Matt. 20:1-16.) In the parable of the wicked husbandmen, his Father is the *Lord of the Vineyard* who sends many servants and finally his own Son—all of which laborers are ill treated or slain by the husbandmen. (Matt. 21:33-46.) In both parables "the vineyard of the Lord of hosts is the house of Israel." (Isa. 5:1-7.)

In this dispensation the Lord's vineyard covers the whole earth, and the laborers are going forth to gather scattered Israel before the appointed day of burning when the vineyard will be purified of corruption. (D. & C. 33:2-7; 72:2; 75:2-5; 101:44-62; 135:6.)

LORD OMNIPOTENT.

See CHRIST, LORD, OMNIPOTENCE. Christ is the *Lord Omnipotent* (Mosiah 3:5, 17-18, 21; 5:2, 15; Rev. 19:6), meaning that as Lord of all he has all power.

LORD OUR RIGHTEOUSNESS.

See CHRIST, LORD, RIGHTEOUSNESS. Christ is known by the name, *The Lord Our Righteousness* (Jer. 23:5-6; 33:16), signifying that as the personification of righteousness himself, he has made it possible, through his atoning sacrifice, for his saints to attain a state of like purity and sanctification.

LORDS.
   See PLURALITY OF GODS.

LORD'S DAY.
   See SABBATH.

LORD'S PRAYER.
   See PRAYER.

LORD'S SCOURGE.
   See SIGNS OF THE TIMES.

LORD'S SUPPER.
   See SACRAMENT.

LORD'S TABLE.
   See SACRAMENT.

LORD'S TIME.
   See TIME.

LOST SCRIPTURE.
   See APOCRYPHA, BIBLE, BOOK OF ENOCH, BOOK OF JOSEPH, BOOK OF MORMON, BOOK OF REMEMBRANCE, BRASS PLATES, DOCTRINE AND COVENANTS, EPISTLES, GOLD PLATES, INSPIRED VERSION OF THE BIBLE, NEW TESTAMENT, OLD TESTAMENT, PEARL OF GREAT PRICE, SCRIPTURE, SEALED BOOK, STANDARD WORKS. Only a small part of the recorded revelations and scriptural writings of the past are now available to men. That great body of revealed truth which is missing—without question a collection of scripture far greater in quantity than the scriptures now extant—is *lost scripture,* meaning that it is lost to the knowledge of men.

Many passages and even whole books of scripture have been lost through the carelessness or wickedness of the record keepers. (1 Ne. 13.) Even some of the revelations given in this dispensation have been lost, as for instance the 116 manuscript pages of the Book of Mormon (D. & C. 10) and the account of the words spoken by the angelic ministrants who restored the Melchizedek Priesthood. There are also many revelations, known in former days, which are lost in the sense that the Lord withholds them from this generation pending such time as men acquire the faith and righteousness which will entitle them to receive the added truths. When men gain the same faith enjoyed by the Brother of Jared, for instance, the sealed portion of the Book of Mormon—a volume of scripture known to the Jaredites and Nephites in certain ages of their histories (Mosiah 28:11-19; Alma 63:12; Ether 4:1-7)—will again be revealed.

Adam kept a Book of Remembrance, only a few fragmentary statements from which have come down to us. (Moses 6:5.) We have no authentic records of the writings of Seth, Enos, Cainan, Mahalaleel, Jared, Methusaleh, or Noah —all of whom lived before the flood and all of whom were great preachers of righteousness. (Moses 6; 8.) The portion of Enoch's prophecies and preachings that has been revealed to us is small. (Moses 6; 7; D. & C. 107:56-57.) Such scriptures as were written or possessed by Shem, Melchizedek, Esaias, Gad, Jeremy, Elihu, Caleb, and Jethro are unknown to us today. (D. & C. 84:7-13.) Indeed there may be many races and peoples, whose very existence is unknown in the modern world, who had revelations and scripture given to them.

We have only a minor part of the scriptures had by the Jaredites. (Ether 1:1-5; 4:1-7.) There were many records in the hands of Mormon when he compiled, abridged, and wrote the Book of Mormon, none of which records are known to us now. (Words of Morm. 1-11.) It is reported by President Brigham Young that there was in the Hill Cumorah a room containing many wagon loads of plates. (*Journal of Discourses,* vol. 19, p. 38.) The Brass Plates contained many passages and books that are not in the Old Testament as we have it. (1 Ne. 13:23.) Among these were the Books of Zenos, Zenock, Neum, and Ezias (1 Ne. 19:10-16; Jac. 5; 6:1; Alma 33:3-17; 34:7; Hela. 8:19-20; 15:11; 3 Ne. 10:16) and also the writings of Joseph who

was sold into Egypt. (2 Ne. 3.)

Reference is made in both the Old and New Testaments to books and epistles which are not now available. These include: Book of the Covenant (Ex. 24:4, 7); Book of the Wars of the Lord (Num. 21:14); Book of Jasher (Josh. 10:13; 2 Sam. 1:18); A Book of Statutes (1 Sam. 10:25); Book of the Acts of Solomon (1 Kings 11:41); Books of Nathan and Gad (1 Chron. 29:29; 2 Chron. 9:29); Prophecy of Ahijah and Visions of Iddo (2 Chron. 9:29; 12:15; 13:22); Book of Shemaiah (2 Chron. 12:15); Book of Jehu (2 Chron. 20:34); Acts of Uzziah, written by Isaiah (2 Chron. 26:22); Sayings of the Seers (2 Chron. 33:19); an epistle of Paul to the Corinthians (1 Cor. 5:9); an epistle of Paul to the Ephesians (Eph. 3:3); an epistle of Paul to the Laodiceans (Col. 4:16); Epistle of Jude (Jude 3); and the Prophecies of Enoch (Jude 14).

The prophecy that Christ should be a Nazarene (Matt. 2:23) and the prediction, known to the scribes in our Lord's day, that Elias must restore all things before the coming of Christ (Matt. 17:10), are illustrations of lost scripture. And there are many apocryphal books now in existence which in their original state were inspired scripture.

This is the great era of restoration and in it all things shall be restored that have been known in all former dispensations. All the truths had in ages past shall be restored, though this does not mean every lost scripture shall again come forth. If substantially identical truths were revealed to successive prophets, there would be no especial need to restore both records.

But many lost scriptures already have been restored, and much more is yet to come. We have already been given the Book of Mormon, and the sealed portion of the plates shall in due course come forth. When the lost tribes of Israel return, they shall bring with them their scriptures. (2 Ne. 29:12-14; D. & C. 133:26-35.) Indeed, the Lord speaks unto "all nations" and they write his word, and when the nations run together their testimonies of the truth run together also. (2 Ne. 29.) This age of restoration is the age in which nations are running together, that is, coming in contact with each other and in many instances becoming one nation.

Some of the restored scriptures have been given again by direct revelation. It was in this way that the Book of Moses came and that the corrections were made in the Inspired Version of the Bible. Other scriptural restorations have taken place by means of inspired translation. The Book of Mormon and the Book of Abraham came in this way. When the Brass Plates come forth, they obviously will come by translation. (Alma 37:1-12.) Presumptively there are many records yet to come forth by means of trans-

lation. (D. & C. 9:2.)

There is no more false or absurd doctrine than the sectarian claim that the Bible (or any other book for that matter) contains all of the word of God. The Bible, great and valuable as it is, is only a part of the great library of revealed truth which the merciful Author of all scripture, in his omniscient wisdom, deigns to give to his children on earth. His voice to those who complain when added scripture is brought to light is: *"Wherefore murmur ye, because that ye shall receive more of my word?"* (2 Ne. 29:8.)

LOST SOULS.
See DESTRUCTION OF THE SOUL.

LOST TRIBES OF ISRAEL.
See GATHERING OF ISRAEL, ISRAEL, KINGDOM OF ISRAEL, SCATTERING OF ISRAEL, TRIBES OF ISRAEL. When Shalmanezer overran the *Kingdom of Israel* (about 721 B.C.), he carried the Ten Tribes comprising that kingdom captive into Assyria. From thence they were led into the lands of the north and have been called the *Lost Tribes* because they are lost to the knowledge of other people. (1 Ne. 22:4.) "We have no knowledge of the location or condition of that part of the Ten Tribes who went into the north country." (*Compendium*, p. 88.)

Esdras, an apocryphal writer,

records this version of their escape from Assyria: "Those are the ten tribes, which were carried away prisoners out of their own land in the time of Osea the king, whom Salmanasar the king of Assyria led away captive, and he carried them over the waters, and so came they into another land. *But they took this counsel among themselves, that they would leave the multitude of the heathen, and go forth into a further country, where never mankind dwelt, That they might there keep their statutes, which they never kept in their own land.* And they entered into Euphrates by the narrow passage of the river. *For the most High then shewed signs for them, and held still the flood, till they were passed over.* For through that country there was a great way to go, namely, of a year and a half: and the same region is called Arsareth. Then dwelt they there until the latter times; and now when they shall begin to come, The Highest shall stay the stream again, that they may go through." (*Apocrypha,* 2 Esdras 13:40-47.)

Commenting on this, Elder George Reynolds has written: "They determined to go to a country where never men dwelt, that they might be free from all contaminating influences. That country could only be found in the north. Southern Asia was already the seat of a comparatively ancient civilization. Egypt flourished in northern Africa, and south-

ern Europe was rapidly filling with the future rulers of the world. They had, therefore, no choice but to turn their faces northward. The first portion of their journey was not however north; according to the account of Esdras, they appear to have at first moved in the direction of their old homes, and it is possible that they originally started with the intention of returning thereto, or probably in order to deceive the Assyrians they started as if to return to Canaan, and when they had crossed the Euphrates, and were out of danger from the hosts of the Medes and Persians, then they turned their journeying feet toward the polar star. Esdras states that they entered in at the narrow passages of the River Euphrates, the Lord staying the springs of the flood until they were passed over. The point on the River Euphrates at which they crossed would necessarily be in its upper portion, as lower down would be too far south for their purpose.

"The upper course of the Euphrates lies among lofty mountains and near the village of Pastash, it plunges through a gorge formed by precipices more than a thousand feet in height and so narrow that it is bridged at the top; it shortly afterward enters the plains of Mesopotamia. How accurately this portion of the river answers the description of Esdras of the narrows, where the Israelites crossed.

"From the Euphrates the wandering host could take but one course in their journey northward, and that was along the back or eastern shore of the Black Sea. All other roads were impassable to them, as the Caucasian range of mountains with only two or three passes throughout its whole extent, ran as a lofty barrier from the Black to the Caspian Sea. To go east would take them back to Media, and a westward journey would carry them through Asia Minor to the coasts of the Mediterranean. Skirting along the Black Sea, they would pass the Caucasian range, cross the Kuban River, be prevented by the Sea of Azof from turning westward and would soon reach the present home of the Don Cossaks." (Reynolds, *Are We of Israel*, pp. 27-28.)

"Is it altogether improbable that in that long journey of one and a half years, as Esdras states it, from Media the land of their captivity to the frozen north, some of the backsliding Israel rebelled, turned aside from the main body, forgot their God, by and by mingled with the Gentiles and became the leaven to leaven with the promised seed all the nations of the earth? The account given in the Book of Mormon of a single family of this same house, its waywardness, its stiffneckedness before God, its internal quarrels and family feuds are, we fear, an example on a small scale of what most probably happened in the vast bodies of Israelites who for so many months wended their tedious way northward. Laman and Lemuel had, no doubt, many counterparts in the journeying Ten Tribes. And who so likely to rebel as stubborn, impetuous, proud and warlike Ephraim? Rebellion and backsliding have been so characteristically the story of Ephraim's career that we can scarcely conceive that it could be otherwise and yet preserve the unities of that people's history. Can it be any wonder then that so much of the blood of Ephraim has been found hidden and unknown in the midst of the nations of northern Europe and other parts until the spirit of prophecy revealed its existence?" (*Are We of Israel,* pp. 10-11.)

The Lost Tribes are not lost unto the Lord. In their northward journeyings they were led by prophets and inspired leaders. They had their Moses and their Lehi, were guided by the spirit of revelation, kept the law of Moses, and carried with them the statutes and judgments which the Lord had given them in ages past. They were still a distinct people many hundreds of years later, for the resurrected Lord visited and ministered among them following his ministry on this continent among the Nephites. (3 Ne. 16:1-4; 17:4.) Obviously he taught them in the same way and gave them the same truths which he gave his followers in Jerusalem and on the American continent; and obviously they recorded his teachings, thus creating volumes of scripture comparable to the Bible and Book of Mormon. (2 Ne. 29:12-14.)

In due course the Lost Tribes of Israel will return and come to the children of Ephraim to receive their blessings. *This great gathering will take place under the direction of the President of The Church of Jesus Christ of Latter-day Saints,* for he holds the keys of "the gathering of Israel from the four parts of the earth, and the leading of the ten tribes from the land of the north." (D. & C. 110:11.) Keys are the right of presidency, the power to direct; and by this power the Lost Tribes will return, with "their prophets" and their scriptures to "be crowned with glory, even in Zion, by the hands of the servants of the Lord, even the children of Ephraim." (D. & C. 133:26-35.)

At the October, 1916, general conference of the Church, Elder James E. Talmage made this prediction: "The tribes shall come; they are not lost unto the Lord; they shall be brought forth as hath been predicted; and I say unto you there are those now living—aye, some here present—who shall live to read the records of the Lost Tribes of Israel, which shall be made one with the record of the Jews, or the Holy Bible, and the record of the Nephites, or the Book of Mormon, even as the Lord hath predicted; and those records, which the tribes lost to man but yet to be found again shall bring, shall tell of the visit of the resurrected Christ to them, after he had mani-

fested himself to the Nephites upon this continent." (*Articles of Faith,* p. 513.)

LOTS.
See Divination, Revelation. In the absence of a direct manifestation of the divine will and when absolute impartiality is desired, it is the approved gospel custom to reach decisions by *casting lots*. In ancient Israel the inheritances of the tribes were determined by lot. (Num. 26:55; 33:54; 36:2.) The same procedure is to be followed in latter-day Israel. (D. & C. 85:7.) Lehi's sons cast lots to see who should go to Laban to get the brass plates. (1 Ne. 3:11.) Obviously the Lord may control where a lot falls, as it appears he did in the case of Laman and his endeavor to get the brass plates.

According to the King James Version of the Bible, Saul asked the Lord, "Give a perfect lot," in determining where guilt lay in connection with his unadvised adjuration. (1 Sam. 14.) If this account is correct, it means that Saul was asking the Lord to give revelation by the casting of lots. Probably the marginal rendition of the statement is much nearer the truth. It reads: "And Saul said: Jahweh, God of Israel, why hast thou not answered thy servant this day? If the guilt be in me or in Jonathan my son, Jahweh, God of Israel, give Urim; but if thus thou say: It is in my people Israel; give Thummim." (1

Sam. 14:41.)

In choosing an apostolic witness to succeed Judas, the other apostles "appointed two," asked the Lord to "shew whether of these two thou hast chosen," and then "gave forth their lots." (Acts 1:20-26.) If this was an actual instance of the casting of lots, then the Lord was revealing by this means that Matthias was his choice to serve in the Council of the Twelve. The statement, "gave forth their lots," however, may well mean that they voted and Matthias was selected. When a high council organizes itself as a court to hear a case, the order in which they speak and for whom is determined by drawing lots, that is, they "cast lots or ballot." (D. & C. 102:12-34.)

LOTTERIES.

See GAMBLING, RAFFLES. *Lotteries* are one of the most flagrant forms of gambling. Ordinarily they are organized enterprises in which lots or chances are sold with prize winners being chosen by drawings. The fact that lotteries are often sponsored by governments, social and civic organizations, and even some churches merely shows how far these organizations have departed from true gospel standards.

LOVE.

See CHARITY, CONDESCENSION OF GOD, GRACE OF GOD, HATRED, LOVING-KINDNESS, MERCY, SERV-ICE. Many attributes and feelings are embraced in *gospel love:* devotion, adoration, reverence, tenderness, mercy, compassion, condescension, grace, service, solicitude, gratitude, kindness. Love's chief manifestation is seen in the grace of God as this is found in the infinite and eternal atonement. "For God so loved the world, that he gave his only begotten Son, that whosoever believeth in him should not perish, but have everlasting life." (John 3:16; D. & C. 34:3.) So infinite and limitless is the love of God, as manifest through the creation and redemption of all things, that John aptly crowned his own teachings on love by saying, "God is love" (1 John 4:7-21), that is, the fulness of perfect love is embodied in him.

The highest manifestation of love on man's part is seen in his devotion to God (Deut. 6:4-9); the next, in his attitude toward his fellow men. (Matt. 22:34-40.) But love of God is found only among those who love their fellow men. "If a man say, I love God, and hateth his brother, he is a liar: for he that loveth not his brother whom he hath seen, how can he love God whom he hath not seen? And this commandment have we from him, That he who loveth God love his brother also." (1 John 4:20-21.)

Love is always associated with and manifest through service. "Thou shalt love the Lord thy God with all thy heart, with all thy might, mind, and strength; and in the name of Jesus Christ thou shalt serve him. Thou shalt love thy neighbor as thyself." (D. & C. 59:5-6.) "If thou lovest me thou shalt serve me and keep all my commandments." (D. & C. 42:29; John 14:15.) "If a man love me, he will keep my words: and my Father will love him, and we will come unto him, and make our abode with him. He that loveth me not keepeth not my sayings." (John 14:23-24; D. & C. 130:3.) "This is love, that we walk after his commandments." (2 John 6.)

Love is the foundation for peace and righteousness in this life and for salvation in the life hereafter. (1 Cor. 2:9; 8:3; 1 John 3:14; D. & C. 76:116.) Faith operates by love. (Gal. 5:6.) The saints of God are recognized by the love they manifest one for another (John 13:34-35), and the absence of love among men is one of the signs of the great apostasy. (Matt. 24:12.) Love is particularly important in the family unit. "Thou shalt love thy wife with all thy heart, and shalt cleave unto her and none else." (D. & C. 42:22; Eph. 5:25, 28, 33; Col. 3:19.)

The members of the Church who keep the commandments have this promise: "Who shall separate us from the love of Christ? shall tribulation, or distress, or persecution, or famine, or nakedness, or peril, or sword? . . . Nay, in all these things we are more than conquerors through him that loved us. For I am persuaded"—Paul is speaking— "that neither death, nor life, nor angels, nor principalities, nor powers, nor things present, nor things to come, Nor height, nor depth, nor any other creature, shall be able to separate us from the love of God, which is in Christ Jesus our Lord." (Rom. 8:35-39.)

LOVING-KINDNESS.

See KINDNESS, LOVE, MERCY. Old Testament reference is found to the *loving-kindness* of the Lord. The connotation is one of steadfast love; it signifies the kindly, merciful, and loving relationship that exists between God and those who keep his commandments. For instance, the saints who abide the day of the Second Coming "shall mention the loving kindness of their Lord, and all that he has bestowed upon them according to his goodness, and according to his loving kindness, forever and ever." (D. & C. 133:52-53; Isa. 63:7-9.)

LOYALTY.

See DEVOTION, LOVE, OBEDIENCE, RIGHTEOUSNESS. Every faithful member of the Church enjoys and cultivates the attribute of *loyalty*—loyalty to the truth, to the Church itself, to the gospel of salvation, to sacred covenants made with the Lord, to the brethren of the priesthood, to the apostles and prophets whom God has sent, to family and friends, to the civil government, and to every righteous principle. Loyalty to true principles is of God, disloyalty of Lucifer. Brethren and sisters who are loyal and true to the Lord's plan and purposes are the ones chosen to administer his affairs on earth and the ones who shall be honored by him in his eternal kingdom hereafter.

LUCIFER.

See DEVIL. This name of Satan means literally *lightbearer* or *shining one*. It is thus intended to convey a realization of his high status of prominence and authority in pre-existence before his rebellion and fall. (D. & C. 76:25-27; Isa. 14:12-20; Luke 10:18; 2 Ne. 2:17-18.)

LUSTS.

See CARNALITY, DEVILISHNESS, FALLEN MAN, PASSIONS, SENSUALITY, SEX IMMORALITY. Lusts are the sinful and impure desires to which fallen man is heir. Mortality is the designated portion of eternity in which man is given the privilege of wrestling with the lusts of the flesh to determine whether he will be worthy of the companionship of pure, righteous, and lust-free personages in eternity. (Gal. 5:16-26; Tit. 3:3; Jas. 1:14-15; 2 Pet. 1:4; 2:10; Jude 18.)

"Abstain from fleshly lusts, which war against the soul." (1 Pet. 2:11.) "Cease . . . from all your lustful desires." (D. & C. 88: 121.) "For all that is in the world, the lust of the flesh, and the lust of the eyes, and the pride of life, is not of the Father, but is of the world. And the world passeth away, and the lust thereof: but he that doeth the will of God abideth for ever." (1 John 2:15-17.)

Of all the lusts of the flesh, those pertaining to sex immorality are the most damning and unholy. "He that looketh on a woman to lust after her, or if any shall commit adultery in their hearts, they shall not have the Spirit, but shall deny the faith and shall fear." (D. & C. 63:16; 42:23; 3 Ne. 12:28; Matt. 5:28.)

LYING.
See LIARS.

MADONNA.

See MARY. *Madonna* (Latin for *my lady*) is a designation originally applied by Catholics to Mary the mother of our Lord. It is a title now in general usage among most

Christians and commonly refers to a picture or statue of Mary, usually with the infant Jesus.

MAGI.

See ASTROLOGY, CHRIST, MAGIC, STAR OF BETHLEHEM. To a priestly caste or order of ancient Media and Persia was applied the name *Magi*. Their religion centered around stargazing and astrology; they worshiped fire, had a religion filled with taboos and spells and were versed in magic. The very word *magic* is one which was used originally to designate the ritual and learning practiced by Persian Magi.

Matthew's account of "wise men from the east" coming to Jerusalem and Bethlehem in search of the Christ Child is sometimes recited as a visit of three Magi. (Matt. 2.) Actually there is no historical basis for the prevailing legend that they were from the apostate Persian cult or that they were three in number. It is much more probable that they were devout men who knew of our Lord's coming advent, including the promise that a new star would arise, and that they came as prophets of any age would have done to worship their King. It is clear that they were in tune with the Lord and were receiving revelation from him, for they were "warned of God in a dream that they should not return to Herod." (Matt. 2:12.)

MAGIC.

See DIVINATION, FORTUNE TELLING, MAGI, MIRACLES, NECROMANCY, SOOTHSAYERS, SORCERY, SPIRITUALISM, SUPERSTITION, WITCHCRAFT, WIZARDS. In imitation of true religion with its miracles, signs, and gifts of the Spirit, Satan has substitute rituals and practices called *magic*. Attempts by unauthorized and therefore powerless ministers to duplicate the miraculous wonders of true religion result in the degenerate worship of magic. In its nature magic is the art which produces effects by the assistance of supernatural beings or by a mastery of secret forces in nature; *magicians* (those skilled in magic) are necromancers, sorcerers, conjurers, and the like.

Magic has flourished among apostate peoples in all ages. The magicians of Pharaoh's court had power given them from Satan to duplicate many of the miracles wrought by Moses. (Gen. 41:8, 24; Ex. 7:11, 22; 8:7, 18-19; 9:11.) The court of Babylon supported a great corps of magicians. (Dan. 1:20; 2: 2-27; 4:7-9; 5:11.) In the latter part of their history, among the Nephites, "there were sorceries, and witchcrafts, and magics; and the power of the evil one was wrought upon all the face of the land." (Morm. 1:19; 2:10.) Among some of the false sects and branches of modern Christendom, particularly as these are found in some of the less advanced nations of the earth, magic plays an extensive role in worship. Special curative and protective powers, for instance, are supposed to attach to items blessed by officials in these churches.

MAGICIANS.
See MAGIC.

MAGNIFICAT.
See MARY. In keeping with their custom of using Latin as their religious language, the Catholics refer to Mary's inspired song of thanksgiving and praise as the *Magnificat.* (Luke 1:46-55.)

MAGOG.
See GOG AND MAGOG.

MAHONRI MORIANCUMER.
See BOOK OF MORMON, JAREDITES. *Mahonri Moriancumer* is the name of the *Brother of Jared,* that mighty prophet who led the Jaredites from the Tower of Babel to their North American promised land. Our present knowledge of the life and ministry of this man, one of the greatest prophets ever to live on earth, is so comparatively slight that we do not even find his name recorded in Moroni's abridgment of the Book of Ether. It was, however, made known by the spirit of inspiration to the Prophet.

Oliver Cowdery, writing during the lifetime of the Prophet, referred to him as *Moriancumer.* (*Times and Seasons,* vol. 2, p. 362; *Juvenile Instructor,* vol. 13, p. 272.) In this connection it is interesting to note that the place on the shore of the great ocean where Jared and his people tarried for four years before crossing to America is known as the land of Moriancumer. (Ether 2:13.)

Elder George Reynolds has left us this account of the circumstances under which the full name was revealed to the Prophet: "While residing in Kirtland, Elder Reynolds Cahoon had a son born to him. One day when President Joseph Smith was passing his door he called the Prophet in and asked him to bless and name the baby. Joseph did so and gave the boy the name of *Mahonri Moriancumer.* When he had finished the blessing, he laid the child on the bed, and turning to Elder Cahoon he said, the name *I have given your son is the name of the Brother of Jared;* the Lord has just shown (*or revealed*) it to me. Elder William F. Cahoon, who was standing near, heard the Prophet make this statement to his father; and this was the first time the name of the Brother of Jared was known in the Church in this dispensation." (*Juvenile Instructor,* vol. 27, p. 282; *Improvement Era,* vol. 8, pp. 704-705.)

In the some 1750 years from Adam to the ministry of Moriancumer, many prophets saw glorious visions and were privileged to see and converse with Christ their Creator. Adam (D. & C. 107:53-57), Seth (Moses 6:3), Enoch to whom Christ, speaking by divine investiture of authority as though he were the Father, appeared and gave many revelations (Moses 6; 7), all those who lived in Enoch's Zion (Moses 7:16), Noah (Moses 8), and undoubtedly others of whom we have no record, all saw the Lord. But the most complete and comprehensive revelation ever given up to that time of the personality of Christ was given to the Brother of Jared.

Moroni's abridgment notes that the Lord "stood in a cloud . . . and for the space of three hours did the Lord talk with the brother of Jared," at the time he was commanded to build the barges for crossing the great ocean. Almost nothing is known of their conversation. (Ether 2:14-16.)

Later, however, when Moriancumer took the 16 stones up on Mount Shelem so that the Lord might touch them, thus causing them to give light in the barges, that great prophet recieved knowledge and revelation greater than that poured out upon the prophets who preceded him. "Behold, I am Jesus Christ," came the voice of God to him. "And never have I showed myself unto man whom I have created, for never has man believed in me as thou hast." Read in context and in the light of other passages, this means that no prior person had ever had so great faith as Moriancumer and that as a consequence none had gained so comprehensive a revelation of Christ's personality. The veil was completely removed where this Jaredite prophet was concerned; the Lord appeared in a more complete manner and form than ever before had been the case. (*Doctrines of Salvation,* vol. 1, p. 37.) Thus we find the Lord saying, "Behold, this body, which ye now behold, is the body of my spirit; and man have I created after the body of my spirit; and even as I appear unto thee to be in the spirit will I appear unto my people in the flesh."

Then Moroni, who is preserving for us only a fraction of the full account, says, "that Jesus showed himself unto this man in the spirit, even after the manner and in the likeness of the same body even as he showed himself unto the Nephites. And he ministered unto him even as he ministered unto the Nephites; and all this, that this man might know that he was God, because of the many great works which the Lord had showed unto him. And because of the knowledge of this man he could not be kept from beholding within the veil; and he saw the finger of Jesus, which, when he saw, he fell with fear; for he knew that it was the finger of the Lord; and he had faith no longer, for he knew, nothing doubting. Wherefore, having this perfect knowledge of God, he could not be kept from within the veil; therefore he saw Jesus; and he did minister unto him." (Ether 3:14-20.)

Also the Lord showed unto the Brother of Jared "all the inhabitants of the earth which had been, and also all that would be; . . . *and there never were greater things made manifest than those which were made manifest unto the brother of Jared.*" (Ether 3:25; 4:4.) All this was written, provision made that it might be read by the Urim and Thummim, and the promise given that in due course it would be revealed to men. "And in that day that they shall exercise faith in me, saith the Lord, even as the brother of Jared did, that they may become sanctified in me, then will I manifest unto them the things which the brother of Jared saw, even to the unfolding unto them all my revelations, saith Jesus Christ, the Son of God, the Father of the heavens and of the earth, and all things that are in them." (Ether 4:7.)

MAJOR PROPHETS.
See PROPHETS.

MAKER.
See CHRIST AS THE FATHER.

MAN.
See ADAM, AHMAN, ANGELS, ANGLO-MAN, DEVIL, DEVILS, GOD, GODHOOD, MAN OF HOLINESS, MORTALITY, PLURALITY OF GODS, PRE-EXISTENCE, WOMAN. Commonly we are in the habit of considering *man* as a human being only and stopping there. Actually the gospel perspective is far broader. In the language of Adam, two of the names of God the Father are, *Man of Holiness,* and *Man of Counsel* (Moses 6:57; 7:35); that is, God is a holy Man, a Man who is perfect in counsel. All beings who are his offspring, who are members of his family, are also men. This applies to the pre-existent spirits, including those who rebelled and were cast out with Lucifer to suffer eternally as sons of perdition (Isa. 14:16); to embodied spirits living on earth as mortal men; to translated beings such as those who are awaiting the day of their resurrection; and to the beings whom we call angels, beings who either as spirits or having tangible bodies are sent as messengers to minister to mortal men.

Even mortal man has a higher status than a finite perspective sometimes gives him. Speaking of such earth-bound creatures the scriptures say: "What is man, that thou art mindful of him? and the son of man, that thou visitest him? For thou hast made him a little lower than the angels, and hast crowned him with glory and honour." (Ps. 8:4-5.) The marginal reading, giving a more accurate translation, reads: "Thou hast made him but little lower than God [meaning Elohim]." Man and

465

God are of the same race, and it is within the power of righteous man to become like his Father, that is to become a holy Man, a Man of Holiness.

MANGER.
See BABE OF BETHLEHEM.

MANIFESTATIONS.
See VISIONS.

MANIFESTO.
See CELESTIAL MARRIAGE, DOCTRINE AND COVENANTS, KEYS OF THE KINGDOM, PLURAL MARRIAGE. President Wilford Woodruff issued an official declaration on October 6, 1890, known as the *Manifesto* which withdrew from the saints the privilege of "contracting any marriage forbidden by the law of the land." (D. & C. pp. 256-257.)

According to the Lord's law the priesthood cannot be used for any purpose without the authorization and approval of the one holding the keys of the kingdom of God on earth. Since these keys are vested in the President of the Church, no person can use that priesthood to seal a plural wife to another person without the approval of the President. (D. & C. 132:7; *Teachings,* p. 324.)

This Manifesto is published in the Doctrine and Covenants. It is a revelation in the sense that the Lord both commanded President Woodruff to write it and told him what to write. It is not, however, the same type of revelation found in most of the sections of the Doctrine and Covenants in that the language, though inspired, is not that of the Lord speaking in the first person.

"The Lord showed me by vision and revelation exactly what would take place if we did not stop this practice," President Woodruff said. *"He has told me exactly what to do. . . .* I saw exactly what would come to pass if there was not something done. I have had this spirit upon me for a long time. But I want to say this: I should have let all the temples go out of our hands; I should have gone to prison myself, and let every other man go there, had not the *God of heaven commanded me to do what I did do;* and when the hour came that I was commanded to do that, it was all clear to me. *I went before the Lord, and I wrote what the Lord told me to write."* (*Discourses of Wilford Woodruff,* pp. 208-218.)

MANKIND.
See MAN.

MANNA.
See BREAD OF LIFE, CHRIST. Upon ancient Israel, *manna* was showered as bread from heaven both to save them temporally and to typify the spiritual salvation they could attain through Christ

who was to come as the Bread of Life. (Ex. 16; Num. 11:6-9.) The partaking of manna by the children of Israel was a sign between them and God "that man doth not live by bread only, but by every word that proceedeth out of the mouth of the Lord doth man live." (Deut. 8:3.)

"I am the bread of life," our Lord said. "He that cometh to me shall never hunger; and he that believeth on me shall never thirst. . . . I am that bread of life. Your fathers did eat manna in the wilderness, and are dead. This is the bread which cometh down from heaven, that a man may eat thereof, and not die. I am the living bread which came down from heaven: if any man eat of this bread, he shall live for ever." (John 6:35, 48-51.) Those who eat of this "hidden manna" shall gain eternal life. (Rev. 2:17.)

MAN OF COUNSEL.

See COUNSELOR, FATHER IN HEAVEN, GOD, MAN OF HOLINESS. One of the revealed names of God the Father is *Man of Counsel* (Moses 7:35), a designation signifying that he is a Man and that the perfection of counsel and direction come from him. In similar manner, he might be called *Man of Wisdom, Man of Righteousness, Man of Power, Man of Love,* or any other name-title which points attention to the perfection and beauty of a particular one of the godly attributes embodied in his Person.

MAN OF GALILEE.
See GALILEAN.

MAN OF HOLINESS.

See FATHER IN HEAVEN, GOD, HOLINESS, HOLY, HOLY ONE, MAN OF COUNSEL, SON OF MAN. God the Father is a *Holy Man,* an exalted, perfected, and glorified Person. Life eternal is gained through a knowledge of the nature and kind of being that he is. Hence, when he revealed himself to Father Adam, the first man, he chose words which, "in the language of Adam," identified him as *"Man of Holiness."* (Moses 6:57.) By this name he signifies both his position as a Man and his status as the embodiment of holiness and perfection. If we still spoke the Adamic language, the words we would use to specify our Father in Heaven would mean *Man of Holiness.*

MAN OF RIGHTEOUSNESS.
See RIGHTEOUSNESS.

MAN OF SIN.

See ANTICHRISTS, APOSTASY, CHURCH OF THE DEVIL, DEVIL. Lucifer is the *man of sin,* spoken of by Paul who was to be revealed in the last days before the Second Coming of our Lord. (2 Thess. 2:1-

12.) He is the one of whom men shall say: "Is this the *man* that made the earth to tremble, that did shake kingdoms; That made the world as a wilderness, and destroyed the cities thereof; that opened not the house of his prisoners?" (Isa. 14:12-20.)

Joseph Smith, by revelation, inserted into Paul's account about the man of sin, these words: *"He it is who now worketh, and Christ suffereth him to work, until the time is fulfilled that he shall be taken out of the way."* (*Inspired Version,* 2 Thess. 2:7.) That is, Satan was then committing havoc among men, and he would continue to do so until the ushering in of the millennial era when he would be bound.

Paul's promise that the man of sin must be revealed before our Lord could return for the millennial era has been abundantly fulfilled. Lucifer's wicked plans, purposes, and works have been revealed or manifest from time to time, from the day of Paul to the present. At a conference of the Church held June 3, 1831, "the man of sin was revealed," in that some of the brethren were overcome by devils whom the Prophet rebuked and cast out. (*History of the Church,* vol. 1, p. 175.)

As far as mortal men are concerned, all those who become the agents and tools of the devil, who are used by him to further his interests and purposes on earth are also *men of sin.*

MAN OF WAR.
See GOD OF BATTLES.

MANSIONS.
See CELESTIAL KINGDOM, HEAVEN, KINGDOM OF GOD, KINGDOMS OF GLORY, SALVATION, TELESTIAL KINGDOM, TERRESTRIAL KINGDOM. To believe that in eternity all men will go either to a heaven of eternal bliss or a hell of eternal torment is a doctrine that offends the sense of justice of every reasonable man. It is in flat contradiction to the revealed principle that men will be judged according to their works and that as their works have varied so will their rewards. (Rev. 20:12-14; Luke 19:16-26.)

Our Lord said, "In my Father's house are many *mansions"*—a truth so self-evident that he added: "If it were not so, I would have told you." (John 14:2.) The Prophet said the meaning of this passage was, "In my Father's kingdom are many kingdoms." Then he added, "I do not believe the Methodist doctrine of sending honest men and nobleminded men to hell, along with the murderer and adulterer. . . . There are mansions for those who obey a celestial law, and there are other mansions for those who come short of the law, every man in his own order." (*Teachings,* p. 366.)

MAN'S TIME.
See TIME.

MARANATHA.
See ANATHEMA.

MARRIAGE.
See CELESTIAL MARRIAGE.

MARRIAGE SUPPER OF THE LAMB.

See BRIDEGROOM, BRIDE OF THE LAMB, CHRIST, HUSBAND. In this dispensation the Bridegroom, who is the Lamb of God, shall come to claim his bride, which is the Church composed of the faithful saints who have watched for his return. As he taught in the parable of the marriage of the king's son, the great *marriage supper of the Lamb* shall then be celebrated. (Matt. 22:1-14.)

The elders of Israel by preaching the message of the restoration are inviting men to come to that supper. "For this cause I have sent you," the Lord says to his missionaries, "that a feast of fat things might be prepared for the poor; yea, a feast of fat things, of wine on the lees well refined, that the earth may know that the mouths of the prophets shall not fail; Yea, *a supper of the house of the Lord,* well prepared, unto which all nations shall be invited. First, the rich and the learned, the wise and the noble; And after that cometh the day of my power; then shall the poor, the lame, and the blind, and the deaf, come in unto the *marriage of the Lamb,* and partake

of the *supper of the Lord,* prepared for the great day to come." (D. & C. 58:6-11; 65:3.)

Soon the scripture shall be fulfilled which saith: "The marriage of the Lamb is come, and his wife hath made herself ready. And to her was granted that she should be arrayed in fine linen, clean and white: for the fine linen is the righteousness of saints. And he saith unto me, Write, *Blessed are they which are called unto the marriage supper of the Lamb."* (Rev. 19:7-9.)

MARTYRDOM.

See APOSTASY, CHURCH OF THE DEVIL, ENDURING TO THE END, PERSECUTION. In the gospel sense, *martyrdom* is the voluntary acceptance of death at the hands of wicked men rather than to forsake Christ and his holy gospel. It is the supreme earthly sacrifice in which a man certifies to his absolute faith and to the desires for righteousness and for eternal life which are in his heart.

Martyrs of religion are found in every age in which there have been both righteous and wicked people on earth. Christ himself was a martyr who voluntarily laid down his life, according to the Father's plan, that immortality and eternal life might become available for his brethren. (John 10:10-18.) "Greater love hath no man than this, that a man lay down his life for his friends." (John 15:13.)

Many apostles, prophets, and saints have been martyred for the gospel cause. (Matt. 23:29-33; Luke 11:47-51; Acts 7; 22:20; Hela. 13:24-28; D. & C. 135.) The Prophet and Patriarch of this dispensation laid down their lives in the gospel cause, as literally thousands of others have done. Men, women, and children, young and old, weak and strong, sick and well, were driven by the thousands from Missouri and Illinois, many to early and untimely deaths as a direct result of the persecutions and diseases thus heaped upon them. Is a saint any less a martyr who is driven from a sick bed into blizzards to freeze and die than he would have been had an assassin's bullet brought merciful death in a brief destroying moment?

Thousands who have lived in this dispensation shall find place with "the martyrs under the altar that John saw." (D. & C. 135:7.) They shall be classed with those who "loved not their lives unto the death" (Rev. 12:11); they are "the souls of them that were slain for the word of God, and for the testimony which they held." (Rev. 6:9.) They shall "rest yet for a little season, until their fellowservants also and their brethren, that should be killed as they were, should be fulfilled." (Rev. 6:11.)

Martyrdom is not a thing of the past only, but of the present and of the future, for Satan has not yet been bound, and the servants of the Lord will not be silenced in this final age of warning and judgment. There are forces and powers in the world today, which would silence the tongue and shed the blood of every true witness of Christ in the world, if they had the power and the means to do it. There are those who would destroy every prophet of God, if they could. Martyrs of true religion are yet to have their blood shed in Jerusalem. "And their dead bodies shall lie in the street of the great city, which spiritually is called Sodom and Egypt, where also our Lord was crucified." (Rev. 11:1-12.) True it is that "the woman," of whom John wrote is and shall be "drunken with the blood of the saints, and with the blood of the martyrs of Jesus." (Rev. 17:6.)

True martyrs of religion receive eternal life. "Whoso layeth down his life in my cause, for my name's sake, shall find it again, even life eternal." (D. & C. 98:13; Mark 8:35; John 12:25; Rev. 2:10.) But the mere laying down of one's life standing alone is not gospel martyrdom. Both the righteous and the wicked have and do sacrifice their lives for friends or country without gaining thereby any hope or assurance of exaltation. Those on the other hand who have the truth and who could escape death by denying it are the martyrs who shall receive a martyr's reward— eternal life. When they seal their testimony with their blood, they are honored and their murderers are condemned. (D. & C. 136:39.)

470

MARY.

See ANNUNCIATION, CHRIST, IMMACULATE CONCEPTION THEORY, MAGNIFICAT, VIRGIN BIRTH. Our Lord's mother, *Mary,* like Christ, was chosen and foreordained in pre-existence for the part she was destined to play in the great plan of salvation. Hers was the commission to provide a temporal body for the Lord Omnipotent, to nurture and cherish him in infancy and youth, and to aid him in preparing for that great mission which he alone could perform. Certainly she was one of the noblest and greatest of all the spirit offspring of the Father.

Mary's name and mission were revealed to holy prophets centuries before her mortal birth. Nephi saw her as, "A virgin, most beautiful and fair above all other virgins." (1 Ne. 11:13-21; 2 Ne. 17:14; Mosiah 3:8; Alma 7:10; Isa. 7:14.) As such a virgin she gave birth to a Son whose Father was the Almighty God. (Matt. 1:18-25; Luke 1:26-38.) While the Holy Ghost rested upon her, she gave forth one of the greatest songs of praise in the scriptures. (Luke 1:46-55.) "She was carried away in the Spirit; and after she had been carried away in the Spirit," she became, "the mother of the Son of God, after the manner of the flesh." (1 Ne. 11:18-20.) As the wife of Joseph, she was the mother of other sons and daughters. (Matt. 13:55-56; Mark 6:3; Gal. 1:19.) She beheld the crucifixion of her Son, and on that dread occasion, by his command, she turned to John the Beloved for her continued support and care. (John 19:25-27.)

MASTER.

See CHRIST, RABBI. Christ is the *Master,* meaning he stood as a teacher, ruler, and commander. "Ye call me Master and Lord: and ye say well," he said, "for so I am." (John 13:13.) After his ascension into heaven, he was called by Paul, the *Master in heaven.* (Eph. 6:9; Col. 4:1.)

MASTER MAHAN.

See CAIN, MURDERERS, SECRET COMBINATIONS. This designation was applied to Cain, Lamech, and others in earliest times, signifying their mastery of the secrets of committing murder and other gross wickedness. Secret combinations began with Cain, Satan first administering the oaths unto him. After taking Satan's oath Cain exulted: "Truly I am *Mahan,* the master of this great secret, that I may murder and get gain." Accordingly, "Cain was called *Master Mahan,* and he gloried in his wickedness." (Moses 5:16-55.) Down through all succeeding ages there have been groups, organizations, churches, and governments having similar secret oaths and objectives —all inspired by Satan and all conferring upon their participants the equivalent of the title, *Master Mahan.*

MASTURBATION.
See SEX IMMORALITY.

MATTER.
See ELEMENTS.

MEATS.
See WORD OF WISDOM.

MEDIATION.
See ADVOCACY, ATONEMENT OF CHRIST, EXPIATION, INTERCESSION, MEDIATOR, PROPITIATION, RECONCILIATION. Our Lord's mission was to bring to pass "the great *mediation of all men,*" meaning that in his capacity as Mediator he had power to intervene between God and man and effect a reconciliation. This mediation or reconciliation was affected through his atoning sacrifice, a sacrifice by means of which sinful men—by the proper use of agency—can wash away their guilt and place themselves in harmony with God. Men "are free to choose liberty and eternal life, through the great mediation of all men, or to choose captivity and death, according to the captivity and power of the devil." (2 Ne. 2: 27.) Those choosing obedience receive the Holy Ghost, are reconciled to God in this world, and

continue in his presence in the world to come.

MEDIATOR.
See ADVOCATE, ATONEMENT OF CHRIST, CHRIST, EXPIATOR, INTERCESSOR, MEDIATION, MOSES, PROPITIATOR, RECONCILER. Just as there are two gospels (the preparatory gospel and the fulness of the gospel), and just as there are two laws (the law of Moses and the law of Christ), so there are two *mediators*—Moses and Christ. "For the law was given through Moses, but life and truth came through Jesus Christ. For the law was after a carnal commandment, to the administration of death; but the gospel was after the power of an endless life, through Jesus Christ, the Only Begotten Son, who is in the bosom of the Father." (*Inspired Version,* John 1:17-18.)

A mediator is one who interposes himself between parties at variance to reconcile them, an office Moses filled as for instance when he pleaded for the people in the golden calf incident (Ex. 32:30-35), and an office which Christ filled as part of his great atoning sacrifice. Hence the revealed statement that Moses *"was ordained by the hand of angels to be a mediator of this first covenant, (the law).* Now this mediator was not a mediator of the new covenant; but *there is one mediator of the new covenant, who is Christ,* as it is written in the law concerning the promises made to

Abraham and his seed. Now *Christ is the mediator of life;* for this is the promise which God made unto Abraham." (*Inspired Version,* Gal. 3:19-20.)

Moses was the mediator of the old covenant or testament; Jesus is the Mediator of the new covenant or testament. (D. & C. 76:69; 107:19; Heb. 8:6; 9:15; 12:24; *Inspired Version,* Heb. 9:15.) But in this age of the earth there is only one law offered to people and that is the law of Christ or the law of the gospel. Hence, to gain salvation, all men must "come unto the knowledge of the truth which is in Christ Jesus, who is the Only Begotten Son of God, and *ordained to be a Mediator between God and man;* who is one God, and hath power over all men. For *there is one God, and one mediator between God and men, the man Christ Jesus;* Who gave himself a ransom for all, to be testified in due time." (*Inspired Version,* 1 Tim. 2:4-6.) Lehi, in teaching the *law of mediation,* spoke similarly: "Look to the great Mediator," he said, "and hearken unto his great commandments; and be faithful unto his words, and choose eternal life, according to the will of his Holy Spirit." (2 Ne. 2:28.)

MEDICINE.

See PHYSICIANS.

MEDICINE MEN.

See AMERICAN INDIANS, APOS-TASY, BOOK OF MORMON, CONJURE MAN, NEPHITES AND LAMANITES. Among the various tribes of American Indians certain men have been or are called *medicine men.* Their functions in the tribes are both spiritual and medicinal. They care for the sick by means of herbs and the like, and they perform chants, "sings," and other ceremonies to ward off evil, entice divine favor, heal the sick, obtain rain, gain victory in battle, and so forth.

Apparently the "ministry" in which these Lamanites are engaged is a degenerate, apostate, and perverted form of the original ministry of elders, patriarchs, and other righteous saints among their ancestors. Many of the chants and "sings" which have been handed down from time immemorial among them are said to tell the stories of Adam and Eve, the flood, the colonization of America by their Hebrew forebears, the ministry of the Great White God among their progenitors, and the like.

MEDIUMS.

See SEANCES, SPIRITUALISM, WITCHCRAFT. *Mediums* are witches; they are persons who have so trained and schooled themselves in sorcery and spiritualism that they have ready access to and communion with evil spirits. In modern spiritualism they are the ones who conduct seances and who profess to call back the dead and receive messages from them. In the main, of course, the messages received are from devils and not from the departed dead.

MEEKNESS.

See HUMILITY, KINDNESS, PATIENCE. In the Sermon on the Mount, as given both to the Jews and to the Nephites, Christ promised that the *meek* shall inherit the earth. (Matt. 5:5; 3 Ne. 12:5.) David gave the same assurance to ancient Israel. (Ps. 37:11.) Few virtues have such inherent worth as *meekness,* for the meek are the godfearing and the righteous. They are the ones who willingly conform to the gospel standards, thus submitting their wills to the will of the Lord. They are not the fearful, the spiritless, the timid. Rather, the most forceful, dynamic personality who ever lived—He who drove the money changers from the temple, and with violence threw down their merchandising equipment (Matt. 21:12-13)—said of Himself, "I am meek and lowly in heart." (Matt. 11:29.)

Meekness is a fruit of the Spirit. (Gal. 5:23.) The Lord has said that his grace is sufficient for the meek in this life (Ether 12:26), and that in eternity they shall have an inheritance in the celestial kingdom. (Ps. 149:4.) When the earth is sanctified, cleansed from all unrighteousness, and prepared for celestial glory, then the meek shall claim their promised inheritance. (D. & C. 88:16-32.)

MEETINGHOUSES.

See CATHEDRALS, CHAPELS, TABERNACLES, TEMPLES. Houses of worship erected in wards and branches of the Church are commonly called *meetinghouses.* Normally they include an assembly hall (or chapel) where sacrament meetings and other meetings of worship are held, a cultural hall (often including gymnasium facilities), class rooms for study purposes, and offices for bishops and other church officers.

MELCHIZEDEK.

See AARON, MELCHIZEDEK PRIESTHOOD. To the man *Melchizedek* goes the honor of having his name used to identify the *Holy Priesthood after the Order of the Son of God,* thus enabling men "to avoid the too frequent repetition" of the name of Deity. (D. & C. 107:2-4.) Of all God's ancient high priests "none were greater." (Alma 13:19.) His position in the priestly hierarchy of God's earthly kingdom was like unto that of Abraham (Heb. 7:4-10), his contemporary whom he blessed (Gen. 14:18-20; Heb. 7:1; *Inspired Version,* Gen. 14:17-40), and upon whom he conferred the priesthood. (D. & C. 84:14.)

Indeed, so exalted and high was the position of Melchizedek in the eyes of the Lord and of his people that he stood as a prototype of the Son of God himself, the Son who was to arise "after the similitude of Melchisedec." (Heb. 7:15.) Both bore the titles, *Prince of Peace* and *King of Heaven*—meaning King of Peace (Alma 13:18; *Inspired Version,* Gen. 14:33, 36)—and both were joint-heirs of the Father's kingdom. "For this Melchizedek was ordained a priest after the order of the Son of God, which order was without father, without mother, without descent, having neither beginning of days, nor end of life. *And all those who are ordained unto this priesthood are made like unto the Son of God, abiding a priest continually."* (*Inspired Version,* Heb. 7:3.)

Alma tells us that "Melchizedek was a king over the land of Salem; and his people had waxed strong in iniquity and abomination; yea, they had all gone astray; they were full of all manner of wickedness; But Melchizedek having exercised mighty faith, and received the office of the high priesthood according to the holy order of God, did preach repentance unto his people. And behold, they did repent; and Melchizedek did establish peace in the land in his days; therefore he was called the prince of peace, for he was the king of Salem; and he did reign under his father." (Alma 13:17-18.)

Paul, very obviously knowing much more about Melchizedek than he happened to record in his epistles, gave as an illustration of great faith some unnamed person who "wrought righteousness, obtained promises, stopped the mouths of lions, Quenched the violence of fire." (Heb. 11:33-34.) From the Prophet's inspired additions to the Old Testament we learn that Paul's reference was to Melchizedek. "Now Melchizedek was a man of faith, who wrought righteousness; and when a child he feared God, and stopped the mouths of lions, and quenched the violence of fire." (*Inspired Version,* Gen. 14: 26.)

There is an unsupported tradition to the effect that Melchizedek was the same person as Shem the son of Noah. That this could hardly have been the case is seen from the revelation which says: "Abraham received the priesthood from Melchizedek, who received it *through the lineage of his fathers, even till Noah."* (D. & C. 84:14.) In other words, there seem to have been at least two generations between Melchizedek and Shem.

MELCHIZEDEK PRIESTHOOD.

See AARONIC PRIESTHOOD, APOSTLES, APOSTOLIC SUCCESSION, CELESTIAL MARRIAGE, CHURCH OF JESUS CHRIST OF LATTER-DAY SAINTS, ELDERS, ENDOWMENTS, EXALTATION, GOSPEL, HIGH PRIESTS, KEYS, MELCHIZEDEK, ORDINATIONS, PATRIARCHS, PERFECTION; PETER, JAMES, AND JOHN; PRIESTHOOD, PRIESTHOOD OFFICES, PRIESTHOOD QUORUMS, QUORUM PRESIDENTS, REST OF THE LORD, SANCTIFICATION, SEVENTIES. To avoid the too frequent repetition of the name of

Deity, *the Holy Priesthood after the Order of the Son of God* is called the *Melchizedek Priesthood.* (D. & C. 107:1-4.) This *"Melchizedek Priesthood comprehends the Aaronic or Levitical Priesthood, and is the grand head, and holds the highest authority which pertains to the priesthood, and the keys of the kingdom of God in all ages of the world to the latest posterity on the earth; and is the channel through which all knowledge, doctrine, the plan of salvation and every important matter is revealed from heaven.*

"Its institution was prior to 'the foundation of this earth, or the morning stars sang together, or the sons of God shouted for joy,' and is the highest and holiest priesthood, and is after the order of the Son of God, and all other priesthoods are only parts, ramifications, powers and blessings belonging to the same, and are held, controlled, and directed by it. It is the channel through which the Almighty commenced revealing his glory at the beginning of the creation of this earth, and through which he has continued to reveal himself to the children of men to the present time, and through which he will make known his purposes to the end of time." (*Teachings,* pp. 166-167.)

"All other authorities or offices in the church are appendages to this priesthood. . . . The Melchizedek Priesthood holds the right of presidency, and has power and authority over all the offices in the church in all ages of the world, to administer in spiritual things. . . . *The power and authority of the higher, or Melchizedek Priesthood, is to hold the keys of all the spiritual blessings of the church—To have the privilege of receiving the mysteries of the kingdom of heaven, to have the heavens opened unto them, to commune with the general assembly and church of the First-born, and to enjoy the communion and presence of God the Father, and Jesus the mediator of the new covenant."* (D. & C. 107:5, 8, 18-19.)

Everything on earth is subject to the power and authority of the Melchizedek Priesthood. When He reigns whose right it is, this power will be manifest without restriction and all nations will bow to the gospel rod. The Melchizedek Priesthood "is *a perfect law of theocracy, and stands as God to give laws to the people, administering endless lives to the sons and daughters of Adam." (Teachings,* p. 322.)

Even under the present circumstances with apostate powers ruling on earth, the Lord's decree is still in force "that *every one being ordained after this order and calling should have power, by faith, to break mountains, to divide the seas, to dry up waters, to turn them out of their course; To put at defiance the armies of nations, to divide the earth, to break every band, to stand in the presence of God; to do all things according to his will, according to his command, subdue principalities and powers; and this by the will of the Son of God which was from before the foundation of the world." (Inspired Version, Gen. 14:30-31.)*

Like God himself, the Melchizedek Priesthood is eternal and everlasting in nature. "The priesthood is an everlasting principle, and existed with God from eternity, and will to eternity, without beginning of days or end of years." (*Teachings,* pp. 157-158, 323; D. & C. 84:17; *Inspired Version,* Heb. 7:1-3.) Adam and others obtained the priesthood "in the creation, before the world was formed." (*Teachings,* p. 157.)

Alma says that those "ordained unto the high priesthood of the holy order of God" were "in the first place," that is in pre-existence, "on the same standing with their brethren," meaning that initially all had equal opportunity to progress through righteousness. But while yet in the eternal worlds, certain of the offspring of God, "having chosen good, and exercising exceeding great faith," were as a consequence "called and prepared from the foundation of the world according to the foreknowledge of God" to enjoy the blessings and powers of the priesthood. These priesthood calls were made "from the foundation of the world," or in other words faithful men held priesthood power and authority first in pre-existence and then again on earth. (Alma 13.) "Every man who has a calling to minister to the inhabitants of the world was or-

dained to that very purpose in the Grand Council of heaven before this world was." (*Teachings,* p. 365.)

As pertaining to mortality, the priesthood was first given to Adam. (Moses 6:67-68.) He stands at the head as the presiding high priest (under Christ) over all the earth for all ages. (*Teachings,* pp. 157-158.) This priesthood of the holy order continued with his worthy descendants until the day of Moses. (D. & C. 84:5 16; 107:41-53.) Through Moses the Lord attempted to set up the house of Israel as a kingdom of priests of the holy order, with each man and his family enjoying the full blessings of the patriarchal order and priesthood. (Ex. 19:5-6; Deut. 7:6.) But Israel rebelled, rejected the higher law, and the Lord took Moses and the fulness of the priesthood from them. (*Inspired Version,* Ex. 34:1-2; D. & C. 84:17-25.) From then until the personal ministry of our Lord among men, the Aaronic Priesthood continued as the most prevalent authority of God on earth. (D. & C. 84:26-28.)

There were at many times, however, and may have been at all times, prophets and worthy men in Israel who held the Melchizedek Priesthood. Joseph Smith said, "All the prophets had the Melchizedek Priesthood and were ordained by God himself," that is, those persons so honored held their authority by special dispensation, for the general priesthood rule found among the people was the Levitical order. (*Teachings,* p. 181; *Doctrines of Salvation,* vol. 3, pp. 80-102.) Among those ancient Israelites who were blessed with the fulness of the higher priesthood were the Nephites. (Alma 13.)

When Christ came, he being a high priest forever after the order of Melchizedek (Heb. 2:17-18; 3:1; 5:6, 10; 6:20; 7:15-17, 21), this holy order was again spread forth among the people. (John 15:16; 1 Pet. 2:5, 9.) Under apostolic direction a kingdom of priests again was found on earth. But *after the apostles ceased to minister among mortals, there was no one left holding the keys to authorize a person to be ordained to any priestly office, and in this manner the Lord took the priesthood from the earth.* (Rev. 12.)

In June, 1829, by divine appointment, Peter, James, and John came to Joseph Smith and Oliver Cowdery and conferred upon them the Melchizedek Priesthood. (D. & C. 27:12-13.) By the hands of Elijah and others of the prophets, also, an additional revelation of the priesthood was given, meaning that these ancient prophets came with keys and powers which authorized the use of the priesthood for additional purposes. (D. & C. 110:11-16; 128:17-21; Jos. Smith 2:38.) This priesthood—with all its powers, parts, keys, orders, and ramifications—is now fully operative among men. Again there is a kingdom of priests on earth, and the divine promise is that this situation will continue, the priesthood never again being lost. (D. & C. 65.)

Those who are faithful in their priesthood callings in this life shall continue on in their holy authorizations in eternity; they shall remain forever "priests and kings"; their destiny is to stand as "priests of the Most High, after the order of Melchizedek, which was after the order of Enoch, which was after the order of the Only Begotten Son." (D. & C. 76:56-57.)

As compared to the Aaronic Priesthood, as administered in ancient Israel, the order of Melchizedek did not come "by descent from father and mother." (*Teachings,* p. 323.) That is, the right to this higher priesthood was not inherited in the same way as was the case with the Levites and sons of Aaron. Righteousness was an absolute requisite for the conferral of the higher priesthood. This "order came, not by man, nor the will of man; neither by father nor mother; neither by beginning of days nor end of years; but of God; And it was delivered unto men by the calling of his own voice, according to his own will, unto as many as believed on his name." (*Inspired Version,* Gen. 14:28-29; Heb. 7:1-3.)

But each righteous spirit called to minister in priestly offices has been ordained to come through a particular lineage. Consequently it has become the right of those holding special inheritance in the Lord's chosen lineage to receive the priesthood, provided they are obedient and faithful. Thus Abraham "sought for the blessings of the fathers," and by righteousness "became a *rightful heir,* a High Priest, holding the *right* belonging to the fathers." The priesthood, he says, "was conferred upon me from the fathers; it came down from the fathers, from the beginning of time, yea, even from the beginning, or before the foundations of the earth to the present time, even the right of the firstborn, on the first man, who is Adam, our first father, through the fathers, unto me. I sought for *mine appointment unto the Priesthood according to the appointment of God unto the fathers concerning the seed."* (Abra. 1:1-4.)

Thereafter Abraham received the promise that his seed after him would be entitled, as of right, to the same priesthood inheritance that he had won. "In thee (that is, in thy Priesthood)," the Lord said to him, "and in thy seed (that is, thy Priesthood), for I give unto thee a promise that *this right shall continue in thee, and in thy seed after thee (that is to say, the literal seed, or the seed of the body)* shall all the families of the earth be blessed, even with the blessings of the Gospel, which are the blessings of salvation, even of life eternal." (Abra. 2:11.)

Accordingly, the seed of Abraham "are *lawful heirs, according to the* flesh," of the priesthood and its blessings. Though they "have

been hid from the world with Christ in God," yet in the restoration of all things the priesthood is again being given to them *because of their "lineage."* (D. & C. 86:8-11.) They are the ones "unto whom rightly belongs the priesthood," and all that appertains to it. (D. & C. 113:6.) But though they are lawful heirs according to the flesh, they do not receive their inheritance until they qualify for it as a result of faith, devotion, and righteous conduct. Personal worthiness is an invarying prerequisite to conferral of the higher priesthood.

Conversely, gospel blessings are denied the rebellious who persecute the saints. "They shall not have *right* to the priesthood, nor their posterity after them from generation to generation." (D. & C. 121: 21.)

Those spirits sent to earth through the lineage of Cain and of Ham were denied the priesthood until June, 1978, when the new revelation on priesthood was received.

Without the Melchizedek Priesthood salvation in the kingdom of God would not be available for men on earth, for the ordinances of salvation—the laying on of hands for the gift of the Holy Ghost, for instance—could not be authoritatively performed. Thus, as far as all religious organizations now existing are concerned, the presence or the absence of this priesthood establishes the divinity or falsity of a professing church. It "continueth in the church of God in all generations," and it "administereth the gospel and holdeth the key of the mysteries of the kingdom, even the key of the knowledge of God" (D. & C. 84:17-19), whom to know is eternal life. (John 17:3.) If there is no Melchizedek Priesthood on earth, the true Church is not here and the gospel of Christ is not available to men. But *where the Melchizedek Priesthood is, there is the kingdom, the Church, and the fulness of the gospel.*

This higher priesthood is designed to enable men to gain exaltation in the highest heaven in eternity. Paul says it is ordained "after the power of an endless life." (Heb. 7:16.) The Prophet says, *"The power of the Melchizedek Priesthood is to have the power of 'endless lives'; for the everlasting covenant cannot be broken."* (*Teachings,* p. 322.) Perfection can be gained only in and through and because of this priesthood. "I advise all to go on to perfection, and search deeper into the mysteries of godliness," the Prophet said. "A man can do nothing for himself unless God direct him in the right way; and *the priesthood is for that purpose."* (*Teachings,* p. 364.) Through this priesthood men become joint-heirs with Christ, receiving and possessing the fulness of the Father's kingdom. *"And all those who are ordained unto this priesthood are made like unto the Son of God, abiding a priest continually."* (*Inspired Version,* Heb. 7:3.)

Indeed, everything connected with the higher priesthood is designed to point man's attention to spiritual things and to mark the course leading to eternal life. By means of it faithful men enter into the rest of the Lord, "which rest is the fulness of his glory." Because of it they have power to sanctify their souls, and the sanctified inherit the celestial world.

Every person upon whom the Melchizedek Priesthood is conferred receives his office and calling in this higher priesthood with an *oath and a covenant.* The *covenant* is to this effect: 1. Man on his part solemnly agrees to magnify his calling in the priesthood, to keep the commandments of God, to live by every word that proceedeth forth from the mouth of Deity, and to walk in paths of righteousness and virtue; and 2. God on his part agrees to give such persons an inheritance of exaltation and godhood in his everlasting presence. The *oath* is the solemn attestation of Deity, his sworn promise, that those who keep their part of the covenant shall come forth and inherit all things according to the promise.

As a holder of the Melchizedek Priesthood, Christ himself is the prototype in this as in all things pertaining to salvation and exaltation. As Paul explained, priests of the Aaronic order receive their calls "without an oath," but Jesus received his priesthood appointment "with an oath by him that said unto him, *The Lord sware and will not repent, Thou art a priest for ever after the order of Melchisedec.*" (Heb. 7:21; *Teachings*, p. 323.) Those who are *priests forever,* who "are priests of the Most High, after the order of Melchizedek, . . . are gods, even the sons of God." (D. & C. 76:57-58.) They have become joint-heirs with Christ, having kept the same covenant and been bound by the same oath.

In revealing the terms and conditions of the oath and covenant of the priesthood in this dispensation, the Lord said: "For whoso is faithful unto the obtaining these two priesthoods of which I have spoken, and the magnifying their calling, are sanctified by the Spirit unto the renewing of their bodies. They become the sons of Moses and of Aaron and the seed of Abraham, and the church and kingdom, and the elect of God. And also all they who receive this priesthood receive me, saith the Lord; For he that receiveth my servants receiveth me; And he that receiveth me receiveth my Father; And he that receiveth my Father receiveth my Father's kingdom; therefore all that my Father hath shall be given unto him. And this is according to the oath and covenant which belongeth to the priesthood. Therefore, all those who receive the priesthood, receive this oath and covenant of my Father, which he cannot break, neither can it be moved. But whoso breaketh this covenant after he hath received it, and altogether turneth therefrom, shall not have forgiveness of sins in this world nor in the world to come. And wo unto all those who come not unto this priesthood which ye have received, which I now confirm upon you who are present this day, by mine own voice out of the heavens; and even I have given the heavenly hosts and mine angels charge concerning you. And I now give unto you a commandment to beware concerning yourselves, to give diligent heed to the words of eternal life. For you shall live by every word that proceedeth forth from the mouth of God." (D. & C. 84:33-44.)

What callings do brethren receive in the priesthood, and how do they go about magnifying them? For convenience of analysis, it might be said that there are two kinds of callings—*ordained callings* and *administrative or set apart callings.* Brethren for instance are ordained elders, seventies, or high priests in the Melchizedek Priesthood; these are ordained callings. Some are set apart to serve as quorum presidents, as high councilors, as members of stake presidencies, or to other positions of administrative responsibility. These are administrative or set apart callings.

Now, to magnify as here used means to enlarge or increase, to improve upon, to hold up to honor and dignity, to make the calling noble and respectable in the eyes of all men by performing the mission which appertains to the calling in an admirable and successful manner. So to magnify a calling in the ministry requires brethren first to learn what duties go with their respective offices and callings and then to go to with their might and do the work assigned them. By doing this, which includes within it the requirement to "give diligent heed to the words of eternal life," and to "live by every word that proceedeth forth from the mouth of God" (D. & C. 84:43-44), they are assured of an eventual inheritance of eternal life in the kingdom of God.

The greatest blessings are reserved for those who obtain "the fulness of the priesthood," meaning the fulness of the blessings of the priesthood. *These blessings are found only in the temples of God.* (D. & C. 124:28, 34, 42; 127:8.) "There are certain key words and signs belonging to the priesthood which must be observed in order to obtain the blessing." (*Teachings,* p. 199.) These, of course, are revealed only in the temples. "Washings, anointings, endowments, and the communication of keys," the Prophet says, are essential to enable one "to secure the *fulness* of those blessings which have been prepared for the Church of the Firstborn, and come up and abide in the presence of Elohim in the eternal worlds." (*Teachings,* p. 237.) Celestial marriage itself is an "order of the priesthood" without which no

one can gain the fulness of glory in the eternal worlds. (D. & C. 131:1-4; 132.) Anciently the elders of Israel who married out of the temple, were said to "have defiled the priesthood, and the covenant of the priesthood." (Neh. 13:25-30.)

"Those holding the fulness of the Melchizedek Priesthood are kings and priests of the Most High God, holding the keys of power and blessing." (Teachings, p. 322.) "If a man gets a fulness of the priesthood of God, he has to get it in the same way that Jesus Christ obtained it, and that was by keeping all the commandments and obeying all the ordinances of the house of the Lord. . . . All men who become heirs of God and joint-heirs with Jesus Christ will have to receive the fulness of the ordinances of his kingdom; and those who will not receive all the ordinances will come short of the fulness of that glory, if they do not lose the whole." (Teachings, pp. 308-309.)

Unfortunately, "there are many called, but few are chosen." That is to say, *many are called to the priesthood, but few are chosen for eternal life.* (D. & C. 95:5-6, 12.) "And why are they not chosen? Because their hearts are set so much upon the things of this world, and aspire to the honors of men, that they do not learn this one lesson—That the rights of the priesthood are inseparably connected with the powers of heaven, and that the powers of heaven cannot be controlled nor handled only upon the principles of righteousness." (D. & C. 121:34-46.)

MEMORY.
See MIND.

MERCY.
See CHARITY, CONDESCENSION OF GOD, GRACE OF GOD, JUDGMENT, JUSTICE, LOVE. In the gospel sense, *mercy* consists in our Lord's forbearance, on certain specified conditions, from imposing punishments that, except for his grace and goodness, would be the just reward of man.

Because mercy is an attribute of Deity (Ex. 33:19; Rom. 9:15-18; 2 Cor. 1:3; Eph. 2:4; 1 Pet. 1:3), men are thereby enabled to have faith in him unto life and salvation. They must have "the idea of the existence of the attribute of mercy in the Deity," the Prophet says, "in order to exercise faith in him for life and salvation; for without the idea of the existence of this attibute in the Deity, the spirits of the saints would faint in the midst of the tribulations, afflictions, and persecutions which they have to endure for righteousness' sake. But when the idea of the existence of this attribute is once established in the mind it gives life and energy to the spirits of the saints, believing that the mercy of God will be poured out upon them in the midst of their afflictions, and that he will com-

passionate them in their sufferings, and that the mercy of God will lay hold of them and secure them in the arms of his love, so that they will receive a full reward for all their sufferings. . . . And as mercy is . . . an attribute of the Deity, his saints can have confidence that it will be exercised towards them, and through the exercise of that attribute towards them comfort and consolation will be administered unto them abundantly, amid all their afflictions and tribulations." (*Lectures on Faith,* pp. 46-47.)

No cry of thanksgiving and relief seems to come more gratefully from the prophetic voice than the comforting exclamation, *"His mercy endureth for ever!"* (1 Chron. 16:34, 41; 2 Chron. 5:13; 7:3, 6; Ezra 3:11; Ps. 106:1; 107:1; 118:1-4; 136; Jer. 33:11.) Certainly his mercy is manifest in all his doings—his creative enterprises and his hand-dealings in all ages with all people. (Ps. 136.)

The atoning sacrifice of our Lord, upon which all things rest, came because of his infinite mercy. (D. & C. 29:1.) Through his condescension, grace, and mercy he has visited the children of men and given great promises to them. (2 Ne. 4:26; 9:53.) The great era of restoration, the era when men again "will hear what God the Lord will speak," the era when "Truth shall spring out of the earth; and righteousness shall look down from heaven," is described as

483

one in which, *"Mercy and truth are met together; righteousness and peace have kissed each other."* (Ps. 85:8-11.) The latter-day gathering of Israel, as part of this great restoration, is to come because of the "great mercies" of the Lord. (Isa. 54:7.) Indeed, the *"voice of mercy"* to scattered Israel and to all men in our day is that the gospel has been restored and the way opened whereby they may escape the calamities to be poured out upon the ungodly. (D. & C. 43:25.)

But mercy is not showered promiscuously upon mankind, except in the general sense that it is manifest in the creation and peopling of the earth and in the granting of immortality to all men as a free gift. Rather, mercy is granted (because of the grace, love, and condescension of God), as it is with all blessings, to those who comply with the law upon which its receipt is predicated. (D. & C. 130:20-21.) That law is the law of righteousness; *those who sow righteousness, reap mercy.* (Hos. 10:12.) There is no promise of mercy to the wicked; rather, as stated in the Ten Commandments, the Lord promises to show mercy unto thousands of them that love him and keep his commandments. (Ex. 20:6; Dan. 9:4; D. & C. 70:18.)

The great Sinaitic proclamation, from the Lord's own mouth, announced: *"The Lord, The Lord God, merciful and gracious, long-suffering, and abundant in goodness and truth, Keeping mercy for thousands, forgiving iniquity and transgression and sin, and that will by no means clear the guilty;* visiting the iniquity of the fathers upon the children, and upon the children's children, unto the third and to the fourth generation." (Ex. 34:6-7.)

Mercy is a gift the Lord reserves for his saints and their weaknesses (D. & C. 38:14; 50:16; 64:4); it is reserved for the meek, they who are the god-fearing and the righteous (D. & C. 97:2); because of it, they will be remembered in the day of wrath. (D. & C. 101:9.) Because of mercy men are enabled to repent (D. & C. 3:10), and when the elders of Israel "confess their sins with humble hearts," a merciful God forgives them of those sins. (D. & C. 61:2.) Indeed, the Lord's people may well ask themselves, "What doth the Lord require of thee, but to do justly, and to love mercy, and to walk humbly with thy God?" (Mic. 6:8.)

Justice demands that for every broken law a penalty must be paid, for "How could there be a law save there was a punishment?" And since all men have sinned, all are in the grasp of justice. Accordingly, all men must pay the penalty for their transgressions unless they can find a supervening power which will wash away their sins and free them from the penalty, unless someone else pays a ransom for them. That ransom is offered to all men in and through the atoning sacrifice of Christ.

"Therefore, according to justice," as Alma explains, "the plan of redemption could not be brought about, only on conditions of repentance of men in this probationary state, yea, this preparatory state; for except it were for these conditions, *mercy could not take effect* except it should destroy the work of justice. Now the work of justice could not be destroyed; if so, God would cease to be God. And thus we see that all mankind were fallen, and they were in the grasp of justice; yea, the justice of God, which consigned them forever to be cut off from his presence. And now, the *plan of mercy could not be brought about except an atonement should be made;* therefore God *himself atoneth for the sins of the world, to bring about the plan of mercy, to appease the demands of justice, that God might be a perfect, just God, and a merciful God also.* . . .

"There is a law given, and a punishment affixed, and a repentance granted; *which repentance, mercy claimeth; otherwise, justice claimeth the creature and executeth the law, and the law inflicteth the punishment;* if not so, the works of justice would be destroyed, and God would cease to be God. But God ceaseth not to be God, and *mercy claimeth the penitent, and mercy cometh because of the atonement;* and the atonement bringeth to pass the resurrection of the dead; and the resurrection of the dead bringeth back men into the presence of God; and thus they are restored into his presence, to be judged according to their works, according to the law and justice. For behold, justice exerciseth all his demands, and also *mercy claimeth all which is her own;* and thus, none but the truly penitent are saved. *What, do ye suppose that mercy can rob justice?* I say unto you, Nay; not one whit. If so, God would cease to be God." (Alma 42: 13-26.)

Because of the atonement, *mercy "overpowereth justice,* and bringeth about means unto men that they may have faith unto repentance. And thus *mercy can satisfy the demands of justice,* and encircles them in the arms of safety, while he that exercises no faith unto repentance is exposed to the whole law of the demands of justice; therefore only unto him that has faith unto repentance is brought about the great and eternal plan of redemption." (Alma 34:15-16.) *"Mercy hath compassion on mercy and claimeth her own; justice continueth its course and claimeth its own."* (D. & C. 88:40.)

"Mercy hath no claim" on any man unless and until he repents and turns to the Lord. (Mosiah 2:38-39.) However, *"If ye will repent, and harden not your hearts,"* saith God, *"then will I have mercy upon you, through mine Only Begotten Son; Therefore, whosoever repenteth, and hardeneth not his heart, he shall have claim on mercy through mine Only Begotten Son,* unto a remission of his sins; and these shall enter into my rest." (Alma 12:33-34.)

Mercy is thus for the repentant, the faithful, the obedient, those who love and serve God. All others fail to escape the clutches of justice. "Blessed are the merciful: for they shall obtain mercy." (Matt. 5:7.) "Be ye therefore merciful, as your Father also is merciful." (Luke 6:36.) Salvation is the reward of those who conform to the plan of mercy. "Surely goodness and mercy shall follow me all the days of my life: and I will dwell in the house of the Lord for ever." (Ps. 23:6.)

So infinite in scope is the plan of mercy that it applies to the living and the dead. Those who do not have the opportunity to subject themselves by repentance to the plan of mercy while in this life, but who would have done so had the opportunity been afforded them, will have their chance in the spirit world; they shall then be saved from the grasp of justice and, reaping the full blessings of mercy, shall go on to celestial reward.

"There is never a time when the spirit is too old to approach God," the Prophet said. *"All are within the reach of pardoning mercy, who have not committed the unpardonable sin, which hath no forgiveness, neither in this world, nor in the world to come. There is a way to release the spirits of the dead; that is by the power and authority of* the priesthood—by binding and loosing on earth. This doctrine appears glorious, inasmuch as it exhibits the *greatness of divine compassion* and benevolence in the extent of the plan of human salvation." (*Teachings,* pp. 191-192.)

MERIDIAN OF TIME.
See DISPENSATIONS, LAST DAYS, MILLENNIUM, TIME. Our Lord's mortal ministry took place in the *meridian of time.* (Moses 5:57; 6: 57; 62; 7:46; D. & C. 20:26; 39:3.) *Time,* as measured by man according to the revolutions of this earth, began after the creation of Adam and his placement in the Garden of Eden. (Abra. 5:13.) The *meridian* is the middle or high point of the day; the sun passes the meridian at noon. Thus the meridian of time is the middle or high point of that portion of eternity which is considered to be mortal time. Since Christ lived, ministered, and worked out the atonement in time's meridian, such era was truly the high point of history.

Many Biblical scholars conclude that from Adam to the birth of Christ was about 4004 years. We know from latter-day revelation that the millennial era is to commence "in the beginning of the seventh thousand years" of this earth's temporal continuance. (D. & C. 77:12.) We know also that between the end of the millennium and the final celestialization of the earth there is to be "a little season" of time, and then time as we measure and know it will cease. (D. & C. 88:110-116.) How long this "little season" will last has not been revealed, but in view of the time periods about which we do have some knowledge, it is not unreasonable to suppose that our Lord's ministry took place somewhere near the meridian of time in the literal sense of the word. (*Doctrines of Salvation,* vol. 1, p. 81.)

MERODACH.

See BEL, FALSE GODS. Apparently *Merodach* is another name for the famous Babylonian god *Bel* or *Belus,* whose downfall Jeremiah predicted. (Jer. 50:1-2.)

MESMERISM.

See HYPNOTISM.

MESSAGE OF THE RESTORATION.

See CHURCH OF JESUS CHRIST OF LATTER-DAY SAINTS, DISPENSATION OF THE FULNESS OF TIMES, GOSPEL, JOSEPH SMITH THE PROPHET, MISSIONARIES, MORMONISM, NEW AND EVERLASTING COVENANT, RESTORATION OF THE GOSPEL, TESTIMONY, TRUTH. Three great truths comprise the *message of the restoration* and must be accepted by all men in this day if they will save themselves in the kingdom of God: 1. That Jesus Christ is the literal Son of God, the Redeemer of the world, he through whom salvation comes for men in all ages; 2. That Joseph Smith is the revealer of the knowledge of Christ and of salvation in this age, that he was called to stand as a legal administrator and hold the keys of salvation for all men of this dispensation; and 3. That The Church of Jesus Christ of Latter-day Saints is the Lord's Church and kingdom on earth, "the only true and living church upon the face of the whole earth" (D. & C. 1:30), the only organization having the power to teach the gospel and administer in its ordinances.

This is the message which our missionaries carry to the world. As far as the printed word is concerned, men gain a testimony that the message is true by studying the Book of Mormon. That book is a witness of the divinity of Christ; hence, anyone who gains the knowledge by revelation from the Holy Ghost that the Book of Mormon is true, also gains at the same time a testimony from the same source that Christ is the Lord. Now if the Book of Mormon is true, then Joseph Smith was a Prophet of God, for the book was translated from plates delivered to him by a resurrected being. And if Joseph Smith was ministered to by one resurrected personage, if he was commanded by revelation to translate the Book of Mormon, and if he was a Prophet, it follows that he received other revelations, that other messengers ministered to him, giving keys and authority, and that he was commanded to set up this Church and kingdom; and therefore, this is the Lord's Church. Thus the whole message of the restoration stands or falls on the truth or falsity of the Book of Mormon.

MESSENGER BEFORE THE LORD.

See CHRIST, ELIAS, GOSPEL, RESTORATION OF THE GOSPEL, SECOND COMING OF CHRIST, SIGNS OF THE TIMES. Before both the first and second comings of our Lord, he sent a *messenger* to prepare the way before him. In the meridian of time that messenger, "the voice of one crying in the wilderness, Make straight the way of the Lord" (John 1:23; Isa. 40:3), was John the Baptist. In the dispensation of the fulness of times that messenger was the Prophet Joseph Smith, to whom John came giving the authority of the preparatory priesthood. (D. & C. 13: Mal. 3:1; *Doctrines of Salvation*, vol. 1, pp. 191-195.) The gospel or message of salvation restored through the Prophet has also been sent to be a messenger before the Lord's face to prepare the way before him. (D. & C. 45:9.)

MESSENGER OF SALVATION.

See ATONEMENT OF CHRIST, CHRIST, MESSENGER OF THE COVE-NANT. Christ is the *Messenger of Salvation,* meaning that he was sent by his Father to bring salvation to men by working out the infinite and eternal atonement. (3 Ne. 27:13-22.)

MESSENGER OF THE COVENANT.

See ANGEL, MESSENGER BEFORE THE LORD, MESSENGER OF SALVATION, NEW AND EVERLASTING COVENANT. Our Lord is the *Messenger of the Covenant.* (Mal. 3:1.) He came in his Father's name (John 5:43), bearing his Father's message (John 7:16-17), to fulfil the covenant of the Father that a Redeemer and Savior would be provided for men. (Moses 4:1-3; Abra. 3:27-28.) Also, through his ministry the terms of the everlasting covenant of salvation became operative; the message he taught was that salvation comes through the gospel covenant.

MESSENGERS.

See ANGELS.

MESSIAH.

See ANOINTED ONE, CHRIST, HOLY MESSIAH, MESSIAHSHIP, MESSIANIC PROPHECIES, MESSIAS. Christ is the *Messiah,* a Hebrew name meaning *Anointed One* and carrying in the popular mind the assurance that he would come as King, Deliverer, and Savior to Israel. He is called the Messiah more then 30 times in the Book of Mormon (1 Ne. 10:4-17; 12:18; 2 Ne. 1:10), but strangely enough the name does not appear in its Hebrew form in the New Testament, and it is found in only one Old Testament passage. (Dan. 9:25-26.) It is found in three different revelations in the Doctrine and Covenants. (D. & C. 13; 19:27; 109:67.)

MESSIAHSHIP.

See CHRIST, JOINT-HEIRS WITH CHRIST, MESSIAH. There is only one Messiah (2 Ne. 25:18), and his status as the Anointed One, the promised Savior, is what constitutes his *Messiahship*. Others do not and cannot attain a status of Messiahship (for they are not born, as Christ was, inheriting life in themselves from an Immortal Parent), though others may become joint-heirs with him in his Father's kingdom.

MESSIANIC PROPHECIES.

See CHRIST, MESSIAH, PROPHECY, PROPHETS. All of the prophets from Adam to John the Baptist foretold the coming of Christ as the Messiah, Savior, King, Deliverer, and Redeemer—the very Son of God. Indeed, the very nature of the prophetic office was and is to bear record of Christ and of the salvation that comes through his atoning sacrifice; and the fact that

the prophets who preceded him spoke, as moved upon by the Holy Ghost, of his coming birth, ministry, mission, death, resurrection, and glorification is the very thing that made them prophets. (Mosiah 13:33.)

The Old Testament abounds in these *Messianic prophecies*, often couching them in language and symbolism which, though seemingly obscure to the spiritually untutored, was plain and clear to those to whom the prophecies came. (2 Ne. 25:4-7.) But perhaps the greatest, plainest, and most glorious Messianic prophecies, were given by the Nephite prophets and are found in the Book of Mormon.

Examples of some of the many Messianic prophecies are found in the following outline:

Many details concerning his birth into mortality were foretold. Isaiah and Nephi foresaw that his mother would be a virgin (Isa. 7: 14; 1 Ne. 11; 14-21; 2 Ne. 17:14); Isaiah also noted particularly the power and dominion to which the new born Child would be heir. (Isa. 9:6-7; 2 Ne. 19:6-7.) King Benjamin and Alma both foretold the name of his mother (Mosiah 3:8; Alma 7:10), and Micah and Alma named the place of his birth. (Mic. 5:1-3; Alma 7:10.) From earliest days it had been foreknown that he would be the Seed of Eve. (Gen. 3:15.) Jacob, Daniel, Nephi, Samuel the Lamanite, and Nephi the grandson of Helaman, each in turn, gave specific prophetic data as to the time of the promised birth. (Gen. 49:10; Dan. 9:25-26; 1 Ne. 19:7-8; Hela. 14; 3 Ne. 1.)

Hosea foretold his sojourn in Egypt (Hos. 11:10), and a prophet whose records have been lost to us specified that he would be called a Nazarene because Nazareth would be the main city of his abode. (Matt. 2:23.)

Assurance that he would come in due course is of frequent scriptural record. (1 Ne. 1; 10; Mosiah 15; Alma 7:7-13.) Balaam, who appears not to have been of Israelitish lineage, gave Israel one of her greatest Messianic prophecies (Num. 24), and Moses spelled out that the coming Messiah would be a prophet like unto Moses himself. (Deut. 18:15-22; Acts 3:22-26; 7:37; 3 Ne. 20:23-26.)

In rather elaborate detail much of his mission and ministry among men was outlined. (Isa. 42:1-7; 52: 13-14; 53; 61:1-3; 1 Ne. 11:28-36; Mosiah 3:5-10.) Provisions of the law of atonement were amply taught. (Isa. 53:4-12; Hos. 13:14; 2 Ne. 9; Mosiah 3; 15; 16; Alma 34.) His position as the Son of God (Alma 33; Hela. 8:14-24; Ps. 2); his rejection by the people (Isa. 8:13-17; 1 Ne. 19:7-13; 2 Ne. 18:13-17; Mosiah 3:5-10); his baptism (1 Ne. 10:7-10; 11:27); his divine kingship (Isa. 32:1; 33:17); his governmental dominion and rights including his heirship to the throne of David (Isa. 9:6-7; 16:5; 2 Ne. 19:6-7); the priesthood he would hold (Ps. 110); his status as the light of the world

(Isa. 9:2; 2 Ne. 19:2); as the rock of offense (Isa. 28:16; Rom. 9:33) and the stone which the builders rejected (Ps. 118:22); and his ministry to the spirits in prison (Isa. 24:22; 42:7; 61:1-3; Moses 7:38-39) —all these things found particular place in the prophetic promises. Indeed the whole law of Moses, and all the ordinances forming part of it, were operated in such a way as to point attention to the coming of the God of Israel in the flesh. (Mosiah 3:14-15; 13:30-35; Hela. 8:14-16.)

Around his crucifixion, death, and resurrection many ancient prophecies are centered. Isaiah, David, Nephi, Nephi the son of Helaman, and Samuel the Lamanite, for instance, speak pointedly of the fact that God himself, having come into mortality, would die. (Ps. 16:10; Isa. 26:19-21; 53:9; Acts 13:35; 1 Ne. 10:11; 11:32-34; Hela. 8:19-20; 14.) That this death should result from crucifixion was fore-revealed by Isaiah, Nephi, Jacob the brother of Nephi, and Enoch, among others. (Isa. 22:21-25; 1 Ne. 11:32-34; 19:10-13; 2 Ne. 10:3; Moses 7:55.) And the glorious resurrection of our Lord was spoken of on many occasions. (Isa. 25:8-9; 26:19-21; Hela. 14.)

MESSIAS.

See CHRIST, MESSIAH. *Messias* is the Greek form of the Hebrew *Messiah,* and it is this Greek rendition that is found in the only

New Testament passages using this particular name of our Lord. (John 1:41; 4:25.) This Greek-inspired translation is not found elsewhere in the scriptures.

MIA.
See MUTUAL IMPROVEMENT ASSOCIATIONS.

MICHAEL THE ARCHANGEL.

See ADAM, ANCIENT OF DAYS, BATTLE OF THE GREAT GOD, WAR IN HEAVEN. Our great prince, *Michael,* known in mortality as *Adam,* stands next to Christ in the eternal plan of salvation and progression. In pre-existence Michael was the most intelligent, powerful, and mighty spirit son of God, who was destined to come to this earth, excepting only the Firstborn, under whose direction and pursuant to whose counsel he worked. "He is the father of the human family, and *presides over the spirits of all men.*" (*Teachings,* p. 157.) The name Michael apparently, and with propriety, means one "who is like God."

In the creation of the earth, Michael played a part second only to that of Christ. When Lucifer rebelled and there was war in heaven, it was Michael who led the hosts of the faithful in casting Satan out. (Rev. 12:7-9.) When the time came to people the earth, the spirit Michael came and inhabited the body formed from the dust of the earth, the living soul thus created being known as *Adam.* As the first man he filled his foreordained destiny of standing as the presiding high priest (under Christ) over all the earth. It is through him that Christ is revealed, that all revelation comes, that the Lord's affairs on earth are directed during the pre-millennial era. (*Teachings,* pp. 157-159, 167-169.) He holds the keys of salvation for all men of all ages. (D. & C. 78:16.)

Three years previous to Adam's mortal death he met in the Valley of Adam-ondi-Ahman with his righteous descendants. "And the Lord appeared unto them, and they rose up and blessed Adam, and called him *Michael, the prince, the archangel.*" (D. & C. 107:54.) He will sit in council at this same place just prior to the great and dreadful day of the Lord; those of all ages who have served under his direction in the ministry will give an accounting of their stewardships; and the Son of Man will come and receive from Adam and all others a final accounting. (D. & C. 116; Dan. 7:9-14, 21-22, 26-27.)

Michael contended with the devil over the body of Moses (Jude 9); ministered comfort to the Prophet Daniel (Dan. 10:13, 21); appeared to Joseph Smith to detect "the devil when he appeared as an angel of light," and to confer keys and authorities (D. & C. 128: 20-21); and will hereafter partake of the sacrament with Christ and other righteous persons on earth. (D. & C. 27:11.)

We know also that he was with Christ in his resurrection (D. & C. 133:54-55); that "at the time of the end" he shall fight the battles of the saints (Dan. 11:40; 12:1); that all the dead shall come forth from their graves at the sound of his trump (D. & C. 29:26); that he will lead the armies of heaven against the hosts of hell in the final great battle when Lucifer is cast out eternally (D. & C. 88: 110-116); and that he does all things "under the counsel and direction of the Holy One, who is without beginning of days or end of life." (D. & C. 78:16.)

MIDDLE AGES.
See DARK AGES.

MIGHTY GOD OF JACOB.
See GOD OF ISRAEL.

MIGHTY ONE OF ISRAEL.
See GOD OF ISRAEL.

MILLENNIUM.
See ADAM-ONDI-AHMAN, DEVIL, EARTH, JUDGMENT DAY, KINGDOM OF GOD, NEW HEAVEN AND NEW EARTH, PEACE, RESURRECTION, REVELATION, SECOND COMING OF CHRIST, SIGNS OF THE TIMES, TIMES OF REFRESHING. Just as *century* means a period of 100 years

so *millennium* means a period of 1000 years. This earth, according to the divine plan, is passing through a mortal or temporal existence of seven millenniums or 7000 years. (D. & C. 77:6-7.) During the first six of these (covering a total period of 6000 years from the time of the fall of Adam) conditions of carnality, corruption, evil, and wickedness of every sort have prevailed upon the earth. Wars, death, destruction and everything incident to the present *telestial state* of existence have held sway over the earth and all life on its face.

When the 7th thousand years commence, however, radical changes will take place both in the earth itself and in the nature and type of existence enjoyed by all forms of life on its face. This will be the long hoped for age of peace when Christ will reign personally upon the earth; when the earth will be renewed and receive its paradisiacal glory; when corruption, death, and disease will cease; and when the kingdom of God on earth will be fully established in all its glory, beauty, and perfection. (Tenth Article of Faith.) This is the period known to the saints of all ages as *the millennium.* Important events and conditions to precede, attend and follow the millennial era include the following:

1. COUNCIL AT ADAM-ONDI-AHMAN PRECEDES MILLENNIUM.— During the first 6000 years of this earth's temporal continuance, the

Lord is administering the affairs of his earthly kingdom through agents, stewards, prophets, and appointed servants to whom he gives the keys and authority to direct such affairs. Adam is the Lord's chief agent in governing the affairs of this earth. The heads of the gospel dispensations and all of the prophets who have served in those blessed eras have been and are subject to this first man of all men.

When the time approaches for Christ to come and reign personally upon earth for the millennial period, then Adam and all those subordinate to him who have held keys and authority will meet in the Valley of Adam-ondi-Ahman. There an accounting will be made of all stewardships; *Christ will come and receive back the keys; and there will be "given him dominion, and glory, and a kingdom, that all people, nations, and languages, should serve him."* (Dan. 7:14.) Following this all will be in readiness for our Lord to reign personally upon the earth, and he will soon thereafter come to usher in the great millennial era.

2. SECOND COMING USHERS IN MILLENNIUM.—We are not living in the millennium now; nor do millennial conditions now prevail upon the earth; nor will they until Christ comes and the earth is renewed and receives its paradisiacal glory. (Tenth Article of Faith.) Christ's coming will mark the beginning of the millennium. The changes in men, all forms of life,

and the earth itself, which will be incident to the new order of things, will take place in the day of that coming.

"In mine own due time," saith the Lord, "will I come upon the earth in judgment, and my people shall be redeemed and shall reign with me on earth. For the great Millennium, of which I have spoken by the mouth of my servants, shall come." (D. & C. 43:29-30.) Again: "I will reveal myself from heaven with power and great glory, with all the hosts thereof, and dwell in righteousness with men on earth a thousand years, and the wicked shall not stand." (D. & C. 29:11.)

3. FIRST RESURRECTION USHERS IN MILLENNIUM.—Many persons have already come forth from the grave in their resurrected and glorified bodies. Righteous saints who lived from the day of Adam to the day of Christ were with him in his resurrection. (Matt. 27:52-53; D. & C. 133:54-55; Hela. 14:25.) To us, however, the first resurrection, the resurrection of the just, will come with the return of our Lord and the commencement of his millennial reign.

"Yea, and blessed are the dead that die in the Lord, from henceforth, *when the Lord shall come,* and old things shall pass away, and *all things become new,* they shall rise from the dead and shall not die after, and shall receive an inheritance before the Lord, in the holy city." (D. & C. 63:49.)

4. RIGHTEOUSNESS WILL NOT

HASTEN MILLENNIUM.—The time for the beginning of the millennium is fixed. It has been definitely set and is known to the Father. It cannot be advanced by the righteousness of the saints nor the repentance of people in the world. Nor can it be postponed either because of increasing wickedness or for any reason. By definition the millennium is the 7th period of 1000 years duration to which this earth is subject. It will commence when Christ comes, and his coming is set by revelation to be in the beginning of the 7th thousand years of this earth's temporal existence. (D. & C. 77:6, 12.)

As a matter of fact, the Second Coming of Christ (and thus the ushering in of the millennial era) will occur in a day of war and wickedness, of carnality, corruption, and abomination such as the world has never before seen. The cup of man's iniquity will be full, and the fury and scourge of the Lord will then be poured out without measure upon all nations. (Ezek. 38; 39; Joel 2; 3; Zech. 12; 13; 14; Mal. 3; 4; D. & C. 29; 45; 64:23-25; 133.)

5. DESTRUCTION OF WICKED AS MILLENNIUM COMMENCES.—Incident to the commencement of the millennial era, the earth (the Lord's vineyard) will be burned. Every corruptible thing will be consumed. (D. & C. 101:24); all the proud and they that do wickedly shall be burned as stubble (Mal. 4:1; D. & C. 29:9; 64:23-25; 133:63-64): the sinners will be destroyed (Isa. 13:9-14); and there will be an entire separation of the righteous and the wicked. (D. & C. 63:54.) Those only shall be able to abide that day who are worthy to live on a paradisiacal or terrestrial sphere.

6. DAY OF JUDGMENT COMMENCES MILLENNIAL ERA.—With the return of our Lord in the clouds of heaven, in all the glory of his Father's kingdom, to usher in the millennial era of peace, will come the first great formal day of judgment. At that day shall be gathered before him all the nations of the living, and he shall separate the sheep from the goats, rewarding the righteous with an inheritance in his Father's kingdom and cursing the wicked with everlasting punishment. (Matt. 25:31-46.) At that day the Twelve who were with the Lord in Jerusalem shall be in glory, even as he, and shall judge the righteous hosts of "the whole house of Israel." (D. & C. 29:9-13.) And beginning at that day, the worthy saints, having been resurrected with celestial bodies, shall live and reign on earth a thousand years. (Rev. 20:4.)

7. RENEWAL OF EARTH TO PARADISIACAL STATE.—With the ushering in of the millennium, "the earth will be *renewed* and receive its *paradisiacal glory*" (Tenth Article of Faith); that is, it will *return* to the edenic, terrestrial state which existed when the Lord God finished the creative enterprise

and pronounced everything that he had made, *"very good."* (Gen. 1:31.) In that primeval day, thorns, thistles, briars, and noxious weeds had not yet made their appearance (Gen. 3:18); there were no deserts and unfruitful places, no barren and unproductive mountains, but the whole earth was a delightful garden; all the earth's land surface was in one place, the seas in another; and death had not entered the scene, but immortality reigned in every department of creation. (2 Ne. 2:22.) Then came the fall of Adam and with it the beginning of the present telestial order of things. (*Man: His Origin and Destiny,* pp. 380-397.)

The millennium is the age of renewal and regeneration when the Lord will "create *new heavens* and a *new earth.*" So sweeping will be the changes, so radical the differences in the order of things, that the former heavens and earth "shall not be remembered, nor come into mind." (Isa. 65:17.) It will be a *"day of transfiguration,"* a day "when *the earth shall be transfigured"* (D. & C. 63:20-21), a day when the continents and islands shall again "become one land," when the mountains and valleys will no longer be found (D. & C. 133:22-24), when all things will return to their state of paradisiacal glory.

Our revelations tell us that when the Lord comes, the "element shall melt with fervent heat; and all things shall become new." (D.

& C. 101:25.) And Peter used this gospel truth as a basis for this powerful exhortation: "But *the day of the Lord* will come as a thief in the night; in the which *the heavens shall pass* away with a great noise, and *the elements shall melt with fervent heat, the earth also and the works that are therein shall be burned up.* Seeing then that all these things shall be dissolved, what manner of persons ought ye to be in all holy conversation and godliness, Looking for and hasting unto the coming of the day of God, wherein the heavens being on fire shall be dissolved, and *the elements shall melt with fervent heat?* Nevertheless we, according to the promise, look for *new heavens* and a *new earth,* wherein dwelleth righteousness. Wherefore, beloved, seeing that ye look for such things, be diligent that ye may be found of him in peace, without spot, and blameless." (2 Pet. 3:10-14.)

8. MILLENNIAL BINDING OF SATAN.—When we speak of the binding of Satan in connection with the millennium, we mean that he will be bound *during* that era, that his powers will be limited *after* that day commences, and not that men will turn to righteousness so as to tie the hands of Satan, thereby bringing millennial conditions to pass. The plan does not call for men to turn voluntarily to righteousness thereby causing the thousand year era of peace to commence. Rather, the

millennium will be brought about by power; the wicked will be destroyed; and those only will remain on earth who are sufficiently righteous to abide the day of the Lord's coming (Mal. 3; 4), a day when the elements shall melt with fervent heat and all things become new.

However, Satan shall be bound (D. & C. 43:31; 45:55; 84:100; 88:110-111; Rev. 20:1-3, 7), and for a thousand years he "shall not have power to tempt any man." (D. & C. 101:28.) Accordingly, "children shall grow up without sin unto salvation" (D. & C. 45:58), and righteousness and peace be everywhere present. It was this concept that caused Nephi to write, speaking of the period *after the commencement* of the millennium, that: "Because of the righteousness of his people, Satan has no power; wherefore, he cannot be loosed for the space of many years; for he hath no power over the hearts of the people, for they dwell in righteousness, and the Holy One of Israel reigneth." (1 Ne. 22:26.)

"And when the thousand years are expired, Satan shall be loosed out of his prison" (Rev. 20:7), "that he may gather together his armies. . . . And then cometh the battle of the great God; and the devil and his armies shall be cast away into their own place, that they shall not have power over the saints any more at all." (D. & C. 88:110-114.)

9. MILLENNIAL ATTAINMENT OF PEACE ON EARTH.—Not until the Prince of Peace comes to reign personally on earth will there be peace, and it will only come then because carnal, wicked, and lustful people have been burned as stubble by the brightness of his coming. (Mal. 3; 4; D. & C. 29:9; 64:23-25; 133:63-64; Jos. Smith 2:37.) It will only come because on the new earth the "enmity of man" shall cease from before the Lord's face. (D. & C. 101:26.) Wars come because of lust (Jas. 4:1-2), and will continue until lustful men are swept from the earth.

When Christ comes "he shall judge among the nations, and shall rebuke many people: and they shall beat their swords into plowshares, and their spears into pruninghooks: nation shall not lift up sword against nation, neither shall they learn war any more." (Isa. 2:4; Micah 4:3; 2 Ne. 12:4.)

10. MILLENNIAL CHANGES IN THE ANIMAL KINGDOM.—On the paradisiacal earth "the enmity of beasts, yea, the enmity of all flesh, shall cease." (D. & C. 101:26.) All animals shall mingle together in peace, and the appetites of the carnivorous beasts shall be changed so that the grass of the field becomes the common diet of the animal world. (Isa. 11:6-9; 65:25.)

11. MORTALITY CONTINUES DURING MILLENNIUM.—Great and marvelous though the changes will be incident to life during the millennial era, yet mortality as such

will continue. Children will be born, grow up, marry, advance to old age, and pass through the equivalent of death. Crops will be planted, harvested, and eaten; industries will be expanded, cities built, and education fostered; men will continue to care for their own needs, handle their own affairs, and enjoy the full endowment of free agency. Speaking a pure language (Zeph. 3:9), dwelling in peace, living without disease, and progressing as the Holy Spirit will guide, the advancement and perfection of society during the millennium will exceed anything men have supposed or expected.

"And he that liveth when the Lord shall come, and hath kept the faith, blessed is he; nevertheless, it is appointed to him to die at the age of man. Wherefore, *children shall grow up until they become old; old men shall die;* but they shall not sleep in the dust, but they shall be changed in the twinkling of an eye." (D. & C. 63:50-51.)

"For they that are wise and have received the truth, and have taken the Holy Spirit for their guide, and have not been deceived—verily I say unto you, they shall not be hewn down and cast into the fire, but shall abide the day. And the earth shall be given unto them for an inheritance; and *they shall multiply and wax strong, and their children shall grow up without sin unto salvation.*" (D. & C. 45:57-58.)

"Be ye glad and rejoice for ever in that which I create: for, behold, I create Jerusalem a rejoicing, and her people a joy. And I will rejoice in Jerusalem, and joy in my people: and the voice of weeping shall be no more heard in her, nor the voice of crying. . . .

"And they shall *build houses,* and *inhabit them;* and they shall *plant vineyards,* and *eat the fruit* of them. They shall not build, and another inhabit; they shall not plant, and another eat: for as the days of a tree are the days of my people, and mine elect shall long enjoy *the work of their hands.* They shall not *labour* in vain, nor bring forth for trouble; for they are the seed of the blessed of the Lord, and their *offspring* with them." (Isa. 65:18-23.)

"But they shall sit every man under his *vine* and under his *fig tree;* and none shall make them afraid: for the mouth of the Lord of hosts hath spoken it." (Micah 4:4.)

12. DEATH, SORROW, DISEASE CEASE DURING MILLENNIUM.— Physical bodies of those living on earth during the millennium will not be subject to the same ills that attend us in our present sphere of existence. Men in that day will still be mortal; children will be born to them; spirits coming into the physical or natural bodies born in that day will then go through their mortal probation as we are now going through ours. Those born during the millennium will not be immortal, that is, their bodies and spirits will not be insep-

arably connected as is the case with resurrected beings. But their bodies will be changed from conditions as they now exist so that disease cannot attack them, and death as we know it cannot intervene to cause a separation of body and spirit.

"There shall be no more thence," the Lord said to Isaiah, "an infant of days, nor an old man that hath not filled his days: for *the child shall die an hundred years old;* but the sinner being an hundred years old shall be accursed." (Isa. 65:20.)

In our day the Lord has revealed: "And there shall be no sorrow because *there is no death.* In that day *an infant shall not die until he is old;* and his life shall be as the age of a tree; And *when he dies* he shall not sleep, that is to say in the earth, but shall be changed in the twinkling of an eye, and shall be caught up, and his rest shall be glorious." (D. & C. 101:29-31.)

13. ALL THINGS REVEALED DURING MILLENNIUM.—In this pre-millennial age we have the fulness of the gospel, meaning that we have the fulness of the authority and sealing power whereby man can be sealed up unto eternal life and become an inheritor of the fulness of eternal reward in our Father's kingdom. But we do not have the fulness of truth; many glorious gospel doctrines have been known and taught in previous dispensations which have not as yet been restored to us. Such was the case, for instance, with Enoch and his people, with certain of the Jaredites, and with the Nephite people following the ministry of Christ among them.

But with the dawning of the millennium, the restoration of all things, "which God hath spoken by the mouth of all his holy prophets since the world began," shall be completed. (Acts 3:21.) As Nephi expressed it, "All things which have been revealed unto the children of men shall at that day be revealed." (2 Ne. 30:15-18; D. & C. 121:26-32.) If the sealed part of the Book of Mormon has not already been revealed, it will come forth in that day.

In addition, millennial revelations will bring to light truths never before manifest to any mortal. "When the Lord shall come, *he shall reveal all things*—Things which have passed, and *hidden things which no man knew,* things of the earth, by which it was made, and the purpose and the end thereof—Things most precious, things that are above, and things that are beneath, things that are in the earth, and upon the earth, and in heaven." (D. & C. 101:32-34.)

14. NONMEMBERS OF CHURCH DURING MILLENNIUM.—Since all who are living at least a terrestrial law—the law of honesty, uprightness, and integrity—will be able to abide the day of our Lord's coming, there will be nonmembers of the

Church on earth during the millennium. (*Doctrines of Salvation,* vol. 1, pp. 86-87; vol 3, pp. 63-64.) Honest and upright people who have been deceived by the false religions and false philosophies of the world will not have their free agency abridged. They will continue to believe their false doctrines until they voluntarily elect to receive gospel light. Speaking of the millennial period, Micah said, *"All people will walk every one in the name of his god,* and we will walk in the name of the Lord our God for ever and ever." (Micah 4:5.)

During the millennium, however, the Lord will use the forces of nature to turn people's attention to the truth. "Whoso will not come up," said Zechariah, "of all the families of the earth unto Jerusalem to worship the King, the Lord of hosts, even upon them shall be no rain." (Zech. 14:16-19.) Joseph Smith said, "The heathen nations who will not come up to worship will be visited with the judgments of God, and must eventually be destroyed from the earth." (*Teachings,* p. 269.)

15. MILLENNIAL CONVERSION OF ALL TO TRUTH.—With the destruction of the wicked and the fall of the great and abominable church (D. & C. 29:21; 88:94)—events destined to accompany the ushering in of the millennium—the conversion of men to the truths of the gospel will become easy. In due course every living soul on earth will come to the knowledge of the truth, "for the earth shall be full of the knowledge of the Lord, as the waters cover the sea." (Isa. 11:9; Hab. 2:14.) This means that when "all things shall be made known unto the children of men" (2 Ne. 30:15-18), they all shall accept the gospel, for the knowledge of God is found only by revelation through the power of the priesthood. (D. & C. 84:19-22.)

This will be the day when the great promise to Israel is fulfilled: "And they shall teach no more every man his neighbour, and every man his brother, saying, Know the Lord: for *they shall all know me,* from the least of them unto the greatest of them, saith the Lord: for I will forgive their iniquity, and I will remember their sin no more." (Jer. 31:34.)

This, also, shall be the day wherein men shall be so close to the Lord that, "Whatsoever *any man* shall ask, it shall be given unto him" (D. & C. 101:27), the day in which before men call, the Lord will answer, and while they are yet speaking, he will hear. (Isa. 65:24.)

16. THE MILLENNIAL KINGDOM OF GOD ON EARTH.—The Church of Jesus Christ of Latter-day Saints is the kingdom of God on earth; it is the kingdom which shall never be destroyed or left to other people; it is the kingdom which shall break in pieces and consume all other kingdoms; and it shall stand forever. (Dan. 2:44.) But for the

present it functions as an ecclesiastical kingdom only.

With the millennial advent, the kingdom of God on earth will step forth and exercise political jurisdiction over all the earth as well as ecclesiastical jurisdiction over its own citizens. When the saints pray, according to the Lord's pattern, "Thy kingdom come. Thy will be done in earth, as it is in heaven" (Matt. 6:10), they are petitioning the Father to send the political or millennial kingdom so that complete righteousness, both civically and religiously, will prevail on earth. That will be the day when, "The kingdom and dominion, and the greatness of the kingdom under the whole heaven, shall be given to the people of the saints of the most High, whose kingdom is an everlasting kingdom, and all dominions shall serve and obey him." (Dan. 7:27; D. & C. 65; *Doctrines of Salvation,* vol. 1, pp. 229-230.)

Until that glorious day when the Lord shall make "a full end of all nations" (D. & C. 87:6), when he shall reign "whose right it is to reign," the saints are commanded to "be subject to the powers that be." (D. & C. 58:22.) But in that day the whole system of government will be changed. Christ having previously come in the clouds of heaven to Adam-ondi-Ahman—where "there was given him dominion, and glory, and a kingdom, that *all people, nations, and languages, should serve him*" (Dan. 7:13-14)—shall then take over the reigns of government personally. *"Ye shall have no laws but my laws when I come, for I am your lawgiver,"* he has said. (D. & C. 38:22.) To the Prophet he said of those who would inhabit the millennial earth: "For the Lord shall be in their midst, and his glory shall be upon them, and *he will be their king and their lawgiver."* (D. & C. 45:59.)

At this time there will be two world capitals, "for out of Zion shall go forth the law, and the word of the Lord from Jerusalem." (Isa. 2:3; *Doctrines of Salvation,* vol. 3, pp. 66-72.) That resurrected personages will have positions of power and responsibility in the kingdom is evident from John's millennial statement: "And hast made us unto our God kings and priests: and *we shall reign on the earth."* (Rev. 5:10; 20:4.) Of this the Prophet Joseph Smith said: "Christ and the resurrected saints will reign over the earth during the thousand years. They will not probably *dwell* upon the earth, but will visit it when they please, or when it is necessary to *govern* it." (*Teachings,* p. 268.) Obviously many governmental offices will be filled by mortal persons living on the earth.

17. TEMPLE WORK DURING MILLENNIUM.—Salvation cannot be gained except through baptism of water and of the Spirit, nor can exaltation be achieved except through temple endowments and the sealing of families together for eternity. These saving and ex-

alting ordinances are performed vicariously in the temples for the worthy dead who did not have opportunity to receive them in this life.

We are commanded to go to with our might, collect all the accurate genealogical data we can, and perform these saving and exalting ordinances for our worthy ancestors. Obviously, due to the frailties, incapacities, and errors of mortal men, and because the records of past ages are often scanty and inaccurate, this great work cannot be completed for every worthy soul without assistance from on high. The millennial era is the time, primarily, when this assistance will be given by resurrected beings. Genealogical records unknown to us will then become available. Errors committed by us in sealings or other ordinances will be rectified, and all things will be arranged in proper order. Temple work will be the great work of the millennium. (*Doctrines of Salvation,* vol. 2, pp. 251-252.)

18. END OF MILLENNIUM AND OF THE EARTH.—When the thousand years are ended Satan shall be loosed, men again shall begin to deny their God, and rebellion shall well up in the hearts of many. For a little season the devil will be free to gather together his armies, even the hosts of hell; and then the final battle will be fought in which Satan (who is Perdition) together with all his sons shall be cast out forever. (D. & C. 29:22-29; 43:31; 88:

110-115; Rev. 20:7-10; 2 Ne. 9:16.) Then will come the end of the earth as it is now constituted, for it will attain its final destiny as a celestial sphere, and the meek shall inherit it forever. (D. & C. 88:16-20.)

MIND.

See CONSCIENCE, GIFT OF THE HOLY GHOST, INTELLIGENCE, LIGHT OF CHRIST, SOUL. The sentient, conscious, and intelligent part of man—the part that perceives, feels, wills, and thinks—is called the *mind.* To those who rule an Omnipotent Creator out of their views, who suppose that all things exist by mere evolutionary chance, the mind of man is an inexplicable mystery. But to those who know about God and his eternal purposes, it is clear that the mind of man rests in the eternal spirit.

The mind was present with the pre-existent spirit; it will be present with the disembodied spirit in the sphere immediately following mortality. Man's intelligence is in his spirit and not in the natural or mortal body. Thus we find the Prophet speaking of "the mind or the intelligence which man possesses," and of using as synonymous terms, "the soul, the mind of man, the immortal spirit [i.e. the intelligence]." (*Teachings,* pp. 352-353.)

In every age the first and great commandment has been: "Thou shalt love the Lord thy God with all thy heart, with all thy might, *mind,* and strength; and in the name of Jesus Christ thou shalt serve him." (D. & C. 59:5; 2 Ne. 25:29; Moro. 10:32; Matt. 22:36-38.) All saints are expected to be of one mind (2 Cor. 13:11; Philip. 1: 27; 1 Pet. 3:8), and that mind is to be "the mind of Christ." (1 Cor. 2:16; Philip. 2:5.) The spirit of revelation consists in having thoughts placed in one's mind by the power of the Holy Ghost (D. & C. 8:2-3; Enos 10), and when anyone speaks under the influence of the Holy Ghost the scriptural expressions thus uttered are "the mind of the Lord." (D. & C. 68:2-4.)

MIND OF CHRIST.
See UNITY.

MINISTERIAL TITLES.
See APOSTASY, BRETHREN, CLERGY, ELDERS, HOLY FATHER, RABBI. Religious leaders among the Jews, glorying in the honors of men, sought "to be called of men, Rabbi, Rabbi," (which is Master). But our Lord, condemning them for their false pride, acclaimed: "Be not ye called Rabbi: for one is your Master, even Christ; and *all ye are brethren.*" (Matt. 23:7-8.) "And call no one your creator upon the earth, or your heavenly Father; for one is your creator and heavenly Father, even he who is in heaven. Neither be ye called masters; for one is your mas-ter, even he whom your heavenly Father sent, which is Christ; for he hath sent him among you that ye might have life. But *he that is greatest among you shall be your servant. And whosoever shall exalt himself shall be abased of him; and he that shall humble himself shall be exalted of him.*" (*Inspired Version,* Matt. 23:6-9.)

Similarly in many ecclesiastical, educational, and governmental circles today it is with some considerable pride that holders of worldly titles are so addressed as to give pointed notice of the titled person's "superior" or at least distinctive status. In churches of Christendom there is no aversion to receiving the deference attached to *ministerial titles.* These titles of honor are sought, and men who should rank themselves as brethren, vie for that pre-eminence presumed to attach to holders of them. But in the true Church, which is the brotherhood of Christ, worldly titles have a hollow ring. Our Lord's true ministers prefer to be greeted by the saints as brethren in the Lord rather than to glory in the honors of men.

Even where the approved and revealed religious titles are concerned, reverence for sacred things dictates that their indiscriminate usage be avoided. A member of the Council of the Twelve, for instance, should not be addressed as *Apostle* Smith, but as *Elder* or *Brother* Smith.

Every male church officer may appropriately be addressed as *Broth-er.* On special and formal occasions there is propriety in calling a member of the First Presidency, or of a stake presidency, or the president of the Council of the Twelve, or a mission president as *President.* A ward bishop or a member of the Presiding Bishopric may properly be addressed as *Bishop.* Members of the Council of the Twelve, the Patriarch to the Church and all stake patriarchs, the assistants to the Twelve, members of the First Council of the Seventy, and all quorum presidents may properly be addressed as *Elder* or *Brother.* (*Doctrines of Salvation,* vol. 3, pp. 120-123.)

MINISTERING OF ANGELS.

See AARONIC PRIESTHOOD, ANGELS, GIFTS OF THE SPIRIT, KEYS OF THE MINISTERING OF ANGELS, MINISTERING SPIRITS, MINISTRY. "Angels speak by the power of the Holy Ghost; wherefore, they speak the words of Christ." (2 Ne. 32:3.) *They are ministers of Christ.* "They are subject unto him, to minister according to the word of his command, showing themselves unto them of strong faith and a firm mind in every form of godliness. And the office of their ministry is to call men unto repentance, and to fulfil and to do the work of the covenants of the Father, which he hath made unto the children of men, to prepare the way among the children of men, by declaring the word of Christ unto the chosen

vessels of the Lord, that they may bear testimony of him." (Moro. 7: 30-31.)

By the *ministering of angels* to men in modern times the Lord's great work of restoration is being accomplished. By this means the Book of Mormon came forth (D. & C. 20:8-12); by it the gospel of salvation was restored to earth. (Rev. 14:6-7; D. & C. 20:35; 133:36-40.) It was under the hands of angelic ministrants that the Aaronic and Melchizedek powers were conferred again upon men (D. & C. 13; 20:12-13); because they heard the voice of angels men again were commissioned to use the keys of the kingdom (D. & C. 110:11-16; 128:20-21); and by the ministering of angels the world is called to repentance. (D. & C. 43:25.)

Indeed, from Adam to the present moment, *whenever men have had sufficient faith, angels have ministered unto them.* So invarying is this principle that it stands forth as the conclusive test of the divinity of any organization on earth. *If angels minister to a people, they are the Lord's people, and his kingdom is with them. If angels do not minister unto them, they are not the Lord's people, and his kingdom is not with them.* (Moro. 7:27-38.) Judged by this standard it is not difficult to find which of all the churches is right and which one men should join if they have a truth-inspired desire to gain eternal salvation. As is well known, angels have and do minister to faithful members of The Church of Jesus Christ of Latter-day Saints.

The practice of the ministering of angels is not limited to mortality. In eternity those in the terrestrial kingdom will be ministered to by those of the celestial, and those in the telestial by angels sent to them from the terrestrial world. (D. & C. 76:86-88.)

MINISTERING SPIRITS.

See MINISTERING OF ANGELS, MINISTERS, MINISTRY, SPIRIT BODIES, TRANSLATED BEINGS. 1. Joseph Smith "explained the difference between an angel and a *ministering spirit:* the one a resurrected or translated body, with its spirit ministering to embodied spirits—the other a *disembodied spirit,* visiting and ministering to disembodied spirits. Jesus Christ became a ministering spirit (while his body was lying in the sepulchre) to the spirits in prison, to fulfil an important part of his mission, without which he could not have perfected his work, or entered into his rest. After his resurrection he appeared as an angel to his disciples." (*Teachings,* p. 191; D. & C. 129.)

The angel who appeared to Adam to query him about his obedience to the law of sacrifice was a ministering spirit (Moses 5:5-8), that is, he was either an *unembodied spirit* from pre-existence or the spirit of some person who had died and

passed into the spirit world to await a future resurrection. This we know because "there are no angels who minister to this earth but those who do belong or have belonged to it" (D. & C. 130:5), and at the time of this particular ministration there were as yet no resurrected or translated personages.

2. After the resurrection is completed, when the spirits and bodies of all personages connected with earth have been inseparably connected, there will no longer be *ministering spirits* within the literal meaning of that term. But at that future day the title will be applied to *resurrected personages* who have assignments to minister to certain other resurrected beings who were their former fellow mortals. For instance, resurrected persons in the terrestrial kingdom will serve as ministering spirits to other resurrected persons in the telestial kingdom. (D. & C. 76:88; Heb. 1:14.)

MINISTER OF SALVATION.

See CHRIST, MINISTERS, SALVATION. Christ is the *Minister of Salvation* (Rom. 15:8; Gal. 2:17; Heb. 8), meaning that through his mediation and atoning sacrifice the whole plan and system of salvation becomes operative.

MINISTERS.

See CLERGY, MINISTERIAL TITLES, MINISTERING OF ANGELS,

MINISTERING SPIRITS, MINISTER OF SALVATION, MINISTRY, OVERSEERS, PASTORS, PRIESTHOOD OFFICES, SHEPHERDS. In the gospel sense, *ministers* are the Lord's authorized and legally commissioned servants whose mission it is to act for the salvation of their fellow men. They are priesthood holders who are directed to preach the gospel and administer the ordinances thereof. (Fifth Article of Faith.) Thus deacons, teachers, and elders are *standing ministers* (D. & C. 84:111; 124:137), seventies are *traveling ministers* (D. & C. 107:97), patriarchs are *evangelical ministers* (D. & C. 107:39), and so on through all the offices of the priesthood, all are designed for a special ministry.

True ministers are called of God by revelation; they hold the priesthood, teach the true gospel, and serve in conformity with the program of the Church. Any professing preachers, ministers, pastors, or ecclesiastical administrators—by whatever designation they may go—who are without the priesthood, and who do not teach the true doctrines of salvation, are false ministers and will be rewarded accordingly.

From the sectarian view, the true Church has a *lay ministry,* meaning that bishops and other church officers do not receive financial compensation for their work; their temporal necessities are provided through secular pursuits. From the Lord's view, his Church is a "kingdom of priests" in which every worthy and qualified man is a minister. (Ex. 19:5-6; Deut. 7:6; 1 Pet. 2:5-9.)

"The ministers of God," Paul wrote, serve "in much patience, in afflictions, in necessities, in distresses, In stripes, in imprisonments, in tumults, in labours, in watchings, in fastings; By pureness, by knowledge, by longsuffering, by kindness, by the Holy Ghost, by love unfeigned, By the word of truth, by the power of God, by the armour of righteousness on the right hand and on the left, By honour and dishonour, by evil report and good report: as deceivers, and yet true; As unknown, and yet well known; as dying, and, behold, we live; as chastened, and not killed; As sorrowful, yet alway rejoicing; as poor, yet making many rich; as having nothing, and yet possessing all things." (2 Cor. 6:4-10; 1 Tim. 4; Mal. 2:5-7.)

MINISTRY.

See CHURCH OF JESUS CHRIST OF LATTER-DAY SAINTS, GOSPEL, MINISTERS, PRIESTHOOD. Brethren holding the priesthood are called to the *ministry.* As the Lord's agents, his ambassadors, they serve him by serving their fellow men. The various offices in the priesthood are so designed that ministers will be available to perform all the diverse and specialized labors which aid the rolling forth of the Lord's purposes. (Eph. 4:11-14.)

Those legally called to the ministry, following in the footsteps of their Master, are sent forth to: Testify of Christ, bear record of Joseph Smith and his successors, and proclaim the divinity of "the only true and living church upon the face of the whole earth" (D. & C. 1:30); to declare glad tidings, preach the gospel, and teach the truths of salvation; to seek the lost, call the wicked to repentance, and leave the unrepentant without excuse; to heal the sick, comfort the bereaved, and refresh the weary; to enlighten the bewildered, enliven the indifferent, and teach the ignorant; to perform the ordinances of salvation, exercise the gifts of the Spirit, and do all things (as directed by their Master) which will spread the hope of salvation among men.

MINOR PROPHETS.
See PROPHETS.

MIRACLES.
See FAITH, GIFTS OF THE SPIRIT, HEALINGS, MAGIC, PRIESTHOOD, SIGNS. In the broadest sense, *miracles* embrace all those events which are beyond the power of any presently known physical power to produce. They are occurrences which deviate from the known laws of nature and which transcend our knowledge of those laws. In this sense atomic explosions, now commonplace, would have been classed as miracles in a less scientifically advanced society; and in this sense the churches of the world accept miracles.

But in the gospel sense, *miracles are those occurrences wrought by the power of God which are wholly beyond the power of man to perform.* Produced by a supernatural power, they are marvels, wonders, and signs, which cannot be duplicated by man's present powers or by any powers which he can obtain by scientific advancements. Miracles in the gospel sense are gifts of the Spirit; they take place when the Lord on his own motion manifests his powers or when man by faith prevails upon Deity to perform supernatural events. In this literal gospel sense the Christian world does not believe in the present performance of miracles; and, for that matter, a large segment of Christendom goes farther and denies completely or spiritualizes away the recorded miracles of the Bible.

"And there were great and marvelous works wrought by the disciples of Jesus," the Book of Mormon record says of gospel miracles during the period following our Lord's ministry among the Nephites, "insomuch that they did heal the sick, and raise the dead, and cause the lame to walk, and the blind to receive their sight, and the deaf to hear; and all manner of miracles did they work among the children of men; and in nothing did they work miracles save it were in the name of Jesus." (4 Ne. 5;

Mosiah 3:5; 15:6.) These events, among others, are typical of those that have always transpired when the true Church has been on earth.

As gifts of the Spirit (D. & C. 46:21; 1 Cor. 12:10, 29; Moro. 10: 12), miracles are always performed among people who have faith. (D. & C. 45:8.) "For I am God, and mine arm is not shortened; and I will show miracles, signs, and wonders, unto all those who believe on my name. *And whoso shall ask it in my name in faith, they shall cast out devils; they shall heal the sick; they shall cause the blind to receive their sight, and the deaf to hear, and the dumb to speak, and the lame to walk.*" (D. & C. 35:8-9.) Indeed, so common is the working of these and other miracles among the true saints of God that the Lord gave this caution by revelation: "Require not miracles, except I shall command you, except casting out devils, healing the sick, and against poisonous serpents, and against deadly poisons; And these things ye shall not do, except it be required of you by them who desire it." (D. & C. 24:13-14.)

Faith and righteousness are the powers by which miracles are wrought (2 Ne. 26:13; Mosiah 8: 18), and miracles are not manifest until after the foundation of faith has been securely built. (Ether 12: 15-16, 18.) Miracles cease when wickedness prevails among a people (Morm. 1:13); their absence is thus conclusive proof of the apostate status of any church or peo-

ple. "There was not any man who could do a miracle in the name of Jesus," the Nephite record states, "save he were cleansed every whit from his iniquity." (3 Ne. 8:1.)

Miracles are one of the great evidences of the divinity of the Lord's work. They are the signs which always follow the true believers. (Mark 16:14-20; Morm. 9:20-25.) Where there are true miracles, there is the true Church; where these miracles are not, there the true Church is not. Our Lord's miracles during his mortal ministry stood as a sign of his divine calling. (John 3:2; Hela. 16:4; 4 Ne. 31.) But miracles standing alone, without other accompaniment, are not conclusive proof that divine approval rests upon a church or people. False and spurious miracles are sometimes wrought by the evil power. (Rev. 13:14; 16:14; 19: 20.)

One of the great identifying characteristics of apostate churches is their denial of miracles. "They deny the power of God, the Holy One of Israel; and they say unto the people: Hearken unto us, and hear ye our precept; for behold there is no God today, for the Lord and the Redeemer hath done his work, and he hath given his power unto men; Behold, hearken ye unto my precept; if they shall say there is a miracle wrought by the hand of the Lord, believe it not; for this day he is not a God of miracles; he hath done his work." (2 Ne. 28:5-6.) The coming forth of the Book of Mormon was reserved for "a day when it shall be said that miracles are done away." (Morm. 8:26.)

But the judgments of God shall rest upon all those who deny his power. "Yea, wo unto him that shall deny the revelations of the Lord, and that shall say the Lord no longer worketh by revelation, or by prophecy, or by gifts, or by tongues, or by healings, or by the power of the Holy Ghost! Yea, and *wo unto him that shall say at that day, to get gain, that there can be no miracle wrought by Jesus Christ;* for he that doeth this shall become like unto the son of perdition, for whom there was no mercy, according to the word of Christ!" (3 Ne. 29:6-7.)

"Do we not read that God is the same yesterday, today, and forever, and in him there is no variableness neither shadow of changing? And now, if ye have imagined up unto yourselves a god who doth vary, and in whom there is shadow of changing, then have ye imagined up unto yourselves a god who is not a God of miracles. . . .

"And who shall say that Jesus Christ did not do many mighty miracles? And there were many mighty miracles wrought by the hands of the apostles. And if there were miracles wrought then, why has God ceased to be a God of miracles and yet be an unchangeable Being? And behold, I say unto you he changeth not; if so he would cease to be God; and he ceaseth not to be God, and is a God of mir-

acles." (Morm. 9:9-20.)

"Has the day of miracles ceased? Or have angels ceased to appear unto the children of men? Or has he withheld the power of the Holy Ghost from them? Or will he, so long as time shall last, or the earth shall stand, or there shall be one man upon the face thereof to be saved? Behold I say unto you, Nay; for it is by faith that miracles are wrought; and it is by faith that angels appear and minister unto men; wherefore, if these things have ceased wo be unto the children of men, for it is because of unbelief, and all is vain." (Moro. 7:28-38.)

MISERY.

See GRIEF, SORROW, WOES. Unrighteousness breeds *misery,* a state of great distress and wretchedness, a state opposite to one of joy and happiness. (2 Ne. 2:11, 23; Alma 3:26; 40:15, 17, 21.) The devil and his angels are miserable creatures (2 Ne. 9:9, 46; D. & C. 76:48), and they seek to drag men down to their own miserable state. (2 Ne. 2:5, 18, 27.) Those who inherit damnation will be miserable forever (Mosiah 3:25; Alma 9:11; 26: 20; 41:4; 42:1, 26; Hela. 3:29; 5:12; 7:16; 12:26; Morm. 8:38), and as a matter of fact an unclean person "would be more miserable to dwell with a holy and just God, under a consciousness" of his filthiness before him, than "to dwell with the damned souls in hell." (Morm. 9:4-

5.) It is through the atoning sacrifice of Christ that men escape eternal misery with the devil and his angels in eternity. (2 Ne. 9:6-9.) And it is through righteousness in this life that they will escape misery in the world to come. "Go to now, ye rich men," James wrote of those who make gold their god, "weep and howl for your miseries that shall come upon you." (Jas. 5:1.)

MISSING SCRIPTURE.
See LOST SCRIPTURE.

MISSIONARIES.
See CONVERSION, ELDERS, GOSPEL, MESSAGE OF THE RESTORATION, MISSIONS, SAVIORS OF MEN, SEVENTIES, TESTIMONY. Every member of the Church is a *missionary,* with the responsibility of teaching the gospel by word and deed to our Father's other children. This responsibility arises through church membership alone, without the receipt of any special call. Church members are under covenant, made in the waters of baptism, "to stand as witnesses of God at all times and in all things, and in all places that ye may be in, even until death." (Mosiah 18:9.) They are subject to the divine pronouncement: "It becometh every man who hath been warned to warn his neighbor." (D. & C. 88:81.)

Further, scores of thousands of the saints have, are, and will serve formally in the stake, regional, and foreign missions. Stake and regional missionaries serve on a part or full-time basis in the stakes. Part-time missionaries are also called from among the local saints in the missions. Foreign missionaries drop their temporal pursuits, travel to the nations of the earth, and for periods of two or three years, without financial help from the Church, devote their full time to proclaiming the message of the restoration.

One of the great evidences of the divinity of the great latter-day work is that hundreds of thousands of the saints have or will go at a moment's notice, at their own expense, to the ends of the earth, to testify of Christ and the restoration of the gospel through Joseph Smith. (D. & C. 133:36-40.) No other church can duplicate or come in any way close to this record of service.

MISSION PRESIDENTS.
See CHURCH ORGANIZATION, MISSIONARIES, MISSIONS. Presiding officers in missions are *mission presidents.* They hold the keys of their ministry and are assisted by two counselors (thus forming a *mission presidency*). *Stake* and *regional mission presidents,* as with other officers in the stakes and wards, devote full church service time to their callings, but are also engaged in the normal temporal pursuits. Presidents of *foreign missions* are called by the First Presi-

dency and devote their full time to the missionary ministry. They direct both the proselyting work and preside over (as a stake president does in a stake) all of the programs of the Church in the missions.

MISSIONS.

See CHURCH ORGANIZATION, DISTRICTS, MISSIONARIES, MISSION PRESIDENTS. *Stake, regional,* and *foreign missions* form a part of the organization of God's earthly kingdom. *Stake missions* are proselyting agencies, within the stakes; *regional missions* are special proselyting agencies, made up of a number of stakes, so that the message of the restoration can be presented with more effect to minority and foreign speaking groups. As the name suggests, *foreign missions* are the ecclesiastical areas of the Church located outside of the stakes. Their purpose is to proselyte and also to carry on the programs of the Church in a manner comparable to the way these things are done in the stakes. For administrative reasons, both stake, regional, and foreign missions are divided into *districts,* and in the case of foreign missions these districts are broken down into *branches.*

MODERN REVELATION.

See REVELATION.

MODESTY.

See CHASTITY, WORLD. *Modesty* in dress is one of the identifying characteristics of true saints. It is an aid in preserving chastity and an outward sign that the modest person is imbued with humility, decency, and propriety. *Immodesty* in dress is worldly, excites passions and lusts, places undue emphasis on sex and lewdness, and frequently encourages and invites petting and other immoral practices. It is an outward sign that the immodest person has become hardened to the finer sensitivites of the Spirit and been overcome by a spirit of vanity and pride. Low-necked dresses and those which do not adequately cover the body, for instance, are obviously destructive of decency.

Extremes of dress of any kind are of doubtful propriety. Costly and elaborate clothing in general is anything but indicative that the wearer has overcome the world and is walking humbly before the Lord. On the other hand old-fashioned, somber, uniform-type clothing worn by fanatical members of some small religious sects is wholly unbecoming in our modern society. Such habits of dress indicate a lack of understanding of sound and true principles of modesty.

Speaking as moved upon by the Spirit, Paul counseled "that women adorn themselves in *modest apparel,* with shamefacedness and sobriety; *not with broided hair, or gold, or pearls, or costly array;* But (which becometh women professing godliness) with good works."

(1 Tim. 2:9-10.) In our day the Lord has spoken similarly: *"Thou shalt not be proud in thy heart; let all thy garments be plain, and their beauty the beauty of the work of thine own hands."* (D. & C. 42: 40.)

MONEY.

See RICHES.

MONOTHEISM.

See ATHEISM, DEISM, GOD, HENOTHEISM, PLURALITY OF GODS, POLYTHEISM, THEISM. *Monotheism* is the doctrine or belief that there is but one God. If this is properly interpreted to mean that the Father, Son, and Holy Ghost—each of whom is a separate and distinct godly personage—are one God, meaning one Godhead, then true saints are monotheists. Professing Christians consider themselves monotheists as distinguished from polytheists, those pagan peoples who believe in a host of gods whose powers are exercised only in their own fields.

It is falsely supposed in the sectarian world that monotheism is the contribution of the Hebrew people to the religious philosophy of the world. They contend that belief in one supreme God began with Abraham, was further established by Moses, but was not fully taught nor understood until Amos and the later prophets. Actually, of course, the true knowledge of God was first revealed to Adam and was known to all the saints from his day to Abraham.

Pagan tribal gods were the creation of the imaginations of apostate peoples, just as the creeds and apostate views of God which prevail in modern Christendom are the result of forsaking the truth. When Moses issued the great proclamation—"Hear, O Israel: *The Lord our God is one Lord"* (Deut. 6:4) —he was but reiterating a great truth known to all the prophets who preceded him.

MONTHS.

See TIME.

MOON.

See ASTRONOMY.

MORALITY.

See CHASTITY.

MORE SURE WORD OF PROPHECY.

See CALLING AND ELECTION SURE.

MORIANCUMER.

See MAHONRI MORIANCUMER.

MORMON BIBLE.

See BIBLE, BOOK OF MORMON, KING JAMES VERSION OF THE

BIBLE, REVELATION, SCRIPTURE, STANDARD WORKS. Almost as soon as the Book of Mormon came from the press in 1830, disbelieving persons began to refer to it as the *Mormon Bible,* a practice which is still current in many places. Generally the purpose and intent of those so designating the Book of Mormon seems to be to belittle the announcement that it is latter-day scripture, and also to further the false notion that Latter-day Saints believe that this volume of American scripture has replaced the traditional Christian Bible among the followers of Joseph Smith.

Since Mormons do in fact believe that the Book of Mormon is a volume of sacred scripture which bears record of Christ and teaches the doctrines of his gospel in plainness, perfection, and purity, it follows that in a purely figurative sense it might be said to be a Mormon Bible. But in the sense that it is in any way intended to replace the Bible itself such a claim is false. In the literal sense of the word the Mormon Bible is the King James Version of the Bible, the same volume that is accepted, believed, and read in most of the Christian sects of the day.

One of the remarkable things about this almost spontaneous practice of designating the Nephite record as the Mormon Bible, and then proclaiming that the traditional Bible is complete and contains all of the word of God that is

needed by men, is the fact that this very reaction and opposition to the truth was foretold in the Book of Mormon itself. In that volume of scripture, speaking of the coming forth of the Nephite record in the last days, the Lord says: "My words shall hiss forth unto the ends of the earth, for a standard unto my people, which are of the house of Israel; And because my words shall hiss forth—many of the Gentiles shall say: A Bible! A Bible! We have got a Bible, and there cannot be any more Bible." (2 Ne. 29:2-10.)

MORMONISM.

See BOOK OF MORMON, CHRISTIANITY, CHURCH OF JESUS CHRIST OF LATTER-DAY SAINTS, GOSPEL, JOSEPH SMITH THE PROPHET, PLAN OF SALVATION, RESTORATION OF THE GOSPEL. To the fulness of the everlasting gospel, revealed anew in this final dispensation, the world has given the nickname *Mormonism.* This name—conferred upon the beliefs and doctrines of the saints and used by its original coiners as an opprobrious epithet —is in no sense offensive to members of The Church of Jesus Christ of Latter-day Saints. In all probability, the term *Christianity* (a synonym for Mormonism) had a similar beginning in the meridian of time.

Since the Latter-day Saints believe the Book of Mormon—a volume which contains the fulness of the gospel, the same gospel which is in the Bible—they do not recoil from the designation of their views as Mormonism. Rather they take every honorable opportunity to herald these views to the world, for they are the pure, unadulterated Christianity of old. *Mormonism is Christianity; Christianity is Mormonism; they are one and the same, and they are not to be distinguished from each other in the minutest detail.*

"Mormonism is . . . a revelation from the heavens to man, introducing a new dispensation to the human family," President John Taylor says. "It is the religion that Adam, Enoch, Noah, Melchizedek, Abraham, Lot, Isaac, Jacob, Moses, Jesus, and the apostles had, . . . and that Lehi, Nephi, Alma, Moroni, Mormon, and a host of others had. . . . It had its origin from God. . . . It is the philosophy of the heavens and the earth, of God, and angels, and saints." (*Gospel Kingdom,* pp. 1-10.)

MORMON PIONEERS.

See MORMONS. "Go as *pioneers* . . . to a land of peace," the Lord commanded Brigham Young and the select group who were going with him to prepare the way for the Mormon colonization of the western frontier. (D. & C. 136.) Arriving in the Salt Lake Valley, July 21-24, 1847, this group (consisting originally of 147 men, three women, and two children) became the first of many. Soon the whole intermountain west was a hive of pioneering activity as the *Mormon Pioneers* laid the foundation for a home for the saints in the tops of the mountains. (*Doctrines of Salvation,* vol. 3, pp. 327-362.) It has become common to refer to all who came west prior to the opening up of the railroad in 1869 as pioneers.

MORMONS.

See BOOK OF MORMON, CHRISTIANS, CHURCH OF JESUS CHRIST OF LATTER-DAY SAINTS, GOSPEL, MORMONISM, SAINTS. *Mormon* was the ancient Nephite prophet who abridged and compiled the sacred records of his people under the title *The Book of Mormon.* This inspired book, containing a record of God's dealings with a people who had the fulness of the gospel, is accepted by The Church of Jesus Christ of Latter-day Saints as scripture. Accordingly, unofficially and by way of nickname, members of this restored Church have become known as *Mormons,* a name which is in no sense offensive or objectionable to them. *Mormons are true Christians; their worship is the pure, unadulterated Christianity authored by Christ and accepted by Peter, James, and John and all the ancient saints.*

MORNING STARS.

See STARS OF HEAVEN.

MORONI.

See ANGELS, BOOK OF MORMON, KEYS OF THE KINGDOM, RESTORATION OF THE GOSPEL, STICK OF EPHRAIM. To *Moroni* the Lord gave the privilege and power to bring to light the Book of Mormon. Following his mortal Nephite ministry, he died and went to the paradise of God. (Moro. 10:34.) Then in modern times, as a resurrected being, because he held "the keys of the record of the stick of Ephraim" (D. & C. 27:5), he came to the Prophet and revealed the Book of Mormon. This coming was in partial fulfilment of John's vision of another angel flying in the midst of heaven to commit the everlasting gospel to man. (Rev. 14: 6-7; D. & C. 133:36-40.)

MORONI'S PROMISE.

See BOOK OF MORMON.

MORTALITY.

See CARNALITY, CORRUPTION, DEATH, DEVILISHNESS, ELEMENTS, FLESH AND BLOOD, IMMORTALITY, MAN, SENSUALITY. Man as now constituted has a mortal body, one subject to death, corruption, and all of the ills of the flesh. *Mortality* is that state of existence during which body and spirit are temporarily joined together; immortality is that future resurrected state in which body and spirit are inseparably connected. (D. & C. 93:33.) In the resurrection all men will be raised from mortality to immortality, from corruption to incorruption. (1 Cor. 15:53-54; Mosiah 16:10; Alma 12:12; 41:4.)

Our present mortal bodies are composed of flesh, blood, and spirit. "The life of the flesh is in the blood" (Lev. 17:11), meaning that if the blood is shed, the spirit leaves the body, death occurs, and the body decays (for it is corruptible) and goes back to the dust from which it was created. By undergoing the experiences of mortality, spirits gain bodies which will be restored to them in the resurrection; also they are tried and tested to see if they will keep the commandments of God while living in this probationary state.

Translated beings live in a state of mortality, but changes are "wrought upon their bodies" so that they will not taste of death. (3 Ne. 28:36-40.) "Ye shall never endure the pains of death," the Lord told the Three Nephites, who like John the Beloved were translated, "but when I shall come in my glory ye shall be changed in the twinkling of an eye from mortality to immortality." (3 Ne. 28: 8.)

Persons continuing to live on earth when Christ comes, and those born during the entire millennial period, will be mortal, but they too will have changes made in their bodies so that disease and death will not affect them as it now affects mortal beings. "Children shall grow up until they become old; old men shall die; but they shall not sleep in the dust, but they shall be changed in the twinkling of an eye." (D. & C. 63: 51; 101:30-31; Isa. 65:20.)

MORTAL SOUL.
See SOUL.

MOSAIC DISPENSATION.
See DISPENSATIONS.

MOSAIC LAW.
See LAW OF MOSES.

MOSES.
See ANGELS, GATHERING OF ISRAEL, KEYS OF THE KINGDOM, LAW OF MOSES, TEN COMMANDMENTS. In prophetic power, spiritual insight, and leadership qualifications, *Moses* ranks with the mightiest men who have ever lived. All succeeding generations have classed him as the great law-giver of Israel. The miracles and majesty attending his ministry can scarcely be duplicated. Indeed, his life and ministry stand as a prototype of the mortal life and ministry of our Lord himself. So great was Moses that even Christ is described as a Prophet like unto this ancient leader of Israel's hosts. (Deut. 18:15-19; Acts 3:22-23; 3 Ne. 20:23.)

We know from the accounts in Exodus, Leviticus, Numbers, and Deuteronomy, and from the Book of Moses, of some of the great works of this ancient seer. Some of the great truths known to him, including his account of the creation (Moses 1; 2; 3; Gen. 1; 2), have been preserved to us. It is clear that he was translated and taken into heaven without tasting death so that, with Elijah, another translated being, he could return on the Mount of Transfiguration and give keys and authority to Peter, James, and John. (Matt. 17:1-13; Alma 45:18-19; *Teachings*, p. 158; *Doctrines of Salvation*, vol. 2, pp. 107-112.) And we know that he had part with Christ in the first resurrection. (D. & C. 133:54-55.)

But the importance of the ministry of Moses to men now living lies primarily in his return to earth in modern times to carry out his part in the great restitution of all things. (Acts 3:19.) On the 3rd of April in 1836 he appeared to Joseph Smith and Oliver Cowdery in the Kirtland Temple and committed unto them the keys of the gathering of Israel and the leading of the Ten Tribes from the land of the north. (D. & C. 110:11.) These were the special powers and endowments that rested with the kingdom in his day, and by virtue of their restoration men are now authorized to use the priesthood for these great purposes. The fact that hundreds of thousands of scattered Israel have been gathered from all nations to the tops of the mountains is visible proof that Moses did return and that the keys which he first exercised in his mortal ministry are again being used by his successors in interest, the modern prophets.

MOST HIGH.

See CHRIST, CHRIST AS THE FATHER, FATHER IN HEAVEN, HIGHEST, SON OF THE HIGHEST. Both the Father and the Son bear the name the *Most High.* (Deut. 32:8-9; Isa. 14:14; Mark 5:7; D. & C. 36:3; 39:19; 76:57.) This designation connotes a state of supreme exaltation in rank, power, and dignity; it indicates that each of these Gods is God above all. Obviously the Father is the Most High God in the literal sense for he is the God of the Son as well as the God of all men. (John 20:17.) The Son, however, is the Most High God in the sense that by divine investiture of authority, he is endowed with the power and authority of the Father, speaks in his name as though he were the Father, and therefore (having the fulness of the Father) he thinks it "not robbery to be equal with God." (Philip. 2:6.)

MOST HIGH GOD.
See MOST HIGH.

MOTHERHOOD.
See MOTHERS IN ISRAEL.

MOTHER IN HEAVEN.

See ETERNAL LIVES, EXALTATION, FATHER IN HEAVEN, MOTHERS IN ISRAEL, PRE-EXISTENCE. Implicit in the Christian verity that all men are the spirit children of an *Eternal Father* is the usually unspoken truth that they are also the offspring of an *Eternal Mother.* An exalted and glorified Man of Holiness (Moses 6:57) could not be a Father unless a Woman of like glory, perfection, and holiness was associated with him as a Mother. The begetting of children makes a man a father and a woman a mother whether we are dealing with man in his mortal or immortal state.

This doctrine that there is a *Mother in Heaven* was affirmed in plainness by the First Presidency of the Church (Joseph F. Smith, John R. Winder, and Anthon H. Lund) when, in speaking of pre-existence and the origin of man, they said that "man, as a spirit, was begotten and born of *heavenly parents,* and reared to maturity in the eternal mansions of the Father," that man is the "offspring of *celestial parentage,*" and that "all men and women are in the similitude of the *universal Father and Mother,* and are literally the sons and daughters of Deity." (*Man: His Origin and Destiny,* pp. 348-355.)

This glorious truth of celestial parentage, including specifically both a Father and a Mother, is heralded forth by song in one of the greatest of Latter-day Saint hymns. *O My Father* by Eliza R. Snow, written in 1843, during the lifetime of the Prophet, includes this teaching:

In the heavens are parents single?
  No; the thought makes reason stare!
Truth is reason, truth eternal,
  Tells me I've a Mother there.

When I leave this frail existence,
  When I lay this mortal by,
Father, Mother, may I meet you
  In your royal courts on high?

Then, at length, when I've completed
  All you sent me forth to do,
With your mutual approbation,
  Let me come and dwell with you.

Mortal persons who overcome all things and gain an ultimate exaltation will live eternally in the family unit and have spirit children, thus becoming Eternal Fathers and Eternal Mothers. (D. & C. 132:19-32.) Indeed, the formal pronouncement of the Church, issued by the First Presidency and the Council of the Twelve, states: "So far as the stages of eternal progression and attainment have been made known through divine revelation, we are to understand that *only resurrected and glorified beings* can become parents of spirit offspring." (*Man: His Origin and Destiny*, p. 129.)

MOTHERS IN ISRAEL.

See CELESTIAL MARRIAGE, EXALTATION, ISRAEL, MOTHER IN HEAVEN, PATRIARCHAL BLESSINGS, PATRIARCHAL ORDER. In the patriarchal blessings of faithful women the inspired promise is sometimes found that they shall be *mothers in Israel*. This expression has reference to either or both of the following states: motherhood in the house of Israel here in mortality; motherhood among exalted beings in eternity, among those for whom the family unit continues, those who shall rule and reign forever in the house of Israel. Motherhood in this life brings forth mortal offspring; in eternity it will bring forth spirit children. (D. & C. 131:1-4; 132:19-32.)

Faith and devotion to the truth on the part of the mothers in Latter-day Israel in rearing their children in light and truth is one of the greatest incentives to righteousness that can be given.

MOUNTAIN OF THE LORD'S HOUSE.

See RESTORATION OF THE GOSPEL, TEMPLES. The *mountain of the Lord's house* is the mountain where the temple of God is built. Isaiah prophesied: *"It shall come to pass in the last days, that the mountain of the Lord's house shall be established in the top of the mountains, and shall be exalted above the hills; and all nations shall flow unto it. And many people shall go and say, Come ye, and let us go up to the mountain of the Lord, to the house of the God of Jacob; and he will teach us of his ways, and we will walk in his paths: for out of Zion shall go forth the law, and the word of the Lord from Jerusalem."* (Isa. 2:2-3; Mic. 4:1-2; 2 Ne. 12:2-3.)

This great prophecy, as is often the case, is subject to the law of multiple fulfilment. 1. In Salt Lake City and other mountain locations temples, in the full and true sense of the word, have been erected, and representatives of all nations are flowing unto them to learn of God and his ways. In this connection and as part of the general fulfilment of Isaiah's prophecy, is the fact that one of the world's greatest genealogical societies has been established in Salt Lake City—a society to which people of all nations come to do the ancestral research which must precede the performance of vicarious temple ordinances. 2. But the day is yet future when the Lord's house is to be built on that "Mount Zion" which is "the city of New Jerusalem" in Jackson County, Missoui. (D. & C. 84:2-4.) Mount Zion, itself, will be the mountain of the Lord's house in the day when that glorious temple is erected. 3. When the Jews flee unto Jerusalem, it will be

"unto the mountains of the Lord's house" (D. & C. 133:13), for a holy temple is to be built there also as part of the work of the great era of restoration. (Ezek. 37:24-28.)

The law cannot go forth from Zion and the word of the Lord from Jerusalem, in the full millennial sense that Isaiah foresaw and specified, until these two great future temples are constructed in the old and new Jerusalems. (Isa. 2; Mic. 4; 2 Ne. 12.)

MOUNT ZION.
See ZION.

MOURNING.
See DEATH, DESPAIR, FASTING, FUNERALS, GNASHING OF TEETH, GRAVES, GRIEF, SACKCLOTH AND ASHES, SIGNS OF THE TIMES, SOLEMN ASSEMBLIES, SORROW, WEEPING. 1. Wholesome and proper *mourning*—mourning based on sound gospel knowledge—is a profitable and ennobling part of life. Men are commanded to fast, and pray, and mourn: all these are essential parts of true worship. (Alma 30:2; Hela. 9:10.)

"Thou shalt live together in love," the Lord says, "insomuch that *thou shalt weep for the loss of them that die,* and more especially for those that have not hope of a glorious resurrection." (D. & C. 42:45.) Thus Abraham mourned for righteous Sarah (Gen. 23:2), and thus all Israel mourned for

Moses. (Deut. 34:8.) At such times of deep sorrow, when death overtakes a loved one, the feelings of a compassionate person become tender, the veil between the living and the dead grows thinner, and things of eternity and of the Spirit sink deeper into the soul. Desires for righteousness are thus built up in the hearts of the bereaved.

Righteous mourning is not confined to periods of great sorrow. It is part of the saintly way of life, and in the waters of baptism the saints make solemn covenant "to mourn with those that mourn." (Mosiah 18:9.) "Call your solemn assembly," the Lord told the early members of the Church, "that your fastings and your mourning might come up into the ears of the Lord." (D. & C. 95:7.) During the periods when righteousness reigned in ancient Israel, that chosen people "walked mournfully before the Lord of hosts." (Mal. 3:14; 3 Ne. 24:14.) And Jacob, speaking of the life of the Nephites, their tribulations and lonely wanderings, said: "We did mourn out our days." (Jac. 7:26.) "Blessed are they that mourn: for they shall be comforted." (Matt. 5:4; 3 Ne. 12:4.)

2. *Mourning* takes place in unrighteousness, and is displeasing to the Lord, when bereaved persons refuse to find comfort and solace in the gospel teachings. Excessive sorrow over the death of a loved one shows spiritual instability. It appears, for example, that the daughters of Ishmael permitted themselves to mourn inordinately over the death of their father. (1 Ne. 16:35-36.) Certainly most of the ritualistic mourning, the elaborate displays of sorrow, the hiring of special mourners, the cutting of the flesh as a sign of sorrow (Lev. 19:28), and so on, are all outside the bounds of decent and dignified mourning. The true gospel perspective is seen in Job's statement: "The Lord gave, and the Lord hath taken away; blessed be the name of the Lord." (Job 1:21.)

One of the signs of the times is the mourning that shall prevail in the last days among the wicked, mourning that will come because of the calamities and plagues that shall be poured out without measure. (D. & C. 45:49; 87:6; 98:9; 112:24; Zech. 12:10-14.) By righteousness the saints have power to escape most of the calamities and mourning of the world. "Let Zion rejoice, while all the wicked shall mourn." (D. & C. 97:18-28; 101:11-14; Isa. 51:11; 2 Ne. 8:11.) Of those who find fault with the Lord's doings, he has said: "Fools mock, but they shall mourn." (Ether 12:26.)

MULEKITES.

See BOOK OF MORMON, JEWS, NEPHITES AND LAMANITES. About 11 years after Lehi left Jerusalem, the city was destroyed by the Babylonians. Zedekiah, king of Judah, was captured, and all his sons except Mulek were slain before his eyes. (2 Kings 25:7; Hela. 8:20-22.) But the Lord led Mulek and a group of other Jews to an inheritance in the American promised land. (Hela. 6:10.) In keeping with Book of Mormon terminology, their nation and people have become known among Latter-day Saints as the *Mulekites,* although that name is not found in the Book of Mormon. They founded the city of Zarahemla, which was discovered in due course by Mosiah and his people, and thereafter the Mulekites were joined with and became known as *Nephites.* (Omni 13-19; Mosiah 25.)

MURDERERS.

See APOSTASY, CAIN, SECRET COMBINATIONS, SIGNS OF THE TIMES. "Thou shalt not kill." (Ex. 20:13.) "Thou shalt do no *murder.*" (Matt. 19:18.) Murder, the unlawful killing of a human being with malice aforethought or under such circumstances of criminality that the malice is presumed, "is a sin unto death" (1 John 5:16-17), a sin for which there is "no forgiveness" (D. & C. 42:79), meaning that a murderer can never gain salvation. "No *murderer* hath eternal life abiding in him." (1 John 3:15.) He cannot join the Church by baptism; he is outside the pale of redeeming grace.

The call to repentance and baptism which includes murderers (3 Ne. 30) has reference to those who took life while engaged in unrighteous wars, as did the Lamanites, because they were compelled to do so, and not because they in their hearts sought the blood of their fellow men. On the other hand, the Jews on whose hands the blood of Christ was found were not invited to repent and be baptized. (Acts 3:19-21.)

Murderers are forgiven eventually but only in the sense that all sins are forgiven except the sin against the Holy Ghost; they are not forgiven in the sense that celestial salvation is made available to them. (Matt. 12:31-32; *Teachings,* p. 356-357.) After they have paid the full penalty for their crime, they shall go on to a telestial inheritance. (Rev. 22:15.)

MUSIC.

See DANCING, PRAYER, SONG OF THE LAMB, WORSHIP. From the beginning, both vocal and instrumental *music* has been a vital and important part of divine worship. Great songs and psalms have come from the pens of inspired poet-prophets in every age to memorialize the mighty works of God in leading and preserving his people. Religious music is by far the greatest music of the ages. What is there to compare—in rhythmic beauty, poetic sublimity, and inspired teachings — with the Psalms of David?

"Praise the Lord with singing,

with music, with dancing, and with a prayer of praise and thanksgiving," is the divine command. (D. & C. 136:28.) "For my soul delighteth in the song of the heart," the Lord says, "yea, *the song of the righteous is a prayer unto me,* and it shall be answered with a blessing upon their heads." (D. & C. 25:12.) One of the great promises of the restoration is: "The righteous shall be gathered out from among all nations, and shall come to Zion, singing with songs of everlasting joy." (D. & C. 45:71; 66:11; 101:18; 109:39; 133:33.)

Good music is eternal. Angelic choirs brightened the pre-existent heavens with their hymns of praise. Who can conceive of the heavenly melodies heard in the courts above, "When the morning stars sang together, and all the sons of God shouted for joy?" (Job 38:7.) Or whose souls would not have been mellowed by the celestial strains announcing the birth of our Lord, "Glory to God in the highest, and on earth peace, good will toward men"? (Luke 2:14.) And what saint is there who does not look forward to the day when his "immortal spirit may join the choirs above in singing the praises of a just God"? (Mosiah 2:28; Morm. 7:7; Rev. 14:2-3.)

Music is given of God to further his purposes. Sweet melodies mellow the souls of men and help prepare them for the gospel. After men receive the truth, songs of praise to Deity help to sanctify and cleanse their souls. It follows that the best and greatest music is that in which, by both note and word, God is praised and his truths are extolled. On the other hand, music can be used for sensuous and carnal purposes. To accomplish the Lord's aims both word and melody must be edifying and lead to wholesome thoughts and emotions. There is vulgar as well as virtuous music.

Wholesome light music designed primarily to entertain has its place. So do the heavy classical presentations that appeal to the more musically gifted. But in meetings set apart to worship the Lord, the saints should sing songs which teach the gospel and enhance faith. Beautiful melodies alone do not suffice; the word-message must also conform to true principles. Truths taught in the hymns should be as accurately presented as they are in the scriptures themselves.

Songs that build faith and testimony and that teach the message of the restoration include such numbers as: *Come, Come Ye Saints; Now Let Us Rejoice; We Thank Thee O God for a Prophet;* and *The Spirit of God.* Many of the great Christian hymns of all churches bear true witness of Christ and teach sound doctrine. Handel's great oratorio, the *Messiah,* is one of the great musical compositions of the ages. Many religious Christmas carols are edifying and ennobling. There is ample appropriate music which furthers the cause of righteousness, without turning to that which only partially meets the proper standard.

MUTUAL IMPROVEMENT ASSOCIATIONS.

See AUXILIARY ORGANIZATIONS, CHURCH ORGANIZATION, GENERAL BOARDS, PRIESTHOOD, RECREATION, STAKE BOARDS. Two great auxiliary organizations are provided to aid the priesthood in leading the youth of Zion to temporal and spiritual salvation. These organizations are the *Young Men's Mutual Improvement Association,* and the *Young Women's Mutual Improvement Association.* Under the direction of their executive heads, as assisted by general and stake boards, these organizations carry on intelligent and comprehensive programs in the wards and branches, programs which are aidful in the development of the personalities and talents of Zion's youth.

President Joseph F. Smith summarized the purposes and work of the *Mutual Improvement Associations* in these words: "The systematic work now being done by the quorums of priesthood provides our young men with the necessary teachings in formal theology and trains them in the duties that pertain to their callings in the priesthood.

"There is, however, a strong need among the young men [and women] of the Church to have an organization and meetings which they themselves conduct: in which they may learn to preside over public assemblies, to obtain a practice necessary to express themselves before the public, and to enjoy themselves in studying and practicing civil, social, scientific, religious and educational affairs.

"The Young Men's [and Women's] Mutual Improvement Associations, therefore, should be strengthened and their efficiency increased in order to offset and counteract the tendency now so prevalent to establish private clubs, secret and social organizations, and select educational societies. . . .

"The field to be occupied is religious, social and educational. The religious work is not to be formally theological in its nature, but rather to be confined to the limits outlined by President Brigham Young, when the organizations were first established: *'Let the keynote of your work be the establishment in the youth of an individual testimony of the truth and magnitude of the great Latter-day work, and the development of the gifts within them.'* In other words, to obtain a testimony of the truth, and to learn to declare and express that testimony, and to develop all noble gifts within them.

"The social includes control of various public and private amusements; musical, dramatic and other entertainments and festivals; field sports, athletic tournaments, excursions and other varieties of social gatherings.

"The educational should include regular class work in ethics and practical religion, literature, science, history, biography, art, music, civil government—supplemented by debates, oratorical and musical contests, lectures, essays, writing for publication, reading and speaking under the auspices of the organization, and if necessary carried on in departments under instructors capable of specializing in their particular lines." (*Gospel Doctrine,* 5th ed., pp. 390-391.)

MYSTERIES.

See Doctrine, First Principles of the Gospel, Gospel, Knowledge, Standard Works. 1. A *mystery* is something which cannot be explained, either because it is beyond human comprehension in general, or because some particular man has not learned enough to understand it. Accordingly, some matters of doctrine, philosophy, or science may be a mystery to one person and not to another. When a thing is understood it is no longer a mystery. In the eternal sense there are no mysteries; all things are known to and understood by Deity; and there will be no mysteries among exalted beings, for they too shall know all things.

A knowledge of the mysteries of God comes by obedience to gospel law. "It is given unto many to know the mysteries of God," Amu-

lek taught. "He that will harden his heart, the same receiveth the lesser portion of the word; and he that will not harden his heart, to him is given the greater portion of the word, until *it is given unto him to know the mysteries of God until he know them in full."* (Alma 12:9-11.)

"If thou shalt ask," the Lord said in this day, "thou shalt receive revelation upon revelation, knowledge upon knowledge, that thou mayest know the mysteries and peaceable things—that which bringeth joy, that which bringeth life eternal. . . . For unto you it is given to know the mysteries of the kingdom, but unto the world it is not given to know them." (D. & C. 42: 61-65; 6:7, 11; 8:11; 11:7.)

"Thus saith the Lord—I, the Lord, am merciful and gracious unto those who fear me, and delight to honor those who serve me in righteousness and in truth unto the end. Great shall be their reward and eternal shall be their glory. *And to them will I reveal all mysteries, yea, all the hidden mysteries of my kingdom from days of old, and for ages to come, will I make known unto them the good pleasure of my will concerning all things pertaining to my kingdom.* Yea, even the wonders of eternity shall they know, and things to come will I show them, even the things of many generations. And their wisdom shall be great, and their understanding reach to heaven; and before them the wisdom of the wise shall perish, and the understanding of the prudent shall come to naught. For by my Spirit will I enlighten them, and by my power will I make known unto them the secrets of my will—yea, even those things which eye has not seen, nor ear heard, nor yet entered into the heart of man." (D. & C. 76:5-10.)

2. There is also a restricted and limited usage of the expression *mysteries;* it is more of a colloquial than a scriptural usage, and it has reference to that body of teachings in the speculative field, those things which the Lord has not revealed in plainness in this day. It is to these things that reference is made when the elders are counseled to leave the mysteries alone.

"Oh, ye elders of Israel, hearken to my voice," the Prophet said, "and when you are sent into the world to preach, tell those things you are sent to tell; preach and cry aloud, 'Repent ye, for the kingdom of heaven is at hand; repent and believe the gospel.' Declare the first principles, and let mysteries alone, lest ye be overthrown. Never meddle with the visions of beasts and subjects you do not understand." (*Teachings,* p. 292.)

MYSTICISM.

See UNITY. *Mysticism* is the belief that direct spiritual union with God is possible through meditation upon him and his laws and through surrender to his will. In theory this is true; man can become one with Deity by learning his laws, surrendering to his will, and keeping his commandments. It is possible to have personal revelation, to gain knowledge from God by direct spiritual insight, to be a prophet of God. But this means accepting Jesus as the Christ and Joseph Smith as his prophet; it means coming into the fold of Christ which is named The Church of Jesus Christ of Latter-day Saints.

In practice, the so-called mystics of the world are seeking union with God through their own mental aberrations and outside the true gospel framework. Their brand of mysticism is an apostate religion, one created in imitation of the true system of salvation, one that will never lead them to their professed goal.

MYTHOLOGY.

See APOSTASY. *Mythology* is a substitute for and a perversion of true religion. It includes the *legends* of a people, their religious beliefs, the notions they have as to their origin, gods, and heroes, and the record of the dramatic events of their history. As long as it is correctly labeled and identified as fiction, it is not particularly harmful; often it forms the basis for great literature, immortal dramas, and interesting study. But unfortunately it also often becomes the set of beliefs to which men adhere in seeking to satisfy their innate desires to worship.

Modern Christians, as part of their various creeds and doctrines, have inherited many myths, legends, and traditions from their ancestors—all of which views they falsely assume are part of true religion. For instance: It is a myth that Adam, Abraham, Moses, and the ancients were uncivilized people; that the knowledge of God came to men by degrees, succeeding prophets each finding new truths about him; that he was first thought to be a God of war and later learned to be a Deity of peace and love; that Christianity had its beginning in the meridian of time, with all those who went before being subject to lesser laws; that the sacrament of the Lord's Supper is an ordinance in which men eat the flesh and drink the blood of Jesus; that men are saved by grace alone, without works; and so on and so on.

Indeed, it would be difficult to assemble a greater number of myths into one philosophical system than are now found in the philosophies of modern Christendom. Except for its ethical teachings, so-called Christianity does not come much nearer the truth in many respects than did the Lamanite legends uncovered by Cortez and his followers, or than the Greek, Romon, or Norse mythology. A myth is a myth whether it parades under Biblical names or openly acclaims itself to be the figment of someone's imagination.

NAME OF CHRIST.

See CHRIST, REVERENCE. Jesus Christ is the *name* given of the Father whereby salvation and all things incident thereto may be attained. (Acts 4:12; Mosiah 3:17.) It is the name the saints take upon them in the waters of baptism (D. & C. 18:21-25; 20:37); the name by which they are called (Alma 5:37-38; 3 Ne. 27:3-10), in which they worship (D. & C. 20:29), and which they use to seal their prayers (D. & C. 50:31); it is the name in which the saints serve God (D. & C. 59:5), work miracles (D. & C. 84:66-73), speak prophecies (D. & C. 130:12), and do all things. (D. & C. 46:31.)

Use of the *name of Christ* centers one's faith in him and constitutes a solemn affirmation as to where all power and authority lies. For God the Father "hath highly exalted him, and given him a name which is above every name: That at the name of Jesus every knee should bow, of things in heaven, and things in earth, and things under the earth; And that every tongue should confess that Jesus Christ is Lord, to the glory of God the Father." (Philip. 2:9-11.)

NAMES OF CHRIST.
See CHRIST.

NAMING OF CHILDREN.
See BLESSING OF CHILDREN.

NATIONS.
See RACES OF MEN.

NATURAL DEATH.
See DEATH.

NATURAL PATRIARCHS.
See PATRIARCHS.

NATURAL RIGHTS.
See INALIENABLE RIGHTS.

NATURE.
See GOD OF NATURE.

NAZARENE.
See CHRIST, JESUS OF NAZARETH. Christ is the Nazarene. Matthew had access to a Messianic prophecy which has not been preserved for our day, which enabled him to write of our Lord: "He came

and dwelt in a city called Nazareth: that it might be fulfilled which was spoken by the prophets, He shall be called a Nazarene." (Matt. 2:23.)

NECKING.
See SEX IMMORALITY.

NECROMANCY.
See DIVINATION, FORTUNE TELLING, MAGIC, OCCULTISM, SOOTHSAYERS, SORCERY, SPIRITUALISM, WITCHCRAFT. Necromancy is that form of divination which attempts to foretell the future by consultation with the dead. Sometimes the term is enlarged to include magic in general. It is and has been a common practice among apostate peoples, but the Lord calls it an abomination and expressly commands Israel to avoid it. (Deut. 18:9-14.)

NEGROES.
See CAIN, HAM, PRE-EXISTENCE, PRIESTHOOD, RACES OF MEN. As with all men, Negroes are the mortal descendants of Adam and the spirit children of the Eternal Father. They come to earth to gain mortal bodies and be subject to the probationary experiences of this present life.

In the providences of the Lord, the gospel and all its attendant blessings are offered to one nation and people after another. During Jesus' mortal ministry he and his disciples took the gospel to the house of Israel only; after his resurrection the word went forth to the Gentiles also. Those who live when the gospel is not on earth may receive its blessings in the spirit world after death.

In all past ages and until recent times in this dispensation, the Lord did not offer the priesthood to the Negroes. However, on June 1, 1978, in the Salt Lake Temple, in the presence of the First Presidency and the Council of the Twelve, President Spencer W. Kimball received a revelation from the Lord directing that the gospel and the priesthood should now go to all men without reference to race or color.

This means that worthy males of all races can now receive the Melchizedek Priesthood, perform ordinances, and hold positions of presidency and responsibility. It means that members of all races may now be married in the temple, although interracial marriages are discouraged by the Brethren, and that the full blessings of the gospel may be made available to their ancestors through vicarious temple ordinances. It also means that Negro members of the Church may now perform missionary service and should bear the burdens of the kingdom equally with all other members of the Church.

This new revelation is one of the signs of the times. It opens the door to the spread of the gospel among all people before the Second Coming in fulfilment of many scriptural promises. It has been received with joy and rejoicing throughout the Church and is one of the evidences of the divinity of the Lord's great latter-day work.

The official document announcing the new revelation, signed by the First Presidency (Spencer W. Kimball, N. Eldon Tanner, and Marion G. Romney) and dated June 8, 1978, is as follows:

"As we have witnessed the expansion of the work of the Lord over the earth, we have been grateful that people of many nations have responded to the message of the restored gospel, and have joined the Church in ever-increasing numbers. This, in turn, has inspired us with a desire to extend to every worthy member of the Church all of the privileges and blessings which the gospel affords.

"Aware of the promises made by the prophets and presidents of the Church who have preceded us that at some time, in God's eternal plan, all of our brethren who are worthy may receive the priesthood, and witnessing the faithfulness of those from whom the priesthood has been withheld, we have pleaded long and earnestly in behalf of these, our faithful brethren, spending many hours in the Upper Room of the Temple supplicating the Lord for divine guidance.

"He has heard our prayers, and by revelation has confirmed that the long-promised day has come when every faithful, worthy man in the Church may receive the holy priesthood, with power to exercise its divine authority, and enjoy with his loved ones every blessing that flows therefrom, including the blessings of the temple. Accordingly, all worthy male members of the Church may be ordained to the priesthood without regard for race or color. Priesthood leaders are instructed to follow the policy of carefully interviewing all candidates for ordination to either the Aaronic or the Melchizedek Priesthood to insure that they meet the established standards for worthiness.

"We declare with soberness that the Lord has now made known His will for the blessing of all His children throughout the earth who will hearken to the voice of His authorized servants, and prepare themselves to receive every blessing of the gospel."

NEPHITE DISPENSATIONS.
See DISPENSATIONS.

NEPHITES AND LAMANITES.
See AMERICAN INDIANS, BOOK OF MORMON, ISHMAELITES, JACOBITES, JAREDITES, JEWS, JOSEPHITES, LAMANITE CURSE, LEMUELITES, MULEKITES, ZORAMITES. Almost from the very day in 600 B.C. in which Lehi, his family and friends, began their journey toward their American promised land, there was a sharp division within the group. Those who were faithful members of the Church, who believed the revelations and sought to keep the commandments of God, chose to call themselves *Nephites* after Nephi their mightiest prophet. Those who were rebellious, whose minds were darkened by unbelief, who were apostates from the Church, chose to call themselves *Lamanites* after Laman, the most forceful and powerful member of their group.

The Nephite group included Lehi and Sariah, Nephi's sisters, and the families of Nephi, Sam, Jacob, and Zoram. (2 Ne. 5.) That portion of the Nephites who were descendants of Jacob, Joseph, and Zoram were sometimes called *Jacobites, Josephites,* and *Zoramites.* The Lamanite group included the families of Laman and Lemuel, and the families of the sons of Ishmael. *Lemuelites* and *Ishmaelites,* accordingly, were portions of the larger colony of Lamanites. (Jac. 1:13-14; 4 Ne. 37-39.) When the *Mulekite* civilization later joined with the Nephites, the whole group were thereafter known by the more prominent name, Nephites. (Mosiah 25.)

Thus the designation Nephites and Lamanites was originally a means of identifying true believers on the one hand and apostates from the faith on the other. After the separation into groups had occurred, however, to avoid intermarriage between them, the Lord placed a curse upon the Lamanites which included a dark skin. (2 Ne. 5:21-25.) Then as large cities and nations developed, the terms Nephite and Lamanite became matters of ancestry and nationality rather than identifications of particular beliefs. Accordingly there were periods when groups of Lamanites were more faithful to the truth than their Nephite kindred. And there were also periods when the believing Lamanites joined with the Nephites, became a white and a delightsome people again, and were again called Nephites. (3 Ne. 2:14-16.)

During the period following the ministry of our Lord among the ancient Americans, the Nephites and Lamanites ceased to exist as separate groups; rather, all men "were in one, the children of Christ, and heirs to the kingdom of God." (4 Ne. 17.) Then when the great apostasy set in "there arose a people who were called the Nephites, and they were true believers in Christ; and among them were those who were called by the Lamanites —Jacobites, and Josephites, and Zoramites; Therefore the true believers in Christ, and the true worshipers of Christ, (among whom were the three disciples of Jesus who should tarry) were called Nephites, and Jacobites, and Josephites, and Zoramites. And it came to pass that they who rejected the gospel were called Lamanites, and Lemuelites, and Ishmaelites." (4 Ne. 36-38.)

In their latter end the Nephites (speaking now of the white skinned group and calling them Nephites from the standpoint of ancestry and nationality) became more cor-rupt and wicked than the Lamanites and were destroyed, as a people and nation, in the great continent-wide wars that came upon them. (Morm. 6.) There were many Nephite groups, however, who were not destroyed in the final conflict, and these (with possible exceptions) have since mingled themselves with the Lamanites, the resulting peoples being known to the world as the *American Indians.* (1 Ne. 13:30; 2 Ne. 3:1-3; 9:53; Alma 45:13-14; D. & C. 3:16-19.)

NEW AND EVERLASTING COVENANT.

See ABRAHAMIC COVENANT, CELESTIAL MARRIAGE, CHILDREN OF THE COVENANT, CHRISTIANITY, CHURCH OF JESUS CHRIST OF LATTER-DAY SAINTS, COVENANTS, DISPENSATION OF THE FULNESS OF TIMES, DISPENSATIONS, EVERLASTING, GOSPEL, JOSEPH SMITH THE PROPHET, MORMONISM, NEW COVENANT, RESTORATION OF THE GOSPEL, SALVATION. God's covenant of salvation is the fulness of the gospel. (D. & C. 39:11; 45:9; 66:2; 133:57.) When men accept the gospel, they thereby agree or covenant to keep the commandments of God, and he promises or covenants to give them salvation in his kingdom.

The gospel is the *everlasting* covenant because it is ordained by Him who is Everlasting and also because it is everlastingly the same. In all past ages salvation was gained by adherence to its terms and conditions, and that same compliance will bring the same reward in all future ages. Each time this everlasting covenant is revealed it is *new* to those of that dispensation. Hence the gospel is the *new and everlasting covenant.*

All covenants between God and man are part of the new and everlasting covenant. (D. & C. 22; 132: 6-7.) Thus celestial marriage is *"a new and an everlasting covenant"* (D. & C. 132:4) or the new and everlasting covenant of *marriage* (*Doctrines of Salvation,* vol. 1, pp. 152-166.) Some covenants, however, have force and validity in all dispensations; baptism is one of these. (D. & C. 22.) Other covenants are made for special purposes in particular dispensations; circumcision is this type of a covenant. (Gen. 17:9-14.)

That the everlasting covenant would be restored in the last days is amply attested in the revelations. (D. & C. 1:22.) Through Jeremiah the Lord promised to "make a new covenant with the house of Israel, and with the house of Judah," a covenant which would lead to that glorious millennial condition in which "they shall teach no more every man his neighbour, and every man his brother, saying, Know the Lord: for they shall all know me, from the least of them unto the greatest of them, saith the Lord." (Jer. 31: 31-34.) Ezekiel said that this would be "an everlasting covenant with them," one that would be made in the day when the Lord set his

sanctuary (temple) "in the midst of them." (Ezek. 37:26.)

Apostasy consists in breaking the everlasting covenant. (D. & C. 1:15.) Isaiah said the universal apostasy would come because men had "transgressed the laws, changed the ordinance, broken the everlasting covenant." (Isa. 24:5.) Those who break their covenants are condemned more severely than they would have been had they never made the initial contract with the Lord. (D. & C. 41:1; 82:2; 132:27.) In covenant-keeping there is salvation; in covenant-breaking, damnation. (D. & C. 76:101; 132:5, 15-27.)

NEW BIRTH.
See BORN AGAIN.

NEW COVENANT.
See BOOK OF MORMON, COVENANTS, LAW OF MOSES, MEDIATOR, NEW AND EVERLASTING COVENANT, NEW TESTAMENT, OLD TESTAMENT. In comparing the old Mosaic covenant with the gospel which had been newly restored in his day, Paul calls the gospel the *new covenant.* Jesus is designated as the Mediator of the new covenant. (Heb. 8; 9; 10; 12:22-24; D. & C. 76:69; 107:19.) From a Biblical standpoint the record of the new covenant is found in the New Testament (which document more literally and accurately might have been called the *New Covenant*). Since the Book of Mormon

also contains the provisions of the new covenant, the covenant which replaced the one previously in force under the law of Moses, it also is called the *new covenant.* (D. & C. 84:57.)

NEW CREATURES OF THE HOLY GHOST.
See BORN AGAIN.

NEW EARTH.
See NEW HEAVEN AND NEW EARTH.

NEW HEAVEN AND NEW EARTH.
See CREATION, EARTH, HEAVEN, MILLENNIUM, RESTORATION OF ALL THINGS, TIMES OF REFRESHING. This expression, *new heaven and new earth,* is used in two distinct senses in the scriptures: 1. It has reference to the millennial, paradisiacal, or renewed earth and heavens that will prevail after the Second Coming of Christ (Tenth Article of Faith, Isa. 65:17-25; 66:22-24; D. & C. 101:23-31); and 2. In other instances it has reference to the celestial heaven and earth that will prevail in the day when the Father and the Son make this planet their habitation. (D. & C. 29:22-25; 77:1; 88:16-32; Rev. 21.)

NEW JERUSALEM.
See HOPE OF ISRAEL, MILLEN- NIUM, NEW HEAVEN AND NEW EARTH, RESURRECTION, TRANSLATED BEINGS, ZION. As far as we now know, *Jerusalem* was first founded as a city after the flood. It is mentioned in Abraham's day under the name *Salem,* a term meaning *peace.* (Gen. 14:18; Ps. 76:2.) Melchizedek was king in the land of Salem, and because he established peace "he was called the prince of peace" (Alma 13:17-18), the "King of peace." (Heb. 7:1-2.) In the original Hebrew the proper name was *Shiloam,* "which signifies righteousness and peace." (*Teachings,* p. 321.) But however designated, Jerusalem was a holy and sacred city to the Lord's people anciently; through all her long history, ancient Israel looked to Jerusalem as the holy city. In due course it became the chief city of our Lord's ministry, and it is now sacred to three great world religions—Judaism, Christianity, and Islam.

During her long history Jerusalem, spiritually, has soared to the heights and sunk to the depths. A great many prophets have ministered in her streets, the visions of eternity have been poured out upon her inhabitants, and the teachings of the gospel have sanctified her inhabitants. On the other hand, in apostate periods, she has slain the living prophets and rejected their teachings, while building the sepulchres of those whom their fathers had rejected and slain. (Matt. 23:13-39; Luke 13:33-35.) Indeed, so great is to be the wickedness in latter-day Jerusalem that "spiritually" she "is called Sodom and Egypt." (Rev. 11:8.)

But even more important than her past glory, her historical position, and her religious influence, is the part (dear to the hearts of the prophets) which Jerusalem is yet to play in the destiny of the world. In the last days the Jerusalem of old is to be rebuilt, a remnant of the Jews is to assemble there, and the final great battles which attend the Second Coming of the Son of Man are to take place at Jerusalem. (*Teachings,* p. 17; Zech. 12; 13; 14.) And then during the millennial era this rebuilt Jerusalem is to be one of two great world capitals, "for out of Zion shall go forth the law, and the word of the Lord from Jerusalem." (Isa. 2:3.)

In addition to the rebuilding of the Jerusalem of old, the latter-days are to see the initial building of a *New Jerusalem* on the American continent, a city which like its ancient counterpart will be a holy city, a Zion, a city of God. (3 Ne. 20:22.) This New Jerusalem is to be built by The Church of Jesus Christ of Latter-day Saints; Jackson County, Missouri, is the spot designated by revelation for its construction. (D. & C. 28; 42:8-9, 30-42; 45:66-67; 52:2, 42-43; 57:1-5; 58:7, 44-58; 84:2-5.) It shall be built when the Lord directs. (*Doctrines of Salvation,* vol. 3, pp. 66-79; D. & C. 124:49-54.)

This New Jerusalem on the American continent will have a dual origin. It will be built by the saints on earth and it will also come down from heaven, and the cities so originating will be united into one holy city. Moroni recorded that America "was the place of *the New Jerusalem, which should come down out of heaven,* and the holy sanctuary of the Lord. Behold, Ether saw the days of Christ, and he spake concerning a New Jerusalem upon this land. And he spake also concerning the house of Israel, and the Jerusalem from whence Lehi should come—after it should be destroyed it should be built up again, a holy city unto the Lord; wherefore, it could not be a new Jerusalem for it had been in a time of old; but it should be built up again, and become a holy city of the Lord; and it should be built unto the house of Israel. And that *a New Jerusalem should be built up upon this land,* unto the remnant of the seed of Joseph. . . .

"The remnant of the house of Joseph shall be built upon this land; and it shall be a land of their inheritance; and *they shall build up a holy city unto the Lord, like unto the Jerusalem of old;* and they shall no more be confounded, until the end come when the earth shall pass away. And there shall be a new heaven and a new earth; and they shall be like unto the old save the old have passed away, and all things have become new.

"And then cometh the New Jerusalem; and blessed are they who

dwell therein, for it is they whose garments are white through the blood of the Lamb; and they are they who are numbered among the remnant of the seed of Joseph, who were of the house of Israel. And then also cometh the Jerusalem of old; and the inhabitants thereof, blessed are they, for they have been washed in the blood of the Lamb; and they are they who were scattered and gathered in from the four quarters of the earth, and from the north countries, and are partakers of the fulfilling of the covenant which God made with their father, Abraham." (Ether 13:3-11.)

Enoch saw the latter-day restoration of the gospel and the subsequent building of the New Jerusalem. "Righteousness and truth will I cause to sweep the earth as with a flood, to gather out mine elect from the four quarters of the earth, unto a place which I shall prepare," the Lord told him, "an Holy City, that my people may gird up their loins, and be looking forth for the time of my coming; for there shall be my tabernacle, and it shall be called Zion, a New Jerusalem. And the Lord said unto Enoch: Then shalt thou and all thy city meet them there, and we will receive them into our bosom, and they shall see us; and we will fall upon their necks, and they shall fall upon our necks, and we will kiss each other." (Moses 7:60-63.) Thus it is that the New Jerusalem shall be built by the saints and shall also come down from heaven.

Events to transpire after the millennial era and before the earth becomes a celestial sphere have not been revealed. We do have an account, however, of "the holy Jerusalem, descending out of heaven from God" a second time, that is, after the earth has become a celestial planet. John refers to this celestial city in Revelation 3:12 and then gives a somewhat detailed description of it in the 21st chapter of the same book.

Having in mind these glorious truths relative to the millennial New Jerusalem and the celestial city of the same name, knowing that Enoch's Zion had been taken to heaven and would return again, the ancient prophets "looked for a city which hath foundations, whose builder and maker is God," confessing the while "that they were strangers and pilgrims on the earth." And God "hath prepared for them a city" (Heb. 11:9-16), that is, he has prepared it for those who gain salvation, for such "come unto mount Sion, and unto the city of the living God, the *heavenly Jerusalem.*" (Heb. 12:22.)

NEW NAME.

See CELESTIAL KINGDOM, CHURCH OF JESUS CHRIST OF LATTER-DAY SAINTS, EXALTATION, RESTORATION OF THE GOSPEL. 1. "Those who come into the celestial kingdom" shall be given a white stone whereon is written a *new name.* The white stone "will become a Urim and Thummim to each individual who receives one, whereby things pertaining to a higher order of kingdoms will be made known. . . . The new name is the key word." (D. & C. 130:10-11; Rev. 2:17.)

2. To latter-day Israel, the scattered remnant destined to be gathered in the great era of restoration, the Lord said: "Thou shalt be called by a *new name,* which the mouth of the Lord shall name." (Isa. 62:2; 65:15.) It may well be that the new name, a name necessarily limited to latter-day usage, is The Church of Jesus Christ *of Latter-day Saints.* (D. & C. 115:4.)

NEW TESTAMENT.

See APOCRYPHA, BIBLE, EPISTLES, GOSPELS, NEW COVENANT, SCRIPTURE, STANDARD WORKS. A *testament* is a solemn covenant. The gospel is the Lord's testament (covenant) of salvation. When the gospel was revealed in the meridian of time, it replaced the old Mosaic covenant—and old testament which had been in force for some 1500 years—and so the new revelation was called the *new testament.* Sectarian religionists today assume, erroneously, that the gospel was being revealed for the first time by Christ and his apostles, and they therefore conclude that the new order was replacing all that had gone before in all ages. Actually, of course, all of the

prophets, patriarchs, and saints from the day of Adam to Moses had the fulness of the gospel, the same gospel which was restored by our Lord and his disciples.

But compared to what the Jews then had, the gospel was a new covenant. Accordingly we find Jesus teaching the symbolism of the sacrament by speaking of his blood "of the new testament." (Matt. 26:28; Mark 14:24; Luke 22:20; 1 Cor. 11:25.) That is, he was instituting a new covenant of sacrament which replaced the old covenant or testament of sacrifice. Thus also we find Paul (as his words have now been preserved in the King James version of the Bible) writing in one place of "Jesus the mediator of the new covenant" (Heb. 12:24) and in another of "the mediator of the new testament." (Heb. 9:15.) The meaning is the same in each case; modern translations of the Bible use the word *covenant* rather than *testament* in nearly every instance.

The authentic records reciting much of the historical development and preserving much of the doctrinal teachings of the early church authorities have come to be known as the *New Testament.* There are in this volume of scripture a total of 27 books. It is common to classify Matthew, Mark, Luke, John, and Acts as historical books, though they abound in doctrinal matters; there are 21 books listed as epistles; and the Book of Revelation is reserved in an apocalyptic category by itself.

All of the books of the New Testament were inspired of the Holy Ghost and were perfect scripture as originally written. Though they have not been preserved to us in their original and perfect form, yet their teachings are to be accepted as true and accurate except in those cases in which matters have been clarified by latter-day revelation. We know from latter-day revelation and from the teachings of the Prophet that the New Testament books were written by the persons whose names they bear, the specious theorizing of higher criticism to the contrary notwithstanding.

NEW WORLD.

See CREATION, EARTH, FLOOD OF NOAH, GARDEN OF EDEN, JAREDITES, NEPHITES AND LAMANITES, WORLD, ZION. Modern scholars call the western hemisphere the *new world,* reaching this conclusion from the fact that civilization to a degree existed on the eastern hemisphere before the discovery of America by Columbus, but presumably did not exist on these western continents. Actually, in the beginning all the land was in one place, and there were no continents or islands. (Gen. 1:9; Moses 2:9; D. & C. 133:22-24.) And from the day of Adam to the flood great civilizations inhabited the lands which now are in the western hemisphere. After the division of the land surface into continents, the inhabitants of the continents had little knowledge of each other. The great Jaredite and Nephite civilizations flourished in what is now called the new world.

NICENE CREED.

See APOSTASY, APOSTLES CREED, ATHANASIAN CREED, CREEDS. Following the military achievements which established him as the sole Roman emperor, and in an attempt further to solidify the empire, politically, civically, and religiously, Constantine called a council of Catholic bishops to meet at Nicaea in 325 A.D. The primary work assigned them was to adopt a creed which would settle the then politically explosive problem of Arianism—a concept that the Son had been created by the Father, was subordinate to him, and was therefore unequal as to eternity, power, and glory.

"The Council was opened by Constantine with the greatest solemnity," says the *Catholic Encyclopedia.* "The emperor waited until all the bishops had taken their seats before making his entry. He was clad in gold and covered with precious stones in the fashion of an Oriental sovereign. A chair of gold had been made ready for him, and when he had taken his place the bishops seated themselves. After he had been addressed in a hurried allocution, the emperor made an address in Latin, expressing *his will* that religious peace should be established."

The following is a literal translation, as published by the Catholic Church, of the *Nicene Creed* then adopted:

"We believe in one God the Father Almighty, Maker of all things visible and invisible; and in one Lord Jesus Christ, the only begotten of the Father, that is, of the substance of the Father, God of God, light of light, true God of true God, begotten not made, of the same substance with the Father, through whom all things were made both in heaven and on earth; who for us men and for our salvation descended, was incarnate, and was made man, suffered and rose again the third day, ascended into heaven and cometh to judge living and dead. And in the Holy Ghost. Those who say: There was a time when He was not, and He was not before He was begotten; and that He was made out of nothing; or who maintain that He is of another hypostasis or another substance [than the Father], or that the Son of God is created, or mutable, or subject to change, [them] the Catholic Church anathematizes."

The Catholic account of the council then gives this statement of the position of Constantine with reference to it: "The business of the Council having been finished, Constantine celebrated the twentieth anniversary of his accession to the empire, and invited the bishops to a splendid repast, at the end of which each of them received rich presents. Several days later *the emperor commanded* that a final session should be held, at which he assisted in order to exhort the bishops to work for the maintenance of peace; he commended himself to their prayers, and *authorized* the fathers to return to their dioceses." (*Catholic Encyclopedia*, vol. 11, pp. 44-45.)

The current version of this creed is called the *Niceno-Constantinopolitan Creed* and was probably adopted by the Council of Constantinople in 381 A.D. The following is a literal translation of this version, the parenthesis indicating words altered or added according to modern Catholic liturgical use:

"We believe (I believe) in one God, the Father Almighty, maker of heaven and earth, and of all things visible and invisible. And in one Lord Jesus Christ, the only begotten Son of God, and born of the Father before all ages. (God of God) light of light, true God of true God. Begotten not made, consubstantial to the Father, by whom all things were made. Who for us men and for our salvation came down from heaven. And was incarnate of the Holy Ghost and of the Virgin Mary and was made man; was crucified also for us under Pontius Pilate, suffered and was buried; and the third day he rose again according to the Scriptures. And ascended into heaven, sitteth at the right hand of the

Father, and shall come again with glory to judge the living and the dead, of whose Kingdom there shall be no end. And (I believe) in the Holy Ghost, the Lord and Giver of life, who proceedeth from the Father (and the Son), who together with the Father and the Son is to be adored and glorified, who spake by the Prophets. And one holy, catholic and apostolic Church. We confess (I Confess) one baptism for the remission of sins. And we look for (I look for) the resurrection of the dead and the life of the world to come. Amen." (*Catholic Encyclopedia,* vol. 11, pp. 49-50.)

NIGHT.

See DAY, SEASONS, TIME. 1. That period from dusk to dawn, when the sun is below our horizon, is called *night*. (Matt. 27:64.)

2. The designation *night* also applies to any period of ignorance, unbelief, or apostasy (such as the dark ages). (Rom. 13:12; D. & C. 112:23.) Periods of adversity and affliction are also so considered. (Isa. 21:12.)

3. Further, *night* is a term applied to death or more accurately the spirit existence that follows life. "After this day of life, which is given us to prepare for eternity, behold, if we do not improve our time while in this life, then cometh the night of darkness wherein there can be no labor performed." (Alma 34:33; John 9:4.)

NOACHIAN DISPENSATION.
See DISPENSATIONS.

NONBELIEVERS.
See BELIEVERS.

NON-CHRISTIANS.
See CHRISTIANS.

NONMORMONS.
See MORMONS.

NURSES.
See PHYSICIANS.

OATH AND COVENANT OF THE PRIESTHOOD.
See MELCHIZEDEK PRIESTHOOD.

OATHS.
See BLASPHEMY, PROFANITY, VOWS. In ancient dispensations,

particularly the Mosaic, the taking of *oaths* was an approved and formal part of the religious lives of the people. These oaths were solemn appeals to Deity, or to some sacred object or thing, in attestation of the truth of a statement or of a sworn determination to keep a promise. These statements, usually made in the name of the Lord, by people who valued their religion and their word above their lives, could be and were relied upon with absolute assurance. (Num. 30.)

Oaths were common among the Nephites, prior to the ministry of the resurrected Lord among them. Nephi guaranteed the freedom of Zoram, for instance, by using in his oath the solemn language, "as the Lord liveth, and as I live." (1 Ne. 4:32-33; Alma 44.) Abraham took an oath of his servant to gain assurance that a proper wife would be selected for Isaac. (Gen. 24.) Joseph bound the children of Israel with an oath to carry his bones out of Egypt. (Gen. 50:24-26.)

While the oaths of the saints have furthered righteous purposes, similar swearing by the wicked has led to great evil. Wicked oaths, made by profane and blasphemous persons, have been the cause of much of the evil that has befallen mankind. These evil oaths, first administered by Satan to Cain (Moses 5:28-33, 49-51), have been preserved in substance and effect in secret, oath-bound organizations ever since. (Hela. 6:30; Ether 9:5.)

Beginning in the meridian of time the law whereunder men might take oaths in righteousness was done away, and the saints were commanded to refrain from their use. "Ye have heard that it hath been said by them of old time, Thou shalt not forswear thyself, but shalt perform unto the Lord thine oaths," Christ said. "But I say unto you, Swear not at all; neither by heaven; for it is God's throne: Nor by the earth; for it is his footstool: neither by Jerusalem; for it is the city of the great King. Neither shalt thou swear by thy head, because thou canst not make one hair white or black. But let your communication be, Yea, yea; Nay, nay: for whatsoever is more then these cometh of evil." (Matt. 5:33-37; 3 Ne. 12:33-37; Jas. 5:12.)

No such restriction on oath taking, however, applies to Deity. Both in ancient and modern times he has spoken to his saints with an oath. (D. & C. 124:47.) The great covenant made with Abraham that in him and in his seed all generations should be blessed was made by God with an oath in which Deity swore in his own name (because he could swear by no higher) that the covenant would be fulfilled. (Gen. 17; Deut. 7:8; 29:10-15; Luke 1:67-75; Heb. 6:13-20.) Similarly, God swore to David, "with an oath, . . . that of the fruit of his loins, according to the flesh, he would raise up Christ to sit on his throne." (Acts 2:29-32.) God also swore, with an oath, that the

Son should be a priest forever after the order of Melchizedek. (Ps. 110: 4; Heb. 7:20-21, 28.)

In similar manner, everyone who has the Melchizedek Priesthood conferred upon him, receives it with an oath and a covenant. (D. & C. 84:33-41.) That is, in each instance, the Lord swears with an oath that the person so honored shall be a priest forever after the order of Melchizedek and shall have eternal life. (D. & C. 76:54-60.) This oath, as well as all others which the Lord makes with men and for their benefit, must be made in righteousness if it is to be binding on earth and in heaven. An oath, to have "efficacy, virtue, or force in and after the resurrection from the dead," must be "sealed by the Holy Spirit of promise," which takes place only in the event of personal righteousness on the part of the one in whose behalf the Lord utters the oath. (D. & C. 132: 7.)

OBEDIENCE.

See AGENCY, CELESTIAL LAW, COMMANDMENTS, DISOBEDIENCE, GOOD WORKS, GOSPEL, LAW, RIGHTEOUSNESS, SALVATION, TELESTIAL LAW, TERRESTRIAL LAW. *Obedience* is the first law of heaven, the cornerstone upon which all righteousness and progression rest. It consists in compliance with divine law, in conformity to the mind and will of Deity, in complete subjection to God and his commands.

To obey gospel law is to yield obedience to the Lord, to execute the commands of and be ruled by him whose we are.

Obedience is possible because of two things: 1. Laws were ordained by Deity so that his spirit children by conformity to them might progress and become like him; and 2. The children of God were endowed with agency, the power and ability to either obey or disobey the divine will. Obedience and disobedience thus had their beginnings in pre-existence, the obedient spirits being the ones who kept their first estate and the disobedient the ones who were cast out with Lucifer and his hosts. The perfect formula for obedience was stated by our Lord in the pre-existent council when he volunteered to follow the Father's plan and be the Redeemer of the world: "Father, thy will be done, and the glory be thine forever." (Moses 4:2.)

The very purpose of the creation of this earth was to provide a place where the spirit children of the Father, having received their mortal bodies, could be tried and tested. "We will prove them herewith," the divine decree reads, "to see if they will do all things whatsoever the Lord their God shall command them." (Abra. 3:25.) The Lord created men, placed them on earth, "And gave unto them commandments that they should love and serve him, the only living and true God, and that he should be the only being whom they should worship." (D. & C. 20:19.) The whole system of creation and existence is thus centered around the eternal principle of obedience to law.

One of Adam's great religious acts has become the classical illustration of perfect obedience. This first man of all men was commanded by the Lord to offer the firstlings of his flocks as a sacrifice, which he did. Thereupon an angel appeared to him and asked: "Why dost thou offer sacrifices unto the Lord? And Adam said unto him: I know not, save the Lord commanded me." Then the angel told him the purpose and significance of sacrifice. (Moses 5:5-8.) It should be noted that obedience preceded receipt of the new revelation.

It is interesting to note, also, that it was in connection with the law of sacrifice that another of the great classical illustrations of obedience was given. Saul, having disobeyed counsel by not destroying the cattle of the Amalekites, choosing rather to offer them in sacrifice to the Lord, received this rebuke from the Prophet Samuel: "Hath the Lord as great delight in burnt offerings and sacrifices, as in obeying the voice of the Lord? Behold, *to obey is better than sacrifice, and to hearken than the fat of rams.* For rebellion is as the sin of witchcraft, and stubbornness is as iniquity and idolatry." (1 Sam. 15:22-23.)

All men are commanded to believe the gospel, repent of their sins, enter in at the gate of baptism, get on the strait and narrow path, and endure to the end in righteousness by obedience to all the laws and ordinances of the gospel. They thereby attain a hope of eternal life in the kingdom of God. (2 Ne. 31; 3 Ne. 27:13-22.) By baptism they make a solemn covenant to serve God "and keep his commandments" (Mosiah 18:7-10), which covenant they renew each time they partake of the sacrament. (D. & C. 20:77-79.)

Man's love of God is measured in terms of obedience and service. "If ye love me, keep my commandments," our Lord proclaimed. (John 14:15.) All blessings flow from obedience to law. (D. & C. 130:18-21.) And since man has been created and redeemed by the Lord, that holy being is certainly entitled to expect his own handiwork to abide by the counsels which he gives from time to time. (Mosiah 2:20-24.)

Christ, himself, set the perfect example of obedience for all his brethren. As the great Exemplar he was baptized to witness "unto the Father that he would be obedient unto him in keeping his commandments." (2 Ne. 31:7.) In all things his obedience was perfect. As Paul wrote: "Though he were a Son, yet learned he obedience by the things which he suffered; And being made perfect, he became the author of eternal salvation unto all them that obey him." (Heb. 5:8-9.)

OBEISANCE.

See PRAYER, REVERENCE, WOR-

SHIP. Showing of *obeisance* consists in bowing down before another person in token of respect, submission, or reverence. Among ancient peoples, with their caste systems, it was an accepted custom. Moses "did obeisance" to his father-in-law (Ex. 18:7), and the sheaves of his brethren "made obeisance" to his sheaf in the dream of Joseph. (Gen. 37:7-9.)

But this practice has little to recommend it in either the church or the civic affairs of a modern, free society. The true saints, members of the earthly kingdom of our Lord, are all brethren and sisters in the Lord; there are no small or mean persons in the Church, no great or exalted personages among those who fellowship each other as the Lord's own peculiar people. Priesthood bearers rejoice in their fellowship in the brotherhood of Christ, quorum officers and members considering themselves as standing on an equal footing. Great as is the reverence and respect of faithful persons for their bishops and stake presidents, or for the General Authorities of the Church, they do not bow to or kneel before them. Cordial handclasps, mutually exchanged, constitute an appropriate greeting, a signal of joint recognition, respect, and acceptance.

Similarly, in a society of free men, in a society built on the proposition that all men are created and stand equal before the law, bowing deference and archaic rituals of obeisance toward government officials seem wholly out of place. Mayors, governors, congressmen, and other officials, are citizens, entitled to the protection of the law and subject to its restraints in the same way and to the same extent as all citizens are. When men are blessed with a government of laws and not of men, then all men are equal before the law.

Obeisance, however, is a true and proper part of the worship of the Eternal King. Faithful people have always bowed down when worshiping the Lord. (Gen. 24:52; Num. 22:31.) Prayer is properly made on bowed knees. (Alma 46:13; Hela. 7:10; 3 Ne. 1:11.) Nephi the disciple bowed himself before Jesus (3 Ne. 11:19), who in turn bowed himself before the Father. (3 Ne. 19:19, 27.) In mocking desecration of sacred worship, the tormentors of our Lord bowed before him as they "platted a crown of thorns" upon his head. (Matt. 27:29; Mark 15:19.) There is a coming day when every knee shall bow to Christ (D. & C. 76:110), even as "all things bow in humble reverence" before the Father. (D. & C. 76:93.)

OBLATIONS.

See FAST OFFERINGS, SABBATH, SACRAMENTS, SACRIFICES, VOWS. Both ancient and modern Israel were commanded to offer their *oblations* unto the Lord. (Lev. 7:38; 2 Chron. 31:14.) In the highest spiritual sense, the offering of an oblation consists in giving full devotion to the Lord, of offering him a broken heart and a contrite spirit. (D. & C. 59:8-12; 3 Ne. 9:19-20.) In a lesser and more temporal sense, an oblation is the offering of sacrifices, or of fast offering, or of any charitable contribution to the Church. (Ezek. 44:30.) Isaiah spoke of *vain oblations* meaning the ritualistic offering of sacrifices when the spirit and meaning of the ordinance and offering had been lost. (Isa. 1:13.) Ezekiel foretold that oblations would again be offered by Israel in the day of gathering. (Ezek. 20:33-44.)

OCCULTISM.

See ALCHEMY, ASTROLOGY, DIVINATION, MAGIC, SORCERY. *Occultism* has reference to the hidden and mysterious powers subject to the control of those who engage in divination, alchemy, astrology, sorcery, and magic. Practice of occultism in any form is contrary to revealed truth and should be avoided.

OFFENSES.

See PERSECUTION, SECOND ESTATE, TRIBULATIONS. 1. As part of their mortal probation, righteous men are called upon to suffer *offenses.* That is, injuries, assaults, affronts, and outrages are committed against them. They suffer because of the sins and crimes of others. But the fact that offenses

must needs be, in no way mitigates the punishment of those guilty of offending the Lord's little ones. (Matt. 18:6-7; Luke 17:1-2.)

2. Speaking of an *offense* as a stumbling block, our Lord was a *Rock of offense* unto the unbelieving and rebellious. (Isa. 8:13-17; Rom. 9:33; 1 Pet. 2:8.)

OFFERINGS.

See OBLATIONS.

OFFICES IN THE PRIESTHOOD.

See PRIESTHOOD OFFICES.

OFFSPRING OF DAVID.

See SON OF DAVID.

OIL.

See CONSECRATION OF OIL.

OLD COVENANT.

See NEW COVENANT.

OLD TESTAMENT.

See APOCRYPHA, BIBLE, LOST SCRIPTURE, NEW TESTAMENT, SCRIPTURE, STANDARD WORKS. Because the records of God's dealings with men from the day of Adam to the coming of Christ were supposed to pertain to an old patriarchal-Mosaic testament or covenant which was done away in Christ, these records were called the *Old Testament.* Choice of the title is said to be based on Paul's statement that the Jews, though engaged "in the reading of the old testament," yet were not able to understand that Mosaic testament. (2 Cor. 3:1-18.)

Actually, of course, the law of carnal commandments, the law of performances and ordinances revealed through Moses, was an old covenant as compared with the gospel restored by Jesus and his apostles. But this new testament or covenant, this restored gospel, was the same testament that had been in force between God and his people from Adam to Moses in both the old and the new worlds. However, so long as it is properly defined and understood the designation *Old Testament* is acceptable for the ancient scriptural record to which it has been applied.

As we now have it the Old Testament contains 39 books, variously classified by analysts as the law, the prophets, the wisdom books, and the historical books; or, as legal, historical, prophetic, wisdom, and devotional literature; or, in some other way. These classifications are artificial, depending on the fancies and views of the critics who create them. The various books themselves are part of a complex and interwoven account of God's dealings with men and their temporal and spiritual needs.

The Book of Mormon and other latter-day revelations throw a great flood of light on Old Testament writings. For instance, these modern scriptures frequently quote, paraphrase, endorse, or interpret specific passages of scripture recorded in the pre-Christian Era. To illustrate: Higher critics teach that there were two or three Isaiahs all of whose writings are combined in the Book of Isaiah. But the Book of Mormon quotes sufficiently from the writings of Isaiah to establish conclusively that one man only is the author of the book of that name. Again: The 38th and 39th chapters of Ezekiel tell of many great events to precede and attend the Second Coming of Christ, and the 29th section of the Doctrine and Covenants pointedly identifies these ancient prophecies as pertaining to the last days. Further: The Book of Moses in the Pearl of Great Price is a revealed confirmation of the authorship and truth of the forepart of the Book of Genesis.

There are in fact, not hundreds, but thousands of instances in which modern revelation confirms the truth of ancient revelation. And when the ancient accounts are read under the inspiration of the Spirit, and in the light of the more perfectly preserved modern revelations, we find a great treasure house of revealed truth. It is no wonder that our Lord told the Nephites "to search . . . the words of Isaiah" and the prophets (3 Ne. 23:1-5), and that he told the Jews to "search the scriptures" (John 5:39), meaning the Old Testament.

OLD WORLD.
See NEW WORLD.

OLIVE OIL.
See CONSECRATION OF OIL.

OMEGA.
See ALPHA AND OMEGA.

OMEGUS.
See ALPHA AND OMEGA, ALPHUS, CHRIST. One of the name-titles of Christ is *Omegus* (D. & C. 95:17), a derivative of the Greek *Omega*. Use of this title emphasizes the eternal continuance of Christ in his exalted station as the Eternal One forever.

OMENS.
See SIGNS.

OMNIPOTENCE.
See EXALTATION, FULNESS OF THE FATHER, GOD, LORD OMNIPOTENT, OMNIPRESENCE, OMNISCIENCE. God is *omnipotent* (*Lectures on Faith,* pp. 9, 43-45, 50-51); he is the Lord Omnipotent (Mosiah 3: 7), the Lord God Omnipotent. (Rev. 19:6.) *Omnipotence* consists in having unlimited power, and God has all power, and there is no power

which he does not have. (D. & C. 19:3, 14, 20; 20:24; 61:1; 93:17; Matt. 28:18; 1 Ne. 9:6; Mosiah 4:9; Alma 12:15; 26:35; Morm. 5:23; Ether 3:4.) Those who obtain exaltation will gain all power and thus themselves be omnipotent. (D. & C. 76:95; 88:107; 132:20.)

OMNIPOTENT GOD.
See LORD OMNIPOTENT.

OMNIPRESENCE.
See GOD, LIGHT OF CHRIST, OMNIPOTENCE, OMNISCIENCE. God is omnipresent (*Lectures on Faith,* p. 9); he is the *Immanent God,* the indwelling Presence in all immensity. "In him we live, and move, and have our being." (Acts 17:28.) "He is above all things, and in all things, and is through all things, and is round about all things; and all things are by him, and of him, even God, forever and ever." (D. & C. 88:41.)

It is by reference to this true doctrine of *omnipresence* that the sectarian world attempts to justify its false creeds which describe Deity as a vague, ethereal, immaterial essence which fills the immensity of space and is everywhere and nowhere in particular present. God himself, of course, is a personal Being in whose image man is created. (Gen. 1:26; 5:1; Moses 2: 26; 6:9), but he is also an immanent Being, meaning that the light of Christ shines forth from him to fill all space. This "light proceedeth forth from the presence of God to fill the immensity of space—The light which is in all things, which giveth life to all things, which is the law by which all things are governed, even the power of *God who sitteth upon his throne,* who is in the bosom of eternity, who is in the midst of all things." (D. & C. 88:12-13.)

God is the *Creator;* the power, light, influence, and spirit that goes forth from his person to fill all immensity is a *creature* of his creating. Thus it was that Paul, speaking of apostate peoples, said they had *"changed the truth of God into a lie, and worshipped and served the creature more than the Creator,* who is blessed for ever." (Rom. 1: 25.)

OMNISCIENCE.

See GOD, KNOWLEDGE, OMNIPOTENCE, OMNIPRESENCE, WISDOM. God is *omniscient. (Lectures on Faith,* pp. 9, 43-45, 50-51; *Doctrines of Salvation,* vol. 1, pp. 5-10.) *Omniscience* consists in having unlimited knowledge. God knows all things (2 Ne. 9:20; D. & C. 38: 1-2; 88:7-13); possesses "a fulness of truth, yea, even of all truth" (D. & C. 93:11, 26); "has all power, all wisdom, and all understanding" (Alma 26:35); is infinite in understanding (Ps. 147:4-5); comprehends all things (Alma 26:35; D. & C. 88: 41); and "hath given a law unto all things." (D. & C. 88:42.)

"It is not because the Lord is ignorant of law and truth that he is able to progress, but *because* of his knowledge and wisdom," President Joseph Fielding Smith has written. "The Lord is constantly using his knowledge in his work. And his great work is in bringing to pass the immortality and eternal life of man. By the creation of worlds and peopling them, by building and extending, he progresses, but *not* because the fulness of truth is not understood by him." (*Doctrines of Salvation,* vol. 1, p. 10; D. & C. 84:38; 93:16-17; Matt. 28:18; Moro. 7:22.)

Joseph Smith said: "Without the knowledge of all things God would not be able to save any portion of his creatures; . . . *and if it were not for the idea existing in the minds of men that God had all knowledge it would be impossible for them to exercise faith in him."* (*Lectures on Faith,* p. 44.)

ONANISM.

See SEX IMMORALITY.

ONE ETERNAL ROUND.

See ETERNAL, ETERNITY TO ETERNITY, EVERLASTING, EVERLASTING TO EVERLASTING, LAW. God governs by law—wholly, completely, invaryingly, and always. He has ordained that identical results always flow from the same causes. There is no respect of persons with him, and he is a Being "with whom is no variableness, neither shadow of turning." (Jas. 1:17; D. & C. 3:1-2.) Hence, the Lord's "course is *one eternal round*, the same today as yesterday, and forever." (D. & C. 35:1.) For example: "He that diligently seeketh shall find; and the mysteries of God shall be unfolded unto them, by the power of the Holy Ghost, as well in these times as in times of old, and as well in times of old as in times to come; wherefore, the course of the Lord is one eternal round." (1 Ne. 10:19.)

ONE HUNDRED FORTY-FOUR THOUSAND.

See CHURCH OF THE FIRST-BORN, EXALTATION, MILLENNIUM, SEALED IN FOREHEAD, SECOND COMING OF CHRIST, ZION. At his Second Coming, "the Lamb shall stand upon Mount Zion, and with him *a hundred and forty-four thousand,* having his Father's name written on their foreheads." (D. & C. 133:18; Rev. 14:1-5.) These 144,-000 are Gods, as the name on their foreheads specifies; their callings and elections have been made sure; they are exalted personages; they are "redeemed from among men, . . . And in their mouth was found no guile: for they are without fault before the throne of God." (Rev. 14:4-5.) They have attained perfection.

These brethren, 12,000 from each of the tribes of Israel—excepting for some unspecified reason the tribe of Dan (Rev. 7:2-8)—"are high priests, ordained unto the holy order of God, to administer the everlasting gospel; for they are they who are ordained out of every nation, kindred, tongue, and people, by the angels to whom is given power over the nations of the earth, to bring as many as will come to the church of the First-born." (D. & C. 77:9-11.) They are part of "a great multitude, which no man could number"—all of whom shall have membership in the Church of the Firstborn and therefore be exalted beings. (Rev. 7:9-17; Heb. 12:22-24.)

ONLY BEGOTTEN.

See ONLY BEGOTTEN SON.

ONLY BEGOTTEN OF THE FATHER.

See ONLY BEGOTTEN SON.

ONLY BEGOTTEN SON.

See BELOVED SON, CHRIST, SON, SON OF GOD. Christ is the *Only Begotten* (Moses 1:6, 17, 21, 33; 2:1, 26-27; 3:18; 4:1), the *Only Begotten Son* (Jac. 4:5, 11; Alma 12:33-34; 13:5; D. & C. 20:21; 29:42; 49:5; 76:13, 25; John 1:18; 3:16), the *Only Begotten of the Father.* (Moses 5:9.) These name-titles all signify that our Lord is the only Son of the Father in the flesh. Each of the words is to be understood literally. Only means *only;*

Begotten means *begotten;* and Son means *son.* Christ was begotten by an Immortal Father in the same way that mortal men are begotten by mortal fathers.

OPEN REBELLION.
See REBELLION.

OPPOSITION IN ALL THINGS.
See AGENCY.

ORACLES.
See FIRST PRESIDENCY, PROPHETS, REVELATION, REVELATORS, SEERS, TEMPLES, VISIONS. 1. Revelations given by God through his prophets are *oracles.* (Acts 7:38; Rom. 3:2; Heb. 5:12.) The First Presidency are appointed "to receive the oracles for the whole church." (D. & C. 124:126.) When these revelations or oracles are given to the people, the recipients are under solemn obligation to walk in the light thus manifest. "And all they who receive the oracles of God, let them beware how they hold them lest they are accounted as a light thing, and are brought under condemnation thereby, and stumble and fall when the storms descend, and the winds blow, and the rains descend, and beat upon their house." (D. & C. 90:5.)

2. Men who receive revelations or oracles for the people are themselves called *oracles.* (2 Sam. 16: 23.) Members of the First Presidency, Council of the Twelve, and the Patriarch to the Church—because they are appointed and sustained as prophets, seers, and revelators to the Church—are known as the *living oracles.* All those who preach the gospel have the obligation to do it by revelation so that they themselves, as they teach, are acting as oracles to their hearers. *"If any man speak,"* Peter said, *"let him speak as the oracles of God."* (1 Pet. 4:11.)

3. In a general sense, any sacred place where oracles are received is called an *oracle.* A temple is an oracle in this sense, with the holy of holies therein being specifically so designated. (1 Kings 6:16; 8:6; 2 Chron. 4:20; Ps. 28:2.) Sacred revelations or oracles given in such places warrant designating the place itself as an oracle, that is, as a house where revelation is received. (D. & C. 124:39.)

ORDAINED PATRIARCHS.
See PATRIARCHS.

ORDER.
See HARMONY, LAW, OBEDIENCE. In the eternal economy of Deity all things are done in wisdom and in *order;* everything is arranged harmoniously, systematically, as part of a perfect pattern. The heavenly bodies, in all their infinite numbers, roll in perfect unity and harmony through bound-

less immensity. (D. & C. 88:42-45.) Earths are created and pass on to their eternal states on the appointed split second of eternal time.

It is the will of the Lord that man, in his sphere, should walk in the same orderly and harmonious way that the Gods walk, without confusion, contention, or irregularity of conduct. (3 Ne. 6:4; Acts 21:24; D. & C. 129:7.) *"Behold, mine house is a house of order, saith the Lord God, and not a house of confusion."* (D. & C. 132:8.) "All things must be done in order." (Mosiah 4:27; D. & C. 20:68; 28:13; 58:55; 107:84.) Men are specifically commanded to set their houses and families in order so that peace and conformity to the Divine will shall result. (D. & C. 90:18; 93:43-44, 50.) The temple itself, according to the Lord's standard, is a "house of order" (D. & C. 88:119; 109:8), so perfectly and properly should all things be done therein.

ORDER OF AARON.
See AARONIC PRIESTHOOD.

ORDER OF ENOCH.
See UNITED ORDER.

ORDER OF MELCHIZEDEK.
See MELCHIZEDEK PRIESTHOOD.

ORDINANCES.

See BAPTISM, BAPTISM FOR THE DEAD, BAPTISM OF FIRE, BLESSING OF CHILDREN, CELESTIAL MARRIAGE, COMMANDMENTS, CONSECRATION OF OIL, DEDICATION OF GRAVES, ENDOWMENTS, GIFT OF THE HOLY GHOST, LAW, LAYING ON OF HANDS, OBEDIENCE, ORDINATIONS, PASSOVER, PATRIARCHAL BLESSINGS, PRAYER, SABBATH, SACRAMENT, SACRIFICES, TEMPLE ORDINANCES, VICARIOUS ORDINANCES, WASHING OF FEET. 1. God's decrees, his laws and commandments, the statutes and judgments that issue from him, are called his *ordinances.* The covenant of the saints, when they "promise to keep all the commandments and statutes of the Lord" is: *"We will walk in all the ordinances of the Lord."* (D. & C. 136:2-4.)

Indeed, the whole world shall be judged by their conformity, or lack of it, to the laws of the Lord. "He that prayeth, whose spirit is contrite, the same is accepted of me if he obey mine ordinances. He that speaketh, whose spirit is contrite, whose language is meek and edifieth, the same is of God if he obey mine ordinances," the Lord says. (D. & C. 52:15-16.) Apostasy is the result when men stray from the Lord's ordinances. (D. & C. 1:15; Isa. 24:5.)

2. Among his laws and commandments, the Lord has provided certain *rites* and *ceremonies* which are also called *ordinances.* These *ordinance-rites* might be pictured

as a small circle within the larger circle of *ordinance-commandments.* Most of these rites and ceremonies, as illustrated by baptism and celestial marriage, are essential to salvation and exaltation in the kingdom of God; some of them, such as the blessing of children and the dedication of graves, are not ordinances of salvation, but are performed for the comfort, consolation, and encouragement of the saints.

ORDINATIONS.

See KEYS, PRESIDENCY, PRIEST-HOOD, QUORUM PRESIDENTS. Proper *modern usage* of terms conforms to this pattern: Priesthood is *conferred* upon an individual; he is *ordained* to office in the priesthood; and he is *set apart* to a position of presidency or administration. Thus a man has the Melchizedek Priesthood conferred upon him; he is ordained an elder in that priesthood; and he is set apart as president of an elders quorum. Similarly a man is ordained an apostle, but set apart a member of the Council of the Twelve; he is ordained a bishop, but set apart to preside over a ward; he is ordained an high priest, but set apart to preside over a stake or to serve as President of the Church.

Keys go with setting apart and not with ordination. A man receives no keys when he is ordained an elder, but he does when set apart as a quorum president. He gains no keys when ordained a seventy, but

such are given to him when he is set apart to serve in the First Council of Seventy or in the presidency of any seventies quorum.

In the early days of this dispensation, however, the word *ordain* was used in a dual sense that included both *ordinations* (as we now classify them) and also the ordinance of *setting apart* to office. Thus the revelations speak of men being ordained high councilors (D. & C. 20:67), or members of the First Presidency (D. & C. 107:22), and women were ordained to executive positions in the auxiliary organizations. Our present usage is that persons are set apart to these positions. (*Doctrines of Salvation,* vol. 3, p. 106.)

Performance of the ordinances of ordination and setting apart are essential parts of church administration. (Fifth Article of Faith.) Secret conferral of authority through these ordinances cannot be. "It shall not be given to any one," the Lord says, "to go forth to preach my gospel, or to build up my church, except he be *ordained by some one who has authority, and it is known to the church that he has authority and has been regularly ordained by the heads of the church.*" (D. & C. 42:11.) Ordinations and settings apart must comply with the law of common consent. (D. & C. 20:65.)

ORGANIZATION.

See CHURCH ORGANIZATION.

ORIGINAL SIN THEORY.

See ACCOUNTABILITY, ADAM, AGENCY, ATONEMENT OF CHRIST, BAPTISM, FALL OF ADAM, IMMACULATE CONCEPTION THEORY, INFANT BAPTISM, REDEMPTION, REPENTANCE, SALVATION, SALVATION OF CHILDREN, YEARS OF ACCOUNTABILITY. In contrast to the doctrines of free agency and personal accountability for sin, modern Christendom has the false doctrine of *original sin.* Although the scriptures abundantly show "that men will be punished for their own sins, and not for Adam's transgression" (Second Article of Faith; *Articles of Faith,* pp. 57-73), the common view is that all men are tainted with sin and denied blessings because of Adam's fall.

"Original sin," according to Catholic theology, is "the hereditary stain with which we are born on account of our origin or descent from Adam. . . . Original sin is the privation of sanctifying grace in consequence of the sin of Adam," and it can only be "effaced by baptism." (*Catholic Encyclopedia,* vol. 11, pp. 312-315.) Infant baptism, therefore, is a necessary corollary to the doctrine of original sin. Since "those who die in original sin are deprived of the happiness of heaven" (*Catholic Encyclopedia,* vol. 2, pp. 258-274), according to their view, it is easy to see why they think infants must be baptized. One false doctrine begets another.

Protestant views about so-called original sin are similar. The Church of England, for instance, teaches that original sin "is the fault and corruption of the Nature of every man, that naturally is ingendered of the offspring of *Adam;* whereby man is very far gone from original righteousness, and is of his own nature inclined to evil, so that the flesh lusteth always contrary to the spirit; and therefore in every person born into this world, it deserveth God's wrath and condemnation." This "condemnation" is removed only "for them that believe and are baptized." (*Book of Common Prayer,* The Anglican Church of Canada, pp. 662-663.)

ORIGIN OF MAN.

See ADAM.

ORTHODOXY.

See BELIEF, BELIEVING BLOOD, FAITH, HERESY, TRUTH. In the true sense, *orthodoxy* consists in believing that which is in harmony with the scriptures. Thus gospel orthodoxy requires belief in the truths of salvation as they have been revealed in this dispensation through Joseph Smith, and as they are understood and interpreted by the living oracles who wear the mantle of the Prophet. Orthodoxy is the opposite of *heterodoxy* or of believing heretical doctrines.

There are degrees of orthodoxy exhibited by members of the

Church. Those who believe the whole law—and who believe it sanely, sensibly, realistically, according to its true meaning and purport—are completely orthodox. Those who intermingle gospel truths with the educational or philosophical theories of the world have not yet attained perfect orthodoxy, the orthodoxy which is essential to salvation.

OUIJA BOARDS.
See MEDIUMS, SEANCES, SPIRITUALISM. *Ouija boards* are trademarked devices used by spiritualist mediums in receiving messages from evil spirits. Marked with the alphabet and various signs, and having a planchette with a pointer instead of a pencil, the boards are used by mediums at seances to spell out words and otherwise receive answers to questions.

Not all professing mediums have communion with evil spirits, and ouija boards might be used by them or others under circumstances in which nothing but false and futile attempts at such communion are involved. But their use, even under circumstances classified wholly as amusement, is extremely unwise. Those who use the devil's tools for any purpose may soon find themselves influenced and controlled by him. In the hands of mediums who have actual contact with evil and unseen forces, the use of ouija boards is a wicked and devilish thing. Wise persons never seek revelation or guidance through communion with Satan.

OUR LORD.
See CHRIST, LORD, REVERENCE. One of the appropriate and reverential titles properly applied to Christ is *Our Lord.* This terminology helps avoid the too frequent repetition of the name of Deity, and it signifies our personal acceptance of him as Lord and God.

OUTER DARKNESS.
See HELL, SPIRIT PRISON. Hell is referred to as *outer darkness.* At death the spirits of the wicked "shall be cast out into outer darkness; there shall be weeping, and wailing, and gnashing of teeth, and this because of their own iniquity, being led captive by the will of the devil. Now this is the state of the souls of the wicked, yea, in darkness, and a state of awful, fearful looking for the fiery indignation of the wrath of God upon them; thus they remain in this state, as well as the righteous in paradise, until the time of their resurrection." (Alma 40:13-14.)

So complete is the darkness prevailing in the minds of these spirits, so wholly has gospel light been shut out of their consciences, that they know little or nothing of the plan of salvation, and have little hope within themselves of advancement and progression through the saving grace of Christ. Hell is literally a place of outer darkness, darkness that hates light, buries truth, and revels in iniquity.

OVERCOMING ALL THINGS.
See EXALTATION.

OVERSEERS.
See BISHOPS, BRANCH PRESIDENTS, MINISTERS, PASTORS, PRIESTS, SHEPHERDS, STAKE PRESIDENTS. An *overseer* in the Church is a bishop, pastor, shepherd, branch president, or stake president—one appointed to superintend the Lord's work in some part of his vineyard, one who overlooks the work of certain laborers therein. To the bishops in his day, Paul said: "Take heed therefore unto yourselves, and to all the flock, over the which the Holy Ghost hath made you overseers, to feed the church of God, which he hath purchased with his own blood." (Acts 20:28.)

P

PAGAN GODS.
See FALSE GODS.

PAGANS.
See HEATHENS.

PAGEANTRY.
See ORDINANCES, RECREATION. Some false churches have worship services in which elaborate *pageantry,* pomp, and display are presented. Included in their rituals are ceremonies involving images, altars, miters, robes, genuflections, and latin incantations. In the true Church pageantry is a form of recreation and entertainment and not of solemn worship. Certain formalities attend the performance of sacred ordinances, but these formalities are beautiful in their simplicity and do not consist in the unsubstantial, empty show and display of those whose worship, in large part, is encased in mystery.

PALMISTRY.
See FORTUNE TELLING.

PALM SUNDAY.
See EASTER, HOSANNA. Sectarians traditionally celebrate the Sunday before Easter as *Palm Sunday* in commemoration of our Lord's triumphal entry into Jerusalem. On that occasion, as Jesus rode upon "a colt the foal of an ass, . . . a very great multitude

spread their garments in the way" (Matt. 21:1-11), and "Took branches of palm trees, and went forth to meet him, and cried, Hosanna: Blessed is the King of Israel that cometh in the name of the Lord." (John 12:12-16; Mark 11:1-11; Luke 19:28-40.)

Among the Latter-day Saints it is the accepted practice to hail Christ as Lord, King, and Messiah, and to shout hosannas to his holy name, on all days and at all times. But it is not the common practice to single out Palm Sunday for any special commemorative worship. Rather the Latter-day Saints memorialize the transcendent events of their era, such things as the coming of John the Baptist, the restoration of the Melchizedek Priesthood, the conferral of the sealing keys by Elijah, and the organization of the Church again on earth.

PANICS.
See SIGNS OF THE TIMES.

PANTHEISM.
See ATHEISM, DEISM, FALSE GODS, GOD. *Pantheism* is in effect the worship of nature. It assumes that the universe and all the phenomena existing in it, including man and nature, are the ever-changing manifestation of God. It is the doctrine that there is no God except the great forces and laws which are manifested in the existing universe. Such apostate concepts are the end result of the philosophy which worships and serves the creature more than the Creator. (Rom. 1:25.)

PARABLES.
See CHRIST, STANDARD WORKS. Our Lord used *parables* on frequent occasions during his ministry to teach gospel truths. His purpose, however, in telling these short stories was *not* to present the truths of his gospel in plainness so that all his hearers would understand. Rather it was so to phrase and hide the doctrine involved that only the spiritually literate would understand it, while those whose understandings were darkened would remain in darkness. (Matt. 13:10-17; *Inspired Version,* Matt. 21:34.) It is never proper to teach any person more than his spiritual capacity qualifies him to assimilate. For instance: Jesus first gave and then partially interpreted the parable of the wheat and the tares (Matt. 13:24-30, 36-43), and yet its full meaning was so obscure that a special interpretive revelation was required in modern times. (D. & C. 86.)

The principle involved which necessitates the policy of teaching by parables is found in Amulek's statement: "It is given unto many to know the mysteries of God; nevertheless they are laid under a strict command that *they shall not impart only according to the portion of his word which he doth grant unto the children of men, according to the heed and diligence which they give unto him."* (Alma 12:9.) The difference in receptiveness to the truth of the Jews, among whom our Lord ministered in mortality, and the Nephites, to whom he went after his resurrection, is nowhere better shown than in the fact that he gave at least 40 parables to the Jews, but he taught the Nephites, not in parables, but in plainness.

PARACLETE.

See ADVOCATE, CHRIST, COMFORTER, HOLY GHOST. The Holy Ghost is considered by scholars to be the *Paraclete,* because the Greek word *paraclete,* as used in John 16:7, is translated Comforter (meaning the Holy Ghost). Literally, this Greek word means, "an advocate or intercessor summoned to aid." The same word, as found in 1 John 2:1, is translated *Advocate,* the context clearly indicating that the Advocate involved is Christ.

If by Paraclete is meant one who aids and helps another, then the Holy Ghost could be so named. But if the intent is to refer to an advocate or intercessor, then the term must apply to Christ. He, and not the Holy Ghost, is the Advocate with the Father. Sectarian views of the Godhead and of the distinguishable missions of the respective members thereof are incomprehensibly garbled.

PARADISE.

See ABRAHAM'S BOSOM, HEAVEN, HELL, SPIRIT PRISON, SPIRIT WORLD. That part of the spirit world inhabited by righteous spirits who are awaiting the day of their resurrection is called *paradise.* It is "a state of happiness, . . . a state of rest, a state of peace, where they shall rest from all their troubles and from all care, and sorrow." (Alma 40:11-14; 4 Ne. 14; Moro. 10:34; D. & C. 77:2, 5.) Then, in the day of the first resurrection, "the spirits of the righteous" shall be reunited with their bodies, and in immortal glory "the righteous shall have a perfect knowledge of their enjoyment, and their righteousness, being clothed with purity, yea, even with the robe of righteousness." (2 Ne. 9:13-14.)

"When men are prepared, they are better off to go hence," the Prophet said. *"The spirits of the just are exalted to a greater and more glorious work; hence they are blessed in their departure to the world of spirits. Enveloped in flaming fire, they are not far from us, and know and understand our thoughts, feelings, and motions, and are often pained therewith."* (*Teachings,* p. 326.)

"To day shalt thou be with me in paradise" (Luke 23:43), is a statement our Lord is purported to have made to the thief on the cross. Actually, as the Prophet explains, "there is nothing in the original word in Greek from which this was taken that signifies paradise; but it was—This day shalt thou be with me in the world of spirits: then I will teach you all about it and answer your inquiries" (*Teachings,* p. 309), meaning, of course, that such teaching and answers would be given, as is nearly always the case, by the mouths of his servants appointed so to serve.

If the Bible is correctly translated, Paul had a spiritual experience in which he was "caught up into paradise" (2 Cor. 12:4), though it may be that this should read that he was caught up to the celestial world, receiving a comparable manifestation to that vouchsafed to by the Three Nephites. (3 Ne. 28:13-15.)

PARADISIACAL EARTH.

See NEW HEAVEN AND NEW EARTH.

PASCHAL LAMB.

See SACRIFICES.

PASSION OF CHRIST.

See ATONEMENT OF CHRIST, CHRIST. Our Lord's sufferings—the pain, torture, crown of thorns, scourging, and final crucifixion—which he endured between the night of the Last Supper and his death on the cross are collectively spoken of as the *Passion of Christ.* (Acts 1:3.) The sectarian world falsely suppose that the climax of his torture and suffering was on the cross (Matt. 27:26-50; Mark 15:1-38; Luke 23:1-46; John 18; 19:1-18)—a view which they keep ever before them by the constant use of the cross as a religious symbol. The fact is that intense and severe as the suffering was on the cross, yet the great pains were endured in the Garden of Gethsemane. (Matt. 26:36-46; Mark 14:32-42; Luke 22:39-46; John 18:1.) It was there that he trembled because of pain, bled at every pore, and suffered both in body and in spirit, and would that he "might not drink the bitter cup." (D. & C. 19:15-19; Mosiah 3:7.) It was there he underwent his greatest suffering for men, taking upon himself, as he did, their sins on conditions of repentance. (D. & C. 18:10-15.)

PASSIONS.

See ANGER, HATRED, LOVE, PASSION OF CHRIST. Emotional feelings of love, ardor, affection, hate, anger, bitterness, and the like, are collectively called *passions.* To exhibit these or kindred emotions is to *show passion.* To be *passionless* is to display neither anger, love, or other emotion; it is to be tranquil and unmoved. Passions are of two kinds: 1. *Holy passions* such as love, hatred of evil, and righteous anger, which incite to godliness; and 2. *Unholy passions* such as jealousy, hate, and unbridled sex desires, which lead men downward.

Passions appertain to and are a part of every stage of existence; spirits in pre-existence, mortal men, and immortal beings all are subject to passions of one sort or another. God himself is the embodiment, in perfection, of every holy and pure passion. He is a jealous God (Ex. 20:5), so much so that *Jealous* is his very name. (Ex. 34:14.) He is a God of love (1 John 4:7-21); he hates evil abominations (Prov. 6: 16-19), and so forth.

The falsity of statements in sectarian creeds that their Deity is without body, parts, and passions, is only exceeded by the absurdity of such assertions. *A God without passions cannot exist, for he would neither love his children, hate their evil ways, or be importuned by their pleas for mercy; he would sit tranquilly by, being neither moved nor affected by any occurrence, reacting neither to good or evil, and hence able to bestow no rewards and impose no penalties.* As Lehi said, he would "have vanished away." (2 Ne. 2:11-13.)

Appetites, desires, and passions which incite to evil are part of the nature of mortal man. (Acts 14:15; Jas. 5:17; Alma 50:30.) Fallen man is by nature carnal, sensual, and devilish. (Moses 5:13; D. & C. 20: 20; Mosiah 3:19; Alma 42:10.) One of the great purposes of mortality is to test him and see if he will bridle his passions. (Alma 38:12.) *Incontinency,* which is lack of restraint and failure to bridle one's passions (particularly where sex desires are concerned), is one of the modern day signs proving the great apostasy. (2 Tim. 3:3.)

PASSOVER.

See DAY OF PENETECOST, SACRAMENT, SACRIFICES. To commemorate Israel's deliverance from Egyptian bondage, the Lord commanded his people to keep the *feast of the passover,* a celebration pointing particularly to the fact that the angel of destruction passed over the homes of the faithful sons of Jacob, when the firstborn in all the families of Egypt were slain. (Ex. 12.)

It was during the week of this feast, some 1500 years after the exodus, that our Lord was crucified. Just before his betrayal he had partaken of the feast with his disciples, using it as the occasion to introduce the ordinance of the sacrament to the Church. (Matt. 26; Mark 14; Luke 22.)

Keeping of the passover, with its sacrifices and unleavend bread, ended (except among apostate peoples) with the sacrifice of "Christ our passover." The saints were to keep the feast only in a spiritual sense, as Paul said: "Let us keep the feast, not with old leaven, neither with the leaven of malice and wickedness; but with the unleav-

ened bread of sincerity and truth."
(1 Cor. 5:6-8.)

PASTORS.

See BISHOPS, BRANCH PRESI-
DENTS, MINISTERS, OVERSEERS,
QUORUM PRESIDENTS, SHEPHERDS,
STAKE PRESIDENTS. A *pastor* is a
shepherd of a flock. As used in the
Church, a pastor is any church
officer or minister who is in charge
of a congregation or ecclesiastical
unit of the Church. When the
scattered sheep of the house of
Israel are gathered in the last days,
then will be fulfilled the Lord's
promise to them: "I will give you
pastors according to mine heart,
which shall feed you with knowledge and understanding." (Jer.
3:15.)

A pastor is not an ordained office in the priesthood. Anyone
serving as a bishop, branch president, stake president, or even
quorum president—being called to
feed his flock with knowledge and
understanding—might properly be
called a pastor. In the early days
of this dispensation, brethren called
pastors were appointed to preside
over two or more mission *conferences* (meaning *districts*) in Great
Britain. (*Doctrines of Salvation,*
vol. 3, pp. 108-109.) There must, of
necessity, be pastors in the true
Church of God. (Eph. 4:11-14;
Sixth Article of Faith.)

PATIENCE.

See HUMILITY, MEEKNESS. To
fill the full measure and purpose
of our mortal probation, we must
have *patience.* This mortal existence is the Lord's sifting sphere,
the time when we are subject to
trials, testing, and tribulations.
Future rewards will be based on
our patient endurance of all things.

"The patience of the saints"
consists in bearing or enduring
pains, trials, and persecutions (even
unto death), without complaint
and with equanimity. (Rev. 13:10;
14:12.) It was the Master himself
who said: "In your patience possess ye your souls" (Luke 21:19),
and anyone who yields his whole
soul and being to the Lord "becometh as a child, submissive,
meek, humble, *patient,* full of love,
willing to submit to all things
which the Lord seeth fit to inflict
upon him, even as a child doth
submit to his father." (Mosiah 3:
19.)

Patience, also, involves an exercise of forbearance under provocation as illustrated in the celestial
principle, "whosoever shall smite
thee on thy right cheek, turn to
him the other also." (Matt. 5:38-
42; 3 Ne. 12:38-42.) Patience in
righteousness leads to perfection
and eternal life. Thus Paul wrote
that "by patient continuance in
well doing" the saints "seek for
glory and honour and immortality,
[and] eternal life." (Rom. 2:7.) And
by revelation in our day the Lord
commanded: *"Continue in patience
until ye are perfected"* (D. & C.
67:13); "And seek the face of the

Lord always, that in patience ye may possess your souls, and ye shall have eternal life." (D. & C. 101:38.)

PATRIARCHAL BLESSINGS.

See EVANGELISTS, PATRIARCHS, PATRIARCH TO THE CHURCH, PROPHECY, REVELATION. Nearly every member of the Church is a literal descendant of Jacob who gave *patriarchal blessings* to his 12 sons, predicting what would happen to them and their posterity after them. (Gen. 49; *Teachings,* p. 151.) As inheritors of the blessings of Jacob, it is the privilege of the gathered remnant of Jacob to receive their own patriarchal blessings and, by faith, to be blessed equally with the ancients. Patriarchal blessings may be given by *natural patriarchs,* that is by fathers in Israel who enjoy the blessings of the patriarchal order, or they may be given by *ordained patriarchs,* specially selected brethren who are appointed to bless worthy church members. (*Doctrines of Salvation,* vol. 3, pp. 169-172; *Gospel Kingdom,* p. 146.)

The First Presidency (David O. McKay, Stephen L Richards, J. Reuben Clark, Jr.), in a letter to all stake presidents, dated June 28, 1957, gave the following definition and explanation: "Patriarchal blessings contemplate an inspired declaration of the lineage of the recipient, and also where so moved upon by the Spirit, an inspired and prophetic statement of the life mission of the recipient, together with such blessings, cautions, and admonitions as the patriarch may be prompted to give for the accomplishment of such life's mission, it being always made clear that the realization of all promised blessings is conditioned upon faithfulness to the gospel of our Lord, whose servant the patriarch is. All such blessings are recorded and generally only one such blessing should be adequate for each person's life. The sacred nature of the patriarchal blessing must of necessity urge all patriarchs to most earnest solicitation of divine guidance for their prophetic utterances and superior wisdom for cautions and admonitions."

PATRIARCHAL CHAIN.

See ADAM-GOD THEORY, ANCIENT OF DAYS, BIRTHRIGHT, CELESTIAL MARRIAGE, EXALTATION, ISRAEL, PATRIARCHAL ORDER. Those who shall hereafter rule and reign in eternity as exalted beings will form a *patriarchal chain* which will begin with Father Adam and spread out until every exalted person is linked in. Exaltation consists in the continuation of the family unit in eternity, and every family which so continues will find its proper place in the eternal organizational framework which the Almighty has ordained. None will be forgotten. Unworthy mortal links will be dropped in eternity, for there is no family in which all generations will attain exaltation; later generations of worthy families will be welded into the links formed by their ancestors who became worthy of a like exaltation with them. All those after the day of Abraham (of whatever literal lineage they may be) who so live as to be worthy of a place in this great patriarchal chain will be welded into Abraham's lineage and shall rise up and bless him as their father. (Abra. 2:9-11.)

PATRIARCHAL ORDER.

See ADAM-GOD THEORY, ANCIENT OF DAYS, BIRTHRIGHT, CELESTIAL MARRIAGE, EXALTATION, ISRAEL, PATRIARCHAL CHAIN, PRIESTHOOD. The Lord's government is patriarchal in nature. The family unit is the center. In pre-existence he was the Father of spirits, and all men are literally brothers and sisters in the spirit. With the placing of man on earth, the Lord began by patterning earthly government after that which is heavenly. A perfect theocratic, patriarchal system was set up with Adam at the head. This system prevailed in large measure among righteous men from Adam to the establishment of Israel in her promised land, when the people prevailed upon the Lord to let them be ruled by kings as were the apostate gentile nations.

In these early days the church government itself was also patriarchal in nature. From Adam to the flood the presiding church officer was always both a high priest and a patriarch, and the office descended from father to son. This order of priesthood itself was called the *patriarchal order.* As an order of the priesthood it is preserved in the Church today only where the office of Patriarch to the Church is concerned. From the days of Aaron to the coming of John the Baptist a modified system of patriarchal administration existed where ecclesiastical affairs were concerned in that Aaron and his descendants, and also the larger group of Levites themselves, administered in certain church affairs. (*Doctrines of Salvation,* vol. 3, pp. 80-87, 101-106, 160-172; *Teachings,* p. 319.)

Administration of church affairs is necessarily on a different basis in our day, but the most important part of the patriarchal order is preserved for worthy members of the Church. Those married in the temple in the new and everlasting covenant of marriage become inheritors of all the blessings of Abraham, Isaac, and Jacob and all the patriarchs and thereby enter into the patriarchal order. If the participating parties abide in the eternal marriage covenant, they shall reap the full blessings of patriarchal heirship in eternity where the patriarchal order will be the order of government and rule.

PATRIARCHS.

See EVANGELISTS, MELCHIZEDEK

PRIESTHOOD, PATRIARCHAL BLESS-
INGS, PATRIARCHAL ORDER, PA-
TRIARCH TO THE CHURCH, PRESI-
DENT OF THE CHURCH, PRIESTHOOD,
PRIESTHOOD OFFICES, PRIEST-
HOOD QUORUMS. 1. One of the ordained offices in the Melchizedek
Priesthood is that of a *patriarch*
or *evangelist.* (D. & C. 107:39.)
This office grows out of and is an
appendage to the higher priesthood.
(D. & C. 107:5.) The office of *patriarch to the Church* is conferred
as a result of lineage and worthiness; *stake patriarchs* are chosen
and ordained by the apostles without respect to lineage. Patriarchs
are also high priests. (D. & C. 107:
39-53.) Their special priestly assignment is to give patriarchal
blessings to members of the
Church, but they can also perform
any duty of a high priest, seventy,
elder, or holder of the Aaronic
Priesthood.

2. In addition to *ordained patriarchs,* there are also *natural patriarchs.* Every holder of the higher
priesthood who has entered into
the patriarchal order of celestial
marriage—thereby receiving for
himself the blessings of the patriarchs Abraham, Isaac, and Jacob—
is a natural patriarch to his
posterity.

Even in the eyes of the world,
the great spiritual leaders, who in
the main lived before the days of
Moses, are known as patriarchs
because of their status as heads or
princes of their families. It is probably in this sense that Peter spoke
of "the patriarch David" (Acts 2:
29), and that Stephen designated
the sons of Jacob as "the twelve
patriarchs." (Acts 7:8-9.) It may
be, however, that all of those before Moses who are considered by
the world to be patriarchs, as
Abraham (Heb. 7:4; Abra. 1:1-4;
2:11; D. & C. 86:8-11), were both ordained and natural patriarchs. (D.
& C. 107:38-53.)

PATRIARCH TO THE CHURCH.
See EVANGELISTS, GENERAL AU-
THORITIES, PATRIARCHAL BLESS-
INGS, PATRIARCHS. Joseph Smith,
Sr., father of the Prophet, was the
first *patriarch to the Church* in this
dispensation. He was chosen by
revelation and ordained on December 18, 1833. "Blessed of the Lord
is my father," the Prophet said
by way of blessing on that occasion, "for he . . . shall be numbered
among those who hold *the right of
patriarchal priesthood, even the
keys of that ministry. . . . .* He shall
be called a prince over his posterity, holding *the keys of the patriarchal priesthood over the kingdom
of God on earth,* even the Church
of the Latter-day Saints, and he
shall sit in the general assembly
of patriarchs, even in council with
the Ancient of Days when he shall
sit and all the patriarchs with him
and shall enjoy his right and authority under the direction of the
Ancient of Days." (*Teachings,* pp.
38-39, 151.)

This ordination marked the restoration of the calling of "evangelical ministers" again on earth, an order of priesthood which "was confirmed to be handed down from father to son," one which "rightly belongs to the literal descendants of the chosen seed, to whom the promises were made." Adam, Seth, Enos, Cainan, Mahalaleel, Jared, Enoch, Methuselah, Lamech, and Noah all enjoyed the rights and powers of this priesthood calling. (D. & C. 107:38-53.) And in modern times it descended from Joseph Smith, Sr., to his son, Hyrum Smith (D. & C. 124:91-96), and has continued on in that rightful lineage to the present time. (*Doctrines of Salvation,* vol. 3, pp. 160-183.)

Of the patriarch to the Church the Lord says: "He shall hold *the keys of the patriarchal blessings* upon the heads of all my people." (D. & C. 124:92.) As one of the General Authorities, the patriarch to the Church stands next in order to the members of the Council of the Twelve.

PATRIOTISM.

See CIVIL GOVERNMENTS, CONSTITUTION OF THE UNITED STATES, KINGCRAFT, LOYALTY. Among the true saints, *patriotism* is a part of religion. Pending that glorious millennial day when theocratic government shall be restored, members of the Church know that they are and necessarily must be subject to and supporters of civil authority.

In its formal declaration regarding governments and laws in general the Church affirms: "We believe that all men are bound to sustain and uphold the respective governments in which they reside, while protected in their inherent and inalienable rights by the laws of such governments. . . . We believe that every man should be honored in his station, rulers and magistrates as such, being placed for the protection of the innocent and the punishment of the guilty; and that to the laws all men owe respect and deference, as without them peace and harmony would be supplanted by anarchy and terror." (D. & C. 134:5-6.)

Patriotic responses of the saints in the payment of taxes, in bearing arms, in obeying the laws of the land, and in responding to government appeals in general, all testify that patriotism is both precept and practice among church members.

PAUL.
See CELIBACY.

PEACE.
See MILLENNIUM, PRINCE OF PEACE, WAR. 1. *Peace,* meaning freedom from war, has been the hope and desire of the righteous among all nations in all ages. They have always been under command to "seek peace, and pursue it" (Ps. 34:14), to "renounce war and proclaim peace" (D. & C. 98:16), and to

"have peace one with another." (Mark 9:50; Rom. 12:18; 1 Tim. 2:2; Mosiah 4:13.) "Blessed are the peacemakers: for they shall be called the children of God." (Matt. 5:9.)

But since this earth is in a fallen or mortal state—so that any who abide on it have power to live a telestial law, which is the law of wickedness and carnality—peace has been found only for limited times among a few of its inhabitants. For two generations there was peace among the Nephites because the wicked had been destroyed. (3 Ne. 10:12; 4 Ne. 1-25.) Righteous as the saints were in the days of Enoch, however, there were wars, for the saints dwelt in the midst of wicked people. (Moses 7: 13-15.)

In the last days, above all other eras, there is to be no peace on earth. On November 1, 1831, the Lord said: "The hour is not yet, but is nigh at hand, when peace shall be taken from the earth, and the devil shall have power over his own dominion." (D. & C. 1:35.) In 1894, President Wilford Woodruff, speaking as the Lord's mouthpiece on earth, announced that peace was taken from the earth and that great wars and desolations would be poured out.

There will be no peace on earth again until the Prince of Peace comes, destroys the wicked, and ushers in the millennial era. There may be a few years of limited peace for a few people; there will

be periods of armed neutrality while men prepare for inevitable conflicts; but universal peace, the era when men "shall beat their swords into plowshares, and their spears into pruninghooks," the day when "nation shall not lift up sword against nation, neither shall they learn war any more" (Isa. 2: 4), shall not come until the wicked are burned as stubble and only the righteous remain. (Mal. 4; *Doctrines of Salvation,* vol. 3, pp. 48-52.)

2. Inner *spiritual peace,* "the peace of God, which passeth all understanding" (Philip. 4:7), is a gift of God to the obedient. (Ps. 37:37; 119:165; Isa. 26:3; 48:18, 22; 57:21; Rom. 8:6; 10:15; 14:17-19; 1 Cor. 14:33; Eph. 6:15.) "Peace I leave with you, my peace I give unto you: not as the world giveth, give I unto you. Let not your heart be troubled, neither let it be afraid." (John 14:27; 16:33.) Those who gain this peace in this life shall die in peace (D. & C. 45:46), continue in peace in the paradise of God (Alma 40:12), and then rise in the resurrection to inherit eternal peace in the kingdom of God. "Learn that he who doeth the works of righteousness shall receive his reward, even peace in this world, and eternal life in the world to come." (D. & C. 59:23.)

3. There is to be no *peace* in the religious field until that millennial day when all men come to a unity of the faith (Eph. 4:11-16), that day when discord and dissension

cease, when Satan is bound and can no longer sow the seeds of false doctrine in the hearts of men.

Pending that day, Paul's language to the Corinthians applies. "For what fellowship hath righteousness with unrighteousness?" he asked, "and what communion hath light with darkness? And what concord hath Christ with Belial? or what part hath he that believeth with an infidel? And what agreement hath the temple of God with idols?" (2 Cor. 6:14-16.) Our Lord affirmed: "Think not that I am come to send peace on earth: I came not to send peace, but a sword. For I am come to set a man at variance against his father, and the daughter against her mother, and the daughter in law against her mother in law. And a man's foes shall be they of his own household." (Matt. 10:34-36; Luke 12:49-53.)

PEARL OF GREAT PRICE.

See BIBLE, BOOK OF MORMON, CHURCH OF JESUS CHRIST OF LATTER-DAY SAINTS, DOCTRINE AND COVENANTS, GOSPEL, KINGDOM OF GOD, SCRIPTURE, STANDARD WORKS. 1. According to our Lord's parable, the kingdom of heaven—that is, the kingdom of God on earth, or in other words The Church of Jesus Christ of Latter-day Saints—is the *pearl of great price.* Because men cannot accept the gospel without also accepting as a divine institution the Lord's Church or kingdom on earth, it is also common to speak of the gospel as the pearl of great price. To gain the money to buy this pearl of exceeding worth, honest truth seekers willingly sell all that they have. (Matt. 13:45-46.) The purpose of this parable is to show the incalculable value of that kingdom through which the gospel of salvation is administered.

2. This expression, *Pearl of Great Price,* has been adopted as the title of a volume of latter-day scripture, a volume containing a choice selection of the revelations, translations, and narrations of the Prophet Joseph Smith. As now published the Pearl of Great Price contains the following:

a. *Book of Moses*—Contrary to the false notions of the higher critics, Moses personally is the author of the Pentateuch or first five books of the Old Testament. (1 Ne. 5:11.) In their present form, however, these five books no longer contain many of the teachings and doctrines originally placed in them by the great lawgiver of ancient Israel. But by direct revelation in modern times the Lord has restored through the Prophet many of the great truths lost from the early Mosaic scriptures.

The Book of Moses, a work containing eight chapters and covering the same general period and events as are found in the first six chapters of Genesis, contains much of this restored truth. The 1st and 7th chapters of Moses are entirely new revelations having no counterpart in Genesis. The other chapters in Moses cover the same events recorded in the first six chapters of Genesis, but the account revealed in latter-days has been so enlarged, contains so much new material, and so radically changes the whole perspective of the Lord's dealings with Adam and the early patriarchs that for all practical purposes it may be considered as entirely new matter. The whole view of the creation of all things; of pre-existence and the purpose of life; of Adam and his fall; of the primeval revelation of the gospel to man; of the terms and conditions in accordance with which salvation is offered to the living and the dead; of Enoch, his ministry and his establishment of Zion; and of Noah, his priesthood and ministry —the whole view and perspective relative to all these things is radically changed by the new revelations in the Book of Moses. This book which is also contained in the Prophet's Inspired Version of the Bible, is one of the most important documents the Lord has ever revealed.

b. *Book of Abraham*—This work was translated by the Prophet from a papyrus record taken from the catacombs of Egypt, a record preserved by the Lord to come forth in this day of restoration. (Milton R. Hunter, *Pearl of Great Price Commentary*, pp. 6-35.) Abraham was the original author, and the scriptural account contains priceless information about the gospel, pre-existence, the nature of Deity, the creation, and priesthood, information which is not otherwise available in any other revelation now extant.

c. *Writings of Joseph Smith*— Three extracts from the Prophet's writings are here included: one, an extract from the Inspired Version of the Bible; the second, extracts from the history of Joseph Smith; and the third, the statement of belief now called the Articles of Faith. The quotation from the Inspired Version is our Lord's discourse on the Second Coming and signs of the times, which begins with the last verse of the 23rd chapter of Matthew and continues through the 24th chapter. The account of the Prophet's own history records his ancestry; recites the events incident to the religious revivalism around Palmyra in the spring of 1820; tells of the appearance of the Father and the Son to him; reports the appearances of Moroni and tells of the coming forth of the Book of Mormon; and records the visitation of John the Baptist and the restoration of the Aaronic Priesthood. The Articles of Faith are a brief summary of some of the basic doctrines of the Church.

Some added items were published in early editions of the Pearl of Great Price. The first edition, published in 1851 in England by Elder Franklin D. Richards, also contained sections 77 and 87 of the Doctrine and Covenants, and extracts from sections 20, 27, and 107, and the hymn, "O Say What Is Truth?" The first American edition, published in 1878, also contained the revelation on marriage, section 132 of the Doctrine and Covenants.

It should be remembered that in the early days of the Church the revelations were not published and disseminated as widely as at present. After the Doctrine and Covenants was brought up to date, it was no longer necessary to publish duplicating items in the Pearl of Great Price. All editions since 1902 of this latter scripture have contained only the books of Moses and Abraham and the extracts from the Prophet's writings. (Milton R. Hunter, *Pearl of Great Price Commentary,* pp. 41-47.)

PEARLY GATES.

See CELESTIAL KINGDOM, KEEPER OF THE GATE, NEW JERUSALEM. To enter the *Pearly Gates* means to gain admittance to the celestial kingdom. The expression is based on John's vision of the celestial earth onto which he saw "the holy Jerusalem, descending out of heaven from God. . . . And the twelve gates were twelve pearls: every several gate was of one pearl." (Rev. 21:10-27.) Since pearls were considered by the ancients as among the most precious of gems and were highly esteemed for their ornamental value, it was quite natural for the Lord so to symbolize the beauty and excellence of admission to his eternal presence.

PECULIAR PEOPLE.

See. HERITAGE, MORMONS, SAINTS. In every age the Lord's people are classified by the world as a *peculiar people,* a designation which the saints accept and in which they rejoice. (Ex. 19:6; Deut. 7:6; 14:1; 1 Pet. 2:5, 9.) They are peculiar, distinctive, unusual, not like any other people, because they have overcome the world. Their doctrines, practices, and whole way of life runs counter to the common course of mankind.

To illustrate: It is peculiar to believe in and receive latter-day revelation; to heal the sick; to raise the dead; to abstain from tea, coffee, tobacco, and liquor; to have visions; to pay one-tenth of one's interest annually as tithing; to marry for eternity; to go on missions; to serve in the ministry without financial pay—and so on through all the beliefs and practices of the true saints.

PEDOBAPTISM.

See INFANT BAPTISM.

PEEP STONES.

See DEVIL, REVELATION, URIM AND THUMMIM. In imitation of the true order of heaven whereby seers receive revelations from God through a Urim and Thummim, the devil gives his own revelations to some of his followers through *peep stones* or *crystal balls*. An instance of this copying of the true order occurred in the early days of this dispensation. Hiram Page had such a stone and was professing to have revelations for the upbuilding of Zion and the governing of the Church. Oliver Cowdery and some others were wrongly influenced thereby in consequence of which Oliver was commanded by revelation: "Thou shalt take thy brother, Hiram Page, between him and thee alone, and tell him that those things which he hath written from that stone are not of me, and that Satan deceiveth him." (D. & C. 28:11.)

PENITENCE.

See CONTRITE SPIRIT, HUMILITY, REMORSE, REPENTANCE. *Penitence* implies sorrow and genuine regret for sins; it is a state of mind that makes a person receptive to the gospel message and to full compliance with the law of repentance. (Alma 32:6-8.) Those who do repent become *truly penitent* in the gospel sense. They are the only ones who are able to know and understand the things of God (Alma 26:21), and to receive that full measure of joy which is available to the saints. (Alma 27:17-18; 29:10.) Mercy shall be granted the penitent in the day

of judgment, and *"none but the truly penitent are saved."* (Alma 42:23-24.)

PENTATEUCH.

See PEARL OF GREAT PRICE.

PENTECOST.

See DAY OF PENTECOST.

PERDITION.

See CAIN, DEVIL, SONS OF PERDITION. Two persons, Cain and Satan, have received the awesome name-title *Perdition*. The name signifies that they have no hope whatever of any degree of salvation, that they have wholly given themselves up to iniquity, and that any feeling of righteousness whatever has been destroyed in their breasts. Both had great administrative ability and persuasive power in pre-existence, but both were rebellious and iniquitous from eternity. (D. & C. 76:25-27; 2 Ne. 2:17-18.) Both came out in open rebellion against God having a perfect knowledge that their course was contrary to all righteousness.

Satan was denied a tabernacle for his spirit body, but Cain has gained one, and as a consequence has a position of pre-eminence over the devil. To Cain the Lord said: "Satan desireth to have thee; . . . and it shall be unto thee according to his desire. And thou shalt rule over him; For from this time forth thou shalt be the father of his lies; thou shalt be called Perdition; for thou wast also before the world." (Moses 5:18-25.)

PERFECTION.

See CELESTIAL MARRIAGE, ETERNAL LIFE, EXALTATION, RIGHTEOUSNESS, SANCTIFICATION. *Perfection is of two kinds—finite or mortal, and infinite or eternal. Finite perfection* may be gained by the righteous saints in this life. It consists in living a godfearing life of devotion to the truth, of walking in complete submission to the will of the Lord, and of putting first in one's life the things of the kingdom of God. *Infinite perfection* is reserved for those who overcome all things and inherit the fulness of the Father in the mansions hereafter. It consists in gaining eternal life, the kind of life which God has in the highest heaven within the celestial world.

Many scriptures exhort the saints to be perfect in this life, an attainment which will lead to eternal perfection hereafter, unless by subsequent rebellion and wickedness a departure is made from the strait and narrow path. Even the sanctified are commanded to beware lest they fall from grace. (D. & C. 20:31-34.)

"He that walketh in a perfect way, he shall serve me," the Lord says. (Ps. 101:6.) Ancient Israel was commanded: "Thou shalt be perfect with the Lord thy God." (Deut.

18:13.) Paul wrote about, "them that are perfect" (1 Cor. 2:6); commanded the living saints to, "Be perfect, be of good comfort, be of one mind, live in peace" (2 Cor. 13:11); said modestly that he himself was not "already perfect," but exhorted "as many as be perfect" to "press toward the mark for the prize of the high calling of God in Christ Jesus." (Philip. 3:12-15.) That is, the perfect saints were to endure to the end in righteousness so as to merit the eternal perfection that is assured by such a course.

The rich young man, desiring to find the course leading to eternal life, was given similar counsel by the Master: "If thou wilt be perfect, go and sell that thou hast, and give to the poor, and thou shalt have treasure in heaven: and come and follow me." (Matt. 19:15-22.) After gaining finite perfection and laying up treasures in heaven, he was yet commanded to follow Christ to gain the ultimate goal.

James gave the saints one practical measuring rod whereby their mortal perfection could be measured: "If any man offend not in word, the same is a perfect man, and able also to bridle the whole body." (Jas. 3:2.)

Noah (Gen. 6:9), Seth (D. & C. 107:43), and Job (Job 1:1) are all listed as perfect men. The same would be true of a host of prophets, apostles, and saints in the various dispensations. Alma says "there were many, exceeding great many" who had walked in the path of perfect righteousness before the Lord. (Alma 13:10-12.)

When our Lord told the Jews, "Be ye therefore perfect, *even as your Father which is in heaven is perfect*" (Matt. 5:48), he was speaking of ultimate eternal perfection in his Father's kingdom. After his own resurrection and when "all power" had been given him "in heaven and in earth" (Matt. 28:18), he amplified his exhortation by saying, "I would that ye should be perfect *even as I, or your Father who is in heaven is perfect.*" (3 Ne. 12:48.)

In this supreme sense no one is perfect except the Lord and those who are like him. Joint-heirs with Christ—those who receive, possess, and inherit equally with him in his Father's kingdom—are thus the only ones who attain unto perfection. *"Every one that is perfect shall be as his master."* (Luke 6:40.) They become possessors of all things because they walked in that light which grows "brighter and brighter until the perfect day." (D. & C. 50:24-29.) They overcome all things, inherit all things, gain all that the Father hath, and enjoy the fulness of his kingdom. (D. & C. 76:54-60; 84:33-40; 93:20-28.)

Joseph Smith taught that the attributes of God are knowledge, faith or power, justice, judgment, mercy, and truth. Then as to his perfections he said: "What we mean by perfections is, the perfections which belong to all the attri-

butes of his nature." (*Lectures on Faith,* pp. 42-50.) Thus God is a perfect being because he is the embodiment of all good attributes in their fulness and perfection. Any being who becomes perfect—*"even as your Father which is in heaven is perfect"* (Matt. 5:48), that is who has the kind and extent of perfection enjoyed by Deity—must be like God.

Christ is the example. "He received a fulness of truth, yea, even of all truth" (D. & C. 93:26), so John tells us. That is, the attribute of truth was perfected in him in the eternal sense and there was not anything which he did not know. If men become perfect, they must do so on the same basis, progressing until they gain all truth, all knowledge, and all the attributes of Deity in their perfection. (D. & C. 93:20-28.) Only those who keep all the commandments and for whom the family unit continues in eternity will merit perfection. (D. & C. 131:1-4; 132:16-32.) This kind of perfection comes not by the Levitical Priesthood (Heb. 7:11), nor can we without our worthy dead attain unto this high status. (Heb. 11:40.)

PERILS.
See SIGNS OF THE TIMES.

PERJURY.
See BEARING FALSE WITNESS.

PERSECUTION.

See APOSTASY, C H A S T E N I N G, CHASTISEMENT, HATRED, SIGNS OF THE TIMES. *Persecution* is the heritage of the faithful. As long as mortal conditions prevail among men, the saints may rest assured that *"all that will live godly in Christ Jesus shall suffer persecution."* (2 Tim. 3:12.) This persecution will consist in ill treatment and oppression, in acts of persistent and cruel hostility, heaped upon them because of their religious beliefs. When the true Church is overcome by the world—as it was in the early days of the Christian Era—harsh and bitter persecution slackens, although the divergent groups of Satan's kingdom still quarrel and fight among themselves.

Persecution is a tool of Satan by which he continues among mortal men the war of rebellion he began in pre-existence. He recognizes the true Church, and in his open rebellion does all he can to persuade those who follow him to fight against the truth and to destroy those who believe it. The restored truth is always preached "in the midst of persecution and wickedness" (D. & C. 99:1), and "the fear of persecution and the care of the world" cause many "to reject the word." (D. & C. 40:2.)

In the ultimate sense, Satan is the father of all persecution. He uses it in an attempt to deny men their agency. Obviously he works through mortal persons who hearken to his enticements and who bow to his decrees. From earliest times, individuals, organizations, governments, and churches have become instruments in his hands to carry on projects of persecution. In modern times Hitler chose to persecute the Jewish people and Stalin chose to heap onerous burdens upon whole nations of non-communistic peoples. Both received their inspiration from beneath.

And similarly, when one group of professing worshipers has poured out the bitter draughts of persecution upon another, the source of direction and guidance has been Lucifer. As the author and father of persecution, Satan has been able to bend mortal men to his will proportionately as they have been willing to serve him. Accordingly, as far as persecutions heaped by one group of religionists upon another are concerned, the severest and most wicked persecutions of all the ages have been fostered, promoted, and carried out by those who have the closest ties with the devil. Indeed, it is of the church of the devil which the revelation speaks when it says, she is *"the great persecutor of the church";* she is "the apostate, the whore, even Babylon, that maketh all nations to drink of her cup, in whose hearts the enemy, even Satan, sitteth to reign"; she is the one, after the apostles were "fallen asleep," who sowed the tares with the wheat. (D. & C. 86.)

Indeed, persecution shall cease at the Second Coming because she shall then be destroyed. "That great church, the mother of abominations, that made all nations drink of the wine of the wrath of her fornication, that *persecuteth the saints of God, that shed their blood*—she who sitteth upon many waters, and upon the islands of the sea—behold, she is the tares of the earth; she is bound in bundles; her bands are made strong, no man can loose them; therefore, she is ready to be burned." (D. & C. 88:94.)

Christ (John 5:16), his apostles (John 15:20), and the prophets of all ages have been particular targets of persecution. *"Blessed are they which are persecuted for righteousness' sake: for theirs is the kingdom of heaven. Blessed are ye, when men shall revile you, and persecute you and shall say all manner of evil against you falsely, for my sake. Rejoice, and be exceeding glad: for great is your reward in heaven: for so persecuted they the prophets which were before you."* (Matt. 5:10-12; 3 Ne. 12:10-12.) On the other hand, one of the marks of a true saint is that he does not engage in the persecution of others. (Matt. 5:44; Rom. 12:14; 1 Cor. 4:12; 3 Ne. 12:44.)

Persecutions have the effect of cleansing and perfecting the saints; they are sometimes permitted to come upon the chosen people "in consequence of their transgressions." Yet the true saints have the assurance that the Lord will own them and "will not utterly cast them off." (D. & C. 101:1-9.)

On the other hand: *"Cursed are all those that shall lift up the heel against mine anointed, saith the Lord,* and cry they have sinned when they have not sinned before me, saith the Lord, but have done that which was meet in mine eyes, and which I commanded them. But those who cry transgression do it because they are the servants of sin, and are the children of disobedience themselves.

"And those who swear falsely against my servants, that they might bring them into bondage and death—Wo unto them; because they have offended my little ones they shall be severed from the ordinances of mine house. Their basket shall not be full, their houses and their barns shall perish, and they themselves shall be despised by those that flattered them. They shall not have right to the priesthood, nor their posterity after them from generation to generation. It had been better for them that a millstone had been hanged about their necks, and they drowned in the depth of the sea.

"Wo unto all those that discomfort my people, and drive, and murder, and testify against them, saith the Lord of Hosts; a generation of vipers shall not escape the damnation of hell. Behold, mine eyes see and know all their works, and I have in reserve a swift judgment in the season thereof, for them all; For there is a time appointed for every man, according

as his works shall be." (D. & C. 121:11-25.)

PERSONIFICATION.

See CHRIST, GOD. Deity frequently uses the principle of *personification* in revealing to men the nature and kind of exalted Beings whom they worship as the Father and the Son. That is, the Lord adopts as his own the names of various inanimate objects, as also those of various abstact ideas or desirable attributes, in order to point up particular aspects of his personality and powers. The inanimate objects so named are not God, nor are the ideas or attributes; rather these things typify something about Deity, or certify that he is the embodiment or incarnation of the particular idea or attribute which he chooses to personify.

Thus "God is love" (1 John 4:8), and "God is light." (1 John 1:5.) Christ is "the way, the truth, and the life" (John 14:6), "the resurrection, and the life" (John 11:25), "the life and the light of the world" (D. & C. 11:28), "the Word" (John 1:1), and "the law." (3 Ne. 15:9.) Christ is also named: Holy (Isa. 57:15), Faithful and True (Rev. 19:11), Chosen (Moses 4:2; 7:39), Righteous (Moses 7:45), Rock (Deut. 32:4), Vine (John 15:1-5), Branch (Jer. 23:5-6), Bread of Life (John 6:35), and the Morning Star. (Rev. 22:16.)

Similarly God is faith, repentance, and baptism; or he is integrity, charity, obedience, and sanctification; or he is honor, decency, cleanliness, and sobriety. But none of these things are literal. Where ideas and attributes are concerned Deity is the embodiment and incarnation of them. Where inanimate objects are chosen as his names, they are chosen to teach that as they perform a certain temporal function, so the Lord of heaven performs a similar spiritual function which is symbolized by the temporal. By virtue of this principle of personification our language is greatly enriched and our knowledge of Deity marvelously expanded.

PESTILENCE.

See SIGNS OF THE TIMES.

PETER, JAMES, AND JOHN.

See ANGELS, ELIAS, KEYS OF THE KINGDOM, MELCHIZEDEK PRIESTHOOD, RESTORATION OF THE GOSPEL. From *Peter, James, and John*—Christ's chief ministers in the meridian of time—have come in modern times the powers, keys, and authorities whereby the affairs of God's earthly kingdom are regulated. These three, who were the First Presidency of the Church in their day (D. & C. 81:1-2), received the keys of the kingdom from the Savior, Moses, and Elias on the Mount of Transfiguration. (Matt. 17:1-13; *Teachings,* p. 158.) Then in June, 1829, they appeared to

571

Joseph Smith and Oliver Cowdery and conferred upon them the following three things: 1. The Melchizedek Priesthood; 2. The keys of the kingdom of God, including the great commission to preach the gospel in all the world; and 3. The keys of the dispensation of the fulness of times. (D. & C. 27:12-13; 128:20.) At that appearance, Peter and James were resurrected beings; John was translated.

PETTING.
See SEX IMMORALITY.

PHANTOMS.
See GHOSTS.

PHILANTHROPY.
See ALMSGIVING, CHARITY. *Philanthropy* is the love of mankind, the desire to help them, to better their condition and status; it is commonly exhibited through organized charitable undertakings. Philanthopic feelings are found among decent and upright people everywhere. But in its highest and most perfect form, philanthropy is found in the gospel and exhibited through the programs of the Church. The gospel of Jesus Christ is the perfect system for bettering mankind temporally, spiritually, physically, morally, and in every respect.

PHILOSOPHY.
See GOSPEL, MORMONISM, PLAN OF SALVATION, SALVATION. *"Philosophy is the account which the human mind gives to itself of the constitution of the world,"* says Emerson, the modern philosopher. (Cited, Orson F. Whitney, *Saturday Night Thoughts,* p. 265.) "We shall define philosophy as total perspective, as *mind overspreading life and forging chaos into unity,"* another modern philosopher, Will Durant, says. It includes *"all questions that vitally affect the worth and significance of human life,"* including "the *realm of ethics,* and . . . the *nature of the good life."* (Will Durant, *Mansions of Philosophy,* p. ix.) *"Only philosophy can give us wisdom,"* he also opines. "Philosophy accepts the hard and hazardous task of dealing with problems . . . like *good and evil, beauty and ugliness, order and freedom, life and death."* (Will Durant, *Story of Philosophy,* pp. 2-3.)

Every basic text on philosophy, such as Mr. Durant's *Mansions of Philosophy,* will contain, among other things, discussions relative to: God and immortality; morals, morality, and immorality; matter, life, and mind; existence, ethics, and truth; reason, instinct, and materialism; life and death; love, marriage, and social relations; the quest of happiness; the elements of character; freedom, the function of religion, and Christianity.

It should be evident to everyone

who has even a casual knowledge of God, the gospel, and the laws of salvation, that *philosophy is in effect a religion which, ruling out revelation, attempts to decide eternal realities by reason alone. In large part it is an attempt to explain, Where we came from, Why we are here, and Where we are going, without reference to the revelations of the Almighty.*

Philosophy is a system of general beliefs and views about God, existence, right and wrong, agency, immortality, and so forth—all of which views rule out the true and living God and the revelations that come through his prophets. Philosophers, it is true, may *profess* to believe in God, but their beliefs will be of the apostate variety; they will worship laws, forces, or the ethereal spirit essence described in the creeds of sectarianism.

True philosophy is found only in and through the gospel of Christ. It is a philosophy revealed from heaven. In it firm answers are found to all of the problems of the philosophers of the world. It answers the eternal, Whence? Why? Whither?, of the speculative thinker, and the answers are true because they are the answers of Deity.

PHRENOLOGY.
See FORTUNE TELLING.

PHYSICAL CREATION.
See CREATION.

PHYSICIANS.
See DISEASES, HEALINGS, HEALTH, WORD OF WISDOM. There are two opposite and almost equally unsound views held by many people as to the value and place of *physicians* in society. Most people rely entirely on doctors and medical science where health is concerned and make no attempt to seek the healing power of the Lord. (2 Chron. 16:12.) Some others reject hospitalization and medicinal aid, supposing that it is only by divine aid that health will or can be restored.

Actually, of course, the Lord intends that men should exercise faith in him so as to be healed, but he also intends that men should use the agency and intelligence he has given them, in both preventing and curing sickness. It is proper that the sick should "be nourished with all tenderness, with herbs and mild food." (D. & C. 42:43.) The Book of Mormon speaks "of the excellent qualities of the many plants and roots which God had prepared to remove the cause of diseases." (Alma 46:40.)

It follows that physicians and *nurses* are a valuable and essential part of our society. Indeed, legitimate healing arts have been practiced from early days, and our Lord in his ministry seems to have countenanced the work of physicians. (Luke 4:23.) His statement, "They that be whole need not a physician, but they that are sick" (Matt. 9:12; Mark 2:17; Luke 5:31;

573

Moro. 8:8), though intended to teach a great truth about repentance and baptism, nonetheless is a direct approval of physicians ministering to the sick.

PILGRIMAGES.
See PILGRIMS, SHRINES, WORSHIP. Journeys to shrines for the purpose of worship are called *pilgrimages*. Neither shrines nor pilgrimages are a part of true worship as practiced by the true saints. God is worshiped in spirit and in truth in all places and at all times. (John 4:24.) After the loss of pure Christianity and before the 4th century, apostate Christendom inaugurated the practice of pilgrimages of worship to Bethlehem, the Mount of Olives, and such places.

Aaronic Priesthood boys and others in this dispensation sometimes take organized excursions to historic sites, but such are for historical and recreational purposes; there is no thought that some special virtue will attach to worship by performing it at these places.

PILGRIMS.
See IDUMEA, PLAN OF SALVATION. Literally, a *pilgrim* is a stranger or traveler passing through a field. Thus men are "strangers and pilgrims on the earth," that is, they are strangers here who are traveling from one eternity to the next, from pre-existence to immortality. (D. & C. 45:11-14; Heb. 11:

8-13; 1 Pet. 2:11.) Man's sojourn on earth consitutes the period of his *pilgrimage*. (Gen. 47:9; Ps. 119:54.)

PIONEERS.
See MORMON PIONEERS.

PIOUSNESS.
See REVERENCE.

PIT.
See BOTTOMLESS PIT, HADES, HELL, SHEOL, SPIRIT PRISON. The term *pit* is used as a synonym for the following terms: *hell, hades, sheol, spirit prison.* (Ps. 30:3; 88:4-6.) Each of these has reference to the prisonlike dwelling place of wicked spirits wherein they await their coming forth in the last resurrection. Terming this place *the pit* lays special emphasis on its nature as a prison, a prison in ancient times commonly having been a pit.

Isaiah said of Satan that he should "be brought down to hell, to the sides of the pit." (Isa. 14:15.) Referring to our Lord's future visit to the spirits in prison while his body lay in the tomb (1 Pet. 3:18-21), Isaiah said of the wicked: "They shall be gathered together, as prisoners are gathered in the pit, and shall be shut up in the prison, and after many days shall they be visited." (Isa. 24:22.) Zechariah alluded to the vicarious baptism that frees repentant spirits from their prison when he said: "By the blood of thy covenant I have sent forth thy prisoners out of the pit wherein is no water." (Zech. 9:11.)

PITY.
See COMPASSION.

PLAGUES.
See SIGNS OF THE TIMES.

PLANETS.
See EARTHS.

PLAN OF EXALTATION.
See PLAN OF SALVATION.

PLAN OF REDEMPTION.
See PLAN OF SALVATION.

PLAN OF SALVATION.
See ATONEMENT OF CHRIST, BAPTISM, ENDURING TO THE END, FAITH, GIFT OF THE HOLY GHOST, GOSPEL, JUDGMENT DAY, KINGDOMS OF GLORY, MORTALITY, OBEDIENCE, PERFECTION, PRE-EXISTENCE, REDEMPTION, REPENTANCE, RESURRECTION, SALVATION, SALVATION FOR THE DEAD. "God himself," the Prophet says, "finding he was in the midst of spirits and glory, because he was more intelligent, saw proper to institute laws whereby the rest could have a privilege to advance like himself.

The relationship we have with God places us in a situation to advance in knowledge. He has power to institute laws to instruct the weaker intelligences, that they may be exalted with himself, so that they might have one glory upon another, and all that knowledge, power, glory, and intelligence, which is requisite in order to save them in the world of spirits." (*Teachings,* p. 354.) Thus the *plan of salvation* (of redemption, and of exaltation) comprises all of the laws, ordinances, principles, and doctrines by conformity to which the spirit offspring of God have power to progress to the high state of exaltation enjoyed by the Father.

The plan of salvation was ordained by the Father. It is not the plan of Christ or of Adam or any of the other of the Father's children. Rather, it was ordained by the Father so that Christ his Firstborn Spirit Son and all the rest of his spirit offspring could progress to exaltation. The Firstborn accepted and conformed to the plan of the Father—"Father, thy will be done, and the glory be thine forever" (Moses 4:2)—as did all the rest of his righteous spirit children; and all played their respective and assigned parts in carrying the great plan forward.

Training for eventual salvation began for each person at the time of his spirit birth. Following a long period of pre-existent, probationary schooling, this earth was created to be a place where the hosts of spirits who kept their first estate might come, receive mortal bodies, and undergo further testing and trials. (Moses 4:1-4; Abra. 3:22-28.)

At death the eternal spirits go to a spirit sphere to gain further experience and then finally they come up in the resurrection, stand before the judgment bar, and are awarded their places in the kingdoms of glory which are prepared. (Alma 40; 41; D. & C. 76.) Christ is the Redeemer as a result of whose atoning sacrifice the terms and conditions of this great plan of redemption become operative for the remainder of mankind, many of whom also play lesser parts in the great scheme and plan of the Father.

The plan of salvation, for men in this life, is the gospel of Jesus Christ. It comprises all of the laws, ordinances, and performances by conformity to which mortal man is empowered to gain eternal life in the kingdom of God. Since the fall of Adam, man has been carnal, sensual, and devilish by nature. (Moses 5:13; 6:49; Alma 42:10; Mosiah 16:1-4; D. & C. 20:20.) By conforming to the plan of salvation, man has power to put off the natural man, to be born again as a new creature of the Holy Ghost, and to become "a saint through the atonement of Christ the Lord." (Mosiah 3:16-19.)

The steps in this plan are: 1. Faith in the Lord Jesus Christ; 2. Repentance; 3. Baptism by immersion under the hands of a legal administrator; 4. The laying on of hands for the gift of the Holy Ghost, also under the hands of a legal administrator; and 5. Enduring in righteousness to the end of the mortal probation. (Fourth Article of Faith; 2 Ne. 9:23-24, 31; 3 Ne. 27:19-21; D. & C. 20:29.)

PLANTS.
See ANIMALS.

PLATES OF ETHER.
See GOLD PLATES.

PLATES OF MORMON.
See GOLD PLATES.

PLATES OF NEPHI.
See GOLD PLATES.

PLAYING CARDS.
See CARD PLAYING.

PLURALITY OF GODS.
See ADAM-GOD THEORY, CHRIST, FALSE GODS, FATHER IN HEAVEN, GODHEAD, GODHOOD, HOLY GHOST, POLYTHEISM. Three separate personages—Father, Son, and Holy Ghost—comprise the Godhead. As each of these persons is a God, it is evident, from this standpoint alone, that a *plurality of Gods* exists. To us, speaking in the proper finite sense, these three are the only Gods

we worship. But in addition there is an infinite number of holy personages, drawn from worlds without number, who have passed on to exaltation and are thus gods.

Paul taught, "There be gods many, and lords many," adding that "to us there is but one God, the Father, of whom are all things, and we in him; and one Lord Jesus Christ, by whom are all things, and we by him. Howbeit there is not in every man that knowledge." (1 Cor. 8:4-7; D. & C. 121:28-32.) The Prophet commenting on this passage said: "Paul had no allusion to the heathen gods. I have it from God, and get over it if you can. I have a witness of the Holy Ghost, and a testimony that Paul had no allusion to the heathen gods in the text." (*Teachings,* p. 371.)

The Prophet also taught—in explaining John's statement, "And hath made us kings and priests unto *God and his Father*" (Rev. 1:6)—that there is "a god above the Father of our Lord Jesus Christ. . . . *If Jesus Christ was the Son of God, and John discovered that God the Father of Jesus Christ had a Father, you may suppose that he had a Father also.* Where was there ever a son without a father? And where was there ever a father without first being a son? Whenever did a tree or anything spring into existence without a progenitor? And everything comes in this way. Paul says that which is earthly is in the likeness of that which is heavenly. Hence

if Jesus had a Father, can we not believe that *he* had a Father also?" (*Teachings,* pp. 370-373.)

Indeed, this doctrine of plurality of Gods is so comprehensive and glorious that it reaches out and embraces every exalted personage. Those who attain exaltation are gods. "Go and read the vision in the Book of Covenants," the Prophet said. "There is clearly illustrated glory upon glory—one glory of the sun, another glory of the moon, and a glory of the stars; and as one star differeth from another star in glory, even so do they of the telestial world differ in glory, and *every man who reigns in celestial glory is a God to his dominions. . . . They who obtain a glorious resurrection from the dead are exalted far above principalities, powers, thrones, dominions, and angels, and are expressly declared to be heirs of God and joint-heirs with Jesus Christ, all having eternal power."* (*Teachings,* p. 374.)

PLURAL MARRIAGE.

See ADULTERY, ARTICLE ON MARRIAGE, CELESTIAL MARRIAGE, CHASTITY, CONCUBINES, KEYS OF THE KINGDOM, MANIFESTO, PRIESTHOOD, SEALING POWER. According to the Lord's law of marriage, it is lawful that a man have only one wife at a time, unless by revelation the Lord commands plurality of wives in the new and everlasting covenant. (D. & C. 49:15-17.) Speaking of "the doctrine of plurality of wives," the Prophet said: "I hold the keys of this power in the last days; for there is never but one on earth at a time on whom the power and its keys are conferred; and I have constantly said *no man shall have but one wife at a time, unless the Lord directs otherwise."* (*Teachings,* p. 324.)

The Lord, by the mouth of his Prophet Jacob, gave similar direction to the Nephites: "For there shall not any man among you have save it be one wife; and concubines he shall have none; For I, the Lord God, delight in the chastity of women. And whoredoms are an abomination before me; thus saith the Lord of Hosts. Wherefore, this people shall keep my commandments, saith the Lord of Hosts, or cursed be the land for their sakes. For *if I will, saith the Lord of Hosts, raise up seed unto me, I will command my people; otherwise they shall hearken unto these things."* (Jacob 2:27-30.)

From such fragmentary scriptural records as are now available, we learn that the Lord did command some of his ancient saints to practice plural marriage. Abraham, Isaac, and Jacob—among others (D. & C. 132)—conformed to this ennobling and exalting principle; the whole history of ancient Israel was one in which plurality of wives was a divinely accepted and approved order of matrimony. Those who entered this order at the Lord's command, and who kept the laws and conditions appertaining to it, have gained for themselves eternal exaltation in the highest heaven of the celestial world.

In the early days of this dispensation, as part of the promised restitution of all things, the Lord revealed the principle of *plural marriage* to the Prophet. Later the Prophet and leading brethren were commanded to enter into the practice, which they did in all virtue and purity of heart despite the consequent animosity and prejudices of worldly people. After Brigham Young led the saints to the Salt Lake Valley, plural marriage was openly taught and practiced until the year 1890. At that time conditions were such that the Lord *by revelation* withdrew the command to continue the practice, and President Wilford Woodruff issued the Manifesto directing that it cease. (*Discourses of Wilford Woodruff,* pp. 213-218.) Obviously the holy practice will commence again after the Second Coming of the Son of Man and the ushering in of the millennium. (Isa. 4.)

Plural marriage is not essential to salvation or exaltation. Nephi and his people were denied the power to have more than one wife and yet they could gain every blessing in eternity that the Lord ever offered to any people. In our day, the Lord summarized by revelation the whole doctrine of exaltation and predicated it upon the marriage of one man to one woman. (D. & C. 132:1-28.) Thereafter he added the principles relative to plurality of wives with the express stipulation that any such marriages would be valid only if authorized by the President of the Church. (D. & C. 132:7, 29-66.)

All who pretend or assume to engage in plural marriage in this day, when the one holding the keys has withdrawn the power by which they are performed, are guilty of gross wickedness.

POLITENESS.
See COURTESY.

POLYGAMY.
See PLURAL MARRIAGE.

POLYTHEISM.
See APOSTASY, ATHEISM, DEISM, FALSE GODS, GOD, HENOTHEISM, MONOTHEISM, PLURALITY OF GODS, THEISM. Primitive and pagan peoples often believe in and worship many supposed gods. They imagine that there are gods of birth, marriage, and death, of war and peace, of the mountains, forests, and plains, and so forth.

It is falsely supposed by uninspired religious scholars that Yahweh or Jehovah was the tribal God of the Hebrew peoples, that he gradually came to have pre-eminence over the gods of other nations, and that he was finally accepted as the One Supreme Being. The fact is, however, that monotheism did not grow out of

polytheism, rather polytheistic concepts are apostate perversions of the original truth about God which was revealed to Adam and the ancient patriarchs.

It should be remembered that polytheism has reference to pagan deities to whom reverence, devotion, and worship are given. It is not to be confused with the gospel truth that there are "gods many, and lords many, But to us there is but one God, the Father, . . . and one Lord Jesus Christ." (1 Cor. 8:4-7.) The saints are not polytheists.

POOR.
See ALMSGIVING, CHURCH WELFARE PLAN, RICHES. In the present worldly state of things, there will always be *poor* people, those who do not have sufficient of this world's goods to satisfy their just needs and wants. Provision is always made by true saints for the care of their less economically fortunate brethren. In modern times this is done primarily through the great Church Welfare Plan.

Whether people are rich or poor ordinarily does not establish whether they are righteous or wicked. The wealthy and the poverty stricken are found both in and out of the Church; and the Lord in his infinite wisdom tests various of his saints with the perils of poorness and others with the snares of worldly riches. It is true, however, as the entire Nephite history testifies, that when the saints become rich in worldly wealth, they frequently become proud and haughty and fall into apostate practices and evils. *It seems to be harder for a rich man to keep the commandments and gain salvation than it is for a poor man.* (Matt. 19:16-26.)

The "poor of this world" who are "rich in faith" are "heirs of the kingdom" and shall be saved (Jas. 2:1-9); the unrighteous poor, however, shall be damned. The righteous poor shall not remain so forever, for in eternity they shall inherit the earth and all things shall be theirs. (D. & C. 88:17-22.) "Wo unto you poor men, whose hearts are not broken, whose spirits are not contrite, and whose bellies are not satisfied, and whose hands are not stayed from laying hold upon other men's goods, whose eyes are full of greediness, and who will not labor with your own hands! *But blessed are the poor who are pure in heart, whose hearts are broken, and whose spirits are contrite, for they shall see the kingdom of God coming in power and great glory unto their deliverance; for the fatness of the earth shall be theirs.* For behold, the Lord shall come, and his recompense shall be with him, and he shall reward every man, and the poor shall rejoice; And their generations shall inherit the earth from generation to generation, forever and ever." (D. & C. 56:17-20.)

POTENTATE.
See CHRIST, KING, RULER. Christ "is the blessed and only *Potentate*" (1 Tim. 6:15), meaning that all earthly power of kings and rulers shall in due course fade away, and he shall stand as the only supreme Sovereign and Ruler of all mankind.

POTTER.
See CHRIST. Christ is the great *Potter* (Jer. 18:1-6), meaning that he governs in the affairs of men so as to mould and shape earthen human vessels into vessels of honor and service to him. "We are the clay, and thou our potter; and we all are the work of thy hand." (Isa. 64:8.) "O house of Israel, cannot I do with you as this potter?" he asked. "Behold, as the clay is in the potter's hand, so are ye in mine hand, O house of Israel." (Jer. 18:6.)

Similarly, as is sometimes done, our Lord might be described as the great Physician, Healer, Engineer, Chief Scout, Foreman, Builder, or the like—all showing his pre-eminence in the field concerned, and all pointing attention to his power to deal in the spiritual field with human souls as these mortal counterparts deal in their temporal pursuits.

POVERTY.
See POOR.

POWER.
See OMNIPOTENCE.

PRAISE THE LORD.
See HALLELUJAH.

PRAYER.
See AMEN, FAITH, FASTING, GOD, HALLELUJAH, MUSIC, NAME OF CHRIST, PRAYER BOOKS, REVERENCE, SACRAMENT MEETINGS, THANKSGIVING, WORSHIP. To *pray* is to speak with God, either vocally or by forming the thoughts involved in the mind. *Prayers* may properly include expressions of praise, thanksgiving, and adoration; they are the solemn occasions during which the children of God petition their Eternal Father for those things, both temporal and spiritual, which they feel are needed to sustain them in all the varied tests of this mortal probation. Prayers are occasions of confession—occasions when in humility and contrition, having broken hearts and contrite spirits, the saints confess their sins to Deity and implore him to grant his cleansing forgiveness.

Prayer has been a part of the gospel from the beginning. "Thou shalt do all that thou doest in the name of the Son," an angel declared to Adam, "and thou shalt repent and *call upon God in the name of the Son forevermore.*"

(Moses 5:8.) This course is essential if men are to be saved; there is no salvation without prayer. How could a man set his heart on righteousness, so as to work out his salvation, without communing by prayer with him who is the author of righteousness?

Prayers of the saints are expected to conform to a prescribed standard of divine excellence; they should fit into the approved pattern of proper prayer. They are to be addressed to the Father, should always be made in the name of Jesus Christ; must be reverential and worshipful in nature, which requirement includes use of the *language of prayer* (the pronouns *thee* and *thine*, for instance, never *you* and *your*); and above all they must be offered in sincerity of heart, with real intent and purpose, and must come from the lips of those who have broken hearts and contrite spirits; and finally, they should be closed with the word *Amen.* As a token of reverence and respect, when occasion permits, they should be made from a kneeling position.

There is nothing in the gospel that is better designed to keep the attention of men centered on God, on righteousness, and on their duties than is prayer. Every thought, word, and act is influenced or governed by the nature and extent of one's communion through prayer with Deity. Over and over again the revelations command: Watch and pray always, lest ye enter into temptation. (Matt. 26:41; Mark 13:33; 14:38; Luke 21:36; 22:40, 46; D. & C. 10:5.) "Ye must pray always, and not faint," Nephi told his brethren. *"Ye must not perform any thing unto the Lord save in the first place ye shall pray unto the Father in the name of Christ, that he will consecrate thy performance unto thee, that thy performance may be for the welfare of thy soul."* (2 Ne. 32:9.)

It is common to classify prayers as *public* and *private* or *secret*. *Family prayers* and those offered as *blessings on the food* at mealtime would be considered private prayers. Those spoken at formal gatherings, and in which one person acts as mouth for the congregation, are *public prayers*. An opening prayer in a formal meeting is sometimes called the *invocation* (because the blessings of the Lord upon that particular meeting are being sought or invoked), and the closing prayer is often referred to as the *benediction* (because a final short statement of blessing and comfort is being made).

Certain proprieties attend the offering of all prayers. Public prayers, in particular, should be *short* and ordinarily should contain no expressions except those which pertain to the needs and circumstances surrounding the particular meeting then involved. They are not sermons or occasions to disclose the oratorical or linguistic abilities of the one acting as mouth.

Unfortunately the all too common practice in the Church in conference sessions, sacrament meetings, and the like, is for those saying the prayers to take entirely too much time and pray about too many matters not directly involved in the particular meeting. One's own *secret prayers* can be as long as the individual cares to make them; Enos, for instance, took occasion to pray all day and on into the night. (Enos 4.)

President Francis M. Lyman, speaking of the proprieties attending the offering of prayers by the saints, gave this wise counsel: "Latter-day Saints, I presume, have learned to feel and appreciate the importance of prayer, equally to any other people. But like the saints in the days of the Savior, we sometimes need some suggestions to aid us in our family prayers, in our prayers for opening and closing meetings of various kinds, our prayers in the blessing of the sacrament, and our prayers in ordaining and confirming. There are a great variety of prayers that the elders of Israel are expected to offer up day after day. In a revelation given to Brother Joseph, the Lord announced that those who did not attend to their prayers in due season, should be had in remembrance before the common judge. (D. & C. 68:33.)

"Family prayers should be attended to in every household, and in these prayers, as in all others, we should remember the injunction of the Savior, that we should not do as the heathen do, indulge in vain repetition, or feel that we are to be heard because of our much speaking.

"Prayers should be offered under the direction and inspiration of the Almighty. Every elder in Israel, should learn to subject himself to the Spirit of the Lord, in all his prayers, and in all the ordinances of the gospel.

"The morning prayer should be suited to the circumstances and conditions of the family, whatever they are. The circumstances of the family differ from morning to morning and from evening to evening, almost as much as our meetings vary. And it is quite suitable that when we meet together, for the transaction of business in the interests of the saints of God, and the interests of the kingdom, we should offer up a prayer to the Lord, and ask his blessings upon us in our labor, and in our counsel. It would not be suitable, of course, for us to offer up a business prayer in the opening of a conference, or in the opening of a ward or a priesthood meeting. *A prayer should be suited to the occasion,* just as we suit an ordination to the circumstances.

"In the opening of meetings, such as conferences, the brother should at one thought and glance take in the situation and ask the Lord to bless us according to what the meeting is.

"In dismissing, we should ask the blessings of the Lord upon the congregation, and what has been said, and commit ourselves to the care of the Lord.

"It is not necessary to offer very long and tedious prayers, either at opening or closing. It is not only not pleasing to the Lord for us to use excess of words, but also it is not pleasing to the Latter-day Saints. *Two minutes will open any kind of meeting, and a half minute will close it.*

"We ought to take into account the occasion, and let the prayer be suited exactly to it. Sometimes our habits may control us more strongly than the Spirit of the Lord, so we should consider these things. *Offer short prayers, and avoid vain repetitions, particularly the repetition of the name of Deity, and the name of the Savior.* It is quite common to open a prayer in the name of Jesus Christ, to close it in his name, and possibly use his name a few times through the prayer. *If we approach the Father, and offer our petitions to him, and then close in the name of Jesus Christ, it is sufficient. There is no prayer so great and important that it is necessary to use more than once the name of the Son of God and of the Father.*

"And let this be a never-forgotten lesson to the young men in Israel, and to all others, that whenever an elder stands up to speak to the people, all hearts of those who have faith in the gospel shall offer up a silent prayer, asking God to bless his servant with the Holy Spirit.

"Avoid praying to be seen or heard of men, but let your prayers be unto the Lord. If you pray to open a meeting, one propriety is to speak loud enough for all to hear. And the same when the sacrament is administered.

"Understand the proprieties in prayer, and shun the improprieties." (*Improvement Era,* vol. 50, pp. 214, 245.)

"Pray in your families unto the Father, always in my name," our Lord said, "that your wives and your children may be blessed." (3 Ne. 18:21.) It is the counsel of the Church that family prayer should take place twice daily, ordinarily before the morning and evening meals.

It is a common practice among the saints, particularly in families having children who need training in praying, to offer one prayer as a family prayer and another one as a blessing on the food. The family prayer is offered while kneeling around the table, the blessing on the food while sitting at the table. There is, of course, no impropriety, particularly where one or two adults only are involved, in including the blessing on the food in the formal family prayer.

Individuals or groups of Latter-day Saints when eating in public places, if conditions are sufficiently quiet and reverential, may with propriety offer a blessing on the food. If circumstances are such that it does not seem appropriate

so to do, however, the food is eaten with a thankful heart, and it is considered that the private prayers of the individuals concerned have already asked for all of the blessings needed for that particular day.

Each individual should, of course, have his own *secret prayers,* ordinarily night and morning. The scriptures speak of prayers "morning, mid-day, and evening." (Alma 34:21; Ps. 55:17; Dan. 6:10.) The command, *Pray always,* means a prayer should always be in the hearts of the faithful and that frequent secret prayers should be spoken.

Our Lord's instruction to the Nephites was: "Verily, verily, I say unto you, ye must *watch and pray always,* lest ye be tempted by the devil, and ye be led away captive by him. And as I have prayed among you even so shall ye pray in my church, among my people who do repent and are baptized in my name. Behold I am the light; I have set an example for you. . . . Behold, verily, verily, I say unto you, ye must watch and pray always lest ye enter into temptation; for Satan desireth to have you, that he may sift you as wheat. Therefore ye must always pray unto the Father in my name; *And whatsoever ye shall ask the Father in my name, which is right, believing that ye shall receive, behold it shall be given unto you."* (3 Ne. 18: 15-20.)

To be binding and efficacious prayer must be offered in faith and with real intent. "For behold, God hath said a man being evil cannot do that which is good; for if he offereth a gift, or prayeth unto God, except he shall do it with real intent it profiteth him nothing. For behold, it is not counted unto him for righteousness. . . . And likewise also is it counted evil unto a man, if he shall pray and not with real intent of heart; yea, and it profiteth him nothing, for *God receiveth none such.*" (Moro. 7:6-9.) Rather men are commanded to "pray unto the Father with all the energy" of their hearts, with all the strength that their whole souls possess. (Moro. 7:48.)

"And when thou prayest thou shalt not do as the hypocrites, for they love to pray, standing in the synagogues and in the corners of the streets, that they may be seen of men. Verily I say unto you, they have their reward. But thou, when thou prayest, enter into thy closet, and when thou hast shut thy door, pray to thy Father who is in secret; and thy Father, who seeth in secret, shall reward thee openly. But when ye pray, *use not vain repetitions,* as the heathen, for they think that they shall be heard for their much speaking. Be not ye therefore like unto them, for your Father knoweth what things ye have need of before ye ask him.

"After this manner therefore pray ye: Our Father who art in heaven, hallowed be thy name. Thy will be done on earth as it is in heaven. And forgive us our debts, as we forgive our debtors. And lead us not into temptation, but deliver us from evil. For thine is the kingdom, and the power, and the glory, forever. Amen." (3 Ne. 13:5-13; Matt. 6:5-13.)

"Do not pray as the Zoramites do, for ye have seen that they pray to be heard of men, and to be praised for their wisdom. Do not say: O God, I thank thee that we are better than our brethren; but rather say: *O Lord, forgive my unworthiness, and remember my brethren in mercy*—yea, acknowledge your unworthiness before God at all times." (Alma 38:13-14.) Further: "Pray for them who despitefully use you and persecute you." (3 Ne. 12:44; Matt. 5:44.)

Those formal, written prayers which are commonly read by ministers, and those recited by lay church members in doing penance or seeking grace, are devoid of the true spirit of prayer and should be shunned. Frequently they are spoken without real intent; and their use keeps men from searching their own hearts in an attempt to pray in faith according to an approved pattern so that actual blessings may be gained from Deity. Not infrequently these prepared prayers are read, recited, or chanted in ritualistic ceremonies in which the speakers do not concentrate all the faculties of their whole souls upon the prayers being offered. As a consequence the words often take on the nature of useless jargon and do not open the door to the receipt of the Lord's blessings.

What blessings should be sought by prayer? Amulek has given this inspired answer: "Call upon his holy name, that he would have mercy upon you; Yea, cry unto him for mercy; for he is mighty to save. Yea, humble yourselves, and continue in prayer unto him. Cry unto him when ye are in your fields, yea, over all your flocks. Cry unto him in your houses, yea, over all your household, both morning, mid-day, and evening. Yea, cry unto him against the power of your enemies. Yea, cry unto him against the devil, who is an enemy to all righteousness. Cry unto him over the crops of your fields, that ye may prosper in them. Cry over the flocks of your fields, that they may increase. But this is not all; ye must pour out your souls in your closets, and your secret places, and in your wilderness. *Yea, and when you do not cry unto the Lord, let your hearts be full, drawn out in prayer unto him continually for your welfare,* and also for the welfare of those who are around you." Then, in effect, he counsels that men must live as they pray and work the works of righteousness in order to gain the blessings for which they pray. (Alma 34:17-29.)

Perfect prayers are those which are inspired, in which the Spirit reveals the words which should be used. (3 Ne. 19:24.) *"And if ye are purified and cleansed from all sin, ye shall ask whatsoever you will in the name of Jesus and it shall be done. But know this, it shall be given you what you shall ask."* (D. & C. 50:29-30.)

Jesus spoke the greatest prayers ever uttered, prayers so much beyond the interpretative power of mere words that they were not recorded. "He himself also knelt upon the earth," the record says, "and behold he prayed unto the Father, and the things which he prayed cannot be written, and the multitude did bear record who heard him. And after this manner do they bear record: The eye hath never seen, neither hath the ear heard, before, so great and marvelous things as we saw and heard Jesus speak unto the Father; And no tongue can speak, neither can there be written by any man, neither can the hearts of men conceive so great and marvelous things as we both saw and heard Jesus speak; and no one can conceive of the joy which filled our souls at the time we heard him pray for us unto the Father." (3 Ne. 17:15-17.)

Among recorded prayers those uttered by our Lord are the greatest. The *Lord's Prayer* stands as a model of perfect expression. (3 Ne. 13:9-13; Matt. 6:9-13.) The *high priestly* or *intercessory prayer,* as it has variously been called, though the record we have is obviously fragmentary, ranks as a superlative example of divine prayer. (John 17.) Similar intercessory pleadings were made on behalf of the Nephites. (3 Ne. 19.)

There are a few approved formal written prayers in the Church. These include *dedicatory prayers* offered when temples are presented to the Lord—the prayer of dedication for the Kirtland Temple being given by direct revelation (D. & C. 109)—and the *sacramental prayers* which are always spoken exactly as found in the revelation. (D. & C. 20:77-79.) Other than formal revealed prayers, it is the practice of the saints to pray extemporaneously, the one acting as mouth striving for the best inspiration he can get in each instance.

Every good gift comes to those who through faith and prayer are enabled to abide the law upon which its receipt is predicated. All things both temporal and spiritual are available in this way. The First Vision and many of the great revelations of this dispensation came as a direct result of fervent prayer. "The Spirit shall be given unto you by the prayer of faith." (D. & C. 42:14.) Salvation itself is a fruit of prayer. "Pray one for another, that ye may be healed. The effectual fervent prayer of a righteous man availeth much." (Jas. 5:16.) "He that observeth not his prayers before the Lord in the season thereof, let him be had in remembrance before the judge of my people." (D. & C. 68:33.)

churches publish *prayer books* containing prayers and other forms for use in public and private worship. These formal prayers violate the true spirit and purpose of prayer, do not lead professing worshipers along the path leading to salvation, and are conducive of that state of mind which keeps praying people from struggling for that faith and inspiration which will benefit them spiritually.

Nearly all prayers recorded in prayer books are formalistic and ritualistic and have little or no application to the personal problems and needs of the penitent persons who seek and desire the Lord's guidance. As an indication of how far removed most of them are from the true form of prayer is the fact that many of them are not made in the name of Christ, while others are addressed directly to Christ or to the Holy Ghost rather than to the Father. In this connection it is worthy of note that among Catholics it is a common, accepted, and approved practice to address prayers to various of their saints with the hope that the advocate so addressed will intercede for or mediate the cause of the petitioner.

PREACHING.
   See SERMONS.

PRAYER BOOKS.
   See APOSTASY, PRAYER. Many

PRE-ADAMITES.
   See FIRST MAN.

PREDESTINATION.

See AGENCY, FOREORDINATION. *Predestination* is a sectarian substitute for the true doctrine of *foreordination*. Just as Lucifer "sought to destroy the agency of man" in pre-existence (Moses 4:3), so through his ministers here he has taught a doctrine, based on scriptural distortions, of salvation and damnation without choice on the part of the individual. Predestination is the false doctrine that from all eternity God has ordered whatever comes to pass, having especial and particular reference to the salvation or damnation of souls. Some souls, according to this false concept, are irrevocably chosen for salvation, others for damnation; and there is said to be nothing any individual can do to escape his predestined inheritance in heaven or in hell as the case may be.

"Predestination to Life is the everlasting purpose of God," say the *Articles of Religion* of the Anglican Church, "whereby (before the foundations of the world were laid) he hath constantly decreed by his counsel secret to us, to deliver from curse and damnation those whom he hath chosen in Christ out of mankind, and to bring them by Christ to everlasting salvation, as vessels made to honour. Wherefore, they which be endued with so excellent a benefit of God be called according to God's purpose by his Spirit working in due season: they through Grace obey the calling: they be justified freely: they be made sons of God by adoption: they be made like the image of his only-begotten Son Jesus Christ: they walk religiously in good works, and at length, by God's mercy, they attain to everlasting felicity.

"As the godly consideration of Predestination, and our Election in Christ, is full of sweet, pleasant, and unspeakable comfort to godly persons, and such as feel in themselves the working of the Spirit of Christ, mortifying the works of the flesh, and their earthly members, and drawing up their mind to high and heavenly things, as well because it doth greatly establish and confirm their faith of eternal Salvation to be enjoyed through Christ, as because it doth fervently kindle their love towards God: So, for curious and carnal persons, lacking the Spirit of Christ, to have continually before their eyes the sentence of God's Predestination, is a most dangerous downfall, whereby the Devil doth thrust them either into desperation, or into wretchlessness of most unclean living, no less perilous than desperation."

Having thus set forth a doctrine, so patently contrary to sense and reason, that men through no acts of their own are predestined either to salvation or damnation, the *Articles of Religion,* almost by way of apologizing for such an absurd concept, conclude with these words: "Furthermore, we must receive

God's promises in such wise, as they be generally set forth to us in holy Scripture: and, in our doings, that Will of God is to be followed, which we have expressly declared unto us in the Word of God." (*Book of Common Prayer,* Anglican Church of Canada, pp. 665-666.)

It is true that the words *predestinate and predestinated* are found in the King James translation of some of Paul's writings (Rom. 8:29-30; Eph. 1:5, 11), but Biblical revisions use the words *foreordain* and *foreordained,* which more accurately convey Paul's views. However, even as the King James Version renders the passages, there is no intimation of any compulsion or denial of free agency, for one of the dictionary definitions of foreordination is predestination, meaning the prior appointment (in pre-existence) of particular persons to perform designated labors or gain particular rewards.

PRE-EXISTENCE.

See AGENCY, COUNCIL IN HEAVEN, ELECTION OF GRACE, FATHER IN HEAVEN, FIRST ESTATE, FOREORDINATION, INTELLIGENCES, MOTHER IN HEAVEN, SPIRIT BIRTH, SPIRIT BODIES, SPIRIT CHILDREN, SPIRIT ELEMENT, STARS OF HEAVEN, WAR IN HEAVEN. *Pre-existence* is the term commonly used to describe the *pre-mortal existence* of the spirit children of God the Father. Speaking of this prior existence in a spirit sphere, the First Presidency of the Church (Joseph F. Smith, John R. Winder, and Anthon H. Lund) said: "All men and women are in the similitude of *the universal Father and Mother,* and are literally the sons and daughters of Deity"; as spirits they were the "offspring of *celestial parentage." (Man: His Origin and Destiny,* pp. 351, 355.) These spirit beings, the offspring of exalted parents, were men and women, appearing in all respects as mortal persons do, excepting only that their spirit bodies were made of a more pure and refined substance than the elements from which mortal bodies are made. (Ether 3:16; D. & C. 131:7-8.)

To understand the doctrine of pre-existence two great truths must be accepted: 1. That God is a personal Being in whose image man is created, an exalted, perfected, and glorified Man of Holiness (Moses 6:57), and not a spirit essence that fills the immensity of space; and 2. That matter or element is self-existent and eternal in nature, creation being merely the organization and reorganization of that substance which "was not created or made, neither indeed can be." (D. & C. 93:29.) Unless God the Father was a personal Being, he could not have begotten spirits in his image, and if there had been no self-existent spirit element, there would have been no substance from which those spirit bodies could have been organized.

From the time of their spirit birth, the Father's pre-existent offspring were endowed with agency and subjected to the provisions of the laws ordained for their government. They had power to obey or disobey and to progress in one field or another. "The first principles of man are self-existent with God," the Prophet said. "God himself, finding he was in the midst of spirits and glory, because he was more intelligent, saw proper to institute laws whereby the rest could have a privilege to advance like himself." (*Teachings,* p. 354.)

The pre-existent life was thus a period—undoubtedly an infinitely long one—of probation, progression, and schooling. The spirit hosts were taught and given experiences in various administrative capacities. Some so exercised their agency and so conformed to law as to become "noble and great"; these were foreordained before their mortal births to perform great missions for the Lord in this life. (Abra. 3:22-28.) Christ, the Firstborn, was the mightiest of all the spirit children of the Father. (D. & C. 93:21-23.) Mortal progression and testing is a continuation of what began in pre-existence.

Every form of life had an existence in a spirit form before being born on this earth. (Moses 3:5-7.) In each instance the spirit creation was "in the likeness of that which is temporal; . . . the spirit of man in the likeness of his person, as also the spirit of the beast, and every other creature which God has created." (D. & C. 77:2.)

PREJUDICE.
See APOSTASY. *Prejudice* is a preconceived judgment, usually unreasoning and biased in nature, which is based on insufficient knowledge. It is one of the chief tools of Satan. By it he keeps the minds of the whole sectarian and pagan worlds so riveted on their false creeds and myths that most people resist the light of restored truth when it shines plainly before them. Indeed, few things are more self-damning, more destructive of progress, more conducive to apostasy and spiritual darkness, than the smothering mantle of prejudice which now envelopes almost the whole earth. The continual prayer of the saints is that the prejudices of the world "may give way before the truth," so that the gospel cause may roll forth. (D. & C. 109:56.)

Unfortunately prejudice exists to some extent even within the Church, with the result that perfect oneness and unity does not yet prevail among the saints; and there are sometimes resultant instances of unfairness and inequity in the operation of certain programs and the treatment of individuals. True saints learn to live above these little difficulties and to cast prejudices out of their minds so that they more effectively may aid in rolling forth the Lord's great latter-day work.

PRE-MORTAL LIFE.
See PRE-EXISTENCE.

PREPARATORY GOSPEL.
See GOSPEL.

PRESBYTERS.
See ELDERS.

PRESIDENCY.
See BISHOPRIC, COUNSELORS, FIRST COUNCIL OF SEVENTY, FIRST PRESIDENCY, GENERAL AUTHORITIES, KEYS OF THE KINGDOM, QUORUM PRESIDENTS, STAKE PRESIDENTS. Operation of the Church and kingdom of God on earth is upon the principle of *presidency*. That is, the Lord selects and the saints sustain presidencies to direct the affairs of the various church organizations. Members of these presidencies are given the keys of their respective callings, by virtue of which they are empowered to preside over and direct the affairs of the organization concerned.

Except in special cases, the powers of presidency are exercised by a president and two counselors. The supreme powers of presidency rest with the First Presidency of the Church. Upon the disorganization (by death of the President) of this highest quorum in the Church, the Council of the Twelve operates as the First Presidency, pending the time that the Presidency as such is formally reorganized.

Stake presidencies preside over stakes, ward bishoprics over wards, quorum presidencies over quorums, and auxiliary organization presidencies (in some instances called superintendencies) over the respective auxiliary organizations. Except where the General Authorities of the Church are concerned, it is the practice of the Church to rotate the privilege and responsibility of organization presidency so that many brethren and sisters of proved worthiness and leadership may enjoy the blessings of service in God's kingdom.

PRESIDENT OF THE AARONIC PRIESTHOOD.
See PRESIDING BISHOP.

PRESIDENT OF THE CHURCH.
See APOSTOLIC SUCCESSION, FIRST PRESIDENCY, HIGH PRIESTS, PROPHETS, REVELATORS, SEERS. Upon the President of the Church the Almighty bestows the highest office and the greatest gifts that mortal man is capable of receiving. He is the earthly head of the kingdom of God, the supreme officer of the Church, the "President of the High Priesthood of the Church; Or, in other words, the Presiding High Priest over the High Priesthood of the Church." (D. & C. 107:65-66.) His duty is "to preside over the whole-church, and to be like unto Moses—Behold, here is wis-

dom; yea, to be a seer, a revelator, a translator, and a prophet, having all the gifts of God which he bestows upon the head of the church." (D. & C. 107:91-92; 21:1.)

He is the one man on earth at a time who can both hold and exercise the keys of the kingdom in their fulness. (D. & C. 132:7.) By the authority vested in him, all ordinances of the gospel are performed, all teaching of the truths of salvation is authorized, and through the keys which he holds, salvation itself is made available to men of his day.

The President of the Church is the mouthpiece of God on earth. Thus saith the Lord: *"Thou shalt give heed unto all his words and commandments which he shall give unto you as he receiveth them, walking in all holiness before me; For his word ye shall receive, as if from mine own mouth, in all patience and faith."* (D. & C. 21:4-5.)

PRESIDING BISHOP.

See AARON, AARONIC PRIESTHOOD, BISHOPS, GENERAL AUTHORITIES, PRIESTHOOD OFFICES. To "the firstborn among the sons of Aaron" belongs the legal right to serve as the President of the Aaronic Priesthood and the *Presiding Bishop* of the Church, *"For the firstborn holds the right of the presidency over this priesthood, and the keys or authority of the same."* This is the office which Aaron held anciently; the right to

it is hereditary; it descends from worthy father to worthy son in the same way that the office of Patriarch to the Church does. But in the absence of a revelation to the President of the Church, designating the lineage and person to hold this high position of bishopric and Levitical presidency, the First Presidency chooses "a high priest of the Melchizedek Priesthood" to hold the office. In this event two counselors are also called to serve in the Presiding Bishopric. (D. & C. 68:14-21; 107:15-17, 68-78.)

As a holder of the keys of presidency over the Aaronic Priesthood of the Church and thus over all other bishops, the Presiding Bishop is one of the General Authorities of the Church. He sits as a judge in Israel, is responsible for many of the temporal concerns of the kingdom (D. & C. 107:68-74), receives consecrations for the care of the Lord's poor (D. & C. 42:31-33; 51: 5, 12-13), and is called to travel and preach as an aid to building up the kingdom. (D. & C. 84:112-116.)

PRESIDING BISHOPRIC.
See BISHOPRIC.

PRESIDING HIGH COUNCIL.
See TRAVELING PRESIDING HIGH COUNCIL.

PRESIDING HIGH PRIESTS.
See HIGH PRIESTS.

PRESIDING PATRIARCH.

See PATRIARCH TO THE CHURCH.

PRIDE.

See HUMILITY, VAINGLORY, VANITY. As spoken of in the revelations, *pride* is the opposite of humility. It is inordinate self-esteem arising because of one's position, achievements, or possessions; and it has the effect of centering a person's heart on the things of the world rather than the things of the Spirit. (1 John 2:15-17.) As humility, which is an attribute of godliness possessed by true saints, leads to salvation, so pride, which is of the devil, leads to damnation. (2 Ne. 28:15.) "God resisteth the proud, but giveth grace unto the humble." (Jas. 4:6; 1 Pet. 5:5.)

Latter-day prevalence of pride in the hearts of men is one of the sure proofs that apostasy and unrighteousness prevail on the earth. (Rom. 1:28-32; 2 Tim. 3:1-7; 2 Ne. 28:10-15; Morm. 8:28-36.) The Lord hates "a proud look." (Prov. 6:16-19.) "Pride goeth before destruction, and an haughty spirit before a fall." (Prov. 16:18.) Pride among the inhabitants of Sodom was one of the chief reasons for her destruction. (Ezek. 16:49.) Pride is wickedness, and those who are proud are living a telestial law and will be utterly destroyed at the Second Coming of Christ. (Isa. 2:12; Mal. 4:1; 1 Ne. 22:15; 3 Ne. 25:1; D. & C. 29:9; 64:24; 133:64.)

Pride is such a gross evil that the scriptures abound in counsels against it. "Be not proud." (Jer. 13:15.) "Beware of pride." (D. & C. 23:1; 25:14; 38:39.) Repent of pride. (D. & C. 56:8.) Cease from pride. (D. & C. 88:121.) "Thou shalt not be proud in thy heart." (D. & C. 42:40.)

PRIESTCRAFT.

See APOSTASY, PRIESTHOOD, PRIESTS. Nephi said that the Lord "commandeth that there shall be no *priestcrafts;* for, behold, *priestcrafts are that men preach and set themselves up for a light unto the world, that they may get gain and praise of the world; but they seek not the welfare of Zion."* (2 Ne. 26:29.) Priesthood and priestcraft are two opposites; one is of God, the other of the devil. When ministers claim but do not possess the priesthood; when they set themselves up as lights to their congregations, but do not preach the pure and full gospel; when their interest is in gaining personal popularity and financial gain, rather than in caring for the poor and ministering to the wants and needs of their fellow men—they are engaged, in a greater or lesser degree, in the practice of priestcrafts.

Apostasy is born of priestcrafts (2 Ne. 10:5; 3 Ne. 16:10; D. & C. 33:4), for those who engage in them follow vain things, teach false doctrines, love riches, and aspire to personal honors. (Alma 1:12, 16.)

Men are commanded to repent of their priestcrafts (3 Ne. 30:2), and eventually, in the millennial day, these great evils will be done away. (3 Ne. 21:19.)

PRIESTESSES.

See CALLING AND ELECTION SURE, CELESTIAL MARRIAGE, ENDOWMENTS, EXALTATION, KINGS, MELCHIZEDEK PRIESTHOOD, PRIESTHOOD, PRIESTS, QUEENS. Women do not have the priesthood conferred upon them and are not ordained to offices therein, but they are entitled to all priesthood blessings. Those women who go on to their exaltation, ruling and reigning with husbands who are kings and priests, will themselves be *queens* and *priestesses.* They will hold positions of power, authority, and preferment in eternity. (*Gospel Kingdom,* pp. 221-222, 229.)

PRIESTHOOD.

See AARONIC PRIESTHOOD, KEYS, KEYS OF THE KINGDOM, LEVITES, MELCHIZEDEK PRIESTHOOD, MINISTERS, ORDINATIONS, PRIESTCRAFT, PRIESTHOOD OFFICES, PRIESTHOOD QUORUMS, QUORUM PRESIDENTS. As pertaining to eternity, priesthood is the eternal power and authority of Deity by which all things exist; by which they are created, governed, and controlled; by which the universe and worlds without number have come rolling into existence; by which the great plan of creation, redemption, and exaltation operates throughout immensity. It is the power of God. (*Discourses,* new ed., p. 130; *Gospel Kingdom,* p. 129.)

As pertaining to man's existence on this earth, priesthood is the power and authority of God delegated to man on earth to act in all things for the salvation of men. It is the power by which the gospel is preached; by which the ordinances of salvation are performed so that they will be binding on earth and in heaven; by which men are sealed up unto eternal life, being assured of the fulness of the Father's kingdom hereafter; and by which in due course the Lord will govern the nations of the earth and all that pertains to them. (*Gospel Doctrine,* 5th ed., pp. 136-200.)

As there is only one God and one power of God, it follows that there is only one priesthood, the eternal priesthood. Thus the Prophet taught: *"All priesthood is Melchizedek, but there are different portions or degrees of it."* (*Teachings,* p. 180.) Also: "Its institution was prior to 'the foundation of this earth, or the morning stars sang together, or sons of God shouted for joy,' and is the highest and holiest priesthood, and is after the order of the Son of God, and *all other priesthoods are only parts, ramifications, powers and blessings belonging to the same and are held, controlled, and directed by it."* (*Teachings,* p. 167.)

It is, however, proper and common to speak of the two great orders of priesthood as priesthoods; hence, the revealed statement, "There are, in the church, two priesthoods, namely, the Melchizedek and Aaronic, including the Levitical Priesthood." (D. & C. 107:1; *Doctrines of Salvation,* vol. 3, pp. 80-183.)

PRIESTHOOD CALLINGS.
See PRIESTHOOD OFFICES.

PRIESTHOOD COVENANT.
See MELCHIZEDEK PRIESTHOOD.

PRIESTHOOD OF AARON.
See AARONIC PRIESTHOOD.

PRIESTHOOD OF ELIAS.
See AARONIC P R I E S T H O O D, ELIAS, PRIESTHOOD. The lesser or Aaronic Priesthood is the *Priesthood of Elias;* that is to say, it is a preparatory priesthood, one that goes before something that is greater (D. & C. 84:107), one that schools and trains a person for the greater or Melchizedek Priesthood. Joseph Smith taught: *"The spirit of Elias is to prepare the way for a greater revelation of God, which is the Priesthood of Elias, or the Priesthood that Aaron was ordained unto. And when God sends a man into the world to prepare for a greater work, holding the*

keys of the power of Elias, it was called the doctrine of Elias, even from the early ages of he world." (*Teachings,* pp. 335-336.)

PRIESTHOOD OFFICES.
See AARONIC PRIESTHOOD, APOSTLES, BISHOPS, COMMON CONSENT, DEACONS, ELDERS, EVANGELISTS, GENERAL AUTHORITIES, HIGH PRIESTS, LEVITES, MELCHIZEDEK PRIESTHOOD, MINISTERS, ORDINATIONS, OVERSEERS, PASTORS, PATRIARCHS, PATRIARCH TO THE CHURCH, PRESIDING BISHOP, PRIESTHOOD QUORUMS, PRIESTS, QUORUM PRESIDENTS, SEVENTIES, SHEPHERDS, TEACHERS. There are in the Melchizedek Priesthood the following *offices:* elder, seventy, high priest, patriarch or evangelist, and apostle; in the Aaronic Priesthood: deacon, teacher, priest, and bishop. Each office is an ordained calling or assignment to serve, on a basis of primary responsibility, in a specified field of priestly responsibility.

The priesthood is greater than any of its offices. No office adds any power, dignity, or authority to the priesthood. All offices derive their rights, prerogatives, graces, and powers from the priesthood. This principle may be diagramed by dividing a circle into segments. The priesthood is the circle; the segments of the circle are the callings or offices in the priesthood. Anyone who serves in a segment of the circle must possess the power of the whole circle. No one can hold an office in the priesthood with out first holding the priesthood.

Thus it is that priesthood is *conferred* upon worthy individuals, and they are then *ordained* to offices in the priesthood; and thus it is that all offices in the priesthood and in the Church are specifically designated as *appendages* to the priesthood; that is, they grow out of the priesthood, they are supplemental to it, they are less than the priesthood in importance. (D. & C. 84:29-30; 107:5.) It follows that it is greater and more important to hold the Melchizedek Priesthood, for instance, than it is to hold any office in that priesthood. It is greater, accordingly, to hold the Melchizedek Priesthood than to hold the office of elder or of an apostle, though, of course, no one could be either an elder or an apostle without first possessing the higher priesthood.

Further, there is *no advancement* from one office to another within the Melchizedek Priesthood. Every elder holds as much priesthood as an apostle or as the President of the Church, though these latter officers hold greater administrative assignments in the kingdom. It follows, also, that any holder of the Melchizedek Priesthood could perform any priestly function he was appointed to do by the one holding the keys of the kingdom. Normally a priesthood bearer works in the particular segment of the priesthood circle in which his primary responsibility lies. (*Gospel Doctrine,* 5th ed., pp. 148-149; *Teachings,* p. 112.)

An elder has all the priesthood he needs to qualify for exaltation in the highest heaven of the celestial world. Indeed, when the ordinances of exaltation are performed vicariously in the temples, those for and on whose behalf they are done, have the Melchizedek Priesthood conferred upon them and are ordained elders; they are not seventies or high priests or some other office.

The multifarious duties to be performed in the Church require specialists in various fields of endeavor; some persons are endowed with talents that permit them to work effectively in one field and some in another. Hence there are offices in the priesthood, all of which are transcendently important; and the eye cannot say to another member of the body, I have no need for thee, or I am greater than thee. (D. & C. 84:106-111; 1 Cor. 12:14-31; *Doctrines of Salvation,* vol. 3, pp. 103-124.)

Joseph Smith and Oliver Cowdery were ordained elders on April 6, 1830, thus obtaining the first ordained offices in the Church in this dispensation. Peter, James, and John had conferred the Melchizedek Priesthood upon them in June, 1829, but there were no offices in the priesthood until after the organization of the Church. It is not possible to hold an office in an organization that does not exist. Later, other offices came as the needs of the ministry required. (*Doctrines of Salvation,* vol. 3, pp. 147-149.) Ordinations to offices must conform to the law of common consent. (D. & C. 20:65.)

Those receiving priesthood offices have the obligation to labor with zeal and energy in their particular callings. (D. & C. 84: 109-110; 107:99-100.) It is by magnifying one's calling in the higher priesthood that men obtain exaltation in the eternal worlds. (D. & C. 84:33-41.) Priesthood offices exist in time and in eternity, and those who magnify their callings in this life will continue on as ministers of Christ holding offices in the priesthood in the realms to come. (Rev. 4; D. & C. 77; 124:130; *Gospel Kingdom,* pp. 182-184.)

PRIESTHOOD OF MELCHIZEDEK.

See MELCHIZEDEK PRIESTHOOD.

PRIESTHOOD ORDINANCES.

See ORDINANCES.

PRIESTHOOD QUORUMS.

See AARONIC PRIESTHOOD, APOSTOLIC SUCCESSION, DEACONS, ELDERS, FIRST PRESIDENCY, HIGH PRIESTS, MELCHIZEDEK PRIESTHOOD, PRIESTHOOD, PRIESTHOOD OFFICES, PRIESTS, QUORUM PRESIDENTS, SEVENTIES, TEACHERS. Bearers of the priesthood living in the various ecclesiastical units of the Church are divided into organizational units called *quorums.* Thus 12 deacons form a *quorum of deacons;* 24 teachers, a *quorum of teachers;* 48 priests, *a quorum of priests;* 96 elders, a *quorum of elders;* 70 seventies, a *quorum of seventy;* the high priests living in a stake area, *a quorum of high priests;* 12 apostles, *the quorum of the Twelve;* and three high priests, *the quorum of the First Presidency.* (D. & C. 107:21-37; 124:125-145.)

Other special groups with administrative responsiblity are also called quorums. Thus "the standing high councils, at the stakes of Zion, form a quorum" with certain specified powers. "The high council in Zion" also is itself a quorum. (D. & C. 107:36-37.) Similarly all stake high councils could be so designated, as also ward bishoprics and the Presiding Bishopric. Indeed, when the Lord named four brethren to direct the affairs of the Nauvoo House he called the group so selected "the quorum of the Nauvoo House." (D. & C. 124:56-63, 117.) In this sense any group of priesthood bearers designated to perform a special labor could be considered a quorum.

There are three great quorums in whose hands the power rests to preside over the Church and direct all its affairs. The first is the "quorum of the Presidency of the Church"; the second is the quorum of the Twelve, "And they form a quorum, equal in authority and power" to the Presidency; and the third is the Seventy, meaning the first quorum of seventy and not just the First Council of the Seventy, "And they form a quorum, equal in authority to that of the Twelve special witnesses or Apostles." (D. & C. 107:21-26.) The meaning of this revelation, setting forth the order of succession in the Church, is that the Twelve are equal with the Presidency in the sense that all the power of the Presidency rests with them in the event there is no Presidency organized at a particular time. The same is true of the Seventy. As long as the superior quorum is organized, there is no equality of powers and authority. There can never be two equal heads in the kingdom of God. The decisions of the Twelve or the Seventy would have to be unanimous to have full validity. (D. & C. 107:27-32.)

PRIESTS.

See AARONIC PRIESTHOOD, CALL-ING AND ELECTION SURE, CE-LESTIAL MARRIAGE, ENDOWMENTS, EXALTATION, HIGH PRIESTS, KINGS, LEVITES, MELCHIZEDEK PRIEST-HOOD, PRIESTHOOD OFFICES, PRIESTHOOD QUORUMS, QUEENS, QUORUM PRESIDENTS, TEACHERS.
1. In general terms a *priest* is a minister. One so designated (if he is a true priest) must in fact hold the priesthood; yet the designation *priest,* when so used, has no reference to any particular office in the priesthood. Thus among the Nephites it was the practice to consecrate priests and teachers, give them administrative responsibility, and send them out to preach, teach, and baptize. (Mosiah 23:17; 25:19; 26:7; Alma 4:7; 15:13; 23:4.) These priests and teachers held the Melchizedek Priesthood (*Doctrines of Salvation,* vol. 3, p. 87.)

Other churches, in imitation of the true gospel order, sometimes refer to their unauthorized ministers as *priests.* Such designations have reference, as the case may be, to particular offices in their organizations or to the general concept that anyone ministering in religious affairs is a priest. Thus we speak of Catholic priests, of the priests of Christendom, of the priests of Baal, or of the priests of wicked King Noah. (Mosiah 11.)

2. Aaron and his sons were appointed *priests* of the Aaronic order. The remainder of the qualified Levites functioned in capacities comparable to present day teachers and deacons. (Ex. 28; 29; Lev. 8; 9; 10; *Doctrines of Salvation,* vol. 3, pp. 83-94, 111-114.) Priests of the Aaronic order served in ancient Israel from the days of Aaron to the coming of John the Baptist. (D. & C. 84:26-27.) Zacharias, the father of John was legally serving as a priest in Israel when Gabriel came to announce the coming birth of the Lord's forerunner. (Luke 1:5-25.) The right to ordination as priests was hereditary; it was confined exclusively to the

designated lineage. Those so ordained offered sacrifices and ministered in the divers ordinances of the law of carnal commandments. One of them served as the high priest (of the Aaronic Priesthood) in Israel, holding an office comparable to that of Presiding Bishop in the Church today.

3. One of the ordained offices in the Aaronic Priesthood in the Church today is that of a *priest*. (D. & C. 18:32; 20:60.) As with "all other authorities or offices in the church," the office of a priest is an appendage to the priesthood. (D. & C. 107:5.) Those so appointed are legal administrators empowered from on high "to preach, teach, expound, exhort, and baptize, and administer the sacrament, And visit the house of each member, and exhort them to pray vocally and in secret and attend to all family duties." They "may also ordain other priests, teachers, and deacons." They "take the lead of meetings when there is no elder present," and can perform any priesthood function that can be done by a teacher or deacon. (D. & C. 20:46-49.)

4. Book of Mormon prophets gave the title *priest* to officers known in this dispensation as *high priests*. That is, they were priests of the Melchizedek Priesthood, or as Alma expressed it, *"the Lord God ordained priests, after his holy order, which was after the order of his Son."* (Alma 13:1-20.) Since there was no Aaronic Priesthood among the Nephites in Alma's day (there being none of the lineage empowered in pre-meridian times to hold that priesthood), there was no need to distinguish between priests of the lesser and greater priesthoods. Similarly, there being no lesser priesthood in Abraham's day, Melchizedek—who held the greater priesthood and in whose name it has ever thereafter been called—was identified as "the priest of the most high God." (Gen. 14:18; Heb. 7:1.) David prophesied similarly of the priesthood which our Lord would hold, saying, "Thou art a priest for ever after the order of Melchizedek." (Ps. 110:4; Heb. 5:6.)

5. Those who endure in perfect faith, who receive the Melchizedek Priesthood, and who gain the blessings of the temple (including celestial marriage) are eventually ordained *kings* and *priests*. These are offices given faithful holders of the Melchizedek Priesthood, and in them they will bear rule as exalted beings during the millennium and in eternity. (Rev. 1:6; 5:10.)

PRIMARY ASSOCIATION.

See AUXILIARY ORGANIZATIONS, CHURCH ORGANIZATION, GENERAL BOARDS, PRIESTHOOD, STAKE BOARDS. Young children receive special guidance, teaching, and social experience through the *Primary Association,* one of the great auxiliary organizations of the Church. Under the direction of its executive heads, as aided by general and stake boards, the Primary operates units in all the wards and branches of the Church. For proselyting purposes primaries are often organized by missionaries without reference to other church organizations. Children are graduated from the primary organizations to the Mutual Improvement Associations and the priesthood quorums.

PRIMITIVE CHURCH.
See CHURCH.

PRINCE.
See PRINCE OF PEACE.

PRINCE OF DEVILS.
See DEVIL. This title for Satan conveys the realization that there is rule and government in the kingdom of the devil. Lucifer is at the head, a *prince of devils,* and under him is an extended and complex organization—all working for the destruction of the souls of men. When our Lord cast out devils, the rebellious Jews accused him of doing it by the power of the prince of devils. (Matt. 9:32-34; 12:22-30; Mark 3:22-27.)

PRINCE OF PEACE.
See CHRIST, PEACE. This title of our Lord signifies one of the most glorious aspects both of his gospel and of his governmental reign. Prophesying in Messianic vein, Isaiah called him the *Prince of Peace* and said, "Of the increase of his government and peace there shall be no end." (Isa. 9:6-7.) The heavenly hosts sang in glorious exultation at his birth, "Glory to God in the highest, and on earth peace, good will toward men" (Luke 2:14); or as the marginal reading, perhaps more accurately, gives it: "On earth peace among men of good will"; or, "On earth peace among men in whom he is well pleased."

In the gospel of the Prince of Peace are found the principles by obedience to which peace can be obtained by any righteous person. Peace comes from the Spirit of the Lord. But the final and enduring peace for all men on earth will not arrive until the Second Coming of the Prince of Peace, his coming in power and glory to usher in the millennial era.

PRINCE OF THE POWER OF THE AIR.
See DEVIL, GOD OF THIS WORLD, WORLD. Paul applies this name to Satan, having apparent reference to his position as the god of this world, that is, the person who rules in worldly and carnal things. Before their conversion, the Ephesian Saints "walked according to the course of this world," he said, "according to the prince of the power of the air, the spirit that now worketh in the chil-

dren of disobedience: Among whom also we all had our conversation in times past in the lusts of our flesh, fulfilling the desires of the flesh and of the mind; and were by nature the children of wrath, even as others." (Eph. 2:2-3.)

This title, *prince of the power of the air,* appears to be an idiomatic expression that no doubt had more pointed meaning to the Ephesians than it does to us. It seems, however, to place emphasis on Satan's influence over persons who live after the manner of the world, those who revel in ths lusts of the flesh. He is the prince of the children of disobedience, the children of wrath.

PRINCE OF THIS WORLD.

See DEVIL, GOD OF THIS WORLD, WORLD. Satan's position of influence and power in the world—the world of carnality, lust, and corruption, the world the saints are commanded to forsake, the world that will end when the millennium commences—is indicated by his title, *prince of this world.* (John 12:31; 14:30; 16:11.) He rules here in this world; it is not without reason that be boasted of having all the kingdoms of the world at his disposal. (Matt. 4:9.)

PRINCIPLES.

See DOCTRINE.

PRINTING.

See SIGNS OF THE TIMES.

PRISONERS.

See SPIRIT PRISON.

PRISONERS OF HOPE.

See BAPTISM FOR THE DEAD, BOTTOMLESS PIT, HOPE, SALVATION FOR THE DEAD, SPIRIT PRISON, SPIRIT WORLD. Zechariah, with apt spritual insight, used the term *"prisoners of hope"* to describe those in the spirit prison, those of whom the Lord said, "By the blood of thy covenant I have sent forth thy prisoners out of the pit wherein is no water." (Zech. 9:11-12.) That is, though held captive in the spirit prison, these prisoners of hope looked forward with desire and expectation to their redemption, a redemption to be wrought out by the blood of Christ as part of the everlasting covenant, a redemption that would be complete only after baptism for the dead had been performed for them in this mortal sphere where there is water.

As part of the great mission of our Lord was the command, "To open the blind eyes, to *bring out the prisoners from the prison,* and them that sit in darkness out of the prison house." (Isa. 42:7; Ps. 142:7; 146:7.) He was sent, "to bind up the brokenhearted, *to proclaim liberty to the captives, and the opening of the prison to them that are bound."* (Isa. 61:1-3; Luke 4:16-21.) And as Peter taught, while our Lord's body lay in the tomb, his Spirit "went and preached unto *the spirits in prison."* (1 Pet. 3:18-22; 4:6; D. & C. 76:73-74; *Gospel Doctrine,* 5th ed., pp. 472-476; *Doctrines of Salvation,* vol. 2, pp. 129-180.) "Let the dead speak forth anthems of eternal praise to the King Immanuel, who hath ordained, before the world was, that which would enable us to redeem them out of their prison; for *the prisoners shall go free."* (D. & C. 128:22.)

PROBATIONARY ESTATE.
See SECOND ESTATE.

PROFANITY.
See APOSTASY, BLASPHEMY, VULGARITY. *Profanity* embraces any language that shows contempt for holy things, that breathes a spirit of irreverence or blasphemy, or that is vulgar in nature, thus leaving a mental impression of unclean and unwholesome things. *Profanity is an evidence of a diseased soul.* "Out of the abundance of the heart the mouth speaketh." (Matt. 12:34; 15:10-20; Mark 7:1-23; Luke 6:45.) The most wicked of all profanity is that which blasphemes the name of Deity, defying the divine injunction: "Thou shalt not take the

name of the Lord thy God in vain; for the Lord will not hold him guiltless that taketh his name in vain." (Ex. 20:7.)

PROGRESSION.
See ETERNAL PROGRESSION.

PROPHECY.
See CALLING AND ELECTION SURE, CHRIST, GIFTS OF THE SPIRIT, HOLY GHOST, PROPHETS, REVELATION, VISIONS, WHITE HORSE PROPHECY. The inspired utterances of prophets are called *prophecy.* These declarations may pertain to the past, present, or future. New truths or unknown events may be revealed in them, or they may contain expressions which confirm and give added witness to truths already revealed and testified to by other prophets. In their most dramatic form they are declarations of things to come, things which no mortal power could have made manifest.

Prophecy is the announcement of something that has been revealed to a prophet; it always comes by the power of the Holy Ghost. The scriptures are recorded prophecy. Peter gave this inspired rule for their interpretation: "Knowing this first, that no prophecy of the scripture is of any private interpretation. For the prophecy came not in old time by the will of man: but holy men of God spake as they were moved by the Holy Ghost." (2 Pet. 1:20-21.) Prophecy is thus a gift of the Spirit (D. & C. 46:22), and wo unto him, the Lord says, who denies the spirit of prophecy. (D. & C. 11:25.)

Belief in and the manifestations of the spirit of prophecy are two of the great evidences of the divinity of the great latter-day work in which the saints are engaged. "We believe in the gift of . . . prophecy" (Seventh Article of Faith), and every legal administrator in the Church who preaches the gospel or administers gospel ordinances must be called of God "by prophecy" (Fifth Article of Faith), meaning that the call must come by revelation from the Holy Ghost.

Every member of the Church—acting in submission to the laws and system which the Lord has ordained—is expected to have the gift of prophecy. It is by this gift that a testimony of the truth comes. "Follow after charity, and desire spiritual gifts," Paul exhorted, "but rather that ye may prophesy. . . . He that prophesieth speaketh unto men to edification, and exhortation, and comfort. . . . *Let the prophets speak* two or three, and let the other judge. If any thing be revealed to another that sitteth by, let the first hold his peace. For *ye may all prophesy* one by one, that all may learn, and all may be comforted. And the spirits of the prophets are subject to the prophets. For God is not the author of confusion, but of peace, as in all churches of the saints. . . . Wherefore brethren, *covet to prophesy,* and forbid not to speak with tongues." (1 Cor. 14.)

PROPHET.

See CHRIST, MESSIANIC PROPHECIES, PROPHECY, PROPHETS. Christ himself is *The Prophet of* Israel. Moses so designated him in one of the great Messianic prophecies. (Deut. 18:15-19.) And our Lord, ministering as a resurrected Personage among the Nephites, said: "Behold, I am he of whom Moses spake, saying: A prophet shall the Lord your God raise up unto you of your brethren, like unto me; him shall ye hear in all things whatsoever he shall say unto you. And it shall come to pass that every soul who will not hear that prophet shall be cut off from among the people." (3 Ne. 20:23; John 6:14; Acts 3:22-23; Jos. Smith 2:40.)

Our Lord made frequent reference to his own prophetic status. For instance: 1. "No prophet is accepted in his own country" (Luke 4:16-30); 2. "A prophet is not without honour, but in his own country, and among his own kin, and in his own house" (Mark 6:1-6; Matt. 13:53-58; John 4:44); and 3. "I must walk to day, and to morrow, and the day following: for it cannot be that a prophet perish out of Jerusalem." (Luke 13:33.) Many of those among whom he ministered ranked him as a prophet (Matt. 14:5; 21:11, 46; John 4:19; 7:40, 52; 9:17), and the believing disciples on the Emmaus Road described him as, "Jesus of Nazareth, which was a prophet mighty in deed and word before God and all the people." (Luke 24:19.)

By every test Christ was the greatest of the prophets. He was a teacher, revealer, and witness of the truth. (John 18:37.) The Holy Ghost was his constant companion. Of him John the Baptist said: "He whom God hath sent speaketh the words of God: for God giveth not the Spirit by measure unto him." (John 3:34.) He had the knowledge and testimony of his own Divine Parentage and mission, and he bore repeated record thereof. (Matt. 26:63-68; 27:40-43; Luke 23:2-3; John 4:24-26; 8:18-29; 9:35-38; 10:7-36.) These are the things that a man must do to be ranked as a prophet.

PROPHET OF THE HIGHEST.

See CHRIST, JOHN THE BAPTIST, PROPHECY, PROPHETS. John the Baptist was specially selected out from among all the prophets to be called *the prophet of the Highest.* (Luke 1:76.) As the forerunner of the Lord, the one chosen in pre-existence to prepare the way before him (1 Ne. 10:5-10), John's prophetic witness of Christ was, "Behold the Lamb of God!" (John 1:29-36.) Our Lord's own testimony of John was: "Among those that

are born of women there is not a greater prophet than John the Baptist: but he that is least in the kingdom of God is greater than he." (Luke 7:28.)

Asked to explain John the Baptist's exalted rank among the prophets, Joseph Smith answered: "First. He was entrusted with a divine mission of preparing the way before the face of the Lord. Whoever had such a trust committed to him before or since? No man.

"Secondly. He was entrusted with the important mission, and it was required at his hands, to baptize the Son of Man. Whoever had the honor of doing that? Whoever had so great a privilege and glory? Whoever led the Son of God into the waters of baptism, and had the privilege of beholding the Holy Ghost descend in the form of a dove, or rather in the *sign* of the dove, in witness of that administration? . . .

"Thirdly. John, at that time, was the only legal administrator in the affairs of the kingdom there was then on the earth, and holding the keys of power. The Jews had to obey his instructions or be damned by their own law; and Christ himself fulfilled all righteousness in becoming obedient to the law which he had given to Moses on the mount, and thereby magnified it and made it honorable, instead of destroying it. The son of Zacharias wrested the keys, the kingdom, the power, the glory from the Jews, by the holy anointing and decree of heaven, and these three reasons constitute him *the greatest prophet born of a woman.*"

Then the Prophet explained how "he that is least in the kingdom of God" is greater than John. "Whom did Jesus have reference to as being the least? Jesus was looked upon as having the least claim in God's kingdom, and [seemingly] was least entitled to their credulity as a prophet; as though he had said —'He that is considered the least among you is greater than John— that is I myself.'" (*Teachings,* pp. 275-276.)

PROPHETS.

See APOSTLES, CHRIST, HOLY GHOST, PROPHECY, PROPHET, PROPHET OF THE HIGHEST, REVELATION, SCHOOL OF THE PROPHETS, SEED OF CHRIST, SEERS, TESTIMONY. A *prophet* is a person who knows by personal revelation from the Holy Ghost that Jesus Christ is the Son of God, "for the testimony of Jesus is the spirit of prophecy." (Rev. 19:10; *Teachings,* pp. 119, 312.) Accordingly, every prophet bears record of Christ. "To him give all the prophets witness" (Acts 10:43; Jac. 4:4), and if a professing minister of salvation is not a witness for Christ, he is not a prophet.

Nothing more than the testimony of Jesus (meaning the receipt of personal revelation from the Holy Ghost certifying that Jesus is the Christ) is needed to make a person a prophet; and if this revealed knowledge has not been received, a person is not a prophet, no matter how many other talents or gifts he may have. But when a person has received revelation from the Spirit certifying to the divinity of Christ, he is then in a position to press forward in righteousness and gain other revelations including those which foretell future events. On this basis, should the necessity arise, those who are prophets are in a position where they "could prophesy of all things." (Mosiah 5:3.)

Prophets in all ages, accordingly, have taken frequent occasion to foretell the future. "Search the revelations of God," Joseph Smith said. "Study the prophecies, and rejoice that God grants unto the world seers and prophets. They are they who saw the mysteries of godliness; they saw the flood before it came; they saw angels ascending and descending upon a ladder that reached from earth to heaven; they saw the stone cut out of the mountain, which filled the whole earth; they saw the Son of God come from the regions of bliss and dwell with men on earth; they saw the Deliverer come out of Zion, and turn away ungodliness from Jacob; they saw the glory of the Lord when he showed the transfiguration of the earth on the mount; they saw every mountain laid low and every valley exalted when the Lord was taking vengeance upon the wicked; they saw truth spring out of the earth, and righteousness look down from heaven in the last days, before the Lord came the second time to gather his elect; they saw the end of wickedness on earth, and the Sabbath of creation crowned with peace; they saw the end of the glorious thousand years, when Satan was loosed for a little season; they saw the day of judgment when all men received according to their works, and they saw the heaven and the earth flee away to make room for the city of God, when the righteous receive an inheritance in eternity, And, fellow sojourners upon earth, it is your privilege to purify yourselves and come up to the same glory, and see for yourselves, and know for yourselves. Ask, and it shall be given you; seek and ye shall find; knock, and it shall be opened unto you." (*Teachings*, pp. 12-13.)

The mission of prophets is not alone to foretell the future. Even more important is the witness they bear to living persons of the divinity of Christ, the teachings they give of the plan of salvation, and the ordinances which they perform for their fellow men. Most of the great prophets are possessors of the Melchizedek Priesthood; as legal administrators some have possessed keys enabling them to administer the fulness of gospel ordinances.

There are, of course, ranks and grades of prophetic responsibility and authority. Every member of the Church should be a prophet as pertaining to his own affairs. "Would God that all the Lord's people were prophets, and that the Lord would put his spirit upon them!" was the prayer of Moses. (Num. 11:29.) Prophecy is one of the gifts of the Spirit to which all the saints are entitled (1 Cor. 12: 10), and faithful members of the Church are exhorted to "covet to prophesy." (1 Cor. 14:39.)

Those who hold offices in the Church, however, should be prophets both as pertaining to their own affairs and the affairs of the organization over which they preside. A quorum president should be a prophet to his quorum, a bishop to his ward, a stake president to his stake. Members of the First Presidency and Council of the Twelve, and the Patriarch to the Church are all sustained as prophets, seers, and revelators to the Church. Any new revelation for the Church would, of course, be presented to the people by the President of the Church, he being the mouthpiece of God on earth. (D. & C. 21:1-7.) "Surely the Lord God will do nothing, but he revealeth his secret unto his servants the prophets." (Amos 3:7.)

Apostles and prophets are the foundation upon which the organization of the true Church rests. (1 Cor. 12:28; Eph. 2:20.) Where there are no apostles and prophets there is no divine Church, but where these officers are found, there is the Church of Christ in all its glory, beauty, and perfection. The inspired promise is that these officers will remain in the Church "Till we all come in the unity of the faith, and of the knowledge of the Son of God, unto a perfect man, unto the measure of the stature of the fulness of Christ." (Eph. 4:13.)

The sectarian practice of calling some of the Old Testament authors *major prophets* and others *minor prophets* is one of the many false notions engulfing erring Christendom. In large part this division is based on the amount and literary excellence of such of the writings of the prophets concerned as have been preserved in the Bible. Elijah and John the Baptist were two of the greatest prophets, and we do not have any of their writings. We know that Adam (Moses 6:5), Enoch, Joseph the son of Jacob (2 Ne. 3), Zenos (Jac. 5), Zenock (Alma 33:15), Neum (1 Ne. 19:10), and many other prophets wrote many things which have not come down to us in our days. We can only speculate as to what Methusaleh, Lamech, Noah, Shem, Melchizedek, Esaias, Gad, Jeremy, Elihu, Caleb, and a great host of known prophets may have written. Further, there are prophets by the thousands who have lived and died of whom we have no knowledge whatever.

The mere statement that there are and have been true prophets is also an assertion that there are and have been false prophets. Our Lord's counsel, "Beware of false prophets" (Matt. 7:15), is pointed instruction to weigh the claims of the prophets, accepting the true, rejecting the false.

"When a man goes about prophesying, and commands men to obey his teachings," the Prophet taught, "he must either be a true or false prophet. False prophets always arise to oppose the true prophets, and they will prophesy so very near the truth that they will deceive almost the very chosen ones." (*Teachings,* p. 365.)

Joseph Smith also said: "If any person should ask me if I were a prophet, I should not deny it, as that would give me the lie; for, according to John, the testimony of Jesus is the spirit of prophecy; therefore, if I profess to be a witness or teacher, and have not the spirit of prophecy, which is the testimony of Jesus, I must be a false witness; but if I be a true teacher and witness, I must possess the spirit of prophecy, and that constitutes a prophet; and *any man who says he is a teacher or preacher of righteousness, and denies the spirit of prophecy, is a liar, and the truth is not in him; and by this key false teachers and impostors may be detected." (Teachings,* p. 269.)

The mere claim on the part of professing religionists that they have the testimony of Jesus does not of itself guarantee or prove that they do in fact have the spirit of prophecy so as to be true prophets. Rather, truth seekers are commanded: *"Believe not every spirit, but try the spirits whether they are of God: because many false prophets are gone out into the world."* (1 John 4:1.) "There are many spirits which are false spirits, which have gone forth in the earth, deceiving the world. . . . But wo unto them that are deceivers and hypocrites, for, thus saith the Lord, I will bring them to judgment." (D. & C. 50:2-6.)

A person claiming to be a true spiritual leader might present such a good imitation of a true prophet as to deceive those who do not themselves have the guidance and inspiration of the Spirit. But in addition to giving lip service to the assertion that Jesus is the Christ, a true prophet must conform his life to the divine pattern; he most conform to the laws and ordinances which the Lord has revealed. "He that speaketh," the Lord says, "whose spirit is contrite, whose language is meek and edifieth, *the same is of God if he obey mine ordinances."* (D. & C. 52:16.)

In this day and age true prophets will be members of The Church of Jesus Christ of Latter-day Saints; they will be persons who have received the right to the constant companionship of the Holy Ghost when they were confirmed members of the Church; they will be persons who have so lived as to merit receiving the promptings and whisperings of the Holy Spirit; they will be people who are in harmony with the prophets and revelators whom God hath chosen to govern and control the affairs of his earthly kingdom. They will not be found in cults or sects which are running counter to the established church order; they will not be in rebellion against the First Presidency and the Twelve, *"for the spirits of the prophets are subject to the prophets."* (1 Cor. 14:32.)

With all their inspiration and greatness, prophets are yet mortal men with imperfections common to mankind in general. They have their opinions and prejudices and are left to work out their own problems without inspiration in many instances. Joseph Smith recorded that he "visited with a brother and sister from Michigan, who thought that 'a prophet is always a prophet'; but I told them that *a prophet was a prophet only when he was acting as such."* (*Teachings,* p. 278.) Thus the opinions and views even of prophets may contain error unless those opinions and views are inspired by the Spirit. Inspired statements are scripture and should be accepted as such. (D. & C. 68:4.)

Since "the spirits of the prophets are subject to the prophets" (1 Cor. 14:32), whatever is announced by the presiding brethren as counsel for the Church will be the voice of inspiration. But the truth or error of any uninspired utterance of an individual will have to be judged by the standard works and the spirit of discernment and inspiration that is in those who actually enjoy the gift of the Holy Ghost.

President Joseph Fielding Smith has said: "It makes no difference what is written or what *anyone* has said, if what has been said is in *conflict* with what the Lord has revealed, we can set it aside. *My words, and the teachings of any other member of the Church, high or low, if they do not square with the revelations, we need not accept them.* Let us have this matter clear. We have accepted the four *standard works* as the measuring yardsticks, or balances, by which we measure every man's doctrine.

"*You cannot accept the books written by the authorities of the Church as standards of doctrine, only in so far as they accord with the revealed word in the standard works.*

"Every man who writes is responsible, not the Church, for what he writes. If Joseph Fielding Smith writes something which is out of harmony with the revelations, then every member of the Church is duty bound to reject it. If he writes that which is in perfect harmony with the revealed word of the Lord, then it should be accepted." (*Doctrines of Salvation,* vol. 3, pp. 203-204.)

PROPHET'S TIME.
See TIME.

PROPITIATION.
See ADVOCACY, ATONEMENT OF

CHRIST, EXPIATION, INTERCESSION, MEDIATION, RECONCILIATION. Our Lord's atoning sacrifice brought the provisions of the *law of propitiation* into full force. That is, he appeased the demands of divine justice and effected a reconciliation between God and man. As John wrote to the saints: "Jesus Christ the righteous . . . is the propitiation for our sins: and not for our's only, but also for the sins of the whole world." (1 John 2:1-2.) Similarly, Paul taught that men are justified freely by God's grace "through the redemption that is in Christ Jesus: Whom God hath set forth to be a *propitiation through faith in his blood,* to declare his righteousness for the remission of sins that are past, through the forbearance of God." (Rom. 3:24-25.)

PROPITIATOR.
See ADVOCATE, ATONEMENT OF CHRIST, CHRIST, EXPIATOR, INTERCESSOR, MEDIATOR, RECONCILER. Christ is the great *Propitiator* in that his mission is one of propitiation, of reconciliation, of appeasing the demands of divine justice by taking upon himself the sins of the repentant.

PROTESTANTS.
See APOSTASY, GOSPEL, RESTORATION OF THE GOSPEL, SECTS. Members of the various sects of that portion of Christendom which broke off from the Roman Catholic Church during the Reformation in the 16th century, as also the

members of those sects which have since broken off from these original dissenting groups, are called *Protestants*. Martin Luther and others, for instance, first remonstrated and protested in the most solemn manner against the practices and doctrine of the Roman Church, and then finally, in good conscience, had no choice but to sever their affiliation with this organization. This Protestant revolution was inspired of God; it was one of the necessary occurrences which prepared the way for the restoration of the gospel.

Members of The Church of Jesus Christ of Latter-day Saints are not Protestants, and the Church itself is not a Protestant church. The true Church is not a dead branch broken from a dead tree; it is a living tree planted again by revelation in the vineyard of the Lord, and it shall grow and flourish long after the vineyard has been burned and every dead branch and vine has been consumed as stubble.

PROXY ORDINANCES.
See VICARIOUS ORDINANCES.

PSALMS.
See MUSIC.

PSYCHIATRY.
See CHURCH OF THE DEVIL, PHYSICIANS. Incident to the development of modern medical practices, there has arisen a new field of specialization called *psychiatry*—a branch of the healing arts which deals with the study and treatment of mental disorders. This matter of the study of the human mind and its effect on the body is one which is as yet only partially explored. In the hands of competent doctors, and when wisely applied, such laws and principles as have been learned may be used for the great benefit and blessing of mentally ailing patients.

Treatment offered by unwise practitioners, however, sometimes has the effect of keeping sinners from repenting, gaining forgiveness, and becoming candidates for salvation.

To illustrate: An individual may go to a psychiatrist for treatment because of a serious guilt complex and consequent mental disorder arising out of some form of sex immorality—masturbation, for instance. It is not uncommon for some psychiatrists in such situations to persuade the patient that masturbation itself is not an evil; that his trouble arises from the false teachings of the Church that such a practice is unclean; and that, therefore, by discarding the teaching of the Church, the guilt complex will cease and mental stability return. In this way iniquity is condoned, and many people are kept from complying with the law whereby they could become clean and spotless before the Lord —in the process of which they would also gain the mental and spiritual peace that overcomes mental disorders.

PULPITS.
See MEETINGHOUSES, TEMPLES. Raised desks or stands called *pulpits* are commonly erected in church buildings to be used as places from which sermons are delivered. In the Kirtland and some other temples built in this dispensation pulpits have been placed on one side of the assembly rooms for officials of the Melchizedek Priesthood and on the other for officers of the Aaronic Priesthood.

PUNISHMENT.
See AGENCY, CHASTENING, CHASTISEMENT, DAMNATION, FIRE AND BRIMSTONE, HELL, JUDGMENT DAY, JUSTICE, KINGDOMS OF GLORY, SPIRIT PRISON, SPIRITUAL DEATH. Implicit in the whole gospel philosophy of free agency, of personal accountability for sins, and of degrees of glory in the eternities, is the doctrine of rewards for righteousness and *punishment* for sin. (Second Article of Faith.)

Punishment implies subjection to a penalty as a result of wrongdoing. The Lord ordains the laws, affixes the punishments, and metes out a just retribution to the disobedient. (Alma 42.) "He has given a law; and where there is no law given there is no punishment; and where there is no punishment

there is no condemnation." (2 Ne. 9:25.) Conversely, where the Lord's law has been given, punishment always follows disobedience. (Amos 3:1-2.)

Penalties are invoked by men for the violation of their laws (Alma 1:17-18; 30:10-11; D. & C. 134) and by God for the violation of his. "Eternal punishment is God's punishment. Endless punishment is God's punishment." (D. & C. 19:11-12; Matt. 25:46.) The unjust shall be punished in the day of judgment (2 Thess. 1:9; 2 Pet. 3: 9), with the sons of perdition reaping the fulness of everlasting punishment. (D. & C. 76:44-48; Heb. 10:29.)

PURIFICATION.
See PURITY.

PURIFIER.
See CHRIST, HOLY GHOST, PURITY, REFINER, SANCTIFIER. 1. Christ is the *Purifier* because it is in and through him and his atoning sacrifice that the righteous become *pure,* clean, spotless, and qualified to dwell in his presence. It is by his power and command that the Holy Ghost operates. (3 Ne. 27:19-21.) He is also the embodiment of the attribute of purity, and the very plan of salvation itself consists in purifying oneself even as he is pure. (1 John 3:1-3; Moro. 7:48; D. & C. 35:21.) At his Second Coming "he shall sit as a refiner and *purifier*

of silver: and he shall purify the sons of Levi" and all others who are worthy to be so cleansed. (Mal. 3:3; 3 Ne. 24:3; D. & C. 128:24.)

2. The Holy Ghost is also a *Purifier* in that, because of Christ and the atonement, this Spirit member of the Godhead has power given him to cleanse, sanctify, and purify the human soul. (3 Ne. 27: 19-21.)

PURITY.

See BAPTISM, CLEANLINESS, FORGIVENESS, PERFECTION, PUR- IFIER, SANCTIFICATION. Those who love the Lord, and who seek to do his will, have as their objective the cleansing, *purifying,* and sancti- fying of their own souls. The *pure in heart* are those who are free from moral defilement or guilt; who have bridled their passions, put off the natural man and be- come saints through the atonement (Mosiah 3:19); who have been born again, becoming the sons and daughters of Christ (Mosiah 5:7); who are walking in paths of up- rightness and virtue and seeking to do all things that further the interests of the Lord's earthly kingdom.

Most of the saints cannot yet be classed among the pure in heart (D. & C. 136:37), but they are all under command to purify their hearts (D. & C. 88:74; 112:28; Jas. 4:8); to be examples in purity (1 Tim. 4:12); to prove themselves worthy "by pureness" (2 Cor. 6:6);

to center their thoughts on "what- soever things are pure" (Philip. 4: 8); and to purify themselves as Christ is pure. (1 John 3:1-3.) It is the Lord's design and purpose to have a pure people. (Tit. 2:14; D. & C. 43:14; 100:16.)

Many of the present day saints and many in former days, however, attained the status of the pure in heart. Those who dwelt in Enoch's Zion attained such a high degree of purity and perfection that the Lord himself dwelt with them, they all in due course being trans- lated and taken up into heaven. (Moses 7:16-21, 67-69.) Many of the Nephite saints yielded themselves to the Lord "even to the purifying and the sanctification of their hearts." (Hela. 3:35.) Alma says that among the ancients "there were many, exceeding great many, who were made pure and entered into the rest of the Lord." (Alma 13:11-12.) Peter said that the hearts of some of the Gentiles were puri- fied by faith (Acts 15:9), and to the saints that same apostle wrote: "Seeing ye have purified your souls in obeying the truth through the Spirit unto unfeigned love of the brethren, see that ye love one an- other with a pure heart fervently." (1 Pet. 1:22.) The hearts of Joseph Smith and Sidney Rigdon were pure at the time they received the vision of the degrees of glory. (D. & C. 76:116.) And eventually, in this life, the hearts of the saints generally will be pure, for Zion is to be redeemed by the pure in heart. (D. & C. 101:18.) Indeed, "this is Zion—the pure in heart." (D. & C. 97:21.)

The very process of working out one's salvation consists in the cleansing and purifying of the human soul. Men must change from their "carnal state" to a pure state in which they have been forgiven of their sins, that is, "purified" through "the atoning blood of Christ." (Mosiah 4:2.) The pure in heart shall see God (Matt. 5:8; 3 Ne. 12:8; D. & C. 97:16), be saved in his kingdom (D. & C. 124:54; 131:8; 2 Ne. 9:14; Alma 5:21, 24; Dan. 12:10), enter into the rest of the Lord (Alma 13:12), possess all things (D. & C. 50:28-29), be one in Christ (3 Ne. 19:28-29), and have exaltation. (1 John 3:1-3; Moro. 7:48; D. & C. 35:21.)

One of the chief identifying characteristics of a saint is that he has a pure mind. (2 Pet. 3:1.) "Unto the pure all things are pure: but unto them that are defiled and unbelieving is nothing pure; but even their mind and conscience is defiled." (Tit. 1:15.)

QUARRELS.
See CONTENTION.

QUEENS.
See CALLING AND ELECTION SURE, CELESTIAL MARRIAGE, ENDOWMENTS, EXALTATION, KINGS, MELCHIZEDEK PRIESTHOOD, PRIESTESSES, PRIESTS. If righteous men have power through the gospel and its crowning ordinance of celestial marriage to become kings and priests to rule in exaltation forever, it follows that the women by their side (without whom they cannot attain exaltation) will be *queens* and priestesses. (Rev. 1:6; 5:10.) Exaltation grows out of the eternal union of a man and his wife. Of those whose marriage endures in eternity, the Lord says, "Then shall *they* be gods" (D. & C. 132:20); that is, each of them, the man and the woman, will be a god. As such they will rule over their dominions forever.

QUETZALCOATL.
See APOSTASY, BOOK OF MORMON, CHRIST, NEPHITES AND LAMANITES. Lamanitish tradition has preserved the account of the ministry among the ancient inhabitants of America of a white God called *Quetzalcoatl*. One of the most accurate and authentic sources of the secular history of America, for the period before Columbus,

was written by Ixtlilxochitl near the close of the 16th century. His material, gained from ancient hieroglyphic writings handed down from his ancestors, contains such statements as these:

"Quetzalcoatl was a favorably disposed man, of grave aspect, *white* and bearded. His dress was a long tunic." He was "just, saintly and good." He taught "by deeds and words the path of virtue . . . forbidding them their vices and sins, giving laws and good doctrine." "He told them that in time to come, . . . he would *return,* and then his doctrine would be received." (Milton R. Hunter and Thomas Stuart Ferguson, *Ancient America and the Book of Mormon,* pp. 195-222; Hunter, *Archaeology and the Book of Mormon,* vol. 2, *Christ in Ancient America.*)

It is well known that one of the chief reasons for the relatively easy conquest of Mexico by Cortez was the belief, almost universal among the Aztecs, that he was the great white God returning as he had promised. (William H. Prescott, *The Conquest of Mexico.*)

Almost without exception Latter-day Saints have associated these traditions with the ministry of the resurrected Christ among the Nephites. President John Taylor, for instance, has written: "The story of the life of the Mexican divinity, Quetzalcoatl, closely resembles that of the Savior; so closely, indeed, that *we can come to no other conclusion than that Quetzalcoatl and Christ are the same being.* But the history of the former has been handed down to us through an impure Lamanitish source, which has sadly disfigured and perverted the original incidents and teachings of the Savior's life and ministry." (*Mediation and Atonement,* p. 194.)

QUORUM OF THE TWELVE.
See APOSTOLIC SUCCESSION.

QUORUM PRESIDENTS.
See AARONIC PRIESTHOOD, APOSTLES, APOSTOLIC SUCCESSION, BISHOPS, COMMON CONSENT, DEACONS, ELDERS, FIRST PRESIDENCY, HIGH PRIESTS, KEYS, MELCHIZEDEK PRIESTHOOD, ORDINATIONS, PRESIDENT OF THE CHURCH, PRESIDING BISHOP, PRIESTHOOD OFFICES, PRIESTS, SEVENTIES, TEACHERS. "Of necessity there are presidents, or presiding officers growing out of, or appointed of or from among those who are ordained to the several offices in these two priesthoods," that is, the Aaronic and Melchizedek Priesthoods. (D. & C. 107:21.) These presidents hold the keys of presidency over their respective quorums and are obligated to sit in council with their fellow quorum members, "teaching them the duties of their office," "edifying one another, as it is given according to the covenants." (D. & C. 107:85-100.) *Quorum presidents* are to help lead their quorum mem-

bers to eternal life in the kingdom of God.

To carry on the diverse duties of the ministry, various provisions exist as to the kind and type of presidents and presidencies there should be in the different quorums and organizations. The President of the Church and his two counselors constitute the First Presidency, and they preside over and direct all the affairs of the kingdom. The president of the Twelve, without counselors, directs the affairs of that quorum. The First Council of the Seventy, consisting of seven presidents, presides over the first quorum of seventy (when such is in existence) and also over all quorums of seventy in the Church. Each quorum of seventy is also presided over by seven equal presidents, with the senior of the group of presidents presiding over the other six.

Quorums of high priests, elders, teachers, and deacons are each presided over by a president and two counselors. Ward bishops serve as presidents of priests quorums; according to the revelation they are entitled to have "counselors for priests." The Presiding Bishopric is the head of the Aaronic Priesthood of the entire Church; ward bishoprics direct their respective wards and are the presidency of the Aaronic Priesthood therein. Stake presidencies preside over their stakes, mission presidencies over their missions, branch presidencies over their branches, and the various auxiliary organization heads over their divers organizations. All things are systematically and properly arranged and organized in God's earthly kingdom. (D. & C. 107:21-37, 85-100; 124:125-145.)

QUORUMS.
See PRIESTHOOD QUORUMS.

QUORUM SECRETARIES.
See CLERKS.

R

RABBI.
See CHRIST, MASTER. Among the ancient Jews three titles of respect, each indicating a different degree of honor, were used to mean master, teacher, doctor, or interpreter of the law. These were: *Rab* meaning *master; Rabbi* meaning *my master;* and *Rabboni* my *lord and master.* Christ was frequently referred to as *Rabbi* (John 1:38, 49; 3:2; 6:25), and on some occasions as *Rabboni.* (John 20:16.)

Our Lord was highly critical of

those who sought honors of men, desiring "to be called of men, Rabbi, Rabbi." To his saints he commanded: "But be not ye called Rabbi: for one is your Master, even Christ; and all ye are brethren." (Matt. 23:7-8.)

RABBONI.
See RABBI.

RACES OF MEN.
See CASTE SYSTEM, GENTILES, HEATHENS, ISRAEL, NEGROES, NEPHITES AND LAMANITES, PRE-EXISTENCE. All *races of men* stem from certain common ancestors. Adam and Eve are our first parents (1 Ne. 5:11), "And they have brought forth children; yea, even *the family of all the earth.*" (2 Ne. 2:20.) Noah occupies a like position of parenthood over humankind. All but the members of his family were destroyed in the flood; and of his three sons, Shem, Ham, and Japheth "was the whole earth overspread." (Gen. 9:19.)

Racial degeneration, resulting in differences in appearance and spiritual aptitude, has arisen since the fall. We know the circumstances under which the posterity of Cain (and later of Ham) were born with the characteristics of the black race. (Moses 5:16-41; 7:8, 12, 22; Abra. 1:20-27.) The Book of Mormon explains why the Lamanites received dark skins and a degenerate status. (2 Ne. 5:21-23.) If we had a full and true history of all races and nations, we would know the origins of all their distinctive characteristics. In the absence of such detailed information, however, we know only the general principle that all these changes from the physical and spiritual perfections of our common parents have been brought about by departure from the gospel truths. (*Doctrines of Salvation,* vol. 1, pp. 148-151; vol. 3, pp. 313-326.)

The race and nation in which men are born in this world is a direct result of their pre-existent life. All the spirit hosts of heaven deemed worthy to receive mortal bodies were foreordained to pass through this earthly probation in the particular race and nation suited to their needs, circumstances, and talents. "When the Most High divided to the nations their inheritance, when he separated the sons of Adam," Moses said with reference to pre-existence, "he set the bounds of the people according to the number of the children of Israel." (Deut. 32:8.) Not only Israel but all groups were thus foreknown and their total memberships designated in the pre-mortal life. Paul spoke similarly when he averred that God "hath made of one blood all nations of men for to dwell on all the face of the earth, and hath determined the times before appointed, and the bounds of their habitation." (Acts 17:26.)

RACIAL SEGREGATION.
See CASTE SYSTEM.

RAFFLES.
See GAMBLING, LOTTERIES.
Raffles are a form of lottery and as such are gambling. Ordinarily raffling practices call for a number of persons to pay, in shares, the value or assumed value of something, and then to determine by chance which one shall have it. President Joseph F. Smith counseled: "No kind of chance game, guessing contest, or raffling device can be approved in any entertainment under the auspices of our church organizations.

"The desire to get something of value for little or nothing is pernicious; and any proceeding that strengthens that desire is an effective aid to the gambling spirit, which has proved a veritable demon of destruction to thousands. Risking a dime in the hope of winning a dollar in any game of chance is a species of gambling.

"Let it not be thought that raffling articles of value, offering prizes to the winners in guessing contests, the use of machines of chance, or any other device of the kind is to be allowed or excused because the money so obtained is to be used for a good purpose. *The Church is not to be supported in any degree by means obtained through gambling. . . .*

"President Young once said to Sister Eliza R. Snow: 'Tell the sisters not to raffle. If the mothers raffle, the children will gamble. Raffling is gambling.' . . . Some say: 'What shall we do? We have quilts on hand—we cannot sell them, and we need means to supply our treasury, which we can obtain by raffling for the benefit to the poor.' *Rather let the quilts rot on the shelves than adopt the old adage,* : 'The end will sanctify the means.' As Latter-day Saints, *we cannot afford to sacrifice moral principle to financial gain."* (*Gospel Doctrine,* 5th ed., p. 327.)

In answer to the query, "Is it proper to raffle property for the benefit of missionaries?" President Smith said emphatically, No. Then he gave this suggestion with reference to a horse involved in a particular case. "Let everybody give a dollar, and let the donors decide by vote to what worthy man, *not of their number,* the horse shall be given. No chance about that—it is pure decision, and it helps the people who wish to buy chances solely for the benefit of the missionary to discourage the gambling propensities of their natures." (*Gospel Doctrine,* 5th ed., p. 326.)

RAISING THE DEAD.
See DEATH.

RAMAH.
See CUMORAH.

RANSOM.
See ATONEMENT OF CHRIST.

RAPE.
See SEX IMMORALITY.

RAPHAEL.
See ANGELS, ARCHANGELS, KEYS OF THE KINGDOM, TRANSLATED BEINGS. As part of the restitution of all things, *Raphael,* an angelic ministrant, a personage who held keys of power during his mortal ministry, returned to earth in modern times and conferred the keys of his dispensation upon Joseph Smith. (D. & C. 128:21.) The Bible contains no mention of Raphael; the apocryphal book of Tobias, however, contains this statement: "I am the Angel Raphael, one of the seven, who stand before the Lord." (Tob. 12:15.)

As to Raphael's mortal identity we can only speculate. We do know the personages, however, who restored the keys exercised in the various great dispensations mentioned in the Bible, with the exception of the dispensation of Enoch. An inference thus arises that Raphael may be Enoch or some other great prophet from his dispensation. If this assumption is correct, then the keys restored by Raphael would be those enjoyed by the saints in Enoch's day including, perhaps, the power whereby men may be translated.

RATIFICATION.
See HOLY SPIRIT OF PROMISE.

REAPING THE EARTH.
See SIGNS OF THE TIMES.

REASON.
See MIND.

REBAPTISM.
See BAPTISM.

REBELLION.
See DAMNATION, DISOBEDIENCE, LAW, SONS OF PERDITION, STUBBORNNESS, WAR IN HEAVEN, WICKEDNESS. *Rebellion* against God is open, wilful resistance to and defiance of his authority. Lucifer and one-third of the hosts of heaven came out in open, organized rebellion in pre-existence. (Rev. 12:7-10.) Those in this life who, having the light before them, succumb to the enticements of the devil become *rebels.* (Mosiah 3:11-12.) *"The Lord redeemeth none such that rebel against him and die in their sins;* yea, even all those that have perished in their sins ever since the world began, that have *wilfully rebelled against God,* that have known the commandments of God, and would not keep them; these are they that have no part in the first resurrection." (Mosiah 15:26.)

Rebellion leads to damnation. There is no mercy for those who know the will of God and who do not do it. "Wo unto him that has the law given," Jacob said, "yea, that has all the commandments of God, like unto us, and that transgresseth them, and that wasteth the days of his probation, for awful is his state!" (2 Ne. 9:27.)

King Benjamin spoke similarly: "After ye have known and have been taught all these things, if ye should transgress and go contrary to that which has been spoken, that ye do withdraw yourselves from the Spirit of the Lord, that it may have no place in you to guide you in wisdom's paths that ye may be blessed, prospered, and preserved—I say unto you, that the man that doeth this, the same cometh out in *open rebellion against God;* therefore he listeth to obey the evil spirit, and becometh an enemy to all righteousness; therefore, the Lord has no place in him, for he dwelleth not in unholy temples. Therefore if that man repenteth not, and remaineth and dieth an enemy to God, the demands of divine justice do awaken his immortal soul to a lively sense of his own guilt, which doth cause him to shrink from the presence of the Lord, and doth fill his breast with guilt, and pain, and anguish, which is like an unquenchable fire, whose flame ascendeth up forever and ever." (Mosiah 2:36-38; Alma 3:18; Morm. 2:15.) Is it any wonder that Samuel said: *"Rebellion is as the sin of witchcraft."* (1 Sam. 15: 23.)

Those saints who traverse the path of rebellion ordinarily do so by defying the will of God in lesser things, and then as their consciences and feelings become hardened, increasing rebellion becomes the established order. For a member of the Church to use tea, coffee, tobacco, or liquor is to rebel against the Lord and his law. Wilful absence from sacrament meeting is a type of rebellion; so likewise is wilful failure to pay an honest tithing.

The degree of condemnation attending rebellion depends upon the nature of the defiance and the light enjoyed by the rebel. The Lord's anger is kindled against all the rebellious. (D. & C. 56:1; 63:2.) In due course they shall be pierced with much sorrow (D. & C. 1:3, 8) and cut off from the land of Zion. "The rebellious are not of the blood of Ephraim." (D. & C. 64:35-36.)

Those who have a perfect knowledge of the truth and who then come out in open rebellion will become sons of perdition. "That which breaketh a law, and abideth not by law, but seeketh to become a law unto itself, and willeth to abide in sin, and altogether abideth in sin, cannot be sanctified by law, neither by mercy, justice, nor judgment. Therefore, they must remain filthy still." (D. & C. 88:35.)

RECOMMENDS.

See EPISTLES OF COMMENDA-

TION. It is the practice of the Church to issue certificates, commonly called *recommends,* in order to identify persons as members of the Church or to certify to their worthiness to receive certain ordinances or blessings. For instance, when a church member moves from one ecclesiastical jurisdiction to another, a recommend is sent to his new presiding officer identifying him as a member of record in the Church; or, when a worthy church member desires to obtain a patriarchal blessing or participate in the sacred ordinances of the temples, he is given a recommend certifying as to his worthiness to gain the desired blessings.

RECONCILER.

See ADVOCATE, ATONEMENT OF CHRIST, CHRIST, EXPIATOR, INTERCESSOR, MEDIATOR, PROPITIATOR. Christ is the great *Reconciler* in that through his atoning sacrifice power is given men to become reconciled to God, to be absolved from all guilt, and to be in harmony with his mind and will.

RECONCILIATION.

See ADVOCACY, ATONEMENT OF CHRIST, EXPIATION, INTERCESSION, MEDIATION, PROPITIATION. Through the Lord's atoning sacrifice, *reconciliation* between God and man is possible. (Jac. 4:11.) In other words, man is ransomed from a state of sin and spiritual darkness and restored to one of harmony and unity with Deity. To those who by faith had become new creatures of the Holy Ghost, Paul wrote: God "hath reconciled us to himself by Jesus Christ, and hath given to us the *ministry of reconciliation;* To wit, that God was in Christ, reconciling the world unto himself, not imputing their trespasses unto them; and hath committed unto us the word of reconciliation. Now then we are ambassadors for Christ, as though God did beseech you by us: we pray you in Christ's stead, *be ye reconciled to God."* (2 Cor. 5: 17-20; Rom. 5:8-12; 11:15; Heb. 2: 17.) Jacob gave similar counsel: "Reconcile yourselves to the will of God, and not to the will of the devil and the flesh; and remember, after ye are reconciled unto God, that it is only in and through the grace of God that ye are saved." (2 Ne. 10:24; 25:23; 33:9.)

RECORDERS.

See RECORD KEEPING.

RECORDING ANGELS.

See ANGELS, BOOK OF LIFE, CELESTIAL BODIES, GUARDIAN ANGELS, TELESTIAL BODIES, TERRESTRIAL BODIES. From the fact that records are kept in heaven (such as the Book of Life), we deduce that there must necessarily be *recording angels;* that is, some ministering servants must be assigned there to keep the records.

Knowing what we do of the importance of record keeping, and knowing that our affairs in this life have been formulated in accordance with a heavenly pattern, we can suppose that many records are kept by those beyond the veil. This view, however, cannot rationally be extended (as it is among some sectarians) to the point of supposing that every word of mortals is recorded. No angel is assigned to follow every person around and keep a record of his every utterance. (*Doctrines of Salvation,* vol. 1, p. 54.)

As a matter of fact, however, *man is his own recording angel* in a very real sense. That is, his thoughts, words, and deeds have a direct and discernible effect on his body. By compliance with a telestial law, a man creates a telestial body; terrestrial and celestial bodies are created by compliance with those respective laws. (D. & C. 88: 16-32.) Thus President John Taylor taught: *"Man himself is a self-registering machine,* his eyes, his ears, his nose, the touch, the taste, and all the various senses of the body are so many media whereby man lays up for himself a record which perhaps nobody else is acquainted with but himself; and when the time comes for that record to be unfolded, all men that have eyes to see, and ears to hear, will be able to read all things as God himself reads them and comprehends them, and all things, we

are told, are naked and open before him." (*Gospel Kingdom,* p. 36.)

RECORD KEEPING.

See BOOK OF LIFE, BOOK OF REMEMBRANCE, BOOK OF THE LAW OF GOD, CHURCH HISTORIAN AND RECORDER, CLERKS, GENEALOGICAL RESEARCH, HISTORY, STANDARD WORKS. Tremendous importance attaches to *record keeping* in the Church and among the families of the saints. From a historical standpoint it is also important among peoples of the world. (*Doctrines of Salvation,* vol. 2, pp. 197-215.) Record keeping began with Adam who learned to read and write by the spirit of inspiration and who kept a book of remembrance in his own language. (Moses 6:5-6.)

Inspired writing is scripture and as such points the direction in which men must travel to gain peace here and salvation hereafter. The Book of Mormon, as an example, is an inspired record of God's dealings with the ancient inhabitants of the American continent. The accounts of the visions and revelations, the doctrinal teachings, the prophecies concerning the last days, the witness which it bears of the divinity of our Lord, together with the historical data contained in it—all this is of inestimable worth to the children of men. That no needful prophecy or teaching should be left out of it, the resurrected Lord commanded the Nephites to add certain prophecies of Samuel the Lamanite which thus far they had failed to record as part of their sacred records. (3 Ne. 23.)

Records of the performance of sacred ordinances must always be kept. Summarizing his explanation of the sealing power—the power that binds on earth and seals in heaven—the Prophet wrote: "In all ages of the world, whenever the Lord has given a dispensation of the priesthood to any man by actual revelation, or any set of men, this power has always been given. Hence, whatsoever those men did in authority, in the name of the Lord, and did it truly and faithfully, *and kept a proper and faithful record of the same,* it became a law on earth and in heaven, and could not be annulled, according to the decrees of the great Jehovah." (D. & C. 128:9.)

From the genealogical standpoint record keeping is vital. Vicarious ordinances can be performed only for those properly identified. Blessings are sometimes denied those whose genealogies are lost. In the days of Ezra, when the Aaronic Priesthood was conferred only upon the Levites, "the children of the priests . . . sought their register among those that were reckoned by genealogy, but they were not found: therefore were they, as polluted, put from the priesthood." (Ezra 2:61-62.)

RECORDS.
See RECORD KEEPING.

RECREATION.
See DANCING, IDLENESS, MUTUAL IMPROVEMENT ASSOCIATIONS, SABBATH, WORK. *Recreation* is an essential and vital part of the gospel of salvation—a gospel which makes provision for every need of man, both temporal and spiritual. After a person has performed his assigned or appointed labors—both in making a living and in service on the Lord's errand—it is edifying, relaxing, and proper to enjoy the diversion of wholesome recreation. The Church itself, through its Mutual Improvement Associations and other organizations, provides and supervises extensive recreational, dancing, and athletic programs.

Wholesome recreation may include parties, banquets, dinners, games, athletic endeavors, and contests, dramas, dances, concerts, radio and television programs, picnics, outings, camping trips, hunting and fishing trips, and vacations in general. But just as there are imitations of all good things, so there are many unwholesome and improper attempts to provide recreation. Diversion sought through cocktail parties, beer halls, saloons, card playing, or vulgar entertainments of whatever sort should be avoided. Excessive participation in even wholesome recreation is also unwise.

REDEEMER.
See CHRIST, DELIVERER, RE-

DEMPTION, SAVIOR. Christ is the *Redeemer* (Isa. 41:14; 54:5; Alma 37:9; 3 Ne. 10:10; D. & C. 15:1; 18:47) because it is he who worked out the redemption, which ransoms and redeems men from the effects of the fall of Adam. He is so named nearly a score of times in both the Old Testament and the Doctrine and Covenants and more than 40 times in the Book of Mormon.

REDEMPTION.

See ATONEMENT OF CHRIST, ETERNAL LIFE, EXALTATION, FALL OF ADAM, IMMORTALITY, INTERCESSION, MEDIATION, REDEEMER, RESURRECTION, SPIRITUAL DEATH. *Redemption* is of two kinds: conditional and unconditional. *Conditional redemption* is synonymous with exaltation or eternal life. It comes by the grace of God coupled with good works and includes redemption from the effects of both the temporal and spiritual fall. Those so redeemed become sons and daughters in the Lord's kingdom and inherit all things. And this is the chief sense in which the term *redemption* is used in the scriptures. (*Doctrines of Salvation,* vol. 2, pp. 9-13.)

Thus: Lehi taught that "redemption cometh in and through the Holy Messiah, . . . *unto all those who have a broken heart and a contrite spirit.*" (2 Ne. 2:6-7.) Alma said that Christ "cometh to redeem *those who will be baptized unto repentance,* through faith on his name." (Alma 9:27.) Nephi explained that though "the Lord surely should come to redeem his people," yet *"he should not come to redeem them in their sins,* but to redeem them from their sins. And he hath power given unto him from the Father to redeem them from their sins *because of repentance;* therefore he hath sent his angels to declare the tidings of the conditions of *repentance,* which *bringeth unto the power of the Redeemer,* unto the salvation of their souls." (Hela. 5:10-11.) Mormon said that the redeemed, being "found guiltless" would "sing ceaseless praises with the choirs above." (Morm. 7:7.) Abinadi explained that those who "dwell with God . . . have *eternal life, being redeemed by the Lord.*" (Mosiah 15:21-25.)

The Lord says that the unbelieving "cannot be redeemed from their *spiritual fall,* because they repent not" (D. & C. 29:42-45), and the Brother of Jared, because of his righteousness, was told by the Lord: "Ye are redeemed from the fall; therefore ye are brought back into my presence; therefore I show myself unto you. Behold, I am he who was prepared from the foundation of the world to redeem my people. Behold, I am Jesus Christ." (Ether 3:13-14.) Full redemption is a blessing reserved for the saints. (D. & C. 35:26; 45:46; 133:52.)

Unconditional redemption is redemption from the effects of the temporal but not the spiritual fall. It consists in obtaining the free gift of immortality but being denied "the eternal life which God giveth unto all the obedient." (Moses 5:11.) It comes by grace alone without works. Speaking in this sense, the Lord says, "The resurrection from the dead is the redemption of the soul." (D. & C. 88:14-17, 99; Alma 12:25; Morm. 9:12-14.) It is in this sense that the Lord redeems or "saves all the works of his hands, except those sons of perdition who deny the Son after the Father has revealed him." (D. & C. 76:43.)

The redemption (meaning the mere fact of resurrection standing alone) saves all others from death, hell, the devil, and endless torment. (2 Ne. 9:25-26.) But the sons of perdition, following their resurrection, are cast out with "the devil and his angels" where "their torment is as a lake of fire and brimstone, whose flame ascendeth up forever and ever and has no end." (2 Ne. 9:13-16.) Then *they shall be as though there had been no redemption made; for they cannot be redeemed according to God's justice; and they cannot die, seeing there is no more corruption."* (Alma 12:18.)

REFINER.

See CHRIST, HOLY GHOST, PURIFIER, SECOND COMING OF CHRIST. Christ is the *Refiner.* (Isa. 48:10; Zech. 13:9; 1 Ne. 20:10.) His mission is to cleanse, purify, and refine the human soul so that it can return to his Father's kingdom in purity, free from dross. (3 Ne. 27: 19-21.) His cleansing power "is like a refiner's fire, . . . And he shall sit as a refiner and purifier of silver" in that great day when he comes to judge the world. (Mal. 3:2-3; 3 Ne. 24:2-3; D. & C. 128:24.)

REFORMATION.
See SIGNS OF THE TIMES.

REGENERATION.

See BAPTISM, BORN AGAIN, TIMES OF REFRESHING. Baptism is called "the washing of *regeneration"* (Tit. 3:5), because it is the ordinance through which sins are washed away and men are regenerated, renewed, or born anew to the things of the Spirit. That is, following baptism in water, faithful and repentant persons receive the baptism of fire by which they are born of the Spirit, or in other words they are regenerated, becoming new creatures of the Holy Ghost. (Mosiah 27:24-26.)

REGENERATION OF THE EARTH.
See TIMES OF REFRESHING.

REINCARNATION.

See PLAN OF SALVATION, PRE-EXISTENCE, RESURRECTION. *Reincarnation* or the *transmigration of souls*—the rebirth of the same spirits in new bodily forms in successive ages—is a false doctrine originating with the devil. (*Teachings*, pp. 104-105.) It runs counter to the whole system and plan of salvation whereunder spirits are born in pre-existence, are permitted to pass through a mortal probation, and then in due course become immortal, incorruptible, and eternal in nature. It is appointed unto man once to be born, "once to die" (Heb. 9:27), once to be resurrected, and thereafter to "die no more." (Alma 11:45; 12:18; D. & C. 63:49.)

REJOICING.
See CHEERFULNESS, J O Y, THANKSGIVING. Faithful saints feel great delight and are uplifted in body and in spirit because of the blessings of the gospel. Theirs is a status of joy and *rejoicing* which comes because of obedience to gospel law. (D. & C. 52:43.) "Lift up thy heart and rejoice." (D. & C. 25:13.) "Rejoice evermore." (1 Thess. 5:16.)

RELIEF.
See CHURCH WELFARE PLAN.

RELIEF SOCIETY.
See AUXILIARY ORGANIZATIONS, CHURCH ORGANIZATION, CHURCH WELFARE PLAN, GENERAL BOARDS, PRIESTHOOD, STAKE BOARDS. Chief among the auxiliary organizations of the Church is the *Relief Society,* a church organization of adult women whose purpose is to work for the temporal and spiritual salvation of all the women of the Church. Under the direction of its executive heads, as aided by general and stake boards, the Relief Society operates units in all the wards and branches of the Church. Many of its charitable works are coordinated with and operated as part of the Church Welfare Plan.

Among its objectives, the Prophet said, "is the relief of the poor, the destitute, the widow and the orphan, and for the exercise of all benevolent purposes." Its membership is made up, he continued, "of some of our most intelligent, humane, philanthropic and respectable ladies; and we are well assured from a knowledge of those pure principles of benevolence that flow spontaneously from their humane and philanthropic bosoms, that with the resources they will have at command, they will fly to the relief of the stranger; they will pour in oil and wine to the wounded heart of the distressed; they will dry up the tears of the orphan and make the widow's heart to rejoice." (*History of the Church,* vol. 4, p. 567.)

"This is a charitable society, and according to your natures," the Prophet said to the members of the Relief Society. "It is natural for females to have feelings of charity and benevolence. You are now placed in a situation in which you can act according to those sympathies which God has planted in your bosoms. . . .

"You will receive instructions through the order of the priesthood which God has established, through the medium of those appointed to lead, guide and direct the affairs of the Church in this last dispensation; and I now turn the key in your behalf in the name of the Lord, and this Society shall rejoice, and knowledge and intelligence shall flow down from this time henceforth; this is the beginning of better days to the poor and needy, who shall be made to rejoice and pour forth blessings on your heads." (*History of the Church,* vol. 4, pp. 605-607.)

"This is an organization that was established by the Prophet Joseph Smith," President Joseph F. Smith said. "It is, therefore, the oldest auxiliary organization of the Church, and it is of the first importance. *It has not only to deal with the necessities of the poor, the sick and the needy, but a part of its duty—and the larger part, too—is to look after the spiritual welfare and salvation of the mothers and daughters of Zion; to see* that none is neglected, but that all are guarded against misfortune, calamity, the powers of darkness, and the evils that threaten them in the world. *It is the duty of the Relief Societies to look after the spiritual welfare of themselves and of all the female members of the Church." (Gospel Doctrine,* 5th ed., p. 385.)

RELIGION.

See CHRISTIANITY, FAITH, GOD, SALVATION, THEOLOGY, WORSHIP. True *religion* is the true and revealed worship of the true God; all other systems of religion are false. In its pure and perfect form religion is found only among those members of the Church who practice their professions, who live the gospel, who walk uprightly before the Lord, who conform their lives to gospel standards, who sanctify their souls, and who thereby gain peace in this life and have a sure hope of eternal life hereafter. To members of the Church who had accepted the knowledge of God and believed the doctrines of salvation, James said: "Pure religion and undefiled before God and the Father is this, To visit the fatherless and widows in their affliction, and to keep himself unspotted from the world." (Jas. 1:27.)

Thus religion is more than theology, more than a knowledge of Deity and the system of salvation revealed by him; it is the actual practice of the revealed precepts. Religious people are "doers of the word, and not hearers only." (Jas. 1:22-26.) "If theology be theory, then religion is practice; if theology be precept, religion is example." (*Articles of Faith,* pp. 3-6.)

True religion, the religion of Jesus Christ, was instituted of God for the benefit of man, and it is found only in The Church of Jesus Christ of Latter-day Saints. (D. & C. 1:30; 134:4; 135:7.) False religion—made of fragments of the truth mixed with error—is found in the Christian sects and among pagan worshipers. There is no salvation in a false religion. Even such good works as may be performed by those who have not accepted the fulness of the truth—though such works will not go unrewarded—are not acts of religion which are accounted unto men for righteousness in the sense of assuring them of a celestial inheritance. (Moro. 7.) But those saints who first profess and believe the true doctrines and who then practice their holy religion shall be saved.

RELIGIOUS EDUCATION.

See AUXILIARY ORGANIZATIONS, KNOWLEDGE, PRIESTHOOD QUORUMS. Since man is saved no faster than he gains knowledge of Christ and the saving principles of his gospel (*Teachings,* p. 217), and since it is impossible for a man to be saved in ignorance of God and his eternal laws (D. & C. 131:6), it follows that the true Church makes extensive and elaborate provision for the *religious education* of its members.

The Church does not maintain theological seminaries, according to the sectarian pattern, in which selected individuals are trained for ministerial careers. There is no paid ministry in the Church, and the salvation of church members depends on individual knowledge of the truths of salvation rather than on the knowledge that a scholarly minister may have. But the Church does maintain *schools, colleges,* and *universities* in which all types of learning are available, and it does maintain *seminaries* and *institutes of religion* in church owned buildings adjacent to public institutions of learning so that students may study gospel truths in their free school periods or at hours before or after the regular school schedules.

But even more important than these special educational provisions is the fact that all of the priesthood quorums and the auxiliary organizations are so set up and arranged that they are teaching agencies for gospel truths. Standing counsel also exists for all individual members of the Church to search the scriptures and study the principles of the gospel in private and on their own initiative.

Taken as a whole, the saints are the best informed group on earth in both religious and secular fields. Their learning is gained "by study and also by faith." (D. & C. 88: 118.) They teach one another the doctrines of the kingdom and the laws of the gospel, and they seek a knowledge of all the sciences, philosophies, and histories, that they may more effectively carry out the great mission assigned to them. (D. & C. 88:77-81.)

Where the true saints are concerned, they excel all others in knowledge and wisdom because they have the mind of Christ (1

Cor. 2); they are taught from on high by the Spirit. "By the unspeakable gift of the Holy Ghost," God gives unto them knowledge, "that has not been revealed since the world was until now." (D. & C. 121:26.) The mysteries of the kingdom are theirs, and the wonders of eternity are distilled upon their souls. (D. & C. 76:1-10; 121:45-46.)

RELIGIOUS HOBBIES.
See GOSPEL HOBBIES.

RELIGIOUS SYNCRETISM.
See APOSTASY, GNOSTICISM. With the exception of the restored gospel, every system of religion in the world today is born of *religious syncretism*. That is, all existing religious systems have resulted from the mingling of previously existing systems; they have been created by the reconciliation and union of a host of different principles, practices, and beliefs.

Revealed religion is the only pure and perfect system of worship. But after the Lord has spoken there are always those who take pleasure in compromising the truth with the ways of the world. Modern Christian sects espouse religious systems that have grown out of revealed Christianity as such was diluted, intermixed, and amalgamated with such worldly philosophies as gnosticism. These very philosophies had themselves been born of previously existing systems as these had intermingled with prior revelations of the gospel. Much of this syncretism has been traced and outlined by Milton R. Hunter in *The Gospel Through the Ages*.

REMISSION OF SINS.
See FORGIVENESS.

REMNANTS OF ISRAEL.
See GATHERING OF ISRAEL.

REMORSE.
See ANGUISH, CONSCIENCE, HELL, REPENTANCE, SORROW. Just as righteousness begets joy, so wickedness breeds *remorse*. (Alma 29:5.) Hence, the ungodly suffer a prolonged and insistent self-reproach; the painful sting of conscience wraps them in intense mental suffering; a poignant uneasiness is born of their sense of personal guilt. Remorse of conscience results from the violation of divine law. (Alma 42:18.) "A man is his own tormentor and his own condemner." (*Teachings,* p. 357.) As Alma taught, the wicked shall be "brought before the tribunal of God" with their "souls filled with guilt and remorse, having a remembrance of all" their "guilt, yea, a perfect remembrance of all" their "wickedness, yea, a remembrance that" they "have set at defiance the commandments of God." (Alma 5:18.)

RENAISSANCE.
See SIGNS OF THE TIMES.

RENEWING OF THE EARTH.
See NEW HEAVEN AND NEW
EARTH.

REORGANITES.
See REORGANIZED CHURCH OF
JESUS CHRIST OF LATTER DAY
SAINTS.

REORGANIZED CHURCH OF
JESUS CHRIST OF LATTER
DAY SAINTS.
See APOSTASY, APOSTOLIC SUC-
CESSION, CHURCH OF JESUS CHRIST
OF LATTER-DAY SAINTS, COMMON
CONSENT. Following the martyrdom of the Prophet and Patriarch,
June 27, 1844 (D. & C. 135), a number of small cults and sects came
into being composed of a few dis-
sident, unfaithful, and apostate
members of the Church—members
who did not have the faith, testimony, and devotion to follow Brigham Young and the Twelve and to
stand firm against the bitter mob-
ocracy of the day. In 1860 a number of these factions and splinter
groups united under the leadership
of "young Joseph," a son of the
martyred seer, to form what has
become known as the *Reorganized
Church of Jesus Christ of Latter
Day Saints,* which now has its
headquarters at Independence, Missouri.

Some of the most unstable and
contentious men of the day—Zenas
H. Gurley, Jason W. Briggs, and
William Marks—became the or-
ganizers of this Reorganized
Church. This so-called Reorganized
Church, now the largest apostate
faction claiming origin in the revelations given Joseph Smith, actually gained so few of the members
from the original Church organized
by the Prophet that it is almost a
misnomer to describe the new organization as a faction of the
original.

President Joseph Fielding Smith
has written: "In 1852, when Jason
W. Briggs and Zenas H. Gurley
combined their Strangite forces,
the membership was about 100
souls, most of whom were converts
made for Mr. Strang. In 1860 when
'young Joseph' assumed the leadership, the membership was 300
souls, most of whom were *converts
that had never belonged to the
Church of Jesus Christ of Latter-
day Saints."* By 1894—50 years
after the death of the Prophet—
according to their own claims, the
Reorganite people had not been
able to induce as many as a thous-
and original church members to
join their cult. By actual count,
"almost the entire membership of
the Church as it stood in 1844, is
accounted for in the following of
President Brigham Young and the
Twelve." (*Doctrines of Salvation,*
vol. 1, pp. 247-273.)

As is commonly the case in the
apostate churches of the world, the

beliefs and doctrines of the Reorganized Church are in a constant state of change and alteration. They have no true apostles and prophets at their head to keep their members from being "tossed to and fro, and carried about with every wind of doctrine." (Eph. 4: 14.) They have deleted more than a score of the revelations in the Doctrine and Covenants, with current agitation among many of their members for additional deletions. Their chief doctrinal stumbling blocks are salvation for the dead, celestial marriage, and temple work in general.

To some degree the spirit of animosity and bitterness manifest by members of the Reorganized Church against the true Church is dying down. "One of a city, and two of a family" (Jer. 3:14), as it were, their more spiritually alert and intelligent members are being converted to the truth and are joining the Church. As the rising generation comes to power and influence it is to be expected that the number of conversions to the truth will increase.

REPENTANCE.

See ATONEMENT OF CHRIST, BAPTISM, CONTRITE SPIRITS, FAITH, FORGIVENESS, JUSTICE, MERCY, PENITENCE, PLAN OF SALVATION, REMORSE, SALVATION, SIN. Because all accountable men are stained by sin (Eccles. 7:20; Rom. 3:10; 1 John 1:8-10), and because no unclean thing can enter into the kingdom of heaven (Alma 11: 37; 3 Ne. 27:19; Moses 6:57), a merciful God has ordained the *law of repentance* whereby the human soul may be cleansed and conditioned for eternal life in his everlasting presence. Repentance is the process whereby a mortal soul —unclean and stained with the guilt of sin—is enabled to cast off the burden of guilt, wash away the filth of iniquity, and become clean every whit, entirely free from the bondage of sin. (D. & C. 58:42-43; 64:3-13; Isa. 1:16-20; Ezek. 18:19-31; 33:7-20.)

To gain forgiveness through repentance a person must have a conviction of guilt, a godly sorrow for sin, and a contrite spirit. He must desire to be relieved of the burden of sin, have a fixed determination to forsake his evil ways, be willing to confess his sins, and forgive those who have trespassed against him; he must accept the cleansing power of the blood of Christ as such is offered through the waters of baptism and the conferral of the Holy Ghost. (*Articles of Faith,* pp. 109-116.)

Repentance is essential to salvation; without it no accountable person can be saved in the kingdom of God. (D. & C. 20:29; Moses 6:52-53, 57; 3 Ne. 9:22.) It is a prerequisite to baptism and hence to membership in the kingdom of God on earth. (D. & C. 18:41; 20:71; 33:11; 49:13.) It is a requirement made of every accountable person, that is of those "having knowledge" (D. & C. 29:49), and parents are obligated to teach repentance to their children to qualify them for baptism when they reach the years of accountability. (D. & C. 68:25-27.)

"Every man must repent or suffer." In the event of repentance, the law of mercy prevails, and the penitent person is saved from suffering. "I, God, have suffered these things for all, that they might not suffer if they would repent; But if they would not repent they must suffer even as I; Which suffering caused myself, even God, the greatest of all, to tremble because of pain, and to bleed at every pore, and to suffer both body and spirit." Hence comes the Lord's imperative command to repent. (D. & C. 19:4-20.) Where there is no repentance, the law of justice takes precedence and remission of sins is gained through suffering rather than as a gift of God through the blood of Christ. (Alma 42:22-24.)

Every encouragement is given to men to repent. The very plan of salvation offered to the world is a "gospel of repentance." (D. & C. 13; 84:27.) The elders of Israel go forth with the command, "Say nothing but repentance unto this generation." (D. & C. 6:9; 11:9; 14:8.) The saints are chastened to bring them to repentance (D. & C. 1:27; 98:21), and scourges and desolation are poured out upon the wicked to humble them as a condition precedent to repentance. (D. & C. 5: 19.) All men everywhere are commanded to repent so that they may gain salvation. (D. & C. 18:9-22; 20:29; 133:16.)

This life is the time that is given for men to repent and prepare to meet God. Those who have opportunity in this life to accept the truth are obligated to take it; otherwise, full salvation will be denied them. Hopes of reward through so-called *death-bed repentance* are vain. As Amulek said: "If ye have procrastinated the day of your repentance even until death, behold, ye have become subjected to the spirit of the devil, and he doth seal you his; therefore, the Spirit of the Lord hath withdrawn from you, and hath no place in you, and the devil hath all power over you; and this is the final state of the wicked." (Alma 34:31-35.)

Repentance is easy or difficult of attainment by various people, depending upon their own attitude and conduct, and upon the seriousness of the sins they have committed. Through rebellion men sometimes place themselves in a position in which the Lord's Spirit will no longer strive with them, and when this occurs there is little hope for them. (D. & C. 1:33; 1 Ne. 7:14; 2 Ne. 26:11; Morm. 5:16; Ether 2:15.) For those who have once basked in the light and who thereafter come out in open rebellion, there is no repentance whatever. (Heb. 6:4-8.) They have sinned unto death, and for such there is no forgiveness. (1 John 5:16.)

REPLENISH THE EARTH.

See CREATION, EVOLUTION, FIRST MAN. Our scriptural accounts, as these are rendered in English, say that God commanded Adam and Eve: "Be fruitful, and multiply, and *replenish the earth,* and subdue it." (Gen. 1:28; Moses 2:28; Abra. 4:28.) Some have falsely concluded from this that Adam and Eve were not the first inhabitants of the earth, that there were pre-Adamites, and that our first parents were being directed to fill up the earth again with posterity.

Actually, there are two accepted and established definitions of replenish. One meaning is to stock with animals or persons *in the first instance,* that is, *to fill;* the other meaning is to *fill again* or *to stock anew.* In the original Hebrew the verb used was *mole,* meaning *fill, to fill,* or *make full.* This same verb is translated *fill* in the command, "Be fruitful, and multiply, and fill the waters in the seas, and let fowl multiply in the earth." (Gen. 1:22.)

Hence the accurate meaning of the command given our first parents was: "Be fruitful, and multiply, and fill the earth with posterity, that is, provide bodies for the spirits in pre-existence." Most translations, other than the King James Version, use the word *fill* rather than *replenish* in this text. Because the word replenish does mean fill, however, and because the Church uses the King James Version of the Bible, it was quite natural for the Prophet to use the same word, that is, replenish, in the books of Moses and of Abraham. (Joseph Fielding Smith, *Answers to Gospel Questions,* vol. 1, pp. 208-211.)

RESPECT OF PERSONS.

See EQUALITY, JUDGMENT, JUSTICE, RIGHTEOUSNESS. God is no *respecter of persons* (D. & C. 1: 35; 38:16), meaning that every person who complies with a law receives the blessing ordained to attend such obedience. For instance, when the Gentiles exercised the requisite faith, they received the Holy Ghost, though that great blessing had theretofore been reserved for the house of Israel. (Acts 10:34-35; 3 Ne. 20:27.) Many of the apostate doctrines of so-called Christendom are based on the assumption that God is a respecter of persons and a partial being, as for instance infant baptism (Moro. 8: 12) and the false teaching that the day of revelation and miracles has ceased. (Morm. 9:7-25.)

Man also is commanded not to respect persons. To Moses the Lord said, "Ye shall not respect persons in judgment" (Deut. 1:17); every person, both great and small, should be treated equally and im-

632

partially. (Lev. 19:15; 2 Chron. 19:7; Job. 34:19.)

RESTITUTION OF ALL THINGS.

See RESTORATION OF ALL THINGS.

REST OF THE LORD.

See CONVERSION, EXALTATION, PRIESTHOOD, TESTIMONY. True saints enter into the *rest of the Lord* while in this life, and by abiding in the truth, they continue in that blessed state until they rest with the Lord in heaven. (Moro. 7:3; D. & C. 84:17-25; Matt. 11:28-30; Heb. 3:7-19; 4:1-11.) The rest of the Lord, where mortals are concerned, is to gain a perfect knowledge of the divinity of the great latter-day work. "It means entering into the knowledge and love of God, having faith in his purpose and in his plan, to such an extent that we know we are right, and that we are not hunting for something else; we are not disturbed by every wind of doctrine, or by the cunning and craftiness of men who lie in wait to deceive." It is "rest from the religious turmoil of the world; from the cry that is going forth, here and there —lo, here is Christ; lo, there is Christ." (*Gospel Doctrine,* 5th ed., pp. 58, 125-126.) The rest of the Lord, in eternity, is to inherit eternal life, to gain the fulness of the Lord's glory. (D. & C. 84:24.)

RESTORATION OF ALL THINGS.

See CREATION, DISPENSATION OF THE FULNESS OF TIMES, EARTH, FALL OF ADAM, MILLENNIUM, RESTORATION OF THE GOSPEL, TIMES OF RESTITUTION. This earth and all that pertains to it, including every form of life on the face thereof, was first created in a terrestrial or paradisiacal state. Incident to the fall of Adam, the earth itself and all life on its face fell to their present telestial state. Since the fall, additional physical degeneracy has occurred in the bodily constitution of man. Also after the fall, the gospel or plan of salvation, in all its beauty and perfection, was revealed to man from time to time in successive dispensations.

Now the great *restoration of all things* is the return of the earth, and all that pertains to it, including every form of life, back to the primeval and perfect state which prevailed when all things first rolled from their Creator's hands and were pronounced, "Very good." (Gen. 1:31.) The most important part of this great restoration of all things is, of course, the restoration of the gospel, but in the eternal sense all of the Lord's dealings are part of his gospel plan. (Joseph Fielding Smith, *The Restoration of All Things,* pp. 6-319.)

"We believe . . . that the earth will be renewed and receive its paradisiacal glory." (Tenth Article of Faith; D. & C. 101:23-31; Isa. 65:

633

17-25.) Thus conditions which prevailed in the Edenic day forecast similar conditions that will again prevail during the millennial era; and a revealed knowledge of millennial conditions gives an understanding of analagous conditions that prevailed when the earth enjoyed its *first* paradisiacal status. The same conditions will not prevail in every detail, but certain basic things will be similarly arranged.

Adam and Eve were placed in Eden in immortality; there was no death for them or for any form of life until after the fall. (2 Ne. 2: 22.) During the millennium, death as we know it will cease, meaning that men will not die until they are an hundred years old; animals will also return to their pristine type of life, the enmity of all forms of life ceasing and the lion eating straw like the ox. (D. & C. 101:24-31; Isa. 11:6-9; 65:17-25.) Sorrow, disease, and sickness were not found in the Garden of Eden, and they will cease again when the millennial era commences.

When the earth was first created all the land was in one place and there were no mountains and valleys of the kind that now exist. At the Second Coming of Christ the sea will be driven back to its place in the north, the continents shall become one land again, every valley shall be exalted, every mountain shall be made low, and the earth shall cease bringing forth thorns and noxious weeds, but

shall become as the garden of the Lord. (D. & C. 133:20-31, 44.)

RESTORATION OF FORMER BLESSINGS.

See EXCOMMUNICATION. Temple and priesthood blessings, as well as all others pertaining to the Church, are lost upon excommunication. In the event of repentance and subsequent rebaptism, all or part of these former blessings—those pertaining to the priesthood, to endowments, and to sealings—may be restored by a member of the Council of the Twelve upon authorization of the President of the Church. Excommunicated men who have not had their endowments receive and advance in the priesthood by conferral and ordination as in the first instance.

RESTORATION OF THE GOSPEL.

See ABRAHAMIC COVENANT, CHURCH OF JESUS CHRIST OF LATTER-DAY SAINTS, DISPENSATION OF THE FULNESS OF TIMES, ELIAS, GATHERING OF ISRAEL, GOSPEL, JOSEPH SMITH THE PROPHET, KINGDOM OF GOD, RESTORATION OF ALL THINGS, TIMES OF RESTITUTION, ZION. Since the gospel was first given to Adam, each time it was thereafter lost by apostasy and then revealed to man again has been a *restoration of the gospel.* Our Lord in his personal ministry, for instance, restored the original gospel, the same plan of salvation which he had revealed to Adam in the beginning. But when men in this day speak of the restoration of the gospel, they mean the final great restoration which has now taken place as part of the restoration of all things. This dispensation is the age of restoration to which all the ancient prophets look forward. In it all things are to be restored "which God hath spoken by the mouth of all his holy prophets since the world began." (Acts 3:19-21.) All things are being gathered together in one in Christ. (Eph. 1:10.)

Gospel restoration is accomplished in the same way in which the gospel was first revealed to Adam; that is: 1. Angelic ministrants are sent from heaven to declare it; 2. God declares its truths by his own voice; and 3. The gift of the Holy Ghost is given to men. (Moses 5:58.) Foreseeing the final great restoration of the gospel, the ancient apostle wrote: "And I saw another angel fly in the midst of heaven, having the everlasting gospel to preach unto them that dwell on the earth, and to every nation, and kindred, and tongue, and people." (Rev. 14:6.)

This angel of the restoration was a *composite angel,* meaning that a number of angels were destined to participate in the events which necessarily must take place to complete the restoration. Moroni came in fulfilment of this promise, because he effected the restoration of the Book of Mormon wherein the doctrines of the true gospel are recorded. (D. & C. 133:36-40.) John the Baptist, Peter, James, and John, Michael, Raphael, Gabriel, Elias, Moses, Elijah, and "divers angels" (D. & C. 128:20-21), all came in fulfilment of this promise because they restored the priesthood and keys whereby the gospel is administered and made operative in the lives of men. (D. & C. 13; 27:12-13; 88:103-104; 110:11-16.)

Among those things to be restored as part of the gospel or as necessary accompaniments to the restoration are the following:

1. GOSPEL KNOWLEDGE.—Until the true doctrines of Christ are known, man cannot conform his life to that high standard of personal righteousness whereby salvation may be gained. Much of this gospel knowledge has already been restored by way of the Book of Mormon, the host of latter-day revelations, and the manifestations of the Spirit to the faithful. Many more gospel truths are, of course, yet to be revealed. (Ninth Article of Faith; D. & C. 101:32-34; 121: 26-32; 132:66.)

2. OPENING OF THE HEAVENS.— This transcendent change from the condition that had prevailed during the long night of apostate darkness took place in the spring of 1820 with the appearance of the Father and the Son to the Prophet. (Jos. Smith 2.) Since then visions, revelations, and the ministering of angels have been the heri-

tage of the faithful, a status which will continue "so long as time shall last, or the earth shall stand, or there shall be one man upon the face thereof to be saved." (Moro. 7:36.)

3. PRIESTHOOD AND KEYS.— These have already come again in their fulness. All of the priesthood and all of the keys needed to save and exalt men in the highest heaven have now been given. (D. & C. 13; 27:12-13; 110:11-16; 128:20-21.)

4. COMING OF ELIAS.—This mighty prophet holds "the keys of bringing to pass the restoration of all things spoken by the mouth of all the holy prophets since the world began, concerning the last days." (D. & C. 27:6; 77:9, 14-15; Matt. 17:11; Mark 9:12.) These keys have already been conferred upon man, and such things as have not already been revealed will be made known "in due time." (D. & C. 132:40, 45.)

5. GIFT OF THE HOLY GHOST. —Receipt of this gift, as far as an individual is concerned, is the heart and core of the restoration, for it is by the power of the Holy Ghost that men are sanctified so as to be qualified for a celestial inheritance. (3 Ne. 27:19-21.) By virtue of the restoration of the higher priesthood and its keys this gift is again bestowed upon faithful converts to the truth.

6. GIFTS OF THE SPIRIT.—These gifts—visions, revelations, miracles, healings, the ministering of angels, tongues, and so forth—are always

showered upon the true saints, and their presence constitutes a sign that the gospel has been restored. (Mark 16:16-20.)

7. TRUE CHURCH AND KINGDOM. —In all ages the gospel has been administered by and through the formal organization of the Church, and until the church organization was perfected the restoration was not complete. (D. & C. 84:2.) The general framework of the organized kingdom was set up on the 6th of April in 1830, and the organization was perfected by about April, 1844, when all of the powers and keys had been conferred upon the Council of the Twelve so that the Church became a self-perpetuating body in accordance with the divine pattern.

8. APOSTLES, PROPHETS, AND CHURCH OFFICERS.—"God hath set some in the church, first apostles, secondarily prophets." (1 Cor. 12:28.) These and other officers are to continue in the true Church as long as there are prospective candidates for salvation who need the guidance of such officers. (Eph. 4:11-14.) Manifestly these officers must serve in the era of restoration. "And I will restore thy judges as at the first, and thy counsellors as at the beginning," saith the Lord, for "Zion shall be redeemed with judgment, and her converts with righteousness." (Isa. 1:26-27.)

9. GATHERING OF ISRAEL.—(1 Ne. 15:19-20; 2 Ne. 3:13, 24; D. & C. 45:17; Acts 1:6.) By this is meant: (a) *Conversion of the scat-*

tered remnants of Jacob to the true Church (2 Ne. 9:2); "And the gospel of Jesus Christ shall be declared among them; wherefore, they shall be restored unto the knowledge of their fathers, and also to the knowledge of Jesus Christ, which was had among their fathers" (2 Ne. 30:5; Morm. 9:36); and they shall come again "unto the knowledge of the covenant" made with their fathers. (3 Ne. 5: 25; 21.) (b) *Their assembling to Zion or Jerusalem as the case may be.* (Tenth Article of Faith; D. & C. 110:11; 2 Ne. 25:11; 30:8; Morm. 5:14.)

10. TEMPLE ORDINANCES.—It is only through the ordinances of his holy house that the Lord deigns to "restore again that which was lost unto you, or which he hath taken away, even the fulness of the priesthood." (D. & C. 124:28; 127:8; 128: 17.)

11. REDEMPTION OF ZION.—(D. & C. 103:13-29.) When this glorious event, the redemption of Zion, has been accomplished, all will be in readiness for the restoration of the Zion of old to the earth. (Moses 7:60-64.)

RESTORED CHURCH.
See CHURCH OF JESUS CHRIST OF LATTER-DAY SAINTS.

RESTORER.
See CHRIST, ELIAS, RESTORATION OF THE GOSPEL. When Christ came in the meridian of time, he came as the great *Restorer,* the one who brought back again to earth the fulness of the gospel, for he then gave again the same truths he had given originally to righteous saints of old. Christianity did not begin a mere 2000 years ago; it existed first in eternity, and then had its beginning on earth with Father Adam.

RESURRECTED LORD.
See RISEN LORD.

RESURRECTION.
See ATONEMENT OF CHRIST, CELESTIAL BODIES, ETERNAL LIFE, FALL OF ADAM, FLESH AND BONES, HELL, IMMORTALITY, INCORRUPTION, JUDGMENT DAY, KINGDOMS OF GLORY, PARADISE, REDEMPTION, SALVATION, SONS OF PERDITION, SPIRITUAL BODIES, SPIRIT WORLD, STILLBORN CHILDREN, TELESTIAL BODIES, TERRESTRIAL BODIES, TRANSLATED BEINGS. The *resurrection* is the creation of an immortal soul; it consists in the uniting or reuniting of body and spirit in immortality. (*Doctrines of Salvation,* vol. 2, pp. 258-301.) A resurrected being is one for whom body and spirit are inseparably connected in a state of incorruption, a state in which there never again can be decay (corruption) or death (separation of body and spirit). (1 Cor. 15; Alma 11:37-46; 12:12-18.) Resur-

rected beings have bodies of flesh and bones, tangible, corporeal bodies, bodies that occupy space, digest food, and have power, outwardly, to appear as mortal bodies do. (Luke 24.)

Nothing is more absolutely universal than the resurrection. Every living being will be resurrected. "As in Adam all die, even so in Christ shall all be made alive." (1 Cor. 15:22.) Those who live and die before the millennial era, all in their proper order, will have their bodies and spirits reunited in resurrected immortality. The righteous who live after the Second Coming shall be changed from mortality to immortality in the twinkling of an eye, their bodies and spirits being united inseparably.

"Yea, and blessed are the dead that die in the Lord, from henceforth, when the Lord shall come, and old things shall pass away, and all things become new, they shall rise from the dead and shall not die after, and shall receive an inheritance before the Lord, in the holy city. And he that liveth when the Lord shall come, and hath kept the faith, blessed is he; nevertheless, it is appointed to him to die at the age of man. Wherefore, children shall grow up until they become old; old men shall die; but they shall not sleep in the dust, but they shall be changed in the twinkling of an eye. Wherefore, for this cause preached the apostles unto the world the resurrection of the dead." (D. & C.

63:49-52.)

Two events of transcendent importance make possible the resurrection: 1. *The fall of Adam;* and 2. *The redemptive sacrifice of the Son of God.* Adam's fall brought temporal or natural death into the world; that is, as a result of Adam's fall mortality was introduced, and mortality is the forerunner of death. Christ's redeeming sacrifice ransomed men from the effects of Adam's fall in that mortality is replaced by immortality, or in other words in that the dead come forth in the resurrection. "For as death hath passed upon all men, to fulfil the merciful plan of the great Creator," Jacob taught, "there must needs be a power of resurrection, and the ressurection must needs come unto man by reason of the fall." (2 Ne. 9:6; Morm. 9:12-13.)

"Behold, the day cometh that all shall rise from the dead and stand before God," Amulek said, "and be judged according to their works. Now, there is a death which is called a temporal death; and the death of Christ shall loose the bands of this temporal death, that all shall be raised from this temporal death." (Alma 11:41-42; 40:2-4.)

This doctrine of a universal resurrection was known and taught from the beginning. (Moses 1:39.) The choice of Christ in the councils of eternity to come down to earth as the Son of God and work out the infinite and eternal atonement was based on the foreknowledge of God—knowledge which he also imparted to his spirit children—that immortality was to be guaranteed and eternal life offered to all men. (Moses 4:1-4.) Immediately after the fall, angels came to Adam teaching that through the promised redemption of the Only Begotten all "might be raised in immortality unto eternal life, even as many as would believe." (D. & C. 29:42-50; Moses 5:6-15.)

Enoch saw the restoration of the gospel in our day and received from the Lord this promise: "And righteousness will I send down out of heaven; and truth will I send forth out of the earth [meaning the Book of Mormon], to bear testimony of mine Only Begotten; his resurrection from the dead; yea, and also the resurrection of all men." (Moses 7:62.) Job (Job 19:25-27), David (Ps. 16:9-11; 17:15), Daniel (Dan. 12:1-3), Ezekiel (Ezek. 37:1-14), and many of the ancient prophets bore testimony of the resurrection. Jehovah (who is Christ), speaking through Isaiah, said of the house of Israel: "Thy dead men shall live, together with my dead body shall they arise. Awake and sing, ye that dwell in dust: for thy dew is as the dew of herbs, and the earth shall cast out the dead." (Isa. 26:19.)

Christ was the firstfruits of the resurrection (1 Cor. 15:23), and because of his resurrection, "by the power of God," all men shall come forth from the grave. (Morm. 9:13.) The righteous dead who lived from the day of Adam to the time when Christ broke the bands of death "were with Christ in his resurrection." (D. & C. 133:54-55.) "And the graves were opened; and many bodies of the saints which slept arose, And came out of the graves after his resurrection, and went into the holy city, and appeared unto many." (Matt. 27:52-53; Hela. 14:25.) All who were with Christ in his resurrection, and all who have so far been resurrected, have come forth with celestial bodies and will have an inheritance in the celestial kingdom. (D. & C. 88:96-102.)

To those who lived before the resurrection of Christ, the day of his coming forth from the dead was known as the *first resurrection*. Abinadi and Alma, for instance, so considered it. (Mosiah 15:21-25; Alma 40.) To those who have lived since that day, the first resurrection is yet future and will take place at the time of the Second Coming. (D. & C. 88:96-102.) We have no knowledge that the resurrection is going on now or that any persons have been resurrected since the day in which Christ came forth excepting Peter, James, and Moroni, all of whom had special labors to perform in this day which necessitated tangible resurrected bodies.

Though all men are assured of a resurrection, all will not be resurrected at the same time, and there will be varying degrees of glory for immortal persons. All will come forth from the grave, "But every man in his own order" (1 Cor. 15: 23), as Paul expresses it. Joseph Smith said: "In the resurrection, some are raised to be angels, others are raised to become gods." (*Teachings,* p. 312.)

Two great resurrections await the inhabitants of the earth: one is the *first resurrection, the resurrection of life, the resurrection of the just;* the other is the *second resurrection, the resurrection of damnation, the resurrection of the unjust.* (John 5:28-29; Rev. 20; D. & C. 76.) But even within these two separate resurrections, there is an order in which the dead will come forth. Those being resurrected with celestial bodies, whose destiny is to inherit a celestial kingdom, will come forth in the *morning* of the first resurrection. Their graves shall be opened and they shall be caught up to meet the Lord at his Second Coming. They are Christ's, the firstfruits, and they shall descend with him to reign as kings and priests during the millennial era. (D. & C. 29:13; 43:18; 76:50-70; 88:97-98; 1 Thess. 4:16-17; Rev. 20: 3-7.)

"And after this another angel shall sound, which is the second trump; and then cometh the redemption of those who are Christ's at his coming; who have received their part in that prison which is prepared for them, that they might receive the gospel, and be judged according to men in the flesh." (D.

& C. 88:99.) This is the *afternoon* of the first resurrection; it takes place after our Lord has ushered in the millennium. Those coming forth at that time do so with terrestrial bodies and are thus destined to inherit a terrestrial glory in eternity. (D. & C. 76:71-80.)

At the end of the millennium, the second resurrection begins. In the forepart of this resurrection of the unjust those destined to come forth will be "the spirits of men who are to be judged, and are found under condemnation; And these are the rest of the dead; and they live not again until the thousand years are ended, neither again, until the end of the earth." (D. & C. 88:100-101.) These are the ones who have earned telestial bodies, who were wicked and carnal in mortality, and who have suffered the wrath of God in hell "until the last resurrection, until the Lord, even Christ the Lamb, shall have finished his work." (D. & C. 76:85.) Their final destiny is to inherit a telestial glory. (D. & C. 76:81-112.)

Finally, in the latter end of the resurrection of damnation, the sons of perdition, those who "remain filthy still" (D. & C. 88:102), shall come forth from their graves. (2 Ne. 9:14-16.) "Then is the time when their torments shall be as a lake of fire and brimstone, whose flame ascendeth up forever and ever; and then is the time that they shall be chained down to an everlasting destruction, according to the power and captivity of Satan, he having subjected them according to his will. Then, I say unto you, they shall be as though there had been no redemption made; for they cannot be redeemed according to God's justice; and they cannot die, seeing there is no more corruption." (Alma 12:17-18.)

Bodily perfection will come to all men as a free gift in the resurrection. But even though all persons are raised from mortality to immortality, from corruption to incorruption, so that disease and physical impairment are no longer found, this mere fact of resurrection does not give peace of mind, the knowledge of God, a hope of eternal life, or any of the great spiritual blessings which flow from gospel obedience. These blessings are not free gifts. Except for the free gift of immortality (which comes by grace alone and includes bodily or physical perfection), all rewards gained in the eternal worlds must be earned. That perfection sought by the saints is both temporal and spiritual and comes only as a result of full obedience.

Amulek taught: "The spirit and the body shall be reunited again in its *perfect form;* both limb and joint shall be restored to its proper frame, even as we now are at this time; and we shall be brought to stand before God, knowing even as we know now, and have a bright recollection of all our guilt. Now, this restoration shall come to all, both old and young, both bond and free, both male and female, both the wicked and the righteous; and even there shall not so much as a hair of their heads be lost; but every thing shall be restored to its perfect frame, as it is now, or in the body, and shall be brought and be arraigned before the bar of Christ the Son, and God the Father, and the Holy Spirit, which is one Eternal God, to be judged according to their works, whether they be good or whether they be evil." (Alma 11:43-44.)

Alma spoke similarly: "The soul shall be restored to the body, and the body to the soul; yea, and every limb and joint shall be restored to its body; yea, even a hair of the head shall not be lost; but all things shall be restored to their proper and perfect frame. . . . And then shall the righteous shine forth in the kingdom of God. But behold, an awful death cometh upon the wicked; for they die as to things pertaining to things of righteousness; for they are unclean, and no unclean thing can inherit the kingdom of God; but they are cast out, and consigned to partake of the fruits of their labors or their works, which have been evil; and they drink the dregs of a bitter cup." (Alma 40:23-26.)

As seen from these scriptures, *the resurrection is a restoration, both a restoration of body and spirit and a restoration to the individual of the same mental and spiritual acquirements and attitudes he had in this life.* As Alma further expressed it, the resurrection or restoration will "bring back again evil for evil, or carnal for carnal, or devilish for devilish— good for that which is good; righteous for that which is righteous; just for that which is just; merciful for that which is merciful. . . . For that which ye do send out shall return unto you again, and be restored; therefore, the word restoration more fully condemneth the sinner, and justifieth him not at all." (Alma 41:13-15.)

It was in accordance with this principle that the Prophet wrote by way of revelation: "Whatever principle of intelligence we attain unto in this life, it will rise with us in the resurrection. And if a person gains more knowledge and intelligence in this life through his diligence and obedience than another, he will have so much the advantage in the world to come." (D. & C. 130:18-19.) Those who "are raised to become gods" (*Teachings,* p. 312) will progress until they receive "a fulness of truth, yea, even of all truth," until they are "glorified in truth" and know "all things." (D. & C. 93:26-28.) The fulness of the Father which includes "all power, both in heaven and on earth" (D. & C. 93:16-17) is not gained by exalted beings until after the resurrection. *Just as the creative and redemptive powers of Christ extend to the earth and all things thereon, as also to the infinite expanse of worlds in immensity, so the power of the resurrection is universal in*

scope. Man, the earth, and all life thereon will come forth in the resurrection. And the resurrection applies to and is going on in other worlds and other galaxies.

Thus saith the Lord: "And the end shall come, and the heaven and the earth shall be consumed and pass away, and there shall be a new heaven and a new earth. For all old things shall pass away, and all things shall become new, even the heaven and the earth, and all the fulness thereof, both *men* and *beasts,* the *fowls* of the air, and the *fishes* of the sea; And not one hair, neither mote, shall be lost, for it is the workmanship of mine hand." (D. & C. 29:23-25.)

John the Revelator saw "the earth, in its sanctified, immortal, and eternal state" (D. & C. 77:1), that is, in its resurrected state. "The earth abideth the law of a celestial kingdom, for it filleth the measure of its creation, and transgresseth not the law—Wherefore, it shall be sanctified; yea, notwithstanding it shall die, it shall be quickened again, and shall abide the power by which it is quickened, and the righteous shall inherit it." (D. & C. 88:25-26.)

John also saw *resurrected beasts in heaven,* and the revelation specifically says they were "individual beasts . . . in their destined order or sphere of creation, in the enjoyment of their *eternal felicity.*" (D. & C. 77:3.) Speaking on this subject the Prophet said: "John saw the actual beast in heaven. . . . John saw beings there of a thousand forms, that had been saved from ten thousand times ten thousand earths like this—strange beasts of which we have no conception: all might be seen in heaven. The grand secret was to show John what there was in heaven. John learned that God glorified himself by saving all that his hands had made, whether beasts, fowls, fishes or men; and he will glorify himself with them.

"Says one, 'I cannot believe in the salvation of beasts.' Any man who would tell you that this could not be, would tell you that the revelations are not true. John heard the words of the beasts giving glory to God, and understood them. God who made the beasts could understand every language spoken by them. The four beasts were four of the most noble animals that had filled the measure of their creation, and had been saved from other worlds, because they were perfect: they were like angels in their sphere. We are not told where they came from, and I do not know; but they were seen and heard by John praising and glorifying God." (*Teachings,* pp. 291-292.)

No man can conceive of the glory that may be attained through the resurrection. God himself, the Father of us all, is a glorified, exalted, immortal, *resurrected Man!* (*Teachings,* pp. 312, 345-346; D. & C. 130:22.)

RESURRECTION AND THE LIFE.

See CHRIST, ETERNAL LIFE, IMMORTALITY, PERSONIFICATION, RESURRECTION. Christ is the *Resurrection and the Life.* This designation points to the fact that *resurrection* (which is immortality) and *life* (which is eternal life) come because of him and his atoning sacrifice. Hence on the principle of personification he could properly say: "I am the resurrection, and the life: he that believeth in me, though he were dead, yet shall he live: And whosoever liveth and believeth in me shall never die." (John 11:25-26.)

RETROGRESSION OF NATIONS.

See APOSTASY.

REVELATION.

See GIFT OF THE HOLY GHOST, INSPIRATION, MINISTERING OF ANGELS, MIRACLES, MORMON BIBLE, ORACLES, PROPHECY, PROPHETS, REVELATOR, REVELATORS, SCRIPTURE, SEERS, SIGNS, SIGNS OF THE TIMES, TESTIMONY, URIM AND THUMMIM, VISIONS, WHITE HORSE PROPHECY. 1. NATURE OF REVELATION.—As used in the gospel, *"revelation* signifies the making known of divine truth by communication from the heavens." (*Articles of Faith,* pp. 296-313.) Revelation comes from God to man in various appointed ways, according to the laws ordained by the Almighty. The Lord appears personally to certain spiritually receptive persons; he speaks audibly by his own voice, on occasions, to those whose ears are attuned to the divine wave length; angels are sent from his presence to minister to deserving individuals; dreams and visions come from him to the faithful; he often speaks by the still small voice, the voice of the Spirit, the voice of prophecy and revelation; he reveals truth by means of the Urim and Thummim; and he gives his mind and will to receptive mortals in whatever ways seem appropriate as circumstances require.

2. PERSONAL REVELATION.—Every devoted, obedient, and righteous person on earth has and does receive revelation from God. Revelation is the natural inheritance of all the faithful. *"No man can receive the Holy Ghost,"* the Prophet said, *"without receiving revelations. The Holy Ghost is a revelator."* (*Teachings,* p. 328.) God is no respecter of persons, meaning that the gift of the Holy Ghost, always and invariably, will be poured out upon all those who abide the law entitling them to that divine companionship. (Acts 10.) That Being "with whom is no variableness, neither shadow of turning" (Jas. 1:17) always bestows the same reward for obedience to the same law.

To the faithful the Lord promises: "Assuredly as the Lord liveth, who is your God and your Redeemer, even so surely shall you receive *a knowledge of whatsoever things you shall ask in faith, with an honest heart, believing that you shall receive. . . .* Yea, behold, *I will tell you in your mind and in your heart, by the Holy Ghost,* which shall come upon you and which shall dwell in your heart. Now, behold, *this is the spirit of revelation."* (D. & C. 8:1-3; 46:7; Matt. 7:7-8; Jas. 1:5.) This is the way testimony is gained, as in the case of Enos (Enos 1-10), and the way all men can learn of the truth of the Book of Mormon. (Moro. 10:3-5.) Missionaries are to bear record of those things which have been revealed to them. (D. & C. 58:63.)

Knowledge is revealed to the saints by the Holy Ghost (D. & C. 121:26-32), and when they speak as moved upon by that member of the Godhead, the resultant expressions are scripture. (D. & C. 68:1-4.) "If thou shalt ask," the Lord said to the Prophet (and it applies in principle to all the saints), *"thou shalt receive revelation upon revelation, knowledge upon knowledge, that thou mayest know the mysteries and peaceable things*—that which bringeth joy, that which bringeth life eternal." (D. & C. 42:61; 59:4.)

"Thus saith the Lord—I, the Lord, am merciful and gracious unto those who fear me, and delight to honor those who serve me in righteousness and in truth unto the end. Great shall be their reward and eternal shall be their glory. And *to them I will reveal all mysteries, yea, all the hidden mysteries of my kingdom from days of old, and for ages to come, will I make known unto them the good pleasure of my will concerning all things pertaining to my kingdom. Yea, even the wonders of eternity shall they know, and things to come will I show them, even the things of many generations. And their wisdom shall be great, and their understanding reach to heaven;* and before them the wisdom of the wise shall perish, and the understanding of the prudent shall come to naught. *For by my Spirit will I enlighten them, and by my power will I make known unto them the secrets of my will*—yea, even those things which eye has not seen, nor ear heard, nor yet entered into the heart of man." (D. & C. 76:5-10.)

Paul wrote: "Eye hath not seen, nor ear heard, neither have entered into the heart of man, the things which God hath prepared for them that love him. *But God hath revealed them unto us by his Spirit: for the Spirit searcheth all things, yea, the deep things of God.* . . . But the natural man receiveth not the things of the Spirit of God: for they are foolishness unto him: neither can he know them, because they are spiritually discerned. But he that is spiritual judgeth all things, yet he himself is judged of no man. For who hath known the mind of the Lord, that he may instruct him? But *we have the mind*

of Christ." (1 Cor. 2:9-10, 14-16; 14:6, 26, 30; 2 Cor. 12:1-4; D. & C. 76:114-118.)

Every person who is sufficiently faithful has the categorical promise that God himself will appear to him. "Verily, thus saith the Lord: It shall come to pass that every soul who forsaketh his sins and cometh unto me, and calleth on my name, and obeyeth my voice, and keepeth my commandments, shall see my face and know that I am." (D. & C. 93:1.) This has reference to the personal appearance of God to mortal beings. (D. & C. 67:10-14.) Many righteous persons have complied with the law of faith involved and received this promised revelation. (Ether 3:19-26.)

With reference to their own personal affairs, the saints are expected (because they have the gift of the Holy Ghost) *to gain personal revelation and guidance rather than to run to the First Presidency or some other church leaders to be told what to do.* "It is a great thing to inquire at the hands of God, or to come into his presence," the Prophet said, "and we feel fearful to approach him on subjects that are of little or no consequence, to satisfy the queries of individuals, especially about things the knowledge of which men ought to obtain in all sincerity, before God, *for themselves,* in humility by the prayer of faith, and more especially a teacher or a high priest in the Church." (*Teach-*

ings, p. 22.)

3. REVELATION FOR THE CHURCH.—Our Lord's true Church is established and founded upon revelation. Its identity as the true Church continues as long as revelation is received to direct its affairs, for the gates of hell can never prevail against that power of faith and righteousness which pulls down revelations from heaven. Jesus commended Peter for his testimony; "flesh and blood hath not revealed it unto thee, but my Father which is in heaven," he said, "and upon this rock I will build my church." (Matt. 16:17-18.) Commenting upon this the Prophet said, "What rock? Revelation." (*Teachings,* p. 274.)

But the Lord's house is a house of order and not a house of confusion. (D. & C. 132:8.) Where the Church is concerned revelation comes only through the appointed channels. No one but the President of the Church, who holds and exercises the fulness of the keys, can announce revelation to the Church. *"No one shall be appointed to receive commandments and revelations in this church excepting my servant Joseph Smith, Jun., for he receiveth them even as Moses. . . . For I have given him the keys* of the mysteries, and the revelations which are sealed, until I shall appoint unto them another in his stead." (D. & C. 28:2-8; 25:9; 90:14; 94:3; 100:11; 107:91-92.)

It is true that all members of the Council of the Twelve are ap-pointed and sustained to serve as prophets, seers, and revelators to the Church (*Teachings,* p. 109), but as with all of the keys of the kingdom which they receive in connection with the holy apostleship, the power to receive and promulgate revelations for the church lies dormant in them unless and until one of them becomes the President of the Church. Since keys are the right of presidency, they can only be exercised in their fulness by one man on earth at a time. (D. & C. 132:7.)

Every person properly appointed and sustained to act in an official capacity in the Church is entitled to the spirit of revelation to guide the particular organization or group over which he presides. The "Presidency are over the Church," the Prophet said, "and *revelations of the mind and will of God to the Church, are to come through the Presidency.* This is the order of heaven, and the power and privilege of this priesthood. *It is also the privilege of any officer in this Church to obtain revelations, so far as relates to his particular calling and duty in the Church."* (*Teachings,* p. 111.)

This system of promulgating revelations through the established head of the Lord's earthly work is so unbending and inflexible that it stands as a test to establish the truth or falsity of purported revelations. *"There is none other appointed unto you to receive commandments and revelations until he be taken,"* the Lord said of the Prophet. *"And this shall be a law unto you, that ye receive not the teachings of any that shall come before you as revelations or commandments; And this I give unto you that you may not be deceived, that you may know they are not of me."* (D. & C. 43:2-7; *Doctrines of Salvation,* vol. 1, pp. 283-289.)

4. NO SALVATION WITHOUT REVELATION.—*"Salvation cannot come without revelation; it is in vain for anyone to minister without it,"* the Prophet taught. (*Teachings,* p. 160.) Without revelation the very existence of God and of the plan of salvation would be unknown, and without revelation there would be no legal administrators to perform the ordinances of salvation with binding effect on earth and in heaven. "Great and marvelous are the works of the Lord," Jacob said. "How unsearchable are the depths of the mysteries of him; and it is impossible that man should find out all his ways. *And no man knoweth of his ways save it be revealed unto him;* wherefore, brethren, despise not the revelations of God." (Jac. 4:8; Jarom 2; Omni 25.)

That revelation must come in the very age and to the very people who are to be saved is also self-evident. "Could we read and comprehend all that has been written from the days of Adam, on the relation of man to God and angels in a future state, we should know

very little about it," said the Prophet. "Reading the experience of others, or the revelations given to *them,* can never give *us* a comprehensive view of our condition and true relation to God. Knowledge of these things can only be obtained by experience through the ordinances of God set forth for that purpose. *Could you gaze into heaven five minutes, you would know more than you would by reading all that ever was written on the subject."* (*Teachings,* p. 324.)

5. REVELATION SAVES OR DAMNS. —The receipt of revelation by individuals or peoples does not assure salvation to the favored recipients. Salvation is gained by enduring in faith and devotion to the end; it is the reward of righteousness. "Although a man may have many revelations, and have power to do many mighty works, yet if he boasts in his own strength, and sets at naught the counsels of God, and follows after the dictates of his own will and carnal desires, he must fall and incur the vengeance of a just God upon him." (D. & C. 3:4.)

Indeed, the receipt of revelation may lead to damnation as well as to salvation. "For of him unto whom much is given much is required; and he who sins against the greater light shall receive the greater condemnation. *Ye call upon my name for revelations, and I give them unto you; and inasmuch as ye keep not my sayings, which I give unto you, ye become trans-*

gressors; and justice and judgment are the penalty which is affixed unto my law." (D. & C. 82:3-4.) In fact the greatest of all penalties, that of being cast out with the devil and his angels in eternity, is reserved for "those sons of perdition who deny the Son after the Father has *revealed him.*" (D. & C. 76:43.)

6. LATTER-DAY REVELATION.— Devout persons of all Christian faiths readily accepted the truth that revelation was poured out upon the faithful, from age to age, from Adam to the days of Christ's apostles. They suppose, however, that since the apostolic era the heavens have been sealed and that revelation has ceased. In reality souls are just as precious in the sight of God today as they ever were, and revelation is still poured out in abundance so that souls may be led to salvation.

"And again I speak unto you who deny the revelations of God," proclaimed Moroni, "and say that they are done away, that there are no revelations, nor prophecies, nor gifts, nor healing, nor speaking with tongues, and the interpretation of tongues; Behold I say unto you, *he that denieth these things knoweth not the gospel of Christ;* yea, he has not read the scriptures; if so, he does not understand them. For do we not read that God is the same yesterday, today, and forever, and in him there is no variableness neither shadow of changing?" (Morm. 9:7-9.)

Nephi wrote: "Wo be unto him that shall say: We have received the word of God, and we need no more of the word of God, for we have enough! For behold, thus saith the Lord God: *I will give unto the children of men line upon line, precept upon precept,* here a little and there a little; and blessed are those who hearken unto my precepts, and lend an ear unto my counsel, for they shall learn wisdom; for unto him that receiveth I will give more; and from them that shall say, We have enough, from them shall be taken away even that which they have." (2 Ne. 28:29-30.)

"Know ye not that there are more nations than one? Know ye not that I, the Lord your God, have created all men, and that I remember those who are upon the isles of the sea; and that I rule in the heavens above and in the earth beneath; and I bring forth my word unto the children of men, yea, even upon all the nations of the earth? *Wherefore murmur ye, because that ye shall receive more of my word?* . . . And because that I have spoken one word ye need not suppose that I cannot speak another; for my work is not yet finished; neither shall it be until the end of man, neither from that time henceforth and forever. Wherefore, because that ye have a Bible ye need not suppose that it contains all my words; neither need ye suppose that I have not caused more to be written." (2 Ne. 29:7-10.)

"Does it remain for a people who never had faith enough to call down one scrap of revelation from heaven, and for all they have now are indebted to the faith of another people who lived hundreds and thousands of years before them, does it remain for them to say how much God has spoken and how much he has not spoken?" the Prophet Joseph Smith asked. "We have what we have, and the Bible contains what it does contain: but to say that God never said anything more to man than is there recorded, would be saying at once that we have at last received a revelation; for it must require one to advance thus far, because it is nowhere said in that volume by the mouth of God, that he would not, after giving what is there contained, speak again; and if any man has found for a fact that the Bible contains all that God ever revealed to man, he has ascertained it by an immediate revelation, other than has been previously written by the prophets and apostles. But through the kind providence of our Father a *portion* of his word which he delivered to his ancient saints, has fallen into our hands, is presented to us with a promise of a reward if obeyed, and with a penalty if disobeyed." (*Teachings*, p. 61.)

Through the whole Bible there are passages of scripture—hundreds and hundreds of them—reciting promises and recording covenants made by God with his chosen people, all of which are to be fulfilled in the last days, and none of which can come to pass without revelation. (*Teachings*, pp. 70-71; *Doctrines of Salvation*, vol. 1, pp. 274-279.) There is no other single subject about which the Bible has as much to say as about the glorious things which are to take place in the dispensation of the fulness of times—all of which things shall be attended by revelation. It is no wonder that the Lord has said: *"Deny not the spirit of revelation, nor the spirit of prophecy, for wo unto him that denieth these things."* (D. & C. 11:25.)

For the future, there is to be new revelation that will dwarf into comparative insignificance all the knowledge now revealed from heaven. When the sealed portion of the Book of Mormon comes forth it will "reveal all things from the foundation of the world unto the end thereof," and in this final dispensation, "all things shall be revealed unto the children of men which ever have been among the children of men, and which ever will be even unto the end of the earth." (2 Ne. 27:10-11, 22; 30:18.) "In that day when the Lord shall come, he shall reveal all things—Things which have passed, and hidden things which no man knew, things of the earth, by which it was made, and the purpose and the end thereof— Things most precious, things that are above, and things that are beneath, things that are in the earth, and upon the earth, and in heaven." (D. & C. 101:32-34.)

7. CHURCH ADMINISTERED BY REVELATION.—Since The Church of Jesus Christ of Latter-day Saints is the Lord's true Church; and since the Lord's Church must be guided by continuous revelation if it is to maintain divine approval; and since we have the unqualified promise that this Church and kingdom is destined to remain on earth and prepare a people for the Second Coming—we could safely conclude (if we had no other evidence) that the Church today is guided by revelation. (*Doctrines of Salvation,* vol. 1, pp. 279-283.) It is true that not many revelations containing doctrinal principles are now being written, because all we are as yet capable and worthy to receive has already been written. But the Spirit is giving direct and daily revelation to the presiding Brethren in the administration of the affairs of the Church. (D. & C. 102: 2, 9, 23; 107:39; 128:11.)

President Wilford Woodruff said: "Where are the revelations of President Young? Do you find them on record? Only a few; but the Holy Ghost and the revelations of God were with Brigham Young from the day that he received this gospel until the day that he laid down his life and his tabernacle was carried to the grave. There was no necessity particularly for Brigham Young to give written revelation, only in a few instances. So with John Taylor. So with Wilford Woodruff. And so in a great measure probably with all who may

follow us, until the coming of the Son of Man. But are we without revelation? We are not. We know our duty, and in a measure we know what lies before us. . . . I traveled with Brigham Young at home and abroad, and I never saw a day in my life but what he had the spirit and power of revelation of God with him. This power was with him when he came to this land. I was with him when he laid the foundations of our temples, and when he laid out the city of Salt Lake. He did all these things by the inspiration and Spirit of Almighty God." (*Discourses of Wilford Woodruff,* pp. 55-56.)

The presence of revelation in the Church is positive proof that it is the kingdom of God on earth. And because the Lord is no respecter of persons he will give to any person, who abides the law entitling him to know, personal revelation of the divinity of the Church and of the fact that it is being led by revelation today. Indeed, for those who accept all the revelations which God gives in any particular day there is peace and joy and a hope of salvation. For those who reject these revelations there awaits the damnation of hell.

From the mouth of the Prophet we have this plain statement: "The plea of many in this day is, that we have no right to receive revelations; but *if we do not get revelations, we do not have the oracles of God; and if they have not the oracles of God, they are not the people of God.* But say you, What will become of the world, or the various professors of religion who do not believe in revelation and the oracles of God as continued in his Church in all ages of the world, when he has a people on earth? I tell you, in the name of Jesus Christ, they will be damned; and when you get into the eternal world, you will find it will be so; they cannot escape the damnation of hell." (*Teachings,* p. 272.)

REVELATOR.

See HOLY GHOST, REVELATION, REVELATORS, TESTATOR, TESTIMONY. "The Holy Ghost is a *Revelator,"* the Prophet said. "No man can receive the Holy Ghost without receiving revelations." (*Teachings,* p. 328.) Those who enjoy the companionship of the Holy Ghost have the spirit of revelation. (D. & C. 8:2-3.) A testimony of the gospel comes from the Holy Ghost. "By the power of the Holy Ghost ye may know the truth of all things." (Moro. 10:5.)

REVELATORS.

See FIRST PRESIDENCY, HOLY GHOST, ORACLES, PROPHETS, REVELATION, SEERS, VISIONS. Anyone who receives revelation from the Lord and conveys the revealed truth to another is a *revelator.* Joseph Smith was a revelator to Sidney Rigdon (D. & C. 100:11); the beloved disciple, because of the great revelations he left for the world, is known as John the Revelator. (D. & C. 77:2; 128:6.) The President of the Church is a revelator for the Church (D. & C. 107:92; 124:94, 125), as also are the members of the First Presidency, the Council of the Twelve, and the Patriarch to the Church.

REVERENCE.

See HONOR, MINISTERIAL TITLES, OBEISANCE, WORSHIP. True and acceptable worship is always attended by feelings of deepest *reverence*—feelings of awe, great respect, and godly fear. Men are to "serve God acceptably with reverence and godly fear." (Heb. 12:28.) Before his throne "all things bow in humble reverence, and give him glory forever and ever." (D. & C. 76:93.) "Holy and reverend is his name." (Ps. 111:9.)

Reverence is due not only to God and his holy name, but to his laws, his gospel, his covenants, his prophets, his ordinances, his temples, his priesthood, and all the things he has revealed and given for the salvation and blessing of his children. It was "out of respect or reverence to the name of the Supreme Being, to avoid the too frequent repetition of his name," that the ancient saints called the Higher Priesthood after Melchizedek. (D. & C. 107:4.)

"Keep my sabbaths, and reverence my sanctuary," is his command to Israel. (Lev. 19:30; 26:2.)

Blessings await "those who shall reverence" him in his house. (D. & C. 109:21.) Obviously the most decorous conduct—unmarred by loud laughter, unnecessary conversation, untoward actions of any sort, or even by evil thoughts—is essential to reverencing the Lord's sanctuary. And what is said of his temples is also true of his meetinghouses.

President Joseph F. Smith said: *"Self-respect requires, among other things, that one shall behave like a true gentleman, in a house of worship. No self-respecting person will go to a house devoted to the service of God to whisper, gossip and visit; rather, it is one's duty to put on self-restraint, to give one's undivided attention to the speaker, and concentrate the mind upon his words that his thoughts may be grasped to one's benefit and profit. . . .*

"Self-respect, deference for sacred things, and personal purity are the beginnings and the essence of widom. The doctrines of the gospel, the church restraint, are like schoolmasters to keep us in the line of duty. If it were not for these schoolmasters, we would perish and be overcome by the evil about us. . . .

"Such a seeming simple thing, then, as proper conduct in a house of worship leads to good results in many respects. Good conduct leads to self-respect, which creates purity of thought and action. Pure thought and noble action lead to a desire to serve God in the strength of manhood and to become subservient to the schoolmasters, church restraint, and the doctrines of the gospel of Christ." (*Gospel Doctrine*, 5th ed., pp. 334-336.)

REVEREND.
See MINISTERIAL TITLES.

RICHES.
See POOR, RICHES OF ETERNITY. As with all men, those who have *riches* will be judged according to their works and gain either salvation or damnation as they may chance to merit. But the nature of fallen man is such that in the overwhelming majority of cases riches are far more of a hindrance than a help in attaining peace in this world and eternal life in the world to come. Accordingly prophets in all ages have warned against "the cares of this world, and the deceitfulness of riches" (Mark 4:19; Matt. 13:22; Luke 8:14), lest men love the things of this world more than the riches of eternity and thereby lose their souls.

"How hardly shall they that have riches enter into the kingdom of God," our Lord taught. "For it is easier for a camel to go through a needle's eye, than for a rich man to enter into the kingdom of God." (Luke 18:18-27; Matt. 19:16-26; Mark 10:17-27.) Also: *"Lay not up for yourselves treasures upon earth,* where moth and rust doth corrupt,

and where thieves break through and steal: But lay up for yourselves treasures in heaven, where neither moth nor rust doth corrupt, and where thieves do not break through nor steal: For where your treasure is, there will your heart be also." (Matt. 6:19-21.)

Paul left us this pointed exhortation: "We brought nothing into this world, and it is certain we can carry nothing out. And having food and raiment let us be therewith content. But they that will be rich fall into temptation and a snare, and into many foolish and hurtful lusts, which drown men in destruction and perdition. For *the love of money is the root of all evil:* which while some coveted after, they have erred from the faith, and pierced themselves through with many sorrows. But thou, O man of God, flee these things; and follow after righteousness, godliness, faith, love, patience, meekness." (1 Tim. 6:7-11.)

James spoke similarly: "Go to now, ye rich men, weep and howl for your miseries that shall come upon you. Your riches are corrupted, and your garments are motheaten. Your gold and silver is cankered; and the rust of them shall be a witness against you, and shall eat your flesh as it were fire. Ye have heaped treasure together for the last days. Behold, the hire of the labourers who have reaped down your fields, which is of you kept back by fraud, crieth: and the cries of them which have reaped are entered into the ears of the Lord of sabaoth." (Jas. 5:1-4.)

An ancient wise man counseled: *"Give me neither poverty nor riches;* feed me with food convenient for me: Lest I be full, and deny thee, and say, Who is the Lord? or lest I be poor, and steal, and take the name of my God in vain." (Prov. 30:8-9.)

The Nephite prophet Jacob warned: "Wo unto the rich, who are rich as to the things of the world. For because they are rich they despise the poor, and they persecute the meek, and their hearts are upon their treasures; wherefore, *their treasure is their God.* And behold, their treasure shall perish with them also." (2 Ne. 9:30, 42.)

On another occasion Jacob taught: "Think of your brethren like unto yourselves, and be familiar with all and free with your substance, that they may be rich like unto you. But *before ye seek for riches, seek ye for the kingdom of God.* And after ye have obtained a hope in Christ ye shall obtain riches, if ye seek them; and ye will seek them for the intent to do good —to clothe the naked, and to feed the hungry, and to liberate the captive, and administer relief to the sick and the afflicted." (Jac. 2:17-19.)

By latter-day revelation the Lord has said: "Wo unto you rich men, that will not give your substance to the poor, for your riches will canker your souls; and this shall be your lamentation in the day of visitation, and of judgment, and of indignation: The harvest is past, the summer is ended, and my soul is not saved! (D. & C. 56:16.)

"Seek not for riches but for wisdom, and behold, the mysteries of God shall be unfolded unto you, and then shall you be made rich. Behold, he that hath eternal life is rich." (D. & C. 6:7.)

RICHES OF ETERNITY.

See ETERNAL LIFE, ETERNITY, RICHES. To the faithful saints the Lord has promised the *riches of eternity.* (D. & C. 38:39; 67:2; 68: 31; 78:18.) These consist in obtaining eternal life and all that is included therein. "Behold, he that hath eternal life is rich." (D. & C. 6:7; 11:7; 43:25.) Accordingly, those who gain the riches of eternity will have a continuation of the family unit in eternity (D. & C. 132); they will progress from grace to grace until they know all things, have all power, and are possessors of all the attributes of godliness in their perfection (D. & C. 50:26-29; 93:6-35); and in addition, because they inherit all that the Father hath (D. & C. 76:50-60; 84:38), they will possess lands and kingdoms and the good things of the earth, the things which we view as wealth and riches from our mortal perspective. (D. & C. 38:20; 88:16-29.)

But the riches of eternity must be earned. "Lay not up for your-selves treasures upon earth," the Lord said, "where moth and rust doth corrupt, and where thieves break through and steal: But lay up for yourselves *treasures in heaven,* where neither moth nor rust doth corrupt, and where thieves do not break through nor steal: For where your treasure is, there will your heart be also." (Matt. 6:19-21.) By developing through gospel obedience the attributes of godliness in this life, man is assured that he will have these godly graces restored to him again in the resurrection (Alma 41:13-15); and thus, having laid up treasures in heaven, he will receive the riches of eternity in the world to come.

RIGHTEOUS.
See PERSONIFICATION.

RIGHTEOUSNESS.

See CELESTIAL LAW, ETERNAL LIFE, EQUITY, FATHER IN HEAVEN, GOD, GOSPEL, INTEGRITY, JUSTICE, LAW, OBEDIENCE, PERFECTION, SALVATION, SANCTIFICATION, SON OF RIGHTEOUSNESS, WICKEDNESS.
1. Plainly and simply stated, *righteousness* is the quality and type of living that results from obedience to the laws and ordinances of the gospel. No persons are wholly righteous; by walking in the light and obeying the celestial law to the extent of their abilities, how-

ever, the saints attain a high degree of righteousness; their conduct becomes blameless, upright, and just; they acquire the attributes of equity, integrity, rectitude, and justice; they attain a state of godliness.

Righteousness brings to pass eternal progression. It was the more righteous portion of the spirits in pre-existence who kept their first estate and gained the right to come to earth and receive bodies. Here in mortality it is the righteous who accept the gospel, live its principles, gain the companionship of the Holy Ghost, and enjoy the peace that passeth understanding. Between death and the resurrection, the souls of the righteous find peace and rest in paradise, while the souls of the wicked— those who are spiritually dead, meaning dead "as to things pertaining unto righteousness" (Alma 12:16; Hela. 14:18)—suffer the damnation of hell in outer darkness. (Alma 40:11-14.) Then in the day of judgment the righteous have righteousness restored to them again. (Alma 41:14; Hela. 14:29; Morm. 9:14.)

Finally, in a state of glorious immortality, "shall the righteous shine forth as the sun in the kingdom of their Father." (Matt. 13: 43; 25:46.) "Behold, the righteous, the saints of the Holy One of Israel, they who have believed in the Holy One of Israel, they who have endured the crosses of the world, and despised the shame of it, they shall inherit the kingdom of God, which was prepared for them from the foundation of the world, and their joy shall be full forever." (2 Ne. 9:18; Alma 34:36; 40:25; 1 Pet. 4:18; D. & C. 29:27; 76:5.) This earth, as a glorified, celestial sphere, shall be the home of the righteous. (D. & C. 88:16-26.)

All of this glory, honor, and possible future reward is attainable because of the atoning sacrifice of Christ. (Rom. 5:18-19.) It is only those who gain the fulness of salvation who will receive the full reward promised by our Lord in the Sermon on the Mount: "Blessed are they which do hunger and thirst after righteousness: for they shall be filled." (Matt. 5:6.)

2. Since Christ is the *Son of Righteousness* (2 Ne. 26:9; 3 Ne. 25:2; Ether 9:22), it follows that God his Father is named *Righteousness*. This is in keeping with the general principle whereunder members of the Godhead reveal themselves under names which point men's attention to characteristics and attributes which are perfected in Deity. Thus God being the embodiment of righteousness chooses that as a name for himself to certify such trust to his children on earth. In like manner he might call himself *Wisdom, Love, Power, Counsel, Faith,* or a great number of such type of names. This is the same practice as that which causes Christ to use the word *Holy* as one of his names. (Isa. 57:15.)

RIGHTS.

See INALIENABLE RIGHTS.

RISEN LORD.

See CHRIST, LORD, RESURRECTION. To point attention to his pre-eminent position as "the firstfruits of them that slept" (1 Cor. 15:20; Col. 1:18), and to emphasize the reality of his resurrection with a tangible body of flesh and bones (Luke 24:36-48), Christ is often called the *Risen Lord.* (Luke 24:34.)

ROBBERY.

See HONESTY, STEALING, WICKEDNESS. 1. To rob is to commit theft; it is to deprive a person of something by force or intimidation. "Thou shalt not defraud thy neighbour, neither rob him." (Lev. 19:13.) *Robbery* should be punished by the law of the land (D. & C. 42:84; 134:8); unless they repent, those guilty of it shall suffer with the damned in hell, be denied a place in the kingdom of God, and find their final destiny in a sphere no higher than the telestial world.

2. In a spiritual sense, persons who seek salvation on some other terms than those the Lord has laid down are classified by him as thieves and *robbers.* They are seeking to gain salvation by deceit and fraud, to rob God of that eternal reward which he has decreed shall be conferred *only* on his terms. "He that entereth not by the door into the sheepfold, but climbeth up some other way, the same is a thief and a robber," Jesus said. (John 10:1-8.) Also, with particular reference to false ministers, he said: *"All that ever came before me who testified not of me are thieves and robbers." (Inspired Version,* John 10:8.)

Describing the degenerate conditions of latter-day churches, Nephi said: "Their churches have become corrupted. . . . They rob the poor because of their fine sanctuaries; they rob the poor because of their fine clothing." (2 Ne. 28:12-13.)

3. Members of the Church and kingdom of God on earth covenant in the waters of baptism that they will keep the commandments of God and serve him with full purpose of heart. (Mosiah 18:10; D. & C. 20:37.) Implicit in this covenant of obedience is the solemn promise to pay an honest tithing, that is, to *give the Lord his tenth of one's increase or interest.* If a member of the Church does not pay an honest tithing, that is, *if he converts the Lord's tenth to his own use,* he is designated in the revelations as a *robber.* Thus we find the Lord saying through Malachi, *"Will a man rob God? Yet ye have robbed me. But ye say, Wherein have we robbed thee? In tithes and offerings. Ye are cursed with a curse: for ye have robbed me, even this whole nation."* (Mal. 3:8-9.)

ROBBING GOD.

See TITHING.

ROBES OF RIGHTEOUSNESS.
See GARMENTS.

ROCK.
See ROCK OF HEAVEN.

ROCK OF AGES.
See ROCK OF HEAVEN.

ROCK OF IIEAVEN.
See CHRIST, LORD OF HOSTS, STONE OF ISRAEL. Christ is the *Rock* (Deut. 32:3-4, 18, 30-31; 1 Cor. 10:1-4), or the *Rock of Heaven.* (Moses 7:53.) Such name-titles carry a connotation of strength and stability (1 Sam. 2:2), as for instance when David exulted: "The Lord is my rock, and my fortress, and my deliverer; The God of my rock, in him will I trust: he is my shield, and the horn of my salvation, my high tower, and my refuge, my saviour." (2 Sam. 22: 1-4; 23:3; Psa. 18:1-3, 31.)

One of Isaiah's great Messianic prophecies was that the promised Messiah would be "for a stone of stumbling and for a *rock of offence* to both the houses of Israel, for a gin and for a snare to the inhabitants of Jerusalem. And many among them shall stumble, and fall, and be broken, and be snared, and be taken." (Isa. 8:14-15.) Both Paul (Rom. 9:33) and Peter (1 Pet. 2:7-8) record the fulfilment of this prophecy.

ROCK OF OFFENCE.
See ROCK OF HEAVEN.

ROOT OF DAVID.
See CHRIST, LION OF THE TRIBE OF JUDAH, SON OF DAVID, SON OF GOD, STEM OF JESSE. Christ is the *Root of David.* (Rev. 5:5; 22:16.) This designation signifies that he who was the Son of David was also before David, was pre-eminent above him, and was the root or source from which the great king in Israel gained his kingdom and power.

ROYAL LAW.
See CHURCH WELFARE PLAN.

RULER.
See CHRIST, GOVERNOR, KING, LAWGIVER, SHILOH. Christ is the *Ruler,* meaning that he has the natural and legal right to rule and reign over the earth and all flesh on its face. (D. & C. 38:21-22; 41:4; 58:20.) It is only because of apostasy and rebellion that he is kept from ruling in the hearts of men in the present state of things. During the millennium he will reign personally upon the earth. (Tenth Article of Faith.)

S

SABAOTH.

See LORD OF SABAOTH.

SABBATH.

See DAY, SACRAMENT MEET-INGS, SYMBOLISMS, TEN COMMAND-MENTS, WORK. Pursuant to divine command men are to rest from all temporal work and to worship the Lord one day in particular each week. This day—no matter which day of the week is involved—is called the *Sabbath,* from the Hebrew *shabbath* meaning *day of rest.* The *rest,* though important, is incidental to the true keeping of the Sabbath. What is more important is that the Sabbath is an *holy day*—a day of worship, one in which men turn their whole souls to the Lord, renew their covenants with him, and feed their souls upon the things of the Spirit.

Sabbath observance is an eternal principle, and the day itself is so ordained and arranged that it bears record of Christ by pointing particular attention to great works he has performed. From the day of Adam to the Exodus from Egypt, the Sabbath commemorated the fact that Christ rested from his creative labors on the 7th day. (Ex. 20:8-11.) From the Exodus to the day of his resurrection, the Sabbath commemorated the deliverance of Israel from Egyptian bondage. (Deut. 5:12-15.) As Samuel Walter Gamble has pointed out in his *Sunday, the True Sabbath of God,* this necessarily means that the Sabbath was kept on a different day each year. From the days of the early apostles to the present, the Sabbath has been the first day of the week, the *Lord's Day,* in commemoration of the fact that Christ came forth from the grave on Sunday. (Acts 20:7.) The Latter-day Saints keep the first day of the week as their Sabbath, not in imitation of what any peoples of the past have done, but because the Lord so commanded them by direct revelation. (D. & C. 59.)

Sabbath observance was a sign between ancient Israel and their God whereby the chosen people might be known (Neh. 13:15-22; Isa. 56:1-8; Jer. 17:19-27; Ezek 46: 1:7); death was the decreed penalty for violation of it. (Ex. 31:12-17.) And the matter of Sabbath observance remains to this day as one of the great tests which divides the righteous from the worldly and wicked.

Sunday being the Lord's Day, it is a day on which men should do the Lord's work, and do it exclusively. There should be no unnecessary work of a temporal nature, no recreation, no unnecessary travel, no joy riding, and the like. The Sabbath is a day for affimative spiritual worship, aside from which, "thou shalt do none other thing, only let thy food be prepared with singleness of heart." (D. & C. 59: 13.)

SACERDOTALISM.

See PRIESTHOOD. *Sacerdotalism* is the doctrine that special powers and rights necessary to the ministry are conferred by ordination. Obviously this is a true principle. "A man must be called of God, by prophecy, and by the laying on of hands, by those who are in authority, to preach the Gospel and administer in the ordinances thereof." (Fifth Article of Faith.)

SACKCLOTH AND ASHES.

See FASTING, MOURNING, SORROW, WEEPING. A coarse, dark cloth made of hair of camels and goats and used anciently for making sacks and bags was called *sackcloth*. It was also used for making the rough garments worn by mourners, and so it became fixed in the prophetic mind as a symbol for sorrow and mourning. It was the custom for mourners, garbed in sackcloth, either to sprinkle *ashes* upon themselves or to sit in piles of ashes, thereby showing their joy had perished or been destroyed. (Gen. 37:34; Esther 4:1-3; Isa. 61:3; Jer. 6:26.)

The use of sackcloth and ashes anciently was also a token of humility and penitence. When righteous persons used the covering of sackcloth and the sprinkling of ashes to aid them in attaining the spiritual strength to commune with Deity, their usage was always accompanied by fasting and prayer. Daniel, for instance, prefaced the record of one of his great petitions to the throne of grace with this explanation: "I set my face unto the Lord God, to seek by prayer and supplications, with fasting, and sackcloth, and ashes: And I prayed unto the Lord my God, and made my confession." (Dan. 9:3-4; Isa. 58:5; 1 Kings 21:17-29.)

Sackcloth and ashes (accompanied by the fasting, prayer, and turning to the Lord that attended their use) became a symbol of the most sincere and humble repentance. By the mouth of Abinadi, the Lord said of King Noah's wicked followers, "Except they repent in sackcloth and ashes, and cry mightily to the Lord their God, I will not hear their prayers, neither will I deliver them out of their afflictions." (Mosiah 11:25; Hela. 11:9.) It was by repenting in sackcloth and ashes that Nineveh was saved following the dire predictions of Jonah. (Jonah 3:5-6.) Our Lord said of Chorazin and Bethsaida, "If the mighty works had been done in Tyre and Sidon, which have been done in you, they had a great while ago repented, sitting in sackcloth and ashes." (Luke 10:13.)

SACRAMENT.

See ATONEMENT OF CHRIST, BAPTISM, PRIESTS, SACRAMENT MEETINGS, SACRAMENTS, SACRIFICES, SYMBOLISMS. To replace the ordinance of sacrifice (which pointed the attention of the saints forward to the coming sacrifice of the Son of God), our Lord during his mortal ministry instituted the ordinance of the *sacrament* (to point the attention of his saints, after his death, back to the great atoning sacrifice which he had wrought).

Assembling his apostles in an upper room on the occasion of the Feast of the Passover (a feast which itself symbolized many of the events which were to attend his coming sacrifice), "And as they were eating, Jesus took bread and brake it, and blessed it, and gave to his disciples, and said, Take, eat; this is in remembrance of my body which I give a ransom for you. And he took the cup, and gave thanks, and gave it to them, saying, Drink ye all of it. For this is in remembrance of my blood of the new testament, which is shed for as many as shall believe on my name, for the remission of their sins." (*Inspired Version*, Matt. 26:22-25; Mark 14:20-25; Luke 22:17-20; *King James Version*, Matt. 26:26-29; Mark 14:22-25; Luke 22:15-20.)

By partaking of the sacrament, worthy saints renew the covenant previously made by them in the waters of baptism (Mosiah 18:7-10); unbaptized children, being without sin, are entitled and expected to partake of the sacrament to prefigure the covenant they will take upon themselves when they arrive at the years of accountability. Worthy partakers of the sacrament put themselves in perfect harmony with the Lord. (3 Ne. 18.) As indicated by our Lord's statement they gain "the remission of their sins." (*Inspired Version*, Matt. 26:24.)

Those who partake of the sacrament worthily thereby put themselves under covenant with the Lord: 1. To always remember the broken body and spilled blood of Him who was crucified for the sins of the world; 2. To take upon themselves the name of Christ and always remember him; and 3. To keep the commandments of God, that is, to "live by every word that proceedeth forth from the mouth of God." (D. & C. 84:44.)

As his part of the contract, the Lord covenants: 1. That such worthy saints shall have his Spirit to be with them; and 2. That in due course they shall inherit eternal life. (D. & C. 20:75-79; Moro. 4; 5.) "Whoso eateth my flesh, and drinketh my blood, hath eternal life; and I will raise him up at the last day." (John 6:54.) In the light of these covenants, promises, and blessings, is it any wonder that the Lord commanded: "It is expedient that the church meet together often to partake of bread and wine in the remembrance of the Lord Jesus." (D. & C. 20:75; *Doctrines of Salva-*

tion, vol. 2, pp. 338-350.)

"Ye shall not suffer any one knowingly to partake of my flesh and blood unworthily, when ye shall minister it," the Lord commanded, "For whoso eateth and drinketh my flesh and blood unworthily eateth and drinketh damnation to his soul." (3 Ne. 8: 28-29.) And Paul added: "For this cause many are weak and sickly among you, and many sleep." (1 Cor. 11:23-30.) Apostates and unrepentant members of the Church thus reap damnation by mocking God in unworthily partaking of the sacrament.

Bread and wine or water are "the emblems of the flesh and blood of Christ" (D. & C. 20:40); expressions relative to the partaking of his flesh and blood are figurative and not literal. The so-called doctrine of transubstantiation which teaches that all who partake of the sacrament are literally eating the body and drinking the blood of Christ is a false doctrine, devised by uninspired men, which helps to hide the true meaning and purport of the sacramental ordinance.

Few ordinances or performances in the Church act as a greater incentive to personal righteousness than worthy partaking of the sacrament. Those who partake of the sacramental emblems—having a comprehension of the covenant involved—are marking for themselves a course which will result in obedience, holiness, and sanctification.

Such persons—having placed themselves in the spirit of prayer, humility, and worship which attend sacramental administrations—become the ones who gain peace in this life and eternal life in the world to come.

SACRAMENT MEETINGS.

See CONFERENCES, FAST MEETINGS, SABBATH, SOLEMN ASSEMBLIES. To comply with the revelation in which the Lord commands his saints, "Go to the house of prayer and offer up thy sacraments upon my holy day" (D. & C. 59:9), the Church directs the holding of weekly *sacrament meetings* in all its organized units. These are the most solemn and sacred meetings in the Church. Their purpose is to enable the saints to renew their covenants by partaking of the sacrament; to receive instuction in the doctrines of the kingdom; to worship the Almighty in song, prayer, and sermon.

Lectures, concerts, talks on any subjects except the doctrines of the gospel, and entertainment of any sort detract from the high degree of spirituality that should prevail in sacrament meetings. These meetings are designed to be reverent, solemn occasions to which the Spirit of the Lord may come without restraint, and as a result of which the saints will be built up in faith, testimony, and desires to serve God and keep his commandments. To the extent that sacrament meetings fall short of these high standards they fail in their purpose and are not what the Lord intended them to be. (*Doctrines of Salvation,* vol. 2, pp. 340-344.)

SACRAMENTS.

See COVENANTS, FASTING, FAST MEETINGS, OBLATIONS, SACRAMENT MEETINGS, VOWS. 1. To his saints the Lord commands: "Go to the house of prayer and offer up thy *sacraments* upon my holy day. . . . On this, the Lord's day, thou shalt offer thine oblations and thy sacraments unto the Most High." (D. & C. 59:9-12; 62:4; 89:5.) *A sacrament is a spiritual covenant between God and man.* In the Church the Lord has provided the ordinance of the sacrament—with the solemn covenants which attend it— as the occasion when these *personal sacraments* shall be offered up, that is when personal covenants shall be made by those who love the Lord.

The saints offer up their sacraments when they covenant with the Lord, as part of the ordinance of the sacrament, to always remember his Son, to take upon them the name of Christ, and to keep the commandments of God. Any personal sacraments, that is, covenants or determinations to serve God, may be included in the vows thus made when one partakes of the sacrament.

2. In Apostate churches, the *sacraments* are said to be certain re-

ligious ceremonies or rites. Both Roman and Greek Catholics name seven so-called sacraments: baptism, confirmation, eucharist, penance, extreme unction, holy orders, and matrimony. Protestants generally name only two: baptism and the Lord's Supper. In the true Church the rites and ceremonies of the gospel are not classified or categorized as sacraments.

SACRED GROVE.

See FIRST VISION, JOSEPH SMITH THE PROPHET, SHRINES. In the spring of 1820, Joseph Smith, Jr., then in his 15th year, was living with his father's family in the township of Palmyra, New York. A short distance west of the family home was a grove of large trees. It was to a secluded spot in this wooded area that the young man was led by the Spirit when he determined within himself to seek wisdom from God as to which of all the churches was right and which he should join. It was there that the Father and the Son personally appeared to him, in accordance with their eternal plan, for the hour had come for the ushering in of the dispensation of the fulness of times. (Jos. Smith 2:15-20.)

Ever since, this chosen site, hallowed by Deity's personal presence, has been known by the saints as the *Sacred Grove*. It is not a shrine in the sense that many denominations have shrines, nor is there any sanctity now attached to the trees and land there located. But it is a spot held sacred in the hearts of those who believe the truths of salvation, because they glory in the transcendent *event* which there took place.

SACRIFICE.

See CONSECRATION, OBEDIENCE, PLAN OF SALVATION, SACRIFICES, SECOND ESTATE. *Sacrifice* is the crowning test of the gospel. Men are tried and tested in this mortal probation to see if they will put first in their lives the things of the kingdom of God. (Matt. 6:33.) To gain eternal life, they must be willing, if called upon, to sacrifice all things for the gospel. "If thou wilt be perfect," Jesus said to the rich young man, "go and sell that thou hast, and give to the poor, and thou shalt have treasure in heaven: and come and follow me."

Hearing this injunction, Peter said: "Behold, we have forsaken all, and followed thee; what shall we have therefore?" To this query our Lord replied: *"Every one that hath forsaken houses, or brethren, or sisters, or father, or mother, or wife, or children, or lands, for my name's sake, shall recieve an hundredfold, and shall inherit everlasting life."* (Matt. 19:16-29; D. & C. 132:55.)

Joseph Smith taught the law of sacrifice in these words: "For a man to *lay down his all,* his character and reputation, his honor, and ap-

plause, his good name among men, his houses, his lands, his brothers and sisters, his wife and children, and even his own life—counting all things but filth and dross for the excellency of the knowledge of Jesus Christ—requires more than mere belief or supposition that he is doing the will of God; but actual knowledge, realizing that, when these sufferings are ended, he will enter into eternal rest; and be a partaker of the glory of God. . . .

"A religion that does not require the sacrifice of all things never has power sufficient to produce the faith necessary [to lead] unto life and salvation; for, from the first existence of man, the faith necessary unto the enjoyment of life and salvation never could be obtained without the *sacrifice of all earthly things. It was through this sacrifice, and this only, that God has ordained that men should enjoy eternal life;* and it is through the medium of the sacrifice of all earthly things that men do actually know that they are doing the things that are well pleasing in the sight of God. When a man has offered in sacrifice all that he has for the truth's sake, not even withholding his life, and believing before God that he has been called to make this sacrifice because he seeks to do his will, he does know, most assuredly, that God does and will accept his sacrifice and offering, and that he has not, nor will not seek his face in vain. Under

these circumstances, then, he can obtain the faith necessary for him to lay hold on eternal life.

"It is vain for persons to fancy to themselves that they are heirs with those, or can be heirs with them, who have offered their all in sacrifice, and by this means obtained faith in God and favor with him so as to obtain eternal life, unless they, in like manner, offer unto him the same sacrifice, and through that offering obtain the knowledge that they are accepted of him. . . .

"From the days of righteous Abel to the present time, the knowledge that men have that they are accepted in the sight of God is obtained by offering sacrifice. . . .

"Those, then, who make the sacrifice, will have the testimony that their course is pleasing in the sight of God; and those who have this testimony will have faith to lay hold on eternal life; and will be enabled, through faith, to endure unto the end, and receive the crown that is laid up for them that love the appearing of our Lord Jesus Christ. But those who do not make the sacrifice cannot enjoy this faith, because men are dependent upon this sacrifice in order to obtain this faith: therefore, they cannot lay hold upon eternal life, because the revelations of God do not guarantee unto them the authority so to do, and without this guarantee faith could not exist." (*Lectures on Faith,* pp. 58-60.)

Sacrifice pertains to mortality; in the eternal sense there is none. Sacrifice involves giving up the things of this world because of the promises of blessings to be gained in a better world. In the eternal perspective there is no sacrifice in giving up all things—even including the laying down of one's life— if eternal life is gained through such a course. (D. & C. 98:13-15.)

SACRIFICES.

See ATONEMENT OF CHRIST, CHRIST, LEVITES, SACRAMENT, SACRIFICE, SYMBOLISMS. After Adam and Eve were cast out of the Garden of Eden, the Lord "gave unto them commandments, that they should worship the Lord their God, and should *offer the firstlings of their flocks,* for an offering unto the Lord. And Adam was obedient unto the commandments of the Lord. And after many days an angel of the Lord appeared unto Adam, saying: Why dost thou offer *sacrifices* unto the Lord? And Adam said unto him: I know not, save the Lord commanded me. And then the angel spake, saying: *This thing is a similitude of the sacrifice of the Only Begotten of the Father, which is full of grace and truth.* Wherefore, thou shalt do all that thou doest in the name of the Son, and thou shalt repent and call upon God in the name of the Son forevermore." (Moses 5:5-8.)

Thus sacrifice was first instituted on earth as a gospel ordinance to be performed by the authority of the priesthood, to typify the coming sacrifice of the Son of God for the sins of the world. From the day of Adam to the death of Christ, sacrifice was practiced by the saints.

The form of the ordinance was always so arranged as to point attention to our Lord's sacrifice. The sacrificial offering made in connection with the Passover, the killing of the Paschal Lamb, for instance, was so arranged that a male lamb of the first year, one without spot or blemish, was chosen; in the offering the blood was spilled and care was taken to break no bones —all symbolical of the manner of Christ's death. (Ex. 12.) Many sacrificial details were added to the law as it operated in the Mosaic dispensation, but the basic principles governing sacrifices are part of the gospel itself and preceded Moses and the lesser order which came through him.

The offering of sacrifices as a generally practiced ordinance of the gospel ended with the sacrifice of Christ; the sacrament became the newly established ordinance which served the same purpose that sacrifices had theretofore served.

Amulek, in teaching the doctrine of the atonement, included this explanation about sacrifice: "It is expedient that there should be a great and last sacrifice; yea, not a sacrifice of man, neither of

beast, neither of any manner of fowl; for it shall not be a human sacrifice; but it must be an infinite and eternal sacrifice. Now there is not any man that can sacrifice his own blood which will atone for the sins of another. Now, if a man murdereth, behold will our law, which is just, take the life of his brother? I say unto you, Nay. But the law requireth the life of him who hath murdered; therefore there can be nothing which is short of an infinite atonement which will suffice for the sins of the world. Therefore, it is expedient that there should be a great and last sacrifice; and then shall there be, or it is expedient there should be, a stop to the shedding of blood; then shall the law of Moses be fulfilled; yea, it shall be all fulfilled, every jot and tittle, and none shall have passed away. And behold, *this is the whole meaning of the law, every whit pointing to that great and last sacrifice;* and that great and last sacrifice will be the Son of God, yea, infinite and eternal." (Alma 34:10-14; 2 Ne. 2:7.) Paul taught at some length, though not so plainly, these same truths. (Heb. 7; 8; 9; 10.)

To the Nephites, the risen Lord commanded: "Ye shall offer up unto me no more the shedding of blood; yea, your sacrifices and your burnt offerings shall be done away, for I will accept none of your sacrifices and your burnt offerings. And ye shall offer for a sacrifice unto me a broken heart and a contrite spirit." (3 Ne. 9:19-20.)

To complete the restoration of all things, apparently on a one-time basis, sacrifices will again be offered in this dispensation. John the Baptist, for instance, brought back the commission and power whereby the sons of Levi shall offer again in righteousness those offerings which they made in ancient days. (D. & C. 13.)

Malachi foretold that such offerings would be attended to again in the day of the Second Coming of Christ. (Mal. 3:1-4.) Joseph Smith, commenting upon Malachi's prophecy, explained how this could be: "It is generally supposed that sacrifice was *entirely* done away when the great sacrifice, the sacrifice of the Lord Jesus was offered up, and that there will be no necessity for the ordinance of sacrifice in [the] future; but those who assert this are certainly not acquainted with the duties, privileges and authority of the priesthood, or with the prophets.

"The offering of sacrifice has ever been connected and forms a part of the duties of the priesthood. It began with the priesthood, and will be continued until after the coming of Christ, from generation to generation. We frequently have mention made of the offering of sacrifice by the servants of the Most High in ancient days, prior to the law of Moses; which ordinances will be continued when the priesthood is restored with all

its authority, power and blessings. . . .

"These sacrifices, as well as every ordinance belonging to the priesthood, will, when the Temple of the Lord shall be built, and the sons of Levi be purified, be fully restored and attended to in all their powers, ramifications, and blessings. This ever did and ever will exist when the powers of the Melchizedek Priesthood are sufficiently manifest; else how can the restitution of all things spoken of by the holy prophets be brought to pass. It is not to be understood that the law of Moses will be established again with all its rites and variety of ceremonies; this has never been spoken of by the prophets; but those things which existed prior to Moses' day, namely sacrifice, will be continued." (*Teachings,* pp. 172-173; *Doctrines of Salvation,* vol. 3, p. 94.)

As a natural historical development, perverted forms of sacrifice have found place among the various portions of humankind. The most abominable of all these perversions of the truth has been the offering of *human sacrifices.* Even the house of Judah, at one period, offered its sons and daughters as sacrifices to the god Molech. (Jer. 7:29-34.) Captive Nephite women and children were offered in sacrifices to idols by the Lamanites in some of the final struggles of those then apostate remnants of Israel. (Morm. 4:14-15, 21.) The Aztecs offered scores of thousands of human sacrifices in the days of Cortez.

False and apostate sacrifices, as with all perversions of the truth, have no saving power. "The things which the Gentiles sacrifice," Paul said, "they sacrifice to devils, and not to God." (1 Cor. 10:20.)

SACRIFICIAL LAMB.
See LAMB OF GOD.

SAINTS.
See BELIEVERS, BRETHREN, CHRISTIANS, CHURCH OF JESUS CHRIST OF LATTER-DAY SAINTS, DISCIPLES, HOLINESS, MORMONS, PROPHETS, SALT OF THE EARTH, SANCTIFICATION. Faithful members of the Church and kingdom of God on earth are called *saints* (1 Ne. 14:12, 14; Acts 9:32, 41; Eph. 1:1), a title signifying that they have been cleansed by baptism and are pure and clean before the Lord. (2 Ne. 9:18.) Ancient Israel, for instance, consisted of a "congregation of saints" (Ps. 149:1), and the term is one of the most frequently used designations of the Lord's people. Paul, in speaking of the Second Coming of our Lord, pointedly recorded that the true believers in the last days would be called saints, for Christ "shall come to be glorified in his saints, and to be admired in all them that believe." (2 Thess. 1:10.) The only true saints in this day are thus members of The Church of Jesus Christ of *Latter-day Saints*. Saints are named nearly 40 times in the Old Testament, over 60 times in the New Testament, about 30 times in the Book of Mormon, and over 70 times in the Doctrine and Covenants.

The plan of salvation consists in putting off "the natural man," who "is an enemy to God," and in becoming "a saint through the atonement of Christ the Lord." Saints are "submissive, meek, humble, patient, full of love, willing to submit to all things which the Lord seeth fit to inflict upon" them. (Mosiah 3:19.)

The saints from the beginning on down who had preceded our Lord in death were with him in his resurrection. (Matt. 27:51-53; Hela. 14:25; 3 Ne. 23:9-11; D. & C. 133:53-55.) Saints who have lived since then will be resurrected in the coming first resurrection (D. & C. 43:18), will be with Christ in the great events incident to his Second Coming (1 Thess. 3:13; Jude 14; D. & C. 133:56), and finally "all the saints shall dwell with God." (Moro. 8:26.)

SALEM.
See NEW JERUSALEM.

SALT OF THE EARTH.
See SACRIFICES, SAINTS. Among the ancient Hebrews *salt* was an indispensable element having both temporal and spiritual uses. It was used as a preservative, in seasoning

food, and in all animal sacrifices. (Lev. 2:13; Ezek. 43:24; Mark 9:49-50.) So essential was it to the sacrificial ordinance that it was the symbol of the covenant made between God and his people in connection with that sacred performance. (Lev. 2:13; Num. 18:19; 2 Chron. 13:5.)

Accordingly, our Lord's statement, made first to the Jews and then to that other great body of Hebrews, the Nephites, that they had power "to be the *salt of the earth*," takes on great significance. (*Inspired Version*, Matt. 5:15; 3 Ne. 12:13.) They had power, in other words, to be the seasoning, savoring, preserving influence in the world, the influence which would bring peace and blessings to all others. It was this concept that caused our Lord to say such things as, "Salt is good: but if the salt have lost his saltness, wherewith will ye season it? Have salt in yourselves, and have peace one with another." (Mark 9:50; Matt. 5:13; Luke 14:34-35; 3 Ne. 12:13.)

Only the saints of God who keep the commandments are the salt of the earth. *"When men are called unto mine everlasting gospel, and covenant with an everlasting covenant,"* the Lord says, *"they are accounted as the salt of the earth and the savor of men;* They are called to be the savor of men; therefore, if that salt of the earth lose its savor, behold, it is thenceforth good for nothing only to be cast out and trodden under the feet of men." (D. & C. 101:39-40; 103:9-10.) Salt is the symbol; "it is a covenant of salt." (Num. 18-19.)

SALUTATIONS.

See OBEISANCE. Among the saints, *salutations* of kindness, respect, and love are the accepted order. (Luke 1:40; Rom. 16; 1 Pet. 5:13.) They are the natural outgrowth of the true fellowship which is part of the brotherhood of Christ. Similar greetings are found among all peoples. The usual greeting in Arabic among Moslems is, "Peace to you"; the reply—"To you, peace."

In commanding the saints to build the Kirtland Temple, the Lord specified that it should be "a house of God; That your incomings may be in the name of the Lord; that your outgoings may be in the name of the Lord; that all your salutations may be in the name of the Lord, with uplifted hands unto the Most High." (D. & C. 88:119-120; 109:9, 19.) Salutations used in the School of the Prophets included these words: "I salute you in the name of the Lord Jesus Christ, in token or remembrance of the everlasting covenant." (D. & C. 88:133-135.) To the Romans, Paul gave the counsel: "Salute one another with an holy kiss." (Rom. 16:16.) Our Lord condemned the scribes and Pharisees for their ostentatious and insincere salutations. (Matt. 23:7; Mark 12:38.)

SALVATION.

See ATONEMENT OF CHRIST, CELESTIAL BODIES, CELESTIAL GLORY, CELESTIAL KINGDOM, CELESTIAL LAW, CELESTIAL SPIRITS, DAMNATION, ELIJAH THE PROPHET, ETERNAL LIFE, ETERNAL LIVES, EXALTATION, GODHOOD, HEAVEN, IMMORTALITY, INTERCESSION, JOSEPH SMITH THE PROPHET, JUDGMENT DAY, KINGDOM OF GOD, KINGDOMS OF GLORY, MANSIONS, MEDIATION, PERFECTION, PLAN OF SALVATION, REDEMPTION, RESURRECTION, SALVATION BY GRACE, SALVATION FOR THE DEAD, SALVATION OF CHILDREN, SAVIOR, SECOND CHANCE THEORY, TELESTIAL BODIES, TELESTIAL GLORY, TELESTIAL KINGDOM, TELESTIAL LAW, TERRESTRIAL BODIES, TERRESTRIAL GLORY, TERRESTRIAL KINGDOM, TERRESTRIAL LAW. 1. *Unconditional or general salvation,* that which comes by grace alone without obedience to gospel law, consists in the mere fact of being resurrected. In this sense salvation is synonymous with immortality; it is the inseparable connection of body and spirit so that the resurrected personage lives forever.

This kind of salvation eventually will come to all mankind, excepting only the sons of perdition. In their case, after their resurrection, "they shall return again to their own place" (D. & C. 88:32); after coming forth in immortality and standing before the judgment bar, because they are "filthy still, . . . they shall go away into ever-lasting fire, prepared for them; and their torment is as a lake of fire and brimstone, whose flame ascendeth up forever and ever and has no end." (2 Ne. 9:13-16.) *They are resurrected, but they are not redeemed from the devil.* "They shall be as though there had been no redemption made; for they cannot be redeemed according to God's justice; and they cannot die, seeing there is no more corruption." (Alma 12:18.) Thus it is that the Lord "saves all the works of his hands, except those sons of perdition who deny the Son after the Father has revealed him." (D. & C. 76:40-48.) All others are saved from death, hell, the devil, and endless torment. (2 Ne. 9:18-27.)

But this is not the salvation of righteousness, the salvation which the saints seek. Those who gain only this general or unconditional salvation will still be judged according to their works and receive their places in a terrestrial or a telestial kingdom. They will, therefore, be damned; their eternal progression will be cut short; they will not fill the full measure of their creation, but in eternity will be ministering servants to more worthy persons.

2. *Conditional or individual salvation,* that which comes by grace coupled with gospel obedience, consists in receiving an inheritance in the celestial kingdom of God. This kind of salvation follows faith, repentance, baptism, receipt of the Holy Ghost, and continued right-

eousness to the end of one's mortal probation. (D. & C. 20:29; 2 Ne. 9:23-24.) All others are damned, for as Amulek said: *"How can ye be saved except ye inherit the kingdom of heaven?"* Further: Christ "shall come into the world to redeem his people; and he shall take upon him the transgressions of those who believe on his name; and these are they that shall have eternal life, and *salvation cometh to none else.* Therefore the wicked remain as though there had been no redemption made, *except it be the loosing of the bands of death;* for behold, the day cometh that all shall rise from the dead and stand before God, and be judged according to their works." (Alma 11:37-41.)

Even those in the celestial kingdom, however, who do not go on to exaltation, will have immortality only and not eternal life. Along with those of the telestial and terrestrial worlds they will be "ministering servants, to minister for those who are worthy of a far more, and an exceeding, and an eternal weight of glory." They will live "separately and singly" in an unmarried state "without exaltation, in their saved condition, to all eternity." (D. & C. 132:16-17.)

3. *Salvation* in its true and full meaning is synonymous with *exaltation* or *eternal life* and consists in gaining an inheritance in the highest of the three heavens within the celestial kingdom. With few exceptions this is the salvation of which the scriptures speak. It is the salvation which the saints seek. It is of this which the Lord says, *"There is no gift greater than the gift of salvation."* (D. & C. 6:13.) This full salvation is obtained in and through the continuation of the family unit in eternity, and those who obtain it are gods. (D. & C. 131:1-4; 132.)

Full salvation is attained by virtue of knowledge, truth, righteousness, and all true principles. Many conditions must exist in order to make such salvation available to men. Without the atonement, the gospel, the priesthood, and the sealing power, there would be no salvation. Without continuous revelation, the ministering of angels, the working of miracles, the prevalence of gifts of the spirit, there would be no salvation. If it had not been for Joseph Smith and the restoration, there would be no salvation. There is no salvation outside The Church of Jesus Christ of Latter-day Saints. (*Doctrines of Salvation,* vol. 2, pp. 1-350.)

SALVATION BY GRACE.

See ATONEMENT OF CHRIST, ETERNAL LIFE, EXALTATION, GRACE OF GOD, IMMORTALITY, RESURRECTION, SALVATION. *Since all good things come by the grace of God (that is, by his love, mercy, and condescension), it follows that salvation itself—in all its forms and degrees—is bestowed because of this infinite goodness.* However, one of the untrue doctrines found in modern Christendom is the concept that man can gain salvation (meaning in the kingdom of God) by grace alone and without obedience. This soul-destroying doctrine has the obvious effect of lessening the determination of an individual to conform to all of the laws and ordinances of the gospel, such conformity being essential if the sought for reward is in reality to be gained.

Immortality is a free gift and comes without works or righteousness of any sort; all men will come forth in the resurrection because of the atoning sacrifice of Christ. (1 Cor. 15:22.) In and of itself the resurrection is a form of salvation meaning that men are thereby saved from death, hell, the devil, and endless torment. (2 Ne. 9:17-27.) "O the wisdom of God, his mercy and grace! For behold, if the flesh should rise no more our spirits must become subject to that angel who fell from before the presence of the Eternal God, and became the devil, to rise no more." (2 Ne. 9: 8.) In this sense, the mere fact of resurrection is called *salvation by grace alone.* Works are not involved, neither the works of the Mosaic law nor the works of righteousness that go with the fulness of the gospel.

Salvation in the celestial kingdom of God, however, is not salvation by grace alone. Rather, it is *salvation by grace coupled with*
obedience to the laws and ordinances of the gospel. (Third Article of Faith.) Those who gain it are "raised in immortality unto eternal life." (D. & C. 29:43; 2 Ne. 9:22-24.) Immortality comes by grace alone, but those who gain it may find themselves damned in eternity. (Alma 11:37-45.) Eternal life, the kind of life enjoyed by eternal beings in the celestial kingdom, comes by grace plus obedience. And the very *opportunity* to follow the course of good works which will lead to that salvation sought by the saints comes also by the grace of God. (*Doctrines of Salvation,* vol. 2, pp. 306-311.)

Thus Nephi wrote: "Be reconciled to God; for we know that *it is by grace that we are saved, after all we can do.*" (2 Ne. 25:23.) Again: "Reconcile yourselves to the will of God, and not to the will of the devil and the flesh; and remember, *after ye are reconciled unto God,* that *it is only in and through the grace of God that ye are saved.*" (2 Ne. 10:24.) And thus Moroni recorded: "Come unto Christ, and be perfected in him, and deny yourselves of all ungodliness; and *if ye shall deny yourselves of all ungodliness, and love God with all your might, mind and strength, then is his grace sufficient for you,* that by his grace ye may be perfect in Christ; and if by the grace of God ye are perfect in Christ, ye can in nowise deny the power of God. And again, if ye by the grace of God are perfect in Christ, and deny not his power, then are ye sanctified in Christ by the grace of God, through the shedding of the blood of Christ, which is in the covenant of the Father unto the remission of your sins, that ye become holy, without spot." (Moro. 10:32-33.)

Paul had occasion to teach the Ephesian Saints that salvation in the kingdom of God did not result from the ordinances and performances (meaning, the works) of the Mosaic dispensation, but that it came because of the grace of God coupled with faith and gospel obedience (meaning, the works inherent in gospel obedience). The passage, though not preserved for us with the same clarity as is common through most of the body of holy writ, is nevertheless plain and clear to those having an understanding of the doctrine of salvation by grace.

"God, who is rich in mercy," Paul explained, "for his great love wherewith he loved us, Even when we were dead in sins, hath quickened us together with Christ, (by grace ye are saved [meaning in the celestial kingdom]); And hath raised us up together, and made us sit together in heavenly places in Christ Jesus [meaning in the celestial kingdom]: That in the ages to come he might shew the exceeding riches of his grace in his kindness toward us through Christ Jesus. For by grace are ye saved through faith [meaning salvation in the celestion kingdom]; and that not

of yourselves: it is the gift of God [meaning that salvation in the kingdom of God is predicated on the atonement of Christ and that man of himself could not bring it to pass]: Not of works, lest any man should boast [meaning that salvation cannot come by the works of man, and specifically not by the works or performances of the Mosaic dispensation]. For we are his workmanship, created in Christ Jesus unto good works, which God hath before ordained that we should walk in them [meaning that obedience is essential to celestial salvation]." Paul then goes on to compare the performances (works) of the Mosaic day, that is, "the law of commandments contained in ordinances," with the gospel requirement that obedience is essential to salvation, explaining that only "by the blood of Christ" can man be reconciled unto God. (Eph. 2.)

SALVATION FOR THE DEAD.

See BAPTISM FOR THE DEAD, ELIJAH THE PROPHET, HELL, PLAN OF SALVATION, SALVATION, SAVIORS ON MOUNT ZION, SECOND CHANCE THEORY, SPIRIT PRISON, SPIRIT WORLD, TEMPLE ORDINANCES, TEMPLES, VICARIOUS ORDINANCES. There is no death, and there are no dead, unto the Lord—all are alive unto him. "God is not the God of the dead, but of the living" (Matt. 22:32), our Lord said with reference to Abraham, Isaac, and

Jacob, who had long before died as men count death, but who were alive as the Lord views things in his eternal perspective.

Since the Lord views man's progress from the pre-existent state to an eventual inheritance in one of the degrees of glory as one continuing course, it is not material (from the eternal perspective) whether the opportunity to accept the gospel of salvation comes in this mortal sphere or in the spirit world hereafter. Sometime after birth into this life and before the resurrection and judgment, every living soul will hear the gospel message and be judged by his reaction thereto. The millions who pass to the spirit world without receiving an opportunity during mortality to hear the truths of salvation will receive their chance subsequent to what men call death.

The great principles and procedures whereby the saving truths of the gospel are offered to, accepted by, and made binding upon the departed dead, comprise the doctrine of *salvation for the dead.* Pursuant to this doctrine the principles of salvation are taught in the spirit world, leaving the ordinances thereof to be performed in this life on a vicarious-proxy basis. By accepting the gospel in the spirit world, and because the ordinances of salvation and exaltation are performed vicariously in this world, the worthy dead can become heirs of the fulness of the Father's kingdom. Salvation for the dead is the system whereunder those who would have accepted the gospel in this life had they been permitted to hear it, will have the chance to accept it in the spirit world, and will then be entitled to all the blessings which passed them by in mortality. (*Doctrines of Salvation,* vol. 2, pp. 100-196.)

SALVATION OF BEASTS.

See RESURRECTION.

SALVATION OF CHILDREN.

See ACCOUNTABILITY, ATONEMENT OF CHRIST, EXALTATION, INFANT BAPTISM, ORIGINAL SIN THEORY, REDEMPTION, REPENTANCE, RESURRECTION, SALVATION, STILLBORN CHILDREN, TEMPTATION, YEARS OF ACCOUNTABILITY. Contrary to the wicked heresies prevailing in modern Christendom, *little children are saved through the atonement of Christ,* without any act on their part or on the part of any other person for them. "Every spirit of man was innocent in the beginning," the Lord says, meaning that in the morning of pre-existence, in the day of their spirit birth, before some began to use their agency to break divine law, all the spirit offspring of the Father were innocent, pure, untainted with sin. Then the Lord adds: "And God *having redeemed man from the fall, men became again, in their infant state, innocent before God.*" (D. & C. 93:38.)

That is, because of the grace of God, manifested through the atoning sacrifice of our Lord, all spirits begin their mortal life in a state of innocence and purity without sin or taint of any sort attaching to them.

"Little children are redeemed from the foundation of the world through mine Only Begotten," the Lord has revealed. "Wherefore, they cannot sin, for power is not given unto Satan to tempt little children, until they begin to become accountable before me." (D. & C. 29:46-47.) Children, as spirits, are in the presence of God before birth, and since they begin their mortal life innocent and free from sin, it follows that if they die before they arrive at the years of accountability, they are still in the state of purity and innocence which entitles them to go back into the presence of God and have salvation.

In recording a glorious vision of the celestial kingdom, received January 21, 1836, the Prophet included this statement: "And I also beheld that *all* children who die before they arrive at the years of accountability, are saved in the celestial kingdom of heaven." (*Teachings,* p. 107.) Obviously, this applies to children of all races and nationalities. (*Doctrines of Salvation,* vol. 2, pp. 49-57.)

The Prophet also taught: "The Lord takes many away, even in infancy, that they may escape the envy of man, and the sorrows and evils of this present world; they were too pure, too lovely, to live on earth; therefore, if rightly considered, instead of mourning we have reason to rejoice as they are delivered from evil, and we shall soon have them again. . . . *All* children are redeemed by the blood of Jesus Christ, and the moment that children leave this world, they are taken to the bosom of Abraham. The only difference between the old and young dying is, one lives longer in heaven and eternal light and glory than the other, and is freed a little sooner from the miserable wicked world. Notwithstanding all this glory, we for a moment lose sight of it, and mourn the loss, but we do not mourn as those without hope." (*Teachings,* pp. 196-197.)

Many scriptures attest to the truth of these principles. "Little children are whole, for they are not capable of committing sin; wherefore the curse of Adam is taken from them in me, that it hath no power over them" (Moro. 8:8), the Lord told Mormon. Speaking of children, the Inspired Version records: "Jesus hath said, Such shall be saved." (*Inspired Version,* Matt. 19:13.) Abinadi taught: "Little children also have eternal life." (Mosiah 15:25.) They are thus in a favored category, much as are the spirits who will be born during the millennium, in the day when "children shall grow up without sin unto salvation." (D. & C. 45:58.)

Not only will little children be saved in the celestial kingdom of

God, but they will be heirs of exaltation in that kingdom. (*Doctrines of Salvation,* vol. 2, pp. 49-57.) On this point the Prophet said: "They will there enjoy the *fulness* of that light, glory and intelligence, which is prepared in the celestial kingdom." (*Teachings,* p. 200.) To inherit the *fulness* is to have exaltation.

Every principle governing the salvation of little children applies with equal force to persons of any age who do not arrive at the years of accountability, for "he that hath no understanding, it remaineth in me to do according as it is written," the Lord says. (D. & C. 29:50.)

SANCTIFICATION.

See BAPTISM OF FIRE, BORN AGAIN, HOLINESS, HOLY GHOST, JUSTIFICATION, SALVATION, SANCTIFIER. To be *sanctified* is to become clean, pure, and spotless; to be free from the blood and sins of the world; to become a new creature of the Holy Ghost, one whose body has been renewed by the rebirth of the Spirit. *Sanctification* is a state of saintliness, a state attained only by conformity to the laws and ordinances of the gospel. The plan of salvation is the system and means provided whereby men may sanctify their souls and thereby become worthy of a celestial inheritance.

Sanctification is a basic doctrine of the gospel (D. & C. 20:31-34); indeed, the very reason men are commanded to believe, repent, and be baptized is so they "may be sanctified by the reception of the Holy Ghost," and thereby be enabled to stand spotless before the judgment bar of Christ. (3 Ne. 27:19-21.)

Moroni summarized the plan of salvation in these words: "Come unto Christ, and be perfected in him, and deny yourselves of all ungodliness; and if ye shall deny yourselves of all ungodliness, and love God with all your might, mind and strength, then is his grace sufficient for you, that by his grace ye may be perfect in Christ; and if by the grace of God ye are perfect in Christ, ye can in nowise deny the power of God. And again, if ye by the grace of God are perfect in Christ, and deny not his power, then are ye *sanctified in Christ by the grace of God,* through the shedding of the blood of Christ, which is in the covenant of the Father unto the remission of your sins, that ye become holy, without spot." (Moro. 10:32-33.)

To the saints the continual cry of the gospel is: *Sanctify yourselves.* (D. & C. 39:18; 43:9, 11, 16; 133:4; Lev. 11:44; 1 Pet. 1:15.) This is accomplished by obedience to the "law of Christ" (D. & C. 88:21, 34-35), and is possible because of his atoning sacrifice. (D. & C. 76:41.) And "all those who will not endure chastening, but deny me," saith the Lord, "cannot be sanctified." (D. & C. 101:5.)

Those who are faithful in magnifying their callings in the Melchizedek Priesthood "are *sanctified by the Spirit unto the renewing of their bodies.*" (D. & C. 84:33.) Speaking of a great host who attained this state of sanctification in early days, Alma said: "They were called after this holy order, and were sanctified, and their garments were washed white through the blood of the Lamb. Now they, after being *sanctified by the Holy Ghost,* having their garments made white, being pure and spotless before God, could not look upon sin save it were with abhorrence; and there were many, exceeding great many, who were made pure and entered into the rest of the Lord their God." (Alma 13:11-12.) Those who attain this state of cleanliness and perfection are able, as occasion may require, to see God and view the things of his kingdom. (D. & C. 84:23; 88:68; Ether 4:7.) The Three Nephites "were sanctified in the flesh, that they were holy, and that the powers of the earth could not hold them." (3 Ne. 28: 39.)

By attaining sanctification in this life (D. & C. 105:31, 35-36), and by continuing to abide in the truth, men attain an eventual inheritance with the sanctified in the celestial world. (D. & C. 76:21; 88:2, 116.) "And unto him that repenteth and sanctifieth himself before the Lord shall be given eternal life." (D. & C. 133:62.) Even sanctified persons, however, have no absolute guarantee that they will be saved. "There

is a possibility that man may fall from grace and depart from the living God; Therefore let the church take heed and pray always, lest they fall into tempation; Yea, and *even let those who are sanctified take heed also.*" (D. & C. 20: 32-34.)

Sanctification is a personal reward that follows personal righteousness. The good works of one person cannot be transferred to another. The unblieving husband is not sanctified by the wife, nor the unbelieving wife by the husband, as it is erroneously supposed that Paul taught. (1 Cor. 7:14.) In reality, as we know from latter-day revelation, Paul was expressing some personal opinions about social conditions in his day, which opinions were designed to controvert the heresy that "little children are unholy." In fact, *"little children are holy, being sanctified through the atonement of Jesus Christ."* (D. & C. 74.)

This earth, in due course, will attain "its sanctified, immortal, and eternal state." (D. & C. 77:1, 12; 130:9.) In that day, when it becomes a celestial sphere, "the poor and the meek of the earth shall inherit it. Therefore, it must needs be sanctified from all unrighteousness, that it may be prepared for the celestial glory." (D. & C. 88:17-26.)

SANCTIFIER.

See BAPTISM OF FIRE, BORN

AGAIN, HOLY GHOST, SANCTIFICA-TION. The Holy Ghost is the *Sanctifier*. It is through his power as a Spirit Being that men may be sanctified and washed clean from all sin. (Alma 13:11-12; 3 Ne. 27: 19-21; D. & C. 84:33.)

SANCTUARIES.
See TEMPLES.

SATAN.
See ADVERSARY, DEVIL. *Satan* is a formal Hebrew name for the devil and means *adversary,* signifying that he wages open war with the truth and all who obey its principles.

SAVAGES.
See APOSTASY.

SAVIOR.
See CHRIST, DELIVERER, REDEEMER, SALVATION, SAVIORS OF MEN, SAVIORS ON MOUNT ZION. Christ is the *Savior*. (Isa. 45:15; Luke 2:11; 1 Ne. 13:40; Morm. 3:14; D. & C. 43:34.) "The Father sent the Son to be the *Saviour of the world*." (1 John 4:14.) He came "to save that which was lost" (Matt. 18:11), not to save people in their sins but from their sins, to bring salvation to all "who believe on his name." (Alma 11:37-45.) He is the Savior because of the atonement; it is that redemptive

sacrifice which guarantees immortality to all and assures the obedient of eternal life.

SAVIOR OF THE WORLD.
See SAVIOR.

SAVIORS OF MEN.
See MESSAGE OF THE RESTORATION, MISSIONARIES, SALVATION, SAVIOR, SAVIORS ON MOUNT ZION. By preaching the gospel of salvation to the world, the saints become the *saviors of men.* Through this message, a message of faith in the Eternal Savior, men may be saved from everlasting destruction and delivered from the evils which are to come upon the wicked. Of his saints the Lord said: "They were set to be a light unto the world, and to be the saviors of men; And inasmuch as they are not the saviors of men, they are as salt that has lost its savor, and is thenceforth good for nothing but to be cast out and trodden under foot of men." (D. & C. 103:9-10.)

SAVIORS ON MOUNT ZION.
See ELIJAH THE PROPHET, SALVATION FOR THE DEAD, SAVIOR, SAVIORS OF MEN, SEALING POWER. Christ our Savior through his atoning sacrifice did for us, vicariously, what we could not do for ourselves. Both literally and figuratively he is to stand upon Mount Zion in glory, receiving honor and

dominion because of his perfectly fulfilled mission. Those of his brethren who perform, vicariously, for others—meaning for those who have died without a knowledge of the gospel—the saving ordinances which they cannot perform for themselves are called *saviors on Mount Zion*. It was of them that Obadiah spoke when he said: "And saviours shall come up on mount Zion; . . . and the kingdom shall be the Lord's." (Obad. 21.)

Speaking of the turning (or binding) of the hearts of the fathers to the children through the mission of Elijah, the Prophet said: "The keys are to be delivered, the spirit of Elijah is to come, the gospel to be established, the saints of God gathered, Zion built up, and the saints to come up as saviors on Mount Zion.

"But how are they to become saviors on Mount Zion? By building their temples, erecting their baptismal fonts, and going forth and receiving all the ordinances, baptisms, confirmations, washings, anointings, ordinations, and sealing powers upon their heads, in behalf of all their progenitors who are dead, and redeem them that they may come forth in the first resurrection and be exalted to thrones of glory with them; and herein is the chain that binds the hearts of the fathers to the children, and the children to the fathers, which fulfils the mission of Elijah." (*Teachings,* p. 330.)

SCAPEGOAT.

See ATONEMENT OF CHRIST, SYMBOLISMS. In ancient Israel, "once a year," the High Priest (of the Aaronic Priesthood) selected a goat by lot to be a *scapegoat*. Then he confessed over the scapegoat's head "all the iniquities of the children of Israel," and sent it away "into the wilderness" to bear "all their iniquities into a land not inhabited." (Lev. 16.) This ordinance was a Mosaic requirement done in similitude of the fact that Christ would atone for the sins of the world and bear the iniquities of those who would repent and confess their sins to the Lord. (Mosiah 13:29-31.)

SCATTERING OF ISRAEL.

See GATHERING OF ISRAEL, ISRAEL, JEWS, LOST TRIBES OF ISRAEL, NEPHITES AND LAMANITES, TRIBES OF ISRAEL. "If a complete history of the house of Israel were written, it would be the history of histories, the key of the world's history for the past twenty centuries" (*Compendium,* p. 85) and more, for Israel has been scattered among all the nations of the earth and has acted as a leavening and enlightening influence wherever her scattered remnants have found lodgement. (*Articles of Faith,* pp. 314-327.) Israel, meaning those comprising all 12 of the tribes, was scattered and afflicted because of unrighteousness and rebellion against the Lord and his covenants. (Lev. 26; Deut. 28; Jer. 16: 11-13.)

The world-wide nature of the dispersion of Israel is foretold and explained in many scriptures. For instance: "I will scatter you among the heathen." (Lev. 26:33.) "The Lord shall cause thee to be smitten before thine enemies: thou . . . shalt be removed into *all the kingdoms of the earth.* . . . And thou shalt become an astonishment, a proverb, and a byword, among *all nations* whither the Lord shall lead thee. . . . And the Lord shall scatter thee among *all people, from the one end of the earth even unto the other;* and there thou shalt serve other gods, which neither thou nor thy fathers have known, even wood and stone." (Deut. 28:25, 37, 64.) "I will sift the house of Israel among *all nations."* (Amos 9:9; Zech. 10:9.) "The house of Israel, sooner or later, will be scattered upon *all the face of the earth, and also among all nations.* And behold, there are many who are already lost from the knowledge of those who are at Jerusalem. Yea, the more part of all the tribes have been led away; and they are scattered to and fro upon the isles of the sea; and whither they are none of us knoweth, save that we know that they have been led away." (1 Ne. 22:3-5.)

SCHISMS.
See SECTS.

SCHOLARSHIP.
See KNOWLEDGE.

SCHOOL OF THE PROPHETS.
See DOCTRINE, KNOWLEDGE, PROPHETS, SALVATION, TRUTH, WASHING OF FEET. In the early days of this dispensation the Lord commanded the brethren to "teach one another the doctrine of the kingdom." They were to learn all things pertaining to the gospel and the kingdom of God that it was expedient for them to know, as also things pertaining to the arts and sciences, and to kingdoms, and nations. They were to "seek learning, even by study and also by faith," and were to build a holy sanctuary or temple in Kirtland, which among other things was to be "a house of learning." (D. & C. 88:74-81, 118-122.)

As part of the then existing arrangement to fulfil these commands, the Lord directed the setting up of the *school of the prophets* (D. & C. 88:122, 127-141), also called "the school of mine apostles" (D. & C. 95:17), meaning apostles who were special witnesses of the name of Christ and not apostles ordained to that office in the Melchizedek Priesthood, for at this time (1833) there were no ordained apostles.

This particular and chief school of the prophets was in fact organized among the leading brethren of the Church in the winter of 1832-1833 in Kirtland with the Prophet

Joseph Smith as its presiding officer. (D. & C. 90:7, 13.) Members of the school were carefully selected; were admitted to membership by the ordinance of washing of feet; were welcomed to the sessions by a special, revealed, and holy salutation; were pronounced "clean from the blood of this generation"; and in the course of their schooling received great knowledge and marvelous spiritual manifestation. (*History of the Church*, vol. 1, pp. 322-323.)

Of the session held March 18, 1833, the Prophet says: "I exhorted the brethren to faithfulness and diligence in keeping the commandments of God, and gave much instruction for the benefit of the saints, with a promise that the pure in heart should see a heavenly vision; and after remaining a short time in secret prayer, the promise was verified; for many present had the eyes of their understanding opened by the Spirit of God, so as to behold many things. I then blessed the bread and wine, and distributed a portion to each. *Many of the brethren saw a heavenly vision of the Savior, and concourses of angels, and many other things,* of which each one has a record of what he saw." (*History of the Church*, vol. 1, pp. 334-335.)

This chief school of the prophets continued in Kirtland for some years. The Prophet wrote of it again in October, 1835 (*History of the Church*, vol. 2, p. 287), and provision was made for its conduct in the Kirtland Temple. (D. & C. 95:17.) Another school of the prophets, or *school of the elders,* or "the school in Zion" (D. & C. 97:1-6), was conducted pursuant to direct revelation, by Elder Parley P. Pratt in Jackson County, Missouri. Concerning this school of the prophets, Elder Pratt says: "In the latter part of the summer (1833) and in the autumn, I devoted almost my entire time in ministering among the churches, holding meetings, visiting the sick, comforting the afflicted and giving counsel. A school of elders was organized, over which I was called to preside. This class, to the number of about 60, met for instructions once a week. The place of meeting was in the open air, under some tall trees, in a retired place in the wilderness, where we prayed, preached and prophesied, and exercised ourselves in the gifts of the Holy Spirit. Here great blessings were poured out, and many great and marvelous things were manifested and taught. The Lord gave me great wisdom, and enabled me to teach and edify the elders, and comfort and encourage them in their preparations for the great work which lay before us. I was also much edified and strengthened. To attend this school I had to travel on foot, and sometimes with bare feet at that, about six miles. This I did once a week besides visiting and preaching in five or six branches a week." (*History of the Church*, vol. 1, pp. 400-401 fn.)

Similar schools were held among the saints in the west, beginning in 1867 and continuing on into the early 70's, although these schools were more in the nature of theological classes, rather than schools of the prophets which followed the formal organizational requirements set forth in the revelation. (D. & C. 88:127-141.) President Brigham Young presided over the school held in Salt Lake City. After a short period these schools in the west were discontinued, and gospel teaching today is done mainly through church schools, priesthood quorums, and the various auxiliary organizations.

SCIENCE AND RELIGION.

See GOSPEL, RELIGION, SIGNS OF THE TIMES, THEOLOGY, TRUTH. Is there a conflict between *science and religion?* The answer to this basic query depends entirely upon what is meant by and accepted as science and as religion. It is common to say there is no such conflict, meaning between true science and true religion—for one truth never conflicts with another, no matter what fields or categories the truths are put in for purposes of study. But there most certainly is a conflict between science and religion, if by science is meant (for instance) the theoretical guesses and postulates of some organic evolutionists, or if by religion is meant the false creeds and dogmas of the sectarian and pagan worlds.

"Oppositions of science falsely so called" were causing people to err "concerning the faith" even in the days of Paul. (1 Tim. 6:20-21.)

There is, of course, no conflict between revealed religion as it has been restored in our day and those scientific realities which have been established as ultimate truth. The mental quagmires in which many students struggle result from the acceptance of unproven scientific theories as ultimate facts, which brings the student to the necessity of rejecting conflicting truths of revealed religion. If, for example, a student accepts the untrue theory that death has been present on the earth for scores of thousands or millions of years, he must reject the revealed truth that there was no death either for man or animals or plants or any form of life until some 6000 years ago when Adam fell.

As a matter of fact, from the eternal perspective, true science is a part of the gospel itself; in its broadest signification the gospel embraces all truth. When the full blessings of the millennium are poured out upon the earth and its inhabitants, *pseudo-science* and *pseudo-religion* will be swept aside, and all supposed conflicts between science and religion will vanish away.

SCIENTIFIC PROGRESS.

See SIGNS OF THE TIMES.

SCOFFERS.
See APOSTASY.

SCRIPTURE.
See BIBLE, BOOK OF MORMON, CANON OF SCRIPTURE, DOCTRINE AND COVENANTS, HOLY GHOST, LOST SCRIPTURE, MORMON BIBLE, PROPHECY, PROPHETS, REVELATION, STANDARD WORKS, WHITE HORSE PROPHECY. Any message, whether written or spoken, that comes from God to man by the power of the Holy Ghost is *scripture*. If it is written and accepted by the Church, it becomes part of the *scriptures or standard works* and ever thereafter may be read and studied with profit. Much of what is in the scriptures was given orally in the first instance and was thereafter recorded either by the uttering prophet or an inspired scribe. Other portions of what is in holy writ were written by the inspired authors by way of revelation and commandment.

The elders of the Church are sent forth "to proclaim the everlasting gospel, by the Spirit of the living God," and they are commanded to "speak as they are moved upon by the Holy Ghost. And *whatsoever they shall speak when moved upon by the Holy Ghost shall be scripture,* shall be the will of the Lord, shall be the mind of the Lord, shall be the word of the Lord, shall be the voice of the Lord, and the power of God unto salvation." (D. & C. 68:1-4.)

SCRIPTURES.
See STANDARD WORKS.

SEALED BOOK.
See BOOK OF MORMON, GOLD PLATES, REVELATION. One of the remarkable prophecies concerning the coming forth of the Book of Mormon is the *sealed book* prophecy. Isaiah foresaw that a portion of the gold plates would be sealed; that the words of the unsealed part would be delivered to a learned man; that the learned man would say he could not read a sealed book; that the book itself would be delivered to an unlearned man; and that it would then be translated by the gift and power of God. (Isa. 29:11-12; *Inspired Version,* Isa. 29:11-26; 2 Ne. 27:6-22.) The fulfilment of this prophecy is found in the circumstances surrounding the translation of the Book of Mormon and the taking of the characters to Professor Charles Anthon who averred, "I cannot read a sealed book." (Jos. Smith 2:63-66.)

In the sealed portion of the plates is recorded a history of the world from the beginning to the end thereof. It shall come forth in that day when the Lord shall see fit "to reveal all things unto the children of men." (2 Ne. 27:7, 10, 22.)

682

SEALED IN FOREHEAD.

See CALLING AND ELECTION SURE, CELESTIAL MARRIAGE, ONE HUNDRED AND FORTY-FOUR THOUSAND, SECOND COMFORTER. John foresaw that in the latter-days the servants of God would plead with the Lord to stay the tide of desolation and destruction "till we have sealed the servants of our God in their foreheads." (Rev. 7:3; 9:4; Ezek. 9:4-6.) With the restoration of the gospel, the power has again been given to seal men up unto eternal life (D. & C. 1:8-9; 68:12; 77:8-9), to place a seal on them so that no matter what happens in the world, no matter what desolation sweeps the earth, yet they shall be saved in the day of the Lord Jesus. (D. & C. 88:84-85; 109:38, 46; 124:124; 131:5; 132: 19, 46, 49.)

Since these sealing blessings are conferred by the laying on of hands of those who hold the keys of this power, it follows that John's description of placing a seal in the forehead is not just apocalyptic imagery but a literal description of what takes place. As with other sacred things, however, the devil has a substitute seal to place; he puts a *mark* in the "foreheads" of his followers also. (Rev. 13:16-18.)

SEALING ANOINTINGS.

See ADMINISTRATIONS.

SEALING POWER.

See CALLING AND ELECTION SURE, CELESTIAL MARRIAGE, ELIJAH THE PROPHET, ENDOWMENTS, ETERNAL LIFE, EXALTATION, KEYS OF THE KINGDOM, PRIESTHOOD, SALVATION FOR THE DEAD, TEMPLES. Whenever the fulness of the gospel is on earth, the Lord has agents to whom he gives power to bind on earth and seal eternally in the heavens. (Matt. 16:19; 18:18; Hela. 10:3-10; D. & C. 132:46-49.) This *sealing power,* restored in this dispensation by Elijah the Prophet (D. & C. 2:1-3; 110:13-16), is the means whereby "All covenants, contracts, bonds, obligations, oaths, vows, performances, connections, associations, or expectations" attain "efficacy, virtue, or force in and after the resurrection from the dead." (D. & C. 132:7.)

All things that are not sealed by this power have an end when men are dead. Unless a baptism has this enduring seal, it will not admit a person to the celestial kingdom; unless an eternal marriage covenant is sealed by this authority, it will not take the participating parties to an exaltation in the highest heaven within the celestial world.

All things gain enduring force and validity because of the sealing power. So comprehensive is this power that it embraces ordinances performed for the living and the dead, seals the children on earth up to their fathers who went before, and forms the enduring patriarchal chain that will exist eternally among exalted beings.

(*Doctrines of Salvation,* vol. 2, pp. 115-128.)

SEA OF GLASS.
See URIM AND THUMMIM.

SEALINGS.

See CELESTIAL MARRIAGE, SEALING POWER, TEMPLE ORDINANCES, VICARIOUS ORDINANCES. Those ordinances performed in the temples whereby husbands and wives are sealed together in the marriage union for time and eternity, and whereby children are sealed eternally to parents, are commonly referred to as *sealings.* In the infinite mercy and justice of an omnipotent God, these ordinances are available for righteous living persons and on a proxy basis for the dead also. Consequently the expressions *sealings for the living* and *sealings for the dead* are in common usage in the Church.

SEALINGS FOR THE DEAD.
See SEALINGS.

SEALINGS FOR THE LIVING.
See SEALINGS.

SEANCES.
See MEDIUMS, SPIRITUALISM, WITCHES SABBATH. Much of the false worship of spiritualists is done at *seances;* these are meetings in which they assemble to receive spirit communications through their mediums.

SEASONS.

See DAY, NIGHT, SIGNS OF THE TIMES, TIME. 1. *Seasons of the year* (summer, fall, winter, and spring) are first referred to in the Bible as being in existence after the flood. "While the earth remaineth" (meaning in its present or fallen state) the Lord promised Noah, "seedtime and harvest, and cold and heat, and summer and winter, and day and night shall not cease." (Gen. 8:22.) The inference is that it was not until after the flood that it became necessary to plant in a particular time so that a harvest might be reaped. Presumptively before that earth-changing event both seedtime and harvest prevailed at all times the year around.

Seasons as we know them with their varied climatic and other conditions come about because the axis of the earth is tilted 23½ degrees. Revealed knowledge of all the great changes the earth has undergone is not presently available to men. We do know that the earth was created in a paradisiacal or terrestrial state; that it fell to its present telestial condition; that it will be renewed and receive again its paradisiacal glory during the millennium; and that eventually it is to become a celestial sphere.

Some have speculated that the

earth's axis tipped, possibly incident to the flood, so that seasons as we know them had their beginning. This speculation would account for some of the so-called pre-historical periods during which, according to geologists and others, climatic conditions on the earth were radically different from those that have prevailed during known time periods. This line of speculation also assumes that when the millennial era commences, when the whole earth again becomes a garden, that the axis thereof will return to its upright position so that seasons in the sense that they now exist will cease.

2. *Seasons* are also periods in which particular events are to occur. Thus the latter-days are the *times and seasons* when the signs of the times will be shown forth, when the great events precedent to the Second Coming of our Lord will take place.

SECOND ADAM.

See ADAM, CHRIST, IMMORTALITY, RESURRECTION. Christ is the *Second Adam*. As the first *mortal* man is called *Adam* (Moses 1:34), so the first Man to come forth in resurrected *immortality* is also called Adam, or more specifically the *Second Adam*. Adam's mortal body was a natural body, Christ's immortal one a spiritual body, meaning a body in which flesh and bones and spirit are inseparably

connected. (D. & C. 88:26-28; 93:33.)

Paul uses this comparison between Adam and Christ to teach some of the basic truths about the resurrection, to teach some of the basic events that take place when a body is sown a natural body and raised a spiritual body. "There is a natural body, and there is a spiritual body," he says. "And so it is written, The first man Adam was made a living soul; the last Adam was made a quickening spirit. . . . The first man is of the earth, earthy: *the second man is the Lord from heaven.* . . . And as we have borne the image of the earthy, we shall also bear the image of the heavenly." (1 Cor. 15:44-49.)

SECOND CHANCE THEORY.

See BAPTISM FOR THE DEAD, GOSPEL, HELL, PLAN OF SALVATION, REPENTANCE, SALVATION, SALVATION FOR THE DEAD, SPIRIT PRISON, SPIRIT WORLD, VICARIOUS ORDINANCES. *There is no such thing as a second chance to gain salvation by accepting the gospel in the spirit world after spurning, declining, or refusing to accept it in this life.* It is true that there may be a second chance to hear and accept the gospel, but those who have thus procrastinated their acceptance of the saving truths will not gain salvation in the celestial kingdom of God.

Salvation for the dead is the

system by means of which those who "die *without a knowledge of the gospel*" (D. & C. 128:5) may gain such knowledge in the spirit world and then, following the vicarious performance of the necessary ordinances, become heirs of salvation on the same basis as though the gospel truths had been obeyed in mortality. *Salvation for the dead is limited expressly to those who do not have opportunity in this life to accept the gospel but who would have taken the opportunity had it come to them.*

"All who have died *without a knowledge of this gospel,*" the Lord said to the Prophet, "who would have received it if they had been permitted to tarry, shall be heirs of the celestial kingdom of God; also all that shall die henceforth *without a knowledge of it, who would have received it with all their hearts,* shall be heirs of that kingdom, for I, the Lord, will judge all men according to their works, according to the desire of their hearts." (*Teachings,* p. 107.)

This is the only revealed principle by means of which the laws pertaining to salvation for the dead can be made effective in the lives of any persons. *There is no promise in any revelation that those who have a fair and just opportunity in this life to accept the gospel, and who do not do it, will have another chance in the spirit world to gain salvation.* On the contrary, there is the express stipulation that men cannot be saved

without accepting the gospel in this life, if they are given opportunity to accept it.

"Now is the time and the day of your salvation," Amulek said. "For behold, *this life is the time for men to prepare to meet God;* yea, behold the day of this life is the day for men to perform their labors. . . . For after this day of life, which is given us to prepare for eternity, behold, if we do not improve our time while in this life, then cometh the night of darkness wherein there can be no labor performed." (Alma 34:31-35; 2 Ne. 9: 27; 3 Ne. 28:34; Luke 9:62.)

An application of this law is seen in the words of the resurrected Christ to the Nephites. "Therefore come unto me and be ye saved," he said in repeating with some variations the Sermon on the Mount he had previously given the Jews, "for verily I say unto you, that *except ye shall keep my commandments, which I have commanded you at this time, ye shall in no case enter into the kingdom of heaven.*" (3 Ne. 12:20.) Thus salvation was forever denied those Nephites unless they gained it by virtue of their obedience during mortality. On the same basis, there is no such thing as salvation for the dead for the Latter-day Saints who have been taught the truths of salvation and had a fair and just opportunity to live them.

Those who have a fair and just opportunity to accept the gospel in this life and who do not do it, but who then do accept it when they hear it in the spirit world will go not to the celestial, but to the terrestrial kingdom. This includes those to whom Noah preached. "These are they . . . who are the spirits of men kept in prison, whom the Son visited, and preached the gospel unto them, that they might be judged according to men in the flesh; Who received not the testimony of Jesus in the flesh, but afterwards received it." (D. & C. 76:72-74.)

Thus the false and heretical doctrine that people who fail to live the law in this life (having had an opportunity so to do) will have a further chance of salvation in the life to come is a soul-destroying doctrine, a doctrine that lulls its adherents into carnal security and thereby denies them a hope of eternal salvation. (*Doctrines of Salvation*, vol. 2, pp. 181-196.)

SECOND COMFORTER.

See CALLING AND ELECTION SURE, COMFORTER, EXALTATION, HOLY GHOST. After a man so devotes himself to righteousness that his calling and election is made sure, "then it will be his privilege to receive the other *Comforter*," the Prophet says. "Now what is this other Comforter? It is no more nor less than the Lord Jesus Christ himself; and this is the sum and substance of the whole matter; that when any man obtains this last Comforter, he will have the

personage of Jesus Christ to attend him, or appear unto him from time to time, and even he will manifest the Father unto him, and they will take up their abode with him, and the visions of the heavens will be opened unto him, and the Lord will teach him face to face, and he may have a perfect knowledge of the mysteries of the kingdom of God; and this is the state and place the ancient saints arrived at when they had such glorious visions—Isaiah, Ezekiel, John upon the Isle of Patmos, St. Paul in the three heavens, and all the saints who held communion with the general assembly and Church of the Firstborn." (*Teachings*, pp. 150-151; John 14: 16:23; D. & C. 88:3-4; 130:3.) "The Holy Spirit of Promise is *not* the Second Comforter." (*Doctrines of Salvation*, vol. 1, p. 55.)

SECOND COMING OF CHRIST.

See ABOMINATION OF DESOLATION, JUDGMENT DAY, LAST DAYS, MILLENNIUM, SIGNS OF THE TIMES, SUPPER OF THE GREAT GOD. No event has transpired on earth, since the very day of creation itself, which is destined to have such a trancendent and recognizable affect on man, the earth, and all created things as the imminent return of the Son of Man will have.

The scriptures detail the events to attend two different appearances of the Lord among men. One appearance came in the meridian of time when he descended below all things, ministered unto his fellow men, and worked out the infinite and eternal atonement. The other is promised for the *last days* when, having ascended above all things, he will return in glory, to reign in the midst of his saints.

At his first coming, Christ was born of Mary; grew to maturity; ministered among men; bore record of his Father; called the Twelve and ordained them; organized his Church; was crucified, died, and rose again the third day; appeared to his disciples as a tangible Being having a body of flesh and bones which he invited them to feel and handle, lest they think him to be only a Spirit.

Finally, in the presence of his disciples, "while they beheld, he was taken up; and a cloud received him out of their sight. And while they looked stedfastly toward heaven as he went up, behold, two men stood by them in white apparel; Which also said, Ye men of Galilee, why stand ye gazing up into heaven? *this same Jesus, which is taken up from you into heaven, shall so come in like manner as ye have seen him go into heaven.*" (Acts 1:9-11.)

This *Second Coming*—a return of the same personal Being who first ministered in humility, meekness, and lowliness (D. & C. 130: 1-2)—will be in power and great glory with the hosts of heaven attending. At that day "the glory of the Lord shall be revealed, and all flesh shall see it together." (Isa. 40:4.) He will come, "not in the form of a woman, neither of a man traveling on the earth" (D. & C. 49:22), but in his might, power, and dominion to take vengeance on the ungodly and reward the righteous.

But before that day, certain promised signs and wonders are to take place, an understanding of which will give those who wait for him an assurance as to the approximate time of his return.

It is true that no man knoweth the day nor the hour of his return —"no, not the angels of heaven, but my Father only" (Matt. 24: 36), as he himself expressed it— but those who treasure up his word will not be deceived as to the time of that glorious day, nor as to the events to precede and to attend it. (Jos. Smith 1:37.) The righteous will be able to read the signs of the times. To those in darkness he will come suddenly, unexpectedly, "as a thief in the night," but to "the children of light" who "are not of the night, nor of darkness," as Paul expressed it, that day will not overtake them "as a thief." They will recognize the signs as certainly as a woman in travail foreknows the approximate time of her child's birth. (1 Thess. 5:1-6.) Now let us list some of the signs and wonders destined to precede and accompany the Second Coming. Among them are the following:

1. UNIVERSAL APOSTASY.—Between the original day of our Lord's

ministry among men and his glorious Second Coming, there was to be a universal falling away from the faith once delivered to the saints. Darkness was to cover the earth and gross darkness the minds of the people, until the earth would be "defiled under the inhabitants thereof." Men were to transgress the laws, change the ordinances, break the everlasting covenant. It would be "as with the people, so with the priest." (Isa. 24.) There were to be false christs, false prophets, and false doctrines, deceiving, if it were possible, even the very elect. (Matt. 24.) "Let no man deceive you by any means," Paul cautioned the Thessalonian Saints who apparently believed that the Second Coming was even then at the door, "for *that day shall not come, except there come a falling away first,* and that man of sin be revealed, the son of perdition; Who opposeth and exalteth himself above all that is called God, or that is worshipped; so that he as God sitteth in the temple of God, shewing himself that he is God." (2 Thess. 2:1-4.)

2. AN ERA OF RESTORATION.— From the beginning prophets have foretold events scheduled to attend the *restoration of all things in the last days.* Peter, for instance, explained that this age of restoration—an age yet future from his day—would commence prior to the Second Advent of our Lord. Speaking of "the times of refreshing"— that is, the day of the Second Com-

ing, the day when the earth is to be renewed (as part of the restoration of all things) and receive again its paradisiacal glory—he said that the Lord, at that day, would "send Jesus Christ, which before was preached unto you: *Whom the heaven must receive until the times of restitution of all things,* which God hath spoken by the mouth of all his holy prophets since the world began." (Acts 3:19-21.) This *era of restoration* is the same as the era or period known as the dispensation of the fulness of times in which the Lord has promised to "gather together in one all things in Christ." (Eph. 1:10.)

3. RESTORATION OF THE GOSPEL. —As part of the restoration of all things, the fulness of the gospel with all its saving powers and graces was to be returned to earth shortly before the great and dreadful day of the Lord. John saw in vision the bringing back of this gospel by angelic ministration and its proclamation among all peoples. This was to take place just before the hour of God's judgment is come, just before the hour of the return of the Son of Man. (Rev. 14:6-7.)

4. GOSPEL WITNESS TO BE HERALDED TO WORLD.—Not only was the one true gospel to be restored in the last days, but *that very gospel*—not some perverted fragment of it to be found in the false churches of the world—was to be preached in all the world. "This Gospel of the Kingdom," our Lord

689

said of the restored gospel, "shall be preached in all the world, for a witness unto all nations, and then shall the end come, or the destruction of the wicked." (Jos. Smith 1:31; Matt. 24:14.)

On November 3, 1831—less than 17 months after the Church and kingdom had been set up again and while it was still a small and unknown organization—the Lord said through the Prophet Joseph Smith: "I have sent forth mine angel flying through the midst of heaven, having the everlasting gospel, who hath appeared unto some and hath committed it unto man, who shall appear unto many that dwell on the earth. And this gospel shall be preached unto every nation, and kindred, and tongue, and people. And the servants of God shall go forth, saying with a loud voice: Fear God and give glory to him, for the hour of his judgment is come; And worship him that made heaven, and earth, and the sea, and the fountains of waters—Calling upon the name of the Lord day and night, saying: O that thou wouldst rend the heavens, that thou wouldst come down, that the mountains might flow down at thy presence." (D. & C. 133:36-40.)

If Joseph Smith had not been a prophet, how would he have dared proclaim, at that day of the yet small beginning of this latter-day work, that the very truths of salvation restored through his instrumentality would be heralded to all the world as a witness unto all

people that the coming of our Lord was near?

5. COMING FORTH OF BOOK OF MORMON.—Also as part of the promised restoration of all things, the Book of Mormon was destined to come forth as a sign that the winding up scene is near. Isaiah links together the apostasy, restoration, and coming forth of the Book of Mormon (Isa. 29); Ezekiel prophesies similarly relative to the Book of Mormon, the latter-day gathering of Israel, and the erection of a holy sanctuary or temple in Jerusalem. (Ezek. 37.) Moroni tells of its coming forth under latter-day conditions that are part of the signs of the times, part of the signs to occur precedent to the coming of our Lord (Morm. 8); and the resurrected Lord himself taught the Nephites that the coming forth of this mighty record to their descendants would be one of the great signs of the fulfilling of the covenants in the last days. (3 Ne. 21.)

6. RESTORATION OF KINGDOM TO ISRAEL.—In part, at least, the gathering of latter-day Israel is pre-millennial. With the restoration of the gospel (the Church itself as organized on April 6, 1830, being *the ecclesiastical kingdom of God on earth*) the scattered remnants of Israel have begun to come to a knowledge of their true Shepherd and to return to his fold. The ancient promise was that when this gathered remnant would establish "the house of the God of Jacob" in

the last days in the tops of the mountains, with the righteous of all nations flowing unto it, then Christ would come, the millennial era commence, and all nations beat their swords into plowshares. (Isa. 2:1-4.)

That will be the day when complete answer will be found to the query, "Lord, wilt thou at this time restore again the kingdom to Israel?" (Acts 1:2-8), for the return of the Messiah will bring *the political kingdom of God on earth;* then the kingdoms of this world will become the kingdom of our God and of his Christ, and he shall reign forever and ever. (Rev. 11: 15.) The restoration of the keys of the gathering of Israel by Moses to Joseph Smith and Oliver Cowdery on April 3, 1836, causes us to know that the fulfilment of all the covenants made to ancient Israel is soon to come to pass. (D. & C. 110:11.)

7. COMING OF ELIJAH.—When Elijah came to Joseph Smith and Oliver Cowdery on April 3, 1836, in fulfilment of the ancient promise (Mal. 4:5-6), that ancient prophet concluded his bestowal of the keys of the sealing power with this assurance: "By this ye may know that *the great and dreadful day of the Lord is near, even at the doors."* (D. & C. 110:13-16.) If that day was near in 1836, how much more so is it today?

8. MESSENGER BEFORE LORD'S FACE.—"Behold, *I will send my messenger,* and he shall prepare the way before me," the Lord declared through Malachi relative to his glorious Second Coming, "even the messenger of the covenant, whom ye delight in: behold, he shall come, saith the Lord of hosts." Thereafter: "The Lord, whom ye seek, shall suddenly come to his temple." (Mal. 3.) Both Joseph Smith through whom the everlasting covenant was restored (and John the Baptist who ministered unto him) and the gospel covenant itself have been sent in fulfilment of this promise. (D. & C. 45:9.)

9. SIGNS OF THE TIMES TO BE FULFILLED.—Many revelations summarize the signs and world conditions, the wars, perils, and commotions of the last days. Preceding our Lord's return, the prophetic word tells of plagues, pestilence, famine, and disease such as the world has never before seen; of scourges, tribulation, calamities, and disasters without parallel; of strife, wars, rumors of wars, blood, carnage, and desolation which overshadow anything of past ages; of the elements being in commotion with resultant floods, storms, fires, whirlwinds, earthquakes—all of a proportion and intensity unknown to men of former days; of evil, iniquity, wickedness, turmoil, rapine, murder, crime, and commotion among men almost beyond comprehension. (Matt. 24; Luke 21; D. & C. 29; 43; 45; 86; 87; 88:86-98; 133; Jos. Smith 1; Mal. 3; 4.)

10. GREAT SIGNS IN HEAVEN AND

ON EARTH.—"He that feareth me shall be looking forth for the great day of the Lord to come, even for the signs of the coming of the Son of Man. And they shall see signs and wonders, for they shall be shown forth in the heavens above, and in the earth beneath. And they shall behold blood, and fire, and vapors of smoke. And before the day of the Lord shall come, the sun shall be darkened, and the moon be turned into blood, and the stars fall from heaven." (D. & C. 45:39-42; 29:14; Joel 2:30-31; Matt. 24:29.)

11. THE GENERATION OF OUR LORD'S RETURN.—True it is that the day and hour of our Lord's coming are and will remain unknown, such being an incentive to all to watch and be ready at all times. But true it also is that *those who watch for that great and dread day are expected to read the signs of the times so as to know the approximate time of his coming.* President Wilford Woodruff taught that we do know the generation when he will come. (*Discourses of Wilford Woodruff,* p. 253.)

"I was once praying very earnestly to know the time of the coming of the Son of Man," the Prophet Joseph Smith recorded on April 2, 1843, "when I heard a voice repeat the following: Joseph, my son, if thou livest until thou art eighty-five years old, thou shalt see the face of the Son of Man; therefore let this suffice, and

trouble me no more on this matter.

"I was left thus, without being able to decide whether this coming referred to the beginning of the millennium or to some previous appearing, or whether I should die and thus see his face. I believe the coming of the Son of Man will not be any sooner than that time." (D. & C. 130:14-17.)

Four days later, April 6, 1843, at the General Conference of the Church, while the Spirit rested upon him, the Prophet said: "Were I going to prophesy, I would say the end would not come in 1844, 5, or 6, or in forty years. *There are those of the rising generation who shall not taste death till Christ comes.*"

The rising generation is the one that has just begun. Thus, technically, children born on April 6, 1843, would be the first members of the rising generation, and all children born, however many years later, to the same parents would still be members of that same rising generation. It is not unreasonable to suppose that many young men had babies at the time of this prophecy and also had other children as much as 50 or 75 years later, assuming for instance that they were married again to younger women. This very probable assumption would bring the date up to, say, the 2nd decade in the 20th century—and the children so born would be members of that same rising generation of which the Prophet spoke. Now if these children lived to the normal age of men generally, they would be alive well past the year 2000 A.D.

This reasoning takes on added significance when considered in connection with the revelation which states categorically that *Christ will come "in the beginning of the seventh thousand years"* of the earth's temporal continuance. (D. & C. 77:6, 12.) We, of course, do not know exactly how many years elapsed between Adam and the birth of Christ, but suppose it to have been 4004; nor can we be certain, from historical sources, how many years have passed since. But reading these inspired statements in connection with the signs of the times which we can interpret, it is plain that the day of the coming of the Son of Man is not far distant.

But back to the sermon of the Prophet. In it he made reference to the voice which spoke to him relative to the time of the Second Coming and then said: "I prophesy in the name of the Lord God, and let it be written—the Son of Man will not come in the clouds of heaven till I am eighty-five years old. . . . *The coming of the Son of Man never will be—never can be till the judgments spoken of for this hour are poured out: which judgments are commenced.* Paul says, Ye are the children of the light, and not of the darkness, that that day should overtake you as a thief in the night. (1 Thess. 5:2-6.) *It is not the design of the Almighty to*

come upon the earth and crush it and grind it to powder, but he will reveal it to his servants the prophets.

"Judah must return, Jerusalem must be rebuilt, and the temple, and water come out from under the temple, and the waters of the Dead Sea be healed. It will take some time to rebuild the walls of the city and the temple, &c.; and all this must be done before the Son of Man will make his appearance. There will be wars and rumors of wars, signs in the heavens above and on the earth beneath, the sun turned into darkness and the moon to blood, earthquakes in divers places, the seas heaving beyond their bounds; *then will appear one grand sign of the Son of Man in heaven.* But what will the world do? They will say it is a planet, a comet, etc. But the Son of Man will come as the sign of the coming of the Son of Man, which will be as the light of the morning cometh out of the east." (*Teachings*, pp. 286-287.)

12. LORD'S SUDDEN COMING TO HIS TEMPLE.—Malachi recorded the promise, speaking of latter-day events, that *"The Lord, whom ye seek, shall suddenly come to his temple."* (Mal. 3:1.) Certainly the Almighty is not limited in the number of appearances and returns to earth needed to fulfil the scriptures, usher in the final dispensation, and consummate his great latter-day work.

This sudden latter-day appearance in the temple does not have reference to his appearance at the great and dreadful day, for that coming will be when he sets his foot upon the Mount of Olivet in the midst of the final great war. The temple appearance was fulfilled, in part at least, by his return to the Kirtland Temple on April 3, 1836; and it may well be that he will come again, suddenly, to others of his temples, more particularly that which will be erected in Jackson County, Missouri.

In this connection it is worthy of note that whenever and wherever the Lord appears, he will come suddenly, that is "quickly, in an hour you think not." (D. & C. 51:20.) His oft repeated warning, "Behold, I come quickly" (D. & C. 35:27), means that when the appointed hour arrives, he will come with a speed and a suddenness which will leave no further time for preparation for that great day.

13. THE COMING AT ADAM-ONDI-AHMAN.—Before the great and dreadful day of the Lord; before the day when Christ is to come and reign personally on earth as King of kings and Lord of lords; before the day when he will administer the affairs of his earthly kingdom in a direct, personal manner, and not through the type of stewardships which now prevail; our Lord will come to receive back the keys and authorities whereunder his stewards have governed for him. This will take place at Adam-ondi-Ahman, which is Spring Hill, Daviess County, Missouri. (D. & C. 116.)

Daniel wrote of the Son of Man being brought before the Ancient of Days (who is Adam, our Father), and there our Lord would have "given him dominion, and glory, and a kingdom, that all people, nations, and languages, should serve him: his dominion is an everlasting dominion, which shall not pass away, and his kingdom that which shall not be destroyed." (Dan. 7:9-14.)

This is the occasion of which the Prophet Joseph Smith speaks when he says that Adam "will call his children together and hold a council with them to prepare them for the coming of the Son of Man. He (Adam) is the father of the human family, and presides over the spirits of all men, and *all that have had the keys must stand before him in the grand council.* This may take place before some of us leave this stage of action. The Son of Man stands before him, and there is given him glory and dominion. Adam delivers up his stewardship to Christ, that which was delivered to him as holding the keys of the universe, but retains his standing as the head of the human family." (*Teachings,* p. 157; *Way to Perfection,* pp. 287-291.) After this has happened Christ will be ready to come and reign personally on earth.

14. PHYSICAL CHANGES OF EARTH AT SECOND COMING.—Great changes are in store for the earth and all things on its face when

our Lord comes in glory. "Not many days hence and the earth shall tremble and reel to and fro as a drunken man." (D. & C. 88:87.) "Every valley shall be exalted, and every mountain and hill shall be made low: and the crooked shall be made straight, and the rough places plain: And the glory of the Lord shall be revealed, and all flesh shall see it together: for the mouth of the Lord hath spoken it." (Isa. 40: 4-5; D. & C. 49:23; Ezek. 38:19-20.)

The Lord "shall command the great deep, and it shall be driven back into the north countries, and the islands shall become one land; And the land of Jerusalem and the land of Zion shall be turned back into their own place, and the earth shall be like as it was in the days before it was divided. And the Lord, even the Savior, shall stand in the midst of his people, and shall reign over all flesh." (D. & C. 133:23-25.) This will be the day when there shall be a new heaven and a new earth, when the earth will be renewed and receive its paradisiacal glory, when the great millennium will be ushered in. (Isa. 65:17-25; D. & C. 101:23-32; Tenth Article of Faith.)

15. ARMAGEDDON: "THE BATTLE OF THAT GREAT DAY OF GOD ALMIGHTY" (Rev. 16:14-21).—The greatest war, slaughter, carnage, bloodshed, and desolation of all the ages will be in full swing at the very hour when Christ returns. *"There shall be a time of trouble,"* says Daniel, *"such as never was*

since there was a nation even to that same time." (Dan. 12:1.)

All the nations of the earth shall be gathered at Jerusalem, at Armageddon, in the valley of Jehoshaphat, the valley of decision. It will be "A day of darkness and of gloominess, a day of clouds and of thick darkness, as the morning spread upon the mountains." The hosts of Gog and Magog, the armies assembled to battle, shall be "a great people and a strong; *there hath not been ever the like, neither shall be any more after it,* even to the years of many generations. A fire devoureth before them; and behind them a flame burneth: *the land is as the garden of Eden before them, and behind them a desolate wilderness; yea, and nothing shall escape them."* (Joel 2:2-3.)

Jerusalem "shall be taken, and the houses rifled, and the women ravished" (Zech. 14:2), and all things shall be in commotion. Then shall the Lord set his foot upon the Mount of Olives, fight the battles of his saints, take vengeance on the wicked, bring peace to the earth, and reign as "king over all the earth." (Ezek. 38; 39; Dan. 11; 12; Joel 2; 3; Zech. 12; 13; 14; D. & C. 133.)

16. THE GREAT AND DREADFUL DAY OF THE LORD.—To the wicked the Second Coming will be a great and dreadful day, a day of sorrow and desolation, a day of burning and vengeance, a day of judgment which the wicked shall not abide. "For the presence of the Lord shall

be as the melting fire that burneth, and as the fire which causeth the waters to boil. O Lord, thou shalt come down to make thy name known to thine adversaries, and all nations shall tremble at thy presence—When thou doest terrible things, things they look not for. . . .

"And it shall be said: Who is this that cometh down from God in heaven with dyed garments; yea, from the regions which are not known, clothed in his glorious apparel, traveling in the greatness of his strength? And he shall say: I am he who spake in righteousness, mighty to save.

"And the Lord shall be red in his apparel, and his garments like him that treadeth in the wine-vat. And so great shall be the glory of his presence that the sun shall hide his face in shame, and the moon shall withhold its light, and the stars shall be hurled from their places.

"And his voice shall be heard: I have trodden the winepress alone, and have brought judgment upon all people; and none were with me; And *I have trampled them in my fury, and I did tread upon them in mine anger, and their blood have I sprinkled upon my garments, and stained all my raiment; for this was the day of vengeance which was in my heart.* (D. & C. 133:41-51.)

17. THE YEAR OF THE LORD'S REDEEMED.—To the righteous who have waited for him and kept his laws, the Second Coming will be a day devoutly to be desired, a day of peace and redemption, a day when injustice will cease and wickedness be banished, a day when the vineyard will be cleansed of corruption and its rightful Ruler reign in the midst of his saints. "Yea, when thou comest down, and the mountains flow down at thy presence, thou shalt meet him who rejoiceth and worketh righteousness, who remembereth thee in thy ways. For since the beginning of the world have not men heard nor perceived by the ear, neither hath any eye seen, O God, besides thee, how great things thou hast prepared for him that waiteth for thee. . . .

"And now the year of my redeemed is come; and they shall mention the loving kindness of their Lord, and all that he has bestowed upon them according to his goodness, and according to his loving kindness, forever and ever." (D. & C. 133:44-62.)

18. PLACES OF THE LORD'S RETURN.—These are many. He has already come suddenly to his temple. (Mal. 3:1; D. & C. 36:8; 110.) Soon he will meet with his stewards, who have held the keys of his kingdom, at Adam-ondi-Ahman. (D. & C. 116; Dan. 7:9-14.) In the midst of the greatest war of all the ages, when all nations are gathered together at Jerusalem, "Then shall the Lord go forth, and fight against those nations, as when he fought in the day of battle. And his feet shall stand in that day upon the mount of Olives, which

is before Jerusalem on the east, and the mount of Olives shall cleave in the midst thereof toward the east and toward the west, and there shall be a very great valley." (Zech. 14:3-4.)

Following this, apparently he will make many successive appearances in all parts of the earth. "For behold, he shall stand upon the mount of Olivet, and upon the mighty ocean, even the great deep, and upon the islands of the sea, and upon the land of Zion. And he shall utter his voice out of Zion, and he shall speak from Jerusalem, and his voice shall be heard among all people." (D. & C. 133:20-21.)

19. VINEYARD TO BE BURNED AT HIS COMING.—Malachi asked: "Who may abide the day of his coming? and who shall stand when he appeareth?" (Mal. 3:2.) In answer he said that Christ would come in judgment and be a swift witness against sorcerers, adulterers, false swearers, and all who live after the manner of the world, all who live a telestial law. All these—the proud and the wicked—would be as stubble when "the day cometh, that shall burn as an oven." (Mal. 3; 4.)

Using the same type of language as Malachi had done, the Lord in our day announced: "Behold, now it is called today until the coming of the Son of Man, and verily it is a day of sacrifice, and a day for the tithing of my people; for *he that is tithed shall not be burned at his coming.* For after today cometh the burning—this is speaking after the manner of the Lord—for verily I say, tomorrow all the proud and they that do wickedly shall be as stubble; and I will burn them up, for I am the Lord of Hosts; and I will not spare any that remain in Babylon. Wherefore, if ye believe me, ye will labor while it is called today." (D. & C. 64:23-25.)

Every corruptible thing shall be consumed in this day of burning. The elements shall melt with fervent heat and all things shall become new, that is, the earth will be renewed and receive its paradisical glory. (D. & C. 101:23-31.)

20. RESURRECTION AND JUDGMENT ATTEND SECOND COMING.—At his coming, the Lord will sit in judgment on all nations, dividing the sheep from the goats, sending some to everlasting punishment and others to life eternal. (Matt. 25:31-46.) At his coming, also, those who have earned the right to come forth in the resurrection of the just will rise from their graves and inherit their places in a celestial or a terrestrial kingdom. (D. & C. 88:95-99.)

21. WATCH AND BE READY.—"And take heed to yourselves, lest at any time your hearts be overcharged with surfeiting, and drunkenness, and cares of this life, and so that day come upon you unawares. For as a snare shall it come on all them that dwell on the face of the whole earth. Watch ye therefore, and pray always, that ye may be accounted worthy to

escape all these things that shall come to pass, and to stand before the Son of man." (Luke 21:34-36.)

SECOND DEATH.

See SPIRITUAL DEATH.

SECOND ESTATE.

See FIRST ESTATE, MORTALITY. As life in our pre-existent home, life as spirit offspring of the Eternal Father, was our first estate or first sphere of life as conscious identities, so this mortal sphere is our *second estate.* Those who were faithful in their first estate earned the right to pass through this second sphere of activity; they were "added upon." Lucifer and his angels have been denied a second estate of existence and are now and will ever remain as spirits. Those who by righteousness and obedience "keep their second estate shall have glory added upon their heads for ever and ever." (Abra. 3:22-28.)

SECOND RESURRECTION.

See RESURRECTION.

SECRETARIES.

See CLERKS.

SECRET COMBINATIONS.

See APOSTASY, CAIN, CHURCH OF THE DEVIL, COMMUNISM, MASTER MAHAN, MURDERERS. Beginning in the days of Cain and continuing through all generations, whenever there have been unrighteous and apostate peoples on earth, Satan has revealed unto them his oaths, vows, and *secret combinations.* Cain first took upon himself the secret oaths as they were administered by Satan; then he killed Abel. Murder, plunder, robbery, power, the destruction of freedom, and the persecution of the saints have been the objectives of these societies ever since. (Moses 5:16-59; 6:15; Hela. 6:17-41.)

These secret societies flourished before the flood; they gained great strength among the Jaredites on this continent; the Gadianton robbers and the Lamanites reveled in them in Nephite days; and they are had in all parts of the earth today. "It hath been made known unto me," Moroni wrote, "that they are had among all people." (Ether 8:20.)

Reliable modern reports describe their existence among gangsters, as part of the governments of communist countries, in some labor organizations, and even in some religious groups. Speaking of these latter-day conditions Moroni said to people now living: "The Lord commandeth you, when ye shall see these things come among you that ye shall awake to a sense of your awful situation, because of this secret combination which shall be among you. . . . For it cometh to pass that whoso buildeth it up seeketh to overthrow the freedom of all lands, nations, and countries." (Ether 8:14-26.)

SECRETS.
See MYSTERIES.

SECTARIANS.
See SECTS.

SECTS.
See APOSTASY, CHRISTIANITY, CREEDS, FIRST VISION, HARLOTS. Division and dissension, contention, confusion and discord—these are among the prevailing characteristics of the *sects* of Christendom. These various sects or *denominations*—all holding to their particular creeds and practices—will never unite, except on one point: all will join hands to fight the truth and stand in opposition to The Church of Jesus Christ of Latter-day Saints. (Jos. Smith 2:20-25.)

Existence of the sects of Christendom is proof positive of the universal apostasy. Truth is one; Christ is not divided; those who enjoy the Spirit, all speak the same things; there are no divisions among them; but they are "perfectly joined together in the same mind and in the same judgment." (1 Cor. 1:10-13.) When Joseph Smith retired to the Sacred Grove, it was to ask the Lord which of all the sects was right and which he should join. The answer: "I must join none of them, for they were all wrong." (Jos. Smith 2:14-20.)

But the apostate nature of the creeds and teachings of the sects in no sense means that all *sectarians,* as individuals, are living in gross unrighteousness without desiring to know and live the truth. "There are many yet on the earth among all sects, parties, and denominations," the Prophet wrote by way of revelation, "who are blinded by the subtle craftiness of men, whereby they lie in wait to deceive, and who are only kept from the truth because they know not where to find it." (D. & C. 123:12.)

SECURITY.
See CHURCH WELFARE PLAN OBEDIENCE, SIGNS OF THE TIMES. It is instinctive for mortal men to seek *security,* to strive for a state of existence in which they will be free from fear, want, danger, and anxiety. Most men rely on riches, power, and influence to give assurance of security, just as nations of men rely on armies, weapons, treaties, and alliances. But all of these can give only a fleeting and partial sense of security. Disasters, disease, plagues, famines, and wars, with all their attendant evils, can sweep man-made security away in one fell swoop. Real security—temporal, physical, spiritual, mental, moral—comes only by obedience to the laws of God. There is no peace of mind or freedom from fear except in righteous living; and

such temporal blessings as can be assured in a wicked world are found in and through the Church Welfare Plan and the economic laws of the Church.

SECURITY PROGRAM.
See CHURCH WELFARE PLAN.

SEDUCTION.
See SEX IMMORALITY.

SEED OF ABRAHAM.
See ISRAEL.

SEED OF CHRIST.
See ADOPTION, CHRIST, MESSIANIC PROPHECIES, SONS OF GOD. One of Isaiah's great Messianic prophecies says of our Lord: "When thou shalt make his soul an offering for sin, he shall see his *seed.*" (Isa. 53:10.) Abinadi quotes this prophecy, asks the question, "Who shall be his seed?" and then gives this inspired answer: "Behold I say unto you, that whosoever has heard the words of the prophets, yea, all the holy prophets who have prophesied concerning the coming of the Lord—I say unto you, that all those who have hearkened unto their words, and believed that the Lord would redeem his people, and have looked forward to that day for a remission of their sins, I say unto you, that these are his seed, or they are the heirs of the king-

dom of God. For these are they whose sins he has borne; these are they for whom he has died, to redeem them from their transgressions. And now, are they not his seed? Yea, and are not the prophets, every one that has opened his mouth to prophesy, that has not fallen into transgression, I mean all the holy prophets ever since the world began? I say unto you that they are his seed." (Mosiah 15:10-13.)

Thus the seed of Christ are those who are adopted into his family, who by faith have become his sons and his daughters. (Mosiah 5:7.) They are the children of Christ in that they are his followers and disciples and keep his commandments. (4 Ne. 17; Morm. 9: 26; Moro. 7:19.)

SEERS.
See FIRST PRESIDENCY, ORACLES, PROPHETS, REVELATION, REVELATORS, URIM AND THUMMIM, VISIONS. From among the Lord's prophets and revelators certain highly spiritual ones have been chosen to act as *seers,* and as such, as occasion has required, they have had the right to use the Urim and Thummim. A seer is a prophet selected and appointed to possess and use these holy interpreters. (Mosiah 8:13; 28:16.) Joseph Smith, the great seer of latter-days (2 Ne. 3:6-11; D. & C. 21:1; 124:125; 127:12; 135:3), for instance, translated the Book of Mormon and received

many revelations by means of the Urim and Thummim.

"A seer is greater than a prophet. . . . A seer is a revelator and a prophet also; and a gift which is greater can no man have, except he should possess the power of God, which no man can; yet a man may have great power given him from God. But a seer can know of things which are past, and also of things which are to come, and by them shall all things be revealed, or, rather, shall secret things be made manifest, and hidden things shall come to light, and things which are not known shall be made known by them, and also things shall be made known by them which otherwise could not be known. Thus God has provided a means that man, through faith, might work mighty miracles; therefore he becometh a great benefit to his fellow beings." (Mosiah 8:15-18.)

The President of the Church holds the office of seership. (D. & C. 107:92; 124:94, 125.) Indeed, the apostolic office itself is one of seership, and the members of the Council of the Twelve, together with the Presidency and Patriarch to the Church, are chosen and sustained as prophets, seers, and revelators to the Church.

If there are seers among a people, that people is the Lord's. Where there are no seers, apostasy prevails. (Isa. 29:10; 2 Ne. 27:5.)

SEER STONES.
See URIM AND THUMMIM.

SEGREGATION.
See CASTE SYSTEM.

SELFISHNESS.
See GREEDINESS. *Selfishness* consists in caring unduly or supremely for oneself; it is one of the lusts of the flesh which must be overcome by those who gain salvation. A selfish person clings to his own comfort, advantage, or position at the expense of others. Men are commanded to repent of their pride and selfishness. (D. & C. 56: 8.) In practice the way to do this is to serve in the Church and make generous financial contributions to sustain its programs.

SELF-RELIANCE.
Properly understood and practiced, *self-reliance* is a desirable saintly virtue; when it leaves the Lord out of the picture, however, it becomes a vice that leads men from the paths of righteousness. The saints, for instance, should have confidence in their own abilities, efforts, and judgments to make a living, to increase in faith and the attributes of godliness, to work out their salvation, to pass all the tests of this mortal probation. They should know that the Lord has not placed his children in

positions beyond their capacities to cope with, that the normal trials and tribulations of life are part of the eternal system. Ordinarily members of the Church should make their own personal decisions, using the agency the Almighty has given them, without running to their bishops or others for direction.

But with it all, man of himself is not wholly self-sufficient. He is not to trust solely in his own strength, nor in the arm of flesh. The Lord is his Counselor and Deliverer, upon whom he must rely for guidance, direction, and inspiration. If the great Creator had not stepped forward to redeem the creatures of his creating, the whole plan of salvation would be void and the most perfect manifestations of self-reliance would have no worth.

SEMINARIES.
See RELIGIOUS EDUCATION.

SENSUALITY.
See CARNALITY, CORRUPTION, DEVILISHNESS, FALLEN MAN, MORTALITY. Natural or sensual men are enemies to God, because they are ruled by passions and appetites rather than by the Spirit. (Mosiah 3:19.) They are friends of the world, and "the friendship of the world is enmity with God." (Jas. 4:4.) That which is sensual is carnal and base; it relates to the body rather than the Spirit. Thus *sensuality* embraces free indulgence in sensual, fleshly pleasures—lewdness, licentiousness, lasciviousness. Since the fall, men in their natural state have been carnal, sensual, and devilish. (D. & C. 20:20; Moses 5:13; 6:49; Mosiah 16:1-4.)

The gospel of salvation is not carnal or sensual. (D. & C. 29:35.) Rather, the plan of salvation consists in overcoming the world, in overcoming carnality and sensuality, in putting off the natural or sensual man and becoming saints. (Mosiah 3:19.)

SEPTUAGINT.
See KING JAMES VERSION OF THE BIBLE.

SEPULCHER.
See GRAVES.

SERAPHIM.
See ANGELS, CHERUBIM, HIERARCHY. *Seraphs* are angels who reside in the presence of God, giving continual glory, honor, and adoration to him. "Praise ye him, all his angels: praise ye him, all his hosts." (Ps. 148:2.) It is clear that seraphs include the unembodied spirits of pre-existence, for our Lord "looked upon the wide expanse of eternity, and *all the seraphic hosts of heaven, before the world was made.*" (D. & C. 38:1.) Whether the name seraphs also applies to perfected and resurrected angels is not clear. While petitioning on behalf of the

saints, the Prophet prayed that "we may mingle our voices with those bright, shining seraphs around thy throne, with acclamations of praise, singing Hosanna to God and the Lamb!" (D. & C. 109:79.)

In Hebrew the plural of seraph is *seraphim* or, as incorrectly recorded in the King James Version of the Bible, *seraphims*. Isaiah saw seraphim in vision and heard them cry one to another, "Holy, holy, holy, is the Lord of hosts; the whole earth is full of his glory." (*Inspired Version,* Isa. 6:1-8.) The fact that these holy beings were shown to him as having wings was simply to symbolize their "power, to move, to act, etc." as was the case also in visions others had received. (D. & C. 77:4.)

SERAPHS.
See SERAPHIM.

SERMON ON THE MOUNT.
See SERMONS.

SERMONS.
See CONFERENCES, EPISTLES, KING FOLLETT SERMON, KNOWLEDGE, PROPHETS, REVELATION, SACRAMENT MEETINGS. Since it pleases God, "by the foolishness of *preaching* to save them that believe" (1 Cor. 1:21), it follows that he sends *preachers* to teach his saving truths. This preaching is presented primarily in *sermons,* but it may be woven into lessons, talks, discourses, speeches, orations, lectures, addresses, and ordinary conversations.

Preaching and gospel sermons have been part of the gospel order from the beginning. After naming the great patriarchs from Adam to Enoch, Moses comments: "And they were *preachers of righteousness,* and spake and prophesied, and called upon all men, everywhere, to repent; and faith was taught unto the children of men." (Moses 6:23.) The Sermon on the Mount (Matt. 5; 6; 7; 3 Ne. 12; 13; 14), the King Follett Sermon (*Teachings,* pp. 342-362), and the angel's sermon to King Benjamin on the atonement of Christ (Mosiah 3) are among the greatest sermons ever delivered. It is the order of the Church that the major portion of the time in conferences and sacrament meetings should be used for sermons.

There are two requisites for a good sermon: 1. The speaker teaches the saving truths of the gospel only; and 2. He speaks by the power of the Holy Ghost. *"Teach the principles of my gospel,"* the Lord commands, *"which are in the Bible and the Book of Mormon, in the which is the fulness of the gospel. . . . And these shall be their teachings, as they shall be directed by the Spirit. And the Spirit shall be given unto you by the prayer of faith; and if ye receive not the Spirit ye shall not teach."* (D. & C. 42:12-14.) Nephi said: "When a man speaketh by the power of the Holy Ghost the power of the Holy Ghost carrieth it unto the hearts of the children of men." (2 Ne. 33:1.)

To qualify as preachers of righteousness the elders of Israel must: 1. Know the doctrines of the gospel; and 2. So live that the Holy Ghost can enlighten their minds and loosen their tongues when they stand before the people. *"Neither take ye thought beforehand what ye shall say,"* is the divine decree, *"but treasure up in your minds continually the words of life, and it shall be given you in the very hour that portion that shall be meted unto every man."* (D. & C. 84:85; Matt. 10:19-20.)

There may be a few instances in which sermons may be read, just as there are a few formal occasions when prayers may be read, as for instance at the dedication of temples. On some radio and television broadcasts written sermons may be appropriate, and there is no impropriety in little children reading written talks. But in the absence of some compelling reason for doing so, those privileged to deliver gospel sermons should: 1. Treasure up those principles of light and truth which it is appropriate to teach from time to time; 2. Manifest sufficient faith to rely on the Lord for guidance as the occasion requires; and 3. Cultivate the ability to attune themselves to the promptings and whisperings of the Spirit when actually standing before the people.

Every experienced elder has spoken on occasions when the spirit of inspiration has rested upon him, when by the power of the Holy Ghost thoughts have come into his mind, and words have fallen from his lips, which were new to him. Many direct revelations are given to the Lord's agents as they stand on their feet, relying on the Spirit, preaching the gospel.

Just as there are false prophets and false Christs, so there are false teachers and *false preachers.* (Words of Morm. 15-16.) Anyone who professes to preach the gospel but who does not have the Spirit, and who does not teach the true principles of salvation, and who is not a legal administrator endowed with power from on high, is a false preacher.

SERPENT.

See DEVIL, DRAGON, SERPENTS. Since the day in which Satan spoke by the mouth of the serpent to entice Eve to partake of the forbidden fruit (Moses 4:5-21), Satan has been called "that old *serpent."* (Rev. 12:9; 20:2; D. & C. 76:28; 88:110.) Choice of the name is excellent, indicating as it does a cunning, sly, subtle, and deceitful craftiness.

SERPENTS.

See BRAZEN SERPENT, DEVIL,

QUETZALCOATL, SERPENT. *Serpents* have been used among both Christian and pagan peoples as a symbol of both good and evil. (Milton R. Hunter, *Archaeology and the Book of Mormon,* vol. 2; *Christ in Ancient America.*) Lucifer, who tempted Eve through the mouth of a serpent (Gen. 3), is called "the great dragon," and "that old serpent" (Rev. 12:7-17; 20:2), thus giving foundation to the use of serpents as an evil symbol. Moses, by command of the Lord raised a brazen serpent before Israel, in similitude of the fact that Christ would be lifted up on the cross (Num. 21:4-9; John 3:14-15; Alma 33:19-22; Hela. 8:14-15), thus giving foundation to the use of serpents as a good symbol. Among the Lamanite descendants of Lehi, Quetzalcoatl, the feathered serpent, became a symbol for the great White God who had ministered among their ancestors.

SERVANT.

See CHRIST, FATHER IN HEAVEN, MINISTER OF SALVATION, SERVANTS OF GOD. Christ is the Father's *Servant.* One of the great Messianic prophecies so designates him. (Isa. 42:1-8; Matt. 12:14-21.) Usage of this term teaches that he is subject to the Father in all things, that he came into the world to do the will of the Father, and that it is by the power of the Father that he accomplished his mission. (3 Ne. 27:13-16; D. & C. 76: 40:43; John 5:30; 6:38.) It should be remembered that in the sense in which the designation is here used, the Servant shall be as his Lord, thus inheriting the fulness of all things for himself. "Where I am, there shall also my servant be." (John 12:26.)

SERVANTS OF GOD.

See ANGELS, CELESTIAL MARRIAGE, DAUGHTERS OF GOD, SONS OF GOD. 1. Those who choose to serve the Lord and who keep his commandments are called his *servants.* After they have been tried and tested and are found faithful and true in all things, they are called no longer servants, but *friends.* (John 15:14-15.) His friends are the ones he will take into his kingdom and with whom he will associate to all eternity. (D. & C. 93:45-46.) They receive the adoption of sonship. "And because ye are sons, God hath sent forth the Spirit of his Son into your hearts, crying, Abba, Father. Wherefore *thou art no more a servant, but a son;* and if a son, then an heir of God through Christ." (Gal. 4:6-7.) Thus those who are servants of God here gain exaltation hereafter.

2. Those who do not choose to serve the Lord, who do not keep his commandments, and who do not receive the ordinances of his house, shall be *servants* to all

SERVICE

did not choose to be his servants
here and so he will require ministering servitude from them in
eternity. Persons for whom the
family unit continues become the
sons of God, members of his family;
those who remain unmarried in
eternity will, as angels and not
gods, be "ministering servants, to
minister for those who are worthy
of a far more, and an exceeding,
and an eternal weight of glory."
(D. & C. 132:16-17, 25.)

SERVICE.
See GOOD WORKS, OBEDIENCE,
RELIGION, RIGHTEOUSNESS, SERV-
ANTS OF GOD. Gospel *service* means
dedication of oneself to righteousness to the extent that a person
accepts the gospel, obeys its laws,
and works in the church organizations.

Service is synonymous with keeping the commandments of God; it
is the child of love. "If thou lovest
me thou shalt serve me and keep
all my commandments." (D. & C.
42:29.) "Thou shalt love the Lord
thy God with all thy heart, with
all thy might, mind, and strength;
and in the name of Jesus Christ
thou shalt serve him." (D. & C.
59:5; 20:19, 31, 37.) Our Lord's
ministry is the perfect example of
service. "I am among you as he
that serveth," he said. (Luke 22:
27; Matt. 20:26-28.) His service was

rendered to his fellow men; and
"when ye are in the service of your
fellow beings ye are only in the
service of your God." (Mosiah 2:
16-17.)

Diligent service in God's earthly
kingdom assures the servant of
eternal life in the kingdom of God
in heaven. (D. & C. 76:5-10.) Those
who serve God are righteous; those
who do not are unrighteous. (Mal.
3:18; 3 Ne. 24:18.) And the Lord
requires the whole heart of a man.
"Therefore, O ye that embark in
the service of God, see that ye
serve him with all your heart,
might, mind and strength, that ye
may stand blameless before God at
the last day. Therefore, if ye have
desires to serve God ye are called to
the work." (D. & C. 4:2-3.)

In the ultimate sense, there are
only two beings to whom service is
rendered, God or the devil. By
keeping the commandments men
serve God and further his interests;
by failing to obey his law, they
"serve the devil, who is the master
of sin." (Mosiah 4:14; Alma 5:37-
42.) "No man can serve two masters: for either he will hate the
one, and love the other, or else he
will hold to the one, and despise
the other. Ye cannot serve God
and mammon." (Matt. 6:24; 3 Ne.
13:24.) When the mammon of this
world takes precedence, in a man's
heart, over the things of righteousness, that man, most assuredly, is
not serving God. "Choose you this
day whom ye will serve." (Josh.
24:15; Alma 30:8.)

SETTING APART.
See ORDINATIONS.

SEVEN PRESIDENTS OF SEVENTIES.
See FIRST COUNCIL OF SEVENTY.

SEVENTIES.
See MELCHIZEDEK PRIESTHOOD, MISSIONARIES, PRIESTHOOD, PRIESTHOOD OFFICES, PRIESTHOOD QUORUMS, QUORUM PRESIDENTS. One of the ordained offices in the Melchizedek Priesthood is that of a *seventy*. Seventies are elders with all the powers of elders, plus a special call and ordination "to preach the gospel, and to be especial witnesses unto the Gentiles and in all the world." (D. & C. 107:25.) As the Lord's "traveling ministers" they are sent "unto the Gentiles first and also unto the Jews." (D. & C. 107:97.) The office of a seventy is an appendage to the higher priesthood. (D. & C. 107:5.)

Speaking of the First Quorum of Seventy, the Lord says: "The Seventy are to act in the name of the Lord, under the direction of the Twelve or the traveling high council, in building up the church and regulating all the affairs of the same in all nations, first unto the Gentiles and then to the Jews. . . . It is the duty of the traveling high council to call upon the Seventy, when they need assistance, to fill the several calls for preaching and administering the gospel, instead of any others." (D. & C. 107:34, 38.)

It appears from the Old Testament account that at least from the days of Moses the elders of Israel have been ordained seventies and given special priesthood blessings and obligations. It was "seventy of the elders of Israel" who went up with Moses, Aaron, Nadab, and Abihu and "saw the God of Israel," thus certainly becoming especial witnesses of his name. (Ex. 24:1-11.) And when the Lord gave Moses additional administrative help to aid in bearing the burdens of the multitudes of Israel, it was the seventy whom he chose. "I will come down and talk with thee," the Lord said to Moses, "and I will take of the spirit which is upon thee, and will put it upon them; and they shall bear the burden of the people with thee, that thou bear it not thyself alone." Those seventy became mighty prophets in Israel. (Num. 11.)

In the meridian of time, our Lord "appointed other seventy also, and sent them two and two before his face into every city and place, whither he himself would come." He gave them pointed missionary direction, they performed their labors, the very devils were subject unto them, and they rejoiced because their names were written in heaven. (Luke 10:1-24.) The indication is clear that these "other seventy" were in addition to previous quorums organized for like purposes. (D. & C. 107:95.)

SEX IMMORALITY.

See ADULTERY, DAMNATION, FORNICATION, TELESTIAL LAW. Every normal person has planted in his physical being certain sexual appetites and desires; one of the chief purposes of this mortal probation is to see whether man will bridle these passions and use them only as authorized and approved by Deity. Hence the commands: On the one hand—"Be fruitful, and multiply, and replenish the earth" (Gen. 1:28); and on the other—"Thou shalt not commit adultery." (Ex. 20:14.) Or, as President Joseph F. Smith expressed it: *"Sexual union is lawful in wedlock, and if participated in with right intent is honorable and sanctifying. But without the bonds of marriage, sexual indulgence is a debasing sin, abominable in the sight of Deity." (Gospel Doctrine, 5th ed., p. 309.)*

Sex immorality is made up of offenses against God of all kinds and degrees. All are evil and damning in their nature, with some, however, being much more so than others. "We are of the opinion there are more grades or degrees of sin associated with the improper relationship of the sexes than of any other wrongdoing of which we have knowledge." President Smith also said. "They all involve a grave offense—the sin against chastity, but in numerous instances this sin is intensified by the breaking of sacred covenants, to which is some-times added deceit, intimidation, or actual violence.

"Much as all these sins are to be denounced and deplored, we can ourselves see a difference both in intent and consequence between the offense of a young couple, who, being betrothed, in an unguarded moment, without premeditation fall into sin, and that of the man, who having entered into holy places and made sacred covenants, plots to rob the wife of his neighbor of her virtue either by cunning or force and [who] accomplishes his vile intent." (*Gospel Doctrine*, 5th ed., p. 310.)

Virtue may be lost by degrees; and chastity may be destroyed a step at a time. Immodesty, necking, and petting, themselves a form of sex immorality, frequently lead to much grosser offenses. Every degree and type of lewdness, lasciviousness, and licentiousness; of concupiscence, prostitution, and whoredoms; of sodomy, onanism, and homosexuality; of masturbation, incontinence, and perversion; of rape, seduction, and infidelity; of adultery, fornication, and uncleanness—all these things, as well as many others, are condemned by divine edict and are among Lucifer's chief means of leading souls to hell. Fine distinctions between them are of no particular moment and are not necessary to observance of the divine laws involved. Counsel in the field of chastity is simply: *Be Chaste!*

"And now we desire with holy zeal to emphasize the *enormity* of sexual sins," President Joseph F. Smith has said. "Though often regarded as insignificant by those not knowing the will of God, they are in his eyes an abomination; and if we are to remain his favored people, they must be shunned as the gates of hell. The evil results of these sins are so patent in vice, crime, misery and disease that it would appear that all, young and old, must perceive and sense them. They are destroying the world. *If we are to be preserved we must abhor them, shun them, not practice the least of them, for they weaken and enervate, they kill man spiritually, they make him unfit for the company of the righteous and the presence of God."* (*Gospel Doctrine*, 5th ed., pp. 275-276.)

Again: *"No more loathsome cancer disfigures the body and soul of society today than the frightful affliction of sexual sin.* It vitiates the very fountains of life, and bequeaths its foul effects to the yet unborn as a legacy of death. It lurks in hamlet and city, in the mansion and in the hovel as a ravening beast in wait for prey; and it skulks through the land in blasphemous defiance of the laws of God and of man." (*Era*, vol. 20, p. 739.)

Further: "Like many bodily diseases, *sexual crime drags with itself a train of other ills.* As the physical effects of drunkenness entail the deterioration of tissue, and disturbance of vital functions, and so render the body receptive of any distemper to which it may be exposed, and at the same time lower the powers of resistance even to fatal deficiency, so does unchastity expose the soul to divers spiritual maladies, and rob it of both resistance and recuperative ability. *The adulterous generation of Christ's day were deaf to the voice of truth, and through their diseased state of mind and heart, sought after signs and preferred empty fable to the message of salvation.*

"We accept without reservation or qualification the affirmation of Deity, through an ancient Nephite prophet: 'For I, the Lord God, delight in the chastity of women. And whoredoms are an abomination before me; thus saith the Lord of Hosts.' (Jac. 2:28.)

"We hold that sexual sin is second only to the shedding of innocent blood in the category of personal crimes; and that the adulterer shall have no part in the exaltation of the blessed." (*Gospel Doctrine*, 5th ed., pp. 309-310.)

SEXUAL DESIRES.
See SEX IMMORALITY.

SEXUAL PERVERSIONS.
See SEX IMMORALITY.

SHAMAN.
See MEDICINE MEN.

SHEEPFOLD OF ISRAEL.
See SHEPHERDS.

SHEOL.
See GEHENNA, GRAVES, HADES, HELL, SPIRIT PRISON, TARTARUS. In Hebrew the word for hell is *sheol;* it is the gloomy abode of departed spirits; it is the place the wicked go to await the day of their eventual resurrection. The Prophet wrote of "the dark and benighted dominion of Sheol" (D. & C. 121:4); the connotation surrounding its usage is one of evil, sorrow, and anguish. In some instances the Authorized Version of the Bible translates sheol as *grave* (Gen. 44: 29, 31; Job 7:9; Ps. 30:3), or *pit.* (Num. 16:30, 33; Job 17:16.)

SHEPHERD.
See GOOD SHEPHERD.

SHEPHERD OF ISRAEL.
See GOOD SHEPHERD.

SHEPHERDS.
See BISHOPS, BRANCH PRESIDENTS, MINISTERS, OVERSEERS, PASTORS, QUORUM PRESIDENTS, STAKE PRESIDENTS. The house of Israel is the choice sheepfold of the Lord, and those appointed to care for the sheep are the Lord's *shepherds.* Thus anyone serving in any capacity in the Church in which he is responsible for the spiritual or temporal well-being of any of the Lord's children is a shepherd to those sheep. The Lord holds his shepherds accountable for the safety (salvation) of his sheep. (Ezek. 34.) To all his shepherds the command is: "Feed my lambs. . . . Feed my sheep." (John 21:15-17; D. & C. 112:14.)

SHILOAM.
See NEW JERUSALEM.

SHILOH.
See CHRIST, LAWGIVER, MESSIAH. Christ is *Shiloh.* (*Inspired Version,* Gen. 50:24.) One of the great Messianic prophecies is found in the patriarchal blessing given by Jacob to Judah in these words: "The sceptre shall not depart from Judah, nor a lawgiver from between his feet, until Shiloh come; and unto him shall the gathering of the people be." (Gen. 49:10.) The sense and meaning is that when kingly authority was conferred in Israel, it would rest with the tribe of Judah "until he come whose right it is" to hold kingly authority, that is until Shiloh the great Lawgiver should inherit the throne of his father David. (Luke 1:32-33.) Jacob's promise saw fulfilment in the normal course of historical events. (*Doctrines of Salvation,* vol. 1, pp. 20-21.)

SHRINES.
See ALTARS, APOSTASY, TEM-

PLES, WORSHIP OF IMAGES. Worshiping at *shrines* is an established part of the religious devotions of some churches in the modern world. These shrines frequently are boxes or altars containing religious relics, or they are special locations where some supernatural event is supposed to have taken place. Images of deities or saints are sometimes placed at these shrines so that they can be adored as part of the worship involved.

Shrines were very common among ancient Mediterranean peoples. Market places in Greek and Roman cities contained many of them. The shrines of "Diana of the Ephesians," which caused Paul so much trouble, were probably miniature silver images of the goddess in her temple. (Acts 19:24-41.)

Shrines play no part in true worship. The saints go to temples and meetinghouses, kneel before holy altars, perform sacred ordinances, and are there taught the doctrines of salvation. But they do not worship at these places because some holy being has once stood there, or because a bone or hank of hair of a dead person has been exhumed and is there displayed. Moses, Elias, Elijah, and the resurrected Lord Jesus himself, have all stood in this dispensation in the Kirtland Temple, but that building is no more a shrine to the saints than is any other building. The Father and the Son both stood in the Sacred Grove in the spring of 1820, but this greatest of all recorded theophanies did not make that grove of trees a shrine.

True worship does not depend upon the place of devotion, but upon the righteousness of the worshiper. As Jesus said to the woman at the well who inquired whether God should be worshiped in that mountain or in Jerusalem: "Woman, believe me, the hour cometh, when ye shall neither in this mountain, nor yet at Jerusalem, worship the Father. . . . But the hour cometh, and now is, when the true worshippers shall worship the Father in spirit and in truth: for the Father seeketh such to worship him." (John 4:20-23.)

SICKNESS.
See DISEASES.

SIGN OF JONAH.
See SIGN OF JONAS.

SIGN OF JONAS.
See CHRIST, RESURRECTION, SYMBOLISMS. Our Lord refused to give the wicked and adulterous Jews any sign proving his divine Sonship, except the *sign of Jonas* (Jonah). This was that "as Jonas was three days and three nights in the whale's belly; so shall the Son of man be three days and three nights in the heart of the earth." (Matt. 12:38-41; 16:4.)

Thus Jonah's burial in and coming forth from the "great fish"

(Jonah 1:15-17; 2) symbolizes the death, burial, and resurrection of Christ, so that "as Jonas was a sign unto the Ninevites, so shall also the Son of man be to this generation." (Luke 11:29-30.) By repenting and believing Jonah, wicked Nineveh was saved; by repenting and believing Christ, the wicked Jews could have freed themselves from sin. And the miracle of the resurrection, symbolized by the sign of Jonas, stands as a witness against them that they rejected their God.

SIGN OF THE CROSS.

See APOSTASY, CHRIST, CROSS. As part of their worship, members and ministers of some modern churches make the *sign of the cross*. In doing so they draw a cross in the air with the right hand beginning at their foreheads. Their purpose is to show devoutness in worship or to consecrate and bless persons or objects. This religious formality is without scriptural or divine warrant. (Rev. 13: 16-17.)

SIGN OF THE DOVE.

See HOLY GHOST. When John baptized Jesus, "he saw the Spirit of God *descending like a dove, and lighting upon him.*" (Matt. 3: 13-17; Mark 1:9-11.) Luke's account says, "The Holy Ghost descended in a bodily shape like a dove upon him." (Luke 3:21-22.) Two Book of Mormon passages speak of the Holy Ghost coming down *"in the form of a dove."* (1 Ne. 11:27; 2 Ne. 31:8.) The Prophet said that John "led the Son of God into the waters of baptism, and had the privilege of beholding the Holy Ghost descend in the form of a dove, or rather *in the sign of the dove,* in witness of that administration."

Then the Prophet gives this explanation: "The sign of the dove was instituted before the creation of the world, a witness for the Holy Ghost, and the devil cannot come in the sign of a dove. *The Holy Ghost is a personage, and is in the form of a personage.* It does not confine itself to the *form* of the dove; but in *sign* of the dove. The Holy Ghost cannot be transformed into a dove; but the sign of a dove was given to John to signify the truth of the deed, as the dove is an emblem or token of truth and innocence." (*Teachings,* pp. 275-276.)

It appears that the sign of the dove was given to John to show that the Holy Ghost had been given; and, if the translation in Luke is correct it also appears that the Holy Ghost (who is a personage of Spirit) descended in "bodily shape," that is having the same shape and bodily form that men have, and that his descent was "like a dove," that is calm, serene, and peaceful.

SIGN OF THE SON OF MAN.

See SECOND COMING OF CHRIST,

SIGNS, SIGN-SEEKING, SIGNS OF
THE TIMES, SON OF MAN. Among
the heavenly signs and wonders of
the last days, one is to stand out
particularly as the harbinger of
the coming of our Lord. It is
singled out and known as the *sign
of the Son of Man.* (Jos. Smith
1:36; Matt. 24:29-30.) "There will
be wars and rumors of wars," the
Prophet said, "signs in the heavens
above and on the earth beneath,
the sun turned into darkness and
the moon to blood, earthquakes in
divers places, the seas heaving beyond their bounds; *then will appear one grand sign of the Son of
Man in heaven. But what will the
world do? They will say it is a
planet, a comet, etc.* But the Son of
Man will come as the sign of the
coming of the Son of Man, which
will be as the light of the morning
cometh out of the east." (*Teachings,* pp. 286-287.) *When this sign
is given, however, it will be known
to and identified by the Prophet
of God on earth. (Teachings,* pp.
279-280.)

SIGNS.

See BELIEF, FAITH, GIFTS OF
THE SPIRIT, HEALINGS, MIRACLES,
SIGN OF THE SON OF MAN, SIGN-
SEEKING, SIGNS OF THE TIMES.
Gifts of the Spirit which the Lord
bestows upon those who believe
and obey the gospel of Christ are
called *signs.* That is, their receipt
stands as an evidence or sign of
the presence of that faith which

results from believing the truth.
Signs are wonders and miracles;
they always and invariably are
manifest to and among the faithful saints.

In every gospel dispensation,
the saints have had this promise:
*"These signs shall follow them that
believe—*in my name shall they
cast out devils; they shall speak
with new tongues; they shall take
up serpents; and if they drink any
deadly thing it shall not hurt them;
they shall lay hands on the sick
and they shall recover; And whosoever shall believe in my name,
doubting nothing, unto him will I
confirm all my words, even unto
the ends of the earth." (Morm. 9:
24-25; Ether 4:18; Mark 16:16-20;
1 Cor. 14:22; D. & C. 68:8-12; 84:
64-72; 124:98.)

Signs flow from faith. They may
incidentally have the effect of
strengthening the faith of those
who are already spiritually inclined, but *their chief purpose is
not to convert people to the truth,
but to reward and bless those already converted.* "Faith cometh
not by signs, but signs follow those
that believe," the Lord says. "Yea,
signs come by faith, not by the will
of men, nor as they please, but by
the will of God. Yea, signs come
by faith, unto mighty works, for
without faith no man pleaseth God;
and with whom God is angry he is
not well pleased; wherefore, unto
such he showeth no signs, only in
wrath unto their condemnation."
(D. & C. 63:9-11.)

Faith that is based on signs alone is weak and ineffective. It continually demands added and greater signs to keep it alive, and those relying on such visible supernatural guidance soon begin "to be less and less astonished at a sign or a wonder from heaven" until they are in danger of disbelieving all they have "heard and seen." (3 Ne. 2:1.) Thus belief based on supernatural experiences is less to be desired than that which stands on its own feet. "Blessed are they that have not seen, and yet have believed." (John 20:29.)

Signs are sacred grants of divine favor reserved for the faithful and concerning which the recipients are commanded not to boast. "A commandment I give unto them," the Lord says, "that they shall not boast themselves of these things, neither speak them before the world; for *these things are given unto you for your profit and for salvation.*" (D. & C. 84:73.)

And as with nearly every good and proper gift, Satan has an evil and ugly substitute. "Signs and lying wonders" (2 Thess. 2:9-12) are the stock in trade of false prophets (Matt. 24:24; Mark 13:22), a fact which establishes the truth that signs, standing alone, do not establish that divine approval rests upon a particular people. Unless there are signs, belief in the true gospel is not established, but the Lord will always have other evidences also to bear record of his work.

Various other usages of the designation *signs* are also of scriptural record. For instance, certain heavenly phenomena are so designated, in order that their promised occurrence will stand as a witness of a future event. (Hela. 14:1-7.) A sign is also something that is performed as a token or memorial of an event which properly should be remembered. The rainbow is given as a sign that the Lord will not again destroy the earth by water. (Gen. 9:8-17.) The feast of unleavened bread was a sign to ancient Israel of their deliverance from Egyptian bondage. (Ex. 13:1-10.)

SIGN-SEEKING.

See ADULTERY, APOSTASY, DEVIL, SIGNS, SIGNS OF THE TIMES. Because signs—miracles, gifts of the Spirit—always follow belief in the true gospel, it is inevitable that nonbelievers who are in open rebellion against the truth (subject as they are to the direction and promptings of Satan) should attempt to disprove the Lord's work by taunting his ministers with the challenge: Show us a sign. Our Lord himself was mocked in this manner. (John 2:18; 6:30.)

Actually, *sign-seeking*—a favorite pastime and enterprise of evilly disposed persons—is an evidence of supreme and gross wickedness on their part. "An evil and adulterous generation seeketh after a sign," the Master said. (Matt. 12:39; 16: 4; Mark 8:12; Luke 11:29.) And from the Prophet we have this account of one of his experiences: "When I was preaching in Philadelphia, a Quaker called out for a sign. I told him to be still. After the sermon, he again asked for a sign. I told the congregation the man was an adulterer; that a wicked and adulterous generation seeketh after a sign; and that *the Lord had said to me in a revelation, that any man who wanted a sign was an adulterous person.* 'It is true,' cried one, 'for I caught him in the very act,' which the man afterwards confessed when he was baptized." (*Teachings,* p. 278.) Sherem (Jac. 7) and Korihor (Alma 30) stand as the classical illustrations of the activities and fate of sign-seekers.

Even among the saints there occasionally are those spiritually weak persons who seek signs. To them the Lord says: "He that seeketh signs shall see signs, but not unto salvation. Verily, I say unto you, there are those among you who seek signs, and there have been such even from the beginning; But, behold, faith cometh not by signs, but signs follow those that believe." As pertaining to those without faith, the Lord "showeth no signs, only in wrath unto their condemnation." (D. & C. 63:7-11; Alma 32:17-18.)

To seek the gifts of the Spirit through faith, humility, and devotion to righteousness is not to be confused with sign-seeking. The saints are commanded to "covet earnestly the best gifts." (1 Cor. 12: 31.) But implicit in this exhortation is the presumption that those so seeking will do so in the way the Lord has ordained. For instance, the gift of testimony is obtained through a course of desire, study, prayer, and practice. Indeed, whenever a person abides the law entitling him to receive a gift, that gift is then freely bestowed upon him.

SIGNS OF THE TIMES.

See ABOMINATION OF DESOLATION, LAST DAYS, SECOND COMING OF CHRIST. In every age the Lord sends forth clearly discernible *signs* and *warnings* so that those who are spiritually inclined can know of his hand-dealings with men. In the meridian of time, when Jewish tempters, members of "a wicked and adulterous generation," came desiring that "he would shew them a sign from heaven," he rebuked and derided them by asking, *"Can ye not discern the signs of the times?"* (Matt. 16:1-4.) To the faithful elders carrying the message of salvation to the world in this dispensation, the Lord has given this promise: "Unto you it shall be given to know the *signs of the times,* and the signs of the coming of the Son of Man." (D. & C. 68: 11.)

As used in these scriptures, *signs* are the recognizable events or occurrences which identify present and which portend future events.

715

They are omens, prodigies, wonders, and marvels of abnormal occurrence. *Times* means the age, era, period, or dispensation involved. Thus the signs of the times for our age or dispensation are the marvelous events—differing in kind, extent, or magnitude from events of past *times*—which identify the dispensation of the fulness of times and presage the Second Advent of our Lord. (Joseph Fielding Smith, *Signs of the Times; Doctrines of Salvation,* vol. 3, pp. 19-37.)

By the power of the Holy Ghost the faithful saints are able to discern the signs of the times, signs preparatory to and part of this final great dispensation, and among them are the following:

1. SPIRIT TO BE POURED OUT ON ALL FLESH.—This promise, as pertaining to the last days, was made by Joel and renewed by Moroni when he appeared to the Prophet Joseph Smith on Sept. 21, 1823. (Joel 2:28-32; Jos. Smith 2:41.) It has reference, not to the Holy Ghost, but to the pouring out of the Spirit of Christ, the spirit or light which enlighteneth every man born into the world. Those who hearken to this spirit and are led by its strivings come to the knowledge of the truth, accept the gospel, and receive the gift of the Holy Ghost. (D. & C. 84:44-48.)

It was this spirit, the Light of Christ, which prepared the way for the opening of the dispensation of the fulness of times. Working in the hearts of men in the dark ages, it caused them to seek light, to translate the Bible, to break away (partially, at least) from the chains of religious darkness which bound their minds. This is the spirit, inspiring good men and honest truth seekers in every nation, which has led to the great discoveries, inventions, and technological advances of our modern civilization —achievements withheld from former dispensations and made known only in the last days.

2. DISCOVERY AND USE OF PRINTING.—Few tools were more effective than printing in paving the way for the great revival of learning, for the religious reformation, and for the breaking away of peoples and nations from religious domination. Without the discovery of movable type in about 1440 A.D. the barrier of gross darkness covering the apostate world could scarce have been pierced. One of the first books published was the Gutenberg Bible in 1456 A.D.

Perhaps no important discovery in world history ever faced such intense and bitter opposition as arose over the use and spread of printing. Civil and ecclesiastical tyrants feared the loss of their ill-held and evilly-exercised powers should knowledge and truth be made available to people generally. "We must root out printing," said the Vicar of Croydon from his pulpit, "or printing will root us out." (*Progress of Man,* pp. 206-215.)

But the destined ascendancy of truth was inevitable. Thomas

Paine's *Rights of Man,* for instance, was one of the major forces in uniting the American colonists in their revolutionary struggle for freedom. But real freedom of the press itself was not assured for any reasonable segment of mankind until the final adoption of the Constitution of the United States in 1789.

3. PROTESTANT REFORMATION AND AGE OF RENAISSANCE.—With the revival of learning and the re-birth in man's breast of a thirst for truth, the dark ages were doomed. Beginning in the 14th century, the Lord began to prepare those social, educational, religious, economic, and governmental conditions under which he could more easily restore the gospel for the last time among men. The spirit of inspiration rested upon Wycliffe, Huss, Luther, Zwingli, Calvin, Knox, and others, causing them to rebel against the religious evils of the day and seek to make the Bible and other truth available to all who would receive such. *The age of Renaissance and Reformation were part of the Lord's program preparatory to ushering in his great latter-day work.* (*Progress of Man,* pp. 196-237.)

4. DISCOVERY AND COLONIZATION OF AMERICA.—The latter-day discovery and colonization of the American nation was part of the divine plan. This land, "choice above all other lands" (Ether 2:7-12), has been reserved in all ages for the particular peoples permitted to inhabit it. In the latter-days these inhabitants were to come from the nations of the Gentiles.

Nephi saw the foundation of a great and abominable church among the nations of the Gentiles —a church "most abominable above all other churches," a church whose foundation was the devil, a church separated from the seed of his brethren, the Lamanites, by many waters. He also beheld that the Spirit of God, meaning the Light of Christ, came down and wrought upon a man among the Gentiles (Columbus), inspiring and impelling him to lead out in the discovery of America.

Then Nephi saw the same spirit, "that it wrought upon other Gentiles; and they went forth out of captivity, upon the many waters." Following this view of the colonization of America, Nephi saw the Revolutionary War, with the new inhabiters of this new land being delivered by "the power of God," while the wrath of God rested upon "their mother Gentiles." (1 Ne. 13: 1-19.)

5. ESTABLISHMENT OF THE AMERICAN NATION.—We know by revelation that the United States was established as a nation by the Lord for two chief reasons: 1. So that the Book of Mormon, containing as it does the fulness of the gospel, might come forth with its message of salvation to both Jew (which includes the Lamanites) and Gentile. 2. So that the Lord's true Church might be set up again

on earth, and thus have the way opened up for the fulfilling of the covenants made by the Lord with the house of Israel.

The resurrected Lord, in speaking to the Nephites of the signs whereby it might be known when the great latter-day work would commence, said that the Gentiles would be established in this land "as a free people by the power of the Father," so that the Book of Mormon record might come forth, and so "that the covenant of the Father may be fulfilled which he hath covenanted with his people, O house of Israel." (3 Ne. 21:4.)

The nation so set up was to be on "a land of liberty unto the Gentiles." It was to be a nation in which no kings would be raised up, a nation which would be fortified "against all other nations," so that all who fought against it "shall perish, saith God. For he that raiseth up a king against me shall perish, for I, the Lord, the king of heaven, will be their king, and I will be a light unto them forever, that hear my words." (2 Ne. 10:9-19.)

6. TRANSLATION AND PRINTING OF BIBLE.—Without a knowledge on the part of the common people of the truths found in the Bible, the Lord could not have brought to pass his latter-day purposes. During the dark ages reading, writing, and a knowledge of the scriptures were confined, almost without exception, to the clergy. Because the people lacked the knowledge of the truth they were more easily kept in bondage by their civil and ecclesiastical overlords. And so the translation and printing of the Bible became a mighty force opening the door to progression and advancement in every field. (J. Paterson Smyth, *How We Got Our Bible.*)

7. ESTABLISHMENT OF U. S. CONSTITUTION.—According to the Lord's plan of agency and freedom, certain "inherent and inalienable rights" belong to "all mankind." Hence, the Lord's interest in civil government; for, "No government can exist in peace, except such laws are framed and held inviolate as will secure to each individual the free exercise of conscience, the right and control of property, and the protection of life." (D. & C. 98:4-10; 134.)

Free agency under law is of God; coercion and anarchy are of Lucifer. The Constitution, as the supreme law of the land, is designed to protect men in their natural and inalienable rights. Hence, it "should be maintained for the rights and protection of all flesh. . . . And for this purpose," saith the Lord, "have I established the Constitution of this land, by the hands of wise men whom I raised up unto this very purpose, and redeemed the land by the shedding of blood." (D. & C. 101:76-80.)

8. LATTER-DAY REVELATION.— *No sign of the times is more dramatic or expressive of such marvelous wonderment as revelation; and no sign is deserving of such*

attentive consideration by man as the opening of the heavens in latter-days. The voice of God is heard again. The Father and the Son appeared personally to the Prophet. Angels again minister to the faithful. The gift of the Holy Ghost is poured out on thousands of righteous church members. The President of the Church stands as a prophet, seer, and revelator to his people. Visions, revelations, gifts of the Spirit abound. By all these means the predictions of the ancient scriptures as pertaining to the last days are being fulfilled. *What could anyone ask more as a sign of the times?*

9. COMING FORTH OF THE BOOK OF MORMON.—One of the great evidences of the Lord's goodness, mercy, and condescension toward his children on earth is found in the coming forth of the Book of Mormon, a book containing a record of God's dealings with peoples and nations on the American continent who had the fulness of the gospel. The price in faith, toil, and blood which first preserved and then brought forth this record in our day is incalculable. Many prophets foretold events surrounding its preparation, preservation, and final coming forth in the latter-days as a sign that the times of restitution of all things had commenced. (Isa. 29; Ezek. 37; 2 Ne. 3; 27; 29; 3 Ne. 21; Morm. 8.)

10. OPPOSITION TO THE BOOK OF MORMON.—Strange as it may seem to present day enemies of the truth, their very opposition to the receipt of more of the word of the Lord by way of the Book of Mormon is one of the signs of the times. Their opposition, summarized in the canting chant, "A Bible! A Bible! We have got a Bible, and there cannot be any more Bible," brings forth this severe rebuke from the Lord: "Thou fool, that shall say: A Bible, we have got a Bible, and we need no more Bible. . . . Wherefore murmur ye, because that ye shall receive more of my word?" (2 Ne. 29.)

11. RESTORATION OF KEYS AND PRIESTHOOD.—*Without priesthood* (which is the power and authority of God delegated to man on earth to act in all things for the salvation of men), *and keys* (which are the right and power of presidency, the right to direct the manner in which priesthood is to be used, and the means by which the door is opened for the gospel cause) *the covenants of the Lord pertaining to the last days could not be fulfilled.* Thus the restoration of the priesthood and its keys becomes a sign that the work reserved for the dispensation of dispensations has commenced. John the Baptist, Peter, James, and John, Michael, Gabriel, Raphael, Elijah, Elias, Moses, and Moroni have all come restoring their keys, powers, and authorities. (D. & C. 13; 27; 128.)

12. RESTORATION OF THE GOSPEL.—From the very beginning the Lord's prophets have known and spoken about the final restoration

of the gospel in the last days. Isaiah devoted so many whole chapters to the great era of restoration and the events to transpire therein that he might well be called the ancient prophet of the restoration. (Isa. 2; 4; 5; 10; 11; 13; 18; 24; 29; 33; 34; 35; 51; 52; 54; 60; 63; 64; 65; 66.)

The promised restoration, destined to come by revelation and angelic ministration, was seen by John as taking place just before the day of judgment. (Rev. 14:6-8; D. & C. 133:36-41.) Indeed, the promised restoration is so extensively intertwined with the whole concept of the last days that no one can really believe these are the last days without believing also that the Lord has spoken again and is bringing to pass his strange act.

13. MESSENGER TO PRECEDE SECOND COMING.—"Behold, I will send my messenger, and he shall prepare the way before me," the Lord said speaking of his Second Coming. (Mal. 3:1-6.) Both John the Baptist and the Prophet Joseph Smith have ministered in our day in fulfilment of this ancient prediction. (*Doctrines of Salvation,* vol. 1, pp. 191-195.) The gospel itself is, also, a messenger preparing the way before the face of the Lord. (D. & C. 45:9.)

14. CHURCH AND KINGDOM SET UP AGAIN.—The Church of Jesus Christ of Latter-day Saints is the kingdom of God on earth. It is the kingdom set up without man's hands (meaning by revelation from

heaven), and it was to come forth in the days of certain kings who reigned subsequent to the days of the Roman Empire; that is, it was to be set up in the last days. (Dan. 2:31-45.) The keys of the kingdom were given to Joseph Smith and Oliver Cowdery in June, 1829, and the formal organization of the kingdom took place on April 6, 1830. (D. & C. 20; 128:20.)

15. GROWTH OF THE CHURCH.— For our day the Church was set up with this decree: It would stand forever; never again would there be universal apostasy; the kingdom would never be destroyed, left to other people, or sink into oblivion. This time the gospel and plan of salvation would remain; the newly established kingdom would in due course break in pieces all earthly kingdoms and would remain forever. (Dan. 2:44.)

Enoch saw that the restored kingdom would remain on earth to prepare a people for the Second Coming of the Lord. (Moses 7:60-66.) In confirming the known truth that the keys of the kingdom had been committed to man on the earth, the Lord gave the irrevocable assurance that the gospel would roll forth "until it has filled the whole earth." (D. & C. 65.) There will be an eventual millennial day when every living soul on earth will belong to the true Church, for the knowledge of God shall cover the earth as the waters cover the sea (Isa. 11:9; Hab. 2:14), and pending that blessed consummation the present marvelous growth, expansion, and stability of the Church will shine forth as one of the signs of the times.

16. GATHERING OF ISRAEL.—After the Church had been organized and perfected in New Testament times, after the apostles had been ordained and commissioned to carry the message of salvation to all the earth, after the resurrected Christ had spent 40 days with his disciples schooling them in all things necessary for their ministry, after all this and more, there yet remained one great promised event about which the disciples had not been informed.

Having in mind the many prophetic declarations relative to the gathering of scattered Israel, and on the occasion of our Lord's ascension into heaven, the apostles asked: "Lord, wilt thou at this time restore again the kingdom to Israel?" In reply the Lord said: "It is not for you to know the times or the seasons, which the Father hath put in his own power." (Acts 1:6-11.) In other words, the promised gathering of Israel was yet *future;* it was to occur in a time *subsequent* to New Testament times; the full restoration of the kingdom to Israel was reserved for the last days.

The keys of that gathering were conferred upon Joseph Smith and Oliver Cowdery by Moses on April 3, 1836, in the Kirtland Temple (D. & C. 110:11), and since that day the scattered remnants of Jacob have been leaving friends and temporal pursuits in all nations, and with the spirit of gathering resting mightily upon them, assembling with the saints who comprise the hosts of Latter-day Israel. *The drawing power of the Church from all nations is one of the marvels of the ages.*

17. TEN TRIBES TO RETURN.—So far, the gathering of Israel has been limited primarily to the scattered sheep of Ephraim (who is ranked as the firstborn and as having the birthright), and to a few of Manasseh, Judah and other tribes. But the time is near when the lost tribes "who are in the north countries shall come in remembrance before the Lord," and shall come to Zion "with songs of everlasting joy," to be crowned with blessings by those of Ephraim who stand at the head. (D. & C. 133:26-34.)

18. TIMES OF GENTILES BEING FULFILLED.—Taking the dispensation of the meridian of time as a starting point, the gospel was preached first to the Jews and thereafter to the Gentiles. Then dropping down to the dispensation of the fulness of times we find the gospel message going first to the Gentiles, with a promise that it will hereafter go to the Jews. Thus the first shall be last and the last first. (1 Ne. 13:42.)

Now this era in which the Gentiles have precedence in receiving the gospel is called the *times of the Gentiles.* In it the non-Jews (meaning the other portions of scattered Israel, the portions found in the great Gentile nations of the earth) have the opportunity to accept the gospel and gain salvation before that right is to be given, in any substantial degree, at least, to the Jews. When the times of the Gentiles are fulfilled, then the gospel will go to the Jews.

Obviously the fulfilling of the times of the Gentiles will not come at a specified moment; it will involve a period of time. We are living in that transition period. Our Lord told his disciples, speaking of the signs of his Second Coming, that "Jerusalem shall be trodden down of the Gentiles, until the times of the Gentiles be fulfilled." (Luke 21:24; D. & C. 45:24-30; *Inspired Version,* Luke 21:24-32.) In December, 1917, General Allenby of Great Britain captured Jerusalem almost without opposition, and for the first time in nearly 1900 years that city came out from under infidel or Gentile domination and was made available for the return of the Jews.

19. RETURN OF JUDAH TO JERUSALEM.—Judah is commanded to flee to Jerusalem in the last days (D. & C. 133:13), and their return is given as one of the signs that the times of the Gentiles is being fulfilled. (D. & C. 45:25.) To effect this return of the Jews to their native Palestine, the Lord has begun to work by what appear to men as natural causes. When England received the mandate of Palestine, Mr. Balfour, secretary of state for foreign affairs, issued a declaration of sympathy with Jewish Zionist aspirations. Great sums were spent by Britain and others to industrialize Palestine, renew the fertility of her soil, and build up her civilization. Hundreds of thousands of Jews returned to the land of their fathers and now an Israeli nation itself has been established there.

20. JEWS TO BEGIN TO BELIEVE IN CHRIST.—"And it shall come to pass that the Jews which are scattered also shall *begin* to believe in Christ; and they shall begin to gather in upon the face of the land." (2 Ne. 30:7.) Much of the old Jewish bitterness against Christ has ceased; many now accept him as a great Rabbi, though not the Son of God. A few have accepted him in the full sense, coming into the true Church along with the gathered remnants of Ephraim and his fellows.

But the great conversion of the Jews, their return to the truth as a nation, is destined to follow the Second Coming of their Messiah. Those able to abide that day, in their extremity and mourning, will ask: "What are these wounds in thine hands and in thy feet? Then shall they know that I am the Lord; for I will say unto them: These wounds are the wounds with which I was wounded in the house of my friends. I am he who was lifted up. I am Jesus that was crucified. I am the Son of God." (D.

& C. 45:51-52; Zech. 12:8-14; 13:6.)

21. BUILDING OF LATTER-DAY TEMPLES.—This final dispensation is now and in greater measure is yet to be the great era of temple work and temple building. Isaiah foretold that the house of the Lord would be established in the tops of the mountains, in the American Zion, and that scattered Israel would flow unto it just before the Second Coming. (Isa. 2:1-5.) Micah repeated the same prophecy. (Micah 4:1-7.) Ezekiel foretold the placing of a similar holy sanctuary among gathered Israel in Palestine in the last days. (Ezekiel 37.) And the Lord has given us renewed assurance that this same temple is to be erected in "the mountains of the Lord's house" in Jerusalem. (D. & C. 133:13.)

This latter-day building of temples—holy sanctuaries apart from the world where sacred ordinances can be performed for the salvation and exaltation of men—even as such temples were built and such ordinances performed anciently (D. & C. 124:25-42), is one of the great evidences of the divinity of this great latter-day work as well as one of the great signs of the last days.

22. LORD TO COME SUDDENLY TO TEMPLE.—Malachi preserved for us the promise that the Lord would suddenly come to his temple in the last days prior to the great and dreadful day of the Lord, an event which actually took place, as far as the Kirtland Temple is concerned, on the 3rd of April in 1836.

(Mal. 3:1; D. & C. 110:1-10.) This is one of those prophetic utterances destined for dual fulfilment, however, and the Lord yet again shall come suddenly to others of his temples, including the great temple to be erected in Jackson County.

23. SPIRIT OF ELIJAH AND GENE-ALOGICAL RESEARCH.—A great change has taken place in this dispensation relative to genealogical research; since the coming of Elijah, the hearts of people everywhere, both in the Church and out, have turned to their fathers. The *time* when genealogical societies were first organized to any appreciable extent ties in so closely with the time of Elijah's return that it constitutes competent and relevant evidence that Elijah actually came. (*Doctrines of Salvation*, vol. 2, pp. 117-128.)

24. PERSECUTION OF THE SAINTS. —Where the gospel is, there will be opposition and persecution, for Lucifer will not stand idly by while the work of God rolls forward. Hence, the saints have been tormented, pushed about, persecuted, reviled. The Missouri persecutions are one of the blackest pages in American history. Persecution is the heritage of the faithful; when men join the Church, it commences; when they leave the truth, their persecutors become their friends.

25. PERSECUTION OF THE JEWS. —Because they rejected the truth

and failed to keep the commandments of the Lord, all the curses enumerated by Moses came upon the Jews. "The Lord shall cause thee to be smitten before thine enemies," he said, so that thou "shalt be removed into all the kingdoms of the earth. . . . And thou shalt become an astonishment, a proverb, and a byword, among all nations whither the Lord shall lead thee." (Deut. 28.) Similar predictions of their scattering and suffering were also made by our Lord during his ministry. (Luke 21:20-24; D. & C. 45:18-32.) And as we view present and past events, in what nations and kingdom have they not become a hiss and a byword? Where have they not been treated as the offscourings of the earth?

Yet with it all a remnant was to be preserved as a peculiar and distinct people. (What a miracle it is that the Jewish people continue as a distinct race in spite of all their persecution and suffering!) And when Jerusalem was no longer trodden down of the Gentiles, when the fulness of the Gentiles was fulfilled, they were to return to the land of their fathers. In Germany, Russia, Poland, and many nations, they have been slaughtered, burned, driven, and scourged; yet they have maintained their distinctive race and are now and will continue to return to Jerusalem. Indeed, their very persecutions have helped cause them to flee unto Jerusalem.

26. TRUE GOSPEL TO BE PREACHED IN ALL THE WORLD.—Mormon missionaries work a modern miracle in carrying again to the world the same identical gospel preached by Christ and his apostles. (Jos. Smith 1:31; D. & C. 133:37.) Where else is there any church or organization which can call upon scores of thousands of its members to volunteer two or three or more years of their lives, pay their own expenses, and go forth carrying a message to the world? "And the voice of warning shall be unto all people, by the mouths of my disciples, whom I have chosen in these last days. And they shall go forth and none shall stay them, for I the Lord have commanded them." (D. & C. 1:4-5.)

27. WORLDLY KNOWLEDGE TO INCREASE.—Never in the entire history of the world has there been anything to compare, even in slight degree, with the great flood of worldly knowledge that has swept the globe in modern times. Marvelous advances have taken place in every field—scientific, historical, sociological, artistic, medicinal, governmental, economic, inventive, atomic, judicial, and so on *ad infinitum*—all of which has been according to the great foreordained plan for man on earth. These advances were withheld and reserved for the final age of the earth's temporal continuance. At "the time of the end," said Daniel, "many shall run to and fro, and *knowledge shall be increased*." (Dan. 12:4.)

But this great increase of latter-day knowledge was not foreseen as leading men to faith, testimony, and ultimate salvation. For "in the last days," said Paul, men shall be "Ever learning, and never able to come to the knowledge of the truth," that is, the truth about God and salvation. (2 Tim. 3:1-7.)

28. SCIENTIFIC AND INVENTIVE PROGRESS.—The promised latter-day increase of knowledge and learning is evidenced by the many inventions, engineering marvels, and mechanical undertakings of modern times. We have already seen the discovery and world-wide use of radio, television, telephones, and wireless; of steam engines, automobiles, airplanes, and railroads; of electricity, atomic energy, and destructive weapons; of medicinal advances, surgical achievements, and wonder drugs. Apparently some of the ancient prophets were even permitted to see the latter-day use of airplanes and armored tanks (Rev. 9:5-10), of trains and automobiles (Nah. 2:3-5), and perhaps other achievements, and to make records of their visions in such descriptive terms as were then available to them.

29. DISEASE, PLAGUE, PESTILENCE TO SWEEP EARTH.—Despite medical advances, people are to suffer from diseases, plagues, and pestilences of undreamed proportions in the last days. Men's hearts shall fail them. (Luke 21:26.) New and unheard of diseases will attack the human system. After the times of the Gentiles comes in there shall be an overflowing scourge, and "a desolating sickness shall cover the land." (D. & C. 45:31.) Also: "I the Lord God will send forth flies upon the face of the earth, which shall take hold of the inhabitants thereof, and shall eat their flesh, and shall cause maggots to come in upon them; And their tongues shall be stayed that they shall not utter against me; and their flesh shall fall from off their bones, and their eyes from their sockets." (D. & C. 29:18-19.) *The plagues and pestilences of the past will be as nothing compared to what is yet to be as the great winding up scene approaches.*

30. ELEMENTS IN COMMOTION.—Our earth has been and will be subject to various physical conditions during the course of its existence. When first created, it came forth in a terrestrial or paradisiacal status, all land being in one place; then came the fall and the resultant telestial conditions now prevailing; and mighty changes were most certainly wrought by the universal flood and in the day when the continents were divided. We are now approaching the day when the earth is to be renewed and returned to its paradisiacal glory and when the islands are to become one land again.

Conditions and circumstances destined to prevail during this final pre-millennial period call for great commotion and upheaval among the very elements. This is the day when "there shall be famines, and pestilences, and earthquakes, in divers places" (Jos. Smith 1:29; D. & C. 45:33); when there shall be "the testimony of earthquakes, that shall cause groanings in the midst of her [the earth], and men shall fall upon the ground and shall not be able to stand." This is the day when we shall hear "the testimony of the voice of thunderings, and the voice of lightnings, and the voice of tempests, and the voice of the waves of the sea heaving themselves beyond their bounds." (D. & C. 88:89-90.) In our day there are to be dust storms, whirlwinds, tornadoes, floods, and "a great hailstorm sent forth to destroy the crops of the earth." (D. & C. 29:16.) And finally, incident to the final change back to its paradisiacal state, the very globe itself shall "tremble and reel to and fro as a drunken man." (D. & C. 88:87.)

31. DISASTERS AND CALAMITIES TO ABOUND.—Perils and calamities, daily instances of turmoil and violent death, and an increasing flood of disasters and dangers are symptomatic of the times. For instance: "There are many dangers upon the waters, and more especially hereafter," the saints learned by revelation back on August 12, 1831, following Elder William W. Phelps' daylight vision of the destroyer riding upon the face of the Missouri River. "For I, the Lord, have decreed in mine anger many destructions upon the waters; yea, and especially upon these waters. . . .

Behold, I, the Lord, in the beginning blessed the waters; but in the last days, by the mouth of my servant John, I cursed the waters. Wherefore, *the days will come that no flesh shall be safe upon the waters."* (D. & C. 61:4-5, 14-15.)

32. STRIKES, ANARCHY, VIOLENCE, TO INCREASE.—Not only do disasters and perils abound because of the unsettled conditions of the elements, but that same spirit of unrest is found among men themselves. The Lord's decree for this age is: *"The whole earth shall be in commotion."* (D. & C. 45:26.) Signs of this commotion are seen daily in the untempered strikes and labor troubles that rock the economic world; in the violence, compulsion, and destruction of property that attend these strikes; in the unholy plots against our freedoms and free institutions; in the anarchy, rebellion, and crime that flow from great political movements which seek to destroy the agency of man and overthrow the governments of the world by force and violence. Communism and every other brutal and evil association or form of government are signs of the times.

33. LATTER-DAY WICKEDNESS.—Our Lord's epigrammatic announcement, *"Iniquity shall abound"* (Jos. Smith 1:30), as he described latter-day conditions, perfectly summarizes the prevailing world condition. Crime and licentiousness of every sort are the common diet of a large portion of the inhabiters of our globe. Murder, robbery, rape,

726

whoredoms, every form of sex immorality, and all forms of crimes against persons and property truly abound. Juvenile delinquency is a problem of substantial magnitude. Birth control is one of the great evils of the day. This is the time when the prediction of the Lord is fulfilled that men should say: "Blessed are the barren, and the wombs that never bare, and the paps which never gave suck." (Luke 23:29.) **And all these iniquities** receive anything but deterrence from the common run of movies, radio and television broadcasts, comic books, and other cheap and degrading so-called literary efforts.

34. SPIRIT CEASING TO STRIVE WITH WICKED.—That spirit which enlightens every person born into the world, which is poured out in abundant measure to guide in bringing about latter-day progress and advancements, is now ceasing to strive with the wicked. "I, the Lord, am angry with the wicked; I am holding my Spirit from the inhabitants of the earth" (D. & C. 63:32), "for my Spirit shall not always strive with man, saith the Lord of Hosts." (D. & C. 1:33.)

Wickedness begets wickedness just as righteousness leads to an increase in righteousness. When men rebel, the spirit ceases to strive with them; finally they are left entirely to their own devices and to the influence of the devil, and then they are ripe for destruction. This is the course that worldly people are now following; the day of destruc-

tion will come at the Second Coming, for then the cup of iniquity of the wicked will be full.

Righteous nations of the past, turning from the Lord to iniquity, have followed this same course. Of the Jaredites it is written: "The Spirit of the Lord had ceased striving with them, and Satan had full power over the hearts of the people; for they were given up unto the hardness of their hearts, and the blindness of their minds that they might be destroyed." (Ether 15:19.) A similar condition came upon the Nephites. (Moro. 8:28; 9:4.) In this day the spirit will continue to be withdrawn until the whole vineyard will be burned, and the righteous only will escape destruction.

35. PEACE TAKEN FROM EARTH. —On November 1, 1831, the Lord said: "The hour is not yet, but is nigh at hand, when peace shall be taken from the earth, and the devil shall have power over his own dominion." (D. & C. 1:35.) Later Elder George A. Smith left us this apt statement: "Peace is taken from the earth, and wrath and indignation among the people is the result; they care not for anything but to quarrel and destroy each other. The same spirit that dwelt in the breasts of the Nephites during the last battles that were fought by them on **this continent, when they continued** to fight until they were exterminated, is again on earth and is in-creasing." (*Journal History*, Sept. 23, 1855.) Never again will there be peace on earth until the Prince of

Peace (returning in power and glory to destroy the warring nations) comes to bring it.

36. ANGELS NOW REAPING THE EARTH.—In a revelation given January 2, 1831, the Lord announced: "The angels are waiting the great command to reap down the earth, to gather the tares that they may be burned; and, behold, the enemy is combined." (D. & C. 38:12.) A similar announcement was repeated on December 6, 1832. (D. & C. 86:5.)

These angels have now begun their work. This we learn through the spirit of inspiration that rested upon President Wilford Woodfuff. June 24, 1894, he said: "God has held the angels of destruction for many years, lest they should reap down the wheat with the tares. But I want to tell you now, that those angels have left the portals of heaven, and they stand over this people and this nation now, and are hovering over the earth waiting to pour out the judgments. And from this very day they shall be poured out. Calamities and troubles are increasing in the earth, and there is a meaning to these things. . . . Great changes are at our doors. The next 20 years will see mighty changes among the nations of the Earth." (*Discourses of Wilford Woodfuff*, p. 230.) It is interesting to note that almost 20 years later to the day, June 28, 1914, the Archduke Ferdinand of Austria was assassinated, thus initiating the first World War.

37. WARS AND RUMORS OF WARS.

—"I have sworn in my wrath, and decreed wars upon the face of the earth," the Lord has said as pertaining to our day, "and the wicked shall slay the wicked, and fear shall come upon every man." (D. & C. 63:33.) Again: "For behold, and lo, vengeance cometh speedily upon the ungodly as the whirlwind; and who shall escape it? The Lord's scourge shall pass over by night and by day, and the report thereof shall vex all people; yea, it shall not be stayed until the Lord come; For the indignation of the Lord is kindled against their abominations and all their wicked works." (D. & C. 97:22-24.)

On Christmas day, 1832, the Lord said that beginning with the rebellion of South Carolina, war would be poured out and would roll forth until it had "made a full end of all nations." (D. & C. 87.) Warfare as we know it, modern warfare, commenced with the Civil War. Probably there has not been a day since April 12, 1861, when the first shots were fired on Fort Sumpter, in which there has not been both war and preparation for war going on at some place on earth. When a shaky peace comes in one place, blood begins to flow in another, which condition will continue until it is climaxed by the great war when the Lord will have gathered all nations together in the Valley of Decision, and he himself will come to fight the battles of the righteous.

38. FAMINES, DEPRESSIONS, AND

ECONOMIC TURMOIL.—Because of iniquity and greed in the hearts of men, there will be depressions, famines, and a frantic search for temporal security—a security sought without turning to the Lord or obeying his precepts. We may expect to see the insatiable desire to get something for nothing result in further class legislation and more socialistic experiments by governments. Economic inequalities will certainly give rise to further class warfare and bickering. There will be riots, bloodshed, hunger, commotion, turmoil, and panics. These are all signs of the times.

39. APOSTATE DARKNESS COVERS EARTH.—With all their vaunted claims of being religious and with all their veneer of piety, the generality of men in the last days are to be in apostate darkness and subject to every form of evil. Any show of godliness is to be in form only, not in substance. As Paul wrote to Timothy: "This know also, that in the last days perilous times shall come. For men shall be lovers of their own selves, covetous, boasters, proud, blasphemers, disobedient to parents, unthankful, unholy, Without natural affection, trucebreakers, false accusers, incontinent, fierce, despisers of those that are good, Traitors, heady, highminded, lovers of pleasures more than lovers of God; Having a form of godliness, but denying the power thereof." (2 Tim. 3:1-5.) Also: "The time will come when they will not endure sound doctrine; but after their own lusts shall they heap to themselves teachers, having itching ears; And they shall turn away their ears from the truth, and shall be turned unto fables." (2 Tim. 4:3-4.)

Nephi spoke similarly in these words: "Behold, in the last days, or in the days of the Gentiles—yea, behold all the nations of the Gentiles and also the Jews, both those who shall come upon this land [America] and those who shall be upon other lands, yea, even upon all the lands of the earth, behold, they will be drunken with iniquity and all manner of abominations— And when that day shall come they shall be visited of the Lord of Hosts, with thunder and with earthquake, and with a great noise, and with storm, and with tempest, and with the flame of devouring fire." (2 Ne. 27:1-2.)

By modern revelation we are told: "Darkness covereth the earth, and gross darkness the minds of the people, and all flesh has become corrupt before my face. Behold, vengeance cometh speedily upon the inhabitants of the earth, a day of wrath, a day of burning, a day of desolation, of weeping, of mourning, and of lamentation; and as a whirlwind it shall come upon all the face of the earth, saith the Lord." (D. & C. 112:23-24.)

Every observant person sees abundant present day evidence that these promised latter-day conditions now prevail. Men are blind to spiritual things because their deeds are evil. The philosophies of men (as, for example, evolution) find followers, while the revealed truths of the gospel are shunned. Who can claim that the "form of godliness" now prevailing has brought men near to that righteousness which is of him who said: "Ye shall be holy: for I the Lord your God am holy"? (Lev. 19:2.)

40. MANY FALSE CHURCHES IN LATTER-DAYS.—This is the great day of Satan's power. It is the day of false Christs, false prophets, false miracles, false religions, false doctrines, false philosophies. It is a day when fables take precedence over facts, when all but the very elect are deceived. Of this day our Lord said: "There shall also arise false Christ, and false prophets, and shall show great signs and wonders, insomuch, that, if possible, they shall deceive the very elect, who are the elect according to the covenant." (Jos. Smith 1:22; Rev. 13:13-14.)

Moroni, writing with fervor and in power, described conditions that would exist when the Book of Mormon should come forth. Among other things he said: "It shall come in a day when it shall be said that miracles are done away; and it shall come even as if one should speak from the dead. And it shall come in a day when the blood of saints shall cry unto the Lord, because of secret combinations and the works of darkness.

"Yea, it shall come in a day when the power of God shall be denied, and churches become defiled and be lifted up in the pride of their hearts; yea, even in a day when leaders of churches and teachers shall rise in the pride of their hearts, even to the envying of them who belong to their churches.

"Yea, it shall come in a day when there shall be heard of fires, and tempests, and vapors of smoke in foreign lands; And there shall also be heard of wars, rumors of wars, and earthquakes in divers places.

"Yea, it shall come in a day when there shall be great pollutions upon the face of the earth; there shall be murders, and robbing, and lying, and deceivings, and whoredoms, and all manner of abominations; when there shall be many who will say, Do this, or do that, and it mattereth not, for the Lord will uphold such at the last day. But wo unto such for they are in the gall of bitterness and in the bonds of iniquity.

"Yea, it shall come in a day when there shall be churches built up that shall say: Come unto me, and for your money you shall be forgiven of your sins." (Morm. 8:26-41.)

41. REFUSAL OF MEN TO BELIEVE SIGNS OF TIMES.—The very fact that men refuse to believe the many signs of the times is itself one of the signs promised to precede the advent of our Lord. Peter prophesied of this, saying: "There shall come in the last days scoffers, walking after their own lusts, And saying, Where is the promise of his coming? for since the fathers fell asleep,

all things continue as they were from the beginning of the creation." (2 Pet. 3:3-4.) That is, in effect, these scoffers are saying, "Why be so gullible as to believe that earthquakes, floods, famines, pestilence, wars, iniquity, and all similar conditions are signs of the last days? Have not these same conditions existed from the beginning of time?"

And how many there are, like the Jews of old, who fail to discern the signs of the times! (Matt. 16:1-4.) "Christ delayeth his coming," they say. (D. & C. 45:26.) Men eat and drink, marry and are given in marriage, the common affairs of day to day living continue, until suddenly ("as it was in the days of Noah, so it shall be also at the coming of the Son of Man") he is here! "For in such an hour as ye think not, the Son of Man cometh." (Jos. Smith 1:40-48.)

42. SIGNS ON EARTH AND IN HEAVENS.—"And it shall come to pass that he that feareth me shall be looking forth for the great day of the Lord to come, even for the signs of the coming of the Son of Man. And they shall see signs and wonders, for they shall be shown forth in the heavens above, and in the earth beneath. And they shall behold blood, and fire, and vapors of smoke. And before the day of the Lord shall come, the sun shall be darkened, and the moon be turned into blood, and the stars fall from heaven." (D. & C. 45:39-42; Joel 2:30-31.)

Perhaps atomic and hydrogen bombs are a prelude to a yet greater fulfilment of this revelation. Certainly modern wonders as now seen in the heavens and on earth—even those created by man's hands without (from the standpoint of the world) divine interposition—had no counterpart either in kind or degree in days of old.

43. LAMANITES TO BLOSSOM AS THE ROSE.—As part of the Lord's covenant people, a part on whom a curse fell because of the iniquity of their fathers, the Lamanites are yet to stand as a sign that the end is near. In March, 1831, the Lord revealed: "Before the great day of the Lord shall come, Jacob shall flourish in the wilderness, and the Lamanites shall blossom as the rose. Zion shall flourish upon the hills and rejoice upon the mountains, and shall be assembled together unto the place which I have appointed." (D. & C. 49:24-25.)

Some Lamanites, gathered into the fold of Christ, have already blossomed forth with all the fruits of righteousness appertaining to the gospel; the scales of darkness have begun to drop from their eyes, according to the promises (2 Ne. 30:6); and they will yet, as a people, become as white, delightsome, and desirable as their Nephite brethren ever were. Already Jacob (with Ephraim at the head) has flourished in the wilderness where Brigham Young led her, a wilderness which has since also begun to blossom as the rose. And already Zion has flourished upon the hills, rejoiced in the mountains, and commenced to assemble together in the appointed places.

44. THE GATHERING AT ADAM-ONDI-AHMAN.—Before the great and dreadful day when the Lord is to return—"In flaming fire taking vengeance on them that know not God, and that obey not the gospel of our Lord Jesus Christ" (2 Thess. 1:8)—there is to be an appearance at a place called *Adam-ondi-Ahman*. There Adam, the Ancient of Days, will sit in council with his children; there Christ will come, and to him shall be given "dominion, and glory, and a kingdom, that all people, nations, and languages, should serve him: his dominion is an everlasting dominion, which shall not pass away, and his kingdom that which shall not be destroyed." (Dan. 7.) The place where this gathering will take place has been specified by revelation (D. & C. 116), and so imminent is its occurrence that the Prophet Joseph Smith was led to remark, "This may take place before some of us leave this stage of action." (*Teachings,* p. 157.)

45. FINAL GREAT WAR TO ATTEND SECOND COMING.—Our Lord will come in the midst of the greatest war the world has ever known. All nations will be gathered together at Jerusalem. The armies of the earth will be assembled in the Valley of Decision. Apparently those engaged in the conflict (possibly counting those in direct support of the fighting forces, meaning those

making the armaments as well as these using them) will total 200,-000,000. This will be the day when again the abomination of desolation will be fulfilled. (Zech. 12; 13; 14; Joel 3; Ezek. 38; 39; Rev. 9; D. & C. 29:14-21; Jos. Smith 1:32.) World conditions which point toward a time when the armies of the world shall wage war in the Holy Land are of great concern to the saints, for at the height of that conflict Christ will come and the great millennial era will be ushered in.

46. SORROW AND FEAR PRECEDE AND ACCOMPANY SECOND COMING.—As the signs of the times unfold, as the plagues and desolations of the last days multiply, "There shall be weeping and wailing among the hosts of men." (D. & C. 29:15.) Fear of the future shall increase in the hearts of the wicked until they shall call on the rocks and the hills to fall on them and hide them "from the face of him that sitteth on the throne, and from the wrath of the Lamb: For the great day of his wrath is come; and who shall be able to stand?" (Rev. 6:12-17; Luke 23:30-31.) After the Lord finally comes, the spirit of grace and supplication shall be poured out on the remaining Jews; they shall learn that they crucified their King; and then "they shall mourn for him, as one mourneth for his only son, and shall be in bitterness for him, as one that is in bitterness for his firstborn." (Zech. 12:10-14.)

47. FALL OF THE GREAT AND ABOMINABLE CHURCH.—One of the

final great events of our age is to be the fall and utter destruction of that great church which is not the Lord's Church, that great church "which is most abominable above all other churches." (1 Ne. 13:5.) "That great church, the mother of abominations, that made all nations drink of the wine of the wrath of her fornication, that persecuteth the saints of God, that shed their blood —she who sitteth upon many waters, and upon the islands of the sea—behold, she is the tares of the earth; she is bound in bundles; her bands are made strong, no man can loose them; therefore, she is ready to be burned." (D. & C. 88:94; 29:21; Ezek. 38; 39; Rev. 17; 18.)

48. SPECIAL MISSION IN JERUSALEM OF TWO LATTER-DAY PROPHETS.—There are to be "two witnesses, . . . two prophets that are to be raised up to the Jewish nation in the last days, at the time of the restoration." They are "to prophesy to the Jews after they are gathered and have built the city of Jerusalem in the land of their fathers." (D. & C. 77:15.) "And I will give power unto my two witnesses," the Lord says, "and they shall prophesy a thousand two hundred and threescore days, clothed in sackcloth."

"These have power to shut heaven," the record continues, "that it rain not in the days of their prophecy: and have power over waters to turn them to blood, and to smite the earth with all plagues, as often as they will. And when they shall have finished their testimony, the beast that ascendeth out of the bottomless pit shall make war against them, and shall overcome them, and kill them. And their dead bodies shall lie in the street of the great city, which spiritually is called Sodom and Egypt, where also our Lord was crucified. And they of the people and kindreds and tongues and nations shall see their dead bodies three days and an half, and shall not suffer their dead bodies to be put in graves. And they that dwell upon the earth shall rejoice over them, and make merry, and shall send gifts one to another; because these two prophets tormented them that dwelt on the earth. And after three days and an half the spirit of life from God entered into them, and they stood upon their feet; and great fear fell upon them which saw them. And they heard a great voice from heaven saying unto them, Come up hither. And they ascended up to heaven in a cloud; and their enemies beheld them." (Rev. 11.)

49. WICKED TO BE BURNED AS STUBBLE.—As the final sign of the times, the final event incident to the ushering in of a new age, the vineyard (earth) is to be burned. The wicked shall be as stubble; every corruptible thing shall be consumed; the elements shall melt with fervent heat; only those living at least a terrestrial law will be permitted to remain on earth. (Mal. 4; D. & C. 29:9-10; 63:34, 54; 101:23-31; 133:63-64.)

50. FINAL RESTITUTION OF ALL THINGS TO BE COMPLETED.—With the ushering of the millennial era, the final restitution of all things will be completed. We will have a new heaven and a new earth—a paradisiacal earth, one in which the sea has returned to its place in the north, with the continents becoming one land again. (D. & C. 101:23-31; 133:22-25; Isa. 65:17-25.)

The New Jerusalem will be built up and Enoch's returning city will join with it, as the Lord said unto Enoch: "Then shalt thou and all thy city meet them there, and we will receive them into our bosom, and they shall see us; and we will fall upon their necks, and they shall fall upon our necks, and we will kiss each other; And there shall be mine abode, and it shall be Zion, which shall come forth out of all the creations which I have made; and for the space of a thousand years the earth shall rest." (Moses 7:63-64.)

51. CHRIST TO REIGN PERSONALLY UPON EARTH.—"I will reveal myself from heaven with power and great glory, with all the hosts thereof, and dwell in righteousness with men on earth a thousand years, and the wicked shall not stand." (D. & C. 29:11.) This will be the final consummation of the age; the world (as now constituted) will end; for "The kingdoms of this world are become the kingdoms of our Lord, and of his Christ; and he shall reign for ever and ever." (Rev. 11:15.)

SIMILITUDES.
See SYMBOLISMS.

SIMONY.
See APOSTASY, CHURCH OF THE DEVIL. *Simony* is the practice of buying church offices and various other forms of ecclesiastical preferment. It is no part of the gospel, has never been practiced in the true Church in any age, but has been found in the false churches of Christendom, from the earliest days of the era of apostasy to the present. The name is derived from Simon the sorcerer (commonly called by the scholars Simon Magus, meaning Simon the magician), because he—having seen miracles performed under the hands of the ancient apostles—sought to buy from Peter the power to confer the gift of the Holy Ghost. (Acts 8:9-24.)

This wicked and worldly practice was particularly prevalent in the dark ages. Strict laws were enacted in England prohibiting and penalizing acts of simony, but in countries such as the United States, where church and state are separated, simony has not been made a criminal offense.

Those who are guilty of this offense are subject to the curse hurled by Peter at the original Simon: "Thy money perish with thee, because thou hast thought that the gift of God may be purchased with money. Thou hast neither part nor lot in this matter:

for thy heart is not right in the sight of God. . . . Thou art in the gall of bitterness, and in the bond of iniquity." (Acts 8:20-23.)

SIN.

See ABOMINATIONS, BAPTISM, FORGIVENESS, INFANT BAPTISM, INIQUITY, ORIGINAL SIN THEORY, REPENTANCE, SIN UNTO DEATH, TRANSGRESSION, UNPARDONABLE SIN, WICKEDNESS. What is *sin?* John said: *"All unrighteousness is sin."* (1 John 5:17.) Also: "Whosoever committeth sin transgresseth also the law: for *sin is the transgression of the law."* (1 John 3:4.) Paul taught: *"Whatsoever is not of faith is sin."* (Rom. 14:23.) James explained: *"To him that knoweth to do good, and doeth it not, to him it is sin."* (Jas. 4:17.) It should be noted that all of these statements were addressed to members of the Church who had received the gospel law.

Elder Orson F. Whitney made this explanation: "Sin is the transgression of divine law, as made known through the conscience or by revelation. A man sins when he violates his conscience, going contrary to light and knowledge—not the light and knowledge that has come to his neighbor, but that which has come to himself. He sins when he does the opposite of what he knows to be right. Up to that point he only blunders. One may suffer painful consequences for only blundering, but he cannot commit sin unless he knows better than to do the thing in which the sin consists. One must have a conscience before he can violate it." (*Saturday Night Thoughts,* p. 239.) "Where there is no law given there is no punishment; and where there is no punishment there is no condemnation." (2 Ne. 9:25.) "He that knoweth not good from evil is blameless." (Alma 29:5.)

Sin cannot be committed unless laws are ordained (Alma 42:17) and unless people have knowledge of those laws so that they can violate them. Adam and Eve could not commit sin while in the Garden of Eden, although laws of conduct had already been established, because the knowledge of good and evil had not yet been given them. Unless they had partaken of the fruit of the tree of the knowledge of good and evil "they would have remained in a state of innocence, having no joy, for they knew no misery; doing no good, for *they knew no sin."* (2 Ne. 2:23.)

This is the same principle used by our Lord in condemning the wicked Pharisees: *"If ye were blind, ye should have no sin: but now ye say, We see; therefore your sin remaineth."* (John 9:41.) It is on this principle also that little children "cannot sin . . . until they begin to become accountable," because in their innocent state they are without "knowledge." (D. & C. 29:46-50; Moro. 8:8.)

Sin is of the devil. "Whatsoever is evil cometh from the devil."

(Alma 5:40.) He is "the master of sin" (Mosiah 4:14), "the author of all sin" (Hela. 6:30); he "is an enemy unto God, and fighteth against him continually and inviteth and enticeth to sin, and to do that which is evil continually." (Moro. 7:12.) During the millennium, when Satan is bound, "children shall grow up without sin unto salvation." (D. & C. 45:58.) By committing sin men place themselves in subjection to Satan (D. & C. 29:40); they become his servants and receive "wages of him." (Alma 5:38-43.) "Whosoever committeth sin is the servant of sin." (John 8:34.)

Christ is the only person who ever lived who was without sin. (D. & C. 45:4; Heb. 4:14-15; 1 Pet. 2:21-22.) "All [others] have sinned, and come short of the glory of God." (Rom. 3:23; 5:12; D. & C. 109:34.) On man's part, the process of gaining salvation is one of cleansing himself from sin so as to stand clean before God at the last day. "Ye cannot be saved in your sins." (Alma 11:37.) Repentance, baptism, and enduring in righteousness to the end comprise the course whereby sins are remitted.

Exaltation consists in inheriting "all things." (D. & C. 76:54-60.) *"But no man is possessor of all things except he be purified and cleansed from all sin."* (D. & C. 50:28.) To those who have gained a remission of their sins, the Lord commands: "Abide ye in the liberty wherewith ye are made free; entangle not yourselves in sins, but let your hands be clean, until the Lord comes." (D. & C. 88:86.)

Forgiveness of sins comes in and through and because of the atoning sacrifice of Christ: "If we walk in the light, as he is in the light, we have fellowship one with another, and the blood of Jesus Christ his Son cleanseth us from all sin. If we say that we have no sin, we deceive ourselves, and the truth is not in us. If we confess our sins, he is faithful and just to forgive us our sins, and to cleanse us from all unrighteousness. If we say that we have not sinned, we make him a liar, and his word is not in us." (1 John 1:7-10.)

For those who love the Lord and desire salvation, Nephi's great cry of exultation is a fitting slogan: *"Awake, my soul! No longer droop in sin. Rejoice, O my heart, and give place no more for the enemy of my soul."* (2 Ne. 4:28.)

SIN AGAINST THE HOLY GHOST.

See UNPARDONABLE SIN.

SINCERITY.

See HONESTY. *Sincerity* is a saving virtue only when it is grounded on truth; gospel sincerity consists in **centering one's whole heart and** mind on the truth. It is the opposite of double-mindedness, deceit, and hypocrisy. (Philip. 1:10; 1 Pet. 2:1-2.) Sincere adherence to false principles keeps a person from salvation. No matter how honestly and genuinely a person may believe, for instance, that Deity is a three-in-one spirit essence that fills the immensity of space, such belief does not make it so. To gain salvation men must "fear the Lord, and serve him in sincerity *and in truth.*" (Josh. 24:14; Eph. 6:24.)

SIN OF ADAM.

See TRANSGRESSION OF ADAM.

SIN UNTO DEATH.

See ADULTERY, MURDERERS, SIN, SONS OF PERDITION, UNPARDONABLE SIN. Those who turn from the light and truth of the gospel, who give themselves up to Satan; who enlist in his cause, supporting and sustaining it; and who thereby become his children—by such a course *sin unto death.* For them there is neither repentance, forgiveness, nor any hope whatever of salvation of any kind. As children of Satan, they are sons of perdition. "Whosoever bringeth forth evil works, the same becometh a child of the devil, for he hearkeneth unto his voice, and doth follow him. And whosoever doeth this must receive his wages of him; therefore, *for his wages he receiveth death, as to things pertaining unto righteousness, being dead unto all good works.*" (Alma 5:41-42.) "The wages of sin is death." (Rom. 6:23.)

"If any man see his brother sin a sin which is not unto death, he shall ask, and he shall give him life for them that sin not unto death. *There is a sin unto death:* I do not say that he shall pray for it. All unrighteousness is sin: and there is a sin not unto death." (1 John 5:16-17.) "I, the Lord, forgive sins unto those who confess their sins before me and ask forgiveness, who have not sinned unto death." (D. & C. 64:7.) *"For if we sin wilfully after that we have received the knowledge of the truth, there remaineth no more sacrifice for sins,* But a certain fearful looking for of judgment and fiery indignation which shall devour the adversaries." (Heb. 10:26-27.) "All manner of sin and blasphemy shall be forgiven unto men: but the blasphemy against the Holy Ghost shall not be forgiven unto men, . . . neither in this world, neither in the world to come." (Matt. 12:31-32.)

In the sense that "no murderer hath eternal life abiding in him" (1 John 3:15), that is, that none guilty of pre-meditated murder can ever gain the celestial kingdom, murder also is a sin unto death. Such persons can never again enjoy spiritual life. It appears that there are some special circumstances under which adultery, in this sense, is also a sin unto death, as witness the Prophet's declaration: "If a man commit adultery, he cannot receive the celestial kingdom of God. Even if he is saved in any kingdom, it cannot be the celestial kingdom." (*History of the Church,* vol. 6, p. 81; *Doctrines of Salvation,* vol. 2, pp. 92-

94.) It may be that there are other abominable things which men in certain circumstances, can do which will bar them eternally from the receipt of spiritual life.

SION.
See ZION.

SISTERS.
See BRETHREN.

SKEPTICISM.
See DOUBT.

SLANDER.
See BACKBITING, BEARING FALSE WITNESS, DEVIL, GOSSIPING. Where the gospel is concerned, *slander* consists in the malicious circulation of lies and false reports about the Church and its members, about the doctrines of salvation as they have been revealed in this day, and about the teachings of the latter-day prophets. (Rom. 3:8.)

Slander is of the devil; the very word devil itself comes from the Greek *diabolos* which means a slanderer. It is natural, therefore, that slanderous reports against the Church have their origin, most generally, among those who are living carnal and sensual lives, whose conduct is such as to cause them to be guided and dominated by Lucifer. Slanderers shall be damned unless they repent. (Ps. 101:5.) "He that uttereth a slander is a fool." (Prov. 10:18.)

SLAVERY.
See AGENCY, BONDAGE, CASTE SYSTEM, FREEDOM. *Human slavery* is not consonant with the principles of agency, freedom, and justice found in the gospel of Christ. "It is not right that any man should be in bondage one to another." (D. & C. 101:79.) It is the great apostate Babylon that makes merchandise of "slaves, and souls of men." (Rev. 18:13.)

The fact that the gospel is in the world in periods when slavery is legally practiced, with the result that the gospel must take cognizance of its existence and make certain regulations with reference thereto, does not mean in the slightest degree that true Christianity approves of slavery. "We believe it just to preach the gospel to the nations of the earth, and warn the righteous to save themselves from the corruption of the world; but we do not believe it right to interfere with bond-servants, neither preach the gospel to, nor baptize them contrary to the will and wish of their masters, nor to meddle with or influence them in the least to cause them to be dissatisfied with their situations in this life, thereby jeopardizing the lives of men; such interference we believe to be unlawful and unjust, and dangerous to the peace of every government allowing human beings to be held in servitude." (D. & C. 134:12.)

SLOTHFULNESS.

See DILIGENCE, IDLENESS, OBEDIENCE. To be slothful is to be lazy, indolent, idle, inactive, sluggish, slow. *Slothfulness* is the opposite of diligence. True saints are not slothful either in their business affairs (Rom. 12:11) or in their spiritual pursuits. (Heb. 6:11-12; Alma 37:41-46.) The slothful servant is classified as unprofitable to the Master because he does not use the talents with which he has been endowed, no matter in what field those talents lie. (Matt. 25:14-30.)

"Set in order your houses; keep slothfulness and uncleanness far from you." (D. & C. 90:18.) Those who keep a commandment with slothfulness are damned. (D. & C. 58:26-29.) Those who are slothful in working in their priesthood callings "shall not be counted worthy to stand," that is stand with the faithful in their celestial inheritance. (D. & C. 107:99-100.)

SMITH, JOSEPH.

See JOSEPH SMITH THE PROPHET.

SOCIALISTIC EXPERIMENTS.

See SIGNS OF THE TIMES.

SMALL PLATES OF NEPHI.

See GOLD PLATES.

SODOMY.

See SEX IMMORALITY.

SOLEMN ASSEMBLIES.

See HOSANNA SHOUT, REVERENCE, SOLEMNITY. 1. In ancient Israel, as part of their Mosaic worship, frequent *solemn assemblies* were held. (Lev. 23:36; Num. 29:35; Deut. 16:8; 2 Chron. 7:9.) They were held in connection with their sacrifices and feasts. (Neh. 8:18; Isa. 1:10-14; Ezek. 45:17; 46:11.) Jerusalem was the city of their solemnities or set feasts. (Isa. 33:20.) The worshipful nature of these assemblies is shown in Joel's cry: "Sanctify ye a fast, call a solemn assembly, gather the elders and all the inhabitants of the land into the house of the Lord your God, and cry unto the Lord." (Joel 1:14; 2:15-17.)

2. In modern Israel *solemn assemblies* have been called in temples from time to time as the Lord has revealed or as his Spirit has indicated. As of old, their purpose is one of solemn worship, when by fasting, prayer, and faith the saints can draw near to the Lord and receive an outpouring of his Spirit. They are not held for the world or before the world, but are for those who have sanctified and purified themselves before the Lord. (D. & C. 88:70-82, 117; 95:7; 108:4; 109:6-10; 124:39; 133:6.) Dedicatory services for temples have always been solemn assemblies.

SOLEMNITY.

See LAUGHTER, LIGHTMINDEDNESS, LIGHT SPEECHES, RECREATION, REVERENCE, SACRAMENT MEETINGS, SOLEMN ASSEMBLIES.

Worship of God is conducive of and should be done in *solemnity*. Proper decorum in sacrament meetings, for instance, is one of solemnity, of formal dignity, of reverence and devotion. The things of God are of eternal import. "Let the solemnities of eternity rest upon your minds." (D. & C. 43:34.) All dealings with Deity should be in solemnity; preaching is to be done "in solemnity of heart." (D. & C. 100:7.) Missionaries are commanded: "Remain steadfast in your minds in solemnity and the spirit of prayer, in bearing testimony to all the world of those things which are communicated unto you." (D. & C. 84:61.) Alma's frequent in injunction to his sons was, "Be sober." (Alma 37:47; 38:15.)

SOLOMON'S TEMPLE.
See TEMPLES.

SON.
See BELOVED SON, CHRIST, FATHER IN HEAVEN, FIRSTBORN, GOD, ONLY BEGOTTEN SON, SON OF GOD. Christ is *The Son,* meaning the Son of God. (2 Ne. 30:2; 31:13, 18; Alma 5:48; 12:33; D. & C. 130:22; Matt. 11:27.) As the Offspring of the Father, inheriting from him the powers of immortality, he was and is able to do all things which his Father commanded. To him all men turn for all that they are or ever hope to be. Into his hands the Father has given all things. "Thou shalt do all that thou doest in the name of the Son, and thou shalt repent and call upon God in the name of the Son forevermore." (Moses 5:8.)

SON AHMAN.
See AHMAN, CHRIST, SON OF MAN, SONS AHMAN. Since *Ahman* is the name of God the Father in the pure language spoken by Adam, *Son Ahman* is the name of his Only Begotten Son. In two of the revelations published in the Doctrine and Covenants he so designates himself. (D. & C. 78:20; 95:17.)

SONG OF THE LAMB.
See CHRIST, LAMB OF GOD, MUSIC. Those who are redeemed by the blood of the Lamb, who gain the fulness of his Father's kingdom, who stand with him in glory on Mount Zion, shall sing a new song (Rev. 14:1-3); "they shall sing the *song of the Lamb,* day and night forever and ever." (D. & C. 133:56.) As revealed to John (Rev. 15:3-4), these are at least some of the words:

Great and marvellous are thy works,
  Lord God Almighty;
Just and true are thy ways,
  Thou King of saints.
Who shall not fear thee, O Lord,
  And glorify thy name?
For thou only art holy:
For all nations shall come
  And worship before thee;
For thy judgments are made manifest.

740

SONGS OF ZION.
See MUSIC.

SON OF DAVID.

See CHRIST, KEY OF DAVID, ROOT OF DAVID, SON OF GOD, SON OF JOSEPH, SON OF MARY. Christ is the *Son of David*, meaning that he was born in mortality as the literal seed and descendant of King David. Our Lord's mortal mother, Mary, was told by Gabriel: "Thou shalt conceive in thy womb, and bring forth a son, and shalt call his name JESUS. He shall be great, and shall be called the Son of the Highest: and the Lord God shall give unto him the throne of *his father David:* And he shall reign over the house of Jacob for ever; and of his kingdom there shall be no end." (Luke 1:31-33.) Both Joseph, his foster father, and Mary, his literal and natural mother, were of the house and lineage of David. (Matt. 1:1-17; Luke 1:26-38; 2:4; 3:23-38.)

That the promised Messiah would be a descendant and heir of David was well known among the Jews in the meridian of time, a fact which caused them falsely to suppose that during his earthly ministry he would reign with temporal power and dominion as David had done. (Matt. 1:1; 9:27; 12:23; 15:22; 20:30-31; 21:9, 15; Mark 10:47-48; 12:35-37; Luke 18:38-39; 20:41-44; John 7:42.) Hence, they were able correctly to answer our Lord's query as to the paternity of Christ

by saying he would be, "The Son of David." But they were completely confounded when he pressed the issue further by referring to David's great Messianic prophecy that Christ would come through David's lineage and also be David's Lord. "How then doth David in spirit," our Lord asked, "call him Lord, saying, The Lord said unto my Lord, Sit thou on my right hand, till I make thine enemies thy footstool? If David then call him Lord, how is he his son?" (Matt. 22:41-46.) In their apostate darkness these Jews were unable to envision the reality that their promised Messiah would be born both as the Son of David and the Son of the Highest.

SON OF GOD.

See BELOVED SON, CARPENTER'S SON, CHRIST, FATHER IN HEAVEN, FIRSTBORN, GOD, ONLY BEGOTTEN SON, SON, SON AHMAN, SON OF DAVID, SON OF JOSEPH, SON OF MAN, SON OF MARY, SON OF RIGHTEOUSNESS, SON OF THE ETERNAL FATHER, SON OF THE EVERLASTING GOD, SON OF THE HIGHEST, SON OF THE LIVING GOD, SONS OF GOD. 1. "What think ye of Christ? whose son is he?" (Matt. 22:42.) The true and revealed answer is: Christ is the *Son of God;* and he has been so designated from the beginning to show the personal, intimate, family relationship that exists between him and his Father. (1 Ne. 10:17; 2 Ne. 25:12, 19; Alma

7:10; 3 Ne. 9:15; D. & C. 6:21; Matt. 27:43; John 10:36; Moses 6:54.)

God the Father is a perfected, glorified, holy Man, an immortal Personage. And Christ was born into the world as the literal Son of this Holy Being; he was born in the same personal, real, and literal sense that any mortal son is born to a mortal father. There is nothing figurative about his paternity; he was begotten, conceived and born in the normal and natural course of events, for he is the Son of God, and that designation means what it says. (1 Ne. 11.)

2. Father Adam, the first man, is also a *son of God* (Luke 3:38; Moses 6:22, 59), a fact that does not change the great truth that Christ is the Only Begotten in the flesh, for Adam's entrance into this world was in immortality. He came here before death had its beginning, with its consequent mortal or flesh-status of existence.

SON OF JOSEPH.

See CARPENTER'S SON, CHRIST, SON OF GOD, SON OF MAN, SON OF MARY. When Jesus began his active ministry he was "about thirty years of age, being (*as was supposed*) the *son of Joseph.*" (Luke 3:23.) That is, he was considered by the people to be "the son of Joseph." (John 1:45.) Though Joseph did sire sons, they were only the half-brothers of our Lord, and the husband of Mary was in reality only the foster and not the natural parent of Jesus. (Matt. 12:46; 13:55; Gal. 1:19.)

SON OF MAN.

See CHRIST, FATHER IN HEAVEN, GOD, MAN OF HOLINESS, SON, SON AHMAN, SON OF GOD. Christ is the *Son of Man,* meaning that his Father (the Eternal God!) is a Holy Man. "In the language of Adam, **Man of Holiness**" is the name of God, "and the name of his Only Begotten is the Son of Man, even Jesus Christ, a righteous Judge, who shall come in the meridian of time." (Moses 6:57.) Thus Christ is the Son of Man of Holiness or more briefly put, the Son of Man. Accordingly, when he asked his disciples, "Whom do men say that I the Son of man am?" (Matt. 16:13), he was conveying precisely the same thought as he would have done by saying, "Whom do men say that I the Son of God am?" for that God who is his Father is a Holy Man.

There are more than 100 instances in which the Old Testament applies the title *son of man* to mortal persons, obviously doing so to emphasize the relative weakness of man as compared to Deity. As a consequence the sectarian world has falsely assumed that the more than 70 New Testament references to Christ as the Son of Man have a similar meaning, that is, that they convey the thought of his manhood rather than of his divinity. Actually all of these scriptures stand as wit-

742

nesses of the kind of Being that his Father is. Latter-day revelation also makes frequent reference to our Lord as the Son of Man, generally in a context telling of his glorious Second Coming. (D. & C. 45:39; 49: 6, 22; 58:65.)

SON OF MARY.

See CHRIST, MARY, SON OF DAVID, SON OF GOD, SON OF JO-SEPH, VIRGIN BIRTH. Christ is the *Son of Mary*. (Matt. 1:18-25; Luke 1:26-38; Mosiah 3:8.) Mary was "the mother of the Son of God, after the manner of the flesh. . . . She was carried away in the Spirit" (1 Ne. 11:18-19), was "overshadowed" and conceived "by the power of the Holy Ghost" (Alma 7:9-10) —but the Holy Ghost is not the Father of Christ—and when the Child was born, he was "the Son of the Eternal Father." (1 Ne. 11: 21.)

SON OF PEACE.

See GOSPEL, LIGHT OF CHRIST, MESSAGE OF THE RESTORATION, PEACE. In instructing the seventies of his day, our Lord said: "Into whatsoever house ye enter, first say, Peace be to this house. And if the *son of peace* be there, your peace shall rest upon it: if not, it shall turn to you again." (Luke 10:5-6.) In other words, the ambassadors of truth were to test the spirits of the people, giving blessings to those who were spiritually inclined and who

sought peace and righteousness and denying those blessings to the rebellious.

Spiritually discerning elders in this dispensation have the same divine insight. When they carry the message of salvation to an honest, upright, truth seeking people, a people in whose hearts the son of peace is found, the elders find a rich harvest. But when they seek to convert those who are not seeking peace and light, the elders can discern the spirit of unbelief. Then their peace returns to them again, and a harvest of souls is not gained.

SON OF RIGHTEOUSNESS.

See CHRIST, RIGHTEOUSNESS, SON OF GOD. Christ is the *Son of Righteousness*. (2 Ne. 26:9; 3 Ne. 25:2; Ether 9:22; Mal. 4:2.) This name-title conveys to the mind that he is the Offspring of him who is the embodiment of righteousness and perfection, whose very name is *Righteousness*.

SON OF THE ETERNAL FATHER.

See CHRIST, SON OF GOD. Christ is the *Son of the Eternal Father* (1 Ne. 11:21; 13:40), a name-title calling attention both to his divine Sonship and to the Eternal nature of his Father.

SON OF THE EVERLASTING GOD.

See CHRIST, SON OF GOD. Christ

is the *Son of the Everlasting God.* (1 Ne. 11:32.) Usage of this designation certifies to his divine Sonship and to the Everlasting pre-eminence and power of the Deity who is his Father.

SON OF THE HIGHEST.

See CHRIST, HIGHEST, MOST HIGH, SON OF GOD. Christ is the *Son of the Highest.* (Luke 1:32.) Gabriel so announced him to Mary. Both his own divine Sonship and the supremacy of the Father in the Godhead are shown by the usage of this name-title.

SON OF THE LIVING GOD.

See CHRIST, SON OF GOD. Christ is the *Son of the Living God.* (D. & C. 42:1; 55:2; 68:25; Morm. 5:14; 9:29; Matt. 16:16.) Use of this appellation bears record of his divine Sonship and of the present, conscious, active existence of his Father. A Living God is one who is alive today, who gives current revelation, and who is just as much interested in the souls of men today as he was anciently—all of which runs counter to the apostate view that the day of revelation has ceased.

SON OF THE MORNING.

See DEVIL, LUCIFER. This name-title of Satan indicates he was one of the early born spirit children of the Father. Always used in association with the name *Lucifer, son of the morning* also apparently signifies *son of light* or *son of prominence,* meaning that Satan held a position of power and authority in pre-existence. (D. & C. 76:25-27; Isa. 14:12-20.)

SONS AHMAN.

See AHMAN, SON AHMAN. As *Ahman* is the name of the Father and Son *Ahman* identifies his Only Begotten in the flesh, so *Sons Ahman* is the name, taken from the pure language, which is given to men. This usage of words is both powerful and expressive. It identifies the Father as a Holy Man, specifies that he has a Son who is like him, and points to the ultimate goal which righteous men may attain, that of becoming joint-heirs with Christ. Men and God are of the same race, and those men who overcome all things, being joint-heirs with Son Ahman, become eventually, as he has become, like their Eternal Father. (Rom. 8:14-17; 1 John 3:1-3; D. & C. 76:50-70; 132.)

SONS OF BELIAL.

See BELIAL, DEVIL, FALSE GODS. In ancient times it was common for the chosen people to refer to those among them who turned to the worship of false gods and the practices of iniquity as *sons* or *children of Belial.* They were sons of Satan in the sense that they followed his enticements and subjected themselves to his will. Our Lord spoke similarly to certain wicked Jews when he said: "Ye are of your father the devil, and the lusts of your father ye will do." (John 8:44.) Moses gave pointed instructions relative to the temporal destruction of those led away by the enticements of the children of Belial. (Deut. 13.)

SONS OF GOD.

See ADOPTION, BASTARDS, CELESTIAL MARRIAGE, CHURCH OF THE FIRSTBORN, DAUGHTERS OF GOD, EXALTATION, FULNESS OF THE FATHER, GODHOOD, JOINT-HEIRS WITH CHRIST, PRE-EXISTENCE, SALVATION, SERVANTS OF GOD. In one sense, the *sons of God* are the spirit offspring of the Father, the ones who "shouted for joy" when "the foundations of the earth" were laid. (Job 38:1-7.) But in a more particular and express sense, they are the ones who accept Christ and his laws and press forward in devotion to truth and righteousness, living "by every word that proceedeth forth from the mouth of God" (D. & C. 84:44), until they become new creatures of the Holy Ghost and are thus spiritually begotten of God. They become by adoption "the children of Christ, his sons, and his daughters" (Mosiah 5:7), and also, through him, they are begotten sons and daughters unto his Father. (D. & C. 76:22-24.)

Those who receive the gospel and join The Church of Jesus Christ of Latter-day Saints have power given them to become the sons of God. (D. & C. 11:30; 35:2; 39:1-6; 45:8; John 1:12.) Sonship does not come from church membership alone, but admission into the Church opens the door to such high status, if it is followed by continued faith and devotion. (Rom. 8:14-18; Gal. 3:26-29; 4:1-7.) The sons of God are members of his family and, hence, are joint-heirs with Christ, inheriting with him the fulness of the Father. (D. & C. 93:17-23.) Before gaining entrance to that glorious household, they must receive the higher priesthood (Moses 6:67-68), magnify their callings therein (D. & C. 84:33-41), enter into the new and everlasting covenant of marriage (D. & C. 131:1-4; 132), and be obedient in all things. (*Doctrines of Salvation,* vol. 2, pp. 8-9, 37-41, 59, 64-65.) Those who become the sons of God in this life (1 John 3:1-3) are the ones who by enduring in continued righteousness will be gods in eternity. (D. & C. 76:58.)

SONS OF LEVI.
See LEVITES.

SONS OF MOSES AND AARON.
See AARON, ADOPTION, MELCHIZEDEK PRIESTHOOD, MOSES. Faithful holders of the Melchizedek Priesthood, no matter what their

natural lineage, become by adoption the *sons of Moses and Aaron*. (D. & C. 84:6, 31-34.)

SONS OF PERDITION.
See Cain, Damnation, Devil, Hell, Perdition, Spiritual Death, Unpardonable Sin. Lucifer is Perdition. He became such by open rebellion against the truth, a rebellion in the face of light and knowledge. Although he knew God and had been taught the provisions of the plan of salvation, he defied the Lord and sought to enthrone himself with the Lord's power. (Moses 4:1-4.) He thus committed the unpardonable sin. In rebellion with him were one-third of the spirit hosts of heaven. These all were thus *followers* (or in other words *sons*) of perdition. They were denied bodies, were cast out onto the earth, and thus came the devil and his angels—a great host of *sons of perdition*.

Those in this life who gain a perfect knowledge of the divinity of the gospel cause, a knowledge that comes only by revelation from the Holy Ghost, and who then link themselves with Lucifer and come out in open rebellion, also become sons of perdition. Their destiny, following their resurrection, is to be cast out with the devil and his angels, to inherit the same kingdom in a state where "their worm dieth not, and the fire is not quenched." (D. & C. 76:32-49; 29:27-30; Heb. 6:4-8; 2 Pet. 2:20-22; 2 Ne. 9:14-16;

Doctrines of Salvation, vol. 1, pp. 47-49; vol. 2, pp. 218-225.)

Joseph Smith said: "All sins shall be forgiven, except the sin against the Holy Ghost; for Jesus will save all except the sons of perdition. (*Teachings,* p. 358.)

SOOTHSAYERS.
See Divination, Fortune Telling, Magic, Necromancy, Prophets, Seers, Sorcery, Spiritualism. A *soothsayer* is one of Satan's substitutes for a seer or a prophet. His mission is to foretell the future by the power of the evil one. Such false prophets were common anciently in the Eastern nations (Isa. 2:6; Dan. 2:27; 5:11; 2 Ne. 12:6), but they were not permitted in Israel (Josh. 13:22), and the penalty for practicing *soothsaying* was death. (Lev. 20:6, 27.) When the final latter-day triumph of Israel is achieved the Lord has promised to cut off witchcrafts and soothsayers out of the land. (3 Ne. 21:16; Mic. 5:12.)

Paul, the apostle, during his ministry, had a dramatic experience with a soothsayer. In this instance the false foreteller was a female, a "damsel possessed with a spirit of divination . . . which brought her masters much gain by soothsaying." To the great embarrassment of Paul and Silas she followed them calling out: "These men are the servants of the most high God, which shew unto us the way of salvation," thus associating her evil practice with the true powers of God's ministers. Of necessity Paul cast the evil spirit out of her, and her power of soothsaying ceased. (Acts 16:16-18.)

SORCERY.

See ASTROLOGY, CHURCH OF THE DEVIL, DIVINATION, EXORCISM, FORTUNE TELLING, MAGIC, NECROMANCY, SOOTHSAYERS, SPIRITUALISM, SUPERSTITION, VOODOOISM, WITCHCRAFT, WIZARDS. Use of power gained from the assistance or control of evil spirits is called *sorcery.* Frequently this power is used in divination, necromancy, and witchcraft. In effect a sorcerer worships Satan rather than God and uses such power as Satan can give him in a vain attempt to imitate the power of God.

Sorcery has been a sinful evil in all ages. It was present in the courts of Pharaoh (Ex. 7:11) and Nebuchadnezzar. (Dan. 2:2.) Israel's prophets inveighed against it. (Isa. 47; 57:3; Jer. 27:9.) Apostate Nephites revelled in its mysteries. (Alma 1:32; Morm. 1:19.) Peter and John fought its evils in their ministries (Acts 8:9-11; 13:6-8), and its power is prevailing with great success over much of the earth today. (Rev. 9:20-21.) Indeed, by her power and sorceries, the great and abominable church has deceived all nations in the last days. (Rev. 18:23.)

But at the Second Coming of the Lord sorcerers will be destroyed (Mal. 3:5; 3 Ne. 24:5); they shall be cast into that hell which is prepared for them (D. & C. 63:17; Rev. 21:8); and finally, having paid the utmost farthing for their crimes, they shall be debased with a telestial inheritance in eternity. (D. & C. 76:103; Rev. 22:15.)

SORROW.

See GRIEF, JOY, MISERY, MOURNING, WEEPING, WOES. As a necessary part of his mortal probation, man is subjected in this life to experiences involving both joy and *sorrow.* (2 Ne. 2:21-23.) In sorrow, as the scriptures frequently use the term, there is an element of suffering and affliction, of toil and labor and trouble, as well as of grief and sadness. "I will greatly multiply thy sorrow and thy conception," the Lord said to Eve. "In sorrow [that is, with suffering attending] thou shalt bring forth children." To Adam he said: "Cursed shall be the ground for thy sake; in sorrow [that is, with toil and labor attending] shalt thou eat of it all the days of thy life." (Moses 4:22-23; Gen. 3:16-17; Jer. 49:24; Hos. 13:13; John 16:21.)

Our Lord himself was "a man of sorrows, and acquainted with grief" (Isa. 53:3-4; Mosiah 14:3-4), meaning that he both suffered pain and had sadness and disappointment caused by the unbelief of his fellow mortals. Similarly the hearts of the saints "flow out with sorrow" because of the calamities and burdens placed upon their number by wicked persecutors. (D. & C. 109:45-48;

123:7.) To his saints, the Lord counsels: "If thou art sorrowful, call on the Lord thy God with supplication, that your souls may be joyful." (D. & C. 136:29.)

Paul speaks of "godly sorrow" which brings to pass repentance and of "the sorrow of the world" which leads to death. (2 Cor. 7:6-16.) Godly sorrow presupposes penitence, and contrition of soul; it is an essential part of repentance and the fogiveness of sins. The sorrow of the world is that which comes to the ungodly whose iniquities are exposed; it is that which comes because a just God sends calamities and destructions upon the wicked.

But sorrow is soon surmounted by the righteous. Sorrows imposed upon the saints by the rebellious are soon swallowed up in the joy of ministerial service. Translated beings are no longer subject to sorrow, "save it be for the sins of the world" (3 Ne. 28:9); the same is true of those who have attained the resurrection of the just. When the spirits of the righteous go to paradise they are in "a state of happiness, . . . a state of rest, a state of peace, where they shall rest from all their troubles and from all care, and sorrow." (Alma 40:12.) During the millennium and for those who come forth in the resurrection of the just, "there shall be no sorrow," as we now know it, "because there is no death." (D. & C. 101:29; Rev. 21:4.)

For the wicked, however, sorrow multiplies. "The rebellious shall be pierced with much sorrow; for their iniquities shall be spoken upon the housetops, and their secret acts shall be revealed." (D. & C. 1:3; 133:70; 136:35.) And then in eternity they shall continue to suffer sorrow to all eternity in the sense of remorse of conscience. (Alma 40:26.)

SOUL.
See INTELLIGENCE, MIND, MORTALITY, PRE-EXISTENCE, RESURRECTION, SPIRIT CHILDREN, SPIRIT WORLD. 1. Spirit beings are *souls;* the two terms are synonymous. The spirits in pre-existence were souls. (Abra. 3:23.) After the spirit leaves the body and goes into the spirit world to await the day of the resurrection, it is still designated as a soul. (Alma 40:11-14.)

2. A *mortal soul,* however, consists of a body and spirit united in a temporary or mortal union. The natural body is the house or tabernacle of the eternal soul or spirit. "The Gods formed man from the dust of the ground, and took his spirit (that is, the man's spirit), and put it into him; and breathed into his nostrils the breath of life, and man became a *living soul.*" (Abra. 5:7.)

3. An *immortal soul* is a resurrected personage, one who has been raised from mortality to immortality, one for whom body and spirit have become inseparably connected. "And the spirit and the body are the soul of man. And the resurrec-

748

tion from the dead is the redemption of the soul." (D. & C. 88:15-16; Alma 40:23.)

SOVEREIGN.
See POTENTATE.

SPAULDING MANUSCRIPT.
See BOOK OF MORMON. One of the early attempts to disprove the divine origin of the Book of Mormon was the specious falsehood—manufactured out of whole cloth without the slightest foundation in fact —that Joseph Smith copied the historical parts of the Book of Mormon from a manuscript written by Solomon Spaulding and that Sidney Rigdon wrote the doctrinal parts. This explanation was fabricated when enemies of the truth began to realize there was great intrinsic merit in the Nephite record, a fact which forced them to change their earlier explanations that the book was made up of senseless jargon written by an ignorant and illiterate farm boy.

Actually, however, it is a known and established historical fact that Sidney Rigdon had nothing whatever to do with the preparation of the Book of Mormon and he never so much as saw Joseph Smith until after the publication of that book. And fortunately the so-called *Spaulding Manuscript,* long lost from the knowledge of men, was found in 1844 among papers that had been in the hands of Mr. E. D.

Howe, publisher of Hurlburt's *Mormonism Unveiled.* (Francis W. Kirkham, *A New Witness for Christ in America,* vol. 1, pp. 130, 298-308, 337-370.)

In 1886 the Deseret News published the entire manuscript, under the title, *The Manuscript Found,* and it is now available to any who care to read it. After comparing this manuscript with the Book of Mormon the publishers concluded: "After carefully perusing both books, we believe we can truthfully assert that there is not one sentence, one incident, or one proper name common to both, and that the oft boasted similarity in matter and nomenclature is utterly false. No two books could be more unlike; in fact Mr. Spaulding's *Manuscript Story* no more resembles the Book of Mormon than *Gulliver's Travels* is like the gospel of St. Matthew."

SPEAKING IN TONGUES.
See TONGUES.

SPECIAL WITNESSES.
See APOSTLES.

SPECTERS.
See GHOSTS.

SPEECHES.
See SERMONS.

SPELLS.
See MAGIC.

SPIRIT.
See SPIRIT ELEMENT.

SPIRIT BIRTH.
See BORN AGAIN, FATHER IN HEAVEN, PRE-EXISTENCE, SPIRIT BODIES, SPIRIT CHILDREN, SPIRIT ELEMENT. 1. In the literal sense, the expression *spirit birth* has reference to the birth of the spirit in pre-existence. Spirits are actually born as the offspring of a Heavenly Father, a glorified and exalted Man. They will be born in a future eternity to future exalted beings for whom the family unit continues. (D. & C. 131:1-4; 132:19-24, 29-32.)

2. In a figurative sense, the expression *spirit birth* has reference to those who are born again of the Spirit, who have become new creatures of the Holy Ghost. (John 3:3-12; Mosiah 27:24-31.)

SPIRIT BODIES.
See PRE-EXISTENCE, SPIRIT BIRTH, SPIRIT CHILDREN, SPIRITUAL BODIES, SPIRIT WORLD. Our *spirit bodies* had their beginning in pre-existence when we were born as the spirit children of God our Father. Through that birth process spirit element was organized into intelligent entities. The bodies so created have all the parts of mortal bodies. The Brother of Jared saw Christ's spirit finger and then his whole spirit body. "I am Jesus Christ," that glorious Personage said. "This body, which ye now behold, is the body of my spirit; . . . and even as I appear unto thee to be in the spirit will I appear unto my people in the flesh." (Ether 3:14-17.)

We had spirit bodies in pre-existence; these bodies are now housed temporarily in mortal tabernacles; during the period between death and the resurrection, we will continue to live as spirits; and finally spirit and body will be inseparably connected in the resurrection to form immortal or spiritual bodies.

Animals, fowls, fishes, plants, and all forms of life were first created as distinct spirit entities in pre-existence before they were created "naturally upon the face of the earth." That is, they lived as spirit entities before coming to this earth; they were spirit animals, spirit birds, and so forth. (Moses 3:1-9.) Each spirit creation had the same form as to outward appearance as it now has in mortality— "the spirit of man," the revelation specifies, being "in the likeness of his person, as also the spirit of the beast, and every other creature which God has created." (D. & C. 77:2.)

SPIRIT CHILDREN.
See ETERNAL LIVES, INTELLIGENCES, PRE-EXISTENCE, SPIRIT BIRTH, SPIRIT BODIES, SPIRIT ELE-

MENT, STARS OF HEAVEN. 1. All men in pre-existence were the *spirit children* of God our Father, an exalted, glorified, and perfected Man. "The Father has a body of flesh and bones as tangible as man's" (D. & C. 130:22); the offspring born to him in that primeval sphere had bodies of *spirit element.* "I was in the beginning with the Father, and am the Firstborn," Christ says of himself; and of all men, his spirit brethren, he says, "Ye were also in the beginning with the Father." (D. & C. 93:21-23.)

2. In a future eternity, *spirit children* will be born to exalted, perfected, glorified couples for whom the family unit continues. The very glory of exalted beings is to have "a fulness and a continuation of the *seeds* forever and ever." (D. & C. 132:19-25, 29-32; 131:1-4.)

SPIRIT CREATION.
See CREATION.

SPIRIT ELEMENT.
See ELEMENTS, INTELLIGENCE, INTELLIGENCES, SPIRIT BIRTH, SPIRIT BODIES, SPIRIT CHILDREN. "There is no such thing as immaterial matter," the Prophet tells us. "All spirit is matter, but it is more fine or pure, and can only be discerned by purer eyes; We cannot see it; but when our bodies are purified we shall see that it is all matter." (D. & C. 131:7-8.) This *spirit element* has always existed; it is co-eternal with God. (*Teachings,* pp. 352-354.) It is also called *intelligence* or *the light of truth,* which "was not created or made, neither indeed can be." (D. & C. 93:29.)

Speaking of pre-existent spirits, Abraham calls them "the intelligences that were organized before the world was." (Abra. 3:22-24.) Thus, portions of the self-existent spirit element are born as spirit children, or in other words the intelligence which cannot be created or made, because it is self-existent, is organized into intelligences.

SPIRIT OF CONTENTION.
See CONTENTION.

SPIRIT OF DISCERNMENT.
See DISCERNMENT.

SPIRIT OF ELIAS.
See ELIAS.

SPIRIT OF ELIJAH.
See ELIJAH THE PROPHET.

SPIRIT OFFSPRING.
See SPIRIT CHILDREN.

SPIRIT OF GOD.
See SPIRIT OF THE LORD.

SPIRIT OF JESUS CHRIST.
See Light of Christ.

SPIRIT OF PROPHECY.
See Prophecy.

SPIRIT OF THE LORD.
See Christ, Firstborn, Holy Ghost, Light of Christ. Three separate and distinct meanings of the title, *Spirit of the Lord,* are found in the revelations: 1. It has reference to the spirit body of Christ our Lord, the body which he had from the time of his birth as the Firstborn of the Father until he was born of Mary in mortality; 2. It is used to mean the Spirit of Jesus Christ, or light of truth, or light of Christ—the Spirit which is impersonal and fills the immensity of space, the Spirit which is the agency by means of which God governs and controls in all things; and 3. It also is a synonym for the Holy Ghost, that Spirit entity or personage of Spirit who is a member of the godhead.

To gain a sound gospel understanding, the truth seeker must determine in each scriptural passage what is meant by such titles as *Spirit, Holy Spirit, Spirit of the Lord, Spirit of God, Spirit of truth.* In many instances this is not difficult; in some cases, however, abbreviated scriptural accounts leave so much room for doubt that nothing short of direct revelation can identify precisely what is meant. We know, for instance, that the Spirit personage who appeared to the Brother of Jared was the Spirit Christ, for he so identified himself. (Ether 3.) But when we read the account of the appearance of "the Spirit of the Lord" to Nephi (1 Ne. 11), we are left to our own interpretive powers to determine whether the messenger is the Spirit Christ or the Holy Ghost. Presumptively it is the Spirit Christ ministering to Nephi much as he did to the Brother of Jared, for such is in keeping with the principle of advocacy, intercession, and mediation, the principle that all personal appearances of Deity to man since the fall of Adam, excepting appearances of the Father and the Son together, have been appearances of Christ.

President Joseph F. Smith said: "The Holy Ghost as a personage of Spirit can no more be omnipresent in person than can the Father or the Son, but by his intelligence, his knowledge, his power and influence, over and through the laws of nature, he is and can be omnipresent throughout all the works of God. It is not the Holy Ghost who in person lighteth every man who is born into the world, but it is the light of Christ, the Spirit of truth, which proceeds from the source of intelligence, which permeates all nature, which lighteth every man and fills the immensity of space. You may call it the Spirit of God, you may call it the influence of God's intelligence, you may call it the substance of his power; no matter what it is called, it is the spirit of intelligence that permeates the universe and gives to the spirits of men understanding, just as Job said. (Job. 32:8; D. & C. 88:3-13.) . . .

"The Holy Ghost is a personage of Spirit, he constitutes the third person in the Trinity, the godhead. The gift or presentation of the Holy Ghost is the authoritative act of conferring him upon man. The Holy Ghost in person may visit men, and will visit those who are worthy, and bear witness to their spirit of God and Christ, but may not tarry with them. The Spirit of God which emanates from Deity may be likened to electricity, . . . which fills the earth and the air, and is everywhere present. It is the power of God, the influence that he exerts throughout all his works, by which he can effect his purposes and execute his will, in consonance with the laws of free agency which he has conferred upon man. By means of his Spirit every man is enlightened, the wicked as well as the good, the intelligent and the ignorant, the high and the low, each in accordance with his capacity to receive the light; and this Spirit or influence which emanates from God may be said to constitute man's consciousness, and will never cease to strive with [righteous] man, until man is brought to the possession of the higher intelligence which can only come through faith, repentance, baptism for the remission of sins, and the gift or the presenta-

tion of the Holy Ghost by one having authority." (*Gospel Doctrine*, 5th ed., pp. 61-62.)

The Spirit which is the Holy Ghost is a revelator; by his power men gain testimonies of the truth. (Moro. 10:3-5; John 14:26; 16:13-14; 1 Cor. 2.) His mission is to bear record of the Father and the Son (John 15:26; 2 Ne. 31:18), and to sanctify and cleanse the souls of the righteous. (3 Ne. 27:19-21.) The Spirit which is the light of Christ is sent to strive with men (D. & C. 1:33), and to give the guidance which reults in the great inventions and discoveries. This is the Spirit which the Lord is withholding from wicked persons in the world (D. & C. 63:32), not the Holy Ghost which the world never had. (John 14:17.) That is, the light of Christ ceases to strive with the wicked in that it no longer guides and entices them to seek gospel light and walk in the course that will prepare them to receive the gospel and all its saving truths. (D. & C. 84:45-48.) This light of Christ is the Spirit which is being poured out upon all flesh in the last days, according to Joel's promise. (Joel 2:28-29; Jos. Smith 2:41.) As a result of this outpouring of the Lord's power the great inventions and advancements of modern times have been made possible. *The light of Christ is the agency or power used by the Holy Ghost in administering his affairs and in sending forth his gifts.* (Moro. 10:17; *Doctrines of Salvation*, vol. 1, pp. 38-55.)

SPIRIT OF TRUTH.

See Christ, Firstborn, Holy Ghost, Intelligence, Light of Christ, Pre-existence, Truth. 1. Christ is the *Spirit of truth,* a title first given him in pre-existence where as the Firstborn Spirit Son of the Father he attained godhood and became the creator of all things. John bore record that our Lord "was in the beginning, before the world was"; that he was "the Spirit of truth, who came into the world, because the world was made by him"; that he was called the Spirit of truth because he was "full of grace and truth." (D. & C. 93:6-11; John 1:1-18; *Inspired Version,* John 1:1-19.) Men partook of some of the same Spirit of truth in pre-existence that filled the Firstborn, for they "were also in the beginning with the Father; that which is Spirit, even the Spirit of truth." (D. & C. 93:23.)

As the Spirit of truth, our Lord is the revealer and dispenser of truth. "My voice," he says, "is Spirit; *my Spirit is truth;* truth abideth and hath no end; and if it be in you it shall abound." (D. & C. 88:66.) And speaking of himself as the Spirit of truth, though now a resurrected and glorified personage, he said: *"The Spirit of truth is of God. I am the Spirit of truth,* and John bore record of me, saying: He received a fulness of truth, yea, even of all truth." (D. & C. 93:26.)

2. The Holy Ghost is the *Spirit of truth,* a title signifying that part of his mission is to guide the saints to all truth, and that by his power the truth of all things may be known. (Moro. 10:5.) He is the "Comforter, . . . the Spirit of truth; whom the world cannot receive" (John 14:16-17), for he manifests himself only to those who keep the commandments. His mission is to testify of Christ. (John 15:26.)

"When he, the Spirit of truth, is come," our Lord said to the apostles of old, "he will guide you into all truth: for he shall not speak of himself; but whatsoever he shall hear, that shall he speak: and he will shew you things to come. He shall glorify me: for he shall receive of mine, and shall shew it unto you." (John 16:13-14; D. & C. 6:15; 107:71.) Indeed, so completely is his mission associated with bearing witness of the truth that John said of him, *"The Spirit is truth."* (1 John 5:6.) The elders are to receive from the Comforter the word of truth, in the Spirit of truth, and to teach it by the same Spirit to those who will receive it "as it is preached by the Spirit of truth." (D. & C. 50:17-21.)

3. In one instance, *spirit of truth* (as contrasted with spirit of error) is used in the scriptures to signify the influence or persuasive power of truth (as contrasted with the similar meaning of spirit of error). (1 John 4:6.)

SPIRIT PRISON.

See Hell, Paradise, Salvation for the Dead, Spirit World.

There are two distinct senses in which the expression spirit prison is used: 1. Since disembodied spirits cannot gain a fulness of joy until their resurrection (D. & C. 93:33-34), they consider their habitation in the spirit world as one of imprisonment, and so the whole spirit world (including both paradise and hell) is a *spirit prison.* It was to the *righteous spirits in prison,* those who were in paradise, that our Lord preached while his body was in the tomb. (1 Pet. 3:18-21; 4:6; D. & C. 76:73-74.)

In the vision of the redemption of the dead, President Joseph F. Smith saw that during his ministry to the spirits in prison, "the Lord went not in person among the wicked and disobedient who had rejected the truth," but that he went "declaring liberty to the *captives who had been faithful,*" to the vast assemblage of the righteous, for they *"had looked upon the long absence of their spirits from their bodies as a bondage." (Gospel Doctrine,* 5th ed., pp. 472-476.)

2. In a more particular sense, however, the *spirit prison* is hell, that portion of the spirit world where the wicked dwell. (Moses 7:37-39.) Before Christ bridged the gulf between paradise and hell—so that the righteous could mingle with the wicked and preach them the gospel—the wicked in hell were confined to locations which precluded them from contact with the righteous in paradise. Abraham told the rich man in hell that between him and Lazarus (who was in paradise) there was a great gulf fixed so that none could go from paradise to hell or from hell to paradise. (Luke 16:19-31.)

Now that the righteous spirits in paradise have been commissioned to carry the message of salvation to the wicked spirits in hell, there is a certain amount of mingling together of the good and bad spirits. Repentance opens the prison doors to the spirits in hell; it enables those bound with the chains of hell to free themselves from darkness, unbelief, ignorance, and sin. As rapidly as they can overcome these obstacles—gain light, believe truth, acquire intelligence, cast off sin, and break the chains of hell—they can leave the hell that imprisons them and dwell with the righteous in the peace of paradise.

SPIRIT RAPPINGS.
See SPIRITUALISM.

SPIRITS (EVIL).
See EVIL SPIRITS.

SPIRITS (FALSE).
See FALSE SPIRITS.

SPIRITS IN PRISON.
See SPIRIT PRISON.

SPIRITUAL BLINDNESS.
See DEAFNESS.

SPIRITUAL BODIES.

See FLESH AND BONES, IMMORTALITY, RESURRECTION, SPIRIT BODIES. Resurrected beings are spiritual personages having bodies of flesh and bones. Mortal bodies are blood bodies, "For the life of the flesh is in the blood" (Lev. 17:11); *immortal bodies are spiritual bodies.* Speaking of death and the resurrection, Paul says: "It is sown a natural body; it is raised a spiritual body. There is a natural body, and there is a spiritual body." (1 Cor. 15:44.) Confirming this truth, we find the Lord saying in latter-day revelation: "For notwithstanding they die, they also shall rise again, a spiritual body." (D. & C. 88:27.) Spiritual bodies are tangible bodies, such as Christ had following his resurrection (Luke 24:36-43); they are not to be confused with *spirit bodies.*

SPIRITUAL DEAFNESS.

See DEAFNESS.

SPIRITUAL DEATH.

See ANNIHILATION, BORN AGAIN, DEATH, ETERNAL LIFE, FALL OF ADAM, FIRE AND BRIMSTONE, GIFT OF THE HOLY GHOST, HELL, SALVATION OF CHILDREN, SONS OF PERDITION, SPIRITUAL LIFE, YEARS OF ACCOUNTABILITY. *Spiritual death* is to be cast out of the presence of the Lord, to die as to the things of righteousness, to die as to the things of the Spirit. Spirit beings as such never die in the sense of annihilation or in the sense that their spirit bodies are disorganized; rather, they continue to live to all eternity either as spirits or as resurrected personages. (*Doctrines of Salvation,* vol. 2, pp. 216-230.)

But those spirit offspring of the Father who do not respond to spiritual impressions, and who are in rebellion against the things of the Spirit, are considered as dead until such time as they progress to the point at which spiritual light can be received. The revelations describe spiritually dead beings who are living in four different estates of existence.

1. SPIRITUALLY DEAD UNEMBODIED SPIRITS.—Lucifer and one third of the spirit hosts of heaven were not receptive to the true order of things in pre-existence. They did not respond to the Spirit of truth, and in due course came out in open rebellion against God. They were thrust down to earth and are dead as pertaining to things of righteousness. Their lot is to wallow in wickedness to all eternity. They are *spiritually dead eternally.* (D. & C. 29:36-40; 76:25-29; 2 Ne. 2:17.)

2. SPIRITUALLY DEAD MORTALS. —By yielding to temptation and partaking of the forbidden fruit, Adam became subject to the will of the devil. For his transgression he was cast out of the Garden of Eden. Thus "he became *spiritually dead,*" because he was out of the presence of the Lord and no longer had communion with Deity either person-

ally or by means of the Spirit. Consequently he was not alive to the things of the Spirit, which are the things of righteousness; and he remained in this state until he was born again of the Spirit through baptism, thus receiving the gift of the Holy Ghost and thereby being again in the presence of God. (D. & C. 29:40-45.)

"Our first parents were cut off both temporally and spiritually from the presence of the Lord," Alma taught. "Therefore, *as the soul could never die, and the fall had brought upon all mankind a spiritual death* as well as a temporal, that is, *they were cut off from the presence of the Lord,* it was expedient that mankind should be reclaimed from this spiritual death. Therefore, as they had become carnal, sensual, and devilish, by nature, this probationary state became a state for them to prepare; it became a preparatory state. And now remember, my son, if it were not for the plan of redemption, (laying it aside) as soon as they were dead their souls were miserable, being cut off from the presence of the Lord." (Alma 42:7-11.) Redemption from this spiritual death is made possible through the atoning sacrifice of Christ.

Thus "all mankind," meaning all who have arrived at the years of accountability, are spiritually dead, and they so remain until they attain unto spiritual life through baptism and the receipt of the gift of the Holy Ghost. Little children,

however, are alive in Christ, meaning spiritually alive (Moro. 8:8-26), "for power is not given unto Satan to tempt little children, until they begin to become accountable" (D. & C. 29:46-50), and where there is no sin there can be no spiritual death.

3. SPIRITUALLY DEAD DISEMBODIED SPIRITS.—When the wicked depart this life, they are "cast out into outer darkness," into hell, where "they have no part nor portion of the Spirit of the Lord," where they are *spiritually dead.* (Alma 40:13-14.) They remain spiritually dead in hell until the day of their resurrection (D. & C. 76:103-112), until "death and hell" deliver up the dead which are in them, so that they may be judged according to their works. (Rev. 20:12-13.)

Speaking of this deliverance, Jacob says that the Lord "prepareth a way for our escape from the grasp of this awful monster; yea, that monster, death and hell, which I call the death of the body, and also *the death of the spirit.* And because of the way of deliverance of our God, the Holy One of Israel, this death, of which I have spoken, which is the temporal, shall deliver up its dead; which death is the grave. And this death of which I have spoken, which is the spiritual death, shall deliver up its dead; which *spiritual death is hell;* wherefore, death and hell must deliver up their dead, and *hell must deliver up its captive spirits,* and the grave must deliver up its captive bodies, and the bodies and the spirits of men will be restored one to the other; and it is by the power of the resurrection of the Holy One of Israel." (2 Ne. 9:10-12.)

4. SPIRITUAL DEATH FOR RESURRECTED PERSONAGES.—*Spiritual death* ceases for those spirits who come up out of hell to receive an inheritance in the telestial world. (D. & C. 76:98-112.) Although those in the telestial world do not receive the fulness of reward, they do receive "of the Holy Spirit through the ministration of the terrestrial," and consequently they are in the presence of the Lord (in this sense) and are no longer spiritually dead. (D. & C. 76:81-88.) Pending the day when they come forth in the second resurrection they are spiritually dead; they "have their part in that lake which burneth with fire and brimstone, which is the second death" (D. & C. 63:17-18), but when they come out of hell, spiritual death ceases for them.

Samuel the Lamanite explained this principle by teaching: Christ "surely must die that salvation may come; yea, it behooveth him and becometh expedient that he dieth, to bring to pass the resurrection of the dead, *that thereby men may be brought into the presence of the Lord.* Yea, behold, this death bringeth to pass the resurrection, and *redeemeth all mankind from the first death—that spiritual death;* for all mankind, by the fall of Adam being cut off from the presence of the Lord, are considered as dead, both as to things temporal and to things spiritual. But behold, *the resurrection of Christ redeemeth mankind, yea, even all mankind, and bringeth them back into the presence of the Lord.* Yea, and it bringeth to pass the condition of repentance, that whosoever repenteth the same is not hewn down and cast into the fire; but whosoever repenteth not is hewn down and cast into the fire; *and there cometh upon them again a spiritual death, yea, a second death, for they are cut off again as to things pertaining to righteousness."* (Hela. 14:15-18.)

Thus, eventually, all are redeemed from spiritual death except those who have "sinned unto death" (D. & C. 64:7), that is, those who are destined to be sons of perdition. John teaches this by saying that after death and hell have delivered up the dead which are in them, then death and hell shall be "cast into the lake of fire. This is the *second death.*" (Rev. 20:12-15.) And thus the Lord said in our day that the sons of perdition are "the only ones on whom the *second death* shall have any power" (D. & C. 76:37), meaning any power *after* the resurrection.

Alma says that after the resurrection the righteous shall "shine forth in the kingdom of God. But behold, an awful death cometh upon the wicked; for they die as to things pertaining to things of righteousness; for they are unclean, and no unclean thing can inherit the kingdom of God; but they are cast out, and consigned to partake of the fruits of their labors or their works, which have been evil; and they drink the dregs of a bitter cup." (Alma 40:25-26.) After the resurrection they "shall be filthy still; . . . and their torment is as a lake of fire and brimstone, whose flame ascendeth up forever and ever and has no end." (2 Ne. 9:14-16.)

SPIRITUAL FALL.
See FALL OF ADAM.

SPIRITUAL GIFTS.
See GIFTS OF THE SPIRIT.

SPIRITUALISM.
See DIVINATION, EVIL SPIRITS, FORTUNE TELLING, GHOSTS, HALLUCINATIONS, HYPNOTISM, MAGIC, MEDIUMS, NECROMANCY, OUIJA BOARDS, SEANCES, SOOTHSAYERS, SORCERY, TRANCES, WITCHCRAFT, WIZARDS. Those religionists who attempt and frequently attain communion (as they suppose) with departed spirits are called *spiritualists*. Their doctrine and belief that mediums and other mortals can actually hold intercourse with the spirits of the dead is called *spiritualism*. Such communion, if and when it occurs, is manifest by means of physical phenomena, such as so-called spirit-rappings, or during abnormal mental states, such as in trances. These commun-

ions are commonly arranged and shown forth through the instrumentality of *mediums*.

It is true that some mediums do make contact with spirits during their *seances*. In most instances, however, such spirits as manifest themselves are probably the demons or devils who were cast out of heaven for rebellion. Such departed spirits as become involved in these spiritualistic orgies would obviously be the spirits of wicked and depraved persons who because of their previous wickedness in mortality had wholly subjected themselves to the dominion of Lucifer. Righteous spirits would have nothing but contempt and pity for the attempts of mediums to make contact with them.

The classical account of Saul resorting to the witch of Endor in a vain attempt to divine the future—because the Lord would no longer answer his queries by revelation—is no exception. (1 Sam. 28.) From the account in the Inspired Version of the Bible it is clear that the witch —who had a familiar spirit and could commune with evil spirits— did not bring up Samuel; and Saul did not see the spirit of that deceased prophet. Samuel did not speak to Saul, as the King James Version erroneously says, but the *medium* told Saul that *she* saw Samuel, and then *she* introduced the message by saying: "These are the words of Samuel unto Saul." That is, the medium was following the common practice of all mediums; she was in contact with devils (who have great knowledge and know some future events), and she reported their message as falsely coming from righteous Samuel. (*Inspired Version,* 1 Sam. 28.)

Isaiah's famous statement on the falsity of spiritualism is: "And when they shall say unto you: Seek unto them that have familiar spirits, and unto wizards that peep and mutter—*should not a people seek unto their God for the living to hear from the dead?* To the law and to the testimony; and if they speak not according to this word, it is because there is no light in them." (2 Ne. 18:19-20; Isa. 8:19-20; *Inspired Version,* Isa. 8:19-20.)

Thus, no matter how sincerely mediums may be deceived into thinking they are following a divinely approved pattern, they are in fact turning to an evil source "for the living to hear from the dead." Those who are truly spiritually inclined know this by personal revelation from the true Spirit; further, the information revealed from spirits through mediums is not according to "the law and to the testimony." Accordingly, though some true facts may be found in it, yet its acceptance and use has the effect of leading souls into the clutches of those evil powers which give the data.

"When thou art come into the land which the Lord thy God giveth thee," Deity said to ancient Israel, "thou shalt not learn to do after the abominations of those nations. There shall not be found among you any one that maketh his son or daughter to pass through the fire, or that useth divination, or an observer of times, or an enchanter, or a witch, Or a charmer, *or a consulter with familiar spirits,* or a wizard, or necromancer. For all that do these things are an abomination unto the Lord: and because of these abominations the Lord thy God doth drive them out from before thee." (Deut. 18:9-12.) Further, in ancient Israel, spiritualistic practices were punishable by death. "A man also or woman that hath a familiar spirit, or that is a wizard, shall surely be put to death." (Lev. 20:27; Ex. 22:18.)

SPIRITUALITY.

See BORN AGAIN, GIFTS OF THE SPIRIT, OBEDIENCE, PERFECTION, RIGHTEOUSNESS. *Spirituality* is that state of holiness, purity, and relative perfection which enables men to enjoy the near-constant companionship of the Lord's Spirit; truly spiritual men walk in the light of personal revelation and enjoy the frequent promptings of the Holy Ghost. They are always sought for to serve as patriarchs and in other positions of church responsibility and leadership. It is not uncommon among the true saints to hear such expressions as, "President McKay is a very spiritual man." The thought behind this is that he has so lived as to overcome worldliness and put himself in tune with spiritual and eternal things. He has been born again.

All men do not come into this world with the same inclination toward or receptiveness of spiritual things. One of the greatest endowments a mortal man can receive is the gift of spirituality, the talent and ability to recognize and cleave unto the truth. "My sheep hear my voice, and I know them, and they follow me," our Lord said. (John 10:27.) That is, his sheep so lived in pre-existence as to develop the gift of spirituality there; then coming to mortality, they brought that talent with them, and consequently they find it easy to believe and follow the true Shepherd.

SPIRITUAL LIFE.

See BORN AGAIN, ETERNAL LIFE, GIFT OF THE HOLY GHOST, SALVATION OF CHILDREN, SPIRITUAL DEATH, YEARS OF ACCOUNTABILITY. "We have passed from death unto life, because we love the brethren," John wrote. "He that loveth not his brother abideth in death." (1 John 3:14.) The life here spoken of is *spiritual life;* the death, spiritual death. In the same sense that spiritual death is to be cast out of the presence of the Lord, to be dead to the things of righteousness, to be dead to the promptings and whisperings of the Spirit, so spiritual life is to be in the presence of the Lord, to be alive to the things of righteousness and of the Spirit. Our Lord had reference not to temporal

but to spiritual life and death when he said to Martha: "I am the resurrection, and the life: he that believeth in me, though he were dead, yet shall he live: And whosoever liveth and believeth in me shall never die." (John 11:25-26.)

Little children are spiritually alive until they arrive at the years of accountability. (Moro. 8:8-26.) Then they die spiritually unless they are born again (D. & C. 29:45-50), unless by baptism they are born of water and of the Spirit (John 3:3-5), unless they become new creatures of the Holy Ghost, gaining the companionship of that member of the Godhead.

Those who enjoy the gift of the Holy Ghost are spiritually alive; they are in the presence of God (for the Holy Ghost is a member of the Godhead and is one with the Father and the Son). If they continue faithful in this life, they will continue to enjoy spiritual life in the world to come, that is they will be in the personal presence of God and have *spiritual* or in other words *eternal* life. (*Doctrines of Salvation,* vol. 2, pp. 216-230.)

SPIRITUOUS LIQUORS.

See WORD OF WISDOM.

SPIRIT WORLD.

See HEAVEN, HELL, PARADISE, SALVATION FOR THE DEAD, SPIRIT PRISON. By *spirit world* is meant the abiding place of disembodied spirits, those who have passed from pre-existence to mortality and have also gone on from this temporal world to another sphere to await the day of their resurrection, final redemption, and judgment. This world is divided into two parts: *paradise* which is the abode of the righteous, and *hell* which is the abode of the wicked. (Alma 40:11-14.)

Until the death of Christ these two spirit abodes were separated by a great gulf, with the intermingling of their respective inhabitants strictly forbidden. (Luke 16:19-31.) After our Lord bridged the gulf between the two (1 Pet. 3:18-21; Moses 7:37-39), the affairs of his kingdom in the spirit world were so arranged that righteous spirits began teaching the gospel to wicked ones. (*Gospel Doctrine*, 5th ed., pp. 472-476.)

Thus, although there are two spheres within the one spirit world, there is now some intermingling of the righteous and the wicked who inhabit those spheres; and when the wicked spirits repent, they leave their prison-hell and join the righteous in paradise. Hence, we find Joseph Smith saying: "Hades, sheol, paradise, spirits in prison, are all one: it is a world of spirits. The righteous and the wicked all go to the same world of spirits until the resurrection." (*Teachings*, p. 310.)

The spirit that enters the body before birth, leaves it at death, and immediately finds itself in the spirit world. That world is upon this earth. (*Discourses*, new ed., pp. 376-381.) Joseph Smith said: "The spirits of the just . . . are not far from us." (*Teachings*, p. 326.) After all men are resurrected, the spirit world will be without inhabitants.

Life and work and activity all continue in the spirit world. Men have the same talents and intelligence there which they had in this life. They possess the same attitudes, inclinations, and feelings there which they had in this life. They believe the same things, as far as eternal truths are concerned; they continue, in effect, to walk in the same path they were following in this life. Amulek said: *"That same spirit which doth possess your bodies at the time that ye go out of this life, that same spirit will have power to possess your body in that eternal world."* (Alma 34:34.) Thus if a man has the spirit of charity and love of the truth in his heart in this life, that same spirit will possess him in the spirit world. If he has the spirit of unbelief and hate in his heart here, so will it be with him when he passes through the door into the spirit world.

The great work in the world of spirits is the preaching of the gospel to those who are imprisoned by sin and false traditions. The faithful elders who depart this life continue their labors for the salvation of their brethren in the spirit world. Those who would have received the gospel in this life, if the opportunity had come to them, will repent and receive it in the next life and will thereby become heirs of salvation.

SPONTANEOUS GENERATION.
See EVOLUTION.

SPOOKS.
See GHOSTS.

SPRITES.
See GHOSTS.

STAKE BOARDS.
See AUXILIARY ORGANIZATIONS, CHURCH ORGANIZATION, GENERAL BOARDS, STAKES. Each auxiliary organization operates its programs within the various stakes with the help and counsel of *stake boards*. These boards consist of worthy and qualified specialists in the various details of the auxiliary work concerned. Board members give aid and counsel and help to train ward auxiliary organization workers in their duties. They do not preside over the ward workers or direct the manner in which the work in the wards shall be done.

STAKE CLERKS.
See CLERKS.

STAKE MISSION PRESIDENTS.
See MISSION PRESIDENTS.

STAKE MISSIONS.
See MISSIONS.

STAKE ORGANIZATION.
See CHURCH ORGANIZATION.

STAKE PATRIARCHS.
See PATRIARCHS.

STAKE PRESIDENCY.
See STAKE PRESIDENTS.

STAKE PRESIDENTS.
See OVERSEERS, PASTORS, SHEP-HERDS, STAKES. Each stake of Zion is presided over by a *stake president* to whom is delegated the keys of the kingdom as pertaining to that stake. He is the presiding high priest in the stake and is responsible for and directs all the programs of the Church within his stake area.

Stake presidents are chosen by the General Authorities as they are moved upon by the Spirit. In accordance with the law of common consent, the name of a person selected is presented to the body of the stake for a sustaining vote, following which the chosen stake head is set apart to his high ministerial position. The *stake presidency* consists of the stake president and two counselors. Stake clerks are not members of this presidency.

STAKES.

See BRANCHES, CHURCH ORGANIZATION, STAKE PRESIDENTS, WARDS, ZION. In prophetic imagery, Zion is pictured as a great tent upheld by cords fastened securely to *stakes*. Thus Isaiah, envisioning the latter-day glory of Israel, gathered to her restored Zion, proclaimed: "Enlarge the place of thy tent, and let them stretch forth the curtains of thine habitations: spare not, lengthen thy cords, and strengthen thy stakes; For thou shalt break forth on the right hand and on the left. . . . For a small moment have I forsaken thee; but with great mercies will I gather thee." (Isa. 54:2-7.) And of the millennial Zion, Isaiah exulted: "Look upon Zion, the city of our solemnities: . . . a tabernacle that shall not be taken down; not one of the stakes thereof shall ever be removed, neither shall any of the cords thereof be broken." (Isa. 33: 20.)

In keeping with this symbolism, the great areas of church population and strength, which sustain and uphold the restored Zion, are called *stakes*. They are the rallying points and the gathering centers for the remnants of scattered Israel. (D. & C. 68:25-26; 82:13-14; 101: 17-21; 115:6, 18; 124:134; 133:9.) In area they cover from a few blocks to many miles; in membership they comprise from a few to several thousand saints; in organization they are divided into smaller units

called *wards* and (in some instances) *branches*.

STANDARDS OF THE GOSPEL.

See OBEDIENCE.

STANDARD TO THE NATIONS.

See ENSIGN TO THE NATIONS.

STANDARD WORKS.

See BIBLE, BOOK OF MORMON, CANON OF SCRIPTURE, DOCTRINE AND COVENANTS, LOST SCRIPTURE, MORMON BIBLE, PEARL OF GREAT PRICE, REVELATION, SCRIPTURE, TRUTH. By the *standard works* of the Church is meant the following four volumes of scripture: The Bible, Book of Mormon, Doctrine and Covenants, and Pearl of Great Price. The Church uses the King James Version of the Bible, but acceptance of the Bible is coupled with a reservation that it is true only insofar as translated correctly. (Eighth Article of Faith.) The other three, having been revealed in modern times in English, are accepted without qualification. Their perfection in any other language, however, is subject to a reservation as to how well the translation actually conveys the original thought.

These four volumes of scripture are the standards, the measuring rods, the gauges by which all things are judged. Since they are the will, mind, word, and voice of the Lord

(D. & C. 68:4), they are true; consequently, all doctrine, all philosophy, all history, and all matters of whatever nature with which they deal are truly and accurately presented. The truth of all things is measured by the scriptures. That which harmonizes with them should be accepted; that which is contrary to their teachings, however plausible it may seem for the moment, will not endure and should be rejected.

The books, writings, explanations, expositions, views, and theories of even the wisest and greatest men, either in or out of the Church, do not rank with the standard works. Even the writings, teachings, and opinions of the prophets of God are acceptable only to the extent they are in harmony with what God has revealed and what is recorded in the standard works. When the living oracles speak in the name of the Lord or as moved upon by the Holy Ghost, however, their utterances are then binding upon all who hear, and whatever is said will without any exception be found to be in harmony with the standard works. The Lord's house is a house of order, and one truth never contradicts another. (*Doctrines of Salvation*, vol. 3, pp. 203-204.)

STARGAZERS.
See ASTROLOGY.

STAR OF BETHLEHEM.
See ASTROLOGY, CHRIST, MAGI.

Our Lord's birth into mortality was accompanied by the appearance of a *new star* in the heavens. One of Samuel the Lamanite's Messianic prophecies foretold this heavenly sign (Hela. 14:5), and the Nephites knew of the promised birth because they saw the new star that arose according to Samuel's word. (3 Ne. 1:21.)

It is apparent that some other prophet in the old world had made a similar prophecy, for when the wise men came from the east to Jerusalem seeking the "King of the Jews," they said, "We have seen his star in the east, and are come to worship him." After these men had been questioned by Herod, the *star of Bethlehem,* "the star, which they saw in the east, went before them, till it came and stood over where the young child was. When they saw the star, they rejoiced with exceeding great joy." (Matt. 2.)

STARS.
See ASTRONOMY.

STARS OF HEAVEN.
See BRIGHT AND MORNING STAR, PRE-EXISTENCE, SPIRIT CHILDREN. In figurative language, the spirit hosts in pre-existence are referred to as the *stars of heaven.* The "third part of the hosts of heaven" who followed Lucifer (D. & C. 29:36) are called by John "the third part of the stars of heaven." (Rev. 12:4.) Isaiah's account of Lucifer's rebel-

lion quotes that powerful spirit as saying in his heart, "I will ascend into heaven, I will exalt my throne above the stars of God. . . . I will be like the most High." (Isa. 14:12-14.) That is, Satan sought pre-eminence over all the spirit children of the Father; he sought to be a ruler over them and to attain the Lord's own honor and glory. (Moses 4:1-4.)

Deity used similar imagery with reference to his spirit children when he queried Job: "Where wast thou when I laid the foundations of the earth? . . . When the *morning stars* sang together, and all the sons of God shouted for joy?" (Job 38:4-7.) The morning stars were the pre-eminent spirits, "the noble and great ones," those who served valiantly in pre-existence and who were "chosen" before they were born to perform mighty works here in mortality. (Abra. 3:22-24.)

STATUTES.
See COMMANDMENTS.

STEALING.
See HONESTY, ROBBERY, TEN COMMANDMENTS, WICKEDNESS. "Thou shalt not *steal;* and he that stealeth and will not repent shall be cast out." (D. & C. 42:20; 59:6; Ex. 20:15; Matt. 19:18; 2 Ne. 26:32.) That is, the unrepentant thief is to be excommunicated from the Church.

Thieves "shall be delivered up unto the law of the land." (D. & C.

42:85.) Unless they repent, they shall not inherit the kingdom of God. (1 Cor. 6:9-11.) Rather, they shall be thrust down to hell to suffer the wrath of God until the resurrection of damnation, at which time they shall come forth to receive the just reward for their ungodly conduct.

STEM OF JESSE.
See BRANCH, CHRIST, SON OF DAVID, SON OF GOD. Christ is the *Stem of Jesse* (Isa. 11:1-5; D. & C. 113:1-2), by which is meant that our Lord came as a descendant of that noble Israelite who sired David the King. (Ruth 4:17.)

STEWARDS.
See STEWARDSHIPS.

STEWARDSHIPS.
See BISHOPS STOREHOUSES, CHURCH WELFARE PLAN, CONSECRATION, TITHING, UNITED ORDER. Under the law of consecration, as it operated through the United Order, church members consecrated, conveyed, and deeded all their property to the Lord's agent. Then they received back to use in supporting their own family a *stewardship* (D. & C. 42:32; 70:3, 9; 72:3; 82:17; 104:11), a *portion* (D. & C. 51:4), or an *inheritance.* (D. & C. 51:4; 57:15.) Each steward managed his own stewardship, conveying back to the Lord's storehouse any surplus which

accrued. (D. & C. 42:33-34, 55; 70: 7-10.)

Underlying this principle of stewardship is the eternal gospel truth that all things belong to the Lord. "I, the Lord, stretched out the heavens, and built the earth, my very handiwork; and all things therein are mine. . . . Behold, all these properties are mine, . . . And if the properties are mine, then ye are stewards; otherwise ye are no stewards." (D. & C. 104:14, 55-56.)

It is by the wise use of one's stewardship that eternal life is won. "It is required of the Lord, at the hand of every steward, to render an account of his stewardship, both in time and in eternity. For he who is faithful and wise in time is accounted worthy to inherit the mansions prepared for him of my Father." (D. & C. 72:3-4; 51:19.)

STICK OF EPHRAIM.

See BOOK OF MORMON, GOLD PLATES, MORONI. Ezekiel, in foretelling the preparation and coming forth of the Book of Mormon, called it *the stick of Ephraim,* and *the stick of Joseph in the hand of Ephraim.* In similar imagery he called the Bible *the stick of Judah.* The promise was that these two records would become one stick in the Lord's hand in the day of the gathering of Israel. (Ezek. 37:15-28.)

"Here then was a symbol," Elder Orson Pratt said, "represented before their eyes in language that could not be misunderstood; it was a symbol of two records; for it is well known that records were kept in ancient times on parchment; rolled upon sticks, the same as we keep our maps at this day. All the prophecies of Jeremiah for many years were written and rolled round a stick, and were called a book; so in Ezekiel these sticks represent two records, one the record of the tribe of Joseph, and the other of Judah." (*Journal of Discourses,* vol. 2, pp. 290-291.) Much interesting speculation has been indulged in to show how logical it was for the Spirit to direct Ezekiel to use the particular imagery here chosen to teach the great truth involved. (Hugh Nibley, *An Approach to the Book of Mormon,* pp. 271-287.)

The Book of Mormon is the *stick of Ephraim* in that it is a record of God's dealings with a people who were of the tribe of Ephraim; it is the stick of Joseph in the hands of Ephraim in that it records God's dealings with a portion of the tribe of Joseph, the record of which came forth by way of latter-day Ephraim and is now in the hands of church members who nearly all are of Ephraim. (D. & C. 27:5.)

STICK OF JOSEPH.

See STICK OF EPHRAIM.

STICK OF JUDAH.

See STICK OF EPRHAIM.

STILLBORN CHILDREN.

See BIRTH, SALVATION OF CHILDREN. When the fetus is born dead, it is said to be a *stillbirth*. Such an occurrence gives rise to anxiety on the part of mothers, in particular, as to whether the *stillborn baby* had in fact become a living soul, whether the partially or nearly formed body had become the home of a pre-existent spirit, and whether such a body will be resurrected. These are matters not clearly answered in the revelation so far available for the guidance of the saints in this dispensation. No doubt such things were plainly set forth in those past dispensations when more of the doctrines of salvation were known and taught than have been revealed so far to us.

That masterful document on the origin of man by the First Presidency of the Church (Joseph F. Smith, John R. Winder, and Anthon H. Lund) appears to bear out the concept that the eternal spirit enters the body prior to a normal birth, and therefore that stillborn children will be resurrected. It states: "The body of man enters upon its career as a tiny germ or embryo, which becomes an infant, *quickened at a certain stage by the spirit whose tabernacle it is*, and the child, after being born, develops into a man." (*Man: His Origin and Destiny,* p. 354.) This interpretation is in harmony with the general knowledge we have of the mercy and justice of that Infinite Being in whose divine economy nothing is ever lost. It would appear that we can look forward with hope and anticipation for the resurrection of stillborn children.

President Brigham Young taught that "when the mother feels life come to her infant, it is the spirit entering the body preparatory to the immortal existence"; and President Joseph Fielding Smith gave it as his opinion "that these little ones will receive a resurrection and then belong to us." "Stillborn children should not be reported nor recorded as births and deaths on the records of the Church," he said, "but it is suggested that parents record in their own family records a name of each such stillborn child." (*Doctrines of Salvation,* vol. 2, pp. 280-281.)

STONE OF ISRAEL.

See CHRIST, ROCK OF HEAVEN, SON OF GOD. Christ is the *Stone of Israel.* (Gen. 49:24.) "I am the good shepherd, and the stone of Israel. He that buildeth upon this rock shall never fall." (D. & C. 50:44.) Christ is thus the stone or foundation upon which all men must build. Of him the psalmist prophesied: "The stone which the builders refused is become the head stone of the corner." (Ps. 118:22; Matt. 21:42; Mark 12:10-11; Luke 20:17-18.) Peter used this truth to teach that the saints "as lively stones" should build "a spiritual house," with Christ, the Stone of Israel, as the foundation. (1 Pet. 2:1-9.)

STOREHOUSES.
See BISHOPS STOREHOUSES.

STRAIGHT AND NARROW PATH.
See BAPTISM, ETERNAL LIFE, EXALTATION, OBEDIENCE, REPENTANCE, SALVATION, STRAIT GATE. The course leading to eternal life is both *strait* and *straight*. It is *straight* because it has an invariable direction—always it is the same. There are no diversions, crooked paths, or tangents leading to the kingdom of God. It is *strait* because it is narrow and restricted, a course where full obedience to the full law is required. Straightness has reference to direction, straitness to width. The gate is *strait;* the path is both *strait* and *straight*. (2 Ne. 9:41; 31:9, 17-18; 33:9; Alma 37:44-45; Hela. 3:29-30; 3 Ne. 14:13-14; 27:33; D. & C. 22; 132:22; Matt. 7:13-14; Luke 13:23-24; Heb. 12:13; Jer. 31:9.)

Thus by entering in at the strait gate (which is repentance and baptism) a person gets on the "straight and narrow path which leads to eternal life." (2 Ne. 31:17-18.) Only members of The Church of Jesus Christ of Latter-day Saints are on the straight and narrow path, and only that portion of them will be saved in the kingdom of God who traverse the path, that is, who endure in obedience to the end. (2 Ne. 31:17-21.)

STRAIT GATE.
See BAPTISM, CELESTIAL MARRIAGE, ETERNAL LIFE, EXALTATION KINGDOM OF GOD, OBEDIENCE, REPENTANCE, SALVATION, STRAIGHT AND NARROW PATH. To enter in at the *strait gate* is to forsake the world, repent of one's sins, and be baptized under the hands of a legal administrator, thus getting on the *straight and narrow path* which leads to eternal life. (2 Ne. 31:17-18; 3 Ne. 14:13-14; 27:33; Matt. 7:13-14; Luke 13:23-24.) The strait gate opens the door or gate to the kingdom of God on earth (which is the Church) and to the kingdom of God in heaven (which is the celestial kingdom). It is a narrow, restricted, limited entrance and "few there be that find it."

Entrance requirements are set by the Lord; "and the keeper of the gate is the Holy One of Israel; and he employeth no servant there; and there is none other way save it be by the gate; for he cannot be deceived, for the Lord God is his name." (2 Ne. 9:41-43.) In April, 1830, when some who had previously been baptized in other churches desired to unite with the Church without rebaptism, the Lord said by way of revelation: "Although a man should be baptized an hundred times it availeth him nothing, for you cannot enter in at the strait gate by the law of Moses, neither by your dead works. . . . Wherefore, enter ye in at the gate, as I have commanded, and seek not

769

to counsel your God." (D. & C. 22.)

In a second and even more particular sense, the Lord uses the term *strait gate* to apply to celestial marriage, such being the ordinance placing one on the path "that leadeth unto the exaltation and continuation of the lives." (D. & C. 132:22; 131:1-4.)

in an unmixed state was in that early day no common commodity, and in fact was scarcely known except to the chemist. The ordinary name for liquids containing alcohol was 'strong drinks', and a plainer designation would have been hard to find." (*Improvement Era,* vol. 20, p. 555.)

STRIFE.

See CONTENTION.

STRIKES.

See SIGNS OF THE TIMES.

STRONG DRINKS.

See HOT DRINKS, WORD OF WISDOM. Elder James E. Talmage has explained the meaning of *strong drinks,* as such expression is used in the Word of Wisdom (D. & C. 89:7), in the following language: "It is evident from a studious reading of the Word of Wisdom and other early revelations in the present dispensation, that the Lord used the language common to the time, such as would be understood without question by the people directly addressed. In the revelation under consideration we read: 'Strong drinks are not for the belly, but for the washing of your bodies'; and the plain meaning is that alcohol in any combination or mixture is injurious to the body when taken internally but may be good for external application. Alcohol

STUBBORNNESS.

See REBELLION, WICKEDNESS. In the gospel sense, *stubbornness* is a fixed, resolute, and unyielding adherence to false principles. It is akin to rebellion and is a form of wickedness. (Deut. 9:27; Judges 2: 19; Ps. 78:8; Prov. 7:11.) Samuel said: "Rebellion is as the sin of witchcraft, and *stubbornness is as iniquity and idolatry."* (1 Sam. 15: 23.) Stubbornness against parental teachings and the standards of Israel was punishable by death under the Mosaic law. (Deut. 21:18-21.)

Stubborn people will be damned, unless they forsake their course of obstinacy, turn to humility, and are "baptized without stubbornness of heart." (Alma 32:14-17.) After baptism, as part of working out their salvation, the saints must strive to shake off every particle of stubbornness against any of the laws and ordinances of the gospel.

SUCCESSION IN THE PRESIDENCY.

See APOSTOLIC SUCCESSION.

SUFFERINGS OF THE UN-
GODLY.
See HELL.

SUICIDES.
See ACCOUNTABILITY. *Suicide* consists in the voluntary and intentional taking of one's own life, particularly where the person involved is accountable and has a sound mind. Mortal life is a gift of God; it comes according to the divine will, is appointed to endure for such time as Deity decrees, and is designed to serve as the chief testing period of man's eternal existence. It is the probationary state or time during which man is tried and tested physically, spiritually, and mentally. No man has the right to run away from these tests, no matter how severe they may be, by taking his own life. Obviously persons subject to great stresses may lose control of themselves and become mentally clouded to the point that they are no longer accountable for their acts. Such are not to be condemned for taking their own lives. It should also be remembered that judgment is the Lord's; he knows the thoughts, intents, and abilities of men; and he in his infinite wisdom will make all things right in due course.

SUN.
See ASTRONOMY.

SUNDAY.
See SABBATH.

SUNDAY SCHOOL.
See AUXILIARY ORGANIZATIONS, CHURCH ORGANIZATION, GENERAL BOARDS, PRIESTHOOD, STAKE BOARDS. Largest among the auxiliary organizations of the Church is the *Sunday School,* a church organization which is designed to teach the truths of the restored gospel in purity and perfection to the whole Church. Under the direction of its executive heads, as aided by general and stake boards, the Sunday School operates units in all the wards and branches of the Church. Every member of the Church, the General Authorities only excepted, from three years and upwards should be a member of the Sunday School organization in his ward or branch.

"The object of our Sunday Schools and the object of our church schools," President Joseph F. Smith said, "the great, the paramount object, is to teach our children the truth, teach them to be honorable, pure-minded, virtuous, honest and upright, and enable them, by our advice and counsel and by our guardianship over them, until they reach the years of accountability [maturity], to become the honorable of the earth, the good and the pure among mankind, the virtuous and the upright, and those who shall be worthy to enter the house of God and not be ashamed of themselves in the presence of angels, if they should come to visit them." (*Gospel Doctrine,* 5th ed., p. 387.)

SUN OF RIGHTEOUSNESS.
See SON OF RIGHTEOUSNESS.

SUPERSTITION.
See DELUSION, DIVINATION, SORCERY, SPIRITUALISM, WITCHCRAFT. Religious beliefs and practices based on fear and credulity (often including belief in the power of omens, signs, charms, and the like) have degenerated into the field of *superstition.* To Paul the mysterious worship of the Athenians was superstition. (Acts 17:22.) From the worldly wise Roman point of view, Christianity itself was falsely supposed to be a superstition. (Acts 25:19.)

Among almost all primitive peoples there are many superstitious beliefs and practices. Even among the supposedly enlightened of modern times much of the same degenerate form of belief and worship prevails. Examples of superstitious beliefs and practices found in modern churches include the use of charms, worship of images, revering of relics, baptism of unborn fetuses, the supposed appearances of spirits and personages to children and others, the presumed changing of the sacramental elements into the literal flesh and blood of Christ, and many other things.

SUPPER OF THE GREAT GOD.
See ABOMINATION OF DESOLATION, SECOND COMING OF CHRIST, SIGNS OF THE TIMES. Those with refined senses find it difficult to conceive of the desolation, destruction, and death that will prevail during the final great battles ushering in Christ's reign of peace. So great shall be the slaughter and mass murder, the carnage and gore, the butchery and violent death of warring men, that their decaying bodies "shall stop the noses of the passengers," and it shall be a task of mammoth proportions merely to dispose of them. Then shall Ezekiel's prophecy be fulfilled that every feathered fowl and every beast of the field shall assemble to "eat the flesh of the mighty, and drink the blood of the princes of the earth." (Ezek. 39.) And then shall the cry go forth of which John wrote: "Come and gather yourselves together unto the *supper of the great God;* That ye may eat the flesh of kings, and the flesh of captains, and the flesh of mighty men, and the flesh of horses, and of them that sit on them, and the flesh of all men, both free and bond, both small and great." (Rev. 19:17-18.) That all this is an actual, literal supper, an horrible but real event yet to be, has been specifically confirmed in latter-day revelation. (D. & C. 29:18-21.)

SUSTAINING OF OFFICERS.
See COMMON CONSENT.

SWEARING.
See PROFANITY.

SWORD.
See WAR.

SYMBOLISMS.
See CHRIST. Gospel understanding and literature is gloriously enhanced and beautified by the abundant use of *symbols* and figurative expressions. Since Christ is the center of the gospel system and the one through whom salvation comes, most of the basic symbolical representations tie into him and his atoning sacrifice. "Behold, *all things have their likeness,* and all things are created and made to bear record of me, both things which are temporal, and things which are spiritual; things which are in the heavens above, and things which are on the earth, and things which are in the earth, and things which are under the earth, both above and beneath: *all things bear record of me.*" (Moses 6:63.)

By way of illustration: *Sacrifices* were performed in "similitude of the sacrifice of the Only Begotten of the Father." (Moses 5:7.) We partake of the *sacrament* in remembrance of the broken flesh and spilled blood of our Lord. (Luke 22:13-20; D. &

C. 20:77-79.) *Baptism* is performed by immersion to typify the death, burial, and resurrection of our Redeemer. (Rom. 6:1-6.) Moses lifted the *brazen serpent* before Israel to point their attention forward to the day when their God would be lifted up upon the cross. (John 3:14-15; Hela. 8:13-15.) The *manna,* or bread from heaven, was sent to foreshadow and bear record of the coming day when Christ, the Bread of Life, would come down from heaven. (John 6:30-58.) Indeed, the *whole Mosaic Law,* in all its parts and portions, was so ordained as to bear record of the future coming of Jehovah in the flesh. (Mosiah 13:29-35.)

Abraham was obedient to the *command to offer up Isaac,* "which is a similitude of God and his Only Begotten Son." (Jac. 4:5.) The *Sabbath Day,* from Adam to Moses, bore record that Christ the Creator had rested from his labors on the 7th day (Ex. 20:8-11); from Moses to Christ's mortal ministry, it pointed attention to the deliverance of Israel from Egyptian bondage by the power of the Holy One of Israel (Deut. 5:12-15); and from the day of his resurrection to the present, the Lord's Day has been holy in commemoration of his coming forth as the firstfruits of them that slept. (D. & C. 59:9-17.) And so illustrations might be multiplied at great length—all showing how various gospel ordinances and performances bear record of Christ or of some great truth that centers in him.

SYMPATHY.
See COMPASSION.

SYNAGOGUES.
See MEETINGHOUSES, TEMPLES. Among ancient Hebrew peoples, houses of worship were called *synagogues*. These buildings were the equivalent of ward meetinghouses or stake tabernacles among the Latter-day Saints. There were said to be 460 or 480 of them in Jerusalem alone, though this may be an exaggeration.

Frequent reference is found in the New Testament to synagogues, but there is only one Old Testament reference (Ps. 74:8), and that is one which the scholars question. That houses of worship among the ancient Jews were called synagogues, however, we learn from the Book of Mormon. (2 Ne. 26:26.) That book makes more than a score of references to them in that part of the record which deals with events preceding the coming of our Lord in the flesh.

SYNCRETISM.
See RELIGIOUS SYNCRETISM.

SYNOPTIC GOSPELS.
See GOSPELS.

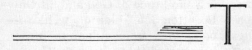

TABERNACLE OF THE CONGREGATION.
See TEMPLES.

TABERNACLES.
See CATHEDRALS, MEETINGHOUSES, TEMPLES. 1. Anciently a *tabernacle* was a tent (Isa. 4:6), and hence a temporary house of worship was a tabernacle. The *tabernacle of the congregation,* however, was a *temple,* a name which it also carried. (1 Sam. 1:9; 3:1-18.) Modern usage has enlarged the term tabernacle to include large permanent houses of worship which in their nature are designed for preaching to assemblies rather than for classroom study. In the early days of the Church in this dispensation it was the practice to erect a stake tabernacle in each stake. The world-famous *Mormon Tabernacle* is located on Temple Square in Salt Lake City.

— 2. To connote the temporary residence of the eternal spirit in a mortal body, that body is referred to as a *mortal tabernacle* or *tabernacle of clay.* (Mosiah 3:5; Alma 7:8; Moro. 9:6.) "The elements are the tabernacle of God; yea, man is the tabernacle of God, even temples; and whatsoever temple is defiled, God shall destroy that temple." (D. & C. 93:35.)

TABOOS.

In imitation of the gospel practice of forbidding certain evil practices and things to the saints for their benefit and blessing, false religions make use of *taboos*. These are supposed to be sacred interdictions laid upon the use of certain words or things or the performance of certain actions. They are found among races of primitive culture and are manifest in many modern sects of so-called Christendom. To illustrate: Servile work on the Sabbath is forbidden to the saints; in contrast, planting crops when the moon is full might be taboo in some primitive tribes. Or, prayers to any but the true God are forbidden by gospel law; but in Babylon prayers to any but the golden image erected to Nebuchadnezzar were taboo. (Dan. 3.)

TACTFULNESS.

See COURTESY, HONESTY, KINDNESS. In the sense of using wisdom and kindness in dealings with others, *tactfulness* is an edifying and desirable quality. It is born of the refining influence of the Spirit. But where deceit, dishonesty, and so-called polite lying

enter the picture, what otherwise might have been a virtue finds itself transformed into a vice.

TALENTS.
See FOREORDINATION.

TARTARUS.

See GEHENNA, HADES, HELL, SHEOL, SPIRIT PRISON. In one instance in the New Testament the classical Greek word *tartarus* is used to mean hell. Peter used it in reference to the abode of "the angels that sinned" and were cast out in the war in heaven (2 Pet. 2:4), perhaps selecting it rather than the usual *hades, sheol,* or *gehenna* because these latter usually designate the abode of wicked mortals in the realm following this life.

TATTOOING.

Tattoos are permanent marks or designs made on the skin by puncuring it and filling the punctures with indelible ink. The practice is a desecration of the human body and should not be permitted, unless all that is involved is the placing of a blood type or an identification number in an obscure place. (Deut. 14: 1.) Latter-day Saint servicemen in particular are counseled to avoid the pitfalls of tattooing. Persons who are tattooed are not, however, denied the ordinances and blessings of the temples.

TEA.
See HOT DRINKS.

TEACHERS.
See AARONIC PRIESTHOOD, LE-
VITES, MELCHIZEDEK PRIESTHOOD,
PRIESTHOOD, PRIESTHOOD OFFICES,
PRIESTHOOD QUORUMS, QUORUM
PRESIDENTS, SERMONS. 1. Those appointed to serve as instructors in
the church organizations—those
whose responsibilities are to conduct classes, present gospel lessons,
guide class members in paths of
righteousness—are called *teachers.*
Both men and women, priesthood
bearers and non-priesthood bearers,
may serve in these positions from
time to time.

2. Among the Nephites, brethren
holding the Melchizedek Priesthood
were selected, consecrated *teachers,*
and given teaching and administrative powers and responsibilities. (1
Ne. 2:22; 2 Ne. 5:19; Mosiah 23:17;
25:19; 26:7; Alma 4:7.) They had
jurisdiction over the churches and,
along with the priests, were "to
preach and to teach the word of
God." (Alma 23:4.) They had power
to baptize (Alma 15:13), a privilege
not enjoyed by teachers in the
Aaronic Priesthood. (D. & C. 20:
58.)

It should be noted that those
consecrated priests and teachers
among the Nephites were not receiving offices in the lesser priesthood, for there was no Aaronic
Priesthood among the Nephites
from the time Lehi left Jerusalem

down to the ministry of Christ
among them. From the time of
Aaron to the coming of our Lord,
the Aaronic Priesthood was an hereditary priesthood; it was conferred
only upon the Levites, none of
whom journeyed with father Lehi
and his colony. (*Doctrines of Salvation,* vol. 3, p. 87.)

3. One of the ordained offices in
the Aaronic Priesthood is that of a
teacher. (D. & C. 18:32; 20:60.) As
with all other authorities or offices
in the church the office of a teacher
is an appendage to the priesthood.
(D. & C. 84:30; 107:5.) Together
with the deacons, teachers are appointed "to watch over the church,
to be standing ministers unto the
church." (D. & C. 84:111.) "The
teacher's duty is to watch over the
church always, and be with and
strengthen them; And see that
there is no iniquity in the church,
neither hardness with each other,
neither lying, backbiting, nor evil
speaking; And see that the church
meet together often, and also see
that all the members do their duty.
. . . They are . . . to warn, expound,
exhort, and teach, and invite all to
come unto Christ." But they do not
"have authority to baptize, administer the sacrament, or lay on
hands." (D. & C. 20:53-59.)

In all things teachers are to be
diligent, working with their might.
(D. & C. 38:40.) They are under express command that their teachings
shall consist of the truths of the
gospel found recorded in the scriptures. (D. & C. 42:12.) Home teach-

ing is one of the assignments given to teachers to enable them to discharge their divinely imposed responsibilities; they can, of course, function also in all of the duties of the deacons.

There is no Biblical passage which makes it plain that persons in Old or New Testament times were ordained to the office of a teacher in either the Aaronic or Melchizedek Priesthood. References to teachers in the Bible apparently refer to persons who acted as preachers or instructors. (Acts 13:1; 1 Cor. 12: 28-29; Eph. 4:11.)

TELEPATHY.

See GIFTS OF THE S P I R I T, THOUGHTS. There is no such thing among mortal beings as mental *telepathy*—that is, the transmission of thoughts from one person to another without communication through the senses. Men's thoughts are secret and cannot be pried into by other men, or for that matter by devils. *"There is none else save God that knowest thy thoughts and the intents of thy heart."* (D. & C. 6:16; 1 Cor. 3:20; Heb. 4:12; Mosiah 24:12.)

However, the Lord can and does on occasion reveal to his prophets the thoughts and intents of the hearts of men. "By the help of the all-powerful Creator of heaven and earth," Jacob said to his Nephite brethren, "I can tell you concerning your thoughts." (Jac. 2:5; Alma 10:17.) This revealing of the thoughts of another is one of the gifts of the Spirit; it is akin to the spirit of prophecy; it comes by the power of God and not of man. (Alma 12:3, 7; 18:16-20, 32; Hela. 9:41.) Our Lord during his ministry frequently exercised the power to read the thoughts of those among whom he labored. (Matt. 9:4; 12: 25; Luke 5:22; 6:8; 9:47; 11:17; 24: 38; 3 Ne. 28:6.)

TELESTIAL BODIES.

See TELESTIAL GLORY, TELESTIAL KINGDOM, TELESTIAL LAW, SALVATION. "All flesh is not the same flesh," Paul says, with reference to the flesh of various forms of life, thus using a self-evident truth to establish in the minds of the Corinthians that there is also a distinction in the kinds of bodies that men have. The fact that some of these are *telestial bodies* has been lost from the King James Version of the Bible. The Inspired Version, however, restores the lost phrases, explaining that there are "celestial bodies, and bodies terrestrial, and bodies telestial; but the glory of the celestial, one; and the terrestrial, another; and the telestial, another." (*Inspired Version,* 1 Cor. 15:40.)

Most accountable men on earth have *telestial bodies* because they live a telestial law, that is the law of carnality and worldliness. These bodies will be quickened in the resurrection with telestial glory, which is found in a telestial kingdom. (D. & C. 76:81-112; 88:16-32.)

TELESTIAL GLORY.

See TELESTIAL BODIES, TELESTIAL KINGDOM, TELESTIAL LAW, SALVATION. That glory granted the inhabitants of the lowest kingdom of glory is called *telestial glory*. In the infinite mercy of a beneficent Father it surpasses all mortal understanding, and yet it is in no way comparable to the glory of the terrestrial and celestial worlds. Telestial glory is typified by the stars of the firmament, and "as one star differs from another star in glory, even so differs one from another in glory in the telestial world" (D. & C. 76:81-112; 1 Cor. 15:41), meaning that all who inherit the telestial kingdom will not receive the same glory.

TELESTIAL KINGDOM.

See TELESTIAL BODIES, TELESTIAL GLORY, TELESTIAL LAW, SALVATION. Most of the adult people who have lived lived from the day of Adam to the present time will go to the *telestial kingdom*. The inhabitants of this lowest kingdom of glory will be "as innumerable as the stars in the firmament of heaven, or as the sand upon the seashore." They will be the endless hosts of people of all ages who have lived after the manner of the world; who have been carnal, sensual, and devilish; who have chosen the vain philosophies of the world rather than accept the testimony of Jesus; who have been liars and thieves, sorcerers and adulterers, blasphem-

ers and murderers. (D. & C. 76:81-112; Rev. 22:15.) Their number will include "all the proud, yea, and all that do wickedly" (Mal. 4:1), for all such have lived a telestial law. "And they shall be servants of the Most High; but where God and Christ dwell they cannot come, worlds without end." (D. & C. 76: 112.)

TELESTIAL LAW.

See TELESTIAL BODIES, TELESTIAL GLORY, TELESTIAL KINGDOM, SALVATION, WORLD. A telestial glory, found only in a telestial kingdom, is reserved for those who develop telestial bodies, such bodies resulting naturally from obedience to *telestial law*. (D. & C. 88:16-32.) This law is the law of the world, and worldly people are conforming to its terms and conditions. Those who refuse to worship the true and living God, who are unclean and immoral, who are proud and rebellious, who walk in paths of wickedness, who are carnal and sensual, who do not maintain standards of decency, uprightness, and integrity, are as a result conforming their lives to the provisions of telestial law. (D. & C. 76:81-112; Mal. 3; 4.)

All the inhabitants of the earth are living at least a telestial law, unless, perchance, there are some who are in open rebellion against the truth, some who wilfully break the law, abide not in it, but seek to become a law unto themselves, choosing to abide in sin, and altogether abiding therein. (D. & C. 88:35.) Such, of course, will be sons of perdition in eternity and will inherit "a kingdom which is not a kingdom of glory." (D. & C. 88:24.)

TEMPESTS.
See SIGNS OF THE TIMES.

TEMPLE MARRIAGE.
See CELESTIAL MARRIAGE.

TEMPLE ORDINANCES.
See BAPTISM FOR THE DEAD, CELESTIAL MARRIAGE, ENDOWMENTS, EXALTATION, ORDINANCES, RECOMMENDS, SALVATION, SALVATION FOR THE DEAD, SEALINGS, TEMPLES, VICARIOUS ORDINANCES. Certain gospel ordinances are of such a sacred and holy nature that the Lord authorizes their performance only in holy sanctuaries prepared and dedicated for that very purpose. Except in circumstances of great poverty and distress, these ordinances can be performed only in temples, and hence they are commonly called *temple ordinances.* Baptism for the dead, an ordinance opening the door to the celestial kingdom to worthy persons not privileged to undergo gospel schooling while in mortality, is a temple ordinance, an ordinance of salvation. All other temple ordinances—washings, anointings, endowments, sealings—pertain to exaltation within the celestial kingdom. Celestial mar-

riage is the gate which puts men on the path leading to the highest of three heavens within the celestial world. (D. & C. 131:1-4.)

All of these ordinances of exaltation are performed in the temples for both the living and the dead. Their essential portions have been the same in all dispensations when the fulness of the sealing power has been exercised by the Lord's prophets. (D. & C. 124:28-41.) They were given in modern times to the Prophet Joseph Smith by revelation, many things connected with them being translated by the Prophet from the papyrus on which the Book of Abraham was recorded. (Book of Abraham, pp. 34-35.)

TEMPLE RECOMMENDS.
See RECOMMENDS.

TEMPLES.
See BAPTISM FOR THE DEAD, CATHEDRALS, CELESTIAL MARRIAGE, ENDOWMENTS, EXALTATION, GENEALOGICAL RESEARCH, MEETINGHOUSES, PRIESTHOOD, RECOMMENDS, SACRIFICES, SALVATION FOR THE DEAD, SEALING POWER, SEALINGS, SIGNS OF THE TIMES, TABERNACLES, TEMPLE ORDINANCES, VICARIOUS ORDINANCES. 1. Holy sanctuaries wherein sacred ordinances, rites, and ceremonies are performed which pertain to salvation and exaltation in the kingdom of God are called *temples.* They are the most sacred places of worship

779

on earth; each one is literally a *House of the Lord,* a house of the great Creator, a house where he and his Spirit may dwell, to which he may come, or send his messengers, to confer priesthood and keys and to give revelation to his people.

From the days of Adam to the present, whenever the Lord has had a people on earth, temples and temple ordinances have been a crowning feature of their worship. "My people are *always* commanded to build" temples, the Lord says, "for the glory, honor, and endowment" of all the saints. (D. & C. 124:39-40.) These temples have been costly and elaborate buildings whenever the abilities of the people have permitted such; nothing is too good for the Lord, and no sacrifice is too great to make in his service. But in the days of poverty, or when the number of true believers has been small, the Lord has used mountains, groves, and wilderness locations for temple purposes. Endowments, for instance, following the latter-day exodus, were first given on Ensign peak. (*Doctrines of Salvation,* vol. 2, pp. 231-257.)

Our knowledge of holy sanctuaries which existed before the day of Moses is slight. We do know that as soon as Moses led Israel out of Egyptian bondage detailed instructions were received to build and use a portable temple or tabernacle, not for general assembly and meetings, but for the performance of holy ordinances. It appears that initially there was in ancient Israel a *provisional tabernacle* (Ex. 33: 7-11); that thereafter the people donated of their riches and the *tabernacle of the congregation* was built (Ex., chapters 25 to 31 and 35 to 40); that this tabernacle was set up at various places in Israel after they entered their promised land (Josh. 18:1-3; Judges 18:31; 21:2; 1 Sam. 1:3, 24; 4; 7:1-2; 21:1-6; 1 Chron. 21:28-30; 2 Chron. 1:3-6); that while the tabernacle was at Gibeon, David erected another tabernacle, in his own city, to house the Ark of the Covenant (1 Sam. 4:10-22; 5; 6; 7:1-2); that with the material collected by David, Solomon built the great temple in Jerusalem (1 Chron. 22:5-19; 1 Kings 5:13-18; 2 Chron., chapters 3 to 7); that Cyrus of Persia sponsored the return of captive Judah from Babylonian bondage to rebuild the temple, a structure called the *temple of Zerubbabel* (Ezra 1:1-4); and that the so-called temple of Herod, the temple in Jerusalem at the time of our Lord's ministry, was in process of being rebuilt at that time. (John 2:20.)

A temple was built among the Nephites shortly after their arrival in America. (2 Ne. 5:16; Jac. 1:17; 2: 2, 11.) Nearly 500 years later the Nephites are known still to have had a temple (Mosiah 1:18; 2:1-7; 7:17; 11:10-12; 19:5), and it was to the temple that the people assembled to await the personal ministry among them of the resurrected

Lord. (Hela. 10:8; 3 Ne. 11:1; James E. Talmage, *The House of the Lord*, pp. 1-333.)

Pursuant to revelation and commandment, the saints built the first temple of this dispensation at Kirtland, Ohio. (D. & C. 88:119.) Therein keys and authorities were restored and a partial endowment was given. (D. & C. 110.) Thereafter temples have been built in Nauvoo, in western America, in foreign lands, and on the islands of the sea; and the day will come when temples will dot the earth, for the great work of the millennial era centers around and in these holy edifices. The temple erected in Salt Lake City was constructed in partial fulfilment of Isaiah's prophecy that "the Lord's house shall be established in the top of the mountains." (Isa. 2:1-4; Micah 4:1-2.) Ezekiel's promise that the Lord's sanctuary will be established in the holy land is yet to be fulfilled. (Ezek. 37:21-28; D. & C. 133:13.)

The inspired erection and proper use of temples is one of the great evidences of the divinity of the Lord's work. Without revelation they can neither be built nor used. Where there are temples, with the spirit of revelation resting upon those who administer therein, there the Lord's people will be found; where these are not, the Church and kingdom and the truth of heaven are not. Temples are to continue until this earth becomes a celestial sphere, when, as it appears from the revelations, their purposes will have been served and they will no longer be needed. (Rev. 21:22.)

2. To point up the sacred and holy nature of the human body, the Lord calls it a *temple*. "Know ye not that ye are the temple of God, and that the Spirit of God dwelleth in you? If any man defile the temple of God, him shall God destroy; for the temple of God is holy, which temple ye are." (1 Cor. 3:16-17; 6:19; 2 Cor. 6:16; D. & C. 93:35; Alma 7:21; 34:36; Hela. 4:24.)

TEMPORAL BODIES.
See MORTALITY.

TEMPORAL DEATH.
See DEATH.

TEMPTATION.
See ACCOUNTABILITY, AGENCY, DEVIL, EVIL, GOOD, PLAN OF SALVATION, SIN, YEARS OF ACCOUNTABILITY. Overcoming *temptation* is an essential and necessary part of working out one's salvation. Mortal man is by nature carnal, sensual, and devilish (Alma 42:10), meaning that he has an inherent and earthly inclination to succumb to the lusts and passions of the flesh. This life is the appointed probationary estate in which it is being determined whether he will fall captive to temptations or rise above the allurement of worldly things so as to merit the riches of eternity.

Christ himself "was in all points

tempted like as we are, yet [he remained] without sin." (Heb. 4:15; D. & C. 20:22; Mosiah 3:7.) Adam was "tempted of the devil," and yielding thereto found himself cast out of the Garden of Eden. (D. & C. 29:36-40.) And all accountable men since his day, in greater or lesser degree, have been overcome by temptation and become sinners. (1 John 1:7-10.) The atonement, the gospel, and the plan of salvation are designed to free men from past sins and give them power to resist temptation in the future.

Temptation—though its *existence* is essential to God's plan—is not of God, but is of the Devil. (Alma 34:39; 3 Ne. 6:17.) "Blessed is the man that endureth temptation: for when he is tried, he shall receive the crown of life, which the Lord hath promised to them that love him. Let no man say when he is tempted, I am tempted of God: for God cannot be tempted with evil, neither tempteth he any man: But every man is tempted, when he is drawn away of his own lust, and enticed. Then when lust hath conceived, it bringeth forth sin: and sin, when it is finished, bringeth forth death." (Jas. 1:12-15.)

The saints should pray always lest they enter into temptation. (3 Ne. 18:18; D. & C. 61:39.) The meaning of the petition, "Lead us not into temptation, but deliver us from evil" (Matt. 6:13; Luke 11: 4; 3 Ne. 13:12), is: Suffer us not to be led into greater temptation than we can bear, but deliver us from evil.

Little children are without sin because "power is not given unto Satan to tempt little children, until they begin to become accountable before me." (D. & C. 29:47.) The Three Nephites, having overcome and being "sanctified in the flesh," are beyond the power of Satan, and he cannot tempt them. (3 Ne. 28: 39.) Similarly, when the righteous saints go to paradise, they will no longer be tempted, but the wicked in hell are subject to the control and torments of Lucifer (D. & C. 132:26.)

TEMPTER.

See DEVIL. Lucifer is the *tempter*. Such name signifies his aim of leading all men to do evil, to forsake righteousness, and to follow that carnal existence which will take them to hell.

TEN COMMANDMENTS.

See ADULTERY, BEARING FALSE WITNESS, COVETOUSNESS, GOD, GOSPEL, LAW OF MOSES, MOSES, MURDERERS, PROFANITY, SABBATH, STEALING, WORSHIP OF IMAGES. In all gospel dispensations, beginning with the Adamic, the Lord has revealed the great governing principles to which all mortal men are subject and by which they will be judged. These revelations have always included the basic laws summarized in what is known as the *Ten Commandments.* These eternal principles have all been ratified and given renewed force by latter-day revelation. (*Doctrines of Salvation,* vol. 1, p. 96.)

Moses received the Ten Commandments twice. (Ex. 20; Deut. 5.) Both times they were written by the finger of the Lord on tablets of stone. The first time they were revealed as part of the fulness of the gospel, but when Moses, returning with the sacred tablets, found Israel reveling in idolatrous worship, he broke the tablets. Thereafter, "The Lord said unto Moses, Hew thee two other tables of stone, like unto the first, and I will write upon them also, the words of the law, according as they were written at the first on the tables which thou brakest; but *it shall not be according to the first, for I will take away the priesthood out of their midst;* therefore my holy order, and the ordinances thereof, shall not go before them; for my presence shall not go up in their midst, lest I destroy them. But I will give unto them the law as at the first, but *it shall be after the law of a carnal commandment;* for I have sworn in my wrath, that they shall not enter into my presence, into my rest, in the days of their pilgrimage." (*Inspired Version,* Ex. 34:1-2.)

Thus the 2nd revelation to Moses of the Ten Commandments was as part of the law of carnal commandments, rather than of the gospel itself. In both instances, however,

the same unchanging, eternal standards of worship and moral conduct were revealed. The two accounts differ in only one major respect and that is in the reason assigned for honoring the Sabbath day. While they lived under the law, the Sabbath was to Israel an occasion to commemorate their deliverance from Egyptian bondage (Deut. 5:12-15) rather than to point their attention back to the hallowed period of rest that followed the six days of creative work when the earth was made. (Ex. 20:8-11.)

TENDERNESS.
See COMPASSION.

TENETS.
See DOCTRINE.

TEN TRIBES OF ISRAEL.
See LOST TRIBES OF ISRAEL.

TERRESTRIAL BODIES.
See TERRESTRIAL GLORY, TERRESTRIAL KINGDOM, TERRESTRIAL LAW, SALVATION. By obedience to terrestrial law men develop *terrestrial bodies and spirits,* thus conditioning themselves to be quickened in the resurrection with terrestrial glory, which is found in a terrestrial kingdom. (D. & C. 76: 71-80; 88:16-32.) As is the case with the development of celestial bodies, those who gain terrestrial ones have

bodies as different from other kinds of flesh as one form of life differs from another. (1 Cor. 15:39-42.)

TERRESTRIAL GLORY.

See TERRESTRIAL BODIES, TERRESTRIAL KINGDOM, TERRESTRIAL LAW, SALVATION. Those attaining a terrestrial kingdom will be inheritors of *terrestrial glory* which differs from celestial glory "as that of the moon differs from the sun in the firmament." (D. & C. 76:71; 1 Cor. 15:41.) In effect they bask, as does the moon, in reflected glory, for there are restrictions and limitations placed on them. They "receive of the presence of the Son, but not of the fulness of the Father" (D. & C. 76:77), and to all eternity they remain unmarried and without exaltation. (D. & C. 132:17.)

TERRESTRIAL KINGDOM.

See TERRESTRIAL BODIES, TERRESTRIAL GLORY, TERRESTRIAL LAW, SALVATION. To the *terrestrial kingdom* will go: 1. Accountable persons who die without law (and who, of course, do not accept the gospel in the spirit world under those particular circumstances which would make them heirs of the celestial kingdom); 2. Those who reject the gospel in this life and who reverse their course and accept it in the spirit world; 3. Honorable men of the earth who are blinded by the craftiness of men and who therefore do not accept and live the gos-

pel law; and 4. Members of The Church of Jesus Christ of Latter-day Saints who have testimonies of Christ and the divinity of the great latter-day work and who are not valiant, but who are instead lukewarm in their devotion to the Church and to righteousness. (D. & C. 76:71-80.)

TERRESTRIAL LAW.

See TERRESTRIAL BODIES, TERRESTRIAL GLORY, TERRESTRIAL KINGDOM, SALVATION. To attain a terrestrial kingdom it is necessary to abide a *terrestrial law,* which consists in living an upright, honorable life but one that does not conform to the standards whereby the human soul is sanctified by the Spirit. (D. & C. 76:71-80; 88:16-32.)

TERRITORY OF DESERET.

See DESERET.

TESTAMENT.

See NEW TESTAMENT.

TESTATOR.

See CHRIST, HOLY GHOST, MEDIATOR. 1. In legal usage, a *testator* is one who leaves a valid will or testament at his death. The will or testament is the written document wherein the testator provides for the disposition of his property. As used in the gospel sense, a *testament* is a covenant. Jesus is the Mediator of the new covenant or testament, that is of the gospel which came to replace the law of Moses. (Heb. 9:15; 12:24; D. & C. 107:19.)

Paul mixed these legal and gospel definitions to teach a basic doctrine. Speaking of Christ's death, and the gifts in effect willed to men in and through that death, he said: "For where a testament is, there must also of necessity be the death of the testator. For a testament is of force after men are dead: otherwise it is of no strength at all while the testator liveth." (Heb. 9:16-17.) In other words, Christ had to die to bring salvation. The testament or covenant of salvation came in force because of the atonement worked out in connection with that death. *Christ is the Testator*. His gift, as would be true of any testator, cannot be inherited until his death. Christ died that salvation might come; without his death, he could not have willed either immortality or eternal life to men.

2. The Holy Ghost is the *Testator*, by which is meant that it is his function to testify and bear record of the Father and the Son. (2 Ne. 31:18.) In Abraham's record this 3rd member of the Godhead was called "God the third, the *witness* or *Testator*." (*Teachings*, p. 190.)

TESTIMONY.

See CONVERSION, FAITH, GIFTS OF THE SPIRIT, GOSPEL, HOLY GHOST, KNOWLEDGE, LAW OF WITNESSES, MORMONISM, PROPHECY, REVELATION, TRUTH. A *testimony* of the gospel is the sure knowledge, received by revelation from the Holy Ghost, of the divinity of the great latter-day work. In former dispensations a testimony was the revealed knowledge of the divinity of the work in that day. A testimony in this day automatically includes the assurance of the truth of the same gospel in all former ages when it has been on earth.

If the sole source of one's knowledge or assurance of the truth of the Lord's work comes from reason, or logic, or persuasive argument that cannot be controverted, it is not a testimony of the gospel. In its nature a testimony consists of knowledge that comes by revelation, "for the testimony of Jesus is the spirit of prophecy" (Rev. 19:10), and anyone gaining that knowledge from the Holy Ghost could, if the Lord willed, receive knowledge of future events also and prophecy of them.

Logic and reason lead truth seekers along the path to a testimony, and they are aids in strengthening the revealed assurances of which a testimony is composed. But the actual sure knowledge which constitutes "the testimony of Jesus" must come by "the spirit of prophecy." This is received when the Holy Spirit speaks to the spirit within men; it comes when the whisperings of the still small voice are heard by the inner man. Receipt of a testimony is accompanied by a feeling of calm, unwavering certainty.

Those who have it can use logic and reason in defending their positions and in bearing their testimonies, but it is the promptings of the Spirit rather than reason alone that is the true foundation upon which the testimony rests.

Three great truths must be included in every valid testimony: 1. That Jesus Christ is the Son of God and the Savior of the world (D. & C. 46:13); 2. That Joseph Smith is the Prophet of God through whom the gospel was restored in this dispensation; and 3. That The Church of Jesus Christ of Latter-day Saints is "the only true and living church upon the face of the whole earth." (D. & C. 1:30.)

Embraced within these great revealed assurances are a host of others, as that the Book of Mormon is true, that holy messengers restored keys and priesthood to men in this day, and that the present leadership of the Church has the right and power to direct the Lord's work on earth. To bear one's testimony is to make a solemn declaration, affirmation or attestation that personal revelation has been received certifying to the truth of those realities which comprise a testimony.

The prophets of all ages have borne testimonies, as for instance: Christ (John 4:25-26; 10:25, 36), Job (Job 19:25), Peter (Matt. 16: 13-20; John 6:68-69), Joseph Smith and Sidney Rigdon. (D. & C. 76:22-24.) After citing the witnesses of other prophets to establish the truth of his teachings, Alma then bore this testimony: "And this is not all. Do ye not suppose that I know of these things myself? Behold, I testify unto you that I do know that these things whereof I have spoken are true. And how do ye suppose that I know of their surety? Behold, I say unto you *they are made known unto me by the Holy Spirit of God.* Behold, I have fasted and prayed many days that I might know these things of myself. And now I do know of myself that they are true; for *the Lord God hath made them manifest unto me by his Holy Spirit; and this is the spirit of revelation which is in me.*" (Alma 5:45-46.)

Any accountable person can gain a testimony of the gospel by obedience to that law upon which the receipt of such knowledge is predicated. This is the formula: 1. He must *desire* to know the truth of the gospel, of the Book of Mormon, of the Church, or of whatever is involved. 2. He must *study* and learn the basic facts relative to the matter involved. "Search the scriptures." (John 5:39.) "Search these commandments." (D. & C. 1:37.) 3. He must *practice* the principles and truths learned, conforming his life to them. "My doctrine is not mine, but his that sent me. If any man will do his will, he shall know of the doctrine, whether it be of God, or whether I speak of myself." (John 7:16-17.) 4. He must *pray* to the Father in the name of Christ, *in faith,* and the truth will then be made manifest by revelation "by the power of the Holy Ghost. And by the power of the Holy Ghost ye may know the truth of all things." (Moro. 10:3-5; 1 Cor. 2.)

With the receipt of a testimony comes the obligation to bear witness to the world of the divinity of the Lord's work. Part of the covenant made in the waters of baptism is that the new converts will "stand as witnesses of God at all times and in all things, and in all places that ye may be in, even until death." (Mosiah 18:9.) "It becometh every man who hath been warned to warn his neighbor." (D. & C. 88:81.) All the elders of Israel have a missionary responsibility. (D. & C. 58: 47; 66:7; 100:10; 124:7.) The apostles and the seventy have a particular and especial responsibility in this field. (D. & C. 107:23-25; 112.) The testimony of the elders is followed by the testimony of calamities. (D. & C. 43:18-29; 88:88-90.) Blessings and cleansing power are given the faithful who bear testimony to the world. (D. & C. 62:3; 84:61; 136:34-40.)

In the justice of God, every person will have the opportunity to gain a testimony of the truth, either in this life or in the spirit world before the day of the resurrection. (D. & C. 1:2.) Those who have a full and complete opportunity in this life, and who do not take it, may receive a second opportunity in the spirit world, but they will not have a second chance to gain salvation by their belated acceptance of the truth. Rather, they will go to a terrestrial kingdom because they "received not the testimony of Jesus in the flesh, but afterwards received it." (D. & C. 76:73-74.)

Men are not saved by virtue of a testimony alone. (D. & C. 3:4.) But a testimony is the beginning of real spiritual progress. With it comes a greater obligation to serve God, keep his commandments, and walk with the light that has been received. (D. & C. 82:2-4.) It is only those who are valiant in testimony who work out their salvation. Those "who are not valiant in the testimony of Jesus" are assigned an inheritance, not in the kingdom of God, but in the terrestrial kingdom. (D. & C. 76:79.)

TESTIMONY MEETINGS.

See FAST MEETINGS, SACRAMENT MEETINGS, TESTIMONY. Those sacrament meetings to which members of the Church are expected to come fasting, and in which they are privileged to bear testimonies of the truth and speak and teach as moved upon by the Spirit, are often called *testimony meetings.*

Missionaries and other special church groups often hold special testimony meetings to promote the special work in which they are engaged. Rich outpourings of the Spirit are frequently manifest in such meetings, and as a result faith and devotion are increased in the hearts of the spiritually inclined who participate in them.

TETRAGRAMMATON.

See ELOHIM, GOD, JEHOVAH. Taken from the word *tetragram,* which means *four letters, tetragrammaton* means the particular four consonant letters used in ancient Hebrew to signify the sacred and "incommunicable name" of Deity. In later Jewish tradition this name was not pronounced except with the vowel points of *Adonai* or *Elohim,* so that according to the scholars the true pronunciation was lost. The four consonants are variously written IHVH, JHVH, JHWH, YHVH, and YHWH, and the words reconstructed by adding vowel points are variously supposed to be Jahaveh, Jahvah, Jahve, Jahveh, Yahve, Yahveh, Yahwe, and Yahweh. The name *Jehovah* is thought by scholars to be a false reconstruction of the incommunicable name. From latter-day revelation, however, we learn that Jehovah is the English form of the actual name by which the Lord Jesus was known anciently. (D. & C. 110:3; Abra. 2:8.)

THANKSGIVING.

See HALLELUJAH, MUSIC, PRAYER, WORSHIP. True worship includes *thanksgiving* to God—the acknowledging and confessing with joy and gladness of the benefits and mercies which he bestows upon his children. "Know ye that the Lord he is God: . . . Enter into his gates with thanksgiving, and into his courts with praise: be thankful unto him, and bless his name." (Ps. 100: 3-4.)

"Blessing, and glory, and wisdom, and thanksgiving, and honour, and power, and might, be unto our God for ever and ever." (Rev. 7:12.)

Men should "live in thanksgiving daily." (Alma 34:38.) In prayer, song, and by walking uprightly before him, they should render thanks to the Lord for the very fact of creation and existence; for the redeeming sacrifice of Christ which ransoms all men from death and offers eternal life to the faithful; for the gospel, the priesthood, the Church and kingdom, and the assurance that the family unit will continue in eternity; for the gift of the Holy Ghost, living oracles to guide the saints, and freedom to worship God according to the dictates of conscience; for temporal and spiritual prosperity and all the good things of life.

"O how you ought to thank your heavenly King!" was the counsel of King Benjamin. "I say unto you, my brethren, that if you should *render all the thanks and praise which your whole soul has power to possess,* to that God who has created you, and has kept and preserved you, and has caused that ye should rejoice, and has granted that ye should live in peace one with another—I say unto you that if ye should serve him who has created you from the beginning, and is preserving you from day to day, by lending you breath, that ye may live and move and do according to your own will, and even supporting you from one moment to another—

I say, if ye should serve him with all your whole souls yet ye would be unprofitable servants." (Mosiah 2:19-21.)

THEARCHY.

See THEOCRACY (THEARCHY).

THEFT.

See STEALING.

THEISM.

See ATHEISM, DEISM, GOD, HENOTHEISM, MONOTHEISM, POLYTHEISM. *Theism* is simply the belief in the existence of a God or gods; it carries a connotation of a belief in monotheism in that it places one god as supreme in the universe.

THEOCENTRIC.

See GOD. That which has God for its center and assumes divine sovereignty is *theocentric,* as a theocentric life or a theocentric universe.

THEOCRACY (THEARCHY).

See GOVERNMENT OF GOD, KINGDOM OF GOD. *Thearchy* or *theocracy* is government by the immediate direction of God through his ministers and representatives. A state governed in this manner is called theocracy. This was the original earthly government, Adam serving as the great presiding high priest through whom the laws of the Lord, both temporal and spiritual, were revealed and administered. This type of government apparently continued among the righteous portion of mankind from the days of Adam to Enoch and the taking of Zion to the Lord's bosom.

The great patriarchs after the flood—Abraham, Isaac, and Jacob, and others—appear to have had this type of government. Righteous portions of the Jareditish peoples were undoubtedly governed on this system. Certainly ancient Israel in the days of Moses and the judges operated on a theocratic basis, and the same system prevailed among the Nephite portion of Lehi's decendants during most of their long history. When Christ comes to reign personally on earth during the millennial era, a perfect theocratic government will prevail. (D. & C. 38:20-22; 58:20-22.)

THEOGONY.

See EXALTATION, GENERATION, GODHOOD, GODS. The term *theogony* has reference to the generation or genealogy of the gods. In view of the revealed latter-day knowledge of how, as the Prophet expressed it, "God came to be God" (*Teachings,* p. 345), and of the power which righteous men have to go on to their exaltation so that they become gods (D. & C. 132:20), the term *theogony* takes on a meaning for the Latter-day Saints which is far beyond anything that the world has supposed.

THEOLOGY.

See GOD, KNOWLEDGE, RELIGION, STANDARD WORKS, WORSHIP. In defining the science of *theology* and in setting forth its comprehensive nature, Elder James E. Talmage has written: "The word *theology* is of Greek origin; it comes to us from *Theos,* meaning God, and *logos*—a treatise, or discourse, signifying by derivation, therefore, collated knowledge of Deity, or the science that teaches us of God, implying also the relation existing between him and his creatures. The term is of ancient usage, and may be traced to pagan sources. Plato and Aristotle speak of theology as the doctrine of Deity and divine things. . . .

"The ultimate boundaries of the science, if boundaries there be, are beyond the capacity of man to survey. Theology deals with Deity, the fountain of knowledge, the source of wisdom; with the proofs of the existence of a Supreme Being, and of other supernatural personalities; with the conditions under which, and the means by which, divine revelation is imparted; with the eternal principles governing the creation of worlds; with the laws of nature in all their varied manifestations. Primarily, theology is the science that deals with God and religion; it presents the facts of observed and revealed truth in orderly array, and indicates the means of their application in the duties of life. Theology then has to do with other facts than those that are specifically called spiritual; *its domain is that of truth.*

"The industrial pursuits that benefit mankind, the arts that please and refine, the sciences that enlarge and exalt the mind—these are but fragments of the great though yet uncompleted volume of truth that has come to earth from a source of eternal and infinite supply. A complete survey of theology, therefore, would embrace all known truths." (*Articles of Faith,* pp. 3-6.)

THEOPHANIES.

See CHRIST, FIRST VISION, GOD, VISIONS. Visible manifestations of God to mortal men are called *theophanies.* That is, in a theophany the Lord is seen in the same literal sense in which he was manifested to the ancient prophets. The appearance of the Father and the Son to Joseph Smith was one of the most glorious theophanies of all the ages. (Jos. Smith 2:16-20.)

From the days of Adam to the present the Lord has freely manifested his personal Self to righteous men. Indeed, because he is no respecter of persons, the same faith and devotion is always rewarded with the same blessing; and so he has said "that every soul who forsaketh his sins and cometh unto me, and calleth on my name, and obeyeth my voice, and keepeth my commandments, shall see my face and know that I am." (D. & C. 93:1; Ether 3; *Teachings,* pp. 149-151.)

THEOSOPHY.

See CHURCH OF THE DEVIL, PHILOSOPHY, REVELATION, SALVATION. *Theosophy* (from the Greek *theos,* God; and *sophia,* wisdom) is the name given to various philosophies which teach that truth is gained from God by direct revelation, intuition, inspiration, or some sort of religious ecstasy. Many of the beliefs are derived from Brahmanism and Buddhism, including the false doctrine of the transmigration of souls.

The principle of receiving revealed truth from Deity is of course part of the very foundation of true religion. But just as there are true and false churches, and true and false prophets, so there are both actual and spurious revelations. Some revelations are of God and some are not. Those purporting to come by contacts made by theosophists are outside the channels which the Lord has set up and are not of God.

THIEF IN THE NIGHT.

See SECOND COMING OF CHRIST.

THIEVES.

See STEALING.

THOUGHTS.

See DESIRES, IDLE WORDS, JUDGMENT DAY, LIGHT-MINDEDNESS. *Thoughts* are the ideas, concepts, judgments, imaginations, fancies, opinions, dispositions, and intentions that arise in the hearts and minds of men. The power to think is an inheritance which all men receive because they are the spirit children of an Omnipotent Father. It is the spirit that thinks, not the mortal tabernacle. The manner in which this power is used (including the thoughts that come into their minds) depends on the manner in which men exercise the agency with which they have been endowed by their Creator.

The thoughts of the Lord are infinite, eternal, and perfect, for he knows all things and has all power. "My thoughts are not your thoughts, neither are your ways my ways, saith the Lord. For as the heavens are higher than the earth, so are my ways higher than your ways, and my thoughts than your thoughts." (Isa. 55:8-9; Ps. 33:11; 92:5.) Man's thoughts are open to the view and knowledge of the Lord. (D. & C. 6:16; 33:1; Mosiah 24:12; Alma 18:32; Job 42:2; Ps. 94:11; 139:2; Heb. 4:12.) To his prophets also this power is given as occasion requires. (Jac. 2:5; Alma 10:17; 12:3, 7; 18:16, 18, 20; Hela.

9:41.) Christ frequently exercised his power to read the thoughts of those among whom he ministered. (Matt. 9:4; 12:25; Luke 5:22; 6:8; 9:47; 11:17; 3 Ne. 28:6.)

Evil thoughts are sinful. (Prov. 15:26; 24:9.) They are an abomination in themselves, and they lead to further wickedness. Evils are not committed until they have been thought out in the heart. "For from within, out of the heart of men, proceed evil thoughts, adulteries, fornications, murders, Thefts, covetousness, wickedness, deceit, lasciviousness, an evil eye, blasphemy, pride, foolishness." (Mark 7:21-22; Matt. 15:19; Luke 6:45.) "Behold, I will bring evil upon this people," saith the Lord, "even the fruit of their thoughts." (Jer. 6:19.) It was only after "God saw that the wickedness of man was great in the earth, and that every imagination of the thoughts of his heart was only evil continually" (Gen. 6:5), that he sent the flood of Noah to cleanse the earth.

On the other hand, "The thoughts of the righteous are right." (Prov. 12:5.) They are at the root of all righteous action; wise words and deeds flow from them; and a righteous judgment will be given because of them. Men are what their thoughts make them. "As he thinketh in his heart, so is he." (Prov. 23:7.) Our thoughts will reward or condemn us before the judgment bar. (Alma 12:12-14.) The righteous and the wicked are divided by their thoughts, and the secret thoughts of men will be revealed in the judgment. (D. & C. 88:109.) Righteous thoughts lead to salvation, wicked thoughts to damnation.

"A fanciful and flowery and heated imagination beware of," the Prophet said, "because the things of God are of deep import; and time, and experience, and careful and ponderous and solemn thoughts can only find them out." (Teachings, p. 137.)

Part of man's mortal probation is to see if he can control his thoughts in accordance with righteous principles. The saints are commanded, "Cast away your idle thoughts" (D. & C. 88:69), which obviously includes all evil thoughts, all those that do not edify, and all that are unproductive. Thoughts are idle if they do not work to further man's peace in this life and eternal reward in the next.

King Benjamin counseled his people: "If ye do not watch yourselves, and your thoughts, and your words, and your deeds, and observe the commandments of God, and continue in the faith of what ye have heard concerning the coming of our Lord, even unto the end of your lives, ye must perish." (Mosiah 4:30.) Paul taught that the saints must bring "into captivity every thought to the obedience of Christ." (2 Cor. 10:5.) To be saved men must repent of their evil thoughts. (Acts 8:18-24.) "Let the wicked forsake his way, and the unrighteous man his thoughts: and let him return unto the Lord, and he will have mercy upon him; and to our God, for he will abundantly pardon." (Isa. 55:7.)

Men should think on the things of righteousness. They should meditate upon the great truths which the Lord has revealed. "Let virtue garnish thy thoughts unceasingly." (D. & C. 121:45.) Above all, men should think of the Lord and his infinite goodness. "Look unto me in every thought" (D. & C. 6:36), is his plea. (Alma 37:36.) "For how knoweth a man the master whom he has not served, and who is a stranger unto him, and is far from the thoughts and intents of his heart?" (Mosiah 5:13.)

Those who "commit" their "works unto the Lord," have power to control and establish their thoughts. (Prov. 16:3.) They have power to gain new thoughts by revelation from the Holy Ghost. When they speak about the Lord and his laws, they are enabled to do so without reading a prepared essay. "Neither take ye thought beforehand what ye shall say; but treasure up in your minds continually the words of life, and it shall be given you in the very hour that portion that shall be meted unto every man." (D. & C. 84:85; 100:5-6; Matt. 10:19; Mark 13:11; Luke 12:11.)

PHITES AND LAMANITES, TRANSLATED BEINGS. Three of the Nephites disciples, desiring to continue their apostolic ministry of bringing souls unto Christ, received this promise from the Lord: "Ye shall never taste of death; but ye shall live to behold all the doings of the Father unto the children of men, even until all things shall be fulfilled according to the will of the Father, when I shall come in my glory with the powers of heaven." (3 Ne. 28:7.)

They were to be free from pain and sorrow (except for the sins of the world), and were to minister, "as the angels of God," unto the Jews, Gentiles, scattered tribes of Israel, "and unto all nations, kindreds, tongues, and people." (3 Ne. 28.) They continued their ministry among the Nephites for some 300 years, until the time of Mormon, when they were finally withdrawn because of the wickedness of the people. (4 Ne. 30-37; Morm. 1:13-16.) Unbeknowns to the world, they are continuing their assigned ministry at this time, and there have been occasions when they have appeared to members of the Church in this final dispensation. It is the common practice in the Church to call them the *Three Nephites*.

THREE NEPHITES.
See BOOK OF MORMON, NE-

THREE WITNESSES.
See WITNESSES OF THE BOOK OF MORMON.

THRIFTINESS.
See EMPLOYMENT, IDLENESS, WORK. Waste is sin, *thriftiness* a virtue. To his saints the Lord has given "the fulness of the earth," including everything in and upon it, with the provision that "all these things" are "to be used, with judgment, not to excess, neither by extortion." (D. & C. 59:16-20.) Accordingly members of the Church should practice economy and exercise good management over their monies and properties.

THRONES.
See CROWNS, EXALTATION, JUDGMENT DAY, KINGS, PRIESTESSES, PRIESTS, QUEENS. In the eternal sense, *thrones* are reserved for exalted persons who rule and reign as kings and queens in the highest heaven of the celestial world. It is in such a sphere that "God, even the Father, reigns upon his throne forever and ever." (D. & C. 76:92; Rev. 20:11.) After Christ has presented up the kingdom to his Father, "Then shall he be crowned with the crown of his glory, to sit on the throne of his power to reign forever and ever." (D. & C. 76:108.)

Then shall all those who are joint-heirs with him—who have been "crowned with the glory of his might," and "made equal with him" (D. & C. 88:107)—then shall they also sit upon their thrones and even sit down with our Lord on his throne. *"To him that overcometh will I grant to sit with me in my* throne, *even as I also overcame, and am set down with my Father in his throne."* (Rev. 3:21.) Enoch foresaw this state of exaltation and said: "Thou art God, . . . thou hast made me, and given unto me a right to thy throne." (Moses 7:59.)

In token of their kingship, sovereignty, and dominion, exalted beings shall sit on thrones in eternity. "All thrones and dominions, principalities and power, shall be revealed and set forth upon all who have endured valiantly for the gospel of Jesus Christ." (D. & C. 121:29.) *"Abraham . . . hath entered into his exaltation and sitteth upon his throne,"* as also have other righteous saints of former ages. (D. & C. 132:29, 37.)

In the day of judgment, when the saints "shall judge angels" (1 Cor. 6:3), they shall sit upon thrones. "I saw thrones, and they sat upon them," John recorded, "and judgment was given unto them." (Rev. 20:4.) The Twelve who were with Christ in his ministry "shall sit upon twelve thrones, judging the twelve tribes of Israel." (Matt. 19:28.)

THUMMIM.
See URIM AND THUMMIM.

TIME.
See DAY, DISPENSATION OF THE FULNESS OF TIMES, ETERNITY, MERIDIAN OF TIME, MORTALITY, NIGHT, SEASONS. 1. Any measurable

part of eternity is referred to as *time*. The periods of duration involved in the rotation and other movements of the various planets and heavenly bodies form the unit of *measurement of time*. Thus a 24 hour period is a day of time on this earth, and 365 days are a year of time. "In answer to the question— Is not the reckoning of *God's time, angel's time, prophet's time,* and *man's time,* according to the planet on which they reside? I answer, Yes," the Prophet said. (D. & C. 130:4-5.)

Time exists and is measured on all planets, and a knowledge of the times and laws governing the heavenly bodies is yet to come forth in this dispensation. "If there be bounds set to the heavens or to the seas, or to the dry land, or to the sun, moon, or stars—All the times of their revolutions, all the appointed days, months, and years, and all the days of their days, months, and years, and all their glories, laws, and set times, shall be revealed in the days of the dispensation of the fulness of times." (D. & C. 121:30-31.)

Some of this revelation has already taken place. For instance: We know that on Kolob, where the Lord's time prevails, a day is 1,000 years of our time. (Abra. 3:4; 2 Pet. 3:8.) Thus it is that the time element in the creation of this earth was reckoned "after the *Lord's time,* which was after the time of Kolob; for as yet the Gods had not ap-pointed unto Adam his reckoning." (Abra. 5:13.)

2. As contrasted with eternity, *time* is the period of mortal probation that begins for each person with birth into this world and ends with the natural or temporal death. (D. & C. 39:22; 72:3; 132:7, 18; Rom. 8:18.)

3. *Time* is also any season, age, or period when a particular event is destined to occur. "The *time* shall come when the knowledge of a Savior shall spread throughout every nation, kindred, tongue, and people." (Mosiah 3:20; Eccles. 3:1-2.) "This life is the time for men to prepare to meet God." (Alma 34:32.)

TIMES.
See TIMES OF RESTITUTION.

TIMES AND SEASONS.
See SIGNS OF THE TIMES.

TIMES OF REFRESHING.
See DISPENSATION OF THE FULNESS OF TIMES, MILLENNIUM, NEW HEAVEN AND NEW EARTH, RESTORATION OF ALL THINGS. Peter spoke of the *times of refreshing* which should come from the presence of the Lord at the Second Coming of Christ. (Acts 3:19-21.) His statement has the same meaning as the one in the Tenth Article of Faith which records that "the earth will be *renewed* and receive

its *paradisiacal glory.*" This occurrence is "the *regeneration*" which shall take place "when the Son of man shall sit in the throne of his glory." (Matt. 19:28.) It is also "the day of *transfiguration* . . . When the earth shall be *transfigured.*" (D. & C. 63:20-21.)

This earth was created in a new or paradisiacal state; then, incident to Adam's transgression, it fell to its present telestial state. At the Second Coming of our Lord, it will be *renewed, regenerated, refreshed, transfigured,* become again *a new earth, a paradisiacal earth.* Its millennial status will be a *return* to its pristine state of beauty and glory, the state that existed before the fall.

TIMES OF RESTITUTION.

See DISPENSATION OF THE FULNESS OF TIMES, MILLENNIUM, RESTORATION OF ALL THINGS, SECOND COMING OF CHRIST. Peter taught that the Second Coming of the Son of Man cannot take place "until the *times of restitution* of all things, which God hath spoken by the mouth of all his holy prophets since the world began." (Acts 3:19-21.) The phrase *times of restitution* means the *age or era of restoration;* it is that *period* in the earth's history known as the dispensation of the fulness of times, for in that era all things are to be restored. (Eph. 1:10.)

It should be noted that Peter does not say that all things must be restored before Christ comes, but that the *age, era, period,* or *times* in the earth's history in which restoration is to take place must itself commence. That era did begin in the spring of 1820, but all things will not be revealed until after Christ comes. (D. & C. 101:32-34.)

TIMES OF THE GENTILES.

See SIGNS OF THE TIMES.

TITHING.

See CHURCH WELFARE PLAN, CONSECRATION, FAST OFFERINGS, TITHING SETTLEMENT. One tenth of the *interest* or *increase* of each member of the Church is payable as *tithing* into the *tithing funds* of the Church *each year.* Salaries, wages, gifts, bequests, inheritances, the increase of flocks, herds, and crops, and all income of whatever nature are subject to the law of tithing. (D. & C. 119.) Payment of the requisite tenth does not comply with the law unless the property and money so donated go into the tithing funds of the Church; it is not left with the individual to choose where his tithing contributions shall be made. (*Gospel Kingdom,* pp. 262-266.)

Tithing is a lesser law, consecration the greater. "The Lord revealed to his people in the incipiency of his work a law which was more perfect than the law of tithing. It comprehended larger things, greater power, and a more speedy accomplishment of the purposes of the Lord. But the people were unprepared to live by it, and the Lord, out of mercy to the people, suspended the more perfect law, and gave the law of tithing, in order that there might be means in the storehouse of the Lord for the carrying out of the purposes he had in view: for the gathering of the poor, for the spreading of the gospel to the nations of the earth, for the maintenance of those who were required to give their constant attention, day in and day out, to the work of the Lord, and for whom it was necessary to make some provision. Without this law these things could not be done, neither could temples be built and maintained, nor the poor fed and clothed. Therefore the law of tithing is necessary for the Church, so much so that the Lord has laid great stress upon it." (*Gospel Doctrine*, 5th ed., p. 225.)

Payment of an honest tithing is essential to the attainment of those great blessings which the Lord has in store for his faithful saints. Indeed, the law of consecration itself is the celestial law of property and money, and to gain the celestial world man must be able to abide this higher law, to say nothing of the lesser law of tithing. (D. & C. 88:21-22; 105:5.)

Accordingly, tithing becomes one of the great tests of the personal righteousness of church members. "By this principle," President Joseph F. Smith says, "the loyalty of the people of this Church shall be put to the test. *By this principle it shall be known who is for the kingdom of God and who is against it.* By this principle it shall be seen whose hearts are set on doing the will of God and keeping his commandments, thereby sanctifying the land of Zion unto God, and who are opposed to this principle and have *cut themselves off from the blessings of Zion.* There is a great deal of importance connected with this principle, for by it it shall be known whether we are *faithful* or *unfaithful.* In this respect it is as essential as faith in God, as repentance of sin, as baptism for the remission of sin, or as the laying on of hands for the gift of the Holy Ghost. For if a man keep all the law save one point, and he offend in that, he is a transgressor of the law, and he is not entitled to the fulness of the blessings of the gospel of Jesus Christ. *But when a man keeps all the law that is revealed, according to his strength, his substance, and his ability, though what he does may be little, it is just as acceptable in the sight of God as if he were able to do a thousand times more.*

"The law of tithing is a test by which the people as individuals shall be proved. Any man who fails to observe this principle shall be known as a man who is indifferent to the welfare of Zion, who neglects his duty as a member of the Church. . . . *He neglects to do that which would entitle him to receive the blessings and ordinances of the gospel.*" (*Gospel Doctrine,* 5th ed., pp. 225-226.)

Both temporal and spiritual blessings are poured out upon the honest tithepayer as a result of his obedience to that law. By such obedience he gains the spirit of inspiration in temporal and spiritual pursuits so that in the end he is ahead financially and temporally, to say nothing of the spiritual growth that always attends such a course. (*Gospel Doctrine,* 5th ed., pp. 226-228.)

Through the mouth of Malachi the Lord said: "Bring ye all the tithes into the storehouse, that there may be meat in mine house, and prove me now herewith, saith the Lord of hosts, if I will not open you the windows of heaven, and pour you out a blessing, that there shall not be room enough to receive it. And I will rebuke the devourer for your sakes, and he shall not destroy the fruits of your ground; neither shall your vine cast her fruit before the time in the field, saith the Lord of hosts. And all nations shall call you blessed: for ye shall be a delightsome land, saith the Lord of hosts." (Mal. 3:10-12.)

Since the Lord is bound to confer promised blessings following obedience and to withhold them in the event of disobedience (D. & C. 82:10), members of the Church who fail or neglect to pay an honest tithing are thereby denying themselves of the receipt of these rich blessings. Further, since all saints are under covenant, made in the waters of baptism (Mosiah 18:8-10), to keep all of the commandments of God, it is a serious defalcation on their part to fail to give Deity his tenth of their income. Is it any wonder, then, that we find the scriptures saying that the saints are robbing God when they fail to pay a full tithing, or that those so defaulting place themselves with those who may be burned at the Second Coming? "Will a man rob God? Yet ye have robbed me. But ye say, Wherein have we robbed thee? In tithes and offerings. Ye are cursed with a curse: for ye have robbed me, even this whole nation." (Mal. 3:8-9.)

"Behold, now it is called today until the coming of the Son of Man, and verily it is a day of sacrifice, and a day for the tithing of my people; for *he that is tithed shall not be burned at his coming.* For after today cometh the burning—this is speaking after the manner of the Lord—for verily I say, tomorrow all the proud and they that do wickedly shall be as stubble; and I will burn them up, for I am the Lord of Hosts; and I will not spare any that remain in Babylon. Wherefore, if ye believe me, ye will labor while it is called today." (D. & C. 64:23-25; Mal. 4:1.)

Strictly speaking there is no such thing as a *part tithing*. Tithing is a tenth, and unless a person contributes the tenth, he has only made a contribution to the tithing funds of the Church. Somewhat inappropriately the term *part-tithepayer* is used with reference to those making such contributions.

TITHING SETTLEMENT.

See TITHING. At the end of each year certain convenient days are set apart for *tithing settlement.* On these days church members are privileged to go over their personal tithing records with their bishop, and to receive counsel from him, so that the tithing status of each member is clearly known both to him and his ecclesiastical judge. As a matter of wisdom, tithing should be paid when income is received, though it is possible to comply with the law by a lump sum contribution at the time of tithing settlement.

TITLES.

See MINISTERIAL TITLES.

TOBACCO.

See WORD OF WISDOM.

TOLERANCE.

See AGENCY, BIGOTRY, BROAD-MINDEDNESS. Gospel *tolerance* tempers the zeal of the saints so that they put up with and allow the false religious beliefs and practices of all people. Men are entitled to worship and believe as they choose, and no matter how false and ab-surd their notions may be, they are tolerated by the saints. (Eleventh Article of Faith.)

All men have weaknesses; none are perfect. Accordingly, in their personal relations with each other, the Lord expects men to bear with the infirmities and shortcomings of each other. (D. & C. 42:43-44, 52; 46:13-14.) But proper tolerance extends, not to sin, but to sinners. Neither the Lord nor the saints can "look upon sin with the least degree of allowance." (D. & C. 1:31.)

TOMBS.

See GRAVES.

TONGUES.

See DAY OF PENTECOST, GIFTS OF THE SPIRIT, MIRACLES, SIGNS. Two of the gifts of the Spirit are *speaking in tongues* and *interpretation of tongues.* (Moro. 10:15-16; D. & C. 46:24-25; 1 Cor. 12:10, 28, 30; 14.) These gifts have been manifest among the saints in every age (Omni 25; Alma 9:21; 3 Ne. 29:6; Morm. 9:7), and they are desirable and useful in the Lord's work. "Let the gift of tongues be poured out upon thy people, even cloven tongues as of fire, and the interpretation thereof," the Prophet prayed at the dedication of the Kirtland Temple. (D. & C. 109:36.)

Tongues and their interpretation are classed among the signs and miracles which always attend the faithful and which stand as evidences of the divinity of the Lord's work. (Morm. 9:24; Mark 16:17; Acts 10:46; 19:6.) In their more dramatic manifestations they consist in speaking or interpreting, by the power of the Spirit, a tongue which is completely unknown to the speaker or interpreter. Sometimes it is the pure Adamic language which is involved. Frequently these gifts are manifest where the ordinary languages of the day are concerned in that the Lord's missionaries learn to speak and interpret foreign languages with ease, thus furthering the spread of the message of the restoration. When the elders of Israel, often in a matter of weeks, gain fluency in a foreign tongue, they have been blessed with the gift of tongues.

An ideal and proper use of tongues was shown forth on the day of Pentecost. By using this gift the apostles were enabled to speak in their own tongue and be understood by persons of many different tongues. (Acts 2:1-18.) Indeed, "the gift of tongues by the power of the Holy Ghost in the Church," as the Prophet said, "is for the benefit of the servants of God *to preach to unbelievers,* as on the day of Pentecost." (*Teachings,* p. 195.) "Be not so curious about tongues," the Prophet also said. *"Do not speak in tongues except there be an interpreter present; the ultimate design of tongues is to speak to foreigners,* and if persons are very anxious to display their intelligence, let them speak to such in their own tongues [that is, in the tongues of the foreigners]." (*Teachings,* pp. 247-248.)

Caution should always attend the use of the gift of tongues. "It is not necessary," for instance, "for tongues to be taught to the Church particularly, for any man that has the Holy Ghost, can speak of the things of God in his own tongue as well as to speak in another; for faith comes not by signs, but by hearing the word of God." (*Teachings,* pp. 148-149.) *"If anything is taught by the gift of tongues, it is not to be received for doctrine."* (*Teachings,* p. 229.) *"Speak not in the gift of tongues without understanding it, or without interpretation. The devil can speak in tongues;* the adversary will come with his work; he can tempt all classes; can speak in English or Dutch. Let no one speak in tongues unless he interpret, except by the consent of the one who is placed to preside; then he may discern or interpret, or another may." (*Teachings,* p. 162, 212.)

Tongues and their interpretation are given for special purposes under special circumstances. There are a host of gifts that are far more important and in the use of which there is less chance for deception. The gifts of exhortation, of preaching, of expounding doctrine, of teaching the gospel—though not nearly so dramatic—are far greater and of more value than tongues. "In the church I had rather speak five words with my understanding, that by my voice I might teach others also," Paul averred, "than ten thousand words in an unknown tongue." (1 Cor. 14:19.)

As with other spiritual gifts, tongues "never will be done away," as long as the earth remains in its present state, "only according to the unbelief of the children of men." (Moro. 10:19.) But in the ultimate perfect day the gifts pertaining to tongues "shall cease." (1 Cor. 13:8.) Obviously in that final glorious day when the saints know all things (which includes a perfect knowledge of all languages) it will no longer be either necessary or possible to speak in tongues and give interpretation thereto.

TORMENT.
See FIRE AND BRIMSTONE.

TORNADOES.
See SIGNS OF THE TIMES.

TOWER OF BABEL.
See JAREDITES.

TRADITIONS.
See DOCTRINE, GOSPEL, REVELATION, SCRIPTURE, STANDARD WORKS, TRUTH. Religious *traditions* are the laws, regulations, beliefs, doctrines and practices which are handed down (usually orally) from one generation to another. Tradi-

tions are either true or false. If they are in accord with the scriptures, they are true; if they go contrary to the written, revealed word, they are false. If they pertain to matters on which the revelations are silent, they may be true or false, and in such cases there is danger in accepting them. The Lord has given sufficient in writing to guide men to salvation without the necessity of turning to fields of religion not covered in the written word.

True gospel teachings which can be amply supported from the revelations are sometimes referred to as traditions whether these teachings are presented orally or in writing. The Book of Mormon frequently contrasts the true traditions of the Nephites, which led to salvation, with the false traditions of the Lamanites, which led to destruction. (Alma 3:8; 23:5; 24:7; 3 Ne. 1:9-11.) Paul exhorted the saints to "stand fast, and hold the traditions which ye have been taught, whether by word, or our epistle." (2 Thess. 2:15; 3:6.)

The most common usage of the term, however, associates it with false and apostate views. (Gal. 1: 14; Col. 2:8; 1 Pet. 1:18; D. & C. 93:39.) In some churches, traditions consist in the code of doctrine and discipline which is independent of the written word, but is considered to be sufficient to refute heresy; it is falsely supposed to have been established originally by Christ and his apostles and to have been handed down from generation to generation from them. It is obvious that the devil can have a real field day in spreading false doctrine when oral traditions are given the force of divine law.

As with all apostate peoples, false traditions existed among the Jews, causing our Lord to ask: "Why do ye also transgress the commandment of God by your tradition?" and then to say of that apostate people that their worship was vain because they taught for doctrine the commandments of men. (Matt. 15:1-9; Mark 7:1-8.) It is interesting to note that one of the false traditions had among the Jews anciently was that "little children are unholy," which is the same apostate concept held by the Catholics and many Protestants at this day.. (D. & C. 74.)

TRAITORS.

See APOSTASY, REBELLION, SONS OF PERDITION, UNPARDONABLE SIN. Gospel *traitors* are those who forsake the truth, betray the cause of Christ, and use their power in the camp of Lucifer the enemy. Traitors are the worst kind of apostates; they not only slip away themselves from the path of righteousness, but they give aid and comfort to the enemy and enlist affimatively in his cause.

Lucifer was a traitor in pre-existence. Judas is the prototype of all mortal traitors. (Luke 6:16.) In large part the persecutions and

trials heaped upon the saints have their origin with apostate-traitors. (*Teachings,* pp. 66-68; D. & C. 122: 3; 135:7.)

Traitors will be damned. Speaking of traitors in general, those who betray any cause no matter what it is, the Prophet said: "As the Lord lives, God never will acknowledge any traitors or apostates. Any man who will betray the Catholics will betray you; and if he will betray me, he will betray you." (*Teachings,* p. 375.)

TRANCES.

See DREAMS, REVELATION, VISIONS. Sometimes prophets go into *trances* in connection with the receipt of visions. That is, they are so completely overshadowed by the Spirit that to all outward appearances normal bodily functions are suspended. Such was the case with Balaam when he saw the coming of Christ and the triumph of Israel. (Num. 24.) Peter "fell into a trance" when he received the vision commanding him to take the gospel to the Gentiles. (Acts 10:9-48.) Paul "was in a trance" when the Lord came to him with the command to leave Jerusalem and carry the message of salvation to the Gentiles. (Acts 22:17-21.)

A similar experience happened to the Prophet Joseph Smith in connection with the First Vision; he was not in control of all his bodily powers when the Father and the Son appeared to him. "When I came to myself again, I found myself lying on my back, looking up into heaven," he said. "When the light had departed, I had no strength; but soon recovering in some degree, I went home." (Jos. Smith 2:20.)

TRANSFIGURATION.

See HOLY GHOST, MILLENNIUM, TIMES OF REFRESHING, TRANSLATED BEINGS. *Transfiguration* is a special change in appearance and nature which is wrought upon a person or thing by the power of God. This divine transformation is from a lower to a higher state; it results in a more exalted, impressive, and glorious condition.

Our Lord "was transfigured before" Peter, James, and John, while on the mount, "and his face did shine as the sun, and his raiment was white as the light." (Matt. 17: 1-13; Mark 9:2-13; 2 Pet. 1:16-19.) Luke describes this event by saying, "As he prayed, the fashion of his countenance was altered, and his raiment was white and glistering." (Luke 9:28-36.) It was on this occasion that Peter, James, and John, also, "were transfigured before" Christ, received from him and from Moses and Elias the keys of the kingdom (*Teachings*, p. 158), and saw in vision the transfiguration of the earth in the millennial day. (D. & C. 63:20-21; *Teachings*, p. 13.)

By the power of the Holy Ghost many prophets have been trans-figured so as to stand in the presence of God and view the visions of eternity. Speaking of such an occasion in his life, Moses recorded: "Now mine own eyes have beheld God; but not my natural, but my spiritual eyes, for my natural eyes could not have beheld; for I should have withered and died in his presence; but his glory was upon me; and I beheld his face, for I was transfigured before him." (Moses 1:11; D. & C. 67:11.) On another occasion, when Moses came down off the mount, having communed with the Lord for 40 days and nights, "the skin of his face shone," so that he had to "put a vail on his face" as he talked with the children of Israel. (Ex. 34:29-35.)

Similarly, when the Three Nephites "were caught up into heaven, and saw and heard unspeakable things," they were transfigured. "Whether they were in the body or out of the body, they could not tell; for it did seem unto them like a transfiguration of them, that they were changed from this body of flesh into an immortal state, that they could behold the things of God." (3 Ne. 28:13-17.) Paul had a similar experience (2 Cor. 12:1-4), as also did Joseph Smith and Sidney Rigdon. (D. & C. 76; *Teachings*, p. 107.)

TRANSFIGURATION OF THE EARTH.

See TIMES OF REFRESHING.

TRANSGRESSION.

See SIN, TRANSGRESSION OF ADAM. In a general sense and in most instances the terms *sin* and *transgression* are synonymous, although the use of the term transgression lays emphasis on the violation of the law or rule involved whereas the term sin points up the wilful nature of the disobedience. There are situations, however, in which it is possible to transgress a law without committing a sin, as in the case of Adam and Eve in the Garden of Eden. (2 Ne. 2:22-23.)

TRANSGRESSION OF ADAM.

See AGENCY, FALL OF ADAM, FORBIDDEN FRUIT, SIN, TRANSGRESSION. It is proper and according to the scriptural pattern to speak of the *transgression of Adam,* but not the *sin of Adam.* (D. & C. 20:20; 29:40; Job 31:33; Rom. 5:14; 1 Tim. 2:14; Alma 12:31; Second Article of Faith.) Lehi says, for instance, "If Adam had not transgressed he would not have fallen." Then he explains that while in their state of innocence in the Garden of Eden, Adam and Eve "knew no sin." (2 Ne. 2:22-23.) Knowledge of good and evil is an essential element in the commision of sin, and our first parents did not have this knowledge until after they had partaken of the fruit of the tree of knowledge of good and evil.

TRANSLATED BEINGS.

See ANGELS, CHURCH OF ENOCH, DEATH, GUARDIAN ANGELS, MINISTERING OF ANGELS, RESURRECTION, THREE NEPHITES. During the first 2200 or so years of the earth's history—that is, from the fall of Adam to the ministry of Melchizedek—it was a not uncommon occurrence for faithful members of the Church to be translated and taken into the heavenly realms without tasting death. Since that time there have been occasional special instances of translation, instances in which a special work of the ministry required it.

Enoch and his people were translated, probably just a few years after Adam's death. (Moses 7:18-21, 31, 63, 69; D. & C. 38:4; 45:11-14; 84:99-100; Gen. 5:22-24; Heb. 11:5.) It is apparent from the abbreviated account of the Lord's dealings with Enoch and his people that Zion was a very great and populous city, having perhaps many thousands or even millions of inhabitants. (Moses 7.) Methuselah, the son of Enoch, was not translated, "that the covenants of the Lord might be fulfilled, which he made to Enoch; for he truly covenanted with Enoch that Noah should be of the fruit of his loins." (Moses 8:2.) But during the nearly 700 years from the translation of Enoch to the flood of Noah, it would appear that nearly all of the faithful members of the Church were translated, for "the Holy Ghost fell on many, and they were caught up by the powers of heaven into Zion." (Moses 7:27.)

That this process of translating

the righteous saints and taking them to heaven was still going on after the flood among the people of Melchizedek is apparent from the account in the Inspired Version of the Bible. Speaking of the faith and righteousness of those holding the Melchizedek Priesthood in that day, the account says: *"And men having this faith, coming up unto this order of God, were translated and taken up into heaven.* And now, Melchizedek was a priest of this order, therefore he obtained peace in Salem, and was called the Prince of peace. *And his people wrought righteousness, and obtained heaven, and sought for the city of Enoch* which God had before taken, separating it from the earth, having reserved it unto the latter days, or the end of the world." (*Inspired Version,* Gen. 14:32-34.)

As far as we know, instances of translation since the day of Melchizedek and his people have been few and far between. After recording that Enoch was translated, Paul says that Abraham, Isaac, and Jacob, and their seed after them (they obviously knowing what had taken place as pertaining to the people of Melchizedek and others) "looked for a city which hath foundations, whose builder and maker is God" (Heb. 11:5-10), that is, they "sought for the city of Enoch which God had before taken." (*Inspired Version,* Gen. 14:34.) But as Paul said, and as the Lord confirmed by latter-day revelation, even these "holy men . . . found it not because

of wickedness and abominations; And confessed they were strangers and pilgrims on the earth; But obtained a promise that they should find it and see it in their flesh." (D. & C. 45:11-14; Heb. 11:11-16.)

Moses, Elijah, and Alma the younger, were translated. The Old Testament account that Moses died and was buried by the hand of the Lord in an unknown grave is an error. (Deut. 34:5-7.) It is true that he may have been "buried by the hand of the Lord," if that expression is a figure of speech which means that he was translated. But the Book of Mormon account, in recording that Alma "was taken up by the Spirit," says, "the scriptures saith the Lord took Moses unto himself; and we suppose that he has also received Alma in the spirit, unto himself." (Alma 45:18-19.) It should be remembered that the Nephites had the Brass Plates, and that they were the "scriptures" which gave the account of Moses being taken by way of translation. As to Elijah, the account of his being taken in "a chariot of fire . . . by a whirlwind into heaven," is majestically set out in the Old Testament. (2 Kings 2.)

Moses and Elijah were translated so that they could come with bodies of flesh and bones to confer keys upon Peter, James, and John on the mount of transfiguration, an event destined to occur prior to the beginning of the resurrection. (Matt. 17:1-6; *Teachings,* p. 158; *Doctrines of Salvation,* vol. 2, pp. 107-111.) The reason for the translation of Alma has not been revealed.

Before our Lord, in the meridian of time, opened the door to the preaching of the gospel to the spirits in prison (Moses 7:36-40; 1 Pet. 3: 18-20), many of the righteous saints were translated and thus given other ministries to perform pending the day of their final redemption. The Prophet says that translated beings are "held in reserve to be ministering angels unto many planets." (*Teachings*, p. 170.) But since the inauguration of the great work of proclaiming the gospel to the spirits in prison, almost every righteous person in the Church has been permitted, in due course, to die and go to an assigned labor in the spirit world.

However, for special purposes a few persons who have lived in the Christian Era have been translated. Our Lord said on one occasion, "There be *some* standing here, which shall not taste of death, till they see the Son of man coming in his kingdom." (Matt. 16:28; Mark 9: 1; Luke 9:27.) The Lord may have had reference to these or other translated persons when he said in March, 1831, "All are under sin, except those which I have reserved unto myself, holy men that ye know not of." (D. & C. 49:8.) Possibly John was present when the original statement was made. In any event John was translated. (John 21:20-23; Rev. 10; D. & C. 7; 77:14.) And on the American continent, among the Nephites, three of the Twelve were also given power over death so that they could continue their ministry until the Second Coming. (3 Ne. 28.)

There are no other known instances of translation during the Christian Era, and unless there is some special reason which has not so far been revealed, it is not likely that there will be any more translations before the Second Coming. During the millennial era, however, all men will live in a state comparable in many respects to the state of translated beings. (D. & C. 101: 23-31; Isa. 11:1-9; 65:17-25.)

"Now the doctrine of translation is a power which belongs to this [the Melchizedek] Priesthood," the Prophet taught. "Many have supposed that the doctrine of translation was a doctrine whereby men were taken immediately into the presence of God, and into an eternal fulness, but this is a mistaken idea. Their place of habitation is that of the *terrestrial order,* and a place prepared for such characters He held in reserve to be ministering angels unto many planets, and who as yet have not entered into so great a fulness as those who are resurrected from the dead. 'Others were tortured, not accepting deliverance; that they might obtain a better resurrection.' (Heb. 11:35.)

"Now it was evident that there was a better resurrection, or else God would not have revealed it unto Paul. Wherein then, can it be said a better resurrection? This distinction is made between the doctrine of the actual resurrection and translation: translation obtains deliverance from the tortures and sufferings of the body, but their existence will prolong as to the labors and toils of the ministry, before they can enter into so great a rest and glory.

"On the other hand, those who were tortured, not accepting deliverance, received an immediate rest from their labors. 'And I heard a voice from heaven saying unto me, Write, Blessed are the dead which die in the Lord from henceforth: Yea, saith the Spirit, that they may rest from their labours; and their works do follow them.' (Rev. 14: 13.)

"They rest from their labors for a long time, and yet their work is held in reserve for them, that they are permitted to do the same work after they receive a resurrection for their bodies." (*Teachings*, pp. 170-171.)

It is from the account of the translation of the Three Nephites that we gain most of our knowledge of the present ministry among men of translated beings. It is very evident that such persons "never taste of death; . . . never endure the pains of death"; that they have undergone a change in their bodies, "that they might not suffer pain nor sorrow save it were for the sins of the world"; that they were holy men, "sanctified in the flesh"; "that the powers of the earth could not hold them"; that "they are as the angels of God," ministering to whomsoever

they will; that they "shall be changed in the twinkling of an eye from mortality to immortality" at the Second Coming; and that they shall then inherit exaltation in the kingdom of God. (3 Ne. 28.)

This final change from mortality to immortality is in effect their death, for all men die, even those who are alive when Christ comes, and those who will live during the millennium. "Children shall grow up until they become old," the Lord says of the millennial era. "Old men shall die; but they shall not sleep in the dust, but they shall be changed in the twinkling of an eye." (D. & C. 63:49-52; 101:23-31.) It is interesting to note that John in recording the Lord's promise to him, apparently knew that he should not "taste" death or "endure" the pains thereof, yet knew that he would pass through a change equivalent to death. "Then went this saying abroad among the brethren, that that disciple should not die," John says, "yet Jesus said not unto him, He shall not die; but, If I will that he tarry till I come, what is that to thee?" (John 21:20-23.)

All translated beings accordingly receive what amounts to an instantaneous death and resurrection. Those who were translated before the resurrection of our Lord "were with Christ in his resurrection." (D. & C. 133:55.) Those who have been translated since the resurrection of Christ shall continue to live as mortals until the Second Coming when they shall receive their immortal glory. It will be resurrected, not translated beings, who shall return with the city of Enoch.

TRANSMIGRATION OF SOULS.
See REINCARNATION.

TRAVELING PRESIDING HIGH COUNCIL.
See APOSTLES, APOSTOLIC SUCCESSION, FIRST PRESIDENCY, HIGH COUNCIL. "The Twelve are a *Traveling Presiding High Council,* to officiate in the name of the Lord, under the direction of the Presidency of the Church, agreeable to the institution of heaven; to build up the church, and regulate all the affairs of the same in all nations, first unto the Gentiles and secondly unto the Jews." (D. & C. 107: 33.)

TREASON.
See TRAITORS.

TREASURES IN HEAVEN.
See RICHES OF ETERNITY.

TRESPASSES.
See TRANSGRESSION.

TRIALS.
See AFFLICTIONS, SECOND ESTATE, SORROW, TEMPTATION, TRIBULATIONS. Man has been placed on earth in a mortal body for the express purpose of undergoing *trials,* including hardship, suffering, and temptation. (Abra. 3:25-26.) This is particularly true of the saints, those who espouse the cause of truth and go forth on the Lord's errand. (2 Cor. 8:2; Heb. 11:36; 1 Pet. 1:6-9; 4:12-13; Ether 12:6; D. & C. 105:19.) "I will prove you in all things," the Lord says, "whether you will abide in my covenant, even unto death, that you may be found worthy." (D. & C. 98:14; 101:4.) "My people must be tried in all things, that they may be prepared to receive the glory that I have for them, even the glory of Zion; and he that will not bear chastisement is not worthy of my kingdom." (D. & C. 136: 31.)

TRIBES OF ISRAEL.
See BIRTHRIGHT, ISRAEL, KINGDOM OF ISRAEL, LOST TRIBES OF ISRAEL, NEPHITES AND LAMANITES. Jacob's 12 sons became the heads of the *tribes of Israel.* They were: Reuben, Simeon, Levi, Judah, Issachar, and Zebulun, the sons of Leah; Dan and Naphtali, the sons of Bilhah; Gad and Asher, the sons of Zilpah; Joseph and Benjamin, the sons of Rachel. (Gen. 29; 30.) These same 12 received from their father Jacob patriarchal blessings, foretelling the destinies of their descendants. (Gen. 49.)

However, Jacob also blessed Ephraim and Manasseh, the sons of Joseph, and adopted them as his own. "Behold, *they are mine,*" the record says, "and the God of my fathers shall bless them; even as Reuben and Simeon they shall be blessed, for they are mine; wherefore *they shall be called after my name.* (Therefore they were called Israel.) And thy issue which thou begettest after them, shall be thine, and shall be called after the name of their brethren in their inheritance, in the tribes; therefore they were called the *tribes of Manasseh and of Ephraim.*" (*Inspired Version,* Gen. 48:5-6.)

Thus Joseph inherited a double portion of Israel, and because the Lord chose the Levites to be his ministers (Ex. 32:25-29; Num. 8) an inheritance was given to both Ephraim and Manasseh in the promised land. (Num. 1; Josh. 13:14, 33; 14:1-5.)

When John recorded his vision of the special mission for 12,000 of each of the tribes of Israel, he named Levi, Manasseh, and Joseph (meaning Ephraim) in the list and for some reason that is not apparent left out the tribe of Dan. (Rev. 7; D. & C. 77:11.) Scholars speculate that "the tribe of Dan is not mentioned, perhaps because of a Jewish tradition that Antichrist was to come from the tribe." (Dummelow, *The One Volume Bible Commentary,* p. 1079.)

TRIBULATIONS.

See AFFLICTIONS, SIGNS OF THE TIMES. As part of their mortal probation the saints are called upon to pass through *tribulations,* that is to undergo severe afflictions, distress, and deep sorrow. (D. & C. 78:14; 109:5; 112:13; 122:5.) "In the world ye shall have tribulation," our Lord said. (John 16:33.)

"Tribulation worketh patience" (Rom. 5:3; 12:12; D. & C. 54:10), and it is only "through much tribulation" that men may "enter into the kingdom of God." (Acts 14:22.) *"He that is faithful in tribulation, the reward of the same is greater in the kingdom of heaven.* Ye cannot behold with your natural eyes, for the present time, the design of your God concerning those things which shall come hereafter, and the glory which shall follow after much tribulation. For *after much tribulation come the blessings.*" (D. & C. 58:2-4; 103:12.) Exalted beings are described in these words: "These are they which came out of great tribulation, and have washed their robes, and made them white in the blood of the Lamb." (Rev. 7:14.) The saints glory in tribulation. (Rom. 5:3; D. & C. 127:2.)

Afflictions are also poured out upon the wicked. (Rom. 2:9.) Particularly is this the case in the last days. (D. & C. 29:8; Matt. 24:29.)

TRIBUNALS.

See CHURCH COURTS.

TRINITY.

See GODHEAD.

TRUE SHEPHERD.
See GOOD SHEPHERD.

TRUE VINE.
See CHRIST, PERSONIFICATION.
Christ is the *True Vine*, his Father
is the *Husbandman,* his prophets
are the branches, and the fruit
which the branches bear is eternal
life for the souls of men. (John 15:1-
8.) Thus without the Father there
would be no Christ, without Christ
there would be no prophets, without prophets there would be no
fruit of eternal life.

TRUTH.
See CHRIST, GOSPEL, HOLY
GHOST, INTELLIGENCE, KNOWL-
EDGE, LIGHT, MORMONISM, REV-
ELATION, SPIRIT OF TRUTH, TESTI-
MONY. 1. Christ is the *Truth,*
meaning that he is the perfect embodiment of all truth. "I am the
way, the truth, and the life" (John
14:6; Ether 4:12); "I am the Spirit
of truth." (D. & C. 93:26.) He is
the champion of truth, the revealer
of truth, the advocate of truth. His
word is truth and all his works conform thereto. "He is full of grace
and truth" (2 Ne. 2:6; John 1:14,
17; D. & C. 93:11), and he came
into the world to "bear witness unto
the truth." (John 18:37.)

2. To Pilate's query, *"What is
truth?"* (John 18:38), there is no
recorded answer. But explicit scriptural definitions are found elsewhere. Truth is an attribute of

Deity, of the "Lord God of truth."
(Ps. 31:5.) He is "longsuffering, and
abundant in goodness and truth"
(Ex. 34:6), "a God of truth and
without iniquity, just and right is
he." (Deut. 32:4; D. & C. 84:102;
109:77; Alma 5:48; 9:26; 13:9.)

The Lord's "law is the truth"
(Ps. 119:142), all his "commandments are truth" (Ps. 119:151), all
his "works are truth" (Dan. 4:37),
his scriptures are truth (Dan. 10:
21), and his "word is truth." (John
17:17.) "The word of the Lord is
truth, and whatsoever is truth is
light, and whatsoever is light is
Spirit, even the Spirit of Jesus
Christ." (D. & C. 84:45.) The Book
of Mormon is an illustration of the
truth, for, "as your Lord and your
God liveth it is true." (D. & C.
17:6; Moses 7:62; Ps. 85:11; D. & C.
128:19.) "Truth is knowledge of
things as they are, and as they
were, and as they are to come." (D.
& C. 93:24.) *Truth thus conforms to
reality, is centered in God, and is
as enduring as Deity himself.*

*Truth is absolute and eternal; it
endureth forever.* (D. & C. 1:39; 88:
66; Ps. 100:5; 117:2.) *It never varies;
what is true in one age is true in
every age.* The theories of men
(scientific or otherwise) vary from
discovery to discovery and are in a
continuing state of flux, unless they
chance on a particular point to
reach ultimate truth. Then there
is no more change, and the truth
discovered is in complete harmony
with every other truth in every

other field. *Truth never conflicts with truth.*

Truth is not relative; it is absolute. What is true in one eternity is true in the next. The knowledge men have of the truth may be great at one time and slight in another, or the reverse, but the quantity of ultimate truth is neither added to nor diminished from by revelations received or discoveries made. For instance: Jesus Christ is the Son of God and salvation is based on his atoning sacrifice. Accountable persons can be saved only on conditions of faith, repentance, baptism, receipt of the gift of the Holy Ghost, and enduring in righteousness to the end. These are eternal, absolute truths. They apply to every living person from Adam to the last man. There is nothing relative about them. Similarly: Joseph Smith was the anointed of the Lord in the restoration of the gospel in latter-days. The Church of Jesus Christ of Latter-day Saints is the Lord's kingdom on earth and the only place where salvation may be found. Again these are absolute, eternal, ultimate truths.

The only field in which men have the assurance that there is any measurable knowledge of ultimate truth is in the field of revealed religion. Certainly there are many scientific discoveries which are pure truth, but there are also many scientific theories in which fact and hypothesis are intermingled. There are also many truths in all

churches, but the measure of truth required to assure salvation is found only in the Church were God has placed it according to his own will. Mormonism, so-called, is thus a synonym for truth. "Have the Presbyterians any truth?" the Prophet asked. "Yes. Have the Baptists, Methodists, etc., any truth? Yes. They all have a little truth mixed with error. We should gather all the good and true principles in the world and treasure them up, or we shall not come out true Mormons." (*Teachings*, p. 316.)

Men are saved if they believe the truth, but damned if they believe not the truth. (2 Thess. 2:11-13.) To gain salvation they must worship, "in spirit and in truth, the true and the living God." (Alma 43:10; John 4:23-24.) Apostasy results when men reject the truth (1 Tim. 6:3-5; 2 Tim. 4:3-4; 2 Pet. 2:1-2; 1 John 1:8), and one of the signs of the times is that men "in the last days" are "Ever learning, and never able to come to the knowledge of the truth." (2 Tim. 3:1-7.)

"The Holy Ghost is a revelator." (*Teachings*, p. 328.) One of his great missions is to reveal truth. (Jac. 4:13; D. & C. 79:2; 91:4-6.) "When he, the Spirit of truth, is come, he will guide you into all truth," our Lord said. (John 16:13.) A testimony of the gospel comes by revelation from the Holy Ghost; the truth of the Book of Mormon is known by this same means; "And by the power of the Holy Ghost ye may know the truth of all things." (Moro. 10:3-5.)

Finally, those who gain exaltation will receive "a fulness of truth, yea, even of all truth," even as Christ did. "And no man receiveth a fulness unless he keepeth his commandments. He that keepeth his commandments receiveth truth and light, until he is glorified in truth and knoweth all things." (D. & C. 93:26-28.)

TRUTHFULNESS.
See HONESTY.

TURMOIL.
See SIGNS OF THE TIMES.

TWELFTH-DAY.
See EPIPHANY.

TWELVE APOSTLES.
See APOSTLES.

TYPES AND SHADOWS.
See SYMBOLISMS.

U

UNBELIEVERS.
See BELIEVERS.

UNCHANGEABLENESS.
See ETERNITY TO ETERNITY.

UNCHASTITY.
See SEX IMMORALITY.

UNCHRISTIAN-LIKE CONDUCT.
See CHRISTIANITY, OBEDIENCE, SEX IMMORALITY. In a general sense, *unchristian-like conduct* means any course of action inharmonious with the high standards of the gospel. It includes dishonesty, cruelty to wives and children, drunkenness, and criminal offenses of all sorts. Specifically, and according to common usage, it is an expression used to refer to adultery or some other gross form of sex immorality, the commission of which warrants excommunication from the true Christian Church.

UNCLEANNESS.
See SEX IMMORALITY.

UNCTION.
See EXTREME UNCTION, GIFT OF THE HOLY GHOST. 1. Literally, an

unction is the act of anointing, as with oil for medicinal purposes; figuratively, it is an anointing from on high, meaning that those so endowed receive the gift of the Holy Ghost. Thus John said of the saints, "Ye have an unction from the Holy One, and ye know all things" (1 John 2:20), that is, they had received the Holy Ghost so that the spirit of revelation and knowledge rested with them.

2. *Unction* has also come to mean that quality in language which excites sober and fervent emotion or religious fervor. Often the result is a simulated fervor or emotional gush. Thus *unctuous speech* is that which breathes a smugly or ingratiatingly sentimental pretense of spirituality or attitude. It is a type of canting, hypocritical exuberance common to a certain class of sectarian ministers and against which Christ's true ministers must be on guard.

UNDERSTANDING.
See KNOWLEDGE.

UNGODLINESS.
See WICKEDNESS.

UNITED ORDER.
See BISHOPS STOREHOUSES, CHURCH WELFARE PLAN, CONSECRATION, STEWARDSHIPS, TITHING. In order to live the law of consecration, the early saints in this dispensation set up the *United Order* as the legal organization to receive consecrations, convey stewardships back to donors, and to regulate the storehouses containing surplus properties.

The United Order is not a communal system; it is not one under which all things are held in common. Rather, after a person has made his consecration, the Lord's agent forthwith reconveys to the donor "as much as is sufficient for himself and family" (D. & C. 42:32), each "according to his family, according to his circumstances and his wants and needs" (D. & C. 51:3), "inasmuch as his wants are just." (D. & C. 82:17.)

Early attempts to operate various united orders failed, but the law of consecration must yet be put into full force, and so the United Order or its equivalent must again be brought into being. It appears that operation of the present Church Welfare Plan may be the beginning of this.

Elder Albert E. Bowen has written: "The Welfare Plan as an integral part of the church organization is a striking counterpart to the pattern laid down in the early revelations concerning the care of the saints. One tenth of the increase annually of members is consecrated to the needs of the Church—a true and irrevocable consecration—augmented by the fast offering. There is not a consecration of all with 'inheritances' given back, but there is a retention of individual poses-

813

sions, with a duty of 'stewardship' reaching out to the tithe, and the fast and the sundry contributions for the building up of the Church, sustaining its missionary system, its temples, houses of worship and the like. There are the storehouses, where are kept something comparable to the 'residues' being surplus accumulations, multiplied by the vast commodity productive power which grows out of free will offerings in time and labor. There are the bishops charged with the same duties of receiving the contributions or consecrations, whichever name we prefer, preserving them and caring for the material needs of the sick or distressed. *It is not asserted that the Welfare Plan is the United Order, but perhaps there is a much greater nearness of approach than we have been accustomed to think.* Safe it is to say that a complete living of the law governing this Plan, and the practice of the principles involved, would make *transition to the organization of the United Order not too difficult.*" (Albert E. Bowen, *The Church Welfare Plan,* p. 145.)

UNITED STATES OF AMERICA.

See CONSTITUTION OF THE UNITED STATES.

UNITY.

See EXALTATION, GODHEAD, PERFECTION, SONS OF GOD. Perfect *unity* is found through the gospel and comes by full obedience to all of the truths of salvation. Our Lord's great plea, made on behalf of his ancient apostles was, "That they all may be one; as thou, Father, art in me, and I in thee, that they also may be one in us: . . . And the glory which thou gavest me I have given them; that they may be one, even as we are one: I in them, and thou in me, that they may be made perfect in one." (John 17:21-23.)

To all his saints he has said in this day: "Be one; and if ye are not one ye are not mine." (D. & C. 38: 27.) Also: That he was crucified for "as many as will believe on my name, that they may become the sons of God, even one in me as I am one in the Father, as the Father is one in me, that we may be one." (D. & C. 35:2.) To the Three Nephites he said: "Ye shall have fulness of joy; and ye shall sit down in the kingdom of my Father; yea, your joy shall be full, even as the Father hath give me fulness of joy; and ye shall be even as I am, and I am even as the Father; and the Father and I are one." (3 Ne. 28:10.)

This unity among all the saints, and between them and the Father and the Son, is reserved for those who gain exaltation and inherit the fulness of the Father's kingdom. Those who attain it will all know the same things; think the same thoughts; exercise the same powers; do the same acts; respond in the same way to the same circum-

stances; beget the same kind of off-spring; rejoice in the same continuation of the seeds forever; create the same type of worlds; enjoy the same eternal fulness; and glory in the same exaltation.

All this is the eventual unity that is to be achieved. But even now in man's feeble mortal state he can yet attain unity in thought, desires, purposes, and the like—such unity coming to those who have the constant companionship of the Holy Ghost. Those so united have, in Paul's expressive language, "the mind of Christ." (1 Cor. 2:16.)

UNIVERSE.

See ASTRONOMY, CREATION, EARTHS, GODHEAD. Except by revelation man has no way of knowing the extent and immensity of the *universe.* We may assume that it consists of that whole system of worlds and galaxies seen in our greatest telescopes, plus much more that remains unknown and undiscovered. But over it all God the Father reigns in supreme omnipotence. Some concept of the extent of his creations may be gained from Enoch's statement, "Were it possible that man could number the particles of the earth, yea millions of earths like this, it would not be a beginning to the number of thy creations; and thy curtains are stretched out still." (Moses 7:30.)

UNKNOWN GOD.

See APOSTASY, CREEDS, FALSE GODS, GOD, IDOLATRY. Finding on Mars hill "an altar with this inscription, TO THE UNKNOWN GOD," Paul took occasion to reveal to the Athenians the_true nature of the living God, as though he were merely giving them a correct understanding of what they already believed. (Acts 17:22-31.) Similarly today, the Elders of Israel go forth among so-called Christian peoples who are worshiping an *Unknown God* (who chances to have the same names as the true and living God), and the elders proceed to reveal the true nature of God, as though they are explaining what the people already believe.

In reality, the God of the saints is a *Known God* who has revealed himself to modern men; the Deity of the sectarian Christians is an *Unknown God,* who does not appear to men, though in some vague way he is supposed to have done so anciently. The saints say that it is life eternal to know the only true God and Jesus Christ whom he hath sent (John 17:3); apostate Christendom says—officially and formally in the accepted and approved creeds—that God is immaterial, uncreated, and *incomprehensible.*

The only similarity between the *Known* and the *Unknown Gods* is that they both bear the same names, and the profession is made that they both have the same characteristics and attributes. For that matter the Athenians probably ascribed to their Unknown God many of the same characteristics and attributes that the sectarians ascribe to the mysterious all-pervading essence which they suppose is their God. Acceptance of the gospel, in large measure, consists in coming to the true knowledge of God, in replacing apostate views about an Unknown God with the light of heaven so that the convert begins to know God and the Son who was sent of God.

UNMORTAL.

See IMMORTALITY, MORTALITY. There are two kinds of *immortality*: 1. Adam was an immortal being in the Garden of Eden because death had not entered the world; this type of immortality was followed by *mortality;* and 2. Resurrected beings are immortal, meaning that their bodies and spirits are inseparably connected, and they can never die.

In an attempt to distinguish the immortality of Eden from the immortality of eternity the word *unmortal* has been coined and applied to Adam's *pre-mortal* state. If this usage helps in understanding conditions as they actually are and were, it has its advantages; but actually, every important word has more than one definition, and the fact that *immortality* is used in more senses than one is not confusing to informed persons.

UNPARDONABLE SIN.

See CHRIST, HOLY GHOST, SIN,

SONS OF PERDITION. Our Lord told the Jews that eventually—either in this world or in the world to come —all sins would be forgiven except the blasphemy against the Holy Ghost. (Matt. 12:31-32; Mark 3:28-30; Luke 12:10.) This sin or blasphemy against the Holy Ghost is thus the *unpardonable sin.*

Particular note should be taken in this connection of the fact that *forgiveness of sins does not thereby confer celestial salvation upon a person.* "All will suffer until they obey Christ himself," the Prophet said. (*Teachings,* p. 357.) The wicked and ungodly will suffer the vengeance of eternal fire in hell until they finally obey Christ, repent of their sins, and gain forgiveness therefrom. Then they shall obtain the resurrection and an inheritance in the telestial and not the celestial kingdom. (D. & C. 76:81-107.) Those who have committed the unpardonable sin, however, will not be redeemed from the devil and instead, after their resurrection, will be cast out as sons of perdition to dwell with the devil and his angels in eternity. (D. & C. 76:30-49.)

Commission of the unpardonable sin consists in crucifying unto oneself the Son of God afresh and putting him to open shame. (Heb. 6:4-8; D. & C. 76:34-35.) To commit this unpardonable crime a man must receive the gospel, gain from the Holy Ghost by revelation the absolute knowledge of the divinity of Christ, and then deny "the new and everlasting covenant by which he was sanctified, calling it an unholy thing, and doing despite to the Spirit of grace." (*Teachings*, p. 128.) He thereby commits murder by assenting unto the Lord's death, that is, having a perfect knowledge of the truth he comes out in open rebellion and places himself in a position wherein he would have crucified Christ knowing perfectly the while that he was the Son of God. Christ is thus crucified afresh and put to open shame. (D. & C. 132:27.)

"What must a man do to commit the unpardonable sin?" the Prophet asked. "He must receive the Holy Ghost, have the heavens opened unto him, and know God, and then sin against him. After a man has sinned against the Holy Ghost, there is no repentance for him. He has got to say that the sun does not shine while he sees it; he has got to deny Jesus Christ when the heavens have been opened unto him, and to deny the plan of salvation with his eyes open to the truth of it; and from that time he begins to be an enemy. This is the case with many apostates of The Church of Jesus Christ of Latter-day Saints.

"When a man begins to be an enemy to this work he hunts me, he seeks to kill me, and never ceases to thirst for my blood. He gets the spirit of the devil—the same spirit that they had who crucified the Lord of Life—the same spirit that sins against the Holy Ghost. You cannot save such persons; you cannot bring them to repentance; they make open war, like the devil, and awful is the consequence." (*Teachings*, p. 358.)

Among other things, this statement from the Prophet, explodes forever the mythical fantasy that the sons of perdition are so few they can be numbered on the fingers of the hand.

UNQUENCHABLE FIRE.
See FIRE AND BRIMSTONE.

UPRIGHTNESS.
See HONESTY, INTEGRITY, JUSTICE, RIGHTEOUSNESS. *Uprightness* is the quality which carries men along a straight path of honesty and duty. Only those who are doing their full duty to their Creator, by keeping his commandments and walking in accordance with his laws, have developed that uprightness which the gospel teaches. Uprightness is an attribute of God. (Ps. 25:8; 92:15.)

Men are commanded to repent, walk uprightly, and sin not. (D. & C. 5:21; 18:31; 46:7.) Parents are to teach their children "to walk uprightly before the Lord." (D. & C. 68:28.) Only the upright will be welcome in Zion (D. & C. 61:16), and all things shall work together for their good. (D. & C. 90:24; 100:15.) Mercy shall be their inheritance (D. & C. 109:1) and salvation their reward. (Ps. 15:1-2; Prov. 28:18; Isa. 33:14-16.)

URIM AND THUMMIM.

See BOOK OF MORMON, GOLD PLATES, PEEP STONES, REVELATION. From time to time, as his purposes require, the Lord personally, or through the ministry of appointed angels, delivers to chosen prophets a *Urim and Thummim* to be used in receiving revelations and in translating ancient records from unknown tongues. With the approval of the Lord these prophets are permitted to pass these instruments on to their mortal successors.

A Urim and Thummim consists of two special stones called *seer stones* or *interpreters.* The Hebrew words *urim* and *thummim,* both plural, mean *lights* and *perfections.* Presumably one of the stones is called Urim and the other Thummim. Ordinarily they are carried in a breastplate over the heart. (Ex. 28:30; Lev. 8:8.)

Because of the sacred nature of these holy instruments, they have not been viewed by most men, and even the times and circumstances under which they have been held by mortals are not clearly set forth. Undoubtedly they were in use before the flood, but the first scriptural reference to them is in connection with the revelations given the Brother of Jared. (Ether 3:21-28.) Abraham had them in his day (Abra. 3:1-4), and Aaron and the priests in Israel had them from generation to generation. (Ex. 28:30; Lev. 8:8; Num. 27:21; Deut. 33:8; 1 Sam. 28:6; Ezra 2:63; Neh. 7:65.) There is no record that Lehi brought a Urim and Thummim to this continent, but King Mosiah had one prior to the discovery of the Book of Ether, and it was handed down from prophet to prophet. (Omni 20-21; Mosiah 8:13-19; 21:26-28; 28:11-20; Alma 63:12; Ether 4:1-7.)

Joseph Smith received the same Urim and Thummim had by the Brother of Jared for it was the one expressly provided for the translation of the Jaredite and Nephite records. (D. & C. 10:1; 17:1; Ether 3:22-28.) It was separate and distinct from the one had by Abraham and the one had by the priests in Israel. The Prophet also had a *seer stone* which was separate and distinct from the Urim and Thummim, and which (speaking loosely) has been called by some a Urim and Thummim. (*Doctrines of Salvation,* vol. 3, pp. 222-226.)

President Joseph Fielding Smith, with reference to the seer stone and the Urim and Thummim, has written: "We have been taught since the days of the Prophet that the Urim and Thummim were returned with the plates to the angel. We have no record of the Prophet having the Urim and Thummim after the organization of the Church. Statements of translations by the Urim and Thummim after that date are evidently errors. The statement has been made that the Urim and Thummim was on the altar in the Manti Tample when that building was dedicated. The Urim and Thummim so spoken of, however, was the seer stone which was in the possession of the Prophet Joseph Smith in early days. This seer stone is now in the possession of the Church." (*Doctrines of Salvation,* vol. 3, p. 225.)

When Moroni first revealed to the Prophet the existence of the gold plates, he also said "that there were two stones in silver bows—and these stones, fastened to a breastplate, constituted what is called the Urim and Thummim—deposited with the plates; and the possession and use of these stones were what constituted 'seers' in ancient or former times; and that God had prepared them for the purpose of translating the book." (Jos. Smith 2:35, 59, 62.) Ammon said of these same stones: "The things are called interpreters, and no man can look in them except he be commanded, lest he should look for that he ought not and he should perish. And whosoever is commanded to look in them, the same is called seer." (Mosiah 8: 13; 28:13-16.)

The existence and use of the Urim and Thummim as an instrument of revelation will continue among exalted beings in eternity. From the inspired writings of the Prophet we learn that angels "reside in the presence of God, on *a globe like a sea of glass and fire, where all things for their glory are manifest, past, present, and future,* and are continually before the Lord. *The place where God resides is a great Urim and Thummim. This earth,* in its sanctified and immortal state, will be made like unto crystal and *will be a Urim and Thummim* to the inhabitants who dwell thereon, whereby all things pertaining to an inferior kingdom, or all kingdoms of a lower order, will be manifest to those who dwell on it; and this earth will be Christ's. Then the *white stone* mentioned in Revelation 2:17, *will become a Urim and Thummim to each individual who receives one,* whereby things pertaining to a higher order of kingdoms will be made known." (D. & C. 130:6-11.)

USURY.
See CHURCH WELFARE PLAN, DEBT. In Biblical times, lending on *usury* was synonymous with charging interest on a loan. Under the social circumstances then prevailing both money and property could be put out to usury, and the payments were made either in produce or money. In modern times usury ordinarily has reference to an unconscionable or exorbitant rate of interest.

Under the old Mosaic law, ancient Israel was forbidden to charge usury when lending to their fellow church members, but there was no such restriction when loans were made to others. This special restriction was part of what we would call the then existing welfare plan; it was one of the ways the more affluent persons in Israel were expected to aid their less fortunate brethren. (Ex 22:25; Lev. 25:35-38; Deut. 23: 19-20.) Our Lord apparently approved the practice of charging usury (Matt. 25:14-30; Luke 19:12-27), and there is no modern day restriction on charging reasonable interest rates.

VAINGLORY.

See BOASTING, PRIDE, VANITY. *Vainglory* is an excessive pride in one's own performances or attainments. It is manifest through boasting or undue vaunting of oneself. "Let nothing be done through strife or vainglory," Paul taught, "but in lowliness of mind let each esteem other better than themselves." (Philip. 2:3.)

VALIANTNESS.

See DEVOTION, ENDURING TO THE END, GOOD WORKS, OBEDIENCE. *Valiant* means fearless, valorous, brave, courageous. Those "who are not valiant in the testimony of Jesus," assuming they are otherwise worthy, go to the terrestrial kingdom. (D. & C. 76:79.) That is, members of the Church who have testimonies, who know by personal revelation from the Holy Ghost that the work is true, but who do not take an affirmative, courageous stand against the world, and in favor of the Church, shall go to the terrestrial kingdom (assuming they are otherwise worthy of such reward). Such persons are "lukewarm,

and neither cold nor hot." (Rev. 3: 14-18.) They belong to the Church but do not magnify their callings in the priesthood, act diligently in the offices to which they are appointed, pay their tithing, honor the Sabbath day, and the like. They are hearers of the word, not doers. (Jas. 1:22.)

On the other hand: "All thrones and dominions, principalities and powers, shall be revealed and set forth upon all who have endured valiantly for the gospel of Jesus Christ." (D. & C. 121:29.)

VALLEY OF DECISION.

See SECOND COMING OF CHRIST.

VANITY.

See BOASTING, PRIDE, VAINGLORY. As commonly used today, *vanity* means shallow pride. Biblical passages relative to vanity, however, have been translated from original words having the meanings of emptiness, fruitlessness, and worthlessness. The Hebrew word translated *vanity* in David's statement, "How long will ye love vanity" (Ps. 4:2), for instance, is one which indicates a sense of empty failure. This same Biblical meaning of vanity seems to have been carried over into the modern revelations. (D. & C. 20:5; 84:54-55.)

VENERATION.
See REVERENCE.

VENGEANCE.
See DAMNATION, PUNISHMENT, REPENTANCE, SECOND COMING OF CHRIST. Vengeance is retribution; it is the infliction of punishment in return for an injury or offense. It is imposed by the Lord (D. & C. 3: 4; Mosiah 17; 3 Ne. 21:20-21), upon the wicked (D. & C. 29:17; 97:22, 26), including specifically those who reject latter-day revelation (Teachings, p. 54), and it may be avoided by repentance. (D. & C. 98:47-48.)

Men are forbidden to execute vengeance upon their fellow men, unless by revelation (acting in the capacity of the Lord's agents) they are sent forth to do his appointed will. (D. & C. 98:23-48.) Ancient Israel, for instance, was commanded to execute the Lord's vengeance upon the Amalekites. (1 Sam. 15: 2-3.) Aside from such unusual and seldom-occurring situations, however, the decree is that vengeance, recompense, and judgment come from the Lord himself. (Morm. 3: 14-15; 8:20; Deut. 32:35, 41: Ps. 94:1; Heb. 10:30.).

It is the wicked, not the right-eous, who swear vengeance upon their enemies. (Alma 25:1.) To the saints, the command is: "Pray for your enemies in the Church and curse not your foes without: for vengeance is mine, saith the Lord, and I will repay. To every ordained member, and to all, we say, be merciful and you shall find mercy. Seek to help save souls, not to destroy them." (Teachings, p. 77.)

When the blood of righteous people is shed, that blood cries from the ground unto the Lord for vengeance. (Alma 1:13; 20:18; 37:30; 60:10; Morm. 8:40-41; Ether 8:22, 24.) And in his own time and way the Lord will recompense those who murder, persecute the saints, and work unrighteousness. They shall "suffer the vengeance of eternal fire." (D. & C. 76:105; Jude 6.) The Second Coming of our Lord is the great day of vengeance; at that day he shall return, "In flaming fire taking vengeance on them that know not God, and that obey not the gospel." (2 Thess. 1:7-9; Isa. 35:4; 63; Luke 21:22; D. & C. 85:3; 112:24; 133:50-51.)

VERACITY.
See HONESTY.

VERSIONS OF THE BIBLE.
See KING JAMES VERSION OF THE BIBLE.

VICARIOUS ORDINANCES.

See ATONEMENT OF CHRIST, BAPTISM FOR THE DEAD, ENDOWMENTS, ORDINANCES, PLAN OF SALVATION, SALVATION, SALVATION FOR THE DEAD, SEALINGS, TEMPLE ORDINANCES, TEMPLES. Salvation itself is based on the vicarious atoning sacrifice of Christ. Through his suffering, death, and resurrection, immortality comes to all men and eternal life to those who obey the full gospel law. He acted on man's behalf, that is, vicariously, paying the penalty for our sins on condition of repentance, ransoming us from the effects of Adam's fall.

In conformity with this pattern of vicarious service, the gospel law enables worthy members of the Church to act on behalf of their dead ancestors in the performance of the ordinances of salvation and exaltation. Baptism is essential to salvation in the celestial kingdom, endowments and sealings to an exaltation therein. The living saints, acting on a proxy basis, perform these ordinances for and in behalf of those who have died and who did not have an opportunity while in this life to receive the ordinances personally. (D. & C. 128; *Doctrines of Salvation*, vol. 2, pp. 129-180.)

VICARIOUS SALVATION.

See SALVATION FOR THE DEAD.

VILENESS.

See WICKEDNESS.

VINE.

See TRUE VINE.

VINEYARD.

See LORD OF THE VINEYARD.

VIOLENCE.

See SIGNS OF THE TIMES.

VIRGIN BIRTH.

See ANNUNCIATION, BIRTH, CHRIST, IMMACULATE CONCEPTION THEORY, MARY. Our Lord is the only mortal person ever born to a *virgin*, because he is the only person who ever had an immortal Father. Mary, his mother, "was carried away in the Spirit" (1 Ne. 11:13-21), was "overshadowed" by the Holy Ghost, and the conception which took place "by the power of the Holy Ghost" resulted in the bringing forth of the literal and personal Son of God the Father. (Alma 7:10; 2 Ne. 17:14; Isa. 7:14; Matt. 1:18-25; Luke 1:26-38.) Christ is not the Son of the Holy Ghost, but of the Father. (*Doctrines of Salvation*, vol. 1, pp. 18-20.) Modernistic teachings denying the *virgin birth* are utterly and completely apostate and false.

VIRGIN MARY.

See MARY.

VISIONS.

See DREAMS, FIRST VISION, GIFT
OF THE HOLY GHOST, GIFTS OF THE
SPIRIT, HOLY GHOST, MINISTERING
OF ANGELS, ORACLES, PROPHECY,
PROPHETS, REVELATION, SEERS,
THEOPHANIES, TRANCES, WHITE
HORSE PROPHECY. Through super-
natural means, by the power of the
Holy Ghost, devout persons are per-
mitted to have *visions* and to see
within the veil. They are enabled
to see spiritual personages and to
view scenes hidden from ordinary
sight. These visions are gifts of the
Spirit. (Seventh Article of Faith.)

They come by faith and vanish
away when faith dies out. (1 Sam.
3:1; Isa. 29:9-14.) Thus they stand
as an evidence of the divinity of the
Lord's work in any age. If the
Lord is giving visions and revelation to a people, such a group constitutes the people of God. If visions
and revelations are not being received by any church or people, then
that group is not the Lord's people.
By this test the identity of the true
Church is known. (Moro. 7:30-38.)

Actual personages from the unseen world frequently appear to
mortals in visions. In the First
Vision, the Prophet beheld and
conversed with the Father and the
Son. (Jos. Smith 2:15-20.) "The
Lord came unto Abram in a vision,"
promised him seed (Gen. 15), and
made covenant with him. (Gen. 17.)
Similarly, "God spake unto Israel in
the visions of the night," authoriz-
ing him "to go down into Egypt."
(Gen. 46:1-4.) Paul saw the risen
Lord in vision (Acts 9:1-9; 26:12-
19), even as the weeping women at
the empty tomb saw "a vision of
angels" saying their Lord had risen
from the dead. (Luke 24:1-23.)

Moses and Elijah personally appeared on the Mount of Transfiguration where they were seen by
Peter, James, and John in vision.
(Matt. 17:1-9.) When Moses, Elijah,
Elias, and the Lord Jehovah stood
before Joseph and Oliver in the
Kirtland Temple, they were seen in
vision because "the veil was taken"
from their mortal eyes. (D. & C.
110.) On August 12, 1831, on the
Missouri River, "Elder William W.
Phelps, in daylight vision, saw the
destroyer riding in power upon the
face of the waters." (Heading, D. &
C. 61.) An angel came to Amulek
"in a vision" and commanded him to
receive Alma. (Alma 8:20.)

Power is also given to the Lord's
prophets to see and converse with
heavenly beings in vision, though
such divine personages are not at
the time in the immediate and personal presence of the one receiving
the vision. Being "overcome with
the Spirit," Lehi, for instance, "was
carried away in a vision, even that
he saw the heavens open, and he
thought he saw God sitting upon
his throne, surrounded with num-
berless concourses of angels in the
attitude of singing and praising
their God." (1 Ne. 1:8.) Joseph
Smith and Sidney Rigdon "beheld
the glory of the Son, on the right
hand of the Father, and received
of his fulness; And saw the holy

angels, and them who are sanctified before his throne, worshiping God, and the Lamb, who worship him forever and ever." (D. & C. 76: 20-21.) Stephen saw "the heavens opened, and the Son of man standing on the right hand of God." (Acts 7:51-56.) In his glorious vision of the celestial world, given January 21, 1836, the Prophet also saw "the blazing throne of God, whereon was seated the Father and the Son." (*Teachings,* p. 107.)

By visions the Lord reveals past, present, and future events. Nephi saw in vision the destruction of Jerusalem after he and his people had left that wicked city. (2 Ne. 1:4.) Moroni opened to the view of the Prophet the hiding place of the plates in Cumorah. (Jos. Smith 2: 42.) Daniel foresaw the great gathering at Adam-ondi-Ahman (Dan. 7:9-14), and Ezekiel saw the resurrection of the house of Israel. (Ezek. 37:1-10.) The kingdoms of glory in the eternal worlds were opened to the view of the Prophet (D. & C. 76); Abraham and Moses beheld the infinite multitude of the Lord's creations (Moses 1; 2; 3; Abra. 3; 4; 5); and Enoch and Abraham saw the hosts of pre-existent spirits. (Moses 6:36; Abra. 3:22-25.)

Images, figures, and symbolical representations are often portrayed in visions as means of conveying gospel truths. Lehi and Nephi both learned much by seeing the tree of life, the rod of iron, the straight and narrow path, and so on. (1 Ne. 8; 11.) Peter learned that the gospel was to go to the Gentiles when the Lord showed him the vision of the unclean animals and commanded him to kill and eat. (Acts 10:9-48; 11:1-18.) Paul learned that he should take the message of salvation to Macedonia when he saw in vision a man praying and asking for gospel light. (Acts 16:9-10.) Daniel was informed of the history of nations and kingdoms by the beasts and figures shown him representing those kingdoms. (Dan. 7; 8; 9; 10.) In contrast, John the Revelator saw actual beasts in heaven to establish in his mind the truth that animals are resurrected and dwell in heavenly spheres. (*Teachings,* pp. 289-292.)

Visions serve the Lord's purposes in preparing men for salvation. By them knowledge is revealed (2 Ne. 4:23), conversions are made (Alma 19:16), the gospel message is spread abroad, the church organization is perfected (D. & C. 107:93), and righteousness is increased in the hearts of men. And visions are to increase and abound in the last days, for the Lord has promised to pour out his "spirit upon all flesh," so that "old men shall dream dreams," and "young men shall see visions." (Joel 2:28-32.)

VOODOOISM.

See SORCERY. *Voodooism* is a barbaric negro religion consisting largely of sorcery. Originating in Africa, it is now found chiefly among Haitian negroes.

VOTING IN THE CHURCH.
See COMMON CONSENT.

VOWS.
See OATHS, OBLATIONS, SACRA-
MENTS. As an incentive to greater
personal righteousness, it is a wholesome and proper thing for the saints
to make frequent *vows* to the Lord.
These are solemn promises to perform some duty, refrain from some
sin, keep some commandment, or
press forward in greater service in
the kingdom. Thus Jacob vowed to
accept Jehovah as his God and to
pay an honest tithing (Gen. 28:20-
22), and Hannah vowed to give
Samuel to the Lord for his service.
(1 Sam. 1:9-18.)

The saints should offer their
vows both on the Lord's day and on
all days (D. & C. 59:8-12); and once
offered, they are to be kept. (D. &
C. 108:3; Num. 30:2; Eccles. 5:4-5.)
When vows are made in righteousness, they are sealed by the Holy
Spirit of promise, and the Lord's
blessings attend their performance.
(D. & C. 132:7.)

As with all true principles, apostate perversion is an ever present
threat where vows are concerned. A
vow to do an evil thing leads to
damnation as rapidly as a vow to
do a righteous thing leads to salvation. Unrighteous Jews, for instance,
avoided the obligation to honor
their parents and provide temporal
sustenance for them (Ex. 20:12; 1
Tim. 5:8) by falsely vowing to use
their property for some other purpose so that it would not be available for parental support. (Matt.
15:3-9; Mark 7:6-13.)

VULGARITY.
See PROFANITY. Refinement,
decency, and an increase in spiritual sensitivity always attend
obedience to divine law; *vulgarity,*
rudeness, and coarseness in conduct
or speech are found where the Spirit
of the Lord has not attained full
sway in the hearts of men. Through
the gospel men have power to overcome that which is vulgar, common,
and worldly, and to attain the state
of refinement and purity which will
enable them to enjoy a celestial
society.

VULGATE.
See KING JAMES VERSION OF
THE BIBLE.

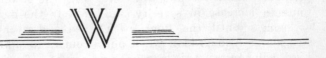

WAGERS.
See GAMBLING.

WAR.
See ARMIES OF HEAVEN, BAT-

TEL OF ARMAGEDDON, BATTLE OF THE GREAT GOD, GOD OF BATTLES, GOG AND MAGOG, PEACE, SECOND COMING OF CHRIST, SIGNS OF THE TIMES, SUPPER OF THE GREAT GOD, WAR IN HEAVEN. *War* is probably the most satanic and evil state of affairs that can or does exist on earth. It is organized and systematic murder, with rapine, robbery, sex immorality and every other evil as a natural attendant. War is of the devil; it is born of lust. (Jas. 4:1.) If all men were righteous, there would be no war; and there will be none during the millennium (Isa. 2:1-5) and in the eternal kingdom of God.

Because Lucifer rebelled and sought the throne of God, there was war in heaven among the pre-existent spirits. (Isa. 14:12-20; Rev. 12:7-9; Moses 4:1-4; Abra. 3:28.) Since the fall of man, lustful and telestial conditions have prevailed and wars have multipled. Words are incapable of expressing the human depravity that has accompanied war in every age, but the era of time known as the last days is the one in which the most extensive and wicked of all wars have been and will be fought. Modern warfare began with the American Civil War, and it has and will continue to increase in severity and wickedness until the final great struggle at Armageddon when our Lord will return to cleanse the earth and usher in the millennial reign of peace.

Although all wars are in their nature evil, yet the fact is that they do exist and that the Lord uses them to further his purposes. Indeed, because of the wickedness of men, he has in his wrath "decreed wars upon the face of the earth, and the wicked shall slay the wicked, and fear shall come upon every man." (D. & C. 63:33.)

Self-defense is as justifiable where war is concerned as where one man seeks to take the life of another, with the obvious conclusion that (from the standpoint of those called upon to engage in armed conflict) some wars are righteous and others are unrighteous. Righteous men are entitled, expected, and obligated to defend themselves; they must engage in battle when there is no other way to preserve their rights and freedoms and to protect their families, homes, land, and the truths of salvation which they have espoused.

In many wars, perhaps most, both sides are equally at fault and neither is justified. But there have been and yet will be wars in which the balances of eternal justice will show that one side had the favor of Deity and the other did not. Obviously when Enoch led the armies of the saints against their enemies, with the power of God being manifest to the degree that mountains fled and rivers turned from their courses to aid the saints, there was a right and a wrong side in the conflict. (Moses 7:13-16.) When Joshua led the armies of Israel against the kings of the Amorites, with the

Lord staying the sun in the heavens so that Israel could carry on the slaughter, there was a right and a wrong side to the war. When Moroni rent his coat and wrote upon it—"In memory of our God, our religion, and freedom, and our peace, our wives, and our children" —and thereby rallied the Nephites to battle, he had the Lord on his side. (Alma 46.)

In the American Revolution the Lord was with the colonists and poured out his wrath upon Great Britain and those who opposed the Americans. (1 Ne. 13:17-19.) The preservation of the American union through the great Civil War was a just cause. World Wars I and II were both righteous wars as far as the allies were concerned, and the Lord's purposes were furthered by the victorious parties. Those nations defending Israel in the coming Armageddon will find the God of Battles allied with them, and the assemblage marching under the banner of Gog and Magog will be the rebels against righteousness.

It must be clearly understood, however, that the responsibility for the loss of life and desolations poured out through warfare will rest upon those who foment and cause the wars. It is true that individual soldiers may be held accountable for needless, brutal killings. War as such is not an open door to unrestricted slaughter. But the soldier who is required to take life and spread desolation will be guiltless before the throne of the Just Judge, whether that single individual fought for or against the Lord's purposes.

WARD BISHOPS.
See BISHOPS.

WARD CLERKS.
See CLERKS.

WARD ORGANIZATION.
See CHURCH ORGANIZATION.

WARDS.
See BRANCHES, CHURCH ORGANIZATION, STAKES. The basic ecclesiastical district or church unit in and through which the programs of the Church are administered is the *ward*. Several wards form a stake of Zion. A bishop is the presiding ward officer; all Aaronic Priesthood quorums are ward quorums: and substantially all of the actual operation of all the programs of the Church takes place in the ward rather than in some larger or higher unit.

Members of a ward form a *congregation* of the saints. They meet together frequently for spiritual and social purposes. It is by faithfulness and service in ward organizations (in the main) that the Lord's saints work out their salvation.

WARD TEACHING.
See HOME TEACHING.

WAR IN HEAVEN.
See AGENCY, ARMIES OF HEAVEN, COUNCIL IN HEAVEN, DEVIL, HEAVEN, MICHAEL THE ARCHANGEL, PLAN OF SALVATION, PRE-EXISTENCE, WAR. Following the pre-existent choosing of Christ and the rejecting of Lucifer to be the Redeemer in the great plan of salvation, Satan and one-third of the spirit hosts destined for life on this earth came out in *open rebellion* against the Father. The rebels "sought to destroy the agency of man" and to modify the Father's plan so that salvation would come automatically to all who passed through mortality. (Moses 4:1-4; Abra. 3:24-28; D. & C. 29:36-38; Isa. 14:12-20; Luke 10:18.) Their rebellion against light and truth and their refusal to subscribe to the terms and condition laid down by the Father whereby salvation might be gained is called by John the *war in heaven.* (Rev. 12:4-9.)

The same inspired writer then goes on to explain that after Satan was cast out onto the earth he was given power "to make *war* with the saints, and to overcome them." (Rev. 12; 13.) *The warfare of the saints on earth* (Eph. 6:10-18; 2 Tim. 4:7-8) *is a continuation of the war in heaven. It is a war between truth and error, between light and darkness, between the Church of the Lamb and the apostate sects of* the world, *between Christ and Satan.* Those who followed Lucifer in pre-existence were the spirits who chose to believe false doctrines about how to gain salvation; those who believe in false systems of salvation in this life, in like manner, are permittng themselves to be overcome by Satan in the *war on earth.*

There were, of course, no neutral spirits in the war in heaven, any more than there are or can be neutrals in this life where choices between righteousness and unrighteousness are involved. "He that is not with me is against me," saith the Lord, "and he that gathereth not with me scattereth abroad." (Matt. 12:30; 1 Ne. 14:10; Alma 5: 38-40.)

WARNING THE WORLD.
See MESSAGE OF THE RESTORATION, MISSIONARIES, RESTORATION OF THE GOSPEL, WATCHMEN, WORLD. In the dispensation of the fulness of times, the members of the true Church are directed by the Lord to *warn the world* of the desolation and destruction that is to be poured out without measure upon the wicked and ungodly. (D. & C. 1:4; 63:37, 57-58; 84:114; 109: 41; 112:5; 124:106; 134:12.) "For this is a day of warning, and not a day of many words. For I, the Lord, am not to be mocked in the last days." (D. & C. 63:58.) "It becometh every man who hath been

warned to warn his neighbor." (D. & C. 88:81.)

Part of the warning message is an invitation to forsake the world, accept the truths of salvation, gather with the saints, and receive the fulness of the blessings of the gospel. "And let your preaching be the warning voice, every man to his neighbor, in mildness and in meekness." (D. & C. 38:41.) When the missionaries or other members of the Church offer the gospel to the people of the world, they thereby raise the warning voice.

All who heed the warning shall escape desolation and misery in the world to come, and many of them have also been freed from the destructions and plagues that are sweeping the earth in the last days. Without even considering the assurance of eternal life that is found only in and through the gospel, what a great temporal blessing it has been to the scores of thousands of converts who have already gathered from the benighted nations of the world to the valleys of the saints!

WARNING VOICE.
See WARNING THE WORLD.

WASHING OF FEET.
See ENDOWMENTS, SCHOOL OF THE PROPHETS, TEMPLE ORDINANCES. 1. Our Lord performed the gospel ordinance of *washing of feet* on the occasion of the last supper.

After the supper, he girded himself with a towel, poured water in a basin, and washed and wiped the feet of the apostles. (John 13:1-17.) The Inspired Version of the Bible inserts the explanation, "Now this was the custom of the Jews under their law; wherefore, Jesus did this that the law might be fulfilled." (*Inspired Version,* John 13:10.)

However, after the ordinance had been performed, our Lord said: "Ye call me Master and Lord: and ye say well; for so I am. If I then, your Lord and Master, have washed your feet; *ye also ought to wash one another's feet.* For I have given you an example, that ye should do as I have done to you. Verily, verily, I say unto you, The servant is not greater than his lord; neither he that is sent greater than he that sent him. If ye know these things, happy are ye if ye do them." (John 13:13-17.)

Thus our Lord did two things in the performance of this ordinance: 1. He fulfilled the old law given to Moses; and 2. He instituted a sacred ordinance which should be performed by legal administrators among his true disciples from that day forward.

As part of the restoration of all things, the ordinance of washing of feet has been restored in the dispensation of the fulness of times. In keeping with the standard pattern of revealing principles and practices line upon line and precept upon precept, the Lord revealed his will concerning the washing of feet little by little until the full knowledge of the endowment and all temple ordinances had been given.

December 27, 1832, this command was given to "the first laborers in this last kingdom": "Sanctify yourselves; yea, purify your hearts, and cleanse your hands and your feet before me, that I may make you clean; That I may testify unto your Father, and your God, and my God, that you are clean from the blood of this wicked generation." (D. & C. 88:74-75.) On that same occasion the command came to organize the school of the prophets, with the express stipulation that "ye shall not receive any among you into this school save he is clean from the blood of this generation; And he shall be received by the ordinance of the washing of feet, for unto this end was the ordinance of the washing of feet instituted." (D. & C. 88:127-141.)

In the case of this school the ordinance is to be performed by the President of the Church. In compliance with this revelation the Prophet on January 23, 1833, washed the feet of the members of the school of the prophets. "By the power of the Holy Ghost I pronounced them all clean from the blood of this generation," he recorded. (*History of the Church*, vol. 1, pp. 322-324; vol. 2, p. 287.)

Later apostles were called and ordained, and on November 12, 1835, the Prophet addressed them, as pertaining to the washing of feet where they were concerned: "The item to which I wish the more particularly to call your attention tonight is the ordinance of washing of feet. This we [meaning the Twelve] have not done as yet, but *it is necessary now, as much as it was in the days of the Savior; and we must have a place prepared, that we may attend to this ordinance aside from the world.*

"We have not desired as much from the hand of the Lord through faith and obedience, as we ought to have done, yet we have enjoyed great blessings, and we are not so sensible of this as we should be. . . . We must have all things prepared, and call our solemn assembly as the Lord has commanded us, that we may be able to accomplish his great work, and it must be done in God's own way. The house of the Lord must be prepared, and the solemn assembly called and organized in it, according to the order of the house of God; and *in it we must attend to the ordinance of washing of feet.* It was never intended for any but official members. It is calculated to unite our hearts, that we may be one in feeling and sentiment, and that our faith may be strong, so that Satan cannot overthrow us, nor have any power over us here.

"The endowment you are so anxious about, you cannot comprehend now, nor could Gabriel explain it to the understanding of your dark minds; but strive to be prepared in your hearts, be faithful in all things, that when we meet in the solemn assembly, that is, when such as

God shall name out of all the official members shall meet, we must be clean every whit. . . . *The order of the house of God has been, and ever will be, the same, even after Christ comes; and after the termination of the thousand years it will be the same; and we shall finally enter into the celestial kingdom of God, and enjoy it forever."* (*History of the Church,* vol. 2, pp. 308-309.)

On Sunday, March 27, 1836, as part of the dedicatory services of the Kirtland Temple, the congregation sang that glorious hymn, "The Spirit of God Like a Fire is Burning!" One verse, as then sung, was:

We'll wash and be washed, and with oil be anointed,
Withal not omitting the washing of feet;
For he that receiveth his penny appointed
Must surely be clean at the harvest of wheat.

On March 29 and 30, 1836, the leading brethren, including the First Presidency, Council of the Twelve, bishoprics, and presidents of quorums, participated in the ordinance of washing of feet. (*History of the Church,* vol. 2, pp. 426, 430-431.)

It should be remembered that the endowment given in the Kirtland Temple was only a partial endowment, and that the full endowment was not performed until the saints had established themselves in Nauvoo. (*Doctrines of Salvation,* vol. 2, pp. 241-242.) The full endowment—referred to in the revelation dated January 19, 1841 (D. & C. 124:36-41) —including washings and anointings, except under unusual circumstances, is designed to be administered in the temples of the Lord.

Thus the knowledge relative to the washing of feet has been revealed step by step in this day until a full knowledge is now incorporated in the revealed ordinances of the Lord's house. Obviously the apostate peoples of the world, being without revelation to guide them, cannot comply with our Lord's command given on the occasion of the last supper.

2. Under certain circumstances, when moved upon by the Spirit but not otherwise, the elders are to cleanse their feet as a witness against those who reject their testimony. "And in whatsoever place ye shall enter, and they receive you not in my name, ye shall leave a cursing instead of a blessing, by casting off the dust of your feet against them as a testimony, and cleansing your feet by the wayside." (D. & C. 24:15; 75:20; Matt. 10:14-15; Mark 6:11; Luke 9:5; 10:10-12; Acts 13:51.)

"He that receiveth you not, go away from him alone by yourselves, and *cleanse your feet even with water,* pure water, whether in heat or in cold, and bear testimony of it unto your Father which is in heaven, and return not again unto that man. And in whatsoever village or city ye enter, do likewise. Nevertheless, search diligently and spare not; and wo unto that house, or that village or city that rejecteth you, or your words, or your testimony concerning me." (D. & C. 84:92-94; 99:4.)

WASHINGS.
See TEMPLE ORDINANCES.

WATCHMEN.
See PRIESTHOOD OFFICES, WARNING THE WORLD. In their capacity as elders, prophets, ambassadors, and ministers, the Lord's agents are *watchmen* upon the tower. Their obligation is to raise the warning voice so that the sheepfold of Israel shall stand secure from the dangers and evils of the world.

"O son of man, I have set thee a watchman unto the house of Israel," the Lord told Ezekiel, for instance, "therefore thou shalt hear the word at my mouth, and warn them from me. When I way unto the wicked, O wicked man, thou shalt surely die; if thou dost not speak to warn the wicked from his way, that wicked man shall die in his iniquity; but his blood will I require at thine hand. Nevertheless, if thou warn the wicked of his way to turn from it; if he do not turn from his way, he shall die in his iniquity; but thou hast delivered thy soul." (Ezek. 33:1-9.)

WATERS OF JUDAH.
See BAPTISM. Isaiah says that the "house of Jacob" has "come forth out of the *waters of Judah*" (Isa. 48:1), a statement of great interest to Latter-day Saints in view of the fact that his words as recorded on the brass plates added the phrase, "*or out of the waters of baptism*" (1 Ne. 20:1), thus preserving in purity an Old Testament text about baptism.

WAY, TRUTH, AND LIFE.
See CHRIST, DOOR OF THE SHEEP, GOD OF TRUTH, KEEPER OF THE GATE, LIGHT OF LIFE, PERSONIFICATION, RESURRECTION AND THE LIFE, SALVATION, TRUTH. "I am *the way, the truth, and the life,*" our Lord proclaimed. He is the *Way* in that it is in and through him that salvation comes; "no man cometh unto the Father, but by me," he said. (John 14:6.) He is the *Truth* because he is the embodiment and personification of that holy attribute. (Alma 5:48.) And he is the *Life* because in him the light of life centers; except for him and his power there would be no existence; should he withdraw the light of life, death would gain an immediate victory; and without him there would be neither immortal life, nor eternal life, which is life in unending glory.

WEAKNESSES.
See HUMILITY, OMNIPOTENCE. All men have *weaknesses*—some in one field, some in another. No

man is strong in every field. "I give unto men weakness that they may be humble," the Lord said, "and my grace is sufficient for all men that humble themselves before me; for if they humble themselves before me, and have faith in me, then will I make weak things become strong unto them." (Ether 12:27, 35-41; D. & C. 50:16; 135:5.)

Those chosen by the Lord to do his work are, in the eyes of the worldly wise, "the weak things of the world"; but they labor with the promise that they shall "confound the things which are mighty." (1 Cor. 1:19-31; D. & C. 1:19, 24; 124:1; 133:58-59.) "I call upon the weak things of the world, those who are unlearned and despised, to thrash the nations by the power of my Spirit; And their arm shall be my arm, and I will be their shield and their buckler; and I will gird up their loins, and they shall fight manfully for me." (D. & C. 35:13-14, 17.)

The fact that all men, even the greatest of the prophets, have weaknesses is in no sense justification for failure to strive for excellence in all fields of endeavor. All men have appetites of one kind or another, but this is no justification, for instance, for using tea, coffee, tobacco, or liquor. The Word of Wisdom is "adapted to the capacity of the weak and the weakest of all saints, who are or can be called saints." (D. & C. 89:3.) Men are obligated to overcome their weaknesses as rapidly as they can.

WEALTH.
See RICHES.

WEEK.
See SABBATH.

WEEPING.
See GNASHING OF TEETH, GRIEF, MOURNING, SACKCLOTH AND ASHES, SIGNS OF THE TIMES, SORROW, WOES. *Weeping* is a part of righteous mourning, as when Abraham wept for Sarah (Gen. 23:2), or as when our Lord wept at the tomb of Lazarus. (John 11:1-46; 20:11.) "There is . . . A time to weep, and a time to laugh." (Eccles. 3:1-4.) "Blessed are ye that weep now: for ye shall laugh. . . . Woe unto you that laugh now! for ye shall mourn and weep." (Luke 6:21-25.) True saints "weep with them that weep." (Rom. 12:15.) God wept, and the heavens wept, when Lucifer and his hosts were cast out. (Moses 7:28-29.)

There are both tears of sorrow and tears of joy. (D. & C. 128:23.) When the heart is touched with feelings of tenderness, compassion, and love, tears of joy may flow. The resurrected Lord, ministering among the Nephites, beholding their supreme faith and devotion, said: "Blessed are ye because of your faith. And now behold, my joy is full. And when he had said these words, *he wept,* and the multitude bare record of it." (3 Ne. 17:20-21.)

Weeping shall prevail among the wicked in the last days, for calamities shall be poured out upon them because of their iniquities. (D. & C. 29:15; 45:53; 112:24.) "Weep not for me, but weep for yourselves, and for your children," our Lord told the daughters of Jerusalem as he foresaw the future desolations that would befall them and their seed. (Luke 23:27-31.) Among the damned souls in hell "there shall be weeping, and wailing, and gnashing of teeth, and this because of their own iniquity, being led captive by the will of the devil." (Alma 40:13-14; Mosiah 16:2; Hela. 13:32-33; Jas. 5:1-6; D. & C. 19:5; 101:89-91; 133: 73.)

WELFARE FARMS.
See CHURCH WELFARE PLAN.

WELFARE PLAN.
See CHURCH WELFARE PLAN.

WELFARE PROJECTS.
See CHURCH WELFARE PLAN.

WELFARE REGIONS.
See CHURCH WELFARE PLAN.

WENTWORTH LETTER.
See ARTICLES OF FAITH, CHURCH OF JESUS CHRIST OF LATTER-DAY SAINTS, FIRST VISION, JOSEPH SMITH THE PROPHET. One of the choicest inspired documents ever written is the Wentworth Letter.

First published in the Times and Seasons of March 1, 1842, it was written by the Prophet Joseph Smith to Mr. Wentworth, editor and proprietor of the Chicago Democrat. "I have written the following sketch of the rise, progress, persecution, and faith of the Latter-day Saints, of which I have the honor, under God, of being the founder," the Prophet said.

It was in this letter that the Prophet left us one of his two recorded accounts of the First Vision; in it he tells of Moroni's visits and the coming forth of the Book of Mormon; it is from this document that we gain the Prophet's description of the gold plates, his account of the Book of Mormon peoples, and of the ministry of apostles and prophets among them; it is here that he recounts the circumstances surrounding the organization of the Church, the inhuman persecutions (particularly in Missouri) that attended the saints, and the founding of Nauvoo.

It is from the Wentworth Letter that we get the 13 concise doctrinal statements known as the Articles of Faith. And it is in this letter that we have recorded one of the Prophet's most plain and expressively worded prophecies: "No unhallowed hand can stop the work from progressing; persecutions may rage, mobs may combine, armies may assemble, calumny may defame, but the truth of God will go forth boldly, nobly, and independent, till it has penetrated every *continent, visited every clime, swept every country, and sounded in every ear, till the purposes of God shall be accomplished, and the Great Jehovah shall say the work is done."* (*History of the Church*, vol. 4, pp. 535-541.)

WESTERN HEMISPHERE.
See NEW WORLD.

WHIRLWINDS.
See SIGNS OF THE TIMES.

WHISKY.
See WORD OF WISDOM.

WHITE HORSE PROPHECY.
See PROPHECY, REVELATION, SCRIPTURE, VISIONS. From time to time, accounts of various supposed visions, revelations, and prophecies are spread forth by and among the Latter-day Saints, who should know better than to believe or spread such false information. One of these false and deceptive documents that has cropped up again and again for over a century is the so-called *White Horse Prophecy.* This supposed prophecy purports to be a long and detailed account by the Prophet Joseph Smith concerning the wars, turmoils, and difficulties which should exist in the last days.

It is a sad commentary on the spiritual insight of professing saints that they will generate intense in-

terest in these supposed prophetic utterances and yet know little of and pay less attention to the volumes of true and sound prophetic writings which delineate authoritatively the course of latter-day world events. It is known by all informed gospel students that whenever revealed truth, new or old, is to be sent forth for the enlightenment of the saints and of the world, it will be announced officially and publicly by the First Presidency.

Speaking, first of the White Horse Prophecy specifically, and then of all such false revelations in general, President Joseph F. Smith said: "The ridiculous story about the 'red horse,' and 'the black horse,' and 'the white horse,' and a lot of trash that has been circu-lated about, and printed, and sent around as a great revelation given by the Prophet Joseph Smith, is a matter that was gotten up, I understand, some ten years after the death of the Prophet Joseph Smith, by two of our brethren, who put together some broken sentences from the Prophet that they may have heard him utter from time to time, and formulated this so-called revelation out of it, and *it was never spoken by the Prophet in the manner in which they have put it forth. It is simply false; that is all there is to it.* . . .

"Now, these stories of revelations that are being circulated around are of no consequence, except for rumor and silly talk by

835

persons that have no authority. The fact of the matter is simply here and this. No man can enter into God's rest unless he will absorb the truth insofar that all error, all falsehood, all misunderstanding and mis-statements, he will be able to sift thoroughly and dissolve, and know that it is error and not truth. When you know God's truth, when you enter into God's rest, you will not be hunting after revelations from Tom, Dick, and Harry all over the world. You will not be following the will of the wisps of the vagaries of men and their own ideas. When you know the truth, you will abide in the truth, and the truth will make you free, and it is only the truth that will free you from the errors of men, and from the falsehood and misrepresentations of the evil one, who lies in wait to deceive and to mislead the people of God from the paths of righteousness and truth." (*Conf. Rep.*, Oct. 1918, p. 58.)

WHITE STONE.
See NEW NAME.

WHITSUNTIDE.
See DAY OF PENTECOST.

WHOREDOMS.
See SEX IMMORALITY.

WHOREMONGERS.
See SEX IMMORALITY.

WICKEDNESS.
See APOSTASY, DAMNATION, DISOBEDIENCE, INIQUITY, REBELLION, SIN, TELESTIAL LAW, TERRESTRIAL LAW. 1. In nearly every scriptural instance, the term *wickedness* is used to describe the sinful, evil, and immoral practices of those who live a telestial law, who are carnal, sensual, and devilish, who live after the manner of the world, being subject to its lusts and passions. The *wicked* are the depraved, the vicious, the evil persons whose conduct is inharmonious with the divine standards. They are living a telestial law because they are doing the things which will assure them of an eventual telestial inheritance.

Wicked acts proceed from the hearts of men, with the result that they contaminate both body and spirit. (Mark 7:20-23.) "There is no peace, saith the Lord, unto the wicked." (Isa. 48:22; 1 Ne. 20:22.) They are "in the gall of bitterness and in the bonds of iniquity; they are without God in the world, and they have gone contrary to the nature of God; therefore, they are in a state contrary to the nature of happiness." In effect they suffer hell on earth. "Wickedness never was happiness." (Alma 41:10-11.)

"God is angry with the wicked." (Ps. 7:11; D. & C. 63:32.) He has promised to take vengeance upon them. (D. & C. 29:17.) "Great destructions await the wicked." (D. & C. 34:9.) At the Second Coming there will be "an entire separation of the righteous and the wicked" (D. & C. 63:54), meaning that every person living a telestial law will be destroyed. (D. & C. 101:24.) That is the day which "shall burn as an oven; and all the proud, yea, and all that do wickedly, shall be stubble" (Mal. 4:1), the day when the Lord "with the breath of his lips," shall "slay the wicked." (Isa. 11:4.)

An awful hell awaits the wicked. (1 Ne. 15:29; Alma 40:14.) "The wicked shall be turned into hell, and all the nations that forget God." (Ps. 9:17.) They "shall go away into unquenchable fire." (D. & C. 43:33.)

But none of the desolations of this life nor the torments of the next need come upon the wicked; if they will but turn to righteousness, they will escape these things. "Let the wicked forsake his way, and the unrighteous man his thoughts: and let him return unto the Lord, and he will have mercy upon him; and to our God, for he will abundantly pardon." (Isa. 55:7.) "Have I any pleasure at all that the wicked should die? saith the Lord God: and not that he should return from his ways, and live?" (Ezek. 18:23.) "If the wicked restore the pledge, give again that he had robbed, walk in the statutes of life, without committing iniquity; he shall surely live, he shall not die. None of his sins that he hath committed shall be mentioned unto him: he hath done that which is lawful and right; he shall surely live." (Ezek. 33:15-16.)

2. In the full gospel sense even those who are living a terrestrial law, and who accordingly will *not* be destroyed at the Second Coming of Christ, are classified as wicked. By living a terrestrial law is meant that they are doing those things which will take them in due course to the terrestrial kingdom. In the full sense, only those who have accepted the gospel and are living its precepts, that is who are living a celestial law, find place among the righteous. It was in this sense that John spoke when he said, "We know that we are of God, and the whole world lieth in wickedness." (1 John 5:19.) That is, the saints who had forsaken the world were righteous; everyone else was wicked; for none but the saints were living a celestial law, the law of the gospel.

It was also in this special sense of the word that Deity spoke in our day: "The whole world lieth in sin, and groaneth under darkness and under the bondage of sin. And by this you may know they are under the bondage of sin, because they come not unto me. For whoso cometh not unto me is under the bondage of sin. And whoso receiveth not my voice is not acquainted with my voice, and is not of me. And *by this you may know the righteous from the wicked,* and that the whole world groaneth under sin and darkness even now." (D. & C. 84:49-53.)

This is the sense in which there will be wickedness on the earth during the millennium. *Telestial wick-*

edness will have ceased with the destruction of every corruptible thing, and those who have lived a terrestrial standard—though not wicked in the full worldly sense— shall be classified as wicked because they have fallen short of the celestial standard.

WISDOM.

See GIFTS OF THE SPIRIT, INTELLIGENCE, KNOWLEDGE, REVELATION, TRUTH, WISDOM BOOKS, WISDOM OF THE WORLD, WORD OF WISDOM. *Wisdom* is knowledge of those true principles by conformity to which men receive divine favor. It presupposes a wise and proper use of knowledge, a sound and discerning judgment in the affairs of life and conduct. It is an attribute of Deity, in whom it is found in its fulness and perfection. "He has all power, all wisdom, and all understanding." (Alma 26:35; 37:12; Mosiah 4:6, 9; D. & C. 76:2; Rev. 5:12; 7:12.)

Wisdom is a gift of the Spirit (D. & C. 46:17); it comes from God by revelation. "He that lacketh wisdom, let him ask of me," the Lord said, "and I will give him liberally and upbraid him not." (D. & C. 42:68.) It was on this principle that Joseph Smith sought the Lord and received the vision which ushered in the dispensation of the fulness of times. (Jos. Smith 2:11-20; Jas. 1:5-6.)

The course of wisdom is the course of obedience; there is no wisdom in wickedness. "The fear of the Lord is the beginning of wisdom: a good understanding have all they that do his commandments." (Ps. 111:10.) "Learn wisdom in thy youth; yea, learn in thy youth to keep the commandments of God." (Alma 37:35.) "Seek not for riches but for wisdom, and behold, the mysteries of God shall be unfolded unto you, and then shall you be made rich. Behold, he that hath eternal life is rich." (D. & C. 6:7; 11:7; Prov. 16:16.) The Lord's promise to the righteous is that "their wisdom shall be great, and their understanding reach to heaven." (D. & C. 76:9.)

Solomon is the symbol of wisdom: "I have given thee a wise and an understanding heart; so that there was none like thee before thee, neither after thee shall any arise like unto thee." (1 Kings 3:12.) As a result Solomon "spake three thousand proverbs: and his songs were a thousand and five. And he spake of trees, from the cedar tree that is in Lebanon even unto the hyssop that springeth out of the wall: he spake also of beasts, and of fowl, and of creeping things, and of fishes. And there came of all people to hear the wisdom of Solomon, from all kings of the earth, which had heard of his wisdom." (1 Kings 4:32-34.)

But Solomon did not endure to the end; his wisdom vanished away. He apostatized from the Church, worshiped false gods, and incurred the wrath of a just God. (1 Kings 11.)

WISDOM BOOKS.

See APOCRYPHA, BIBLE, WISDOM. It appears to have been a popular ancient custom for the accepted wise men of the day to formulate gems of wisdom in proverb form and to record their discourses on moral and ethical problems. These writings are commonly called the *wisdom books.* They include: Job, Proverbs, and Ecclesiastes—from the Bible; Wisdom of Jesus the Son of Sirach or Ecclesiasticus, and Wisdom of Solomon—from the Apocrypha.

WISDOM OF THE WORLD.

See APOSTASY, EVOLUTION, HIGHER CRITICISM, KNOWLEDGE, WISDOM, WORLD. Two kinds of wisdom are described in the scriptures: 1. True wisdom, that which is revealed by the Spirit and leads to righteousness and peace; 2. False wisdom, the *wisdom of the world,* which leads in carnal paths and away from the things of eternal worth.

The wisdom of the world results from the uninspired reflections, research, and discoveries of men. It is composed of partial and fragmentary truths mixed with error. Theorizing and hypothecating commonly accompany it. This type of wisdom includes the philosophies and learning of men which are destructive of faith. Astrology, organic evolution, the so-called higher criticism which denies the divinity of Christ, and any supposed knowledge which rules God out of the picture, falls in this category.

The wisdom of the world is transitory; it will vanish away. But the wisdom of God is eternal; it will endure forever. Scientific theories change with every new discovery, but the wisdom revealed from God is eternal truth. (*Doctrines of Salvation,* vol. 1, pp. 320-324.)

"Hath not God made foolish the wisdom of this world?" Paul asked. Then with great inspiration he explained how the things of the Spirit take precedence over the learning of men. (1 Cor. 1:18-31; 2; 3:18-23.) Jacob wrote similarly: "O that cunning plan of the evil one! O the vainness, and the frailties, and the foolishness of men! When they are learned they think they are wise, and they hearken not unto the counsel of God, for they set it aside, supposing they know of themselves, wherefore, their wisdom is foolishness and it profiteth them not. And they shall perish. But to be learned is good if they hearken unto the counsels of God." (2 Ne. 9:28-29, 41-43.)

WISE MEN.
See MAGI.

WITCHCRAFT.

See CONJURE MAN, DIVINATION, EVIL SPIRITS, EXORCISM, FORTUNE TELLING, HYPNOTISM, INCANTATIONS, MAGIC, MEDICINE MEN, MEDIUMS, NECROMANCY, SOOTH-

SAYERS, SORCERY, SPIRITUALISM, SUPERSTITION, WITCH DOCTORS, WITCHES SABBATH, WIZARDS. One of the most evil and wicked sects supported by Satan is that which practices *witchcraft,* such craft involving as it does actual intercourse with evil spirits. A *witch* is one who engages in this craft, who practices the black art of magic, who has entered into a compact with Satan, who is a sorcerer or sorceress. Modernly the term witch has been limited in application to women.

There are no witches, of course, in the sense of old hags flying on broomsticks through October skies; such mythology is a modernistic spoofing of a little understood practice that prevailed in all the apostate kingdoms of the past and which even now is found among many peoples. (Deut. 18:9-14; 2 Kings 9:22; 21:6; 2 Chron. 33:6; Isa. 19:3; Gal. 5:20; Morm. 1:19; 2:10.)

"When thou art come into the land which the Lord thy God giveth thee," the God of Israel said to his people, "thou shalt not learn to do after the abominations of those nations. There shall not be found among you any one that maketh his son or his daughter to pass through the fire, or that useth *divination,* or an *observer of times,* or an *enchanter,* or a *witch,* Or *a charmer, or a consulter with familiar spirits, or a wizard, or a necromancer.* For all that do these things are an abomination unto the Lord: and because of these abominations the Lord thy God doth drive them out from before thee. Thou shalt be perfect with the Lord thy God. For these nations, which thou shalt possess, hearkened unto observers of times, and unto diviners: but as for thee, the Lord thy God hath not suffered thee so to do." (Deut. 18:9-14.)

Lest his people Israel be led to hell by practicing all these abominations—and all of them are part and portion of the craft of witches —the Lord decreed: "Thou shalt not suffer a witch to live." (Ex. 22:18.) First excommunication and then death by stoning was the penalty. (Lev. 20:6, 27.) It should be noted that the trying, convicting, and executing of so-called witches during the middle ages and in early American history was a wholly apostate and unwarranted practice. It is probable that none, or almost none, of those unhappily dealt with as supposed witches were persons in actual communion with evil spirits. Their deaths illustrate the deadly extremes to which the principles of true religion can be put when administered by uninspired persons.

Witchcraft is one of the "works of the flesh" (Gal. 5:19-20), and in that day when the glory of Israel is fully restored the Lord has promised to cut off witchcrafts and to destroy soothsayers out of the land. (3 Ne. 21:16; Mic. 5:12.)

WITCH DOCTORS.
See CONJURE MAN, MAGIC, MEDICINE MEN, SORCERY, WITCHCRAFT.

So-called *witch doctors* are found among primitive peoples. These ministers of false religious principles frequently engage in practices of magic and sorcery. Their ostensible aim is one of detecting or "smelling out" witches and of counteracting their magic spells and influence.

WITCHES.
See WITCHCRAFT.

WITCHES SABBATH.
See MEDIUMS, SEANCES, SORCERY, WITCHCRAFT. A *witches sabbath,* according to medieval demonology, was imagined to be a midnight assembly in which witches, sorcerers, and demons joined together to celebrate their evil orgies. Such orgies no doubt have taken place among peoples steeped in the mysteries of witchcraft. Probably the nearest thing to them among modern and supposedly civilized peoples are the seances in which mediums actually hold intercourse with devils.

WITNESSES.
See LAW OF WITNESSES.

WITNESSES OF THE BOOK OF MORMON.
See BOOK OF MORMON, GOLD PLATES, LAW OF WITNESSES. To fulfil the law of witnesses, the Lord commanded others in addition to the Prophet to bear record of the divinity of the Book of Mormon. Two groups, known as the *Three Witnesses* and as the *Eight Witnesses,* have left their solemn testimonies, testimonies which are published with each copy of the book itself. The Three Witnesses were shown the Gold Plates by the Angel Moroni, and they heard the voice of God bear record that the translation was correct. They also saw the breastplate, the sword of Laban, the Urim and Thummim, and the Liahona. The Eight Witnesses were shown the Plates by the Prophet, and they left their testimony of what their eyes had seen and their hands had felt.

In the Book of Mormon itself the promise is made that witnesses would be provided. (2 Ne. 11:3; 27: 12; Ether 5:2-4.) Knowing this, Oliver Cowdery, David Whitmer, and Martin Harris were moved by an inspired desire to be chosen as such special witnesses of the book's divinity. The Prophet, at their solicitation, inquired of the Lord and received a reply that these brethren could have the desire of their hearts. (D. & C. 17.)

"Not many days after the above commandment was given," the Prophet says of the revelation naming the Three Witnesses, "we four, viz., Martin Harris, David Whitmer, Oliver Cowdery and myself, agreed to retire into the woods, and try to obtain, by fervent and humble prayer, the fulfilment of the promises given in the above revelation—that they should have a view of the plates. We accordingly made choice of a piece of woods convenient to Mr. Whitmer's house, to which we retired, and having knelt down, we began to pray in much faith to Almighty God to bestow upon us a realization of these promises.

"According to previous arrangement, I commenced by vocal prayer to our Heavenly Father, and was followed by each of the others in succession. We did not at the first trial, however, obtain any answer or manifestation of divine favor in our behalf. We again observed the same order of prayer, each calling on and praying fervently to God in rotation, but with the same result as before.

"Upon this, our second failure, Martin Harris proposed that he should withdraw himself from us, believing, as he expressed himself, that his presence was the cause of our not obtaining what we wished for. He accordingly withdrew from us, and we knelt down again, and had not been many minutes engaged in prayer, when presently we beheld a light above us in the air, of exceeding brightness; and behold, *an angel stood before us. In his hands he held the plates which we had been praying for these to have a view of. He turned over the leaves one by one, so that we could see them, and discern the engravings thereon distinctly.* He then addressed himself to David Whitmer, and said, 'David, blessed is the Lord, and he that keeps his commandments'; when, immediately afterwards, *we heard a voice from out of the bright light above us, saying, 'These plates have been revealed by the power of God, and they have been translated by the power of God. The translation of them which you have seen is correct, and I command you to bear record of what you now see and hear.'*

"I now left David and Oliver, and went in pursuit of Martin Harris, whom I found at a considerable distance, fervently engaged in prayer. He soon told me, however, that he had not yet prevailed with the Lord, and earnestly requested me to join him in prayer, that he also might realize the same blessings which we had just received. We accordingly joined in prayer, and ultimately obtained our desires, for before we had yet finished, *the same vision was opened to our view,* at least it was again opened to me, and I once more beheld and heard the same things; whilst at the same moment, Martin Harris cried out, apparently in an ecstasy of joy, "'Tis enough; 'tis enough; mine eyes have beheld; mine eyes have beheld'; and jumping up, he shouted, 'Hosanna,' blessing God and otherwise rejoiced exceedingly." (*History of the Church,* vol. 1, pp. 54-55.)

These Three Witnesses later left the Church and became enemies of the Prophet, but throughout their entire lives each of them remained steadfast in bearing testimony of the divinity of the Book of Mormon. Oliver Cowdery and Martin Harris, in their latter years, returned to the Church and died in full fellowship. (*Doctrines of Salvation,* vol. 1, pp. 222-228.)

Although the Three Witnesses and the Eight Witnesses are in a class by themselves—for their testimonies shall rise up to condemn the unbelieving and rebellious before the judgment seat of Christ—yet there are or will be 10,000 times 10,000 other witnesses to testify with equal surety of the truth of the Book of Mormon. Every person who will abide the law entitling him to know of the truth of this Nephite record shall gain personal revelation from the Holy Ghost of its divinity, thus becoming a personal witness of its truth. (Moro. 10:3-5.)

WIZARDRY.
See WIZARDS.

WIZARDS.
See DIVINATION, MAGIC, SORCERY, SPIRITUALISM, WITCHCRAFT. A *wizard* is a sorcerer, one who has magical skills, who engages in witchcraft, who communes with familiar spirits. The practice of wizardry is an abomination (Lev. 19:31; Deut. 18:9-12), and in an-

cient Israel the penalty therefor was death. (Lev. 20:6, 27.)

WOES.
See GRIEF, MISERY, SORROW. In a host of scriptures the Lord and his prophets speak of *woes* coming upon individuals or multitudes because of failure to abide some prescribed standard of divine excellence. The meaning is that deep or inconsolable grief or misery will attend the commission of some proscribed act, the omission of some required duty, or that such penalty will grow out of an ungodly course of conduct. For instance: "Wo unto the liar, for he shall be thrust down to hell." (2 Ne. 9:34.) "Wo unto that house, or that village or city that rejecteth you, or your words, or your testimony concerning me." (D. & C. 84:94.) "Woe is unto me, if I preach not the gospel!" (1 Cor. 9:16.) "Woes shall go forth, weeping, wailing and gnashing of teeth, yea, to those who are found on my left hand." (D. & C. 19:5.)

WOMAN.
See EVE, MAN. As Adam was the first man of all men, the primal parent of the human race (Moses 1:34), so Eve his wife, was "the mother of all living," and "the first of all *women*." (Moses 4:26.) The figurative account of her creation says, "She shall be called Woman, because she was taken out of man." (Moses 3:23.)

Setting the pattern for all her daughters for all ages, Eve's mortal mission included two special assignments: 1. She was to be an help meet for her husband (Moses 3:20); and 2. She was to bring forth children. "I will greatly multiply thy sorrow and thy conception," the Lord said. "In sorrow thou shalt bring forth children, and thy desire shall be to thy husband, and he shall rule over thee." (Moses 4:22.) Thus woman's primary place is in the home, where she is to rear children and abide by the righteous counsel of her husband.

Peter counseled: "Ye wives, be in subjection to your own husbands," wearing simple, unadorned apparel, "For after this manner in the old time the holy women also, who trusted in God, adorned themselves, being in subjection unto their own husbands: Even as Sara obeyed Abraham, calling him lord: whose daughters ye are, as long as ye do well." (1 Pet. 3:1-6.)

Paul taught: Man "is the image and glory of God: but the woman is the glory of the man. For the man is not of the woman; but the woman of the man. Neither was the man created for the woman; but the woman for the man. . . . Nevertheless neither is the man without the woman, neither the woman without the man, in the Lord. For as the woman is of the man, even so is the man also by the woman; but all things of God." (1 Cor. 11:7-12.)

In the true Patriarchal Order man holds the priesthood and is the head of the household of faith, but he cannot attain a fulness of joy here or of eternal reward hereafter alone. Woman stands at his side a joint-inheritor with him in the fulness of all things. Exaltation and eternal increase is her lot as well as his. (D. & C. 131:1-4.) Godhood is not for men only; it is for men and women together. (D. & C. 132:19-20.)

WORD.
See WORD OF GOD.

WORD OF GOD.
See CHRIST, CREATOR, LOGOS, REVELATION, SCRIPTURE. 1. Christ is the *Word* (John 1:1-5, 14), the *Word of Life* (1 John 1:1), the *Word of God* (Rev. 19:11-16), the *Word of God's Power* (Moses 1:32) —all of which titles signify that the words of salvation are in him; that he carries his Father's word to all men; that he is the executive and administrator who does the will of the Father; that the Father speaks and his word is executed by the Son. (D. & C. 93:8.)

Use of the title, *Word of God,* is usually in connection with the creative enterprises of the Son. (John 1:1-5; Moses 1:32-35.) The clear meaning is that God speaks his word, which the Son, by the power of the Spirit, puts into operation, and thereby becomes himself the *Word.* (Moses 2:5, 16; 3:7; 4:3; Jac.

4:9; Morm. 9:17; D. & C. 29:30.)

2. By the *word of God* is also meant the scriptures, the revelations, the message of salvation which God sends by the mouths of holy men called to his ministry. Hence, we find such counsel as that given by Paul to Timothy: *"Preach the word;* be instant in season, out of season; reprove, rebuke, exhort with all longsuffering and doctrine." (2 Tim. 4:2.)

WORD OF LIFE.
See WORD OF GOD.

WORD OF WISDOM.

See DISEASES, DRUNKENNESS, HEALTH, HOT DRINKS, PHYSICIANS, STRONG DRINKS. A revelation given to Joseph Smith, February 27, 1833, containing a *part* of the revealed counsel in the field of health, because it begins, "A Word of Wisdom, for the benefit of . . . the church" (D. & C. 89:1), is now commonly known as the *Word of Wisdom.* As a revealed law of health, dealing particularly with dietary matters, it contains both positive and negative instructions. Its affimative provision gives directions for the use of meat and grain by both man and animals; its prohibitions direct man to refrain from the use of certain specified harmful things. (D. & C. 89.)

Three types of things are prohibited to man by the Word of Wisdom—tobacco, strong drinks, and hot drinks. By strong drinks is meant alcoholic beverages; hot drinks, according to the Prophet's own statement, mean tea and coffee. Accordingly the negative side of the Word of Wisdom is a command to abstain from *tea, coffee, tobacco,* and *liquor.*

Abstinence from these four things has been accepted by the Church as a measuring rod to determine in part the personal worthiness of church members. When decisions are made relative to the granting of temple recommends or approving brethren for church positions or ordinations, inquiry is made relative to these four items.

Obviously the standard of judgment must be uniform throughout the Church, and local officers are not at liberty to add other items to this list. However, there are many other substances which have a harmful effect on the human body, though such particular things are not specifically prohibited by the Word of Wisdom. Certainly the partaking of cola drinks, though not included within the measuring standard here set out, is in violation of the spirit of the Word of Wisdom. Harmful drugs of any sort are in a like category.

Some unstable people become cranks with reference to this law of health. It should be understood that the Word of Wisdom is not the gospel, and the gospel is not the Word of Wisdom. As Paul said, "The kingdom of God is not meat and drink; but righteousness, and peace, and joy in the Holy Ghost." (Rom. 14:17.)

There is no prohibition in Section 89, for instance, as to the eating of white bread, using white flour, white sugar, cocoa, chocolate, eggs, milk, meat, or anything else, except items classified under the headings, tea, coffee, tobacco, and liquor. As a matter of fact those who command that men should not eat meat, are not ordained of God, such counsel being listed by Paul as an evidence of apostasy. God has created "meats," he says, *"to be received with thanksgiving of them which believe and know the truth."* (1 Tim. 4:3.) If some particular food or drink disagrees with an individual, then that person should act accordingly without reference to the prohibitions in this particular law of health.

Actually, the Word of Wisdom is only a small part of the revealed truth relative to health and the use of food and drink. For instance, months before the Word of Wisdom was revealed, the Lord said this to his saints: "The fulness of the earth is yours, the beasts of the field and the fowls of the air, and that which climbeth upon the trees and walketh upon the earth; Yea, and the herb, and the good things which come of the earth, whether for food or for raiment, or for houses, or for barns, or for orchards, or for gardens, or for vineyards; Yea, *all things which come of the earth, in the season thereof, are made for the benefit and the use of man, both to* *please the eye and to gladden the heart; Yea for food and for raiment, for taste and for smell, to strengthen the body and to enliven the soul.* And it pleaseth God that he hath given all these things unto man; for unto this end were they made to be used, with judgment, not to excess, neither by extortion." (D. & C. 59:16-20.)

When first given the Word of Wisdom was not a commandment, but it has since been made one. "Give heed to this Word of Wisdom," President Joseph F. Smith said. *"It was given unto us 'not by commandment'; but by the word of President Brigham Young, it was made a commandment unto the saints." (Gospel Doctrine,* 5th ed., p. 365.) The Prophet himself gave this decision: *"No official member in this Church is worthy to hold an office after having the Word of Wisdom properly taught him, and he, the official member, neglecting to comply with and obey it." (Teachings,* p. 117.)

Obedience to this divine law brings many temporal and spiritual blessings. Physical well-being and increased temporal prosperity are among the temporal advantages. In the spiritual field, those who observe this law "shall find wisdom and great treasures of knowledge, even hidden treasures." (D. & C. 89:19.) In other words, through the cleanliness resulting from keeping this law of health, and by "walking in obedience to the commandments" (D. & C. 89:18), the saints will qualify for the companionship of the Holy Spirit, with great spiritual endowments coming as a result thereof. (*Gospel Doctrine*, 5th ed., pp. 365-368.)

WORDS.
See IDLE WORDS.

WORK.
See CHURCH WELFARE PLAN, DOLE, EMPLOYMENT, GOOD WORKS. *Work* is the great basic principle which makes all things possible both in time and in eternity. Men, spirits, angels, and Gods use their physical and mental powers in work. "My Father worketh hitherto, and I work," Jesus announced. (John 5:17.) Also: "I must work the works of him that sent me, while it is day." (John 9:4.)

Without work there would be neither existence, creation, redemption, salvation, or temporal necessities for mortal man. Deity worked six days in the creation of this earth and then rested on the seventh. (Ex. 20:8-11.) The Father's work and glory is to bring to pass the immortality and eternal life of man. (Moses 1:39.) Our Lord's mission was to work out the infinite and eternal atonement. (3 Ne. 27:13-17.) Man is commanded to work both temporally and spiritually—to work out his salvation with fear and trembling before God (Philip. 2:12), and to earn his living by the sweat of his face until he returns

to the ground. (Gen. 3:19.) *Work is a blessing that brings salvation, idleness a curse that assures damnation.*

WORKS.
See GOOD WORKS.

WORLD.
See BABYLON, EARTH, EARTHS, MILLENNIUM, SECOND COMING OF CHRIST. At least two distinct meanings are found in the scripture for *the world*. 1. The earth or planet upon which we dwell (Moses 1:33); 2. The social conditions created by such of the inhabitants of the earth as live carnal, sensuous, lustful lives, and who have not put off the natural man by obedience to the laws and ordinances of the gospel.

Christ said: "I am not of the world." (John 17:16.) "I have overcome the world." (John 16:33.) To his apostles he said: "If ye were of the world, the world would love his own: but because ye are not of the world, but I have chosen you out of the world, therefore the world hateth you." (John 15:19.)

All mortals who arrive at the years of accountability are of the world unless they put off the natural man, become new creatures of the Holy Ghost, and gain the rebirth of the Spirit. Alma taught that since the fall of Adam all mankind has "become carnal, sensual, and devilish, by nature." (Alma 42:10.)

The angelic ministrant to King Benjamin said: "The *natural man is an enemy to God,* and has been from the fall of Adam, and will be, forever and ever, unless he yields to the enticings of the Holy Spirit, and putteth off the natural man and becometh a saint through the atonement of Christ the Lord." (Mosiah 3:19.)

Members of the Church have the goal of overcoming the world. *"Love not the world,"* John said, "neither the things that are in the world. If any man love the world, the love of the Father is not in him. For all that is in the world, the lust of the flesh, and the lust of the eyes, and the pride of life, is not of the Father, but is of the world. And *the world passeth away,* and the lust thereof: but he that doeth the will of God abideth for ever." (1 John 2: 15-17.)

James wrote: "Ye adulterers and adulteresses, know ye not that *the friendship of the world is enmity with God?* whosoever therefore will be a friend of the world is the enemy of God." (Jas. 4:4.)

The end of the world is the end of unrighteousness or of worldliness as we know it, and this will be brought about by "the destruction of the wicked." (Jos. Smith 1:4.) When our world ends and the millennial era begins, there will be a new heaven and a new earth. (Isa. 65:17-25; D. & C. 101:23-24.) Lust, carnality, and sensuousness of every sort will cease, for it will be *the end of the world.*

WORLDS.
See EARTHS.

WORSHIP.
See HONOR, OBEISANCE, PRAYER, REVERENCE, THANKSGIVING, WORSHIP OF IMAGES. *Worship* consists in paying divine honors to a deity. This religious reverence and homage falls into two categories—*true worship* and *false worship,* the one based on gospel truth and leading to salvation, the other consisting of an intermixture of truth and error and leading to damnation.

The Father and the Son are the objects of all true worship. "Thou shalt worship the Lord thy God, and him only shalt thou serve." (Matt. 4:10; Luke 4:8; Ex. 34:14; Mosiah 18:25; D. & C. 20:17-19.) No one can worship the Father without also worshiping the Son. "All men should honour the Son, even as they honour the Father. He that honoureth not the Son honoureth not the Father which hath sent him." (John 5:23.) It is proper to worship the Father, in the name of the Son, and also to worship the Son. "Believe in Christ, and deny him not; and Christ is the Holy One of Israel; wherefore ye must bow down before him, and worship him with all your might, mind, and strength, and your whole soul; and if ye do this ye shall in nowise be cast out." (2 Ne. 25:16, 29.)

True worship presupposes a knowledge of the truth about God and his laws. Jesus told the Samaritan woman at the well: "Ye worship ye know not what: we know what we worship: for salvation is of the Jews." (John 4:22.) Our Lord revealed anew some of the writings of John—writings which explained how Christ himself had worked out his own salvation, finally receiving all power in heaven and on earth—and then he said: "I give unto you these sayings that you may understand and know *how to worship,* and know *what you worship,* that you may come unto the Father in my name, and in due time receive of his fulness." (D. & C. 93:6-20.) *Unless men know God and his laws they cannot "worship him in spirit and in truth"* (John 4:24), *and there is no salvation in any other kind of worship.*

Deity is worshiped in prayer, song, sermon, and testimony; by the making of covenants, offering of sacrifices, performance of ordinances, and the participation in religious rituals and ceremonies; he is worshiped by man's act of believing divine truths, by his being converted to them in their fulness; he may be worshiped in thought, word, and deed. But the most perfect of all worship comes from those who first believe the gospel, who then participate in its outward forms, and who finally keep the standards of personal righteousness that appertain to it.

Obedience is the true measure of true worship. "In vain they do worship me, teaching for doctrines the commandments of men." (Matt. 15:

9; Mark 7:6-8.) "Give unto the Lord the glory due unto his name; worship the Lord in the beauty of holiness." (Ps. 29:2.) Without personal righteousness, without the beauty of holiness, there is no true worship.

Most of the worship in the world is *false worship* because it rejects the fulness of the restored truth, does not cling to Christ and his gospel standards, substituting rather a form of godliness which denies the power thereof. (Jos. Smith 2:19.) To the extent that false worship turns away from God, it turns to the devil, so that men actually (though often unknowingly, for they are in apostate darkness) worship the dragon (Rev. 13:4, 15; 14:9), idols (Isa. 2:8), money, and the like.

WORSHIP OF IMAGES.

See APOSTASY, FALSE GODS, IDOLATRY, TEN COMMANDMENTS. According to their own official statement, Catholics *worship images*—not just false gods or a concept of Deity which is false and untrue—but out and out, plainly and simply stated, they worship the actual images of the so-called saints which are everywhere found in their cathedrals and other buildings. In their own encyclopedia they make careful recitation of their belief that there are two kinds of worship, the supreme adoraton reserved for Deity only and the lesser adoration and worship given the images of their saints and such symbols as the cross.

"Something must be said about the Catholic principles concerning the worship of sacred images," the *Catholic Encyclopedia* says under the subheading, *Principles of Image-Worship*, in an article entitled *Images*. "Worship by no means implies only the supreme adoration that may be given only to God."

Then consideration is given to the command, *"Thou shalt not make unto thee any graven image, or any likeness of any thing that is in heaven above, or that is in the earth beneath, or that is in the water under the earth: Thou shalt not bow down thyself to them, nor serve them"* (Ex. 20:4-5), and it is explained that this part of the Ten Commandments has been abolished. They say it is not part of natural law and was discontinued along with the law of Moses. The reason given is that no one can "prove the inherent wickedness of making a graven thing."

Their analysis is summarized with these four principles: 1. "It is forbidden to give divine honour or worship to the angels and saints, for this belongs to God alone." 2. *"We should pay the angels and saints an inferior honour or worship, for this is due to them as the servants and special friends of God."* 3. "We should give to relics, crucifixes and holy pictures a relative honour, as they relate to Christ and his saints and are memorials of

them." 4. "We do not pray to relics or images, for they can neither see nor hear nor help us."

In spite of this formal assertion that the worship of images should not include the offering of prayers to them, it is well known that in practice great hosts of Catholics have prayed and do now pray to the image itself. Even the *Catholic Encyclopedia* itself admits: "The customs by which we show our 'respect and worshipful honour' for holy images naturally *vary in different countries and at different times*. Only the authority of the Church has occasionally stepped in, sometimes to prevent a spasmodic return to Iconoclasm, *more often to forbid excesses of such signs of reverence as would be misunderstood and give scandal.*"

In other words, when the level of intelligence has been such among the people of a nation as to cause them to revolt at the pagan absurdity of praying to the image itself, the Catholic hierarchy has forbidden the excesses which consisted in praying to the image itself. It is, of course, well understood that Catholic prayers are addressed to the saint, before whose image the worshiper kneels, with the hope that such saint will intercede with Mary and with the Lord. (*Catholic Encyclopedia,* vol. 7, pp. 670-672.)

WORTHINESS.

See OBEDIENCE, RIGHTEOUSNESS, SALVATION. In gospel usage, *worth-*

iness has reference to meriting a blessing or reward because of obedience to that law upon which its receipt is predicated. Worthiness is determined solely on the basis of personal righteousness. (D. & C. 41:6; 50:34; 51:4-5; 67:14; 90:26.) For instance: Accountable persons who have faith and repent of their sins are worthy of baptism; church members who have "a godly walk and conversation" are worthy to partake of the sacrament (D. & C. 20:69); and those who keep all of the standards of the Church are worthy of the blessings of the temple.

Salvation itself is the crowning reward of worthiness (Rev. 3:4; D. & C. 105:35-36; 107:100), and it is Christ himself—together with those, who being "like him" (1 John 3:1-3) are "joint-heirs" with him (Rom. 8:14-17)—who are and shall be "Worthy . . . to receive power, and riches, and wisdom, and strength, and honour, and glory, and blessing." (Rev. 5:12.)

On the other hand unworthiness deprives men of blessings; those who attempt to gain blessings in unworthiness are damned. "Whoso eateth and drinketh my flesh and blood unworthily eateth and drinketh damnation to his soul." (3 Ne. 18:29; 1 Cor. 11:29.) "See that ye are not baptized unworthily; see that ye partake not of the sacrament of Christ unworthily; but *see that ye do all things in worthiness.*" (Morm. 9:29.)

WRATH.

See ANGER, INDIGNATION. Deity manifests *wrath* as one of his attributes. It is an accompaniment of anger; indignation is its emotional basis; inherent in it is the purpose and intent of meting out a just punishment upon those whose acts have caused it to be aroused. The wrath of God does not fall upon the righteous, but upon the wicked. (D. & C. 1:9; 59:21.) "Instead of blessings, ye, by your own works, bring cursings, wrath, indignation, and judgments upon your own heads, by your follies, and by all your abominations, which you practise before me, saith the Lord." (D. & C. 124:48.)

When men are "ripened in iniquity," then the fulness of the Lord's wrath comes upon them, and they are destroyed in the flesh. (Ether 2:8-9; 14:25.) Such was the case with the Jaredites, the Nephites, and the inhabitants of Sodom and Gomorrah, for instance; such will be the case with the wicked at the Second Coming. The "fiery indignation of the wrath of God" will continue to be poured out upon the wicked in hell until the day of their resurrection. (Alma 40:14; Rev. 14:10; D. & C. 19:15; 76:106-107.) Then, to all eternity, those subject to the second death shall be "vessels of wrath, doomed to suffer the wrath of God, with the devil and his angels in eternity." (D. & C. 76:33, 38.)

When exhibited by mortals,

wrath frequently implies rage and leads those so emotionally exercised to seek revenge for real or supposed wrongs. Paul lists wrath as one of the works of the flesh (Gal. 5:19-20) and counsels, "Let not the sun go down upon your wrath." (Eph. 4:26, 31; 6:4; Col. 3:8.) Obviously, no matter what the provocation, the gospel is not to be preached with strife or in wrath. (D. & C. 60:7, 14.)

WRITING.
See ADAMIC LANGUAGE.

WRONGDOING.
See SIN.

XMAS.
See CHRISTMAS. Since the letter X has been accepted as an abbreviation for Christ, it is not uncommon to find Christmas abbreviated as *Xmas,* Christian as *Xn* or *Xtian,* and Christianity as *Xty.* These abbreviations do not partake of the real spirit of reverence that should attend a reference to Deity, or to something closely associated with him, and accordingly their use should be discouraged.

YAHWEH.
See CHRIST, JAH, JEHOVAH, LORD, TETRAGRAMMATON. *Yahweh* is believed to be the most accurate reconstruction of the Hebrew word meaning *Jehovah* (who is Christ). Other reconstructions of this name of Deity are: *Yahwe, Yahve, Yahveh, Jahweh,* and *Jahveh.*

YEARS.
See TIME.

YEARS OF ACCOUNTABILITY.
See ACCOUNTABILITY, AGENCY, BAPTISM, INFANT BAPTISM, ORIGINAL SIN THEORY, SALVATION OF CHILDREN, TEMPTATION. When a child reaches the age at which he has sufficient mental, spiritual, and physical maturity to be held accountable before God for his acts, he is said to have arrived at the *years of accountability.* He then knows right from wrong and can

exercise his agency to do good or evil. Accordingly he must pay the penalty for his sins, unless he gains a remission of them through repentance and baptism, "For all men must repent and be baptized, and not only men, but women, and children who have arrived at the years of accountability." (D. & C. 18:42.) "No one can be received into the church of Christ unless he has arrived unto the years of accountability before God, and is capable of repentance." (D. & C. 20:71.)

Attainment of the age and state of accountability is a gradual process. Thus the Lord says that "power is not given unto Satan to tempt little children, until they begin to become accountable before me." (D. & C. 29:47.) Children who develop normally become accountable "when eight years old" (D. & C. 68:27), and they are then subject to the law of baptism. Obviously if children or adults do not develop mentally to the point where they know right from wrong and have the normal intellect of an accountable person, they never arrive at the years of accountability no matter how many actual years they may live. Such persons, though they may be adults, are without the law, cannot repent, are under no condemnation, "and unto such baptism availeth nothing." (Moro. 8:22.) Because they have no "understanding" it remains for the Lord "to do according as it is written" concerning them (D. & C. 29:48-50), that is, save them through the power of his redemptive sacrifice. (Moro. 8:22.)

YMMIA.
See MUTUAL IMPROVEMENT ASSOCIATIONS.

YOKE OF CHRIST.
See CHRIST, GOSPEL, OBEDIENCE, SERVICE. To keep the commandments and serve with fidelity and devotion in the Church is to wear the *Yoke of Christ*, the yoke of service and devotion. Those who love the Lord and desire salvation willingly shoulder this yoke, thereby finding rest to their souls (Matt. 11:28-30) and discovering that the Lord's commandments are not grievous. (1 John 5:3.)

YOUNG MEN'S MUTUAL IMPROVEMENT ASSOCIATION.
See MUTUAL IMPROVEMENT ASSOCIATIONS.

YOUNG WOMEN'S MUTUAL IMPROVEMENT ASSOCIATION.
See MUTUAL IMPROVEMENT ASSOCIATIONS.

YULETIDE.
See CHRISTMAS.

YWMIA.
See MUTUAL IMPROVEMENT ASSOCIATIONS.

Z

ZEAL.

See DEVOTION, DILIGENCE, DUTY, ENDURING TO THE END, FANATICISM, OBEDIENCE. True *zeal* is an attribute of godliness which men acquire through participation in the cause of righteousness. It consists in being earnestly, intensely, and "anxiously engaged in a good cause." (D. & C. 58:27; Gal. 4:18.) It is acquired following acceptance of the truth, godly sorrow for sin, and true repentance. (2 Cor. 7:10-11.) Members of the Church are obligated to "be zealous" in the cause of Christ. (Rev. 3:19.)

False zeal is that religious devotion and enthusiasm which is not based on truth. A zeal toward God which is "not according to knowledge," meaning the true knowledge of salvation, is false and unprofitable. (Rom. 10:2.) Before his conversion Paul manifested zeal "not according to knowledge" when he persecuted the Church. (Philip. 3:4-7.)

ZION.

See HOLY ONE OF ZION, MILLENNIUM, SECOND COMING OF CHRIST, STAKES, TRANSLATED BEINGS, ZIONISM. 1. *Zion* is the name given by the Lord to his saints; it is the name by which the Lord's people are always identified. Of the saints in Enoch's day the record says: *"And the Lord called his people ZION, because they were of one heart and one mind, and dwelt in righteousness; and there was no poor among them."* (Moses 7:18.) *"This is Zion—THE PURE IN HEART,"* he said in this day. (D. & C. 97:21.) Thus The Church of Jesus Christ of Latter-day Saints is Zion. Joining the Church is becoming a citizen of Zion.

Many revelations speak of Zion in this sense. Before the organization of the Church, the command was given to a number of brethren, "Seek to bring forth and establish the cause of Zion." (D. & C. 6:6; 11:6; 12:6; 14:6.) On the day of its organization, the Lord commended The Prophet for his diligence, prayers, and labors in bringing forth Zion. (D. & C. 21:7-8.) After its organization various brethren were commanded to labor in Zion with all their power and strength. (D. & C. 24:7; 30:11; 93:53.)

2. After the Lord had called his people Zion, Enoch "built a city that was called the *City of Holiness, even Zion.*" This "Zion, in process of time," after 365 years, "was taken up into heaven, . . . for God received it up into his own bosom; and from thence went forth the saying, ZION IS FLED." Between

that time and the flood "many" persons "were caught up by the powers of heaven into Zion." It is this City of Zion which is to return in the last days, probably shortly after the ushering in of the millennial era. (Moses 7:18-69; D. & C. 38:4.)

3. At least from the days of King David, the name *Zion* was applied to one of the hills upon which Jerusalem is built or (later) to the entire city. (2 Sam. 5:6-7; 1 Kings 8:1.) Solomon built his temple in Zion.

4. The New Jerusalem to be built in Jackson County, Missouri, is also called the *City of Zion* or *Zion.* Dozens of revelations in the Doctrine and Covenants speak about this Zion. (*Doctrines of Salvation,* vol. 3, pp. 66-79.) Isaiah and other of the ancient prophets have much to say both about it and about the Jerusalem of old which shall be restored in grandeur and beauty in the last days. These two great cities, dual world capitals, are needed to fulfil the great millennial promise: "Out of Zion shall go forth the law, and the word of the Lord from Jerusalem." (Isa. 2:3.)

5. Joseph Smith announced at the April, 1844, general conference of the Church that all of North and South America comprise the *land of Zion* (*Teachings,* p. 362), a land "choice above all other lands" (1 Ne. 2:20; Ether 1:42), a land upon which the scattered remnant of Israel is commanded to gather. (D. & C. 133; *Doctrines of Salva-*

tion, vol. 3, pp. 72-75.)

6. At the Second Coming, "the Lamb shall stand upon *Mount Zion,* and with him a hundred and forty-four thousand, having his Father's name written on their foreheards." (D. & C. 133:18; Rev. 14: 1-5.) The Mount Zion spoken of is identified by latter-day revelation as the New Jerusalem to be built in Jackson County, Missouri. (D. & C. 84:1-4.)

7. Paul uses the term *Mount Zion* to refer to the abode of exalted beings, those who overcome all things and inherit the fulness of the Father's kingdom. To them he says: *"Ye are come unto mount Sion, and unto the city of the living God, the heavenly Jerusalem, and to an innumerable company of angels, To the general assembly and church of the firstborn."* (Heb. 12:22-24.)

ZIONISM.

See GATHERING OF ISRAEL, JEWS, MILLENNIUM, SECOND COMING OF CHRIST, SIGNS OF THE TIMES, ZION. One of the living miracles of the ages is the preservation of the Jewish people as a distinct race and the restless anxiety in the hearts of so many of them to return to the land of their fathers. This modern movement to resettle the house of Judah in Palestine is called *Zionism.* It gains impetus from the many Old Testament prophecies which tell of the latter-day return of Judah to their homeland.

Governing in the affairs of men

and controlling the destinies of nations, as he does, the Lord is using this Zionism movement to prepare the way for the great gathering of Judah that is yet to be. In the midst of World War I (Nov. 2, 1917), in the Balfour Declaration, the British government went on record as favoring, "the establishment in Palestine of a national home for the Jewish people." On November 29, 1947, the General Assembly of the United Nations proposed the partition of Palestine into an Arab and a Jewish state. Then on May 14, 1948, the Jewish National Council proclaimed a Jewish state in Palestine to be called Israel. Since then there has been considerable tumult and difficulty in that area—all but a prelude of greater difficulties destined to take place there.

All this is a harbinger of the great gathering which will involve the ultimate conversion and sanctification of the chosen of Judah. (D. & C. 133:35.) The great day is ahead, a day in which the Jewish people will be gathered because they believe in the very Messiah whom their forbears rejected, a day in which they will be gathered into the sheepfold of Israel, join The Church of Jesus Christ of Latter-day Saints, and build a temple in Jerusalem from which the word of the Lord can go forth. The great and coming gathering will be under the direction of him who holds the keys of the gathering of Israel, the President of the Church.

ZORAMITES.

See BOOK OF MORMON, NEPHITES AND LAMANITES. 1. That portion of the Nephites who were lineal descendants of Zoram, the servant of Laban, were sometimes called *Zoramites*. (Jac. 1:13-14; 4 Ne. 37-39.)

2. An apostate Nephite named Zoram (possibly a descendant of the original Zoram) founded a sect called *Zoramites* in the days of the Republic, about 74 B.C. (Alma 30: 59; 31:1.) Alma and Amulek labored as missionaries among the Zoramites (Alma 31; 32; 33; 34; 35), Amulek delivering to them that great sermon which spells out the doctrine that there is no second chance for salvation in the next life for those who do not take their opportunity to receive the truth in this life. (Alma 34:31-35.)